Lecture Notes in Computer Science 10603

Commenced Publication in 1973
Founding and Former Series Editors:
Gerhard Goos, Juris Hartmanis, and Jan van Leeuwen

More information about this series at http://www.springer.com/series/7409

Xingming Sun · Han-Chieh Chao
Xingang You · Elisa Bertino (Eds.)

Cloud Computing and Security

Third International Conference, ICCCS 2017
Nanjing, China, June 16–18, 2017
Revised Selected Papers, Part II

Editors
Xingming Sun
Nanjing University of Information Science and Technology
Nanjing
China

Xingang You
China Information Technology Security Evaluation Center
Nanjing
China

Han-Chieh Chao
National Dong Hwa University
Shoufeng
Taiwan

Elisa Bertino
Department of Computer Science
Purdue University
West Lafayette, IN
USA

ISSN 0302-9743 ISSN 1611-3349 (electronic)
Lecture Notes in Computer Science
ISBN 978-3-319-68541-0 ISBN 978-3-319-68542-7 (eBook)
https://doi.org/10.1007/978-3-319-68542-7

Library of Congress Control Number: 2017956776

LNCS Sublibrary: SL3 – Information Systems and Applications, incl. Internet/Web, and HCI

Printed on acid-free paper

This Springer imprint is published by Springer Nature
The registered company is Springer International Publishing AG
The registered company address is: Gewerbestrasse 11, 6330 Cham, Switzerland

Preface

The two-volume set of proceedings (LNCS 10602 and 10603) contains the papers presented at ICCCS 2017: the Third International Conference on Cloud Computing and Security held during June 16–18, 2017, in Nanjing, China. The conference was hosted by the College of Computer and Software at the Nanjing University of Information Science and Technology, who provided the wonderful facilities and material support. We made use of the excellent EasyChair submission and reviewing software.

The aim of this conference is to provide an international forum for the latest results of research, development, and applications in the field of cloud computing and information security. This year we received more than 391 submissions from 15 countries and regions, including USA, UK, France, Australia, Ireland, South Korea, South Africa, India, Iraq, Kazakhstan, Indonesia, Vietnam, Ghana, China, and Taiwan. Each submission was allocated to three Program Committee (PC) members and each paper received on average three reviews. The committee decided to accept 116 papers, yielding an acceptance rate of 29.7%.

The program also included six distinguished talks. "Green Networking and Computing: New Perspectives and Challenges Within Energy-Oriented Infrastructures and Devices" by Dr. Aniello Castiglione, University of Salerno, Italy; "Content-Based Search over Encrypted Text Data in Cloud" by Dr. Zhangjie Fu, Nanjing University of Information Science and Technology, China; "Error Correcting Codes in Data Hiding and Secret Image Sharing" by Dr. Ching-Nung Yang, National Dong Hwa University, Taiwan; "Cloud-of-Things and Edge Computing: Recent Advances and Future Trends" by Dr. Mohammad Mehedi Hassan, King Saud University (KSU), Kingdom of Saudi Arabia; "SDN-Enabled Cloud Data Center" by Prof. Ren-Hung Hwang, National Chung Cheng University, Taiwan; and "Exploring the Geospatial Data: When Visualization Meets Query Processing" by Dr. Zhifeng Bao, RMIT University, Australia.

We would like to extend our sincere thanks to all authors who submitted papers to ICCCS 2017 and to all PC members. It was a truly great experience to work with such talented and hard-working researchers. We also appreciate the external reviewers for assisting the PC members in their particular areas of expertise. Finally, we would like to thank all attendees for their active participation and the organizing team who nicely managed this conference. We look forward to seeing you again at next year's ICCCS.

June 2017

Xingming Sun
Han-Chieh Chao
Xingang You
Elisa Bertino

Organization

General Chairs

Xingming Sun	Nanjing University of Information Science and Technology, China
Han-Chieh Chao	National Dong Hwa University, Taiwan
Xingang You	China Information Technology Security Evaluation Center, China
Elisa Bertino	University of Purdue, USA

Organizing Committee Chairs

Jian Shen	Nanjing University of Information Science and Technology, China
Kuan-Ching Li	Providence University, Taiwan
Chih-Hsien Hsia	Chinese Culture University, Taiwan
Shuangkui Xia	Beijing Institute of Electronics Technology and Application, China

Technical Program Committee Chairs

Chin-Feng Lai	National Cheng Kung University, Taiwan
Yang Xiao	The University of Alabama, USA
Aniello Castiglione	University of Salerno, Italy
Yunbiao Guo	China Information Technology Security Evaluation Center, China
Zhangjie Fu	Nanjing University of Information Science and Technology, China

Steering Committee Chairs

Xingming Sun	Nanjing University of Information Science and Technology, China
Han-Chieh Chao	National Dong Hwa University, Taiwan
Alex Liu	Michigan State University, USA
Yang Xiao	The University of Alabama, USA
Zhiqiu Huang	Nanjing University of Aeronautics and Astronautics, China

Technical Program Committee

Ming Yin	Harvard University, USA
Saeed Arif	University of Algeria, Algeria
Zhifeng Bao	Royal Melbourne Institute of Technology University, Australia
Hanhua Chen	Huazhong University of Science and Technology, China
Jie Chen	East China Normal University, China
Xiaofeng Chen	Xidian University, China
Ilyong Chung	Chosun University, South Korea
Jintai Ding	University of Cincinnati, USA
Zhangjie Fu	Nanjing University of Information Science and Technology, China
Jinguang Han	Nanjing University of Finance and Economics, China
Jiguo Li	Hohai University, China
Kuan-Ching Li	Providence University, Taiwan, China
Zhe Liu	University of Waterloo, Canada
Sungyoung Lee	Kyung Hee University, South Korea
Mohammad Mehedi Hassan	King Saud University, Saudi Arabia
Debiao He	Wuhan University, China
Wien Hong	Nanfang College of Sun Yat-Sen University, China
Qiong Huang	South China Agricultural University, China
Xinyi Huang	Fujian Normal University, China
Yongfeng Huang	Tsinghua University, China
Zhiqiu Huang	Nanjing University of Aeronautics and Astronautics, China
Patrick C.K. Hung	University of Ontario Institute of Technology, Canada
Hai Jin	Huazhong University of Science and Technology, China
Sam Tak Wu Kwong	City University of Hong Kong, SAR China
Xiangyang Li	Illinois Institute of Technology, USA
Yangming Li	University of Washington, USA
Quansheng Liu	University of South Britanny, France
Junzhou Luo	Southeast University, China
Yonglong Luo	Anhui Normal University, China
Sangman Moh	Chosun University, South Korea
Yi Mu	University of Wollongong, Australia
Zemin Ning	Wellcome Trust Sanger Institute, UK
Shaozhang Niu	Beijing University of Posts and Telecommunications, China
Jeff Z. Pan	University of Aberdeen, UK
Wei Pang	University of Aberdeen, UK
Rong Peng	Wuhan University, China
Jiaohua Qin	Central South University of Forestry and Technology, China
Yanzhen Qu	Colorado Technical University, USA
Kui Ren	State University of New York, USA
Shengli Sheng	University of Central Arkansas, USA

Organizing Committee

Contents – Part II

Information Security

Optimization and Classification

Short Paper

Contents – Part I

IoT Applications

Information Security

Practical Privacy-Preserving Outsourcing of Large-Scale Matrix Determinant Computation in the Cloud

Shaojing Fu[1,2,3](✉), Yunpeng Yu[1], and Ming Xu[1]

[1] College of Computer, National University of Defense Technology, Changsha, China
shaojing1984@163.com, {yuyunpeng,xuming}@nudt.edu.cn
[2] Sate Key Laboratory of Cryptology, Beijing, China
[3] Science and Technology on Information Assurance Laboratory, Beijing, China

Abstract. Large-Scale matrix determinant computation (LMDC) is a common scientific and engineering computational task and has a number of applications. But such computation involves enormous computing resources, which is burdensome for the clients. Cloud computing enables computational resource-constrained clients to economically outsource such computations to the cloud server. In this paper, we investigate the privacy-preserving large-scale matrix determinant computation outsourcing problem, where the clients can outsource LMDC to the untrusted cloud server, relieving the clients from computation burden. We propose a new privacy-preserving algorithm for outsourcing LMDC, which substantially reduces the computation burden on the client side. Our algorithm builds on a series of carefully-designed pseudorandom matrices, which can hide the original matrix from the cloud server with low computational complexity. The extensive security analysis shows that our algorithm is practically-secure, and offers a higher level of privacy protection than the state-of-the-art on LMDC outsourcing. We provide extensive theoretical analysis and experimental evaluation to show its high-efficiency and security compared to the previous works.

Keywords: Cloud computing · Privacy-preserving · Matrix determinant computation · Outsourcing computation

1 Introduction

With the emergence of the big data, many large-scale systems and applications have to deal with the enormous data. However, analyzing large-scale data is often too expensive for resource-limited clients. Nowadays, cloud computing provides a new approach to efficiently and economically solve such computing tasks for individuals, companies and governments [1–4]. In cloud computing, the computational resource-constraint clients can outsource their computing tasks to the cloud server which contains plenty of computing resources in a pay-per-use manner [5].

X. Sun et al. (Eds.): ICCCS 2017, Part II, LNCS 10603, pp. 3–15, 2017.
https://doi.org/10.1007/978-3-319-68542-7_1

Large-scale matrix determinant computation (LMDC) is one of the most basic algebraic problems in common scientific and engineering computing task and has a number of applications which include hyper volume [6], anharmonic oscillator analysis [7] etc. In practice, solving LMDC requires too much computation and storage resources for the ordinary clients. The economical solution is to outsource LMDC to the cloud server. Despite the tremendous benefits of cloud computing. Directly outsourcing computation to the cloud inevitably brings in new security concerns and challenges [8]. The computational problems and their results usually contain sensitive information. But the cloud is not fully trusted. To protect the privacy of sensitive data, the client should encrypt the sensitive data before outsourcing and decrypt the returned results from the cloud after outsourcing. Mohassel [9] proposed a secure protocol for outsourcing linear algebra computation tasks including matrix determinant, however, Mohassel protocols utilize the existing homomorphic encryption schemes which have higher computational complexity. Recently, Lei et al. [10] proposed a secure algorithm of secure outsourcing of large-scale matrix determinant computation to the cloud. Their algorithm is based on the disguising technique. They claimed the cloud has a negligible probability of correct guess of the number of zero elements in original matrix. However, the security arguments given for Lei et al.'s work do not hold, the cloud can obtain the number of zero elements in original matrix from the encrypted matrix. According to privacy requirement proposed by Gennaro et al. [11], Lei et al.'s scheme cannot protect the privacy of the original matrix X. Therefore, we are motivated to design a new algorithm that enables clients to outsource privacy-preserving large-scale matrix determinant computation to the cloud server while apparently relieving the client of its high computation burden.

In this paper, we propose a new secure algorithm that supports privacy-preserving LMDC outsourcing in cloud computing. Our algorithm is designed to meet the efficiency and security requirements under the computation outsourcing model. Our design delegates the most expensive computation for solving LMDC to the cloud to get rid of computation costs. To protect the data privacy, the original matrix is permuted and masked by a series of carefully-designed pseudorandom matrices. Security analysis proves that our algorithm can properly protect the privacy of input/output data of outsourced LMDC. The contributions of this paper can be summarized as follows:

(1) We propose a privacy-preserving algorithm for secure outsourcing of LMDC in cloud systems, which reduces the computation burden on the client side. The computation complexity for the client is no more than $O(n^2)$.
(2) Through a series of disguise-based techniques, our algorithm can protect data privacy of LMDC, especially the number of zero elements in original matrix.
(3) We provide extensive theoretical analysis to demonstrate its high efficiency and security compared to the previous work.

The rest of this paper is organized as follows: In Sect. 2, we present the system and threat model together with the design goals of our scheme. Section 3 gives the preliminaries and notations that are used in our paper. Section 4 provides the detailed construction of our scheme together with the theoretical analysis. Section 5 analyzes the performance of our scheme in experiments. Finally, we conclude our work in Sect. 6.

2 Problem Formulation

In this section, we present the system and threat model for secure outsourcing of LMDC, and introduce our design goals (Fig. 1).

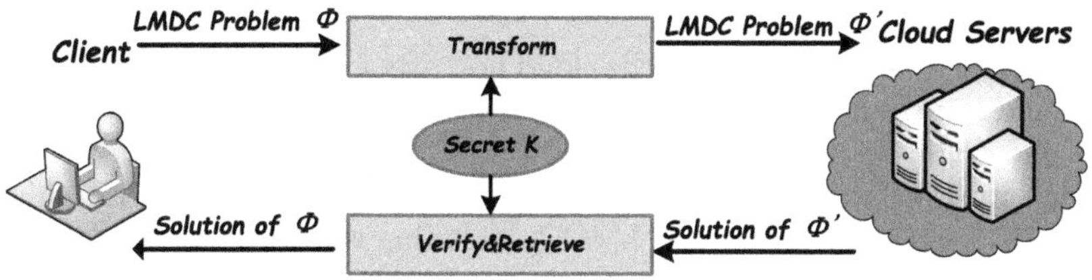

Fig. 1. A secure system model for outsourcing LMDC

2.1 System Model

We consider an asymmetric computing outsourcing architecture involving two different parties, as shown in Fig. 2. The cloud server contains the unlimited computing resources in a pay-per-use manner. Meanwhile, the computational resource-limited client cannot carry out the heavy computation of solving LMDC locally, where the complexity is usually $(O(n^{\rho})(2 < \rho \leqslant 3))$. Therefore, the client can outsource the LMDC problem to the cloud server. During the outsourcing process, the client outsources the most expensive computation to the cloud server and retrieves the solution from the returned results. The client has to preserve the input and output data privacy.

In this work, we pay more attention on finding a scheme to securely and effectively outsource the LMDC $\Phi : X$, where $X \in \mathbb{R}^{n \times n}$ is the original matrix. Instead of directly sending the original LMDC Φ to the cloud server, the client first uses a secret key K to transform the LMDC $\Phi : X$ into the encrypted version $\Phi' : X'$. The encrypted version Φ' is sent to the cloud server. The cloud sever is expected to help the client finding the desired answer of Φ'. And the cloud server is supposed to obtain as little as possible on the sensitive information contained in Φ. After receiving the returned result of encrypted problem Φ' from the cloud server, the client should be able to first verify whether the result is correct. If the returned result is correct, the client then uses the secret K to get the desired solution for the original problem Φ.

2.2 Threat Model

In this paper, we consider an *honest-but-curious* cloud server [12], where the server honestly conducts the process of solving LMDC, but it may attempt to derive sensitive information from the input/output data of the processing. Specifically, the privacy threats for outsourced LMDC come from the sensitive information in the original matrix A, and the solution $det(A)$.

2.3 Design Goals

In this paper, we identify the following goals that the outsourcing scheme should achieve:

(1) Correctness: If the client and the cloud honestly follow the scheme, the cloud should return the correct solution and the client can obtain the correct result of the original LMDC problem.
(2) Security: The cloud cannot derive any sensitive information of the original LMDC from the transformed LMDC, including the number of zero element in original matrix during outsourcing the LMDC computation.
(3) The local computation done by the client (including key generation and transformation computation) should be substantially less than solving the original LMDC computation on his own. In particular, the overall computational complexity for the client is no more than $O(n^2)$.

3 Preliminaries and Notations

In this section, we describe some preliminaries and notations that are used in this paper.

3.1 Computational Indistinguishability

To enable the client to securely delegate computing tasks to the cloud server, the outsourced data should appear random. The notion of privacy is defined as computational indistinguishability [13].

Definition 1. *Two probability ensembles [13]* $X = \{X_{\mathrm{n}}\}_{n \in N}$ *and* $Y = \{Y_{\mathrm{n}}\}_{n \in N}$ *are computationally indistinguishable if for every probabilistic polynomial time distinguisher* D *there exists a negligible function* $negl(n)$ *such that*

$$|Pr[D(X_{\mathrm{n}}) = 1] - Pr[D(Y_{\mathrm{n}}) = 1]| < negl(n) \tag{1}$$

The probability ensemble $X = \{X_{\mathrm{n}}\}_{n \in N}$ is consisted by a series of random variables $X_1, X_2, \cdots$. The notation $D(X_{\mathrm{n}})$ denotes that x is distinguished from distribution X_{n}. Distinguisher $D(X)$ outputs 1 if it can distinguish x form distribution X_{n} in a probabilistic polynomial-time.

3.2 Privacy-Preserving Matrix Transformation

Privacy-preserving Matrix Transformation is first proposed by Salinas et al. [14], which allows the client to hide the data of the matrix in the sense of computational indistinguishability [13]. Specifically, assume that the values of matrix A are within the range $[-K, K]$, where $K = 2^l (l > 0)$ is a positive constant. Then the client hides the privacy of matrix A by adding a random matrix as $\hat{A} = A + Z$, where the random matrix Z is constructed as follows:

$$Z = uv^T \tag{2}$$

where $u \in \mathbb{R}^{m\times 1}$ is a vector of uniformly distributed random variables ranging from -2^p and 2^p $(p > 0)$, $v \in \mathbb{R}^{n\times 1}$ is a vector of arbitrary positive constants ranging from 2^l and 2^{l+q} $(q > 0)$. Salinas et al. [14] have proved that the matrix $\hat{A}$ is computational indistinguishable from a random matrix R whose elements in its jth column are sampled from a uniform distribution with interval $[-2^p v_j, 2^p v_j]$ $(\forall j \in [1, n])$.

The important property of the determinant of matrix includes the following lemma [15].

Lemma 1. Suppose that $A, B, 0$ and D are matrices of dimension $n \times n$, $n \times m$, $m \times n$, $m \times m$, respectively, then

$$\det \begin{bmatrix} A & B \\ 0 & D \end{bmatrix} = \det(A)det(D) \tag{3}$$

4 Scheme Construction

In this section, we first give a general framework of our scheme and then we present the detailed construction of our scheme. In the end, we give a theoretical analysis on its correctness, security and efficiency.

4.1 The General Framework

Now, we present a privacy-preserving outsourcing computation scheme that contains the following five phases:

(1) $KeyGen(1^\lambda)$: The client initializes a random key generation algorithm which generates some random parameters for the problem transformation. The random parameters are kept secret by the client.
(2) $ProbTrans(\Phi, parameters)$: The client uses the transformation algorithm to transform the original LMDC problem Φ into transformed LMDC Φ' via the parameters for phase *ProbSolve*.
(3) $ProbSolve(\Phi')$: Given the transformed LMDC Φ', the cloud gets matrices L and U by invoking any existing LU decomposition algorithm. Then, the cloud server sends L and U back to the client.

(4) *SolRetri*(L, U): The client uses the result verification algorithm to check the correctness of the returned result matrices L and U. If the results pass the check, accepts the results; Otherwise, rejects them.
(5) *ResultVerify*$(L, U, parameters)$: The client uses the solution retrieval algorithm to retrieve a correct solution of the original LMDC Φ from the returned result of the transformed LMDC Φ'.

4.2 Scheme Description

The input data of LMDC is a full rank matrix $X \in \mathbb{R}^{n\times n}$. The output data of LMDC is $\det(X)$. In the following, we introduce how to securely outsource the LMDC to the cloud with result verifiability.

***KeyGen*:** Given a security parameter 1^λ, the client specifies key space K_d, and selects a set of non-zero random numbers:$\{d_1, d_2 \cdots, d_n\} \leftarrow K_d$.

Then, the client specifies a positive integer m and picks $3m$ vectors $b_1, \cdots, b_m \in \mathbb{R}^{n\times 1}$, $c_1, \cdots, c_m \in \mathbb{R}^{m\times 1}$ and $s_1, \cdots, s_m \in \mathbb{R}^{(n+m)\times 1}$, where $b_1 = [b_{1,1}, \cdots, b_{n,1}]^T$, $\cdots$, $b_m = [b_{1,m}, \cdots, b_{n,m}]^T$, $c_1 = [c_{1,1}, \cdots, c_{m,1}]^T$, $\cdots$, $c_m = [c_{1,m}, \cdots, c_{m,m}]^T$ are constructed as u shown in Sect. 3.2, and $s_1 = [s_{1,1}, \cdots, s_{1,n}, s_{1,n+1}, \cdots, s_{1,n+m}]^T$, $\cdots$, $s_m = [s_{m,1}, \cdots, s_{m,n}, s_{m,n+1}, \cdots, s_{m,n+m}]^T$ are constructed as v shown in Sect. 3.2.

***ProbTrans*:** The client first generates matrix $D = \text{diag}(d_1, d_2, \cdots d_n)$.The client computes $X'' = XD$.

Then, the client generates matrices $B = [b_1 \cdots b_m]$ and $C = [c_1 \cdots c_m]$ of dimension $n \times m$, $m \times m$, respectively. Then, the client generates a ***Well-designed Privacy-preserving Matrix*** S of dimension $(n + m) \times (n + m)$ as

$$S = \begin{bmatrix} 1 & & & 0 & \cdots & 0 \\ & \ddots & & \vdots & \ddots & \vdots \\ & & 1 & 0 & \cdots & 0 \\ s_{1,1} & \cdots & s_{1,n} & s_{1,n+1} & \cdots & s_{1,n+m} \\ \vdots & \ddots & \vdots & \vdots & \ddots & \vdots \\ s_{m,1} & \cdots & s_{m,n} & s_{m,n+1} & \cdots & s_{m,n+m} \end{bmatrix} = \begin{bmatrix} E & 0 \\ S_1 & S_2 \end{bmatrix}.$$

where E is an $n \times n$ identity matrix, 0 is an $m \times n$ zero matrix,

$$S_1 = \begin{bmatrix} s_{1,1} & \cdots & s_{1,n} \\ \vdots & \ddots & \vdots \\ s_{m,1} & \cdots & s_{m,n} \end{bmatrix}, S_2 = \begin{bmatrix} s_{1,n+1} & \cdots & s_{1,n+m} \\ \vdots & \ddots & \vdots \\ s_{m,n+1} & \cdots & s_{m,n+m} \end{bmatrix}.$$

After that, the client generates a matrix $T = \begin{bmatrix} X'' & B \\ 0 & C \end{bmatrix}$, where 0 is a $m \times n$ zero matrix. The client computes $Y = T \times S$. According to Eq. 9, the client can efficiently compute Y with $O(n^2)$ computation complexity. Later, the encrypted matrix Y will be sent to the cloud server.

***ProbSolve*:** On input the encrypted matrix Y, the cloud server computes a lower triangular matrix L and an upper triangular matrix U such that $Y = LU$ by invoking any existing LU decomposition algorithm. Then, the cloud server sends L and U back to the client.

***ResultVerify*:** Handling result verification can be addressed by Lei et al. [10]. That is, the client first generates l random vectors $r_i \in \mathbb{R}^{(n+m)\times 1}$ $(i \in [1,l])$, and then verifies whether the equation $L \times (U \times r_i) = Y \times r_i$ holds. If the equations hold, the client accepts L and U as the correct results; Otherwise, rejects them and claims a failure to the cloud server.

***SolRetri*:** Given the returned matrices L and U from the cloud, the client computes det(X):

$$\det(X) = \frac{\prod_{i=1}^{n+m}(L_{i,i}U_{i,i})}{\prod_{i=1}^{n} d_i \times \det(C) \times det(S_2)}$$

Remark 1. Note that the dimension of C and S_2 is $m \times m$ $(2 \leq m \ll n)$. Therefore, $det(C)$ and $det(S_2)$ can be directly calculated on the client side. As show in Table 2, ***SolRetri*** phase in our algorithm is extremely fast.

4.3 Correctness Analysis

Our scheme is designed to return the correct solution $\det(X)$ of LMDC to the client. Thus in the following, we prove that if the cloud follows the algorithm honestly, the $\det(X)$ can be computed as

$$\det(X) = \frac{\prod_{i=1}^{n+m}(L_{i,i}U_{i,i})}{\prod_{i=1}^{n} d_i \times \det(C) \times det(S_2)} \tag{4}$$

Since $X'' = XD$, $\det(X) = \frac{\det(X'')}{\det(D)}$, where the determinant of matrix D is computed as

$$\det(D) = \prod_{i=1}^{n} d_i \tag{5}$$

Following from Lemma 1, $T = \begin{bmatrix} X' & B \\ 0 & C \end{bmatrix}$, $S = \begin{bmatrix} E & 0 \\ S_1 & S_2 \end{bmatrix}$, this leads to

$$\det(X') = \det(T)/\det(C)\det(S) = \det(E)det(S_2) = \det(S_2). \tag{6}$$

$Y = T \times S$, $Y = L \times U$, this leads to $T = LUS^{-1}$. This result in $\det(T) = \det(L)det(U)det(S)^{-1}$. For triangle matrices L and U, we have

$$\det(L) = \prod_{i=1}^{n+2} L_{i,i}, \det(U) = \prod_{i=1}^{n+2} U_{i,i}\,. \tag{7}$$

Based on Eqs. 5, 6, 7, we conclude that our construction is correct for solving the LMDC problem.

4.4 Security Analysis

Output Privacy: The proposed scheme is supposed to protect output data privacy if given the returned matrices L and U, the cloud cannot derive information about the solution determinant $\det(X)$ of the original X. Given matrices L and U, the cloud can compute $\det(Y) = det(L)det(U) = \prod_{i=1}^{n+2}(L_{ii}U_{ii})$. According to (5), $\det(X) = \frac{\det(Y)}{det(D)\times\det(C)\times\det(S_2)}$. By keeping matrices D, C and S_2 private, the client prevents the cloud server to recover $\det(X)$ from $\det(Y)$.

Remark 2. In the whole process, the cloud only has the knowledge of the transformed matrix Y. Due to $C \times S_2$ is presented in Y, so the cloud server can brute force of m (note that m is small). Once the cloud server knows the value of m, the cloud server can obtain the $\det(C) \times \det(S_2) = \det(C \times S_2)$. By keeping matrix D private, the client prevents the cloud server to recover $\det(X)$ from $\det(Y)$.

Input Privacy: The proposed scheme can preserve input data privacy if the cloud cannot retrieve any information of the original matrix X from the encrypted matrix Y, including the number of zero element in the original matrix.

Proof. The original matrix X is encrypted by the following two phases:

Phase 1: Let $X'' = XD$. Each element in X is disguised by multiplying a factor. That is, $X''(i,j) = d_j X(i,j)$.

Phase 2: Let X'' serve as a building block of matrix T, i.e., $T = \begin{bmatrix} X'' & B \\ 0 & C \end{bmatrix}$. The client computes $Y = TS$. That is,

$$\begin{aligned} Y = T \times S &= \begin{bmatrix} X'' & B \\ 0 & C \end{bmatrix} \times \begin{bmatrix} E & 0 \\ S_1 & S_2 \end{bmatrix} \\ &= \begin{bmatrix} X'' + B \times S_1 & B \times S_2 \\ C \times S_1 & C \times S_2 \end{bmatrix} = \begin{bmatrix} X' & B' \\ 0' & C' \end{bmatrix} \end{aligned} \tag{8}$$

In Phase 1, there are $(K_d)^n$ cases to guess $\{d_1, d_2, \cdots, d_n\}$. Through the diagonal matrix D, the client protect the privacy of the determinant of the matrix X.

In Phase 2, Let

$$\begin{aligned} X' &= X'' + BS_1 \\ &= \begin{bmatrix} x''_{1,1} + b_{1,1}s_{1,1} + \cdots + b_{1,m}s_{m,1} & \cdots & x''_{1,n} + b_{1,1}s_{1,n} + \cdots + b_{1,m}s_{m,n} \\ \vdots & \ddots & \vdots \\ x''_{n,1} + b_{n,1}s_{1,1} + \cdots + b_{n,m}s_{m,1} & \cdots & x''_{n,n} + b_{n,1}s_{1,n} + \cdots + b_{n,m}s_{m,n} \end{bmatrix} \\ &= X'' + b_1 s_1{}' + \cdots + b_m s_m{}' \end{aligned} \tag{9}$$

where $s_{11}{}' = [s_{1,1}, \cdots, s_{1,n}]$, $\cdots$, $s_{1m}{}' = [s_{m,1}, \cdots, s_{m,n}]$. When $m = 1$, $BS_1 = b_1 s_1{}'$, which is the same as the definition of Privacy-preserving Matrix Transformation in [14]. As proved in [14], the disguised X' are computational indistinguishable with a random matrix R, whose elements in each column are sampled from a uniform distribution with variable intervals. However, the disguise can leak the linear relation between the rows and columns of BS_1 if the X is a large sparse matrix. That is, when $m = 1$, it still leaks the numbers of the zero element. In our scheme, let $2 \leq m \ll n$, there is no linear relation between the row and columns of BS_1. It can protect the number of zero element while keeping computational indistinguishability.

Let

$$B' = B \times S_2 = \mathrm{b}_1\mathrm{s}_{21}{}' + \mathrm{b}_2\mathrm{s}_{22}{}' + \cdots b_m s_{2m}{}' = B'' + \mathrm{b}_2\mathrm{s}_{22}{}' + \cdots b_m s_{2m}{}' \tag{10}$$

where $B'' = \mathrm{b}_2 s_{21}$, $\mathrm{s}_{21}{}' = [s_{1,n+1}, \cdots, s_{1,n+m}]$, $\cdots$, $s_{1m}{}' = [s_{m,n+1}, \cdots, s_{m,n+m}]$. Matrix B' is computational indistinguishable with a random matrix R. Similarly, Matrices $0'$ and C' are also computational indistinguishable with random matrices. Therefore, the Y is computational indistinguishable with a random matrix R.

Let D, B, C, $S = (s_{ij})$, D', B', C', $S' = (s'_{ij})$ be eight random matrices generated by the client. Given two matrices $X = (x_{ij})$ and $S' = (s'_{ij})$ which are chosen by the cloud server, the client generates $T = \begin{bmatrix} XD & B \\ 0 & C \end{bmatrix} = (t_{ij})$ and $T' = \begin{bmatrix} X'D' & B' \\ 0 & C' \end{bmatrix} = (t'_{ij})$, and computes $Y = TS = (y_{ij})$ and $Y' = T'S' = (y'_{ij})$, where

$$y_{ij} = \sum_{i=1}^{n}\sum_{j=1}^{n} t_{ij} \cdot s_{ij}$$

and

$$y'_{ij} = \sum_{i=1}^{n}\sum_{j=1}^{n} t'_{ij} \cdot s'_{ij}.$$

The B, C, $S = (s_{ij})$, B', C', $S' = (s'_{ij})$ are constructed as shown in Sect. 4.2, thus y_{ij} and y'_{ij} are computationally indistinguishable. Therefore, the advantage of the cloud server to distinguish between Y and Y' is negligible.

Consider the above, the cloud cannot retrieve any information of X from Y.

Remark 3. Note that D, B, C, S, r_i, in our scheme can be only used one time. Thus such parameters are freshly generated for each time of outsourcing LMDC.

4.5 Efficiency Analysis

In this section, we present the computational complexity analysis for the proposed scheme in theory. Our efficiency analysis follows the methodology of Serigo et al. [14], which defines the computational complexity of a party as the number of floating-point (flops) operations (additions, subtractions, multiplications, and divisions), bitwise operations and encryptions that the party needs to perform.

To analyze the overall computational complexity for the client, we have to look into every phase of our scheme in detail. In the ***KeyGen***, the client takes

$n \cdot S$ to generate one set of non-zero random numbers $\{d_1, d_2, \cdots, d_n\}$, where S is the number of bitwise operations to generate a random number by methods such as Mersenne Twister [16]. Then, the client gets the random vectors $b_1, \cdots, b_m, c_1, \cdots, c_m$, and $s_1, \cdots, s_m$, the client takes $(2m(n+m)) \cdot S$ bitwise operations. In the ***ProbTrans***, the client computes $X'' = XD$, which takes n^2 floating-point operations. According to (9), the client computes $X + BS_1$, which takes mn^2 additions and mn^2 floating-point operations. Therefore, the client computes $Y = T \times S$, which takes $(2m-1)(n+\mathrm{m})^2 + n^2$ floating-point operations, including $(m-1)(n+\mathrm{m})^2$ additions and $m(n+\mathrm{m})^2$ floating-point operations. The ***ProbSolve*** is conducted by the cloud. In the ***ResultVerify***, the client firstly generates l random vectors $r_i (i \in [1, l])$, which takes $l(n+m) \cdot S$ bitwise operations. Then, the client takes $3(n+m)^2$ floating-point operations to verify the result. In the ***SolRetri***, the client performs $2(2n+m)+3+2m^3$ floating-point operations to retrieve $\det(X)$. Therefore, the total computational complexity for the client side is $(2(m+1)(n+m)^2 + 2n^2 + 3n + 2m + 1 + 2m^3) \cdot flops + ((2m+1)(n+m)+n) \cdot S$. That is, there are $O(n^2) \cdot flops$ and $O(n^2) \cdot S$ bitwise operations for this scheme (Table 1).

Remark 4. Note that the client takes $2m^3$ floating-point operations to compute the determinant $det(C)$ and $det(S_2)$. Since $m \ll n$, we assume that the computational complexity of solving the determinant of C and S_2 is $O(n) \cdot flops$ operations.

Table 1. Comparison of securely outsourcing LMDC

	Lei et al. [10]	Our scheme
KeyGen	$(m(n+1) + 2(n+m-1)) \cdot S + 2(n+m) \cdot flops$	$(2m(n+m) + 2n) \cdot S$
ProbTrans	$(5n + 2m + 2(n+m)^2) \cdot flops$	$((2m-1)(n+\mathrm{m})^2 + 2n^2) \cdot flops$
ResultVerify	$l(n+m) \cdot S + 3(n+m)^2 \cdot flops$	$l(n+m) \cdot S + 3(n+m)^2 \cdot flops$
SolRetri	$(4n + 5m) \cdot flops$	$(3n + 2m + 1 + 2m^3) \cdot flops$
Privacy-preserving	×	✓

5 Performance Evaluation

In this section, we evaluate the performance of our proposed scheme through extensive experiments. The algorithms are all programmed with Matlab R2014a. Following the experiments of Lei et al. [10], both the client-side and the cloud server computations in our experiments are implemented on the same workstation which is configured as a virtual machine equipped with a 64 GB RAM and 8 cores (each runs at 2.1 GHz) with the software suite of VMware ESXi. In the experiment, dimension n changes from 5000 to 25000. All of matrix instances are generated to be full rank with each element randomly located in (0, 1).

5.1 Evaluationof KeyGen and ProbTrans

We first explore the computation cost for the client in the ***KeyGen*** phase. In the ***KeyGen*** phase, the client has to generate some random parameters. These random parameters in our scheme can be only used one time. Thus such parameters are freshly generated for each time of outsourcing LMDC. We set $m = 50$ in the experiment.

In the ***ProbTrans*** phase, the original LMDC Φ is transformed into Φ'. As shown in Sect. 4.2, the main computation cost in ***ProbTrans*** is dominated by the computation of $Y = T \times S$.

The computation cost of ***KeyGen*** and ***ProbTrans*** for different scale of the original matrix is shown in Table 2. Table 2 shows that the time cost of ***ProbTrans*** is the most.

5.2 Cost of ResultVerify and SolRetri

In the ***ResultVerify*** phase, the client can verify whether the equation $L \times (U \times r_i) = Y \times r_i (i \in [1, l])$ holds. The computation cost of ***ResultVerify*** is dominated by the matrix-vector multiplication with complexity $O(n^2)$. In the experiments, let $l = 1$. Table 2 shows that the time cost of ***ResultVerify*** is fast. The time cost of the ***ResultVerify*** phase is monotonically increasing with the value of l. Since the result verification is not the main focus of this work, we refer the readers to other experiments for more detailed analysis.

In the ***SolRetri*** phase, the client computes $\det(X) = \frac{\det(Y)}{\det(D) \times \det(C) \times det(S_2)}$. The client can directly compute the $det(C)$ and $det(S_2)$ by himself. Table 2 shows that the time cost of ***SolRetri*** is extremely fast.

Table 2. Computation cost of our scheme for the different problem size

Benchmark		Time cost for client side			
Matrix size	Storage	***KeyGen***	***ProbTrans***	***ResultVerify***	***SolRetri***
n = 5,000	0.2 GB	0.157 s	0.645 s	0.036 s	0.317 ms
n = 1,0000	0.5 GB	0.581 s	2.580 s	0.122 s	0.333 ms
n = 15,000	0.8 GB	1.268 s	6.062 s	0.272 s	0.354 ms
n = 20,000	1.1 GB	2.227 s	10.889 s	0.517 s	0.389 ms
n = 25,000	1.8 GB	3.464 s	16.694 s	0.830 s	0.485 ms

5.3 Comparison

In the experiment, the m is set as $m = 50$. Figure 5.3 clearly compares the totaling running time of the client side with that of [10]. As expected in our theoretical results, the experiment results demonstrate that our algorithm is more efficient compared to that of [10].

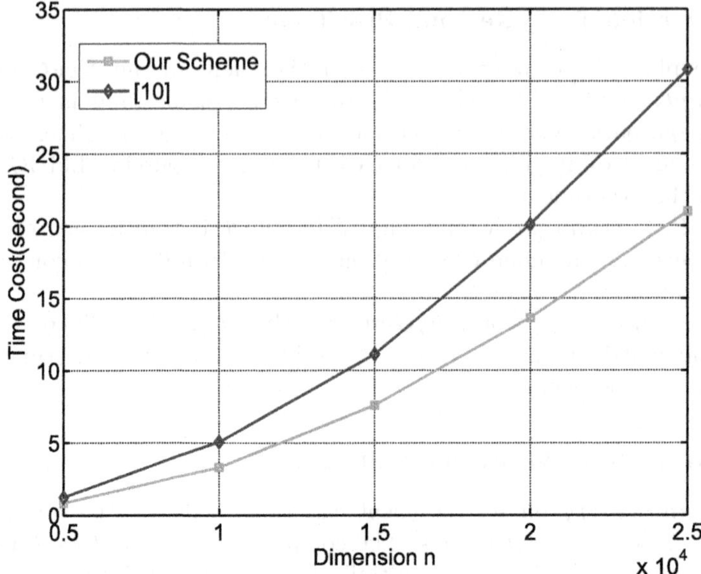

Fig. 2. The total running time in client side of our scheme compared with that of [10]

6 Conclusions

In this paper, we propose a new privacy-preserving algorithm for outsourcing large-scale matrix determinant computation (LMDC) to the cloud. By delegating the most expensive computation of solving LMDC to the cloud, our algorithm relieves the client of its high computation burden. Moreover, with a series of carefully-designed pseudorandom matrices, our algorithm can properly protect the privacy of input/output data of outsourced LMDC. Particularly, it can hide the number privacy of zero elements in the original matrix. Extensive experiments demonstrate that our algorithm achieves higher efficiency than the existing scheme in the client-side computation.

Acknowledgments. This work is supported by the Open Foundation of State Key Laboratory of Cryptology (No: MMKFKT201617), National Nature Science Foundation of China under grant 61572026, 61672195 and 61379144, the Foundation of Science and Technology on Information Assurance Laboratory (No: KJ-15-001).

References

1. Demirkan, H., Delen, D.: Leveraging the capabilities of service-oriented decision support systems: putting analytics and big data in cloud. Decis. Support Sys. **55**, 412–421 (2013)

2. Wang, Q., Hu, S., Ren, K., He, M., Du, M., Wang, Z.: CloudBI: practical privacy-preserving outsourcing of biometric identification in the cloud. In: Pernul, G., Ryan, P.Y.A., Weippl, E. (eds.) ESORICS 2015. LNCS, vol. 9327, pp. 186–205. Springer, Cham (2015). doi:10.1007/978-3-319-24177-7_10
3. Fu, Z., Ren, K., Shu, J., et al.: Enabling personalized search over encrypted outsourced data with efficiency improvement. IEEE Trans. Parallel Distrib. Syst. **27**, 2546–2559 (2016)
4. Xia, Z., Wang, X., et al.: A privacy-preserving and copy-deterrence content-based image retrieval scheme in cloud computing. IEEE Trans. Inf. Forensics Secur. **11**, 2594–2608 (2016)
5. Sakr, S., et al.: A survey of large scale data management approaches in cloud environments. IEEE Commun. Surv. Tutor. **13**, 311–336 (2011)
6. Peng, B.: The Determinant: A Means to Calculate Volume (2011)
7. Biswas, S.N., et al.: The hill determinant: an application to the anharmonic oscillator. Phys. Rev. D **4**, 3617–3620 (1971)
8. Seccombe, A., et al.: Security guidance for critical areas of focus in cloud computing. Evidence and Cloud Computing the VMI Approach Poisel Malzer and Tjoa (2009)
9. Mohassel, P.: Efficient and Secure Delegation of Linear Algebra. IACR Cryptology Eprint Archive (2011)
10. Lei, X., et al.: Cloud computing service: the case of large matrix determinant computation. IEEE Trans. Serv. Comput. **8**, 688–700 (2015)
11. Gennaro, R., Gentry, C., Parno, B.: Non-interactive verifiable computing: outsourcing computation to untrusted workers. In: Rabin, T. (ed.) CRYPTO 2010. LNCS, vol. 6223, pp. 465–482. Springer, Heidelberg (2010). doi:10.1007/978-3-642-14623-7_25
12. Yu, Y., et al.: Efficient, secure and non-iterative outsourcing of large-scale systems of linear equations. In: 2016 IEEE International Conference on Communications, pp. 1–6. IEEE Press, Kuala Lumpur (2016)
13. Katz, J., Lindell, Y.: Introduction to Modern Cryptography: Principles and Protocols. Chapman & Hall/CRC, Boca Raton (2007)
14. Salinas, S., et al.: Efficient secure outsourcing of large-scale linear systems of equations. In: 2015 International Conference on Computer Communications, pp. 1035–1043. IEEE Press, Hong Kong (2015)
15. Meyer, C.D.: Matrix Analysis and Applied Linear Algebra. Society for Industrial and Applied Mathematics, Philadelphia (2000)
16. Matsumoto, M., Nishimura, T.: Mersenne twister: a 623-dimensionally equidistributed uniform pseudo-random number generator. ACM Trans. Model Comput. Simul. **8**, 3–30 (1998)

Probability-p Order-Preserving Encryption

Ce Yang, Weiming Zhang(✉), Jiachen Ding, and Nenghai Yu

CAS Key Laboratory of Electro-magnetic Space Information,
University of Science and Technology of China, Hefei, China
{zhangwm,ynh}@ustc.edu.cn

Abstract. Order-Preserving Encryption (OPE) is an encryption preserving the order relationship of the plaintexts to support efficient range query on ciphertexts. Other than traditional symmetric encryption aiming at absolute security, OPE sacrifices some security for the ability to search on ciphertext. In this paper, we propose a new cryptographic primitive, Probability-p Order-Preserving Encryption (p-OPE), which preserves the order of plaintexts with probability p. When $p = 1$, p-OPE becomes OPE, thus p-OPE is an extension of OPE. We define and analyse the security and precision of the novel primitive, then we propose a construction of p-OPE and conduct experiments to show its performance. As shown in the theoretical analysis and experiment results, p-OPE can improve the security at the cost of some precision sacrifice.

Keywords: Searchable encryption · Order-Preserving Encryption · Range query

1 Introduction

Cloud computing is widely used nowadays. By outsourcing data to the cloud, customers can utilize the computing and storage resources provided by cloud server and reduce maintenance costs. With the rapid development of cloud computing, more and more sensitive information, such as customer information and transaction records, are stored in the cloud. Usually, cloud service can provide better security supportance than individual or small corporation. Nevertheless, the attackers may be willing to spend more resources to intrude the cloud server because of its potential interest. Sometimes, even the administrator of the cloud provider is in collusion with the attackers.

Therefore, sensitive data should be encrypted before outsourcing to the cloud. The mainstream approach used to protect data privacy is cryptography. Data are protected from unauthorized access after encryption. While protecting data privacy, encryption makes data hard to use. For example, traditional plaintext search methods fail on encrypted data. To solve this problem, searchable encryption systems [4,6–9,19–23] have been proposed. Searchable encryption enables searches on ciphertexts without decryption or decryption key, thus the plaintext of sensitive data is protected from attackers, even malicious cloud administrator.

X. Sun et al. (Eds.): ICCCS 2017, Part II, LNCS 10603, pp. 16–28, 2017.
https://doi.org/10.1007/978-3-319-68542-7_2

Order-Preserving Encryption (OPE) [1] is one of the cryptographic primitives enabling search on encrypted data. OPE is a secret-key encryption whose encryption function preserves numerical ordering of the plaintexts. OPE can be used to build an encrypted index supporting range query on numeric data, thus it has been used in encrypted database systems such as CryptDB [16] developed by MIT; Encrypted Bigquery client [10] developed by Google; and other secure retrieval systems [17].

OPE was first proposed by Agrawal et al. [1]. Boldyreva et al. [2] and Popa et al. [15] proved that any practical immutable OPE scheme leaks more than orders. Then, Boldyreva constructed an OPE scheme that uses hypergeometric distribution to lazy-sample a random order-preserving function. Popa et al. [15] designed an order-preserving encoding scheme that leaks at most the order through an interactive protocol. Boneh et al. [3] extended OPE to a more general concept as order-revealing encryption, of which the ciphertexts can be compared by an arbitrary algorithm other than the standard comparison operation as in the case of OPE, and they built a construction that leaks at most the order.

Though OPE provides efficient search ability for range query, it becomes vulnerable in some situation as shown in recent works.

Naveed et al. [14] considered the security of searchable encryption and presented four different attacks that recover the plaintext from property preserving encryption. Two of the attacks, sorting attack and cumulative attack, are applied to OPE and can recover plaintext with high probability. The sorting attack assumed that the plaintext was dense, which is not a typical situation for OPE. The cumulative attack utilized additional information about the distribution of plaintext.

Li et al. [11] developed a differential attack on OPE. Their attack reveals the leakage of distribution by exploiting the difference between ciphertexts. When OPE is used on the inverted index of an encrypted document dataset, experiments shows that the attacker can infer the encrypted keywords using differential attack if the attacker has some background information.

Durak et al. [5] studied the information leakage of ORE and OPE. They considered two issues: First, they showed that ORE may reveal additional information when multiple columns of correlated data are encrypted using OPE. Second, they discussed the leakage of concrete OPE schemes on non-uniform data.

These researches motivates us to propose a novel cryptographic primitive, which has better security than OPE while preserving the high efficiency of range query. Our contribution includes:

1. We propose a new cryptographic primitive, Probability-p Order-Preserving Encryption (p-OPE), which is an extension of OPE and aims at improving security. We define the security and precision metrics of p-OPE based on realistic situation, and we make a theoretical analysis of it.
2. We propose a construction of p-OPE and conduct experiments to show its performance. The experiment results show that the user can achieve a balance between security and query accuracy by adjusting the order-preserving probability p.

2 Probability-p Order-Preserving Encryption

In this section, we propose the concept of Probability-p Order-Preserving Encryption (p-OPE), which is an extension of OPE scheme. First, we define the novel cryptographic primitive. Then, we study the security and precision of p-OPE.

2.1 Definition

To improve the security of OPE, we propose the concept p-OPE.

Informally, a p-OPE $f : [1, n] \to [1, m]$ is an encryption scheme which preserves the order of the plaintext with probability not less than p when the plaintext follows a uniform distribution, i.e.

$$P(f(x_1) < f(x_2)|x_1 < x_2) \geq p. \tag{1}$$

When $p = 1$, p-OPE becomes OPE.

We give a definition which does not rely on the plaintext distribution. Considering an encryption $f : [1, n] \to [1, m]$, we say a pair of plaintext (x_1, x_2) is an ordered pair if $x_1 < x_2$, and an ordered pair (x_1, x_2) is a reverse pair if $f(x_1) > f(x_2)$. We define reverse number n_r as the number of reverse pairs, i.e. $n_r = |\{(x_1, x_2)|x_1 < x_2 \wedge f(x_1) > f(x_2)\}|$. An encryption f is a p-OPE, if the proportion of reverse pairs in all ordered pairs is smaller than $1 - p$, i.e. f is a p-OPE, if

$$n_r \leq (1 - p)\left(\frac{1}{2}n(n - 1)\right), \tag{2}$$

where n_r is the reverse number, n is the size of plaintext space. We can prove that the formal definition is in accordance with our intuitive definition:

Theorem 1. *If f is a p-OPE, x_1, x_2 are randomly picked from a uniform distribution on X, then*

$$P(f(x_1) < f(x_2)|x_1 < x_2) \geq p. \tag{3}$$

Proof

$$\begin{aligned} P(f(x_1) < f(x_1)|x_1 < x_2) &= \frac{P(f(x_1) < f(x_2) \wedge x_1 < x_2)}{P(x_1 < x_2)} \\ &= 1 - \frac{P(f(x_1) < f(x_2) \wedge x_1 > x_2)}{P(x_1 < x_2)} \\ &= 1 - \frac{|\{(x_1, x_2)|x_1 < x_2 \wedge f(x_1) > f(x_2)\}|}{|\{(x_1, x_2)|x_1 < x_2\}|} \\ &= 1 - \frac{|\{(x_1, x_2)|x_1 < x_2 \wedge f(x_1) > f(x_2)\}|}{\frac{1}{2}n(n-1)} \\ &\geq 1 - (1 - p) \\ &= p. \end{aligned} \tag{4}$$

Thus the theorem is proved. □

To discuss the property of p-OPE, we start from a special p-OPE named as permutation function, which has a ciphertext space of the same size as the plaintext space. More precisely, a permutation function g is a bijection on integer interval $[1, n]$.

Every general p-OPE f is a composition of a permutation function g and an order-preserving function h. Order-preserving function h can be generated by mapping from i to the ciphertext of the i-th smallest ciphertext, and $g(x) = h_d(g(x))$, where h_d is the corresponding decryption function of the order-preserving function h.

Any p-OPE can do such a decomposition, and any permutation function and any OPE can be combined to build a p-OPE. Based on this, we can analyse the security and precision of p-OPE.

2.2 Security

Researchers have proposed different security metrics for OPE. Here we use *mean absolute error* (MAE) [13] to measure the security. MAE applies to scenarios that not only the accurate recovery but also a close estimation of plaintext is acceptable, which holds for most application of OPE. For example, if the encrypted data is salary, the adversary usually does not care the difference between 10,000 and 10,100.

We define MAE formally here. For a p-OPE $f : [1, n] \to [1, m]$ with decryption function f_d, the MAE of an adversary is defined as:

$$d_{\text{MAE}}(f_d, f_d') = \sum_{y} |f_d(y) - f_d'(y)| P_y, \tag{5}$$

where $f_d(y)$ is the decryption function, $f_d'(y)$ is the approximation of the adversary, and P_y is the probability of ciphertext y. When the order-preserving function is a continuous function, the definition will be an integral. When the plaintext follows a uniform distribution, MAE is equivalent to $d_m = \sum_x |x - f_d'(f(x))|$.

We consider two different attack scenarios.

The first one is the scenario in which the adversary knows the plaintext distribution. Previous work [14] shows that an adversary can recover the plaintext of an OPE with high precision in this scenario. As discussed in previous subsection, f is a composition of a permutation function g and an order-preserving function h. Here we consider the situation that the order-preserving function is insecure, i.e. the adversary knows $h(x)$, thus the security of p-OPE relies on the permutation function.

When the adversary knows $h(x)$ and has no knowledge of $g(x)$, an option for the adversary is to estimate plaintext as: $f_d'(y) = h_d(y)$, where $h_d(y)$ is the decryption function of OPE $h(x)$. We have $f_d'(y) = f_d'(h(g(x))) = h_d(h(g(x))) = g(x)$, i.e. $f_d(y) - f_d'(y) = x - g(x)$. Thus, the security of p-OPE is determined by the permutation function $g(x)$ in our assumption.

Now we analyse the relationship between order-preserving probability p and MAE d_m. We have:

Theorem 2. *For a permutation function $g : [1, n] \to [1, n]$ with reverse number n_r, if the adversary uses the identity function $g'_d(k) = k$ as the estimation and the plaintext follows a uniform distribution, then MAE d_m satisfies*

$$n_r \le d_m \le 2n_r. \tag{6}$$

Proof. The reverse pairs can be split to four different parts as:

$$\begin{aligned} &f(x_1) > x_1, f(x_2) > x_2,\\ &f(x_1) > x_1, f(x_2) = x_2,\\ &f(x_1) > x_1, f(x_2) < x_2,\\ &f(x_1) \le x_1, f(x_2) < x_2. \end{aligned} \tag{7}$$

We abbreviate subscription 1, 2 and denote them with $n(>, >), n(>, =), n(>, <)$, $n(\le, <)$.

Consider x_i such that $f(x_i) > x_i$ and $f(x_i) - x_i$ gets maximum. For $x < x_i$, we have $f(x) - x \le f(x_i) - x_i$, thus

$$f(x) \le f(x_i) + x - x_i < f(x_i), \tag{8}$$

we know that x, x_i cannot be a reverse pair for $x < x_i$.

For $x > x_i$, (x_i, x) is a reverse pair if $f(x) < f(x_i)$. Because the number of x satisfying $f(x) < f(x_i)$ is $f(x_i) - 1$, and the number of x satisfying $x < x_i$ and $x_i - 1$ is $x_i - 1$. Thus the number of x with $x_i < x$ and $f(x_i) > f(x)$ is $f(x_i) - x_i$, i.e.,

$$|\{x | x > x_i \wedge f(x) < f(x_i)\}| = f(x_i) - x_i. \tag{9}$$

and we have the number of reverse pairs related with x_i is $f(x_i) - x_i$.

We can remove x_i from points of interested, and repeat it. Thus for all x with $f(x) > x$, the sum of number of reverse pairs related with x is

$$N(f(x) > x) = \sum_{f(x) > x} f(x) - x. \tag{10}$$

i.e.

$$n(>, >) + n(>, =) + n(>, <) = \sum_{f(x) > x} f(x) - x. \tag{11}$$

For x satisfying $f(x) < x$, we have a similar conclusion,

$$N(f(x) < x) = \sum_{f(x) < x} x - f(x). \tag{12}$$

i.e.

$$n(>,<) + n(\leq,<) = \sum_{f(x)<x} x - f(x). \tag{13}$$

Thus

$$\begin{aligned} n_r &= n(>,>) + n(>,=) + n(>,<) + n(\leq,<) \\ &\leq n(>,>) + n(>,=) + n(>,<) + n(>,<) + n(\leq,<) \\ &= \sum_x |f(x) - x| \\ &= d_m, \end{aligned} \tag{14}$$

and similarly,

$$2n_r \geq d_m. \tag{15}$$

In conclusion, the theorem is proved. □

Because order-preserving probability p is determined by n_r, this theorem shows the relationship between p and security. The security increases with the reverse number, and $d = 0$ when $p = 1$.

The second one is the adversary knows several plaintext-ciphertext pairs. In this scenario, the adversary can use interpolation to estimate the decryption function. We show the performance of p-OPE and compare it with OPE constructions using experiments in the latter.

2.3 Precision

Precision is related with applications. We consider the precision of range query. Here we adopt the false positive and false negative from the evaluation of plaintext information retrieval [12] to illustrate the precision of ciphertext query. For a plaintext query Q_X and the corresponding ciphertext query Q_Y, a false negative is a plaintext x appear in the plaintext query but the corresponding ciphertext not in the ciphertext query, i.e. $x \in Q_X$ and $f(x) \notin Q_Y$; a false positive is the opposite, i.e. $x \notin Q_X$ and $f(x) \in Q_Y$.

We measure the precision using the ratio of right results and errors. For a range query, if the query result contains n_e related results and n_{fp} false positives, and the number of false negatives is n_{fn}, then we define the precision as:

$$P_e = \frac{n_e}{n_e + n_{fp} + n_{fn}}. \tag{16}$$

The precision of a p-OPE is the average of precision of all possible range queries.

In term of range query, different query distribution will lead to different precision. A simple way to generate query is randomly pick two plaintext uniformly and make them the endpoint of query interval. However, interval generated such way is somewhat not uniform. Assume the plaintext chosen is x_1, x_2, then the probability of plaintext x in the interval $[x_1, x_2]$ or $[x_2, x_1]$ is

$$\begin{aligned} P &= P(x_1 \le x \wedge x_2 \ge x) + P(x_1 > x \wedge x_2 \le x) \\ &= P(x_1 \le x)P(x_2 \ge x) + P(x_1 > x)P(x_2 \le x) \\ &= \frac{x}{N}\frac{N-x+1}{N} + \frac{N-x}{N}\frac{x}{N}. \end{aligned} \tag{17}$$

Obviously, different plaintext will be queried with different probability, and the midpoint of plaintext space will be queried in half of the queries. Because we assume the plaintext follows a uniform distribution, we also hope that each plaintext will be queried equiprobablely. We generate intervals with the same length and different centers as queries. The queries is generated as $[x, x+k]$, where x obeys a uniform distribution, and k is a fixed number.

For each plaintext interval $[x_1, x_2]$, the user can traverse different ciphertext intervals to find the most suitable ciphertext query $[y_1', y_2']$ to minimize the error. Here we propose a more simple way to response the query. For plaintext interval $[x_1, x_2]$, we use $[x_1 - e, x_2 + e]$ as ciphertext query, where e is a constant chosen by user.

Now we analyse the precision of our ciphertext query. We have

Theorem 3. *Assume p-OPE $g(x) : [1, n] \to [1, n]$ is a permutation function. If range query is generated as $[x, x+k]$, where x follows a uniform distribution on $[1-k, n]$, then the precision of g satisfies*

$$P_e \ge \frac{k+1}{(n+k)(k+2e+1)}\left(n - \left\lceil \frac{d_m}{k+e+1} \right\rceil\right). \tag{18}$$

Proof. We say a plaintext x matches an plaintext interval query $[x_1, x_2]$, if the plaintext x is in the plaintext interval $[x_1, x_2]$, and the corresponding ciphertext $g(x)$ is in the corresponding ciphertext query $[x_1 - e, x_2 + e]$.

Denote the set of plaintexts matching a interval $[x_1, x_2]$ as $Q_e([x_1, x_2])$, i.e. if $x \in [x_1, x_2]$ and $g(x) \in [x_1 - e, x_2 + e]$, then $x \in Q_e([x_1, x_2])$, and vice versa.

For each plaintext x, we can calculate $n_q(x)$, the number of intervals it matches. The definition of $n_q(x)$ is

$$n_q(x) = |\{(x_1, x_2) | x_2 - x_1 = s \wedge x \in Q_e([x_1, x_2])\}|. \tag{19}$$

For plaintext x with $|x - f(x)| \le e$, x matches each interval $[x_1, x_2]$ it in. For plaintext x with $e < |x - f(x)| \le k + e$, x matches $s + 1 + d - |x - f(x)|$ different intervals. For plaintext x with $k + e < |x - f(x)|$, x matches none interval. Thus, if we define function $f_r(k)$ as

$$f_r(i) = \begin{cases} k+1, & i \le e \\ k+1+e-i, & e \le i \le e+k+1 \\ 0, & e+k+1 \le k \end{cases} \tag{20}$$

then $n_q(x) = f_r(|x - f(x)|)$.

According to the definition of precision, the precision of g is

$$\begin{aligned} P_e &= \sum_{x=1-k}^{n} P_e(x)\frac{1}{n+k} \\ &= \frac{1}{n+k}\sum_{i=1-k}^{n}\frac{n_e}{k+2e+1} \\ &= \frac{1}{n+k}\sum_{i=1-k}^{n}\frac{|\{x|x \in Q_e([i,i+k])\}|}{k+2e+1} \\ &= \frac{1}{(n+k)(k+2e+1)}\sum_{x=1}^{n} n_q(x). \end{aligned} \tag{21}$$

Now we discuss the relationship between $\sum n_q$ and MAE d_m. When the MAE of two sequences is a fixed num, we estimate the precision between them.

For two numbers k_1, k_2 with fixed sum, we calculate $f_r(k_1) + f_r(k_2)$. It is easy to know, if $k_1 + k_2 > k + e + 1$, then $f_r(k_1) + f_r(k_2)$ get minimum when $k_1 = k + e + 1$; if $k_1 + k_2 < k + e + 1$, then $f_r(k_1) + f_r(k_2)$ get minimum when $k_1 = 0$.

Thus for n different numbers, the sum of their precision function will greater than the sequence of $(k+e+1, k+e+1, \ldots, k+e+1, s_r, 0, \ldots, 0)$, where $0 \le s_r \le k+e+1$. If $(k+e+1)(n_l - 1) < d_m \le (k+e+1)n_l$, we have $\sum n_r(x) > (n - n_l)(k+1)$, i.e.

$$\sum n_r(x) \ge \left(n - \left\lceil \frac{d_m}{k+e+1} \right\rceil\right)(k+1). \tag{22}$$

Thus, we have

$$\begin{aligned} P_e &= \frac{\sum n_q(x)}{(n+k)(k+2e+1)} \\ &\ge \frac{k+1}{(n+k)(k+2e+1)}\left(n - \left\lceil \frac{d_m}{k+e+1} \right\rceil\right). \end{aligned} \tag{23}$$

□

Theorem 3 shows the relationship between precision and security. The lower bound ensures the precision in the worst case. When the size of plaintext space is large enough, the probability of precision reaching lower bound is small. Thus, in most situation, actual precision is better than the lower bound.

3 Construction

In this section we give a construction of p-OPE based on the framework in previous section. First, we give the algorithm of our construction, then we show its actual security and precision performance.

3.1 Construction

As discussed in previous section, a p-OPE can be constructed from a permutation function and an order-preserving function. The OPE scheme has been discussed by many previous researchers, and ready-made schemes such as random-partition scheme or OPE based on hypergeometric distribution can be adopted.

Thus, we focus on the permutation scheme. If the size of plaintext space is n, the targeted order-preserving probability is p, then we use a random-shift algorithm to generate a permutation function.

The algorithm runs in a loop. Based on the size of p, the algorithm execute multiple rounds of interval-shift operations to adjust the order relationship of the sequence. A right interval-shift on an sequence $(x_1, x_2, \ldots, x_n)$ is to move the first element to the last position, and move other elements to the left position next to it, i.e. $(x_1, x_2, \ldots, x_n) \rightarrow (x_2, x_3, \ldots, x_n, x_1)$. A left interval-shift is a similar operation in the opposite direction, i.e. $(x_1, x_2, \ldots, x_n) \rightarrow (x_n, x_1, x_2, \ldots, x_{n-1})$. In each round of the algorithm, the algorithm randomly choose a continuous subsequence of x^n, and evaluate the reverse number after interval-shift. If the reverse number decreases with the interval-shift, the operation will not be executed but discarded. The same operation is repeated until the actual order-preserving probability is close to p enough.

The detailed algorithm is shown in Algorithm 1.

3.2 Experiments

In this subsection, we conduct experiments to show the performance of our constructions. First, we verify the theoretical analysis.

The security and precision of proposed construction is shown in Fig. 1. As we expect, MAE d_m increases with the increase of reverse number n_r, and precision decreases with the decrease of order-preserving probability. Figure 1 also shows that a linear function of n_r is a close enough approximation of d_m when the size of plaintext space n is large enough.

Second, we compare the security of p-OPE with three different OPE constructions, random order-preserving function proposed by Boldyreva [2], random uniform sampling proposed by Wozniak [18], and order-revealing encryption proposed by Boneh [3]. We consider the scenario that the attacker knows k plaintext-ciphertext pairs and he uses linear interpolation to estimate the plaintext. The results of proposed method, Boldyreva, and Wozniak are shown in Fig. 2. A point at rate r and MAE d means the number of ciphertext which has a MAE smaller than d is nr when the experiment repeats n times. The proposed method improves the security significantly. With the increase of k, the security of OPE decreases.

Because the ciphertext of ORE is not number, we map the ciphertext of ORE to integers according to the orders before we use interpolation. For example, when the ciphertext sequence is (y_1, y_2, y_3) and $y_2 < y_3 < y_1$, we map the ciphertexts to $(3, 1, 2)$. We compare proposed method of different order-preserving probability with Boneh. The experiment result is shown in Fig. 3. As

Algorithm 1. Random-Shift algorithm

```
Input the size of plaintext space n, expected order-preserving probability p.
Output permutated sequence x^n.
n_r = ⌊(1/2) n(n − 1) ∗ p⌋.
Initialize x^n = (1, 2, ..., n).
while n_r > 3 do
    Choose l from a uniform distribution on [1, n].
    Choose k from a uniform distribution on [1, n_r].
    Randomly choose d from {−1, 1}.
    if d < 0 then
        flip the sequence x^n
    end if
    if x + k > n then
        k = n − x.
    end if
    s = 0
    for i in [l + 1, l + k] do
        if x_l < x_i then
            s = s + d
        else
            s = s − d
        end if
    end for
    if s > 0 then
        x = x_l
        for i in [l + 1, l + k] do
            x_{i−1} = x_i
        end for
        x_{l+k} = x
    end if
    n_r = n_r − s
    if d < 0 then
        flip the sequence x^n
    end if
end while
```

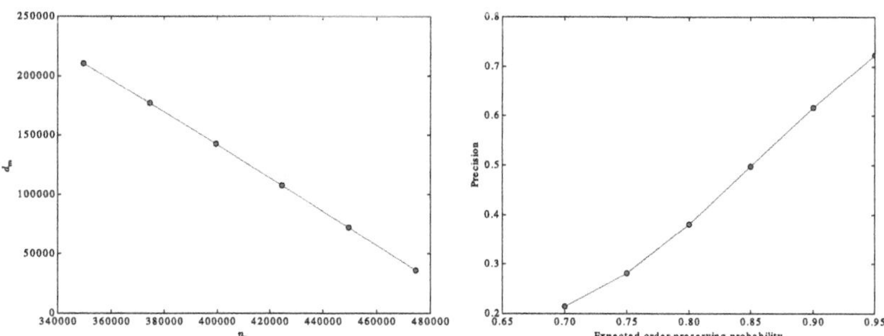

Fig. 1. The security and precision of p-OPE. The size of plaintext space is 1000. Left figure shows the relationship between reverse number n_r and MAE d_m, and right figure shows the relationship between order-preserving probability and query precision.

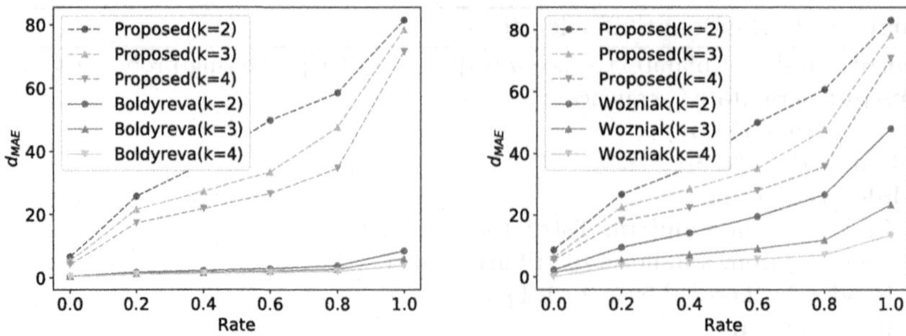

Fig. 2. The security of proposed method (p = 0.80) and Boldyreva, Wozniak.

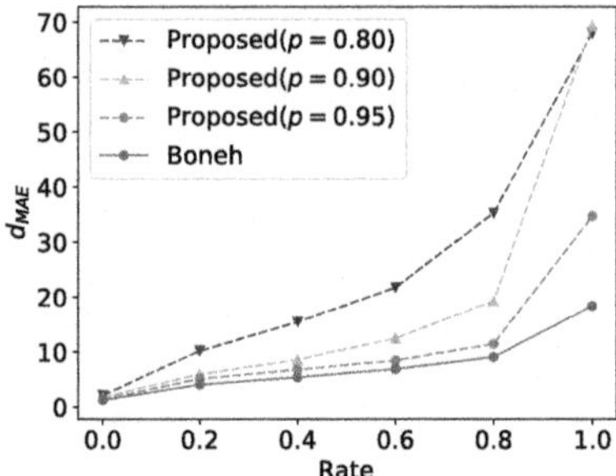

Fig. 3. The security of proposed method and Boneh.

we expected, the attack accuracy of proposed method is lower than Boneh, which leaks only orders, and the security improves with the decrease of order-preserving probability.

4 Conclusion

In this paper, we propose a new cryptographic primitive p-OPE, aiming at improving the security of OPE while preserving searching efficiency. We analyse the security and precision of p-OPE, which is an extension of OPE. We also propose a construction of p-OPE and conduct experiment to verify its performance. The experiment results are in accordance with the theoretical analysis.

Acknowledgements. This work was supported in part by the Natural Science Foundation of China under Grant U1636201 and 61572452.

References

1. Agrawal, R., Kiernan, J., Srikant, R., Xu, Y.: Order preserving encryption for numeric data. In: Proceedings of the 2004 ACM SIGMOD International Conference on Management of Data, SIGMOD 2004, NY, USA, pp. 563–574. ACM, New York (2004)

2. Boldyreva, A., Chenette, N., Lee, Y., O'Neill, A.: Order-preserving symmetric encryption. In: Joux, A. (ed.) EUROCRYPT 2009. LNCS, vol. 5479, pp. 224–241. Springer, Heidelberg (2009). doi:10.1007/978-3-642-01001-9_13
3. Boneh, D., Lewi, K., Raykova, M., Sahai, A., Zhandry, M., Zimmerman, J.: Semantically secure order-revealing encryption: multi-input functional encryption without obfuscation. In: Oswald, E., Fischlin, M. (eds.) EUROCRYPT 2015. LNCS, vol. 9057, pp. 563–594. Springer, Heidelberg (2015). doi:10.1007/978-3-662-46803-6_19
4. Chen, C., Zhu, X., Shen, P., Hu, J., Guo, S., Tari, Z., Zomaya, A.Y.: An efficient privacy-preserving ranked keyword search method. IEEE Trans. Parallel Distrib. Syst. **27**(4), 951–963 (2016)
5. Durak, F.B., DuBuisson, T.M., Cash, D.: What else is revealed by order-revealing encryption? In: Proceedings of the 2016 ACM SIGSAC Conference on Computer and Communications Security, CCS 2016, NY, USA, pp. 1155–1166 (2016). http://doi.acm.org/10.1145/2976749.2978379
6. Fu, Z., Huang, F., Sun, X., Vasilakos, A., Yang, C.N.: Enabling semantic search based on conceptual graphs over encrypted outsourced data. IEEE Trans. Serv. Comput. **PP**(99), 1 (2016)
7. Fu, Z., Ren, K., Shu, J., Sun, X., Huang, F.: Enabling personalized search over encrypted outsourced data with efficiency improvement. IEEE Trans. Parallel Distrib. Syst. **PP**(99), 1 (2015)
8. Fu, Z., Sun, X., Ji, S., Xie, G.: Towards efficient content-aware search over encrypted outsourced data in cloud. In: IEEE INFOCOM 2016 - The 35th Annual IEEE International Conference on Computer Communications, pp. 1–9, April 2016
9. Fu, Z., Wu, X., Guan, C., Sun, X., Ren, K.: Toward efficient multi-keyword fuzzy search over encrypted outsourced data with accuracy improvement. IEEE Trans. Inf. Forensics Secur. **11**(12), 2706–2716 (2016)
10. Google: The encrypted bigquery client. https://github.com/google/encrypted-bigquery-client
11. Li, K., Zhang, W., Yang, C., Yu, N.: Security analysis on one-to-many order preserving encryption-based cloud data search. IEEE Trans. Inf. Forensics Secur. **10**(9), 1918–1926 (2015)
12. Manning, C.D., Raghavan, P., Schütze, H., et al.: Introduction to Information Retrieval, vol. 1. Cambridge University Press, Cambridge (2008)
13. Martınez, S., Miret, J.M., Tomas, R., Valls, M.: Security analysis of order preserving symmetric cryptography. Appl. Math. Inf. Sci. (AMIS) **7**(4), 1285–1295 (2013)
14. Naveed, M., Kamara, S., Wright, C.V.: Inference attacks on property-preserving encrypted databases. In: Proceedings of the 22nd ACM SIGSAC Conference on Computer and Communications Security, CCS 2015, NY, USA, pp. 644–655. ACM, New York (2015)
15. Popa, R., Li, F., Zeldovich, N.: An ideal-security protocol for order-preserving encoding. In: 2013 IEEE Symposium on Security and Privacy (SP), pp. 463–477, May 2013
16. Popa, R.A., Redfield, C.M.S., Zeldovich, N., Balakrishnan, H.: Cryptdb: protecting confidentiality with encrypted query processing. In: Proceedings of the Twenty-Third ACM Symposium on Operating Systems Principles, SOSP 2011, NY, USA, pp. 85–100. ACM, New York (2011)
17. Wang, C., Cao, N., Ren, K., Lou, W.: Enabling secure and efficient ranked keyword search over outsourced cloud data. IEEE Trans. Parallel Distrib. Syst. **23**(8), 1467–1479 (2012)

18. Wozniak, S., Rossberg, M., Grau, S., Alshawish, A., Schaefer, G.: Beyond the ideal object: towards disclosure-resilient order-preserving encryption schemes. In: Proceedings of the 2013 ACM Workshop on Cloud Computing Security Workshop, CCSW 2013, NY, USA, pp. 89–100. ACM, New York (2013)
19. Xia, Z., Wang, X., Sun, X., Wang, Q.: A secure and dynamic multi-keyword ranked search scheme over encrypted cloud data. IEEE Trans. Parallel Distrib. Syst. **27**(2), 340–352 (2016)
20. Xia, Z., Wang, X., Zhang, L., Qin, Z., Sun, X., Ren, K.: A privacy-preserving and copy-deterrence content-based image retrieval scheme in cloud computing. IEEE Trans. Inf. Forensics Secur. **11**(11), 2594–2608 (2016)
21. Xia, Z., Zhu, Y., Sun, X., Qin, Z., Ren, K.: Towards privacy-preserving content-based image retrieval in cloud computing. IEEE Trans. Cloud Comput. **PP**(99), 1 (2015)
22. Xia, Z., Xiong, N.N., Vasilakos, A.V., Sun, X.: EPCBIR: an efficient and privacy-preserving content-based image retrieval scheme in cloud computing. Inf. Sci. **387**, 195–204 (2017). http://www.sciencedirect.com/science/article/pii/S0020025516321971
23. Zhangjie, F., Xingming, S., Qi, L., Lu, Z., Jiangang, S.: Achieving efficient cloud search services: multi-keyword ranked search over encrypted cloud data supporting parallel computing. IEICE Trans. Commun. **98**(1), 190–200 (2015)

DLPDS: Learning Users' Information Sharing Behaviors for Privacy Default Setting in Recommender System

Hongchen Wu(✉) and Huaxiang Zhang

School of Information Science and Engineering, Shandong Normal University, Jinan 250358, China
{wuhongchen, huaxzhang}@sdnu.edu.cn

Abstract. The proliferation of Internet of things has allowed users to provide preference feedback and maintain profiles in multiple websites, which could indicate tastes covering several kinds of domains but focus on small number of topics. Leveraging all the user information available in several sites or domains may be beneficial for knowing the users better and generating higher-quality recommendations. However, aggregating all users' information globally could trigger users' awareness on privacy concerns, which further cause users refuse to share the information so that the recommendation quality is reduced. We provide evidence that a recommender system could mitigate the privacy-integration problem, when it is applied with our novel model, called disclosure-learning privacy default setting (DLPDS), which transfer the pattern of users' past information sharing behaviors into privacy default settings. The result of the experiment support that our DLPDS model could gain users' trust and aggregate more users information, and that adapting the privacy default settings to the user information sharing pattern may results in positive feedback that promoting better prediction accuracy of the recommender system.

Keywords: Machine learning · Privacy default setting · Information sharing · Cross-domain recommender system

1 Introduction

With the proliferation of Internet of things, the majority of recommender systems suggest recommendations for items belonging to a single domain, e.g. Facebook recommend people, Youtube recommends videos and TV programs, and Last.fm recommends music albums. The frameworks of these domain-specific recommender systems have been successfully deployed by numerous websites, and the single-domain recommendation is pitched as a focus on a certain market.

However, large social media sites like Tencent Wechat and Sina Microblog often store user feedback and comments for items from multiple sites, and users often express their tastes and interests for a variety of themes. It could be beneficial to leverage and aggregate all the available user data provided in various websites, in order to generate more encompassing user models and better recommendations. Instead of analyzing each site (e.g., movies, books, and music) independently, knowledge trained in a source

X. Sun et al. (Eds.): ICCCS 2017, Part II, LNCS 10603, pp. 29–39, 2017.
https://doi.org/10.1007/978-3-319-68542-7_3

domain could be transferred to and exploited in another target domain. The research challenge of transferring knowledge, and the business potential of delivering recommendations spanning across multiple sites, have triggered an increasing interest in cross-domain recommendation.

Single-domain recommendation is suffering the problem of cold-start, which hinders the recommendation generation due to the lack of sufficient information about users. In contrast, cross-sites recommendations may draw on information acquired from site to another, to alleviate the cold-start problem. The website which owns a larger number of users and understands its users better, could transfer the user knowledge to the newly-construct website. For example, a user's favorite book genres may be derived from her favorite music genres. If a user has accounts in multiple websites, his/her tastes could be more focused on the topics that commonly fitting the major trend in these websites.

These cases are underpinned by an intuitive assumption that there are correspondences between user and item profiles in the source and target domains, which means that users have multiple accounts in the websites for different types of recommendations. This assumption has been validated in the studies where only strong dependencies are uncovered between different domains [1–3]. Recommender system collects user preferences in ways analogous to statistical database queries and could raise privacy problems [4–7], which can be exploited to identify information about a particular user [8], although it is an important tool in social media for individuals in making choices without sufficient experiences of the alternatives by providing suggestions for items to be of use [9–14]. Cross-domain recommender systems leverage these dependencies through considering, e.g. the overlaps between different types of item sets, correlations between user preferences in multiple accounts, and similarities of item attributes. After that, they apply a variety of methods and techniques for fusing the knowledge of the source domain and the target domain, and improving the quality of recommendations from the enriched knowledge.

This has raised great conflicts from users' privacy concern [15–17], since people may not want their habits or views widely known. Readers would raise their privacy concerns evaluation-sharing system if the refereeing process was not blinded in the review [18]. Although the Internet offers teenagers great opportunities for entertainment, information, and marketplace exchange, some practices of interactive marketing have raised public concerns about harms the Internet allegedly poses to teenagers [19]. On one hand, theories of self-disclosure suggest that consumers' willingness to disclose personal information is based on their assessments of the costs and benefits. Thus, companies who interact with consumers over the Internet use a number of approaches to alter this cost-benefit tradeoff and encourage consumers to self-disclosure [20]; On the other hand, people are hesitated to disclosing personal information due to risk of unexpected outcomes. This privacy contradiction is still an interesting topic in cross-domain recommendation problem.

As a result, privacy is still a challenging and largely under-explored topic in cross-domain recommendation. This paper illustrates our disclosure-learning privacy default setting (DLPDS) model, which learning users' information sharing behaviors from the cross-domain environment, could use the learned knowledge for privacy default settings, and reduce the effect of cold-start as well as increase the prediction accuracy. In the experiment, we have observed that a recommender system applying our DLPDS model has received better prediction accuracy in the early stage, compared with a baseline recommender system without the privacy default settings. We believe this phenomenon is beneficial for users feel less concerned about their privacy and disclose more information for better recommendation. This findings of this paper could be a good reference for any researchers and website managers who want to make better user-centric strategies in privacy issues and want to reduce the cold-start effect for the newly-built recommender system.

This paper is organized as follows. Section 2 proposes our basic data structure, algorithm implementation, and default-formation model. The experiment that applying the model and A/B testing are presented in Sect. 3, and we also forward the possible explanation on why the reduced cold-start effect could happen. We draw the conclusion and future works in Sect. 4.

2 Model Implementation

2.1 Basic Model Elements

Since our analysis lies in users information sharing behaviors, it is needed to show the basic data structure of our model that used as input of the experiment:

Questions (char *RequestedItem*$_1$[*Coin*], char *RequestedItem*$_2$[*Coin*], …, char *RequestedItem*$_n$[*Coin*])

The *RequestedItem* is the information requested from users, such as "would you mind let us know how much time you use in your phone browser?", "would you mind let us know what is your homepage in your browser?", "how many cars you own?", "would you mind let us know your kids' name?", etc. There is an indicator that shows this question's sensitiveness is high or low, and we call that "*Coin*". *Coin* = 1 indicates this is a high sensitive request, which means most users would prefer not to share that information to a recommender engine; otherwise this is a low sensitive question, which most users would probably share that personal information.

User (bool *Answer*$_1$, bool *Answer*$_2$, …, bool *Answer*$_n$)

This is data structure for users, and would only exist after they finished answering their questions sheet. We ask real answers from users, and only those correct answers will be marked as "YES". The denied requests and fake answers will be marked as "NO". For easy recording, $Answer_x$ ($x = 1, 2, \ldots, n$) is noted as "0" (No, I would rather not share my information to this question) or "1" (Yes, I can disclose my information to this question). Also, the number of *Answer*s that one user provided should be exactly the same number as the requested questions in the survey sheet that s(he) had viewed, otherwise we would remove his/her answers due to incompleteness of the sheet, and disqualify his/her eligibility of payment. Furthermore, the total number of "0"s and "1"s from all users for answering the question *X* will determine its value of *Coin*.

UserSensitiveness (bool[] *Answers*, bool I_c, bool I_d)

This data structure is the core concept of our DLPDS model, which showing the sensitiveness of a user in answering questions and the overall denies to their information receiver, and by which we cluster each user's information sharing pattern. The indicator I_c shows this user's sensitiveness to questions by learning from the previous disclosures, and "1" stands for high sensitiveness, while "0" presents low sensitiveness. The indicator $I_d = 0$ stands for users are eager to disclose the information to a receiver whom he don't know, and $I_d = 1$ means he only disclose the information to the people he is familiar with. For example: $X(Answers[30], 0, 1)$ means the user X has demonstrated low sensitive behaviors to the previous 30 requests, and the information receivers are his friends. With more questions answered by this user, more Boolean values will be added into *Answers*[] list, and the two indicators would change overtime. Once user's *UserSensitiveness* structure is created, the two indicators start to track user's sensitiveness by machine learning algorithms e.g., K-means, and every parameter stop changing when this user finished answering the questions. General overflow of our DLPDS model can be seen in Fig. 1., at the beginning, all types of users are mixed in a group, and K-means clustering could divide all users into four groups according to their sharing behaviors of how sensitive the information are and whom could receive the information. Users from (0, 0) group will disclose the low sensitive information to a stranger, (0, 1) group contains users will disclose low sensitive information to a friend, (1, 0) group means the contained users could disclose high sensitive information to a stranger, and (1, 1) group consisting of users could disclose high sensitive information to a friend. In the process of users disclosing their information, K-means constantly tracks their ***Answers[]*** ***{A_1, A_2, …, A_n}***, and once the change of the value of I_c or I_d is detected, users will be reassigned to a correct group.

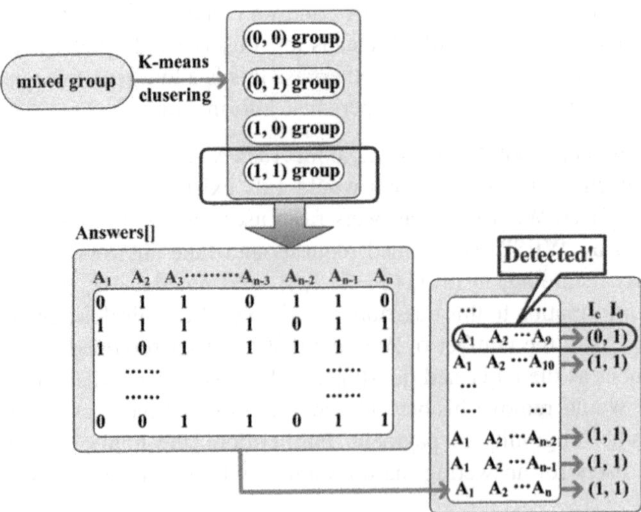

Fig. 1. Model of indicators-training, user disclosure-change detection and K-means clustering techniques

2.2 Clustering Method for User Grouping

If one user's indicator changed due to some reason, it is needed to compare his/her past behavior with similar one's behavior whose indicator did not changed, and clustering method can help. We mainly classify people into 4 groups with K-means clustering method, because the two indicators ($\boldsymbol{I_c}$, $\boldsymbol{I_d}$) can only take the value of {(0, 0), (0, 1), (1, 0), (1, 1)}, Its implementation of K-means clustering method is given below, for each user who attends our study labeled as User X ($a_1(x)$, $a_2(x)$,..., $a_n(x)$), where $a_r(x)$ stands for user X's answer towards No. r question ($r = 1, 2, 3 \ldots n$), and the distance between two users x_i and x_j can be defined as follows:

$$\mathrm{d}(x_i, x_j) = \sqrt{\sum_{r=1}^{n} \left(a_r(x_i) - a_r(x_j)\right)^2} \tag{1}$$

Based on the definition of distance, the K-means clustering implementation is:

Algorithm 1 2Coins-Based K-means Clustering

Input: the participants dataset X {x< $a_1(x)$, $a_2(x)$,…,$a_n(x)$>}
Output: (0, 0) group, (0, 1) group, (1, 0) group, (1, 1) group

```
for j = 1, 2, …, n do
    {training_samples} ← a_j(x)
end for
Set P_00 = ∅
Set P_01 = ∅
Set P_10 = ∅
Set P_11 = ∅
draw a_i(x), a_k(x), a_l(x), a_m(x) from {training_samples} randomly
    where j, k, l, m ϵ {1, n}
P_00 = a_i(x)
P_01 = a_k(x)
P_10 = a_l(x)
P_11 = a_m(x)
{training_samples} = {training_samples} - {a_i(x), a_k(x), a_l(x), a_m(x)}
for a_q(x) in {training_samples}
   find min {d(a_q(x), P_XY)},
              where XY = {(00), (01), (1,0), (1,1)}
   P_XY = P_XY + a_q(x)
   {training_samples} ← {training_samples} - a_q(x)
   recalculate P_XY
              where for a_p(x) in P_XY
                     find min {Σ d(a_p(x), P_XY)}
                     end for
   until {training_samples} = ∅
end for
```

This algorithm is used to proof two users' similarity after their information sharing behavior are detected as "first same then different" in the experiment process.

2.3 Formation of Users' Privacy Default

The connections between users and their information receivers can be cast into graphical model, which represents the elements of a social media network and their mutual relationships. The model is represented as a $G = (V, E)$ network where V represents the set of users. E represents a set of edges. Each edge connects two vertices and it represents a type of relationship between them. Edges can be weighted as the times that sharing behaviors happened or the total amount of disclosures, which represents the strength of friendship between a user and the information receiver.

The friendship can take many forms. A user might have talked with someone and find that they share a common interest, so they become friends. A friendship can also be formed due to the introductions throughout friends in social media community. If a user u has an edge connection with a user u', u' will be defined as a friend of u. Friendship indicate possible happenings of information sharing, and can be divided into three levels depending on to how many times the disclosures happened and the total amount of information has been shared. Shown in Fig. 2, each node represents a user, and its size indicates how many close friends this user have. The biggest node stands for a globally trusted user. The maximum of disclosure volume may represent the friendship between close friends, while the lowest volume represents the amount of information being shared with a stranger.

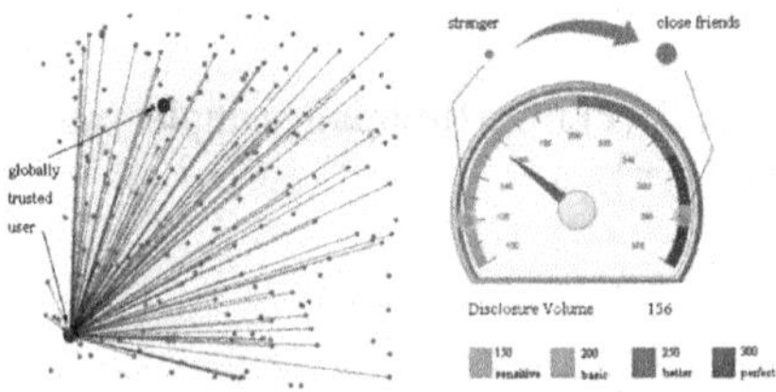

Fig. 2. Users' relationship in the social media network could be casted into a $G = (V, E)$ network, and the disclosure volume between them indicate how close they are

Generally, a friend from the level A is closely connected to the user u and they share the most amount of information. Friends from level B are less connected with user u, and u should consider the risk before sharing the information. Friends from level C might be used for reference, but they should take greater risk when trusting them. Here we give the formal definition of **Friendship** and **Disclosure**.

Friendship of user *u* (User *u'*, String *group*, float *strength score*)

Each user u has a friend list that maintains their information receiver. It holds the set of users $U_{u'}$ that contains all users such as u' that have a connection with u. *group* represents the level of friendship that u' belongs to, e.g., A, B, or C. *strength score* indicates the level of proximity to user u' in the same group, where a higher score represents a closer relation with user u, whom this users may share more information with.

When the sensitiveness of two disclosures *i* and *i'* are the same, they can be placed into a same cluster to show their level of sensitiveness are the same. When a user *u* can disclose the content *i*, *u* may also disclose another content *i'*, if *i* and *i'* are belonging to the same cluster. Our implemented definition of a **Disclosure** is given below:

Disclosure *d* (Cluster *c*, float *sensitiveness score*)
For each **Disclosure** *d*, similar items can be determined such as *d'* depending on their clusters. Furthermore, the *sensitiveness score* can show the similarity between **Disclosures** *d* and *d'*, where a higher score shows that users are less likely to share the information. The privacy default settings are settled as the **Disclosures** $\{D\}$ and information receivers $\{U\}$ whose clusters containing the same level of **Friendship** and **Disclosure**. For example, we found that user *u* has disclosed the content *d* to the friend type *A*, and the default settings will be settled as disclose *d'* to *u'*, where *u'* and *u* are friend in type strength of *A*, and *d* and *d'* belong to same cluster of sensitiveness.

3 Experiment

3.1 Data Description

We hire users who have at least 5 accounts in social media websites, e.g. Tencent Wechat, Sina Microblog, etc., to join our experiment. Our data are collected from a crowdsourcing platform Sojump, which is a website providing online survey services that connects more than 2 million members throughout China and enables individuals and businesses to coordinate the use of human intelligence to perform tasks that computers are currently unable to complete. Users will be assigned into a recommender system in two conditions, in the first condition the recommender system is applied with our disclosure-learning privacy default setting in the cross-domain environment (DLPDS), while in the second condition the recommender system is regarded as the baseline, which do not applied with the disclosure-learning privacy default setting (nDLPDS) and it require users to sign the user privacy agreement before login.

The recommender system in both conditions provides suggestions of what is currently most famous item throughout the social media websites where the users have accounts in. It collects the most frequent keywords that overlapping the websites, and ranks the related item in the descending order. The items rank top will be recommended to the users in the first priority:

$$\{HK\}_{common} = \{HK\}_{weibo} ※ \{HK\}_{wechat} ※ \ldots = \{P_{1c}, P_{2c}, \ldots, P_{xc}\} \tag{2}$$

where $\{HK\}$ represents the frequent keywords in a specific website, and P_{xc} stands for the keywords that are currently ranking top in overall websites:

$$|R_{ic,w_1}| + |R_{ic,w_2}| + \ldots |R_{ic,w_y}| \geq |R_{jc,w_1}| + |R_{jc,w_2}| + \ldots |R_{ic,w_y}| \tag{3}$$

where $R_{ic,w1}$ represents the ranking value of keyword *ic* in the website w_1, and $1 \leq i < j \leq x$.

3.2 Results

The experiment ran from 20 Nov 2016 to 20 Dec 2016; 717 participants from Sojump with unique IP addresses responded to our study, 693 of whom were qualified for further analysis, and the others did not pass the cheating test since they provide fake information of their multiple accounts in social media websites. The qualified users were assigned to the two conditions DLPDS and nDLPDS randomly (N1 = 351, N2 = 342).

In the condition DLPDS shown in Fig. 3A, users share more information (average disclosures = 13) than the users in the condition nDLPDS (average disclosures = 3) in Fig. 3B, especially in the first 16 days (item 1–16). As a result, the prediction accuracy for recommending the items is comparatively higher of the recommender system in condition DLPDS (average prediction accuracy = 33.71%) than the recommender system in condition nDLPDS (average prediction accuracy = 19.85%). We believe the enrich information has promoted the recommendation accuracy. As a result, our DLPDS model of learning users' past sharing behaviors for the privacy default settings has somehow reduced the effect of cold start. On this basis, in the later 15 days (item 17–31), users demonstrate higher disclosure volume (average disclosures 70 > 38) and the recommender system performs better recommendation accuracy (average prediction accuracy 85.61% > 63.2%).

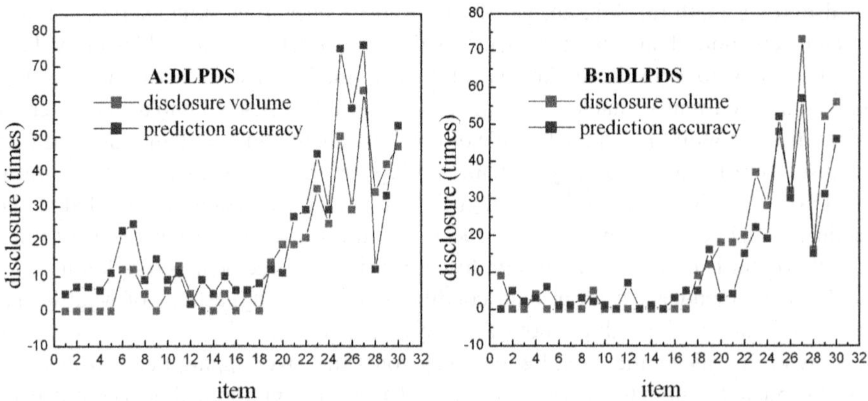

Fig. 3. The information sharing volume and prediction accuracy in DLPDS and nDLPDS

In order to know what makes the phenomenon happen, we require the users to forward their comments during they are participating the experiment in both conditions. The comments could be positive: e.g. "I believe the privacy requesting strategies is good" or negative: e.g. "The information requesting is terrible and offensive". We use the nature language processing techniques to distinguish the each comment is positive, negative, or neutral. Two counters *P* and *N* are initialized as 0 to record the times of positive and negative comments. Whenever there detects a positive (negative) comment, the counter *P.counter* (*N.counter*) will +1.

We regard the negative comments as users' awareness of potential risk. Shown in Fig. 4A, users' risk awareness is generally decreasing in both conditions, which support that recommender system has provide good suggestions of what items to view, and help users gain trust from the recommendation benefits. Comparatively, in the condition DLPDS the recommender system, where the default privacy setting is applied, has successfully ease the effect of cold start problem with low rate of negative comment. In contrast, the recommender system in condition nDLPDS has demonstrated the confronted problem of cold start, which should be caused by the one-for-all privacy collection strategy.

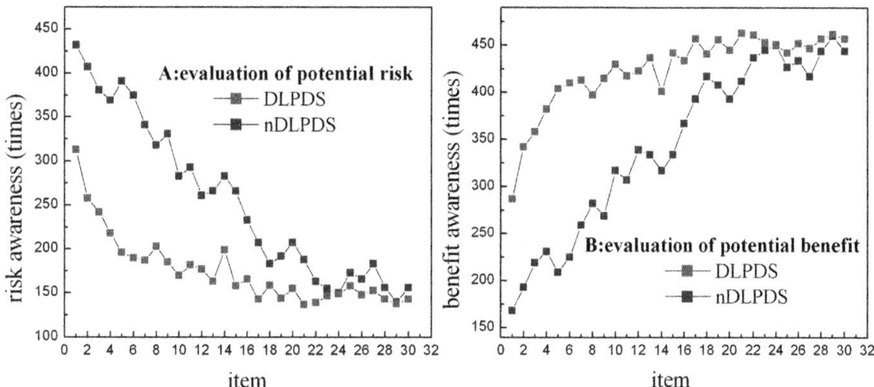

Fig. 4. Users' evaluation of potential risk in A and potential benefit in B

Similarly, we regard a positive comment from each user as his/her awareness of potential benefit, shown in Fig. 4B. Recommender system has applied the DLPDS model so that the prediction accuracy is increasing. This has persuaded users to comment better and disclose more information. In comparison, in condition DLPDS, recommender system has learned users' sharing behaviors and provided better privacy personalized collection strategies by privacy default setting than the recommender system in condition nDLPDS. As a result, we believe our privacy default setting has gained more trust from users by accustoming the requesting strategy to their intended information-sharing pattern.

We forward possible explanation of why the disclosure-learning default privacy settings could work better than the "one-fits-all" privacy collection agreement. We further look at those users who demonstrate negative comments in the condition nDLPDS, and more than 87% of them follow what their friends are doing against the information collection: just reject the collection request when they have no idea of evaluating the risks and benefits. This phenomenon has approved that bad collection strategy, such as request whoever to sign the privacy agreement before login, will make users upset and raise their privacy concerns, which will further cause them to disclose less information and lower the prediction accuracy of recommender systems.

4 Conclusion and Future Works

This paper aimed to show that users' information sharing behaviors could be adapted from their previous behaviors in the Internet of things, where the cross-domain environment has created an opportunity to transfer and fuse knowledge of users from multiple website account. Our DLPDS model has learned users past information-sharing pattern, and settles the transferred pattern as the privacy default setting. In the experiment we have proved that this privacy default setting technique work better than the one-fit-all privacy collection strategy, both on the volume of privacy collection and users' evaluation of potential risks and benefits. The technique called DLPDS could reduce the effect of cold-start problem and increase the prediction accuracy of recommendation. The findings of this paper has provide evidence that the best method of knowing the users better is not requesting users to sign the privacy agreement, but is adapting to their information sharing behaviors. As a result, this paper could be a good reference for scholars and website mangers to want to collect users' information for increasing the recommendation accuracy without raising their privacy concern. In the future work, we will further check out the factors that influencing users' decision of privacy disclosure in all possible aspects, and other issues could affect the prediction accuracy of a recommender systems in social media and cross-domain environments. Hopefully more interesting phenomenon will be found.

Acknowledgement. This work was supported by the National Natural Science Foundation of China (Nos. 61373081, 61572298); and a project of Shandong province Higher Educational Science and Technology program (No. J17KB178); and Young science and technology project raising fund of Shandong Normal University; and the author Hongchen Wu thanks for the financial support from the China Scholarship Council (CSC, File No. 201306220132).

References

1. Shapira, B., Rokach, L., Freilikhman, S.: Facebook single and cross domain data for recommendation systems. User Model. User-Adap. Interact. **23**, 211–247 (2013)
2. Winoto, P., Tang, T.: If you like the devil wears prada the book, will you also enjoy the devil wears prada the movie? a study of cross-domain recommendations. New Gener. Comput. **26**, 209–225 (2008)
3. Gallina, B., Kashiyarandi, S., Zugsbratl, K., Geven, A.: Enabling cross-domain reuse of tool qualification certification artefacts. In: Bondavalli, A., Ceccarelli, A., Ortmeier, F. (eds.) SAFECOMP 2014. LNCS, vol. 8696, pp. 255–266. Springer, Cham (2014). doi:10.1007/978-3-319-10557-4_28
4. Benisch, M., Kelley, P.G., Sadeh, N., Cranor, L.F.: Capturing location-privacy preferences: quantifying accuracy and user-burden tradeoffs. Pers. Ubiquit. Comput. **15**, 679–694 (2011)
5. Betsch, T., Haberstroh, S., Glöckner, A., Haar, T., Fiedler, K.: The effects of routine strength on adaptation and information search in recurrent decision making. Organ. Behav. Hum. Decis. Process. **84**, 23–53 (2001)
6. Buchanan, T., Paine, C., Joinson, A.N., Reips, U.-D.: Development of measures of online privacy concern and protection for use on the internet. J. Am. Soc. Inf. Sc. Technol. **58**, 157–165 (2007)

7. Compañó, R., Lusoli, W.: The policy maker's anguish: regulating personal data behavior between paradoxes and dilemmas. In: Moore, T., Pym, D., Ioannidis, C. (eds.) Economics of Information Security and Privacy, pp. 169–185. Springer, Heidelberg (2010). doi:10.1007/978-1-4419-6967-5_9
8. Sousa, L.: Facebook and your privacy: who sees the data you share on the biggest social network. Consumer Reports magazine (2012)
9. Fang, L., LeFevre, K.: Privacy wizards for social networking sites. In: Proceedings of the 19th International Conference on World wide web, pp. 351–360 (2010)
10. Baloian, N., Galdames, P., Collazos, C.A., Guerrero, L.A.: A model for a collaborative recommender system for multimedia learning material. In: de Vreede, G.-J., Guerrero, L.A., Marín Raventós, G. (eds.) CRIWG 2004. LNCS, vol. 3198, pp. 281–288. Springer, Heidelberg (2004). doi:10.1007/978-3-540-30112-7_24
11. Kelley, P.G., Cranor, L.F., Sadeh, N.: Privacy as part of the app decision-making process. In: Proceedings of the SIGCHI Conference on Human Factors in Computing Systems. pp. 3393–3402 (2013)
12. Knijnenburg, B.P.: Simplifying privacy decisions: towards interactive and adaptive solutions.In: Proceedings of the RecSys 2013 Workshop on Human Decision Making in Recommender Systems, ACM RecSys 2013, pp. 40–41 (2013)
13. Knijnenburg, B.P., Jin, H.: The persuasive effect of privacy recommendations. In: Twelfth Annual Workshop on HCI Research in MIS, Paper 16 (2013)
14. Knijnenburg, B.P., Kobsa, A.: Making decisions about privacy: information disclosure in context-aware recommender systems. ACM Trans. Interact. Intell. Syst. **3**, 1–23 (2013)
15. Yu, H., Ali, A., Virendra, C., Marsh, S.: Keyphrase-Based Information Sharing in the ACORN Multi-agent Architecture. In: Horlait, E. (ed.) MATA 2000. LNCS, vol. 1931, pp. 243–256. Springer, Heidelberg (2000). doi:10.1007/3-540-45391-1_20
16. Yuan, H., Li, S., Rusconi, P., Aljaffan, N.: When eye-tracking meets cognitive modeling: applications to cyber security systems. In: Tryfonas, T. (ed.) HAS 2017. LNCS, vol. 10292, pp. 251–264. Springer, Cham (2017). doi:10.1007/978-3-319-58460-7_17
17. Aly, A., Van Vyve, M.: Practically efficient secure single-commodity multi-market auctions. In: Grossklags, J., Preneel, B. (eds.) FC 2016. LNCS, vol. 9603, pp. 110–129. Springer, Heidelberg (2017). doi:10.1007/978-3-662-54970-4_7
18. Lipford, H.R., Besmer, A., Watson, J.: Understanding privacy settings in facebook with an audience view. In: Proceedings of the 1st Conference on Usability, Psychology, and Security (2008)
19. Liu, B., Lin, J., Sadeh, N.: Reconciling mobile app privacy and usability on smartphones: could user privacy profiles help? In: Proceedings of the 23rd International Conference on World Wide Web, pp. 201–212 (2014)
20. Madden, M.: Privacy management on social media sites. Pew Internet Report, pp. 1–20 (2012)

New Construction of Low-Hit-Zone Frequency Hopping Sequence Sets with Optimal Partial Hamming Correlation

Zhengqian Li[1], Pinhui Ke[1(✉)], and Zhifan Ye[2]

[1] Fujian Provincial Key Laboratory of Network Security and Cryptology, College of Mathematics and Informatics, Fujian Normal University, Fuzhou 350117, Fujian, People's Republic of China
keph@fjnu.edu.cn

[2] Department of Mathematics and Physics, Fujian Jiangxia University, Fuzhou 350108, Fujian, People's Republic of China

Abstract. A new construction of low-hit-zone (LHZ) frequency hopping sequence (FHS) sets with optimal partial Hamming correlation (PPHC) is proposed in this paper. Our construction yields LHZ FHS sets with optimal PPHC by interleaving techniques, in which short FHSs with good Hamming correlation are used as base sequences while certain appropriate sequences are chosen as shift sequences. The LHZ FHS sets proposed in this paper have new parameters not covered in the literature.

Keywords: Frequency hopping sequence sets · Low-hit-zone · Partial Hamming correlation · Decimated sequence · Interleaving techniques

1 Introduction

Frequency-hopping multiple accesses (FHMA) spread spectrum systems have been applied to Bluetooth, mobile communications, military radio communications, and sonar echolocation systems [3,6,16,17]. In asynchronous FHMA systems, FHS sets are required to have low Hamming correlation throughout the whole period and their optimality is formulated by the Peng-Fan-Lee bound [13] and Niu-Peng-Liu-Liu bound [10]. For a survey of optimal FHSs with respect to these bounds, we refer to [1,2,7,20]. Thus, it is important to design the FHS set with good Hamming correlation properties.

In this paper, we only pay attention to the partial correlation of LHZ FHSs. The FHS design with no-hit-zone (NHZ) or low-hit-zone (LHZ) aims at making Hamming correlation values equal to zero or a very low value within a correlation zone [15]. In recent years, a little progress on the study of the partial Hamming correlation of LHZ FHSs has been made. The first research on constructions of optimal or near optimal LHZ FHS sets was presented by Ma et al. [9] in 2011, after which Niu et al. [12] got two constructions of optimal LHZ FHS sets by

X. Sun et al. (Eds.): ICCCS 2017, Part II, LNCS 10603, pp. 40–49, 2017.
https://doi.org/10.1007/978-3-319-68542-7_4

Table 1. Comparison of the parameters of known LHZ FHS sets with optimal PPHC

Parameters $(L, N, Q, Z_{\text{PH}}, W, H_{\text{LHZ}}(X;W))$	Constrains	Reference
$(N_0N_1, p_1, p_0p_1, \min(N_0, N_1)-1, \frac{i\lambda\omega_0 N_1}{\lambda+\alpha-1} < W \le (i+1)\omega_0 N_1, i+1)$	$\omega_0 \mid N_1, \gcd(N_0, N_1)=1, 0 \le i \le \lambda-1, 0<\alpha<1, p_0(\lambda+\alpha-1)(\min(N_0, N_1)p_1-1) = N_0N_1(\min(N_0,N_1)-p_0)$	Theorem 4 in [14]
$(\frac{q^{n-1}}{l}, T, q^{n-1}, L_z, W, \lceil\frac{W}{M}\rceil)$	$n \ge 1, k=n-1, q^{n-1} = T(L_z+1), l>0, \gcd(l,n)=1, l \mid q-1$	Theorem 2 in [18]
$(W(q^n-1), K, q, v-1, sL_c, s\frac{q^{n-1}-1}{q-1})$	$2 \le W < \frac{(q^n-2)q}{q-1}, Kv = q^n-1, \gcd(r, q^n-1)=1, \gcd((v+1)r^{-1}(\text{mod } q^n-1), L_c)=1, W = r(\text{mod } v), (v+1)Wr^{-1} \equiv 1(\text{mod } q^n-1), 1 \le s \le (q-1)W$	Theorem 2 in [5]
$(T\frac{q^n-1}{l}, M, q^k, v-1, rd, r\frac{q^{n-k}-1}{q-1})$	$2 \le T < \frac{q^k(q^n-1-l)l}{(q^k-1)(q^nl-q^n+1)}, \gcd(l,n)=1, l \mid q-1, Mv = \frac{q^n-1}{l}, \gcd(t, q^n-1) = 1, T \equiv t(\text{mod } v), \gcd\big((v+1)t^{-1}(\text{mod } q^n-1), d\big)=1, (v+1)Tt^{-1} = 1(\text{mod } q^n-1)$	This paper

interleaving techniques in 2012. Besides, Zhou et al. [18] and Han et al. [5] also got some constructions of LHZ FHS sets with optimal PPHC property in 2016 (Table 1).

The outline of this paper is as follows. In Sect. 2, we give some preliminaries on LHZ FHS sets. In Sect. 3, we give some brief introductions to the interleaving techniques and l-decimated sequences. In Sect. 4, we present a construction of LHZ FHS sets with optimal PPHC property, then we give some remarks and illustrate an example. Finally, some conclusions are given in Sect. 5.

2 Preliminaries

Let $\mathcal{F} = \{f_0, f_1, \cdots, f_{Q-1}\}$ be a frequency slot set with Q available frequency slots, also called an alphabet. A set $X = \{x_0, x_1, \cdots, x_{N-1}\}$ be an FHS set with N frequency hopping sequences of length L over $\mathcal{F}$ if $x_i \in X$ for all $0 \le i < N$.

For any two frequency slots $x_i, x_j \in X$, let $x_i = \{x_i(0), x_i(1), \cdots, x_i(L-1)\}$, $x_j = \{x_j(0), x_j(1), \cdots, x_j(L-1)\}$, $0 \le i, j < N$. For any integer τ, $0 \le \tau < L$, the periodic Hamming correlation function of x_i and x_j at a time delay τ is defined by

$$H_{x_i,x_j}(\tau) = \sum_{t=0}^{L-1} h[x_i(t), x_j(t+\tau)],$$

where

$$h[x_i(t), x_j(t+\tau)] = \begin{cases} 1, & \text{if } x_i(t) = x_j(t+\tau); \\ 0, & \text{otherwise}, \end{cases}$$

and all operations among the position indices are performed modulo L. When $x_i = x_j$, $H_{x_i,x_j}(\tau)$ is called periodic Hamming autocorrelation of x_i, and denoted by $H_{x_i}(\tau)$ for short.

The maximum periodic Hamming autocorrelation $H(x_i)$ of sequence x_i is defined by

$$H(x_i) = \max_{1 \le \tau < L} \{H_{x_i}(\tau)\}.$$

For simplicity, we denote an FHS of length L over an alphabet of size Q with maximum periodic Hamming autocorrelation H as an (L, Q, H) FHS.

Early in 1974, Lempel and Greenberger established a lower bound on the maximum periodic Hamming autocorrelation as follows [8].

Lemma 1 (Lempel-Greenberger bound). *Let x_i be an (L, Q, H) FHS. Then we have*

$$H \ge \left\lceil \frac{(L-r)(L+r-Q)}{(L-1)Q} \right\rceil \tag{1}$$

where r is the least nonnegative meeting $L \equiv r \pmod{Q}$, and $\lceil t \rceil$ means the least integer greater than or equal to t.

Definition 1. *For an FHS x_i, when the formula above is valid with equality, it is called an optimal FHS.*

For two FHSs $x_i, x_j \in X$, the partial Hamming correlation with a correlation window length W starting at k is defined by

$$H_{x_i,x_j}(k \mid W; \tau) = \sum_{t=k}^{k+W-1} h[x_i(t), x_j(t+\tau)], \; 0 \le \tau, k < L, \; 1 \le W \le L,$$

where all the operations among the position indices are performed modulo L.

For the FHS set X with window W $(1 \le W < L)$, let $H_{\mathrm{LHZ}}(X; L)$ be a given nonnegative integer. Then the LHZ Z_{PH} with respect to partial Hamming correlation is defined by $Z_{\mathrm{PH}} = \min\{Z_{\mathrm{P}_1}, Z_{\mathrm{P}_2}\}$, where Z_{P_1} and Z_{P_2} are defined as follows.

$$\begin{aligned} Z_{\mathrm{P}_1} &= \max\big\{\delta \mid H_{x_i}(k \mid W; \tau) \le H_{\mathrm{LHZ}}(X; W), \text{ for} \\ &\qquad 0 \le k < L, 1 \le \tau \le \delta, \forall x_i \in X\big\}, \\ Z_{\mathrm{P}_2} &= \max\big\{\delta \mid H_{x_i,x_j}(k \mid W; \tau) \le H_{\mathrm{LHZ}}(X; W), \text{ for} \\ &\qquad 0 \le k < L, 0 \le \tau \le \delta, \forall x_i, x_j \in X, x_i \ne x_j\big\}. \end{aligned}$$

We denote an LHZ FHS set X with N FHSs of length L over an alphabet of size Q, and maximum partial Hamming correlation $H_{\mathrm{LHZ}}(X; W)$ over all correlation windows of length W within the LHZ Z_{PH} as $(L, N, Q, Z_{\mathrm{PH}}, W, H_{\mathrm{LHZ}}(X; W))$ LHZ FHS set.

In 2010, Niu et al. [10] obtained the following lower bound on the maximum partial Hamming correlation within the correlation window length W of an LHZ FHS set.

Lemma 2 (Niu-Peng-Liu-Liu bound). *Let X be an FHS set with the above mentioned parameters, then we have*

$$H_{\mathrm{LHZ}}(X;W) \geq \left\lceil \frac{(NZ_{\mathrm{PH}}+N-Q)W}{(NZ_{\mathrm{PH}}+N-1)Q} \right\rceil. \tag{2}$$

Definition 2. *For any FHS set X, when the formular above is valid with equality for the given correlation window length W. It is called an LHZ FHS set with optimal partial Hamming correlation.*

3 Interleaving Techniques and l-decimated Sequence

Firstly, we give a brief introduction to the interleaving techniques. The interleaving techniques were introduced by Gong in [4].

3.1 Interleaving Techniques

Let $\boldsymbol{a} = (a(0), a(1), \cdots, a(L-1))$ be an (L, Q, H) FHS, and $\boldsymbol{e} = (e_0, e_1, \cdots, e_{T-1})$ be a shift sequence of length T over $\mathbb{Z}_L$, i.e., $e_i \in \mathbb{Z}_L$, $0 \leq i < T$. An $L \times T$ matrix is formed by placing the shifts of sequence $\boldsymbol{a}$ referred to $\boldsymbol{e}$ as follows

$$A = \begin{pmatrix} a(0+e_0) & a(0+e_1) & \cdots & a(0+e_{T-1}) \\ a(1+e_0) & a(1+e_1) & \cdots & a(1+e_{T-1}) \\ \vdots & \vdots & \ddots & \vdots \\ a(L-1+e_0) & a(L-1+e_1) & \cdots & a(L-1+e_{T-1}) \end{pmatrix},$$

where the additions in parentheses are computed modulo L. By reading the elements in A row by row, we get a sequence $A^{'} = (a_0, a_1, \cdots, a_{LT-1})$ of period LT. We say $A^{'}$ an (L, T) interleaved sequence associated with $(\boldsymbol{a}, \boldsymbol{e})$, where $\boldsymbol{a}$ and $\boldsymbol{e}$ are called the base sequence and the shift sequence, respectively. For short, we write the interleaved sequence as

$$A^{'} = \boldsymbol{I}(\boldsymbol{L}^{e_0}(a), \boldsymbol{L}^{e_1}(a), \cdots, \boldsymbol{L}^{e_{T-1}}(a)),$$

where $\boldsymbol{I}$ is interleaving operator, and $\boldsymbol{L}$ is shift operator, i.e., $L^i(a) = (a(i), a(i+1), \cdots, a(0), a(1), \cdots, a(i-1))$.

3.2 l-decimated Sequence

For an m-sequence $s = \{s(x) | 0 \leq x < q^n - 1\}$ over $\mathbb{F}_q$ of degree n, there exists $\beta \in \mathbb{F}_{q^n}^*$ such that each element of s can be represented as

$$s(x) = tr_{q^n/q}(\beta\alpha^x),\ 0 \leq x < q^n - 1,$$

where $tr_{q^n/q}(x) = \sum\limits_{i=0}^{n-1} x^{q^i}$ is the trace function from $\mathbb{F}_{q^n}$ to $\mathbb{F}_q$.

Lemma 3 (Shift-and-add property [3]). *Let s be a sequence over $\mathbb{F}_q$ of degree n. Then s is an m-sequence if and only if for each pair (i,j), $0 \le i,j \le q^n - 1$, and $c,d \in \mathbb{F}_q$, either there exists some k, $0 \le k \le q^n - 2$ such that*

$$c\boldsymbol{L}^i s + d\boldsymbol{L}^j s = \boldsymbol{L}^k s$$

or $c\boldsymbol{L}^i s + d\boldsymbol{L}^j s$ is the zero sequence.

Definition 3. *Let l be any positive integer with $l \mid (q-1)$ and $gcd(l,n) = 1$, and s be any m-sequence over F_q of degree n. Then the l-decimated sequence $a_s = \{a_s(x) \mid 0 \le x < \frac{q^n-1}{l}\}$ of s can be defined as*

$$a_s(x) = s(lx),\ 0 \le x < \tfrac{q^n-1}{l}.$$

Definition 4. *Let s be an m-sequence over $\mathbb{F}_q$ of degree n. Then we can define a sequence*

$$c = \{c(x) : 0 \le x < \frac{q^n-1}{l}\} = \{g^k_{a_s}(x) : 0 \le x < \frac{q^n-1}{l}\} \tag{3}$$

over $\mathbb{F}_q^k$ as where $g^k_{a_s}(x) = (s(lx), s(l(x+1)), \cdots, s(l(x+k-1)))$, $0 \le x < \frac{q^n-1}{l}$.

Lemma 4 [19]. *Let a_s be the l-decimated sequence of m-sequence s of length $q^n - 1$. Then there are $q^{n-k} - 1$ and $\frac{q^{n-k}-1}{l}$ zero element $\boldsymbol{0}^k$ in $g^k_s(x)$ and $g^k_{a_s}(x)$, respectively.*

Lemma 5. *For any sequence $c = g^k_{a_s}(x)$ of length $\frac{q^n-1}{l}$ over $\mathbb{F}_q^k$, every segment of $\frac{q^n-1}{q-1}$ consecutive symbols contains exactly $\frac{q^{n-k}-1}{q-1}$ zeros.*

Proof. Let α be a primitive element of $\mathbb{F}_{q^n}$ and $d = \frac{q^n-1}{q-1}$, then $\beta = \alpha^d$ is a primitive element of $\mathbb{F}_q$. For the sequence c in Definition 4, we can write it as

$$c(x) = \big(tr_{q^n/q}(\gamma\alpha^{lx}), tr_{q^n/q}(\gamma\alpha^{l(x+1)}), \cdots, tr_{q^n/q}(\gamma\alpha^{l(x+k-1)})\big),$$

where $0 \le x < \frac{q^n-1}{l}$. Let $x = id + j$, $d = \frac{q^n-1}{q-1}$, $0 \le i < \frac{q-1}{l}$, $0 \le j < d$. Then we have

$$\begin{aligned} c(x) &= \big(tr_{q^n/q}(\gamma\alpha^{idl+jl}), tr_{q^n/q}(\gamma\alpha^{idl+(j+1)l}), \cdots, tr_{q^n/q}(\gamma\alpha^{idl+(j+k-1)l})\big) \\ &= \alpha^{idl}\big(tr_{q^n/q}(\gamma\alpha^{jl}), tr_{q^n/q}(\gamma\alpha^{(j+1)l}), \cdots, tr_{q^n/q}(\gamma\alpha^{(j+k-1)l})\big) \\ &= \eta^i c(j), \end{aligned}$$

where $\eta = \alpha^{dl} \in \mathbb{F}_q^*$. Thus, if we arrange the sequence c into a $\frac{q-1}{l} \times d$ array, then c has the array structure defined by Zhou et al. in [19]. Then the conclusion follows. □

4 Construction of Optimal Partial LHZ FHS Sets

In this section, by using of interleaving techniques and one l-decimated sequence of m-sequence, we will introduce a construction of LHZ FHS sets with optimal partial Hamming correlation.

Lemma 6. *Let c be a sequence of length $\frac{q^n-1}{l}$ over $\mathbb{F}_q^k$ in* (3). *Then c is an optimal* $(\frac{q^n-1}{l}, q^k, \frac{q^{n-k}-1}{l})$ *FHS with respect to the Lempel-Greenberger bound.*

Proof. Put $\frac{q^n-1}{l}$ and q^k, which are just the length and alphabet size of the sequence c into the bound (1). We know that the maximum periodic Hamming autocorrelation

$$H \geq \left\lceil \frac{(\frac{q^n-1}{l} - r)(\frac{q^n-1}{l} + r - q^k)}{(\frac{q^n-1}{l} - 1)q^k} \right\rceil$$

$$\geq \left\lceil \frac{(q^n - 1 - rl)(q^n - 1 + rl - q^k l)}{(q^n - 1 - l)q^k l} \right\rceil$$

$$= \left\lceil \frac{q^{n-k} - 1}{l} - \frac{(q^k - 1)(q^n l - q^n - rl^2 + 1) + rl^2(r - 1)}{q^k(q^n l - l - l^2)} \right\rceil,$$

where r is the least nonnegative residue of $\frac{q^k-1}{l}$ modulo q^k. Clearly, we have

$$0 < \frac{(q^k - 1)(q^n l - q^n - rl^2 + 1) + rl^2(r - 1)}{q^k(q^n l - l - l^2)} < \frac{(q^k - 1)(q^n l - q^n + 1)}{q^k(q^n l - l - l^2)} < 1,$$

where the last inequality follows from the assumption that $l|(q-1)$. Then it follows that

$$H \geq \frac{q^{n-k} - 1}{l}.$$

Therefore, sequence c is a $(\frac{q^n-1}{l}, q^k, \frac{q^{n-k}-1}{l})$ FHS meeting the Lempel-Greenberger bound. □

New Construction:

Step 1: Select a $(\frac{q^n-1}{l}, q^k, \frac{q^{n-k}-1}{l})$ FHS $c = \big(c(0), c(1), \cdots, c(\frac{q^n-1}{l} - 1)\big)$ in (3).
Step 2: Let M, v, T and t be four positive integers such that $2 \leq T < \frac{q^k(q^n-1-l)l}{(q^k-1)(q^n l - q^n + 1)}$, $Mv = \frac{q^n-1}{l}$, $\gcd(t, q^n - 1) = 1$, $\gcd\big((v+1)t^{-1} (\mathrm{mod}\ q^n - 1), d\big) = 1$, and $(v+1)Tt^{-1} = 1 (\mathrm{mod}\ q^n - 1)$.
Generate a shift sequence set $E = \{e^i \mid 0 \leq i < M\}$, where for each $0 \leq i < M$, $e^i = (e_0^i, e_1^i, \cdots, e_{T-1}^i) = \big(ivt^{-1} (\mathrm{mod}\ \frac{q^n-1}{l}), (iv + (v+1)t^{-1}) (\mathrm{mod}\ \frac{q^n-1}{l}), \cdots, (iv + (v+1)(T-1))t^{-1} (\mathrm{mod}\ \frac{q^n-1}{l})\big)$.
Step 3: Construct FHS set $C = \{c^i = c^i(x) \mid 0 \leq i < M, 0 \leq x < T\frac{q^n-1}{l}\}$, where for each $0 \leq i < M$, $c^i = \big(c^i(0), c^i(1), \cdots, c^i(T\frac{q^n-1}{l} - 1)\big) = \boldsymbol{I}\big(\boldsymbol{L}^{ivt^{-1} (\mathrm{mod}\ \frac{q^n-1}{l})}(c), \boldsymbol{L}^{(iv+(v+1)t^{-1}) (\mathrm{mod}\ \frac{q^n-1}{l})}(c), \cdots, \boldsymbol{L}^{(iv+(v+1)(T-1))t^{-1} (\mathrm{mod}\ \frac{q^n-1}{l})}(c)\big)$.

Theorem 1. *The FHS set C obtained by above Construction is a $(T\frac{q^n-1}{l}, M, q^k, v-1, rd, r\frac{q^{n-k}-1}{q-1})$ LHZ FHS set with optimal partial Hamming correlation if T satisfies $T \equiv t (mod\ v)$, where $d = \frac{q^n-1}{q-1}$.*

Proof. By Theorem 2 in [11], we know that C is an $(T\frac{q^n-1}{l}, M, q^k, v-1, T\frac{q^{n-k}-1}{l})$ LHZ FHS set when $T \equiv t(\text{mod } v)$. So we only need to prove that the sequence set C possesses optimal partial Hamming correlation.

By the matrix representation, the FHS c^i can be written as

$$\begin{pmatrix} C(ivt^{-1}) & C((iv+(v+1)t^{-1})) & \cdots & C((iv+(v+1)j)t^{-1}) & \cdots & C((iv+(v+1)(T-1))t^{-1}) \\ C(ivt^{-1}+1) & C((iv+(v+1)t^{-1})+1) & \cdots & C((iv+(v+1)j)t^{-1}+1) & \cdots & C((iv+(v+1)(T-1))t^{-1}+1) \\ \vdots & \vdots & \ddots & \vdots & \ddots & \vdots \\ C(ivt^{-1}+y) & C((iv+(v+1)t^{-1})+y) & \cdots & C((iv+(v+1)j)t^{-1}+y) & \cdots & C((iv+(v+1)(T-1))t^{-1}+y) \\ \vdots & \vdots & \ddots & \vdots & \ddots & \vdots \\ C(ivt^{-1}-1) & C((iv+(v+1)t^{-1})-1) & \cdots & C((iv+(v+1)j)t^{-1}-1) & \cdots & C((iv+(v+1)(T-1))t^{-1}-1) \end{pmatrix}$$

where the additions in parentheses are computed modulo $\frac{q^n-1}{l}$.

Let $x = yT+j, 0 \le y < \frac{q^n-1}{l}, 0 \le j < T$. From $(v+1)Tt^{-1} \equiv 1(\mod q^n-1)$, we have

$$\begin{aligned} c^i(x) &= c\big((iv+(v+1)j)t^{-1}+y)\big) \\ &= c\big((iv+(v+1)(x-yT))t^{-1}+y)\big) \\ &= c\big((iv+(v+1)x)t^{-1}+[1-(v+1)Tt^{-1}]y)\big) \\ &= c\big((iv+(v+1)x)t^{-1}\big). \end{aligned}$$

Then the partial Hamming correlation between two sequence $c^{i_1}, c^{i_2} \in C$, $0 \le i_1, i_2 < M$ with the correlation window length rd starting at w is

$$\begin{aligned} & H_{c^{i_1},c^{i_2}}(w \mid rd) \\ &= \sum_{x=w}^{w+rd-1} h\big[c\big((i_1v+(v+1)x)t^{-1}\big), c\big((i_2v+(v+1)(x+\tau))t^{-1}\big)\big] \\ &= \sum_{x=w}^{w+rd-1} h\big[g^k_{a_s}\big((i_1v+(v+1)x)t^{-1}\big), g^k_{a_s}\big((i_2v+(v+1)(x+\tau))t^{-1}\big)\big] \\ &= \sum_{x=w}^{w+rd-1} h\big[g^k_{a_s}\big((i_1v+(v+1)x)t^{-1}\big) - g^k_{\mathbf{L}^{\tau(v+1)t^{-1}}a_s}\big((i_2v+(v+1)x)t^{-1}\big), \mathbf{0}^k\big] \\ &= \sum_{x=w}^{w+rd-1} h\big[g^k_{\mathbf{L}^{i_1vt^{-1}}a_s}\big((v+1)xt^{-1}\big) - g^k_{\mathbf{L}^{(\tau(v+1)+i_2v)t^{-1}}a_s}\big((v+1)xt^{-1}\big), \mathbf{0}^k\big] \\ &= \sum_{x=w}^{w+rd-1} h\big[g^k_{\mathbf{L}^{i_1vt^{-1}}a_s - \mathbf{L}^{(\tau(v+1)+i_2v)t^{-1}}a_s}(x'), \mathbf{0}^k\big]. \quad (\textit{Let } x' = (v+1)t^{-1}x) \end{aligned}$$

And

$$\begin{aligned}\boldsymbol{L}^{i_1vt^{-1}}a_s(x') - \boldsymbol{L}^{(\tau(v+1)+i_2v)t^{-1}}a_s(x') &= \boldsymbol{L}^{i_1vt^{-1}}s(lx') - \boldsymbol{L}^{(\tau(v+1)+i_2v)t^{-1}}s(lx')\\ &= \left(\boldsymbol{L}^{i_1vt^{-1}} - \boldsymbol{L}^{(\tau(v+1)+i_2v)t^{-1}}\right)s(lx')\\ &= \left(\boldsymbol{L}^{i_1vt^{-1}}s - \boldsymbol{L}^{(\tau(v+1)+i_2v)t^{-1}}s\right)(lx')\\ &= a_{\boldsymbol{L}^{i_1vt^{-1}}s-\boldsymbol{L}^{(\tau(v+1)+i_2v)t^{-1}}s}(x').\end{aligned}$$

In the light of Lemma 3, $\boldsymbol{L}^{i_1vt^{-1}}s - \boldsymbol{L}^{(\tau(v+1)+i_2v)t^{-1}}s$ is always the zero sequence if $(i_1-i_2)vt^{-1}+\tau(v+1)t^{-1} \equiv 0 \mod (q^n-1)$, while it equals $\boldsymbol{L}^{i'}$, $0 \le i' < q^n-1$ if $(i_1-i_2)vt^{-1}+\tau(v+1)t^{-1} \not\equiv 0 \mod (q^n-1)$.

Case 1. $i_1 = i_2$ and $1 \le \tau \le v-1$. In this case, $(i_1-i_2)vt^{-1}+\tau(v+1)t^{-1} \not\equiv 0 \mod (q^n-1)$ is always true. Then $H_{c^{i_1}}(w \mid rd; \tau)$ equals to

$$\left|\left\{x \mid g^k_{\boldsymbol{L}^{i_1vt^{-1}}a_s - \boldsymbol{L}^{(\tau(v+1)+i_2v)t^{-1}}a_s}((v+1)t^{-1}x) = 0, x = w, w+1, \cdots, w+rd-1\right\}\right|.$$

Let $x' = w_0d + w_1$, where $w_0 > 0$, $0 \le w_1 < d$, i.e. $(v+1)t^{-1}x = w_0d + w_1$. Since $\gcd\big((v+1)t^{-1}(\text{mod } q^n-1), d\big) = 1$, w_1 traverses all the elements in $\{0, 1, \cdots, d\}$ r times as x takes all the elements in $\{w, w+1, \cdots, w+rd-1\}$. Then by Lemma 5, we have $H_{c^{i_1}}(w \mid rd; \tau) = r\frac{q^{n-k}-1}{q-1}$.

Case 2. $i_1 \ne i_2$, $0 \le \tau \le v-1$. Similar to the proof of Case 1, we can get

$$H_{c^{i_1},c^{i_2}}(w \mid rd; \tau) = \begin{cases} rd, & \text{if } (i_1-i_2)vt^{-1}+\tau(v+1)t^{-1} \equiv 0 \text{ mod}(q^n-1);\\ r\frac{q^{n-k}-1}{q-1}, & \text{otherwise.}\end{cases}$$

It is obvious that $H_{c^{i_1},c^{i_2}}(w \mid rd; \tau) = rd$ is impossible for $0 \le \tau \le v-1$. In brief, we have $H_{c^{i_1},c^{i_2}}(w \mid rd; \tau) = r\frac{q^{n-k}-1}{q-1}$, $1 \le r \le T\frac{q-1}{l}$, for $1 \le \tau \le v-1$ when $i_1 = i_2$, and for $0 \le \tau \le v-1$, $i_1 \ne i_2$. Thus C is an $(T\frac{q^n-1}{l}, M, q^k, v-1, rd, r\frac{q^{n-k}-1}{q-1})$ LHZ FHS set.

We then check the optimality of C with respect to the bound (2)

$$\begin{aligned}H_{LHZ}(C; rd) &\ge \left\lceil \frac{(M(v-1)+M-q^k)rd}{(M(v-1)+M-1)q^k} \right\rceil\\ &= \left\lceil \frac{(q^n-1-q^kl)(q^n-1)r}{(q^n-1-l)(q-1))q^k} \right\rceil\\ &= \left\lceil r\frac{q^{n-k}-1}{q-1} - \frac{(q^k-1)(q^nl-q^n+1)r}{q^k(q^n-1-l)(q-1)} \right\rceil.\end{aligned}$$

Since $1 \le r \le T\frac{q-1}{l}$, and $2 \le T < \frac{q^k(q^n-1-l)l}{(q^k-1)(q^nl-q^n+1)}$, then we have $0 < \frac{(q^k-1)(q^nl-q^n+1)r}{q^k(q^n-1-l)(q-1)} < 1$. It follows that $H_{LHZ}(C; rd) \ge r\frac{q^{n-k}-1}{q-1}$.

According to Definition 2, C is a $(T\frac{q^n-1}{l}, M, q^k, v-1, rd, r\frac{q^{n-k}-1}{q-1})$ LHZ FHS set with optimal partial Hamming correlation. □

Remark 1. Our construction yields LHZ FHS sets with optimal PPHC and its parameters is not covered in the literature. Specially, when $k = 1$ and $l = 1$, the FHS set c is a $(W(q^n - 1), K, q, v - 1, sL_c, s\frac{q^{n-1}-1}{q-1})$ FHS set constructed by Han et al. [5].

Remark 2. For any positive integer $1 \leq k \leq n$, we presented a construction of LHZ FHS sets with optimal PPHC. In addition, when $k = n - 1$, $(\frac{q^n-1}{l}, T, q^{n-1}, W, L_Z, \lceil\frac{W}{M}\rceil)$ LHZ FHS sets with optimal PPHC was presented by Zhou and Peng et al. in [18]. In our construction, it holds for any $1 \leq k \leq n$ by Lemma 5.

Finally, we give an example to illustrate our construction.

Example 1. Let $q = 5$, $n = 3$, $l = 2$, $k = 2$, and α be the primitive element of F_{5^3} with $\alpha^3 = 4\alpha^2 + 3$. Then we can get an m-sequence $s = \{120332224243340432042342201003231044111212442024102142110300414302233313122101230132133040023240114443431130314034134402001 4\}$.

We select an $(62, 25, 2)$ FHS $c = \{c(x) \mid 0 \leq x < 62\}$, then $c = \{(1, 0), (0, 3), (3, 2), (2, 4), (4, 4), (4, 3), (3, 0), (0, 3), \cdots\}$. Generate a shift sequence set $E = \{e^i \mid 0 \leq i < 2\}$, such that $e^0 = (0, 16)$, $e^1 = (31, 47)$, where $M = 2$, $v = 31$, $T = 2$, and $t = 33$ $(t^{-1} = 47)$.

We construct the FHS set $C = \{c^0, c^1\}$ by the Construction, where

$$c^0 = \{(1,0), (1,4), (0,3), (4,1), (3,2), (1,1), (2,4), (1,1), (4,4), \cdots\},$$
$$c^1 = \{(4,0), (4,1), (0,2), (1,4), (2,3), (4,4), (3,1), (4,4), (1,1), \cdots\}.$$

For all τ $(\tau \leq 30)$, it can be verified that the maximum partial Hamming correlation of FHS set C is given by $H_{\mathrm{LHZ}}(C; 31r) = r$, where $W = 31r$, $1 \leq r \leq 4$. It is easy to check that $(124, 2, 25, 30, 31r, r)$ LHZ FHS set C meets the bound in (2). That is, the set C is an LHZ FHS set with optimal PPHC.

5 Conclusions

Using an m-sequence and its decimation, we presented a new construction of LHZ FHS sets with optimal partial Hamming correlation. The construction in this paper includes the construction given by Han et al. in 2016 as a special case by taking $k = 1$ and $l = 1$. The proposed FHS sets will be useful as signature sequence to reduce the mutual interference for the quasi-synchronous FHMA systems in practice.

Acknowledgements. The authors would like to thank the reviewers and editors for their detailed and constructive comments, which substantially improved the presentation of the paper. This research was supported by Natural Science Foundation of Fujian Province (No. 2015J01237) and Fujian Normal University Innovative Research Team (IRTL1207).

References

1. Chu, W., Colbourn, C.J.: Optimal frequency-hopping sequences via cyclotomy. IEEE Trans. Inf. Theory **51**(3), 1139–1141 (2005)
2. Chung, J.H., Han, Y.K., Yang, K.: New classes of optimal frequency-hopping sequences by interleaving techniques. IEEE Trans. Inf. Theory **55**(12), 5783–5791 (2009)
3. Golomb, S.W., Gong, G.: Signal Design for Good Correlation: For Wireless Communication, Cryptography, and Radar. Cambridge University Press, Cambridge (2005)
4. Gong, G.: Theory and applications of q-ary interleaved sequences. IEEE Trans. Inf. Theory **41**(2), 400–411 (1995)
5. Han, H., Peng, D., Parampalli, U., Ma, Z., Liang, H.: Construction of low-hit-zone frequency hopping sequences with optimal partial hamming correlation by interleaving techniques. Des. Codes Cryptogr. **84**, 1–14 (2016)
6. Kong, Y., Zhang, M., Ye, D.: A belief propagation-based method for task allocation in open and dynamic cloud environments. Knowl.-Based Syst. **115**, 123–132 (2017)
7. Kumar, P.V.: Frequency-hopping code sequence designs having large linear span. IEEE Trans. Inf. Theory **34**(1), 146–151 (1988)
8. Lempel, A., Greenberger, H.: Families of sequences with optimal hamming-correlation properties. IEEE Trans. Inf. Theory **20**(1), 90–94 (1974)
9. Ma, W., Sun, S.: New designs of frequency hopping sequences with low hit zone. Des. Codes Cryptogr. **60**(2), 145–153 (2011)
10. Niu, X., Peng, D., Liu, F., Liu, X.: Lower bounds on the maximum partial correlations of frequency hopping sequence set with low hit zone. IEICE Trans. Fundam. Electron. Commun. Comput. Sci. **93–A**(11), 2227–2231 (2010)
11. Niu, X., Peng, D., Zhou, Z.: New classes of optimal frequency hopping sequences with low hit zone. Adv. Math. Commun. **7**(3), 111–114 (2011)
12. Niu, X., Zhou, Z.: New classes of optimal low hit zone frequency hopping sequences with new parameters. IEICE Trans. Fundam. Electron. Commun. Comput. Sci. **E95–A**(11), 1835–1842 (2014)
13. Peng, D., Fan, P., Ho, L.M.: Lower bounds on the periodic hamming correlations of frequency hopping sequences with low hit zone. Sci. Chin. Inf. Sci. **93–A**(2), 1569–1572 (2006)
14. Wang, C.Y., Peng, D.Y., Han, H.Y., Zhou, L.M.: New sets of low-hit-zone frequency-hopping sequence with optimal maximum periodic partial hamming correlation. Sci. Chin. Inf. Sci. **58**(12), 1–15 (2015)
15. Wang, X., Fan, P.: A class of frequency hopping sequences with no hit zone. In: International Conference on Parallel and Distributed Computing, Applications and Technologies, pp. 896–898 (2003)
16. Xia, Z., Wang, X., Sun, X., Wang, B.: Steganalysis of least significant bit matching using multiorder differences. Secur. Commun. Netw. **7**(8), 1283–1291 (2014)
17. Yuan, C., Xia, Z., Sun, X.: Coverless image steganography based on SIFT and BOF. J. Internet Technol. **18**(2), 209–216 (2017)
18. Zhou, L., Peng, D., Liang, H., Wang, C., Ma, Z.: Constructions of optimal low-hit-zone frequency hopping sequence sets. Des. Codes Cryptogr. **85**, 1–14 (2016)
19. Zhou, Z., Tang, X., Niu, X., Parampalli, U.: New classes of frequency-hopping sequences with optimal partial correlation. IEEE Trans. Inf. Theory **58**(1), 453–458 (2012)
20. Zhou, Z., Tang, X., Peng, D., Parampalli, U.: New constructions for optimal sets of frequency-hopping sequences. IEEE Trans. Inf. Theory **57**(6), 3831–3840 (2011)

Detecting and Preventing DDoS Attacks in SDN-Based Data Center Networks

Po-Ching Lin(✉), Yu-Ting Hsu, and Ren-Hung Hwang

Department of Computer Science and Information Engineering, National Chung Cheng University, Chiayi, Taiwan
{pclin,rhhwang}@cs.ccu.edu.tw, pisces19930209@gmail.com

Abstract. Distributed denial-of-service (DDoS) attacks are deemed a serious threat to Internet services. A common solution to mitigate the attacks is to redirect traffic to scrubbing centers (SCs) for traffic classification and DDoS filtering. However, the capacity and locations of SCs should be pre-determined, and traffic redirection to SCs also give rise to extra network footprint and long latency. In this work, we present a solution based on network function virtualization (NFV) to launch scrubbing functions on demand and software-defined networking (SDN) to redirect traffic to these functions. We propose a lightweight probing strategy to identify anomalous traffic and the victim, and allocate virtual scrubbing functions close to the victim to minimize network footprint and network latency. We simulate a proof-of-concept design in Mininet to demonstrate its operation. The evaluation shows 96.6% of DDoS packets can be mitigated with the response time of one second.

Keywords: DDoS · SDN · NFV · Virtual scrubbing function · Traffic redirection

1 Introduction

Distributed denial-of-service (DDoS) is a well-known and long-lived attack type in the Internet. The attack can flood a target service with an enormous amount of network traffic from numerous attack sources to easily disrupt a service for various purposes such as extortion and revenge. For defense, the target should be equipped with at least similar amount of capacity to resist the attack. Unfortunately, attackers have an edge in the arms race nowadays due to the existence of botnets, which involve a large number of compromised hosts for generating DDoS traffic [1]. The largest DDoS attack has reached over 1Tbps recently [2]. Therefore, the cost of defense by capacity provisioning becomes prohibitively high and impractical.

To remove DDoS traffic from network traffic, a common practice is deploying *scrubbing centers* (SCs) for traffic cleansing (e.g., [3]). When DDoS attacks are suspected to happen, network traffic will be redirected to an SC, which will filter out DDoS traffic after classification, and forward only normal traffic back

X. Sun et al. (Eds.): ICCCS 2017, Part II, LNCS 10603, pp. 50–61, 2017.
https://doi.org/10.1007/978-3-319-68542-7_5

to the original destination. The computation and network capacity of an SC, which is usually pre-allocated, should be over-provisioned to accommodate a potentially huge amount of DDoS traffic. The locations of SCs should be also strategically determined in advance [4]. However, since the sources and amount of DDoS traffic cannot be predicted before the attack happens, optimizing the deployment locations of SCs is difficult in practice, and a sub-optimal deployment will result in large network footprint and long latency due to traffic detouring. The latter is particularly unacceptable for interactive or delay sensitive network applications.

Due to evolution of cloud computing, computation capacity can be provisioned on demand. Not only many network services have been deployed in a cloud environment for high availability and scalability, but also network functions can. This concept known as network function virtualization (NFV), which allows network functions to be deployed as virtualized devices (known as virtualized network function, i.e., VNF), has motivated intensive study in recent years [5]. The traffic scrubbing function, like other network functions, can be also virtualized, and its total capacity can be expanded *on demand* in NFV to deal with the ever-increasing amount of DDoS traffic. Therefore, the spare computation and network resources in a cloud environment can be allocated to virtualized scrubbing functions (VSFs), and suspicious traffic towards a service in the same environment will be redirected to them for scrubbing DDoS traffic.

In this work, we present use of VSFs in a data center network (DCN) to protect cloud services from DDoS attacks. This design is a solution complementary to deploying global SCs, if the spare capacity of a DCN is sufficient to deal with a DDoS attack. The benefits are that the network footprint can be minimized and the latency due to traffic redirection can be also shortened. Nonetheless, a few questions arise immediately from the promising idea. (1) How is the amount of network traffic in the DCN monitored, and how is suspicious traffic determined? (2) How many VSFs should be allocated or de-allocated based on the amount of DDoS traffic? (3) How should network traffic be redirected and distributed among the VSFs? We assume the DCN is based on software-defined networking (SDN). The switches are OpenFlow capable ones in a hierarchical structure such as a multi-rooted tree and a fat tree [6]. The controller owns a global view of the entire network. It keeps probing the switches for abnormal network traffic surge in the DCN, and configures them to redirect traffic to VSFs if necessary. However, the controller-switch polling and responses in a large DCN will result in a large overhead. Installing per-flow monitoring rules for traffic statistics is also apparently not scalable. Not only the flow table size in the switches is typically limited, but also DDoS attacks usually come with IP spoofing, which will lead to a large number of "flows" and overflow the flow tables easily.

To reduce the number of probes, we design a strategy that probes the switches in higher levels in the DCN hierarchy with higher frequency, and those in lower levels with lower frequency. It is noted that we do not install extra monitoring rules on the switches to count the number of per-flow or per-destination packets, but instead watch the traffic out from the egress ports and monitor how its volume changes over time by entropy analysis. The design focuses on probing in the top level (i.e., having fewer switches), and follows the path of flooding downward to pinpoint the victim virtual machine (VM) *only when traffic flooding is detected in a higher level.* This approach will save the probing overhead in a large DCN. After the victim is identified, the system will launch VSFs surrounding it based on available system resources. The VSFs will be launched and scale proportionally to the amount of DDoS flooding. The switches on the path of flooding will distribute the flooding traffic to the VSFs by using the group tables on the switches. The traffic of the same flows will be distributed to the same VSFs for stateful analysis. After analysis, the VSFs will scrub flooding traffic, while forwarding only normal traffic back to the victim.

The DDoS detection in this design is very lightweight with only few overheads. Only necessary rules for traffic redirection will be installed during DDoS attacks in the design. During a peaceful period, the only overhead to the DCN is the probing packets for DDoS traffic, and it is minimized due to the proposed probing strategy.

The rest of this work is organized as follows. Section 2 reviews existing work that detects and defends DDoS attacks by using SDN/NFV in literature. Section 3 describes the design details, including DDoS detection, dynamic deployment of VSFs and traffic redirection. Section 4 evaluates the method by simulation. This work is concluded in Sect. 5.

2 Related Work

Although DDoS defense is a well studied topic, due to recent development of SDN and NFV, researchers have started to explore approaches to leverage their advanatages of flexible resource allocation and elastic scaling for DDoS defense [7–11]. We focus on reviewing SDN/NFV-based methods for DDoS defense in this section, while referring readers to other good surveys such as [12] for generic DDoS defense issues.

- Based on SDN
  The architecture in [8] is divided into two parts: monitor and correlator. The former is responsible for monitoring and raising an alert, and the latter is responsible for feature identification. Once the form of attack is confirmed, the SDN controller will execute attack containment actions. The work in [9] separates the data collection process from the control plane to reduce the burden, and keeps monitoring data with the employment of sFlow. Once network anomaly is detected, the attack can be effectively mitigated by modifying flow table. BroFlow [10] uses an optimization algorithm to select the locations of sensors and allocate required machines on demand. It can detect and respond in real time, drop malicious traffic from the source as close as it can to significantly reduce the latency caused by the attack.
- Based on NFV
  The work in [7] tackles different types of DDoS attacks with the flexibility of NFV to launch several defensive VMs, and steers traffic to these VMs for

processing via dynamic configuration of SDN. In VGuard [11], the incoming flows are assigned to different tunnels by prioritization to ensure service quality for users, and it redirects traffic to firewall VNFs or DDoS VNFs according to service demand.

In industry, Amazon recently have offered a new DDoS protection service called AWS Shield [13], which claims to block 96% of most common DDoS attacks and will be automatically deployed to protect customers' Elastic Load Balancers, CloudFront and Route 53 services. In addition, customers with AWS Shield Advanced have the flexibility to write customized rules in order to mitigate sophisticated application layer attacks.

3 System Design

In this work, we propose a lightweight NFV-based solution to defend DDoS attacks targeted at services in a DCN. We bear in mind the following features when designing the method. (1) The controller queries for only output port statistics, and no monitoring rules are installed for traffic statistics. The extra flow rules are only those necessary for traffic redirection to the VSFs to save the limited flow table sizes. (2) The probes for traffic statistics focus on the top level of switches, and follow the path of flooding downward from the top level for detailed statistics only when traffic anomaly is detected in a higher level of switches until the victim service is located. (3) The VSFs are launched surrounding the victim to minimize network footprint and latency. The number of VSFs is proportional to the amount of traffic to be analyzed, and can be dynamically allocated or de-allocated on demand. The detail of the method will be described in the following subsections.

3.1 Entropy-Based DDoS Detection

The controller probes for the egress port statistics of a switch and detects traffic anomaly of DDoS by entropy analysis. The probing is feasible by requesting the switch with the `OFPMP_PORT_STATS` multi-part type in the OpenFlow protocol [14] or by polling the sFlow interface counters (www.sflow.org). After getting the traffic statistics from each port, the controller performs the entropy-based analysis similar to the methods presented in [9,15]. However, the entropy is computed on a per-port instead of per-destination-IP basis. The computation is easier because the number of ports is usually much smaller than that of destination IP addresses. Suppose the proportion of the number of packets output to port i among all the ports of the switch in a time interval t is defined as follows:

$$p_i = \frac{n_i}{\sum_{j=1}^{N} n_j}, \tag{1}$$

where N is the number of egress ports and n_j is the number of packets output of port j. We consider using the normalized entropy H_t in the time interval defined as follows:

$$H_t = \frac{-\sum_{i=1}^{N} p_i \log p_i}{\log N}. \tag{2}$$

When a DDoS attack occurs, the entropy will be lower than that in a normal period because the number of packets out from an egress port will dominate the numbers from the other ports. Let H_a and H_n denote the entropy in an interval with and without DDoS attacks. We can assert the occurrence of a DDoS attack if $H_n - H_a > \delta$, where δ is a threshold to specify the amount of decrease in the entropy. To be adapted to the latest traffic status, we let H_n be the moving average of the entropies in the past K time intervals, and δ be $\lambda\rho$, where λ is a multiplicative factor and ρ is the standard deviation of the entropies in the past time intervals. If the decrease is larger than the threshold δ, the controller will configure necessary flow rules to redirect packets targeted at the victim for scrubbing (to be described in Sect. 3.4).

An attacker may evade the entropy-based detection by two strategies. First, he may slowly increase the traffic volume to the victim. Since the detection criterion is adapted to the latest traffic status, there will be no abrupt change in the traffic volume to raise the alarm. Second, he may distribute attack traffic to multiple hosts (including the victim) evenly, so that no traffic volume from a single egress port will dominate the others. To counter the first evasion, we still need to set an upper bound to the traffic volume to a victim. The bounds can be specified according to the capacity of each service. It is noted that if the upper bound is exceeded, the design should redirect the traffic to the VSFs for classification instead of enforcing rate limitation indiscriminately by mechanisms such as meter [14]; otherwise, normal traffic will be also incorrectly filtered out. For the second evasion, if the attack traffic is distributed to multiple victims close to each other (e.g., connected to the same edge switch), this attack can be detected because the entropy in upper-level switches is still low. If the hosts are distributed across the DCN, the entropy in lower-level switches will be low. However, because the probing frequency in lower-level switches is low, the response time in the detection will be slower than that without this evasion. This problem is an inevitable tradeoff between the probing overhead and the response time. Nonetheless, the attacker must send much more attack traffic than targeting at a single victim for the second evasion. In other words, the attacker will pay for the second evasion.

3.2 Probing Strategy

To reduce the probing overhead, we focus primarily on the top-level switches by probing them with higher frequency than those in low levels. Since the switches in the top level are relatively few, the overall probing overhead will be rather low. Consider the scenario in Fig. 1, in which the DDoS traffic follows the red arrows to attack the victim in the second rack from the left. At first thought, the controller can probe the switches only in the top level, and go to the next level only if traffic anomaly is detected on some switch (i.e., the left core switch in this example). In the second level, only the switch connected to the egress port to which the DDoS traffic is forwarded (i.e., the leftmost aggregate switch in this example) is probed. The process goes on by making the probing follow the path of traffic anomaly until the victim is located. The complexity of probing is just $O(h)$, where h is the height of the DCN hierarchy. However, if the controller probes only the top-level switches in a normal period, the controller will be unable to track the decrease of entropy on the lower-level switches in the past time intervals. Therefore, the controller still needs to probe the lower-level switches in a normal period, but with lower frequency.

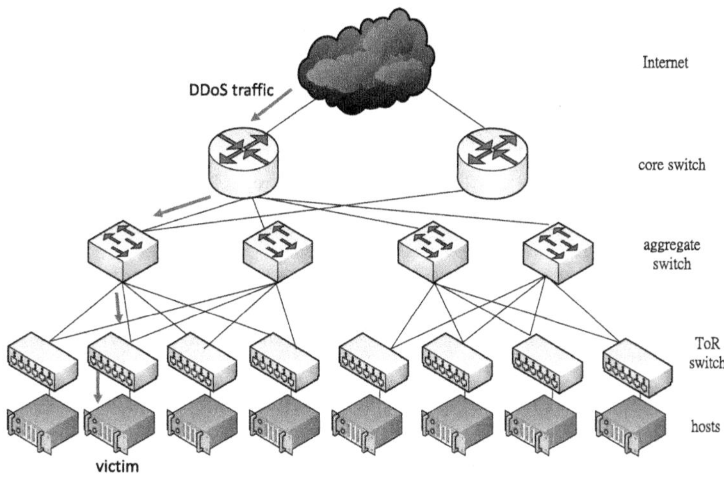

Fig. 1. The attack path of DDoS traffic in a DCN (Color figure online).

We use the following rule of thumb to determine the probing frequency. Suppose the number of switches in the $(i + 1)$-th level in the DCN hierarchy is k times that in the i-th level, where the level is numbered from the top. In a normal period, if the controller probes every switch in the i-th level every t seconds, then it will probe the switches in the next level every αkt seconds, where $\alpha \geq 1$. Thus, the probes to the $(i+1)$-th level will be no more than those to the i-th level. In this period, since there is no abrupt change in the traffic from the upper level, it is fine to probe the lower levels with lower frequency.

3.3 VSF Allocation

The VSFs are allocated and launched to scrub DDoS traffic once it is detected from probing. The positions of VSFs should be near the victim to reduce network footprint and latency. Let the total traffic volume, including normal and DDoS traffic, to the victim be b_v. $c(p)$ denotes the total traffic volume that can be handled by the VSFs on physical machine (PM) p, and the volume is proportional to the available capacity of p. For simplicity, we assume the VSFs have the same capacity (i.e., being allocated with identical resources), and the PMs with different capacity will be allocated with different number of VSFs. We order the PMs by their distance to the victim as $p_1, p_2, \ldots$, from short to long. The distance is calculated by the number of switches on the shortest path from a PM to the victim. For example, if the PM is on the same rack as the victim, the distance is 1. Then, we allocate and launch VSFs on m PMs surrounding the victim according to this order until $\sum_{i=1}^{m} c(p_i) \geq b_v$.

3.4 Traffic Redirection and Scrubbing

Figure 2 illustrates how normal and DDoS traffic is redirected and distributed to the VSFs on the underlying PMs. According to Sect. 3.3, the VSFs are allocated around the victim and their number is sufficient to accommodate the total traffic, which will be distributed to them according to their scrubbing capacity. The software switches on the PMs are virtual ones to distribute the traffic to the VSFs. After scrubbing, only normal traffic will be redirected back to the victim. We do not assume how the VSFs classify and filter DDoS traffic, as that mechanism is beyond the scope of this work.

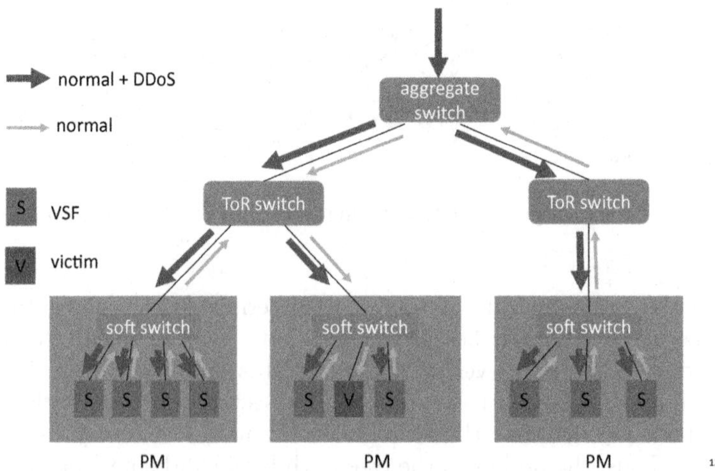

Fig. 2. Traffic redirection for DDoS scrubbing.

We use the `select` group type in the group table to distribute traffic to the VSFs. Upon detecting traffic anomaly, the controller will configure a flow entry in the flow table to forward the packets from the uplink port and destined for the victim to a group entry in the group table on the switches in the path toward the VSFs. The flow entry is basically in the following format:

```
if in_port==uplink_port and ipv4_dst==victim
then actions=some group entry
```

The target group entry contains the action buckets with weights to forward the packets to the VSFs. For each packet, the switch selects a single action bucket by symmetric hashing (i.e., exchanging the source and destination addresses does not affect the bucket selection) to ensure packets of the same flow will go to the same VSFs for stateful analysis. A packet will be forwarded to some VSF according to the output instruction in the selected bucket.

After the flow entry to forward the packets destined for the victim to the group table has been installed on each switch, the weights for the egress ports are configured proportional to the capacity of the underlying VSFs in a bottom-up approach as follows. (1) In the software switches, the number of buckets are the number of VSFs on that PM. Since we assume all the VSFs have the same capacity, the bucket weights are all 1. The design can be easily extended for different weights. For normal traffic after scrubbing, we install a rule that specifies packets from the port linked to a VSF and destined for the victim to be forwarded to the egress port according to shortest path computation. The rule looks like the aforementioned format, but the action becomes output to the egress port. (2) In the top-of-rack (ToR) switches, the number of buckets are the number of PMs that have VSFs allocated. The bucket weight for an egress port is set to w if the port is linked to a PM with w VSFs. Like the software switches, we also install a rule for the ports linked to the PMs with VSFs, and the rule is defined similarly. (3) In the aggregate or core switches, the weight of a bucket is the number of underlying VSFs from the egress port specified in that bucket. The rest is defined similarly.

4 Evaluation

We simulate the DDoS defense architecture in Mininet (mininet.org). The embedded Open vSwitch (openvswitch.org) in Mininet is upgraded to the latest version 2.7.0 for better support of the group table. Because Mininet does not support simulating VMs within PMs, we eliminate the level of software switches in the simulation, and make the hosts in the bottom level play as the roles of VMs in the design. The simulated DCN hierarchy involves three levels. From the top level to the edge (i.e., top of rack) are 1, 4 and 16 switches, and under each top-of-rack switch are 5 hosts. Thus, totally 80 hosts are in the simulated DCN. Despite the minor change, the simulation is still similar to the illustration in Fig. 2, if we consider the hosts as VMs, top-of-rack switches as software switches, and so on. The link capacities are all 1 Gb/s. Although the simulated environment is much smaller than a real one, it is a proof-of-concept design to evaluate the correctness of the presented idea and the efficiency of DDoS mitigation.

Figure 3 illustrates part of the DCN topology in the simulation. Like Fig. 2, V denotes the victim, S denotes the VSFs, and H denotes the hosts used by other tenants. An external host sends DDoS packets with IP spoofing to simulate distributed attacks. Suppose four VSFs surrounding the victim are sufficient in capacity to handle the DDoS traffic plus normal traffic. The group tables are configured for traffic distribution according to the descriptions in Sect. 3.4. For example, the weights of the action buckets on S6 are all 1's to distribute traffic uniformly to the VSFs under it, and the weights of the action buckets on S2 are 3 and 1 for S6 and S7 due to the number of allocated VSFs under the two switches. In the VSFs, the kernel option `ip_forward` (for acting as a router) is enabled to simulate redirecting normal traffic back to the victim, and `rp_filter` (for reverse path filtering [16]) is disabled to simulate all incoming traffic, including IP spoofed packets, will be handled by the classification function in the VSFs, rather than by the Linux kernel.

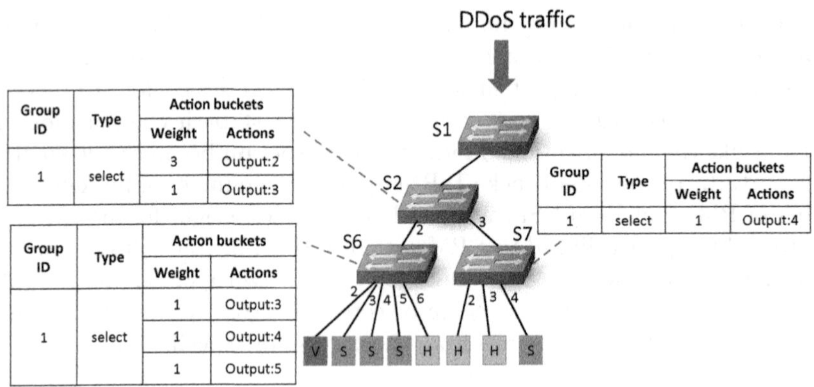

Fig. 3. Group table setup.

4.1 Traffic Distribution

After setting up the topology, the hosts ping each other for the switches to learn the position of each host. We then randomly select 29 hosts to generate arbitrary UDP packets from iperf to simulate normal traffic for five minutes, and run hping3 from an external host to generate SYN flooding packets with IP spoofing for one minute before iperf stops; thus, the dominant DDoS traffic is mixed with the normal traffic. The speed of flooding is set by the `faster` command option (i.e., inter-arrival time of 1μs, but subject to the performance of the system running hping3), and each SYN flooding packet has 40 bytes in the payload. Table 1 summarizes the load distribution to the VSFs. Given the weights on the switches, the ideal distribution on S_2 is 75%:25%, while that on S_6 is 33%:33%:33%. We find that the actual load distribution does not conform exactly to that specified by the weights, but the difference is within 8%.

Nonetheless, we also notice that if we add one more VSF to $S7$, and adjust the number of action buckets and their weights on S_2 and S_7 according to the

Table 1. Load distribution among VSFs

Switch	Weight setup	Percentages of distribution
S_2	weight = 3	83%:17%
	weight = 1	
S_6	weight = 1	40%:26%:34%
	weight = 1	
	weight = 1	
S_7	weight = 1	100%

descriptions in Sect. 3.4 (e.g., the weights on S_2 become 3:2), the load distribution on S_7 will be highly biased to one of the VSFs (less than 1% of the packets or even zero to the other VSF). According to a similar observation in [17], we speculate that the imbalance is because the packets forwarded to S_7, when their hash values are computed for load distribution on S_2, have almost or all the same hash values. If S_7 and S_2 use the same hash functions, the hash values computed for those packets on S_7 will be almost or all the same again. However, in exactly what conditions will this imbalance happen deserves further investigation in future work.

4.2 Impact of Response Time

The probing frequency is certainly a tradeoff between probing overhead and response time to DDoS attacks. In the evaluation, we probe the switch in the top level every 5 s, those in the second level every 20 s, and those in the third level every 80 s, according to the descriptions in Sect. 3.2.

We define the response time as the time gap between the start of DDoS attacks and the traffic redirection right after the DDoS detection by the controller. We consider the number of packets that are handled in the group table on S_2 (implying that the architecture starts the traffic redirection and scrubbing after finding traffic anomaly by probing) to measure the impact of response time on the amount of DDoS traffic to be scrubbed. Figure 4 compares the number of such packets for different response time. Given that the controller probes S_2 every five seconds, if the response time is 4.5 s, 20.9% of the DDoS packets will not be redirected to the VSFs and go to the victim, where 258,795 out of the handled packets in the group table are DDoS packets. Otherwise, if the response time is reduced to one second, only 3.4% of the DDoS packets will go to the victim, where 262,863 out of the handled packets are DDoS packets. These results demonstrate that DDoS attacks can be efficiently mitigated if the response time is short.

Increasing the probing frequency can shorten the response time and mitigate DDoS traffic more efficiently, but this means also increases the probing overhead. Two approaches can improve the mitigation efficiency further. First, the controller can configure the meter table on the switches to limit the traffic rate

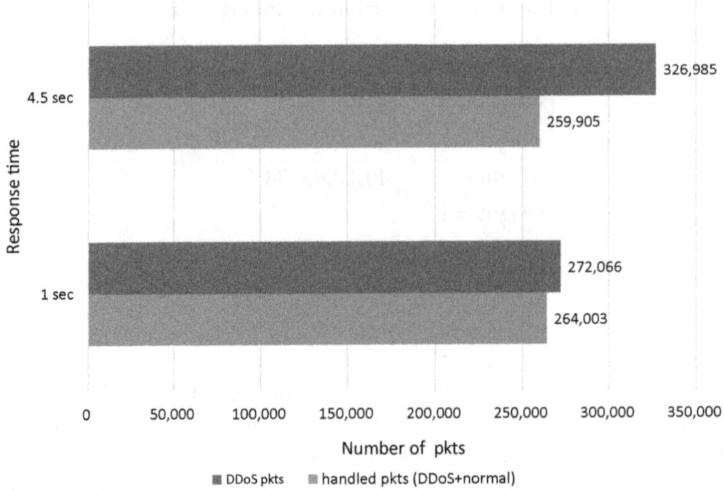

Fig. 4. Number of handled packets vs. response time.

to the victim beforehand, but the meter table will also drop normal traffic indiscriminately when DDoS attacks occur. This means should be only temporary, and the VSFs still must take over the mitigation soon to avoid affecting normal users. Moreover, the meter table has not been implemented on Open vSwitch so far; thus, we cannot evaluate its performance in the evaluation yet. Second, we suggest the OpenFlow standard could support the capability of reporting asynchronously an event of excessive traffic volume larger than a specified threshold. This capability can minimize the response time without probing overhead. A feasible means could extend the meter bands to support such an asynchronous report when the traffic exceeds the target rate.

5 Conclusion

DDoS attacks are still a serious threat to Internet services at present. In this work, we present an SDN/NFV-based architecture to leverage available resources in a data center for DDoS defense. This architecture features a lightweight probing strategy, dynamic deployment of VSFs, and traffic redirection with load distribution. This solution can complement the mainstream solution to DDoS attacks by deploying global scrubbing centers, but has lesser network footprint and shorter latency. We also have a proof-of-concept simulation to demonstrate the feasibility of this architecture, which can mitigate 96.6% of DDoS packets if the response time is as short as one second. This simulation is a preliminary attempt. We will soon carry the simulation to a more high-end hardware platform, demonstrate the feasibility in a much larger topology, and analyze the factors that affect the performance in depth.

References

1. Hoque, N., Bhattacharyya, D.K., Kalita, J.K.: Botnet in DDoS attacks: trends and challenges. IEEE Commu. Surv. Tutor. **17**(4), 2242–2270 (2015)
2. Hilton, S.: Dyn analysis summary of friday october 21 attack (2016). http://dyn.com/blog/dyn-analysis-summary-of-friday-october-21-attack
3. Why akamai cloud security for DDoS protection (2016). https://www.akamai.com/us/en/solutions/products/cloud-security/ddos-protection-service.jsp
4. Ziberman, P., Puzis, R., Elovici, Y.: On network footprint of traffic inspection and filtering at global scrubbing centers. IEEE Trans. Dependable Secure Comput. **14**(5), 521–534 (2017)
5. Mijumbi, R., Serrat, J., Gorricho, J.L., Bouten, N., Turck, F.D., Boutaba, R.: Network function virtualization: state-of-the-art and research challenges. IEEE Commun. Surv. Tutor. **18**(1), 236–262 (2016)
6. Bari, M.F., Boutaba, R., Esteves, R., Granville, L.Z., Podlesny, M., Rabbani, M.G., Zhang, Q., Zhani, M.F.: Data center network virtualization: a survey. IEEE Commun. Surv. Tutor. **15**(2), 909–928 (2013)
7. Fayaz, S.K., Tobioka, Y., Sekar, V., Bailey, M.: Bohatei: flexible and elastic DDoS defense. In: USENIX Security Symposium (2015)
8. Chin, T., Mountrouidou, X., Li, X., Xiong, K.: An SDN-supported collaborative approach for DDoS flooding detection and containment. In: IEEE Military Communications Conference (MILCOM) (2015)
9. Giotis, K., Argyropoulos, C., Androulidakis, G., Kalogeras, D., Maglaris, V.: Combining OpenFlow and sFlow for an effective and scalable anomaly detection and mitigation mechanism on SDN environments. Comput. Netw. **62**, 122–136 (2014)
10. Lopez, M.A., Duarte, O.C.M.B.: Providing elasticity to intrusion detection systems in virtualized software defined networks. In: IEEE International Conference on Communications (ICC) (2015)
11. Fung, C.J., McCormick, B.: VGuard: a distributed denial of service attack mitigation method using network function virtualization. In: International Conference on Network and Service Management (CNSM) (2015)
12. Zargar, S.T., Joshi, J., Tipper, D.: A survey of defense mechanisms against distributed denial of service (DDoS) flooding attacks. IEEE Commu. Surv. Tutor. **15**(4), 2046–2069 (2013)
13. AWS Shield (2016). https://aws.amazon.com/tw/shield
14. OpenFlow Switch Version 1.5.1 Specification (2015). https://www.opennetworking.org/images//openflow-switch-v1.5.1.pdf
15. Wang, R., Jia, Z., Ju, L.: An entropy-based distributed DDoS detection mechanism in software-defined networking. In: IEEE Trustcom/BigDataSE/ISPA (2015)
16. Linux Advanced Routing & Traffic Control HOWTO. http://tldp.org/HOWTO/Adv-Routing-HOWTO/lartc.kernel.rpf.html
17. Lin, P.C., Lin, Y.D., Wu, C.Y., Lai, Y.C., Kao, Y.C.: Balanced service chaining with traffic steering in software defined networks with network function virtualization. IEEE Comput. **49**(11), 68–76 (2016)

Bayesian Game Based Pseudo Honeypot Model in Social Networks

Miao Du[1(✉)], Yongzhong Li[1], Qing Lu[2], and Kun Wang[2]

[1] Jiangsu University of Science and Technology, Zhenjiang 212003, China
dumiao0118@163.com, liyongzhong61@163.com

[2] Nanjing University of Posts and Telecommunications, Nanjing 210003, China
luqing1016@foxmail.com, kwang@njupt.edu.cn

Abstract. In this paper, we study applying honeypots to protect social networks against DDoS attacks. Different from previous works that study honeypots for DDoS attacks, we consider attackers are rational and know to optimize attacking strategies based on the defender's strategy. To deal with such strategic attackers, we propose a novel pseudo honeypot game model following the Bayesian game setting. In addition, we rigorously prove the existence of Bayesian Nash equilibriums (BNEs) and show how to find them in all different cases. Simulations show the BNEs achieved in the games not only reduce energy consumption but also improve efficiency of the defense.

Keywords: Social networks · Distributed denial of service · Bayesian game · Pseudo honeypot · Optimal active detection · Network security

1 Introduction

Social Networks (SNs) have been experiencing explosive developments in decade years, and playing a significant role in people's lives. Recently, social networks have gained tremendous popularity in the cyber space. SNs are now among the most popular sites on the Web. For instance, recent database shows that about 4 out of 5 users visit SNs [1]. Similarly, Facebook, for example, claims that it owns about 1.2 billion active users in a month [2]. The wide variety of SNs and huge amount of information available in these networks introduce unprecedented research challenges to efficiently handle such data but they do also represent a great research opportunity for understanding the nature and evolution of social networks at massive scale.

With the development of SNs, the security problems of SNs are becoming critical. Distributed Denial of Service (DDoS) attack [3] can directly consume system resources, so that the target system cannot provide normal service. In DDoS attacks, the intruder attempts to make the resource cannot be used by legitimate users [4].

DDOS attacks mainly rely on many bots, they sent a large number of seemingly legitimate network packets to the victim host, resulting in network congestion or server resource depletion. DDoS attack once implemented, malicious data packet will be sent to the victim host like a flood, which leads to the legitimate users' data packets cannot transmit normally [5]. In this paper, we introduce a novel pseudo honeypot defense mechanism to prevent DDoS attacks using Bayesian game.

X. Sun et al. (Eds.): ICCCS 2017, Part II, LNCS 10603, pp. 62–71, 2017.
https://doi.org/10.1007/978-3-319-68542-7_6

We study DDoS attacks in SNs and set a pseudo honeypot game model based on Bayesian game, forming a game environment through the study of honeypot trapping mechanism, and using game theory to formally describe the honeypot participants' strategies and payoffs, so that the reasonable analysis proves the validity and effectiveness of the game model.

To this end, our main contributions in this paper can be listed as follows:

- We propose a pseudo honeypot game to solve the DDoS attack in SNs, which makes the defense mechanism more active, effective and deceptive. Moreover, we analyze groups of portfolio strategies to achieve an optimal equilibrium between legitimate users and attackers.
- We utilize a game tree approach to analyze the payoffs of attackers and legitimate users in the pseudo honeypot game model, thus visually displaying the strategies and making them easy to understand.
- We conduct various experiments to evaluate the performance compared with the existing models. Experimental results demonstrated that the proposed model can increase legitimate users' payoffs, reduce energy consumption and improve safety and stability.

The rest of the paper is organized as follows. In Sect. 2, we present state-of-the-art from three aspects. The detailed theoretical derivations of the pseudo honeypot game model are presented in Sect. 3. Section 4 provides simulation results to validate the performance of the proposed model. Finally, we draw the main conclusions in Sect. 5.

2 Related Work

In this section, we present the state-of-the art on DDoS in SNs, honeypot for DDoS and game theory. Then, we compare our work with the literature.

2.1 DDoS in SNs

Distributed Denial-of-Service (DDoS) attacks have been a big threat to the network space for a long time [6]. According to a survey [7], more than half of the companies have been persecuted by DDoS attacks, and the average cost of resisting DDoS attacks was expected as much as 2.5 million dollars [8]. To deal with DDoS attacks in SNs, Wang and Wu [9] proposed an active defense mechanism against DDoS attack. Peng et al. [10] presented a traffic detection approach to solve the DDoS attack.

2.2 Honeypot for DDoS

Honeypots are designed to attract, detect, and collect attack information. Traditional single honeypot is generally used to capture and attack investigation [11]. Honeypots are deployed in the defense system to confuse the attacker [12]. Honeypot is actually a trap, once the attackers mistakenly believe that the honeypot is a normal server, its attack behavior will be recorded and traced by the honeypot [13, 14]. Nowadays, large number of honeypots can work together as a Honeynet for large-scale defense scenarios [15].

2.3 Game Theory in DDoS

The threat of DDoS attacks has led researchers to consider the use of game theory to try to solve these problems. Wang et al. [16] proposed a bertrand game approach to address DDoS attacks, and Luo et al. [17] presented a mathematical model for low-rate shrew DDoS. Wang et al. [18] proposed a game theory-based method to solve DDoS attacks in smart grid. Garfinkeli et al. [19] surveyed previous works on applying game-theoretic techniques to address security and privacy problems.

We propose a novel pseudo honeypot game model against DDoS attacks using a Bayesian game approach. We prevent the DDoS attacks by the decoy performance of the honeypots, and utilize a Bayesian game approach to analyze and prove the effect of the honeypots.

3 Game Model

In this section, we first setup the pseudo honeypot game (PHG) model and define the payoffs function, followed by, the derivation of the Nash equilibrium is in detail. Then, we present the theoretical analysis of the game. Finally, we analyse the payoffs of legitimate users and attackers via game trees.

3.1 Pseudo Honeypot Game Model

Figure 1 shows the novel PHG model. In this figure, we define the game G as $G \triangleq \{\{Q, H\}, \{S_Q, S_H\}, U_Q, U_H\}$, where $\{Q, H\}$ is the finite collection of players $N \triangleq \{Q_1, Q_2, \ldots, Q_n; H_1, H_2, \ldots, H_n\}$, wherein $Q \triangleq \{Q_\kappa, Q_\tau, Q_\omega\}$ represents real service, honeypot service and pseudo honeypot service, and $H \triangleq \{H_\kappa, H_\tau\}$ represents legitimate users and attackers respectively. $\{S_Q, S_H\}$ is an offensive and defensive strategy collection of players, wherein $S_Q \triangleq \{\partial_1, \partial_2\}$ represents the service-side's strategies of providing service or not. $S_H \triangleq \{\vartheta_1, \vartheta_2\}$ represents the visitors' strategies of providing access or not. $\{U_Q, U_H\}$ is the payoffs' collection of the game, wherein U_Q represents the service-side's strategy payoffs and U_H represents the visitors' strategy payoffs.

Next, we explain the payoffs for the three cases.

- **CASE 1.** Service-side provides real service. If providing service for legitimate users, the payoff is ε ($\varepsilon > 0$) for both sides, otherwise it is $-\varepsilon$. If providing service for attackers, the service performance will deteriorate, the service-side's payoff is $-\varsigma\varepsilon$, attackers' payoff is $\varsigma\varepsilon - \sigma$ ($\varsigma \geq 1$ and $\varepsilon \gg \sigma > 0$), or else services' payoff is $-\sigma$ and attackers' payoff is 0.
- **CASE 2.** Service-side provides honeypot service. For legitimate users, no matter whether the service-side provides honeypot service, they are unable to obtain normal service, consequently the payoff is $-\varepsilon$. If the services provide effective honeypot service to decoy attackers successfully, the service-side's payoff is $\xi_1\varphi$ ($\varphi > 0$ and $\xi_1 \geq 1$), the attackers' payoff is $-\xi_1\varphi - \sigma$.

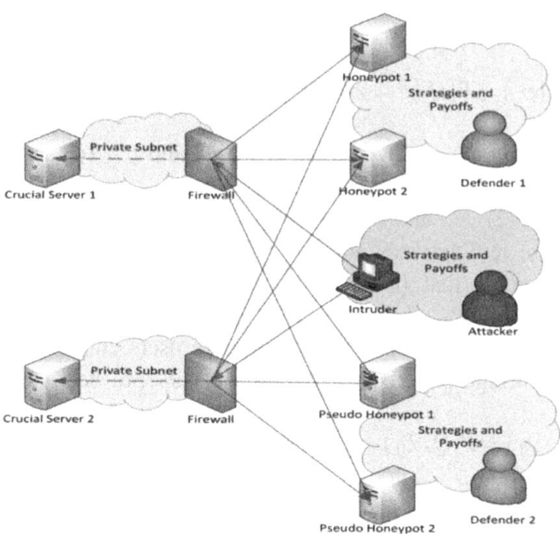

Fig. 1. Pseudo honeypot game mode. l

- **CASE 3.** Service-side provides pseudo honeypot service. For legitimate users, pseudo honeypot service is similar to normal service, they are able to obtain normal service, consequently the payoff is ε. If providing service for attackers, the service performance will deteriorate, the service-side's payoff is $-\varsigma\varepsilon$, attackers' payoff is $\varsigma\varepsilon$ - $\xi_2\varphi - \sigma$ (ξ_2 represents pseudo honeypot decoy factor and $\xi_2 \geq 1$). If the services provide effective pseudo honeypot service to decoy attackers successfully, the service-side's payoff is $\xi_2\varphi$.

Here, we have $\{P(H_\tau) = \mu, P(H_\kappa) = 1 - \mu\}$. Since visitors need a priori probability judgment for the type of services, we consider $\{P(Q_\tau) = v, P(Q_\kappa) = 1 - v - v', P(Q_\omega) = v'\}$.

Theorem 1. *A Bayesian-Nash Equilibrium strategy* $\{(\partial_1,\ \partial_1,\ \partial_1),\ (\vartheta_1,\ \vartheta_1)\}$ *exists in the pseudo honeypot game model.*

Proof: The payoff of the real services for the strategy ∂_1 can be defined as $U_{Q_\kappa}(\partial_1)$, we have

$$U_{Q_\kappa}(\partial_1) = P(H_\tau|\vartheta_1) * (-\varsigma\varepsilon) + P(H_\kappa|\vartheta_1) * \varepsilon = -\varsigma\varepsilon\mu + (1-\mu)\varepsilon \tag{1}$$

when the real services choose strategy ∂_1, we can obtain the average payoff $U_{Q_\kappa}(\partial_1)$ by integrating (1).

$$U_{Q_\kappa}(\partial_2) = P(H_\tau|\vartheta_1) * 0 + P(H_\kappa|\vartheta_1) * (-\varepsilon) = (\mu - 1)\varepsilon \tag{2}$$

where the average payoff $U_{Q_\kappa}(\partial_2)$ is obtained by real services' strategy ∂_2.

$$U_{Q_\omega}(\partial_1) = P(H_\tau|\vartheta_1) * (-\varsigma\varepsilon) + P(H_\kappa|\vartheta_1) * \varepsilon = -\varsigma\varepsilon\mu + (1-\mu)\varepsilon \tag{3}$$

$$U_{Q_\omega}(\partial_2) = P(H_\tau|\vartheta_1) * 0 + P(H_\kappa|\vartheta_1) * (-\varepsilon) = (\mu - 1)\varepsilon \tag{4}$$

similarly, we can obtain the average payoff $U_{Q_\omega}(\partial_1)$ and $U_{Q_\omega}(\partial_2)$ by pseudo honeypot services' strategy ∂_1 and ∂_2, respectively.

According to (1), (2), (3) and (4), when $\mu < 2/(2+\varsigma)$ is attackers, the dominant strategy for both the real services and the pseudo honeypots is ∂_1, otherwise is ∂_2. Therefore, we can argue that $(\partial_1, \partial_1, \partial_1)$ is the dominant strategy for the visitors' portfolio strategy $(\vartheta_1, \vartheta_1)$ when $\mu < 2/(2+\varsigma)$, and the dominant strategy is $(\partial_2, \partial_1, \partial_2)$ if $\mu > 2/(2+\varsigma)$. When the legitimate users choose strategy ϑ_1 and ϑ_2, we can obtain the average payoff $U_{H_\kappa}(\vartheta_1)$ and $U_{H_\kappa}(\vartheta_2)$, respectively, as

$$\begin{aligned} U_{H_\kappa}(\vartheta_1) &= P(Q_\tau|\partial_1) * (-\varepsilon) + P(Q_\kappa|\partial_1) * \varepsilon + P(Q_\omega|\partial_1) * \varepsilon \\ &= v(-\varepsilon) + (1 - v - v')\varepsilon + v'\varepsilon = (1-2v)\varepsilon \end{aligned} \tag{5}$$

$$U_{H_\kappa}(\vartheta_2) = P(Q_\tau|\partial_1) * 0 + P(Q_\kappa|\partial_1) * 0 + P(Q_\omega|\partial_1) * 0 = 0 \tag{6}$$

similarly, we can obtain the average payoff $U_{H_\tau}(\vartheta_1)$ and $U_{H_\tau}(\vartheta_2)$ for the attackers.

$$\begin{aligned} U_{H_\tau}(\vartheta_1) &= P(Q_\tau|\partial_1) * (-\xi_1\varphi - \sigma) + P(Q_\kappa|\partial_1) * (\varsigma\varepsilon - \sigma) + P(Q_\omega|\partial_1) * (\varsigma\varepsilon - \xi_2\varphi - \sigma) \\ &= v(-\xi_1\varphi - \sigma) + (1 - v - v')(\varsigma\varepsilon - \sigma) + v'(\varsigma\varepsilon - \xi_2\varphi - \sigma) \\ &= (1-v)\varsigma\varepsilon - \sigma - (v\xi_1 + v'\xi_2)\varphi \end{aligned} \tag{7}$$

and

$$U_{H_\tau}(\vartheta_2) = P(Q_\tau|\partial_1) * 0 + P(Q_\kappa|\partial_1) * 0 + P(Q_\omega|\partial_1) * 0 = 0 \tag{8}$$

where the average payoff $U_{H_\tau}(\vartheta_1)$ and $U_{H_\tau}(\vartheta_2)$ can be obtained for the attackers' strategy ϑ_1 and ϑ_2, respectively. We consider that $U_{H_\kappa}(\vartheta_1) = U_{H_\kappa}(\vartheta_2)$ and $U_{H_\tau}(\vartheta_1) = U_{H_\tau}(\vartheta_2)$. Then, we have $v = \frac{1}{2}$.

$$\begin{cases} v + v' = \frac{(1-v)\varsigma\varepsilon - \sigma}{\xi\varphi} \\ \xi\varphi = \frac{v}{(v+v')\xi_1\varphi} + \frac{v'}{(v+v')\xi_2\varphi} \end{cases} \tag{9}$$

if

$$v + v' < \frac{(1-v)\varsigma\varepsilon - \sigma}{\xi\varphi} < \frac{1}{2} \tag{10}$$

we have $\varsigma\varepsilon - 2\sigma < \xi\varphi$, then $P(Q_\kappa) = 1 - v - v' > \frac{1}{2}$, and thus

$$\begin{cases} P(Q_\kappa) = 1 - \nu - \nu' > \nu = P(Q_\tau) \\ P(Q_\kappa) = 1 - \nu - \nu' > \nu' = P(Q_\omega) \end{cases} \tag{11}$$

In this case, we obtain a condition $\nu' < 1 - 2\nu$, if $\frac{1}{2} < \frac{(1-\nu)\varsigma\varepsilon - \sigma}{\xi\varphi} < \nu + \nu'$, and we have $\varsigma\varepsilon - 2\sigma > \xi\varphi$. According to this, we get $\frac{\xi\varphi - [(1-\nu)\varsigma\varepsilon - \sigma]}{\xi\varphi} < 1 - (\nu + \nu') < \frac{1}{2}$.

Then, we can obtain

$$\begin{aligned} \frac{\xi\varphi - [(1-\nu)\varsigma\varepsilon - \sigma]}{\xi\varphi} = \frac{(\nu - 1)\varsigma\varepsilon + \sigma + \xi\varphi}{\xi\varphi} > \frac{(\nu - 1)\varsigma\varepsilon + \xi\varphi}{\xi\varphi} \\ > \frac{(\nu - 1)(\xi\varphi + 2\sigma) + \xi\varphi}{\xi\varphi} > \nu \end{aligned} \tag{12}$$

Thus we have

$$\begin{cases} \mu < \frac{2}{2+\varsigma} \\ \nu < \frac{1}{2} \\ \nu\xi_1\varphi + \nu'\xi_2\varphi < (1 - \nu)\varsigma\varepsilon - \sigma \end{cases} \tag{13}$$

Therefore, we can obtain a BNE strategy $\{ (\partial_1, \partial_1, \partial_1), (\vartheta_1, \vartheta_1)\}$ in the game under the condition (13).

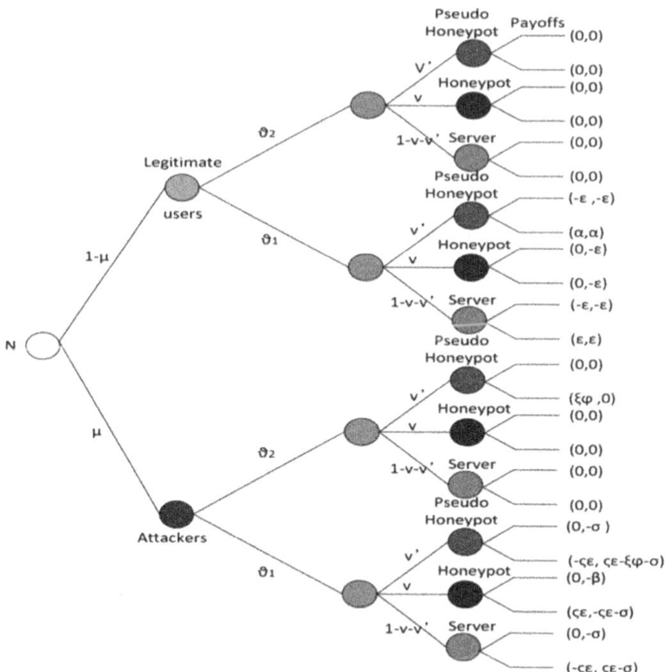

Fig. 2. The game tree from legitimate user' perspective

3.2 Nash Equilibrium Analysis in Pseudo Honeypot Game Model

The PHG model is flexible and deceptive to the attackers, as it introduces the psuedo honeypot in the game, the equilibrium conditions are related to v and v', which makes the BNE conditions more diversified.

Figure 2 is the game tree from the legitimate user's perspective. From the figures it is clear that the game equilibrium conditions relate to the probabilities of the honeypot and the pseudo honeypot, v and v', as well as decoy factors ξ_1 and ξ_2. Therefore, the result of the game is completely controlled by the services. Importantly, the PHG model makes the strategies increase so that the defenders can adjust v and v', or ξ_1 and ξ_2 flexibly to improve the defense mechanism and achieve different BNEs according to different strategies.

4 Performance Evaluations

In this section, the performance of the PHG model are analysed and compared to existing Honeypot game (HG) model [20], All Monitor (AM) model [21] and Cluster Head (CH) monitor model [22]. The simulation consists of two different parts: average residual energy performance and safety performance. In the first part, we setup the experimental platform to verify the effect of the game-theoretic PHG model according to actual network models. Then we compare the performance of our proposed game model with existing models.

4.1 Simulation Results Analysis

The simulation scenario is a two-dimensional monitoring area, whose edges are 400 m long. 500 nodes are scattered randomly. The initial energy of each node is 5 J. Detailed simulation settings are list in Table 1.

Table 1. Simulation settings

Scene Parameter	Parameter Values
Network scale	400 m * 400 m
Number of nodes	500
Simulation times	10 min
Nodes placement strategy	Random placement
Promiscuous mode	Yes
Nodes movement	No
Initial energy of nodes	5 J
Wireless broadcast model	Standard radio
Radio signal energy	25.0 dBm
Wireless receiving packet mode	Error free reception
Compared model	HG model, CH monitor model, all monitor model

We firstly consider that μ is fixed μ, then we deploy the PHG model $\{(v, v') = (0.2, 0.2), (0.4, 0.4)\}$ respectively to simulate energy consumptions compared to the AM model and the CH monitor model. Subsequently, we assume honeypot and pseudo honeypot's decoy factor $\xi_1 = \xi_2 = 5$ is a definite value, then we setup six groups of different service deployments, i.e., {S = 12, H = 2, PH = 6}, S, H, PH represents number of servers, honeypots and pseudo honeypots to simulate the attack flow on services and service flow on legitimate users according to the six groups of different service deployments under different preconditions $\varsigma = 1$, respectively.

Figures 3 show that the slopes of the energy consumption curves of the HG model are relatively smooth, which means the change in the energy consumption is relatively slow. When the frequency of the HG and PHG is low, AM model's energy consumption outweighs the HG and the PHG models. However, the PHG model will consume more energy with the frequency increase of honeypot and pseudo honeypot, prompting that we need to adjust and deploy pseudo honeypot more reasonably. Otherwise, it may result in unnecessary waste of resources. Therefore, if we deploy the pseudo honeypot methodology, our proposed model can incorporate both intrusion detection and cyber resource efficiency.

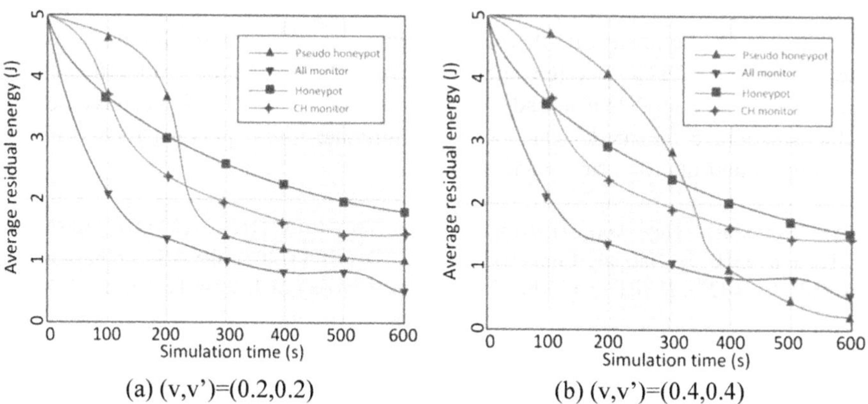

Fig. 3. Energy consumptions in deploying honeypot and pseudo honeypot when (v, v') = (0.2, 0.2), and (v, v') = (0.4, 0.4)

Figure 4 show that as the attack damage factor ς increases, the intruders are more likely to launch attacks. In addition, if there is no pseudo honeypot in the model, the defenders will be more likely to be attacked. However, if pseudo honeypots are effectively deployed in the model, they can greatly reduce the probability of the attacks and ensure the service for legitimate users at the same time. Therefore, the PHG model can be an effective defense mechanism against DDoS attacks.

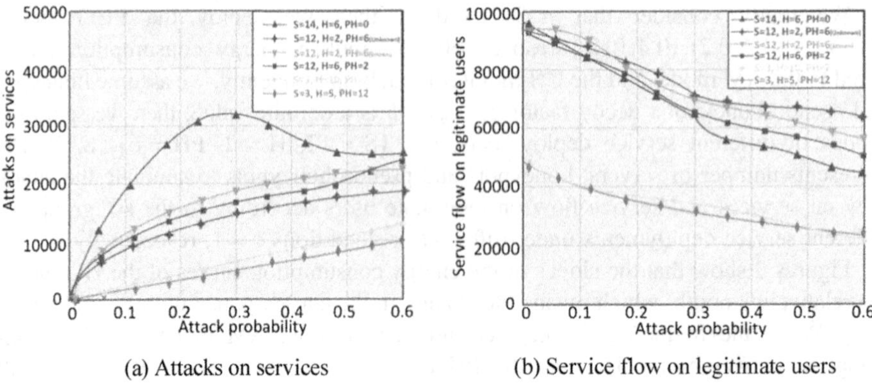

(a) Attacks on services

(b) Service flow on legitimate users

Fig. 4. Attacks on services and Service flow on legitimate users in attack damage factor $\varsigma=1$

5 Conclusions

In this paper, we proposed the pseudo honeypot game model to prevent DDoS attacks for SNs. The pseudo honeypot game model can improve the deceptiveness and increase the strategies geometrically. Furthermore, multiple equilibrium conditions in pseudo honeypot game model can interfere attackers' strategies. Simulation results showed that the proposed game models can lead to a more active, effective and deceptive defense mechanism, where the model can increase legitimate users' payoffs, reduce energy consumption and improve safety and stability.

Acknowledgments. This work is supported by NSFC (61572262, 61533010, 61373135, 61571233, 61532013); National China 973 Project (2015CB352401); the NSF of Jiangsu Province (BK20141427); NUPT (NY214097); The Qinlan Project of Jiangsu Province.

References

1. The State of Social Media 2011: Social is the new normal (2011). http://www.briansolis.com/2011/10/state-of-social-media-2011/
2. Facebook Statistics. http://www.statisticbrain.com/facebook-statistics/
3. Wang, K., Yu, J., Liu, X., Guo, S.: A pre-authentication approach to proxy re-encryption in big data context. IEEE Trans. Big Data **PP**(99), 1 (2017)
4. Jin, T., Yu, C., Yong, H., Wei, S.: SIP flooding attack detection with a multi-dimensional sketch design. IEEE Trans. Dependable Secure Comput. **11**(6), 582–595 (2014)
5. Du, M., Wang, K., Liu, X., Guo, S., Zhang, Y.: A differential privacy-based query model for sustainable fog data centers. IEEE Trans. Sustain. Comput. **PP**(99), 1 (2017)
6. Zargar, S.T., Joshi, J., Tipper, D.: A survey of defense mechanisms against DDoS flooding attacks. IEEE Commun. Surveys Tuts. **15**(4), 2046–2069 (2013)
7. Wang, K., Du, M., Yang, D., Zhu, C., Shen, J., Zhang, Y.: Game theory-based active defense for intrusion detection in cyber-physical embedded systems. ACM Trans. Embedded Comput. Syst. **16**(1), 18 (2016)

8. How Much Does a DDoS Attack Cost.html. http://www.internetnews.com/security/article.php/3933046/
9. Wang, K., Wu, M.: Nash equilibrium of node cooperation based on metamodel for MANETs. J. Inf. Sci. Eng. **28**(2), 317–333 (2012)
10. Peng, T., Leckie, C., Ramamohanarao, K.: Survey of networkbased defense mechanisms countering the DoS and DDoS problems. ACM Comput. Surv. **39**(1), 60–67 (2007)
11. Wang, K., Zhuo, L., Shao, Y., Yue, D., Tsang, K.F.: Toward distributed data processing on intelligent leakpoints prediction in petrochemical industries. IEEE Trans. Ind. Inf. **12**(6), 2091–2102 (2016)
12. Chun-Jen, C., Khatkar, P., Tianyi, X., Jeongkeun, L., Dijiang, H.: NICE: network intrusion detection and countermeasure selection in virtual network systems. IEEE Trans. Dependable Secure Comput. **10**(4), 198–211 (2013)
13. Jiang, H., Wang, K., Wang, Y., Gao, M., Zhang, Y.: Energy big data: a survey. IEEE Access **4**, 3844–3861 (2016)
14. Wang, K., Wang, Y., Sun, Y., Guo, S., Wu, J.: Green industrial Internet of Things architecture: an energy-efficient perspective. IEEE Commun. Mag. **54**(12), 48–54 (2016)
15. Beham, M., Vlad, M., Reiser, H.P.: Intrusion detection and honeypots in nested virtualization environments. In: Proceeding of IEEE/IFIP International Conference on Dependable Systems and Networks, pp. 1–6 (2016)
16. Wang, K., Yuan, L., Mizayaki, T., Sun, Y., Guo, S.: Anti-eavesdropping with selfish jamming in wireless networks: a bertrand game approach. IEEE Trans. Veh. Technol. (2016). doi:10.1109/TVT.2016.2639827
17. Luo, J., Yang, X., Wang, J., Xu, J., Sun, J., Long, K.: On a mathematical model for low-rate shrew DDoS. IEEE Trans. Inf. Forensics Secur. **9**(7), 1069–1083 (2014)
18. Wang, K., Ouyang, Z., Krishnan, R., Shu, L., He, L.: A game theory based energy management system using price elasticity for smart grids. IEEE Trans. Ind. Inf. **11**(6), 1607–1616 (2015)
19. Garfinkel, T., Rosenblum, M.: A virtual machine introspection based architecture for intrusion detection. In: Proceeding of Network and Distributed Systems Security, pp. 191–206 (2003)
20. Wang, K., Du, M., Sun, Y., Vinel, A., Zhang, Y.: Attack detection and distributed forensics in M2M networks. IEEE Netw. **30**(6), 49–55 (2016)
21. Zhan, Z., Xu, M., Xu, S.: Characterizing honeypot-captured cyber attacks: Statistical framework and case study. IEEE Trans. Inf. Forensics Security **8**(11), 1775–1789 (2013)
22. Wang, K., Du, M., Maharjan, S., Sun, Y.: Strategic honeypot game model for distributed denial of service attacks in the smart grid. IEEE Trans. Smart Grid (2017). doi:10.1109/TSG.2017.2670144

Conducting Correlated Laplace Mechanism for Differential Privacy

Hao Wang[1,2], Zhengquan Xu[1,2(✉)], Lizhi Xiong[3], and Tao Wang[1,2]

[1] State Key Laboratory of Information Engineering in Surveying, Mapping and Remote Sensing, Wuhan University, Wuhan 430079, China
{haowang354,xuzq,wangtao.mac}@whu.edu.cn

[2] Collaborative Innovation Center for Geospatial Technology, Wuhan 430079, China

[3] School of Computer and Software, Nanjing University of Information Science and Technology, Nanjing 210044, China
lzxiong16@163.com

Abstract. Recently, differential privacy achieves good trade-offs between data publishing and sensitive information hiding. But in data publishing for correlated data, the independent Laplace noise implemented in current differential privacy preserving methods can be detected and sanitized, reducing privacy level. In prior work, we have proposed a correlated Laplace mechanism (CLM) to remedy this problem. But the concrete steps and detailed parameters to imply CLM and the complete proof has not been discussed. In this paper, we provide the complete proof and specific steps to conduct CLM. Also, we have verified the error of our implement method. Experimental results show that our method can retain small error to generate correlated Laplace noise for large quantities of queries.

Keywords: Correlated data · Data publishing · Privacy preserving · Differential privacy · Correlated Laplace noise

1 Introduction

With advances in internet of things, data collection and curation technology, research topics such as Privacy Preserving Data Mining (PPDM) and Privacy Preserving Data Release (PPDR) can provide outstanding benefits for the governments, commerce and social public services [1–3]. However, data publishers or owners may not willing to reveal their true data because of various reasons, most probably privacy considerations [4–6].

The problem of privacy preserving data publishing has attracted interests of researchers spanning multiple disciplines. In the literature, random perturbation induces uncertainty (e.g., random noise) about individual values and becomes a widely accepted and practical approach for data privacy preserving. Among the alternatives, differential privacy is state-of-the-art standard privacy notion [7]. Specifically, differential privacy requires the effect a single record has on the statistic results of the data is significantly little.

X. Sun et al. (Eds.): ICCCS 2017, Part II, LNCS 10603, pp. 72–85, 2017.
https://doi.org/10.1007/978-3-319-68542-7_7

Although differential privacy has been widely employed as a robust standard, previous studies [8–15] have demonstrated that individual privacy may be disclosed when data are correlated. Current differential privacy preserving methods for correlated data publication primarily represent themselves into two natural solutions: establishing correlation models, or transforming a correlated series into an independent form. The first approaches establish a model to describe the relations of the correlated data, while the idea of the other type, transform-based methods, is to transform a correlated data series into an independent series in another domain.

However, for correlated data publishing, the method to introduce IID noise (usually Laplace noise) into correlated data leading to the correlation of original data different with that of noise series. Then the attacker can take advantage of the background knowledge of the different correlations to filter out part of the noise, resulting in a decline of the effective noise level in practice and further leading to a decline in the actual strength of privacy protection. Therefore, the current two categories of differential privacy preserving algorithms can not be directly applied to the correlated data. The ideas of both are increasing the independent noise added in the correlated data to offset the decline of privacy degree caused by the filtering attack. But the extra noise will destroy data utility.

These challenges imply that current differential privacy mechanisms are not appropriate for correlated data publication in a straightforward manner. Thus, a novel approach to address these challenges is in high demand. In fact, the key problem of existing mechanisms is that the correlation of IID noise is not consistent with that of original data. That is to say, if we make the correlation of the noise series match with that of original series, then the refinement attacks will make no sense. Based on this idea, in literature [16], we have proposed a correlated Laplace mechanism (CLM), which makes the noise series and original series similar to an adversary, to address these challenges and publish correlated data. But [16] has not discussed the specific method to imply CLM. In this paper, we provide the concrete steps and detailed parameters to conduct CLM and give complete proof for CLM. Our contributions are threefold:

- Concrete steps and detailed parameters are discussed to conduct CLM, including the design of filter and detailed parameters.
- We provide the complete proof for CLM. Since [16] only discussed the design principle of CLM, in this paper, we theoretically prove the correctness of CLM.
- We empirically evaluate the error of the correlation between generating noise and original data over three real datasets, namely, GPS traces, Flu and Unemployment. Experiments show that our method retains small error to generate correlated Laplace noise for large quantities of queries.

The remainder of this paper is organized as follows. In Sect. 2, we summarize related work on differentially private publication over correlated data and describe the limitations of existing methods. We then briefly introduce the notations adopted in this work and state the problem definition in Sect. 3. Our approaches and experiments are described in Sects. 4 and 5, respectively, followed by our conclusions in Sect. 6.

2 Related Work

Existing differential privacy mechanisms for correlated data publishing can be classified into two types. One type is model-based methods and the other type is transform-based methods.

2.1 Correlation Model

The first type takes advantage of a model to describe the correlation of the data. The correlation can be modeled in various ways. Borrow the idea from cryptography, Gehrke et al. [22] dealt with correlated data and proposed a privacy model assuming the adversary has zero-knowledge. To satisfy this criterion, a perturbation mechanism was proposed to preserve the privacy of correlated data, while the aggregate functions need to be carefully selected. Consider the background knowledge the adversary has, Shen and Yu [18] proposed a framework based on sampling and probability transition property, called Markov Chain Monte Carlo (MCMC) algorithm. The MCMC framework can conduct frequent graph pattern mining tasks, meanwhile guaranteeing differential privacy. Bayesian differential privacy [19] is another definition of privacy based on Pufferfish. It presented a Gaussian model to accurately describe the correlations of the data in the series and analyzed the privacy level of different perturbation algorithms. Zhu et al. [17] utilized correlation coefficient matrix to describe the correlation of series. Then they calculated the sensitivity function of differential privacy considering the correlation coefficient as the weight. In [17], a query over a network structure, which is unknown to adversaries, was proposed. However, the problem setting in [20] is different from that in this paper, in which the correlation structure is assumed to be exactly known to adversaries.

With the development of correlation modeling methods, we believe that there will be more mechanisms attempt to achieve the goal of this paper by establishing more accurate correlation models.

2.2 Series Transformation

The idea of the other type transforms the correlated data into independent form while maintaining its major characteristic. Rastogi et al. [21] proposed a Fourier Perturbation Algorithm (FPA) to address this issue. Discrete Fourier Transformation (DFT) in FPA is conducted to transform the correlated data into independent Fourier domain. FPA perturbed the DFT coefficients which can (approximately) reconstruct the original data. Furthermore, in order to overcome the shortcomings of FPA addressing short-term and non-stationary series, Discrete Wavelet Transform (DWT) is introduced by [22–24]. DWT extends the scope of FPA and maintains more features of the series. Despite of the difficulty to achieve differential privacy guarantee, [25] extracted the features of dataset to another dimension utilizing Principal Component Analysis (PCA). Then they published the perturbed data that are useful for a number of common statistical learning applications.

Despite the benefits in data utility, transform-based approaches destroy the correlation of the data to a certain extent.

3 Preliminaries

In this section, we review the theory of differential privacy and formalize the CLM mechanism.

3.1 Differential Privacy

Differential privacy is a currently recognized preservation model that can guarantee stricter security. It is essentially a kind of noise perturbed mechanism. By adding noise to the raw data or statistical results, differential privacy can guarantee that the value changing of a single record has a minimal effect on the statistical output results. Thus, differential privacy can not only preserve privacy of sensitive data, but also support data mining on statistical results. Its formal definition is as follows:

Definition 1 (ε-Differential Privacy): We give two neighboring datasets, D and $D^{'}$, which have the same cardinality but differ in only one record. A random perturbation mechanism, M, ensures ε-differential privacy if M makes every set of outcomes, S, for any pair of D and $D^{'}$ satisfy:

$$Pr[M(D) \in S] \leq exp(\varepsilon) \times Pr[M(D^{'}) \in S] \tag{1}$$

where $S \subseteq Range(M)$, $Range(M)$ is value range of M. $Pr[\cdot]$ and ε denote probability density function (PDF) and privacy budget parameters, respectively. A smaller ε means better privacy. Figure 1 depicts the output probability distribution of randomized algorithm M satisfying ε-differential privacy on D and $D^{'}$.

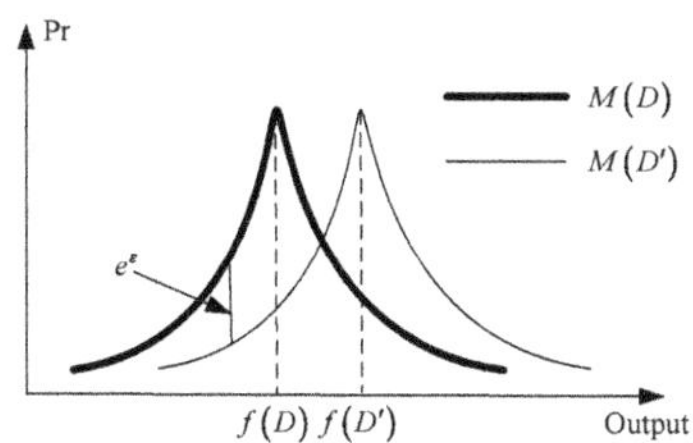

Fig. 1. Output probability density of random algorithm M on D and $D^{'}$

Privacy budget ε is mainly restricted by randomized algorithm M. In practice applications, M is generally realized by a Laplace mechanism. The definition of the Laplace mechanism is as follows:

Definition 2 (Laplace Mechanism): Assuming that $f(\cdot)$ is the statistical output function, then a noise sequence $Y \sim Lap(\lambda)$, which obeys Laplace distribution, can make randomized algorithm $M(D) = f(D) + Y$ satisfy ε-differential privacy. λ is the scale parameter of Laplace distribution, and the PDF of Laplace distribution is:

$$\rho(x) = \frac{1}{2\lambda} exp(-\frac{|x|}{\lambda}) \tag{2}$$

The scale parameter λ is determined by sensitivity function Δf and privacy preserving intensity ε:

$$\lambda = \frac{\Delta f}{\varepsilon} \tag{3}$$

where Δf is the maximum effect of the statistical output function a single record has on:

$$\Delta f = \max_{D'} \|f(D) - f(D^{'})\|_1 \tag{4}$$

As an example, consider a dataset whose sensitivity of a query is 1. According to differential privacy, the noise added to the true answer, which distributed according to $Lap(1/\varepsilon)$, suffices to guarantee ε-differential privacy.

3.2 CLM

As shown in Fig. 2, because of the strong correlation between neighboring locations, Amy's trajectory can be abstracted as a stationary series. To achieve differential privacy for her location data, current approaches added independent noise into her true value. But the independent noise can not resist some refinement attacks (e.g., filtering). After filtering, the series obtained by the adversary is quite precise to the original trajectory.

On the contrary, if the correlation of noise series matches with that of original series, then the refinement methods can not filter the added noise. In this case, noise series can guarantee the auto-correlation function of the noise same as that of the original series. Thus, an attacker cannot make use of refinement methods to sanitize noise from publishing time-series.

Therefore, the drop of privacy level is caused by the difference of autocorrelations between noise and original series. Since the correlation of a time-series can be represented by its auto-correlation function, assume that the original time-series is X and the noise series is Z. Intuitively, if we make the autocorrelation of the noise match with that of the original series, i.e.,

$$R_Z(\tau) = R_{XX}(\tau) \tag{5}$$

this serious issue can be solved.

CLM is based on this idea. In addition, literature [21] discussed the scheme to produce IID Laplace noise series from Gauss noise series in a distributed

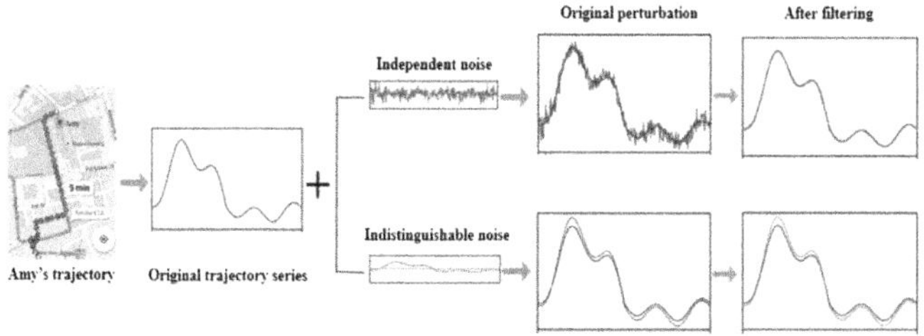

Fig. 2. Diagram of attack model for correlated time-series

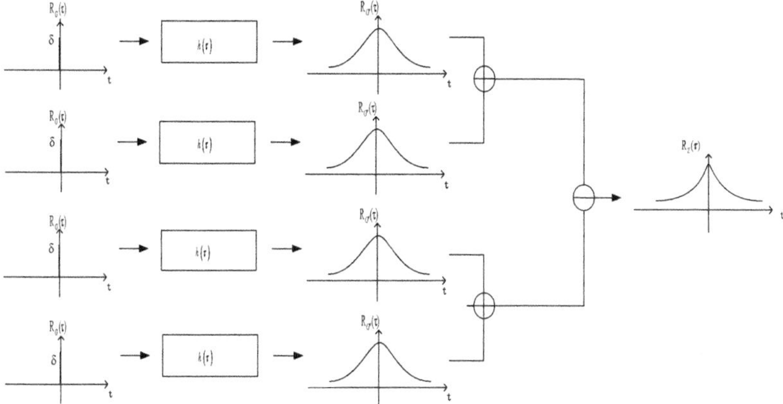

Fig. 3. Framework of CLM

system. Inspired by their work, we let four Gauss white noise series pass through a specific linear system with a certain impulse response to produce correlated Laplace noise series. The framework of CLM is illustrated in Fig. 3.

As shown in Fig. 3, first of all, four IID Gauss white noise series are generated, whose parameters are determined by the sensitivity function and protection intensity. Then the white noise series pass through a specific filter (which is one of the typical linear systems) and correlated Gauss series are obtained. Finally, a correlated Laplace series is produced according the principle to generate Laplace series from Gauss series.

4 Methodology

In this section, we first prove the correctness of problem definition and CLM. Then we describe the design principle of filter and other parameters.

4.1 Correctness of Problem Definition

We firstly demonstrate that the condition in Eq. (6) satisfies the definition of differential privacy.

Theorem 1. If the auto-correlation functions of noise and original series, $R_Z(\tau)$ and $R_{XX}(\tau)$, satisfy

$$R_Z(\tau) = R_{XX}(\tau)$$

Then $X^{'} = X + Z$ satisfies ε-differential privacy.

Proof. From Definition 1 we know that

$$\begin{aligned}
&CLM(M) \\
&= \sup_{x_i, x_i^{'}, R_{XX}(\tau), S} \ln \frac{Pr[M(X) \in S|X^{'}] \cdot Pr[X^{'}|R_{XX}(\tau)]}{Pr[M(X^{'}) \in S|X^{'}] \cdot Pr[X^{'}|R_{X^{'}X^{'}}(\tau)]} \\
&= \sup_{x_i, x_i^{'}, S} \ln \frac{Pr[M(X) \in S|X^{'}]}{Pr[M(X^{'}) \in S|X^{'}]} \\
&\quad + \sup_{x_i, x_i^{'}, R_{XX}(\tau), R_{X^{'}X^{'}}(\tau)} \ln \frac{Pr[X^{'}|R_{XX}(\tau)]}{Pr[X^{'}|R_{X^{'}X^{'}}(\tau)]}
\end{aligned}$$

Considering the right hand side,

$$\begin{aligned}
&\sup_{x_i, x_i^{'}, R_{XX}(\tau), R_{X^{'}X^{'}}(\tau)} \ln \frac{Pr[X^{'}|R_{XX}(\tau)]}{Pr[X^{'}|R_{X^{'}X^{'}}(\tau)]} \\
&= \sup_{x_i, x_i^{'}, R_{XX}(\tau), R_{X^{'}X^{'}}(\tau)} \\
&\quad \ln \frac{Pr[X^{'}|R_{XX}(\tau)]}{Pr[X^{'}|R_{XX}(\tau)] \cdot Pr[R_{XX}(\tau)|R_{X^{'}X^{'}}(\tau)]} \\
&= \sup_{x_i, x_i^{'}, R_{XX}(\tau), R_{X^{'}X^{'}}(\tau)} \ln \frac{1}{Pr[R_{XX}(\tau)|R_{X^{'}X^{'}}(\tau)]}
\end{aligned}$$

If $R_Z(\tau) = R_{XX}(\tau)$, then

$$\begin{aligned}
&\sup_{x_i, x_i^{'}, R_{XX}(\tau), R_{X^{'}X^{'}}(\tau)} \ln \frac{1}{Pr[R_{XX}(\tau)|R_{X^{'}X^{'}}(\tau)]} \\
&\leq \sup_{x_i, x_i^{'}, R_{XX}(\tau), R_{X^{'}X^{'}}(\tau)} \ln \frac{1}{Pr[R_{X^{'}X^{'}}(\tau)|R_{X^{'}X^{'}}(\tau)]} \\
&= \sup_{x_i, x_i^{'}, R_{XX}(\tau), R_{X^{'}X^{'}}(\tau)} \ln(1) \\
&= 0
\end{aligned}$$

Then we have

$$CTS - DP(M) = \sup \ln \frac{Pr[M(X) \in S|X^{'}]}{Pr[M(X^{'}) \in S|X^{'}]}$$

In addition,

$$\sup_{x_i, x_i^{'}, S} \ln \frac{Pr[M(X) \in S|X^{'}]}{Pr[M(X^{'}) \in S|X^{'}]} \leq \varepsilon$$

Then $CLM(M)$ satisfies ε-differential privacy.

4.2 Proof of CLM

In this section, we demonstrate the correctness of CLM, i.e., satisfies the condition in Eq. (6).

Theorem 2. If the auto-correlation function of $G_i^{'}$, $R_{G'}(\tau)$, satisfies that

$$R_{G'}(\tau) = \sqrt{\frac{R_{XX}(\tau)}{8}} \tag{6}$$

then the auto-correlation function of the noise series Z, calculated by $Z = {G_1^{'}}^2 + {G_2^{'}}^2 - {G_3^{'}}^2 - {G_4^{'}}^2$, satisfies $R_Z(\tau) = R_{XX}(\tau)$.

Proof sketch. Since $Z = {G_1^{'}}^2 + {G_2^{'}}^2 - {G_3^{'}}^2 - {G_4^{'}}^2$, then

$$\begin{aligned} R_Z(\tau) &= E[(g_1^{'2}(t) + g_2^{'2}(t) - g_3^{'2}(t) - g_4^{'2}(t)) \\ &\quad (g_1^{'2}(t+\tau) + g_2^{'2}(t+\tau) - g_3^{'2}(t+\tau) - g_4^{'2}(t+\tau))] \\ &= 4[R^2_{G_1^{'}}(\tau) + R^2_{G_2^{'}}(\tau) - R^2_{G_3^{'}}(\tau) - R^2_{G_4^{'}}(\tau)] \\ &= 8R^2_{G'}(\tau) \end{aligned}$$

if $R_{G'}(\tau) = \sqrt{\frac{R_{XX}(\tau)}{8}}$, then

$$R_Z(\tau) = R_{XX}(\tau)$$

4.3 Impulse Function of Filter

Theorem 2 shows the condition that $R_{G'}(\tau)$ should satisfy, then the parameters (mainly the impulse response) of the filter can be obtained according to the condition, as demonstrated in Theorem 3.

Theorem 3. If the pulse response of the filter $h(\tau)$ satisfies that

$$h(\tau) = \sqrt{\frac{R_{XX}(\tau)}{16\pi N_0}} \tag{7}$$

then the auto-correlation function of $G_i^{'}$, $R_{G'}(\tau)$, satisfies the condition in Eq. (7), where N_0 is the Power Spectral Density (PSD) of Z, $\delta(\tau)$ is the impulse function of white noise.

Proof. According to Theorem 2, the auto-correlation function $R_{G'}(\tau)$ of $G_i^{'}$ should satisfy:

$$R_{G'}(\tau) = \sqrt{\frac{R_{XX}(\tau)}{8}} \tag{8}$$

If we conduct Fourier transform of Eq. (9), we can obtain the PSD, $P_{G'}(\omega)$, of the correlated Gauss series $G_i^{'}$:

$$P_{G'}(\omega) = 2\pi\sqrt{\frac{R_{XX}(\tau)}{8}} \cdot \delta(\omega) \tag{9}$$

Because $G^{'}$ is the Gauss white noise series, the PSD of $G^{'}$, $P_G(\omega)$ is:

$$P_G(\omega) = N_0 \tag{10}$$

Since the filter is a linear system, the expression of $R_{G'}(\tau)$ is

$$R_{G'}(\tau) = R_G(\tau) * [h(\tau) * h(-\tau)] \tag{11}$$

where $R_G(\tau)$ represents the auto-correlation function of the Gauss white noise and the symbol $*$ denotes convolution. Furthermore, the auto-correlation function and the PSD are a pair of Fourier transformation. In order to facilitate the solution, Eq. (10) is performed by Fourier transform, then the PSD of the correlated Gauss series, $P_{G'}(\omega)$ is:

$$P_{G'}(\omega) = P_G(\omega) \cdot |H(\omega)|^2 \tag{12}$$

If the pulse response $h(\tau)$ of the filter is:

$$h(\tau) = \sqrt{\frac{R_{XX}(\tau)}{16\pi N_0}} \tag{13}$$

Then the system function of the filter is:

$$|H(\omega)|^2 = \frac{1}{N_0} 2\pi\sqrt{\frac{R_{XX}(\tau)}{8}} \cdot \delta(\omega) \tag{14}$$

Combine Eqs. (12) and (13), the auto-correlation function of correlated Gauss noise satisfies Theorem 2.

4.4 Order of Filter

The impulse response of the filter is obtained in Sect. 4.3. Theoretically, it can be realized using an infinite impulse response (IIR) filter, but IIR filters are not practical for use in mobile equipment with limited computation power. In order to address discrete correlated time-series efficiently, we simplify the filter model and use a second-order filter as an example to describe the design principle. A second-order filter can be used to approximately build the correlation instead of an IIR filter. Specifically, the formula for the impulse response $h(n)$ in a discrete system is

$$h(n) = \frac{[x^{'}(n) - \sum_{m=0}^{n-1} h(m)x(n-m)]}{x(0)} \tag{15}$$

After sequential iteration of Eq. (21), we obtain the impulse response $h(n)$ of the filter

$$h(n) = \sum_{k=0}^{\infty} \sqrt{R_{XX}(n)}\delta(n-k) \tag{16}$$

If it is a second-order filter, then its impulse response is

$$h(n) = R_{XX}(0)\delta(n) + R_{XX}(1)\delta(n-1) \tag{17}$$

Theorem 3 demonstrates the design principle of the filter. Now we summarize the complete procedure of CLM in Algorithm 1.

Algorithm 1. $X^{'} = CLM(X)$

Input:
Original time-series X;
Output:
Publishing time-series $X^{'}$.
1: The data owner calculates the auto-correlation function $R_{XX}(\tau)$ of the time-series X to be released.
2: The data owner generates four IID Gauss white noise series G_1, G_2, G_3, G_4, which have the same length with X. In addition, $G_i \sim N(0, \sqrt{2\lambda})$, $i \in \{1, 2, 3, 4\}$.
3: Let G_1, G_2, G_3, G_4 pass through a filter whose impulse response $h(\tau)$ is $\sqrt{\frac{R_{XX}(\tau)}{16\pi N_0}}$ and obtain four new Gauss noise series $G_1^{'}$, $G_2^{'}$, $G_3^{'}$, $G_4^{'}$ with the auto-correlation function $R_{G^{'}}(\tau) = \sqrt{\frac{R_{XX}(\tau)}{8}}$.
4: Calculate $Z = G_1^2 + G_2^2 - G_3^2 - G_4^2$.
5: Add noise series Z into X and obtain the publishing time-series $X^{'} = X + Z$.
6: return $X^{'}$.

5 Experimental Evaluation

In this section, we evaluate the performance of our method to conduct mechanism CLM. Specifically, security, utility of CLM are evaluated by our method.

5.1 Datasets and Configuration

We conducted our experiments on three real-world datasets, including Trajectory [26], Flu and Unemployment [27]. Each experiment was run 100 times.

In the three datasets, trajectory and unemployment datasets covering a longer timestamp have stronger correlation than the other two datasets. In order to collect various different types of statistical query results, a query set Q containing 1,000 random queries was conducted on every dataset. The data utility was measured by the index-Mean Squared Error (MSE):

$$MSE = \frac{1}{N} \sum_{x_i \in X} |x_i^{'} - x_i| \tag{18}$$

where N denotes the length of the series. A lower MSE implies a better utility.

5.2 Privacy Evaluation

The performance of the CLM mechanism was examined through comparison with five state-of-the-art approaches. We calculate the PDF of the queries and obtain the real privacy degree $\varepsilon^{'}$ under the setting privacy budgets, which vary from 0.1 to 0.9 with a step 0.2.

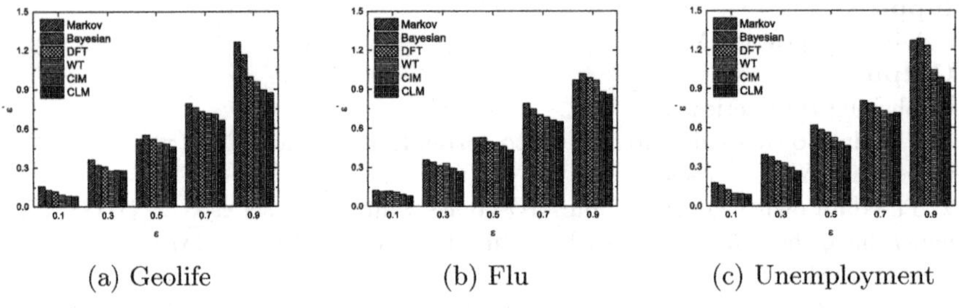

(a) Geolife (b) Flu (c) Unemployment

Fig. 4. Comparison results of privacy degree. (a) Geolife. (b) Flu. (c) Unemployment

Figure 4 illustrates the comparison results of privacy degree on all datasets. We observe that the $\varepsilon^{'}$ of CLM is lower than our setting value, which means stronger protect intensity. In Fig. 4a, when $\varepsilon = 0.1$, the $\varepsilon^{'}$ of CLM is 0.081 while the CIM is 0.086, with an improvement by 5.8%. When $\varepsilon = 0.9$, CLM achieves an $\varepsilon^{'}$ of 0.873 while CIM achieves 0.895, with an improvement by 2.5%. We observe that the privacy degree of CLM and CIM is smaller than our setting while the other algorithms exceed it. It demonstrates the effectiveness on privacy degree of our solution.

Moreover, the privacy degree of different schemes in Fig. 4b and c is closer than that in Fig. 4a. The reason is caused by the stronger correlation of the data in Fig. 4b and c. The biggest difference of $\varepsilon^{'}$ in different schemes appears in Fig. 4a, when $\varepsilon = 0.9$, the performance of CLM improves 30.9% than Markov. The results illustrate that the correlation of time-series actually has effect on the privacy degree. Because of the different description of correlation model and processing methods, the noise size added by these mechanisms are not the same, resulting in different privacy degree.

5.3 Utility Evaluation

To evaluate the effect of our solution on data utility, we report the Mean Squared Error of CLM and compare it with state-of-the-art mechanisms. The privacy budget ε varies from 0.1 to 0.9 with a 0.2 step and the MSE of different approaches is illustrated in Fig. 5.

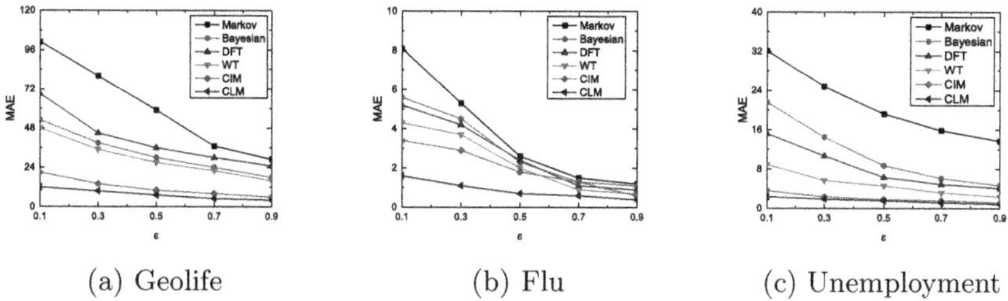

(a) Geolife (b) Flu (c) Unemployment

Fig. 5. Comparison results of utility. (a) Geolife. (b) Flu. (c) Unemployment

As shown in Fig. 5, we observe that CLM has lower MSE than any other methods on all datasets. Specifically, because of the strong correlation in datasets (a), the MSE is larger than that in Fig. 5b and c. In Fig. 5a, when $\varepsilon = 0.1$, CLM achieves a MSE of 12.1 while the existing best mechanism CIM achieves 21.6, with an improvement by 44.0%. When $\varepsilon = 0.9$, CLM achieves a MSE of 6.0 while CIM achieves 4.1, with an improvement by 31.7%. The improvement by CLM can also be observed in Fig. 5b and c, which shows that for correlated time-series data publication, CLM performs better than the other algorithms in data utility. This is because the perturbed noise in CLM maintains the same size with that in standard differential privacy, while the noise in correlation model based methods is generated according to the model, this actually leads to inaccurate publishing data. DFT and WT outperform model based algorithms but the utility of them depends on the transformation coefficients reserved. The results imply the effectiveness of CLM on correlated time-series data publication.

In terms of differential privacy, privacy budget ε is the decisive factor to determine privacy degree. According to Dwork, the reasonable value of ε for privacy preserving purposes is less than 1, and this criterion is followed in our experiments. In order to have a comprehensive evaluation, we evaluate CLM's performance under different privacy preserving degrees. Specifically, the privacy budget ε varies from 0.1 to 0.9 with a 0.2 step.

6 Conclusions

In our prior work, we have proposed a corrected Laplace noise mechanism (CLM) to differentially private publishing corrected data. But we have not given the proof and detailed steps to conduct CLM. In this paper, we provide the concrete steps and detailed parameters to imply CLM and prove the correctness of

CLM completely. Extensive experiments on real-life datasets demonstrate our implement method is effective for large amount of queries.

Acknowledgements. This work was supported in part by the National Natural Science Foundation of China (41671443), Applied Basic Research Program of Wuhan (2016010101010024), the Open Funding of NUIST, PAPD, CICAEET and Startup Foundation for Introducing Talent of Nanjing University of Information Science and Technology under Grant 2016r055, the Fundamental Research Funds for the Central Universities (2042017kf0044), China Postdoctoral Science Foundation (Grant No. 2017M612511) and LIESMARS Special Research Funding. The authors are grateful for the anonymous reviewers who made constructive comments and improvements.

References

1. Chanda, A.K., Saha, S., Nishi, M.A.: An efficient approach to mine flexible periodic patterns in time series databases. Eng. Appl. Artif. Intell. **44**, 46–63 (2015)
2. Fu, Z., Ren, K., Shu, J., Sun, X., Huang, F.: Enabling personalized search over encrypted outsourced data with efficiency improvement. IEEE Trans. Parall. Distrib. **27**, 2546–2559 (2016)
3. Qu, Z., Keeney, J., Robitzsch, S., Zaman, F., Wang, X.: Multilevel pattern mining architecture for automatic network monitoring in heterogeneous wireless communication networks. China Commun. **13**, 108–116 (2016)
4. Xue, Y., Jiang, J., Zhao, B., Ma, T.: A self-adaptive artificial bee colony algorithm based on global best for global optimization. Soft Comput. (2017). doi:10.1007/s00500-017-2547-1
5. Fu, Z., Sun, X., Ji, S., Xie, G.: Towards efficient content-aware search over encrypted outsourced data in cloud. In: 35th IEEE International Conference on Computer Communications. IEEE Press, San Francisco (2016). doi:10.1109/INFOCOM.2016.7524606
6. Laforet, F., Buchmann, E., Bohm, K.: Individual privacy constraints on time-series data. Inf. Syst. **54**, 74–91 (2015)
7. Dwork, C.: Differential privacy. In: Bugliesi, M., Preneel, B., Sassone, V., Wegener, I. (eds.) ICALP 2006. LNCS, vol. 4052, pp. 1–12. Springer, Heidelberg (2006). doi:10.1007/11787006_1
8. Kifer, D., Machanavajjhala, A.: No free lunch in data privacy. In: 35th ACM SIGMOD International Conference on Management of Data, pp. 1513–1522. ACM, New York (2011)
9. Kifer, D., Machanavajjhala, A.: Pufferfish: a framework for mathematical privacy definitions. ACM Trans. Database Syst. **39**, 1–36 (2014)
10. Xia, Z., Zhu, Y., Sun, X., Qin, Z., Ren, K.: Towards privacy-preserving content-based image retrieval in cloud computing. IEEE Trans. Cloud Comput. **99**, 1–1 (2015)
11. Xia, Z., Wang, X., Zhang, L., Qin, Z., Sun, X., Ren, K.: A privacy-preserving and copy-deterrence content-based image retrieval scheme in cloud computing. IEEE Trans. Inf. Forensics Secur. **11**, 2594–2608 (2016)
12. Xia, Z., Xiong, N., Vasilakos, A.V., Sun, X.: EPCBIR: an efficient and privacy-preserving content-based image retrieval scheme in cloud computing. Inf. Sci. **387**, 195–204 (2017)

13. Xia, Z., Lv, R., Zhu, Y., Ji, P., Sun, H., Shi, Y.: Fingerprint liveness detection using gradient-based texture features. Sig. Image. Video Process. **11**, 381–388 (2017)
14. Xiong, L., Xu, Z., Xu, Y.: A secure re-encryption scheme for data services in a cloud computing environment. Concurr. Comput. Pract. Exp. **27**, 4573–4585 (2015)
15. Chen, X.: Reversible watermarking method based on asymmetric-histogram shifting of prediction errors. J. Syst. Soft. **86**, 2620–2626 (2013)
16. Wang, H., Xu, Z.: CTS-DP: publishing correlated time-series data via differential privacy. Knowl.-Based Syst. **122**, 167–179 (2017)
17. Zhu, T., Xiong, P., Li, G.: Correlated differential privacy: hiding information in non-IID data set. IEEE Trans. Inf. Forensics Secur. **10**, 229–242 (2015)
18. Shen, E., Yu, T.: Mining frequent graph patterns with differential privacy. In: 19th ACM SIGKDD International Conference on Knowledge Discovery and Data Mining, pp. 545–553. ACM, New York (2013)
19. Yang, B., Sato, I., Nakagawa, H.: Bayesian differential privacy on correlated data. In: 21th ACM SIGMOD International Conference on Management of Data, pp. 747–762. ACM, New York (2015)
20. Jiang, W., Xie, C., Zhang, Z.: Wishart mechanism for differentially private principal components analysis. Comput. Sci. **9285**, 458–473 (2015)
21. Rastogi, V., Nath, S.: Differentially private aggregation of distributed time-series with transformation and encryption. In: 15th ACM SIGMOD International Conference on Management of Data, pp. 735–746. ACM, New York (2010)
22. Gehrke, J., Lui, E., Pass, R.: Towards privacy for social networks: a zero-knowledge based definition of privacy. In: 8th Theory of Cryptography Conference, pp. 432–449. ACM, New York (2011)
23. He, X., Machanavajjhala, A., Ding, B.: Blowfish privacy: tuning privacy-utility trade-offs using policies. In: 21th ACM SIGMOD International Conference on Management of Data, pp. 1447–1458. ACM, New York (2014)
24. Xiao, X., Wang, G., Gehrke, J.: Differential privacy via wavelet transforms. IEEE Trans. Knowl. Data Eng. **23**, 1200–1214 (2009)
25. Cynthia, D., Thakurta, K., Talwar, A.: Analyze gauss: optimal bounds for privacy-preserving PCA. In: 46th ACM Symposium on Theory of Computing, pp. 11–20. ACM, New York (2014)
26. Zheng, Y., Asia, M., Building, F.S.: Geolife: a collaborative social networking service among user, location and trajectory. Bull. Tech. Comm. Data Eng. **33**, 32–39 (2010)
27. Fan, L., Xiong, L., Sunderam, V.: FAST: differentially private real-time aggregate monitor with filtering and adaptive sampling. In: 18th ACM SIGMOD International Conference on Management of Data, pp. 1065–1068. ACM, New York (2013)

A Symmetric Authenticated Proxy Re-encryption Scheme with Provable Security

Zhiniang Peng[1], Shaohua Tang[1(✉)], and Linzhi Jiang[2,3]

[1] School of Computer Science and Engineering, South China University of Technology, Guangzhou 510006, China
246003@qq.com , shtang@ieee.org

[2] University of Electronic Science and Technology of China, Chengdu 611731, China
linzjiang@hotmail.com

[3] West Anhui University, Liuan 237012, China

Abstract. In crypto 2013, Dan et al. proposed a symmetric proxy re-encryption scheme based on key homomorphic PRF. It can be used to ensure the data privacy in cloud storage systems. However, it only focuses on preventing a honest-but-curious proxy from learning anything about the encrypted data. Although it can be made to provide integrity without disrupting the key homomorphism property by using MAC then encrypt with counter-mode, it's not a symmetric authenticated proxy re-encryption scheme because only the data owner can verify the integrity of some encrypted data. In this paper, we propose a symmetric authenticated proxy re-encryption scheme which can prevent a malicious proxy from tampering users' data. It can update the authentication tag as well as the ciphertext so that any intended user can verify the integrity of the encrypted data.

Keywords: Symmetric proxy re-encryption · Key homomorphic PRF · Cloud storage · Encryption-and-Mac

1 Introduction

Proxy re-encryption (PRE) [1,7] allows a proxy to transform a ciphertext encrypted under Alices key into one that can be decrypted by Bobs key. It has many useful applications in cloud storage [15,25]. Many proxy re-encryption schemes have been proposed in the asymmetric crypto world [8,11,14].

In many applications, data is always encrypted using symmetric cipher for better efficiency. Although an asymmetric PRE scheme can be efficiently used to re-encrypt the key which is used to encrypt the data with symmetric cipher [1], there is a weakness [23] that re-encrypting the key does not update the actual key used to encrypt data (the key of the symmetric encryption) and users who have the previous key can use the same key to decrypt the data.

For example, a company stores some data encrypted under a key sk_1 on a cloud based storage system and any employee who knows sk_1 has access to it.

X. Sun et al. (Eds.): ICCCS 2017, Part II, LNCS 10603, pp. 86–99, 2017.
https://doi.org/10.1007/978-3-319-68542-7_8

As employees leave the company, there is a need to re-encrypt it using a new key sk_2. To prevent the cloud from obtaining any information about the data, a naive way is to download the entire ciphertext from the cloud, re-encrypt under a new key, and upload the new ciphertext to the cloud. Unfortunately, downloading and re-uploading all the data from the cloud just for the purpose of key rotation results in considerable wasted bandwidth and cost. Asymmetric PRE schemes are not practical in this case especially when the size of the data to be encrypted is large.

Typically, there are two ways to solve this problem. The first one is using double encryption strategy proposed in [9], but its computation overhead is doubled and it's inflexible for many scenarios. The second one is to encrypt the data using a symmetric proxy re-encryption scheme (S-PRE) and use the cloud as the proxy holding the company's encrypted data. Now, by simply sending to the cloud the re-encryption key, the cloud can translate the ciphertext from key sk_1 to key sk_2 without doing any large data transfers.

There are S-PRE schemes based on some primitive with algebraic property such as ANOT [21,23], but those basic primitives are always inefficient. In crypto 2013, Dan et al. proposed a S-PRE [5] based on key homomorphic pseudorandom function (KH-PRF) [2]. It provides IND-CPA security and has various applications in cloud based systems.

The complete system model in cloud computing [10] or clouding storage should involve three different entities: the data owner, the data user and the cloud server [24,26]. Dan's scheme can be made to provide integrity without disrupting the key homomorphism property by using MAC-then-encrypt with counter-mode [12]. This can ensure that the data owner can verify the integrity of outsourced data. However, data users can not verify the integrity of encrypted data. One way to provide integrity for data users is to use digital signature schemes, but it will introduce asymmetric cryptography and it's not suitable for some applications where the data owner wants to hide his identity. To prevent the malicious proxy (cloud server) to tamper users' data, a better solution is to build a symmetric authenticated proxy re-encryption scheme where every user has independent MAC key and encryption key, the re-encryption algorithm can update the encryption key as well as the MAC key to make sure every intended data user can verify the integrity of some encrypted data with his/her own key.

Our Contributions: In this paper, we propose a symmetric authenticated proxy re-encryption (SA-PRE) scheme with provable security in random oracle model. It's the first SA-PRE scheme based on KH-PRF and it can re-encrypt the authentication tag as well as the ciphertext. Our scheme provides indistinguishability under chosen plaintext attack (IND-CPA) and ciphertext integrity (INT-CTXT) against any malicious user and malicious proxy. Our work also shows that generic Encryption-and-Mac composition [3] can be used to get an authenticated encryption scheme if nonce is used and the MAC is based on PRF.

2 Preliminaries

2.1 Key Homomorphic Pseudorandom Function

Definition 1. *Key homomorphic PRF Consider an efficiently computable function* $F : \mathcal{K} \times \mathcal{X} \rightarrow \mathcal{Y}$ *such that* $(\mathcal{K}, \oplus)$ *and* $(\mathcal{Y}, \otimes)$ *are both groups. We say that* $(F, \oplus, \otimes)$ *is a key homomorphic PRF if the following properties hold:*

(1) F *is a secure pseudorandom function.*
(2) For every $k_1, k_2 \in \mathcal{K}$ *and every* $x \in \mathcal{X}$, $F(k_1, x) \otimes F(k_2, x) = F(k_1 \oplus k_2, x)$.

Let $\mathcal{G}$ be a finite cyclic group of prime order q and let $H_1 : \mathcal{X} \rightarrow \mathcal{G}$ be a hash function modeled as random oracle. Then we define function $F_m : Z_q \times \mathcal{X} \rightarrow \mathcal{G}$ as:

$$F_m(k, x) \leftarrow H_1(x)^k.$$

If the Decision Diffe-Hellman (DDH) [4] assumption holds in $\mathcal{G}$, then F_m is a secure PRF in random oracle model [18]. As we can see that $F_m(k_1 + k_2, x) = F_m(k_1, x) \times F_m(k_2, x)$, this PRF is clearly key homomorphic. KH-PRF has many applications in cloud storage systems [19]. It can sometimes be replaced by a y-almost KH-PRF [6,13] which can be constructed based on LWE [20] or Ring-LWE problems [16,17].

2.2 Symmetric Proxy Re-encryption from KH-PRF

Let $F_e : \mathcal{K}_e \times \mathcal{X} \rightarrow \mathcal{Y}_e$ be a KH-PRF, the symmetric proxy re-encryption scheme proposed in [5] consists of the following algorithms.

Setup$(1^k) \rightarrow$ *pp*: According to the security parameter 1^k, the setup algorithm chooses appropriate parameters *pp* for F_e.

KeyGen$(pp) \rightarrow sk$: The key generation algorithm outputs a random key $sk \in F_e$.

ReKeyGen$(sk_i, sk_j) \rightarrow rk_{ij}$: The re-encryption key generation algorithm takes two secret key sk_i and sk_j as inputs and returns $rk_{ij} = sk_j - sk_i$ as re-encryption key.

Enc$(sk, m) \rightarrow C$: The encryption algorithm chooses a random r from X and computes $c = m + F_e(sk, r)$. Then it outputs (r, c).

ReEnc$(rk_{ij}, C_i) \rightarrow C_j$: The re-encryption algorithm takes ciphertext $C_i = (r_i, c_i)$ and re-encryption key rk_{ij} as inputs. It Outputs $(r_i, c_i + F_e(rk_{ij}, r_i))$.

Dec$(sk, C) :\rightarrow m$: The decryption algorithm takes ciphertext $C = (r, c)$ as inputs, it outputs $c - F(sk, r)$.

If F_e is a secure KH-PRF, then this scheme provides IND-CPA security against various adversaries.

3 Our Scheme

Our proposal is based on the S-PRE in [5]. We introduce an updatable MAC to it and prove its security in random oracle model. Let $F_e : \mathcal{K}_e \times \mathcal{X} \rightarrow \mathcal{Y}_e$ be a KH-PRF and $F_m : \mathcal{K}_m \times \mathcal{X} \rightarrow \mathcal{Y}_m$ be the KH-PRF based on DDH assumption. Suppose message $m \in \mathcal{Y}_e$, our SA-PRE scheme consists of the following six algorithms:

$Setup(1^k) \rightarrow pp$: According to the security parameter 1^k, the setup algorithm chooses appropriate parameters pp for F_e and F_m.
$KeyGen(pp) \rightarrow sk$: The key generation algorithm takes public parameters pp and outputs a random key sk as follows:

- Randomly choose a key $k_e \in \mathcal{K}_e$ for F_e.
- Randomly choose a key $k_m \in \mathcal{K}_m$ for F_m.
- Let $sk = (k_e, k_m)$.

$ReKeyGen(sk_i, sk_j) \rightarrow rk_{ij}$: The re-encryption key generation algorithm takes two secret key sk_i and sk_j as input. It outputs the re-encryption key rk_{ij} as follows:

- Compute $rk_{e_{ij}} = k_{e_j} - k_{e_i}$.
- Compute $rk_{m_{ij}} = k_{m_j}/k_{m_i}$.
- Let $rk_{ij} = (rk_{e_{ij}}, rk_{m_{ij}})$.

$Enc(sk, m) \rightarrow C$: The encryption algorithm takes message m and secret key $sk = (k_e, k_m)$ as input. It computes the ciphertext C as follows:

- Randomly choose nonce r.
- Compute $c = F_e(k_e, r) + m$.
- Compute $t = F_m(k_m, r||m)$.
- Let $C = (r, c, t)$.

$ReEnc(rk_{ij}, C_i) \rightarrow C_j$: The re-encryption algorithm takes ciphertext $C_i = (r_i, c_i, t_i)$ and re-encryption key $rk_{ij} = (rk_{e_{ij}}, rk_{m_{ij}})$ as input. It computes the ciphertext C_j as follows:

- Let $r_j = r_i$.
- Compute $c_j = c_i + F_e(rk_{e_{ij}}, r_j)$.
- Compute $t_j = (t_i)^{rk_{m_{ij}}}$.
- Let $C_j = (r_j, c_j, t_j)$.

$Dec(sk, C) :\rightarrow m$ or $\perp$: The decryption algorithm takes ciphertext $C = (r, c, t)$ and secret key $sk = (k_e, k_m)$ as input. It computes the results as follows:

- Compute $m = c - F_e(k_e, r)$.
- Return $\perp$ if $t \neq F_m(k_m, r||m)$.
- Otherwise return m

Correctness. Let $pp \leftarrow Setup(1^k)$, $sk \leftarrow KeyGen(pp)$ and $m \in \mathcal{Y}_e$. Then $Dec(sk, Enc(sk, m)) = m + F_e(k_e, r) - F_e(k_e, r) = m$ as desired for all nonce r. Let $sk_i \leftarrow KeyGen(pp)$, $sk_j \leftarrow KeyGen(pp)$ and $rk_{ij} \leftarrow ReKeyGen(sk_i, sk_j)$. Then $Dec(sk_j, ReEnc(rk_{ij}, Enc(sk_i, m))) = m$ holds for all nonce r.

If message m is too large to fit in an element of $\mathcal{Y}_e$, we can convert it to a vector over $\mathcal{Y}_e$ and extend the length of $F_e(k_e, r)$ by introducing a counter in r. Similar technique are used in the updatable encryption scheme in [5].

4 Security Analysis

In this section, we will prove that our SA-PRE scheme is a secure authenticated encryption against any malicious user and malicious proxy. Our scheme is designed by generic Encryption-and-Mac composition, meaning that we use an IND-CPA secure symmetric encryption scheme and a SUF-CMA secure MAC scheme in a black box way. In a ciphertext $C = (r, c, t)$, r is a nonce; c can be considered as a ciphertext encrypted by a stream cipher based on PRF F_e; t can be considered as a authentication tag computed by a MAC scheme based on PRF F_m.

However, Bellare and Namprempre proved that generic Encryption-and-Mac can only guarantee plaintext integrity (INT-PTXT) in paper [3]. This is because that MAC could reveal information about the plaintext. But this does not mean that our scheme is insecure. In fact, our work shows that generic Encryption-and-Mac composition can be used to get an INT-CTXT $\wedge$ IND-CPA secure authenticated encryption if nonce is introduced and the MAC is based on PRF.

4.1 Security Against Any Malicious User

We considered a security model inspired by the work of Canetti and Hohenberger [7]. A malicious user can access re-encryption oracle as well as encryption oracle. The encryption oracle ($C \leftarrow Enc(i, m)$) takes an user's index i and plaintext m as inputs and outputs the ciphertext C encrypted under user i's sk_i. The re-encrypt oracle ($C_j \leftarrow Re(C_i, sk_j)$) takes an ciphertext C_i and an new secret key sk_j as inputs and transforms the ciphertext encrypted under sk_i to a new ciphertext encrypted under sk_j.

INT-CTXT Against Any Malicious User

Theorem 1. *The advantage of any malicious user $\mathcal{A}$ in INT-CTXT game against our scheme $\mathcal{E}$ is less than ϵ_m, where ϵ_m is the advantage of some efficient algorithm against PRF F_m.*

Proof. We construct an adversary $\mathcal{B}$ which uses $\mathcal{A}$ to break the PRF F_m. The game between the challenger and the adversary $\mathcal{B}$ starts with the challenger first randomly chooses a PRF key $k_m \in K_m$. $\mathcal{B}$ can asks $F_m(k_m, r)$ for different r. Then $\mathcal{B}$ is supposed to output a PRF pair $(r, F_m(k_m, r))$ which has not been asked before. For simplicity, we suppose nonce r will never repeat.

$\mathcal{B}$ works by interacting with $\mathcal{A}$ in an INT-CTXT game as follows ($\mathcal{B}$ simulates the challenger for $\mathcal{A}$):

Setup: $\mathcal{B}$ chooses appropriate parameter pp and gives it to $\mathcal{A}$. $\mathcal{B}$ creates empty lists $\mathcal{SK}$ and $\mathcal{C}$.

Enc: When $\mathcal{A}$ asks the encryption oracle for user i and plaintext m_k, $\mathcal{B}$ responds as follows:

- If i is not in $\mathcal{SK}$, then randomly choose $k_{e_i} \in \mathcal{K}_e$ and $k_{m_i} \in \mathcal{K}_m$ for user i. Add (i, k_{e_i}, k_{m_i}) to $\mathcal{SK}$.
- Randomly choose r_k, and ask PRF challenger for $v_k = F_m(k_m, r_k||m_k)$.
- Let $c_k = m_k + F_e(k_{e_i}, r_k)$ and $t_k = {v_k}^{k_{m_i}}$.
- Add (r_k, c_k, t_k, m_k) to list $\mathcal{C}$ and respond to $\mathcal{A}$ with (r_k, c_k, t_k).

ReEnc: When $\mathcal{A}$ asks the re-encryption oracle to convert ciphertext $C = (r, c, t)$ encrypted under user i's secret key into ciphertext under secret key $sk_j = (k_{e_j}, k_{m_j})$, $\mathcal{B}$ responds as follows:

- If i is not in $\mathcal{SK}$:
  Return $\perp$, and stop the simulation.
- If C is in $\mathcal{C}$:
  Get the corresponding message m.
  Let $c_j = m + F_e(k_{e_j}, r)$, $t_j = F_m(k_{m_j}, r_j||m)$
  Respond to $\mathcal{A}$ with (r, c_j, t_j).
- If (r, t) is not in $\mathcal{C}$:
  Get the user i's key (i, k_{e_i}, k_{m_i}) from list $\mathcal{SK}$.
  Compute $m = c - F_e(k_{e_i}, r)$.
  Compute $t = t^{\frac{1}{k_{m_i}}}$.
  Output PRF pair $(r||m, t)$ to PRF challenger.
- If (r, t) is in $\mathcal{C}$, but c is not in $\mathcal{C}$:
  Compute $m = c - F_e(k_{e_i}, r)$.
  Get (m', c') from $\mathcal{C}[r, t]$.
  m certainly not equal to m', otherwise c will equal to c'.
  Compute $t = t^{\frac{1}{k_{m_i}}}$.
  Output PRF pair $(r||m, t)$ to PRF challenger.

Forge: Eventually, $\mathcal{A}$ outputs a forged ciphertext $C = (r, c, t)$ for user i. $\mathcal{B}$ outputs a PRF pair as follows:

- Get the user i's key (i, k_{e_i}, k_{m_i}) from list $\mathcal{SK}$.
- Compute $m = c - F_e(k_{e_i}, r)$.
- Compute $t = t^{\frac{1}{k_{m_i}}}$.
- Output PRF pair $(r||m, t)$ to PRF challenger.

Claim: During the simulation, $\mathcal{A}$'s view is identical to that in the real attack. If $\mathcal{A}$ can forge a valid ciphertext during ReEnc phase or Forge phase, $\mathcal{B}$ can use it to break PRF F_m with at least the some advantage. So we can conclude that

$$Adv_{\mathcal{E}}^{INT-CTXT}(\mathcal{A}) \leq Adv_{PRF}(\mathcal{B}) \leq \epsilon_{F_m}.$$

IND-CPA Against Any Malicious User

Theorem 2. *The advantage of any malicious user in IND-CPA game against our scheme* $\mathcal{E}$ *is less than* $2 * \epsilon_{F_m} + \epsilon_{F_e}$*, where* ϵ_{F_m} *is the advantage of some efficient algorithm against PRF* F_m *and* ϵ_{F_e} *is the advantage of some efficient algorithm against PRF* F_e*.*

Proof. Our proof uses a sequence of games [22].

Game 0: Fix a malicious user $\mathcal{A}$. Let us define Game 0 to be the real attack game in the definition of IND-CPA. We describe the attack game using Fig. 1 and define S_i to be the event that Game i return true, then $\mathcal{A}$'s advantage in Game 0 is $|Pr[S_0] - 1/2|$.

```
Game(1^k,b):
  pp ← Setup(1^k)
  (k_e, k_m) ← K
  m_0, m_1 ← A^{Re,Enc}(pp)
  r ← R
  c = F_e(k_e, r) + m_b
  t = F_m(k_m, r||m_b)
  b' ← A(r, c, t)
  return (b = b')

Enc(m):
  r ← R
  c = F_e(k_e, r) + m
  t = F_m(k_m, r||m)
  C[(r, c, t)] = m
  return: (r, c, t)

Re(C,ŝk):
  (r, c, t) = C
  m = c − F_e(k_e, r)
  If t ≠ F_m(k_m, r||m)
    return: ⊥
  (k̂_e, k̂_m) = ŝk
  c = m + F_e(k̂_e, r)
  t = F_m(k̂_m, r||m)
  return: (r, c, t)
```

Fig. 1. Game 0.

Game 1: [This is a transition based on INT-CTXT of $\mathcal{E}$.] We now make a small change to Game 0. The differences between Game 0 and Game 1 are boxed up in Fig. 2. Instead of re-encrypting every valid ciphertext, we only re-encrypt the ciphertext recorded in a list $\mathcal{C}$. Define E_{01} as the event that $\mathcal{A}$ produces a new valid ciphertext and asks re-encryption oracle to re-encrypt it. Game 0 and Game 1 are identical for $\mathcal{A}$ unless E_{01} happens. If E_{01} happens, it means that INT-CTXT of $\mathcal{E}$ is broken.

```
Game(1^k,b):
  pp ← Setup(1^k)
  (k_e, k_m) ← K
  m_0, m_1 ← A^{Re,Enc}(pp)
  r ← R
  c = F_e(k_e, r) + m_b
  t = F_m(k_m, r||m_b)
  b' ← A(r, c, t)
  return (b = b')

Enc(m):
  r ← R
  c = F(k_e, r) + m
  t = F(k_m, r||m)
  C[(r, c, t)] = m
  return: (r, c, t)

Re(C,ŝk):
  (r, c, t) = C
  [ m = C[c, r, t] ]
  [ If C[c, r, t] = ⊥ ]
    return: ⊥
  (k̂_e, k̂_m) = ŝk
  c = m + F_e(k̂_e, r)
  t = F_m(k̂_m, r||m)
  return: (r, c, t)
```

Fig. 2. Game 1.

If $\mathcal{A}$ can distinguish Game 0 and Game 1, then we can construct an adversary $\mathcal{F}$ that can break the INT-CTXT of $\mathcal{E}$ with at least the same advantage. Then we can get that

$$|Pr[S_0] - Pr[S_1]| \leq Pr[E_{01}] \leq Adv_{\mathcal{E}}^{INT-CTXT}(\mathcal{F}) \leq \epsilon_{F_m}. \quad (1)$$

Game 2: [This is a transition based on the indistinguishability of PRF F_e.] In Game 2, we use real random function $\mathcal{U}$ instead of PRF F_e during encryption and challenge ciphertext generation. Differences between Game 1 and Game 2 are boxed up in Fig. 3. If $\mathcal{A}$ can distinguish Game 1 and Game 2, then we can construct an adversary $\mathcal{F}_e$ that can break the indistinguishability of PRF F_e with at least the same advantage. Then we can get that

$$|Pr[S_2] - Pr[S_1]| \leq \epsilon_{F_e}. \tag{2}$$

Game$(1^k$,b):
$pp \leftarrow Setup(1^k)$
$(k_e, k_m) \leftarrow \mathcal{K}$
$m_0, m_1 \leftarrow \mathcal{A}^{Re,Enc}(pp)$
$r \leftarrow \mathcal{R}$
$\boxed{c = \mathcal{U} + m_b}$
$t = F_m(k_m, r||m_b)$
$b' \leftarrow \mathcal{A}(r, c, t)$
return $(b = b')$

Enc(m):
$r \leftarrow \mathcal{R}$
$\boxed{c = \mathcal{U} + m}$
$t = F(k_m, r||m)$
$\mathcal{C}[(r, c, t)] = m$
return: (r, c, t)

Re$(C,\hat{sk})$:
$(r, c, t) = C$
$m = \mathcal{C}[c, r, t]$
If $C[c, r, t] = \bot$
return: $\bot$
$(\hat{k_e}, \hat{k_m}) = \hat{sk}$
$c = m + F_e(\hat{k_e}, r)$
$t = F_m(\hat{k_m}, r||m)$
return: (r, c, t)

Fig. 3. Game 2.

Game$(1^k$,b):
$pp \leftarrow Setup(1^k)$
$(k_e, k_m) \leftarrow \mathcal{K}$
$m_0, m_1 \leftarrow \mathcal{A}^{Re,Enc}(pp)$
$r \leftarrow \mathcal{R}$
$c = \mathcal{U} + m_b$
$\boxed{t = \mathcal{U}}$
$b' \leftarrow \mathcal{A}(r, c, t)$
return $(b = b')$

Enc(m):
$r \leftarrow \mathcal{R}$
$c = \mathcal{U} + m$
$\boxed{t = \mathcal{U}}$
$\mathcal{C}[(r, c, t)] = m$
return: (r, c, t)

Re$(C,\hat{sk})$:
$(r, c, t) = C$
If $C[c, r, t] = \bot$
return: $\bot$
$(\hat{k_e}, \hat{k_m}) = \hat{sk}$
$m = C[c, r, t]$
$c = m + F_e(\hat{k_e}, r)$
$t = F_m(\hat{k_m}, r||m)$
return: (r, c, t)

Fig. 4. Game 3.

Game 3: [This is a transition based on the indistinguishability of PRF F_m.] In Game 3, we use real random function $\mathcal{U}$ instead of PRF F_m during encryption and challenge ciphertext generation. Differences between Game 2 and Game 3 are boxed up in Fig. 4. If $\mathcal{A}$ can distinguish Game 2 and Game 3, then we can construct an adversary $\mathcal{F}_m$ that can break the indistinguishability of PRF F_m with at least the same advantage. Then we can get that

$$|Pr[S_3] - Pr[S_2]| \leq \epsilon_{F_m}. \tag{3}$$

Combining 1, 2, and 3, we can get that

$$|Pr[S_0] - Pr[S_3]| \leq 2 * \epsilon_{F_m} + \epsilon_{F_e}.$$

In Game 3, all the ciphertexts leak no information about the secret key sk. The challenge ciphertext is independent of messages m_0 and m_1. This means that the adversary's advantage in Game 3 is $|Pr[S_3] - 1/2| = 0$. Then we can conclude that the advantage of any malicious user in IND-CPA game of our scheme is less than $2 * \epsilon_{F_m} + \epsilon_{F_e}$.

4.2 Security Against Any Malicious Proxy

A malicious proxy can access encryption oracle as well as re-encryption key generation oracle. The re-encryption key generation oracle ($C \leftarrow ReK(i,j)$) takes two users' index i and j and outputs the re-encryption key rk_{ij}, which can be used to convert a ciphertext originally encrypted under sk_i into a new ciphertext encrypted under sk_j.

INT-CTXT Against Any Malicious Proxy

Theorem 3. *The advantage of a malicious proxy in INT-CTXT game against our scheme $\mathcal{E}$ is less than ϵ_m, where ϵ_m is the advantage of some efficient algorithm against PRF F_m.*

Proof. We construct an adversary $\mathcal{B}$ using $\mathcal{A}$ to break the PRF F_m. The game between the challenger and the adversary $\mathcal{B}$ starts with the challenger first randomly chooses a PRF key $k_m \in \mathcal{K}_m$. $\mathcal{B}$ asks $F_m(k_m, r)$ for different r. Then $\mathcal{B}$ is supposed to output a PRF pair $(r, F_m(k_m, r))$ which was not asked before.

$\mathcal{B}$ works by interacting with $\mathcal{A}$ in an INT-CTXT game as follows ($\mathcal{B}$ simulates the challenger for $\mathcal{A}$):

Setup: $\mathcal{B}$ chooses appropriate parameters *pp* and gives it to $\mathcal{A}$. Then $\mathcal{B}$ creates empty lists $\mathcal{SK}$ and $\mathcal{C}$.

Enc: When $\mathcal{A}$ asks the encryption oracle for user i and plaintext m_k, $\mathcal{B}$ responds as follows:

- If i is not in $\mathcal{SK}$, then randomly choose $k_{e_i} \in \mathcal{K}_e$ and $k_{m_i} \in \mathcal{K}_m$ for user i and add (i, k_{e_i}, k_{m_i}) to $\mathcal{SK}$.
- Randomly choose r_k, and ask PRF challenger for $v_k = F_m(k_m, r_k || m_k)$.
- Let $c_k = m_k + F_e(k_{e_i}, r_k)$ and $t_k = {v_k}^{k_{m_i}}$.
- Respond to A with (r_k, c_k, t_k).

ReK: When $\mathcal{A}$ asks the re-encryption key generation oracle for a re-encryption key from user i to user j, $\mathcal{B}$ responds as follows:

- If i or j is not in $\mathcal{SK}$:
  Return $\perp$, and stop the simulation.
- Get (k_{e_i}, k_{m_i}) and (k_{e_j}, k_{m_j}).
- Let $rk_{e_{ij}} = k_{e_j} - k_{e_i}$ and $rk_{m_{ij}} = k_{m_j}/k_{m_i}$.
- Respond to $\mathcal{A}$ with $(rk_{e_{ij}}, rk_{m_{ij}})$.

Forge: Eventually, $\mathcal{A}$ outputs a forged ciphertext $C = (r, c, t)$ for user i. $\mathcal{B}$ outputs a PRF pair as follows:

- Get the user i's key (k_{e_i}, k_{m_i}) from list $\mathcal{SK}$.
- Compute $m = c - F_e(k_{e_i}, r)$.
- Compute $t = t^{\frac{1}{k_{m_i}}}$.
- Output PRF pair $(r||m, t)$ to PRF challenger.

Claim: During the simulation, $\mathcal{A}$'s view is identical to that in the real attack. If $\mathcal{A}$ can forge a valid ciphertext, $\mathcal{B}$ can use it to break PRF F_m. So we can conclude that

$$Adv_{\mathcal{E}}^{INT-CTXT}(\mathcal{A}) \leq Adv_{PRF}(\mathcal{B}) \leq \epsilon_{F_m}.$$

IND-CPA Against Any Malicious Proxy

Theorem 4. *The advantage of a malicious proxy in IND-CPA game against our scheme $\mathcal{E}$ is less than $\epsilon_{F_m} + \epsilon_{F_e}$, where ϵ_{F_m} is the advantage of some efficient algorithm against PRF F_m and ϵ_{F_e} is the advantage of some efficient algorithm against PRF F_e.*

Proof. We use a sequence of games in our proof.

Game $\hat{0}$: Fix a malicious proxy $\mathcal{A}$. Let us define Game $\hat{0}$ to be the real attack game against $\mathcal{A}$ in the definition of IND-CPA. We describe it in Fig. 5. We define $\hat{S}_i$ to be the event that Game $\hat{i}$ return true, then $\mathcal{A}$'s advantage in Game $\hat{0}$ is $|Pr[\hat{S}_0] - 1/2|$.

Game(1^k,b):	**Enc(i, m)**:	**Re(i, j)**:
$pp \leftarrow Setup(1^k)$ $(k_e, k_m) \leftarrow \mathcal{K}$ $i, m_0, m_1 \leftarrow \mathcal{A}^{Re,Enc}(pp)$ $r \leftarrow \mathcal{R}$ $(k_{e_i}, k_{m_i}) = SK[i]$ $c = F_e(k_e, r) + m_b$ $c = c + F(k_{e_i}, r)$ $t = F_m(k_m, r\|\|m_b)^{k_{m_i}}$ $b' \leftarrow \mathcal{A}(r, c, t)$ **return** $(b = b')$	If $SK[i] = \perp$ $(k_{e_i}, k_{m_i}) \leftarrow \mathcal{K}$ $SK[i] = (k_{e_i}, k_{m_i})$ $r \leftarrow \mathcal{R}$ $c = F(k_e, r) + m$ $c = c + F(k_{e_i}, r)$ $t = F(k_m, r\|\|m)^{k_{m_i}}$ **return:** (r, c, t)	If $SK[i] = \perp$ or $SK[j] = \perp$ **return:** $\perp$ $(k_{e_i}, k_{m_i}) = SK[i]$ $(k_{e_j}, k_{m_j}) = SK[j]$ $rk_{e_{ij}} = k_{e_j} - k_{e_i}$ $rk_{m_{ij}} = k_{m_j}/k_{m_i}$ **return:** $(rk_{e_{ij}}, rk_{m_{ij}})$

Fig. 5. Game $\hat{0}$.

Game $\hat{1}$: [This is a transition based on the indistinguishability of PRF F_e.] In Game $\hat{0}$, we use real random function $\mathcal{U}$ instead of PRF during encryption and challenge ciphertext generation. Differences between Game $\hat{0}$ and Game $\hat{1}$ are boxed up in Fig. 6. If $\mathcal{A}$ can distinguish Game $\hat{0}$ and Game $\hat{1}$, then we can construct an adversary $\mathcal{F}_m$ that can break the indistinguishability of PRF F_e with at least the same advantage. Then we can get that

$$|Pr[\hat{S}_0] - Pr[\hat{S}_1]| \leq \epsilon_{F_m}. \tag{4}$$

Game $\hat{2}$ [This is a transition based on the indistinguishability of PRF F_m.] In Game $\hat{2}$, we use real random function $\mathcal{U}$ instead of PRF F_m during encryption and challenge ciphertext generation. Differences between Game $\hat{2}$ and Game $\hat{1}$ are boxed up in Fig. 7. If there is an adversary $\mathcal{A}$ which can distinguish Game $\hat{2}$ and Game $\hat{1}$, then we can construct an adversary $\mathcal{F}_m$ that can break the indistinguishability of PRF F_m with at least the same advantage. Then we can get that

$$|Pr[\hat{S}_2] - Pr[\hat{S}_1]| \leq \epsilon_{F_m}. \tag{5}$$

Combining 4 and 5, we can get that

$$|Pr[\hat{S}_0] - Pr[\hat{S}_2] \leq |Pr[\hat{S}_0] - Pr[\hat{S}_1] + Pr[\hat{S}_1] - Pr[\hat{S}_2]| \leq \epsilon_{F_m} + \epsilon_{F_e}.$$

Game(1^k,b):	**Enc(i, m):**	**Re(i, j):**
$pp \leftarrow Setup(1^k)$ $(k_e, k_m) \leftarrow \mathcal{K}$ $i, m_0, m_1 \leftarrow \mathcal{A}^{Re,Enc}(pp)$ $r \leftarrow \mathcal{R}$ $(k_{e_i}, k_{m_i}) = SK[i]$ $\boxed{c = \mathcal{U} + m_b}$ $c = c + F_e(k_{e_i}, r)$ $t = F_m(k_m, r\|\|m_b)^{k_{m_i}}$ $b' \leftarrow \mathcal{A}(r, c, t)$ **return** $(b = b')$	If $SK[i] = \perp$ $(k_{e_i}, k_{m_i}) \leftarrow \mathcal{K}$ $SK[i] = (k_{e_i}, k_{m_i})$ $r \leftarrow R$ $\boxed{c = \mathcal{U} + m_0}$ $c = c + F_e(k_{e_i}, r)$ $t = F(k_m, r\|\|m)^{k_{m_i}}$ **return:** (r, c, t)	If $SK[i] = \perp$ or $SK[j] = \perp$ **return:** $\perp$ $(k_{e_i}, k_{m_i}) = SK[i]$ $(k_{e_j}, k_{m_j}) = SK[j]$ $rk_{e_{ij}} = k_{e_j} - k_{e_i}$ $rk_{m_{ij}} = k_{m_j} / k_{m_i}$ **return:** $(rk_{e_{ij}}, rk_{m_{ij}})$

Fig. 6. Game $\hat{1}$.

Game(1^k,b):	**Enc(i, m):**	**Re(i, j):**
$pp \leftarrow Setup(1^k)$ $(k_e, k_m) \leftarrow \mathcal{K}$ $i, m_0, m_1 \leftarrow \mathcal{A}^{Re,Enc}(pp)$ $r \leftarrow \mathcal{R}$ $(k_{e_i}, k_{m_i}) = SK[i]$ $c = \mathcal{U} + m_b$ $c = c + F_e(k_{e_i}, r)$ $\boxed{t = \mathcal{U}^{k_{m_i}}}$ $b' \leftarrow \mathcal{A}(r, c, t)$ **return** $(b = b')$	If $SK[i] = \perp$ $(k_{e_i}, k_{m_i}) \leftarrow \mathcal{K}$ $SK[i] = (k_{e_i}, k_{m_i})$ $r \leftarrow R$ $c = \mathcal{U} + m_0$ $c = c + F_e(k_{e_i}, r)$ $\boxed{t = \mathcal{U}^{k_{m_i}}}$ **return:** (r, c, t)	If $SK[i] = \perp$ or $SK[j] = \perp$ **return:** $\perp$ $(k_{e_i}, k_{m_i}) = SK[i]$ $(k_{e_j}, k_{m_j}) = SK[j]$ $rk_{e_{ij}} = k_{e_j} - k_{e_i}$ $rk_{m_{ij}} = k_{m_j} / k_{m_i}$ **return:** $(rk_{e_{ij}}, rk_{m_{ij}})$

Fig. 7. Game $\hat{2}$.

In Game $\hat{2}$, all the ciphertexts leak no information about secret key sk. The challenge ciphertext is independent of messages m_0 and m_1. This means that $\mathcal{A}$'s advantage in Game $\hat{2}$ is $|Pr[\hat{S}_2] - 1/2| = 0$. Then we can conclude that the advantage of any malicious proxy in IND-CPA game of our scheme is less than $\epsilon_{F_m} + \epsilon_{F_e}$.

4.3 IND-CCA Security

According to theorem 3.2 in [3], an encryption scheme that is both IND-CPA secure and IND-CTXT secure is also IND-CCA secure (INT-CPA $\wedge$ INT-CTXT $\rightarrow$ IND-CCA). Combining above theorems, we can conclude that our SA-PRE $\mathcal{E}$ is IND-CCA secure against any malicious user and any malicious proxy.

In fact, our security reduction shows that generic Encryption-and-Mac composition can be used to get an authenticated encryption scheme if nonce is used and the MAC is based on PRF.

5 Comparison and Conclusions

The most costly parts of our scheme are evaluations of KH-PRFs. So we compare our SA-PRE with Dan's S-PRE by counting the number of KH-PRFs need to be evaluated. Suppose we want to encrypt a message with size of n times the size of KH-PRF, we need to evaluate n KH-PRFs to mask the plaintext and 1 KH-PRF to compute the authentication tag. We give a comparison of our SA-PRE with Dan's S-PRE in Table 1.

Table 1. Comparison of our SA-PRE with Dan's S-PRE.

	Dan's S-PRF	Our SA-PRF
Security	IND-CPA	IND-CCA
Key size	Size of a KH-PRF key	Size of two KH-PRF keys
Encryption	n KH-PRF evaluations	n + 1 KH-PRF evaluations
Decryption	n KH-PRF evaluations	n + 1 KH-PRF evaluations
ReKeyGen	1 KH-PRF basic operation	2 KH-PRF basic operations
Re-encryption	n KH-PRF evaluations	n + 1 KH-PRF evaluations

From Table 1, we can observe that the key size and re-encryption key generating time of our SA-PRE are doubled compared with the Dan's S-PRE and our SA-PRE need one more KH-PRE evaluations in encryption, decryption and re-encryption compared with Dan's S-PRE. When n become larger, the performance gap between our SA-PRE will be negligible. So we can conclude that our SA-PRE is comparable to Dan's S-PRE in performance.

In this paper, we propose a SA-PRE by introducing an updatable MAC into Dan's S-PRE to provide authentication. The re-encryption process can update the authentication key as well as the encryption key. We prove that it's IND-CPA and INT-CTXT secure against any malicious user or any malicious proxy. Our work also shows that the generic Encryption-and-Mac composition can be used to get an authenticated encryption scheme if nonce is used and the MAC is based on PRF.

Acknowledgments. This work was supported by the National Natural Science Foundation of China (Nos. 61632013, U1135004 and 61170080), 973 Program (No. 2014CB360501), Guangdong Provincial Natural Science Foundation (No. 2014A030308006), and Guangdong Provincial Project of Science and Technology (No. 2016B090920081).

References

1. Ateniese, G., Fu, K., Green, M., Hohenberger, S.: Improved proxy re-encryption schemes with applications to secure distributed storage. ACM Trans. Inf. Syst. Secur. (TISSEC) **9**(1), 1–30 (2006). ACM, New York
2. Banerjee, A., Peikert, C.: New and improved key-homomorphic pseudorandom functions. In: Garay, J.A., Gennaro, R. (eds.) CRYPTO 2014. LNCS, vol. 8616, pp. 353–370. Springer, Heidelberg (2014). doi:10.1007/978-3-662-44371-2_20

3. Bellare, M., Namprempre, C.: Authenticated encryption: relations among notions and analysis of the generic composition paradigm. In: Okamoto, T. (ed.) ASIACRYPT 2000. LNCS, vol. 1976, pp. 531–545. Springer, Heidelberg (2000). doi:10.1007/3-540-44448-3_41
4. Boneh, D.: The decision Diffie-Hellman problem. In: Buhler, J.P. (ed.) ANTS 1998. LNCS, vol. 1423, pp. 48–63. Springer, Heidelberg (1998). doi:10.1007/BFb0054851
5. Boneh, D., Lewi, K., Montgomery, H., Raghunathan, A.: Key homomorphic PRFs and their applications. In: Canetti, R., Garay, J.A. (eds.) CRYPTO 2013. LNCS, vol. 8042, pp. 410–428. Springer, Heidelberg (2013). doi:10.1007/978-3-642-40041-4_23
6. Brakerski, Z., Vaikuntanathan, V.: Constrained key-homomorphic PRFs from standard lattice assumptions. In: Dodis, Y., Nielsen, J.B. (eds.) TCC 2015. LNCS, vol. 9015, pp. 1–30. Springer, Heidelberg (2015). doi:10.1007/978-3-662-46497-7_1
7. Canetti, R., Hohenberger, S.: Chosen-ciphertext secure proxy re-encryption. In: Proceedings of the 14th ACM Conference on Computer and Communications Security, pp. 185–194. ACM, New York (2007)
8. Chow, S.S.M., Weng, J., Yang, Y., Deng, R.H.: Efficient unidirectional proxy re-encryption. In: Bernstein, D.J., Lange, T. (eds.) AFRICACRYPT 2010. LNCS, vol. 6055, pp. 316–332. Springer, Heidelberg (2010). doi:10.1007/978-3-642-12678-9_19
9. Cool, D., Keromytis, A.D.: Conversion and proxy functions for symmetric key ciphers. In: International Conference on Information Technology: Coding and Computing (ITCC 2005)-Volume II, vol. 1, pp. 662–667. IEEE (2005)
10. Fu, Z., Ren, K., Shu, J., Sun, X., Huang, F.: Enabling personalized search over encrypted outsourced data with efficiency improvement. IEEE Trans. Parallel Distrib. Syst. **27**(9), 2546–2559 (2016)
11. Green, M., Ateniese, G.: Identity-based proxy re-encryption. In: Katz, J., Yung, M. (eds.) ACNS 2007. LNCS, vol. 4521, pp. 288–306. Springer, Heidelberg (2007). doi:10.1007/978-3-540-72738-5_19
12. Krawczyk, H.: The order of encryption and authentication for protecting communications (or: how secure is SSL?). In: Kilian, J. (ed.) CRYPTO 2001. LNCS, vol. 2139, pp. 310–331. Springer, Heidelberg (2001). doi:10.1007/3-540-44647-8_19
13. Lewi, K., Montgomery, H., Raghunathan, A.: Improved constructions of PRFs secure against related-key attacks. In: Boureanu, I., Owesarski, P., Vaudenay, S. (eds.) ACNS 2014. LNCS, vol. 8479, pp. 44–61. Springer, Cham (2014). doi:10.1007/978-3-319-07536-5_4
14. Libert, B., Vergnaud, D.: Unidirectional chosen-ciphertext secure proxy re-encryption. In: Cramer, R. (ed.) PKC 2008. LNCS, vol. 4939, pp. 360–379. Springer, Heidelberg (2008). doi:10.1007/978-3-540-78440-1_21
15. Liu, Q., Wang, G., Wu, J.: Time-based proxy re-encryption scheme for secure data sharing in a cloud environment. Inf. Sci. **258**, 355–370 (2014). Elsevier
16. Lyubashevsky, V., Peikert, C., Regev, O.: On ideal lattices and learning with errors over rings. In: Gilbert, H. (ed.) EUROCRYPT 2010. LNCS, vol. 6110, pp. 1–23. Springer, Heidelberg (2010). doi:10.1007/978-3-642-13190-5_1
17. Lyubashevsky, V., Peikert, C., Regev, O.: A toolkit for ring-LWE cryptography. In: Johansson, T., Nguyen, P.Q. (eds.) EUROCRYPT 2013. LNCS, vol. 7881, pp. 35–54. Springer, Heidelberg (2013). doi:10.1007/978-3-642-38348-9_3
18. Naor, M., Pinkas, B., Reingold, O.: Distributed pseudo-random functions and KDCs. In: Stern, J. (ed.) EUROCRYPT 1999. LNCS, vol. 1592, pp. 327–346. Springer, Heidelberg (1999). doi:10.1007/3-540-48910-X_23

19. Parra, J.R., Chan, T., Ho, S.-W.: A noiseless key-homomorphic PRF: application on distributed storage systems. In: Liu, J.K., Steinfeld, R. (eds.) ACISP 2016. LNCS, vol. 9723, pp. 505–513. Springer, Cham (2016). doi:10.1007/978-3-319-40367-0_34
20. Regev, O.: The learning with errors problem. In: Invited Survey in CCC, p. 15 (2010)
21. Rivest, R.L.: All-or-nothing encryption and the package transform. In: Biham, E. (ed.) FSE 1997. LNCS, vol. 1267, pp. 210–218. Springer, Heidelberg (1997). doi:10.1007/BFb0052348
22. Shoup, V.: Sequences of games: a tool for taming complexity in security proofs. IACR Cryptology ePrint Archive 2004, 332 (2004)
23. Syalim, A., Nishide, T., Sakurai, K.: Realizing proxy re-encryption in the symmetric world. In: Abd Manaf, A., Zeki, A., Zamani, M., Chuprat, S., El-Qawasmeh, E. (eds.) ICIEIS 2011. CCIS, vol. 251, pp. 259–274. Springer, Heidelberg (2011). doi:10.1007/978-3-642-25327-0_23
24. Xia, Z., Wang, X., Sun, X., Wang, Q.: A secure and dynamic multi-keyword ranked search scheme over encrypted cloud data. IEEE Trans. Parallel Distrib. Syst. **27**(2), 340–352 (2016)
25. Xu, L., Wu, X., Zhang, X.: CL-PRE: a certificateless proxy re-encryption scheme for secure data sharing with public cloud. In: Proceedings of the 7th ACM Symposium on Information, Computer and Communications Security, pp. 87–88. ACM, New York (2012)
26. Zhangjie, F., Xingming, S., Qi, L., Lu, Z., Jiangang, S.: Achieving efficient cloud search services: multi-keyword ranked search over encrypted cloud data supporting parallel computing. IEICE Trans. Commun. **98**(1), 190–200 (2015)

Quantum Secret Sharing in Noisy Environment

Ming-Ming Wang[1,2(✉)], Zhi-Guo Qu[2], and Mohamed Elhoseny[3]

[1] School of Computer Science, Xi'an Polytechnic University, Xi'an 710048, China
bluess1982@126.com
[2] Jiangsu Engineering Center of Network Monitoring,
Nanjing University of Information Science and Technology, Nanjing 210044, China
[3] Faculty of Computers and Information Sciences, Mansoura University,
Mansoura, Egypt

Abstract. As an unavoidable factor of real-world implementation of quantum cryptograph, quantum noise severally affects the security and reliability of the quantum system. In this paper, we study how QSS, an important branch of quantum cryptograph, is affected by noise or decoherence. QSS protocols for sharing classical information and quantum states are studied in four types of noise that usually encountered in real-world, i.e., the bit-flip, phase-flip (phase-damping), depolarizing and amplitude-damping noise, respectively. Two methods are introduced to evaluate the effect of noise. For the QSS protocol sharing classical information, the efficiency for generating secret key is used. Our results show that the efficiencies are quiet different from each other in four types of noise. While for the protocol sharing quantum states, the output states and the state-independent average fidelity are studied, respectively. It indicates that the players will get two different output states in the amplitude-damping noise, but get one output state in the other three types of noise. Besides, the state-independent average fidelity behaves differently from each other. Our study will be helpful for analyzing and improving quantum secure communications protocols in real-world.

Keywords: Quantum secure communications · Quantum noise · Quantum secret sharing · Fidelity · Efficiency

1 Introduction

In the past few decades, quantum physics has great promoted the development of communications and computations. Quantum cryptograph, especially quantum key distribution [1], can achieve a high-level security [2–4] than classical ones [5–8]. Besides, quantum algorithms, such as Grovers search algorithm [9], can solve a certain problem much faster than classical algorithms [10–12]. In cryptograph, secret sharing is a basic primitive protocol that could be used to protect highly sensitive information. A typical secret sharing protocol is the (k, n) threshold protocol [5,13], where a secret can be split into n pieces in such a way that any set of k pieces is enough to reconstruct the secret, but any set less than k pieces cannot get any information of the secret. With the development

X. Sun et al. (Eds.): ICCCS 2017, Part II, LNCS 10603, pp. 100–112, 2017.
https://doi.org/10.1007/978-3-319-68542-7_9

of quantum cryptography, secret sharing has been presented in quantum setting, which is known as quantum secret sharing (QSS). In 1999, Hillary et al. [2] proposed the first QSS protocol by using Greenberger-Horne-Zeilinger (GHZ) states for eavesdropping detection and secret splitting, which is also called the HBB-QSS protocol. In the HBB-QSS protocol, a dealer named Alice can create a random secret for two players Bob and Charlie, where the secret can only be recovered by two of the players, while one cannot get anything meaningful. After that, the HBB-QSS protocol has been generalized to multiparty [14] and high-dimensional system [15]. Besides of entanglement-based protocols, QSS protocols without entanglement have also been developed [16,17]. These above QSS protocols deal with sharing classical information among players. Apart from QSS protocols for sharing classical information, there exists another type of QSS protocols for sharing quantum states among a set of players [18,19], which is also known as quantum state sharing (QSTS) [20]. It should be mentioned that Hillary et al. also proposed a QSTS protocol in Ref. [2], which will be called as the HBB-QSTS protocol hereafter.

Most of quantum communications protocols were studied in ideal situation where no outside interaction was considered. But in real-world, a quantum system will unavoidably interact with its surrounding environment. For example, transmission or storage of a qubit will suffer from decoherence with the environment and produce the pure state into the mixed one. Different quantum noise models have been established to describe this interaction. In recent years, some quantum communications protocols subjected to noisy environment have been studied, including quantum teleportation [21–24], remote state preparation [25–29] and quantum cryptograph [30,31], etc.

To our knowledge, there is a few discussions of QSS and QSTS protocols in noisy environment [32]. In this paper, we will study the effect of quantum noise on QSS protocols, not only QSS protocols for sharing classical information, but also QSTS protocols for sharing quantum state. And we will consider all types of noise usually encountered in real-world implementation of quantum communications protocols, namely, the bit-flip, phase-flip (phase-damping), depolarizing, and amplitude-damping noise. Taking the most prestigious HBB-QSS protocol and HBB-QSTS protocol of a single-qubit as examples, we will show that for different types of noise, the efficiency of QSS, the output state and fidelity of QSTS vary quite different from each other. The rest of this paper is organized as follows. The noise models of different types of noise are presented in Sect. 2. The HBB-QSS protocol in noisy environment is studied in Sect. 3. While the HBB-QSTS protocol of a single-qubit in noisy environment is studied in Sect. 4. The paper is discussed and concluded in Sect. 5.

2 Noise Models

To begin with, we will give a brief introduction of the noise models used in the paper. There are four types of noise usually encountered in real-world quantum communications protocols, namely the bit-flip, phase-flip or phase-damping, depolarizing and amplitude-damping noise [33].

2.1 The Bit-Flip Noise

The bit-flip noise changes the state of a qubit from $|0\rangle$ to $|1\rangle$ or from $|1\rangle$ to $|0\rangle$ with probability λ and its Kraus operators are

$$E_0 = \sqrt{1-\lambda}\, I,\ E_1 = \sqrt{\lambda}\, X, \tag{1}$$

where I is identity matrix, X is the Pauli matrix and $0 \le \lambda \le 1$ is the noise parameter.

2.2 The Phase-Flip or Phase-Damping Noise

The phase-flip noise changes the phase of the qubit $|1\rangle$ to $-|1\rangle$ with probability λ and it can be described by Kraus operators as

$$E_0 = \sqrt{1-\lambda}\, I,\ E_1 = \sqrt{\lambda}\, Z, \tag{2}$$

where Z is the Pauli matrix and $0 \le \lambda \le 1$. Note that the phase-flip noise is equivalent to the phase-damping noise [33], which describes the loss of quantum information without energy dissipation.

2.3 The Depolarizing Noise

The depolarizing noise takes a qubit and replaces it with a completely mixed state $\frac{I}{2}$ with probability λ and its Kraus operators are

$$E_0 = \sqrt{1-\lambda}\, I,\ E_1 = \sqrt{\frac{\lambda}{3}}\, X,\ E_2 = \sqrt{\frac{\lambda}{3}}\, Z,\ E_3 = \sqrt{\frac{\lambda}{3}}\, Y, \tag{3}$$

where X, Z, Y are Pauli matrices and $0 \le \lambda \le 1$.

2.4 The Amplitude-Damping Noise

The amplitude-damping noise describes the energy dissipation effects due to loss of energy from a quantum system and its Kraus operators are as follows

$$E_0 = \begin{pmatrix} 1 & 0 \\ 0 & \sqrt{1-\lambda} \end{pmatrix},\ E_1 = \begin{pmatrix} 0 & \sqrt{\lambda} \\ 0 & 0 \end{pmatrix}, \tag{4}$$

where $0 \le \lambda \le 1$ indicates the noise parameter.

3 Quantum Secret Sharing of Classical Information in Noisy Environment

In ideal situation, it is assumed that an entangled quantum resource has been shared among participants. However, in real situation, there must be a source generator who generates the entangled states and distributes each qubit to relevant player. For one thing, each distribution quantum channel will inevitably be affected by quantum noise in real-world implementation. Besides, the storage of qubits will also be affected by quantum noise. In the following, we will discuss how the HBB-QSS protocol [2] is affected by noise.

3.1 The HBB-QSS Protocol in Density Matrix Form

In the three-party HBB-QSS protocol, the quantum resource used is a set of three-qubit GHZ states, each of which has the form

$$|\mathrm{GHZ_3}\rangle = \frac{1}{\sqrt{2}}(|000\rangle + |111\rangle)_{\mathrm{ABC}}, \tag{5}$$

where subscripts A, B and C are qubits of the GHZ triplet. To be specific, Alice holds qubit A, Bob holds B and Charlie holds C.

Two Pauli measurement bases X and Y are introduced in the protocol, where their eigenstates are

$$|x_\pm\rangle = \frac{1}{\sqrt{2}}(|0\rangle \pm |1\rangle), |y_\pm\rangle = \frac{1}{\sqrt{2}}(|0\rangle \pm \mathrm{i}|1\rangle). \tag{6}$$

In the HBB-QSS protocol, each player measures his/her qubit either in the X basis or the Y basis randomly. If the measurement bases chosen by three parties are in the set of $\{XXX, XYY, YXY, YYX\}$, their outcomes are correlated and can be used for secret key generating or eavesdropping detection. While the GHZ carrier becomes useless if the chosen measurement bases are in $\{XXY, XYX, YXX, YYY\}$. Therefore, the efficiency of the protocol is 50% and half of the entangled GHZ states have to be discarded.

In quantum noisy environment, it is more convenient to represent the system in the form of density operator. To simplify the analysis, suppose the noise type on each qubit is identical. In this case, the entangled source shared among three players after interaction with the noisy environment can be rewritten as

$$\rho_{\mathrm{source}} = \sum_{i,j,k} E_i^{\mathrm{A}} E_j^{\mathrm{B}} E_k^{\mathrm{C}} * |\mathrm{GHZ_3}\rangle\langle \mathrm{GHZ_3}| * E_i^{\mathrm{A}\dagger} E_j^{\mathrm{B}\dagger} E_k^{\mathrm{C}\dagger}, \tag{7}$$

where E_i represents the noise operator that acts on qubit A, E_j represents the noise operator on qubit B and E_k represents the noise operator on qubit C.

Note that only if the measurement bases chosen by three parties are in $\{XXX, XYY, YXY, YYX\}$, their outcomes become correlated. For each of these four bases, only half of the results are useful for secret key generating. It is necessary to calculate the probability of each useful results in noisy environment, respectively. For example, if Alice, Bob and Charlie have choose their measurement bases as XXX, only the following four measurement results are useful, that is $|x_+\rangle|x_+\rangle|x_+\rangle$, $|x_+\rangle|x_-\rangle|x_-\rangle$, $|x_-\rangle|x_+\rangle|x_-\rangle$ and $|x_-\rangle|x_-\rangle|x_+\rangle$. And one of the probabilities that Alice gets $|x_+\rangle$, Bob gets $|x_+\rangle$ and Charlie gets $|x_+\rangle$ on condition that measurement bases XXX are chosen will be

$$p\{x_+x_+x_+|XXX\} = \mathrm{tr}\left[(M_{x_+} \otimes M_{x_+} \otimes M_{x_+}) * \rho_{\mathrm{source}}\right], \tag{8}$$

where $M_{x_+} = |x_+\rangle\langle x_+|$.

The efficiency that Bob and Charlie get a useful bit from Alice can be represented as

$$\begin{aligned}\eta = \frac{1}{4}\,[&p(x_+x_+x_+|XXX) + p(x_+x_-x_-|XXX)\\&+p(x_-x_+x_-|XXX) + p(x_-x_-x_+|XXX)\\&+p(x_+y_+y_-|XYY) + p(x_+y_-y_+|XYY)\\&+p(x_-y_+y_+|XYY) + p(x_-y_-y_-|XYY)\\&+p(y_+x_+y_-|YXY) + p(y_+x_-y_+|YXY)\\&+p(y_-x_+y_+|YXY) + p(y_-x_-y_-|YXY)\\&+p(y_+y_+x_-|YYX) + p\{y_+y_-x_+|YYX)\\&+p(y_-y_+x_+|YYX) + p(y_-y_-x_-|YYX)]\,,\end{aligned} \tag{9}$$

since $p(XXX) = p(XYY) = p(YXY) = p(YYX) = \frac{1}{4}$ is the probability that useful measurement bases are chosen.

3.2 The Efficiency of HBB-QSS Protocol in Noisy Environment

The efficiencies of the HBB-QSS protocol in four types of noise can be calculated as follows. In the bit-flip noise, one will get the efficiency as

$$\eta^{\mathrm{BF}} = \frac{1}{2}(2 - 3\lambda + 3\lambda^2). \tag{10}$$

In the phase-flip noise, the efficiency is

$$\eta^{\mathrm{PF}} = 1 - 3\lambda + 6\lambda^2 - 4\lambda^3. \tag{11}$$

In the depolarizing noise, the efficiency is

$$\eta^{\mathrm{DE}} = 1 - 2\lambda + \frac{8\lambda^2}{3} - \frac{32\lambda^3}{27}. \tag{12}$$

In the amplitude-damping noise, one will get

$$\eta^{\mathrm{AM}} = \frac{1}{2}[1 + (1-\lambda)^{\frac{3}{2}}]. \tag{13}$$

The efficiencies of the HBB-QSS protocol in different types of noise are plotted in Fig. 1. As is shown, the maximal efficiency is η^{AM} when $\lambda < 0.582$, and η^{BF} when $\lambda > 0.582$, which means the amplitude-damping or the bit-flip noise has the slightest effect on the HBB-QSS protocol depending on the value of λ. The minimal efficiency is always η^{PF} and it will be 0 when $\lambda = 1$, which means the phase-flip noise has the worst effect on the HBB-QSS protocol and the protocol will totally fail in a complete phase-flip noise. Different from the others, the efficiency η^{BF} decreases when $\lambda < \frac{1}{2}$ and increases to 1 when $\lambda > \frac{1}{2}$ and its minimal value is $\frac{5}{8}$.

Besides, η^{PF}, η^{AM} and η^{DE} decrease with the increase of the noise rate λ. But η^{PF} decreases rapidly towards 0 with the increase of λ. While η^{DE} and η^{AM} will get their minimal values as $\frac{13}{27}$ and $\frac{1}{2}$ respectively when $\lambda = 1$. η^{DE} is always less than η^{AM}, which means the effect of the depolarizing noise on quantum system is more serious than the amplitude-damping noise.

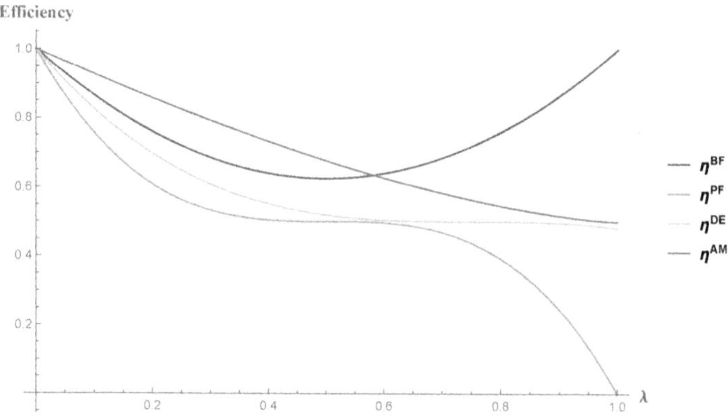

Fig. 1. The efficiencies of the HBB-QSS protocol in four different types of noise with noise parameter λ, where η^{BF} represents the efficiency in the bit-flip noise, η^{PF} in the phase-flip noise, η^{DE} in the depolarizing noise and η^{AM} in the amplitude-damping noise.

4 Quantum State Sharing in Noisy Environment

In the following, we are going to study the effect of noise on the HBB-QSTS protocol of a single-qubit, which was also appeared in [2].

4.1 The HBB-QSTS Protocol in Density Matrix Form

In the HBB-QSTS protocol, the dealer Alice has a secret state and she wants to share it with Bob and Charlie. The qubit has the form

$$|\phi\rangle_{\mathrm{T}} = a|0\rangle + be^{\mathrm{i}c}|1\rangle, \tag{14}$$

with $a, b, c \in \mathcal{R}$, $c \in [0, 2\pi]$ and $a^2 + b^2 = 1$. Note that the above form is different from the form in [2] where complex coefficients was considered, but they only differ by a global phase with no physical significance.

Alice, Bob and Charlie use a three-qubit GHZ state as entangled resource, where each party holds one qubit. Then, the quantum system can be presented as

$$\rho_{\mathrm{sys}} = |\phi\rangle\langle\phi|_{\mathrm{T}} \otimes |\mathrm{GHZ}_3\rangle\langle\mathrm{GHZ}_3|_{\mathrm{ABC}}. \tag{15}$$

To simplify the analysis, suppose the noise type on each qubit is identical. In this case, the quantum system among three players after interaction with noisy environment can be rewritten as

$$\xi(\rho_{\mathrm{sys}}) = \sum_{i,j,k,l} E_i^{\mathrm{T}} E_j^{\mathrm{A}} E_k^{\mathrm{B}} E_l^{\mathrm{C}} * \rho_{\mathrm{sys}} * E_i^{\mathrm{T}\dagger} E_j^{\mathrm{A}\dagger} E_k^{\mathrm{B}\dagger} E_l^{\mathrm{C}\dagger}. \tag{16}$$

To begin with, Alice performs a Bell-basis measurement on qubits T and A, where the Bell-basis has the form

$$\begin{aligned}|\varPhi_0\rangle &= \frac{1}{\sqrt{2}}(|00\rangle + |11\rangle),\ |\varPhi_1\rangle = \frac{1}{\sqrt{2}}(|00\rangle - |11\rangle),\\ |\varPhi_2\rangle &= \frac{1}{\sqrt{2}}(|00\rangle + |11\rangle),\ |\varPhi_3\rangle = \frac{1}{\sqrt{2}}(|00\rangle + |11\rangle).\end{aligned} \tag{17}$$

And the related measurement projectors are represented as

$$\mathcal{B}_m = |\varPhi_m\rangle\langle\varPhi_m|,\ m = 0, 1, 2, 3. \tag{18}$$

After this measurement, the total system changes to

$$\widetilde{\rho}_m = \frac{\left(\mathcal{B}_m \otimes I^{\otimes 2}\right)\xi(\rho_{\text{sys}})\left(\mathcal{B}_m \otimes I^{\otimes 2}\right)}{\operatorname{tr}\left[\left(\mathcal{B}_m \otimes I^{\otimes 2}\right)\xi(\rho_{\text{sys}})\right]}. \tag{19}$$

The probability of occurrence of a particular $\widetilde{\rho}_m$ is

$$\mathcal{Q}_m = \operatorname{tr}\left[\left(\mathcal{B}_m \otimes I^{\otimes 2}\right)\xi(\rho_{\text{sys}})\right]. \tag{20}$$

The system of Bob and Charlie becomes

$$\widetilde{\rho}_{\text{BC}_m} = \operatorname{tr}_{\text{TA}}(\widetilde{\rho}_m). \tag{21}$$

Either Bob or Charlie can get the secret state with the help of others. Suppose that Bob agrees to help Charlie to recover the secret state. He performs a X-basis measurement on qubit B, where the measurement operators are

$$\mathcal{X}_0 = |x_+\rangle\langle x_+|,\ \mathcal{X}_1 = |x_-\rangle\langle x_-|. \tag{22}$$

After Bob's measurement, the system of qubits B and C changes to

$$\widetilde{\rho'}_{\text{BC}_{mn}} = \frac{(\mathcal{X}_n \otimes I)\,\widetilde{\rho}_{\text{BC}_m}\,(\mathcal{X}_n \otimes I)}{\operatorname{tr}\left[(\mathcal{X}_n \otimes I)\,\widetilde{\rho}_{\text{BC}_m}\right]}. \tag{23}$$

The probability of getting $\widetilde{\rho'}_{\text{BC}_{mn}}$ is

$$\mathcal{Q}'_{mn} = \operatorname{tr}\left[(\mathcal{X}_n \otimes I)\,\widetilde{\rho}_{\text{BC}_m}\right]. \tag{24}$$

In this case, the system of qubit C in Charlie's side becomes

$$\widetilde{\rho}_{\text{C}_{mn}} = \operatorname{tr}_{\text{B}}(\widetilde{\rho'}_{\text{BC}_{mn}}). \tag{25}$$

Now Charlie can reconstruct the secret qubit by performing a recovery operator on qubit C if he gets both Alice's and Bob's measurement outcomes, where their relation can be found in Table 1. The recovery operation can be described as follows

$$\rho_{\text{out}}^{mn} = U_{mn}\widetilde{\rho}_{\text{C}_{mn}}U_{mn}^{\dagger}. \tag{26}$$

Table 1. The recovery operator U_{mn} with Alice's measurement result (MR) $|\Phi_m\rangle$ and Bob's MR $|x_n\rangle$.

Alice's MR	Bob's MR	U_{mn}
$\|\Phi_0\rangle$	$\|x_+\rangle$	σ_x
$\|\Phi_0\rangle$	$\|x_-\rangle$	$\sigma_x\sigma_z$
$\|\Phi_1\rangle$	$\|x_+\rangle$	$\sigma_x\sigma_z$
$\|\Phi_1\rangle$	$\|x_-\rangle$	σ_x
$\|\Phi_2\rangle$	$\|x_+\rangle$	I
$\|\Phi_2\rangle$	$\|x_-\rangle$	σ_z
$\|\Phi_3\rangle$	$\|x_+\rangle$	σ_z
$\|\Phi_3\rangle$	$\|x_-\rangle$	I

4.2 Efficiency of the QSTS Protocol in Noisy Environment

Since the effect of quantum noise, the output state ρ_{out}^{mn} in Charlie's side might not be the ideal secret state. For each m and n, the fidelity of the output state can be defined as

$$F_{m,n} = \langle\phi|\rho_{\text{out}}^{m,n}|\phi\rangle. \tag{27}$$

Each output state may occur with different probabilities. We can define the average fidelity as

$$\overline{F} = \sum_{m,n} Q_m Q'_{mn} F_{m,n}. \tag{28}$$

Note that the average fidelity is related to the parameters of the secret state $|\phi\rangle_{\text{T}}$ in Eq. 14. To eliminate parameters a, b and c of the secret state and compute the average fidelity over all possible prepared states, we define the state-independent average fidelity as [24]

$$\langle\overline{F}\rangle = \frac{1}{2\pi}\int_0^{2\pi}\int_0^1 \overline{F} da^2 dc. \tag{29}$$

4.3 The Output State and the Fidelity in Noisy Environment

In the bit-flip noise, the output state has the form

$$\begin{aligned}
\rho_{\text{out}}^{\text{BF}} = &\left(b^2(2\lambda-1)^3 - 4\lambda^3 + 6\lambda^2 - 3\lambda + 1\right)|0\rangle\langle 0| \\
&+ abe^{-\text{i}c}\left(4\left(-1+e^{2\text{i}c}\right)\lambda^3 - 6\left(-1+e^{2\text{i}c}\right)\lambda^2 + 3\left(-1+e^{2\text{i}c}\right)\lambda + 1\right)|0\rangle\langle 1| \\
&+ abe^{-\text{i}c}\lambda\left(\left(4\lambda^2 - 6\lambda + 3\right) + e^{2\text{i}c}\left(-4\lambda^3 + 6\lambda^2 - 3\lambda + 1\right)\right))|1\rangle\langle 0| \\
&+ \left(\lambda\left(4\lambda^2 - 6\lambda + 3\right) - b^2(2\lambda-1)^3\right)|1\rangle\langle 1|.
\end{aligned} \tag{30}$$

which is irrelevant to m and n. Accordingly, the state-independent average fidelity is

$$\langle\overline{F_{\text{BF}}}\rangle = \frac{1}{3}\left(3 - 6\lambda + 12\lambda^2 - 8\lambda^3\right). \tag{31}$$

In the phase-flip noise, the output state is

$$\rho_{\text{out}}^{\text{PF}} = a^2 \left|0\right\rangle \left\langle 0\right| + abe^{-\text{i}c}(1-2\lambda)^4 \left|0\right\rangle \left\langle 1\right| + abe^{\text{i}c}(1-2\lambda)^4 \left|1\right\rangle \left\langle 0\right| + b^2 \left|1\right\rangle \left\langle 1\right|. \tag{32}$$

which is also irrelevant to m and n. And the fidelity is

$$\langle \overline{F_{\text{PF}}} \rangle = \frac{1}{3}\left(3 - 8\lambda + 24\lambda^2 - 32\lambda^3 + 16\lambda^4\right). \tag{33}$$

In the depolarizing noise, the output state is

$$\begin{aligned}\rho_{\text{out}}^{\text{DE}} &= \frac{1}{27}(b^2(4\lambda-3)^3 - 32\lambda^3 + 72\lambda^2 - 54\lambda + 27)|0\rangle\langle 0| \\ &+ \frac{1}{81}(abe^{-\text{i}c}(3-4\lambda)^4)|0\rangle\langle 1| + \frac{1}{81}(abe^{\text{i}c}(3-4\lambda)^4)|1\rangle\langle 0| \\ &+ \frac{1}{27}(2\lambda\left(16\lambda^2 - 36\lambda + 27\right) - b^2(4\lambda-3)^3)|1\rangle\langle 1|.\end{aligned} \tag{34}$$

which is still the same one. The fidelity is

$$\langle \overline{F_{\text{DE}}} \rangle = \frac{1}{243}\left(243 - 594\lambda + 1080\lambda^2 - 864\lambda^3 + 256\lambda^4\right). \tag{35}$$

In the amplitude-damping noise, there are two different output states depending on the result of m. For $m = 0, 1$, the output state will be

$$\begin{aligned}\rho_{\text{out}}^{\text{AM1}} &= \frac{b^2\left(2\lambda^3 - 3\lambda^2 + 2\lambda - 1\right) + \lambda^2 + 1}{2b^2(\lambda-1)\lambda + \lambda + 1}|0\rangle\langle 0| + \frac{abe^{-\text{i}c}(\lambda-1)^2}{2b^2(\lambda-1)\lambda + \lambda + 1}|0\rangle\langle 1| \\ &+ \frac{abe^{\text{i}c}(\lambda-1)^2}{2b^2(\lambda-1)\lambda + \lambda + 1}|1\rangle\langle 0| - \frac{\lambda - 1b^2\left(2\lambda^2 - 3\lambda + 1\right) + \lambda}{2b^2(\lambda-1)\lambda + \lambda + 1}|1\rangle\langle 1|.\end{aligned} \tag{36}$$

While for $m = 2, 3$, the output state will be

$$\begin{aligned}\rho_{\text{out}}^{\text{AM2}} &= \frac{(1-\lambda)(1+b^2(2\lambda-1))}{1+2b^2\lambda}|0\rangle\langle 0| + \frac{abe^{-\text{i}c}(1-\lambda)}{1+2b^2\lambda}|0\rangle\langle 1| \\ &+ \frac{abe^{\text{i}c}(1-\lambda)}{1+2b^2\lambda}|1\rangle\langle 0| + \frac{b^2\left(2\lambda^2 - \lambda + 1\right) + \lambda}{1+2b^2\lambda}|1\rangle\langle 1|.\end{aligned} \tag{37}$$

The state-independent average fidelity is

$$\langle \overline{F_{\text{AM}}} \rangle = \frac{1}{6}\left(6 - 7\lambda + 6\lambda^2 - 2\lambda^3\right). \tag{38}$$

The state-independent average fidelities of the HBB-QSTS protocol in different types of noise are plotted in Fig. 2. After a simple calculation, it can be concluded that $\langle \overline{F_{\text{AM}}} \rangle$ is the maximal fidelity when $\lambda < 0.406$, $\langle \overline{F_{\text{BF}}} \rangle$ is the maximal when $0.406 > \lambda > 0.409$, and $\langle \overline{F_{\text{PF}}} \rangle$ is the maximal when $\lambda > 0.409$. While $\langle \overline{F_{\text{DE}}} \rangle$ is the minimal fidelity when $\lambda < 0.897$, and $\langle \overline{F_{\text{BF}}} \rangle$ is the minimal fidelity when $\lambda > 0.897$.

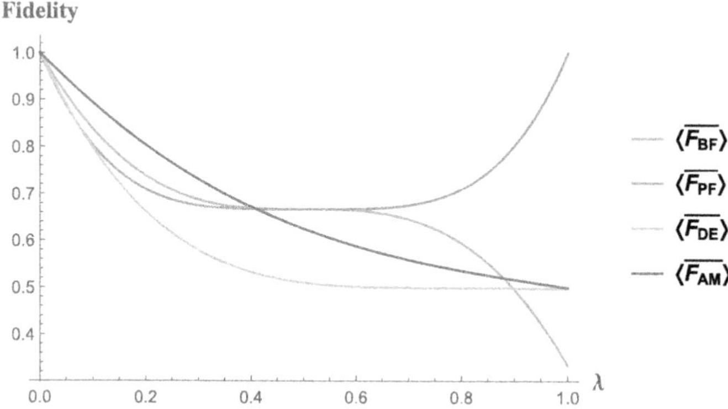

Fig. 2. The state-independent average fidelities of the HBB-QSTS protocol in different types of noise with noise parameter λ, where $\langle\overline{F_{\rm BF}}\rangle$ is the state-independent average fidelity in the bit-flip noise, $\langle\overline{F_{\rm PF}}\rangle$ the phase-flip noise, $\langle\overline{F_{\rm DE}}\rangle$ the depolarizing noise and $\langle\overline{F_{\rm AM}}\rangle$ the amplitude-damping noise.

Besides, the fidelity $\langle\overline{F_{\rm PF}}\rangle$ decreases when $\lambda < \frac{1}{2}$, while increases towards 1 when $\lambda > \frac{1}{2}$, and its minimal value is $\frac{2}{3}$. While $\langle\overline{F_{\rm BF}}\rangle$, $\langle\overline{F_{\rm AM}}\rangle$ and $\langle\overline{F_{\rm DE}}\rangle$ decrease with the increase of the noise rate λ. But $\langle\overline{F_{\rm BF}}\rangle$ decreases rapidly towards $\frac{1}{3}$ when λ increases towards 1. Besides, $\langle\overline{F_{\rm DE}}\rangle$ is always less than $\langle\overline{F_{\rm AM}}\rangle$, which indicates that the depolarizing noise has stronger effect than the amplitude-damping noise. And when $\lambda = 1$, $\langle\overline{F_{\rm DE}}\rangle$ and $\langle\overline{F_{\rm AM}}\rangle$ will get their minimal values as $\frac{121}{243}$ and $\frac{1}{2}$, respectively.

5 Discussions and Conclusions

Someone may concern the security of QSS protocols, which is the basic requirement of their implementations. The security of the HBB-QSS protocol has been studied extensively [2,34,35] in ideal situation. It is shown that an attack can be detected with a very high probability if we choose enough amount of checking or detecting qubits. In a practical implementation of HBB-QSS, similar to QKD [36], the security of the HBB-QSS protocol can be guaranteed as long as the error caused by the attacker can be distinguished from the error cause by noise. That is, the QSS protocol in noise environment is secure if the error caused by noise can be controlled under a certain threshold. In this case, we can say that the QSS protocol is safe if the error is below the threshold, while we can conclude there exists an attacker if the error is above the threshold. For HBB-QSTS protocol, similar results can also be got since the attacker exists only in the procedures of entanglement distribution, where security check can be performed like the HBB-QSS.

We have investigated two types of QSS protocols in four types of noise, respectively. As is discussed, some information of the secret is lost since the interaction with quantum noise in the processes of qubits transmission or storage.

Two different methods are presented to evaluate how a protocol is affected by quantum noise. For the HBB-QSS protocol sharing classical information, the efficiency for generating secret key or detecting eavesdropping is used. It is shown that the efficiencies are quiet different from each other in four types of noise. In the bit-flip noise, the efficiency gets its minimal value as $\frac{5}{8}$ when $\lambda = \frac{1}{2}$ and gets its maximal value as 1 when $\lambda = 0$ or 1. While in the phase-flip, depolarizing and amplitude-damping noise, the efficiencies decrease with the increase of λ. The minimal efficiency is 0 in the phase-flip noise, but the minimal values are near $\frac{1}{2}$ in the depolarizing and amplitude-damping noise.

While for the HBB-QSTS protocol sharing quantum states, the state-independent average fidelity is utilized. We calculate both the output state and the state-independent average fidelity in different types of noise, respectively. On the one hand, it indicates that the receiver will get two different output states depending on the Alice's result m in the amplitude-damping noise. But he will get the same output state in the other three types of noise, which is irrelevant to m. The can be explained by the symmetry of geometric picture of noise operators on the Bloch sphere [33]. Besides, the fidelity behaves differently from each other. In the phase-flip noise, the state-independent average fidelity gets its minimal value as $\frac{2}{3}$ when $\lambda = \frac{1}{2}$. But in the bit-flip, depolarizing and amplitude-damping noise, the fidelities decrease with the increase of λ. The minimal fidelities in the bit-flip, depolarizing and amplitude-damping noise are $\frac{1}{3}$, $\frac{121}{243}$ and $\frac{1}{2}$, respectively.

In summary, we have studied the HBB-QSS and HBB-QSTS protocols in noisy environment and shown how these protocols are affected by all types of noise usually encountered in real-world. Our results will be helpful for analyzing and improving quantum secure communications in real implementation. To explain our ideas, we considered simple cases where three players were involved and the same type of noise acted on the system. In the future, it is interesting to study cases where multiplayers are involved or different types of noise act simultaneously.

Acknowledgments. This project was supported by NSFC (Grant Nos. 61601358, 61373131), PAPD and CICAEET.

References

1. Bennett, C.H., Brassard, G.: Quantum cryptography: public key distribution and coin tossing. In: Proceedings of IEEE International Conference on Computers Systems and Signal Processing, New York, pp. 175–179. IEEE (1984)
2. Hillery, M., Bužek, V., Berthiaume, A.: Quantum secret sharing. Phys. Rev. A **59**(3), 1829 (1999)
3. Terhal, B.M., DiVincenzo, D.P., Leung, D.W.: Hiding bits in bell states. Phys. Rev. Lett. **86**(25), 5807 (2001)
4. Wang, M.M., Chen, X.B., Yang, Y.X.: A blind quantum signature protocol using the GHZ states. Sci. China Phys. Mech. Astron. **56**(9), 1636 (2013)
5. Shamir, A.: How to share a secret. Commun. ACM **22**(11), 612 (1979)

6. Xia, Z., Wang, X., Sun, X., Wang, B.: Steganalysis of least significant bit matching using multi-order differences. Secur. Commun. Netw. **7**(8), 1283 (2014)
7. Xia, Z., Wang, X., Sun, X., Liu, Q., Xiong, N.: Steganalysis of LSB matching using differences between nonadjacent pixels. Multimed. Tools Appl. **75**(4), 1947 (2016)
8. Ma, T., Zhou, J., Tang, M., Tian, Y., Al-Dhelaan, A., Al-Rodhaan, M., Lee, S.: Social network and tag sources based augmenting collaborative recommender system. IEICE Trans. Inf. Syst. **E98–D**(4), 902 (2015)
9. Grover, L.K.: Quantum mechanics helps in searching for a needle in a haystack. Phys. Rev. Lett. **79**(2), 325 (1997)
10. Xia, Z., Wang, X., Sun, X., Wang, Q.: A secure and dynamic multi-keyword ranked search scheme over encrypted cloud data. IEEE Trans. Parallel Distrib. Syst. **27**(2), 340 (2016)
11. Fu, Z., Sun, X., Liu, Q., Zhou, L., Shu, J.: Achieving efficient cloud search services: multi-keyword ranked search over encrypted cloud data supporting parallel computing. IEICE Trans. Commun. **E98.B**(1), 190 (2015)
12. Fu, Z., Ren, K., Shu, J., Sun, X., Huang, F.: Enabling personalized search over encrypted outsourced data with efficiency improvement. IEEE Trans. Parallel Distrib. Syst. **27**(9), 2546 (2016)
13. Blakley, G.R.: Safeguarding cryptographic key. In: Proceedings of the 1979 AFIPS National Computer Conference, Monval, NJ, USA, pp. 313–317. AFIPS Press (1979)
14. Xiao, L., Long, G.L., Deng, F.G., Pan, J.W.: Efficient multiparty quantum-secret-sharing schemes. Phys. Rev. A **69**(5), 052307 (2004)
15. Yu, I.C., Lin, F.L., Huang, C.Y.: Quantum secret sharing with multilevel mutually (un) biased bases. Phys. Rev. A **78**, 12344 (2008)
16. Guo, G.P., Guo, G.C.: Quantum secret sharing without entanglement. Phys. Lett. A **310**(4), 247 (2003)
17. Zhang, Z.J., Li, Y., Man, Z.X.: Multiparty quantum secret sharing. Phys. Rev. A **71**(4), 044301 (2005)
18. Cleve, R., Gottesman, D., Lo, H.K.: How to share a quantum secret. Phys. Rev. Lett. **83**(3), 648 (1999)
19. Gottesman, D.: Theory of quantum secret sharing. Phys. Rev. A **61**(4), 042311 (2000)
20. Lance, A.M., Symul, T., Bowen, W.P., Sanders, B.C., Lam, P.K.: Tripartite quantum state sharing. Phys. Rev. Lett. **92**(17), 177903 (2004)
21. Badziąg, P., Horodecki, M., Horodecki, P., Horodecki, R.: Local environment can enhance fidelity of quantum teleportation. Phys. Rev. A **62**(1), 012311 (2000)
22. Taketani, B.G., de Melo, F., de Matos Filho, R.L.: Optimal teleportation with a noisy source. Phys. Rev. A **85**(2), 020301 (2012)
23. Knoll, L.T., Schmiegelow, C.T., Larotonda, M.A.: Noisy quantum teleportation: an experimental study on the influence of local environments. Phys. Rev. A **90**(4), 042332 (2014)
24. Rigolin, G., Fortes, R.: Fighting noise with noise in realistic quantum teleportation. Phys. Rev. A **92**(1), 012338 (2015)
25. Xiang, G.Y., Li, J., Yu, B., Guo, G.C.: Remote preparation of mixed states via noisy entanglement. Phys. Rev. A **72**(1), 012315 (2005)
26. Chen, A.X., Deng, L., Li, J.H., Zhan, Z.M.: Remote preparation of an entangled state in nonideal conditions. Commun. Theor. Phys. **46**(2), 221 (2006)
27. Guan, X.W., Chen, X.B., Wang, L.C., Yang, Y.X.: Joint remote preparation of an arbitrary two-qubit state in noisy environments. Int. J. Theor. Phys. **53**(7), 2236 (2014)

28. Liang, H.Q., Liu, J.M., Feng, S.S., Chen, J.G., Xu, X.Y.: Effects of noises on joint remote state preparation via a GHZ-class channel. Quantum Inf. Process. **14**(10), 3857 (2015)
29. Wang, M.M., Qu, Z.G.: Effect of quantum noise on deterministic joint remote state preparation of a qubit state via a GHZ channel. Quantum Inf. Process. **15**(11), 4805 (2016)
30. Thapliyal, K., Pathak, A., Banerjee, S.: Quantum cryptography over non-Markovian channels (2016). arXiv:1608.06071
31. Sharma, V., Thapliyal, K., Pathak, A., Banerjee, S.: A comparative study of protocols for secure quantum communication under noisy environment: single-qubit-based protocols versus entangled-state-based protocols. Quantum Inf. Process. **15**(11), 4681 (2016)
32. Wang, M.M., Wang, W., Chen, J.G., Farouk, A.: Secret sharing of a known arbitrary quantum state with noisy environment. Quantum Inf. Process. **14**(1), 4211 (2015)
33. Nielsen, M.A., Chuang, I.L.: Quantum Computation and Quantum Information. Cambridge University Press, Cambridge (2000)
34. Karlsson, A., Koashi, M., Imoto, N.: Quantum entanglement for secret sharing and secret splitting. Phys. Rev. A **59**(1), 162 (1999)
35. Qin, S.J., Gao, F., Wen, Q.Y., Zhu, F.C.: Cryptanalysis of the Hillery-Buzcaronek-Berthiaume quantum secret-sharing protocol. Phys. Rev. A **76**(6), 062324 (2007)
36. Gisin, N., Ribordy, G., Tittel, W., Zbinden, H.: Quantum cryptography. Rev. Mod. Phys. **74**, 145 (2002)

SimHash-Based Similar Neighbor Finding for Scalable and Privacy-Preserving Service Recommendation

Yanwei Xu and Lianyong Qi(✉)

School of Information Science and Engineering,
Qufu Normal University, Rizhao 276826, China
lianyongqi@gmail.com

Abstract. With the ever-increasing number of web services on the Web, various service recommendation techniques, e.g., User-based Collaborative Filtering (UCF) have been developed to alleviate the service selection burden of a target user. In traditional UCF-based recommendation approaches, the first key step is to find the candidate users who have the largest invoked-service intersection with the target user, as a larger invoked-service intersection often means higher probability that two users are similar friends (i.e., neighbors). However, the above similar-neighbor finding process is often time-consuming and vulnerable to privacy, especially when the number of candidate users is huge. In view of these challenges, a scalable and privacy-preserving similar-neighbor finding approach based on SimHash, i.e., $SNF_{SimHash}$ is proposed in this paper. Finally, a set of experiments are conducted on *WS-DREAM* dataset to validate the feasibility of $SNF_{SimHash}$. Experiment results show that our proposal can achieve a good tradeoff between accuracy and efficiency while guaranteeing privacy-preservation.

Keywords: Service recommendation · Service intersection · SimHash · Privacy · Scalability · Collaborative filtering

1 Introduction

With the increasing popularity of service-oriented computing technology, a huge amount of web services are emerging on the Web to provide a light-weight resolution to satisfy the complex computation requirements from various users [1, 2]. However, the big volume of candidate web services also place a heavy burden on the service selection decisions of a target user, as it is often difficult and tedious to determine the optimal services that satisfy the target user most [3, 4].

In this situation, various recommendation techniques are put forward to alleviate the service selection burden of target users, e.g., the User-based Collaborative Filtering (UCF) that is widely adopted in existing recommender systems [5]. In traditional UCF recommendation approaches, the similar friends (i.e., neighbors) of a target user could be determined first based on the historical user-service quality data; afterwards, the services preferred by the similar neighbors of a target user are recommended to the target user so as to finish the whole service recommendation process.

X. Sun et al. (Eds.): ICCCS 2017, Part II, LNCS 10603, pp. 113–122, 2017.
https://doi.org/10.1007/978-3-319-68542-7_10

According to the above UCF recommendation approaches, the similarity between two users depends on the service intersection that is commonly invoked by these two users. For example, suppose there are a target user u_{taregt} and two users A and B. If A and u_{taregt} invoked two common services while B and u_{taregt} invoked 100 common services in the past, then B is more probably a similar neighbor of u_{target} than A is. Therefore, in UCF recommendation process, one key step is to determine the candidate users who have invoked the most services that are common with the target user, as more "commonly invoked services" often mean high probability that two users are similar neighbors.

However, two challenges are present in the above similar-neighbor finding process.

(1) It is often time-consuming to calculate the size of service intersection commonly invoked by two users, especially when the candidate service space is large. In this situation, the service recommendation efficiency and scalability are decreased considerably.
(2) User privacy (e.g., the information of services invoked by a user) cannot be always guaranteed, when the service intersection size of two users are calculated. In this situation, a user is probably reluctant to release his/her data to other users, which makes the UCF recommendation infeasible.

In view of the above two challenges, a novel similar-neighbor finding approach based on SimHash, i.e., $SNF_{SimHash}$ is put forward in this paper. Through $SNF_{SimHash}$, we can determine the similar neighbors who have invoked the most services that are common with the target user, in a scalable and privacy-preserving manner.

The rest of this paper is organized as follows: Related work is presented in Sect. 2. The motivation of our paper is introduced in Sect. 3. In Sect. 4, we introduce the details of our proposed similar-neighbor finding approach $SNF_{SimHash}$. In Sect. 5, a set of experiments are conducted on *WS-DREAM* dataset to validate the feasibility of our proposal. And finally, in Sect. 6, we summarize the paper and point out the future research directions.

2 Related Work

Collaborative Filtering (CF) has become one of the most effective techniques in existing recommender systems. User-based CF and item-based CF are brought forth for high-quality service recommendation in [5, 6], respectively. In order to integrate the advantages of these two approaches, a hybrid CF recommendation approach is introduced in [7]. Experiment results indicate that the hybrid CF recommendation approach improves the recommendation performance significantly. As the quality of a web service often depends on the service execution context (e.g., time, location), the authors in [8, 9] put forward time-aware CF and location-aware CF, respectively, to improve the accuracy of recommended results. However, the above approaches only take the objective service quality as recommendation basis, while neglect the subjective preferences of users. Considering this drawback, a user preference-aware CF recommendation approach is proposed in [10], to aid the personalized recommendation requirements from different users.

However, the above CF recommendation approaches do not consider the size of service intersection between different users. In view of this drawback, in [11, 12], the authors introduce the size of service intersection invoked by two users into the user similarity calculation process, respectively. Also, the authors argue that the more "commonly-invoked" services there are, the more similar two users are. Similarly, the authors in [13] combine the size of service intersection and Matrix Factorization technique for accurate service recommendation. However, two challenges are present in these approaches. First, it is often time-consuming to calculate the size of service intersection by two users, especially when the web service space is very large. Second, user privacy cannot always be guaranteed during the calculation process of service intersection size, which often blocks a user's willingness of data sharing with other users.

In view of these challenges, a SimHash-based approach called $SNF_{SimHash}$ is proposed in this paper, to find the similar neighbors who have the most commonly-invoked services with a target user, in a scalable and privacy-preserving manner.

3 Research Motivation

In this section, a concrete example (in Fig. 1) is provided to demonstrate the motivation of our paper. Here, symbol u_{target} represents a target user to who the recommender system intends to recommend services, $U = \{u_1, \ldots, u_m\}$ and $WS = \{ws_1, \ldots, ws_n\}$ denote the user set and web service set, respectively. Besides, the user-service invocation relationships are also presented in Fig. 1.

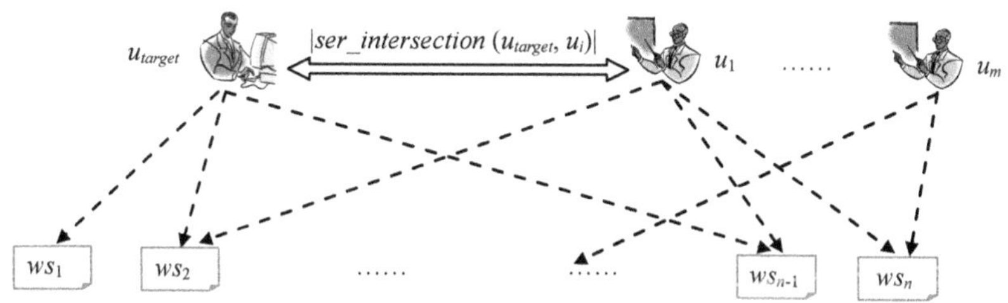

Fig. 1. Calculate the size of service intersection between different users: an example

According to UCF recommendation approaches, in order to find the similar neighbors of target user u_{target}, we need to first count the number of services commonly invoked by u_{target} and any other user $u_i \in U$, so as to find the candidate users who have the most commonly-invoked services with u_{target}. Namely, we need to calculate the size of service intersection (denoted by $ser\_intersection\left(u_{target}, u_i\right)$), i.e., $\left|ser\_intersection\left(u_{target}, u_i\right)\right|$. However, it is often time-consuming to obtain all the values of $\left|ser\_intersection\left(u_{target}, u_i\right)\right| (1 \leq i \leq m)$ when m (the number of users) or n (the number of web services) is large. Besides, user u_i dare not release his/her "invoked services" data to u_{target} due to privacy concerns, which makes the calculation of $\left|ser\_intersection\left(u_{target}, u_i\right)\right|$ infeasible.

In this situation, it is a great challenge to find the candidate users who have the most commonly-invoked services with u_{target} in a scalable and privacy-preserving way. In view of this challenge, a novel SimHash-based similar-neighbor finding approach called $SNF_{SimHash}$ is put forward in this paper, which will be elaborated in the next section.

4 SimHash-Based Similar Neighbor Finding

Generally, we proposed $SNF_{SimHash}$ approach consists of the three steps in Fig. 2. Here, u_{target} denotes a target user.

Step 1: Buliding user index offline. For each user $u_i \in U$, calculate his/her hash value (i.e., user index) $H(u_i)$ based on the SimHash theory.

Step 2: Finding similar neighbors of u_{target}. According to the same hash function in Step 1, determine target user u_{target}'s hash value $H(u_{target})$. If the Hamming distance between $H(u_{target})$ and $H(u_i)$ is smaller than a threshold, then calculate the similarity between u_{target} and u_i and further determine the similar neighbors of u_{target}.

Fig. 2. Two steps of our proposed $SNF_{SimHash}$ approach

Step 1: Building user index offline

In this step, we build user index $H(u_i)$ offline for user $u_i \in U$ based on the SimHash technique [14], whose major procedure is elaborated in Fig. 3. Next, we introduce the details of user index building procedure. Here, m and n denote the number of users and number of services, respectively.

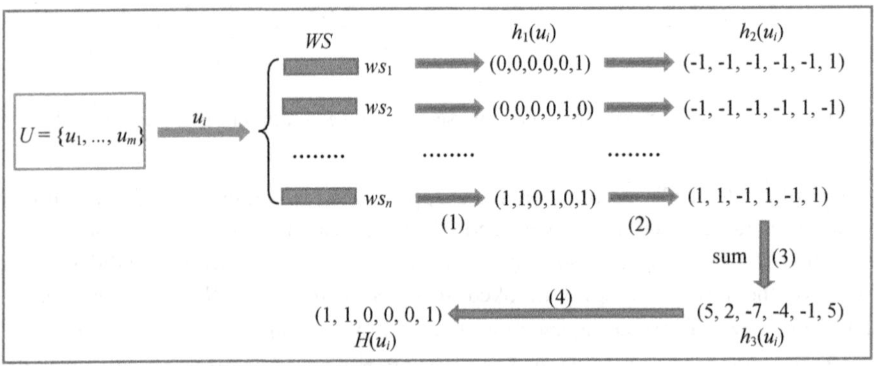

Fig. 3. User index building procedure in step 1

(1) For each service $ws_j \in WS$, we transform its number (i.e., j) into a r-dimensional 0–1 index $g(ws_j)$ where $r = log_2^n$(taking Fig. 3(1) for example, $r = 6$ and $g(ws_1) = (0, 0, 0, 0, 0, 1)$ hold). Then user u_i can be denoted by the n-dimensional vector $h_1(u_i) = (v_1, \ldots, v_n)$ in (1), where $v_j = g(ws_j)$ if u_i has ever invoked service ws_j before.

$$v_j = \begin{cases} g(ws_j) & \text{if } u_i \text{ has ever invoked } ws_j \text{ before} \\ Null & \text{if } u_i \text{ has never invoked } ws_j \text{ before} \end{cases} \tag{1}$$

Next, we drop the *Null* element v_j in vector $h_1(u_i)$ and convert the value "0" in remaining v_j vector to be "−1", thus a new vector $h_2(u_i)$ is achieved (see Fig. 3(2)). Afterwards, for each column in Fig. 3(2), we calculate the sum of all its elements and then a new vector $h_3(u_i)$ is obtained (see Fig. 3(3)). Finally, in $h_3(u_i)$, the positive values are replaced by 1 and the negative values are replaced by 0, respectively. Thus we derive a r-dimensional 0–1 vector $H(u_i)$ (see Fig. 3(4)). Finally, according to the SimHash theory, $H(u_i)$ can be considered as the index for user u_i.

The above process for building user index has two advantages: first, it can be completed offline so that the time cost is reduced; second, user privacy information (e.g., the service set invoked by a user) could be protected very well due to the adopted hashing technique.

Step 2: Finding similar neighbors of u_{target}

According to Step 1, we can obtain the index for target user u_{target}, i.e., $H(u_{target})$. Next, we calculate the Hamming Distance between $H(u_{target})$ and $H(u_i)$ $(1 \le i \le m)$, i.e., $D(H(u_{target}), H(u_i))$. Suppose $H(u_{target})$ and $H(u_i)$ are denoted by r-dimensional vectors $(v_{target-1}, \ldots, v_{target-r})$ and $(v_{i-1}, \ldots, v_{i-r})$, respectively. Then the Hamming Distance $D(H(u_{target}), H(u_i))$ could be calculated by (2), where a_k is obtained by (3). In (3), symbol "⊕" denotes the XOR operation.

$$D(H(u_{target}), H(u_i)) = \sum a_k (1 \le k \le r) \tag{2}$$

$$a_k = v_{target-k} \oplus v_{i-k} = \begin{cases} 1 & \text{if } v_{target-k} \neq v_{i-k} \\ 0 & \text{if } v_{target-k} = v_{i-k} \end{cases} \tag{3}$$

Then according to the SimHash theory, if $D(H(u_{target}), H(u_i)) < 3$ holds, we can conclude that the services invoked by u_{target} and the services invoked by u_i are approximately the same. In other words, u_i is a similar neighbor of u_{target} with high probability. Next, we calculate the Pearson Correlation Coefficient (PCC) between u_{target} and u_i, i.e., $sim(u_{target}, u_i)$ based on existing approaches (the PCC calculation formula is out of the scope of this paper; please refer to [11] for more details). Finally, the users u_i with the highest similarity $MAX\{sim(u_{target}, u_i)\}$ are regarded the similar neighbors of u_{target}, and could be recruited for further service recommendation.

5 Experiments

5.1 Experiment Configurations

In this section, a set of experiments are conducted to validate the feasibility of our proposed $SNF_{SimHash}$ approach. The experiments are based on a real-world service quality dataset *WS-DREAM* [15], which collects a huge amount of service quality data (e.g., response time) from 339 users on 5825 web services. In order to prove the advantages of our proposal, we compare our proposal with the benchmark method, i.e., the traversal method (i.e., for each candidate user in set *U*, we calculate the size of his/her service intersection with the target user, and finally obtain the maximal value of service intersection size). Besides, the following two evaluation measures are tested and compared, respectively (as user privacy can be protected well by the intrinsic nature of SimHash, we will not evaluate the capability of privacy-preservation of our proposal here).

(1) *time cost*: the consumed time for determine the candidate users who have invoked the most services that are common with the target user.
(2) *accuracy*: suppose $max\text{-}size_{benchmark}$ and $max\text{-}size_{SimHash}$ denote the maximal values of service intersection size between target user and other users based on the benchmark approach and our proposed $SNF_{SimHash}$ approach, respectively. Then we utilize their ratio in (4) to measure the accuracy of similar neighbor finding in our proposal (the larger the better).

$$accuracy = (max\text{-}size_{SimHash} / max\text{-}size_{benchmark}) * 100\% \tag{4}$$

The user-service matrix density is 10% and the experiments are conducted on a Lenovo laptop with 2.40 GHz processor and 12.0 GB RAM. The laptop is running under Windows 10 and JAVA 8. Each experiment is repeated 10 times and the average experiment results are taken.

5.2 Experiment Results and Analyses

Concretely, the following four profiles are tested and compared, respectively. Here, *m* and *n* denote the number of users and number of web services, respectively.

Profile 1: Efficiency comparison between $SNF_{SimHash}$ and benchmark (w.r.t. *n*)
In this profile, we test the time cost of our proposal with respective to the number of web services, i.e., *n*, and compare it with the benchmark method. The experiment parameters are set as follows: $m = 300$, *n* is varied from 1000 to 5000. The concrete experiment results are shown in Fig. 4. As can be seen from Fig. 4, the time cost of benchmark method increases approximately linearly with the growth of *n*, this is because the benchmark method is actually a traversal method in which each web service is considered. While our proposed $SNF_{SimHash}$ approach outperforms the benchmark method in terms of time cost as most jobs (e.g., user index building) in our approach could be finished offline, which improves the algorithm efficiency and scalability significantly.

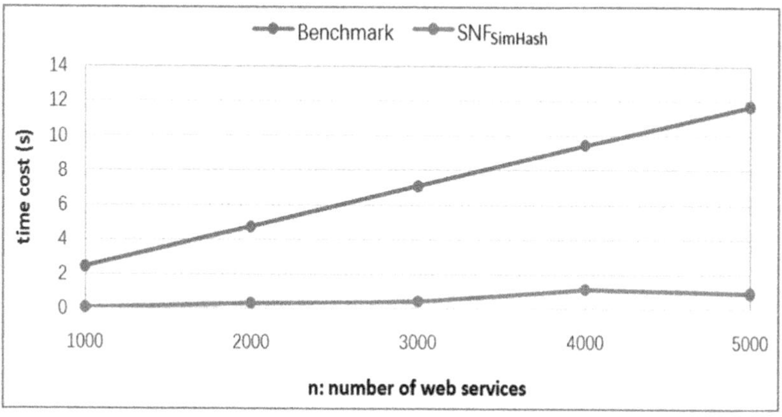

Fig. 4. Efficiency comparison between $SNF_{SimHash}$ and benchmark (w.r.t. n)

Profile 2: Efficiency comparison between $SNF_{SimHash}$ and benchmark (w.r.t. m) In this profile, we test the time cost of our proposal with respective to the number of users, i.e., m, and compare it with the benchmark method. The concrete experiment parameters are set as below: m is varied from 50 to 300, n = 5000. The concrete experiment results are presented in Fig. 5. As shown in Fig. 5, the time cost of benchmark method increases approximately linearly with the growth of m, this is because the benchmark method is actually a traversal method in which each user is considered. While in our proposed $SNF_{SimHash}$ approach, most jobs (e.g., user index building) could be done in an offline manner, therefore, the time cost of our proposal outperforms that of the benchmark method. Besides, similar to Profile 1, the time cost of our proposal stays approximately stable and increases slowly with the growth of m, which means that our approach can generally satisfy the quick response requirements from most users.

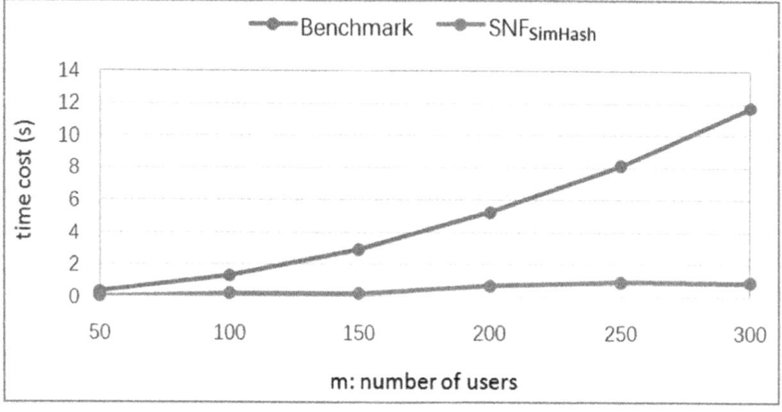

Fig. 5. Efficiency comparison between $SNF_{SimHash}$ and benchmark (w.r.t. m)

Profile 3: Accuracy of $SNF_{SimHash}$ with respect to n

In this profile, we test the accuracy of $SNF_{SimHash}$ with respective to the number of web services, i.e., n. The concrete experiment parameters are set as follows: m = 300, n is varied from 1000 to 5000. The concrete experiment results are shown in Fig. 6. As Fig. 6 indicates, the accuracy values of our approach are higher than 85% in most cases (i.e., when $n > 1000$), this is because more web services often mean more valuable recommendation information and hence, the accuracy is higher. Besides, the accuracy of our approach stays approximately stable; this is because the adopted SimHash technique can guarantee to find the near-to-optimal similar neighbors who have invoked the most services that are common with the target user.

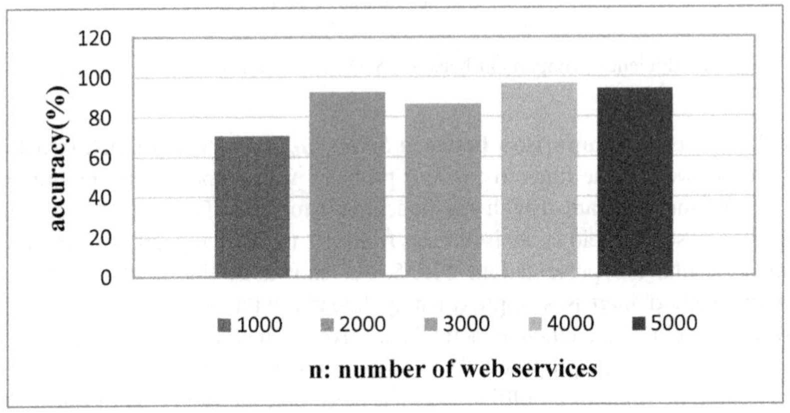

Fig. 6. Accuracy of $SNF_{SimHash}$ w.r.t. n

Profile 4: Accuracy of $SNF_{SimHash}$ with respect to m

In this profile, we test the accuracy of $SNF_{SimHash}$ with respective to the number of users, i.e., m. The concrete experiment parameters are set as follows: m is varied from 50 to 300, n = 5000. The concrete experiment results are shown in Fig. 7. As Fig. 7 shows, the accuracy values of our approach are higher than 80% in all cases, and the accuracy is near 100% when m = 200 holds. Besides, the accuracy of our approach increases approximately with the growth of m, this is because more users often mean more valuable recommendation information and hence, the accuracy value is raised correspondingly.

With the below experiment results and analyses, we can conclude that our proposed $SNF_{SimHash}$ approach achieves a good tradeoff among the accuracy and time cost of similar neighbor finding while guarantee the privacy-preservation in the service recommendation process.

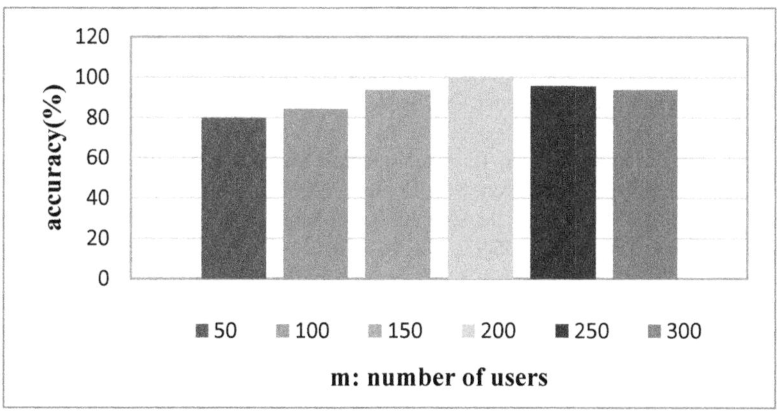

Fig. 7. Accuracy of $SNF_{SimHash}$ w.r.t. m

6 Conclusions

Collaborative Filtering has become one of the most effective service recommendation techniques that are widely adopted in various recommender systems to alleviate the target users' service selection burden. As one key step in CF-based recommendation approaches, finding the similar neighbors who have invoked the most web services that are common with the target user is crucial to the subsequent service recommendation process. However, the traditional similar-neighbor finding approaches often suffer from low scalability and privacy risks. In view of this drawback, a novel SimHash-based approach called $SNF_{SimHash}$ is put forward in this paper, to find the similar neighbors of a target user in a scalable and privacy-preserving manner. Finally, through a set of experiments deployed on a real-world service quality dataset *WS-DREAM*, we validate the feasibility of our proposal in terms of accuracy and efficiency while guaranteeing the privacy-preservation.

In the future, we will further improve the accuracy of our approach by considering more service invocation context, e.g., service invocation time, location and frequency. Besides, space complexity optimization is still an open problem in big data environment, which calls for intensive study in the future.

Acknowledgements. This paper is partially supported by Natural Science Foundation of China (No. 61402258), Open Project of State Key Laboratory for Novel Software Technology (No. KFKT2016B22).

References

1. Fu, Z., Ren, K., Shu, J., Sun, X., Huang, F.: Enabling personalized search over encrypted outsourced data with efficiency improvement. IEEE Trans. Parallel Distrib. Syst. **27**(9), 2546–2559 (2016)

2. Qi, L., Dou, W., Chen, J.: Weighted principal component analysis-based service selection method for multimedia services in cloud. Computing **98**(1–2), 195–214 (2016)
3. Ma, Y., Wang, S., Hung, P.C.K., Hsu, C.-H., Sun, Q., Yang, F.: A highly accurate prediction algorithm for unknown web service QoS values. IEEE Trans. Serv. Comput. **9**(4), 911–923 (2016)
4. Xue, Y., Jiang, J., Zhao, B., Ma, T.: A self-adaptive articial bee colony algorithm based on global best for global optimization. Soft Comput. (2017)
5. Rong, H., Huo, S., Hu, C., Mo, J.: User similarity-based collaborative filtering recommendation algorithm. J. Commun. **35**(2), 16–24 (2014)
6. Chung, K.-Y., Lee, D., Kuinam, K.J.: Categorization for grouping associative items using data mining in item-based collaborative filtering. Multimedia Tools Appl. **71**(2), 889–904 (2014)
7. Jiang, C., Duan, R., Jain, H.K., Liu, S., Liang, K.: Hybrid collaborative filtering for high-involvement products: a solution to opinion sparsity and dynamics. Decis. Support Syst. **79**, 195–208 (2015)
8. Wang, X., Zhu, J., Zheng, Z., Song, W., Shen, Y., Lyu, M.R.: A spatial-temporal QoS prediction approach for time-aware web service recommendation. ACM Trans. Web **10**(1), 7 (2016)
9. Yu, C., Huang, L.: A web service QoS prediction approach based on time- and location-aware collaborative filtering. Serv. Oriented Comput. Appl. **10**(2), 135–149 (2016)
10. Fletcher, K.K., Liu, X.F.: A collaborative filtering method for personalized preference-based service recommendation. In: IEEE International Conference on Web Services, pp. 400–407 (2015)
11. Zheng, Z., Ma, H., Lyu, M.R., King, I.: QoS-aware web service recommendation by collaborative filtering. IEEE Trans. Serv. Comput. **4**(2), 140–152 (2011)
12. Chen, X., Zheng, Z., Yu, Q., Lyu, M.R.: Web service recommendation via exploiting location and QoS information. IEEE Trans. Parallel Distrib. Syst. **25**(7), 1913–1924 (2014)
13. Xie, Q., Zhao, S., Zheng, Z., Zhu, J., Lyu, M.R.: Asymmetric correlation regularized matrix factorization for web service recommendation. In: IEEE International Conference on Web Services, pp. 204–211 (2016)
14. Sadowski, C., Levin, G.: Simhash: hash-based similarity detection (2007). www.googlecode.com/sun/trunk/paper/SimHashwithBib.pdf
15. Zheng, Z., Zhang, Y., Lyu, M.R.: Investigating QoS of real world web services. IEEE Trans. Serv. Comput. **7**(1), 32–39 (2014)

Universally Composable Three-Party Password Authenticated Key Exchange

Qihui Zhang, Xuexian Hu(✉), Jianghong Wei, and Wenfen Liu

State Key Laboratory of Mathematical Engineering and Advanced Computing, Zhengzhou 450002, China
xuexian_hu@hotmail.com

Abstract. Three-party password authenticated key exchange (3PAKE) allows two clients, each sharing a password with a trusted server, to establish a session key with the help of the server. It is a quite practical mechanism for establishing secure channels in large communication network. However, most current 3PAKE protocols are analyzed in security models that don't adequately address protocol composition problem. In this paper, a direct definition of security for 3PAKE within the universal composability framework is proposed, which captures the basic security requirements of the problem and is proven to be stronger than the commonly used security notions. To further justify our formulation of 3PAKE, we prove that a slight variant of a generic 3PAKE protocol by Wang and Hu securely realizes the new security definition.

Keywords: Password authentication · Key exchange · Universal composability · Provable security

1 Introduction

Establishing secure session keys is critical to many practical security system [1–9]. Password authenticated key exchange (PAKE) allows parties sharing only a low-entropy, human-memorable password to securely establish a common session key over an insecure channel. Due to its simplicity and ease to use, which does not rely on dedicated hardware for storing high entropy secrets [10], PAKE has become an important cryptographic primitive.

The early solutions for the problem aim for two-party password authenticated key exchange (2PAKE), such as the well-known encrypted key exchange (EKE) protocol [11], in which two parties identify their communicating partner using a shared password. Since then many 2PAKE protocols have been proposed [12–16]. However, in communication environment where only 2PAKE protocols are available, every party has to remember many passwords, one for each entity with whom he might want to establish a session key. It is impractical when the network is relatively large, since the number of strings one person can remember is limited. To solve this problem, three-party PAKE (3PAKE) was proposed, in which each client shares a password with the trusted server, and two clients

X. Sun et al. (Eds.): ICCCS 2017, Part II, LNCS 10603, pp. 123–137, 2017.
https://doi.org/10.1007/978-3-319-68542-7_11

establish a common session key with the aid of the server. This solution is quite realistic in practical setting, since it provides each client user with the capability of exchanging secure cryptographic keys with all the other client users, while only requiring it to remember one single password.

Security Models. In 2005, Abdalla et al. presented the first formal security model for 3PAKE [17], called the Real-Or-Random (ROR) model, as an extension of the model of [12,18]. Along with the ROR model, they also gave a model in the traditional Find-Then-Guess (FTG) setting, and proved that the ROR model is strictly stronger than this definition. From then on, numerous 3PAKE protocols [19–21] have been proven secure in the ROR/FTG models.

However, as pointed out by Canetti et al. [22], none of these models considers the realistic setting in which the 3PAKE protocols are used as components of some larger protocols. That is, they cannot provide meaningful security guarantees under protocol composition. Moreover, these security models usually assume the passwords are mutually independent. They fail to deal with the scenarios in which possibly related passwords are used for different protocol executions [23,24]. To overcome these deficiencies, Deng et al. presented a security definition along with a new 3PAKE protocol [25] within the UC framework [26], which tries to provide stronger security guarantees. Unfortunately, their formalization doesn't achieve mutual authentication between the clients and the server, which is an essential security requirement for 3PAKE to resist undetectable on-line dictionary attacks. Moreover, it is pointed out by Yuan et al. [27] that Deng et al.'s scheme, which was proven secure under their definition in [25], is vulnerable to dictionary attacks. Recently, a formulation is provided by Hu et al. [28] by utilizing split functionality. However, although the security definition is conceptually simple, the resulting scheme, which has to compute and send additional commitment values prior to actual message exchange, is not very efficient.

Related Work. The first ideal functionality for 2PAKE protocols [22] in the UC framework [26] was proposed by Canetti et al., which is built on the known UC formulation of standard key exchange. Later on, this definition is improved to include explicit client authentication by Abdalla et al. in [29] and to include explicit mutual authentication by Groce and Katz in [30]. Along with the first 2PAKE functionality in UC framework, Canetti et al. [22] also provided a slight variant of the KOY protocol [13] and Gennaro et al.'s framework [31], and proved that it UC securely realizes their 2PAKE functionality in static corruption model. After that, many UC secure 2PAKE protocols have been presented, either in the random oracle model [29] or in the standard model with continuously improved security or efficiency [30,32,33]. As mentioned before, these 2PAKE protocols are not enough for large scale communication network because of practical considerations. Nevertheless, they can be used as underlying primitives for constructing 3PAKE protocols (see below), and the latter could benefit from the efficiency improvement of the former.

Contributions. There are two main contributions in this paper. First, we propose a new definition of security for 3PAKE protocols within the UC security framework [26], by directly formulating an ideal functionality for 3PAKE that captures the security requirement of this problem. Our formulation additionally achieves explicit mutual authentication between clients and the trusted server, which provides security guarantees for 3PAKE against undetectable on-line dictionary attacks. Next, we demonstrate that this 3PAKE security notion within the UC framework is actually stronger than the commonly used Real-Or-Random model [17], in the sense that any protocol secure with respect to our definition is also secure in the ROR model. Second, as an additional justification for our definition, we prove that the generic construction of 3PAKE protocols by Wang and Hu [34], with slight variation, securely realizes the new security definition within the UC framework. The proof allows this protocol to benefit from the universal composition theorem, which provides the instantiated protocols with security guarantees under arbitrary composition with other protocols.

2 The 3PAKE Functionality

In this section, we present our formulation of the ideal functionality $\mathcal{F}_{3PAKE}$ for three-party password authenticated key exchange with mutual authentication between the clients and the server. The starting points are the 2PAKE functionality described in [22,29,30] and the security model given in [17].

2.1 Functionality Definition

The functionality $\mathcal{F}_{3PAKE}$ is parameterized by a security parameter k. It interacts with an adversary $\mathcal{S}$ and a set of parties $\mathbf{P} = \{P_l\}_{l \in I}$ as follows:

- **Upon receiving** $(\texttt{NewSession}, sid, Pid, P_l, pw_l, \texttt{client})$ **from party** P_l**:** If this is the first NewSession-query for P_l, where Pid is an ordered set of the form $Pid = PidC \cup PidS = \{P_i, P_j\} \cup \{P_s\}$ and $P_l \in PidC$, record $(sid, Pid, P_l, pw_l, \texttt{client})$, mark it with $\texttt{status}_l = \texttt{fresh}$, and send $(sid, Pid, P_l, \texttt{client})$ to $\mathcal{S}$. Ignore any subsequent NewSession-queries with a different Pid set. If all the players involved in Pid have submitted their NewSession-queries, then record (sid, Pid, ready) and send it to $\mathcal{S}$.
- **Upon receiving** $(\texttt{NewSession}, sid, Pid, P_s, pw_i, pw_j, \texttt{server})$ **from party** P_s**:** If this is the first NewSession-query for P_s, where Pid is an ordered set of the form $Pid = PidC \cup PidS = \{P_i, P_j\} \cup \{P_s\}$ and $P_s \in PidS$, record $(sid, Pid, P_s, pw_i, pw_j, \texttt{server})$, mark it with $\texttt{status}_i^s = \texttt{status}_j^s = \texttt{fresh}$ and send $(sid, Pid, P_s, \texttt{server})$ to $\mathcal{S}$. Ignore any subsequent NewSession-queries with a different Pid set. If all the players involved in Pid have submitted their NewSession-queries, record (sid, Pid, ready) and send it to $\mathcal{S}$.
- **Upon receiving** $(\texttt{TestPwd}, sid, Pid, P_l, pw'_l, \texttt{client})$ **from the adversary** $\mathcal{S}$**:** If there is a record of the form $(sid, Pid, P_l, pw_l, \texttt{client})$ which is fresh, then do:
  - If $pw_l = pw'_l$, mark $\texttt{status}_l = \texttt{compromised}$ and reply to $\mathcal{S}$ with "correct guess".

  - If $pw_l \neq pw'_l$, mark $\texttt{status}_l = \texttt{interrupted}$ and reply to $\mathcal{S}$ with "wrong guess".
- **Upon receiving** $(\texttt{TestPwd}, sid, Pid, P_s, pw'_l, l, \texttt{server})$ **with** $l \in \{i, j\}$ **from the adversary** $\mathcal{S}$**:** If there is a record of the form $(sid, Pid, P_s, pw_i, pw_j, \texttt{server})$ with $\texttt{status}_l^s = \texttt{fresh}$, then do:
  - If $pw_l = pw'_l$, mark $\texttt{status}_l^s = \texttt{compromised}$ and reply to $\mathcal{S}$ with "correct guess".
  - If $pw_l \neq pw'_l$, mark $\texttt{status}_l^s = \texttt{interrupted}$ and reply to $\mathcal{S}$ with "wrong guess".
- **Upon receiving** $(\texttt{NewKey}, sid, Pid, P_s, \alpha)$ **from** $\mathcal{S}$**, where** $\alpha \in \{\texttt{completed}, \texttt{error}\}$**:** If there exists a record of the form $(sid, Pid, P_s, pw'_i, pw'_j, \texttt{server})$, and this is the first NewKey query for P_s, then:
  - If one of the statuses corresponding to this record is interrupted, i.e., either $\texttt{status}_i^s$ or $\texttt{status}_j^s$ is $\texttt{interrupted}$, then output $(sid, Pid, P_s, \texttt{error})$ to P_s.
  - If this record is fresh, i.e., $\texttt{status}_i^s = \texttt{status}_j^s = \texttt{fresh}$, and there exist $(sid, Pid, P_i, pw_i, \texttt{client}), (sid, Pid, P_j, pw_j, \texttt{client})$ but either $pw_i \neq pw'_i$ or $pw_j \neq pw'_j$, then output $(sid, Pid, P_s, \texttt{error})$ to P_s.
  - In any other case, output (sid, Pid, P_s, α) to P_s.

  Finally, report the result (either error or completed) to $\mathcal{S}$. Moreover, if the result is error, report the reasons causing this (e.g., $pw_i \neq pw'_i$).
- **Upon receiving** $(\texttt{NewKey}, sid, Pid, P_l, sk, d)$ **from** $\mathcal{S}$**, where** $sk \in \{0,1\}^k$, $d \in \{\texttt{yes}, \texttt{no}\}$**:** If there exists a record of the form $(sid, Pid, P_l, pw_l, \texttt{client})$, and this is the first NewKey query for P_l, then do: if $d = \texttt{no}$, send $(sid, Pid, P_l, \texttt{error})$ to P_l; otherwise, set $\widetilde{l} = \{i, j\} \setminus \{l\}$ and do the following:
  - If either of the following events happens, output (sid, Pid, P_l, sk) to P_l.
    (1) P_l is corrupted, or the record $(sid, Pid, P_l, pw_l, \texttt{client})$ is compromised;
    (2) there exists $(sid, Pid, P_s, pw'_i, pw'_j, \texttt{server})$ with $pw_l = pw'_l$, and either P_s is corrupted or $\texttt{status}_{\widetilde{l}}^s = \texttt{compromised}$;
    (3) there exist $(sid, Pid, P_s, pw'_i, pw'_j, \texttt{server}), (sid, Pid, P_{\widetilde{l}}, pw_{\widetilde{l}}, \texttt{client})$ with $pw_l = pw'_l, pw_{\widetilde{l}} = pw'_{\widetilde{l}}$, and $P_{\widetilde{l}}$ is corrupted.
  - Else, if the record $(sid, Pid, P_l, pw_l, \texttt{client})$ is fresh, and there exists a record $(sid, Pid, P_s, pw'_i, pw'_j, \texttt{server})$ with $pw_l = pw'_l$ and $\texttt{status}_l^s = \texttt{fresh}$, then
    (1) If there exists a record $(sid, Pid, P_{\widetilde{l}}, pw_{\widetilde{l}}, \texttt{client})$ with $pw_{\widetilde{l}} = pw'_{\widetilde{l}}$, and a key sk' was sent to $P_{\widetilde{l}}$, and $\texttt{status}_{\widetilde{l}}^s, \texttt{status}_{\widetilde{l}}$ were fresh at that time, then output (sid, Pid, P_l, sk') to P_l.
    (2) Otherwise, if an output $(sid, Pid, P_s, \texttt{completed})$ was sent to P_s, pick a new random key sk' of length k and output (sid, Pid, P_l, sk') to P_l.
  - In other cases, output $(sid, Pid, P_l, \texttt{error})$ to P_l.

  Either way, mark the record $(sid, Pid, P_l, pw_l, \texttt{client})$ as error is a error was sent to P_l and as completed otherwise, and report the result to $\mathcal{S}$.

2.2 Design Rationales

The functionality starts with an initialization step, in which each player provides an input to notify its interest in participating into the protocol. We assume that every client starts a new session with input (NewSession, sid, Pid, P_l, pw_l, client), where P_l is the identity of the client and pw_l is its password, $Pid = PidC \cup PidS = \{P_i, P_j\} \cup \{P_s\}$ represents the ordered set of identities of players (the clients and the server) with whom it intends to interactive. Accordingly, the server starts a new session with input (NewSession, sid, Pid, P_s, pw_i, pw_j, server), where P_s is the identity of the server and pw_i, pw_j are the passwords it shares with clients in $PidC$ respectively.

The queries TestPwd are dealt with in the same manner as usual. However, when a NewKey query is asked, the answer seems a little complex. Firstly, there are three parties involved and many cases for each session should be considered. Secondly, since we want to achieve mutual authentication property, the order of the NewKey queries should be dealt with felicitously. In fact, we need to make it mandatory for the adversary to ask the NewKey queries for the clients after the corresponding query for the server. Thirdly, note that the adversary can always just modify or discard the last acknowledge message to a session, we endow the adversary with the ability to cause an instance to an error state.

More specifically, when a NewKey query is asked for a server instance, it is given an error message in the failure cases, such as the session is interrupted or it does not share the same password with some of the clients. In other cases, the instance might receive a completed or error message up to the adversary's schedule. For example, if record ($sid, Pid, P_s, pw'_i, pw'_j$, server) is fresh, and there exist two fresh records (sid, Pid, P_i, pw_i, client), (sid, Pid, P_j, pw_j, client) with $pw_i = pw'_i$ and $pw_j = pw'_j$, the server instance should come to the completed state at first glance. However, note that an adversary can always modify or omit just the last flows sent to the server, then it in fact can choose whether this instance is completed or not, i.e., error.

When a NewKey query is asked for a client instance, three different cases are considered. If the client instance is compromised or, very informally, some of the parties are corrupted, the adversary is given the power to fully determine the resulting session key. If the instance is interrupted, or it does not share the same password with the server, or an error message was sent to the server, then output (sid, Pid, P_l, error) to P_l. In the other case, if all involved instances are fresh, the target client instance is given a random session key or the same session key as its peer if one has already been sent to the latter.

Remark 1. Note that an ideal functionality for three-party password-based key exchange was proposed by Deng et al. in [25]. However, we opt to not use their formulation but to define a new one for the following reasons. Firstly, their formulation doesn't achieve mutual authentication between the clients and the server. As we known, lack of explicit authentication is the major reason for the undetectable on-line dictionary attacks against 3PAKE protocols. Hence, it would be better to include mutual authentication explicitly in the security definition.

Secondly, in Deng et al.'s formulation, the adversary is given the power to fully determine the session key "if one of the three parties P_i, P_j or P_s is corrupted". We do not agree with this and stress that the adversary who has corrupted the intended peers (i.e., P_j, P_s) of the target instance P_i can only be given this power when these instances have consistent passwords.

3 Relations Between Security Definitions

In this section, we compare the security definition presented in Sect. 2 with prior related security definitions. More precisely, we show that our 3PAKE security definition within the UC framework is actually stronger than the commonly used Real-Or-Random (ROR) model of Abdalla *et al.* [17], in the sense that any protocol securely realizing our functionality is also secure within the ROR model.

3.1 Security Comparison

First of all, in order to eliminate the discrepancy between these two communication models in the ways they use session IDs (SIDs), a trivial transformation is adopted. For any 3PAKE protocol Π that assumes unique pre-determined SIDs, we define a related protocol Π^t as follows: Π^t first has the participants exchange nonces, then it uses the concatenation of these nonces as a SID to execute an instance of the original protocol Π.

Theorem 1. *Let Π be a 3PAKE protocol that assumes unique pre-determined SIDs and Π^t be the corresponding transformed protocol. If Π securely realizes the multi-session extension $\widehat{\mathcal{F}}_{3PAKE}$ in the presence of static corruption adversaries, then Π^t is semantically secure (with forward secrecy) in the ROR model.*

Proof. Given an adversary $\mathcal{M}$ against semantical security within the ROR model, we would construct an environment $\mathcal{Z}$, which either interacts with the dummy adversary $\mathcal{A}$ and parties executing the real protocol Π, or with a simulator $\mathcal{S}$ and the multi-session extension functionality $\widehat{\mathcal{F}}_{3PAKE}$. Next we show that if the environment $\mathcal{Z}$ can only distinguish the real and ideal execution with probability negligible in security parameter k, the advantage of the adversary $\mathcal{M}$ in violating the semantic security is also negligible.

The environment $\mathcal{Z}$, which essentially runs $\mathcal{M}$ as a subroutine, simulates the executions of protocol Π^t for $\mathcal{M}$ as in the ROR model. At the beginning, $\mathcal{Z}$ first selects a random password pw_U uniformly from the dictionary D for every client $U \in \mathbf{U}$, and gives the passwords of malicious clients to the adversary $\mathcal{M}$. Then it chooses a uniformly random bit $b \in \{0, 1\}$ which will be used in answering the *Test* queries. When a common reference string (CRS) is used, $\mathcal{Z}$ also obtains from the dummy adversary $\mathcal{A}$ the CRS used for protocol Π, and gives this string to $\mathcal{M}$ as it is the CRS for protocol Π^t. It then starts the protocol execution by answering adversary $\mathcal{M}$'s oracle queries as follows.

- `Execute`$(U_1^{i_1}, S^j, U_2^{i_2})$: The environment $\mathcal{Z}$ sets $P_{U_1,i_1} = U_1||i_1, P_{U_2,i_2} = U_2||i_2, P_{S,j} = S||j$ and $Pid = PidC \cup PidS = \{P_{U_1,i_1}, P_{U_2,i_2}\} \cup \{P_{S,j}\}$, chooses random nonces $n_{U_1,i_1}, n_{U_2,i_2}, n_{S,j}$ of length k and sets $sid = n_{U_1,i_1}||n_{S,j}|| n_{U_2,i_2}$. It then gives input $(\texttt{NewSession}, sid, Pid, P_{U_1,i_1}, pw_{U_1}, \texttt{client})$ to party P_{U_1,i_1}, $(\texttt{NewSession}, sid, Pid, P_{U_2,i_2}, pw_{U_2}, \texttt{client})$ to party P_{U_2,i_2}, $(\texttt{NewSession}, sid, Pid, P_{S,j}, pw_{U_1}, pw_{U_2}, \texttt{server})$ to party $P_{S,j}$, as well as the command $(\texttt{Execute}, sid, Pid)$ to the adversary $\mathcal{A}$ instructing it to pass messages between these parties unmodified. When the resulting transcript `Trans` is returned to $\mathcal{Z}$, it hands $\mathcal{M}$ the transcript $(n_{U_1,i_1}, n_{S,j}, n_{U_2,i_2}, \texttt{Trans})$.
- `SendClient`$(U_1^{i_1}, m)$ or `SendServer`(S^j, m): If m is of appropriate form, such as command `start` or nonce n, informing the party to initiate a new interaction with some other parties, the environment $\mathcal{Z}$ chooses random nonce n_{U_1,i_1} (resp. $n_{S,j}$) and hands it to $\mathcal{M}$ as it comes from session $U_1^{i_1}$ (resp. S^j). Once all nonces, say $n_{U_1,i_1}, n_{S,j}, n_{U_2,i_2}$, corresponding to different parties involved in the interaction are known, $\mathcal{Z}$ sets $sid = n_{U_1,i_1}||n_{S,j}||n_{U_2,i_2}$, provides input $(\texttt{NewSession}, sid, Pid, P_{U_1,i_1}, pw_{U_1}, \texttt{client})$ to party P_{U_1,i_1} (resp. $(\texttt{NewSession}, sid, Pid, P_{S,j}, pw_{U_1}, pw_{U_2}, \texttt{server})$ to party $P_{S,j}$) and the command $(\texttt{Send}, sid, Pid, P_{U_1,i_1})$ (resp. $(\texttt{Send}, sid, Pid, P_{S,j})$) to the adversary $\mathcal{A}$. The adversary $\mathcal{A}$ then forwards messages to and from this party P_{U_1,i_1} (resp. $P_{S,j}$) and the environment $\mathcal{Z}$, while $\mathcal{Z}$ in turn forwards these messages to and from the adversary $\mathcal{M}$.
- `Corrupt`(U): Recall that the environment $\mathcal{Z}$ chose the passwords for all the clients in $\mathcal{U}$, then it can simply respond to $\mathcal{M}$ with the right password pw_U.
- `Test`(U^i): Note that, according to the definition, environment $\mathcal{Z}$ would obtain all the session keys of completed sessions as subroutine outputs. If the session key is not defined yet, it returns $\perp$. When $\mathcal{M}$ makes a `Test`(U^i) query and the session U^i is completed, which means that party $P_{U,i}$ is completed and a session key $sk_{U,i}$ has been outputted, the environment $\mathcal{Z}$ finds the corresponding session key. If client U or Pid_U^i is dishonest, then it returns the real session key. Otherwise, it returns either the session key held by instance U^i if $b = 1$ or a random number of the same size if $b = 0$. However, in the random case, the same random value should be returned for `Test` queries that are asked to two instances which are partners.

Assume that the bit outputted by adversary $\mathcal{M}$ is b', then environment $\mathcal{Z}$ outputs 1 when $b' = b$, and outputs 0 otherwise. Consequently, when the environment is interacting with the dummy adversary $\mathcal{A}$ and parties executing the real protocol Π, $\mathcal{M}$'s view is exactly the same as that in the ROR model. Thus the probability that $\mathcal{Z}$ outputs 1 in this case, denoted as $P\{\text{EXEC}_{\Pi,\mathcal{A},\mathcal{Z}} = 1\}$, is equal to $\Pr\{\text{EXEC}_{\Pi,\mathcal{A},\mathcal{Z}} = 1\} = \Pr[Succ^{ror}] = Adv_{\Pi^\iota,D}^{ror-ake}(\mathcal{M})/2 + 1/2$.

Next, we bound the probability that $\mathcal{Z}$ outputs 1 when it is interacting with a simulator $\mathcal{S}$ and the functionality $\widehat{\mathcal{F}}_{3PAKE}$. Two subcases are considered. On the one hand, if $\mathcal{S}$ asks at most q_S `TestPwd` queries, the probability it makes at least one correct guess is limited by $q_S/|D|$; on the other hand, if $\mathcal{S}$ never correctly guesses a password, the session keys generated by the functionality are all random values, independent of the view of $\mathcal{S}$ and thus the view of $\mathcal{M}$, which implies that $\mathcal{M}$ can only guess b correctly with probability 1/2. Therefore,

$$\Pr\{\text{EXEC}_{\widehat{\mathcal{F}}_{3PAKE},\mathcal{S},\mathcal{Z}} = 1\} \leq \frac{q_\mathcal{S}}{|D|} + \frac{1}{2}\left(1 - \frac{q_\mathcal{S}}{|D|}\right) = \frac{q_\mathcal{S}}{2|D|} + \frac{1}{2}. \quad (1)$$

Since it is assumed that Π securely realizes $\widehat{\mathcal{F}}_{3PAKE}$, there exists a simulator $\mathcal{S}$ for the dummy adversary $\mathcal{A}$, such that any environment $\mathcal{Z}$ can only distinguish the real and ideal execution with negligible probability. That is

$$|\Pr\{\text{EXEC}_{\Pi,\mathcal{A},\mathcal{Z}} = 1\} - \Pr\{\text{EXEC}_{\widehat{\mathcal{F}}_{3PAKE},\mathcal{S},\mathcal{Z}} = 1\}| \leq negl(k), \quad (2)$$

which in turn implies that

$$Adv_{\Pi^t,D}^{ror-ake}(\mathcal{M}) \leq \frac{q_\mathcal{S}}{|D|} + negl(k). \quad (3)$$

Finally, since $\mathcal{S}$ is the simulator for $\mathcal{A}$, it is easy to prove that the number of `TestPwd` queries asked by $\mathcal{S}$ is less than or equal to the number of `Send` commands received by $\mathcal{A}$, thus the number $q_\mathcal{M}$ of `Send` queries made by $\mathcal{M}$ (see Lemma A.1 in [22]). Combining the result in inequality (3), we have $Adv_{\Pi^t,D}^{ror-ake}(\mathcal{M}) \leq q_\mathcal{M}/|D| + negl(k)$ and then complete the proof of Theorem 1.

4 UC Secure 3PAKE Protocols

In this section, we show that a slight variant of the generic construction of 3PAKE protocols by Wang and Hu [34] securely realizes the new security definition within the UC framework, as a justification for our definition of the ideal functionality $\mathcal{F}_{3PAKE}$ in Sect. 2.

4.1 Cryptographic Tools

We first briefly recall the cryptographic tools needed in the generic construction of 3PAKE protocol: UC secure 2PAKE protocol (without explicit mutual authentication) and message authentication code.

UC Secure 2PAKE Protocols. The definition of the 2PAKE functionality is first given by Canetti et al. in [22], along with the first protocol to achieve such a level of security. Later on, this definition is improved to include client authentication by Abdalla et al. in [29] and to include explicit mutual authentication by Groce and Katz in [30]. Since the 2PAKE functionality does not need to achieve mutual authentication in the following generic construction, we only recall the basic 2PAKE functionality by Canetti et al. [22] in this section.

Message Authentication Codes. A message authentication code $MAC = (Mac, Ver)$ consists of two algorithms. The message authentication code generation algorithm Mac is a randomized algorithm. It takes as inputs a MAC key k and a a message m, and returns a MAC tag $t = Mac(k, m)$. The verification algorithm Ver is a deterministic algorithm. It takes as input a MAC key k, a message m and a candidate MAC tag t for m, then returns a bit $b = Ver(k, m, t)$, which is 1 if t is a valid MAC tag for message m under MAC key k; and it is 0 in the other cases. We say that a message authentication code MAC is existentially unforgeable under adaptive chosen message attacks (EUF-CMA secure) if, for every uniformly random key k, all adversaries can only forge a new valid message-tag pair with probability negligible in the security parameter, even after seeing polynomial many valid message-tag pairs.

4.2 Description of the Protocol

The detailed description of the general construction of 3PAKE protocol is presented in the below. One difference must be taken care of is that, for the sake of simplicity, we assume session identifiers are uniquely determined in advance, other than obtained at the end of the protocol execution. Moreover, since different sessions of the protocol share the same common reference string (CRS), we actually have to resort to the UC framework with joint state proposed by Canetti and Rabin [35]. Therefore, sub-session identifiers (ssids) are used instead of session identifiers (sids) in the following specification.

The protocol, denoted by Π_{3PAKE}, is parameterized by a security parameter k and a set of parties $\mathbf{P} = \{P_l\}_{l \in I}$. As a generic construction, it is described as a hybrid protocol in which the parties also make calls to as well as obtains temporary (session) keys from instances of an ideal 2PAKE functionality $\mathcal{F}_{2PAKE}$. Assume that two clients P_i and P_j are activated to establish a shared session key with the help of the sever P_s, the concrete steps are as follows.

(1) When client P_i receives an input ($\texttt{NewSession}, ssid, Pid, P_i, pw_i, \texttt{client}$) from the environment $\mathcal{Z}$ where $Pid = PidC \cup PidS = \{P_i, P_j\} \cup \{P_s\}$, it invokes an instance of 2PAKE functionality $\mathcal{F}_{2PAKE}$. More precisely, P_i defines $ssid_i = ssid||P_i||P_s$ and sends input ($\texttt{NewSession}$, $ssid_i$, $P_i, P_s, pw_i, \texttt{client}$) to the instance of 2PAKE functionality with session identifier $ssid_i$, denoted as $\mathcal{F}_{2PAKE}^{ssid_i}$; if no such instance exists, a new instance is activated. When client P_j receives a $\texttt{NewSession}$ query, it proceeds similarly in a symmetrical way, with session identifier $ssid_j = ssid||P_j||P_s$.

(2) When server P_s receives an input ($\texttt{NewSession}, ssid, Pid, P_s, pw_i, pw_j$, $\texttt{server}$) from the environment $\mathcal{Z}$ where $Pid = PidC \cup PidS = \{P_i, P_j\} \cup \{P_s\}$, it sets $ssid_i = ssid||P_i||P_s$ and $ssid_j = ssid||P_j||P_s$. Then, P_s sends input ($\texttt{NewSession}, ssid_i, P_s, P_i, pw_i, \texttt{server}$) to the instance of 2PAKE functionality $\mathcal{F}_{2PAKE}^{ssid_i}$, and sends ($\texttt{NewSession}, ssid_j, P_s, P_j, pw_j, \texttt{server}$) to the instance of 2PAKE functionality $\mathcal{F}_{2PAKE}^{ssid_j}$.

(3) Upon receiving a temporary key sk_{is} from the 2PAKE functionality $\mathcal{F}_{2PAKE}^{ssid_i}$ as a subroutine output, client P_i selects a random value $x_i \in Z_p^*$ and

computes $X_i = g^{x_i}$ and $tag_{is} = Mac(sk_{is}, ssid, Pid, P_i, X_i)$, then it sends message $(ssid, Pid, P_i, X_i, tag_{is})$ to the server P_s. Upon receiving a temporary key sk_{js} from the 2PAKE functionality $\mathcal{F}_{2PAKE}^{ssid_j}$, client P_j proceeds similarly, by choosing $x_j \in Z_p^*$, computing $X_j = g^{x_j}, tag_{js} = Mac(sk_{js}, ssid, Pid, P_j, X_j)$ and sending message $(ssid, Pid, P_j, X_j, tag_{js})$ to the server P_s.

(4) When server P_s receives $(ssid, Pid, P_i, X_i, tag_{is})$ and $(ssid, Pid, P_j, X_j, tag_{js})$, it first checks whether the MAC tags tag_{is} and tag_{js} contained in these messages are valid, using the temporary keys sk_{si} and sk_{sj} received from the underlying 2PAKE functionalities, respectively. If any of the checks is invalid, it outputs $(ssid, Pid, P_s, \texttt{error})$ and aborts this session. Otherwise, if all checks are valid, it computes $tag_{si} = Mac(sk_{si}, ssid, Pid, P_s, X_j), tag_{sj} = Mac(sk_{sj}, ssid, Pid, P_s, X_i)$, sends $(ssid, Pid, P_s, X_j, tag_{si})$ and $(ssid, Pid, P_s, X_i, tag_{sj})$ to P_i and P_j respectively, and outputs $(ssid, Pid, P_s, \texttt{completed})$.

(5) Upon receiving message $(ssid, Pid, P_s, X_j, tag_{si})$, P_i first checks whether $Ver(sk_{is}, ssid, Pid, P_s, X_j, tag_{si}) = 1$. If it is valid, P_i computes $sk_i = X_j^{x_i} = g^{x_i x_j}$; otherwise, it sets $sk_i = \texttt{error}$. At last, it outputs $(ssid, Pid, P_i, sk_i)$.

(6) Symmetrically, upon receiving message $(ssid, Pid, P_s, X_i, tag_{sj})$, P_j checks whether $Ver(sk_{js}, ssid, Pid, P_s, X_i, tag_{sj}) = 1$. If it is valid, P_j computes $sk_j = X_i^{x_j} = g^{x_i x_j}$; otherwise, it sets $sk_j = \texttt{error}$. Finally, it outputs $(ssid, Pid, P_j, sk_j)$.

4.3 Security Proof

Let $\widehat{\mathcal{F}}_{3PAKE}$ be the multi-session extension of the 3PAKE functionality $\mathcal{F}_{3PAKE}$ presented in Sect. 2. Let $\mathcal{F}_{CRS}$ be a CRS functionality that provides a CRS to all the participants, and let $\mathcal{F}_{2PAKE}$ be the 2PAKE functionality as described in Sect. 4.1. The following theorem implies that the generic construction of 3PAKE protocols presented in the last section is UC secure in the presence of static corruption adversaries, who may corrupt some of the participants but only prior to the beginning of a protocol execution. Although this is a relatively weak assumption in the UC framework, as Theorem 1 shows that, the weak corruption model of [17] is implied by this definition.

Theorem 2. *Assume that (Mac, Ver) is an EUF-CMA secure message authentication scheme, and suppose that the DDH assumption holds in the group G, then the protocol Π_{3PAKE} presented in Sect. 4.2 securely realizes $\widehat{\mathcal{F}}_{3PAKE}$ in the $(\mathcal{F}_{CRS}, \mathcal{F}_{2PAKE})$-hybrid model, in the sense of static corruption.*

In order to prove the we have to show that for any real adversary $\mathcal{A}$, there exists an ideal world adversary (a.k.a. a simulator) $\mathcal{S}$ such that, all environment can only distinguish between an execution with $\mathcal{A}$ in the real world and an execution with $\mathcal{S}$ in the ideal world with at most negligible probability.

Construction of the Simulator. The ideal world adversary $\mathcal{S}$ (interacting with the functionality $\widehat{\mathcal{F}}_{3PAKE}$ and the environment $\mathcal{Z}$), which is also known as the simulator, is constructed as follows.

Informally, the simulator $\mathcal{S}$ activates the real-world adversary $\mathcal{A}$ and constructs for it a simulated environment, by utilizing the information provided by the ideal functionality $\widehat{\mathcal{F}}_{3PAKE}$ through oracle accesses, such as `TestPwd` and `NewKey` queries. On the other hand, the simulator $\mathcal{S}$ replies to the queries of the environment $\mathcal{Z}$ with the help of subroutine calls to the real-world adversary $\mathcal{A}$. On the whole, the simulation is implemented by $\mathcal{S}$ just forwarding the environment's instructions and following the adversary's actions. However, since the simulator does not know the password used by the parties without asking `TestPwd` calls, it has to simulate these parties for $\mathcal{A}$ in such scenarios.

Specifically, the simulator first chooses randomly a dummy password $\hat{w}$. Then, it makes interface between the real-world adversary $\mathcal{A}$ and the functionality $\widehat{\mathcal{F}}_{3PAKE}$ as follows.

(1) On message $(ssid, Pid, P_l, \texttt{client})$ from $\widehat{\mathcal{F}}_{3PAKE}$, $\mathcal{S}$ first makes sure that Pid is of the form $Pid = PidC \cup PidS = \{P_i, P_j\} \cup \{P_s\}$ and $P_l \in PidC$, then it starts to simulate a new session of the protocol Π_{3PAKE} for client P_l by using the dummy password $\hat{w}$. We denote this session $(ssid, Pid, P_l)$. More specifically, the simulator sends $(\texttt{NewSession}, ssid, Pid, P_l, \hat{w}, \texttt{client})$ to P_l as input. The party P_l in turn defines $ssid_l = ssid||P_l||P_s$ and sends input $(\texttt{NewSession}, ssid_i, P_l, P_s, \hat{w}, \texttt{client})$ to the instance of 2PAKE functionality with session identifier $ssid_l$, denote as $\mathcal{F}^{ssid_l}_{2PAKE}$; if no such instance exists, a new instance is activated.

(2) Upon receiving a message $(ssid, Pid, P_s, \texttt{server})$ from $\widehat{\mathcal{F}}_{3PAKE}$, $\mathcal{S}$ makes sure that Pid is of the right form and starts a new session for P_s, by inputting $(\texttt{NewSession}, ssid, Pid, P_s, \hat{w}, \hat{w}, \texttt{server})$, denoted by $(ssid, Pid, P_s)$. It first sets $ssid_i = ssid||P_i||P_s$ and $ssid_j = ssid||P_j||P_s$, then sends input $(\texttt{NewSession}, ssid_i, P_s, P_i, \hat{w}, \texttt{server})$ to $\mathcal{F}^{ssid_i}_{2PAKE}$, and sends input $(\texttt{NewSession}, ssid_j, P_s, P_j, \hat{w}, \texttt{server})$ to $\mathcal{F}^{ssid_j}_{2PAKE}$.

(3) If the adversary $\mathcal{A}$ makes `TestPwd` queries to instances of 2PAKE functionality, the simulator makes `TestPwd` queries to instances of functionality $\widehat{\mathcal{F}}_{3PAKE}$ and replies according to the response it received. For example, without loss of generality, assume that $\mathcal{A}$ makes a query $(\texttt{TestPwd}, ssid_i, P_s, pw)$ to $\mathcal{F}^{ssid_i}_{2PAKE}$. Then, $\mathcal{S}$ asks query $(\texttt{TestPwd}, ssid, Pid, P_s, pw, i, \texttt{server})$ to $\widehat{\mathcal{F}}_{3PAKE}$. If this is a "correct guess", then $\mathcal{S}$ resets the password of this server session within $\mathcal{F}^{ssid_i}_{2PAKE}$ to pw, and replies to $\mathcal{A}$ with "correct guess"; If this is a "wrong guess", then $\mathcal{S}$ keeps the password unchanged as $\hat{w}$ and replies to $\mathcal{A}$ with "wrong guess".

(4) If the adversary $\mathcal{A}$ makes `NewKey` queries to instances of 2PAKE functionality, then $\mathcal{S}$ simulates the instances of 2PAKE functionality and responses to the queries as specification. Note that a new password other than the dummy one should be used when a "correct guess" has been made by $\mathcal{A}$.

(5) Assume that an honest client P_l with $l \in \{i, j\}$ receives a subroutine output $(ssid_l, sk_{ls})$ from the underlying 2PAKE functionality, the

party P_l simulated by $\mathcal{S}$ selects a random value $x_l \in Z_p^*$ and computes $X_l = g^{x_l}$ and $tag_{ls} = Mac(sk_{ls}, ssid, Pid, P_l, X_l)$, then it sends message $(ssid, Pid, P_l, X_l, tag_{ls})$ to the server P_s.

(6) When $\mathcal{A}$ delivers a message of the form $(ssid, Pid, P_l, X_l, tag_{ls})$ to P_s who is simulated by $\mathcal{S}$, do nothing until all the messages corresponding to the two clients in $PidC = \{P_i, P_j\}$ have been received. Then, if the party P_s is `corrupted`, `compromised` or `interrupted`, or P_s is `fresh` but the message related to P_l is not generated by P_l while P_l is an honest instance, check the tag tag_{ls} and reply to this message using the temporary key sk_{sl}; Otherwise, $\mathcal{S}$ makes a query of the form $(\texttt{NewKey}, sid, Pid, P_s, \texttt{completed})$ to $\widehat{\mathcal{F}}_{3PAKE}$. If an error happens and $\mathcal{S}$ learns that some passwords are inconsistent, say $pw_i \neq pw_i^{'}$, it changes the corresponding temporary key sk_{si} to an independent random value $sk_{si}^{'}$, and uses this new temporary key $sk_{si}^{'}$ for the verification of tag_{is}; If the response to the `NewKey` query indicates that P_i, P_j have consistent passwords with P_s respectively, then $\mathcal{S}$ simulates P_s faithfully to reply these message, using unchanged temporary keys sk_{si}, sk_{sj}.

(7) When a simulated client $P_l \in \{P_i, P_j\}$ receives message $(ssid, Pid, P_s, X_{\bar{l}}, tag_{sl})$, if the party P_l is `corrupted`, `compromised` or `interrupted`, or P_l is `fresh` but this message is not generated by P_s while P_s is an honest instance, check the tag tag_{sl} and reply to this message using the temporary key sk_{is}; otherwise, $\mathcal{S}$ asks `NewKey` query for P_l to $\widehat{\mathcal{F}}_{3PAKE}$ and replies to the messages as follows. If an error occurs and the response indicates that P_l and P_s have inconsistent password, then change the temporary key sk_{ls} to an independent random value $sk_{ls}^{'}$, and uses this new temporary key for the verification of tag_{sl}; Otherwise, the original temporary key sk_{ls} is used to reply the message.

Proof of Indistinguishability. In order to prove that every environment can only distinguish the interaction with a real adversary and a real protocol execution from the interaction with an ideal adversary and an ideal protocol with at most negligible probability, we define a sequence of "hybrid games". Due to limitation of space, we only list the game sequence below. The proof of indistinguishability between adjacent games could be found in the full version.

We denote G_0 the real world game, in which all the honest players are simulated faithfully according to the protocol, using the right passwords obtained from the environment.

Game G_1: First of all, we reject MAC tags that are non-oracle-generated, whereas both the sender and the intended receiver are honest parties.

Game G_2: In this game, we change the passwords used by honest players into dummy ones.

Game G_3: From this game, we begin to deal with the final session keys. More specifically, we change the simulation to avoid relying on the knowledge of Diffie-Hellman exponents x and y, through embedding a single random Diffie-Hellman triple(X_0, Y_0, Z_0) into the protocol execution via the classical random self-reducibility of the Diffie-Hellman problem.

Game G_4: This game is similar to the previous one, except that the simulator is given a triple (X_0, Y_0, Z_0) sampled uniformly random from G^3, instead of a Diffie-Hellman triple.

Note that, in Game G_4, as all the session keys are changed into random values which are independent of the message exchanged, it is indistinguishable from the protocol execution in the ideal world.

5 Conclusions

In this paper, we present a formulation of the ideal functionality for three-party password authenticated key exchange with mutual authentication, and demonstrate that this 3PAKE security notion within the UC framework is actually stronger than the commonly used Real-Or-Random model. Moreover, we prove that a slight variant of the generic construction of 3PAKE protocols by Wang et al. securely realizes the new security definition within the UC framework.

Acknowledgments. This work is supported by the National Natural Science Foundation of China (Grant Nos. 61502527 and 61379150).

References

1. Yuan, C., Sun, X., Lv, R.: Fingerprint liveness detection based on multi-scale LPQ and PCA. China Commun. **13**(7), 60–65 (2016)
2. Fu, Z., Sun, X., Ji, S., et al.: Towards efficient content-aware search over encrypted outsourced data in cloud. In: Proceedings of the INFOCOM, San Francisco, CA (2016)
3. Xia, Z., Zhu, Y., Sun, X., et al.: Towards privacy-preserving content-based image retrieval in cloud computing. IEEE Trans. Cloud Comput. (in press)
4. Xia, Z., Wang, X., Zhang, L., et al.: A privacy-preserving and copy-deterrence content-based image retrieval scheme in cloud computing. IEEE Trans. Inf. Forensics Secur. **11**(11), 2594–2608 (2016)
5. Xia, Z., Xiong, N., Vasilakos, A., et al.: EPCBIR: an efficient and privacy-preserving content-based image retrieval scheme in cloud computing. Inf. Sci. **387**, 195–204 (2017)
6. Xia, Z., Lv, R., Zhu, Y., et al.: Fingerprint liveness detection using gradient-based texture features. SIViP **11**(2), 381–388 (2017)
7. Xiong, L., Xu, Z., Xu, Y.: A secure re-encryption scheme for data services in a cloud computing environment. Concurr. Comput.: Pract. Exp. **27**(17), 4573–4585 (2015)
8. Chen, X., et al.: Reversible watermarking method based on asymmetric-histogram shifting of prediction errors. J. Syst. Softw. **86**(10), 2620–2626 (2013)
9. Fu, Z., Ren, K., et al.: Enabling personalized search over encrypted outsourced data with efficiency improvement. IEEE TPDS **27**(9), 2546–2559 (2016)
10. Zhang, Z., Yang, K., Hu, X., et al.: Practical anonymous password authentication and TLS with anonymous client authentication. In: Proceedings of the CCS 2016, pp. 1179–1191 (2016)

11. Bellovin, S.M., Merritt, M.: Encrypted key exchange: password-based protocols secure against dictionary attacks. In: Proceedings of the IEEE S&P 1992, pp. 72–84 (1992)
12. Bellare, M., Pointcheval, D., Rogaway, P.: Authenticated key exchange secure against dictionary attacks. In: Preneel, B. (ed.) EUROCRYPT 2000. LNCS, vol. 1807, pp. 139–155. Springer, Heidelberg (2000). doi:10.1007/3-540-45539-6_11
13. Katz, J., Ostrovsky, R., Yung, M.: Efficient password-authenticated key exchange using human-memorable passwords. In: Pfitzmann, B. (ed.) EUROCRYPT 2001. LNCS, vol. 2045, pp. 475–494. Springer, Heidelberg (2001). doi:10.1007/3-540-44987-6_29
14. Jiang, S., Gong, G.: Password based key exchange with mutual authentication. In: Handschuh, H., Hasan, M.A. (eds.) SAC 2004. LNCS, vol. 3357, pp. 267–279. Springer, Heidelberg (2004). doi:10.1007/978-3-540-30564-4_19
15. Benhamouda, F., Blazy, O., Chevalier, C., Pointcheval, D., Vergnaud, D.: New techniques for SPHFs and efficient one-round PAKE protocols. In: Canetti, R., Garay, J.A. (eds.) CRYPTO 2013. LNCS, vol. 8042, pp. 449–475. Springer, Heidelberg (2013). doi:10.1007/978-3-642-40041-4_25
16. Hu, X., Zhang, J., et al.: Universally composable anonymous password authenticated key exchange. Sci. China Inf. Sci. **60**(5), 52107 (2017)
17. Abdalla, M., Fouque, P.-A., Pointcheval, D.: Password-based authenticated key exchange in the three-party setting. In: Vaudenay, S. (ed.) PKC 2005. LNCS, vol. 3386, pp. 65–84. Springer, Heidelberg (2005). doi:10.1007/978-3-540-30580-4_6
18. Bellare, M., Rogaway, P.: Provably secure session key distribution: the three party case. In: Proceedings of the STOC 1995, pp. 57–66 (1995)
19. Chang, T., Hwang, M., Yang, W.: A communication-efficient three-party password authenticated key exchange protocol. Inf. Sci. **181**, 217–226 (2011)
20. Xiong, H., Chen, Y., Guan, Z., et al.: Finding and fixing vulnerabilities in several three-party password authenticated key exchange protocols without server public keys. Inf. Sci. **235**, 329–340 (2013)
21. He, D., Chen, Y., Chen, J.: An ID-based three-party authenticated key exchange protocol using elliptic curve cryptography for mobile-commerce environments. Arab. J. Sci. Eng. **38**(8), 2055–2061 (2013)
22. Canetti, R., Halevi, S., Katz, J., Lindell, Y., MacKenzie, P.: Universally composable password-based key exchange. In: Cramer, R. (ed.) EUROCRYPT 2005. LNCS, vol. 3494, pp. 404–421. Springer, Heidelberg (2005). doi:10.1007/11426639_24
23. Wang, D., Wang, P.: On the implications of Zipf's law in passwords. In: Askoxylakis, I., Ioannidis, S., Katsikas, S., Meadows, C. (eds.) ESORICS 2016. LNCS, vol. 9878, pp. 111–131. Springer, Cham (2016). doi:10.1007/978-3-319-45744-4_6
24. Wang, D., Zhang, Z., Wang, P., et al.: Targeted online password guessing: an underestimated threat. In: Proceedings of the ACM CCS 2016, pp. 1242–1254 (2016)
25. Deng, M., Ma, J., Le, F.: Universally composable three party password-based key exchange protocol. China Commun. **6**(3), 150–155 (2009)
26. Canetti, R.: Universally composable security: a new paradigm for cryptographic protocols. In: Proceedings of the FOCS 2001, pp. 136–145 (2001)
27. Yuan, W., Hu, L., Li, H., et al.: Offline dictionary attack on a universally composable three-party password-based key exchange protocol. Procedia Eng. **15**, 1691–1694 (2011)
28. Hu, X., Zhang, Z., Zhang, Q.: Universally composable three-party password-authenticated key exchange with contributiveness. Int. J. Commun Syst **28**(6), 1100–1111 (2015)

29. Abdalla, M., Catalano, D., Chevalier, C., Pointcheval, D.: Efficient two-party password-based key exchange protocols in the UC framework. In: Malkin, T. (ed.) CT-RSA 2008. LNCS, vol. 4964, pp. 335–351. Springer, Heidelberg (2008). doi:10.1007/978-3-540-79263-5_22
30. Groce, A., Katz, J.: A new framework for efficient password-based authenticated key exchange. In: Proceedings of the ACM CCS 2010, pp. 516–525 (2010)
31. Gennaro, R., Lindell, Y.: A framework for password-based authenticated key exchange. In: Biham, E. (ed.) EUROCRYPT 2003. LNCS, vol. 2656, pp. 524–543. Springer, Heidelberg (2003). doi:10.1007/3-540-39200-9_33
32. Abdalla, M., Chevalier, C., Pointcheval, D.: Smooth projective hashing for conditionally extractable commitments. In: Halevi, S. (ed.) CRYPTO 2009. LNCS, vol. 5677, pp. 671–689. Springer, Heidelberg (2009). doi:10.1007/978-3-642-03356-8_39
33. Abdalla, M., Benhamouda, F., Blazy, O., Chevalier, C., Pointcheval, D.: SPHF-friendly non-interactive commitments. In: Sako, K., Sarkar, P. (eds.) ASIACRYPT 2013. LNCS, vol. 8269, pp. 214–234. Springer, Heidelberg (2013). doi:10.1007/978-3-642-42033-7_12
34. Wang, W., Hu, L.: Efficient and provably secure generic construction of three-party password-based authenticated key exchange protocols. In: Barua, R., Lange, T. (eds.) INDOCRYPT 2006. LNCS, vol. 4329, pp. 118–132. Springer, Heidelberg (2006). doi:10.1007/11941378_10
35. Canetti, R., Rabin, T.: Universal composition with joint state. In: Boneh, D. (ed.) CRYPTO 2003. LNCS, vol. 2729, pp. 265–281. Springer, Heidelberg (2003). doi:10.1007/978-3-540-45146-4_16

A High-Capacity Quantum Secret Sharing Protocol Based on Single D-Level Particles

Xiang Lin[1], Juan Xu[1,2(✉)], Hu Liu[1], Xuwei Tang[1], and Maomao Fu[1]

[1] College of Computer Science and Technology, Nanjing University of Aeronautics and Astronautics, Nanjing 211106, People's Republic of China
{xianglinlx, juanxu}@nuaa.edu.cn, zhudaipopo@sina.cn, xuweitang@163.com

[2] Key Laboratory of Computer Network and Information Integration, Southeast University, Ministry of Education, Nanjing 211189, People's Republic of China

Abstract. A new quantum secret sharing protocol is proposed to share a private key based on single d-level particles. A generalized definition of capacity is also given to weigh the total efficiency of such QSS protocols. It is shown that the capacity of this protocol is $\log_2 d$, higher than the ones using single two-level particles (the maximum capacity is 1) and the similar ones proposed by Tavakoli et al. and Karimipour et al. (the capacities are $\log_2 d/d$ and $\log_2 d/2$ respectively). Besides, it is secure against several common attacks and feasible with present-day technology.

Keywords: Quantum cryptography · Quantum secret sharing · D-level · Capacity · Efficiency

1 Introduction

As quantum computers ready to leap out the lab [1], some classical cryptographic [30] algorithms and protocols are threatened by the power of quantum computers with quantum algorithms, such as Shor's parallel algorithm [2] and Grover's search algorithm [3]. Contemporarily, quantum cryptography attracts growing attention since it can be safe against quantum technologies. Quantum secret sharing (QSS) [4] is an important branch of quantum cryptography, which plays a central role in various secure multiparty computation and keys management tasks, and will be increasingly important in an era with quantum computers, more specifically, quantum network.

Nowadays, QSS protocols broadly fit into two categories: those to share classical messages [5, 6, 16–21, 27, 28] and those to share quantum information (such as quantum state and quantum operation) [7–14, 29]. Entangled states are essential for quantum information sharing, but not for classical message sharing. So single-particle states are widely used in QSS protocols sharing classical information in virtue of low cost and high efficiency of preparation compared to multi-particle entangled states [15]. Two-level single particles are mainly used in such protocols. The qubit capacity [16] of such QSS protocols is $1/n$ [17, 18] to 1 [16, 19].

X. Sun et al. (Eds.): ICCCS 2017, Part II, LNCS 10603, pp. 138–146, 2017.
https://doi.org/10.1007/978-3-319-68542-7_12

In this paper, we propose a new QSS protocol based on single multi-level particles to share a private key. Meanwhile, a generalized definition of capacity is given to weigh the total efficiency of such QSS protocols. It is shown that the capacity is further increased due to multi-level single particles. Recently, two QSS protocols with single d-level particles are proposed in 2015: the capacity of the protocol introduced by Tavakoli et al. [20] is $\log_2 d/d$, and the capacity of Karimipour and Asoudeh's [21] is $\log_2 d/2$. Compared with these two protocols, our protocol is more efficient since the capacity is $\log_2 d$. Besides, our protocol is also secure against some common attacks and can be realized with the state of the art technology.

The rest of this paper is organized as follows. Section 2 introduces the new QSS protocol using single multi-level particles. An extended capacity is defined and analyzed in Sect. 3. Section 4 discusses the security. Finally, a conclusion is drawn in Sect. 5.

2 The High-Capacity QSS Protocol

An orthonormal basis of a d-level quantum system ($d \geq 3$) is $B_Z = \{|0\rangle, |1\rangle, \ldots, |d-1\rangle\}$. It can be converted to another orthonormal basis $B_F = \{F|0\rangle, F|1\rangle, \ldots F|d-1\rangle\}$ by Fourier transform, where $F(j) = \frac{1}{\sqrt{d}} \sum_{k=0}^{d-1} e^{2\pi ijk/d}|k, j = 0, 1, \ldots, d-1$.. Obviously, B_Z and B_F are mutual unbiased bases.

A d-level unitary operation set is defined as follows:

$$\left\{U_x | U_x = \sum\nolimits_{k=0}^{d-1} e^{\frac{2\pi ix(x+k)}{d}} |x \oplus k\rangle\langle k|, x = 0, 1, \ldots, d-1\right\}, \tag{1}$$

where $'\oplus'$ denotes modulo-d addition. Then the following formulas can be derived:

$$U_x|j\rangle = e^{2\pi ix(x+j)/d}|j \oplus x\rangle, j = 0, 1, \ldots, d-1; \tag{2}$$

$$U_x F|j\rangle = e^{-2\pi ijx/d}|j \oplus x\rangle, j = 0, 1, \ldots, d-1. \tag{3}$$

It should be noticed that the global phase will not affect the measuring results.

Suppose the dealer, Alice, wants to distribute a private key, which can be thought of as a bit string, to Bob 1, Bob 2, …, and Bob $n (n \geq 3)$, and hopes the Bobs can obtain the key only if all of them cooperate honestly. The specific procedure of our protocol is described as follows.

(a) First of all, Alice and Bob n share a N-bit key $K = \{k_1, k_2, \ldots, k_N\}$, where $k_i \in \{0, 1\}$ according to the steps of BB84 [22].
(b) Alice prepares a random string $A^0 = \{a_1^0, a_2^0, \ldots, a_N^0\}$, where $a_i^0 \in \{0, 1, \ldots, d-1\}$. Then she prepares N single d-level particles according to the values of K and A^0. That is, the i-th particle state is $|a_i^0\rangle$ if $k_i = 0$, and $F|a_i^0\rangle$ if $k_i = 1$. As a result, Alice holds N qudits, each of which is one of the following $2d$ states:

$$\{|0\rangle, |1\rangle, \ldots, |d-1\rangle, F|0\rangle, F|1\rangle, \ldots F|d-1\rangle\}. \tag{4}$$

Afterwards, she inserts enough decoy particles, randomly in one of the $2d$ states, into the qudits and sends this sequence S_0 in known time slots to Bob 1. Alice broadcasts the position of decoy particles after Bob 1 announces his receipt of all the particles.

(c) Bob 1 discards the decoy particles after measuring them randomly in B_Z or B_F basis, and compares the results based on proper bases with Alice. If the rate of the results unmatched is above expected, the process is terminated. Otherwise, Bob 1 produces a random string $A^1 = a_1^1, a_2^1, \ldots, a_N^1$, where $a_i^1 \in \{0, 1, \ldots, d-1\}$, and then performs unitary operation $U_{a_i^1}$ on the i-th particle. Subsequently, he inserts enough decoy particles, randomly in one of the $2d$ states, into the qudits and sends this sequence S_1 in known time slots to Bob 2. After Bob 2 announces that he has received all of the signals, Bob 1 publishes the position of decoy particles.
(d) Bob $k (2 \leq k \leq n-1)$ does the same in turn as Bob 1 has done in Step (c).
(e) Bob n discards the decoy signals after measuring them in bases chosen at random, and compares the results from proper bases with Bob $n-1$. If the rate of disagreement is above a certain bound, the communication is aborted. Otherwise, Bob n measures each particle using the correct basis according to K (that is, using B_Z basis if $k_i = 0$ and using B_F basis if $k_i = 1$, and gets the result $R = \{0, 1, \ldots, d-1\}^N$, which is equal to $\oplus_{j=0}^{n-1} A^j$.
(f) Bobs can obtain the raw secret A^0 while they cooperate honestly to get the result of $\left[R - \oplus_{j=1}^{n-1} A^j\right] modd$.
(g) Alice announces the position of M bits chosen at random $(M \ll N)$ and compares the values with Bobs. If the rate of disagreement is higher than acceptable, they abandon the raw secret. Otherwise, the remaining are used as a private key, totally $(N-M)\log_2 d$ bits.

The above procedure is depicted briefly in Fig. 1.

It should be noticed that an initial authentication procedure is required between each sender-and-receiver pair, but omitted in this protocol. Error correction and privacy amplification can also be used to generate the final highly secret key.

3 Capacity Analysis

In Reference [16], we defined qubit capacity as the number of bits that can be shared from one qubit (ignore the qubits for detection), i.e.,

$$c_{q=}\frac{b_s}{q_p}, \tag{5}$$

where q_p denotes the number of qubits prepared, and b_s stands for the number of bits shared as the raw secret.

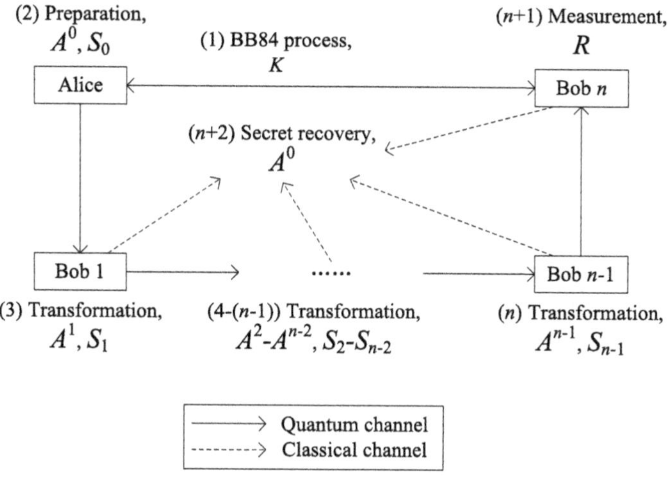

Fig. 1. Schematic diagram of our QSS protocol. K is a random value determining the measuring bases. A^0 is the raw shared secret. $A^i(1 \leq i \leq n-1)$ is a random value determining the transformation. $S_i(0 \leq i \leq n-1)$ is the single d-level particle sequence. R is the measuring result.

Take the protocols in [17, 18] as an example, the dealer sends N single photons to n players and the players finally obtain the shared key by bitwise XOR of their measuring results of qubits. Neglecting the photons for detecting eavesdropping, the dealer and players can finally share N/n bits classical information. So the qubit capacity of the protocols is $1/n$ (n indicates the number of players). To increase the qubit capacity, bitwise Exclusive OR operations on qubits' measuring results are removed in some protocols, say [16, 19], so the qubit capacity reach maximum 1.

To measure the efficiency of QSS protocol using single d-level states, the generalized definition of capacity is given as follows (neglect the detecting qudits):

$$C = \frac{B}{Q}\log_2 d, \tag{6}$$

where d indicates the level of the used qudits, B expresses the number of bits shared as the raw secret, and Q denotes the number of qudits prepared.

In 2015, Tavakoli et al. proposed a QSS protocol using sequential manipulation of single d-level states only when d is prime [20]. According to formula (6), since the number of valid rounds is $1/d$, the corresponding dimensions can be regarded as d/d. And the number of bits shared as the raw secret is 1, the number of qudits prepared is 1 as well. So we can know that the capacity is $\log_2 d/d$. Subsequently, Karimipour and Asoudeh introduced a similar protocol for any d using the idea of the analogy with a random walk performed by a particle through a lattice of states. The number of valid rounds is $1/2$, then the corresponding dimensions can be regarded as $d/2$. And same to the previous protocol, the number of bits shared as the raw secret and the number of qudits prepared is both 1. The capacity is increased to $\log_2 d/2$.

Obviously, the capacity of our protocol is $C = (N/N)\log_2 d = \log_2 d$ (ignore the detecting qudits and qubits used in BB84 process). It is higher than the above mentioned protocols. That is, our protocol needs less quantum resources to produce a certain amount of bits, which will make it more applicable than those need more quantum resource. In addition, it is difficult to prepare and maintain entangled states nowadays, especially when a large number of particles are needed to be entangled. Our protocol does not exploit entangled states, so it can be readily realized with current technology. In a word, this protocol is more feasible than other protocols because of the absence of entanglement as well as much less need for quantum resources, especially there are a large number of players.

4 Security Discussion

Theoretically, unconditional security can be achieved in a quantum cryptography algorithm or protocol, owning to the quantum characteristics such as quantum no-cloning theorem and quantum uncertainty principle. However, it may be intercepted without being detected by a dishonest participant or an eavesdropper, conventionally referred to as Eve, via some subtle classical or quantum attack strategies. Thus each practicable QSS protocol should be designed carefully.

In our protocol, BB84 process is firstly performed. BB84 protocol has been proved to be unconditionally secure [23]. The brief analysis of security against several common attacks is provided below.

(1) Intercept-resend and tampering attacks: During the transmission procedure between each sender-and-receiver pair, Eve intercepts the sequence and resends another one to Bob k, or performs some operations directly on intercepted photons, that is, tampers the states, and sends the sequence to Bob k. This protocol utilizes decoy particles to test these two kinds of attacks. The error rate will be abnormally high owing to any of the two attacks; thus the communication should be aborted.

For simplicity, suppose there is no channel noise and each decoy particle is in one of the $2d$ states $\{|0\rangle, |1\rangle, \ldots, |d-1\rangle, F|0\rangle, F|1\rangle, \ldots F|d-1\rangle\}$ with equal probability $1/2d$. If no attack is launched during transmission, the error rate will be 0. If intercept-resend or tampering attack is launched, and each changed decoy particle is in one of the $2d$ states with equal probability $1/2d$, the error rate will be $(1/2d) * [0 + 1 * (d-1) + (1/d) * d] = 1/2$. So the receiver can be aware of such attacks easily from the error rate and abort the communication decidedly.

Furthermore, since bit 0 or 1 is corresponding to four state $|0\rangle, |1\rangle, |+\rangle$ or $|-\rangle$, there are 8 kinds of situation altogether. And the probabilities of each situation are identical. We can calculate the average quantity of information Eve can gain from every bit k_i(denoting by I_{k_i}).

$$\begin{aligned} I_{k_i} &= H(k_i) - H\left(k_i \middle| A^i\right) \\ &= 1 + \frac{8}{8} \times \left(4 \times \frac{1}{4} log \frac{1}{4}\right) \\ &= 1 + log \frac{1}{4} \approx 0.398, \end{aligned} \tag{7}$$

where A^i donate the state of Bob i's particle. It is shown that the intercept-resend and tampering attack can only gain a little information about the secret message.

(2) Intercept-measure-resend attack: During the transmission process, Eve intercepts and measures the sequence randomly in B_Z or B_F basis, and then resends the sequence to the legal receiver. In this case, Eve will use the wrong basis with probability $1/2$. Then during the detection procedure, the legal receiver compares the results from 'right' (actually wrong after this attack) bases with the sender. Consequently, the error rate will be $(1/2) * [(2d - 1)/2d] = (2d - 1)/4d \geq 5/12$ (as $d \geq 3$). So this kind of attack will be detected by the legal correspondents.

Here we can also calculate the average quantity of information Eve can gain from every bit k_j(denoting by I_{k_j}, in order to be different from, I_{k_i}). The calculation is same to that of intercept-resend and tampering attacks, expect the probabilities of the final state. While the qubit is 0, if Eve measures the particle in B_Z basis, the probability of the result in state 0 is $1/2$. Else if Eve measures the particle in B_Z basis, the probability of the result in state $|+\rangle$ or $|-\rangle$ is $\frac{1}{4}$ respectively.

$$\begin{aligned} I_{k_j}k\_\{i\} &= H(k_j) - H\left(k_j \middle| A^j\right) \\ &= 1 + \frac{8}{8} \times \left(2 \times \frac{1}{4} log \frac{1}{4} + \frac{1}{2} log \frac{1}{2}\right) \\ &= 1 - \frac{3}{2} log 2 \approx 0.548 \end{aligned} \tag{8}$$

where A^j donate the state of Bob j's particle. Here we have shown that the receiver can take the intercept-measure-resend attack to gain some information about the secret message without the controller's permission. But it's still secure with this kind of attack.

(3) Misstatement attack: Bob $i(1 \leq i \leq n - 1)$ misstates his A^i so that none of other Bobs but he can obtain the secret information. A sample test is conducted to discover such an attack in Step (g).
(4) Participant attack: Some dishonest Bobs try to recovery the secret with the absence of the rest. Suppose the number of these Bobs is $m(m < n)$. If Bob n is not one of the dishonest, they can only get the value $(\oplus_m A^j) mod\, d$. If Bob n is among them, they can get the value $[R - (\oplus_{m-1} A^j)] mod\, d$, but not the secret $\left[R - \oplus_{j=1}^{n-1} A^j\right] mod\, d$. They also cannot obtain the effective information about the secret.

In practice, there are some attacks due to imperfect equipment, for example, invisible-photon attack [24], Trojan-horse attack [25]. As we have proposed in [26], a special filter can be used to defend invisible-photon attack and a 50-50 photon number splitter (that is, the photon number splitter reflects the photon and transmits the photon with half probability respectively) can be used against Trojan-horse attack. Suppose the particles are photons. An example of Bob *i*'s operating procedures against invisible-photon attack and Trojan-horse attack is given in Fig. 2. We can see that each decoy photon passing through a filter, a 50–50 photon number splitter and one polarizing photon number splitter will be finally detected by one single photon detector. The photon in state $|0\rangle$ or $|+\rangle$ will detected by DET1 or DET4, and $|1\rangle$ or $|-\rangle$ by DET2 or DET3. If an incorrect basis is chosen, one photon can be detected by any one of the four detectors. In a word, it implies the existence of Trojan-horse attack if more than one photon is detected at the same time.

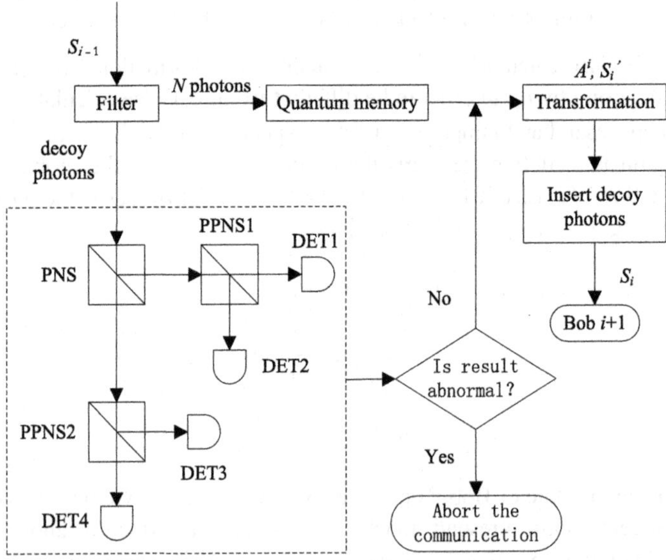

Fig. 2. Schematic illustration of Bob *i*'s operation against invisible-photon attack and Trojan-horse attack. Classical information and inspection between Bob *i* and the sender is omitted. PNS: 50–50 Photon Number Splitter; PPNS: Polarizing Photon Number Splitter; DET: Single Photon Detector.

It is shown that in theory our protocol is safe against some common attack because of the effective measures, and in practice, it can be also secure by the aid of special measures.

5 Conclusions

We propose a one-to-many QSS protocol using single d-level particles to share a pri vate key. The dealer Alice and the players Bobs are involved in this protocol. Firstly, Alice establishes the preparing and measuring bases with the last Bob. Then she prepares single d-level particles in known states and sends them to Bobs, who performs random unitary transformations on each particle in turn, except that the last Bob performs measurements instead of transformations. Bobs can cooperate to obtain the key from the knowledge of their respective local operations and the measuring result of the last Bob. The analysis shows that the protocol has obvious advantage in capacity. Clearly, having less use for quantum resources as well as no use for entanglement, it is more feasible with present-day technology. Besides, it also takes some effective measures to prevent several common attacks.

Acknowledgements. This work is supported by Natural Science Foundation of Jiangsu Province, China (Grant No. BK20140823), Chinese Postdoctoral Science Foundation (Grant No. 2013M531353), National Natural Science Foundation of China (Grant No. 61571226), Prospective Joint Research Project of Jiangsu Province (Grant No. BY2016003-11), and Fundamental Research Funds for the Central Universities (Grant No. NS2014096).

References

1. Castelvecchi, D.: Quantum computers ready to leap out the lab. Nature **541**, 9–10 (2017)
2. Shor, P.: Algorithms for quantum computation: discrete logarithms and factoring. In: FOCS (1994)
3. Grover, L.: Quantum mechanics helps in searching for a needle in a haystack. Phys. Rev. Lett. **79**(2), 325–328 (1997)
4. Hillery, M., Bužek, V., Berthiaume, A.: Quantum secret sharing. Phys. Rev. A **59**(3), 1829–1834 (1999)
5. Xu, J., Yuan, J.: Improvement and extension of quantum secret sharing using orthogonal product states. Int. J. Quantum Inf. **12**(1), 1450008 (2014)
6. Maitra, A., De, S., Paul, G., Pal, A.: Proposal for quantum rational secret sharing. Phys. Rev. A **92**(2), 022305 (2015)
7. Liu, Z., Chen, H., Xu, J., Liu, W., Li, Z.: High-dimensional deterministic multiparty quantum secret sharing without unitary operations. Quantum Inf. Process. **11**(6), 1785–1795 (2012)
8. Gao, G.: Secure multiparty quantum secret sharing with the collective eavesdropping-check character. Quantum Inf. Process. **12**(1), 55–68 (2013)
9. Hsu, J., Chong, S., Hwang, T., Tsai, W.: Dynamic quantum secret sharing. Quantum Inf. Process. **12**(1), 331–344 (2013)
10. Chen, X., Niu, X., Zhou, X., Yang, Y.: Multi-party quantum secret sharing with the single-particle quantum state to encode the information. Quantum Inf. Process. **12**(1), 365–380 (2013)
11. Ji, Q., Liu, Y., Xie, C., Yin, X., Zhang, Z.: Tripartite quantum operation sharing with two asymmetric three-qubit W states in five entanglement structures. Quantum Inf. Process. **13**, 1659–1676 (2014)

12. Liao, C., Yang, C., Hwang, T.: Dynamic quantum secret sharing protocol based on GHZ state. Quantum Inf. Process. **13**(8), 1907–1916 (2014)
13. He, X., Yang, C.: Deterministic transfer of multiqubit GHZ entangled states and quantum secret sharing between different cavities. Quantum Inf. Process. **14**(12), 4461–4474 (2015)
14. Xie, C., Liu, Y., Xing, H., Zhang, Z.: Probabilistic three-party sharing of operation on a remote qubit. Entropy **17**(2), 841–851 (2015)
15. Wagenknecht, C., Li, C., Reingruber, A., Bao, X., Goebel, A., Chen, Y., Zhang, Q., Chen, K., Pan, J.: Experimental demonstration of a heralded entanglement source. Nat. Photonics **4**, 549–552 (2010)
16. Xu, J.: Quantum secret sharing with shared key dependent on receivers. In: ICNC (2011)
17. Yan, F., Gao, T.: Quantum secret sharing between multiparty and multiparty without entanglement. Phys. Rev. A **72**(1), 012304 (2005)
18. Deng, F., Li, X., Zhou, H.: Efficient high-capacity quantum secret sharing with two-photon entanglement. Phys. Lett. A **372**, 1957–1962 (2008)
19. Xu, J., Chen, H., Liu, Z., Ruan, Y., Zhu, W.: Quantum secret sharing without exclusive OR of qubits' measuring results. In: IEEE CEC (2012)
20. Tavakoli, A., Herbauts, I., Zukowski, M., Bourennane, M.: Secret sharing with a single *d*-level quantum system. Phys. Rev. A **92**, 030302(R) (2015)
21. Karimipour, V., Asoudeh, M.: Quantum secret sharing and random hopping: using single states instead of entanglement. Phys. Rev. A **92**, 030301(R) (2015)
22. Bennett, C., Brassard, G.: Quantum cryptography: public key distribution and coin tossing. In: IEEE ICCSSP (1984)
23. Shor, P., Preskill, J.: Simple proof of security of the BB84 quantum key distribution protocol. Phys. Rev. Lett. **85**(2), 441–444 (2000)
24. Cai, Q.Y.: Eavesdropping on the two-way quantum communication protocols with invisible photons. Phys. Lett. A **351**, 23–25 (2006)
25. Deng, F.G., Li, X.H., Zhou, H.Y., Zhang, Z.J.: Erratum: improving the security of multiparty quantum secret sharing against Trojan horse attack. Phys. Rev. A **73**, 049901(E) (2006). (Phys. Rev. A 72, 044302 (2005))
26. Xu, J., Chen, H., Liu, Z., Ruan, Y., and Zhu, W.: Quantum secret sharing without exclusive OR of qubits' measuring results. In: WCCI 2012 IEEE World Congress on Computational Intelligence, New York, pp. 613–616. IEEE, (2012)
27. Lin, S., Guo, G., Xu, Y., Sun, Y., Liu, X.: Cryptanalysis of quantum secret sharing with d-level single particles. Phys. Rev. A **93**, 062343 (2016)
28. Mohajer, R., Eslami, Z.: Quantum secret sharing using single states. In: 8th International Symposium on Telecommunications (IST) (2016)
29. Xu, T., Li, Z., Bai, C., Ma, M.: A new improving quantum secret sharing scheme. Int. J. Theor. Phys. **56**, 1308 (2017)
30. Fu, Z., Ren, K., Shu, J., Sun, X., Huang, F.: Enabling personalized search over encrypted outsourced data with efficiency improvement. IEEE Trans. Parallel Distrib. Syst. **27**(9), 2546–2559 (2016)

An Inconsistency Detection Method for Security Policy and Firewall Policy Based on CSP Solver

Yi Yin[1,2(✉)], Yuichiro Tateiwa[3], Yun Wang[1], Yoshiaki Katayama[3], and Naohisa Takahashi[3]

[1] School of Computer Science and Engineering, Southeast University, Nanjing, China
yi837@hotmail.com, 101004974@seu.edu.cn
[2] School of Computer Science and Technology, Nanjing Normal University, Nanjing, China
[3] Department of Computer Science and Engineering, Graduate School of Engineering, Nagoya Institute of Technology, Nagoya, Japan
{tateiwa,katayama,naohisa}@nitech.ac.jp

Abstract. Packet filtering in firewall either accepts or denies network packets based upon a set of pre-defined rules called firewall policy. Firewall policy always designed under the instruction of security policy, which is a generic document that outlines the needs for network access permissions. The design of firewall policy should be consistent with security policy.

If firewall policy is not consistent with security policy, firewall policy may violate the intentions of security policy, which is the reason that result in critical security vulnerabilities. This paper extends our previous method, which represented security policy and firewall policy as Constraint Satisfaction Problem (CSP) and used a CSP solver *Sugar* only to verify whether they are consistent. In this paper, we propose a method to detect and resolve inconsistencies of firewall policy and security policy. We have implemented a prototype system to verify our proposed method, experimental results show the effectiveness.

Keywords: Security policy · Firewall policy · CSP problem

1 Introduction

Firewall is a traditional and very important component for network security. When packets come to firewall, they are accepted or denied based on a set of pre-defined rules called **firewall policy** (represented as ***FP***). *FP* is usually designed under the instruction of some generic rules for network access permissions, which is called **security policy** (represented as ***SP***). *SP* is an essential directory document in an organization, it defines the broad boundaries of information security. The design of *FP* should be consistent with *SP*, if they are not consistent, the inconsistencies may bring about security hole and even lead to irreparable consequences. Therefore, it is very important to detect and resolve the inconsistencies of *SP* and *FP*. However, *SP* and *FP* are always described in

X. Sun et al. (Eds.): ICCCS 2017, Part II, LNCS 10603, pp. 147–161, 2017.
https://doi.org/10.1007/978-3-319-68542-7_13

different forms and abstractions, correctly verifying whether *SP* and *FP* are consistent and detecting inconsistencies is by no means easy.

We have proposed some methods to verify whether *SP* and *FP* are consistent [1, 2]. In previous work [1], we developed a geometric analysis method and interpreted *SP* and *FP* as a set of packets respectively, then we compared two sets of packets to decide whether *SP* and *FP* are consistent. In previous work [2], we proposed a method that represents *SP* and *FP* as Constraint Satisfaction Problem (**CSP**) and constructs a consistency decision model, then uses CSP solver *Sugar* [3] to verify the consistency of *SP* and *FP*. Our two previous works could only verify whether *SP* and *FP* are consistent, when they are not consistent, previous two works could not detect and deal with the inconsistencies. To resolve this problem, in this paper, also by using CSP solver *Sugar*, we propose a method that can detect and deal with the inconsistencies of *SP* and *FP*.

The major contributions of this paper are stated as follows:

1. This paper constructs some logical formulas and uses CSP solver *Sugar* to verify them, the inconsistencies of *SP* and *FP* could be decided based on the verification results of *Sugar*. There is no need to interpret the meanings of *SP* and *FP* rules by means of additional complex analysis technology.
2. Since the CSP solver *Sugar* supports arithmetic, normal, logic and so on, which makes our proposed method easily introduce set operators of "*not*", "*and*", "*or*" and so on. For this reason, the description of *SP* rules becomes more intuitively.
3. We have developed a prototype system for the proposed method. Experimental results show the effectiveness.

This paper is organized as follows. Section 2 introduces specifications of *SP* and *FP*. Section 3 describes what is CSP and how to represent *SP* and *FP* as CSP files. Section 4 presents our proposed method and its implementation. Section 5 introduces our prototype system and experiments. Section 6 discusses relevant works in the similar areas. Finally, Sect. 7 draws the conclusions and future works.

2 *SP* and *FP*

2.1 *SP* Specification

SP is a generic instruction scenario for network access permissions, it is a specification for *FP* rules design. We have designed a model in previous works [1], which included network specification, network services and rules specification.

To represent network, we divided the target network into several disjoint subnetworks (called **regions**). Each region is a range of IP addresses or an address. For example, the region "DMZ" shown in Fig. 1 is represented as 166.68.13.0/28. We use **Host List** (shown in Table 1) to show all the available hosts and use a Region Definition Table (**RDT**, shown in Table 4) to represent all the divided regions of the network. In addition, we permit to use set operators to represent *SP*, such as "!(*not*)", "*and*", and so on, where "!(*not*)" represents other than a certain subnet or a region, "*and*" represents the union of two regions or subnets.

To represent network services, we use a Service Definition Table (**SDT**, shown in Table 2) and a Protocol Definition Table (**PDT**, shown in Table 3) to represent all the services provided in the network.

To represent *SP* rules, we suppose that *SP* consists of *m* rules $\{s_1, s_2, \ldots\ldots, s_m\}$ and each rule s_i ($i \in [1, m]$) is described as follows. Each *SP* rule s_i represents that firewall takes the action A_i (*accept* or *deny*) to the access, which comes from the region of R_{i2} to the service S_i in the region of R_{i1}.

$$s_i\text{: if } S_i \text{ in } R_{i1} \text{ from } R_{i2} \text{ then } A_i$$

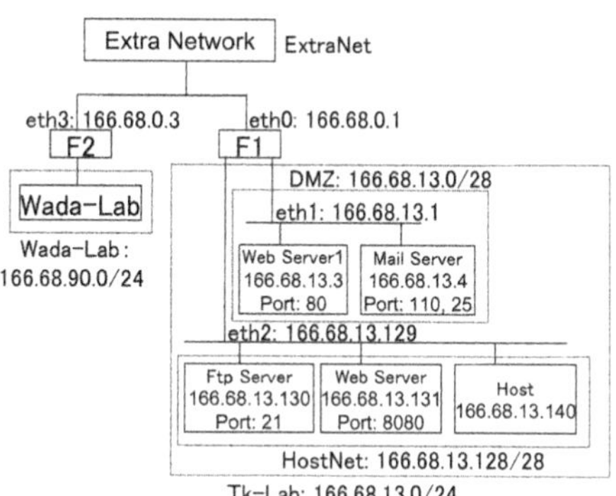

Fig. 1. Network example

Table 1. Host List

Host List
166.68.90.0/24
166.68.13.0/24

Table 2. Service Definition Table

Service name	Protocol	Des Port
WEBserver	tcp	80
FTPserver	tcp	21

Table 3. Protocol Definition Table

Protocol	Protocol number
tcp	6
udp	17
any	0–255

Table 4. Region Definition Table

Region name	IP address of region
DMZ	166.68.13.0/28
HostNet	166.68.13.128/28
Tk-Lab	166.68.13.0/24
ExtraNet	!166.68.13.0/24 and !166.68.90.0/24

2.2 *FP* Specification

A firewall policy *FP* usually consists of an ordered set of *n* rules $\{f_1, f_2, \ldots\ldots, f_n\}$. Each rule f_i includes *t* predicates, $p_1, p_2, \ldots, p_t$, and an *action* shown as follows:

$$f_i\text{:}\, p_{i1}, p_{i2}, \ldots\ldots, p_{it}, action,$$

where t is the number of key fields of header used in packet filtering. The commonly used header fields are: protocol, source IP (**SrcIP**), destination IP (**DesIP**), source port (**SrcPort**) and destination port (**DesPort**). Each predicate p_{ij} ($i \in [1, n], j \in [1, t]$) in a rule, is a matching condition for a packet header field.

3 CSP Problem and Policy Representation

3.1 CSP Problem and CSP Solver

Formally speaking, a **Constraint Satisfaction Problem** (CSP) is always defined as a triple $<V, D, C>$. V is a finite set of variables $\{V_1, V_2, \ldots, V_n\}$, D is a set of domains $\{D_1, D_2, \ldots, D_n\}$ for the variables, C is a set of constraints $\{C_1, C_2, \ldots\ldots, C_n\}$.

A CSP is the problem of assigning values to variables that satisfy some constraints. The values assigned to variables that satisfy all the constraints are called the **solution** of a CSP problem. The program to get the solutions of CSP problem is called **CSP solver**. ***Sugar*** is a kind of CSP solver, it solves a finite linear CSP by translating it into a SAT problem by using order encoding method [4] and solving the translated SAT problem by the *MiniSat* solver [5].

3.2 Syntax of *Sugar*

CSP solver accepts **CSP file** [6] as input. A CSP file describes three elements V, D, C in Lisp-like list format, where includes variable definitions and constraints definitions. Variable definition is the description of elements V, D, it supports Boolean and integer variables. Constraint definition is the description of element C.

A CSP file example is shown in Fig. 2. The first two lines defines $x \in \{1, 2, \ldots, 10\}$, $y \in \{1, 3, 5, \ldots, 7\}$. The third line defines the formula of $(x+2 \leqslant y) \bigvee (y+3 \leqslant x)$. The last two lines is a totality. The forth line defines extensional constraint r of two variables. The last line is the utilization of the defined relation r, which is equivalent to $(x, y) \in \{(1, 3), (2, 5), (3, 7)\}$. Here, the key word *support* means that which set of values are available. Each line is called as a **CSP sentence**.

```
(int x 1 10)
(int y (1 3 5..7))
(or (<= (+ x 2) y) (<= (+ y 3) x))
(relation r 2 (support (1 3) (2 5) (3 7)))
(r x y)
```

Fig. 2. Example of CSP file

3.3 Representations of *SP* and *FP* as CSP Files

According to Sect. 3.1, each CSP is modeled as a three tuple of $<V, D, C>$. Therefore, how to represent three elements V, D, C is the main task of *SP* and *FP* rules representation. In previous work [2], we have explained representation steps of *FP* and *SP* rules in detail, here we simply describe these steps.

***FP* Representation:** If *FP* consists of *n* rules $\{f_1, f_2, \ldots\ldots, f_n\}$, the set of packets that *FP* could be filtered is represented as the disjunction formula (1). According to Sect. 2.2, the predicates for packet filtering of each rule f_i is represented as the conjunction formula (2). The commonly used header fields of packets are *protocol*, *SrcIP*, *DesIP*, *SrcPort* and *DesPort*, therefore, formula (2) is equivalent to formula (3).

$$FP = f_1 \vee f_2 \vee \ldots \vee f_n \tag{1}$$

$$f_i = p_{i1} \wedge p_{i2} \wedge \ldots \wedge p_{it} \tag{2}$$

$$f_i = protocol \wedge SrcIP \wedge SrcPort \wedge DesIP \wedge DesPort. \tag{3}$$

The steps to represent *FP* rules as CSP file are shown as follows:

Step1: Lets *V* be a set of integer variables, the elements in *V* are shown as follows:

$$V\text{: } \{pr, sip_1, sip_2, sip_3, sip_4, ps, dip_1, dip_2, dip_3, dip_4, pd\},$$

where *pr* represents *protocol* number, sip_1–sip_4 and dip_1–dip_4 represent *SrcIP* and *DesIP* respectively, *ps* and *pd* represent *SrcPort* and *DesPort* respectively.
Step2: Determines the range value of each variable in *V*.
Step3: We represent predicates of each f_i as Lisp-like list format, then connect all the predicates by the conjunctive operation according to formula (3).
Step4: We connect all the conditions of *FP* rules by the disjunctive operation.

For example, Fig. 4 shows the corresponding CSP file of two rules shown in Fig. 3.

	Protocol	SrcIP	SrcPort	DesIP	DesPort	Action
f1	tcp	129.8.50.200	>1023	123.4.5.*	25	Accept
f2	*	*	*	*	*	Deny

Fig. 3. Rules example

```
(int pr  0  255)
(int sip1  0  255) (int sip2  0  255) (int sip3  0  255) (int sip4  0  255)
(int dip1  0  255) (int dip2  0  255) (int dip3  0  255) (int dip4  0  255)
(int ps  0  65535) (int pd  0  65535)

( or  ( and   (= pr 6)  (= sip1 129)(= sip2 8)(= sip3 50)(= sip4 200)
              (and (>= ps 1023)(<= ps 65535))
              (= dip1 123)(= dip2 4)(= dip3 5)(and (>= dip4 0)(<= dip4 255))
              (= pd 25)
      )
      ( and   (and (>= pr 0)(<= pr 255))
              (and (>= sip1 0)(<= sip1 255))(and (>= sip2 0)(<= sip2 255))
                  (and (>= sip3 0)(<= sip3 255))(and (>= sip4 0)(<= sip4 255))
              (and (>= ps 0)(<= ps 65535))
              (and (>= dip1 0)(<= dip1 255))(and (>= dip2 0)(<= dip2 255))
                  (and (>= dip3 0)(<= dip3 255))(and (>= dip4 0)(<= dip4 255))
              (and (>= pd 0)(<= pd 65535))
      )
)
```

Fig. 4. CSP file of rules shown in Fig. 3

***SP* Representation:** If *SP* consists of *m* rules $\{s_1, s_2, \ldots, s_m\}$, the set of packets that *SP* could be filtered is represented as the following disjunction formula (4),

$$SP = s_1 \vee s_2 \vee \ldots \vee s_m \tag{4}$$

According to the form of *SP* rule described in Sect. 2.1, the condition for packet filtering of each *SP* rule s_i could be represented as following conjunction formula (5),

$$s_i = S_i \wedge R_{i1} \wedge R_{i2} \tag{5}$$

The steps to represent *SP* rules as CSP file are shown as follows:

Step1–Step2: Decides the needed variables and the range value of each variable that used to represent *SP* rules, it is the same as *FP* representation.
Step3: According to *SP* rules and Tables 1, 2, 3 and 4, we represent the condition part of each *SP* rule s_i into Lisp-like list format, and then connect it as a conjunctive formula.
Step4: According to formula (4), we connect all *SP* rules by the disjunctive operation.

4 Inconsistency Detection of *SP* and *FP*

4.1 Inclusion Relations Between *SP* and *FP*

We define ***S*** to represent a set of rules and **P(*S*)** to represent the set of packets that match *S*. Despite the description forms of *SP* and *FP* are different, they both stipulate some conditions for filtering packets. Therefore, *SP* and *FP* rules could be viewed as a set of packets that satisfy some conditions. We use **P(*SP*)** to represent the set of packets that match *SP*, and use **P(*FP*)** to represent the set of packets that match *FP*. We also define **R (*SP*, *FP*)** to represent the inclusion relations between P(*SP*) and P(*FP*). According to set theory, R(*SP*, *FP*) could be classified as five kinds shown in formula (6).

$$R(SP, FP) = \begin{cases} Equal & when\, P(SP) = P(FP) \\ Cover & when\, P(SP) \supseteq P(FP) \\ Inside & when\, P(SP) \subseteq P(FP) \\ Disjoint & when\, P(SP) \cap P(FP) = \emptyset \\ Overlap & Otherwise \end{cases} \tag{6}$$

4.2 Consistency Decision of *SP* and *FP*

According to set theory, two sets *A* and *B* are equal if and only if they have the same elements, which also could be represented as the following identity.

$$A = B \quad if\ and\ only\ if\ A \subseteq B\ \text{and}\ B \subseteq A \tag{7}$$

Suppose *SP* consists of *m* rules $\{s_1, s_2, \ldots, s_m\}$ and *FP* consists of *n* rules $\{f_1, f_2, \ldots, f_n\}$. To verify the consistency of *SP* and *FP*, we constructed the following two formulas P_1 and P_2. We can use "*not*" operator to unify the actions of rules. Here, for the simplicity, we suppose actions of *SP* or *FP* rules are all *accept*.

$$P_1 = (\neg s_1) \wedge (\neg s_2) \wedge \ldots \wedge (\neg s_m) \wedge (f_1 \vee f_2 \ldots \vee f_n) \quad (8)$$

$$P_2 = (\neg f_1) \wedge (\neg f_2) \wedge \ldots \wedge (\neg f_n) \wedge (s_1 \vee s_2 \vee \ldots \vee s_m) \quad (9)$$

The formula P_1 wants to check whether the set of packets denied by *SP* rules have intersection with the set of packets accepted by the *FP* rules. Similarly, the formula P_2 wants to check whether the set of packets denied by *FP* rules have intersection with the set of packets accepted by the *SP* rules.

Then we use CSP solver *sugar* to verify P_1 and P_2. If the *Sugar*'s output of P_1 is *UNSATISFIABLE*, which means that the set of packets denied by *SP* have no intersection with the packets accepted by *FP*. So, conversely, we can think that the set of packets accepted by *SP* includes or equals to the set of packets accepted by *FP*, that is, P(*SP*) $\supseteq$ P(*FP*). Similarly, if *Sugar*'s output of P_2 is *UNSATISFIABLE*, which means P(*FP*) $\supseteq$ P(*SP*). According to the formula (7), when *Sugar*'s outputs of P_1 and P_2 are both *UNSATISFIABLE*, we can decided that P(*FP*) = P(*SP*). That is to say, R(*SP*, *FP*) could be decided according to *Sugar*'s outputs of P_1 and P_2.

4.3 Classification of Inconsistency Between *SP* and *FP*

When R(*SP*, *FP*) is not *Equal*, we think that there have inconsistencies between *SP* and *FP*. In our previous work [2], how to detect and deal with the inconsistencies are not resolved. To resolve this problem, we considered that *SP* is an abstract demands outline for firewall design, once *SP* is constructed, it does not change frequently. For this reason, we take *SP* as the reference, the inconsistencies are viewed as the differences of *FP* compared with *SP*. To resolve these inconsistencies, we should make *FP* to be the same as *SP*. We also suppose that there have no anomalies in individual *SP* or *FP*. We classify the inconsistencies of *FP* and *SP* as the following three kinds.

(1) **Redundancies:** If we take *SP* as the reference, *FP* have redundant rules. To resolve this inconsistency, redundant rules should be deleted from *FP*.
(2) **Insufficiencies:** If we take *SP* as the reference, *FP* have insufficient rules. To resolve this inconsistency, *SP* rules that are not included in *FP* should be added in *FP*.
(3) **Warnings:** If we take *SP* as the reference, *FP* have some especial rules, which are not completely redundant rules. Especially if we delete them from *FP*, which may affect the original intentions of *SP*. To resolve this inconsistency, we detect and show them to the network administrator.

4.4 Inconsistency Decision Analysis

We think that *SP* and *FP* have inconsistencies when R(*SP*, *FP*) are *Inside*, *Cover*, *Overlap*, and *Disjoint*. We explain how to detect the corresponding inconsistency for each inclusion relation as follows.

When R(*SP*, *FP*) is *Cover*, that is, P(*SP*) $\supseteq$ P(*FP*), which means that there exist some rules in *SP* but not in *FP*, therefore, *FP* has insufficient rules compared with *SP*. We should check each *SP* rule s_i (i $\in$ [1, *m*]) to decide whether it is an insufficient rule in *FP*. To implement the detection, we define **R(*s*$_i$, *FP*)** to represent the inclusion relations between each *SP* rule s_i and *FP*. Similar as formula (6), R(s_i, *FP*) also have the five inclusion relations shown in formula (10), the corresponding inconsistency of each inclusion relation and resolving method are summarized as in Table 5.

$$R(si, FP) = \begin{cases} Equal & when\, P(si) = P(FP) \\ Inside & when\, P(si) \subseteq P(FP) \\ Cover & when\, P(si) \supseteq P(FP) \\ Disjoint & when\, P(si) \cap P(FP) = \emptyset \\ Overlap & Otherwise \end{cases} \quad (10)$$

When R(*SP, FP*) is *Inside*, that is, P(*SP*) ⊆ P(*FP*), which means that there exist warning or redundant rules in *FP*. To check each *FP* rule f_i (i ∈ [1, *n*]) and decide which rules are warnings or redundancies, we define **R(f_i, *SP*)** to represent the inclusion relations between each *FP* rule f_i and *SP*. R(f_i, *SP*) also have the five inclusion relations shown as in formula (11), the corresponding inconsistency of each inclusion relation and resolving method are summarized as in Table 6.

Table 5. Insufficiency analysis

R(s_i, *FP*)	Inconsistency	Resolving inconsistency
Disjoint	Insufficiency	Add s_i in *FP*
Inside	No inconsistency	–
Cover	Insufficiency	Add s_i in *FP*
Overlap	Insufficiency	Add s_i in *FP*
Equal	No inconsistency	–

$$R(fi, SP) = \begin{cases} Equal & when\, P(fi) = P(SP) \\ Inside & when\, P(fi) \subseteq P(SP) \\ Cover & when\, P(fi) \supseteq P(SP) \\ Disjoint & when\, P(fi) \cap P(SP) = \emptyset \\ Overlap & Otherwise \end{cases} \quad (11)$$

Table 6. Redundancy or warning analysis

R(f_i, *SP*)	Inconsistency	Resolving inconsistency
Disjoint	Redundancy	Delete f_i from *FP*
Inside	No inconsistency	–
Cover	Warning	Show f_i to administrator
Overlap	Warning	Show f_i to administrator
Equal	No inconsistency	–

When R(*SP*, *FP*) are *Overlap* and *Disjoint* relations, the inconsistency detection could be divided into insufficiency analysis and redundancy or warning analysis, that is, we can firstly check whether exist insufficient rules, and then check whether exist redundant or warning rules.

4.5 Algorithms for Inconsistency Decision

From the analysis in Sect. 4.4, if we get R(s_i, *FP*) and R(f_i, *SP*), we can decide which rules caused inconsistencies. The following pseudo-code is *Inconsistency_Detection* algorithm, which describes the whole processes of inconsistency detection.

```
1:  Input:  SP, FP      Output:  NewFP
2:  Algorithm  RuleSet  Inconsistency_Detection(SP, FP)
3:  { RuleSet    NewFP,   FP_Temp;
4:    NewFP=FP;   FP_Temp=FP;
5:    Construct P1=(¬s1)∧(¬s2)∧...∧(¬sm)∧(f1∨f2∨...∨fn),
6:              P2=(¬f1)∧(¬f2)∧...∧(¬fn)∧(s1∨s2∨...∨sm);
7:    Use Sugar to verify P1 and P2 ;
8:    if( (Sugar(P1)==UNSAT) && ( (Sugar(P2)==UNSAT) )
9:            SP = FP,  then exit;
10:   else if(Sugar(P1)==UNSAT)
11:           NewFP = Insufficiency (SP, FP);
12:   else if(Sugar(P2)==UNSAT)
13:           NewFP = Redundancy_Warning (SP, FP);
14:   else
15:   {   FP_Temp = Insufficiency (SP, FP);
16:       NewFP = Redundancy_Warning (SP, FP_Temp);  }
17:   Return NewFP;  }
18:  End of Algorithm
```

According to Sect. 4.2, we firstly construct formulas P_1 and P_2, then we use *Sugar* to verify whether they are *SATISFIABLE* (*SAT*) or *UNSATISFIABLE* (*UNSAT*). If P_1 and P_2 are both *UNSAT*, which means that *SP* is equal to *FP* and then exit. If only *Sugar*'s output of P_1 is *UNSAT*, which means that $SP \supseteq FP$. In line 11, we call *Insufficiency* function to detect insufficient rules. If only *Sugar*'s output of P_2 is *UNSAT*, which means that $SP \subseteq FP$. In line 13, we call *Redundancy_Warning* function to detect redundant or warning rules. Otherwise, we call *Insufficiency* function and *Redundancy_Warning* function in turn.

The following pseudo-code is *Insufficiency* detection algorithm. We firstly constructed T_1 shown as in formula (12), then use *Sugar* to verify it. If *Sugar*'s output of T_1 is *UNSAT*, which means that s_i and *FP* have no intersections, R(s_i, *FP*) is *disjoint*. According to Table 5, s_i is an insufficient rule to *FP*, it should be added in *FP*. If Sugar's output of T_1 is *SAT*, which means that s_i and *FP* have intersections, R(s_i, *FP*) is one of the *Overlap*, *Inside*, *Cover* or *Equal* relations. To implement further detection, we change the parameters of formulas P_1 and P_2 and construct T_2 and T_3 shown as in formulas (13), (14), then we use *Sugar* to verify them. The *Sugar*'s outputs of T_2 and T_3 are the same as P_1 and P_2. R(s_i, *FP*) can be decided by *Sugar*'s outputs of T_1–T_3, their relations are summarized in Table 7. Then, we can deal with s_i according to Table 5.

```
Input: SP, FP            Output: NewFP
Algorithm RuleSet   Insufficiency ( SP,   FP )
{  RuleSet     NewFP;
   NewFP=FP;
   for each si in SP do
   { Construct T1=(si)∧(f1∨f2∨...∨fn),
                T2=(¬si)∧(f1∨f2∨...∨fn),
                T3=(¬f1)∧(¬f2)∧...∧(¬fn)∧(si);
     if( Sugar(T1)==UNSAT )
        Add si in NewFP;
     if ( Sugar(T1)==SAT )
     {if ((Sugar(T2)==UNSAT) && (Sugar(T3)==UNSAT) )
                Continue;
      else if(Sugar(T2)==UNSAT)  Add si into NewFP;
      else if(Sugar(T3)==UNSAT)  Continue;
      else                      Add si into NewFP;  }
   }
   Return NewFP;
 }
 End of Insufficiency Algorithm
```

$$T_1 = (s_i) \wedge (f_1 \vee f_2 \vee \ldots \vee f_n) \tag{12}$$

$$T_2 = (\neg s_i) \wedge (f_1 \vee f_2 \vee \ldots \vee f_n) \tag{13}$$

$$T_3 = (\neg f_1) \wedge (\neg f_2) \wedge \ldots \wedge (\neg f_n) \wedge (s_i) \tag{14}$$

Table 7. *Sugar*'s outputs of T_1–T_3 and R(s_i, *FP*)

T_1	T_2	T_3	R(s_i, *FP*)
UNSAT	SAT	SAT	*Disjoint* when $P(s_i) \cap P(FP) = \emptyset$
SAT	UNSAT	SAT	*Cover* when $P(s_i) \supseteq P(FP)$
SAT	SAT	UNSAT	*Inside* when $P(s_i) \subseteq P(FP)$
SAT	UNSAT	UNSAT	*Equal* when $P(s_i) = P(FP)$
SAT	SAT	SAT	*Overlap* when $P(s_i) \cap P(FP) \neq \emptyset$

The following pseudo-code is *Redundancy_Warning* detection algorithm. We firstly construct T_4 shown as in formula (15) to verify whether R(f_i, *SP*) is *disjoint*. If *Sugar*'s output of T_4 is *UNSAT*, which means that R(f_i, *SP*) is *disjoint*. According to Table 6, f_i is a redundant rule to *SP*, it should be deleted from *FP*. If *Sugar*'s output of T_4 is *SAT*, we construct T_5 and T_6 shown as in formulas (16), (17) to implement further detection, and then we use *Sugar* to verify them. The *Sugar*'s outputs of T_5–T_6 are the same as P_1 and P_2. R(f_i, *SP*) can be decided by *Sugar*'s outputs of T_4–T_6, their relations are summarized as in Table 8. Then, we can deal with each f_i according to Table 6.

```
Input: SP, FP        Output: NewFP
Algorithm RuleSet  Redundancy_Warning(SP, FP)
{RuleSet    NewFP;
 NewFP = FP;
 for each fi in FP do
 { Construct T4=(fi)∧(s1∨s2∨...∨sm),
             T5=(¬fi)∧(s1∨s2∨...∨sm),
             T6=(¬s1)∧(¬s2)∧...∧(¬sm)∧(fi);
   if (Sugar(T4)==UNSAT)      Delete fi from NewFP;
   if (Sugar(T4)==SAT)
   { if ( (Sugar(T5)==UNSAT) && (Sugar(T6)==UNSAT) )
                  Continue;
    else if(Sugar(T5)==UNSAT) Show fi to Administrator;
    else if(Sugar(T6)==UNSAT)  Continue;
    else                     Show fi to Administrator; }
  }
  Return  NewFP;
}
End of Redundancy_Warning Algorithm
```

$$T_4 = (f_i) \wedge (s_1 \vee s_2 \vee \ldots \vee s_n) \tag{15}$$

$$T_5 = (\neg f_i) \wedge (s_1 \vee s_2 \vee \ldots \vee s_n) \tag{16}$$

$$T_6 = (\neg s_1) \wedge (\neg s_2) \wedge \ldots \wedge (\neg s_n) \wedge (f_i) \tag{17}$$

Table 8. *Sugar*'s outputs of T_4–T_6 and R(f_i, *SP*)

T_4	T_5	T_6	R(f_i, *SP*)
UNSAT	SAT	SAT	*Disjoint* when $P(f_i) \cap P(SP) = \emptyset$
SAT	UNSAT	SAT	*Cover* when $P(f_i) \supseteq P(SP)$
SAT	SAT	UNSAT	*Inside* when $P(f_i) \subseteq P(SP)$
SAT	UNSAT	UNSAT	*Equal* when $P(f_i) = P(SP)$
SAT	SAT	SAT	*Overlap* when $P(f_i) \cap P(SP) \neq \emptyset$

5 Implementation and Experiments

5.1 Prototype System

According to the proposed inconsistency detection method, we implemented a prototype system. The architecture of the prototype system is shown as in Fig. 5. The inputs are: abstract *SP* rules, network topology information, and *FP* rules. According to network topology, *SP* rules are represented as the same form with *FP* rules. Then the prototype system constructs formulas P_1 and P_2 and uses *Sugar* to verify them. According to *Sugar*'s results of P_1 and P_2, insufficiency detection and redundancy or warning detection functions are used to decide and deal with inconsistencies. The dashed line rectangle in Fig. 5 is our proposed inconsistency decision procedures.

5.2 Experiments and Considerations

The prototype system implemented in C language. Experiments were performed using a computer equipped with an Intel Core i5 (3.2 GHz) and 8 GB RAM, running Windows OS, Cygwin, and CSP solver *Sugar*. To evaluate the feasibility of our proposed method, we manually designed *SP* and *FP* rules ranged from 10–100 respectively, then did the following four experiments. The experimental results are shown in Fig. 6.

1. Measure the time for verifying whether *SP* is equal to *FP*.
2. Measure the time for detecting only insufficiencies of *FP*.
3. Measure the time for detecting only redundancies or warnings of *FP*.
4. Measure the time for detecting insufficiencies, redundancies or warnings of *FP*.

The execution time of each experiment includes: the time of making formulas P_1, P_2, and T_1–T_6 of each loop; the time of using *Sugar* to verify P_1, P_2, T_1–T_6; the time of inconsistencies decision and resolving. *Sugar*'s input is CSP file, therefore, formulas P_1, P_2, and T_1–T_6 are all written in files, that is, the execution time of each experiment involves many files I/O cost.

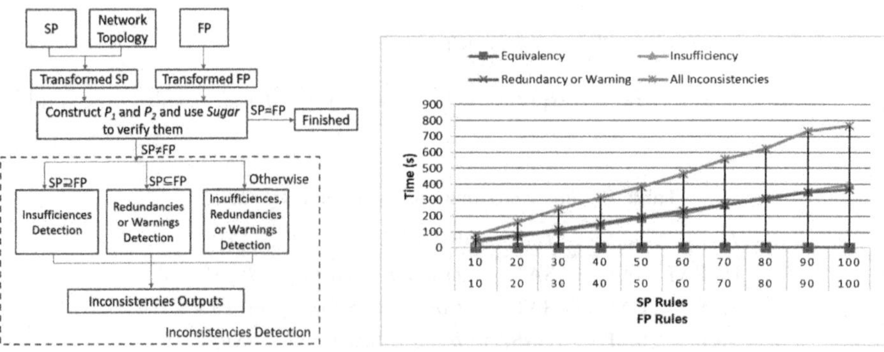

Fig. 5. Architecture of prototype system

Fig. 6. Experimental results

The results in Fig. 6 show that when *SP* and *FP* have 100 rules respectively, in the worst case, if *R*(*SP*, *FP*) are *Disjoint* and *Overlap* relations, it took about 780 s to detect and resolve all inconsistencies. When we only detect and resolve insufficiencies, or when we only detect and resolve redundancies or warnings will take similar time, they both took about 400 s. If we only verify whether *SP* and *FP* are consistent, it only took about 3 s. In average, the prototype system needs about 2 s to check whether a single rule should be added in *FP* or be deleted from *FP*.

6 Related Works

The anomalies classification and discovery of *FP* have gained a lot of attention. Wool [7] recently inspected firewall policies collected from different organizations and indicated that all examined firewall policies have security flaws. Al-Shaer and Hamed [8] reported comprehensive and in-depth study of automated firewall policy analysis for designing, configuring and managing distributed firewalls. It also provided methodologies, techniques, tools and case studies. Work [9] proposed a novel anomaly management framework that facilitates systematic detection and resolution of firewall policy anomalies. Research [10] presented a *FP* checking model, then used SAT solver to analyze reachability of policy definition. It also did some experiments and compared the proposed model with BDD-based configuration analysis approaches. The above works took aim at anomalies detection methods only in *FP*, these methods could not directly used to detect inconsistencies detection between *SP* and *FP*.

Some similar works use formal representation to model *FP* and *SP* [11–13]. Work [11] presented a Firewall Policy Query Engine (FPQE) that renders the whole process of anomaly resolution in a fully automated one, and which does not require any human intervention. Instead of prompting the administrator for inserting the proper order corrective actions, FPQE executed those queries against a high level firewall policy. FPQE used *MiniSat* solver to check whether *FP* rules are correct and complete with respect to a *SP*. Work [12] defined Boolean formula representation of *SP* and *FP*, and formulated the condition that ensures correctness of firewall configuration. Then, it also used *MiniSat* solver to check the validity of the condition. If the configuration is not correct, this work produced an example of packet to help users to correct the configuration. The above two works both used *MiniSat* solver, which does not support arithmetical or normal calculation. For this reason, these two works did not support to represent rules intuitively, for example, they could not deal with IP addresses with set operator (e.g. *not, and*), and so on. Work [13] proposed a formal method and used SMT solver *Yices* [14] to certify automatically that a *FP* is sound and complete with respect to a *SP*. Although this work explained that it provide some information helping users to correct *FP* errors, it could not directly detect and show which rules cause inconsistencies between *SP* and *FP*.

Work [15] provided the methods automatically perform comparisons algebraically of two *FP*s. It used algebraic structure to determine the semantics required of a policy language, and to make comparisons rule-order and firewall implementation independent. It also provided a formalism to compute the composition of rule sets. However, this work only took two *FP*s comparison as a goal. Because the descriptions of *SP* and *FP* have different abstractions, the proposed method in work [15] could not directly used to detect inconsistencies between *SP* and *FP*.

7 Conclusion and Future Work

In this paper, we propose a method to detect the inconsistencies between *SP* and *FP*. We firstly construct consistency decision model and use CSP solver *Sugar* to verify whether *SP* and *FP* are consistent. If *SP* and *FP* are not consistent, to implement the inconsistency decision, we construct some logical formulas and use *Sugar* to verify them. We also implemented a prototype system and did some experiments to show the effectiveness of our proposed method.

Our future work includes optimization of our proposed method and results visualization. We also would like to extend our method to handle other types of rule-based systems, such as stateful firewall rules, IDS rules, and so on. We will also extend our research to the cloud security applications [16–18].

Acknowledgments. This research was partially supported by National scholarship for studying abroad of China Scholarship Council (CSC); National Natural Science Foundation of China (No. 60973122, 61572256).

References

1. Yin, Y., Xu, X., Katayama, Y., Takahashi, N.: Inconsistency detection system for security policy and firewall policy. In: 2010 First International Conference on Networking and Computing, pp. 294–297. IEEE (2011)
2. Yin, Y., Xu, J., Takahashi, N.: Verifying consistency between security policy and firewall policy by using a constraint satisfaction problem server. In: Zhang, Y. (ed.) Future Wireless Networks and Information Systems. LNEE, vol. 144, pp. 135–145. Springer, Heidelberg (2012). doi:10.1007/978-3-642-27326-1_18
3. Sugar: a SAT-based Constraint Solver. http://bach.istc.kobe-u.ac.jp/sugar/
4. Tamura, N., Banbara, M.: Sugar: a CSP to SAT translator based on order encoding. In: Proceedings of the Second International CSP Solver Competition, pp. 65–69 (2008)
5. The MiniSat Page. http://minisat.se/MiniSat.html
6. Syntax of Sugar CSP description. http://bach.istc.kobe-u.ac.jp/sugar/current/docs/syntax.html
7. Wool, A.: Trends in firewall configuration errors: measuring the holes in Swiss cheese. IEEE Internet Comput. **14**(4), 58–65 (2010)
8. Al-Shaer, E.: Automated Firewall Analytics-Design, Configuration and Optimization. Springer International Publishing, Basel (2014). doi:10.1007/978-3-319-10371-6
9. Hu, H., Ahn, G., Kulkarni, K.: Detecting and resolving firewall policy anomalies. IEEE Trans. Secure Comput. **9**(3), 318–331 (2012)
10. Jeffrey, A., Samak, T.: Model checking firewall policy configurations. In: IEEE International Symposium on Policies for Distributed Systems and Networks, pp. 60–67. IEEE (2009)

11. Bouhoula, A., Yazidi, A.: A security policy query engine for fully automated resolution of anomalies in firewall configurations. In: IEEE 15th International Symposium on Network Computing and Applications, pp. 76–80 (2016)
12. Matsumoto, S., Bouhoula, A.: Automatic verification of firewall configuration with respect to security policy requirements. In: Corchado, E., Zunino, R., Gastaldo, P., Herrero, Á. (eds.) Proceedings of the International Workshop on Computational Intelligence in Security for Information Systems, pp. 123–130. Springer, Berlin (2009)
13. Youssef, N.B., Bouhoula, A., Jacquemard, F.: Automatic verification of conformance of firewall configurations to security policies. In: IEEE Symposium on Computers and Communications, pp. 526–531. IEEE (2009)
14. Dutertre, B., de Moura, L.: The YICES SMT Solver. http://gauss.ececs.uc.edu/Courses/c626/lectures/SMT/tool-paper.pdf
15. Ranathunga, D., Roughan, M., Kernick, P., Falkner, N.: Malachite: firewall policy comparison. In: 2016 IEEE Symposium on Computers and Communication, pp. 310–317. IEEE (2016)
16. Yuan, C.S., Xia, Z.H., Sun, X.M.: Coverless image steganography based on SIFT and BOF. J. Internet Technol. **18**(2), 209–216 (2017)
17. Liu, Q., Cai, W.D., Shen, J., Fu, Z.J., Liu, X.D., Linge, N.: A speculative approach to spatial-temporal efficiency with multi-objective optimization in a heterogeneous cloud environment. Secur. Commun. Netw. **9**(17), 4002–4012 (2016)
18. Xia, Z.H., Wang, X.H., Sun, X.M., Wang, B.W.: Steganalysis of least significant bit matching using multi-order differences. Secur. Commun. Netw. **7**(8), 1283–1291 (2014)

Reversible Data Hiding in Encrypted Image Based on Block Classification Scrambling

Fan Chen[1], Hongjie He[1(✉)], Tinghuai Ma[2], and Shu Yan[1]

[1] School of Information Science and Technology, Southwest Jiaotong University, Chengdu 611756, China
fchen@swjtu.edu.cn, hehojie@126.com

[2] School of Computer and Software, Nanjing University of Information Science and Technology, Nanjing 210044, China

Abstract. To improve the security and the quality of decrypted image, this work proposes a reversible data hiding in encrypted image based on block classification scrambling. In image encryption phase, all 8×8 blocks are firstly classified into the smooth blocks and texture ones and the corresponding block-type matrix is generated according to their most significant bits (MSB). And then the XOR-encrypted smooth and texture blocks are scrambled by the encryption key, respectively. At last, the encrypted image is generated by scanning the scrambled smooth and texture blocks in order. The risk of content disclosure of encrypted image obtained by the proposed method is reduced since the value and location of each pixel are both protected. Experimental results demonstrate that the probability for lossless recovery of proposed method is 100% even if for texture image Baboon at a high embedding rate of 0.15 bpp.

Keywords: Reversible data hiding · Block classification · Scrambling encryption

1 Introduction

With the development of the imaging devices, such as digital cameras and smartphones, our world has been witnessing a tremendous growth in quantity, availability and importance of images [1, 2]. Furthermore, the cloud computing provides a storage resources through the Internet [3, 4]. Cloud storage services enable users to access their outsourced images remotely from a variety of places, rather than having to stay nearby their computers. However, the image privacy becomes the biggest problem in open and heterogeneous cloud environment [5–8]. For example, the patients may not want to disclose their medical images to any others except a specific doctor in medical applications [5]. To minimize the risk of image content leakage, the images are encrypted before outsourcing to the cloud. On the other hand, to manage the outsourced images, the cloud server may embed some additional data into the encrypted images, such as image category and notation information, and use such additional data to identify the ownership or verify the integrity of images [9]. Obviously, the cloud server has no right to introduce permanent distortion during data embedding into the encrypted images [10].

X. Sun et al. (Eds.): ICCCS 2017, Part II, LNCS 10603, pp. 162–174, 2017.
https://doi.org/10.1007/978-3-319-68542-7_14

As a result, the reversible data hiding in encrypted images (RDH-EI) becomes a hotspot in reversible data hiding field.

According to image encryption mechanism, the RDH-EI can be classified into the reversible data hiding in symmetric encryption domain and asymmetric (public key) encryption domain. The RDH-EI methods based on public key cryptosystem utilize the holomorphic property of encryption algorithm to embed secret information [11, 12], or create information redundancy by image encryption [13, 14]. The RDH-EI methods based on symmetric cryptosystem generally encrypt original image with stream cipher, and utilize the spatial correlation in natural image to reconstruct the original image. In 2011, Zhang [15] proposed a RDH-EI method based on stream cipher. According to the encryption key, a content owner encrypts an original image by the bitwise exclusive-or (XOR) operation, and data hider flips 3 LSB (least significant bit) of part of encrypted pixels to hide secret data. A receiver use a fluctuation function to infer the secret data and recover the original image. Some improved schemes [16–18] were proposed to reduce the error rate of data extraction by modifying the fluctuation function from different viewpoint. These RDH-EI methods proposed in [15–18] have a common feature: the data extraction and image recovery are conducted at the same time after image decryption. In other words, the data extraction needs both encryption key and data-hiding key. These methods are called the joint RDH-EI. On the contrary, the RDH_EI methods that data extraction and image recovery can be performed separately are called the separable RDH-EI.

Compared with the joint RDH-EI, the data extraction in the separable RDH-EI only needs data-hiding key, which realizes the independent operation of content owner and data-hider. Existing separable RDH-EI can be divided into two categories: one is to preprocess original image to reserve room before encryption for data hiding [19–21]. In [19], the three LSBs of the selected pixels before encryption was emptied out by shifting the histogram of estimating errors of another pixels and used to data hiding. The RDH-EI methods based on reserving-room-before-encryption can achieve a high data hiding capacity and error free for data extraction and image recovery. Another category of separable RDH-EI is to directly embed secret data into an encrypted image. In 2012, Zhang [22] proposed a RDH-EI method based on compression, in which a content-owner encrypts an original image by bitwise XOR operation using the encryption key, and a data-hider may compress the least significant bits of the encrypted image to create a sparse space for data hiding. Zhang's method [22] achieves separable between data extraction and image decryption, error free for data extraction, and high quality of decrypted and recovered images. However, it is difficult to recover the original content without any error if the amount of additional data is larger than 0.04 bpp (bit per pixel). To improve the probability of lossless recovery of recovered image, Wu and Sun [23] proposed a separable method based on prediction error, in which an additional data was embedded to more significant bit (MSB) of encrypted pixels by bit replacement, and the original image content was recovered based on prediction error. Wu's method provides an improved reversibility and good visual quality of recovered image for higher payload embedding. However, the existing RDH-EI methods including reserving room before encryption and vacating room after encryption are a potential security risks due to the fact that the encrypted image is generated by XOR-encryption [24]. The XOR-encryption makes the encrypted pixels value randomly distribute in the range [0, 255], but the position of original pixel is not changed. If an attacker obtain a pair of the original image and encrypted one, the used key-stream can be estimated without knowing the encryption key. In this case, the content of encrypted image by adopting the same encryption key could be disclosed due to the feature of XOR-encryption.

To improve the security of RDH-EI method, this work proposes a RDH-EI method based on block classification permutation. All 8 × 8 blocks in an original image are firstly classified into the smooth blocks and texture ones and the corresponding block type-mark is generated according to their most significant bits (MSB). The XOR operation is applied on all the pixels to protect image content, and the block classification scrambling is designed to further protect position information of the encrypted image. Furthermore, the data hider can easy find the smooth pixels in the encrypted image without knowing the original image content. Experimental results demonstrate that the original image content can be reconstructed without any error for all tested image including the texture Baboon with the different embedding rates.

2 Block Classification Scrambling Based RDH_EI

In this section, a RDH-EI scheme based on block classification scramble is proposed, which is made up of image encryption, data hiding, data extraction, image decryption and image recovery.

2.1 Image Encryption

Assume an original image X with a size of $8M \times 8N$ pixels is in uncompressed format and each pixel with gray value falling into [0, 255] is represented by 8 bits. The original image X is firstly partitioned into non-overlapping 8 × 8 block,

$$X = \{X_{ij} | i = 1, 2, \ldots, M, j = 1, 2, \ldots, N\} \tag{1}$$

According to a certain scanning order, each 8 × 8 block X_{ij} can be expressed as,

$$X_{ij} = \left\{x_{ij1}, x_{ij2}, \ldots, x_{ij64}\right\} \tag{2}$$

In this work, we use a binary matrix $T = \{t_{ij} | 1 \leq i \leq M, 1 \leq i \leq N\}$ called the type-mark to represent the type of corresponding block in the original image. In other words, it $t_{ij} = 0$, the all pixels in the corresponding block X_{ij} is smooth pixel; otherwise, all pixels in the corresponding block X_{ij} is non-smooth pixel. For each block X_{ij} in the original image X, if the MSBs of all pixels are same, we consider the block X_{ij} as smooth block; otherwise it is considered as non-smooth. That is,

$$t_{ij} = \begin{cases} 0, & \text{if all pixels in } X_{ij} \geq 128 \\ 0, & \text{if all pixels in } X_{ij} < 128 \\ 1, & \text{otherwise} \end{cases} \tag{3}$$

If the MSB of smooth pixel is used to embed the additional data, it is easy to deduce the original MSB of embedded pixel in the decryption phase and recovery phase. This makes the quality of decrypted and recovered images be improved. In order to facilitate the hider to find the smooth pixels in encrypted image, we should separate the smooth blocks from the texture blocks. According to the type-mark T, the smooth-block table L^s and texture-block table L^t are generated by scanning order from top to bottom, left to right, respectively.

$$\begin{cases} L^s = \{L^s_m = X_{ij}|t_{ij} = 0, m = 1, 2, \ldots, N_s\} \\ L^t = \{L^t_k = X_{ij}|t_{ij} = 1, k = 1, 2, \ldots, N_t\} \end{cases} \quad (4)$$

where N_s and N_t is the number of smooth blocks and texture blocks, respectively, and $N_s + N_n = M \times N$. Since an 8×8 block can be considered as a linear table with of 64 pixels according to (2), the L^s and L^t can be considered as the one-dimensional sequence with length of $64N_s$ and $64N_n$ pixels, respectively. In other words, the L^s and L^t can also be expressed as,

$$\begin{cases} L^s = \{l^s_i|i = 1, 2, \ldots, 64N_s\} \\ L^t = \{l^t_i|i = 1, 2, \ldots, 64N_t\} \end{cases} \quad (5)$$

To ensure the secrecy of the image content, the XOR-encryption version of the L^s and L^t, denoted as $[\![L^s]\!]$ and $[\![L^t]\!]$, are easily obtained by the exclusive-or of the original bits and pseudo-random bits which is generated using the encryption key K_e. That is,

$$\begin{cases} [\![L^s]\!] = \{[\![l^s_i]\!] = Xor(l^s_i, K_e)|i = 1, 2, \ldots, 64N_s\} \\ [\![L^t]\!] = \{[\![l^t_i]\!] = Xor(l^t_i, K_e)|i = 1, 2, \ldots, 64N_t\} \end{cases} \quad (6)$$

where *Xor (.)* is the exclusive-or encryption function of pixel with gray value falling into [0, 255]. The detailed exclusive-or encryption method refers Zhang's scheme [22]. Compared the smooth-block table L^s with the corresponding encryption version $[\![L^s]\!]$, the value of pixels is changed but the position of pixels is unchanged. The relationship between L^t and $[\![L^s]\!]$ is the same too. To further protect the position information of pixels in encrypted image, the pixels in the XOR-encryption sequences $[\![L^s]\!]$ and $[\![L^t]\!]$ are scrambled based on the encryption key K_e, respectively.

In the following, taking $[\![L^s]\!]$ as an example, we describle how to obtained the corresponding scrambled sequence of $[\![L^s]\!]$, denoted as $[\![L^s]\!]' = \{[\![l^s_i]\!]'|i = 1, 2, \ldots, 64N_s\}$. Firstly, one pseudorandom sequence with size of $64N_s$, denoted as $R = \{r_i|i = 1, 2, \ldots, 64N_s\}$, is firstly produced based on the encryption key K_e, where r_i is the real in interval [0, 1]. And then the index sequence A is obtained by sorting the real pseudorandom sequence R,

$$A = \{a_i|i = 1, 2, \ldots, 64N_s\}, \; such\, that \; r_{a_1} \le r_{a_2} \le \ldots \le r_{a_{64N_s}} \quad (7)$$

Obviously, a_i is the integer in interval $[1, 64N_s]$ and the inequalities $a_i \ne a_j$ for $\forall\, i \ne j$ [25]. Each pixel in the corresponding scrambled sequence $[\![L^s]\!]'$ can be obtained by,

$$[\![l_i^s]\!]' = [\![l_{a_i}^s]\!], i = 1, 2, \ldots, 64N_s \tag{8}$$

Using the same method, the scrambled sequence $[\![L^t]\!]'$ of the XOR-encryption sequences $[\![L^t]\!]$ can be obtained. Two scrambled sequences $[\![L_i^s]\!]'$ and $[\![L^t]\!]'$ are connected to produce a sequence L,

$$L = [\![L_i^s]\!]' || [\![L^t]\!]' \tag{9}$$

The encrypted image E is generated by scanning the linear table L into two-dimensional with the size of $8M \times 8N$ pixels. Finally, we embed the binary-code of N_s into the MSB of the first pixels in encrypted version E to tell data-hider the number of smooth blocks in which he can embed additional information. It implies that the maximum embedding rate is N_s/MN bpp. Note that after image encryption, the data hider and other third party can not access the content of original image without the encryption key, thus the privacy of the content owner being protected.

To help understand the proposed image encryption process, Fig. 1 shows the flow chart of the proposed image encryption. Figure 1(a) is an original image including 3×3 blocks. According to formula (3), we can obtain the type-mark of the original image, as shown in Fig. 1(b). From Fig. 1(b) we can know that there are four smooth blocks marked by black background in Fig. 1(a) and five texture blocks marked by gray background in Fig. 1(a) in the original image since the corresponding type-mark consists of four zero and five one. According to the original and the type-mark, the smooth-block table L^s and the texture one L^t can be obtained by formula (4), as shown in Fig. 1(c). Figure 1(d) is the corresponding XOR-encryption version of the L^s and L^t. Compared Fig. 1(c) with Fig. 1(d), the value of pixels in the XOR-encryption versions is different from that of corresponding pixels in the original versions, but the position of pixels is the same as that of the corresponding ones. According to the scrambling encryption described by formula (8), the corresponding scrambled sequences of the XOR-encryption tables shown in Fig. 1(e) is achieved, where the position of pixels is different from that of the corresponding ones in the XOR-encryption tables. At last, the encrypted image E with size of 3×3 blocks, as shown in Fig. 1(f), is generated by scanning the scrambled sequences $[\![L_i^s]\!]'$ and $[\![L^t]\!]'$ in turn.

Compared Fig. 1(a) with Fig. 1(f), it is observed that the value and position of each pixel in the encrypted image are different from that in the original image. In other words, both value and position of each pixel in the encrypted image are protected. In this case, the used key-stream cannot be estimated without knowing the encryption key even if an attacker obtain a pair of the original image and encrypted one. This is because the position of all pixels in encrypted image obtained by the proposed method is also disrupted. On the other hand, it is easily know from Fig. 1(f) that all pixels in the 4 smooth-blocks are placed in the top of the encrypted image and all pixels in the texture blocks are arranged in the back of the encrypted image. As a result, the data-hider can easy find the smooth pixels in the encrypted image without knowing the original image content. The number of smooth blocks in which the data-hider can embed additional data should be 4 in term of the maximum embedding rate is *4/9* bpp.

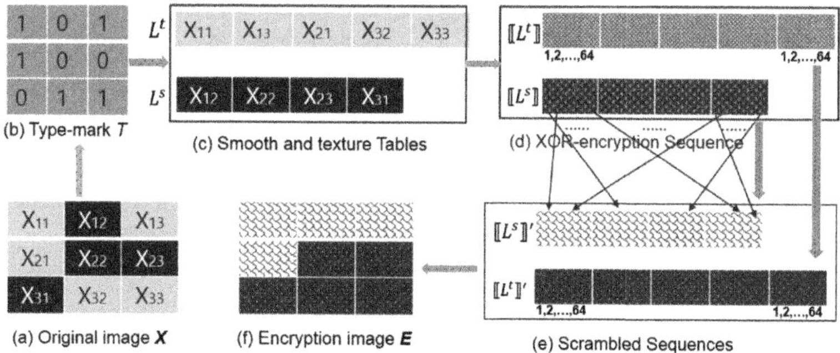

Fig. 1. Flow chart of the proposed encryption method

Note that, the type-mark as part of the encryption key is also shared between the content owner and the receiver in the proposed encryption method. This makes the security of encrypted image be improved. The cost is to increase some extra burden of storage and transmission. Fortunately, this cost is accepted especially for the content owner who requires a higher security of image content since the additional storage space is not too much. In fact, the type-mark can also be embedded the MSB of the last $M \times N$ smooth pixels in the encrypted image, and the maximum embedding rate would be reduced from N_s/MN bpp to $N_s/MN - (1/64)$ bpp.

2.2 Data Hiding

When a data-hider receives the encrypted image E, he can embed some additional data for the certain purpose such as integrity authentication, media notation and fast retrieval so on if he possesses the data-hiding key K_h.

Let $D = \{d_k | k = 1, 2, \ldots, N_d\}$ be a binary additional data to be embedded in the encrypted image, where N_d be the number of bits in the additional data. Firstly, the data-hider reads the number of smooth blocks, denoted as C_{max}, by extracting the MSB of the first pixels in the encrypted image. It's important to note that the value of N_d should be not more than that of $64C_{max}$. And then, the data-hider pseudo-randomly selects N_d encrypted pixels that will be used to carry the additional data. To make the selected encrypted pixels be smooth pixels and nearly uniform distributed, the index sequence $A = \{a_i | i = 1, 2, \ldots, C_{max}\}$ with size of $64C_{max}$ is generated by adopting the same method of formula (7) according to the data-hiding key K_h. The kth ($k = 1, 2, \ldots, N_d$) bit in the additional data, i.e. d_k, is embedded by modifying the MSB of the pixel $e_{i_k j_k}$ in the encrypted image,

$$e_{i_k j_k} = 128 \times d_k + mod\left(e_{i_k j_k}, 128\right), \ k = 1, 2, \ldots, N_d \tag{10}$$

where, mod (,) is modulus after division, i_k and j_k denote the row and column coordinates of the pixel and are computed by,

$$\begin{cases} i_k = \lfloor a_k/8N \rfloor + 1 \\ j_k = mod(a_k, 8N) + 1 \end{cases}, k = 1, 2, \ldots, N_d \tag{11}$$

where $\lfloor \cdot \rfloor$ is the largest integer less than or equal to the given parameter. When all the bits are embedded, a marked-encrypted image is constructed. Since the pixel $e_{i_k j_k}$ used to embed the additional data d_k is randomly selected based on the data-hiding key, a potential attacker cannot extract the embedded data.

2.3 Data Extraction

In the data extraction phase, we consider that the receiver only has the marked-encrypted image and the data hiding key. The N_d pixels, denoted as $e_{i_k j_k}$, in the marked encrypted image are obtained according to the data hiding key by adopting the same method of data hiding. The extracted data $D' = \{d_k' | k = 1, 2, \ldots, N_d\}$ are achieved by,

$$d_k' = \lfloor e_{i_k j_k}/128 \rfloor, k = 1, 2, \ldots, N_d \tag{12}$$

2.4 Image Decryption

When the receiver only has the encryption key (including the corresponding type-mark *T*), the inverse process of the encryption process is performed to obtain the marked decrypted image $Z^0 = \{Z_{ij}^0 | 1 \le i \le M, 1 \le i \le N\}$, in which there are some pixels whose MSB may be error. The decrypted image $Z = \{Z_{ij} | 1 \le i \le 8M, 1 \le i \le 8N\}$ is firstly initialized to the marked decrypted image Z^0. To obtain the good quality of decrypted image, the value of the pixel Z_{ij} such that $t_{ij} = 0$ is adjusted by estimating its MSB,

$$Z_{ij} = \begin{cases} 128 + mod(Z_{ij}, 128), & if \sum_{\delta \in Z_{ij}^0} \lfloor \delta/128 \rfloor \ge 32 \\ mod(d_{ij}, 128), & otherwise \end{cases} \tag{13}$$

2.5 Image Recovery

When the receiver has the data hiding and encryption keys, he can extract the embedded bits and obtain the recovered image $R = \{r_{ij} | 1 \le i \le 8M, 1 \le i \le 8N\}$ with superior quality. This is due to the fact that the pixels with embedding additional bits can be clearly known.

According to the data hiding and formula (11), the receiver can compute the position of pixels with additional data in the encrypted image $\{i_k, j_k | k = 1, 2, \ldots, N_d\}$. It is easily achieve the position mark matrix of encrypted image $P^E = \{p_{ij}^E | 1 \le i \le 8M, 1 \le i \le 8N\}$

$$p_{ij}^E = \begin{cases} 1, & for(i_k, j_k), k = 1, 2, \ldots, N_d \\ 0, & otherwise \end{cases} \quad (14)$$

The position matrix of decrypted image, denoted as $P = \{p_{ij}|1 \leq i \leq 8M, 1 \leq i \leq 8N\}$, can be obtained by performing the inverse process of the classification permutation for P^E. According the position matrix of decrypted image and the marked decrypted image $D^0 = \{d_{ij}^0|1 \leq i \leq M, 1 \leq i \leq N\}$, we can reconstruct the recovered image R = $\{r_{ij}|1 \leq i \leq M, 1 \leq i \leq N\}$.

$$r_{ij} = \begin{cases} d_{ij}^0, & if\, p_{ij=0} \\ 128 \times \mu_{ij} + \bmod(d_{ij}^0, 128), & otherwise \end{cases} \quad (15)$$

where, the value of μ_{ij} is computed by,

$$u_{ij} = \begin{cases} 1, & if\, d_{mn}^0 \geq 128 \text{ such that } p_{mn} = 0 \\ 0, & otherwise \end{cases} \quad (16)$$

The range of the parameters m and n are,

$$\begin{cases} m \in [\lfloor (i-1)/8 \rfloor \times 8 + 1, \lfloor (i-1)/8 \rfloor \times 8 + 8] \\ n \in [\lfloor (j-1)/8 \rfloor \times 8 + 1, \lfloor (j-1)/8 \rfloor \times 8 + 8] \end{cases} \quad (17)$$

3 Experiment Results

In all of our experiments, the secret message bits are randomly generated. Four images with the size of 512 × 512 pixels are utilized, which are popularly used in the testing the efficiency of RDH schemes by other researchers. The tested images including Lena, Airplane, Lake and Baboon are shown in Fig. 2. For the separable methods, the extracted bits are completely correct since data extraction and image recovery are separated. Therefore, only the embedding rate and visual quality of the decrypted image and recovered image are concerned for the following experiments.

3.1 Performance Analysis

To validate the performance of the proposed scheme, two test image Lena and Baboon, shown as in Fig. 2(a) and (d), were used as the original image in this experiment. Figure 3(a) is the type-mark of Lena and Baboon images, where the number of the smooth blocks in them are respectively 2652 and 852, which means the maximum embedding rate of Lena and Baboon images are 0.65 bpp and 0.21 bpp.

Figure 3(b) is the encrypted images containing the additional bits, where the 16384 additional bits are embedded and the embedding rate is about 0.0625 (=16384/(512 × 512)) bpp. As can be seen from Fig. 3(b), it looks like a random noise image due to the fact that the pixel values in the marked-encrypted image randomly distribute

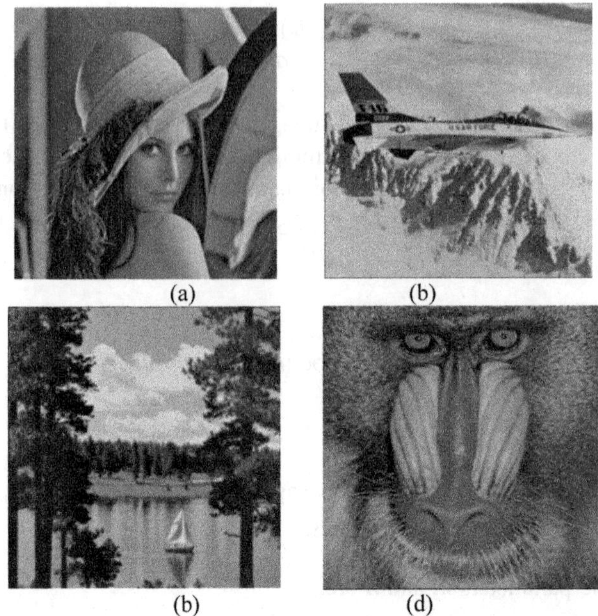

Fig. 2. Tested images (a) Lena, (b) Airplane, (c) Lake, (d) Baboon

in the range [0, 255] and the position of pixels is also be changed. Since the containing-encrypted images were contained the embedded data, the additional data could be easily extracted using the data-hiding key. We directly decrypted the containing-encrypted image using the encryption key including its corresponding type-mark, the decrypted images are obtained and given in Fig. 3(c). The value of PSNR (Peak Signal-to-Noise Patio) in the decrypted images of Lena and Baboon are $+\infty$ dB. That is, the decrypted images of Lena and Baboon are the same as the corresponding original image when the number of embedded data is 16384 bits. On the other hand, by using both the data-hiding key and the encryption key including the type-mark, the embedded data could be successfully extracted and the original images could be perfectly recovered from the encrypted images containing embedded data, evidenced by the $+\infty$ dB PSNR. That is, when embedding rate is about 0.0625 bpp, the proposed scheme could lossless reconstructed the original content of Lena and Baboon images even if only encryption key is used.

3.2 Performance Comparison

In this subsection, performance comparisons among the proposed method, Zhang's method [22] and Wu's method [23] is demonstrated in Tables 1 and 2 including the embedding rate (ER), the quality of decrypted and the quality of the recovered one. In this experiment, the four tested images and 100 different keys are adopted, and the embedding rates are 4096, 16384 and 40960 bits in term of 0.0156, 0.0625 and 0.15.63 bpp, respectively.

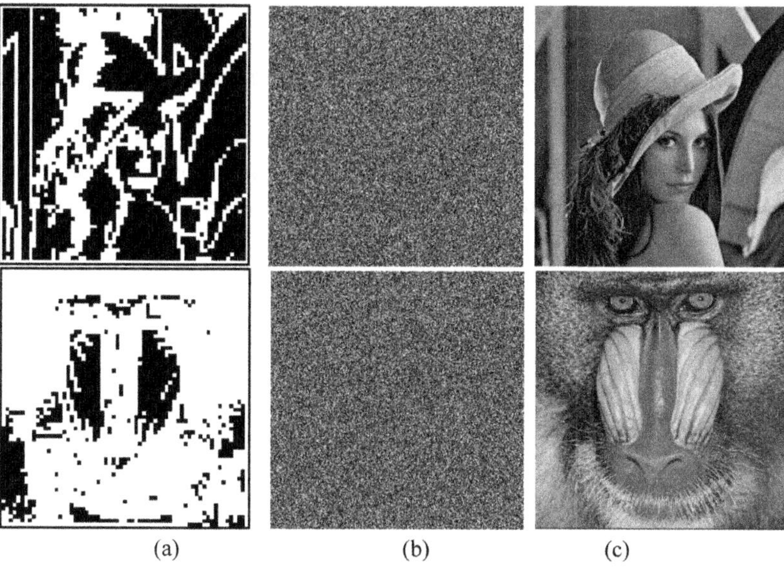

Fig. 3. Experimental results by the proposed method with 16384 bits embedded (a) Type mark, (b) Encrypted images containing embedded data with 16384 bits, (c) decrypted images with PSNR +∞ dB

The quality of encrypted images with different embedding rate are shown in Table 1. As can be seen from Table 1, it is easy to know that the quality of decrypted images is related to the complexity of the image itself and the embedding rate. When the embedding rate is 0.0156 and 0.06.25 bpp, PSNR of decrypted image by the proposed method is +∞ dB. It implies that the probabilities for lossess decryption of the proposed method are 1 for the four test images when embedding rate is not more

Table 1. Quality comparison of decrypted images between proposed, Zhang [22] and Wu [23]

ER (bpp)	Images	Wu (%/dB)	Zhang (%/dB)	Proposed (%/dB)
0.015.6	Lena	0/35.27	0/54.18	1/+∞
	Airplane	0/34.43	0/54.36	1/+∞
	Lake	0/30.60	0/54.51	1/+∞
	Baboon	0/23.68	0/54.15	1/+∞
0.06.25	Lena	0/34.46	0/38.32	1/+∞
	Airplane	0/33.76	0/38.15	1/+∞
	Lake	0/30.23	0/38.19	1/+∞
	Baboon	0/23.48	0/38.28	1/+∞
0.1563	Lena	0/32.58	0/38.01	1/+∞
	Airplane	0/31.77	0/38.28	1/+∞
	Lake	0/29.10	0/37.91	1/+∞
	Baboon	0/22.98	0/37.92	0/28.99

than 0.0625 bpp. When embedding rate is 0.1563 bpp, the proposed method can obtained the error-free decrypted images for Lena, Airplane and Lake images, however the PSNR of decrypted Baboon image by the proposed method is less than that by Zhang's method. Fortunately, the probability for lossless recovery of proposed method is 100% even if for texture image Baboon at a high embedding rate of 0.0156 bpp as shown in Table 2. In other words, for four test image including the texture Baboon image, the complete reversibility (i.e., prob for lossless recovery is 1) is provided by the proposed method.

Table 2. Quality comparison of recovered images between proposed, Zhang [22] and Wu [23]

ER (bpp)	Images	Wu (%/dB)	Zhang (%/dB)	Proposed (%/dB)
1.56%	Lena	1/–	0/65.89	1/+∞
	Airplane	0.99/60.17	0/60.14	1/+∞
	Lake	0.73/59.39	0/56.32	1/+∞
	Baboon	0/51.01	0/55.14	1/+∞
6.25%	Lena	1/–	0/55.63	1/+∞
	Airplane	0.93/60.17	0/48.66	1/+∞
	Lake	0.26/58.32	0/42.63	1/+∞
	Baboon	0/44.69	0/40.01	1/+∞
15.63%	Lena	1/–	0/44.65	1/+∞
	Airplane	0.74/60.17	0/42.08	1/+∞
	Lake	0.04/54.84	0/39.88	1/+∞
	Baboon	0/40.57	0/38.78	1/+∞

4 Conclusion and Future Work

In this paper, a block classification scrambling based separable reversible data hiding in encrypted image is proposed, which consists of image encryption, data embedding, data extraction, image decryption and image recovery. In the image encryption phase, the type-mark is firstly generated according to the MSB of each 8×8 blocks in the original image, and then a block classification permutation encryption is designed. Combining with the XOR-encryption, the content privacy of an encrypted image is improved since the value and location of each pixel in encrypted image are both protected. Moreover, it is easy for the data hider to find the smooth pixels in the encrypted image without the original content of a test image. When the receiver has both of the keys, he can recover the original content without any error for all tested image including the texture Baboon and all tested embedding rates ranged from 0.01 to 0.15 bpp. In the future, the relationship between the maximum embedding rata and the quality of decrypted and recovered images should be theoretically analyzed.

Acknowledgments. The research is supported by the National Natural Science Foundation of China (61373180, U1536110).

References

1. Xia, Z., Wang, X., Zhang, L., Qin, Z., Sun, X., Ren, K.: A privacy-preserving and copy-deterrence content-based image retrieval scheme in cloud computing. IEEE Trans. Inf. Forensics Secur. **11**(11), 2594–2608 (2016)
2. Fu, Z., Wu, X., Guan, C., Sun, X., Ren, K.: Toward efficient multi-keyword fuzzy search over encrypted outsourced data with accuracy improvement. IEEE Trans. Inf. Forensics Secur. **11**(12), 2706–2716 (2016)
3. Kong, Y., Zhang, M., Ye, D.: A belief propagation-based method for task allocation in open and dynamic cloud environments. Knowl.-Based Syst. **115**, 123–132 (2016)
4. Liu, Q., Cai, W., Shen, J., Fu, Z., Liu, X., Linge, N.: A speculative approach to spatial-temporal efficiency with multi-objective optimization in a heterogeneous cloud environment. Secur. Commun. Netw. **9**(17), 4002–4012 (2016)
5. Xia, Z., Xiong, N., Vasilakos, A.V., Sun, X.: EPCBIR: an efficient and privacy-preserving content-based image retrieval scheme in cloud computing. Inf. Sci. **387**, 195–204 (2017)
6. Xia, Z., Zhu, Y., Sun, X., Qin, Z., Ren, K.: Towards privacy-preserving content-based image retrieval in cloud computing. IEEE Trans. Cloud Comput. (2015). doi:10.1109/TCC.2015.2491933
7. Fu, Z., Ren, K., Shu, J., Sun, X., Huang, F.: Enabling personalized search over encrypted outsourced data with efficiency improvement. IEEE Trans. Parallel Distrib. Syst. **27**(9), 2546–2559 (2016)
8. Xia, Z., Wang, X., Sun, X., Wang, Q.: A secure and dynamic multi-keyword ranked search scheme over encrypted cloud data. IEEE Trans. Parallel Distrib. Syst. **27**(2), 340–352 (2015)
9. Yu, Y., MH, Au, Ateniese, G., Huang, X., Susilo, W., et al.: Identity-based remote data integrity checking with perfect data privacy preserving for cloud storage. IEEE Trans. Inf. Forensics Secur. **12**(4), 767–778 (2017)
10. Zhang, W., Wang, H., Hou, D., Yu, N.: Reversible data hiding in encrypted images by reversible image transformation. IEEE Trans. Multimed. **18**(8), 1469 (2016)
11. Zhang, X., Long, J., Wang, Z., Cheng, H.: Lossless and reversible data hiding in encrypted images with public key cryptography. IEEE Trans. Circuits Syst. Video Technol. **26**(9), 1622–1631 (2016)
12. Xian, S., Lou, X.: Reversible data hiding in encrypted image based on homomorphic public key cryptosystem. J. Softw. **27**(6), 1592–1601 (2016)
13. Zhang, M., Ke, Y., Su, T.: Steganography in encrypted domain based on LWE. J. Electron. Inf. Technol. **38**(2), 354–360 (2016)
14. Ke, Y., Zhang, M., Su, T.: A novel multiple bits reversible data hiding in encrypted domain based on R-LWE. J. Comput. Res. Dev. **53**(10), 2307–2322 (2016)
15. Zhang, X.: Reversible data hiding in encrypted image. IEEE Signal Process. Lett. **18**(4), 255–258 (2011)
16. Hong, W., Chen, T., Wu, H.: An improved reversible data hiding in encrypted images using side match. IEEE Signal Process. Lett. **19**(4), 199–202 (2012)
17. Liao, X., Shu, C.: Reversible data hiding in encrypted images based on absolute mean difference of neighboring pixels. J. Vis. Commun. Image Represent. **28**, 21–27 (2015)
18. Qian, C., Zhang, X.: Effective reversible data hiding in encrypted image with privacy protection for image content. J. Vis. Commun. Image Represent. **31**, 154–164 (2015)
19. Ma, K., Zhang, W., Zhao, X., et al.: Reversible data hiding in encrypted images by reserving room before encryption. IEEE Trans. Inf. Forensics Secur. **8**(3), 553–562 (2013)
20. Xu, D., Wang, R.: Separable and error-free reversible data hiding in encrypted images. Signal Process. **123**, 9–21 (2016)

21. Nguyen, T., Chang, C., Chang, W.: High capacity reversible data hiding scheme for encrypted images. Signal Process.: Image Commun. **44**, 84–91 (2016)
22. Zhang, X.: Separable reversible data hiding in encrypted image. IEEE Trans. Inf. Forensics Secur. **7**(2), 826–832 (2012)
23. Wu, X., Sun, W.: High-capacity reversible data hiding in encrypted images by prediction error. Signal Process. **104**, 387–400 (2014)
24. Huang, F., Huang, J., Shi, Y.: New framework for reversible data hiding in encrypted domain. IEEE Trans. Inf. Forensics Secur. **11**(12), 2777–2789 (2016)
25. Chen, F., He, H., Huo, Y.: Self-embedding watermarking scheme against JPEG compression with superior imperceptibility. Multimed. Tools Appl. (2016). doi:10.1007/s11042-016-3574-0

A Mutation Approach of Detecting SQL Injection Vulnerabilities

Yanyu Huang, Chuan Fu, Xuan Chen, Hao Guo, Xiaoyu He, Jin Li, and Zheli Liu(✉)

Nankai University, Tianjin, China
onlyerir@163.com, 267451153@qq.com, waffer@yeah.net, {guohao,hexiaoyun}@geiri.sgcc.com.cn, jinli71@gmail.com, liuzheli@nankai.edu.cn
http://www.springer.com/lncs

Abstract. As Internet is increasingly prosperous, Web services become more common in our social life. As users can access pages on the Web directly, Web application plays a vital role in various domains such as e-finance and public-services. Inevitably, it will be followed by unprecedented amount of attacks and exploitations. Amongst all of those attacks, SQL injection attacks have consistently high rank in last years due to corresponding vulnerabilities. It is crucial to checking this vulnerabilities before web services being public. In our paper we present an effective approach for testing, MOSA, and mutation operators set to its underpinning. Using this approach we can produce test inputs that cause executable and malignant SQL statement efficiently. Besides that, we do numerous experiments and the results demonstrate that the mutation approach can detect SQL injection vulnerabilities and generate inputs that bypass web application firewalls.

Keywords: Vulnerability · Test generation · Mutation operators

1 Introduction

In recent years, the world wide web developed from a traditional information medium to a vital application bench. Finance, retailing, education, societal network and government work have been more convenient due to the web [1]. The amount is more than before assuming including private web services are arranged within this system.

Service Oriented Architecture applications are prevailing, and the situation of which can be owed to the incessant practicability, interoperability, and manoeuvrability. And yet, there are some malevolent users who are interested in those

Zheli Liu received the BSc and MSc degrees in computer science from Jilin University, China, in 2002 and 2005, respectively. He received the PhD degree in computer application from Jilin University in 2009. After a postdoctoral fellowship in Nankai University, he joined the College of Computer and Control Engineering of Nankai University in 2011.

X. Sun et al. (Eds.): ICCCS 2017, Part II, LNCS 10603, pp. 175–188, 2017.
https://doi.org/10.1007/978-3-319-68542-7_15

applications. The amount of known web vulnerabilities is increasing radically. Up-to-date security reports show that web-based systems suffer nearly 26 attacks per minute [2]. Like Microsoft and Google, some vulnerability survey found that at lowest 8% of services including vulnerabilities. The investigations that we mentioned, among with time-cost stress of market, make the requirement of effective detecting approaches that can handle the growing web risks and the finite time and resources limited by testing [13].

SQL injection attack is different from other attack, which does not squander system resource. At the same time, due to SQL injection attack is able to achieve or modify confidential information, it is a vital imperil to military or banking database servers. SQLi target database drive system by the SQL code fragments into fragile input parameters is not correct inspection and disinfection. The injected code snippet can change the behavior of the application when they show or modify the system information into SQL statements. The SQLi attack is top-ranked within threatening web services security risk in 2013 which analyse by the Open Web Application Security Project (OWASP) [14]. Under such circumstances, some ways are proposed by investigator to detect SQLi attacks like automatic deficient encoding techniques, static and dynamic vulnerability analysis, and runtime SQLi attack detection and prevention [12].

At the remnant part of this paper is composed by follows: Sect. 2 describes a background on SQLi attack and corresponding vulnerabilities and some related work. Section 3 expounds our approach based on mutation operators and tools. Section 4 states treatment and appraisal with results and threats to validity. Eventually, Sect. 5 summarizes the work.

2 Background and Related Work

This section presents a sententious background on web applications and SQLi vulnerabilities and summarizes previous work about SQLi detecting.

2.1 Background

In spite of a web application is working on a web browser as a program barely, the construction of the application is formed of three tier, and the specific structure is shown in Fig. 1. In Fig. 1, by request of the browser presentation tier is sent to a web browser [3].

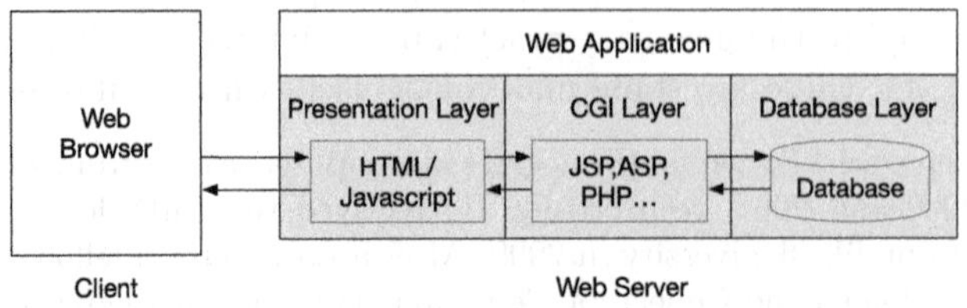

Fig. 1. Web application architecture.

(1) Presentation Tier: The user input is sent to this tier and the result of user processing is shown.
(2) CGI Tier: A.k.a, the Server Script Process, this is situated in mid tier
(3) Database Tier: All of the data will be saved and retrieved by this tier.

SQL Injection Attack is based on code injection technique which detects a security vulnerability existing in the database layer of an application. Supposing this situation, input of user is also erroneously screening for string literal escape characters which are inserted in SQL statements or the input is not strongly typed, the vulnerability will turn up [11].

Tautology
A website would be wide open to SQLi attack if which uses the origin. For instance, assuming that a user enters"' OR 1=1–" and"", in place of username ="Admin" and password = "admin", the resulting of query will be:

SELECT * from FROM userdata WHERE username=' ' OR 1=1 –' AND password =''

After WHERE token as a qualified statement, the database analysis every character, and the "OR 1=1" clause's inclusion turns conditional into tautology. Therefore, database will return the specific data of all user information. A malignant user could embed numerous SQL commands by using this vulnerability, even there will be some commands could modify or destroy private information of database [10].

Remote execution of stored procedures. The type of attack stored early by web application developer is conducted by implementing the programs. An example is shown as follows: "'; SHUTDOWN; – ", so that the query will be built as:

Query = "Select accounts from Userinformation WHERE username = "; SHUTDOWN; – password=";

Illegal Queries
Critical users collect enough data from error display so that the users can obtain more database information, which will assist the users to enter the web applications system by utilizing SQL injection vulnerability [4].

Within this paper we take SQL vulnerabilities about the input parameters into under test: the parameter of SQLi attacks is in peril of assuming that is inserted in any statement of specific implementation as well if, an attacker can submit critical inputs can transform the original logic of SQL statement. Attacker tries to summit inputs that lead to performable SQL statements to mine available vulnerabilities. If not, the database will reject final statements, which are possible that there is not existing such actions like visiting or modifying data.

2.2 Related Work

Due to all kinds of web vulnerabilities and program without rigid check, the reason of malignant attacks was increasing, which is mainly by ASP or PHP scripting injection for instance a chief assault method. With development of

Web station quantity being fast, building by SQL injection has turned into the mainstream of web attack. While the Web server compilation process trendy the script writer disregard programming safety standard phenomenon, giving rise to a wide variety of interactive operation loopholes in Web server. Consisting of at least 70% of SQL injection point exists, the vitium of malevolent attackers can use the server, database allotment the shortcomings and complicated formation of unlawful statements through procedures or scripts intruding server acquire website legal permissions and gain the related database substance, severe still is able to achieve all server where the connection system data. A severe risk to data from a database, and so much so that threat system security and users.

There are two forms of SQL injection attack: rely on the time when the malignant attackers enter inputs, and the attacks appear. The one of form about SQL injection is that attackers embed malignant inputs, and the attacks turn up immediately, with the malignant inputs being concatenated with the SQL statement [8]. The other is that attackers seed malignant inputs into the database, which is applied at a later time, to indirectly trigger SQL injection attack. The former is called a first order SQLi, and the latter is called a second order SQLi [5].

Most study authors developed many process to check and prevent SQL injection attacks; the most widely used method is static analysis, dynamic analysis, combined static and dynamic analysis, web framework, protective programming and machine study-type skill [7]. Early study about SQLi inspection made use of both white-box and black-box ways to mining vulnerabilities. Some white-box technology applied taint analysis to discriminate invalidated inputs inserted into SQL statements [6]. There are so many researchers suggesting to using symbolic execution to discriminate the constraints that need to be content to resulting in a SQLi attack. All sorts of academic and online security sources have enumerated and discussed foregone SQLi patterns. All the same, it is not enough to check an application as malicious users by relying on these patterns, which is all the time finding new approaches to mine vulnerabilities. The mutation operators we propose in this paper change inputs to raise the likelihood of triggering vulnerabilities rather than the program under test to evaluate the effectiveness of test suites in finding faults [9].

Our approach differs in following aspects: (1) targeting SQL injection vulnerabilities that needs diverse mutation operators and inputs generation approached; (2) It is much more challenging for the failures observability in the case of SQL injection vulnerabilities to searching crashes. We need to intercept communication between a SUT and its database to analyse SQL statements for executability and vulnerability detection.

3 Approach

We put forward an efficient automatic approach, namely MOSA, for mining SQLi vulnerabilities. Our approach is based on a set of mutation operators that control user inputs to generate fresh test inputs to trigger SQLi attacks. Furthermore, these operators can be linked by diverse ways and multiple operators can be applied to the same one. So it could be possible to create inputs including fresh attack patterns, thus increasing the likelihood of mining vulnerabilities.

Particularly, we would like to create tests that are able to bypass web application firewalls and lead to performable SQL statements. A WAF may restraint SQLi attacks and prevent a vulnerable service from being exploited. Therefore, effective test inputs need to get through the WAF so that it can reach the service. Besides, they are able to bring about performable SQL statements as otherwise, security problems are almost impossible to appear because the database engine will refuse them and therefore there will be no information would be leaked or came to terms.

This section presents our proposed mutation operators to create message for testing. A specific case is afforded to each mutation operator. In some operators we also discuss their preconditions with reference to input and previously operators which have been applied. Afterwards we will probe the test generating approach and the automated tool that we employed to sustain the approach.

3.1 Mutation Operators

According to the purpose of mutation operators we can sort them into the following three types: Behaviour-transforming, syntax-repairing and obfuscation. Table 1 displays a summary of all mutation operators.

Table 1. Summary of mutation operators classified into behaviour-transforming, syntax-repairing, and ob- fuscation operators

Pattern name	Description
Behaviour-transforming operators	
or	Adds an OR-clause to the input
and	Adds an AND-clause to the input
semi	Adds a semicolon followed by an additional SQL statement
Syntax-repairing operators	
par	Appends a parenthesis to a legal input
cmt	Adds a comment command (– or #) to an input
qot	Adds a single or double quote to an input
Obfuscation operators	
wsp	Changes the encoding of whitespaces
chr	Changes the encoding of a character literal en- closed
in	quotes
html	Changes the encoding of an input to HTML entity encoding
per	Changes the encoding of an input to percent- age encoding
bool	Rewrites a boolean expression while preserving it's truth value
keyw	Obfuscates SQL keywords by randomising the capitalisation and inserting comments

Behaviour-Transforming. This type of mutation operators changes inputs for changing the expected behaviour of application when there is existing SQL injection vulnerability. For instance, the application could return more database rows than expected caused by a mutated input, as a result the application may reveal sensitive information to a potential attacker or unexpected user. We define the following behaviour-transforming operators:

Pattern or

Adds *OR* $x = x$ to the *WHERE* clause of a SQL statement where x is a random number or a character enclosed in single or double quotes.

Pattern and

Adds *AND* $x = y$ to the *WHERE* clause of a SQL statement where x and y are random numbers or single characters enclosed in single or double quotes and x is not equal to y.

Preconditions of pattern and: MO_or has not been applied.

Pattern semi

Adds a semicolon (;) followed by an additional SQL statement to the input. The resulting query has the form *sql_stmt1*; *sql_stmt2*, where *sql_stmt1* is the original SQL statement and *sql_stmt2* is a randomly chosen SQL statement from a predefined list.

Sytax-Repairing. This type of mutation operators changes inputs with the aim of repairing SQL syntax errors when they might show up. As mentioned before, a SQLi attack tries to change the behaviour of the application by injecting malignant inputs. Hence, the malignant input itself is expected to include SQL statement fragments. Different from the regular legal inputs, this type of input could give rise to SQL syntax errors when being combined with its targets, i.e., predefined SQL statements. Because the approach that we propose is a black-box technique, it is challenging to generate inputs that do not cause syntax errors when the predefined SQL statement syntax is unbeknown to the test generator. The mutation operators we define in this class are the following:

Pattern par

Appends a closing parenthesis to the end of an input.

Preconditions of pattern par: A behaviour-transforming mutation operator has been previously applied.

Pattern cmt

Adds a SQL comment command (double dashes – and the hash character #) to the input. Any SQL that follows a comment command is not executed.

Pattern qot

Adds either a single quote (') or a double quote (") to the mutant.

Preconditions of pattern: A behaviour-transforming mutation operator, which contains a character literal, has been previously applied.

Obfuscation. There are some applications that may employ input filters, e.g., a web application firewall, to prevent themselves from SQLi attacks. In essence, a WAF inspects every input to check for suspicious and typical string patterns which are used in SQLi attacks, such as SQL key- words, and blocks them. For example, a WAF uses a blacklist with including forbidden characters or strings to decide if an input is suspicious or not. In practice, almost all security-critical systems are protected by such filters, like a software system, which handles credit card information, having to employ a WAF to prevent attacks with obeying with industry security standards. Obfuscation mutation operators try to avoid filtering by mutating an input to a semantically equivalent input but in a different form. This might prevent the filter from recognising the forbidden characters or strings in the mutated input. We define the following obfuscation mutation operators:

Pattern wsp

Replaces a whitespace with a semantically equivalent character (+, /**/, or unicode encodings: %20, %09,%0a, %0b, %0c, %0d and %a0).

Preconditions: The input contains at least one whitespace.

Pattern chr

Replaces a character literal enclosed in quotes ('c') with an equivalent representation, where c is an arbitrary printable ASCII character. Equivalent representations are:

- Short binary representation, for example, '*a*' is replaced with *b'1100001'*.
- Long binary representation, for example, '*a*' is replaced with *_binary'1100001'*.
- Unicode representation, for example, '*a*' is re- placed with *n'a'*.
- Hexadecimal representation, for example, '*a*' is replaced with *x'61'*.

Preconditions of pattern chr: A behaviour-transforming mutation operator, which contains a character literal, has been previously applied.

Pattern html

Changes the encoding of a mutant using HTML entity encoding. In HTML entity encoding, a character can be encoded in two ways: (i) numeric character reference in the form *&#N* where *N* is the character's code position in the used character set in decimal or hexadecimal representation; (ii) Character entity reference [32] in the form *&SymbolicName*. For example, *"* is the encoding for the single quote character (').

Preconditions of pattern html: For character entity reference encoding, only characters with symbolic names can be encoded.

Pattern per

Changes the encoding of a mutant using percent en- coding: *%HH*, where *HH* is a two digit hexadecimal value referring to the character's ASCII code. For example, the single quote character (') is encoded as *%27*.

Pattern bool

Replaces a boolean expression with an equivalent boolean expression. For example, the boolean expression *1=1* which is used in MO_or could be obfuscated as *not false=!!1*. Both expressions evaluate to true, which maintains the same semantic meaning of the mutant after obfuscation.

Preconditions of pattern bool: Can only be applied to input values that contain a boolean expression.

Pattern keyw

Obfuscates SQL keywords and operators using different techniques: Randomly changing the case of some letters, adding comments in the middle of a keyword or replacing a keyword with an alternative representation. Most SQL parsers are case insensitive, e.g. the keyword *select*, *SELECT* or *SeLeCt* are all legal. Some parsers accept keywords which contain a comment in the middle of the keyword (e.g. *sel/*comment here*/ect*). Finally, some keywords have alternative forms, e.g. *OR* can also be expressed as ||.

Preconditions of pattern keyw: The input value contains at least one SQL keyword.

3.2 Test Generation

Different types of single or multiple mutation operator can be applied to a simple input parameters, to produce the expected input. The latter one aims to check the tiny vulnerabilities, which only can be generated by combining multiple mutation operator input to trigger.

Each restraint conditions of mutations has to start from a legal test example, which meets the application criteria under test. As legitimate test inputs in an initial part, which guarantees we will avoid to produce directly be applied to refuse the test case on account of correlation between inputs or complex ones which are not likely to be created at random. In addition, the advantage of legal test example is more possible to content input legitimacy and can get to critical parts of the application lightly. For instance, if an program anticipates a user information combined with other inputs that we hope to change, a well-defined format must be observed by the user information; or the test case would be refused immediately. With the existing technology, legal test cases from present functional suites can be recycled or if there are not such test suites, legal test cases can be manually generated by using SoapUI[4] and analogous means.

The test generation algorithm is defined officially by Algorithm 1: beginning with a legal test case, each input is changed a predefined amount of times. The function Apply MO (Line 4) uses one or more mutation operators to generate a input at random. A simple grammar defined the different legal means to link operators is used by the function and the function makes sure that all of the preconditions for the used operators are contented. The manipulate under test is known as the updated test case TC0. If the oracle marks a vulnerability, all of the SQL statements that were announced owing to the call are detected. Assuming that the percentage of performable SQL statements is above a predefined threshold P, the input is informed as vulnerable and the test case is preserved to assist the test creator in debugging and fixing the vulnerability (Line 5–8). In this test we select P = 100%, implying that all SQL statements that are triggered must be executed.

Algorithm 1. Test Generation Algorithm:

Input TC: A test case: ArrayOf($Input$)
OP: A web service operation to be tested
Output TS: Test Suite for SQLi vulnerabilities
V: Set of vulnerable inputs

```
T = ∅
for each Input ∈ TC do
    while max_tries_not_reached do
        TC' = apply_MO(TC,Input)
        if call(OP,TC') = VulnrFlagged then
            if performable_SQL ≥ P then
                V = V ∪ Input
                TS = TS ∪ TC'
            end if
        end if
    end while
end for
return TS, V
```

3.3 Test Oracle

It may lead to making the application erroneous if it succeeds when a malignant input is sent to a target application. In most situations, the representation of anomalous behaviour can be observed from the results of the target system returns or from the surrounding environment. In our tests, according to interest SQL injections, a database proxy aims at intercepting the communication can be deployed between the target system and its database, to make sure whether an input is potentially critical. For instance, GreenSQL 5 can be applied for this purpose. An early research that contrasted GreenSQL to five alike tools has found such technology is the most valid in checking SQL injection attacks. Particulars of using a database proxy as oracle have been talked over before. Normal database accesses deploy and train a database proxy in typical. The results of normal employ of the systems or the execution of present functional test ones. The proxy masters normal patterns of legal SQL statements in view of the training information. Once the proxy has been trained, it will proceed to examine the exchange between the system and its database, furthermore, enhance alarms when discriminating dubious database queries. Each alarm accords with a SQL statement of database, and one test case can bring about multiple SQL statements and consequently multiple alarms. Manual test may be needed to confirm that all SQL statements flagged in fact make clear a vulnerability in the application for avoiding error positives according to imperfect practice.

3.4 Tool

The pivotal components of a Java tool (Test generator and Monitor) have been presented by Fig. 2, and the usage of that is displayed in practice. Test generator

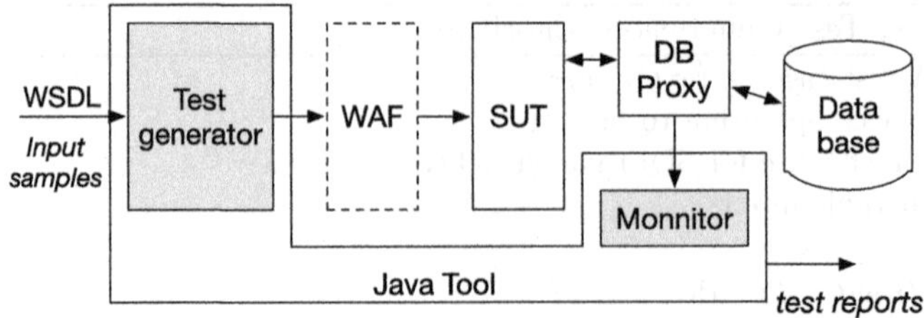

Fig. 2. Components of Java Tool and how it is used in practice.

takes the WSDL file of the web service under test and a sample test for each web service manipulation tested as inputs. There are lots of professional tools and present approaches can create the sample test with ease. The sample test can be examined by the tool to search all input parameters for an manipulation and supersedes each one at a turn, with a SQLi attack created by our mutation approach. Afterwards this approach will send the modified test case to the web service under test. A web application firewall may be arranged in between the test generator and the SUT in some settings. In the figure the proxy component examines the communication between the SUT and its database to check malignant SQL statements. At last, the Monitor component of Java Tool constantly queries the oracle component to realize if created inputs expose a SQLi vulnerability or not.

In Xavier, we use GreenSQL to intercept SQL statements. A learning approach is applied by the database proxy to check SQLi vulnerabilities. So it has to be drilled in a learning phase to distinguish legal SQL statements. In the phase of detection, all intercepted statements are considered by the proxy, which have not been learned early as SQLi attacks.

If each doubtful malignant statement forms syntactically correct SQL, it is further analysed. An attacker can only find a SQLi vulnerability, when he injects the malignant input in the way that the result of SQL statement is free to syntax errors. Or else the attacker can not attain targets, for instance, to gain or modify information and transform the control flow of application, assuming that the malignant statement is not performing. MySQL-Proxy7 is used to keep watch on if a SQL statement has been performing or if there existed a false message in execution.

4 Experiments and Results

We have to comment on the validity of the two methods of open source system, and in two different settings: whether there is a web application firewall. In most cases, including those of our industry partners, the firewall for the attacker is a protective layer of the first layer and is representative by the attacker, this is the main motivation of the latter. Therefore, this is considered to be more realistic. We use the ModSecurity firewall OWASP core which is a collection of rules to deploy in our experiment architecture. We consider a known SQLi attack model, which is a comprehensive list of commonly used penetration testers, as a benchmark for our evaluation in practice.

4.1 Treatments

The baseline method we refer to as a standard attack model for the 137 has been found. This pattern is merged in a repository that holds the SQLi attack mode. This repository includes different types of attacks such as modern, UNION query based on Boolean-based. We test the performance of SqlMap, and come to the conclusion that it is an advanced penetration testing tool, and we find that we can more effectively dig holes by using the Std method. In the specific content of our research, a set of attack mode Std are suitable for each input parameters.

4.2 Variables

We use T as the total number of test cases to generate a SQL statement that is marked by a database agent, by which a set of parameters for a set of test cases for a particular web service is given. In these tests, we further investigate whether the resulting SQL statements are executable. We refer to Te as the total number of SQL statements that can be generated and executed. We compared the Std and MOSA in two ways, as we will see like, we need to consider T and Te, when individual attention will come to the conclusion that to some extent different, the conclusion can only use executable SQL statement. Because there is a corresponding input, you can generate non executable statement, after processing the completion of a target, will produce a syntax error in the SQL statement. Because the database engine will reject them, they are difficult to cause a certain degree of security impact, therefore, there will be no data leakage or compromise occurs.

If there is a higher yield of Te technology, it will be regarded as an effective method for detection of exploitable vulnerabilities. That is to say, the Te value is high, it is more likely to detect available, the size of a test suite bug fixed. In addition, it may also be found faster is the vulnerability, we need a small number of tests to find loopholes in the implementation stage. Large number of service and input parameters is very important in practice.

As a test case can give multiple SQL statements, we need to determine how to calculate the time of Te is a feasible and the combination of the executable statement. Because, in practice, a single tag and executable statements produced by a specific input can lead to serious consequences, as more SQL statements are executable, which have the opportunity to find vulnerabilities is high. In our analysis, the conservative intention by our results shows that a test is considered if and only if all the tags statements of T are executable.

4.3 Results

We ran MOSA, Std in each of the parameters of the two selected topics, SugarCRM HotelRS. There are a total of 108 input parameters for all of their web service. As mentioned earlier, Std requires 137 test execution for each parameter, and the MOSA, because of its non determinism, we should test execution randomly. In order to make the experiment more efficiently, we consider the amount of execution time for each parameter generation and test 1000 times. Then we use the guide way (back, sampling) form 10K test suite and each one has 137 test 1000 sampling from these tests, so that each test suite with Std of Te. In Table 2, we reported the percentage of T and Te Std subjects applying WAF protection and their mean percentage MOSA over 10K test suites. We report only the results of the fragile input parameters of two test techniques and confirmed after the manual inspection.

Table 2. Results of Std and MOSA on the subject applications protected by the WAF

Subject	Parameter	Std		MOSA	
		% T	% T_e	% T (avg)	% T_e (avg)
HotelRS	country	0.73	0.0	36.84	20.69
	arrDate	2.19	0.0	35.91	9.11
	depDate	5.84	0.0	36.59	11.42
	name	6.57	0.0	38.34	11.72
	address	7.30	0.0	39.67	9.64
	email	6.57	0.0	36.33	9.88
SugerCRM	value	2.19	0.0	37.42	20.48
	add_user_id	2.19	0.0	29.35	6.89
	query1	0.73	0.0	8.97	0.20
	query2	3.65	0.0	76.56	31.43
	order_by	7.30	0.0	80.08	31.96
	rel_mod_qry	6.57	0.0	44.82	0.0

4.4 Threats to Validity

The underlying risks to correctness of our consequences get bogged down in the both internal and external classification:

Internal Aspect: Owing to the intrinsic characters of the approach, this part discusses if we can assuredly explain the relevance has been inspect between manipulation and executed SQL statements or not. In the case of MOSA, because of explaining for randomness is nondeterministic, we created and ran almost 1000 tests with each parameter, after that selected specimen of 10K suites for testing of 137 test situations to achieve a statistical contrast with criterion attacks. As well we have deleted any wrong warning by checking the surveys of GreenSQL.

We chose ModSecurity which is applied in lots of production systems as the WAF and meanwhile employed the OWASP Core Rule Set.

External aspect: Following introduction is about the summarization of the results. Even if we barely employ two programs in the experiments, the estimation expense of working this test is partly high, and actual users employ SugarCRM as the amount of downloads result. Though we contrast just two test approaches, those are typical of state within black-box SQL injection test, as the retrospect of relevant operation result.

5 Conclusion

Within the most usual classification of vulnerabilities SQL injections are top-ranked. Attacks of exploiting such type of vulnerabilities rise swiftly with the passage of time. Due to mentioned situation, automatic mining approaches are vital, not only to find vulnerabilities in web applications before being used, but also to reduce testing effort in contexts where the amount of services and their input parameters are large. Especially there exists a requirement of black-box techniques that do not need to access the source code, as this is a usual constraint when third party components are applied or software implementation is outsourced. Living techniques that have investigated this specific problem are bounded to known attack patterns that become antiquated very rapidly, particularly given the quick progress of web application and their underpinning approach. Their performance may be limited by the existence of application prevention mechanisms as well, like WAF, which may block foregone attacks. Our results of test experiments acknowledge above facts by displaying that state-of-practice, standard attacks do not, in most situations, bypass the WAF. Furthermore, the part of not blocking by the firewall will bring about non-executable SQL statements due to syntax errors.

Among this paper we proposed an efficient mutation approach for mining SQL injection vulnerabilities, supported by a tool that concentrates on mutating the input values of web service parameters. The technique applies a union of mutation operators, the functions of which are (1) generating inputs with a high likelihood of distorting the behaviour of applications, (2) amending inputs to eliminate possible syntax errors according to mutations, and (3) obfuscating attacks to increase their likelihood to bypass the WAF. The ultimate aim of our approach is to create randomised inputs to check SQL vulnerabilities in the way of SQL statements through the firewall that are executable and leaking or compromising information in the database. Our experimental results have displayed our approach and tool implemented much better than state-of-practice standard attack patterns, and that the likelihood of finding SQL injection vulnerabilities is high, even there may still exist a firewall, and with a rational amount of test input executions for every parameter in each service.

Acknowledgments. This work was supported by the National Natural Science Foundation of China (Nos. 61672300, 91438117, 91538202), and National Natural Science Foundation of Tianjin (No. 16JCYBJC15500).

References

1. Appelt, D., Alshahwan, N., Briand, L.: Assessing the impact of firewalls and database proxies on SQL injection testing. In: Vos, T.E.J., Lakhotia, K., Bauersfeld, S. (eds.) FITTEST 2013. LNCS, vol. 8432, pp. 32–47. Springer, Cham (2014). doi:10.1007/978-3-319-07785-7_2
2. Beery, T., Niv, N.: Web application attack report (2013)
3. Lee, I., Jeong, S., Yeo, S., Moon, J.: A novel method for SQL injection attack detection based on removing SQL query attribute values. Math. Comput. Model. **55**, 58–68 (2012)
4. Balasundaram, I., Ramaraj, E.: An efficient technique for detection and prevention of SQL injection attack using ASCII based string matching. Procedia Eng. **30**, 183–190 (2012). SciVerse ScienceDirect
5. Kim, M.-Y., Lee, D.H.: Data-mining based SQL injection attack detection using internal query trees. Expert Syst. Appl. **41**, 5416–5430 (2014)
6. Jang, Y.-S., Choi, J.-Y.: Detecting SQL injection attacks using query result size. Comput. Secur. **44**, 104–118 (2014). ScienceDirect
7. SQL Injection Wiki: SQL injection cheat sheet. http://www.sqlinjectionwiki.com/
8. Natarajana, K., Subramanib, S.: Generation of SQL-injection free secure algorithm to detect and prevent SQL-injection attacks. Procedia Technol. **4**, 790–796 (2012). SciVerse ScienceDirect
9. Pinzón, C.I., De Paz, J.F., Herrero, Á., Corchado, E., Bajo, J., Corchado, J.M.: idMAS-SQL: intrusion detection based on MAS to detect and block SQL injection through data mining. Inf. Sci. **231**, 15–31 (2013)
10. Shar, L.K., Tan, H.B.K., Briand, L.C.: Mining SQL injection and cross site scripting vulnerabilities using hybrid program analysis. In: Proceedings of the 2013 International Conference on Software Engineering, pp. 642–651 (2013)
11. Appelt, D., Nguyen, C.D., Briand, L.C., Alshahwan, N.: Automated testing for SQL injection vulnerabilities: an input mutation approach. In: Proceedings of the 2014 International Symposium on Software Testing and Analysis, pp. 259–269 (2014)
12. Xue, P.-C.: SQL injection attack and guard technical research. Procedia Eng. **15**, 4131–4135 (2011). SciVerse ScienceDirect
13. Chung, Y.-C., Wu, M.-C., Chen, Y.-C., Chang, W.-K.: A hot query bank approach to improve detection performance against SQL injection attacks. Comput. Secur. **31**, 233–248 (2012). SciVerse ScienceDirect
14. Williams, J., Wichers, D.: WASP Top. 10 2013rcl: the ten most critical web application security risks. In: The Open Wep Application Security Project (2013)

A Chaotic Map-Based Authentication and Key Agreement Scheme with User Anonymity for Cloud Computing

Fan Wu[1(✉)] and Lili Xu[2]

[1] Department of Computer Science and Engineering, Xiamen Institute of Technology, Xiamen 361021, China
conjurer1981@gmail.com

[2] School of Information Science and Technology, Xiamen University, Xiamen 361005, China

Abstract. Cloud computing is a hot issue mentioned more and more nowadays. Vast information for every domain are stored in cloud servers. Security issue is accompanied with the fast development of cloud application. On the other hand, many authentication schemes with different methods have been presented over the last decades. To guarantee the valid access to remote server, smart cards are used on the client side. Moreover, user anonymity becomes a hot issue in such schemes. We present a chaotic-map based mutual authentication scheme for cloud computing. After our concrete analysis, the new scheme not only makes user anonymous but also performs well in basic aspects compared with recent schemes. The new scheme is practical and efficient via our comparison and it overcomes various attacks and meets security requirements in public opinion. ...

Keywords: User anonymity · Bergamo et al.'s attack · Chaotic maps · Off-line guessing attack

1 Introduction

Cloud computing is a popular notion in the last few years. In such environment, resources for computing and storage are supported by the third party to guarantee cost reduction. Users do not worry about the maintenance of hardware and software but only need to pay for the rent fee or even be free of charge. They can access and share their own data whenever they want with the help of network. But with more and more attacks appearing on the Internet, protecting information in communication channel becomes an important topic. Authentication is an important way to be used [3,4,17,26]. On one hand, in 1991, Chang and Wu gave the first smart-card-authentication scheme [2]. Many protocols with the storage device have been proposed, like [7,22–25]. In other words, the user can be authenticated by the server with messages depending on his password and a smart card released by the remote server. On the other hand, researchers

X. Sun et al. (Eds.): ICCCS 2017, Part II, LNCS 10603, pp. 189–200, 2017.
https://doi.org/10.1007/978-3-319-68542-7_16

employ chaotic maps to build authentication schemes. Chaos is a well-defined robust and random-like phenomenon. Chaotic systems are unpredictable and sensitive to initial system conditions and parameters. So chaos becomes a way in the field of cryptography. Many such schemes have appeared [8,16].

1.1 Relative Work

In 2009, Tseng et al. [21] proposed a new key agreement protocol using chaotic maps. They claimed that their scheme had advantages including mutual authentication and user anonymity. But Niu et al. [19] showed that Tseng et al.'s scheme was under the insider attack and in fact with no user anonymity or perfect forward security. Then they presented a new scheme. However, Xue et al. [27] presented that Niu et al.'s scheme had low efficiency and was under the man-in-middle attack. Later Tan [20] pointed out that Xue et al.'s scheme could not resist the man-in-middle attack and in fact it was without user anonymity.

Recently, smart cards are added into authentication schemes based on chaotic maps [5,6,11,20]. In 2013, Guo et al. [5] presented a key agreement scheme based on chaotic map using smart cards. But Hao et al. [6] presented Guo et al.'s scheme had two weaknesses: no user anonymity and inefficiency of two secret keys. Then they presented a new protocol to overcome the weaknesses. Unfortunately, Yau et al. [28] found that Hao et al.'s scheme was under the off-line password guessing attack, the user impersonation attack, the parallel attack and the de-synchronization attack. We make an explanation here: we change the name DoS attack in [28] into de-synchronization attack since the name DoS attack may make readers confused. In fact they have the same meaning that the attacker can change data transmitted in the public channel to make the user's subsequent legal logins failed. In 2015, Lin [16] pointed out that Guo et al.'s scheme [5] could not resist Bergamo et al.'s attack and it had the disadvantage of user-traceability. Then Lin proposed a new scheme and he claimed that his solution avoided the above mentioned problems. But Lin's scheme can not resist Bergamo et al.'s attack, the off-line password guessing attack, the user impersonation attack and the de-synchronization attack.

Such authentication technology is also applied in cloud computing [9,10,15]. Here we give a secure key agreement and mutual authentication scheme with chaotic maps for cloud computing. With security analysis, all can see that our scheme is robust enough to resist all attacks and owns the usual security requirements.

The rest part of our paper is arranged as follows: Sect. 2 shows some basic knowledge of Chebyshev polynomial in cryptosystem, notations and premises for analyzing the scheme. Our scheme is in Sect. 3. We show the concrete security analysis in Sect. 4 and list the comparison of performance between our scheme and recent schemes also based on chaos in Sect. 5. At last, the conclusion is in Sect. 6.

2 Preliminaries

In this section, first we review some knowledge of Chebyshev chaotic maps in cryptosystem. Then we list the terminology of this paper and some assumptions to analyze the security of schemes.

2.1 Basic Knowledge of Chebyshev Polynomial in Cryptosystem

Definition 1. *Our scheme employs the enhanced Chebyshev polynomial in cryptosystem: according to [12], s is an integer variable and* $s \in (-\infty, +\infty)$. *p is a large prime. The Chebyshev polynomial* $T_n(s)$ *is presented as follows:*

$$T_n(s) = \begin{cases} 1 & n = 0 \\ s \mod p & n = 1 \\ 2sT_{n-1}(s) - T_{n-2}(s) \mod p & n \geq 2 \end{cases}$$

According to [29], the semigroup property holds for the Chebyshev polynomial defined in real number field. i.e., given $s \in (-\infty, +\infty)$ and two random positive integers u and v, the equation $T_u(T_v(s)) = T_v(T_u(s))$ holds. So in the above two cases, this property is the basis of constructing the session key.

Definition 2. *Let* $s \in Z_p^*$, *then* $T_n(s)$ *mod p is defined as the sequence produced by the Chebyshev polynomial. The period of* $(T_n(s) \mod p)$ *is d, for* $n = 0, 1, 2 \ldots$, *if* $T_{n+d}(s) = T_n(s)$.

Definition 3. *From [12] we know: if we call* d_{min} *as the minimal period of* $T_n(s) \mod p$, d_{min} *is a divisor of either* $p - 1$ *or* $p + 1$.

2.2 Notations

Here we list the notations used in the whole paper.

- U_i, ID_i, PW_i: the $i-th$ user with his identity and password
- S, x: the remote server and its secret key
- $h(.)$, $h_1(.)$: one-way hash functions
- $E_k(.)/D_k(.)$: a symmetric encryption/decryption function with key k
- sk_u, sk_s: the session key formed by U_i and S respectively
- $a \oplus b$: the X-OR computation with a and b
- $a||b$: the concatenation of a and b
- $a? = b$: whether a is equal to b
- A: a malicious attacker
- l_s: the security length
- u, v: the degrees of Chebyshev polynomials

2.3 Assumptions for Analysis

Assumptions 1 and 2 are in accord with [12]. And Assumptions 3, 4 and 5 are the attacker's model for informal analysis. Here we care for the adversary's abilities but not for how to make them true.

Assumption 1. The discrete logarithm (DL) problem is: Given a number y, it's hard to find the Discrete Logarithm (DL) n where $T_n(s) = y$.

Assumption 2. The Chebyshev polynomial computational Diffie-Hellman (CPCDH) problem is: Given three elements s, $T_u(s)$ and $T_v(s)$, it's difficult to compute the number $T_{uv}(s)$.

Assumption 3. The quantity of passwords can be used by U_i is finite. In other words, A can guess it in polynomial time.

Assumption 4. S's secret key, the result of hash function and the ciphertext produced by the symmetric cryptosystem are secure. They cannot be cracked by A in polynomial time.

Assumption 5. A can get all information from U_i's smart card [14,18]. Also, A can eavesdrop, intercept and forge all the messages between U_i and S in public communication channel. A can do attacks, e.g., off-line password guessing attack, by the above data.

3 Details of Our Scheme

There are four phases in our scheme: system initialization, registration, authentication and password change.

3.1 System Initialization

We use the Definitions 1, 2 and 3 in Sect. 2.

S generates the secret key x, a random positive integer $s \in Z_p^*$, a symmetric key cryptosystem with $E_k(.)$ and $D_k(.)$ and two one-way hash functions $h(.)$ and $h_1(.)$. Moreover, we define the minimal period of $T_n(s)$ is $p+1$.

3.2 Registration

The process is in Table 1.

1. U_i selects ID_i, PW_i and b_i, computes $HPW_i = h(PW_i||b_i)$ and sends ID_i with HPW_i to S via a secure channel.
2. S selects a random number r_i, computes $IM_i = E_x((ID_i \oplus r_i)||r_i)$ and $B_1 = h(ID_i||HPW_i) \oplus HPW_i \oplus h(x||IM_i)$, and stores IM_i, B_1, $h(.)$, $E_k(.)/D_k(.)$, s and p into a smart card. Then S issues it to U_i via a secure way.
3. When U_i gets the smart card, he computes $B_2 = h(ID_i||PW_i) \oplus b_i$ and stores B_2 into the card. Now U_i's smart card contains IM_i, B_1, B_2, s, p, $h(.)$ and $E_k(.)/D_k(.)$.

3.3 Authentication

1. U_i inserts the smart card into a terminal and enters ID_i and PW_i. The smart card calculates $b_i^{'} = B_2 \oplus h(ID_i||PW_i)$. Then the smart card selects two random integers $u \in [1, p+1]$ and r_u, computes

$$HPW_i = h(PW_i||b_i^{'})$$
$$C_1 = T_u(s)$$
$$C_2 = B_1 \oplus h(ID_i||HPW_i) \oplus HPW_i$$
$$C_3 = h(ID_i||C_1||C_2||r_u)$$
$$C_4 = C_2 \oplus C_3$$
$$C_5 = E_{C_3}(ID_i||C_1||r_u)$$

and sends $M_1 = \{C_4, IM_i, C_5\}$ to S.

2. When S receives M_1, it decrypts IM_i and gets $ID_i^{'}$ and $r_i^{'}$. Then S computes $C_2^{'} = h(x||IM_i)$, $C_3^{'} = C_4 \oplus C_2^{'}$, decrypts C_5 and obtains $ID_i^{''}$, $C_1^{'}$, and $r_u^{'}$. S checks if $ID_i^{'}? = ID_i^{''}$. Then S checks $C_3^{'}? = h(ID_i^{'}||C_1^{'}||C_2^{'}||r_u^{'})$. If all above verifications are correct, S will goes on the next step. Otherwise, S rejects the session.
3. S chooses three random integers $v \in [1, p+1]$, r_s and r_i^{new}, computes

$$IM_i^{'} = E_x((ID_i^{'} \oplus r_i^{new})||r_i^{new})$$
$$C_6 = T_v(s)$$
$$sk_s = T_v(C_1^{'})$$
$$C_7 = h(x||IM_i^{'})$$
$$C_8 = h_1(ID_i^{'}||IM_i^{'}||C_1^{'}||C_2^{'}||C_6||C_7||sk_s||r_s)$$
$$C_9 = C_2^{'} \oplus C_8$$
$$C_{10} = E_{C_8}(IM_i^{'}||C_6||C_7||r_s)$$

and sends $M_2 = \{C_9, C_{10}\}$ to U_i and uses sk_s as its session key.

4. The smart card calculates $C_8^{'} = C_9 \oplus C_2$, decrypts C_{10} and gets $IM_i^{''}$, $C_6^{'}$, $C_7^{'}$ and $r_s^{'}$. Then the card computes $sk_u = T_u(C_6^{'})$ and checks $C_8^{'}? = h_1(ID_i||IM_i^{''}||C_1||C_2||C_6^{'}||C_7^{'}||sk_u||r_s^{'})$. If the equation is incorrect, U_i rejects the session. Otherwise, the card computes $B_1^{'} = C_2 \oplus C_7^{'} \oplus B_1$ and replaces (B_1, IM_i) with $(B_1^{'}, IM_i^{''})$. Finally, U_i uses sk_u as the session key.

Table 1. Registration

U_i		S
select ID_i, PW_i and b_i		
compute $HPW_i = h(PW_i\|\|b_i)$		
	$\xrightarrow{ID_i, HPW_i}$	
		select r_i, compute $IM_i = E_x((ID_i \oplus r_i)\|\|r_i)$
		$B_1 = h(ID_i\|\|HPW_i) \oplus HPW_i \oplus h(x\|\|IM_i)$
		store IM_i, B_1, $h(.)$, $E_k(.)/D_k(.)$, s and p into a smart card
	$\xleftarrow{smartcard}$	
compute $B_2 = h(ID_i\|\|PW_i) \oplus b_i$ and store B_2		

3.4 Password Change

1. The first three steps are the same as step 1 to 3 of Authentication phase.
2. After S's successful checking, S sends $C_{11} = h(a_i||ID_i^{'}||IM_i||C_1^{'}||C_2^{'}||C_4||C_5)$ with a password changing grant. U_i checks $C_{11}? = h(a_i||ID_i||IM_i||C_1||C_2||C_4||C_5)$. If it is incorrect, U_i rejects the session. Otherwise, U_i is requested to input a new password PW_i^{new}. The card then produces a nonce b_i^{new}, and computes the following data: $HPW_i = h(PW_i||b_i^{'})$, $HPW_i^{new} = h(PW_i^{new}||b_i^{new}$, $B_1^{new} = B_1 \oplus h(ID_i||HPW_i) \oplus HPW_i \oplus h(ID_i||HPW_i^{new}) \oplus HPW_i^{new}$ and $B_2^{new} = h(ID_i||PW_i^{new}) \oplus b_i^{new}$. Finally the card substitutes B_1^{new} and B_2^{new} for B_1 and B_2.

4 Analysis of Our Scheme

We give the concrete security analysis of our scheme in this section and compare it with some recent schemes of the same kind in [6,8,11,16].The results are listed in Table 2.

Table 2. Comparison of Security Characters

	Ours	[6]	[11]	[16]	[8]
Resistance to Bergamo et al.'s attack	✓	✓	✓	×	✓
Resistance to the insider attack	✓	✓	✓	✓	✓
Resistance to the off-line password guessing attack	✓	×	✓	×	✓
Resistance to the user impersonation attack	✓	×	✓	×	✓
Resistance to the server spoofing attack	✓	✓	✓	✓	✓
Resistance to the parallel attack	✓	×	✓	✓	✓
Resistance to the replay attack	✓	✓	✓	✓	✓
Resistance to the de-synchronization attck	✓	×	×	×	×
Resistance to the known-key attack	✓	✓	✓	✓	✓
User anonymity & mutual authentication	✓	✓	✓	✓	✓
Password changeability & strong forward security	✓	✓	✓	✓	✓

4.1 Resistance to the Insider Attack

It's obvious that U_i submits HPW_i to S in the registration phase. Here the password is in $h(PW_i||b_i)$. The administrator of the server does not know the random number b_i and cannot directly get PW_i. So our scheme is not vulnerable to this attack.

4.2 Resistance to Bergamo et al.'s Attack

In our scheme, $s \in Z_p^*$, not $[-1, 1]$. So the attacker cannot use inverse cosine function to get a number to threaten the session. It is obvious that Bergamo et al.'s attack can be avoided. Also, we should say that this attack occurs in Lin's scheme [16]. According to premises in Sect. 2.3, a malicious user A may retrieve the data from his own smart card, and get $s||T_r(s) = h(PW_A||b_A) \oplus D_A$ where PW_A is A's password and b_A and D_A are data in A's smart card. Then he obtains $T_{r_u}(s)$ from the communication channel. According to [1], A can compute $r_u^* = \frac{arccos(T_{r_u}(s))+2k\pi}{arccos(s)}|_{k \in Z}$. In fact $T_{r_u^*}(s) = T_{r_u}(s)$. A can go on calculating $C = T_{r_u^*}(T_r(s)) = T_r(T_{r_u^*}(s))$ and decrypt the second message to get $T_{r_s}(s)$. So the session key $sk = T_{r_u^*}(T_{r_s}(s))$ can be calculated by the attacker A.

4.3 Resistance to the Off-line Password Guessing Attack

We suppose A gets all information from U_i's smart card and eavesdrops all messages between U_i and S and we list two cases to analyze this attack:

1. For M_1, $C_2 (= C_4 \oplus C_3)$ has some connection to the password. In order to get C_2 from B_1, A should know ID_i, PW_i and b_i. But we do not make b_i stored in smart card directly and ID_i is protected in $IM_i = E_x((ID_i \oplus r)||r)$ and $C_5 = E_{C_3}(ID_i||C_1||r_u)$. A cannot check whether guessed PW^* is right using the eavesdropped C_4, IM_i and C_5. For M_2, C_{10} is encrypted by C_8. Anyone can get C_8 in only one way: computes $C_9 \oplus C_2$ without guessing x. The above situation appears again.
2. If A uses his own smart card with ID_A and PW_A, he can get $C_{2A} = h(x||IM_A) = B_{1A} \oplus h(ID_A||HPW_A) \oplus HPW_A$. Unfortunately, C_2 for each user is different from others due to different ID and IM. So the information of A himself is useless to crack passwords of others.

Above all, our scheme can resist off-line password guessing attack. But Lin's scheme [16] has weakness for such attack. If A gets D_i and b_i from U_i's smart card in 4.2, we know that A has already got $s||T_r(s)$, and can calculate $HPW_i = D_i \oplus (s||T_r(s))$. Then A retrieves a password PW^* from the dictionary and checks $HPW_i ?= h(PW^*||b_i)$. At last A can find the right password.

4.4 Resistance to the User Impersonation Attack

If the attacker A wants to forge a legal user, he must compute a suitable C_4 and a corresponding number C_5. Suppose A gets all information from U_i's smart card, it is hard to do this. As we explain in Sect. 4.3, A cannot calculate $C_2 = h(x||IM_i)$, not to say $C_3 = h(ID_i||C_1||C_2||r_u)$. So he cannot generate a right message M_1 and this attack could not succeed. But for 4.2, the attacker can calculate C, decrypt $E_C(Q_i||R_i||T_1)$ and get Q_i, R_i and T_1 after Bergamo et al.'s attack. In fact, Q_i and R_i are constant numbers unless U_i changes the password. To forge U_i, A selects a random number r_A and gets the timestamp T_A, computes

$C_A = T_{r_A}(T_r(s))$ and sends $T_{r_A}(s), E_{C_A}(Q_i||R_i||T_A)$ to S. Once A receives the message from S, he decrypts it with C_A and gets $T_{r_s}(s)$. It is easy to see that the session key $sk_A = T_{r_A}(T_{r_s}(s))$ can be calculated by A. So A can finish this attack successfully.

4.5 Resistance to the Server Spoofing Attack

A should calculate a corresponding message (C_9, C_{10}) to pretend to be S. Due to lack of x, it's hard for A to calculate $C_2 = h(x||IM_i)$ and $IM' = E_x((ID_i \oplus r_i^{new})||r_i^{new})$, not to say C_8, which is used to construct C_9. And it is impossible to compute C_{10} without C_8. So A cannot forge the right M_2.

4.6 Resistance to the Parallel Attack and the Replay Attack

Messages from U_i and S have different structures. And the two participants use different data to encrypt information. Each time U_i and S choose fresh numbers u and v to produce the session key $T_u(T_v(s))$, which is verified in C_8. Furthermore, every message has a random number r_u or r_s. So the two attacks can be avoided.

4.7 Resistance to the De-synchronization Attack

In our scheme, after U_i inputs ID_i and PW_i, the two elements should be checked in Authentication and Password change phases. Once either of them happens to be wrong, it can be detected by S and the data in smart card will not be changed by mistake. The next login will not be affected. We also note that schemes in [8,11,16] are under this attack since no checking mechanism is used in password change phase in any of them. So the three schemes cannot resist this attack while ours avoids it.

4.8 Resistance to the Known-Key Attack

We can clearly see that if A knows some session keys, he cannot get others via his knowledge. Each session key $T_u(T_v(s))$ is built on CPCDH problem and different from others. So there is no relation among the different session keys.

4.9 User Anonymity

Every session U_i uses a new IM_i to denote his identity in communication. It only can be decrypted by x. Moreover, C_5 is encrypted by C_3 and in fact $C_3 = C_4 \oplus h(x||IM_i)$. A does not know x, so he could not calculate $h(x||IM_i)$. According to the analysis in Sect. 4.3, A could not obtain $h(x||IM_i)$ via U_i's messages and smart card. We can get the conclusion that the user keeps anonymous.

Moreover, every time U_i uses a new IM_i, so the adversary cannot trace any legal user in authentication.

4.10 Freely Choose Password and Change Password

It's clear to see that the right of selecting and changing password is mastered by the user in registration and password change phases. So our scheme is friendly for the users to select and update their own passwords.

4.11 Mutual Authentication

S can verify U_i's identity by decrypting IM_i and checking C_3, the hash result containing $h(x||IM_i)$ in M_1. On the user side, U_i can check C_8 and C_9 to see if the other side owns x to generate the information.

4.12 Strong Forward Security

If all public and private information owned by both participants is obtained by A, he can get $T_u(s)$ and $T_v(s)$ from the messages. But it is hard to obtain the session key $sk_u = sk_s = T_u(T_v(s))$ which is based on CPCDH problem.

5 Performance Comparison

We list the results of the performance comparison among our scheme and recent schemes of the same sort. First we define the lengths of relative parameters in Table 3. Then we test the time cost of referred cryptographic operations. The results are in Table 4. Some basic conditions are explained below:

1. To solve the Chebyshev polynomial, we use the method in [12], which deals every bit of the exponent n from "left to right". We use 1024 bits as the length of Chebyshev polynomial degree and value, as referred in [12].
2. The symmetric encryption/decryption algorithm we test is AES and the hash function we use is SHA1.

Table 3. Lengths of parameters (bits)

ID_i, $h(,)$, $h_1(.)$ sn (in [8])	Random number	n, s, p	Point in elliptic curves (x, y)
160	160	1024	320

Table 4. Time cost of computations (ms)

CPU: Intel(R) Core(TM)2 T6570 2.1GHz Memory:4G Win7(32-bit) Visual C++ 2008 MIRACL C/C++ Library	
T_c time of one Chebyshev map operation	140.4110
T_s time of one symmetric encryption/decryption operation	0.1303
T_h time of one hash function operation	0.0004

From the table we can see that $T_c \gg T_s \gg T_h$. Moreover, some standards are illustrated to compare the schemes:

- To use Chebyshev polynomial, s and p should be saved in U_i's smart card during the registration phase. Furthermore, the basic point P and the public key should also be stored in the card if U_i needs scalar multiplication in elliptic curve group. Schemes in [5,6] miss p.
- However, to analyze scheme in [16], we use 2048 bits as the length of Chebyshev polynomial degree and value in [13] to calculate smart card storage cost and communication cost. According to [13], the 2048-bit precision of floating point implies the Chebyshev polynomial degree and value smaller than 2^{970}.

According to the above premises, we show the performance comparison in Table 5 and present each aspect of Table 5 below.

- According to the order of the four kinds of time cost, our scheme takes a bit more time on user side than [6,16], but is better than others. On server side, our scheme costs a little more time than [6,8,16]. The reason is our scheme needs the server's secret key x to decrypt IM_i and produce a new $IM_i^{'}$.
- The storage cost in smart card on user side is the second point. Our scheme takes more than schemes in [6,8], but better than others.

Table 5. Performance comparison

	Time cost (ms)	Smart card storage cost (bits)	Communication cost (bits)	Transmission times	Security
Ours	$U{:}2T_c+2T_s+4T_h = 281.0842$ $S{:}2T_c+4T_s+4T_h = 281.3448$	2624	3748	2	✓
[6]	$U{:}2T_c+T_s+3T_h = 280.9535$ $S{:}2T_c+4T_s+2T_h = 281.3432$	2464	3232	2	×
[11]	$U{:}3T_c+T_s+2T_h = 421.3641$ $S{:}3T_c+2T_s+T_h = 421.494$	3616	3072	2	×
[16]	$U{:}2T_c+2T_s+3T_h = 281.0838$ $S{:}2T_c+3T_s+2T_h = 281.2137$	4640	5228	2	×
[8]	$U{:}2T_c+2T_s+7T_h = 281.0854$ $S{:}2T_c+3T_s+4T_h = 281.2145$	2528	6112	3	×

- The communication cost of our scheme is in the middle. It is less than [8,16].
- The transmission times in our scheme is no more than others. In detail, there are two in our scheme. The number is equal to [6,11,16] and less than [8].
- Security is the most important aspect. Only our scheme has the formal proof to support security. Also, schemes in [6,8,11,16] are all insecure as we mentioned before in Sects. 1 and 4 while our scheme is secure via our informal analysis.

According to the above analysis, our scheme is secure and performs well among schemes referred in Table 5.

6 Conclusion

In this paper, we present a novel chaotic-map based authentication scheme for cloud computing. After concrete analysis, our scheme overcomes the common disadvantages and performs well. It is fit for practical applications.

References

1. Bergamo, P., D'Arco, P., De Santis, A., Kocarev, L.: Security of public-key cryptosystems based on chebyshev polynomials. IEEE Trans. Circ. Syst. I: Regul. Pap. **52**(7), 1382–1393 (2005)
2. Chang, C.C., Wu, T.C.: Remote password authentication with smart cards. IEE Proc.-Comput. Digit. Tech. **138**(3), 165–168 (1991)
3. Fu, Z., Ren, K., Shu, J., Sun, X., Huang, F.: Enabling personalized search over encrypted outsourced data with efficiency improvement. IEEE Trans. Parallel Distrib. Syst. **27**(9), 2546–2559 (2016)
4. Fu, Z., Wu, X., Guan, C., Sun, X., Ren, K.: Toward efficient multi-keyword fuzzy search over encrypted outsourced data with accuracy improvement. IEEE Trans. Inf. Forensics Secur. **11**(12), 2706–2716 (2016)
5. Guo, C., Chang, C.C.: Chaotic maps-based password-authenticated key agreement using smart cards. Commun. Nonlinear Sci. Numer. Simul. **18**(6), 1433–1440 (2013)
6. Hao, X., Wang, J., Yang, Q., Yan, X., Li, P.: A chaotic map-based authentication scheme for telecare medicine information systems. J. Med. Syst. **37**(2), 9919 (2013)
7. He, D., Wang, D.: Robust biometrics-based authentication scheme for multiserver environment. IEEE Syst. J. **9**(3), 816–823 (2015)
8. Jabbari, A., Bagherzadeh, J.: A revised key agreement protocol based on chaotic maps. Nonlinear Dyn. **78**(1), 669–680 (2014)
9. Jiang, Q., Khan, M.K., Lu, X., Ma, J., He, D.: A privacy preserving three-factor authentication protocol for e-health clouds. J. Supercomput. **72**(10), 3826–3849 (2016)
10. Jiang, Q., Li, B., Ma, J., Tian, Y., Yang, Y.: Cryptanalysis and improvement of a smart card based mutual authentication scheme in cloud computing. In: Sun, X., Liu, A., Chao, H.-C., Bertino, E. (eds.) ICCCS 2016. LNCS, vol. 10039, pp. 311–321. Springer, Cham (2016). doi:10.1007/978-3-319-48671-0_28
11. Jiang, Q., Ma, J., Lu, X., Tian, Y.: Robust chaotic map-based authentication and key agreement scheme with strong anonymity for telecare medicine information systems. J. Med. Syst. **38**(2), 12 (2014)

12. Kocarev, L., Lian, S.: Chaos-Based Cryptography: Theory, Algorithms and Applications, vol. 354. Springer, Heidelberg (2011). doi:10.1007/978-3-642-20542-2
13. Kocarev, L., Tasev, Z.: Public-key encryption based on Chebyshev maps. In: Proceedings of the 2003 International Symposium on Circuits and Systems, ISCAS 2003, vol. 3, pp. 28–31. IEEE (2003)
14. Kocher, P., Jaffe, J., Jun, B.: Differential power analysis. In: Wiener, M. (ed.) CRYPTO 1999. LNCS, vol. 1666, pp. 388–397. Springer, Heidelberg (1999). doi:10.1007/3-540-48405-1_25
15. Li, X., Liao, J., Liang, W., Zhao, J.: An extended chaotic maps based authenticated key agreement protocol without using password. In: Sun, X., Liu, A., Chao, H.-C., Bertino, E. (eds.) ICCCS 2016. LNCS, vol. 10039, pp. 421–431. Springer, Cham (2016). doi:10.1007/978-3-319-48671-0_37
16. Lin, H.Y.: Improved chaotic maps-based password-authenticated key agreement using smart cards. Commun. Nonlinear Sci. Numer. Simul. **20**(2), 482–488 (2015)
17. Liu, Q., Cai, W., Shen, J., Fu, Z., Liu, X., Linge, N.: A speculative approach to spatial-temporal efficiency with multi-objective optimization in a heterogeneous cloud environment. Secur. Commun. Netw. **9**(17), 4002–4012 (2016)
18. Messerges, T.S., Dabbish, E.A., Sloan, R.H.: Examining smart-card security under the threat of power analysis attacks. IEEE Trans. Comput. **51**(5), 541–552 (2002)
19. Niu, Y., Wang, X.: An anonymous key agreement protocol based on chaotic maps. Commun. Nonlinear Sci. Numer. Simul. **16**(4), 1986–1992 (2011)
20. Tan, Z.: A chaotic maps-based authenticated key agreement protocol with strong anonymity. Nonlinear Dyn. **72**(1–2), 311–320 (2013)
21. Tseng, H.R., Jan, R.H., Yang, W.: A chaotic maps-based key agreement protocol that preserves user anonymity. In: IEEE International Conference on Communications, ICC 2009, pp. 1–6. IEEE (2009)
22. Wang, D., Gu, Q., Cheng, H., Wang, P.: The request for better measurement: a comparative evaluation of two-factor authentication schemes. In: Proceedings of the 11th ACM on Asia Conference on Computer and Communications Security, pp. 475–486. ACM (2016)
23. Wang, D., He, D., Wang, P., Chu, C.H.: Anonymous two-factor authentication in distributed systems: certain goals are beyond attainment. IEEE Trans. Dependable Secur. Comput. **12**(4), 428–442 (2015)
24. Wang, D., Wang, P.: On the usability of two-factor authentication. In: Tian, J., Jing, J., Srivatsa, M. (eds.) SecureComm 2014. LNICSSITE, vol. 152, pp. 141–150. Springer, Cham (2015). doi:10.1007/978-3-319-23829-6_11
25. Wang, D., Wang, P.: Two birds with one stone: two-factor authentication with security beyond conventional bound. IEEE Trans. Dependable Secur. Comput. (2016). doi:10.1109/TDSC.2016.2605087
26. Xia, Z., Wang, X., Zhang, L., Qin, Z., Sun, X., Ren, K.: A privacy-preserving and copy-deterrence content-based image retrieval scheme in cloud computing. IEEE Trans. Inf. Forensics Secur. **11**(11), 2594–2608 (2016)
27. Xue, K., Hong, P.: Security improvement on an anonymous key agreement protocol based on chaotic maps. Commun. Nonlinear Sci. Numer. Simul. **17**(7), 2969–2977 (2012)
28. Yau, W.C., Phan, R.C.W.: Security analysis of a chaotic map-based authentication scheme for telecare medicine information systems. J. Med. Syst. **37**(6), 9993 (2013)
29. Zhang, L.: Cryptanalysis of the public key encryption based on multiple chaotic systems. Chaos, Solitons Fractals **37**(3), 669–674 (2008)

An Anonymous User Authentication and Key Distribution Protocol for Heterogenous Wireless Sensor Network

Xin Zhang and Fengtong Wen(✉)

School of Mathematical Sciences, University of Jinan, Jinan 250022, China
zhangxin_9zy@163.com, wftwq@163.com

Abstract. With the development of the Internet of Things (IOT), peoples' lifestyle and social inter-communication have been changed greatly. As a part of the IOT, wireless sensor network (WSN) also attracts many researchers to pay close attention. In this paper, we investigate one latest scheme (Farash et al.'s scheme) that provides an efficient user authentication and key agreement scheme for heterogeneous wireless sensor network tailored for the Internet of Things environment. However, we find some shortcomings and weaknesses in this scheme. It cannot supply anonymity for users and sensors and cannot protect stolen smart card attack. So our work is to eliminate the threat of cryptographic attack and to improve security.

Keywords: Wireless sensor networks · Anonymity · Authentication · Security · BAN-logic

1 Introduction

With the development of information technologies, there are more and more Wireless Sensor Networks (WSN) be used in our real life, such as vehicular ad hoc network, smart home environment and health care system [1]. In the WSN environment, because of sensor nodes' low processing ability, the main data processes are afforded by gateway node (GWN) [2,3]. Due to limited resource of sensor, we know that traditional session key establishment schemes need too much energy consumption to fit the WSN [2,3]. Therefore, lightweight and security schemes are urgently needed.

In 2006, the first lightweight scheme was proposed by Wong et al., in which only hash function and XOR computation are used [4]. It is a mutual authentication scheme, but is proved to be vulnerable to replay attack and impersonation attack. In 2009, Das [5] proposed an improved scheme used GWN, in which the GWN has bigger data processing ability than sensor nodes. Their scheme is still lightweight, but does not provide key agreement. After that, other scholars study Das et al.'s scheme [6,7].

All above are based on symmetric scheme. Recently, there have been many other schemes [9–12,16–19] for WSN. Taking the Yeh et al.'s scheme [8] as an

X. Sun et al. (Eds.): ICCCS 2017, Part II, LNCS 10603, pp. 201–215, 2017.
https://doi.org/10.1007/978-3-319-68542-7_17

example, it is the first ECC-based scheme. But its large consumption of memory is not desirable. However, this is the most asymmetric-based schemes' common weakness.

In 2015, Farash et al. [13] proposed an efficient user authentication and key agreement scheme for HWSN to eliminate the shortcomings of Turkanović et al.'s scheme [14]. The authors also illustrated that their scheme could free from potential network attacks, including user impersonation attack, password guessing attack. Their scheme seems to be efficient and feasible for practical applications. Unfortunately, we find that their scheme is insecure, for it can not resist password guessing attack or be anonymous. Therefore we strengthen the weak links of their scheme.

The remainder of this paper is organized as follow. Section 2 presents a brief review and cryptanalysis of Farash et al.'s scheme. Then, we proceed with analyzing its weaknesses in Sect. 3. Subsequently, we present a new anonymous scheme in Sect. 4. And we prove that our scheme is more efficient and security in Sect. 5. Section 6 concludes the paper.

2 Overview of Farash et al.'s Scheme

In this section, we review Farash et al.'s scheme (2015). Their scheme is made up of five phases: pre-deployment phase, registration phase, which consists of two parts-users' and sensors', login and authentication phase and password change phase. The notations mentioned in Farash et al.'s scheme are showed in Table 1.

Table 1. Notations

Notation	Meaning
GWN	Gateway node
U_i	The ith user
S_j	The jth sensor node
ID_i	The identity of U_i
PW_i	The password of U_i
SID_j	The identity of S_j
r_i, r_j	Secret random nonces of user and sensor node
T_x	Timestamp
ΔT	Time interval for the allowed transmission delay
$X =?Y$	Comparing valued X with Y
SK	The session key shared among user and sensor node
$h(\cdot)$	An hash function
$\|$	String concatenation operation
$\oplus$	Exclusive-OR operation

2.1 Pre-deployment Phase

According to the attributes of Farash et al.'s define of WSN, the pre-deployment phase is essential. This phase is done by an administrator off line, who shared a key X_{GWN-S_j} $1 < i < m$ between every sensor node and the gateway node. The m means the number of the sensor nodes.

2.2 Registration Phase

Sensor Node Registration Phase. Every sensor node shares a pair of X_{GWN-S_j}-SID_j with GWN. Their communication is through insecure channel.

Step 1. Firstly S_j chooses a random r_j and masks SID_j by computing $MP_j = h(X_{GWN-S_j}\|r_j\|SID_j\|T_1)$ and $MN_j = r_j \oplus X_{GWN-S_j}$. Then it sends the massage $\{SID_j, MP_j, MN_j, T_1\}$ to GWN.

Step 2. Once received the massage, GWN would check if T_1 is in the permitted time. If T_1 meets the request, GWN finds the corresponding X_{GWN-S_j} according to SID_j. Nextly, GWN computes its own version of $r_j' = MN_j \oplus X_{GWN-S_j}$ and $MP_j' = h(X_{GWN-S_j}\|r_j'\|SID_j\|T_1)$ and compares MP_j' with the received MP_j. If the verification is correct, GWN computes $x_j = h(SID_j\|X_{GWN})$, $e_j = x_j \oplus X_{GWN-S_j}$, $d_j = h(X_{GWN}\|1) \oplus h(X_{GWN-S_j}\|T_2)$ and $f_j = h(x_j\|d_j\|X_{GWN-S_j}\|T_2)$.

Step 3. GWN sends the message $\{e_j, f_j, d_j, T_2\}$ to sensor node.

Step 4. Sensor also needs to check $|T_2 - T_c| < \Delta T$ and f_j. Then, the sensor node computes its secret values $x_j = e_j \oplus X_{GWN-S_j}$ and $h(X_{GWN}\|1) = d_j \oplus h(X_{GWN-S_j}\|T_2)$, then stores them into its memory. At the same time, it needs to delete the X_{GWN-S_j} and to give the announcement to GWN.

Step 5. Finally GWN deletes the pair of X_{GWN-S_j}-SID_j from its memory.

User Registration Phase

Step 1. User have to choose their ID (ID_i) and password (PW_i). Then it masks the PW_i by computing $MP_i = h(r_i\|PW_i)$ with a pre-select random r_i. After that, U_i sends the message $\{MP_i, ID_i\}$ to GWN through secure channel.

Step 2. After receiving the message, GWN computes $e_i = h(MP_i\|ID_i)$, $d_i = h(ID_i\|X_{GWN})$, $g_i = h(X_{GWN}) \oplus h(MP_i\|d_i)$ and $f_i = d_i \oplus h(MP_i\|e_i)$. Nextly, GWN stores the e_i, f_i, g_i into user's smart card(SC)and sends the SC to user. Finally, U_i inserts the r_i into the SC.

2.3 Login and Authentication Phase

The login and authentication can be roughly divided into five steps as follow.

Step 1. U_i attaches his/her smart card into a terminal and keys ID_i', PW_i'. Then the smart card computes $MP_i' = h(r_i\|PW_i')$, $e_i' = h(MP_i'\|ID_i')$ and verifies if the e_i' is same as the e_i stored in it. If the verification holds, SC continues to compute $d_i = f_i \oplus h(MP_i'\|e_i)$ and $h(X_{GWN}) = g_i \oplus h(MP_i'\|d_i)$. Then the SC sends the message T_i, $M_1 = ID_i' \oplus h(h(X_{GWN})\|T_1)$, $M_2 = K_i \oplus h(d_i\|T_1)$, $M_3 = h(M_1\|M_2\|K_i\|T_1)$ to sensor node where the K_i is a random nonce chose by SC.

Step 2. Upon receiving message, S_j verifies the freshness of T_1. If it is invalid, S_j terminates the session. Otherwise, S_j masks SID_j by computing $ESID_j = SID_j \oplus h(h(X_{GWN}\|1)\|T_2)$. Then S_j sends the message M_1, M_2, M_3, T_1 (from U_i) added with $ESID_j$, T_2, $M_4 = h(x_j\|T_1\|T_2) \oplus K_j$, $M_5 = h(SID_j\|M_4\| T_1\|T_2\|K_j)$ to GWN where the K_j is a random nonce chose by S_j.

Step 3. After receiving message, GWN verifies the freshness of T_2. If the T_2 is valid, GWN computes $SID_j' = ESID_j \oplus h(h(X_{GWN}\|1)\|T_2)$ and $ID_i' = M_1 \oplus h(h(X_{GWN})\|T_1)$. GWN further computes $x_j' = h(SID_j'\|X_{GWN})$, $d_i' = h(ID_i'\|X_{GWN})$. Subsequently GWN obtains K_j' and K_i' by computing $K_j = h(x_j\|T_1\|T_2) \oplus M_4$ and $K_i = M_2 \oplus h(d_i\|T_1)$. GWN authenticates S_j and U_i by testing whether the equations $M_5 = h(SID_j'\|M_4\|T_1\|T_2\|K_j')$ and $M_3 = h(M_1\|M_2\|K_i'\|T_1)$ are established or not, respectively. If they are valid, GWN masks K_j' for U_i by computing $M_6 = K_j' \oplus h(d_i'\|T_3)$, as well as masks K_i' for S_j by computing $M_7 = K_i' \oplus h(x_j'\|T_3)$. Finally GWN computes $M_8 = h(M_6\|d_i'\|T3)$ and $M_9 = h(M_7\|x_j'\|T3)$ to maintain the integrity of information. GWN sends the message $\{M_6, M_7, M_8, M_9, T_3\}$ to the S_j.

Step 4. After receiving the response message from GWN, S_j verifies the validity of the timestamp T_3. If T_3 is invalid, S_j terminates the communication. Otherwise, it computes $h(M_7\|x_j\|T3)$ and checks whether it equals to the received M_9 or not. If true, GWN is authentic. S_j gets the $K_i' = M_7 \oplus h(x_j\|T_3)$ and $SK = h(K_i' \oplus K_j)$. Otherwise, the procedure is terminated. Lastly, S_j computes $M_{10} = h(SK\|M_6\|M_8\|T_3\|T_4)$, then sends the message $\{M_6, M_8, M_{10}, T_3, T_4\}$ to U_i.

Step 5. Upon receiving message, U_i verifies the validity M_8 and T_4 and attains K_j' just like S_j. Then U_i computes $SK = h(K_i \oplus K_j')$. Finally U_i checks whether $h(SK\|M_6\|M_8\|T_3\|T_4)$ equals to the received M_{10} to decided whether he/she believes the session key.

After finishing mutual authentication, U_i and S_j share a common session key $SK = h(K_i \oplus K_j')$.

3 Cryptanalysis of Farash et al.'s Scheme

3.1 No User Anonymity Attack

A legitimate user U_i stores r_i, f_i, g_i, and e_i in her/his SC. Then U_i can computes her/his own $MP_i = h(r_i\|PW_i)$, $d_i = f_i \oplus h(MP_i\|e_i)$. Finally U_i can obtain $h(X_{GWN}) = g_i \oplus h(MP_i\|d_i)$ where the $h(X_{GWN})$ is a common value for every user to compute $M_1 = ID_i \oplus h(h(X_{GWN})\|T_1)$. Therefore, a legitimate user can find every user's ID by computing $ID_i' = M_1' \oplus h(h(X_{GWN})\|T_1)$, in which the M_1' and T_1 are sent via insecure channel.

3.2 No Sensor Node Anonymity Attack

Every legitimate sensor node stores $h(X_{GWN}\|1)$, then a sensor node can compute every sensor node's real ID by computing $SID_j = ESID'_j \oplus h(h(X_{GWN}\|1)\|T_2)$ where the $ESID'_j$ and T_2 are sent through insecure channel.

3.3 Stolen Smart Card Attack

As we know the smart card is a tamper resistant hardware. It can be stolen. When a legitimate user stole other's SC. He/She can get a lot of information.

Guess PW_i. There are two ways to guess PW_i. On the one hand, he/she can obtain other's ID_i, then guess PW_i in the equation $e'_i = h(MP'_i\|ID'_i) = h(h(r'_i\|PW_i)\|ID'_i)$ where r_i and e_i are stored in the SC. On the other hand, he/she can obtain other's PW_i by computing $M_1 \oplus M'_1 = h(h(X_{GWN})\|T_1) \oplus h(h(X_{GWN})\|T_1)' = h(g_i \oplus h(h(r_i\|PW_i)\|f_i \oplus h(h(r_i\|PW_i)\|e_i))\|T_1) \oplus h(h(r_i\| PW_i)\|f_i \oplus h(h(r_i\|PW_i)\|e_i))\|T'_1)$ where the r_i, e_i, f_i are stored in the SC. M_1 and T_1 are sent via insecure channel in one time. M'_1 and T'_1 are supported to be in another time.

A malevolent legitimate user can obtain other's ID through the same method showed in Sect. 3.1, then guess PW'_i by the way that is mentioned previously in Sect. 3.3. Futhermore, he/she can compute the vital secret value d'_i by computing $d'_i = f'_i \oplus h(MP'_i\|e'_i)$ and $MP'_i = h(r'_i\|PW'_i)$. In the former two equations, r'_i, e'_i, f'_i are stored in the SC and PW'_i can be guessed. As a result, all information of the other user (U'_i), if the malevolent legitimate user had stolen the other user's smart card. He/She can further get K_i, K'_j by computing $K_i = M_2 \oplus h(d'_i\|T_1)$ and $K'_j = M_6 \oplus h(d'_i\|T_3)$. Then it is easy to gain $SK = h(K_i \oplus K'_j)$. When a malevolent legitimate user obtained all values of other users, he/she could launch impersonation attack, man-in-the-middle attack and so on.

4 Our Proposed Scheme

In this section, we propose an improved anonymous user authentication and key distribution protocol for HWSN. Our protocol ensures conditional privacy-preserving of user and sensor node, which means that only GWN could obtain the real ID of them. It is a very important feature for a security HWSN. The protocol has high feasible efficiency based on the simple calculation such as XOR and hash. In addition, GWN does not need the storage space for $h(X_{GWN-S_j})$ for every sensor node.

Our protocol aims to overcome the shortcomings in Farash et al.'s scheme and alters the key agreement to a simple key distribution. There are four parts in our protocol: initial phase, registration phase, login and authentication phase and password-change phase. And the abbreviations in our protocol are the same as Table 1. In this protocol, addition of new node also needs to register.

4.1 Initialization Phase

Initially, GWN dispatches every sensor node a token T off line, which allows sensors to take part in this HWSN.

4.2 Registration Phase

This phase is divided into two sub-phases: sensor node registration phase and user registration phase. They are all through secure channel.

Sensor Node Registration Phase

Step 1. Firstly S_j chooses a random m_j and sends the massage $\{SID_j, m_j, T\}$ to GWN via a secure channel.

Step 2. Once received the massage, GWN would check if the T is valid. If T meets the request, GWN computes $x_j = h(X_{GWN}\|SID_j)$ and $y_j = h(X_{GWN}\|m_j)$ and sends x_j and y_j to S_j.

Step 3. Finally S_j stores m_j, x_j and y_j in its memory. The registration of sensor node is finished.

User Registration Phase

Step 1. Firstly U_i chooses two random values r_i and m_i and masks ID_i and PW_i by computing $MP_i = h(ID_i\|r_i)$ and $MQ_i = h(PW_i\|r_i)$. Then U_i sends ID_i and m_i to GWN through secure channel.

Step 2. After receiving the message, GWN computes $d_i = h(X_{GWN}\|ID_i)$ and $bi = h(X_{GWN}\|m_i)$ and stores them in SC of U_i, then sends the SC to U_i.

Step 3. Upon receiving the SC, U_i computes $e_i = MP_i \oplus MQ_i$, $g_i = d_i \oplus h(MP_i)$ and $f_i = b_i \oplus h(MQ_i)$ and stores the message $\{e_i, f_i, g_i, r_i, m_i\}$ instead of the previous message in the SC. The registration of user is finished.

4.3 Login and Authentication Phase

As shown in Fig. 1, there are six steps in login and authentication phase.

Step 1. U_i inserts his/her smart card into a terminal and keys ID_i', PW_i'. Then the smart card computes $MP_i' = h(ID_i'\|r_i)$, $MQ_i' = h(PW_i'\|r_i)$ and $e_i' = MP_i' \oplus MQ_i'$ and verifies if the e_i' is the same as e_i stored in it. If the verification holds, SC continues to compute $d_i = g_i \oplus h(MP_i')$ and $b_i = f_i \oplus h(MQ_i')$ with the stored values, then sends the message $\{T1, m_i, M_1 = h(b_i\|T_1) \oplus ID_i', M_2 = h(M_1\|m_i\|d_i\|T_1)\}$ where the m_i is stored in the SC to S_j.

Step 2. Upon receiving message, S_j verifies the freshness of T_1. If it is invalid, S_j terminates the session. Otherwise, S_j masks SID_j by computing $ESID_j = SID_j \oplus h(y_j\|T_2)$, as well as computes $z_j = h(x_j\|SID_j)$. Then S_j sends a message M_1, M_2, m_i, T_1 (from U_i) added with $ESID_j$, T_2, $M_3 = h(T_1\|T_2\|m_j\|z_j)$ where the m_j is stored by S_j to GWN.

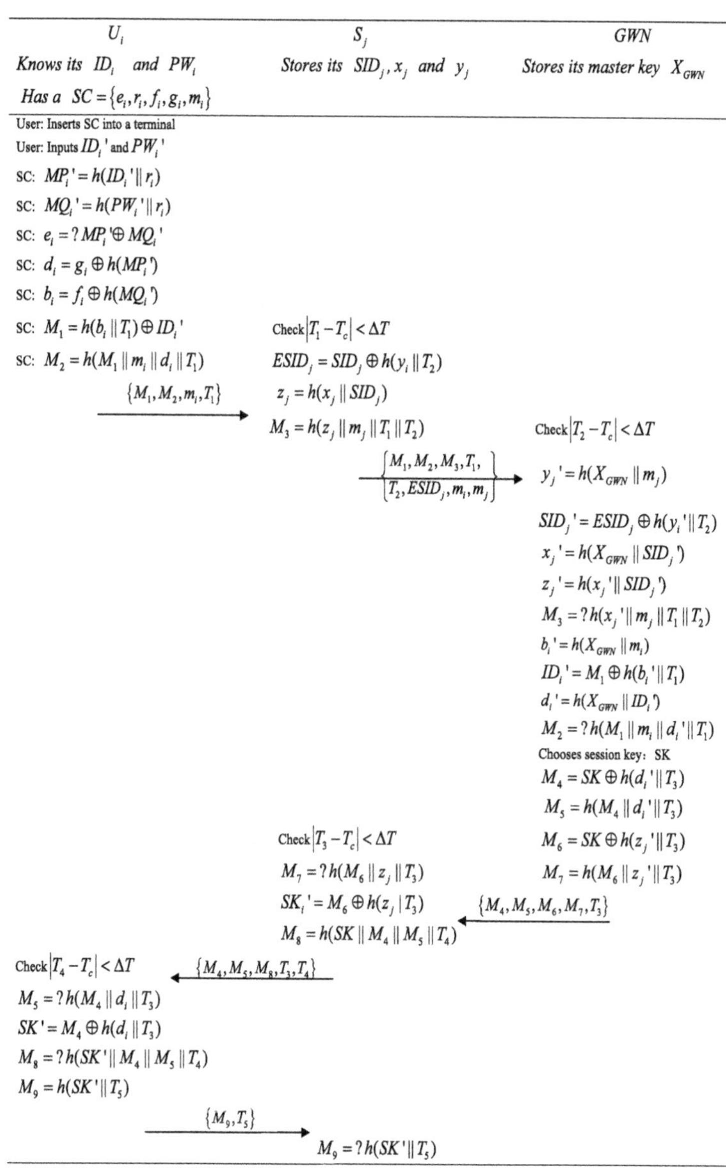

Fig. 1. Login and authentication phase

Step 3. After receiving message, GWN verifies the freshness of T_2. If the T_2 is valid, GWN computes $y_j' = h(X_{GWN}\|m_j)$, $SID_j' = ESID_j \oplus h(y_j'\|T_2)$ and $b_i' = h(X_{GWN}\|m_i)$, $ID_i' = M_1 \oplus h(b_i\|T_1)$. Then GWN further computes $x_j' = h(X_{GWN}\|SID_j')$, $d_i' = h(X_{GWN}\|ID_i')$. GWN obtains $z_j' = h(x_j\|SID_j)$. At the same time, GWN authenticates S_j and U_i by testing whether the equations $M_3 = h(T_1\|T_2\|m_j\|z_j')$ and $M_2 = h(M_1\|m_i\|d_i'\|T_1)$ are established or not, respectively. If the equations are established, GWN chooses a session key(SK) for S_j and U_i, then GWN masks SK for U_i by computing $M_4 = SK \oplus h(d'_i \| T_3)$, as well as masks SK for S_j by computing $M_6 = SK \oplus h(z'_j \| T_3)$. Finally GWN computes $M_5 = h(M_4 \| d'_i \| T3)$ and $M_7 = h(M_6 \| z'_j \| T3)$ to preserve the integrity of information. GWN sends the message $\{M_4, M_5, M_6, M_7, T_3\}$ to S_j.

Step 4. After receiving the response message from GWN, S_j verifies the validity of the timestamp T_3. If T_3 is invalid, S_j terminates the communication; otherwise, it computes $h(M_6 \| z_j \| T3)$ and checks whether it equals to the received M_7 or not. If it is valid, GWN is authentic. Furthermore S_j gets $SK' = M_6 \oplus h(z_j \| T_3)$. Otherwise, the procedure is terminated. Lastly, S_j computes $M_8 = h(SK' \| M_4 \| M_5 \| T_4)$, then sends a message $\{M_4, M_5, M_8, T_3, T_4\}$ to U_i.

Step 5. Upon receiving message, U_i verifies the validity T_4. If it is permitted, U_i checks if $M_5 = h(M_4 \| d_i \| T3)$ is held. If it is, GWN is authentic and U_i obtains $SK' = h(d_i \| T_3) \oplus M_4$. Subsequently, U_i checks whether $h(SK' \| M_4 \| M_5 \| T_4)$ equals to the received M_8 to decided whether accept the session key. Finally, U_i computes $M_9 = h(SK \| T_5)$ and sends it with T_5 to S_j.

Step 6. Once received the message from U_i, S_j would check T_5. After that S_j computes $M'_9 = h(SK \| T_5)$ and checks whether it is equal to the M_9. If it is equal, S_j will believe that there is a session key between S_j and U_i. The login and authentication phase are finished.

4.4 Password Change Phase

When a user U_i wants to update his/her password off-line and does not want to modify other data in sensor node and GWN, he/she can make a request to smart card and enter his/her identity ID_i, old password PW_i and new password PW_i^{new} to smart card. The steps are showed in Fig. 2.

U_i

Knows its ID_i *and* PW_i

Has a $SC = \{e_i, r_i, f_i, g_i, m_i\}$

User: Inserts SC into a terminal

User: Inputs ID_i and PW_i

SC: $MP_i = h(ID_i \| r_i)$

SC: $MQ_i = h(PW_i \| r_i)$

SC: $e_i = ?\ MP_i \oplus MQ_i$

SC: $b_i = f_i \oplus h(MQ_i)$

User: Chooses and inputs new password PW_i'

SC: $MQ_i' = h(PW_i' \| r_i)$

SC: $e_i' = MP_i \oplus MQ_i'$

SC: $f_i' = b_i \oplus h(MQ_i')$

SC: Changes e_i' with e_i

SC: Changes f_i' with f_i

Fig. 2. Password-change phase

Step 1. U_i needs to login SC by keying ID_i, PW_i. To finish the login phase, SC needs to compute $MP_i = h(ID_i \| r_i)$, $MQ_i = h(PW_i \| r_i)$ and $e_i = MP_i \oplus MQ_i$ and to verify if the e_i' is the same as e_i stored in it.

Step 2. If the login is successful, SC computes $b_i = f_i \oplus h(MQ_i)$. Then, U_i needs to input a new password PW_i^{new}. SC computes new $MQ_i' = h(PW_i^{new} \| r_i)$, $e_i' = MP_i \oplus MQ_i'$ and $f_i' = b_i \oplus h(MQ_i')$. Finally SC uses the new e_i' and f_i' to take the place of e_i and f_i in its memory.

5 Security Analysis of Our Scheme

In this section, we will give the security analysis in detail. In Sect. 3, we have proved that Farash et al.'s scheme is vulnerable to the stolen of SC attack and is not anonymous. But, our protocol provides attributes to resist attacks mentioned before. The comparation of security features between Farash et al.'s scheme and our scheme is showed in Table 2.

Table 2. Compare between the two scheme

Security feature	Farash et al.'s scheme	Proposed scheme
Mutual authentication	Yes	Yes
Password protection	No	Yes
Offline password change	Yes	Yes
Dynamic node addition	Yes	Yes
User anonymity	No	Yes
Sensor node anonymity	No	Yes
Resilience against replay attack	Yes	Yes
Privileged-insider attack	No	Yes
Man-in-the-middle attack	Yes	Yes
Smart card attack	No	Yes
User impersonation attack	Yes	Yes

5.1 Mutual Authentication Between All Parties

GWN obtain ID_i' by computing $ID_i' = M_1 \oplus h(b_i \| T_1)$, then obtain $d_i' = h(X_{GWN} \| ID_i)$, which is the same as the user's secret value d_i. At the same time, GWN compares the M_2 and $h(M_1 \| T_1 \| m_i \| d_i')$ to authenticate U_i. User can also authenticate GWN by computing the M_5, which has the secret d_i only known by GWN and the user. The authentication between S_j and GWN is similar to the authentication between U_i and GWN. The vital difference is the secret value is x_j or z_j. U_i authenticates S_j indirectly by comparing the M_8 and the $h(SK \| M_4 \| M_5 \| T_4)$. S_j authenticates U_i indirectly by comparing the M_9 and the $h(SK \| T_5)$.

5.2 Authentication Proof Based on BAN-Logic

Our scheme is proved to be security by using the Burrows-Abadi-Needham Logic(BAN-logic) [15]. We will illustrate that the key establishment between the user U_i and the sensor node S_j is successful. Here are the three items of BAN-logic. X and Y are symbols for statements. P and Q are symbols for principals, K is a symbol for cryptographic encryption key.

The notations and postulates of BAN-logic are showed as follow:

$P| \equiv X$: P believes X.
$P \triangleleft X$: P sees/receive X.
$P| \sim X$: P once said X.
$P| \Rightarrow X$: P controls X.
$\sharp X$: X is fresh.
$P \overset{K}{\longleftrightarrow} Q$: P and Q communicate using shared key K.
(X): The hashed value of X.
$(X, Y)_K$: The hashed value of X and Y using K as key.
$\langle X, Y \rangle_Y$: X and Y are combined using K as key.
SK: The session key used in the current authentication session.
R1: $\frac{P|\equiv P \overset{K}{\longleftrightarrow} Q, P \triangleleft \{X\}_K}{P|\equiv Q|\sim X}$
R2: $\frac{P|\equiv \sharp X, P|\equiv Q|\sim X}{P|\equiv Q|\equiv X}$
R3: $\frac{P|\equiv Q|\Rightarrow X, P|\equiv Q|\equiv X}{P|\equiv X}$
R4: $\frac{P|\equiv \sharp X}{P|\equiv \sharp(X,Y)}$
R5: $\frac{P|\equiv Q|\equiv (X,Y)}{P|\equiv Q|\equiv X}$

The proposed scheme's goal:

$U_i| \equiv (U_i \overset{SK}{\longleftrightarrow} S_j)$
$U_i| \equiv S_j| \equiv (U_i \overset{SK}{\longleftrightarrow} S_j)$
$S_j| \equiv (U_i \overset{SK}{\longleftrightarrow} S_j)$
$S_j| \equiv U_i| \equiv (U_i \overset{SK}{\longleftrightarrow} S_j)$

Here are the idealized messages exchange and some assumptions for our protocol:

M1: $U_i \overset{S_j}{\longleftrightarrow} GWN : \langle ID_i, T_1, (U_i \overset{ID_i}{\longleftrightarrow} GWN)\rangle_{b_i}$
M2: $S_j \longrightarrow GWN : \langle SID_j, T_2, (S_j \overset{SID_j}{\longleftrightarrow} GWN)\rangle_{y_j}$
M3: $GWN \longrightarrow S_j : (SK, M_6, T_3, (S_j \overset{SID_j}{\longleftrightarrow} GWN), (S_j \overset{SK}{\longleftrightarrow} GWN))_{z'_j = z_j}$
M4: $U_i \overset{GWN}{\longleftrightarrow} S_j : \langle SK, T_3, (S_j \overset{SID_j}{\longleftrightarrow} GWN), (S_j \overset{SK}{\longleftrightarrow} GWN), (U_i \overset{SK}{\longleftrightarrow} S_j)\rangle_{z'_j = z_j}$
M5: $GWN \overset{S_j}{\longleftrightarrow} U_i : \langle SK, T_3, M_4, (U_i \overset{ID_i}{\longleftrightarrow} GWN), (U_i \overset{SK}{\longleftrightarrow} GWN)\rangle_{d'_j = d_j}$
M6: $S_j \longrightarrow U_i : (M_4, M_5, T_3, T_4, (U_i \overset{ID_i}{\longleftrightarrow} GWN), (U_i \overset{d_i}{\longleftrightarrow} GWN), (U_i \overset{SK}{\longleftrightarrow} GWN), (U_i \overset{SK}{\longleftrightarrow} S_j))_{SK}$

M7: $U_i \longrightarrow S_j : (T_5)_{SK}$
A1: $GWN| \equiv \sharp(T_1)$
A2: $GWN| \equiv \sharp(T_2)$
A3: $S_j| \equiv \sharp(T_3)$
A4: $U_i| \equiv \sharp(T_4)$
A5: $U_i| \equiv GWN \Rightarrow (U_i \stackrel{SK}{\longleftrightarrow} S_j)$
A6: $S_j| \equiv GWN \Rightarrow (U_i \stackrel{SK}{\longleftrightarrow} S_j)$
A7: $U_i| \equiv (U_i \stackrel{b_i,d_i}{\longleftrightarrow} GWN)$
A8: $S_j| \equiv (S_j \stackrel{z_j,y_j}{\longleftrightarrow} GWN)$
A9: $GWN| \equiv (U_i \stackrel{b_i,d_i}{\longleftrightarrow} GWN)$
A10: $GWN| \equiv (S_j \stackrel{z_j,y_j}{\longleftrightarrow} GWN)$
A11: $U_i| \equiv \sharp(T_3)$ Now we will give proof.

In the M1:

Step 1: We have
$GWN \triangleleft \langle ID_i, T_1, (U_i \stackrel{ID_i}{\longleftrightarrow} GWN)\rangle_{b_i}$
Step 2: Refer to Step 1, A9, M1, we get
$GWN| \equiv U_i| \sim \langle ID_i, T_1, (U_i \stackrel{ID_i}{\longleftrightarrow} GWN)\rangle$
Step 3: Refer to A1, M4, we obtain
$GWN| \equiv \sharp\langle ID_i, T_1, (U_i \stackrel{ID_i}{\longleftrightarrow} GWN)\rangle$
Step 4: Refer to Step 2, Step 3, M2, we infer
$GWN| \equiv U_i| \equiv \langle ID_i, T_1, (U_i \stackrel{ID_i}{\longleftrightarrow} GWN)\rangle$
Step 5: Refer to Step 4, M5, we deduce
$GWN| \equiv U_i| \equiv (U_i \stackrel{ID_i}{\longleftrightarrow} GWN)$
Step 6: Refer to Step 5, A9, we gain
$GWN| \equiv (U_i \stackrel{ID_i}{\longleftrightarrow} GWN)$

In the M2:

Step 1: We have
$GWN \triangleleft \langle SID_j, T_2, (S_j \stackrel{SID_j}{\longleftrightarrow} GWN)\rangle_{y_j}$
Step 2: Refer to Step 1, A10, M1, we get
$GWN| \equiv S_j| \sim \langle SID_j, T_2, (S_j \stackrel{SID_j}{\longleftrightarrow} GWN)\rangle$
Step 3: Refer to A2, M4, we obtain
$GWN| \equiv \sharp\langle SID_j, T_2, (S_j \stackrel{SID_j}{\longleftrightarrow} GWN)\rangle$
Step 4: Refer to Step 2, Step 3, M2, we infer
$GWN| \equiv S_j| \equiv \langle SID_j, T_2, (S_j \stackrel{SID_j}{\longleftrightarrow} GWN)\rangle$
Step 5: Refer to Step 4, M5, we deduce
$GWN| \equiv S_j| \equiv (S_j \stackrel{SID_j}{\longleftrightarrow} GWN)$
Step 6: Refer to Step 5, A10, we gain
$GWN| \equiv ((S_j \stackrel{SID_j}{\longleftrightarrow} GWN)$

In the M3:

Step 1: We have
$S_j \triangleleft (SK, M_6, T_3, (S_j \stackrel{SID_j}{\longleftrightarrow} GWN), (S_j \stackrel{SK}{\longleftrightarrow} GWN))_{z_j'=z_j}$
Step 2: Refer to Step 1, A8, M1, we get
$S_j| \equiv GWN| \sim (SK, M_6, T_3, (S_j \stackrel{SID_j}{\longleftrightarrow} GWN), (S_j \stackrel{SK}{\longleftrightarrow} GWN))_{z_j'=z_j}$
Step 3: Refer to A3, M4, we obtain
$S_j| \equiv \sharp(SK, M_6, T_3, (S_j \stackrel{SID_j}{\longleftrightarrow} GWN), (S_j \stackrel{SK}{\longleftrightarrow} GWN))$
Step 4: Refer to Step 2, Step 3, M2, we infer
$S_j| \equiv GWN| \equiv (SK, M_6, T_3, (S_j \stackrel{SID_j}{\longleftrightarrow} GWN), (S_j \stackrel{SK}{\longleftrightarrow} GWN))$
Step 5: Refer to Step 4, M5, we deduce
$S_j| \equiv GWN| \equiv ((S_j \stackrel{SK}{\longleftrightarrow} GWN)$
Step 6: Refer to Step 5, A6, we gain
$S_j| \equiv ((S_j \stackrel{SK}{\longleftrightarrow} GWN)$

In the M4:

Step 1: We have
$S_j \triangleleft \langle SK, T_3, (S_j \stackrel{SID_j}{\longleftrightarrow} GWN), (S_j \stackrel{SK}{\longleftrightarrow} GWN), (U_i \stackrel{SK}{\longleftrightarrow} S_j)\rangle_{z_j'=z_j}$
Step 2: Refer to Step 1, A8, M1, we get
$S_j| \equiv U_i| \sim \langle SK, T_3, (S_j \stackrel{SID_j}{\longleftrightarrow} GWN), (S_j \stackrel{SK}{\longleftrightarrow} GWN), (U_i \stackrel{SK}{\longleftrightarrow} S_j)\rangle_{z_j'=z_j}$
Step 3: Refer to A3, M4, we obtain
$S_j| \equiv \sharp\langle SK, T_3, (S_j \stackrel{SID_j}{\longleftrightarrow} GWN), (S_j \stackrel{SK}{\longleftrightarrow} GWN), (U_i \stackrel{SK}{\longleftrightarrow} S_j)\rangle$
Step 4: Refer to Step 2, Step 3, M2, we infer
$S_j| \equiv U_i| \equiv \langle SK, T_3, (S_j \stackrel{SID_j}{\longleftrightarrow} GWN), (S_j \stackrel{SK}{\longleftrightarrow} GWN), (U_i \stackrel{SK}{\longleftrightarrow} S_j)\rangle$
Step 5: Refer to Step 4, M5, we deduce
$S_j| \equiv U_i| \equiv (U_i \stackrel{SK}{\longleftrightarrow} S_j)$
Step 6: Refer to Step 5, A6, we gain
$S_j| \equiv (U_i \stackrel{SK}{\longleftrightarrow} S_j)$

In the M5:

Step 1: We have
$U_i \triangleleft (SK, M_4, T_3, (U_i \stackrel{ID_i}{\longleftrightarrow} GWN), (U_i \stackrel{SK}{\longleftrightarrow} GWN))_{d_i'=d_i}$
Step 2: Refer to Step 1, A7, M1, we get
$U_i| \equiv GWN| \sim (SK, M_4, T_3, (U_i \stackrel{ID_i}{\longleftrightarrow} GWN), (U_i \stackrel{SK}{\longleftrightarrow} GWN))_{d_i'=d_i}$
Step 3: Refer to A11, M4, we obtain
$U_i| \equiv \sharp(SK, M_4, T_3, (U_i \stackrel{ID_i}{\longleftrightarrow} GWN), (U_i \stackrel{SK}{\longleftrightarrow} GWN))$
Step 4: Refer to Step 2, Step 3, M2, we infer
$U_i| \equiv GWN| \equiv (SK, M_4, T_3, (U_i \stackrel{ID_i}{\longleftrightarrow} GWN), (U_i \stackrel{SK}{\longleftrightarrow} GWN))$
Step 5: Refer to Step 4, M5, we deduce
$U_i| \equiv GWN| \equiv ((U_i \stackrel{SK}{\longleftrightarrow} GWN)$
Step 6: Refer to Step 5, A5, we gain
$U_i| \equiv ((U_i \stackrel{SK}{\longleftrightarrow} GWN)$

In the M6:

Step 1: We have
$U_i \lhd (M_4, M_5, T_3, T_4, (U_i \overset{ID_i}{\longleftrightarrow} GWN), (U_i \overset{d_i}{\longleftrightarrow} GWN), (U_i \overset{SK}{\longleftrightarrow} GWN), (U_i \overset{SK}{\longleftrightarrow} S_j))_{SK}$
Step 2: Refer to Step 1, A7, M1, we get
$U_i| \equiv S_j| \sim (M_4, M_5, T_3, T_4, (U_i \overset{ID_i}{\longleftrightarrow} GWN), (U_i \overset{d_i}{\longleftrightarrow} GWN), (U_i \overset{SK}{\longleftrightarrow} GWN), (U_i \overset{SK}{\longleftrightarrow} S_j))_{SK}$
Step 3: Refer to A4, M4, we obtain
$U_i| \equiv \sharp(M_4, M_5, T_3, T_4, (U_i \overset{ID_i}{\longleftrightarrow} GWN), (U_i \overset{d_i}{\longleftrightarrow} GWN), (U_i \overset{SK}{\longleftrightarrow} GWN), (U_i \overset{SK}{\longleftrightarrow} S_j))$
Step 4: Refer to Step 2, Step 3, M2, we infer
$U_i| \equiv S_j| \equiv (M_4, M_5, T_3, T_4, (U_i \overset{ID_i}{\longleftrightarrow} GWN), (U_i \overset{d_i}{\longleftrightarrow} GWN), (U_i \overset{SK}{\longleftrightarrow} GWN), (U_i \overset{SK}{\longleftrightarrow} S_j))$
Step 5: Refer to Step 4, M5, we deduce
$U_i| \equiv S_j| \equiv (U_i \overset{SK}{\longleftrightarrow} S_j)$
Step 6: Refer to Step 5, Step 2, A5, we gain
$U_i| \equiv (U_i \overset{SK}{\longleftrightarrow} GWN)$

5.3 Discussion on the Possible Attacks

5.4 Anonymity

The user's ID is in e_i and M_1. The e_i has two unknown values for an attacker. So it is not easy to obtain ID_i. $M_1 = h(b_i \| T_1) \oplus ID_i = h(h(X_{GWN} \| m_i) \| T_1) \oplus ID_i$, where X_{GWN} is only known by GWN. So it is also difficult for attackers to get ID_i. The sensor's ID is masked in the $ESID_j = SID_j \oplus h(y_j \| T_2)$ where $y_j = h(X_{GWN} \| m_j)$ has X_{GWN} only known by GWN. So it is hard to know SID_j for an attacker.

5.5 Smart Card Attacks

There are five values stored in SC, of which $g_i = h(X_{GWN} \| ID_i) \oplus h(MP_i)$ and $f_i = h(X_{GWN} \| m_i) \oplus h(MQ_i)$ both contain X_{GWN} only known by GWN. e_i has two unknown values for an attacker. So it is not easy to attack. r_i is only used in $e_i = MP_i \oplus MQ_i$. It is not used in communication among user, sensor node and GWN. In proposed protocol m_i is a public random value sent through insecure channel. So an attacker does not get any information or impact the protocol, if he/she got one's SC.

6 Conclusion

In this paper, we investigated an user authentication schemes proposed by Farash et al. Furthermore, we show that their scheme is susceptible to password guessing attack and fails to satisfy their security claims. We therefore conclude that their scheme cannot be practically used in networks.

Therefore, we propose an improved protocol, which can overcome all the drawbacks of Farash et al.'s scheme. But a vital difference between the two scheme is that session key's generation. While, our scheme's security is better than the Farash et al.'s, which can be concluded by the proof-of-concept implementation. Moreover, we also provide the BAN-logic to prove the practicability of our protocol. In our protocol, there is no extra information that needs to be stored in GWN for every sensor node. And the change of user's password dose not influence any sensor node or GWN.

References

1. Römer, K., Mattern, F.: The design space of wireless sensor networks. IEEE Wirel. Commun. **11**(6), 54–61 (2004)
2. Akyildiz, I.F., Su, W., Sankarasubramaniam, Y., et al.: A survey on sensor networks. Commun. Mag. IEEE **40**(8), 102–114 (2002)
3. Akyildiz, I.F., Su, W., Sankarasubramaniam, Y., et al.: Wireless sensor networks: a survey. Comput. Netw. **38**(4), 393–422 (2002)
4. Wong, K.H.M., Zheng, Y., Cao, J., et al.: A dynamic user authentication scheme for wireless sensor networks. In: International Conference on Sensor Networks, vol. 1, pp. 244–251. IEEE Press (2006)
5. Das, M.L.: Two-factor user authentication in wireless sensor networks. Trans. Wirel. Commun. **8**(3), 1086–1090 (2009). IEEE Press
6. He, D.J., Gao, Y., Chan, S., Chen, C., Bu, J.: An enhanced two-factor user authentication scheme in wireless sensor networks. Ad Hoc Sens. Wirel. Netw. **10**(4), 361–371 (2010)
7. Nyang, D.H., Lee, M.K.: Improvement of Dass two-factor authentication protocol in wireless sensor networks. In: CORD Conference Proceedings, p. 631 (2009)
8. Yeh, H.L., et al.: A secured authentication protocol for wireless sensor networks using elliptic curves cryptography. Sensors **11**(5), 4767–4779 (2011)
9. Chen, T.H., Shih, W.K.: A robust mutual authentication protocol for wireless sensor networks. ETRI J. **32**(5), 704–712 (2010)
10. Wen, F., Li, X.: An improved dynamic ID-based remote user authentication with key agreement scheme. Comput. Electr. Eng. **38**(2), 381–387 (2011)
11. Wen, F., Susilo, W., Yang, G.: A robust smart card based anonymous user authentication protocol for wireless communications. Secur. Commun. Netw. **7**(6), 897–993 (2014)
12. Eschenauer, L., Gligor, V.D.: A key-management scheme for distributed sensor networks. In: ACM Conference on Computer and Communications Security, CCS, vol. 2, pp. 41–47 (2002)
13. Farash, M.S., Turkanović, M., Kumari, S., Hölbl, M.: An efficient user authentication and key agreement scheme for heterogeneous wireless sensor network tailored for the internet of things environment. Ad Hoc Netw. **36**, 152–176 (2015)
14. Turkanović, M., Brumen, B., Hölbl, M.: A novel user authentication and key agreement scheme for heterogeneous ad hoc wireless sensor networks, based on the internet of things notion. Ad Hoc Netw. **20**(2), 96–112 (2014)
15. Michael, B., Martin, A., Roger, N.: A logic of authentication. ACM Trans. Comput. Syst. **8**(1), 18–36 (1990)

16. Zhang, Y., Sun, X., Wang, B.: efficient algorithm for k-barrier coverage based on integer linear programming. China Commun. **13**(7), 16–23 (2016)
17. Liu, Q., Cai, W., Shen, J., Fu, Z., Liu, X., Linge, N.: A speculative approach to spatial-temporal efficiency with multi-objective optimization in a heterogeneous cloud environment. Secur. Commun. Netw. **9**(17), 4002–4012 (2016)
18. Wang, B., Gu, X., Ma, L., Yan, S.: Temperature error correction based on BP neural network in meteorological WSN. Int. J. Sens. Netw. **23**(4), 265–278 (2017)
19. Qu, Z., Keeney, J., Robitzsch, S., Zaman, F., Wang, X.: Multilevel pattern mining architecture for automatic network monitoring in heterogeneous wireless communication networks. China Commun. **13**(7), 108–116 (2016)

Privacy-Preserving Multi-party Aggregate Signcryption for Heterogeneous Systems

Shufen Niu(✉), Zhenbin Li, and Caifen Wang

College of Computer Science and Engineering, Northwest Normal University, Lanzhou 730070, Gansu, People's Republic of China
{shufen76,zhenbinli,wangcf}@nwnu.edu.cn
http://www.nwnu.edu.cn/?version=en

Abstract. To achieve heterogeneous communication from certificateless cryptography (CLC) to identity-based cryptography (IBC), we present a heterogeneous scheme that enables m senders in the CLC to transmit m message to n receivers in the IBC. In the proposed signcryption scheme, each sender is mapped to a distinct pseudo identity, so the sender's identity privacy preservation can be guaranteed. At the same time, to ensure the receiver's identity privacy, the identity information of all authorized recipients is mixed by the Lagrange interpolation polynomial during the signcryption process, which prevents the receiver's identity from being exposed. Compared with existing schemes, the proposed scheme presents efficient computational overhead and is suitable for heterogeneous environments. In addition, our scheme has the indistinguishability against adaptive chosen ciphertext attacks and existential unforgeability against adaptive chosen-message attacks in the random oracle model.

Keywords: Heterogeneous cryptography systems · Aggregate signcryption · Certificateless cryptography · Identity-based cryptography

1 Introduction

In 1984, Shamir [1] introduced identity-based cryptography, which is considered as one of the most important primitives in modern cryptography. In 2003, the notion of certificateless cryptography was introduced by Al-Riyami and Paterson [2]. Signcryption, first proposed by Zheng [3], is a new cryptographic primitive that fulfills both the functions of digital signature and public key encryption in a logical single step, at a cost significantly lower than that required by the traditional signature-then-encryption approach.

In 2000, Bellare et al. [4] introduced the notion of multi-receiver public key encryption. Duan and Cao [5] proposed a multi-receiver signcryption scheme that needs only one pairing operation in the signcryption stage, and the validity of message can be verified by any receiver. In 2013, Pang et al. [6] proposed an anonymous multi-receiver signcryption scheme.

The signcryption schemes described are implemented in the same cryptography environment. However, using one kind of cryptography syetem in different

X. Sun et al. (Eds.): ICCCS 2017, Part II, LNCS 10603, pp. 216–229, 2017.
https://doi.org/10.1007/978-3-319-68542-7_18

network environments is impossible. A plausible approach to solve this problem is to utilize heterogeneous signcryption. Sun and Li [7] proposed a heterogeneous signcryption schemes; however, these schemes can only achieve outsider security. In 2011, Huang et al. [8] proposed a signcryption scheme with internal security.

Related studies have been conducted to achieve security and privacy through on asymmetric cryptography. He et al. [9] utilized IBC to provide mutual authentication and privacy protection for vehicular ad hoc networks. Kamat et al. [10] utilized IBC to ensure security for vehicular networks. Horng et al. [11] used CLC to achieve security for vehicular sensor networks. Zhang et al. [12] adopted CLC for mobile ad hoc network security. All the four schemes operate effectively based on IBC and CLC, respectively. However, we suppose that we would like to achieve secure communications from a vehicular ad hoc network to a mobile ad hoc network, using only one type of cryptography environment is insufficient. Owing to the practical application requirements, it is necessary to design a security scheme that is fit for heterogeneous environments.

This paper presents a new heterogeneous aggregate signcryption scheme for multi-sender and multi-receiver network environment. That is, the proposed scheme allows multiple senders in CLC system to use the signcryption algorithm to send m messages to multiple receivers in IBC system (CLC $\rightarrow$ IBC MHAS). The main contributions of this paper are the following:

(1) We study the heterogeneous multi-party signcryption between certificateless cryptography and identity-based cryptography, and we demonstrate that the proposed scheme is more practical in the heterogeneous environment.
(2) Our scheme can ensure the privacy of the sender's identity by mapping the sender's messages to a distinct pseudo identity. Moreover, the proposed scheme can ensure the privacy of the receiver's identity by mixing the identity information of all authorized recipients through the Lagrange interpolation polynomial during the signcryption process.
(3) The verification equation of de-signcryption procedure in our scheme needs only a small constant number of pairing computations that are independent of the number of aggregated signatures. Compared with previous signcryption schemes, our scheme is efficient in computational cost.

2 Framework and Security Model for CLC $\rightarrow$ IBC MHAS

In this paper, CLC $\rightarrow$ IBC MHAS simply indicates that m senders in the CLC cryptosystem transmit m messages to n receivers in the IBC cryptosystem. In this section, we provide the formal definition and security models for the CLC $\rightarrow$ IBC MHAS scheme.

2.1 Framework for CLC $\rightarrow$ IBC MHAS

Definition 3. A CLC $\rightarrow$ IBC MHAS scheme consists of the following seven algorithms:

- **Setup:** Taken a security parameter k as input, the trusted authorities (TA) and PKG generate its own master public/secret keys and system parameter *paramas*, respectively.
- **CLC-KG:** This algorithm generates the partial private key and user key for CLC users.
- **IBC-KG:** This algorithm generates the private key for IBC users, inputting a user's identity IDr_i, PKG compute the corresponding private key Dr_i.
- **Signcrypt:** Given a sender's pseudo identity IDs_j, n receivers' identities $\{IDr_i\}_{i=1}^{n}$ and message M_j, a sender IDs_j run *signcrypt* algorithm to output a ciphertext σ_j.
- **Individual de-signcrypt:** Given a sender's pseudo identity IDs_j, the private key Dr_i of the receiver and a ciphertext σ_j, the receiver outputs the plaintext M_j, or the symbol $\perp$.
- **Aggregate:** For an aggregating set $\mathcal{S}$ of m senders with pseudo identities $\{IDs_j\}_{j=1}^{m}$ corresponding public keys $\{Qs_j\}_{j=1}^{m}$ and ciphertext $\{\sigma_j = (R_j, C_j, S_j, T_j)\}_{j=1}^{m}$ from $\mathcal{S}_j$ respectively, the receiver calculates $S = \sum_{j=1}^{m} S_j$ and outputs $\sigma = (\{R_j, C_j, T_j\}_{j=1}^{m}, S)$ as a aggregate signcryption.
- **Aggregate de-signcrypt:** Given an aggregating set $\mathcal{S}$ of m senders, the pseudo identity IDs_j of each sender $\mathcal{S}_j$, the corresponding public key Ps_j of $\mathcal{S}_j$ and the aggregate signcryption σ, outputs true if the aggregate designcrypt is valid, or false otherwise.

2.2 Security Models for CLC → IBC MHAS

In this paper, we extend certificateless signcryption [13], multi-recipient signcryption [6] and heterogeneous signcryption [14] security models for our CLC → IBC MHAS scheme. In the following, we describe the adversaries' model of the multiparty heterogeneous signcryption scheme (CLC → IBC MHS) and the multiparty heterogeneous aggregate signcryption scheme (CLC → IBC MHAS).

Confidentiality requirement. The confidentiality property is defined based on the concept of indistinguishability of encryptions under adaptively chosen ciphertext attacks (IND-CCA2). We define Game I as follows:

Game I: The game is performed by a challenger $\mathcal{B}$ and an adversary $\mathcal{A}$.

Setup: The challenger $\mathcal{B}$ first runs the *Setup* algorithm. It sends public parameters *params* to $\mathcal{A}$, while the master keys are kept secret. When $\mathcal{A}$ receives *params*, $\mathcal{A}$ outputs target identities $L^* = \{IDr_i{}^*\}_{i=1}^{n}$.

Phase 1: $\mathcal{A}$ performs a number of queries to $\mathcal{B}$:

- **Key extraction query:** When $\mathcal{A}$ asks a key extraction query corresponding to an identity IDr, $IDr \neq IDr_i^* (i = 1, 2, \ldots, n)$, $\mathcal{B}$ executes the *IBC-KG* algorithm to compute the private key Dr.
- **Signcryption query:** $\mathcal{A}$ chooses a target plaintext M, a list of receivers' identity information $L = \{IDr_i\}_{i=1}^{n}$ and gives them to $\mathcal{B}$. $\mathcal{B}$ randomly chooses an identity $IDs_j \in \{IDs_j\}_{j=1}^{m}$, calculates the private key Ds_j, and generates the ciphertext σ_j and returns it to $\mathcal{A}$.

- **Individual de-signcryption query:** $\mathcal{A}$ submits a ciphertext σ_j with pseudo identities IDs_j, and a set of receivers identities $L^* = \{IDr_i{}^*\}_{i=1}^n$, $\mathcal{B}$ randomly chooses an identity $IDr_i^* \in L^*$ and calculates the private key Dr_i^* using the *IBC-KG* algorithm. $\mathcal{A}$ checks the validity of σ_j and if it is a valid ciphertext, $\mathcal{A}$ returns the result of running the*Individual de-signcrypt* algorithm on the ciphertext M_j.

Challenge: When *Phase 1* ends, the adversary outputs a pseudo identity $\{IDs_j^*\}$, n distinct receivers identities $\{IDr_i^*\}_{i=1}^n$ and two messages M_{j0}^*, M_{j1}^*. Upon receiving M_{j0}^*, M_{j1}^*, $\mathcal{B}$ picks up a random bit $\beta \in \{0,1\}$ and creates a target ciphertext σ^* as the signcryption of messages $M_{j,\beta}^*$ using the private keys corresponding to IDs_j^* and the public key of $\{IDr_i^*\}_{i=1}^n$. The challenger returns σ_j^* to the adversary.

Phase 2: $\mathcal{A}$ can continue to probe the challenger as in *Phase 1* with the following restrictions:

(1) $\mathcal{A}$ should not query the key extraction for the target identities $L^* = \{IDr_i^*\}_{i=1}^n$.
(2) In *Phase 2*, $\mathcal{A}$ cannot make an *Individual de-signcrypt query* for the challenge ciphertext σ_j^* under IDs_j^* and $\{IDr_i^*\}_{i=1}^n$.

Response: Finally, $\mathcal{A}$ outputs its guess $\beta' \in \{0,1\}$. If $\beta' = \beta$, $\mathcal{A}$ wins this game. The advantage of $\mathcal{A}$ is defined as $Succ(\mathcal{A}) := 2Pr[\beta' = \beta] - 1$.

Definition 4 (Confidentiality in CLC$\rightarrow$IBC MHS). A CLC$\rightarrow$IBC MHS scheme is said to be the IND-CCA2 property if no probabilistic polynomial-time adversary $\mathcal{A}$ has a non-negligible advantage in Game I.

Authenticity requirement. The authenticity property is defined on the basis of existential unforgeability against chosen message attacks (EUF-CMA).

Game II: The game is performed by a challenger $\mathcal{B}$ and an adversary $\mathcal{F}$.

Setup: The challenger $\mathcal{B}$ first runs the *Setup* algorithm. It sends public parameters *params* to the adversary $\mathcal{F}$, while the master keys are kept secret. When $\mathcal{F}$ receives *params*, outputs target identity IDs^*.

Attack: $\mathcal{F}$ issues a number of queries $\mathcal{B}$:

- **Extract Partial Private Key:** $\mathcal{F}$ produces an identity IDs_j, and then $\mathcal{B}$ calculates the partial private key Ds_j from the partial private key extraction algorithm, and transmits it to $\mathcal{F}$.
- **Extract Secret Key:** $\mathcal{F}$ produces an identity IDs_i, $\mathcal{B}$ calculates the secret key Xs_j the from the *CLC-KG* algorithm, and transmits it to $\mathcal{F}$.
- **Request Public Key:** When $\mathcal{F}$ receives a public key extraction query for an identity IDs_j, $\mathcal{B}$ calculates the corresponding public key Ps_j using the *CLC-KG* algorithm, and transmits it to $\mathcal{F}$.

- **Replace Public Key:** For any identity IDs_j and a valid public key Ps'_j, $\mathcal{B}$ replaces Ps_j with a value Ps'_j.
- **Signcryption query, Individual de-signcryption query:** This is the same as in *Game I.*

Forgery: $\mathcal{F}$ outputs identities IDs^*_j, $\{IDr^*_i\}^n_{i=1}$, corresponding public keys Ps^*_j and $\{Qr^*_i\}^n_{i=1}$, a message M^*_j and a ciphertext σ^*_j. The restriction is that $\mathcal{F}$ cannot ask for private key extraction on IDs^*_j, and σ^*_j cannot be produced by the *Signcrypt* algorithm.

Definition 5 (Unforgeability in CLC → IBC MHS). A CLC → IBC MHS scheme is said to be EUF-CMA, if no probabilistic polynomial-time forger $\mathcal{F}_I$ has a non-negligible advantage against a challenger in Game II.

Game III: The game is performed by a challenger $\mathcal{B}$ and an adversary $\mathcal{F}_I$.

Setup: The challenger $\mathcal{B}$ first runs the *Setup* algorithm. It sends public parameters *params* to the adversary $\mathcal{F}_I$, while the master keys are kept secret. When $\mathcal{F}_I$ receives *params*, outputs m target identities $\{IDs_j{}^*\}^m_{j=1}$.

Attack: $\mathcal{F}_I$ issues a number of queries $\mathcal{B}$:

- **Extract Partial Private Key, Extract Secret Key, Request Public Key, Replace Public Key, Signcryption query:** There are the same as in *Game II.*
- **Aggregate De-signcryption query:** $\mathcal{A}$ submits an aggregate ciphertext σ, senders with pseudo identities $\{IDs_i\}^m_{i=1}$ and a set of receivers identities $L^* = \{IDr_i{}^*\}^n_{i=1}$, $\mathcal{B}$ calculates the private key $\{Dr_i\}^n_{i=1}$ using *IBC-KG* algorithm. $\mathcal{A}$ checks the validity of σ and if it is a valid ciphertext, then $\mathcal{A}$ returns the result of running the *Aggregate de-signcrypt* algorithm on the ciphertext σ.

Forgery: $\mathcal{F}_I$ outputs identities $\{IDs^*_j\}^m_{j=1}$, $\{IDr^*_i\}^n_{i=1}$ and corresponding public keys $\{Ps^*_j\}^m_{j=1}$ and $\{Qr^*_i\}^m_{i=1}$, m messages $\{M^*_j\}^m_{j=1}$, and an aggregate ciphertext σ^*. The restriction here is that $\mathcal{F}_I$ cannot ask for private key extraction on IDs^*_j, and σ^* cannot be produced by the *Signcrypt*algorithm.

Definition 6 (Unforgeability in CLC → IBC MHAS). A CLC → IBC MHAS scheme is said to be EUF-CMA, if no probabilistic polynomial-time forger $\mathcal{F}_I$ has a non-negligible advantage against a challenger in the Game III.

3 CLC → IBC MHAS Scheme

Our scheme allows m senders in the CLC system and n receivers in the IBC system. Our construction consists of four entities, i.e., TA, KGC, m senders, and n receivers. The KGC is responsible for creating partial private keys for senders and receivers.

Setup: The TA runs the parameter generator to input a security parameter k to construct the following system parameters. Let $\mathbb{G}_1$ and $\mathbb{G}_2$ be two cyclic groups with prime order q, where $\mathbb{G}_1$ is additive and $\mathbb{G}_2$ is multiplicative. P and Q are two different generators of $\mathbb{G}_1$. Furthermore, let e be an admissible bilinear map. The KGC randomly chooses $s \in \mathbb{Z}_q^*$ and calculates $P_{pub} = sP$, where s is a master secret for partial key extraction, which is only known to the KGC. The KGC chooses four hash functions: $H_1 : \{0,1\}^* \rightarrow \mathbb{G}_1, H_2 : \mathbb{G}_2 \rightarrow \{0,1\}^{l_m}, H_3, H_4 : \{0,1\}^* \rightarrow \mathbb{Z}_q{}^*$, where l_m denotes the length of a message. Then, the public system parameters are $Params = <q, \mathbb{G}_1, \mathbb{G}_2, e, P, Q, P_{pub}, H_0, H_1, H_2, H_3, H_4>$.

CLC-KG: A sender $\mathcal{S}_j (j \in \{1, 2, \ldots, m\})$ in CLC system with an identity IDs_j calculates the private key by working as follows:

∘ **Pseudo-Identity-Generation/Partial-Private-Key-Extraction:**

(1) A sender calculates $ID_{j,1} = k_j P$ for a random number $k_j \in \mathbb{Z}_q^*$ and transmits $(RID_j, ID_{j,1})$ to the KGC in a secure way.
(2) The KGC calculates $ID_{j,2} = RID_j \oplus H_0(sID_{j,1})$, where $H_0(\cdot)$ is a cryptographic hash function $H_0 : \{0,1\}^* \rightarrow \mathbb{Z}_q^*$. Then, a sender's pseudo identity is $IDs_j = (ID_{j,1}, ID_{j,2})$.
(3) For a given pseudo identity IDs_j, the KGC calculates the partial private key $Ds_j = sQs_j$, where s is the master secret of the KGC and $Qs_j = H_1(IDs_j)$.
(4) The KGC secretly transmits the partial private key as Ds_j to the sender S_j.

∘ **User-Key-Generation:** The sender picks a secret value Xs_j as her/his secret key, and calculates her/his public key $Ps_j = Xs_j \cdot P$.

IBC-KG: To generate the private key for n receivers in IBC system, KGC compute the private key of an identity $IDr_i (i = 1, 2, \ldots, n)$ as $Dr_i = s \cdot Qr_i$, where $Qr_i = H_1(IDr_i)$.

Signcrypt: Inputing the message M_j, a list of receivers' identities $L = \{IDr_i\}_{i=1}^n$; A sender $\mathcal{S}_j$ does the following:

(1) Randomly picks a number $r_j \in \mathbb{Z}_q^*$, $P_j \in \mathbb{G}_1$, calculates $R_j = r_j P$, $\omega_j = e(P_{pub}, P_j)^{r_j}$, and $C_j = H_2(\omega_j) \oplus M_j$.
(2) For $i = 1, 2, \ldots, n$, calculates $x_i = H_3(IDr_i)$, and $f_i(x) = \prod_{1 \leq i \neq j \leq n} \frac{x - x_j}{x_i - x_j} = a_{i,1} + a_{i,2}x + \ldots + a_{i,n}x^{n-1}$, where $a_{i,1}, a_{i,2}, \ldots, a_{i,n} \in \mathbb{Z}_q$, and then calculates $y_{ij} = r_j(P_j + Qr_i)$.
(3) For $i = 1, 2, \ldots, n$, calculates $T_{ij} = \sum_{k=1}^n a_{k,i} y_{k,j}$ and then let $\mathcal{T}_j = (T_{1j}, T_{2j}, \ldots, T_{nj})$.
(4) Calculates $h_j = H_4(C_j, R_j, Ps_j, IDs_j)$ and $S_j = Ds_j + (Xs_j + h_j r_j) \cdot Q$.
(5) $\mathcal{S}_j$ transmits the final ciphertext $\sigma_j = (R_j, C_j, S_j, \mathcal{T}_j)$ to the receivers.

Individual De-signcrypt: After receiving m ciphertext $\{\sigma_j = (R_j, C_j, S_j, \mathcal{T}_j)\}_{j=1}^m$, the receiver with an identity $IDr_i (i \in \{1, 2, \ldots, n\})$ decrypts the ciphertext σ_j as follows:

(1) Calculates $Qs_j = H_1(IDs_j)$, $h_j = H_4(C_j, R_j, Ps_j, IDs_j)$.
(2) Checks whether

$$e(S_j, P) = e(Qs_j, P_{pub}) e(Ps_j + h_j \cdot R_j, Q)$$

holds or not. If it holds, the ciphertext is valid; otherwise, reject the ciphertext.

(3) Calculates $x_i = H_3(IDr_i)$ and $y'_{ij} = T_{1j} + x_i T_{2j} + \ldots + x_i^{n-1} T_{nj} (j = 1, 2, \ldots, m)$.
(4) Calculates $\omega'_j = e(P_{pub}, y'_{ij}) e(R_j, Dr_i)^{-1}$.
(5) Recovers message M_j as $M_j = H_2(\omega'_j) \oplus C_j (j = 1, 2, \ldots, m)$.

Aggregate: Considering m senders with pseudo identities $\{IDs_j\}_{j=1}^m$ and the corresponding public keys $\{Qs_j\}_{j=1}^m$, and ciphertext $\{\sigma_j = (R_j, C_j, S_j, T_j)\}_{j=1}^m$, the receiver calculates $S = \sum_{j=1}^m S_j$ and outputs $\sigma = (\{R_j, C_j, T_j\}_{j=1}^m, S)$ as an aggregate signcryption.

Aggregate de-signcrypt: Each receiver can verify the validity of the aggregate signcryption as follows

(1) Calculates $Qs_j = H_1(IDs_j)$, $h_j = H_4(C_j, R_j, Ps_j, IDs_j)$.
(2) Checks whether

$$e(S, P) = e(\sum_{j=1}^{m} Qs_j, P_{pub}) e(\sum_{j=1}^{m} (Ps_j + h_j \cdot R_j), Q)$$

holds or not. If it holds, the ciphertext is valid, then each receiver can recover message $M_j (j = 1, 2, \ldots, m)$ in a manner similar to Individual de-signcrypt; otherwise, reject the ciphertext.

3.1 Correctness

(**1**) : Correctness of the verification algorithm
Let $Qs_j = H_1(IDs_j)$, $h_j = H_4(C_j, R_j, Ps_j, IDs_j)$, we have

$$\begin{aligned} e(S_j, P) &= e(Ds_j + (Xs_j + h_j r_j) \cdot Q, P) \\ &= e(Ds_j, P) e((Xs_j + h_j r_j) \cdot Q, P) \\ &= e(Qs_j, P_{pub}) e(Ps_j + h_j R_j, Q) \end{aligned}$$

(**2**) : Correctness of the decryption algorithm

$$\begin{aligned} y'_{ij} &= T_{1j} + x_i T_{2j} + \cdots + {x_i}^{n-1} T_{nj} \\ &= a_{1,1} \times r_1(P_1 + Qr_1) + \cdots + a_{n,1} \times r_j(P_j + Qr_n) \\ &+ x_i(a_{1,2} \times r_j(P_j + Qr_1) + \cdots + a_{n,2} \times r_j(P_j + Qr_n)) \\ &+ \cdots + {x_i}^{n-1}(a_{1,n} \times r_j(P_j + Qr_1) + \cdots \\ &+ a_{n,n} \times r_j(P_j + Qr_n)) \\ &= (a_{1,1} + \cdots + a_{1,n}{x_i}^{n-1}) \times r_j(P_j + Qr_1) + \cdots \\ &+ (a_{i,1} + \cdots + a_{i,n}{x_i}^{n-1}) \times r_j(P_j + Qr_i) + \cdots \\ &+ (a_{n,1} + \cdots + a_{n,n}{x_i}^{n-1}) \times r_j(P_j + Qr_n) \\ &= r_j(P_j + Qr_i) \end{aligned}$$

Thus, we can get

$$\begin{aligned}\omega_j' &= e(P_{pub}, y_{ij}') \times e(R_j, Dr_i)^{-1} \\ &= e(P_{pub}, r_j(P_j + Qr_i)) \times e(R_j, Dr_i)^{-1} \\ &= e(P_{pub}, r_jP_j)e(P_{pub}, r_jQr_i) \times e(R_j, Dr_i)^{-1} \\ &= e(P_{pub}, P_j)^{r_j}\end{aligned}$$

Then, we have $M_j = H_2(\omega_j') \oplus C_j$.

4 Security Proof

To demonstrate the security of our scheme, we assume $H_i(i = 1, 2, 3, 4)$ as random oracles. We assume that the adversary asks q_{H_i} queries to H_i for $i = 1, 2, 3, 4$, q_d queries to unsigncryption, q_s queries to signcryption, q_{ppk} queries to partial private key extraction, q_{sk} queries to secret key extraction, q_{pk} queries to public key extraction and q_{pkr} queries to public key replacement.

4.1 Confidentiality

Theorem 1. *In the random oracle, if there is an IND-CCA2 adversary $\mathcal{A}$ has an advantage ϵ against CLC→IBC MHS, then there is an algorithm $\mathcal{B}$ that solves the DBDH problem with an advantage $\epsilon' \geq \epsilon - \frac{nq_{H_1}q_d}{2^k}$.*

Proof. We construct a simulator $\mathcal{B}$ that makes use of $\mathcal{A}$ to compute $e(P, P)^{abc}$ from an instance (P, aP, bP, cP) of the DBDH problem.

Setup: At the beginning, challenger $\mathcal{B}$ runs the Setup algorithm. $\mathcal{B}$ sets $P_{pub} = bP$, $P_j = cP$ for a given pseudo identity IDs_j, and gives the public parameters $params = \langle \mathbb{G}_1, \mathbb{G}_2, e, P, P_0, P_1, H_1, H_2, H_3, H_4 \rangle$ to the attacker $\mathcal{A}$, then $\mathcal{A}$ outputs n target identities $\{IDr_1{}^*, IDr_2{}^*, \cdots, IDr_n{}^*\}$.

Phase 1. $\mathcal{A}$ can request a number of queries. To respond to these queries, H_1, H_2, H_3 and H_4 are random oracles controlled by $\mathcal{B}$ as follows. $\mathcal{B}$ keeps lists H_i-list $(i = 1, 2, 3, 4)$ which are used to record answers to the corresponding H_i query.

- H_1-**query:** Input an identity ID_i to H_1. If there exists (ID_i, t_i, Q_i) in H_1-list, $\mathcal{B}$ returns Q_i; otherwise, does as follows:
  (1) If $ID_i \neq IDr_k{}^*, k \in \{1, 2, \cdots, n\}$, choose $t_i \in \mathbb{Z}_q{}^*$ at random, calculates $Q_i = t_iP$; otherwise, calculates $Q_i = t_iP - P_j$.
  (2) Put (ID_i, t_i, Q_i) into H_1-list; return Q_i.
- $H_i(i = 2, 3, 4)$-**query:** Upon receiving a query, if the corresponding query exists in H_i-list, return it to $\mathcal{A}$. Otherwise, $\mathcal{B}$ randomly chooses an integer as the query result and returns it to $\mathcal{A}$. Meanwhile, $\mathcal{B}$ puts the query result into H_i-list.

- **Key extraction query:** For a key extraction query on identity IDr_i. If $IDr_i \neq IDr_k{}^*, k \in \{1, 2, \cdots, n\}$, $\mathcal{B}$ finds (IDr_i, t_i, Qr_i) from H_1-list. $\mathcal{B}$ recovers (IDr_i, t_i, Qr_i) from H_1-query, and then calculates the corresponding private key $Dr_i = t_i P_{pub}$, $\mathcal{B}$ returns it to $\mathcal{A}$; otherwise, $\mathcal{B}$ aborts and outputs failure.
- **Individual de-signcryption query:** When receiving a sender with a pseudo identity $IDs_j, j \in \{1, 2, \cdots, m\}$, a receiver with an identity IDr_i and the ciphertext σ_j, $\mathcal{B}$ follows the steps below:
  (1) If $IDr_i = IDr_k{}^*, k \in \{1, 2, \cdots, n\}$, $\mathcal{B}$ aborts and outputs failure.
  (2) If $IDr_i \neq IDr_k{}^*, k \in \{1, 2, \cdots, n\}$, $\mathcal{B}$ calculates $h_j = H_4(C_j, R_j, Ps_j, IDs_j)$, and verifies whether the equation $e(S_j, P) = e(Qs_j, P_{pub})e(Ps_j + h_j \cdot R_j, Q)$ holds. If it does not hold, the ciphertext is not valid; otherwise, $\mathcal{B}$ calculates the de-signcryption as follows:
    (a) Find the secret key Dr_i corresponding to IDr_i from the H_1-list.
    (b) Calculates $y'_{ij} = T_{1j} + x_i T_{2j} + \ldots + x_i^{n-1} T_{nj} (j \in \{1, 2, \ldots, m\})$.
    (c) Calculates $\omega'_j = e(P_{pub}, y'_{ij}) e(R_j, Dr_i)^{-1}$ and then get the plaintext as $M_j = H_2(\omega'_j) \oplus C_j$.

Finally, $\mathcal{B}$ answers to $\mathcal{A}$ with $\sigma_j = (R_j, C_j, S_j, T_j)$.

Challenge: $\mathcal{A}$ outputs two plaintext M_{j0}, M_{j1} and an arbitrary sender's private key $Ds_j, j \in 1, 2, \ldots, m$ to the challenger $\mathcal{B}$. $\mathcal{B}$ randomly chooses bit $\beta \in \{0, 1\}$ and computes the signcryption of the message $M_{j\beta}$. Firstly, $\mathcal{B}$ searches H_1-list to get t_i^* related to $IDr_i^*, i = 1, 2, \ldots, n$, and their public key $Qr_i = t_i^* P - P_j$, then computes $y_{ij} = a(P_j + Qr_i) = a(P_j + t_i^* P - P_j) = at_i^* P$ to get $T_i^*, i = 1, 2, \ldots, n$. $\mathcal{B}$ produces the challenged ciphertext $\sigma_j^* = (R_j^*, C_j^*, S_j^*, T_j^*)$ where $R_j^* = aP, S_j^* = t_j bP + (v_j + ah'_j) \cdot Q$ and $P_j = cP$, and then returns σ_j^* to $\mathcal{A}$.

Phase 2. $\mathcal{A}$ performs a number of queries as Phase 1.

Guess. Finally, $\mathcal{A}$ outputs a bit $\beta' \in \{0, 1\}$ as its guess. If $\beta' = \beta$, $\mathcal{B}$ wins this game as the answer of DBDH problem because $\omega'_j = e(P_{pub}, P_j)^{r_j} = e(bP, cP)^a = e(P, P)^{abc}$.

For q_d Individual de-signcrypt queries, the probability to reject a valid ciphertext is not greater than $\frac{nq_d}{2^k}$. If $\mathcal{A}$ wins the IND-CCA2 game, the advantage of $\mathcal{B}$ is $\epsilon' \geq \epsilon - \frac{nq_{H_1} q_d}{2^k}$.

4.2 Unforgeability

Theorem 2. *In the random oracle model, if there is a EUF-CMA adversary $\mathcal{F}$ has an advantage ϵ against CLC→ IBC MHS, then there exists an algorithm $\mathcal{B}$ that solves the CDH problem with an advantage $\epsilon' \geq (\epsilon - \frac{q_s}{2^k})(1 - \frac{1}{q_{ppk}})^{q_{ppk}}$.*

Proof. We construct a simulator $\mathcal{B}$ that makes use of $\mathcal{F}$ to compute abP from an instance (P, aP, bP) of the CDH problem.

Setup: The challenger $\mathcal{B}$ runs the Setup algorithm. It randomly selects a number $t \in \mathbb{Z}_q^*$, and sets $P_{pub} = aP, Q = tP$, and then sends the system parameters

$params = \langle \mathbb{G}_1, \mathbb{G}_2, e, P, P_{pub}, Q, H_i(i = 1, 2, 3, 4)\rangle$ to $\mathcal{F}$. $\mathcal{F}$ outputs a challenge a pseudo identity IDs^*.

- H_1**-query:** When $\mathcal{B}$ receives a query (IDs_j, w_{1j}, Qs_j). If (IDs_j, w_{1j}, Qs_j) exists in H_1-list, return Qs_j; otherwise, does as follows:
  (1) If $IDs_j \neq IDs^*$, chooses $w_{1j} \in \mathbb{Z}_q{}^*$ at random, computes $Qs_j = w_{1j}P$; otherwise, $\mathcal{B}$ sets $Qs_j = w_{1j}bP$.
  (2) Put (IDs_j, w_{1j}, Qs_j) into H_1-list.
- H_2**-query:** When $\mathcal{B}$ receives a query for H_2, $\mathcal{B}$ selects a random number $w_{2j} \in \mathbb{Z}_q{}^*$ and responds $w_{2j} \in \mathbb{Z}_q{}^*$ as a hash value of H_2.
- $H_i(i = 3, 4)$**-query:** When $\mathcal{B}$ receives a query, if the corresponding query exists in H_i-list, $\mathcal{B}$ returns it to $\mathcal{F}$. Otherwise, $\mathcal{B}$ randomly chooses an integer as the query result and return it to $\mathcal{F}$. Meanwhile, $\mathcal{B}$ puts the query result into H_i-list.
- **Public key query:** When $\mathcal{B}$ receives a query (IDs_j, x_j, Ps_j). If there exists (IDs_j, x_j, Ps_j) in public key-list, then $\mathcal{B}$ returns Ps_j; otherwise, $\mathcal{B}$ chooses $x_j \in \mathbb{Z}_q{}^*$ at random, computes $Ps_j = x_jP$, puts (IDs_j, x_j, Ps_j) into public key-list; returns Ps_j as answer.
- **Extract secret key query:** When $\mathcal{B}$ receives a query IDs_j. If $\mathcal{B}$ replaces public key of IDs_j, $\mathcal{B}$ returns $\perp$; otherwise, there exists $(IDs_j, x_j, Ps_j = x_jP)$ in public key-list, returns x_j as answer.
- **Extract partial private key query:** When $\mathcal{B}$ receives a query on IDs_j, $\mathcal{B}$ retrieves the corresponding (IDs_j, w_{1j}, Qs_j) from the H_1-list, and sets $Ds_j = w_{1j}aP$, and puts (ID_j, w_{1j}, Ds_j) into partial private key-list; return Ds_j.
- **Replace public key query:** When $\mathcal{B}$ receives a replace public key query (IDs_j, Ps'_j), $\mathcal{B}$ first finds (IDs_j, x_j, Ps_j) on public key-list, then $\mathcal{B}$ updates public key-list with tuple $(IDs_j, \perp, Ps'_j)$, and sets $x_j = \perp, Ps_j = Ps'_j$.
- **Signcryption query:** When $\mathcal{B}$ receives a signcryption query on (M_j, IDs_j, L), where $L = \{IDr_1, IDr_2, \cdots, IDr_n\}$, $\mathcal{B}$ does as follows:
  (1) If $IDs_j \neq IDs^*$, then $\mathcal{B}$ proceeds the signcryption algorithm, because $\mathcal{B}$ knows the sender's private key.
  (2) If $IDs_j = IDs^*$, $\mathcal{B}$ simulates the signcrypt algorithm to create a signcryption in the following steps:
    (a) $\mathcal{B}$ randomly chooses $r_j, h_j \in \mathbb{Z}_q{}^*$, calculates $R_j = r_jP - h_j^{-1}Ps_j$, $\omega_j = e(P_{pub}, P_j)^{r_j}$ and $c = H_2(\omega_j) \oplus M_j$.
    (b) Calculates $x_i = H_3(IDr_i)$ and $y_{ij} = r_j(P_j + Qr_i)$, where $i = 1, 2, \cdots, n$ and $Qr_i = H_1(IDr_i)$.
    (c) Calculates $p_i(x) = \prod_{1 \leq j \neq i \leq n} \frac{x - x_j}{x_i - x_j} = a_{i,1} + a_{i,2}x + \cdots + a_{i,n}x^{n-1}$, and $T_{ij} = \sum_{k=1}^{n} a_{k,i}y_{k,j}$, where $i = 1, 2, \cdots, n$ and $b_{i,1}, b_{i,2}, \cdots, b_{i,n} \in \mathbb{Z}_q$.
    (d) Calculates $S_j = Ps_j + h_jr_jQ$

Finally, $\mathcal{B}$ answers to $\mathcal{F}$ with $\sigma_j = (R_j, C_j, S_j, T_j)$.

Attack: $\mathcal{F}$ adaptively performs polynomially bounded number of queries to the various oracles in this phase.

Forge: Eventually, $\mathcal{F}$ outputs a tuple $(M_j^*, \sigma_j^*, IDs_j{}^*, Ps_j{}^*)$. If $IDs_j{}^* \neq IDs^*$, $\mathcal{B}$ aborts; otherwise, by forking lemma, $\mathcal{B}$ chooses different hash function h'^* and interacts with $\mathcal{F}$ with the same random tape, then the adversary can give a different forger $\sigma_j'^*$. Finally, $\mathcal{F}$ outputs abPas a solution to the CDH instance by calculating

$$abP = (((h_j^*)^{-1}S_j^* - (h_j'^*)^{-1}S_j'^*)((h_j^*)^{-1} - h_j'^*)^{-1}))^{-1} - x_j^* tP)(w_{1j}^*)^{-1}$$

During signcryption queries, the probability that $\mathcal{B}$ fails is at most $\frac{q_s}{2^k}$, the probability that $\mathcal{B}$ aborts when $\mathcal{F}$ makes a partial private key extraction is at most $\frac{1}{q_{ppk}}$. Consequently, we obtain $\epsilon' \geq (\epsilon - \frac{q_s}{2^k})(1 - \frac{1}{q_{ppk}})^{q_{ppk}}$.

Theorem 3. *In the random oracle model, if there is a EUF-CMA adversary $\mathcal{F}_I$ has an advantage ϵ against CLC→ IBC MHAS, then there exists an algorithm $\mathcal{B}$ that solves the CDH problem with an advantage $\epsilon' \geq (\epsilon - \frac{q_s}{2^k})(1 - \frac{1}{q_{sk}+m})^{q_{sk}+m-1}$.*

Proof. We construct a simulator $\mathcal{B}$ that makes use of $\mathcal{F}_I$ to compute abP from an instance (P, aP, bP) of the CDH problem.

- **Extract Partial Private Key, Extract Secret Key, Request Public Key, Replace Public Key.** There are the same as in *Game II.*
- **Aggregate De-signcryption query:** $\mathcal{A}$ submits an aggregate ciphertext σ, senders with pseudo identities $\{IDs_j\}_{j=1}^m$ and a set of receivers identities $L^* = \{IDr_i{}^*\}_{i=1}^n$, $\mathcal{B}$ calculates the private key $\{Dr_i\}_{i=1}^n$ using IBC-KG algorithm. $\mathcal{A}$ checks the validity of σ and if it is a valid ciphertext, then $\mathcal{A}$ returns the result of running the Aggregate de-signcrypt algorithm on the ciphertext σ.

Forgery: $\mathcal{F}_I$ outputs identities $\{IDs_j^*\}_{j=1}^m$ and $\{IDr_i^*\}_{i=1}^n$ and corresponding public keys $\{Ps_j^*\}_{j=1}^m$ and $\{Qr_i^*\}_{i=1}^n$, m messages $\{M_j^*\}_{j=1}^m$ and an aggregate ciphertext $\sigma^* = (R_j^*, C_j^*, T_j^*, S^*)$. The forged aggregate signcryption ciphertext must be verified by *Aggregate de-signcrypt*, namely:

$$e(S^*, P) = e(\sum_{j=1}^m Qs_j^*, P_{pub})e(\sum_{j=1}^m (Ps_j^* + h_j^* \cdot R_j^*), Q)$$

where $P_{pub} = aP, Q = tP, Qs_j^* = w_{1j}bP$. $\mathcal{B}$ can solve CDH problem as follows:

$$abP = (S^* - t \cdot \sum_{j=1}^m (x_j^* P + h_j^* \cdot R_j^*))(\sum_{j=1}^m w_{1j})^{-1}$$

We estimate the probability that $\mathcal{F}_I$ succeeds in solving CDH. In *signcryption queries*, the probability that $\mathcal{B}$ fails is at most $\frac{q_s}{2^k}$, the probability that $\mathcal{B}$ aborts when $\mathcal{F}_I$ makes a secret key extraction is at most $\frac{1}{q_{sk}+m}$. Consequently, we obtain $\epsilon' \geq (\epsilon - \frac{q_s}{2^k})(1 - \frac{1}{q_{sk}+m})^{q_{sk}+m-1}$.

5 Numerical Analysis

We evaluate the performance analysis of the proposed scheme. To provide numerical results, we implement our scheme and [6,16] by measuring the performance of the signcryption and de-signcryption operations. Our implementation is written in C by using the Pairing-Based Cryptography Library (Libpbc) [17]. For the comparisons, we use the curve groups implemented in the Libpbc library. The computations are run on a PC with 2.9 GHz CPU frequency and 4 GB of RAM, using Linux operating system. In the experiment, we used elliptic curves with a base field size of 512 bits and an embedding degree 2. The security levels are chosen as $|p| = 512$.

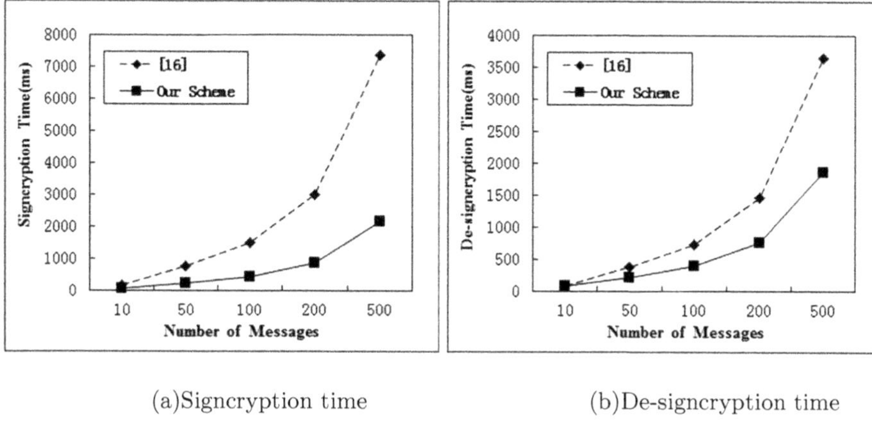

(a)Signcryption time (b)De-signcryption time

Fig. 1. Signcryption (a) and de-signcryption (b) time (ms) when the number of messages $m = 10, 50, 100, 200, 500$.

Figure 1 presents a comparison of our scheme with the multi-sender scheme [16] in terms of performance of the signcryption and de-signcryption operations. We fix the number of receivers $n = 50$, and the number of messages or senders is set to $m = 10, 50, 100, 200, 500$. As shown in Fig. 1, the computation overhead efficiency of our scheme is better than that of the scheme proposed by Eslami et al. [16] for the signcryption and de-signcryption process.

Then, we compare our scheme with the multi-receiver scheme [6] in terms of performance of the de-signcryption operations. In this experiment, we first set the number of senders at $m = 1$ and the number of receivers n at $10, 50, 100, 200, 500$ (Fig. 2c). Second, the number of senders is set at $m = 50$, and the number of receivers n is set at $10, 50, 100, 200, 500$ (Fig. 2d). As illustrated in Fig. 2c, when the number of senders is fixed at $m = 1$, the computational cost of our scheme is less efficient than that of the scheme proposed by Pang et al. [6]. However, when the number of receivers is greater than 2, the computation overhead is significantly reduced when compared with Pang et al.'s scheme.

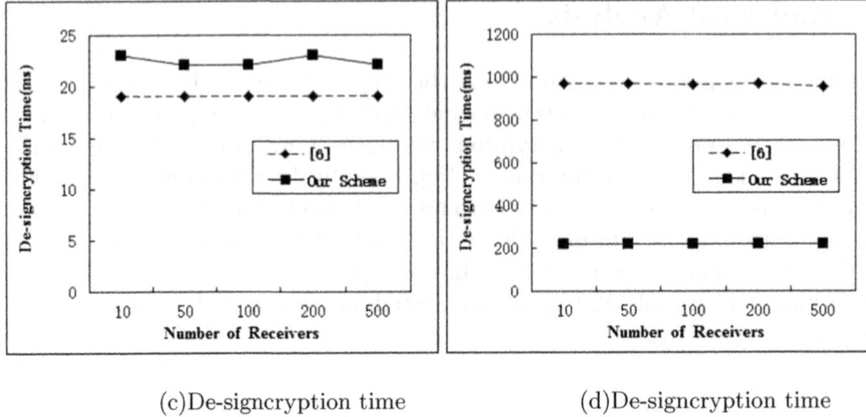

(c)De-signcryption time (d)De-signcryption time

Fig. 2. De-signcryption time (ms) when the number of senders is set to $m = 1(c), m = 50(d)$, respectively, whereas the number of receivers $n = 10, 50, 100, 200, 500$.

6 Conclusion

We propose a novel privacy-preserving multi-party signcryption scheme for CLC to IBC heterogeneous systems. Our scheme can ensure privacy preservation for all users in heterogeneous systems. Our scheme can also provide confidentiality and unforgeability in the random oracle model. Furthermore, the proposed scheme presents efficient computational complexity in relation to existing well-known schemes.

Acknowledgments. The work was supported by the National Natural Science Foundation of China under grant 61562077, 61462077, 61662071, 61662069.

References

1. Shamir, A.: Identity-based cryptosystems and signature schemes. In: Blakley, G.R., Chaum, D. (eds.) CRYPTO 1984. LNCS, vol. 196, pp. 47–53. Springer, Heidelberg (1985). doi:10.1007/3-540-39568-7_5
2. Al-Riyami, S.S., Paterson, K.G.: Certificateless public key cryptography. In: Laih, C.-S. (ed.) ASIACRYPT 2003. LNCS, vol. 2894, pp. 452–473. Springer, Heidelberg (2003). doi:10.1007/978-3-540-40061-5_29
3. Zheng, Y.: Digital signcryption or how to achieve cost(signature & encryption) ≪ cost(signature) + cost(encryption). In: Kaliski, B.S. (ed.) CRYPTO 1997. LNCS, vol. 1294, pp. 165–179. Springer, Heidelberg (1997). doi:10.1007/BFb0052234
4. Bellare, M., Boldyreva, A., Micali, S.: Public-key encryption in a multi-user setting: security proofs and improvements. In: Preneel, B. (ed.) EUROCRYPT 2000. LNCS, vol. 1807, pp. 259–274. Springer, Heidelberg (2000). doi:10.1007/3-540-45539-6_18
5. Duan, S., Cao, Z.: Efficient and provably secure multi-receiver identity-based signcryption. In: Batten, L.M., Safavi-Naini, R. (eds.) ACISP 2006. LNCS, vol. 4058, pp. 195–206. Springer, Heidelberg (2006). doi:10.1007/11780656_17

6. Pang, L., Li, H., Gao, L., Wang, Y.: Completely anonymous multi-recipient signcryption scheme with public verification. PLoS ONE **8**(5), e63562 (2013)
7. Sun, Y., Li, H.: Efficient signcryption between TPKC and IDPKC and its multi-receiver construction. Sci. China Inf. Sci. **53**(3), 557–566 (2010)
8. Huang, Q., Wong, D.S., Yang, G.: Heterogeneous signcryption with key privacy. Comput. J. **54**(4), 525–536 (2011)
9. He, D., Zeadally, S., Xu, B., Huang, X.: An efficient identity-based conditional privacy-preserving authentication scheme for vehicular ad hoc networks. IEEE Trans. Inf. Forensics Secur. **10**(12), 2681–2691 (2015)
10. Kamat, P., Baliga, A., Trappe, W.: Secure, pseudonymous, and auditable communication in vehicular ad hoc networks. Secur. Commun. Netw. **1**(3), 233–244 (2008)
11. Horng, S.J., Tzeng, S.F., Huang, P.H., Wang, X., Li, T., Khan, M.K.: An efficient certificateless aggregate signature with conditional privacy-preserving for vehicular sensor networks. Inf. Sci. **317**(C), 48–66 (2015)
12. Zhang, Z., Susilo, W., Raad, R.: Mobile ad-hoc network key management with certificateless cryptography. In: ICSPCS, pp. 1–10. IEEE Xplore (2008)
13. Barbosa, M., Farshim, P.: Certificateless signcryption. In: ACM Symposium on Information, Computer and Communications Security (ASIACCS), pp. 369–372 (2008)
14. Li, F., Zhang, H., Takagi, T.: Efficient signcryption for heterogeneous systems. IEEE Syst. J. **7**(3), 420–429 (2013)
15. Xia, Z., Wang, X., Zhang, L., Qin, Z., Sun, X., Ren, K.: A privacy-preserving and copy-deterrence content-based image retrieval scheme in cloud computing. IEEE Trans. Inf. Forensics Secur. **11**(11), 2594–2608 (2016)
16. Eslami, Z., Pakniat, N.: Certificateless aggregate signcryption. J. King Saud Univ. - Comput. Inf. Sci. **26**, 276–286 (2014)
17. The Pairing-based Cryptography Library. http://crypto.stanford.edu/pbc/

An Enhanced Method of Trajectory Privacy Preservation Through Trajectory Reconstruction

Yan Dai and Jie Shao(✉)

School of Computer Science and Engineering, Center for Future Media, University of Electronic Science and Technology of China, Chengdu, China
daiyan@std.uestc.edu.cn, shaojie@uestc.edu.cn

Abstract. Trajectory data of mobile users contain plenty of sensitive spatial and temporal information, and can support many applications through data analysing and mining. However, re-identification attack and inference attack on such data may cause serious personal privacy leakage. Existing privacy preserving techniques cannot protect trajectory privacy well or largely scarify data utility. In view of these issues, in this paper we propose an enhanced trajectory privacy preserving method which can protect the trajectory privacy preferably while maintaining a high utility of the trajectory in data publishing. A mechanism is proposed to protect the privacy through replacing stop points in the trajectory and an effective trajectory reconstruction algorithm is introduced to avoid the mutations of trajectory, and also deal with the possible presence of obstacles around trajectories. The performance of our proposal is comprehensively evaluated on a real trajectory dataset. The results show that our method achieves a high privacy level and improves the utility of trajectory data greatly, compared with the state-of-the-art method.

Keywords: Trajectory data · Privacy preservation · Replacement of stop points · Trajectory reconstruction

1 Introduction

In recent years, the widespread usage of mobile positioning techniques and location-aware devices makes massive trajectory data easy to obtain. These trajectory data support many applications related to moving objects through data analysing and mining. However, while published trajectory data can bring people huge benefits, *re-identification attack* and *inference attack* on such data may cause serious personal privacy leakage. Here, re-identification attack means attackers can link a specific trajectory with an unique victim and then obtain his whole trajectory, and inference attack can be explained as attackers try to obtain the sensitive attributes of users' trajectory and hence infer users' personal privacy, such as health condition and lifestyle. The attackers then may send unsolicited advertising messages or even threaten the security of users. Therefore, privacy protection of trajectories becomes an urgent and challenging research problem.

X. Sun et al. (Eds.): ICCCS 2017, Part II, LNCS 10603, pp. 230–243, 2017.
https://doi.org/10.1007/978-3-319-68542-7_19

In this paper, we focus on protecting the trajectory privacy in a data publishing scenario, in which location service providers or other organizations publish the data to third parties for different purposes. However, if attackers get these data, the users' personal information will be fully exposed. A trajectory of sequential data can be considered as a user's database, and each sampling position in the trajectory as one individual record. For each individual trajectory, most of these studies concentrate on protection of the whole trajectory's footprints. Although such an approach can meet the requirement of trajectory privacy protection, it leads to a large computational burden and a huge storage overhead. More importantly, through this approach, the reconstructed trajectory will greatly deviate from the real trajectory, leading to a very poor data utility.

For privacy protection, users care more about long-stayed locations and frequently visited locations (we mark these locations as "stop points"), but not all locations where they just passed by. Because these stop points can reveal the purpose and meaning of a trip [8], attackers can easily infer the user's personal privacy with them. Therefore, to be simple but effective, trajectory privacy protection can be realized through protecting these stop points [9]. This method can not only ensure the level of privacy protection, but also avoid serious trajectory information loss. To protect the stop points, some researchers propose to coarsen their locations [6]. However, through this method, attackers can easily find the repeated coarse zones and then the re-identification attacks always occur. Thus, another method [9] is proposed to protect the stop points. It means to replace stop points with less sensitive points of interest (POIs), and then publish reconstructed trajectories.

As for POI selection process, there are two strategies: searching all the POIs in the whole user space, or iteratively searching a suitable POI on each trajectory segment. However, these approaches will lead to a large distortion and heavy computation cost. In this paper, we propose a different POI searching method based on stop point. We will compare our method with searching method based on trajectory segment discussed in [9]. Finally, for trajectory reconstruction, we further consider the effect of obstacles and mutations. We develop an effective trajectory reconstruction algorithm which can avoid the mutations of trajectory in the real environment with obstacles. Through experiments we can see that our proposal can achieve the degree of trajectory protection as similar as the baseline approach of [9], but gain higher trajectory utility while considering the obstacles in user space.

The contributions of our work are mainly as follows:

- We propose an enhanced POI selection method based on stop point. It selects an POI in an expanding circle whose center is the corresponding stop point.
- We propose an effective reconstruction algorithm of trajectory, which avoids the inference attack caused by the mutations of trajectory, and further considers the effect of obstacles until a reasonable trajectory is reconstructed.
- Our proposed method is evaluated on a real-world dataset. The results show that it achieves a high privacy level and improves the utility of trajectory data greatly.

The rest of the paper is organized as follows. In Sect. 2, we review trajectory privacy protection techniques. In Sect. 3, we introduce some concepts and system architecture. In Sect. 4, we present our enhanced method. The experimental study is reported in Sects. 5 and 6 concludes.

2 Related Work

Existing trajectory privacy protection methods can be divided into four categories.

- The first category is *fake trajectory* method. It means that the initial trajectory is published with several fake trajectories to confuse attackers. Note that some attributes of fake trajectories cannot deviate too much from actual trajectory, because severe distortion may cause attackers infer users' true trajectory easily [7]. This method is simple but not very effective. Firstly, the fake trajectory may go through existing obstacles, so attackers can easily get rid of this obviously unreasonable trajectory. Secondly, the storage of fake trajectories can cause a large expense. Thirdly, the utility of trajectory data is poor due to the published fake trajectories, and it will affect the quality of queries or applications based on these data.
- The second category is *cloaking trajectory* method. It means that the points on the trajectory are generalized into some regions [4,10]. This method ensures that the published data are real, and also achieves a balance between privacy and utility to some degree. However, attackers can obtain the rough trajectory of user by connecting these regions easily. In addition, cloaking all the sampling points would cause a huge computational overhead.
- The third category is *selectively releasing trajectory* method. It means ignoring those points of a high sensitivity or visited frequently in the trajectory publishing and only publish locations with less sensitivity [3,5]. This method is simple and effective, but it may cause a sudden change of trajectory and lead to severe data distortion. More importantly, as a result, the usability can be rapidly decreased.
- The forth category is *differential privacy* method. It becomes widely used to protect privacy nowadays [1,2]. The main idea is to add Laplace noise to a database so that an adversary cannot decide weather a particular trajectory record is included in the database or not. Although it provides provable guarantees independent of an adversary's background knowledge and computational power, the noise is unbounded, so the variance of Laplace sampling is quite large due to the high sensitivity of trajectory publishing. Thus, the amount of noise to add could be too large to provide any information with good utility.

3 Problem Statement

3.1 Definitions

The definitions and symbols we use are defined as follows.

Definition 1 (Trajectory). *A spatio-temporal trajectory* T *can be described as* $T = \{q_i, (x_1, y_1, t_1), (x_2, y_2, t_2), \cdots, (x_n, y_n, t_n)\}$. q_i *is identifier of the trajectory.* $(x_i, y_i, t_i)(1 \leq i \leq n)$ *is a point on the trajectory, where* (x_i, y_i) *is the location of this point, and* t_i *is the timestamp.*

For a moving object, its trajectory is a set of location points at a certain sampling interval.

Definition 2 (Sensitivity). *The sensitivity of a POI can be expressed as a number* $s, 0 \leq s \leq 1$. *The value of* s *is set by users.*

A higher value of s means the more sensitive the corresponding location is. In addition, the sensitivities of POIs are not equal for different users, as they are set by users themselves.

3.2 System Architecture

Our work focuses on trajectory privacy protection in the case of data publishing. Firstly, we assume that location-based service providers or organizations which have direct access to users' original trajectory data are trusted, and they can also acquire the related background knowledge of space environment such as POIs and obstacles' distribution. Secondly, we assume that malicious attackers can not only obtain users' reconstructed trajectory data published, but also know the related background. Finally, we assume that the attackers know that users' trajectory data may have been changed, but they do not know the specific process of the trajectory reconstruction.

Figure 1 gives our system architecture. The inputs are initial trajectory, POI distribution and obstacle distribution. First, we divide all sampling points into two parts: move points and stop points [6]. Besides, there are two kinds of stop points: the first is the point at which user stays for a long time, and the second is the point around which user wanders for a long time. Then, based on the stop points, we determine the area to retrieve POIs. In this work, in order to make a contrast, we adopt the segment-based method and point-based method respectively to determine the searching area. After this step, we will select a less sensitive POI from the area to replace the corresponding stop point. Finally, we reconstruct the trajectory to avoid the mutations of trajectory. We also need to check whether the reconstructed trajectory segment has passed through obstacles. If yes, we will reselect other POIs until the reconstructed trajectory does not go through any obstacle.

3.3 Attack Models

We assume that the trajectory is already anonymized by replacing the true trajectory identifier with a random pseudonym. We can find that after this protection step, threatens of trajectory privacy leakage still exist as following attacks:

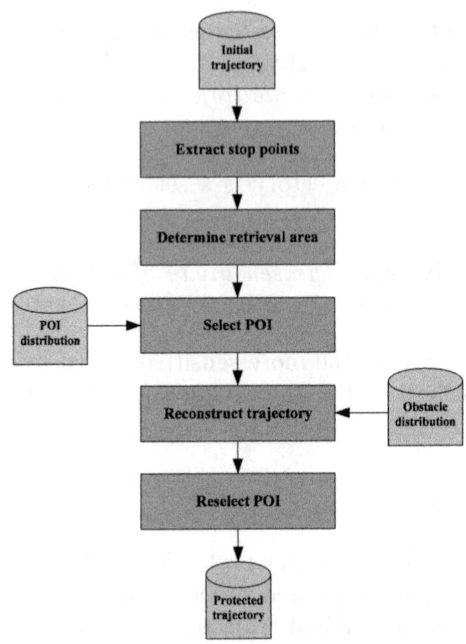

Fig. 1. System architecture of trajectory privacy preservation.

- *Re-identification attack:* If a trajectory is specific in the user's database so that not many records can match it, attackers can easily identify the victim's trajectory with the help of the background information. Suppose attackers know a user q_i would will be at location l_i at time t_i and at the same time, (l_i, t_i) happens to be a point in q_i's trajectory in the published database. An attacker can easily re-identify the whole trajectory of the user q_i and his sensitive information. In this situation, we assume there exists only one trajectory matches the background information.
- *Inference attack:* Through matching a specific sampling point and attacker's side information, there could be more than one trajectories matching the background information. In this situation, if a sensitive attribute of trajectories occurs frequently in these matched traces, even though the record of the victim cannot be uniquely identified, the probability that the victim has the sensitive attribute can be inferred. For example, assume the database is about medical records, and through some specific sampling points we can infer there exist three traces associated to a user named Bill, and two of the three traces including a diagnosis, HIV, the attacker then can infer that Bill has HIV with $2/3 \approx 66.7\%$ confidence.

Although attackers can obtain a lot side information about user's whereabouts through many ways, the obtained trajectories have already been changed. Thus, attackers can only match the replaced trajectory sequence and its side information to re-identify the victim or to infer the sensitive value of the victim. Clearly, such attacks cannot cause too many damages.

3.4 Evaluation Criteria

Trajectory protection requires us to avoid the leakage of users' personal privacy and also maintain a relatively high data utility. Therefore, both aspects of *privacy level* and *data utility* need to be evaluated for the algorithm performance.

Privacy Level: In Definition 2, we have mentioned that the sensitivity of a POI is expressed as s, so we can measure the privacy level of a method using the total difference of the sensitivity between initial trajectory and reconstructed trajectory. If the difference is larger, the performance is better. Reasonably, we use average difference rather than total difference to represent privacy level we will gain. For example, we assume A, B, C are the stop points on a trajectory, and $A^{'}, B^{'}, C^{'}$ are the corresponding selected POIs to replace them. We can measure the privacy level as:

$$Privacy = \frac{(s_A - s_{A'}) + (s_B - s_{B'}) + (s_C - s_{C'})}{3} \tag{1}$$

Utility of Trajectory Data: We measure the utility of trajectory data by measuring the similarity between reconstructed trajectory and initial trajectory. In our trajectory reconstruction process, as well as replacing stop points, we also reasonably replace some moving points on the trajectory, which can effectively avoid the inference attack caused by the mutations of reconstructed trajectory. Thus, we consider all the points on the published trajectory which have been replaced, rather than only stop points. In this paper, we characterize the similarity of two curves using the average value of Euclidean distance between the changed points and their original points. More importantly, in order to facilitate evaluation, we take the step of normalization. Assuming there are six points to be replaced, the distances of replaced points and initial points are denoted as $d_1, d_2, d_3, d_4, d_5, d_6$, and d_4 is the largest of these distances, the utility then can be measured as:

$$Utility = 1 - \frac{\frac{1}{6}(d_1 + d_2 + d_3 + d_4 + d_5 + d_6)}{d_4} \tag{2}$$

Therefore, we can get the value of utility in the range of $[0, 1]$. The larger the value is, the smaller the deviation is, and the performance is better.

4 The Algorithm

Our algorithm can be divided into three steps: extracting stop points, selecting suitable POI, and reconstructing trajectory. Detailed descriptions are given as follows.

Algorithm 1. Extracting stop points

Input: Original trajectory of mobile users ξ, time threshold th_{time}, distance threshold th_{dist}
Output: A set of stop points δ_{stop}

1: $i \leftarrow 1$;
2: $k \leftarrow 1$;
3: **while** $i < SizeOf(\xi)$ **do**
4:     **if** $(\xi[i+1][t] - \xi[i][t]) > th_{time}$ **then**
5:         $\delta_{stop}[k] \leftarrow \xi[i]$;
6:         $k \leftarrow k+1$;
7:     **end if**
8:     $i \leftarrow 1$;
9: **end while**
10: $i \leftarrow 1$;
11: **while** $i < SizeOf(\xi)$ **and** $\xi[i] \notin \delta_{stop}$ **do**
12:     $j \leftarrow i+1$;
13:     **while** $j < SizeOf(\xi)$ **do**
14:         **if** $(\xi[j][l] - \xi[i][l]) > th_{dist}$ **then**
15:             $\Delta_{time} \leftarrow \xi[j][t] - \xi[i][t]$;
16:             **if** $\Delta_{time} > th_{time}$ **then**
17:                 $\delta_{stop}[k] \leftarrow CenterPointOf(\xi[i] \rightarrow \xi[j])$;
18:                 $k \leftarrow k+1$;
19:             **end if**
20:         **end if**
21:         $j \leftarrow j+1$;
22:     **end while**
23:     $i \leftarrow i+1$;
24: **end while**

4.1 Extraction of Stop Points

As mentioned before, stop points are divided into two categories: long-stayed points and wondering points. For long-stayed points, e.g., the GPS device loses signals or is turned off, we adopt a duration-based strategy. Thus, the stop points are these points which have a large time interval with their subsequent point. Therefore, to extract them, a time threshold parameter th_{time} is introduced. If the duration which a moving object stays at a certain location exceeds th_{time}, this point can be regarded as a stop point. That is to say, given a trajectory $T = \{(l_1, t_1), (l_2, t_2), \cdots, (l_n, t_n)\}$, if $|t_{i+1} - t_i| > th_{time}, l_i$ can be determined to be a stop point. For wondering points, we introduce a distance threshold parameter th_{dist}. For a sampling point on the trajectory, if each of distance between it and its subsequent points is less than th_{dist}, and the duration of these points is longer than th_{time}, we regard the center of these points as the stop point.

Related pseudo code is shown in Algorithm 1. The input includes the user's original trajectory sequence ξ, a user-defined time threshold th_{time}, and a user-defined distance threshold th_{dist}. The output is a set of stop points δ_{stop}. Lines 3–9 of Algorithm 1 extract the long-stayed points and lines 11–24 extract the wondering points. These marked stop points are put into δ_{stop} and they need to be replaced next.

4.2 Selection of Suitable POI with Less Sensitivity

Our work mainly compares the searching method based on trajectory segment with the searching method based on stop point.

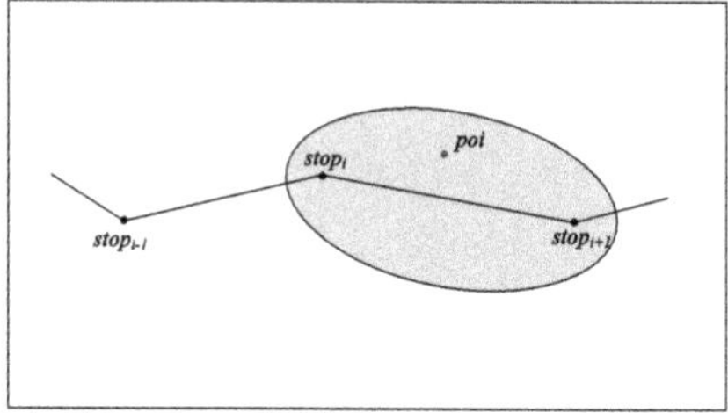

(a) Selecting POI based on trajectory segment.

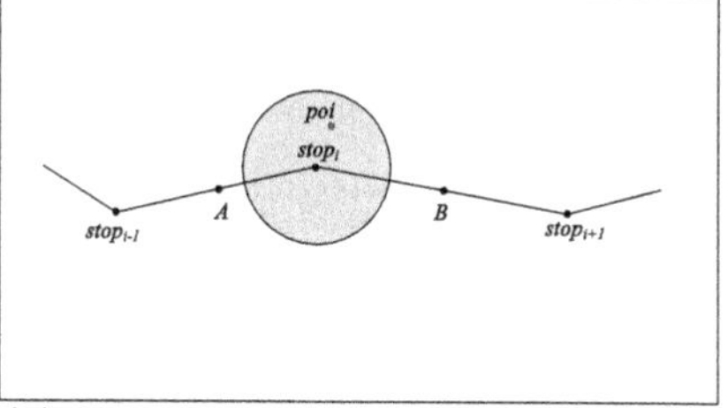

(b) Selecting POI based on stop point.

Fig. 2. Schemes for POI selection.

Algorithm 2. Retrieving POI based on trajectory segment

Input: The set of stop points δ_{stop}, the set of POIs P
Output: The selected POI poi

```
1: i ← 1;
2: while i < SizeOf(δ_stop) do
3:     StartStop ← δ_stop[i][ID];
4:     EndStop ← δ_stop[i + 1][ID];
5:     ξ_seg ← ξ[StartStop : EndStop];
6:     P_seg ← filter(routePOI(ξ_seg, P))];
7:     if SizeOf(P_seg) > 0 then
8:         poi ← LeastSensitive(P_seg);
9:     else
10:        foci_1, foci_2 ← StartStop, EndStop;
11:        Axis ← DistanceOf(StartStop, EndStop);
12:        P_seg ← filter(regionPOI(foci_1, foci_2, Axis, P, Boundary, Increment));
13:        poi ← LeastSensitive(P_seg);
14:    end if
15:    i ← i + 1;
16: end while
```

Selecting POI based on Trajectory Segment: As Fig. 2(a) shows, for every trajectory segment, such as $stop_i \rightarrow stop_{i+1}$, we firstly search POIs on the current trajectory segment. If it succeeds, we use the selected POI with the lowest sensitivity to replace the first stop point $stop_i$. If it fails, we continue to search suitable POIs in the area determined by the trajectory segment. The area is determined as an expanding ellipse whose two focus are the stop points $stop_i$ and $stop_{i+1}$. The ellipse continues to expand until a suitable POI is found. It is also necessary to set a boundary of the ellipse to limit the expansion of elliptical searching area. If exceeding, it means the searching fails, and in this case, we directly publish the stop point.

Related pseudo code is shown in Algorithm 2. The input includes the set of stop points δ_{stop} and the set of POIs P. The output is the selected POI poi. Lines 3–5 of Algorithm 2 segment the trajectory into episodes according to stop points. Lines 6–8 show that if we can retrieve POIs on the trajectory segment, the POI with the lowest sensitivity is then chosen to replace stop point. Lines 9–14 show that if it fails, we then search the less sensitive POI in the ellipse as defined.

Algorithm 3. Retrieving POI based on stop point

Input: The sets of stop points δ_{stop}, the set of POIs P

Output: The selected POI poi

```
1: i ← 1;
2: while 1 <= i <= SizeOf(δ_stop) do
3:     ξ_1 ← ξ[δ_stop[i − 1] : δ_stop[i]];
4:     ξ_2 ← ξ[δ_stop[i] : δ_stop[i + 1]];
5:     A ← MidPointOf(ξ_1);
6:     B ← MidPointOf(ξ_2);
7:     ξ_seg ← ξ[A : B];
8:     P_seg ← filter(routePOI(ξ_seg, P));
9:     if SizeOf(P_seg > 0) then
10:        poi ← LeastSensitive(P_seg);
11:    else
12:        CenterOfCircle ← δ_stop[i];
13:        Radius ← 0;
14:        P_seg ← filter(regionPOI(CenterOfCircle, Radius, P, Boundary, Increment));
15:        poi ← LeastSensitive(P_seg);
16:    end if
17:    i ← i + 1;
18: end while
```

Selecting POI based on Stop Point: In our work, we pay more attention to the searching method based on stop point. As Fig. 2(b) shows, for every stop point $stop_i$ on the trajectory, we mark the midpoint between $stop_i$ and the previous stop point $stop_{i-1}$ as A. As the same, we mark the midpoint between $stop_i$ and the next stop point $stop_{i+1}$ as B. Firstly, we try to search a less sensitive POI on the trajectory segment $A \rightarrow B$. If it succeeds, we use the selected POI to replace the stop point $stop_i$. This situation also only involves temporal modification and does not change the route of trajectory segment. If it fails, we retrieve POIs in the area determined by stop point $stop_i$. The area is determined as an expanding circle whose center is $stop_i$. Similar to trajectory segments, the circle also cannot expand unlimitedly and we should set a boundary of the circle. This searching method is simple, and we can ensure the selected POI is as close as possible to the initial trajectory.

Related pseudo code is shown in Algorithm 3. The input includes the set of stop points δ_{stop} and the set of POIs P. The output is the selected POI poi. Lines 3–7 of Algorithm 3 label the two midpoints. Lines 8–10 show that if we can retrieve POIs on the trajectory $A \rightarrow B$, the POI with the lowest sensitivity is then chosen for replacement. Lines 11–16 show that if it fails, we search a less sensitive POI in the circle as defined.

4.3 Reconstruction of Trajectory

After selecting a suitable POI, we proceed to reconstruct the trajectory. As Fig. 3 shows, for ease of description we label the stop point $stop_i$ as O, and label the selected POI poi as O'. Similarly, we mark the midpoint between $stop_i$ and $stop_{i-1}$ as A and the midpoint between $stop_i$ and $stop_{i+1}$ as B. The trajectory reconstruction algorithm can be expressed as follows: firstly, we try to find a moving point in the trajectory segment $A \rightarrow O$, namely C. The point C must satisfy that the difference between the length of trajectory segment $C \rightarrow O$

and the length of trajectory segment $C \rightarrow O^{'}$ is minimal. After selecting C, we should uniformly generate points on the segment $C \rightarrow O^{'}$ with the same number of moving points on the trajectory segment $C \rightarrow O$. The rationale is that this can avoid the sudden change of velocity. Similarly, we find a point D on the segment $O \rightarrow B$ and generate a certain number of points on the segment $O^{'} \rightarrow D$. Finally, for the stop point O, we use the trajectory segment $A \rightarrow C \rightarrow O^{'} \rightarrow D \rightarrow B$ to take the place of the original trajectory segment $A \rightarrow O \rightarrow B$. This reconstruction process is applied to every stop point until the reconstruction of the whole trajectory is completed.

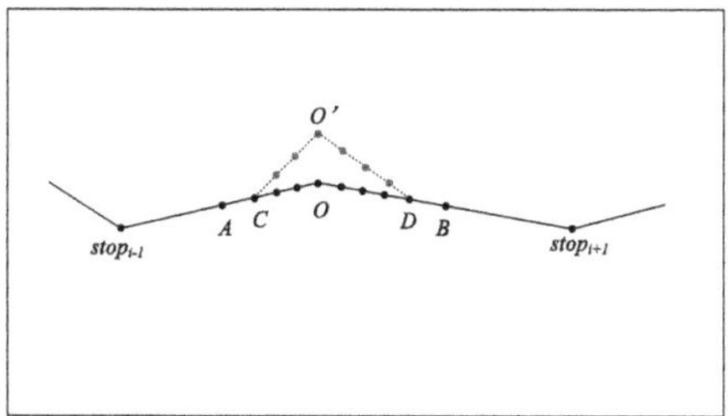

Fig. 3. Trajectory reconstruction process.

Through the observation of Fig. 3, we also replace some moving points on the trajectory. This can effectively avoid the sudden change of locations on the reconstructed trajectory. If not, third parties or malicious attackers can easily find such special locations on the published trajectory, so that they can mine users' personal privacy according to the sensitive information of these special locations.

What we also should take note is that our proposed algorithm needs to detect whether the reconstructed trajectory goes through obstacles. If it does, we need to reselect a suitable POI. Assume that we directly publish the trajectory which goes through an obstacle, then malicious attackers can quickly find this special trajectory segment.

Related pseudo code is shown in Algorithm 4. The input includes the original trajectory ξ, the selected POI poi, the set of stop points δ_{stop} and the set of obstacles φ. The output is the reconstructed trajectory ξ^{*}. Lines 5–6 look for the points A and B. Lines 7–11 uniformly generate moving points on the reconstructed trajectory segments. Lines 12–14 check whether the reconstructed trajectory segment has gone through obstacles. If yes, it reselects another suitable POI.

5 Experiments

In this section, we show the comparison results of segment-based method and our point-based method.

Algorithm 4. Trajectory reconstruction with obstacles

Input: The original trajectory of mobile users ξ, the selected POI poi, the set of stop points δ_{stop}, the set of obstacles ϕ
Output: The reconstructed trajectory ξ^*
$i \leftarrow 2$;
while $i < SizeOf(\delta_{stop})$ **do**
  $\xi_{seg1} \leftarrow \xi[A : \delta_{stop}[i]]$;
  $\xi_{seg2} \leftarrow \xi[\delta_{stop}[i] : B]$;
  select a point $\psi_1 \in \xi_{seg1}$ *making that* $Dis \leftarrow DistanceOf(\psi_1, poi) - DistanceOf(\psi_1, \delta_{stop}[i])$ *is minimal*;
  select a point $\psi_2 \in \xi_{seg2}$ *making that* $Dis \leftarrow DistanceOf(\psi_2, poi) - DistanceOf(\psi_2, \delta_{stop}[i])$ *is minimal*;
  $sum1 \leftarrow SumPointBetween(\psi_1, \delta_{stop}[i])$;
  $sum2 \leftarrow SumPointBetween(\psi_2, \delta_{stop}[i])$;
  generate sum1 points between ψ_1 *and poi uniformly*;
  generate sum2 points between ψ_2 *and poi uniformly*;
  $\xi^* \leftarrow [A : \psi_1 : poi : \psi_2 : B]$;
  if $\xi^* \cap \phi \neq \emptyset$ **then**
    reselect poi;
  end if
end while

5.1 Experimental Setup

We run our experiments on a real-world dataset. This GPS trajectory dataset was collected by Microsoft Research Asia *Geolife* project[1] by 182 users in a period of over five years (from April 2007 to August 2012), which contains 17,621 trajectories with a total distance of 1,292,951 km and a total duration of 50,176 h. The majority of the data was created in Beijing, China.

During the process of extracting stop points, we set the duration threshold th_{time} as 20 min. We also set the distance threshold th_{dist} as 200 m. During the process of extracting POIs, we set the parameter of the two methods, segment-based method proposed in [9] and point-based method proposed in this paper. For the former, we set the boundary of elliptical axis as 1000 m. Once exceeding 1000 m, the replacement process fails. For the latter, we also set the boundary of circle's radius as 1000 m. Both the ellipse and circle expand 100 m each time if a POI cannot be found.

In order to contrast the two methods comprehensively under different conditions, we test with different numbers of POIs respectively. For each number of POIs, we run the experiment 20 times to obtain the average result. Moreover, we consider the effect of obstacles. Therefore, The experiment is performed repeatedly by changing the number of obstacles. In the experiments, we generate POIs at random in the area determined by the trajectory dataset. The number of POIs is set to 1000, 3000, $\cdots$, 9000 respectively. For each obstacle, we represent their shape as a circle. The center of circle is produced at random in the area, while the radius is set to a random number between 10 m and 100 m. Similarly, the number of obstacles is set to 0, 1000, 3000, $\cdots$, 9000.

Note that, the privacy sensitivities of stop points and POIs need to be set by users. In the experiments, we set the sensitivity of stop points to 1 and set the sensitivity of POIs to a random number between 0 and 1.

[1] https://www.microsoft.com/en-us/download/details.aspx?id=52367.

5.2 Experimental Results

Study on Privacy: Figure 4 shows the privacy of the two methods with the different numbers of POIs. Figure 4(a)–(f) represent the experimental results of different number of obstacles. We can see that the difference of two methods is very small in terms of privacy, regardless of the number of POIs or obstacles. The reason is that for both two methods, we select the POI with the smallest sensitivity for replacement. Thus, the privacy only depends on the distribution of POIs and it has little to do with the POI selection method. The slight difference between them is only caused by the reason that the sensitivities of the most sensitive POI in two methods may be not equal.

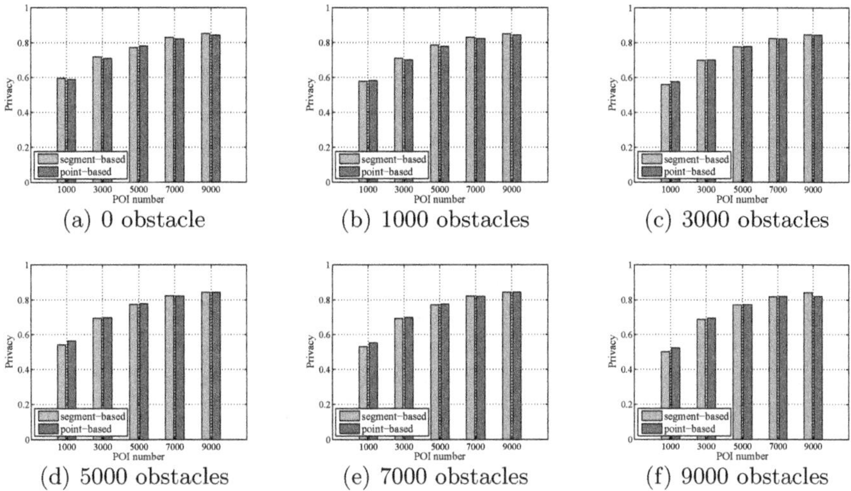

(a) 0 obstacle (b) 1000 obstacles (c) 3000 obstacles

(d) 5000 obstacles (e) 7000 obstacles (f) 9000 obstacles

Fig. 4. Comparison of privacy with different numbers of POIs and obstacles for segment-based method and point-based method.

Moreover, every figure in Fig. 4 shows that the privacy will rise with the increase of number of POIs. This is reasonable because more POIs will lead to a larger probability of finding a substitute with low sensitivity.

From another perspective, if we compare the privacy of two methods with the change of obstacles, we can find that the change of privacy is small. This is a good news for us because it shows that the introduced obstacles will not lead to a great decrease of privacy, which makes our method more practical.

Study on Utility: Figure 5 shows the utility of the two methods with the different numbers of POIs. Similarly, Fig. 5(a)–(f) represent the results when the number of obstacles is 0, 1000, 3000, $\cdots$, 9000 respectively. Different from the results of privacy, the difference of two methods is large in terms of utility, especially when the number of obstacles is small. From Fig. 5 we can see that the proposed point-based method performs much better than the segment-based

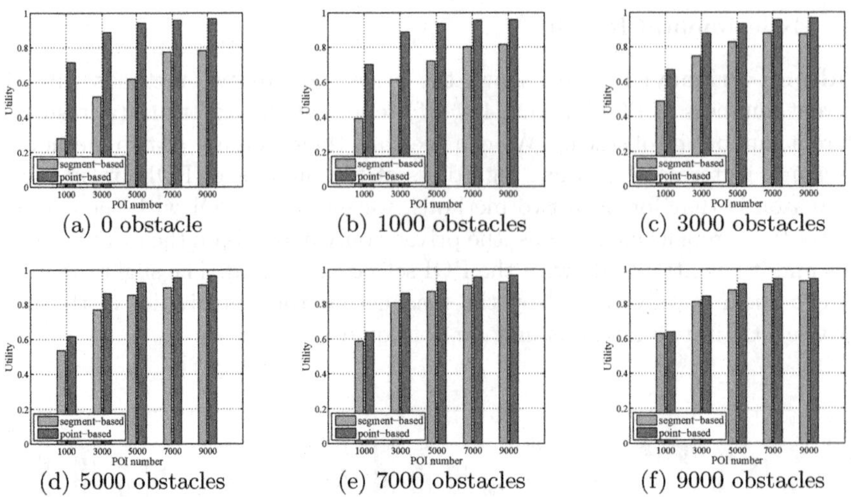

(a) 0 obstacle (b) 1000 obstacles (c) 3000 obstacles

(d) 5000 obstacles (e) 7000 obstacles (f) 9000 obstacles

Fig. 5. Comparison of utility with different numbers of POIs and obstacles for segment-based method and point-based method.

method in terms of utility. The reason is that in segment-based method, what we should replace with the selected POI is the first stop point. If the trajectory segment is very long and the selected less sensitive POI is near the second stop point on the segment, there will be a very large deviation between initial trajectory and reconstructed trajectory. However, as Fig. 5 shows, this situation will disappear gradually with the increase of obstacles. The reason is that the POI which is far from stop point may go through obstacles with high possibility, so these farther POIs are more likely to be reselected and the reselected POIs would be more close to the stop point. Therefore, with the increase of number of obstacles, more farther POIs will be reselected and the utility will rise continuously. In addition, from these figures, we can see that the utility also will rise with the increase of number of POIs. If the number of POIs is large, it is highly likely to retrieve suitable POI in a smaller area, and thus the deviation is smaller.

6 Conclusions

In this work, an enhanced method of trajectory privacy preservation is proposed through trajectory reconstruction. Our main contributions contain three parts. Firstly, we proposed an enhanced point-based method. Secondly, we investigated the effect of obstacles. Thirdly, we developed a reasonable reconstruction of trajectory. We conducted comprehensive experiments on a real-world dataset, and the results verified that our point-based method can improve the utility of trajectory data compared with segment-based method. Moreover, the introduced obstacles not only make the method more practical, but also improve the utility of segment-based method.

Acknowledgments. This work is supported by the National Natural Science Foundation of China (grants No. 61672133 and No. 61632007), the Fundamental Research Funds for the Central Universities (grants No. ZYGX2015J058 and No. ZYGX2014Z007), and a project funded by the Priority Academic Program Development of Jiangsu Higher Education Institutions and Jiangsu Collaborative Innovation Center on Atmospheric Environment and Equipment Technology.

References

1. Chen, R., Ács, G., Castelluccia, C.: Differentially private sequential data publication via variable-length n-grams. In: The ACM Conference on Computer and Communications Security, CCS 2012, Raleigh, NC, USA, 16–18 October 2012, pp. 638–649 (2012)
2. Chen, R., Fung, B.C.M., Desai, B.C., Sossou, N.M.: Differentially private transit data publication: a case study on the montreal transportation system. In: The 18th ACM SIGKDD International Conference on Knowledge Discovery and Data Mining, KDD 2012, Beijing, China, 12–16 August 2012, pp. 213–221 (2012)
3. Gidófalvi, G., Huang, X., Pedersen, T.B.: Privacy: preserving trajectory collection. In: Proceedings of the 16th ACM SIGSPATIAL International Symposium on Advances in Geographic Information Systems, ACM-GIS 2008, Irvine, California, USA, 5–7 November 2008, p. 46 (2008)
4. Gkoulalas-Divanis, A., Verykios, V.S., Mokbel, M.F.: Identifying unsafe routes for network-based trajectory privacy. In: Proceedings of the SIAM International Conference on Data Mining, SDM 2009, Sparks, Nevada, USA, 30 April–2 May 2009, pp. 942–953 (2009)
5. Gruteser, M., Liu, X.: Protecting privacy in continuous location-tracking applications. IEEE Secur. Priv. **2**(2), 28–34 (2004)
6. Huo, Z., Meng, X., Hu, H., Huang, Y.: You Can Walk Alone: trajectory privacy-preserving through significant stays protection. In: Lee, S., Peng, Z., Zhou, X., Moon, Y.-S., Unland, R., Yoo, J. (eds.) DASFAA 2012. LNCS, vol. 7238, pp. 351–366. Springer, Heidelberg (2012). doi:10.1007/978-3-642-29038-1_26
7. Luper, D., Cameron, D., Miller, J., Arabnia, H.R.: Spatial and temporal target association through semantic analysis and GPS data mining. In: Proceedings of the 2007 International Conference on Information and Knowledge Engineering, IKE 2007, Las Vegas, Nevada, USA, 25–28 June 2007, pp. 251–257 (2007)
8. Monreale, A., Trasarti, R., Renso, C., Pedreschi, D., Bogorny, V.: Preserving privacy in semantic-rich trajectories of human mobility. In: Proceedings of the 3rd ACM SIGSPATIAL International Workshop on Security and Privacy in GIS and LBS, SPRINGL 2010, San Jose, California, USA, 2 November 2010, pp. 47–54 (2010)
9. Naghizade, E., Kulik, L., Tanin, E.: Protection of sensitive trajectory datasets through spatial and temporal exchange. In: Conference on Scientific and Statistical Database Management, SSDBM 2014, Aalborg, Denmark, 30 June–02 July 2014, pp. 40:1–40:4 (2014)
10. Nergiz, M.E., Atzori, M., Saygin, Y., Güç, B.: Towards trajectory anonymization: a generalization-based approach. Trans. Data Priv. **2**(1), 47–75 (2009)

Efficient and Short Identity-Based Deniable Authenticated Encryption

Chunhua Jin(✉) and Jianyang Zhao

Faculty of Computer and Software Engineering, Huaiyin Institute of Technology, Huai'an 233003, China
xajch0206@163.com

Abstract. Deniable authentication is an important security requirement for many applications that require user privacy protection, since the sender can deny that he/she has signed the message. Considering the importance of communication efficiency, in this paper, we explore the novel deniable authenticated encryption, which outperforms the existing ones in terms of communication costs and ciphertext size. Our protocol meets all the security requirement of message confidentiality and deniable message authentication. Our protocol is based on identity cryptography and can avoid the public key certificates based public key infrastructure (PKI). Our protocol is provably secure in the random oracle model.

Keywords: Deniable authenticated encryption · Identity-based cryptography · Random oracle model

1 Introduction

Security is an essential part of computer networks. As two basic security requirements, message confidentiality and message authentication should be considered in secure communication. Message confidentiality is achieved usually through symmetric cryptography technology. The participants first share a secret session key through a key distribution protocol, and then the sender encrypts a messages using the session key and sends the resultant ciphertext to the receiver. Message authentication is usually achieved through asymmetric cryptography, where digital signatures are the primary choice. However, considering user privacy, there could be a potential privacy issue on the signer/sender, because any third party can verify the validity of the digital signature. Moreover, the receiver could forward the received message and the corresponding digital signature to any third party without the consent of the sender and the sender cannot deny sending the message to the receiver due to the non-repudiation of signature. However, this is an undesired security requirement when a user's privacy needs to be preserved (e.g., some email requirements). Therefore, deniable authentication was proposed to overcome this privacy issue.

Deniable authentication protocol is a special type of authentication protocol. Compared with traditional authentication protocol, deniable authentication protocol has two properties: (1) only the designated receiver can identify the source

X. Sun et al. (Eds.): ICCCS 2017, Part II, LNCS 10603, pp. 244–255, 2017.
https://doi.org/10.1007/978-3-319-68542-7_20

of the given message; (2) the designated receiver cannot prove the source of the given message to any third party. Therefore, deniable authentication protocol plays an important role in actual application scenarios, such as electronic voting system, secure internet shopping and internet negotiation [1].

1.1 Related Work

In 2009, Wang and Song [2] defined a formal security model for non-interactive deniable authentication protocol. Then they presented a non-interactive deniable authentication protocol based on designated verifier proofs and proved its security in their model. Raimondo and Gennaro [3] proposed two new approaches for deniable authentication. Their scheme does not require the use of CCA-secure encryption, thus showing a different generic approach to the problem of deniable authentication. In 2011, Tian et al. [4] put forward a non-interactive deniable authentication protocol and proved its security in their model. Youn et al. [5] presented a non-interactive deniable authentication scheme based on trapdoor commitment scheme. They give the security proof of their scheme under firmly formalized security model. In 2013, Chen and Chou [6] proposed a non-interactive deniable authentication protocol based on elliptic curve. They claimed that their protocol can achieve full deniability and have high efficiency. Subsequently, Li et al. [7] proposed an efficient identity-based deniable authentication and proved its security in random oracle model. In the same year, Gambs et al. [8] proposed a prover anonymous and deniable distance-bounding authentication. They formally model and define prover anonymity. This property makes the verifiers infer only the legitimacy of the prover but not his identity. For deniability, they ensure that the back-end server cannot distinguish prover behavior from malicious verifier behavior. Shi et al. [9] proposed a quantum deniable authentication protocol based on single photons. this protocol has the remarkable advantages of the higher qubit efficiency and consuming fewer quantum resources. Security analysis results show that this scheme satisfies known key security and withstands forgery attack, impersonation attack and inter-resend attack. Recently, Zeng et al. [10] proposed a deniable ring authentication protocol to handle concurrent scenario. They construct a CCA2-secure multi-receiver encryption scheme to support this protocol and it requires only 2 communication rounds, which is round-optimal in fully deniable ring authentications. Li et al. [11] proposed two heterogeneous deniable authentication protocols for pervasive computing environments using bilinear pairings. The first protocol allows a sender in a public key infrastructure (PKI) environment to send a message to a receiver in an identity based cryptography (IBC) environment. The second protocol allows a sender in the IBC environment to send a message to a receiver in the PKI environment.

However, when we carefully look at these above protocols, the messages are all transmitted in plaintexts. This may reveal some privacy identity information about the sender and the receiver. In order to achieve confidentiality, messages should be protected. In 2008, Harn and Ren [12] showed that the deniable authentication has important applications in email services. Lu et al. [13] proposed a deniable authentication protocol based on the Diffie-Hellman algorithm.

Their protocol can achieve deniable authentication, mutual authentication and confidentiality. Later, Yoon et al. [14] proposed a robust deniable authentication protocol based on ElGamal's algorithms and claimed that their protocol can satisfy the properties of deniable authentication, mutual authentication and confidentiality. However, Li and Takagi [15] showed that in Yoon et al.'s protocol, the receiver can prove the source of the given message to a third party. Subsequently, Hwang and Sung [16] proposed a deniable authenticated encryption based on the concept of signcryption. Their protocol can achieve confidentiality, sender anonymity and sender protection. In the same year, Harn et al. [17] proposed a full deniability message authentication scheme. Since there are an infinite number of possible message generators, their scheme allows the originator of the message to deny its behavior. All transmitted messages can be protected and authenticated between the sender and the designated receiver. In 2013, Hwang et al. [18] proposed a non-interactive deniable authentication protocol with anonymity and fair protection. In 2016, Li et al. [19] proposed a deniable authenticated encryption scheme with confidentiality and deniable authentication in a logical single step. They also designed an E-mail protocol using the proposed deniable authenticated encryption scheme. However, the above protocols are based on PKI. A main difficulty against PKI technology is how to manage the public key certificates including distribution, storage, revocation and computational cost of certificates verification. In order to eliminate public key certificates and simplify the key management, identity-based deniable authentication encryption was proposed [20,21]. In [20], Wu et al. first proposed an identity-based deniable authentication encryption protocol which can satisfy confidentiality, deniablity and authentication. In [21], Li et al. presented an identity-based deniable authenticated encryption protocol using tag-key encapsulation mechanism and data encapsulation mechanism hybrid techniques.

1.2 Motivation and Contribution

In order to reduce the computational and communication cost generated in signature-then-encryption schemes, Zheng [22] proposed the concept of signcryption. However, the signcryption scheme still has non-repudiation property. While our goal is to make our scheme satisfy the deniability property. Motivated by the above mentioned, in this paper, we design an efficient ID-based deniable authenticated encryption (IBDAE) protocol. Our protocol is a new non-interactive IBDAE protocol using the bilinear pairings. It can be proven secure in the random oracle model under the Decisional Bilinear Differ-Hellman (DBDH) and the Bilinear Differ-Hellman (BDH) assumptions. Our protocol is more efficient than other related protocols since it has lower computational cost and communication overhead. Our protocol can achieve deniable authentication and confidentiality.

1.3 Organization of the Paper

The rest of this paper is organized as follows. Section 2 describes some preliminary works. The formal security model for IBDAE is defined in Sect. 3. Our protocol is proposed in Sect. 4. In Sect. 5, we analyze our protocol and show that our protocol is provable secure in the random oracle model. Section 6 gives the performance of our proposed protocol. We conclude the paper in Sect. 7.

2 Preliminaries

In this section, we briefly introduce the basic definition and properties of the bilinear pairings.

Let G_1 be a cycle additive group generated by P and G_2 be a cycle multiplication group. G_1 and G_2 have the same prime order q. A bilinear pairing is a map $e : G_1 \times G_1 \rightarrow G_2$ with the following properties:

- Bilinearity: For all $P, Q \in G_1, a, b \in \mathbb{Z}_q^*$, $e(aP, bQ) = e(P, Q)^{ab}$.
- Non-degeneracy: There exists $P, Q \in G_1$ such that $e(P, Q) \neq 1$.
- Computability: There exists an efficient algorithm to compute $e(P, Q)$ for all $P, Q \in G_1$.

The modified Weil pairing and the Tate pairing are admissible maps of this kind. Please see [23,24] for more details. The security of this scheme described here relies on the hardness of the following problems.

Definition 1. *Given two groups G_1 and G_2 of the same prime order q, a bilinear map $e : G_1 \times G_1 \rightarrow G_2$ and a generator P of G_1, the Decisional Bilinear Diffie-Hellman Problem (DBDHP) in (G_1, G_2, e) is, given quadruples of the form (P, aP, bP, cP) and an element $h \in G_2$, to decide whether $h = e(P, P)^{abc}$ or not.*

Definition 2. *Given two groups G_1 and G_2 of the same prime order q, a bilinear map $e : G_1 \times G_1 \rightarrow G_2$ and a generator P of G_1, the Bilinear Diffie-Hellman Problem (BDHP) in (G_1, G_2, e) is to compute $e(P, P)^{abc}$ given (P, aP, bP, cP).*

3 Formal Model for IBDAE Protocol

In this section, we give the framework and security notion for IBDAE protocols.

3.1 Framework of IBDAE Protocols

An IBDAE protocol is made of four algorithms as the following.

Setup: Given a security parameter k, the PKG generates the system public parameters *params* and a master private key s. Here, for simplification, we do not need to include *params* in other algorithms.

Extract: Given an identity ID and the master key s, the PKG computes the corresponding private key S_{ID} and transmits it to its owner in a secure way.

Deniable authenticated encrypt (DAE): Given a message m, a sender's private key S_{ID_s} and a receiver's identity ID_r, the sender computes DAE(m, S_{ID_s}, ID_r) to obtain the ciphertext σ.

Deniable authenticated decrypt (DAD): Given the ciphertext σ, a sender's identity ID_s and a receiver's private key S_{ID_r}, the receiver computes DAD(σ, S_{ID_r}, ID_s) to obtain the message m or the symbol $\perp$ if σ is not a valid ciphertext between the sender and the receiver.

For consistency, we require that if σ = DAE(m, S_{ID_s}, ID_r), then we have m = DAD(σ, S_{ID_r}, ID_s).

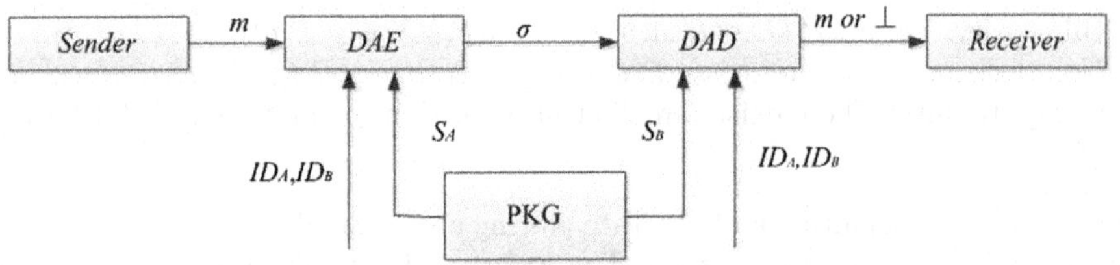

Fig. 1. Secure communication of our scheme

Figure 1 shows secure communication of our scheme, where the sender generates deniable authenticated ciphertext σ for message m using his/her identity ID_s, private key S_{ID_s} and the receiver's identity ID_r. The receiver decrypts σ by means of his/her identity ID_r and corresponding private key S_{ID_r} and the sender's identity. He/she gets the message m or $\perp$. Note that S_{ID_s} and S_{ID_r} are obtained from the PKG.

3.2 Security Notion

An IBDAE scheme needs to satisfy the following security characteristics:

- Confidentiality: it is computationally infeasible for an adaptive attacker to obtain any information from a ciphertext.
- Deniable authentication: the sender can deny its action since the receiver can also generate a valid deniable authenticator, and only the receiver can identify the source of the given message.

We borrow the security notion of digital signature to define the security notion for deniable authentication of the IBDAE scheme. However, the security notion for deniable authentication and digital signature are different. In a digital signature scheme, only the sender can generate a valid signature. It means that no one except the sender can forge a signature for a message. However, for deniable authentication of IBDAE scheme, both the sender and the receiver can generate a valid deniable authenticator for a message, which ensures the deniable authentication of IBDAE scheme. The confidentiality for IBDAE schemes is similar to the confidentiality for ID-based signcryption schemes. These notions are semantical security (that is, deniable authentication against adaptive chosen messages attacks and indistinguishability against adaptive chosen ciphertexts attacks).

Definition 3. *We say that an IBDAE scheme has the indistinguishability property against adaptive chosen ciphertexts attacks (IND-IBDAE-CCA2) if no polynomially bounded adversary has a non-negligeable advantage in the following game.*

Setup: The challenger $\mathcal{C}$ runs Setup algorithm with a security parameter k to generate the system parameters param and the master private key s. $\mathcal{C}$ sends param to the adversary $\mathcal{A}$.

Phase 1: The adversary $\mathcal{A}$ can perform a polynomially bounded number of queries in an adaptive manner(i.e. every query may depend on the answers to the previous queries). The types of allowed queries are described below.

- *Extract: $\mathcal{A}$ chooses an identity ID, $\mathcal{C}$ runs Extract algorithm and sends the corresponding private key S_{ID} to $\mathcal{A}$.*
- *DAE: $\mathcal{A}$ chooses two identities ID_i, ID_j and a message m. $\mathcal{C}$ first runs Extract algorithm to get the sender's private key S_{ID_i}. Then it sends the result of $DAE(m, S_{ID_i}, ID_j)$ to $\mathcal{A}$.*
- *DAD: $\mathcal{A}$ chooses two identities ID_i, ID_j and a ciphertext σ. $\mathcal{C}$ first runs the Extract algorithm to get the receiver's private key S_{ID_j}. Then it sends the result of $DAD(\sigma, ID_i, S_{ID_j})$ to $\mathcal{A}$ (If σ is an invalid ciphertext, the result can be the symbol $\perp$).*

Challenge: $\mathcal{A}$ decides when Phase 1 ends. Then it outputs two equal length messages m_0 and m_1, and two challenged identities ID_A and ID_B. It cannot ask the private key corresponding to the identities ID_A nor ID_B in Phase 1. $\mathcal{C}$ chooses a random bit b from $\{0, 1\}$, computes $\sigma = DAE(m_b, S_{ID_A}, ID_B)$ and sends σ to $\mathcal{A}$.

Phase 2: $\mathcal{A}$ can ask a polynomially bounded number of queries as in Phase 1. In this phase, it cannot make an Extract query on identities ID_A nor ID_B and it cannot ask a DAD query on (σ, ID_A, S_{ID_B}) to get the message m for σ.

Guess: $\mathcal{A}$ outputs a guess b' and wins the game if $b = b'$.

The advantage of $\mathcal{A}$ is defined as $Adv(A) = |2P[b' = b] - 1|$ where $P[b' = b]$ denotes the probability that $b' = b$.

Definition 4. *We say that an IBDAE scheme has the deniable authentication property against adaptive chosen messages attacks (DA-IBDAE-CMA) if no polynomially bounded adversary has a non-negligeable advantage in the following game.*

Setup: The challenger $\mathcal{C}$ runs Setup algorithm with a security parameter k to generate the system parameters param and the master private key s. $\mathcal{C}$ sends param to the adversary $\mathcal{A}$.

Attack: $\mathcal{A}$ can perform a polynomially bounded number of queries in an adaptive manner (i.e., every query may depend on the answers to the previous queries). The types of allowed queries are described below.

- *Extract: $\mathcal{A}$ chooses an identity ID, $\mathcal{C}$ runs Extract algorithm and sends the corresponding private key S_{ID} to $\mathcal{A}$.*
- *DAE: $\mathcal{A}$ chooses two identities ID_i, ID_j and a message m. $\mathcal{C}$ first runs Extract algorithm to get the sender's private key S_{ID_i}. Then it sends the result of $DAE(m, S_{ID_i}, ID_j)$ to $\mathcal{A}$.*
- *DAD: $\mathcal{A}$ chooses two identities ID_i, ID_j and a ciphertext σ. $\mathcal{C}$ first runs Extract algorithm to get the receiver's private key S_{ID_j}. Then it sends the result of $DAD(\sigma, ID_i, S_{ID_j})$to $\mathcal{A}$ (If σ is an invalid ciphertext, the result is the symbol $\perp$).*

Forgery: $\mathcal{A}$ outputs a ciphertext σ and two identities ID_A, ID_B, in which ID_A and ID_B did not appear in any Extract query in the Attack phase. It wins the game if the result of $DAD(\sigma^*, ID_A, S_{ID_B})$ is not the symbol $\perp$.

The advantage of $\mathcal{A}$ is defined as the probability that it wins.

In the above definition, the adversary is not allowed to make an *Extract* query on identity ID_B. This condition is necessary to get the deniable property. The sender can deny its behavior because the receiver can also produce a valid ciphertext.

4 A New IBDAE Protocol

In this section, we present a new IBDAE protocol with pairings. The following shows the construction of the protocol.

Setup: Given security parameters k, n and l, the PKG chooses groups G_1 and G_2 of prime order q, a bilinear map $e : G_1 \times G_1 \rightarrow G_2$ and three hash functions $H_1 : \{0,1\}^* \rightarrow G_1$, $H_2 : G_2 \rightarrow \mathbb{Z}_q$, $H_3 : \{0,1\}^n \times \mathbb{Z}_q \rightarrow \{0,1\}^l$. E and D is the symmetric encryption algorithm and symmetric decryption algorithm, respectively. It picks a master key $s \in \mathbb{Z}_q^*$ randomly and computes $P_{pub} = sP$. The PKG publishes system parameters $(G_1, G_2, n, l, e, P, q, P_{pub}, H_1, H_2, H_3, E, D)$

and keeps s secret. The plaintexts must have a fixed bitlength of n with $n + l < k \approx log_2^q$.

Extract: Given an identity ID, The PKG sets the user's public key $Q_{ID} = H_1(ID) \in G_1$ and computes the corresponding private key $S_{ID} = sQ_{ID}$ which is sent to the owner in a secure way.

Deniable authenticated encrypt (DAE): Given a message $m \in \{0,1\}^n$, a sender's private key S_{ID_s} and a receiver's identity ID_r, the sender follows the steps below.

- Choose x from $\mathbb{Z}_q^*$ randomly.
- Compute $\tau = e(P_{pub}, Q_{ID_r})^x$
- Compute $k_2 = H_2(\tau)$.
- Compute $r = E_{k_2}(m \parallel H_3(m, k_2))$.
- Compute $S = xP_{pub} - rS_{ID_s}$.
- Compute $V = e(S, Q_{ID_r})$.
- The ciphertext is $\sigma = (r, V)$.

Deniable authenticated decrypt (DAD): Given a ciphertext σ, a sender's identity ID_s and a receiver's private key S_{ID_r}, the receiver follows the steps below.

- Compute $\tau = Ve(Q_{ID_s}, S_{ID_r})^r$.
- Compute $k_2 = H_2(\tau)$.
- Compute $m' = D_{k_2}(r)$.
- Take m as the first n bits of m' if and only if $(m, H_3(m, k_2))$ are the first $n+l$ bits of m'.

5 Analysis of the Protocol

In this section, we analyze the security of the proposed protocol.We show that our protocol is provable security. The following two theorems show that the proposed protocol is both IND-IBDAE-CCA2 and DA-IBDAE-CMA secure.

Theorem 1. *In the random oracle model, if an adversary $\mathcal{A}$ can win the IND-IBDAE-CCA2 game, with an advantage ε within a time t and asking at most q_{H_i} queries to oracle $H_i (i = 1, 2, 3)$, at most q_K key extraction queries, q_E DAE queries and q_D DAD queries. Then there exists a distinguisher $\mathcal{C}$ that can solve the DBDH problem in a time $O(t + (2q_{H_3}^2 + q_D)T_e)$ with an advantage*

$$Adv(\mathcal{C}^{DBDH(G_1,P)}) > \frac{2(\varepsilon - q_D/2^{k-1})}{q_{H_1}^4}$$

where T_e denotes the computation time of the bilinear map.

Proof. This proof is omitted because of page limitation. Please contact the corresponding author for the full version.

Theorem 2. *In the random oracle model, if an adversary $\mathcal{A}$ can win the DA-IBDAE-CMA game, with an advantage $\varepsilon \geq 5(q_E+1)(q_E+q_{H_3})q_{H_1}/(2^k-1)$ within a time t and asking at most q_{H_i} queries to oracle $H_i (i = 1, 2, 3)$, at most q_K key extraction queries, q_E DAE queries and q_D DAD queries. Then there exists a challenger $\mathcal{C}$ that can solve the BDH problem in expected time $t' \leq 60343 q_{H_3} q_{H_1} 2^k t/\varepsilon(2^k-1)$.*

Proof. This proof is omitted because of page limitation. Please contact the corresponding author for the full version.

6 Performance

In this section, we will compare the computational cost, key size, ciphertext size, interactive mode, formal security proof and type of our protocol with those of existing protocols [15,16,20,21] in Table 1. We denoted by A, P, E, M, PM, CV, the point add operation in G_1, the bilinear pairing operation, the modular exponentiation operation in finite field, multiplication operation in finite field, point multiplication operation in G_1, a certificate verification (CV) operation(which normally costs about two E computation). We note that modular exponentiation operation in finite field is equivalent to point multiplication operation in Elliptic Curve Cryptosystem (ECC)(i.e. E = PM), and multiplication operation in finite field is equivalent to point addition peration in ECC(i.e. M = A). We can omit hash function operation, XOR operation and add operation in finite field since they have fast computational speeds. In addition, we assume that $|G_1| = 160$ bits, $|G_2| = 1024$ bits, $|p| = 512$ bits, $|q| = 160$ bits, $|m| = 160$ bits, $|cert| = 320$ bits, hash value = 160 bits. Here the key size is the sum of public key and secret key. From Table 1, for key size and ciphertext length, we have the great advantage. In addition, scheme [15] is interactive and lack of formal security proof. Our protocol is deniable authenticated encryption protocol based on ID-based cryptography. Therefore, our protocol has no the management of public key certificates problem.

Table 1. Performance comparison

Schemes	Computational cost		Key size (bits)	Ciphertext size (bits)	Interactive mode	Formal security proof	Type
	DAE	DAD					
[15]	4E + CV = 6E	4E + CV = 6E	672	832 + $\|cert\|$ = 1252	Interactive	No	PKI
[16]	3E + 1M + CV = 5E + 1M	2E + 1M + CV = 4E + 1M	672	992 + $\|cert\|$ = 1312	Non-interactive	Yes	PKI
[20]	2P + E + 2PM	2P + A + PM	320	1856	Non-interactive	Yes	ID-based
[21]	2P + A + 3PM	1P + 2PM	320	1536	Non-interactive	Yes	ID-based
Ours	2P + 3PM + 1A	1P + 1PM	320	1184	Non-interactive	Yes	ID-based

We adopt the experiment on PBC library with an embedding degree 2 on an Intel Pentium(R) Dual-Core processor running 2.69 GHz, 2,048 MB of RAM(2,007.04 MB available). A point add operation and a point multiplication

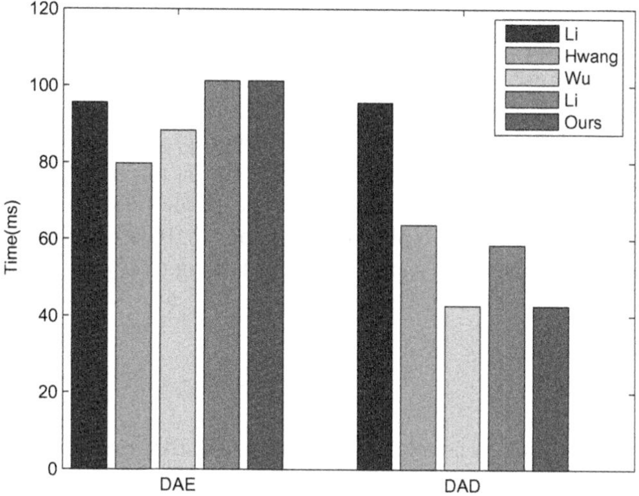

Fig. 2. The main computational cost of deniable authenticated encryption

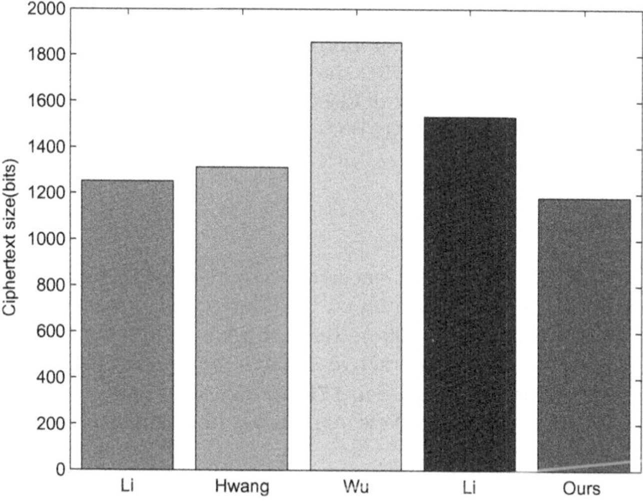

Fig. 3. The communication overhead of deniable authenticated encryption

need 0.065 ms and 15.927 ms using an ECC with 160 bits q, respectively. A pairing computation and an exponential computation need 26.68 ms and 3.126 ms, respectively. DAE and DAD in [15] need 95.562 ms and 95.562 ms, respectively. DAE and DAD in [16] need 79.7 ms and 63.773 ms, respectively. DAE and DAD in [20] need 88.34 ms and 42.672 ms, respectively. DAE and DAD in [21] need 101.206 ms and 58.534 ms, respectively. DAE and DAD in our scheme need 101.206 ms and 42.607 ms, respectively. Figure 2 shows the time for DAE and

DAD in [15,16,20,21] and our scheme. As compared with [15,16,20,21], the computational cost for DAE of our protocol is the same as [21] but a little high than [15,16,20] because two pairings are needed which belongs to G_2. The computational cost for DAD of our protocol is the lowest although we need one pairing. For type, [15,16] are based on PKI cryptography, which has the public key certificate management problem, while [20,21] and our protocol is based on ID-based cryptography, which can avoid the public key certificate management problem. Figure 3 shows ciphertext size for [15,16,20,21] and our scheme. Although our protocol needs to send V which is belong to G_2, the communication overhead of our protocol is still the least.

7 Conclusion

In this paper, we propose a novel non-interactive IBDAE protocol using pairings with formal security proof. Our protocol has more advantages in computational cost and communication overhead than the related protocols. In addition, our protocol can achieve both deniable authentication and confidentiality. Our protocol has potential applications in privacy enhanced communication networks.

Acknowledgements. This work is supported by the National Natural Science Foundation of China (grant no. 61073176), the Natural Science Foundation of Jiangsu Province (grant no. BK20161302) and Electric Power Company Technology Project of Jiangsu Province (grant no. J2017123)

References

1. Dwork, C., Naor, M., Sahai, A.: Concurrent zero-knowledge. In: Proceedings of the Thirtieth Annual ACM Symposium on the Theory of Computing Symposium on Theory of Computing (STOC 1998), Texas, USA, pp. 409–418 (1998)
2. Wang, B., Song, Z.: A non-interactive deniable authentication scheme based on designated verifier proofs. J. Inf. Sci. **179**(6), 858–865 (2009)
3. Raimondo, M., Gennaro, R.: New approaches for deniable authentication. J. Crypto. **22**(4), 572–615 (2009)
4. Tian, H., Chen, X., Jiang, Z.: Non-interactive deniable authentication protocols. In: Wu, C.-K., Yung, M., Lin, D. (eds.) Inscrypt 2011. LNCS, vol. 7537, pp. 142–159. Springer, Heidelberg (2012). doi:10.1007/978-3-642-34704-7_12
5. Youn, T., Lee, C., Park, Y.: An efficient non-interactive deniable authentication scheme based on trapdoor commitment schemes. Comput. Commun. **34**(3), 353–357 (2011)
6. Chen, Y., Chou, J.: ECC-Based non-interactive deniable authentication with designated verifier. IACR Cryptology ePrint Archive, p. 783 (2013)
7. Li, F., Xiong, P., Jin, C.: Identity-based deniable authentication for Ad Hoc networks. Computing **96**(9), 843–853 (2014)
8. Gambs, S., Onete, C., Robert, J.: Prover anonymous and deniable distance-bounding authentication. In: Proceedings of the 9th ACM Symposium on Information, Computer and Communications Security, pp. 501–506. ACM (2014)

9. Shi, W., Zhang, J., Zhou, Y., Yang, Y.G.: A novel quantum deniable authentication protocol without entanglement. Quantum Inf. Process. **14**(6), 2183–2193 (2015)
10. Zeng, S., Chen, Y., Tan, S., He, M.: Concurrently deniable ring authentication and its application to LBS in VANETs. Peer-to-Peer Netw. Appl. **10**, 1–13 (2016)
11. Li, F., Hong, J., Omala, A.: Practical deniable authentication for pervasive computing environments. Wireless Netw. 1–11 (2016)
12. Harn, L., Ren, J.: Design of fully deniable authentication service for e-mail applications. Commun. Lett. **12**(3), 219–221 (2008)
13. Lu, R., Lin, X., Cao, Z., Qin, L., Liang, X.: A simple deniable authentication protocol based on the Diffie-Hellman algorithm. Int. J. Comput. Math. **85**(9), 1315–1323 (2008)
14. Yoon, E., Yoo, K., Yeo, S., Lee, C.: Robust deniable authentication protocol. Wireless Pers. Commun. **55**(1), 81–90 (2010)
15. Li, F., Takagi, T.: Cryptanalysis and improvement of robust deniable authentication protocol. Wireless Pers. Commun. **69**(4), 1391–1398 (2013)
16. Hwang, S., Sung, Y.: Confidential deniable authentication using promised signcryption. J. Syst. Softw. **84**(10), 1652–1659 (2011)
17. Harn, L., Lee, C., Lin, C., Chang, C.C.: Fully deniable message authentication protocols preserving confidentiality. Comput. J. **54**(10), 1688–1699 (2011)
18. Hwang, S., Sung, Y., Chi, J.: Deniable authentication protocols with confidentiality and anonymous fair protections. In: Pan, J.S., Yang, C.N., Lin, C.C. (eds.) Advances in Intelligent Systems and Applications, vol. 21, pp. 41–51. Springer, Heidelberg (2012). doi:10.1007/978-3-642-35473-1_5
19. Li, F., Zhong, D., Takagi, T.: Efficient deniably authenticated encryption and its application to e-mail. IEEE Trans. Inf. Forensics Secur. **11**(11), 2477–2486 (2016)
20. Wu, W., Li, F.: An efficient identity-based deniable authenticated encryption scheme. KSII Trans. Internet Inf. Syst. (TIIS) **9**(5), 1904–1919 (2015)
21. Li, F., Zheng, Z., Jin, C.: Identity-based deniable authenticated encryption and its application to e-mail system. Telecommun. Syst. **62**(4), 625–639 (2016)
22. Zheng, Y.: Digital signcryption or how to achieve cost(signature & encryption) $\ll$ cost(signature) + cost(encryption). In: Kaliski, B.S. (ed.) CRYPTO 1997. LNCS, pp. 165–179. Springer, Heidelberg (1997). doi:10.1007/BFb0052234
23. Choon, J.C., Hee Cheon, J.: An identity-based signature from gap Diffie-Hellman groups. In: Desmedt, Y.G. (ed.) PKC 2003. LNCS, vol. 2567, pp. 18–30. Springer, Heidelberg (2003). doi:10.1007/3-540-36288-6_2
24. Boneh, D., Franklin, M.: Identity-based encryption from the Weil pairing. In: Kilian, J. (ed.) CRYPTO 2001. LNCS, vol. 2139, pp. 213–229. Springer, Heidelberg (2001). doi:10.1007/3-540-44647-8_13
25. Pointcheval, D., Stern, J.: Security arguments for digital signatures and blind signatures. J. Crypto. **13**(3), 61–396 (2003)

Towards Fully Homomorphic Encryption From Gentry-Peikert-Vaikuntanathan Scheme

Gang Du[1], Chunguang Ma[1(✉)], Zengpeng Li[1], and Ding Wang[2]

[1] College of Computer Science and Technology, Harbin Engineering University, Harbin, China
{dugang,machunguang,lizengpeng}@hrbeu.edu.cn

[2] School of Electronics Engineering and Computer Science, Peking University, Beijing, China
wangdingg@pku.edu.cn

Abstract. Despite the convenience brought by cloud computing, internet users, meanwhile, are faced with risks of data theft, tampering, forgery, etc. Fully homomorphic encryption (FHE) has the ability to deal with the ciphertext directly, which can solve the problem of data security in cloud computing. Therefore, fully homomorphic encryption (FHE) has been widely used in cloud computing as well as multiparty computing, functional encryption and private information retrieval, etc. However, previous FHE schemes are based on standard (ring) learning with errors (LWE) assumption and the most typical schemes were created by Brakerski (CRYPTO2012) and Gentry-Sahai-Waters (GSW) (CRYPTO2013). Moreover, inspired by the work of Li et al. at ICPADS2016, they made use of Brakerski's scale-invariant technology and constructed a new FHE scheme with errorless key switching under Dual-First-is-errorless LWE (Dual-Ferr.LWE) problem. Hence, armed with Li et al.'s work, in this paper, we use Gentry-Peikert-Vaikuntanathan's scheme (i.e., under dual LWE assumption) as building block to construct a FHE scheme. Lastly, under the assumption of decisional learning with errors (LWE), we prove that our scheme is CPA (chosen-plaintext-attack) secure.

Keywords: Cloud computing · Lattice based cryptography · Fully homomorphic encryption · Dual learning with errors · First of errorless LWE

1 Introduction

As a new mode of commercial applications, cloud computing services have greatly changed people's way of life. Cloud computing can be understood as a process in which the user gives the computing task to the cloud server, and then, the server returns the results of the computation to the user [23,24]. With the rapid development of cloud computing, increasingly more people store data in the cloud, but it cannot be overlooked that applications of cloud computing are also accompanied by security risks, such as data storage, transmission security and

X. Sun et al. (Eds.): ICCCS 2017, Part II, LNCS 10603, pp. 256–267, 2017.
https://doi.org/10.1007/978-3-319-68542-7_21

user privacy [8,25,26]. The security problem of cloud computing which exerts a negative effect on its application and popularization is a crucial issue in cloud computing research. Fully homomorphic encryption is a new cryptographic technology based on computational complexity theory of mathematical problems, which can provide a method to protect the privacy of the outsourcing data.

Moreover, the hard problem of lattice-based cryptography is considered as a useful tool for the foundation of secure cryptographic constructions. Attractive features of lattice cryptography include apparent resistance to quantum attacks (in contrast with most number-theoretic cryptography), high asymptotic efficiency and parallelism, security under worst-case intractability assumptions, and solutions to long-standing open problems in cryptography.

FHE has long been a holy grail in cryptography [20]. However, it is only in the past few years that candidate FHE schemes have been proposed. The first scheme was constructed by Gentry [9], and his work inspired a tremendous amount of research showing efficient improvements to his scheme (e.g. [21,22]), realizations of FHE based on different assumptions (e.g. [2–7,12,15]), implementations of FHE (e.g. [10,13,14]), etc.

1.1 Our Contribution and Techniques

We note that most of existing FHE schemes are constructed based on LWE assumption. However, the FHE scheme based on dual LWE has only been proposed by Brakerski [2] and just two constructions proposed by Li et al. [17–19]. Therefore, it is an interesting work to construct a FHE based on dual LWE roughly following their novel techniques.

The main observation is that the errorless key-switching procedure [17] doesn't have noise elements and not against key recovery attack [16].

$$<\mathbf{c}_{out}, sk_{out}> = <\mathbf{c}_{in}, sk_{in}> \ (mod\ q)$$

Hence, we propose a variant of Key-Switching procedure based on Dual LWE

$$<\mathbf{c}_{out}, sk_{out}> = <\mathbf{c}_{in}, sk_{in}> + <\mathbf{c}_{in}, \mathbf{x}_{in\to out}> \ (mod\ q)$$

We add some noise to the *KeySwitch* phase to make it work more efficiently and security.

2 Preminary

In this section we introduce some notations and learning with errors problem for both the search and decision variants. More details are as follows:

2.1 Notation

We use bold lower-case letters like $\mathbf{x}$ to denote column vectors; for row vectors we use the transpose $\mathbf{x}^T$. We use bold upper-case letters like $\mathbf{A}$ to denote matrices and sometimes identify a matrix with its ordered set of column vectors. We will be using norms in many of the inequalities in this work. For that reason, we will give three well known norms and inequalities related to norms that we will use in the following sections. l_∞ norm is: $||\mathbf{v}||_\infty = max\{|v_1|, \cdots, |v_n|\}$; l_1 norm is: $||\mathbf{v}||_1 = \sum_{i=1}^{n} |v_i|$ and Euclidean norm is: $||\mathbf{v}||_2 = \sqrt{\sum_{i=1}^{n} |v_i|^2}$.

Lemma 1 *([1] Lemma 12). Let vector* $\mathbf{x}$ *be some vector in* $\mathbb{Z}^m$ *and let* $\mathbf{e} \leftarrow D_{\mathbb{Z}^m,r}$*. Then the quantity* $| \mathbf{x}^T \cdot \mathbf{e} |$ *when treated as an integer in* $[0, \cdots, q-1]$ *satisfies*

$$| \mathbf{x}^T \cdot \mathbf{e} | \leq ||\mathbf{x}|| r\omega(\sqrt{log\ m}) + ||\mathbf{x}||\sqrt{m}/2$$

with all but negligible probability in m.

Lemma 2 *([11] Corollary 5.4). Let* n *and* q *be positive integers with* q *prime, and let* $m \geq 2nlg\ q$*. Then for all but a* $2q^n$ *fraction of all* $\mathbf{A} \in \mathbb{Z}_q^{n\times m}$ *and for any* $r \geq \omega(\sqrt{log\ m})$*, the distribution of the syndrome* $\mathbf{u} = \mathbf{A} \cdot \mathbf{e}\ mod\ q$ *is statistically close to uniform over* $\mathbb{Z}_q^n$*, where* $\mathbf{e} \leftarrow D_{\mathbb{Z}^m,r}$.

2.2 Learning with Errors

We survey the main foundational work that directly underlies most modern lattice-based cryptographic schemes. Here we just describe LWE, its hardness, and a basic LWE-based cryptosystem in some detail.

Definition 1 *(Learning with Errors Distribution). For a vector* $\mathbf{s} \in \mathbb{Z}_q^n$ *called the secret, the LWE distribution* $\mathcal{A}_{\mathbf{s},\chi}$ *over* $\mathbb{Z}_q^n \times \mathbb{Z}_q$ *is sampled by choosing* $\mathbf{a} \in \mathbb{Z}_q$ *uniformly at random, choosing* $\mathbf{e} \leftarrow \chi$*, and outputting* $(\mathbf{a}, b = \langle\mathbf{s}, \mathbf{a}\rangle + e\ (mod\ q))$.

There are two versions of the LWE problem: search version, which is to find the secret given LWE samples, and decision version, which is to distinguish between LWE samples and uniformly random ones.

Definition 2 *(Search* $-\ LWE_{n,q,\chi,m}$*). Given* m *independent samples* $(\mathbf{a}_i, b_i) \in \mathbb{Z}_q^n \times \mathbb{Z}_q$ *drawn from* $\mathcal{A}_{\mathbf{s},\chi}$ *for a uniformly random* $\mathbf{s} \in \mathbb{Z}_q^n$ *(fixed for all samples), find* $\mathbf{s}$.

Definition 3 *(Decision* $-\ LWE_{n,q,\chi,m}$*). Given* m *independent samples* $(\mathbf{a}_i, b_i) \in \mathbb{Z}_q^n \times \mathbb{Z}_q$ *where every sample is distributed according to either: (1)* $\mathcal{A}_{\mathbf{s},\chi}$ *for a uniformly random* $\mathbf{s} \in \mathbb{Z}_q^n$ *(fixed for all samples), or (2) the uniform distribution, distinguish which is the case (with non-negligible advantage).*

3 Fully Homomorphic Encryption from GPV Scheme

In this section, we use GPV scheme [11] as a building block to construct a variant of FHE scheme.

3.1 New Key Switching

In this subsection, we construct a new key switching procedure.

- **SwitchKeyGen**: $\mathbf{P}_{sk_{in} \Rightarrow sk_{out}} \leftarrow SwitchKeyGen(sk_{in}, sk_{out})$:
  1. For the input secret key $sk_{in} = [1, \mathbf{e}_{in}]^T \in D_{\mathbb{Z}_q^{n_{in} \times 1}, r}$ and the output secret key $sk_{out} = [1, \mathbf{e}_{out}]^T \in D_{\mathbb{Z}_q^{n_{out} \times 1}, r}$, where the input secret key $\mathbf{e}_{in} \in D_{\mathbb{Z}_2^{(n_{in}-1) \times 1}}$ and the output secret key $\mathbf{e}_{out} \in D_{\mathbb{Z}_2^{(n_{out}-1) \times 1}}$;
  2. Compute $\mathbf{u}_{in \Rightarrow out} = \mathbf{A}_{in \Rightarrow out} \cdot \mathbf{e}_{out} \in \mathbb{Z}_q^{\hat{n}_{in} \times 1}$, let $\hat{n_{in}} = n_{in} \times \lfloor log\ q \rfloor$. $Powerof2_q(sk_{in}) \in \mathbb{Z}_q^{\hat{n}_{in}}$, and choose a random matrix $\mathbf{A}_{in \Rightarrow out}$ which from $\mathbb{Z}_q^{\hat{n}_{in} \times (n_{out}-1)}$;
  3. Here in order to get the secure scheme and prevent one from learning all the secret keys, we add some noise $\mathbf{x} \leftarrow \chi^{n_{in} \times 1} (\mathbf{x}_{in \Rightarrow out} := Powerof2_q(\mathbf{x}) \in \chi^{\hat{n_{in}} \times 1})$ to the $\mathbf{u}_{in \Rightarrow out}$. Then compute:

  $$\mathbf{b}_{in \Rightarrow out} = \mathbf{A}_{in \Rightarrow out} \cdot \mathbf{e}_{out} + Powerof2_q\left(sk_{in} + \mathbf{x}\right) \in \mathbb{Z}_q^{\hat{n}_{in} \times 1};$$

  4. Output $\mathbf{P}_{in \Rightarrow out} = [\mathbf{b}_{in \Rightarrow out} \mid -\mathbf{A}_{in \Rightarrow out}] \in \mathbb{Z}_q^{\hat{n}_{in} \times n_{out}}$.
- **SwitchKey** $\mathbf{c}_{out} \leftarrow SwitchKey(\mathbf{P}_{in \Rightarrow out}, BitDecomp(\mathbf{c}_{in}))$:
  1. To switch a ciphertext from a secret key sk_{in} to sk_{out}, first compute

  $$\mathbf{P}_{in \Rightarrow out} \cdot (sk_{out}) = \mathbf{b}_{in \Rightarrow out} - \mathbf{A}_{in \Rightarrow out} \cdot \mathbf{e}_{out} = Powerof2_q(sk_{in} + \mathbf{x}) \quad (1)$$

  2. Then output $\mathbf{c}_{out} = \mathbf{P}_{in \Rightarrow out}^T \cdot BitDecomp(\mathbf{c}_{in}) \in \mathbb{Z}_q^{n_{out} \times 1}$, where we note that $BitDecomp(\mathbf{c}_{in}) \in \mathbb{Z}_q^{\hat{n}_{in} \times 1}$.

  We usually omit the subscripts when they are clear in the context.

Lemma 3 *(Correctness). Let $sk_{in} \in \mathbb{Z}^{n_{in}}$, $sk_{out} \in \mathbb{Z}^{n_{out}}$ and $\mathbf{c}_{in} \in \mathbb{Z}_q^{n_{in}}$ be any vectors. Let $\mathbf{P}_{in \Rightarrow out} \leftarrow SwitchKeyGen(sk_{in}, sk_{out})$ and set $\mathbf{c}_{out} \leftarrow SwitchKey(\mathbf{P}_{in \Rightarrow out}, \mathbf{c}_{in})$. Then:*

$$<\mathbf{c}_{out}, sk_{out}> = <\mathbf{c}_{in}, sk_{in}> + <\mathbf{c}_{in}, \mathbf{x}> \ (mod\ q) \quad (2)$$

Proof. We will give a more detailed proof than that of [2] and [5].

$$\begin{aligned} <\mathbf{c}_{out}, sk_{out}> &= BitDecomp(\mathbf{c}_{in})^T \cdot Powerof2_q(sk_{in} + \mathbf{x}) \\ &= <\mathbf{c}_{in}, sk_{in}> + <\mathbf{c}_{in}, \mathbf{x}> \ (mod\ q) \end{aligned}$$

Lemma 4. *$|\pounds|$ is the noise inflicted by the key switching process, We bound $|\pounds|$ using the bound on χ, therefore $|\pounds| := |<\mathbf{c}_{in}, \mathbf{x}>| \leq n_{in} \cdot B = O((m\lceil log\ q \rceil)^2)B$, where $\mathbf{x} \leftarrow \chi^{n_{in}}$.*

Lemma 5 *(Security). Let the input secret key $sk_{in} \in \mathbb{Z}^{n_{in}}$ be any vector.If we generate the output secret key $sk_{out} \leftarrow GPV.SecretKeyGen(params)$ and $\mathbf{P}_{sk_{in} \Rightarrow sk_{out}} \leftarrow SwitchKeyGen(sk_{in}, sk_{out})$: then $\mathbf{P}_{sk_{in} \Rightarrow sk_{out}}$ is computationally indistinguishable from uniform random distribution over $\mathbb{Z}_q^{\hat{n}_{in} \times n_{out}}$ under $DLWE_{n,q,\chi}$ assumption.*

3.2 Our Construction

In this subsection, we use the new key-switching procedure as described in Sect. 3.1 to construct a variant of FHE (vFHE) scheme which is based on GPV scheme.

- $params \leftarrow vFHE.Setup(1^\lambda, 1^L)$:
  We choose security parameter λ, the number of level L and output the scheme parameters $params := (m, n, q, \chi)$;
- $(pk, evk, sk) \leftarrow vFHE.KeyGen(params)$:

1. For $i = L$ down to 0, we sample $L+1$ secret vector $\mathbf{e}_i \leftarrow D_{\mathbb{Z}_q^m, r}$ and output: $sk := \mathbf{e}_L$.
2. Set $\mathbf{u}_i = f_{\mathbf{A}}(\mathbf{e}_i) = \mathbf{A} \cdot \mathbf{e}_i$ and compute $pk_i := \mathbf{P}_i = (\mathbf{u}_i \mid -\mathbf{A}) = (\mathbf{A}\mathbf{e}_i \mid -\mathbf{A})$;
3. For user's secret key sk, for the convenience, we define $\hat{sk}_i$:

$$\begin{aligned}\hat{sk}_{i-1} = (1, \hat{\mathbf{e}}_{i-1})^T &= \big(BitDecomp(sk_{i-1} \otimes sk_{i-1})\big) \in \{0,1\}^{((m+1)\cdot\lceil log\ q\rceil)^2} \\ &= BitDecomp\Big((1, \mathbf{e}_{i-1})^T\Big) \otimes BitDecomp\Big((1, \mathbf{e}_{i-1})^T\Big)\end{aligned}$$

   Compute:

$$\begin{aligned}\mathbf{P}_{\hat{sk}_{i-1} \Rightarrow sk_i} &\leftarrow SwitchKeyGen(\hat{sk}_{i-1}, sk_i) \\ &= SwitchKeyGen\Big((1, \hat{\mathbf{e}}_{i-1})^T, (1, \hat{\mathbf{e}}_i)^T\Big)\end{aligned}$$

4. Output: $pk = \mathbf{P}_0$, $sk = (1, \mathbf{e}_L)^T$, $evk = \mathbf{P}_{\hat{sk}_{i-1} \Rightarrow sk_i}$, $i \in [L]$.

- $\mathbf{c} \leftarrow vFHE.Encrypt(params, pk, m)$:
  1. Set $\mathbf{m} = (m, 0, \cdots, 0) \in \mathbb{Z}_q^{(m+1)\times 1}$, $m \in \{0,1\}$, then choose $\mathbf{s} \leftarrow \mathbb{Z}_q^{n\times 1}$, $\mathbf{x}^T := (x \leftarrow \{0\}, \mathbf{x}_1^T \leftarrow \chi^{1\times m}) \in D_{\mathbb{Z}^{1\times(m+1)}}$;
  2. Compute $\mathbf{c} := \mathbf{P}^T \cdot \mathbf{s} + \lfloor \frac{q}{2} \rfloor \cdot \mathbf{m} + \mathbf{x} \in \mathbb{Z}_q^{(m+1)\times 1}$, where the size of ciphertext is $O((m+1)log^2\ q)$.
- $m' \leftarrow vFHE.Decrypt(params, sk, \mathbf{c})$:
  1. Compute $<\mathbf{c}, \tilde{\mathbf{e}}> = \lfloor \frac{q}{2} \rfloor \cdot m + small\ (mod\ q)$, where secret keys $sk := \tilde{\mathbf{e}} = (1, \mathbf{e})^T$.
- $vFHE.Evaluate(params, evk, \mathbf{c}_1, \cdots, \mathbf{c}_l)$:
  - $Eval.Add(evk, \mathbf{c}_1, \mathbf{c}_2)$, $\mathbf{c}_{add} \leftarrow SwitchKey(\mathbf{P}_{(\mathbf{i-1})\Rightarrow \mathbf{i}}, \hat{\mathbf{c}}_{add}) \in \mathbb{Z}_q^{n+1}$:
    Assume w.l.o.g that both input ciphertexts are encrypted under the same secret key sk_{i-1}. Where $\hat{\mathbf{c}}_{add} := Powerof2(\mathbf{c}_1 + \mathbf{c}_2) \otimes Powerof2((1, 0, \cdots, 0))$.
  - $Eval.Mult(evk, \mathbf{c}_1, \mathbf{c}_2)$, $\mathbf{c}_{mult} \leftarrow SwitchKey(\mathbf{P}_{(\mathbf{i-1})\Rightarrow \mathbf{i}}, \hat{\mathbf{c}}_{mult}) \in \mathbb{Z}_q^{n+1}$:
    Assume w.l.o.g that both input ciphertexts are encrypted under the same secret key sk_{i-1}. Where $\hat{\mathbf{c}}_{mult} = \lfloor \frac{2}{q} \cdot (Powerof2(\mathbf{c}_1 \otimes \mathbf{c}_2)) \rceil = \lfloor \frac{2}{q} \cdot (Powerof2(\mathbf{c}_1) \otimes Powerof2(\mathbf{c}_2)) \rceil$.

Lemma 6 *(Correctness). Suppose the parameters* $r := B \geq \omega(\sqrt{log\ n}) \cdot \sqrt{n}$ *(refer to [2]),* $m = nlog\ q + 2\lambda$. *A E-noise ciphertext of some message* $m \in \{0,1\}$ *under secret key* $sk := \tilde{\mathbf{e}} \in \mathbb{Z}_q^{(m+1)\times 1}$ *under ciphertext vector* $\mathbf{c} := \mathbf{P}^T \cdot \mathbf{s} + \lfloor \frac{q}{2} \rfloor \cdot \mathbf{m} + \mathbf{x}\ (mod\ q) \in \mathbb{Z}_q^{(m+1)\times 1}$. *It holds that:*

$$\mathbf{c}^T \cdot \tilde{\mathbf{e}} := \lfloor \frac{q}{2} \rfloor \cdot m + \underbrace{x + \mathbf{x}_1^T \cdot \mathbf{e}}_{small}\ (mod\ q)$$

with $m \in \{0,1\}$ *and* $|small| < E \leq \lfloor q/2 \rfloor / 2$. *Then* $m \leftarrow Decrypt(sk, \mathbf{m})$.

Proof. Where $\mathbf{x} \leftarrow \{0\} \times \chi^m$. Then For $\forall x_i \leftarrow \chi, i \neq 1$, $|x_i| \leq B$(where $B \ll q$ is a bound on the values of χ), $\mathbf{x}_1 \leftarrow \chi^m$. By definition, We can get

$$\begin{aligned} <\mathbf{c}, \tilde{\mathbf{e}}> &= \mathbf{s}^T \cdot \mathbf{P} \cdot \tilde{\mathbf{e}} + \lfloor \frac{q}{2} \rfloor \cdot m + \underbrace{x + \mathbf{x}_1^T \cdot \mathbf{e}}_{small}, (By\ Lemma\ 1) \\ &= \lfloor \frac{q}{2} \rfloor \cdot m + small\ (mod\ q) \end{aligned}$$

with $||small|| \leq ||x|| + ||\mathbf{x}_1^T \cdot \mathbf{e}|| \leq E$, the norm of the error elements is bounded by $B_\chi \cdot r \cdot \omega(\sqrt{log\ m}) + B_\chi \sqrt{m}/2$, i.e. $||B_\chi \cdot r\omega(\sqrt{log\ m}) + B_\chi \sqrt{m}/2|| < E \leq \frac{q}{4}$, for the sake of simplicity we set the norm of error elements expressed by E. □

3.3 Homomorphic Operation Analysis

Choose $m_0, m_1 \in \{0,1\}$, then generate the $\mathbf{m}_0 = (m_0, 0, \cdots, 0) \in \mathbb{Z}_q^{(m+1)\times 1}$ and $\mathbf{m}_1 = (m_1, 0, \cdots, 0) \in \mathbb{Z}_q^{(m+1)\times 1}$ separately. Run the *Encrypt*$(params, pk, \mathbf{m}_i)$, $i \in \{0,1\}$:

$$\mathbf{c}_0 = \mathbf{P}^T \cdot \mathbf{s} + \lfloor \frac{q}{2} \rfloor \cdot \mathbf{m} + \mathbf{x} \in \mathbb{Z}_q^{(m+1)\times 1}; \mathbf{c}_1 = \mathbf{P}^T \cdot \mathbf{s} + \lfloor \frac{q}{2} \rfloor \cdot \mathbf{m} + \mathbf{x} \in \mathbb{Z}_q^{(m+1)\times 1};$$

Then run the *Decrypt*$(params, sk, \mathbf{c}_i), \in \{0,1\}$ separately, we get:

$$\begin{aligned} <\mathbf{c}_0, \tilde{\mathbf{e}}_0> &= <\mathbf{c}_0, (1, \mathbf{e}_0)^T> = \lfloor \frac{q}{2} \rfloor \cdot m_2 + small_0; \\ <\mathbf{c}_1, \tilde{\mathbf{e}}_1> &= <\mathbf{c}_1, (1, \mathbf{e}_1)^T> = \lfloor \frac{q}{2} \rfloor \cdot m_1 + small_1 \end{aligned}$$

Homomorphic Addition Analysis

Lemma 7. *For Eval.Add*$(evk, \mathbf{c}_0, \mathbf{c}_1)$, *we have*

$$\hat{\mathbf{c}}_{add} := Powerof2(\mathbf{c}_0 + \mathbf{c}_1) \otimes Powerof2((1, 0, \cdots, 0)) \in \mathbb{Z}_q^{\left((m+1)\lceil log\ q \rceil\right)^2}$$

then we get $\mathbf{c}_{add} \leftarrow SwitchKey(\mathbf{P}_{(\mathbf{i-1})\Rightarrow \mathbf{i}}, \hat{\mathbf{c}}_{add}) \in \mathbb{Z}_q^{n+1} := [\mathbf{P}_{(\mathbf{i-1})\Rightarrow \mathbf{i}}^T \cdot \hat{\mathbf{c}}_{add}]_q$, *for* $<\mathbf{c}_{add}, (1, \mathbf{e}_{add})> = <\hat{\mathbf{c}}_{add}, (1, \hat{\mathbf{e}}_{add})> + <\hat{\mathbf{c}}_{add}, \mathbf{x}>\ (mod\ q)$, *there exists:*

$$<\hat{\mathbf{c}}_{add}, (1, \hat{\mathbf{e}}_{add})> (mod\ q) = \lfloor \frac{q}{2} \rfloor \cdot (m_0 + m_1) + error^{Add} + k' \cdot q$$

where the $|error^{Add} + <\hat{\mathbf{c}}_{add}, \mathbf{x}>| \leq 2E + O\big((m\lceil log\ q \rceil)^2\big) \cdot B < \lfloor q/2 \rfloor / 2$.

Proof. For $||<\hat{\mathbf{c}}_{add}, \mathbf{x}>|| \leq (n_{in} log\ q)^2 \cdot B = O((m\lceil log\ q\rceil)^2) \cdot B$, where $\mathbf{x} \leftarrow \chi^{\left((m+1)\lceil log\ q\rceil\right)^2}$, by Lemma 4. For $\mathbf{c}_{add} = \mathbf{c}_1 + \mathbf{c}_2$, by Lemma 3 there exists:

$$\begin{aligned} <\hat{\mathbf{c}}_{add}, \hat{sk}_{i-1}> &= \lfloor\frac{q}{2}\rfloor(m_1+m_2) + \underbrace{(small_1 + small_2)}_{error^{Add}} + \underbrace{(k_1+k_2)}_{k'} \cdot q \\ &= \lfloor\frac{q}{2}\rfloor(m_1+m_2) + error^{Add} + k' \cdot q. \end{aligned}$$

The above Lemma 7 is proven using the Lemma 6 and Triangle-Inequality, $||error^{Add}|| \leq ||small_1|| + ||small_2|| \leq 2E$. By Lemmas 4 and 6, putting it together, the bound on error of addition is $|<\mathbf{c}, \mathbf{x}> + error^{Add}| \leq 2E + O((m\lceil log\ q\rceil)^2)B \leq \frac{q}{4}$.

Homomorphic Multiplication Analysis. Homomorphic multiplication has an even more significant problem than the error growth: the dimension of the ciphertext also grows extremely fast, i.e., exponentially with the number of multiplied ciphertexts, due to the use of the tensor product. To resolve this issue, [5] introduced a clever dimension reduction—also called key switching technique. But we make a little modification to the technique, as shown in the new key switching procedure Subsect. 3.1, so that the new key switching procedure will help us analyze the behave of error elements.

Lemma 8. *If $|k| \leq O(m \log q)$, then there exists:*

$$\begin{aligned} \left\langle (Powerof2(\mathbf{c}), BitDecomp\left((1, \mathbf{e}_{i-1})^T \right) \right\rangle &= \langle \mathbf{c}, (1, \mathbf{e}_{i-1})^T \rangle \\ &= \left\lfloor \frac{q}{2} \right\rfloor \cdot m + small + kq. \end{aligned}$$

Proof

$$\begin{aligned} |k| &= \frac{\left|\left\langle (Powerof2(\mathbf{c}), BitDecomp\left((1, \mathbf{e}_{i-1})^T \right) \right\rangle - \lfloor\frac{q}{2}\rfloor \cdot m - small\right|}{q} \\ &\leq \frac{1}{2} \cdot (m+1)\lceil log\ q\rceil + 1 = O(mlog\ q) \end{aligned}$$

Lemma 9. *For $Eval.Mult(evk, \mathbf{c}_0, \mathbf{c}_1)$, we have $\hat{\mathbf{c}}_{mult} = \lfloor\frac{2}{q}(Powerof2(\mathbf{c}_1 \otimes \mathbf{c}_2))\rceil = \lfloor\frac{2}{q}(Powerof2(\mathbf{c}_1) \otimes Powerof2(\mathbf{c}_2))\rceil$, then we get*

$$\mathbf{c}_{mult} \leftarrow SwitchKey(\mathbf{P}_{(\mathbf{i-1})\Rightarrow\mathbf{i}}, \hat{\mathbf{c}}_{mult}) := [\mathbf{P}^T_{(\mathbf{i-1})\Rightarrow\mathbf{i}} \cdot \hat{\mathbf{c}}_{mult}]_q \in \mathbb{Z}_q^{n+1}.$$

Hence for $<\mathbf{c}_{mult}, (1, \mathbf{e}_{mult})> = <\hat{\mathbf{c}}_{mult}, (1, \hat{\mathbf{e}}_{mult})> + <\hat{\mathbf{c}}_{mult}, \mathbf{x}>(mod\ q)$, there exists:

$$<\hat{\mathbf{c}}_{mult}, (1, \hat{\mathbf{e}}_{mult})>(mod\ q) = \lfloor\frac{q}{2}\rfloor \cdot (m_0 m_1) + error^{Mult}(mod\ q)$$

where the $||error^{Mult} + \langle\hat{\mathbf{c}}_{mult}, \mathbf{x}\rangle|| \leq 2E + 2 \cdot O(m \log\ q)E + \frac{E^2}{q} + O((m\lceil log\ q\rceil)^2) \cdot B \leq \frac{q}{4}$.

Proof. By Lemma 4, we get $||<\hat{\mathbf{c}}_{mult}, \mathbf{x}>|| \leq O\big((m\lceil log\ q\rceil)^2\big) \cdot B$. For $\hat{\mathbf{c}}_{mult} = \lfloor \frac{2}{q} \cdot (Powerof2(\mathbf{c}_1 \otimes \mathbf{c}_2))\rceil = \lfloor \frac{2}{q} \cdot (Powerof2(\mathbf{c}_1) \otimes Powerof2(\mathbf{c}_2))\rceil$ by Lemma 3, there exits

$$\begin{aligned}
<\hat{\mathbf{c}}_{mult}, \hat{sk}_{mult}> :=& \Big\langle \lfloor \frac{2}{q} \cdot (Powerof2(\mathbf{c}_1) \otimes Powerof2(\mathbf{c}_2))\rceil, \\
& BitDecomp\Big((1, \mathbf{e}_{i-1})^T \Big) \otimes BitDecomp\Big((1, \mathbf{e}_{i-1})^T \Big) \Big\rangle \\
=& \Big\langle \Big(\frac{2}{q} \cdot (Powerof2(\mathbf{c}_1 \otimes \mathbf{c}_2)) + \mathbf{c}_\delta \Big), \\
& BitDecomp\Big((1, \mathbf{e}_{i-1})^T \otimes (1, \mathbf{e}_{i-1})^T \Big) \Big\rangle
\end{aligned}$$

Observe that $\mathbf{c}^*_{mult} = \frac{2}{q} \cdot \mathbf{c}_{mult} = \frac{2}{q} \cdot \mathbf{c}_1 \otimes \mathbf{c}_2$ since $\mathbf{c}_{mult} = 2 \cdot \mathbf{c}_1 \otimes \mathbf{c}_2$, therefore:

$$\begin{aligned}
\langle \mathbf{c}^*_{mult}, sk_{mult} \rangle =& \Big\langle \Big(\frac{2}{q} \cdot \big(Powerof2(\mathbf{c}_1 \otimes \mathbf{c}_2)\big) \Big), \\
& BitDecomp\Big((1, \mathbf{e}_{i-1})^T \otimes (1, \mathbf{e}_{i-1})^T \Big) \Big\rangle \\
=& \frac{2}{q} \left\lfloor \frac{q}{2} \right\rfloor^2 \cdot \underbrace{m_1 m_2}_{Eq.1} + \frac{2}{q} \left\lfloor \frac{q}{2} \right\rfloor \cdot Eq.2 + \frac{2}{q} q Eq.3 + \frac{2}{q} \cdot Eq.4 + 2 \cdot Eq.5 \\
=& \left\lfloor \frac{q}{2} \right\rfloor \cdot m_1 m_2 + error^{Mult}\ (mod\ q)
\end{aligned}$$

For further convenience, we denote $Eq.2 = \Big((m_1 \cdot small_2 + m_2 \cdot small_1) \Big)$, $Eq.3 = (small_1 k_2 + small_2 k_1)$, $Eq.4 = (small_1 small_2)$ and $Eq.5 = qk_1k_2 + \left\lfloor \frac{q}{2} \right\rfloor (m_1k_2 + m_2k_1)$. Hence, we easily observe that $error^{Mult} := \frac{2}{q} \cdot \left\lfloor \frac{q}{2} \right\rfloor \cdot Eq.2 + \frac{2}{q} q \cdot Eq.3 + \frac{2}{q} \cdot Eq.4 + 2 \cdot Eq.5$.

We can get the result of $||error^{Mult}|| \leq 2E + 2 \cdot O(m \log\ q)E + E^2 \leq \frac{q}{4}$ by Lemmas 6 and 8.

Lemma 10. *By definition:*

$$\begin{aligned}
\Delta :=& \Big\langle \mathbf{c}_\delta, \hat{sk}_{i-1} \Big\rangle \\
=& \Big\langle \underbrace{\Big(\lfloor \frac{2}{q} \cdot (Powerof2(\mathbf{c}_1 \otimes \mathbf{c}_2))\rceil - \frac{2}{q} \cdot (Powerof2(\mathbf{c}_1 \otimes \mathbf{c}_2)) \Big)}_{\mathbf{c}_\delta}, \hat{sk}_{i-1} \Big\rangle
\end{aligned}$$

Now, since $||\mathbf{c}_\delta||_\infty \leq \frac{1}{2}$ *and since* $\hat{sk}_{i-1} \in \{0,1\}^{\left((m+1)\lceil log\ q\rceil\right)^2}$*, then* $||\hat{sk}_{i-1}||_1 \leq \big((m+1)\lceil log\ q\rceil\big)^2$*. It follows that* $|\Delta| \leq ||\mathbf{c}_\delta|| \cdot ||\hat{sk}_{i-1}|| \leq \frac{1}{2} \cdot \big((m+1)\lceil log\ q\rceil\big)^2 = O(m^2 log^2 q)$.

Proof. Because $\left\langle \hat{\mathbf{c}}_{mult}, \hat{sk}_{i-1} \right\rangle =: \left\langle \lfloor \frac{2}{q} \cdot (Powerof2(\mathbf{c}_1 \otimes \mathbf{c}_2)) \rceil, \hat{sk}_{i-1} \right\rangle$, therefore:

$$\left\langle \hat{\mathbf{c}}_{mult}, \hat{sk}_{i-1} \right\rangle - \Delta = \left\langle \frac{2}{q} \cdot (Powerof2(\mathbf{c}_1 \otimes \mathbf{c}_2)), \hat{sk}_{i-1} \right\rangle$$
$$= \frac{2}{q} <\mathbf{c}_1, (1, \mathbf{e}_1)^T > \cdot <\mathbf{c}_2, (1, \mathbf{e}_2)^T >$$

By Lemmas 4, 6 and 9, putting them together, the bound of multiplication noise is $|| \lfloor error^{mult} \rceil || + || <\mathbf{c}_{mult}, \mathbf{x}> || \leq ||\Delta|| + ||error^{mult}|| = O((m \lceil log\ q \rceil)^2) + 2E + 2 \cdot O(m \log\ q)E + E^2 \leq \frac{q}{4}$.

Theorem 1. *The decryption works correctly as long as*

$$||error|| = max\{2E + O((m\lceil \log q \rceil)^2) \cdot B,$$
$$O((m\lceil \log q \rceil)^2) + 2E + 2 \cdot O(m \log q)E + E^2\} \leq \frac{q}{4}$$

Proof. The proof of Theorem 1 is deferred to Lemmas 7 and 9. We omit further details here.

Theorem 2. *If the scheme vFHE with parameters $n, q, |\chi| \leq B$, L, then we say the scheme vFHE is L-homomorphic.*

Proof. Set the L is the circuit depth, then let E_i be a bound on the noise in the ciphertext after the evaluation of i-th ($i \in [L]$) level of gates. Firstly, assume that $E_0 := (r \cdot \omega(\sqrt{log\ m}) + \sqrt{m}/2) \cdot B_\chi$, it hold that $E_{i+1} = (r \cdot \omega(\sqrt{log\ m}) + \sqrt{m}/2) \cdot E_i$. Then, we get $E_L = (r \cdot \omega(\sqrt{log\ m}) + \sqrt{m}/2)^{L+O(1)} \cdot B_\chi$. Lastly, if $E_L < \lfloor q/2 \rfloor / 2$ by Lemma 6, the scheme can decrypted successfully. □

3.4 Security Analysis

We now sketch the security proof.

Theorem 3. *The above system is IND-CPA-secure and anonymous, assuming that LWE is hard.*

Proof. The proof contains three steps:

- Firstly, we argue that the distribution of the syndrome $\mathbf{u} = \mathbf{A}\mathbf{e}$ is statistically close to uniform over $\mathbb{Z}_q^n$ follows directly from Lemma 2 and the public key $\mathbf{P}_0 := [\mathbf{u}_0, -\mathbf{A}]$ is computationally indistinguishable from uniform distribution based on Lemma 5.
- Secondly, we argue that the evaluate key $\mathbf{P}_{sk_0:sk_1}, \cdots, \mathbf{P}_{sk_{L-1}:sk_L}$, we replace all $\mathbf{P}_{sk_{i-1}:sk_i}$, $i \in [L]$ with uniform distribution in descending order (one by one).
- Finally, we can use the leftover hash lemma to replace the ciphertext $\mathbf{c}$ with a uniformly random value $\mathbf{c}'$, which are indistinguishable from uniform assuming the hardness of $LWE_{n,m,q,\chi}$. In this case, the challenge ciphertext is statistically independent of the encrypted message.

This concludes the proof of the theorem. □

4 Conclusion

In Table 1, we provide a comparison between our scheme and the FHE schemes [2,17], where all of the schemes are adaptive indistinguishable chosen plaintext security and can be proved secure under the LWE assumption.

In this work, we revisited Brakerski's key-Switching approach from LWE-based FHE cryptosystems and constructed a Brakerski style of FHE scheme based on dual LWE assumption. Besides, we also conducted a theoretical comparison of Brakerski [2] scheme and our scheme.

Table 1. Comparison four scheme

Scheme	$\|pk\|$	$\|sk\|$	$\|evk\|$	$\|bit\|$	$\|Ct\|$	Assumption
[2]	$O(mnlog\ q)$	$O(nlog\ q)$	$O(n^2 log\ q)$	1	$O(n \cdot log\ q)$	LWE
[17]	$O(mnlog\ q)$	$O(mlog\ q)$	$O(m^2 log^2\ q)$	1	$O(m \cdot log\ q)$	Dual-Ferr-LWE
vFHE	$O(mnlog\ q)$	$O(mlog\ q)$	$O(m^2 log^2\ q)$	1	$O(m \cdot log\ q)$	Dual-LWE

Acknowledgements. We would like to thank all anonymous reviewers for their helpful advice and comments. This work is supported by the National Natural Science Foundation of China (Grant No. 61472097) and Fujian Provincial Key Laboratory of Network Security and Cryptology Research Fund (Fujian Normal University) (No. 15003).

References

1. Agrawal, S., Boneh, D., Boyen, X.: Efficient lattice (H)IBE in the standard model. In: Gilbert, H. (ed.) EUROCRYPT 2010. LNCS, vol. 6110, pp. 553–572. Springer, Heidelberg (2010). doi:10.1007/978-3-642-13190-5_28
2. Brakerski, Z.: Fully homomorphic encryption without modulus switching from classical GapSVP. In: Safavi-Naini, R., Canetti, R. (eds.) CRYPTO 2012. LNCS, vol. 7417, pp. 868–886. Springer, Heidelberg (2012). doi:10.1007/978-3-642-32009-5_50
3. Brakerski, Z., Gentry, C., Halevi, S.: Packed ciphertexts in LWE-based homomorphic encryption. In: Kurosawa, K., Hanaoka, G. (eds.) PKC 2013. LNCS, vol. 7778, pp. 1–13. Springer, Heidelberg (2013). doi:10.1007/978-3-642-36362-7_1
4. Brakerski, Z., Gentry, C., Vaikuntanathan, V.: (Leveled) fully homomorphic encryption without bootstrapping. In Proceedings of the 3rd Innovations in Theoretical Computer Science Conference, pp. 309–325, ACM (2012)
5. Brakerski, Z., Vaikuntanathan, V.: Efficient fully homomorphic encryption from (standard) LWE. In: 2011 IEEE 52nd Annual Symposium on Foundations of Computer Science, pp. 97–106. IEEE (2011)
6. Brakerski, Z., Vaikuntanathan, V.: Fully homomorphic encryption from ring-LWE and security for key dependent messages. In: Rogaway, P. (ed.) CRYPTO 2011. LNCS, vol. 6841, pp. 505–524. Springer, Heidelberg (2011). doi:10.1007/978-3-642-22792-9_29

7. Brakerski, Z., Vaikuntanathan, V.: Lattice-based the as secure as PKE. In: Proceedings of the 5th Conference on Innovations in Theoretical Computer Science, pp. 1–12 (2014)
8. Fu, Z., Ren, K., Shu, J., Sun, X., Huang, F.: Enabling personalized search over encrypted outsourced data with efficiency improvement. IEEE Trans. Parallel Distrib. Syst. **27**(9), 2546–2559 (2016)
9. Gentry, C., et al.: Fully homomorphic encryption using ideal lattices. STOC **9**, 169–178 (2009)
10. Gentry, C., Halevi, S., Smart, N.P.: Homomorphic evaluation of the AES circuit. In: Safavi-Naini, R., Canetti, R. (eds.) CRYPTO 2012. LNCS, vol. 7417, pp. 850–867. Springer, Heidelberg (2012). doi:10.1007/978-3-642-32009-5_49
11. Gentry, C., Peikert, C., Vaikuntanathan, V.: Trapdoors for hard lattices and new cryptographic constructions. In: Proceedings of the Fortieth Annual ACM Symposium on Theory of Computing, pp. 197–206. ACM (2008)
12. Gentry, C., Sahai, A., Waters, B.: Homomorphic encryption from learning with errors: conceptually-simpler, asymptotically-faster, attribute-based. In: Canetti, R., Garay, J.A. (eds.) CRYPTO 2013. LNCS, vol. 8042, pp. 75–92. Springer, Heidelberg (2013). doi:10.1007/978-3-642-40041-4_5
13. Halevi, S., Shoup, V.: Algorithms in HElib. In: Garay, J.A., Gennaro, R. (eds.) CRYPTO 2014. LNCS, vol. 8616, pp. 554–571. Springer, Heidelberg (2014). doi:10.1007/978-3-662-44371-2_31
14. Halevi, S., Shoup, V.: Bootstrapping for `HElib`. In: Oswald, E., Fischlin, M. (eds.) EUROCRYPT 2015. LNCS, vol. 9056, pp. 641–670. Springer, Heidelberg (2015). doi:10.1007/978-3-662-46800-5_25
15. Hiromasa, R., Abe, M., Okamoto, T.: Packing messages and optimizing bootstrapping in GSW-FHE. In: Katz, J. (ed.) PKC 2015. LNCS, vol. 9020, pp. 699–715. Springer, Heidelberg (2015). doi:10.1007/978-3-662-46447-2_31
16. Li, Z., Galbraith, S.D., Ma, C.: Preventing adaptive key recovery attacks on the GSW levelled homomorphic encryption scheme. In: Proceedings of the Provable Security - 10th International Conference, ProvSec 2016, Nanjing, China, 10–11 November 2016, pp. 373–383 (2016)
17. Li, Z., Ma, C., Du, G., Ouyang, W.: Dual LWE-based fully homomorphic encryption with errorless key switching. In: IEEE ICPADS 2016, pp. 1169–1174 (2016)
18. Li, Z., Ma, C., Morais, E., Du, G.: Multi-bit leveled homomorphic encryption via mathsf dual.LWE-based. In: Proceedings Inscrypt 2016, Revised Selected Papers, Beijing, China, 4–6 November 2016, pp. 221–242 (2016)
19. Li, Z., Ma, C., Wang, D.: Leakage resilient leveled the on multiple bit message. IEEE Trans. Big Data (2017)
20. Rivest, R.L., Adleman, L., Dertouzos, M.L.: On data banks and privacy homomorphisms. Found. Secure Comput. **4**(11), 169–180 (1978)
21. Smart, N.P., Vercauteren, F.: Fully homomorphic encryption with relatively small key and ciphertext sizes. In: Nguyen, P.Q., Pointcheval, D. (eds.) PKC 2010. LNCS, vol. 6056, pp. 420–443. Springer, Heidelberg (2010). doi:10.1007/978-3-642-13013-7_25
22. Stehlé, D., Steinfeld, R.: Faster fully homomorphic encryption. In: Abe, M. (ed.) ASIACRYPT 2010. LNCS, vol. 6477, pp. 377–394. Springer, Heidelberg (2010). doi:10.1007/978-3-642-17373-8_22
23. Wang, D., He, D., Wang, P., Chu, C.-H.: Anonymous two-factor authentication in distributed systems: certain goals are beyond attainment. IEEE Trans. Dependable Secure Comput. **12**(4), 428–442 (2015)

24. Wang, D., Wang, N., Wang, P., Qing, S.: Preserving privacy for free: efficient and provably secure two-factor authentication scheme with user anonymity. Inf. Sci. **321**, 162–178 (2015)
25. Xia, Z., Wang, X., Sun, X., Wang, Q.: A secure and dynamic multi-keyword ranked search scheme over encrypted cloud data. IEEE Trans. Parallel Distrib. Syst. **27**(2), 340–352 (2016)
26. Xia, Z., Wang, X., Zhang, L., Qin, Z., Sun, X., Ren, K.: A privacy-preserving and copy-deterrence content-based image retrieval scheme in cloud computing. IEEE Trans. Inf. Forensics Secur. **1**(11), 2594–2608 (2016)

Privacy-Preserving Medical Information Systems Using Multi-authority Content-Based Encryption in Cloud

Rui Guo[1,2], Xiong Li[3(✉)], and Dong Zheng[1]

[1] National Engineering Laboratory for Wireless Security, Xi'an University of Posts and Telecommunications, Xi'an 710121, China
{guorui,zhengdong}@xupt.edu.cn

[2] State Key Laboratory of Networking and Switching Technology, Beijing University of Posts and Telecommunications, Beijing 100876, China

[3] School of Computer Science and Engineering, Hunan University of Science and Technology, Xiangtan 411201, China
lixiongzhq@163.com

Abstract. In the Medical Information Systems (MIS), the patient outsources his e-health records, a dramatically huge amount of health data, to a third party like cloud service provider. The Internet providing host-to-host communication using TCP/IP network topology has not satisfied the growing demands of data processing in MIS. Based on the content-to-consumer paradigm, content-centric networking architecture was proposed for simple easy-to-manage caching features to users. In this paper, we proposed a privacy-preserving e-health records scheme that protects name and content simultaneously. Our proposal has multi-authority without a trusted single or central authority to distribute secret keys, which avoids the key escrow problem and meets the distributed features of MIS. As we know, this scheme is the first multi-authority content-based encryption (MA-CBE). Furthermore, this MA-CBE resists up to (N-1) corrupted authorities collusion attack, and the security is proven to be semantically secure based on the standard decisional bilinear Diffie-Hellman assumption. Our comparison analysis reports that the proposal gives a better performance than other related schemes.

Keywords: Medical Information Systems · Cloud computing · Multi-authority · Content-centric network · Privacy-preserving

1 Introduction

Medical Information Systems (MIS) promote the traditional medical and healthcare services by information and communication technology. In MIS, the patient is allowed to create, manage, control, and share his e-health records with family, friends, doctors, healthcare providers and other authorized users. With the development of cloud computing, the patient's e-health records, including HD

X. Sun et al. (Eds.): ICCCS 2017, Part II, LNCS 10603, pp. 268–279, 2017.
https://doi.org/10.1007/978-3-319-68542-7_22

color Doppler Ultrasound, Electrocardiogram and other supplementary, are outsourced to be stored at the third parties like medical cloud service providers, such as Microsoft Health Vault [1] and Google Health [2]. After that, the related specialists all over the world are able to achieve this material and make an accurate treatment, which facilitates the patient and saves the medical resources.

Due to the rising demand for medical services, a huge amount of data is transmitted on Internet that provides host-to-host communication using IP addresses. Cisco predicts the global IP traffic will grow with a compound annual growth rate of 23%, the global mobile data traffic will increase nearly 10-fold from 2014 to 2019 [3]. With such fast data proliferation, researchers have paid more attention to a new Internet architecture, called Content-Centric Networking (CCN) [4], to distribute and store the content efficiently instead of host-centric.

In the content-centric architectures of MIS, medical content is searched using names (such as keywords of e-health records) and cached on demand to be distributed. Users can request medical content according to their names rather than their locations, and routers could respond these requests directly instead of forwarding to the medical content servers. Hence, the CCN applied in cloud offers much advantage for content distribution service, including reducing download delay, conserving network resources, balancing loud traffic and so on, which fits the speciality of MIS [5].

However, a promising network CCN is also facing many challenges at present [6–10]. The content name is semantically tied to user preferences, so that the name in plaintext may leak the sensitive information to malicious CCN nodes which could easily profile the interests and privacy of user. Even if the name is protected, by using of the content returned to the user, curious CCN nodes can deduce their private information as well [11]. Therefore, all names and contents related to user should be protected in order to preserve privacy in CCN.

There have been several research works contributed to the design of protecting name and content [12–17]. In 2013, ref filters, Chaabane et al. [12] solve the problem of name privacy firstly, but they do not analysis the security of the proposal and the bloom filters may return false positive. Fotiou et al. [13] propose a lookup using homomorphic encryption to preserve the privacy, and model the problem as Private Information Retrieved. Because of the homomorphic operation, this scheme is infeasible for large scale environment due to the high computational complexity. At the same time, Mannes et al. [14] proposed a proxy-encryption scheme for addressing the problem of content privacy, but ignores the name privacy. The scheme in [15] protects the name by an anti-censorship mechanism based on Huffman coding that shows a better performance. In order to protect name and content simultaneously, Tsudik et al. [16] adopts the method of anonymous communication to prevent monitoring activities. However, this solution ties requests to the end user and are unusable to serve new quest, losing the benefits from in-network caching. In 2016, Wang and Mu [17] give a new paradigm for content based encryption and apply this scheme to construct a secure content delivery protocol in CCN, but this work is just one-to-one encryption model that is unsuitable for distributed system.

In this paper, considering the multi-authority in cloud storage [18] (such as in Fig. 1), we propose a content-based encryption for MIS in cloud. There are N authorities to generate the private key all together, which avoids the key escrow problem in single or central authority system. We also share a pseudorandom function seed in every two authorities and keep it secretly, add authority's private key into user's secret key to resist up to $(N-1)$ corrupted authorities attack. As we know, our proposal is the first multi-authority content-based encryption (MA-CBE), and it can protect the name and content of e-health records simultaneously. Under the Decisional Bilinear Diffie-Hellman (DBDH) assumption, we also prove this scheme is semantic security in the random oracle model. Furthermore, after comparing with related schemes, we find that our protocol offers a better performance.

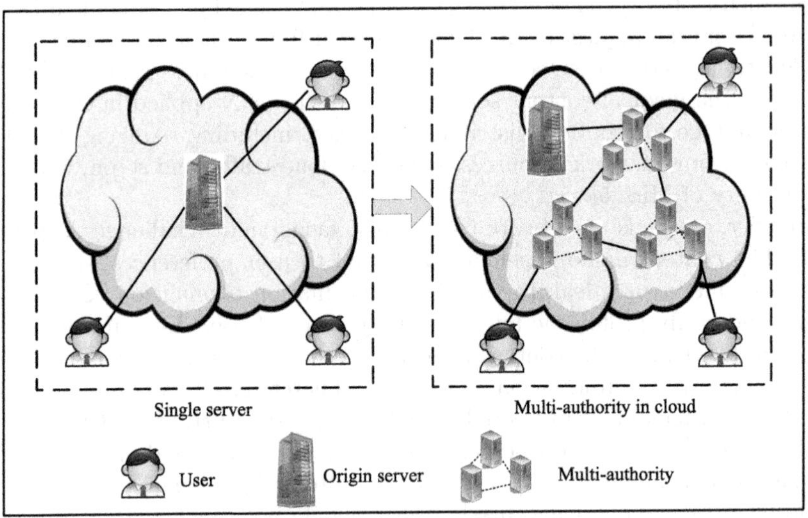

Fig. 1. Multi-authority in cloud storage

The rest of the paper is organized as follows. Section 2 provides a brief overview of bilinear maps, related complexity assumption and some definitions including formal definition of MA-CBE, and security model. In Sect. 3, we present a MA-CBE protocol for MIS. In Sect. 4, we analyze the security of proposal and compare the performance with related schemes. We conclude the paper in Sect. 5.

2 Preliminaries

2.1 Bilinear Maps

Let (G, G_T) be two multiplicative cyclic groups of prime order p. A bilinear map $\hat{e}: G \times G \rightarrow G_T$ with generator g of G satisfies the following properties:

(a) *Bilinearity*: for all $g, h \in G$, $a, b \in Z_p$, we have $\hat{e}(g^a, h^b) = \hat{e}(g, h)^{ab}$.
(b) *Non-Degeneracy*: $\hat{e}(g, g) \neq 1 \in G_T$.
(c) *Computability*: there is efficient algorithm to compute $\hat{e}(g, h)$, where $g, h \in G$.

2.2 Complexity Assumption

The security of this protocol is based on the decisional bilinear Diffie-Hellman (DBDH) problem, which is defined as follows.

Let g be a generator of G, a, b, c, z are chosen at random in Z_p. Given $A = g^a, B = g^b, C = g^c$, decide whether $\hat{e}(g, g)^z = \hat{e}(g, g)^{abc}$.

We define that a probabilistic polynomial-time algorithm $\mathcal{B}$ with an output $b' \in \{0, 1\}$ has advantage ε in solving the DBDH problem if

$$Adv_{\mathcal{B}}^{DBDH} = \mid \Pr[\mathcal{B}(A, B, C, \hat{e}(g, g)^{abc}) = 1] - \Pr[\mathcal{B}(A, B, C, \hat{e}(g, g)^z) = 1] \mid \geq \varepsilon$$

We say that the DBDH assumption holds if no polynomial-time adversary has non-negligible advantage in solving the DBDH problem.

2.3 Definitions

Definition 1. A multi-authority content-based encryption (MA-CBE) contains the following five algorithms.

Setup $(1^\lambda) \rightarrow (params)$: This algorithm takes a security parameter 1^λ as input and generates the system public parameter $params$.

Authority Setup $(1^\lambda) \rightarrow (SK_k, PK_k)$: This algorithm is run by authority. Every authority A_k generates his secret key SK_k and public key PK_k for $k \in \{1, 2, \cdots, N\}$. There are N authorities in this system.

KeyGen $(SK_k, \mathsf{name}) \rightarrow SK_U$: This algorithm is run by each authority A_k and user U to generate user's secret key SK_U. It takes the secret key SK_k of authority A_k, a unique identifier name of content $C \in G_T$ as input, and outputs user's secret key SK_U.

Encryption $(PK_k, C) \rightarrow CT$: This algorithm takes a content C, public key PK_k of each authority A_k as inputs, returns the ciphertext CT. Each content has a unique name.

Decryption $(SK_U, CT) \rightarrow C$: This algorithm takes user's secret key SK_U and the ciphertext CT as input, returns the content C.

According to this model, we can construct the MA-CBE for preserving the privacy in MIS.

Definition 2. Let $\mathcal{A}$ be an adversary and Π be a CBE scheme with multi-authority. $\mathcal{A}$ interacts with a challenger $\mathcal{C}$ in the following game.

Setup: Adversary $\mathcal{A}$ submits a list of corrupted authorities L_A to algorithm $\mathcal{B}$. Challenger $\mathcal{C}$ runs the algorithm **Setup** and returns the system parameters $params$ to the adversary $\mathcal{A}$.

Authority Setup: For the corrupted authorities, the challenger $\mathcal{C}$ sends the public and secret key (PK_k, SK_k) to adversary $\mathcal{A}$. For the honest authority, the challenger $\mathcal{C}$ sends his public key PK_k to adversary $\mathcal{A}$.

Phase 1: The adversary $\mathcal{A}$ queries **KeyGen** to generate a private decryption key SK_U corresponding to name, sends SK_U to the adversary $\mathcal{A}$.

Challenge: The adversary $\mathcal{A}$ submits two equal length content C_0 and C_1, the challenger flips a random coin $\beta \in \{0,1\}$ and runs the algorithm **Encryption** to send ciphertext CT^* to adversary $\mathcal{A}$.

Phase 2: $\mathcal{A}$ issues a sequence of queries in *Phase 1*.

Guess: Adversary $\mathcal{A}$ outputs his guess β' on β.

The advantage of an adversary $\mathcal{A}$ in this game is defined as

$$Adv(\mathcal{A}) = \mid \Pr[\beta' = \beta] - \frac{1}{2} \mid .$$

Definition 3. A MA-CBE scheme is (q, ε)-secure in the above model if no probabilistic polynomial-time adversary $\mathcal{A}$ making q secret key queries has advantage at least

$$Adv_{\mathcal{A}}^{MA-CBE} = \mid \Pr[\beta' = \beta] - \frac{1}{2} \mid .$$

3 Our Construction

In this section, we give the multi-authority MIS model and then describe the detailed construction of our scheme.

3.1 MIS Model

In this MIS model, there are four parties: MIS Server, N Authorities, Patient and Doctor. MIS Server is a cloud storage server, which is responsible for storing the encrypted e-health records. N Authorities are various different organizations, such as hospital, center of medical insurance and so on, which are responsible for exchanging the patient's information. Patient can create, manage and control his e-health records, and Doctor is allowed to access this information. All the patient's data in this system might be considered as content. Different contents is labeled with different names. The MIS model is illustrated in Fig. 2.

3.2 The Proposed Scheme

In this subsection, we will present our detailed MA-CBE scheme as follows.

Setup: Given the security parameter 1^λ, MIS Server outputs a bilinear map $\hat{e} : G \times G \rightarrow G_T$, where G and G_T are two multiplicative cyclic groups with prime order p, and g is the generator of group G. It chooses a random number $\alpha \in Z_p^*$ and computes $h = g^\alpha \in G$, and a collision-resistant hash function $H : \{0,1\}^* \rightarrow Z_p^*$. Suppose that there are N authorities in MIS, named $A_1, A_2, \cdots, A_N$. The public parameters are $params = <\hat{e}, p, g, h, G, G_T>$.

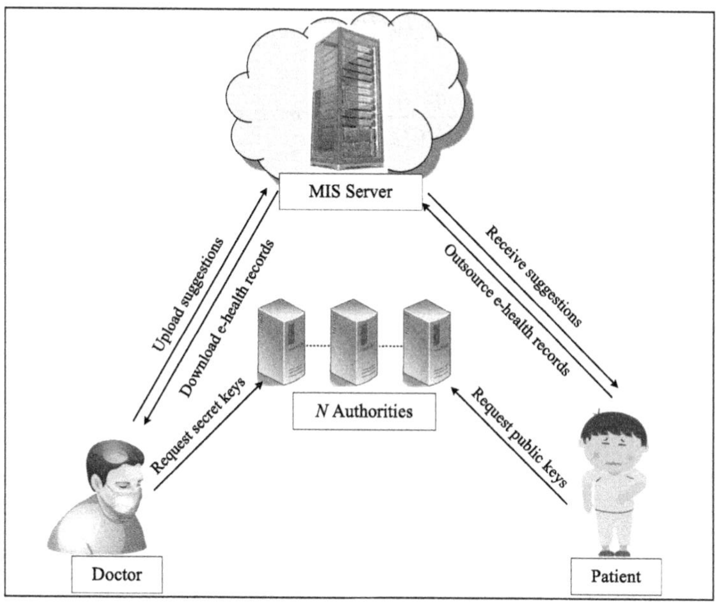

Fig. 2. MIS model

Authority Setup: For each authority A_k, it chooses $\alpha_k \in Z_p^*$ at random, computes $Y_k = \hat{e}(g, g)^{\alpha_k}$. For every user U_i, where $i \in \{1, 2, \cdots, n\}$, chooses a random number $t_{ki} \in Z_p^*$ and computes $T_{ki} = g^{t_{ki}}$. A_k also chooses $x_k \in Z_p^*$ at random and computes $y_k = h^{x_k}$. Two authorities A_k and A_j pick $s_{kj} \in Z_p^*$ randomly and share it between them as a secret pseudorandom function (PRF) seed through a 2-party key exchange channel, it obviously that $s_{kj} = s_{jk}$. They define a PRF as

$$PRF_{kj}(u) = h^{\frac{x_k x_j}{(s_{kj}+u)}},$$

where $u = H(\mathsf{name})$ for each content $C \in G_T$ with its unique identifier $\mathsf{name} \in \{0, 1\}^*$, which can only be computed by A_k and A_j. Authority A_k outputs his public key as

$$PK_k = <Y_k, y_k, \{T_{ki}\}_{i \in \{1,2,\cdots,n\}}>,$$

and his private key as

$$SK_k = <\alpha_k, x_k, \{s_{kj}\}_{j \in \{1,2,\cdots,N\} \setminus \{k\}}, \{t_{ki}\}_{i \in \{1,2,\cdots,n\}}>.$$

KeyGen: Each authority A_k chooses a random number $r_k \in Z_p^*$, computes $S_{ki} = h^{\frac{r_k}{t_{ki}}}$. User U_i interacts with each authority A_k in $N - 1$ times to finish the anonymous key issuing introduced in [19], and computes

$$D_{kj} = g^{\alpha_k} \cdot h^{r_k} \cdot PRF_{kj}(u) \ \ for \ \ k > j,$$

and

$$D_{kj} = \frac{g^{\alpha_k} \cdot h^{r_k}}{PRF_{kj}(u)} \ \ for \ \ k < j.$$

Finally, user U_i can computes

$$D_{U_i} = \prod_{(k,j)\in\{1,2,\cdots,N\}\times(\{1,2,\cdots,N\}\setminus\{k\})} D_{kj} = g^{\sum_{k\in\{1,2,\cdots,N\}}(N-1)\alpha_k} . h^{\sum_{k\in\{1,2,\cdots,N\}}(N-1)r_k}.$$

Therefore, the secret key of U_i is

$$SK_{U_i} = <D_{U_i}, \{S_{ki}\}_{k\in\{1,2,\cdots,N\}}>.$$

Encryption: To encrypt the content C with unique identifier name $\in \{0,1\}^*$, such as the patient's e-health records. The sender picks $s \in Z_p^*$ at random, and computes

$$CT_1 = C \cdot (\prod_{k\in\{1,2,\cdots,N\}} Y_k)^s, CT_2 = g^s, CT_3 = \{(T_{ki})^s\}_{k\in\{1,2,\cdots,N\}}.$$

The ciphertext is constructed as $CT = <CT_1, CT_2, CT_3>$ and transmitted to users.

Decryption: In order to decrypt the ciphertext CT, the user, such as the Doctor, computes the following $<V, W>$ at first,

$$\begin{aligned} V &= \prod_{k\in\{1,2,\cdots,N\}} \hat{e}(CT_3, S_{ki}) \\ &= \prod_{k\in\{1,2,\cdots,N\}} \hat{e}((T_{ki})^s, h^{\frac{r_k}{t_{ki}}}) \\ &= \prod_{k\in\{1,2,\cdots,N\}} \hat{e}(g^{t_{ki}\cdot s}, h^{\frac{r_k}{t_{ki}}}) \\ &= \prod_{k\in\{1,2,\cdots,N\}} \hat{e}(g,h)^{s\cdot r_k} \\ &= \hat{e}(g,h)^{s\cdot\sum_{k\in\{1,2,\cdots,N\}} r_k}, \end{aligned}$$

and

$$\begin{aligned} W &= \hat{e}(D_{U_i}, CT_2) \\ &= \hat{e}(\prod_{(k,j)\in\{1,2,\cdots,N\}\times(\{1,2,\cdots,N\}\setminus\{k\})} D_{kj}, g^s) \\ &= \hat{e}(g^{\sum_{k\in\{1,2,\cdots,N\}}(N-1)\alpha_k} \cdot h^{\sum_{k\in\{1,2,\cdots,N\}}(N-1)r_k}, g^s) \\ &= \hat{e}(g^{\sum_{k\in\{1,2,\cdots,N\}}(N-1)\alpha_k}, g^s) \cdot \hat{e}(h^{\sum_{k\in\{1,2,\cdots,N\}}(N-1)r_k}, g^s) \\ &= \hat{e}(g,g)^{s\cdot\sum_{k\in\{1,2,\cdots,N\}}(N-1)\alpha_k} \cdot \hat{e}(g,h)^{s\cdot\sum_{k\in\{1,2,\cdots,N\}}(N-1)r_k}. \end{aligned}$$

Then, the user obtain the content as $C = CT_1 \cdot \frac{V}{W^{\frac{1}{N-1}}}$.

Correctness: Consistency of this scheme is clear since that

$$\begin{aligned} CT_1 \cdot \frac{V}{W^{\frac{1}{N-1}}} &= C \cdot (\prod_{k\in\{1,2,\cdots,N\}} Y_k)^s \\ &\cdot \frac{\hat{e}(g,h)^{s\cdot\sum_{k\in\{1,2,\cdots,N\}} r_k}}{(\hat{e}(g,g)^{s\cdot\sum_{k\in\{1,2,\cdots,N\}}(N-1)\alpha_k} \cdot \hat{e}(g,h)^{s\cdot\sum_{k\in\{1,2,\cdots,N\}}(N-1)r_k})^{\frac{1}{N-1}}} \\ &= C \cdot (\prod_{k\in\{1,2,\cdots,N\}} \hat{e}(g,g)^{\alpha_k})^s \cdot \frac{1}{\hat{e}(g,g)^{s\cdot\sum_{k\in\{1,2,\cdots,N\}} \alpha_k}} \\ &= C \cdot \hat{e}(g,g)^{s\cdot\sum_{k\in\{1,2,\cdots,N\}} \alpha_k} \cdot \frac{1}{\hat{e}(g,g)^{s\cdot\sum_{k\in\{1,2,\cdots,N\}} \alpha_k}} \\ &= C. \end{aligned}$$

4 Security Analysis and Comparisons

4.1 Security Analysis

Collusion resistance: In this scheme, authorities A_k and A_j share a PRF seed s_{kj} and keep it secretly between them. Therefore, one PRF seed is still unknown to malicious authority at least, even if there is up to $(N-2)$ corrupted authorities. In the procession of **KeyGen**, authority's private key α_k is inserted into user's secret key D_{U_i}. If only one authority is honest, the other malicious authorities still get nothing about D_{U_i}. It means that this scheme can resist up to $(N-1)$ corrupted authorities attack. In order to preserve the privacy of patient and doctor in MIS in cloud computing environment, the secret key is generated according to the anonymous key issuing protocol, the name and content are protected simultaneously, and thus avoiding the leakage of privacy.

Theorem 1. *Given H is a collision resistant hash function, our MA-CBE scheme is (p, ε) semantically secure assume that the ε'-DBDH assumption holds, where*

$$\varepsilon' \geq \frac{\varepsilon}{2} \cdot \prod_{k\in\{1,2,\cdots,N\}} (1 - \frac{n_k - 2}{(p-1)^2}).$$

Proof. Assume that a polynomial-time adversary $\mathcal{A}$ can break this scheme according to the security model in Sec.2 with advantage ε. We can then construct an algorithm $\mathcal{B}$ that will break the DBDH assumption with advantage $\frac{\varepsilon}{2} \cdot \prod_{k\in\{1,2,\cdots,N\}}(1 - \frac{n_k-2}{(p-1)^2})$, where n_k is the number of totally secret key from A_k.

Challenger $\mathcal{C}$ generates the bilinear group $<G, G_T>$ with prime order p and chooses a generator $g \in G$. It flips a coin δ. If $\delta = 0$, sends $<g^a, g^b, g^c, g^{abc},>$ to $\mathcal{B}$. Otherwise, sends $<g^a, g^b, g^c, g^z,>$ to $\mathcal{B}$, where $a, b, c, z \in Z_p^*$ at random.

Setup: Adversary $\mathcal{A}$ submits a list of corrupted authorities L_A to $\mathcal{B}$, where $|L_A| < N$, $\mathcal{B}$ chooses $\eta \in Z_p^*$ and sets $h = g^{a+\eta}$.

H-Query: $\mathcal{B}$ maintains a list L of a tuple $<\mathsf{name}_i, u_i>$. The list is initially empty. Upon receiving a hash query for name_i, $\mathcal{B}$ looks up the list L to find the hash value of name_i and returns u_i to $\mathcal{A}$. If name_i is not in the list L, $\mathcal{B}$ randomly chooses $u_i \in Z_p^*$ and adds a new tuple $<\mathsf{name}_i, u_i>$ to L and $\mathcal{B}$ returns u_i.

Authority Setup: $\mathcal{B}$ randomly chooses $A_k^* \in \{A_1, A_2, \cdots, A_N\} \backslash L_A$,

(a) For $A_k \in L_A$, $\mathcal{B}$ chooses $v_k, w_{ki} \in Z_p^*$ at random and computes $T_{ki} = g^{w_{ki}}$ for each user U_i. Then, $\mathcal{B}$ chooses a value $x_k \in Z_p^*$, a PRF seed $s_{kj} \in Z_p^*$ for corrupted authorities A_k and A_j, and computes $y_k = h^{x_k}$. $\mathcal{B}$ sends $<v_k, x_k, s_{kj}, w_{ki},>$ and $<Y_k, y_k, T_{ki}>$ to adversary $\mathcal{A}$, where $Y_k = \hat{e}(g,g)^{v_k}$.

(b) For $A_k \notin L_A$, $\mathcal{B}$ chooses $v_k, w_{ki} \in Z_p^*$ at random and computes $T_{ki} = g^{w_{ki}}$. Then, $\mathcal{B}$ chooses a value $x_k \in Z_p^*$ and computes $y_k = h^{x_k}$, $Y_k = \hat{e}(g,g)^{ab} \cdot \prod_{A_k \in L_A} \hat{e}(g,g)^{-v_k} \cdot \prod_{A_k \notin L_A, A_k \neq A_k^*} \hat{e}(g,g)^{-bv_k}$. For two honest authority A_k and A_j, $\mathcal{B}$ chooses a PRF seed $s_{kj} \in Z_p^*$ for them and sends $<Y_k, y_k, T_{ki}>$ to adversary $\mathcal{A}$.

Phase 1: $\mathcal{A}$ makes **KeyGen** queries for secret key as follows,

(a) For $A_k \in L_A$, $\mathcal{B}$ chooses u_i corresponding to w_{ki} from L and uses $<v_k, x_k, s_{kj}, w_{ki},>$ to compute secret key.
(b) For $A_k \notin L_A$, $\mathcal{B}$ chooses $r_k \in Z_p^*$ at random and computes $\{S_{ki} = h^{\frac{r_k}{w_{ki}}}\}$, secret key D_{kj} is computed by $\mathcal{B}$ in two different situations as follows:

(i) $A_k \neq A_k^*$: For $k > j$, sets $D_{kj} = (g^b)^{v_k} \cdot h^{r_k} \cdot PRF_{kj}(u_i)$. Otherwise, sets $D_{kj} = \frac{(g^b)^{v_k} \cdot h^{r_k}}{PRF_{kj}(u_i)}$.
(ii) $A_k = A_k^*$: For $k > j$, sets $D_{kj} = (g^b)^{-\eta} \cdot \prod_{A_k \in L_A} g^{-v_k} \cdot \prod_{A_k \notin L_A, A_k \neq A_k^*} (g^b)^{-v_k} \cdot h^{r_k} \cdot PRF_{kj}(u_i)$. Otherwise, sets $D_{kj} = \frac{(g^b)^{-\eta} \cdot \prod_{A_k \in L_A} g^{-v_k} \cdot \prod_{A_k \notin L_A, A_k \neq A_k^*} (g^b)^{-v_k} \cdot h^{r_k}}{PRF_{kj}(u_i)}$.

We claim that D_{kj} is correctly distributed. Here, we only describe the situation when $k > j$ since the situation $k < j$ is as simple as the situation when $k > j$.

$$\begin{aligned}
D_{kj} &= (g^b)^{-\eta} \cdot \prod_{A_k \in L_A} g^{-v_k} \cdot \prod_{A_k \notin L_A, A_k \neq A_k^*} (g^b)^{-v_k} \cdot h^{r_k} \cdot PRF_{kj}(u_i) \\
&= g^{-b\eta} \cdot (g^{a+\eta})^{r_k} \cdot g^{-(\sum_{A_k \in L_A} v_k + \sum_{A_k \notin L_A, A_k \neq A_k^*} bv_k)} \cdot PRF_{kj}(u_i) \\
&= (g^{a+\eta})^{-b} \cdot g^{ab} \cdot (g^{a+\eta})^{r_k} \cdot g^{-(\sum_{A_k \in L_A} v_k + \sum_{A_k \notin L_A, A_k \neq A_k^*} bv_k)} \cdot PRF_{kj}(u_i) \\
&= g^{ab} \cdot (g^a g^\eta)^{r_k - b} \cdot g^{-(\sum_{A_k \in L_A} v_k + \sum_{A_k \notin L_A, A_k \neq A_k^*} bv_k)} \cdot PRF_{kj}(u_i) \\
&= g^{ab - (\sum_{A_k \in L_A} v_k + \sum_{A_k \notin L_A, A_k \neq A_k^*} bv_k)} \cdot h^{r_k - b} \cdot PRF_{kj}(u_i).
\end{aligned}$$

Let $r'_k = r_k - b$, we have

$$D_{kj} = g^{ab-(\sum_{A_k \in L_A} v_k + \sum_{A_k \notin L_A, A_k \neq A_k^*} bv_k)} \cdot h^{r'_k} \cdot PRF_{kj}(u_i).$$

Challenge: Adversary $\mathcal{A}$ submits two equal-length content C_0 and C_1 with unique identifiers name_0^* and name_1^* respectively to the simulator $\mathcal{B}$. Then, $\mathcal{B}$ flips a random coin $\beta \in \{0,1\}$ and computes $CT_1^* = C_\beta \cdot Z$, $CT_2^* = g^c$, $CT_3^* = \{(T_{ki})^s\}_{k\in\{1,2,\cdots,N\}}$. $\mathcal{B}$ sends the challenge ciphertext $C_{T,\beta}^* = <CT_1^*, CT_2^*, CT_3^*>$ to the adversary $\mathcal{A}$. If $\delta = 0$, then $Z = g^{abc}$. Let $s = c$, we can compute $\prod_{k\in\{1,2,\cdots,N\}} Y_k^c = \prod_{A_k\in L_A} \hat{e}(g,g)^{cv_k} \cdot \prod_{A_k\notin L_A, A_k\neq A_k^*} \hat{e}(g,g)^{cbv_k} \cdot (\hat{e}(g,g)^{abc} \cdot \prod_{A_k\in L_A} \hat{e}(g,g)^{-cv_k} \cdot \prod_{A_k\notin L_A, A_k\neq A_k^*} \hat{e}(g,g)^{-cbv_k}) = \hat{e}(g,g)^{abc} = Z$. Therefore, $C_{T,\beta}^*$ is a valid ciphertext of content C.

Phase 2: $\mathcal{A}$ makes **KeyGen** queries, $\mathcal{B}$ responds as in *Phase 1*.

Guess: Finally, adversary $\mathcal{A}$ outputs his guess β'. If $\beta' = \beta$, $\mathcal{B}$ outputs his guess $\delta' = 0$ on δ. Otherwise, $\mathcal{B}$ outputs his guess $\delta' = 1$ on δ. Since the input of Z is a random number z when $\delta = 1$, adversary $\mathcal{A}$ gains nothing about β. Therefore, $\mathcal{A}$ can distinguish with no advantage, namely $\Pr[\beta' \neq \beta \mid \delta = 1] = \frac{1}{2}$, $\mathcal{B}$ outputs his guess $\delta' = 1$ when $\beta' = \beta$, thus we have $\Pr[\delta' = \delta \mid \delta = 1] = \frac{1}{2}$. If $\delta = 0$, then the advantage of adversary $\mathcal{A}$ outputs $\beta' = \beta$ is at least ε by definition. Hence, we have $\Pr[\beta' = \beta \mid \delta = 0] \geq \frac{1}{2} + \varepsilon$. When $\beta' = \beta$, $\mathcal{B}$ outputs his guess $\delta' = 0$, so we have $\Pr[\delta' = \delta \mid \delta = 0] \geq \frac{1}{2} + \varepsilon$.

Suppose that N_i is the number of situations that a valid secret key can be computed when adversary chooses i secret keys. Hence, the worst case when adversary possesses $n_k - 1$ secret keys out of total n_k secret keys that authority A_k monitors. Then, we can get the probability of succession is

$$\frac{1}{p-1}\left(\frac{N_2}{C_{p-1}^2} + \frac{N_3}{C_{p-1}^3} + \cdots + \frac{N_{n_k-1}}{C_{p-1}^{n_k-1}}\right) < \frac{1}{p-1} \cdot \frac{N_2(n_k-2)}{C_{p-1}^2} < \frac{n_k-2}{(p-1)^2}.$$

Therefore, $\mathcal{B}$'s advantage to break DBDH assumption is

$$\prod_{k\in\{1,2,\cdots,N\}} \left(\frac{n_k-2}{(p-1)^2}\right) \mid \frac{1}{2}\Pr[\delta' = \delta \mid \delta = 0] + \frac{1}{2}\Pr[\delta' = \delta \mid \delta = 1] \mid \geq \frac{\varepsilon}{2} \cdot \prod_{k\in\{1,2,\cdots,N\}} \left(1 - \frac{n_k-2}{(p-1)^2}\right).$$

4.2 Comparisons

In this subsection, we discuss some crucial features which will affect the practicability of this scheme. Comparing with other related schemes, from Tables 1 and 2, we can see that our proposal is a multi-authority content-based encryption without central authority who is responsible for issuing public and private keys to users and thus is able to decrypt all ciphertext in the system. This scheme can resist up to $(N-1)$ malicious authorities collusion. Moreover, the protocol achieves a high privacy in protecting both name and content, avoiding leakage of the patient and doctor's preferences. Meanwhile, it adopts the mode of many-to-many in procession of encrypting, which fits the distributed characteristic of

Table 1. Comparing with other related schemes

Scheme	Multi-authority	Collusion resistance	Privacy-preserving	Encryption model
[12]	No	Not against collusion	No	One-to-many
[13]	No	Not against collusion	Yes	One-to-many
[15]	No	Not against collusion	No	One-to-many
[17]	No	N/A	Yes	One-to-one
Ours	Yes	Against collusion	Yes	Many-to-many

Table 2. Comparison on computing and communication cost

Component	[17]	Ours
Encryption time	$2G + 2G_T$	$(N+1)G + NG_T$
Decryption time	$G + 2G_T$	$(N+1)G_T$
The size of authority's PK	$2L_G + 2L_{G_T}$	$(n+1)L_G + L_{G_T}$
The size of authority's SK	L_{Z_p}	$(N+n+1)L_{Z_p}$
The size of Uuser's SK	$2L_G$	$(N+1)L_G$
The size of CT	$2L_G + 2L_{G_T}$	$(N+1)L_G + L_{G_T}$

MIS in cloud computing environment. As for the cost, we can conclude that the computational time and the size of communication increase linearly with the number of authority N and user n. In summary, our proposal offers a better performance.

5 Conclusions

In this paper, we propose the notion of multi-authority content-based encryption scheme that can be used in preserving the privacy of user in MIS under the cloud computing circumstances, and define the corresponding security model. Our proposal can protect the name and content of e-health records simultaneously to preserve the privacy. Moreover, $(N-1)$ corrupted authorities can get nothing about user's privacy for the reason of PRF seeds and the secret key of authority. We prove the security of our scheme under the DBDH assumption and make a comparison at last.

Acknowledgements. This study was supported by the Open Foundation of State key Laboratory of Networking and Switching Technology (Beijing University of Posts and Telecommunications) under grant SKLNST-2016-2-11.

References

1. Microsoft HealthVault. http://www.healthvault.com
2. Google Health. http://www.healthgoogle.com

3. Cisco: Cisco Visual Networking Index: Global Mobile Data Traffic Forecast Updata, 2014–2019. Cisco White Paper (2015)
4. Jacobson, V., Smetters, D.K., Thomton, J.D., Plass, M.F., Briggs, N.H., Braynard, R.L.: Networing named content. In: 5th International Conference on Emerging and Technologies, pp. 1–12. ACM, New York (2009)
5. Tang, J.H., Quek, T.Q.S.: The role of cloud computing in content-centric mobile networking. IEEE Commun. Mag. **54**, 52–59 (2016)
6. Li, B., Ma, M.D., Yang, X.B.: Perceptive forwaiding in content-centric networks. IEEE Access. **5**, 4595–4605 (2017)
7. Asghar, M.R., Bernardini, C., Crispo, B.: PROTECTOR: privacy-preserving information lookup in content-centric networks. In: IEEE International Conference on Communications, pp. 1–7. IEEE Press, New York (2016)
8. Xia, Z., Zhu, Y., Sun, X., Qin, Z., Ren, K.: Towards privacy-preserving content-based image retrieval in cloud computing. IEEE Trans. Cloud Comput. **99**, 1–1 (2015)
9. Xia, Z., Wang, X., Zhang, L., Qin, Z., Sun, X., Ren, K.: A privacy-preserving and copy-deterrence content-based image retrieval scheme in cloud computing. IEEE Trans. Inf. Forensics Secur. **11**, 2594–2608 (2016)
10. Xia, Z., Xiong, N.N., Vasilakos, A.V., Sun, X.: An efficient and privacy-preserving content-based image retrieval scheme in cloud computing. Inf. Sci. **387**, 195–204 (2017)
11. Goel, P., Holmberg, E., Konezny, M., Ayyagari, R., Sillman, D.: CCNx packet processing on PARC router platform. In: 2nd ACM Conference on Information-Centric Networking, pp. 211–212. ACM, New York (2015)
12. Chaabane, A., Cristofaro, E.D., Kaafar, M.A., Uzun, E.: Privacy in content-oriented networking: threats and contermesures. ACM SIGCOMM Comput. Commun. Rev. **43**, 25–33 (2013)
13. Fotiou, N., Trossen, D., Marias, G.F., Kostopoulos, A., Polyzos, G.C.: Enhancing information lookup privacy through homomorphic encryption. Secur. Commun. Netw. **7**, 2804–2814 (2013)
14. Mannes, E., Maziero, C., Lassance, L.C., Borges, F.: Controle de acesso baseado em reencriptação por proxy em Redes Centradas em Informação. In: 14th Brazilian Symposium on Information and Computing Systems Security, pp. 2–15. SBC Press (2014)
15. Tournai, R., Misra, S., Kliewer, J., Ortegel, S., Mick, T.: Catch me if you can: a practial framwork to evade censorship in information certirc networks. In: 2nd ACM Conference on Information-Centric Networking, pp. 167–176. ACM, New York (2015)
16. Tsudik, G., Uzun, E., Wood, C.A.: AC3N: anonymous communication in content-centric networking. In: 13rd IEEE Annual Consumer Communications & Networking Conference, pp. 988–991. IEEE Press, New York (2016)
17. Wang, X., Mu, Y.: Content-based encryption. In: Liu, J.K., Steinfeld, R. (eds.) ACISP 2016. LNCS, vol. 9723, pp. 57–72. Springer, Cham (2016). doi:10.1007/978-3-319-40367-0_4
18. Lin, X.Y., Tang, S.H., Xu, L.L., Wang, H.Q., Chen, J.: Two-factor data access control with efficient revocation for multi-authority cloud storage systems. IEEE Access **5**, 393–405 (2017)
19. Qian, H.L., Li, J.G., Zhang, Y.C., Han, G.: Privacy-preserving personal health record using multi-authority attribute-based encryption with revocation. Int. J. Inf. Secur. **14**, 487–497 (2015)

Detect Storage Vulnerability of User-Input Privacy in Android Applications with Static and Dynamic Analysis

Li Jiang and Yi Zhuang(✉)

College of Computer Science and Technology,
Nanjing University of Aeronautics and Astronautics, Nanjing, China
{nuaa_jiangli, zyl6}@nuaa.edu.cn

Abstract. In recent years Android has become the most popular operating system in mobile phone, and a variety of apps bring people great convenience in our daily life and work. Due to the resource constraints in mobile phone and user experience considerations, a large number of private data are stored in the phone itself. Privacy Leaks will bring huge losses to us. EditText, which is designed for Android developers to input the sensitive data (e.g. username, password, search keywords etc.) to the apps, carries much *User-Input Privacy* (UIP) data. So, whether these UIP data is stored in the phone safely becomes the key to protect the privacy. In this paper, we do the research about the UIP data in EditText widget, and detect whether the data entered by the user is safely stored through static taint analysis and dynamic Smali Instrumentation. Experiments show that some of the apps store the UIP data in EditText at an unsafe location or store them in a weak way, which will bring the risk of privacy leakage.

Keywords: Android security · Privacy protection · Static and dynamic analysis · Smali instrumentation · Storage vulnerability

1 Introduction

Because of its openness, Android, which is favored by the major mobile phone manufacturers, has become the most widely used mobile operating system. At the same time, a variety of applications are pouring into the App Store. Due to the large number of private data the smart phone carries, once such data is subjected to leak, that would bring its user a huge lose. Traditional detection of privacy leaks focus on the mobile phone itself, and these privacy data is called the *System Center Privacy* (SCP) data, which is generated by the operating system and can get through a specific system calls under the corresponding permission, such as IMEI, phone number, GPS locations, etc. However, privacy data is not limited to this. The content that user enters to a mobile app through its user interface (UI) also contains the user's privacy, which is called the *User-Input Privacy* (UIP) data. To make the app more convenient for users to use, developers usually store lots of user-related data in the phone. These inputs are actually entered by the users at an app's runtime closely linked with the privacy of users. For example, a mobile phone stores various data, such as the search history in the mobile

X. Sun et al. (Eds.): ICCCS 2017, Part II, LNCS 10603, pp. 280–291, 2017.
https://doi.org/10.1007/978-3-319-68542-7_23

browser, the communication records of the chat apps, the video player's playback records etc. Malware can get the user's habits and sensitive information through those data.

Under the pressure of development cycle, many developers directly store those UIP data as plaintext in the phone without any awareness of security, which will bring the risk of privacy leaks. To promote development efficiency, Android SDK provides both internal and external storage mode. But the security of external storage is low and any app can read and write all external storage data with the permission: <uses-permission android: name = "*android.permission.WRITE_EXTERNAL_STORAGE*"/> in AndroidManifest.XML; Rather than external storage, internal storage is the place where private date of apps are stored. Android deny any other apps to read this private data by the file access mechanism in Linux. But if only rely on that mechanism to limit the file access to internal storage, there will be a huge security risk. An attacker can use the system vulnerabilities and other methods to obtain root privilege, and then access all the data in the phone. The statistics of CVE Details show that: Android, Debian Linux and Ubuntu become the most attacked operating system in 2016 [1]. There are a large number of privilege escalation vulnerabilities to break through the restrictions to achieve the purpose of reading private data. Such as WeChat, a popular social app, has been disclosed exists access control vulnerability (CNNVD-201701-100) [2], in January 2017. Dirty COW (CVE-2016-5195) [3] is a privilege escalation vulnerability in the Linux Kernel. It has been proved that app can get the root privilege in the almost all of Android operating systems. This indicates that the boundary between internal and external storage becomes blurred.

The purpose of this paper is to detect whether the UIP data in EditText has been stored safely in the process of using the app. Consider the following scenario as shown in Fig. 1: users input the content of the item that needs to be searched in searchbox of a shopping app (Amazon Shopping), and then the server returns the result of the product. EditText is widely used to input information in app designing. To provide a better user experience in the second query, developers store those historical input data in the phone

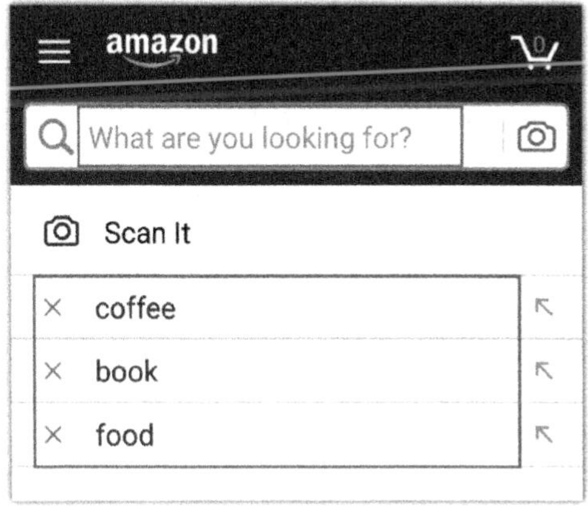

Fig. 1. Product search interface of Amazon

itself. However, once such historical data is stored in an unsafe place, the malware can read the corresponding data to understand the user's recent activities, that causes privacy leaks, such as "the acquaintance to change the password event" in Alipay [4, 5], 2017. This paper found that a large number of apps store those UIP data in an unsafe way, and this can lead to privacy issues.

2 Related Work

The current researches on privacy leaks mainly include static and dynamic analysis. Static analysis means scan the app by the way of information flow analysis, control flow analysis, and parsing, so that we can infer the behaviors of the app. Many systems are designed for static analysis, such as the AndroidLeaks system [6] proposed by Gibler et al. in 2012, the SCANDAL system [7] designed by Di Cerbo et al. in 2010 and FlowDroid [8] proposed by Fritz et al. in 2014. Dynamic analysis mainly use dynamic taint analysis technology, which according the characteristics of sensitive information transmission to dynamic monitoring android system through taint tracking to detect privacy leaks. Enck et al. presented TaintDroid [9] to achieve the taint trace on DVM, and Sun et al. designed TaintArt [10] to trace taint on ART.

In recent years, more and more researchers pay attention to the study of UIP. Huang et al. design and implement SUPOR [11], a static mobile app analysis tool, to automatically examines the UIs to identify sensitive user inputs containing critical user data. And this work is similar to UIPicker [12], which designed to detect the semantic information within the application layout resources and program code. Both of them do this work with the help of machine learning techniques, but UIPicker focuses on both UI and program code while SUPOR not. As for UIP data input through EditText, Cox et al. present SpanDex [13], which is a set of extensions of Android's Dalvik virtual machine, to ensures apps do not leak users' passwords.

Although the previous work make a very huge contribution to the research of UIP, if used to solve the problem in the above situation, there are some inadequacies: (1) the analysis of cryptographic functions is missing in static taint analysis to determine whether there is encryption in the path from source to sink and the strength of the encryption. (2) Dynamic taint analysis methods need to modify the Android system, so it is difficult to widely used in the Android fragmentation market.

This paper focuses on the UIP data in EditText. We design and implement a prototype system to the detect Storage Vulnerability of UIP data by combining with the static and dynamic analysis method on Android. The system consists of static analysis and dynamic verification. Static analysis is designed to obtain the basic information of the app and to build the risk storage paths; Then inject the security code to monitor its internal data process by Smali Instrumentation technology; Install the modified apk in your phone to dynamic verify. Finally, we design an algorithm to detect whether the EditText data is stored at an unsafe location and whether the app uses a weak storage method at the running time.

3 System Overview

In order to trace the data input by the Editext and solve the problems and challenges in the above scenario, we use the static and dynamic analysis to examine apps. The proposed system is divided into two parts: (1) static analysis and apk repackage. This part is designed for the static analysis of the apk to obtain the basic information of the app and build the risk storage path in the background. Then inject the security code to monitor its internal data process by Smali Instrumentation technology. Finally, output the modified apk. (2) Android EditText Privacy Management. This is an app that is designed and implemented to collects the UIP data in EditText as well as TraceView data at dynamic runtime. In the end, the app notifies the detection results through the algorithm proposed in Sect. 3.2.

3.1 Static Analysis and Apk Repackage

Static analysis and apk repacking is designed for the static analysis of the original apk. As the Fig. 2 shows, the framework consists of three parts.

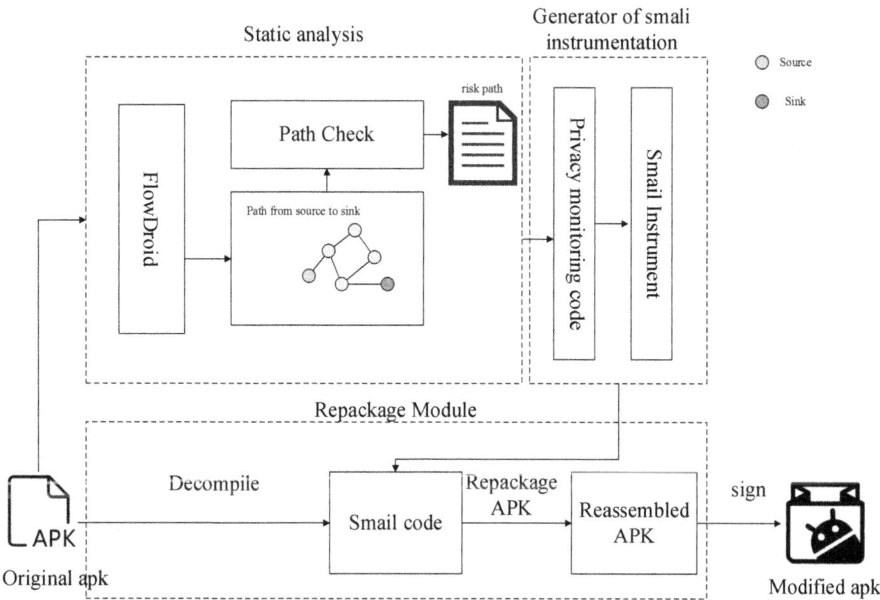

Fig. 2. Framework of static analysis and repacking

- **Static Analysis**

This phase is developed based on FlowDroid [8] which provides static taint analysis and supports redefine source and sink method to obtain taint transmission path of an apk. Source is defined as the corresponding apis which is used to get the data in EditText and the sink is defined as apis of read and write operations on a file. In this paper, we select the source and sink as follows (Table 1).

Table 1. Source and sink defined in this paper

Source	<android.widget.EditText: android.text.Editable getText()>
Sink	<java.io.OutputStream: void write(byte[])> <java.io.OutputStream: void write(byte[],int,int)> <java.io.OutputStream: void write(int)> <java.io.FileOutputStream: void write(byte[])> <java.io.FileOutputStream: void write(byte[],int,int)> <java.io.FileOutputStream: void write(int)> <java.io.Writer: void write(char[])> ...... <java.io.Writer: void write(java.lang.String,int,int)> <java.io.Writer: java.io.Writer append(java.lang.CharSequence)> <java.io.OutputStreamWriter: java.io.Writer append(java.lang.CharSequence)>

Note: The defined functions of the sink include all types of file access related apis in the table. Due to the limited number of pages, the functions are not all listed.

However, FlowDroid lacks the components to detect whether the data is encrypted though the path in the scenario. So we design a path check module based on FlowDroid. The purpose of this module is to analyze the path from source to sink to judge whether it uses encryption and the strength of the encryption. The path is divided into the following 4 levels (Table 2).

Table 2. Rules of path level

Path type	Storage location	Encrypted	The level of encryption
Danger	External	No	–
Medium	Internal	No	–
Fine	Internal	Yes	Java level
Safe	Internal	Yes	Native level

The hierarchy of encryption is divided into Java layer and Native layer. In the Java layer, Android development libraries have provided most of the encryption algorithms. Only need to import the corresponding algorithm packages, can the developer directly call the relevant encryption functions. So the identification to determine whether it is encrypted is mainly through the string match of the function in the Java layer. In the experiment, we list the major cryptographic algorithms including AES, DES, TEA, RC2, RC4, RC5 and Blowfish. While in Native layer, the C/C++ code is compiled to *.so* file and Java layer calls the corresponding native methods via JNI. To identify whether the function in the *.so* file is encryption function, we use the Findcrypt2 plugin in IDA [14, 15] to do this job.

The result of static analysis is a set of source-to-sink paths in which collects the risk storage paths of EditText data. Those apis associated with the sink method will guide the subsequent smali instrumentation.

- **Generator of smali instrumentation**

The results of apk static analysis is used to smail instrumentation. The purposes of instrumentation are as follows: (1) Get the data entered in EditText. (2) Inject TraceView monitor code in the app to get the call stack information at real-time. EditText is widely used for UI in Android development [16] including Plain Text, Person Name, Password etc. Although EditText is widely used in the UI, the frequency of it is low. Generally, it exists on the interface of inputting username and password, commenting information and searching box. Its Smail code is Landroid/widget/EditText.

TraceView [17] is provided to debug your application and profile its performance by Google. Using *start Method Tracing* to start Android monitor and *stop Method Tracing* to stop, then we can get a *.trace* file. It can dynamically generate at runtime and show the real behavior of the app very accurately. How to use *.trace* file to detect privacy leak and the communication method between the modified app and the client of EditText privacy management is described in Sect. 3.2.

- **Repackage Module**

This module is designed for apk repackaging. Finally we sign and release the modified apk. This part is developed upon Open source project Baksmali/Smali [18].

3.2 Android EditText Privacy Management

This part is an app running on the client's phone (Android EditText Privacy Management, AEPM), which is similar to the App Store. The modified apps are installed in the mobile phone and they are running under the monitoring of AEPM which communicates to them through IPC. The AEPM can record the log and sent messages to remind the user during the real-time monitoring. The implementation of its framework is shown in Fig. 3:

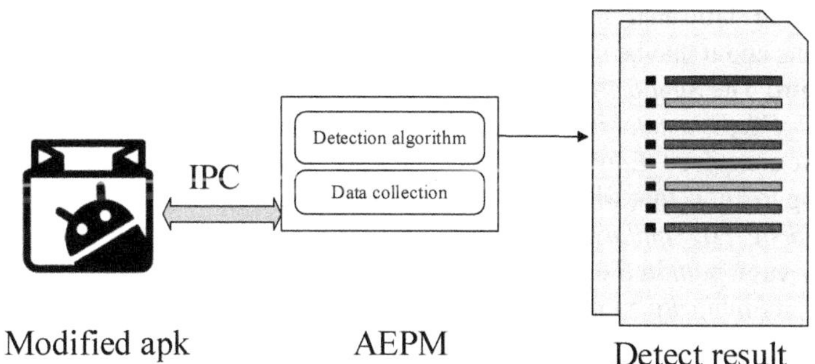

Fig. 3. Framework of AEPM

- **Data collection**

Data collection is a module of AEPM and user can set the type of file to monitor in the app. The AEPM communicates with the modified apps by IPC (in this paper we use LocalSocket). The process of collection includes:

(1) Collect UIP data in EditText and start Method Tracing

The purpose of this part is to get the UIP data in EditText by the Smali Instrumentation code technology and open the TraceView monitor switch to start Method Tracing at the same time. The benefit of this step is to capture the event sequences of the app more accurately when users are inputting data in EditText at real-time and then prepare for the subsequent analysis.

(2) Stop Method Tracing

This step is to stop TraceView and generate a *.trace* file for later processing. Truncated functions are the file access operations at the risk path of static analysis in this paper. Meanwhile we can obtain specific parameters of file access operations, such as file name, storage location etc. In order to prevent a case that the app uses the EditText widget without file access operations, we set a threshold time. Stop TraceView monitoring automatically when reaching the threshold.

- **Detection algorithm**

This module describes how to use the information given above to detect privacy leaks in EditText data. Using the repackaging method proposed in Sect. 3.1, the TraceView file we get is the monitoring information of the app in real time. The behavior of the function calls are stored by the structure of the tree. From the above process, we can accurately get the TraceView data during the time between users input data in EditText and store them in the system. And we can also get the content in EditText and the final data of the read or write operations on a file. Finally we generate the detection report by matching the call stack information and the leak paths obtained in the static analysis. The matching algorithm is as follows.

Algorithm 1 Matching algorithm

Input: *I_Edit* as the UIP data in EditText, *T* as the TraceView data, *S* as a set of risk paths in static analysis, *I_Fileparameter* as the parameters of file access operations and it maybe *null*.

Output: The *SimilarityPath* of detection

if *I_Fileparameter* is *null* return *null*

else compare *I_Edit* with *I_Fileparameter* using Approximate String Matching to know that whether *I_Edit* is in *I_Fileparameter*

Similarity = 0, *SimilarityPath=null*

for each *path* **in** *S* **do**

    if *Similarity* > LevenshteinDistance(*path*,*T*)//use Levenshtein distance to calculate

        Similarity = LevenshteinDistance(*path*,T)

        SimilarityPath=path

    end if

end for

return *SimilarityPath*

- **Detect result**

This section is designed to record and alert the storage vulnerability of the UIP data in EditText by the way of notification messages.

4 Experiment and Result Analysis

4.1 Environment

With an Intel Core i5-6300HQ 2.30 GHz and 64 GB RAM on window10, we build and develop Flowdroid with Eclipse Kepler Service Release 2 on 64-bit JVM with a maximum heap space of 16 GB.

4.2 Experimental Methods and Results

We use the apps collected from Google Play and Chinese App Store in browser, social, shopping, news and reading apps in top 20. Finally, the number of apps is 100 and we analyze 87 apps successfully. The reasons for the unsuccess are the following: (1) some apps use the anti-reverse reinforcement technology to protect the integrity of it. That can lead to errors in the process of static analysis. (2) Due to the size of some apps is so larger, the static analysis of app costs too much memory and time to get the result in a tolerable time. Table 3 shows the results of static analysis for five classifications.

Table 3. The results of static analysis for five classifications

Type of apps	Browser	Social	Shopping	News	Reading
Average risk paths	2.17	1.23	0.58	5.40	6.18
Storage location	Internal	Internal	Internal	Internal/External	Internal/External
Is encrypted	Yes	Yes	Partly	No	No

Figure 4 shows the type of storage used in the apps and it can be seen that the sqlite-based database files occupy the vast majority of the storage.

In the successful analysis of the apps, 82.3% of the apps store the UIP data in EditText in the internal storage without encrypting, and mostly use sqlite to store. From the results in Table 3, we can see that the social and shopping apps have the least risk storage path, while the news and reading apps have the most dangerous storage path. This is also consistent with the reality of the situation that there are a large number of privacy chat records stored in social apps so they have a stronger security policy than News and Reading apps.

Table 4 lists the memory and time consumption of the typical app in the five categories.

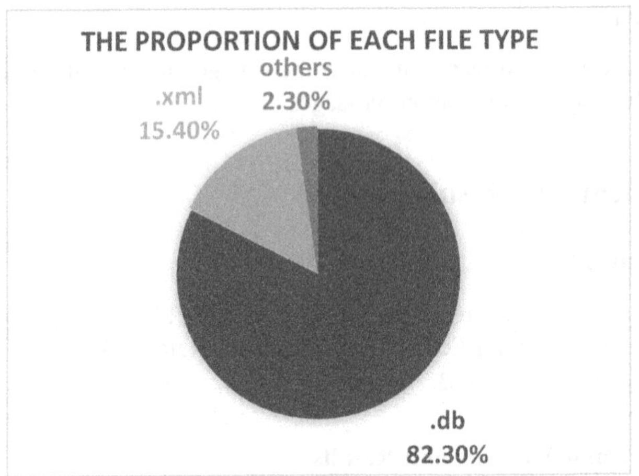

Fig. 4. The type of storage used in the apps

Table 4. The result of static analysis for 5 typical apps

Name	UC Browser	WeChat	Amazon Shopping	Daily News	QQReader
Original apk size (M)	28.0	38.6	22.38	11.9	19.0
Modified apk size (M)	30.2	–	24.5	12.2	20.1
Time of static analysis (S)	867	–	479	382	525
Memory (GB)	3.01	–	1.0	0.75	0.83
Risk paths	6	–	5	10	6
Storage location	Internal	–	Internal	Internal	External

Note: In the typical apps of the selected 5 group listed in the table, the analysis of WeChat is failed. The main reason for that is the app uses anti-reverse reinforcement technology to make the app analysis exceptionally exit. Because the size of current app is very large, static analysis costs much time. So we recommend to achieve the static analysis with the help of large-scale computers in the background.

In order to verify the effect of dynamic analysis, we install the typical apps in the mobile phone and observe the dynamic effect of AEPM at running time. We use those apps and input some UIP data through EditText including login, search, comment and other operations. The figure shows the notifications of AEPM after normally use those apps in 30 min.

Figure 5 shows the risk paths triggered by the typical apps in 30 min. Through the analysis, we find that: (1) These apps store the UIP data in login EditText through confusing or encrypting method. And the most apps support Third-Party Login (Such as WeChat, QQ, Micro-Blogging, Alipay, etc.), so the user's account is relatively stored safely. (2) The apps trigger the most dangerous path when using similar "search" and "comment" functions.

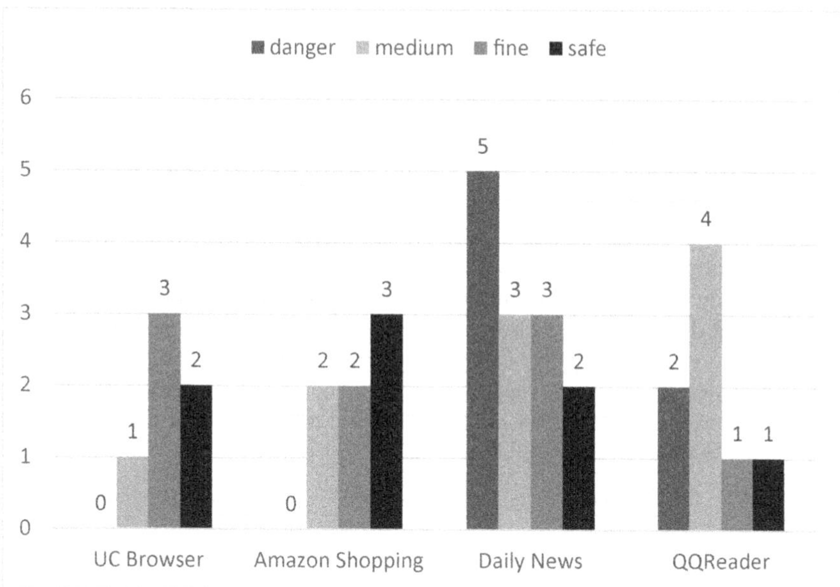

Fig. 5. The number of triggered risk paths in 30 min

Figure 6 shows that AEPM detects the QQ reader stores the historical query data which user inputs in EditText at external storage in plaintext. So any app can read the history query data and know "What books are users viewing recently!".

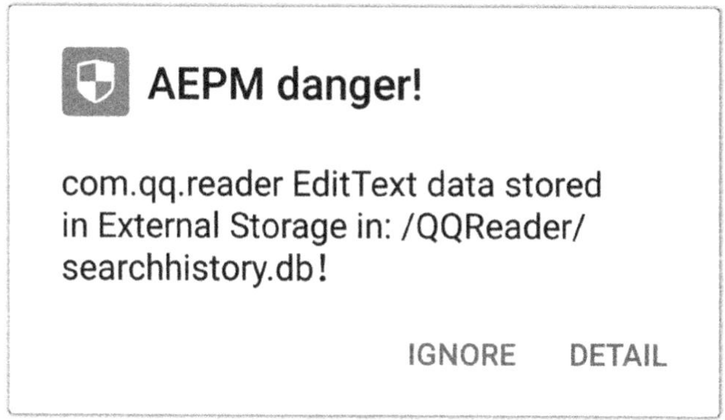

Fig. 6. An example of AEPM notification

5 Discussion

Through this experimental analysis, we find that a large number of popular apps store some UIP data in EditText at internal storage without encrypting. Once the malware gets root privilege, the data will be completely exposed. Those data are generated by the user when using the apps and contain the user's privacy. We recommend that developers try to use encryption methods when store UIP data in EditText, and it is better to use encryption on native layer. When the app releases, programmers should use the anti-reverse technologies to prevent malicious get the key of encryption.

6 Further Work

User input information is not always privacy. So we will do some work on the definition of privacy and non-private information which will be difficult. And in order to protect the UIP data mentioned above, we will propose a solution in our next paper.

Acknowledgments. This work is supported by the National Natural Science Foundation of China (General Program) under Grant No. 61572253, and the Aeronautical Science Foundation of China under Grant No. 2016ZC52030.

References

1. Android Was 2016's Most Vulnerable Product. https://www.bleepingcomputer.com/news/security/android-was-2016s-most-vulnerable-product/
2. CNNVD-201701-100. https://www.easyaq.com/news/1117126844.shtml
3. Dirty COW (CVE-2016-5195). https://dirtycow.ninja/
4. Alipay is now a major loophole: single password can be falsified! Get tied up with a bank card! http://thechinesenews.net/Today-News/47729.html
5. Alipay is acquaintance of tampering with a password vulnerabilities, user delete friends, the official said the problem has been solved. http://www.thechinesenews.net/Today-News/47977.html
6. Gibler, C., Crussell, J., Erickson, J., Chen, H.: AndroidLeaks: automatically detecting potential privacy leaks in android applications on a large scale. In: Katzenbeisser, S., Weippl, E., Camp, L.J., Volkamer, M., Reiter, M., Zhang, X. (eds.) Trust 2012. LNCS, vol. 7344, pp. 291–307. Springer, Heidelberg (2012). doi:10.1007/978-3-642-30921-2_17
7. Di Cerbo, F., Girardello, A., Michahelles, F., Voronkova, S.: Detection of malicious applications on android OS. In: Sako, H., Franke, K.Y., Saitoh, S. (eds.) IWCF 2010. LNCS, vol. 6540, pp. 138–149. Springer, Heidelberg (2010). doi:10.1007/978-3-642-19376-7_12
8. Arzt, S., Rasthofer, S., Fritz, C., Bodden, E., Bartel, A., Klein, J., Le Traon, Y., Octeau, D., McDaniel, P.: Flowdroid: precise context, flow, field, object-sensitive and lifecycle-aware taint analysis for android apps. ACM Sigplan Not. **49**(6), 259–269 (2014)
9. Enck, W., Gilbert, P., Han, S., Tendulkar, V., Chun, B.-G., Cox, L.P., Jung, J., McDaniel, P., Sheth, A.N.: TaintDroid: an information-flow tracking system for realtime privacy monitoring on smartphones. ACM Trans. Comput. Syst. (TOCS) **32**(2), 5 (2014)
10. Sun, M., Wei, T., Lui, J.: Taintart: a practical multi-level information-flow tracking system for android runtime. In: Proceedings of the 2016 ACM SIGSAC Conference on Computer and Communications Security 2016, pp. 331–342. ACM (2016)
11. Huang, J., Li, Z., Xiao, X., Wu, Z., Lu, K., Zhang, X., Jiang, G.: SUPOR: precise and scalable sensitive user input detection for android apps. In: USENIX Security (2015)
12. Nan, Y., Yang, M., Yang, Z., Zhou, S., Gu, G., Wang, X.: UIPicker: user-input privacy identification in mobile applications. In: USENIX Security (2015)

13. Cox, L.P., Gilbert, P., Lawler, G., Pistol, V., Razeen, A., Wu, B., Cheemalapati, S.: SpanDex: secure password tracking for android. In: USENIX Security (2014)
14. IDA. https://www.hex-rays.com/products/ida/
15. FindCrypt2. http://www.hexblog.com/?p=28
16. EditText | Android Developers. https://developer.android.com/reference/android/widget/EditText.html
17. Profiling with Traceview and dmtracedump | Android Studio. https://developer.android.com/studio/profile/traceview.html#knownissues
18. JesusFreke/smali: smali/baksmali. https://github.com/JesusFreke/smali

Certificateless Cryptography with KGC Trust Level 3 Revisited

Fei Li[1,2,3], Wei Gao[1,2,3](✉), Dongqing Xie[1], and Chunming Tang[1]

[1] School of Mathematics, Guangzhou University, Guangzhou 510000, China
miss_lifei@163.com, mygaowei@163.com, dongqing_xie@hotmail.com, ctang@gzhu.edu.cn

[2] Nanjing University of Information Science and Technology, Nanjing 210044, China

[3] School of Mathematics and Statistics, Ludong University, Yantai 264025, China

Abstract. This paper revisits the issue of obtaining KGC (Key Generator Center) trust level 3 in certificateless cryptography. The AP (Al-Riyami-Paterson) binding technique can modularly construct the certificateless encryption/signature scheme with trust level 3 from that with trust level 2. However, its security proof has been an open problem. Yang and Tan improved the AP framework by adding extra cryptographic tools: random oracles for security proof in the random oracle model or trapdoor hash functions for security proof in the standard model. This paper aims to prove secure the original AP binding technique. The basic technique for achieving this security proof depends on the improved security model for certificateless encryption (or signature) schemes. As an application example, one key dependent certificateless encryption scheme with both authority trust level 3 and provable security in the standard model is modularly constructed by applying the AP binding framework to one conventional certificateless encryption scheme.

Keywords: Certificateless cryptography · Provable security · Trust level

1 Introduction

Certificateless cryptography (CLC) proposed by Al-Riyami and Paterson [1] lies between identity based cryptography (IBC) and conventional public key cryptography (PKC) based on PKI. It tries to solve both the key escrow issue in IBC and the certificate management issue in PKC. In CLC, the entity's full private key fsk is computed from the partial private key ppk generated by Key Generation Centre (KGC) and the user self-generated secret key usk (also known as secret value) which corresponds to the user's public key upk. The ciphertext is generated based on the identity and the entity public key. There exists no certificate to authenticate the entity public key in CL-PKC. As a result, an adversary in CLC can use any public key of its choice to replace the original public key and certificateless cryptosystems should be secure against such an attack. Attackers for CLC are usually divided into two types in the security model [1].

X. Sun et al. (Eds.): ICCCS 2017, Part II, LNCS 10603, pp. 292–304, 2017.
https://doi.org/10.1007/978-3-319-68542-7_24

The attacker of Type I is used to capture an ordinary adversary that can replace the user public keys. The attacker of Type II is used to capture an honest-but-curious KGC that knows the master secret key but never replaces public keys. In fact, the KGC can impersonate any user once if it can arbitrarily change the public key. Since the notion of certificateless cryptography was proposed, there are some important improvements in the security models. In [10], to prevent the Denial-of-Decryption attacks, the concept of self-generated-certificate public key cryptography was proposed. The attack model called the malicious-but-passive KGC in certificateless cryptosystems was developed by Au et al. [2], and further studied in [8,15]. In [7], Hu et al. formalized the KGC trust level 3 security. In [14], for reaching KGC trust level 3, the notion of the key dependent certificateless encryption/signature schemes was developed and the generic construction for key dependent CLE and CLS schemes was presented.

Next, we focus on the issue of KGC trust level 3. The trust hierarchy for public key cryptography is divided into 3 levels by Girault [6]. (1) For level 1, as in identity-based cryptography [3], the trusted authority knows the private key of any user; (2) For level 2, as in conventional certificateless cryptography, the authority cannot figure out the secret key, but can first generate false guarantees and then impersonate the user. (3) For level 3, as in public key cryptography based on PKI, the authority cannot figure out the secret key, and it has to face the proof for generating false guarantees of the user once if it does such fraud. To address the KGC trust level problem in CLC, Yang and Tan [14] developed the concept called Key Dependent Certificateless encryption/signature (KD-CLE and KD-CLS) which naturally obtain the KGC trust level and proposed the way for transforming any conventional certificateless cryptosystem into its key dependent counterparts. In fact, as early as in the first paper on certificateless cryptography, the authors had noticed the issue of KGC trust level and introduced the AP (Al-Riyami-Paterson) binding technique which can lift the authority trust level of any certificateless encryption/signature scheme from 2 to 3. However, they did not provide the formal security proof. This AP binding technique looks very reasonable and has been informally showed secure. However, whether it can be formally prove secure has been an open problem [14]. Yang and Tan [14] explained why the security proof for the AP binding method can not be obtained, then bypassed the security proof for the original AP binding technique, and turned to expand the AP binding technique by involving extra cryptographic tools: random oracles for obtaining security proof in the random oracle model or trapdoor hash functions for obtaining security proof in the standard model.

Our Work. Following Yang and Tan's work [14], this paper tries to solve the above open problem. As the starting point, we improve the security model of conventional certificateless encryption and key dependent certificateless encryption. In fact, the improved points in our new security model focus on replaced public keys. In previous security models such as those in [1,14], for the replaced public key, the relative secret key (also known as secret value in [1,14]) is thought to be known by the attacker and unknown by the challenger. In contrast, we find some contrary cases where the secret key relative to the replaced public key is unknown by the attacker and known by the challenger. In other words, in our improved security model, "being replaced" for public keys will not be used as the criterion for "being known" for the secret key as before. With this discovery, we improve the security model for conventional/key dependent certificateless encryption. With this improved security model, the AP binding technique is formally proved to be one secure generic framework which can generate one secure KD-CLE scheme if the underlying CLE is assumed to be secure. As an application example, one key dependent certificateless encryption scheme with both authority trust level 3 and provable security in the standard model is modularly constructed from the existing conventional certificateless encryption scheme due to Dent et al. [4] through the AP binding framework. We also show that our results can also be naturally extended to other certificateless cryptosystems such as certificateless signatures.

Paper Organization. In Sect. 2, we present the improved security model for conventional CLE and key dependent CLE and review the AP binding technique. In Sect. 3, we show that the AP binding technique is provably secure in our improved security model. In Sect. 4, one key dependent certificateless encryption scheme is modularly constructed by applying the AP binding technique. Some observations on our result are presented in Sect. 5. The conclusion is in Sect. 6.

2 Preliminaries

2.1 Syntax Definitions for CLE and KD-CLE

Following previous works [1,5], we present the syntax definition as follows.

Definition 1. A ("Key Dependent" or "Conventional") certificateless encryption scheme has the following seven algorithms. Here note that conventional CLE and KD-CLE are defined in one syntax framework with the differences pointed out by the notation $[\cdot]_{KD}$.

- $\mathsf{Setup}(1^k) \rightarrow (mpk, msk)$, run by the KGC, takes as input the security parameter 1^k, and then returns a master public/secret key pair (mpk, msk).
- $\mathsf{GenUSK}(mpk) \rightarrow usk$, run by the user, takes mpk as inputs, and returns a user secret key usk. In some previous works, the "user secret key" is also called "secret value".
- $\mathsf{GenUPK}(mpk, usk) \rightarrow upk$, run by the user, takes as input the master public key mpk and the user secret key usk and then returns a user public key upk.
- $\mathsf{GenPPK}(msk, ID, [upk]_{KD}) \rightarrow ppk$, run by KGC, takes as input the master secret key msk, the *optional* user public key upk and the entity identity ID, and then returns the partial private key ppk for the user.

Remark 1: The notation $[\cdot]_{KD}$ means that: (1) upk is not taken as input for "*conventional*" certificateless encryption schemes, but taken as input for "*key dependent*" certificateless encryption schemes (KD-CLE).

- $\mathsf{GenFPK}(mpk, usk, ppk) \to fpk$, run by the entity, takes as input the master public key mpk, the entity secret key usk, and the partial private key ppk, and then returns the full private key fpk.
- $\mathsf{Encrypt}(mpk, ID, upk, m) \to c$, run by the sender, takes as input the master public key mpk, the identity ID, the public key upk and one message m, and then outputs the ciphertext c.
- $\mathsf{Decrypt}(mpk, fpk, c) \to m$, run by the receiver, takes the master public key mpk, the full private key fpk, and a ciphertext c as input, and then outputs the plaintext m.

2.2 Security Models for CLE and KD-CLE

The following steps constitute the common game framework to define CCA (Chosen Ciphertext Attack) security of certificateless encryption schemes (CLE or KD-CLE) for the attacker $\mathcal{A}$ being of Type I or II. After this game, respectively for Type I and Type II attackers, the oracle sets and the oracle query restrictions will be further described in details.

1. $(mpk, msk) \leftarrow \mathsf{Setup}(1^k)$.
   The setup algorithm $\mathsf{Setup}(1^k)$ is run the challenger.
2. $(ID^*, upk^*_{ID^*}, m_0, m_1) \leftarrow \mathcal{A}^{\mathcal{O}}(mpk)$.
   With the master public key and the oracle access to all oracles in the set $\mathcal{O}$, the attacker $\mathcal{A}$ finally sends the target identity with the public key and message pair $(ID^*, upk^*_{ID^*}, m_0, m_1)$ to the challenger. Different instantiation of the oracle set $\mathcal{O}$, being $\mathcal{O}_I$ or $\mathcal{O}_{II}$, defines the attack type being of Type I or II. The set of oracles ($\mathcal{O}_I$ and $\mathcal{O}_{II}$) will be further described after this game.
3. $c^* \leftarrow \mathsf{Encrypt}(mpk, ID^*, upk^*_{ID^*}, m_b)$, where $b \xleftarrow{R} \{0,1\}$.
   The challenger chooses a random bit $b \in \{0,1\}$ and sends ciphertext $c^* \leftarrow \mathsf{Encrypt}(mpk, ID^*, upk^*_{ID^*}, m_b)$ to the attacker. Here note that $upk^*_{ID^*}$ refers to ID^*'s *current* public key.
4. $b' \leftarrow \mathcal{A}^{\mathcal{O}}(c^*)$.
   Given the challenged ciphertext c^*, with access to the oracle set $\mathcal{O}$ restrictively as will be described below, the attacker finally returns a guessed bit b' for b.

<u>The adversary advantage</u> for winning the game is defined to be

$$\mathrm{Adv}^{CCA}_{CLE,\mathcal{A}} = |\Pr[b = b'] - 1/2|.$$

A certificateless encryption scheme is said to be CCA (chosen ciphertext attack) secure, if $Adv^{CCA}_{CLE,\mathcal{A}}(k)$ is negligible in the parameter k for both cases: (1)$\mathcal{A}$ is of Type I, denoted by $\mathcal{A}_I$; (2) $\mathcal{A}$ is of type II, denoted by $\mathcal{A}_{II}$. According to the oracle sets and oracle query restrictions, $\mathcal{A}_{II}$ and $\mathcal{A}_I$ are determined as follows. <u>Oracle set $\mathcal{O}$</u>, instantiated with $\mathcal{O}_I$ for type I attackers or $\mathcal{O}_{II}$ for Type II attackers, consists of some oracles as below:

- $O^{MSK}(mpk)$ presents the master secret key msk corresponding to the master public key. In previous security models [1], the presence of msk of the challenger to the adversary is directly expressed. For expression convenience and without essential difference, here the presence of msk is formalized by this specific oracle.
- $O^{UPK}(ID)$ returns ID's original public key upk_{ID}. The set of all original public keys provided by the challenger for the adversary is denoted by $\mathcal{OPK}$.
- $O^{RPK}(ID, upk)$ changes ID's public key into the value upk. Without loss of generality, for the input ID, the oracle query $O^{UPK}(ID)$ is assumed to be made previously.
- $O^{PPK}(ID, [upk]_{KD})$ outputs the partial private key ppk_{ID} for the identity ID. Just as before mentioned in the syntax definition, only for KD-CLE schemes, the optional parameter of public key upk should be included.
- $O^{FPK}(ID, upk)$ outputs the user's full private key fpk_{ID} for the identity ID and the public key upk. Without loss of generality, upk is assumed to be the current public key of the input identity ID. We also assume that this oracle O^{FPK} will first make the oracle query $O^{RPK}(ID, upk)$ to set upk as ID's user public key, if ID's current public key is not upk.
- $O^{DEC}(ID, upk, c)$ outputs the decryption of c for the identity ID and the current public key upk. This oracle O^{DEC} is assumed to first make the oracle query $O^{RPK}(ID, upk)$ to set upk as ID's user public key, if ID's current public key is not upk.

Remark 2. For the two oracles of O^{FPK} and O^{DEC}, in previous works [1,14], the current public key upk is usually not explicitly included as input. For convenience of expression and without essential difference, here upk is explicitly taken as input.

For Type I adversaries, the oracle set $\mathcal{O}$ is instantiated with

$$\mathcal{O}_I = \{O^{PPK}, O^{FPK}, O^{UPK}, O^{RPK}, O^{DEC}\}$$

under the following restrictions:

I.1 $\mathcal{A}$ cannot make the full private key query $O^{FPK}(ID, upk)$ for $upk \notin \mathcal{OPK}$, since there is no way for the challenger to know the corresponding indispensable secret key.

I.2 $\mathcal{A}$ cannot make the full private key query $O^{FPK}(ID^*, upk^*_{ID^*})$, since this will help $\mathcal{A}$ to trivially succeed.

I.3 $\mathcal{A}$ cannot make the decryption query $O^{DEC}(ID^*, upk^*_{ID^*}, c^*)$, since this will help $\mathcal{A}$ to trivially succeed.

I.4 $\mathcal{A}$ can not make the query for the partial private key $O^{PPK}(ID^*, upk^*_{ID^*})$ for $upk^*_{ID^*} \notin \mathcal{OPK}$, since this will help $\mathcal{A}$ to know the partial private key and the secret key together, and then trivially succeed.

For Type II adversaries, the oracle set $\mathcal{O}$ is instantiated with

$$\mathcal{O}_{II} = \{O^{MSK}, O^{FPK}, O^{UPK}, O^{RPK}, O^{DEC}\}$$

under the following restrictions:

II.1, II.2, II.3 are the same to the above restriction rules I.1, I.2, I.3 respectively.

II.4 $upk^*_{ID^*} \in \mathcal{OPK}$. Otherwise, the Type II adversary, which is able to compute the partial private key by itself, can further get known the target user secret key, and hence can trivially succeed in computing the target full private key.

Remark 3. In the above restriction I.1, for one identity ID and its "current" public key upk, the condition $upk \notin \mathcal{OPK}$ means that the current user secret key usk is known by the adversary and not known by the challenger. In contrast, in previous works [1], the corresponding restriction usually requires that, $\mathcal{A}$ is not allowed to query the full private key of any identity if the corresponding public key has ever been replaced. Similar analysis works for the condition $upk^*_{ID^*} \notin \mathcal{OPK}$ in the restriction I.4 and $upk^*_{ID^*} \in \mathcal{OPK}$ in the restriction II.4.

2.3 Al-Riyami-Paterson Binding Technique

Al-Riyami-Paterson binding method is as follows: for a traditional certificateless encryption scheme $\mathcal{CLE}$ = (Setup, GenUSK, GenUPK, GenPPK, GenFPK, Encrypt, Decrypt), construct a key dependent CLE scheme $\mathcal{KD}$-$\mathcal{CLE}$ = (Setup', GenUSK', GenUPK', GenPPK', GenFPK', Encrypt', Decrypt') as follows:

- (Setup', GenUSK', GenPPK', GenFPK', Decrypt') are same as (Setup, GenUSK, GenUPK, GenFPK, Decrypt) respectively.
- GenPPK'(msk, ID, upk): let $ID' = ID||upk$, run $usk \leftarrow$ GenPPK(msk, ID') and return usk.
- Encrypt'(mpk, ID, upk, m): let $ID' = ID||upk$, run $c \leftarrow$ Encrypt(mpk, ID', upk, m) and return c.

In [14], Yang and Tan analyzed difficulties in developing a generic proof for the above AP binding technique. To get provable security, they proposed two modified versions of the AP binding technique: in stead of using the original AP binding $ID' = ID||upk$, they used (1) $ID' = H(ID||upk)$ for provable security in random oracle model, where $H(\cdot)$ is a cryptographic hash function taken as one random oracle; or (2) $ID' = H_{pk}(ID||upk)$ in the standard model, where $H_{pk}(\cdot)$ is a trapdoor hash function. At the end, they proposed the open problem that, whether the Al-Riyami-Paterson binding technique can be proved to be secure as a generic transformation.

3 Security Proof for AP Binding Technique

Theorem 1. If the conventional certificateless encryption scheme $\mathcal{CLE}$ is CCA secure against PPT adversaries of type I, then the corresponding key dependent certificateless encryption scheme $\mathcal{KD}$-$\mathcal{CLE}$ is also CCA secure against PPT adversaries of type I.

Proof. We prove it by contradiction. We assume that there is an adversary $\mathcal{A}$ (against $\mathcal{KD}$-$\mathcal{CLE}$) who wins a non-negligible advantage. We try to construct one adversary $\mathcal{B}$ (against $\mathcal{CLE}$) whose advantage is non-negligible. $\mathcal{B}$ simulates the game for $\mathcal{A}$. $\mathcal{B}$ first passes mpk to $\mathcal{A}$ and answers $\mathcal{A}$'s queries as below. Here note that, without loss of generality, each oracle for $\mathcal{A}$ against $\mathcal{KD}$-$\mathcal{CLE}$ and its counterpart oracle for $\mathcal{B}$ against $\mathcal{CLE}$ use the same notation. For example, the decryption oracle for $\mathcal{KD}$-$\mathcal{CLE}$ and the decryption oracle for $\mathcal{CLE}$ both use the notation $O^{DEC}(\cdot)$.

- $O^{UPK}(ID)$: If the user ID has ever been queried by $\mathcal{A}$, then the corresponding original public key is returned according to the below recording list L_{opk}. Otherwise, $\mathcal{B}$ selects a random valid CLE identity string ID'', makes a $O^{UPK}(ID'')$ query to its own oracle, and returns the original public key $upk_{ID''}$ of ID'' as the answer for $O^{UPK}(ID)$. To record the case that ID and ID'' has the same original public key, adds (ID, ID'') to the initially empty list L_{opk}.
- $O^{RPK}(ID, upk)$: For $ID' = ID||upk$, $\mathcal{B}$ makes a query $O^{RPK}(ID', upk)$ to its own challenger. After this oracle query, ID for $\mathcal{KD}$-$\mathcal{CLE}$ and ID' for $\mathcal{CLE}$ have the same current public key and full private key.
- $O^{PPK}(ID, upk)$: For $ID' = ID||upk$, $\mathcal{B}$ makes a query $O^{PPK}(ID')$ to its own challenger, and transfers the answer to $\mathcal{A}$.
- $O^{FPK}(ID, upk)$: For $ID' = ID||upk$, $\mathcal{B}$ first makes a public key replacing oracle query $O^{RPK}(ID', upk)$ to ensure that the current public key of ID' is upk, and then issues a query $O^{FPK}(ID', upk)$ to the challenger of itself, and transfers the answer to $\mathcal{A}$.
- $O^{DEC}(ID, upk, c)$: For $ID' = ID||upk$, $\mathcal{B}$ first makes a public key replacing oracle query $O^{RPK}(ID', upk)$ to ensure that the current public key of ID' is upk, and then makes a $O^{DEC}(ID', upk, c)$ query to its own challenger, and transfers the answer to $\mathcal{A}$.

During these oracle queries, when $\mathcal{A}$ outputs $(ID^*, upk^*_{ID^*}, m_0, m_1)$ as the challenge, $\mathcal{B}$ first makes a public key replacing oracle query $O^{RPK}(ID^{*\prime}, upk^*_{ID^*})$ to ensure that the current public key of $ID^{*\prime}$ is $upk^*_{ID^*}$, and then transfers $(ID^{*\prime}, upk^*_{ID^*}, m_0, m_1)$ to its own challenger for $ID^{*\prime} = ID^*||upk^*_{ID^*}$. After the target ciphertext c^* is returned from the challenger, $\mathcal{B}$ then transfers c^* to $\mathcal{A}$ as the challenging ciphertext. Then $\mathcal{B}$ answers the oracle queries as before. At the end, when $\mathcal{A}$ gives a bit b' to $\mathcal{B}$, $\mathcal{B}$ transfers b' to its own challenger.

Next, we analyze the restrictions on oracle access.

I.1 For $\mathcal{A}$'s full private query $O^{FPK}(ID, upk)$, according to the restriction, upk should be an original public key of one certain identity generated by its challenger (simulated by $\mathcal{B}$). However, $\mathcal{B}$ never generates any public key by itself. Hence upk must be ever gotten from $\mathcal{B}$'s challenger and then transferred to $\mathcal{A}$. Hence $\mathcal{B}$ also never violate restriction I.1.

I.2 According to $\mathcal{B}$'s simulation of O^{FPK}, since $\mathcal{A}$ don't violates this restriction to make the query $O^{FPK}(ID^*, pk^*_{ID^*})$, $\mathcal{B}$ will not make the query $O^{FPK}(ID^{*\prime}, pk^*_{ID^*}) = O^{FPK}(ID^* \, || pk^*_{ID^*}, pk^*_{ID^*})$. Hence, $\mathcal{B}$ will not violates this rule.

I.3 According to $\mathcal{B}$'s simulation of O^{DEC}, since $\mathcal{A}$ don't violates this rule to make the query $O^{DEC}(ID^*, pk^*_{ID^*}, c^*)$, $\mathcal{B}$ will not make the query $O^{DEC}(ID^{*\prime}, pk^*_{ID^*}, c^*) = O^{DEC}(ID^* \, || pk^*_{ID^*}, pk^*_{ID^*}, c^*)$. Hence, $\mathcal{B}$ will not violates this rule.

I.4 According to $\mathcal{B}$'s simulation of O^{PPK}, since $\mathcal{A}$ don't violates this rule to make a partial private key query $O^{PPK}(ID^*,\ upk^*_{ID^*})$ for $upk^*_{ID^*} \notin \mathcal{OPK}$ (This means $upk^*_{ID^*}$ is generated by $\mathcal{A}$) and $\mathcal{B}$ never generates any public key by itself. Hence, $\mathcal{B}$ will not violates this rule.

Based on the above description, it can be seen that $\mathcal{B}$ makes the successful simulation for $\mathcal{A}$ without violating any restriction and wins the game only if $\mathcal{A}$ succeeds. Additionally, $\mathcal{B}$'s running time is equal to that of $\mathcal{A}$ without considering some trivial differences. Now, the proof is completed.

Theorem 2. If the conventional certificateless encryption scheme $\mathcal{CLE}$ is CCA secure against PPT adversaries of type II, then the corresponding key dependent certificateless encryption scheme $\mathcal{KD}$-$\mathcal{CLE}$ is CCA secure against PPT adversaries of type II.

Proof. We prove it by contradiction. Assume we have a Type II adversary $\mathcal{A}$ (against $\mathcal{KD}$-$\mathcal{CLE}$) whose advantage is non-negligible, we try to construct one Type II adversary $\mathcal{B}$ (against $\mathcal{CLE}$) whose advantage is also non-negligible. $\mathcal{B}$ simulates the game for $\mathcal{A}$. $\mathcal{B}$ first passes mpk to $\mathcal{A}$ and answers $\mathcal{A}$'s queries as below.

- $O^{MSK}(mpk)$: $\mathcal{B}$ makes the query $O^{MSK}(mpk)$ to its own challenger, and transfer the answer to $\mathcal{A}$.
- $O^{UPK}(ID)$, $O^{RPK}(ID, upk)$, $O^{FPK}(ID, upk)$, $O^{DEC}(ID, upk, c)$: $\mathcal{B}$ simulates these oracle queries just as in the proof for Theorem 1.

During these oracle queries, when $\mathcal{A}$ outputs $(ID^*, upk^*_{ID^*}, m_0, m_1)$ as the target, $\mathcal{B}$ sends $(ID^{*\prime}, upk^*_{ID^*}, m_0, m_1)$ to its challenger for $ID^{*\prime} = ID^* || upk^*_{ID^*}$. After the target ciphertext c^* is received from the challenger, B transfers c^* to $\mathcal{A}$ as the target ciphertext. B then answers the oracle queries as before. At the end, when $\mathcal{A}$ provides a bit b' to $\mathcal{B}$, $\mathcal{B}$ transfers b' to its own challenger.

Just as analyzed in the proof for Theorem 1, $\mathcal{B}$ will not violates the restriction rules II.1, II.2, II.3. According to the restriction rule II.4, $upk^*_{ID^*}$ should be generated by $\mathcal{A}$'s challenger (here simulated by $\mathcal{B}$). However during the whole simulation process, $\mathcal{B}$ never generated any public key by itself. Hence $upk^*_{ID^*}$ is not generated by $\mathcal{A}$ or $\mathcal{B}$, but be generated by $\mathcal{B}$'s challenger and then given to $\mathcal{B}$. Hence $\mathcal{B}$ does not violates the restriction rule II.4.

Based on the above description, it can be seen that $\mathcal{B}$ makes the successful simulation for $\mathcal{A}$ without violating any restriction and wins the game only if $\mathcal{A}$ succeeds. Additionally, $\mathcal{B}$'s running time is same to that of $\mathcal{A}$ without considering some trivial differences. Now, the proof is completed.

4 KD-CLE Scheme Secure in the Standard Model

When the AP binding technique is applied to the Dent-Libert-Paterson conventional CLE scheme, the following KD-CLE scheme is constructed. The KD-CLE scheme works as follows.

First, we present bilinear pairing which is used for our KD-CLE construction. Let $\mathbb{G}, \mathbb{G}_T$ be the prime q-order groups and let g be $\mathbb{G}$'s generator, where $\mathbb{G}$ and $\mathbb{G}_T$ are multiplicatively represented. A map $e : \mathbb{G} \times \mathbb{G} \rightarrow \mathbb{G}_T$ is called a bilinear pairing, if the below conditions all hold: (1) e is bilinear: $e(g^a, g^b) = e(g, g)^{ab}$ where $a, b \in \mathbb{Z}_q^*$; (2) e is non-degenerate: $e(g, g) \neq 1$, where 1 is $\mathbb{G}_T$'s identity; (3) e can be efficiently computed.

- $\mathsf{Setup}(1^k)$: Let $(\mathbb{G}, \mathbb{G}_T)$ be bilinear pairing groups of order $q > 2^k$ and let g a generator of $\mathbb{G}$. Set $g_1 = g^\gamma$, where γ is randomly chosen from $\mathbb{Z}_p^*$, and randomly pick $g_2, u', u_1, u_2, \ldots, u_n, v', v_1, v_2, \ldots, v_n \in \mathbb{G}$. For $i = i_1 i_2 \ldots i_n$ and $w = w_1 w_2 \ldots w_n$, the two functions are as below.

$$F_u(i) = u' \prod_{j=1}^{n} u_j^{i_j} \text{ and } F_v(w) = v' \prod_{j=1}^{n} v_j^{w_j}$$

  The hash function $H : \{0,1\}^* \leftarrow \{0,1\}^n$ is collision resistant (here note, H will not be assumed as the random oracle in the security proof). Let the master public key be

$$mpk \leftarrow (g, g_1, g_2, u', u_1, \ldots, u_n, v', v_1, \ldots, v_n)$$

  and the master secret key be $msk \leftarrow g_2^\gamma$.
- $\mathsf{GenUSK}(mpk)$: Return the user secret key x_{ID} which is randomly chosen from $\mathbb{Z}_p^*$.
- $\mathsf{GenUPK}(x_{ID}, mpk)$: Return $upk_{ID} = (X, Y) = (g^{x_{ID}}, g_1^{x_{ID}})$.
- $\mathsf{GenPPK}(mpk, \gamma, ID, upk_{ID})$: Pick $r \leftarrow \mathbb{Z}_p^*$ and return $d_{ID} = (d_1, d_2) = (g_2^\gamma \cdot F_u(i)^r, g^r)$, where $i = H(ID||upk_{ID})$.
- $\mathsf{GenFPK}(x_{ID}, d_{ID}, mpk)$: Randomly choose r' from $\mathbb{Z}_q^*$ and set the private key as

$$sk_{ID} = (s_1, s_2) = (d_1^{x_{ID}} \cdot F_u(i)^{r'}, d_2^{x_{ID}} \cdot g^{r'}) = (g_2^{\gamma x_{ID}} \cdot F_u(i)^t, g^t)$$

  where $i = H(ID||upk_{ID}), t = r x_{ID} + r'$.

- $\mathsf{Encrypt}(m, upk_{ID}, ID, mpk)$: If upk_{ID} is correctly shaped, randomly chooses s from $\mathbb{Z}_q^*$ and then computes

$$C = (C_0, C_1, C_2, C_3) = (m \cdot e(Y, g_2)^s, g^s, F_u(i)^s, F_v(w)^s),$$

where $i = H(ID||upk_{ID}), w \leftarrow H(C_0, C_1, C_2, ID, pk_{ID})$.
- $\mathsf{Decrypt}(C, sk_{ID}, mpk)$: If

$$e(C_1, F_u(i) \cdot F_v(w)) = e(g, C_2 \cdot C_3), \text{where } i = H(ID||upk_{ID}),$$

then return $m \leftarrow C_0 \cdot \frac{e(C_2, s_2)}{e(C_1, s_1)}$.

Lemma 1. The Dent-Libert-Paterson conventional CLE scheme [4] is CCA secure in our improved security model, if the 3-DDH assumption holds in the group $\mathbb{G}$.

Proof. In [4], for Type I attackers and Type II attackers, Theorems 2 and 3 respectively described the CCA provable security of the Dent-Libert-Paterson conventional CLE scheme in their security model. Now, we show that their security proof can be modified into the security proof in our new security model. First, revisit Remark 3 which explains the differences between our security model and that in [4]: with the *same* purpose to formally capture the case that the secret key of one identity ID is unknown by the adversary (or known by the challenger), we require that the public key should be the original one of **ANY** identity (ID or $ID' \neq ID$), while the public key should be the original (never replaced) one of **ONLY** ID in the security model of [4]. In other words, as said in Remark 3, for the case that the current secret key is known by the challenger, the previous security model ignored the subcase that the current public key of ID is not the original public key of itself, but is the original public key of the other identity ID'. Following this observation on security model differences, during checking and modifying the original security proof in [4], we only need to focus on the steps where the security proof aims to use the case that the challenger (or adversary) knows (or does not know) the secret key for the current public key, but uses the criterion whether the public key is the replaced one. We modifies these places by using the new criterion whether the public key has been original one of any identity, to decide whether the challenger (or adversary) knows (or does not know) the secret key for the current public key. In fact, at these places in the security proof, the relative logic is based on not how to ensure that the challenger (or adversary) knows (or unknows) the current secret key, but the ultimate result that the challenger (or adversary) knows (or unknows) the current secret key. For example, the case $c_{mode} = 1$ in Game 9 in the security proof of Theorem 2 in [4] only associates with whether the secret key is unknown by adversary (or known by the challenger). Hence, these modifications do not affect the logics of the original security proof in [4], but use the more reasonable criterion to fit the logics of the security proof. By this analysis, the security proof in [4] can be directly used as that for the above lemma with a few trivial modifications. Here we omit the detailed the proof.

Following Theorems 1, 2 and Lemma 1, the following corollary can be directly obtained.

Theorem 3. The above KD-CLE scheme is CCA secure if the 3-DDH problem is assumed to be intractable in the group $\mathbb{G}$.

5 Further Discussions

Now we point out the following observations. Firstly, many existing CLE schemes, provably secure in their "old" security model, can remain provably secure in our new security model. For example, as shown in Lemma 1, the Dent-Libert-Paterson conventional CLE scheme [4] remains provably secure in our new security model, by slightly or even trivially modifying the previous proof in the "old" security model. In the security proof of Lemma 1, the reasons why these modifications work has been concretely explained.

Secondly, many efficient KD-CLE schemes can be modularly constructed from existing conventional CLE schemes. In fact, the security proof in our new security model helps to "revive" the "perfect" and "old" generic transforming method from conventional CLE to KD-CLE due to Al-Rayami and Paterson. "Perfect" means that, unlike the results in [14], the AP transformation can construct KD-CLE from conventional CLE with almost no cost.

Thirdly, similar results for key-dependent certificateless signatures can be obviously obtained [11,14], following the results on modularly transforming conventional CLE into KD-CLE. Since this further extension is trivial, we omitted these detailed descriptions for KD-CLS. Additionally, following the results for key dependent encryption and signatures, other certificateless primitives, such as signcryption and authentication [13] in the key dependent sense can also be trivially obtained.

At last, our improved security model is more comprehensive and may be technically significant in basic theory for certificateless cryptography. In fact, there are many works on improving the security model for certificateless primitives [2,5,9,10,12,14,16]. However, to capture "whether the current secret key is unknown by the adversary" (simultaneously known by the challenger), all previous security models use the standard "whether the public key has been replaced" while our security model uses the standard "whether the public key has been generated by the challenger (denoted by $upk \in \mathcal{OPK}$)".

6 Conclusion

We positively answered the open problem whether the AP binding technique [1,14] is provably secure. This result means that any provably secure conventional CLE/CLS scheme with KGC trust level 2 can be almost directly transformed into the corresponding provably secure key dependent CLE/CLS scheme with KGC trust level 3. As a example, we modularly constructed one key dependent CLE scheme with KGC trust level 3 and provable security in the stand model.

Although the improved CLE security is proposed for proving security for the AP binding technique, it may have independent significance in certificateless cryptography.

Acknowledgements. This work is partially supported by National Natural Science Foundation of China (Nos. 61202475, 61133014, 61472114), the Priority Academic Program Development of Jiangsu Higher Education Institutions (PAPD, Nanjing University of Information Science & Technology), Jiangsu Collaborative Innovation Center on Atmospheric Environment and Equipment Technology (CICAEET, Nanjing University of Information Science & Technology), and the open foundation of Key Laboratory of Information Security, School of Mathematics and Information Science.

References

1. Al-Riyami, S.S., Paterson, K.G.: Certificateless public key cryptography. In: Laih, C.-S. (ed.) ASIACRYPT 2003. LNCS, vol. 2894, pp. 452–473. Springer, Heidelberg (2003). doi:10.1007/978-3-540-40061-5_29
2. Au, M.H., Chen, J., Liu, J.K., Mu, Y., Wong, D.S., Yang, G.: Malicious KGC attack in certificateless cryptography. In: Proceedings of the 2nd ACM Symposium on Information, Computer and Communications Security, pp. 302–311. ACM (2007)
3. Dan, B., Franklin, M.: Identity-based encryption from the weil pairing. SIAM J. Comput. **32**(3), 213–229 (2003)
4. Dent, A.W., Libert, B., Paterson, K.G.: Certificateless encryption schemes strongly secure in the standard model. In: Cramer, R. (ed.) PKC 2008. LNCS, vol. 4939, pp. 344–359. Springer, Heidelberg (2008). doi:10.1007/978-3-540-78440-1_20
5. Dent, A.W.: A survey of certificateless encryption schemes and security models. Int. J. Inf. Secur. **7**(5), 349–377 (2008)
6. Girault, M.: Self-certified public keys. In: Davies, D.W. (ed.) EUROCRYPT 1991. LNCS, vol. 547, pp. 490–497. Springer, Heidelberg (1991). doi:10.1007/3-540-46416-6_42
7. Hu, B.C., Wong, D.S., Zhang, Z., Deng, X.: Certificateless signature: a new security model and an improved generic construction. Des. Codes Cryptogr. **42**(2), 109–126 (2007)
8. Huang, Q., Wong, D.S.: Generic certificateless encryption secure against malicious-but-passive kgc attacks in the standard model. J. Comput. Sci. Technol. **25**(4), 807–826 (2010)
9. Huang, X., Mu, Y., Susilo, W., Wong, D.S., Wu, W.: Certificateless signatures: new schemes and security models. Comput. J. **55**(4), 457–474 (2012)
10. Liu, J.K., Au, M.H., Susilo, W.: Self-generated-certificate public key cryptography and certificateless signature/encryption scheme in the standard model. In: Proceedings of the 2nd ACM Symposium on Information, Computer and Communications Security, pp. 273–283. ACM (2007)
11. Pang, L., Hu, Y., Liu, Y., Xu, K., Li, H.: Efficient and secure certificateless signature scheme in the standard model. Theoret. Comput. Sci. **30**(5), 3025–3041 (2017)
12. Wang, X.A., Huang, X., Yang, X.: Further observations on certificateless public key encryption. In: Yung, M., Liu, P., Lin, D. (eds.) Inscrypt 2008. LNCS, vol. 5487, pp. 217–239. Springer, Heidelberg (2009). doi:10.1007/978-3-642-01440-6_18

13. Xiong, H.: Cost-effective scalable and anonymous certificateless remote authentication protocol. IEEE Trans. Inf. Forensics Secur. **9**(12), 2327–2339 (2014)
14. Yang, G., Tan, C.H.: Certificateless cryptography with KGC trust level 3. Theor. Comput. Sci. **412**(39), 5446–5457 (2011)
15. Yang, W., Zhang, F., Shen, L.: Efficient certificateless encryption withstanding attacks from malicious KGC without using random oracles. Secur. Commun. Netw. **7**(2), 445–454 (2014)
16. Zhang, F., Shen, L., Wu, G.: Notes on the security of certificateless aggregate signature schemes. Inf. Sci. **287**, 32–37 (2014)

Server-Less Lightweight Authentication Protocol for RFID System

Jing Li, Zhiping Zhou(✉), and Ping Wang

Engineering Research Center of Internet of Things Technology, Applications Ministry of Education, Jiangsu 214122, China
{6141913003,6151913006}@vip.jiangnan.edu.cn, zzp@jiangnan.edu.cn

Abstract. The design of secure authentication protocols for RFID system is still a great challenging problem. Many authentication protocols for RFID have been presented, but most have security flaws. We analyzes the security of scheme proposed by Deng et al., and point out that this scheme can't resist location tracking attack, and the low efficiency of the reader searches a target tag. Based on this, an improved protocol to overcome the security vulnerability of Deng's protocol is presented. The formal proof of correctness of the improved protocol is given based on GNY logic which is one of the model logics, and finally experiments shows the improved protocol has the good efficiency of time complexity.

Keywords: RFID · Authentication protocol · Location tracking attack · Time complexity

1 Introduction

With the development of RFID system technology, RFID system has been applied in different scenarios. Several researchers have proposed authentication protocol for RFID tag and reader without backend server. Ref [1] firstly proposed server-less authentication protocol for RFID, authorization stage of this scheme of the reader communication with the Central Server (*CS*) to download the access list L_i of the authorized tags. But through the security analysis shows that the proposed protocol only meets the one-way authentication, namely the reader authenticates a tag, while the tag does not authenticate the reader, which is vulnerable to reader impersonation attack, and it is possible to leak the location privacy of the user using the reader. In addition, Ref [2] also pointed out that the proposed scheme of Ref [1] has the problem of tag tracking attack and tag impersonation attack. Ref [3] proposed a lightweight and server-less RFID authentication protocol, but Ref [4] showed that this scheme is vulnerable to impersonation attack and reply attack, and based on this, an improved protocol is proposed. They claim the improved scheme meets mutual authentication, anonymity, untraceability and resists Dos attack. However, Ref [5] pointed that the improved scheme of Ref [4] is vulnerable to tag tracking attack, as the tag uses a constant value challenge-response to the reader, which causes an attacker simulate a reader to track a target tag. And at last, an improved protocol was proposed. But, through security

X. Sun et al. (Eds.): ICCCS 2017, Part II, LNCS 10603, pp. 305–314, 2017.
https://doi.org/10.1007/978-3-319-68542-7_25

analysis, the improved scheme still exist reply attack, tracking attack and only meets only one side authentication. Ref [6] put forward a enhancing privacy RFID system with server-less authentication protocol, while Ref [7] showed the scheme of Ref [6] has de-synchronization attack problem, and an improved protocol was proposed to overcome this attack. But in this paper we show that protocol of Ref [7] is vulnerability against location tracking attack. Ref [8] put forward server-less RFID mutual authentication and secure tag search protocols, and Ref [9] put forward a version of a hash-based RFID server-less security scheme, their schemes have a good security attribute. But we find that the above schemes of design exist in common properties, i.e. the readers of these schemes require $O(N)$ work to identify and authenticate a tag, which is not suitable for large-scale environment. In order to identify and authenticate a target tag quickly, the tree-based hash RFID authentication protocols with server-less were proposed [11–13], which make the reader search tag time complexity from $O(N)$ to $O(\log_{\alpha} N)$, where α is the branching factor at each level of the tree, N is the total number of RFID tags. Ref [11–13] in search time complexity is greatly reduced, but tags of these schemes once compromised by an attacker to obtain its inner information, which cause the key information of other tags been exposed. That is to say, the tree structure of authentication schemes has information leakage problems. Ref [14] proposed an efficient detection of counterfeit products in large-scale RFID systems using batch authenticating protocol, this scheme adopted the idea of grouping to improve the efficiency of system. Base on this, this paper adopt the idea of grouping applied to improved protocol to improve the efficiency of system. Moreover, changing the mode of the reader updates key to solve the de-synchronization attack, and when key is updated, it introduces random numbers to resist to tracking attack.

Through analysis show that the above schemes based on server-less RFID security authentication protocol has some problems: (1) time complexity, in order to provide anonymous, the tag can't directly provide their own identifier, rather than they send their identifier to reader by encrypted, and then the reader tries key of all tags to match messages. In other words, the cost of validation tag is linear with the number of tags, which seriously affect the efficiency of RFID system; (2) location privacy, an attacker obtains key information of tag by violent attack, and then makes the tag put into circulation, which can track the tag after each round of authentication by the attacker; (3) unable to resist common attacks, such as impersonation attack, reply attack, de-synchronization attack and so on; Based on this, a server-less RFID security authentication protocol is proposed based on Ref [7], the improved scheme not only solves location tracking attack, but also reduces the reader's time complexity to improve the efficiency of RFID system.

2 Vulnerability of Deng et al.'s Protocol

Deng et al. proposed authentication scheme based on proposed protocol by Hoque et al.'s [6] to avoid the de-synchronization attack, and the design of scheme referred to Ref. [7]. However, through Ouafi-Phan privacy model finds this scheme of Ref. [7] has location tracking attack problem. Besides, the search time complexity of the reader is $O(N)$, which is not suitable for large-scale RFID system. The details of three vulnerabilities are described in the following subsections.

2.1 Location Tracking Attack

Learning phase: In the l round of communication interaction, an attacker calls *Corrupt query*(T_0, k) to obtain the tag's inner information $seed_{T_0}^{l}$, and then the attacker computes message $\alpha = M(M(seed_{T_0}^{l}))$ according to obtain information of the tag T_0.

Challenge phase: The attacker selects two fresh tags T_0 and T_1 for test, and calls a *Test query*$(T_0, T_1, l+1)$. According to the randomly chosen a bit $b \in \{0, 1\}$, the attacker is given a tag $T_b \in \{T_0, T_1\}$. Afterwards, the attacker calls *Execute query*$(R, T_b, l+1)$ to obtain communication messages $< rand_i^{l+1}, rand_j^{l+1}, n_j^{l+1} >$ between the entities.

Guess phase: The attacker stops the game G, and outputs a bit $b' \in \{0, 1\}$ as a guess of bit b as follows.

$$b' = \begin{cases} 0 & if\ C_{i+1}^{T_b} = C_i^{T_0} \\ 1 & otherwise \end{cases} \tag{1}$$

Stick out a mile, we have:

$$\begin{aligned} Adv_A^{upriv}(k) &= |pr(b' = b) - pr(random\ coin\ flip)| \\ &= |pr(b' = b) - \frac{1}{2}| \\ &= |1 - \frac{1}{2}| = \frac{1}{2} \gg \varepsilon \end{aligned} \tag{2}$$

Proof: if $T_b = T_0$, then

$$\begin{aligned} n_j^{l+1} &= P(seed_{T_0}^{l+1} \oplus (rand_i^{l+1} || rand_j^{l+1})) \\ &= P(M(M(seed_{T_0}^{l})) \oplus (rand_i^{l+1} || rand_j^{l+1})) \\ &= PRNG(\alpha \oplus (rand_i^{l+1} || rand_j^{l+1})) \end{aligned} \tag{3}$$

The security of Deng et al.'s scheme depends on the key seed shared by reader and tag. If the interactive authentication is successful, the reader and tag side update key seeds through the hash function, as $Seed = M(M(seed))$, where $M(.)$ is denotes the one-way hash function. Once the tag is compromised by an attacker, the attacker can obtain tag's inner information, and the probability of obtaining the key seed after each successful authentication is 1. The attacker can compute n_j through intercepting random numbers $rand_i$, $rand_j$ between reader and tag sides, so the attacker can track the target tag.

2.2 Time Complexity

After the reader receives the tag's challenge-response message, it searches each tag's directory information from database list to match, and its time complexity is $O(N)$, where N is denotes total number of tags. In the worst case, the reader is exhaustive search, as it operates N times pseudo random number generator operation to match transform message from tag. Therefore, with the increase number of storage tags, the reader search time also increase linearly.

3 Improved Protocol

3.1 The Improved Protocol Description

Similar to proposed protocol by Deng et al. has two stages: initialization phase and authentication phase.

Initialization phase: The reader and the tag store the information needed to perform the authentication process, which differs from protocol of Deng et al. lie in: tags of the improved protocol are divided into τ disjoint groups, and each group size is $n = N/\tau$. Each group is associated with a unique key that we refer to as a group key ID_G, as every tag shares this group key with other members of the given group. Each tag is assigned a unique key that is only available for the tag and the reader.

Authentication phase: The improved protocol authentication process as shown in Fig. 1, the specific process is as follows:

Step 1 $R_i \rightarrow T_j$: The reader R_i generates random number $rand_i$, and sending a query command and $rand_i$ to tag T_j;

Step 2 $T_j \rightarrow R_i$: Receiving the generated random number $rand_i$ from R_i, the tag T_j generates random number $rand_j$ and computes $a_j = P(ID_{Gi} \oplus (rand_j || rand_i))$, $n_j = P(Seed_{Tj} \oplus (rand_i || rand_j))$, and sending the message $<a_j, n_j, rand_j>$ as a response message to the reader R_i;

Step 3 $R_i \rightarrow T_j$: Receiving the tag's message, the reader R_i search ID_{Gi} from data directory to make $a_q = P(ID_{Gi} \oplus (rand_j || rand_i))$, where $q \in \{1, 2, \ldots, \tau\}$. If $a_q = a_j$, it stands for that the target tag belongs to the q group tag.
The reader R_i continues searches $Seed_{Tj}$ from data directory of the q group tag to make $n_m = P(Seed_{Tj} \oplus (rand_i || rand_j))$, where $m \in \{1, 2, \ldots, n\}$. If $n_m == n_j$, the reader updates key $Seed_{PTj} = Seed_{Tj}$, $Seed_{Tj} = M(Seed_{Tj} \oplus (rand_j || rand_i))$. The reader R_i completes the update key after computes $s = M(Seed_{Tj} \oplus rand_j)$, $n_i = P(s)$.
If $n_m \neq n_j$, the reader R_i searches $Seed_{PTj}$ from data directory of the q group tag to make $n_m = P(Seed_{pTj} \oplus (rand_i || rand_j))$, where $m \in \{1, 2, \ldots, n\}$. When $n_m == n_j$, the reader updates key, as $Seed_{Tj} = M(Seed_{Tj} \oplus (rand_j || rand_i))$. The reader R_i computes $s = M(Seed_{pTj} \oplus rand_j)$, $n_i = P(s)$ after completing the update key. At last, the reader R_i sends message n_i to the tag T_j.

(1) $R_i \rightarrow T_j$: request, rand$_i$
(2) $T_j : a_j = P(ID_{Gi} \oplus (rand_j \| rand_i))$
(3) $\quad n_j = P(Seed_{Tj} \oplus (rand_i \| rand_j))$
(4) $T_j \rightarrow R_i : a_j, n_j, rand_j$
(5) $R_i : n_i = rand_i$
(6) $\quad$ *for all q from* 1 *to* τ
(7) $\qquad$ *Let* $a_q = P(ID_{Gi} \oplus (rand_j \| rand_i))$
(8) $\quad$ *for all m from* 1 *to n*
(9) $\qquad$ *Let* $n_m = P(Seed_{Tj} \oplus (rand_i \| rand_j))$
(10) $\qquad$ *if* $(n_m == n_j)$ *then*
(11) $\qquad\quad$ *Let* $Seed_{PTj} \leftarrow Seed_{Tj} \leftarrow M(Seed_{Tj} \oplus (rand_j \| rand_i))$
(12) $\qquad\quad s = M(Seed_{Tj})$
(13) $\qquad\quad n_i = P(s)$
(14) $\qquad\quad R_i \rightarrow T_j : n_i$
(15) $\quad$ *else for all m from* 1 *to n*
(16) $\qquad$ *Let* $n_m = P(Seed_{pTj} \oplus (rand_i \| rand_j))$
(17) $\qquad$ *if* $(n_m == n_j)$ *then*
(18) $\qquad\quad$ *Let* $Seed_{Tj} \leftarrow M(Seed_{pTj} \oplus (rand_j \| rand_i))$
(19) $\qquad\quad s = M(Seed_{pTj})$
(20) $\qquad\quad n_i = P(s)$
(21) $\qquad\quad R_i \rightarrow T_j : n_i$
(22) T_j : *Let* $k = M(Seed_{Tj})$
(23) $\qquad b = P(k)$
(24) $\quad$ *if* $(b == n_i)$ *then*
(25) $\qquad$ *Let* $Seed_{Tj} \leftarrow M(Seed_{Tj} \oplus (rand_j \| rand_i))$
(26) $\quad$ *else* Reader is not authorized
Or is an adversary

Fig. 1. The improved RFID authentication protocol

Step 4 T_j: Receiving the message from the reader R_i, the tag T_j computes $k = M(Seed_{Tj})$, $b = P(k)$. If $b == n_i$, the tag updates its own key $Seed_{Tj} = M(Seed_{Tj} \oplus (rand_j \| rand_i))$, else the tag doesn't update its own key.

3.2 Innovation Description

In order to prevent an attacker in some way to make a tag compromise to obtain the tag's inner information, resulting in tracking the target tag. The key of the improved scheme updates key and introduces the reader and tag side's random number $rand_i$, $rand_j$ in each round of communication successfully. The two random numbers are added to the input parameters of the pseudo random number generator function, in this way, making the key is random and fresh.

To improve the efficiency of the large-scale RFID system, the improved scheme adopts the idea of Ref. [14] which based on the group. Suppose, N is the total number of tags in the system and τ is the number of groups, then the group size is $n = N/\tau$. Hence, the reader searches time complexity from $O(N)$ to $O(\tau + n)$. This ways prevents the exhaustive search of the reader and improves the efficiency of RFID authentication system.

4 Security Analysis

This section analyzes the security performance of the proposed scheme.

Resistant replay attack: Replay attack, that is, an attacker sends session message to the next round of conversation through eavesdropping and interception of the previous session. An arbitrary authentication process in the improved scheme, the reader and tag generate different random numbers and adopt pseudo random number generator to encrypt the message, making the interactive authentication of an arbitrary authentication process no rules, namely the communication message is random. Assume an attacker replies message $<a_j, n_j, rand_j>$ to reader, due to each round of interactive authentication process introducing fresh random number, the attacker can't adopt the way of replaying to obtain the possibility of the other party validation by intercepting message. This is a way to prevent an attacker from completing the authentication process successfully.

Mutual authentication: For the reader, the reader first verifies that the tag belongs to which groups of tags, as verifies $a_q = ?P(ID_{Gi} \oplus (rand_j||rand_i))$. If equal, the reader is deemed to have the target tag in this group tag, and continues to verify $n_m = ?P(Seed_{Tj} \oplus (rand_i||rand_j))$ or $n_m = ?P(Seed_{pTj} \oplus (rand_i||rand_j))$. If equal, the reader looks the tag as a legal tag and updates the key of the tag. For the tag, the tag verifies $n_i = ?P(M(Seed_{Tj}))$ after receiving the reader's message. If equal, the tag looks the reader as a legal reader and updates its own key. This way to achieve strategy and means of mutual authentication between tag and reader, not only effectively prevent attackers from simulating the behavior of legal tag, but also can avoid attackers simulate authorized reader which malicious tracking the legal tag, improving RFID system security and resist aggression.

Resistant tracking attack: Tracking attack, that is, an attacker can distinguish between different tags by interactive communication of RFID authentication protocol. In the scheme of Deng et al., this key of construction method is $Seed_{Tj} = M(M(Seed_{Tj}))$, where M represents Hash function. Assume that a attacker can completely control over the communication channel. The Attacker can observe all interactive messages, modify interactive messages, delete interactive messages, delay interactive messages, and reply any messages during transmission [17]. Even, the attacker calls $Corrupt\ query(T_j, k)$ to obtain inner information $Seed_{Tj}$ of tag T_j, moreover, One-way Hash function is a function of the public, so people can obtain its algorithms. We can find that attackers can obtain the key of later each round, and then tracking the target the tag.

Resistant de-synchronization attack: The reader of the improved protocol stores the current and previous key, and judges the received message from tag match with which round key to calculate. If matches with the previous round key by the encryption operation, then the reader only updates and stores the current key, as $Seed_{Tj} = M(Seed_{Tj} \oplus (rand_j||rand_i))$; If matches with the current round key by the encryption operation, the reader updates and stores two round keys, as $Seed_{PTj} = Seed_{Tj}$, $Seed_{Tj} = M(Seed_{Tj} \oplus (rand_j||rand_i))$. Therefore, the method to solve the de-synchronization attack is as follows: the tag only updates key after receiving the reader's reply message and verifying successfully, meanwhile, the reader keeps the tag's key of the previous round. In this way, the attacker regardless of by what way to attack, this protocol can resist de-synchronization attack.

To contrast clearly compare with existing protocols based on server-less RFID authentication protocol in the aspect of security and privacy, as shown in Table 1. By comparison, Ref [1, 5–7] has tracking attack problems, making the holder tag is always followed by an attacker. Ref [1, 5] didn't realize mutual authentication, and were vulnerable to common attacks. Ref [6] is vulnerable to de-synchronization attack, making the tag itself stored data information is inconsistent with stored tags' data information of the reader, causing the tag lose authentication qualification. Ref [9] and the improved scheme have a good security attribute.

Table 1. Security comparison

	Ref [1]	Ref [5]	Ref [6]	Ref [7]	Ref [9]	Improved scheme
Replay attack	√	✗	√	√	√	√
Mutual authentication	✗	✗	√	√	√	√
Tracking attack	✗	✗	✗	✗	√	√
De-synchronization attack	√	√	✗	√	√	√

5 Performance Evaluations

5.1 Compare with Time Complexity

In order to improve the reader's efficiency of the proposed protocol, we adopt the idea of grouping based on the Ref [14]. This section compares with the existing protocols [6, 7, 9, 14] and improved protocol in the aspect of searching time. The simulation environment is as follows: Intel Core i3-2.10 GHz, RAM-6 GB. Because each run time has small differences, we have run various operations 30 times respectively to get the average results, then the pseudo-random number generator function (*PRNG*) takes about 0.021 ms, the hash function takes about 0.25 ms. In order to facilitate comparison, we use a reader searches a target tag in the worst case time. In addition, the Ref [14] and the improved protocol make the total number of tag N divided into $\tau = 2$ groups, and the each group has N/τ tags. As shown in Fig. 2, the number of group tags increase from 0 to 100000, Ref [6, 7, 9, 14] and improved scheme of reader search target tag required time consuming rises with the number of tags increased, but the improved scheme of reader searching target tag required time consuming is smaller than proposed scheme by Ref [6, 7, 9, 14]. The Ref [14] and improved scheme use the idea based-group, but Ref [14] adopts hash function for each directory to match transmission messages. Ref [9] proposed scheme based on the Ref [6], and also uses hash function to instead of *PRNG* function to increase security level, but time consuming of one-way hash function takes about 10 times as much as the *PRNG* function. As a result, the rising speed of Ref [9, 14] is faster than that of Ref [7] and the improved scheme.

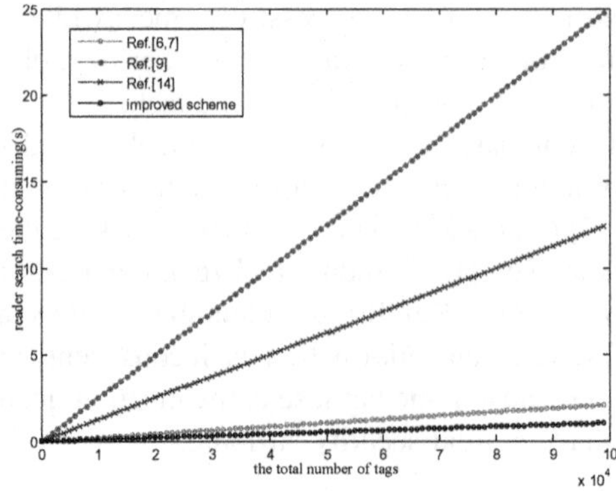

Fig. 2. Time-consuming contrast of the reader searching target tag

5.2 The Effect of Grouping on Search Time

In the improved scheme, when the total number of tags N is fixed, the change of group numbers will causes changes of the reader search target tag time-consuming. As shown in Fig. 3, when $N = 10000$ or $N = 100000$ or $N = 200000$, the reader search time-consuming curve is decline first, then reaches the minimum, and then rise. When $N = 10000$ and $\tau = 100$, the reader search time at least, is 4.2 ms; when $N = 100000$, $\tau = 316$, the reader search time at least, is 13.2816 ms; when $N = 200000$, $\tau = 447$, the reader search time at least, is 18.783 ms. This is due to the reader's search time associated with $(\tau + N/\tau)$. In order to make the reader search time consuming least, then make $t = \arg\min_{\tau}(\tau + N/\tau)$, where $1 \leq \tau \leq N$, we can find that when $\tau = \sqrt{N}$, t takes the minimum value. However, since the number of τ is an integer, when $\tau = ceil(\sqrt{N})$, the reader search time at least. The composite Figs. 2 and 3 show that we can find when τ is fixed value, the reader search targert time required

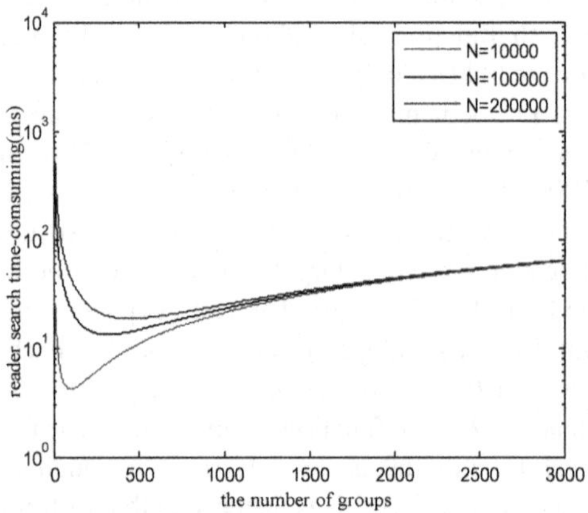

Fig. 3. The effect of grouping on reader search time-consuming

time-consuming increase linearly with the number of tags increased. When N is fixed value, the reader search time-consuming curve is decline first, then reaches the minimum, and then rise. Therefore, in the improved scheme, we must determine the total number of tags first, and according to the tatal number of tags to determine the number of groups, so that the reader search target tag of time-consuming at least in the worst case.

6 Conclusion

Designing of a secure authentication scheme for low-cost RFID tags is still an open and challenging problem. In this paper, we first cryptanalysis a recent lightweight RFID authentication protocol and an improved server-less RFID security authentication protocol is presented. By security analysis and experimental results show that the proposed protocol not only resist various attacks, but also improve the efficiency of RFID system.

Acknowledgements. This work is supported by the Special Funds of Basic Research Business Expenses of Central University under Grant No. JUSRP51510.

References

1. Tan, C.C., Sheng, B., Li, Q.: Serverless search and authentication protocols for RFID. In: 5th Annual IEEE International Conference on Pervasive Computing and Communications, pp. 3–12. IEEE Press, White Plains (2007)
2. Safkhani, M., Peris-Lopez, P., Bagheri, N., Naderi, M., Hernandez-Castro, J.C.: On the Security of Tan et al. Serverless RFID Authentication and Search Protocols. In: Hoepman, J.-H., Verbauwhede, I. (eds.) RFIDSec 2012. LNCS, vol. 7739, pp. 1–19. Springer, Heidelberg (2013). doi:10.1007/978-3-642-36140-1_1
3. Lin, L.C., Tsaur, S.C., Chang, K.P.: Lightweight and serverless RFID authentication and search protocol. In: 2nd IEEE International Conference on Computer and Electrical Engineering, pp. 95–99. IEEE Press, Dubai (2010)
4. Lee, C.F., Chien, H.Y., Laih, C.S.: Server-less RFID authentication and searching protocol with enhanced security. J. Inter. J. Commun. Syst. **25**(3), 376–385 (2012)
5. He, J.L., Xu, Y.J., Xu, Z.Q.: Secure and private protocols for server-less RFID systems. J. Inter. J. Control Autom. **7**(2), 131–142 (2014)
6. Hoque, M.E., Rahman, F., Ahamed, S.I., et al.: Enhancing privacy and security of RFID system with server-less authentication and search protocols in pervasive environments. J. Wirel. Per. Commun. **55**(1), 65–79 (2010)
7. Deng, M., Yang, W., Zhu, W.: Weakness in a server-less authentication protocol for radio frequency identification. J. Mechatron. Autom. Control Syst. **237**, 1055–1061 (2014)
8. Mtita, C., Laurent, M., Delort, J.: Efficient server-less radio-frequency identification mutual authentication and secure tag search protocols with untrusted readers. J. IET. Info. Secur. **10** (5), 262–271 (2016)
9. Abdolmaleky, S., Atapoor, S., Hajighasemlou, M., et al.: A strengthened version of a Hash-based RFID server-less security scheme. J. Adv. Comput. Sci. **4**(3), 18–23 (2015)

10. Kumar, N., Kaur, K., Misra, S.C., et al.: An intelligent RFID-enabled authentication scheme for healthcare applications in vehicular mobile cloud. J. Peer-to-Peer Netw. Appl. **9**(5), 824–840 (2015)
11. Nohl, K., Evans, D.: Quantifying information leakage in tree-based Hash protocols. In: Ning, P., Qing, S., Li, N. (eds.) ICICS 2006. LNCS, vol. 4307, pp. 228–237. Springer, Heidelberg (2006). doi:10.1007/11935308_16
12. Bringer, J., Chabanne, H., Icart, T.: Improved privacy of the tree-based hash protocols using physically unclonable function. In: Ostrovsky, R., De-Prisco, R., Visconti, I. (eds.) SCN 2008. LNCS, vol. 5229, pp. 77–91. Springer, Heidelberg (2008). doi:10.1007/978-3-540-85855-3_6
13. Alabrah, A., Bassiouni, M.: A tree-based authentication scheme for a cloud toll/traffic RFID system. In: 2015 IEEE Vehicular Networking Conference, pp. 108–111. IEEE Press, Kyoto (2016)
14. Rahman, F., Ahamed, S.I.: Efficient detection of counterfeit products in large-scale RFID systems using batch authentication protocols. J. Pers. Ubiquit. Comput. **18**(1), 177–188 (2014)
15. Chen, Y., Chou, J.S.: ECC-based untraceable authentication for large-scale active-tag RFID systems. J. Electron. Commer. Res. **15**(1), 97–120 (2015)
16. Qu, Z., Keeney, J., Robitzsch, S., et al.: Multilevel pattern mining architecture for automatic network monitoring in heterogeneous wireless communication networks. J. China Commun. **13**(7), 108–116 (2016)
17. Ouafi, K., Phan, R.C.W.: Privacy of recent RFID authentication protocols. In: Chen, L., Mu, Y., Susilo, W. (eds.) ISPEC 2008. LNCS, vol. 4991, pp. 263–277. Springer, Berlin Heidelberg (2008). doi:10.1007/978-3-540-79104-1_19
18. Zhang, Y., Sun, X., Wang, B.: Efficient algorithm for K-barrier coverage based on integer linear programming. J. China Commun. **13**(7), 16–23 (2016)
19. Wang, B., Gu, X., Ma, L., et al.: Temperature error correction based on BP neural network in meteorological wireless sensor network. In: Sun, X., Liu, A., Chao, H.C., Bertino, E. (eds.) ICCCS 2016. LNCS, vol. 10040, pp. 117–132. Springer, Cham (2016). doi:10.1007/978-3-319-48674-1_11
20. Liu, Q., Cai, W., Shen, J., et al.: A speculative approach to spatial-temporal efficiency with multi-objective optimization in a heterogeneous cloud environment. J. Secur. Commun. Netw. **9**(17), 4002–4012 (2016)

Efficient CP-ABE with Non-monotonic Access Structures

Yong Cheng(✉), Huaizhe Zhou, Jun Ma, and Zhiying Wang

Computer School, National University of Defense Technology, Changsha, China
{ycheng,huaizhezhou,majun,zywang}@nudt.edu.cn

Abstract. Ciphertext policy attribute based encryption (CP-ABE) systems are suitable for supporting access control with complex attribute-based policies. But there is a few CP-ABE systems that support non-monotonic access structures. In this paper we present an efficient CP-ABE construction which supports **NOT** operation as well as m-of-n threshold gates. This construction is proved to be selectively secure under decisional bilinear Diffie-Hellman assumption. The comparison between our scheme and other similar systems shows that our construction is an efficient and expressive CP-ABE construction that supports the negation of attributes.

Keywords: CP-ABE · Access control · Non-monotonic access structures

1 Introduction

Nowadays, there is an emerging trend that more and more customers are using the public infrastructure (e.g. cloud storage) for online data sharing. However, these public service providers are "untrusted"and may compromise users' data. So customers are trend to adopt the public key encryption as a powerful mechanism for protecting the data confidentiality [1]. Generally speaking, traditional public key encryption algorithms are not suitable for supporting data sharing with complex access control policies [2]. The reasons are resided in two aspects. First, the data sender has to define an exact list of all receivers and obtain their public key before encrypting data. Second, the data need to be encrypted to each particular receiver's public key, which will increase the sender's computational cost significantly.

Sahai and Waters [3] introduced a new vision of public key encryption named Attribute Based Encryption (ABE). ABE algorithm enables the data sender to express how he/she wants to share the data as follows. First, every data

Y. Cheng is an engineer at National University of Defense Technology, Changsha, P. R. China. His current research interests include the storage security in public cloud services, trusted computing in public cloud or other un-trusted devices, cryptographic algorithm design for data security, data leakage prevention, etc.

X. Sun et al. (Eds.): ICCCS 2017, Part II, LNCS 10603, pp. 315–325, 2017.
https://doi.org/10.1007/978-3-319-68542-7_26

receiver is represented by a set of string called "attributes". Then a private key is generated for each receiver associated with his/her attributes. Last, the data sender describes the data access control policy through a formula over all receivers' attributes. A receiver can decrypt the ciphertext if and only if his/her attributes satisfy the access formula. The main drawback of Sahai-Water approach is that the access control policy can only be expressed in a monotone access formula consisting of one threshold gate.

Goyal et al. [4] proposed a variant of ABE named Key-Policy ABE (KP-ABE) which can greatly increase the expressibility of access structures. In KP-ABE scheme, the users' private keys can express any monotone access formula consisting of m-of-n ($1 \leq m \leq n$, $m, n \in \mathbb{Z}_+$) threshold gates. Notice that **AND** gates can be expressed as n-of-n threshold gates and **OR** gates as 1-of-n threshold gates. Another variant of ABE proposed by Bethencourt et al. [5] is Ciphertext-Policy ABE (CP-ABE). On the contrary, CP-ABE's ciphertexts is associated with a threshold access structure. The CP-ABE algorithm also supports any monotone access formula consisting of **AND**, **OR**, or threshold gates. Although the KP-ABE and CP-ABE are more expressive than the ABE initial construction, there is still a fundamental limitation that the monotone access formula cannot express *negative* constraints.

To address the problem of non-monotonic access formulas, Ostrovsky et al. [6] (OSW) proposed a KP-ABE scheme that supports any access formula over attributes, including non-monotonic access structures. The OSW construction employs the idea of broadcast revocation scheme [7] to support the expression of both negative and non negative attributes. But its public parameter is consisted of $O(n)$ group elements and its private keys are consisted of $O(t\log(n))$ group elements, where t represents the amount of shares generated by Linear Secret Sharing Schemes [8] (LSSS), and n is the size of the universal attributes set. Lewko et al. [9] (LSW) proposed a more efficient scheme over OSW for non-monotonic ABE, in which the public parameter will be only $O(1)$ group elements and private keys will be of size $O(t)$. Both the OSW scheme and the promoted one have the ciphertext consisting of $O(n)$ group elements. The first work to explicitly support non-monotonic in CP-ABE was proposed by Cheung and Newport [10](CN). They described a provably secure CP-ABE scheme which obtains chosen ciphertext security by using one-time signatures. But their access structures are consisted of only **AND** gates on positive and negative attributes, in other words, they only support **NOT** and **AND** operations.

1.1 Our Contribution

In this work, we present an efficient CP-ABE construction under Decisional Bilinear Diffie-Hellman (DBDH) assumption. Access structures in this scheme can be any formula involving **NOT**, **AND**, **OR**, and threshold gates. The security proof of the efficient construction is under DBDH assumption.

In this construction, the negation of an attribute is treated as a separate negative attribute beside the original one (positive attribute). At a high level, this technique implicitly makes a secret share available to the user if and only

Table 1. Comparison of ABE systems with non-monotonic access structures.

System	Type	Access structure	Supported policy
OSW [6]	KP-ABE	LSSS matrix	AND, OR, threshold, NOT
LSW [9]	KP-ABE	LSSS matrix	AND, OR, threshold, NOT
CN [10]	CP-ABE	AND gates	AND, NOT
Our scheme	CP-ABE	LSSS matrix	AND, OR, threshold, NOT

if the given attribute is not present among his/her attributes. Therefore, the system can support monotonic access structures with negative attributes. The main disadvantage of adapting negative attributes is that the number of users' attributes may be increased significantly. Suppose the size of universal attributes is n, we have to expand every user's attributes set to size n by adding negative attributes.

We find that the size of private keys can be reduced by applying primes theory. A fundamental theorem of arithmetic is that every integer greater than 1 can be expressed uniquely as a product of primes (no considering the order). Suppose that each attribute is "mapped" to an unique prime, then the attributes set can be expressed uniquely by the product of these primes. We can determine whether an attribute is in (belongs to) a set in such a way an attribute ("mapping" to prime p) belongs to a set (the product is s) if and only if $s \bmod p = 0$.

In Table 1 we summarize the comparisons between our scheme and the OSW, LSW and CN systems in terms of type, access structure, and supported policy. Taken all together our scheme is the first constructions of expressive CP-ABE algorithm that support non-monotonic access structures.

1.2 Related Work

ABE is derived from Identity-Based Encryption [11] (IBE), where IBE can be viewed as a special case of ABE actually. Sahai and Waters [3] introduced fuzzy identity-based encryption as a primitive work of ABE. And later the ABE systems are divided into KP-ABE and CP-ABE by Goyal et al. [4]. In KP-ABE systems, an encrypted ciphertext is associated with a set of attributes, and a user's private key represents the access structure over attributes. Contrary to KP-ABE, in CP-ABE systems a user's private key is associated with attributes and an encrypted ciphertext will reflect the access policy. Both in KP-ABE and CP-ABE systems, a user will be able to decrypt ciphertext if and only if the attributes set satisfies the access policy.

To date, a number of different constructions [6,9,10,12–14,16,21] of ABE have been proposed. Most of their constructions are based on Secret Sharing Schemes [17,18] (SSS); the exception is constructed through **AND** gates [10]. In these SSS-based systems, a randomness (or the system's master key [3,4]) is divided into shares by using SSS; and then these shares are embedded into user secret keys (KP-ABE) or ciphertext components (CP-ABE). In the **AND** gates based system, the master key is embedded into private key and ciphertext components directly. Generally speaking, the SSS based scheme is more expressive than the other one. The SSS based ABE algorithm usually takes access tree [5,19] or LSSS matrix [14] as the access structure. Because SSS are limited to expressing monotonic access structures (since a participating party can always choose not to contribute his share), the corresponding ABE scheme can only support **AND**, **OR**, or threshold gates. At the same time, the **AND** gates based system can support **NOT** gates naturally, but it can not support m-of-n threshold gates.

Ostrovsky et al. [6] introduced the first construction based on LSSS matrix which can support **NOT** gates as well as threshold ones. The OSW scheme transform the non-monotonic access structures into a monotonic one only with **NOT** gates on leaf nodes. And then the negative attribute is supported by make a share "available" to the decryptor if and only if the corresponding attribute is not presented. The OSW basic construction requires that every ciphertext has exactly d attributes. And at the expense of efficiency, this constraint can be removed by using "filler" attributes and parallel encryption systems. As a stepping optimization, Lewko et al. [9] directly remove the bound on the maximum number of attributes by adopting a random oracle model.

2 Background

Most existing ABE schemes only consider monotone access structures. Our constructions also will use monotone access structures, and we give the definition adopted from [8].

Definition 1 (Access Structure). *Let $\{P_1, ..., P_n\}$ denote a set of parties. A collection $\mathbb{A} \subseteq 2^{\{P_1,...,P_n\}}$ is monotone if $\forall B, C$: if $B \subseteq C$ and $B \in \mathbb{A}$, then $C \in \mathbb{A}$. An access structure (resp., monotonic access structure) is a collection (resp., monotone collection) $\mathbb{A}$ of non-empty subsets of $\{P_1, ..., P_n\}$, i.e., $\mathbb{A} \subseteq 2^{\{P_1,...,P_n\}} \backslash \{\varnothing\}$. The sets in $\mathbb{A}$ are called the authorized sets, and the sets not in $\mathbb{A}$ are called the unauthorized sets.*

We will also make essential use of linear secret-sharing schemes. The monotonic access structure can be presented in LSSS matrix and we adopt the definitions from those given in [8].

Definition 2 (Linear Secret Sharing Schemes). *A secret sharing scheme Π over a set of parties $\mathcal{P}$ is called linear (over $\mathbb{Z}_p$) if*
1. The shares for each party form a vector over $\mathbb{Z}_p$.
2. There exists a matrix M with l rows and n columns called the share-generating matrix for Π. For all $i \in \{1, 2, ..., l\}$, the i'th row of M is labeled with an party $\rho(i)$ where ρ is a mapping function. When we consider the column vector $v = (s, r_2, r_3, ..., r_n)$, where $s \in \mathbb{Z}_p$ is the secret to be shared and $r_2, r_3, ..., r_n \in \mathbb{Z}_p$ are randomly chosen. Then Mv is the vector of l shares of the secret s according to Π, and the share $(Mv)_i$ belongs to party $\rho(i)$.

It is proved in [8] that every linear secret sharing scheme enjoys the linear reconstruction property, defined as follows: Suppose that $\{\Pi_{\mathbb{A}}\}$ is an LSSS for the access structure $\mathbb{A}$. Let $S \in \mathbb{A}$ be any authorized set, an let $I \subseteq \{1, 2, ..., l\}$ be defined as $I = \{i : \rho(i) \in S\}$. Then, there exist constants $\{\omega_i \in \mathbb{Z}\}_{i \in I}$ such that, if $\{\lambda_i\}$ are valid shares of any secret s according to Π, then $s = \Sigma_{i \in I} \omega_i \lambda_i$. Furthermore, these constants $\{\omega_i\}$ can be found in time polynomial in the size of the share generating matrix M. In our construction, the target vector is set to $(1, 0, 0, ..., 0)$ for any linear secret sharing scheme, and we will have $(1, 0, 0, ..., 0) \in span(\{M_i\}_{i \in I})$.

In the NM-CPABE scheme, parties are equivalent to attributes. Our constructions support **NOT** gates by transforming non-monotonic access structures into monotonic ones. We introduce the definition of non-monotonic access structures from [6].

Definition 3 (Non-monotonic Access Structure). *Let $\mathcal{P}$ denote a set of attributes. The attributes in $\mathcal{P}$ may be divided into positive (like x) and negative (like $\neg x$) ones. And if $x \in \mathcal{P}$ then $\neg x \in \mathcal{P}$ and vice versa. $\breve{x}$ refer to an attribute that may be positive or negative (i.e., x or $\neg x$). Let $\{\Pi_{\mathbb{A}}\}_{\mathbb{A} \in \mathcal{A}}$ represent a given family of linear secret-sharing schemes for a set of possible monotone access structures $\mathcal{A}$. The set of possibly non-monotone access structures $\widetilde{\mathcal{A}}$ is defined as follows.*

For each access structure $\mathbb{A} \in \mathcal{A}$ over a set of attributes $\mathcal{P}$, a possibly non-monotonic access structure $NM(\mathbb{A})$ is defined over the set of attributes $\widetilde{\mathcal{P}}$, where $\widetilde{\mathcal{P}}$ is the set of all positive attributes in $\mathcal{P}$. $\widetilde{\mathcal{A}}$ is defined as the set of these $NM(\mathbb{A})$ access structures. And $NM(\mathbb{A})$ is defined by specifying that $\widetilde{S}$ is authorized in $NM(\mathbb{A})$ if and only if $N(\widetilde{S})$ is authorized in $\mathbb{A}$, where $\widetilde{S} \subseteq \widetilde{\mathcal{P}}$ and $N(\widetilde{S}) \subseteq \mathcal{P}$ is defined as follows: First, all attributes in $\widetilde{S}$ are in $N(\widetilde{S})$, so $\widetilde{S} \subset N(\widetilde{S})$; Second, for each attribute $x \in \widetilde{\mathcal{P}}$ such that $x \notin \widetilde{S}$, let $\neg x \in N(\widetilde{S})$.

3 Efficient Construction

The main technical novelty in this efficient construction lies in finding a way to "integrate" a certain number of attributes into one attribute. Learning from primes and divisibility theory, we know that any positive integer $N > 1$ can be uniquely written as $N = \prod_i p_i^{e_i}$, where $\{P_i\}$ are distinct primes and e_i is the exponent of p_i and $e_i \geq 1$. We first define a special random oracle only mapping strings to "primed" elements. Then in the private key generating stage, we only create the secret component corresponding to the product of all "primes".

The Setup, Encrypt, KeyGen, and Decrypt algorithms are described as follows.

Setup(λ). This algorithm takes security parameter λ as input. And it selects $\mathbb{G}_1, \mathbb{G}_2, e, g$ for system startup. This algorithm chooses random exponents $\alpha, a \in \mathbb{Z}_p$.

A special hash function $H' : \{0,1\}^* \rightarrow \mathbb{Z}_{\leq p}$, where $\mathbb{Z}_{\leq p}$ means the set of all prime positive integers less than or equal to p. We define another hash function

$H : \{0,1\}^* = g^{H'(*)} \rightarrow \mathbb{G}_1$ for generating random elements in $\mathbb{G}_1$. Let $H'(*) = o$, we have $H(*) = g^o$.

The public parameters PK and the master secret key MK is generated as

$$\text{PK} = \{g, e(g,g)^\alpha, g^a\}, \text{MK} = g^\alpha.$$

Encrypt(PK, $NM(\mathbb{A})$, $\mathcal{M}$**).** As before, Encrypt algorithm convert $NM(\mathbb{A})$ into monotonic form (M, ρ), where M is an $l \times n_c$ LSSS matrix. l is also the number of leaf nodes in access structure $\mathbb{A}$ and n_c is the number of nodes. As discussed in [8], l will not exceed the number of all positive attributes, n, and the number of columns of M is at most the number of rows of M. That is $n_c \leq l \leq n$, so we can reduce the size of ciphertext.

This algorithm first chooses a random vector $v = (s, r_2, ..., r_{n_c}) \in Z_p^{n_c}$, and then publishes the ciphertext as

$$\text{CT} = \{C = \mathcal{M}e(g,g)^{\alpha s}, C' = g^s, \\ \{C_{i,j} = g^{aM_{i,j}v_j} H(j + \rho(i))^{-s}\}_{1 \leq i \leq l, 1 \leq j \leq n_c}\}.$$

KeyGen(MK, S**).** KeyGen first obtains attributes set S_u from S, and then chooses an random element $t \in \mathbb{Z}_p$. Let $H(j + x) = g^{o_{j,x}}$ where $1 \leq j \leq n_c$ and $x \in S_u$.

The private key is presented as

$$\text{SK} = \{K = g^\alpha g^{at}, L = g^t, O_{S_u} = \prod_{1 \leq j \leq n_c, x \in S_u} o_{j,x}\}.$$

Decrypt(CT, SK**).** As before, let $I = \{i : \rho(i) \in S_u\}$, and $\{w_i \in \mathbb{Z}_p\}_{i \in I}$ be a set of constants satisfies that $s = \sum_{i \in I} w_i \lambda_i$ where $\{\lambda_i\}_{i \in I}$ are valid shares according to M. And we define a new binary operation $\widehat{\%}$ as follows.

$$a \widehat{\%} b = \begin{cases} 0, b \bmod a == 0; \\ a, \text{otherwise}. \end{cases}$$

Decrypt algorithm first computes

$$\begin{aligned}
& e(C', K) / \prod_{1 \leq j \leq n_c} e(L, \prod_{i \in I} C_{i,j}^{\omega_i \widehat{\%} O_{S_u}}) \\
&= e(C', K) / \prod_{1 \leq j \leq n_c} \left(e(g^t, g^{\sum_{i \in I} aM_{i,j} v_j \omega_i \widehat{\%} O_{S_u}}) \cdot e(g^t, \prod_{i \in I} h_{j,\rho(i)}^{-s\omega_i \widehat{\%} O_{S_u}}) \right) \\
&= e(C', K) / \prod_{1 \leq j \leq n_c} e(g^t, g^{\sum_{i \in I} aM_{i,j} v_j \omega_i}) \\
&= e(C', K) / e(g^t, g^{\sum_{i \in I} aM_{i,1} v_1 \omega_i}) \\
&= e(C', K) / e(g,g)^{ats} \\
&= e(g,g)^{\alpha s}.
\end{aligned}$$

Then the message is computed as

$$\mathcal{M} = C / e(g,g)^{\alpha s}.$$

4 Proof of Security

The efficient construction's security can be also proved under DBDH assumption. In this section, we will prove the following theorem.

Theorem 1. *Suppose the DBDH assumption holds, there is no polynomial time adversary can selectively break the last construction.*

Proof :

Suppose there is a polynomial time adversary $\mathcal{A}$ that can selectively break the last construction with non-negligible advantage ϵ. We build a simulator $\mathcal{B}$ that can play the DBDH game with non-negligible advantage.

The simulation proceeds as follows.

First, the challenger startups the system and generates $\mathbb{G}_1, \mathbb{G}_2, g, e$. Then the challenger flips a fair binary coin $\nu \in \{0,1\}$, outside of $\mathcal{B}$'s view. If $\nu = 1$, the challenger sets $T = e(g,g)^{abc}$; otherwise, $T = e(g,g)^z$. Finally, the challenger sends g, g^a, g^b, g^c and T to the simulator $\mathcal{B}$.

Init. The simulator runs $\mathcal{A}$'s algorithm. The adversary selects the challenge access structure $NM(\mathbb{A})^*$, which is equivalent to (M^*, ρ^*). M is an $l^* \times n_c^*$ LSSS matrix.

Setup. The simulator $\mathcal{B}$ chooses a random element $\alpha' \in \mathbb{Z}_p$ and sets $\alpha = ab + \alpha'$, which means $e(g,g)^\alpha = e(g^a, g^b) \cdot e(g,g)^{\alpha'}$.

The random oracles H' and H is programmed as follows.

The hash function H' returns the same answer as before. If there exists an index i which satisfies $\rho^*(i) = x$ and $i \le n^*$, let $H'(j+x) = o_{j,x}$, then we have

$$H(j+x) = g^{o_{j,x} + aM^*_{i,j}}.$$

Otherwise, $H(j+x)$ returns the same answer as before.

Phase 1. In this phase $\mathcal{B}$ answers any private key query. We consider the situation where(/in which) $\mathcal{B}$ is required to generate the private key for an attributes set S where S does not satisfy M^*.

$\mathcal{B}$ first chooses random elements $r \in \mathbb{Z}_p$. The private key components K and L is defined as

$$K = g^{\alpha'} g^{ar}, L = g^r.$$

We also expand the attributes set S to S_u as before. In the challenger's construction, let $O_x = \prod_{1 \le j \le n_c^*} o_{j,x}$, then we have $O_{S_u} = \prod_{x \in S_u} O_x$. We calculate O_{S_u} as follows.

For each $x \in S_u$ without index i such as $\rho^*(i) = x$, we can simply obtain O_x by letting $O'_x = \prod_{1 \le j \le n_c^*} o_{j,x}$.

For other attributes x existing in the access structure, we have to make sure that each exponent $o_{j,x}$ is not the prime divisor of O_{S_u}. That we calculate $O'_x = \prod_{1 \le j \le n_c^*} (o_{j,x} + b)$ in this situation.

Finally we calculate O_{S_u} as $O_{S_u} = \prod_{x \in S_u} O'_x$.

Challenge. In this stage, $\mathcal{A}$ submits two challenge equal length messages $\mathcal{M}_0$, $\mathcal{M}_1$ to the simulator. $\mathcal{B}$ flips a fair binary coin $\mu \in \{0,1\}$, and then creates $C = \mathcal{M}_\mu Te(g,g)^{\alpha' s}$ and $C' = g^s$. By the definition of a LSSS, we can find a vector $\omega = (\omega_1, ..., \omega_{n_c^*}) \in Z_p^{n_c^*}$, such that $\omega_1 = -1$ and $\omega_i \cdot M_i^* = 0$ for all i where $\rho^*(i) \in S_u$.

To simulate the $C_{i,j}$ values, $\mathcal{B}$ selects random elements $r'_2, ..., r'_{n_c^*}$ and lets

$$v^* = (s, s + r'_2, ..., s + r'_{n_c}) \in Z_p^{n_c^*}.$$

The ciphertext components $C_{i,j}$ is calculated as

$$C_{i,j} = g^{aM_{i,j}^* v_j^* \omega_j} H(j + \rho(i))^{-s}\}_{1 \le i \le l, 1 \le j \le n_c^*}.$$

Phase 2. Same as Phase 1.

Guess. If the adversary gives out a correct guess $\mu' = \mu$, then $\mathcal{B}$ outputs $\nu' = 1$ to guesses that $T = e(g,g)^{abc}$; otherwise, it outputs $\nu' = 0$ to indicate that $T = e(g,g)^z$.

Now we calculate the advantage of $\mathcal{B}$ as follows.

If $v = 0$, the adversary can not get any information about $\mathcal{B}_\mu$. Then we have

$$\Pr[\mu' \neq \mu | \nu = 0] = \Pr[\mu' = \mu | \nu = 0] = \frac{1}{2}.$$

Because $\mathcal{B}$ outputs $\nu' = 0$ when $\mu' \neq \mu$, that is

$$\Pr[\nu' = \nu | \nu = 0] = \Pr[\mu' \neq \mu | \nu = 0] = \frac{1}{2}.$$

If $v = 1$, the adversary can get some exact information about $\mathcal{B}_\mu$. As described in the supposition before, $\mathcal{A}$ can output a correct μ' with non-negligible advantage. The probability of $\mathcal{A}$ in this case is

$$\Pr[\mu' = \mu | \nu = 1] = \frac{1}{2} + \epsilon.$$

Because $\mathcal{B}$ outputs $\nu' = 1$ when $\mu' = \mu$, that we have

$$\Pr[\nu' = \nu | \nu = 1] = \Pr[\mu' = \mu | \nu = 1] = \frac{1}{2} + \epsilon.$$

Finally, we can calculate the probability of $\mathcal{B}$ that output a correct guess $\nu' = \nu$ as

$$\begin{aligned} \Pr[\nu' = \nu] &= \Pr[\nu' = \nu, \nu = 0] + \Pr[\nu' = \nu, \nu = 1] \\ &= \frac{1}{2}\Pr[\nu' = \nu | \nu = 0] + \frac{1}{2}\Pr[\nu' = \nu | \nu = 1] \\ &= \frac{1}{2} + \frac{1}{2}\epsilon. \end{aligned}$$

Therefore, $\mathcal{B}$ can play the DBDH game with non-negligible advantage. So there is no polynomial time adversary $\mathcal{A}$ that can selectively break the last construction with non-negligible advantage. Theorem 1 holds. $\square$

5 Comparison

In this section we compare our scheme with other systems in terms of the size of keys and ciphertext and computational time. To avoid the impact of different security assumption, we only consider these constructions under the DBDH assumption.

Let L_* denote the bit length of any element in $*$, T_* denote the time of $*$ operations. Suppose that n is the number of attributes in the system, l is the number of leaf nodes in the access structures, n_c is the number of nodes in the access formulas, n_S is the size of users' attributes set, and I is the size of minimal attributes set that satisfies the access structures.

We summarize the comparisons between our scheme and the CN, Waters systems in terms of the sizes of PK, MK, SK, and CT in Table 2. Note that we do not count the size of the message, the access policy, the bilinear map and other fundamental components. In the efficient construction, the size of PK is reduced to $\mathcal{O}(1)$ by adopting random oracle, which is suitable for large universe construction. Benefiting from primes theory, the size of SK is also reduced to $\mathcal{O}(1)$.

Table 2. Comparison of size of PK, MK, SK, and CT in CP-ABE systems.

System	PK	MK	SK	CT
CN [10]	$(3n+1)L_{\mathbb{G}_1} + L_{\mathbb{G}_2}$	$(3n+1)L_{\mathbb{Z}_p}$	$(2n+1)L_{\mathbb{G}_1}$	$(n+1)L_{\mathbb{G}_1} + L_{\mathbb{G}_2}$
Waters [14]	$(n^2+2)L_{\mathbb{G}_1} + L_{\mathbb{G}_2}$	$L_{\mathbb{G}_1}$	$(n+n_S+1)L_{\mathbb{G}_1}$	$(nl+1)L_{\mathbb{G}_1}$
Our construction	$2L_{\mathbb{G}_1} + L_{\mathbb{G}_2}$	$L_{\mathbb{G}_1}$	$2L_{\mathbb{G}_1} + L_{\mathbb{Z}_p}$	$(n_c l+1)L_{\mathbb{G}_1}$

Table 3. Comparison of computational time in CP-ABE systems.

System	Key generation	Encryption	Decryption
CN [10]	$(2n+1)T_{\mathbb{G}_1}$	$(n+1)T_{\mathbb{G}_1} + 2T_{\mathbb{G}_2}$	$(n+1)T_{\mathbb{G}_2} + 2T_e$
Waters [14]	$(nn_S+n+1)T_{\mathbb{G}_1}$	$(nl+1)T_{\mathbb{G}_1} + 2T_{\mathbb{G}_2}$	$nIT_{\mathbb{G}_1} + (n+I+1)T_{\mathbb{G}_2}$
Our construction	$4T_{\mathbb{G}_1}$	$(n_c l+1)T_{\mathbb{G}_1} + 2T_{\mathbb{G}_2}$	$n_c IT_{\mathbb{G}_1} + (n_c+1)T_{\mathbb{G}_2}$

The comparisons of computational time of private key generation, encryption, and decryption between our scheme and the CN, Waters systems is given out in Table 3. In the efficient construction, the time of private key generation is reduced significantly because we adopt exponents multiplying instead of group operations. We notice that the time of encryption and decryption in the efficient scheme is longer than in the CN system, the reason is that our construction introduces LSSS matrix as the access structure that can support **NOT**, **AND**, **OR**, and threshold operations.

6 Conclusions

In this paper, we present a CP-ABE system that support non-monotonic access structures. The construction is proved to be selectively secure under DBDH assumption.

We compare our construction with other systems that support non-monotonic access structures. The result shows that our scheme are expressive CP-ABE constructions that support negation of attributes. We also compare our construction with other systems which are proved secure under DBDH assumption. Generally speaking, the efficiency of our construction is better than CN and Waters systems.

Acknowledgments. The authors would like to thank anonymous reviewers for their suggestions. Besides, this work was supported by the National Natural Science Foundation of China under Grant Nos. 61303191, 61402504 and 61402508.

References

1. Nag, A., Choudhary, S., Dawn, S., Basu, S.: Secure data outsourcing in the cloud using multi-secret sharing scheme. In: Mandal, J., Satapathy, S., Sanyal, M., Bhateja, V. (eds.) AISC, vol. 458, pp. 337–343. Springer, Singapore (2017). doi:10.1007/978-981-10-2035-3_34
2. Athira, R., Tina, S., Arun, R., Suvanam, S.: A survey on attribute based encryption schemes for data sharing. In: Proceedings of the 2016 International Conference on Emerging Trends in Engineering and Management, pp. 19–23 (2016)
3. Sahai, A., Waters, B.: Fuzzy identity-based encryption. In: Cramer, R. (ed.) EUROCRYPT 2005. LNCS, vol. 3494, pp. 457–473. Springer, Heidelberg (2005). doi:10.1007/11426639_27
4. Goyal, V., Pandey, O., Sahai, A., Waters, B.: Attribute-based encryption for fine-grained access control of encrypted data. In: Proceedings of the 13th ACM Conference on Computer and Communications Security, pp. 89–98. ACM (2006)
5. Bethencourt, J., Sahai, A., Waters, B.: Ciphertext-policy attribute-based encryption. In: Proceedings of the 2007 IEEE Symposium on Security and Privacy, pp. 321–334. IEEE (2007)
6. Ostrovsky, R., Sahai, A., Waters, B.: Attribute-based encryption with non-monotonic access structures. In: Proceedings of the 14th ACM Conference on Computer and Communications Security, pp. 195–203. ACM (2007)
7. Naor, M., Pinkas, B.: Efficient trace and revoke schemes. In: Frankel, Y. (ed.) FC 2000. LNCS, vol. 1962, pp. 1–20. Springer, Heidelberg (2001). doi:10.1007/3-540-45472-1_1
8. Beimel, A.: Secure schemes for secret sharing and key distribution. Phd thesis, Israel Institute of Technology, Technion, Haifa, Israel (1996)
9. Lewko, A., Sahai, A., Waters, B.: Revocation systems with very small private keys. In: Proceedings of the 2010 IEEE Symposium on Security and Privacy, pp. 273–285. IEEE (2010)
10. Cheung, L., Newport, C.: Provably secure ciphertext policy ABE. In: Proceedings of the 14th ACM Conference on Computer and Communications Security, pp. 456–465. ACM (2007)

11. Boneh, D., Gentry, C., Waters, B.: Collusion resistant broadcast encryption with short ciphertexts and private keys. In: Shoup, V. (ed.) CRYPTO 2005. LNCS, vol. 3621, pp. 258–275. Springer, Heidelberg (2005). doi:10.1007/11535218_16
12. Vaikuntanathan, V., Voulgaris, P.: Attribute based encryption using lattices. U.S. Patent 9,281,944 (2016)
13. Brakerski, Z., Cash, D., Tsabary, R., Wee, H.: Targeted homomorphic attribute-based encryption. In: Hirt, M., Smith, A. (eds.) TCC 2016. LNCS, vol. 9986, pp. 330–360. Springer, Heidelberg (2016). doi:10.1007/978-3-662-53644-5_13
14. Waters, B.: Ciphertext-policy attribute-based encryption: an expressive, efficient, and provably secure realization. In: Catalano, D., Fazio, N., Gennaro, R., Nicolosi, A. (eds.) PKC 2011. LNCS, vol. 6571, pp. 53–70. Springer, Heidelberg (2011). doi:10.1007/978-3-642-19379-8_4
15. Ramanna, S.C.: More efficient constructions for inner-product encryption. In: Manulis, M., Sadeghi, A.R., Schneider, S. (eds.) ACNS 2016. LNCS, vol. 9696, pp. 231–248. Springer, Cham (2016). doi:10.1007/978-3-319-39555-5_13
16. Attrapadung, N., Hanaoka, G., Matsumoto, T., Teruya, T., Yamada, S.: Attribute based encryption with direct efficiency tradeoff. In: Manulis, M., Sadeghi, A.R., Schneider, S. (eds.) ACNS 2016. LNCS, vol. 9696, pp. 249–266. Springer, Cham (2016). doi:10.1007/978-3-319-39555-5_14
17. Asmuth, C., Bloom, J.: A modular approach to key safeguarding. IEEE Trans. Inf. Theory **29**(2), 208–210 (1983)
18. Shamir, A.: How to share a secret. Commun. ACM **22**(11), 612–613 (1979)
19. Ibraimi, L., Tang, Q., Hartel, P., Jonker, W.: Efficient and provable secure ciphertext-policy attribute-based encryption schemes. In: Bao, F., Li, H., Wang, G. (eds.) ISPEC 2009. LNCS, vol. 5451, pp. 1–12. Springer, Heidelberg (2009). doi:10.1007/978-3-642-00843-6_1
20. Lewko, A., Waters, B.: Decentralizing attribute-based encryption. In: Paterson, K.G. (ed.) EUROCRYPT 2011. LNCS, vol. 6632, pp. 568–588. Springer, Heidelberg (2011). doi:10.1007/978-3-642-20465-4_31
21. Fu, Z., Ren, K., Jiangang, S., Sun, X., Huang, F.: Enabling personalized search over encrypted outsourced data with efficiency improvement. In: IEEE Transactions on Parallel and Distributed Systems, vol. 27, no. 9, pp. 2546–2559 (2016)

Image Authentication Based on Least Significant Bit Hiding and Double Random Phase Encoding Technique

Faliu Yi[1], Yousun Jeoung[2], Ruili Geng[3], and Inkyu Moon[2(✉)]

[1] School of Computer and Software, Nanjing University of Information Science and Technology, Nanjing, China
yifaliu@hotmail.com

[2] School of Computer Engineering, Chosun University, 309 Pilmun-daero, Dong-gu, Gwangju 61452, South Korea
ysl128f@naver.com, inkyu.moon@chosun.ac.kr

[3] Spectral MD, Inc, 2515 Mckinney Ave #1000, Dallas, TX 75201, USA
ruiligeng@gmail.com

Abstract. In this paper, we proposed an image authentication method based on least significant bit (LSB) hiding and double random phase encoding (DRPE) technique. An image that needs to be authenticated is first encrypted using DRPE algorithm. All amplitude information in this encrypted image is discarded and the phase mask is reserved. Then, the phase image is converted into a binary image by setting phase values less than zero as zero and other values as one. The binary image is hided in a host image with the LSB hiding approach. The recipient extracts the hiding binary image from the host image and then sets the zero-values as $-\pi$ and one-values as π. Finally, the retrieved phase mask is decrypted and authenticated using DRPE and non-linear cross correlation algorithm, respectively. The proposed authentication scheme can provide another layer of security because the retrieved phase mask cannot reveal any original image information. Furthermore, the decrypted image from phase mask cannot be visually recognized with naked eyes which can distract the attention of attackers. Experimental results have shown the feasibility of the proposed authentication algorithm.

Keywords: Image authentication · Lease significant bit hiding · Double random phase encoding · Non-linear cross correlation

1 Introduction

Hiding information into digital image or other media is a kind of steganography techniques such that people from both the sender and recipient rarely realize that there has hidden information in the host image or video [1–3]. However, the secret information would be extracted and analyzed from host image by attacker when the useful information is directly hidden in the image, i.e. using least significant bit (LSB) hiding technique to hide a binary image without any manipulation would be easily attacked because the attacker can visualize the extracted information directly [4, 5]. As a result,

X. Sun et al. (Eds.): ICCCS 2017, Part II, LNCS 10603, pp. 326–335, 2017.
https://doi.org/10.1007/978-3-319-68542-7_27

two kinds of approach are proposed to solve the aforementioned problem. The first one is to modify the embedded image (host image with information hidden) such as encrypting the embedded image and transmitting the encrypted embedded image via the internet. The other one is to encrypt or shuffle the hidden information first before hiding them into a host image [6, 7]. The embedded image in the first approach is a disordered and confusing message that would make suspicious enough to attacker [1]. On the other hand, the modified information hidden in the host image or video in the second approach does not create any special attention to attackers [1, 6]. In this paper, the second type of scheme is utilized to hide image for image authentication that is widely needed to prevent unauthorized access in various e-commerce application fields.

Double random phase encoding (DRPE) technique as an encryption approaches has been widely used in the fields of image authentication, watermarking, and encryption since it was proposed by Refregier and Javidi in 1995 because it can convert an image into stationary white noise which cannot be predicted by using any part of its information [8–13]. Moreover, DRPE algorithm can be achieved quickly due to its parallel property [12, 13]. As a result, it is a good idea to hide an encrypted image resulted from DRPE into a host image to enhance the security. However, the pixel value in encrypted image from DRPE becomes complex value that greatly increases the storage size and makes the data transmission burdens. In addition, it is difficult to hide all of the complex value into a host image using LSB hiding due to the big size of encrypted image. In order to solve these problems, we proposed to use only the phase information and discard all the amplitude information in the encrypted image. Moreover, we convert the phase image into a binary image and hide it into a host image using LSB hiding technique. In this case, even the attackers get the binary image from the embedded image; they cannot get the original image information because they do not have the keys used in DRPE algorithm. Even if the attackers happen to know the DRPE keys, it is also difficult to visualize the decrypted image because the binary image only preserves partial phase information and the decrypted image will be not easily recognized with naked eyes, which can enhance the image security in another level. However, the decrypted image can be authenticated with a statistical nonlinear cross correlation method [14, 15].

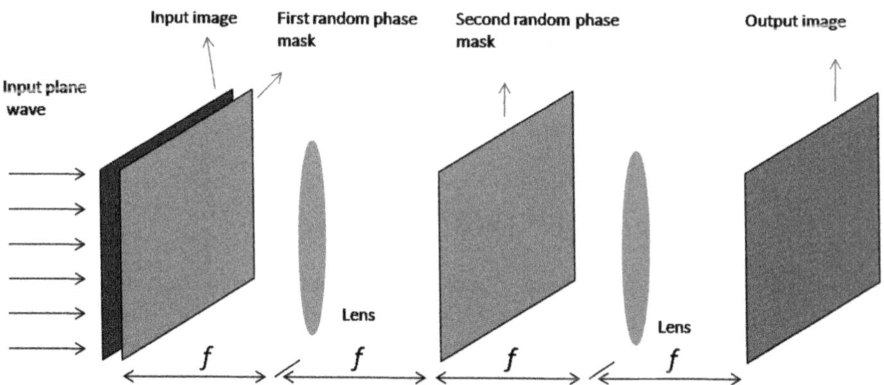

Fig. 1. Schematic diagram of DRPE system in the Fourier domain

This image authentication algorithm can be briefly described as follows: a secret image that needs to be verified is firstly encrypted with DRPE algorithm. All the amplitude information in encrypted image is discarded while the phase information is kept and converted into a binary image by using rule such as setting phase value between $-\pi$ and 0 as 0 and others as 1. The binary image is then hidden into a host image by using LBS hiding technique. As a result, the embedded image can be transmitted in the internet without creating attention of attackers. When the recipient gets the embedded image, the last bit of each pixel in embedded image is extracted and a binary image is formed. A phase image is obtained by conducting the reverse operation such as setting 0 values as $-\pi$ and others as π. In this step, a lot of phase information is lost. Then, the partial phase image is decrypted with DRPE algorithm. In this step, the decrypted image would be not easily recognized with naked eyes which can enhance the data security because it will distract the attention of attackers. Fortunately, the encrypted image from partial phase image can be successfully authenticated with a nonlinear cross correlation algorithm. The proposed image authentication algorithm is easily implemented and the image security is enhanced as well.

2 Methodology

In this section, the DRPE algorithm, LSB hiding technique, statistical non-linear cross correlation method and procedure of proposed image authentication are presented.

2.1 Double Random Phase Encoding

Figure 1 is the schematic diagram of a DRPE system in the Fourier domain. A primary image *f(x, y)* is firstly encrypted into a stationary white noise image $e(\xi, \eta)$ using two random phase masks p_1 = exp(j2πm(x, y)) and p_2 = exp(j2πn(μ, ν)) where *m(x, y)* and *n*(μ, ν) are uniformly distributed between 0 and 1, *j* is an imaginary unit, and *exp* means the natural exponential function. As shown in Fig. 1, the first phase mask p_1 is placed in the input image plane and the second mask p_2 is in the Fourier domain. The DRPE process can be further expressed as following equation [8, 11–13].

$$\mathrm{e}(\xi,\eta) = \zeta^{-1}[\zeta[f(x,y)\exp(j2\pi m(x,y))]\exp(j2\pi n(\mu,v))] \tag{1}$$

where ζ and ζ^{-1} denote a 2D Fourier transform and an inverse Fourier transform, respectively. The double random phase decoding is the inverse process of DRPE which is described as follows [8, 11–13]:

$$d(x,y) = \left|\zeta^{-1}[\zeta[e(\xi,\eta)]][exp(j2\pi n(\mu,v))]^*\right| \tag{2}$$

where *d(x,y)* is the decrypted image, * expresses the complex conjugate, and $|\cdot|$ is the modulus operation. The DRPE system is not only implemented in the Fourier domain, it is successfully conducted in the other domains such as Fresnel domain [9], the fractional Fourier domain [16], and the Gyator domain [17]. In addition, many DRPE-based algorithms are proposed for image encryption, authentication and watermarking [18–24].

2.2 Least Significant Bit Hiding

Least significant bit hiding is to embed a secret image or text in the least significant bits of the pixel value in host image. Since the hiding process is conducted in the LSB of the image pixels, the altered image with slight variation in its pixel values will be indistinguishable from the original by a human being [1, 4, 25–30]. Therefore, the host image quality will not be changed a lot and thus rarely make the attention of attackers. The simple LSB hiding technique based on a gray scale image is shown in Fig. 2. The gray level for a gray scale image is 256 and each pixel value is represented with 8 bits. The last 1, 2 or 3 bits of each pixel value can be used to embed the secret image or text. In Fig. 3, a binary image (middle) with the same size of host image (left) is embedded into the last bit of pixel value in host image and get the embedded image (right).

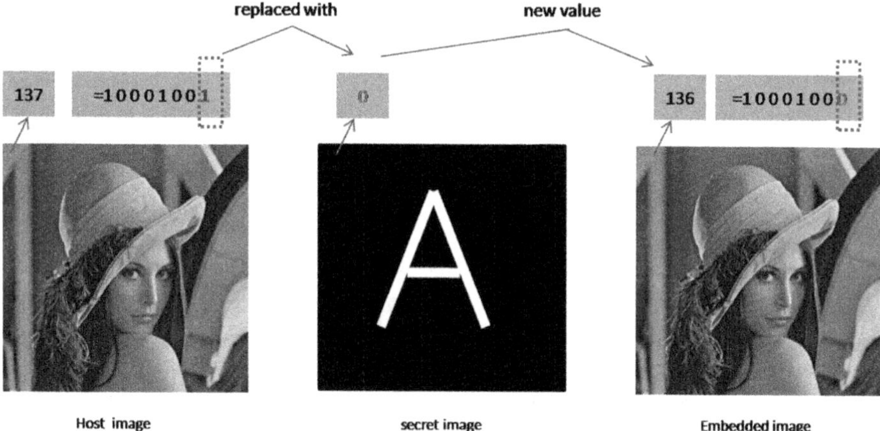

Fig. 2. Illustration of least significant bit hiding method

2.3 Statistical Non-linear Cross Correlation

Statistical non-linear cross correlation is a kind of correlation transforms between two images, i.e. reference and decrypted image [10, 14, 15]. It can verify some images that are even unrecognized by naked eyes [14, 18]. The mathematically expression of a statistical non-linear cross correlation transform *c(x, y)* between reference image *r(x, y)* and decrypted image *d(x, y)* is given as follows [14, 18]:

$$c(x,y) = \zeta^{-1}\left\{|r(\mu,\eta)d(\mu,\eta)|^{k}\exp[i(\phi_r(\mu,\eta) - \phi_d(\mu,\eta))]\right\} \tag{3}$$

where $r(\mu,\eta)$ and $d(\mu,\eta)$ are the 2D Fourier transforms of the reference and decrypted images, $\phi_r(\mu,\eta)$ and $\phi_d(\mu,\eta)$ are the phase part of $r(\mu,\eta)$ and $d(\mu,\eta)$, respectively, parameter k is the strength of applied nonlinearity that is usually measured by the best peak-to-correlation energy (PCE) that is defined as following equation [14, 18].

$$PCE = \frac{max\left[|c(x,y)|^2\right]}{\sum_{i=1}^{M}\sum_{j=1}^{N}|c(x,y)|^2} \tag{4}$$

where M and N are the image size and $c(x, y)$ is the statistical non-linear cross correlation transform result between two images. PCE can be used as a metric to evaluate the statistical non-linear cross correlation between two images and a higher PCE value means a good nonlinear correlation result. In this paper, the parameter k is set to 0.3 which is verified a good value for non-linear cross correlation evaluation [14, 18].

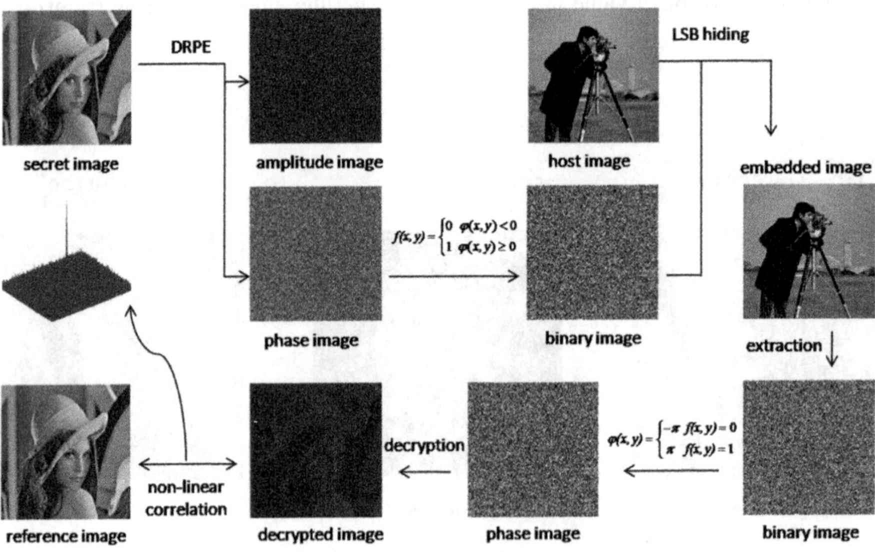

Fig. 3. Image authentication procedure

2.4 Image Authentication Procedure

The proposed image authentication method is based on LSB hiding and DRPE algorithm. Firstly, a secret image is encrypted by DRPE algorithm and only the phase image in encrypted image is kept. Moreover, the phase image is converted into a binary image by setting pixel values between $-\pi$ and 0 to 0, and other pixel values (between 0 and π) to 1. Then, the binary image is embedded into a host image using LSB hiding technique. The recipient extracts the binary image from the embedded image and converts it into a phase image by setting 0 value to $-\pi$ and 1 value to π. Later, the secret image is decrypted by using the extracted phase image and double random phase decoding method. Finally, the decrypted image is verified with the statistical non-linear cross correlation approach. The whole procedure is shown in Fig. 3. In this image authentication method, the extracted image from embedded image is not recognized and the decrypted image is not easily recognized by naked eyes either, which can distract the attention of attackers and enhance the system security.

3 Experimental Results

All results are obtained from numerical simulation based on Matlab (R2012a) that is executed on a 64-bit Windows 7 OS computer with a 3.3 GHz Intel Core i5-2500 k processor and 4 GB of RAM. The secret image including true and false class and host image are all with size of 500 × 500. Figure 4 presents the true, false, and host image. The Fig. 4(a) which is a true class image is also viewed as a reference image for image authentication.

Fig. 4. Images used for testing

The secret images (both true and false class images) are firstly encrypted with DRPE algorithm and their amplitude information in encrypted images is discarded while the corresponding phase images are preserved. The phase information in encrypted images for both true (see Fig. 4(a)) and false (see Fig. 4(b)) class secret images are shown in Fig. 5.

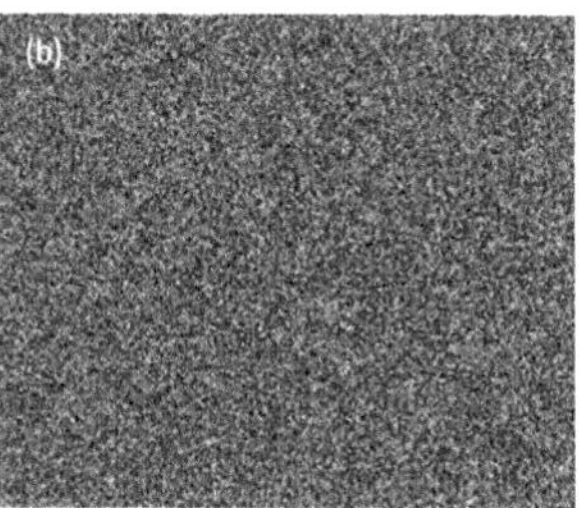

Fig. 5. Phase information in encrypted images for true (a) and false (b) class secret image

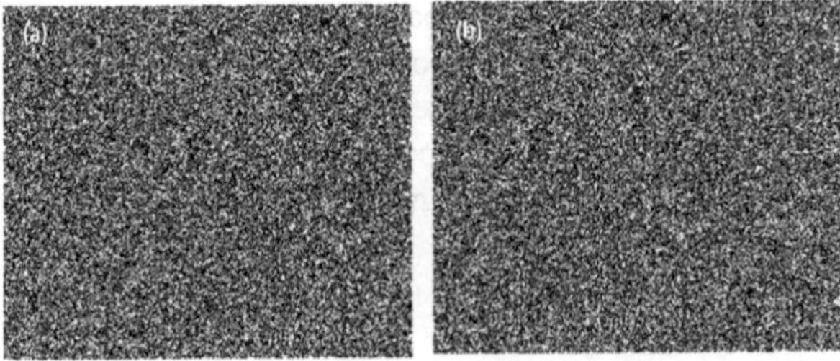

Fig. 6. Converted binary images for true (a) and false (b) class secret image

The type of pixel value in phase image is double which occupies 64 bits and it is difficult to embed so many bits into a host image. Therefore, the phase image is converted into binary image by setting pixel that has value smaller than 0 to 0 and others to 1. Figure 6 shows the binary images obtained from this transformation. Consequently, these binary images are embedded into the host image using LSB hiding method. Here, the binary image is embedded into the host image by replacing only the last bit of each pixel value in the host image. The embedded images for true and false class secret images are shown in Fig. 7. It is noted from Fig. 7 that the embedded images look the same as the original host image with naked eyes. The peak signal-to-noise ratio (PSNR) values between host image (Fig. 4(c)) and embedded image for true (Fig. 7(a)) and false (Fig. 7(b)) secret image are measured to be 51.14 and 53.33, respectively, which means the embedded image has high quality compared to the original host image.

Fig. 7. Embedded images for true (a) and false (b) class secret image

The embedded images are then transmitted in the internet. Because the embedded image looks the same as the host image, it can distract the attention of attackers. In the recipient part, the binary image hidden in the host image is extracted and converted into phase image by setting 0 value as $-\pi$ and 1 value as π. It can be noted that this process will lose some phase information because it is not a totally inverse operation. Fortunately, the original image can be derived from the partial phase information. The phase image derived from the binary image hidden in the host image is present in Fig. 8. It is noted that these phase images still look like white noise and cannot be recognized by attackers.

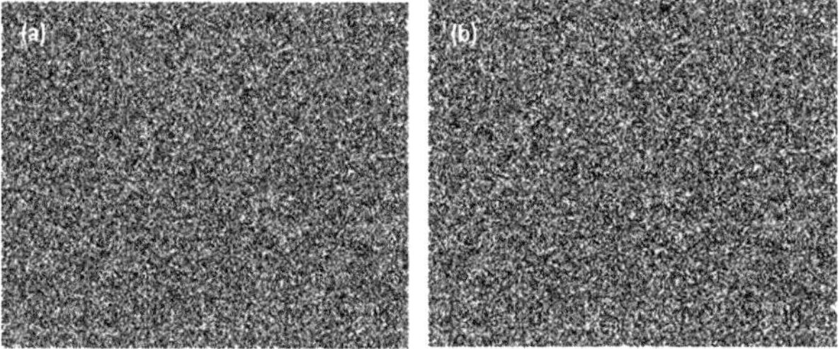

Fig. 8. Phase images derived from embedded images for true (a) and false secret image

Then, the double random phase decoding approach is applied to the extracted phase images as shown in Fig. 8 to get the decrypted images. Figure 9 shows the decrypted images for both true and false class secret image. It is found that the decrypted image from the proposed system is not easily recognized by naked eyes because it is decrypted from partial phase information. Consequently, this can enhance the security of system in another level [14, 18] because it can distract the attackers' attention.

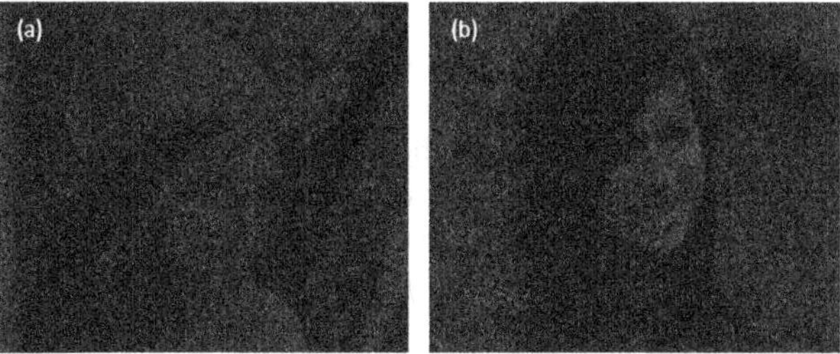

Fig. 9. Decrypted images for true (a) and false (b) class secret image

Even though the decrypted image cannot be easily recognized with naked eyes, it can be verified with statistical non-linear cross correlation transform as defined in Subsect. 2.3. The non-linear correlation planes between reference image and true and false class secret image are shown in Fig. 10. It is obvious that the true class image has high peak in the center of correlation plane while that peak is not apparent for false class secret image, which means the statistical non-linear cross correlation transform can successfully distinguish true class image from the false class image and achieve the image authentication. In addition, the PCE value is calculated to be 0.0037 between reference and true class image while it is 7.99×10^{-5} between reference and false class image. These simulation results reveal that our proposed method can achieve the image authentication based on LSB hiding technique and DRPE algorithm. Moreover, our proposed method is very suitable to distract the attention of attackers which can enhance the security of authentication system.

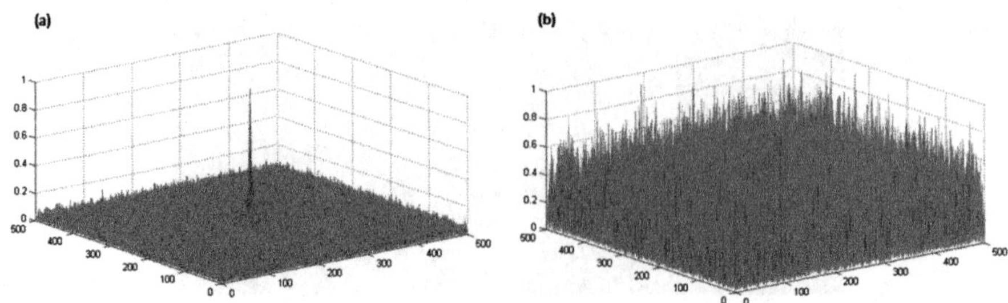

Fig. 10. Non-linear correlation plane between reference and true (a) and false (b) class image

4 Conclusions

In this paper, an image authentication algorithm was proposed based on least significant bit hiding and double random phase encoding approach. The proposed scheme uses simple hiding technique to hide complex encrypted image resulted from double random phase encoding and fulfills the image authentication with non-linear cross correlation method. This image authentication approach can distract the attention of attackers in two ways. First, the secret image hidden in a host image cannot be recognized because it is a binary image from encrypted image. Second, the decrypted image from hidden information cannot be easily recognized with naked eyes even correct keys are given. On the other hand, the vague image can be authenticated using a statistical non-linear cross correlation algorithm. Experimental results have verified the feasibility of the proposed image authentication algorithm.

Acknowledgements. This research was supported by Basic Science Research Program through the National Research Foundation of Korea (NRF) funded by the Ministry of Science, ICT and Future Planning (NRF-2015R1A2A1A10052566).

References

1. Ghoshal, N., Mandal, J.K.: Image authentication technique in frequency domain based on discrete Fourier transformation (IATFDDFT). arXiv preprint arXiv:1212.3371 (2012)
2. Bartolini, F., et al.: Image authentication techniques for surveillance applications. Proc. IEEE **89**, 1403–1418 (2011)
3. Petitcolas, F., Ross, J.A., Markus, G.K.: Information hiding-a survey. Proc. IEEE **87**, 1062–1078 (1999)
4. Champakamala, N., Padmini, K., Radhika, D.K.: Least significant bit algorithm for image steganography. Int. J. Adv. Comput. Technol. **3**, 3–38 (2013)
5. Rey, C., Dugelay, J.L.: A survey of watermarking algorithms for image authentication. EURASIP J. Adv. Signal Process. **6**, 218932 (2002)
6. Gupta, S., Ankur, G., Bharat, B.: Information hiding using least significant bit steganography and cryptography. Int. J. Modern Educ. Comput. Sci. **4**, 27 (2012)
7. Asad, M., Gilani, J., Khalid, A.: An enhanced least significant bit modification technique for audio steganography. In: International Conference on Computer Networks and Information Technology (ICCNIT). IEEE (2011)

8. Refregier, P., Javidi, B.: Optical image encryption based on input plane and Fourier plane random encoding. Opt. Lett. **20**, 767–769 (1995)
9. Situ, G., Zhang, J.: Double random-phase encoding in the Fresnel domain. Opt. Lett. **29**, 1584–1586 (2004)
10. Yi, F., Moon, I., Lee, Y.H.: A multispectral photon-counting double random phase encoding scheme for image authentication. Sensors **14**, 8877–8894 (2014)
11. Moon, I., et al.: Avalanche and bit independence characteristics of double random phase encoding in the Fourier and Fresnel domains. JOSA A **31**, 110–1111 (2014)
12. Lee, J., et al.: Graphics processing unit–accelerated double random phase encoding for fast image encryption. Opt. Eng. **53**, 112308 (2014)
13. Moon, I., et al.: Efficient asymmetric image authentication schemes based on photon counting-double random phase encoding and RSA algorithms. Appl. Opt. **55**, 4328–4335 (2016)
14. Javidi, B.: Nonlinear joint power spectrum based optical correlation. Appl. Opt. **28**, 2358–2367 (1989)
15. Yi, F.: Photon-counting double-random-phase image authentication in the Fresnel domain. In: Sun, X., Liu, A., Chao, H.-C., Bertino, E. (eds.) ICCCS 2016. LNCS, vol. 10040, pp. 487–497. Springer, Cham (2016). doi:10.1007/978-3-319-48674-1_43
16. Unnikrishnan, G., Joseph, J., Singh, K.: Optical encryption by double-random phase encoding in the fractional Fourier domain. Opt. Lett. **25**, 887–889 (2000)
17. Li, H., Wang, Y.: Double-image encryption based on iterative gyrator transform. Opt. Commun. **281**, 5745–5749 (2008)
18. Pérez-Cabré, E., Cho, M., Javidi, B.: Information authentication using photon-counting double-random-phase encrypted images. Opt. Lett. **36**, 22–24 (2011)
19. Cho, M., Javidi, B.: Three-dimensional photon counting double-random-phase encryption. Opt. Lett. **38**, 3198–3201 (2013)
20. Chen, Y., et al.: An improved watermarking method based on double random phase encoding technique. Opt. Laser Technol. **42**, 617–623 (2010)
21. Sheng, Y., et al.: Information hiding based on double random-phase encoding and public-key cryptography. Opt. Express **17**, 3270–3284 (2009)
22. Cai, L., et al.: Digital image encryption and watermarking by phase-shifting interferometry. Appl. Opt. **43**, 3078–3084 (2004)
23. Chen, W., Chen, X.: Double random phase encoding using phase reservation and compression. J. Opt. **16**, 025402 (2014)
24. Chen, W., et al.: Phase-modulated optical system with sparse representation for information encoding and authentication. IEEE Photonics J. **5**, 6900113 (2013)
25. Chan, C., Cheng, L.: Hiding data in images by simple LSB substitution. Pattern Recogn. **37**, 469–474 (2004)
26. Fillatre, L.: Adaptive steganalysis of least significant bit replacement in grayscale natural images. IEEE Trans. Signal Process. **60**, 556–569 (2012)
27. Xia, Z., et al.: A privacy-preserving and copy-deterrence content-based image retrieval scheme in cloud computing. IEEE Trans. Inf. Forensics Secur. **11**, 2594–2608 (2016)
28. Yuan, C., Sun, X., Lv, R.: Fingerprint liveness detection based on multi-scale LPQ and PCA. China Commun. **13**, 60–65 (2016)
29. Wan, J., et al.: Forensics feature analysis in quaternion wavelet domain for distinguishing photographic images and computer graphics. Multimedia Tools Appl. 1–7 (2016)
30. Huang, L., et al.: AutoODC: automated generation of orthogonal defect classifications. Autom. Softw. Eng. **22**, 3–46 (2015)

On-Line Intrusion Detection Model Based on Approximate Linear Dependent Condition with Linear Latent Feature Extraction

Jian Tang[1(✉)], Meijuan Jia[2], Jian Zhang[3], and Meiying Jia[4]

[1] Faculty of Information Technology, Beijing University of Technology, Beijing 100124, China
freeflytang@126.com
[2] Inner Mongolia University of Technology, Inner Mongolia, Hohhot 010051, China
2922334030@qq.com
[3] School of Computer & Software, Nanjing University of Information Science & Technology (NUIST), Nanjing 210044, China
jianzhang_neu@163.com
[4] Research Institute of Computing Technology, Beifang Jiaotong University, Beijing 100029, China
jmy100@tom.com

Abstract. Most of the intrusion detection models (IDM) are constructed with off-line training data. Time-variance characteristic of the practical network system cannot be embodied in the off-line constructed IDM. On-line updating of the off-line IDM with the valued new samples is very necessary. In this paper, a new on-line instruction detection model based on approximate linear dependent (ALD) condition with linear latent feature extraction is proposed to address this problem. Specifically, the valued samples which can represent drift of the practical network are indentified with ALD and prior knowledge. Then, these selected samples are used to update the off-line IDM based on on-line latent feature extraction method and fast machine learning algorithm with sample-based updating strategy. Experiments based on KDD99 data are used to validate the proposed approach.

Keywords: Intrusion detection model · On-line updating · Approximate linear dependent · Latent feature extraction · Fast machine learning algorithm

1 Introduction

Intrusion detection techniques for national network fundamental infrastructures have become one of the most essential issues. It is very important to construct intrusion detection model (IDM) with high detection accuracy and low training time for these intrusion detection system (IDS). In fact, this is a kind of classified identification problem faced with detailed application problem [1]. Thus, various machine learning methods and modeling strategies widely used in many studies can be employed to build IDM [2–6].

X. Sun et al. (Eds.): ICCCS 2017, Part II, LNCS 10603, pp. 336–345, 2017.
https://doi.org/10.1007/978-3-319-68542-7_28

As an effective classifier should has simple structure and fewer inputs, latent feature extraction approaches are always used in high dimensional data modeling [7, 8]. Latent features extracted by project to latent structure or partial least squares (PLS) are used popularly duo to its correlative to the modeling input and output space jointly [9]. Artificial neural network (ANN) and support vector machines (SVM) are the most used construction methods of IDM [10]. Random weights neural network (RWNN) approach has fast learning speed in terms of its randomly assignment of the input weights and biases [11]. Thus, nonlinear latent features-based RWNN algorithm is used to construct IMD; results show that there isn't much improvement of the prediction accuracy from the linear latent features to the nonlinear ones. Thus, PLS is used as the latent feature extraction method in this paper.

In nature, the practical network systems have characteristic of dynamic time-variance, which is same as that of industrial processes. That is to say, concept drift in machine learning domain should also be focused in IMD. Some adaptive mechanisms are used to address the concept drift problem, such as moving window, recursive updating and on-line ensemble learning approach [12]. Both sample-based and batch-based updating strategies can be used in the above adaptive mechanisms, and the former method can adaptive the concept drift more quickly than the later. However, using every new coming sample to update the off-line model is not reasonable [13]. The indentify methods of the valued new samples include: based on square prediction error (SPE) and Hotelling's T^2 of principal component analysis (PCA), based on approximate linear dependence (ALD) on kernel feature space and original data space, based on prediction error band (PEB), and based on fusion condition of ALD and PEB [14]. However, these updating samples' identification strategies have not been used in IDM.

Motivated by the above problems, an on-line instruction detection model based on approximate linear dependent (ALD) condition with linear latent feature extraction is proposed. At first, off-line IDM is constructed based on the latent feature extraction method using PLS and fast machine learning algorithm using RWNN. Then, ALD condition is used to judge the new coming samples' ALD condition with these off-line training samples, and a manual pre-set threshold is used to determine which new sample can be used to update the old IMD. Thirdly, the latent features of the selected new sample are on-line extracted. Finally, the IDM-based on RWNN is re-trained with these new extracted latent features. Simulation based on KDD99 data are used to validate the proposed approach.

2 On-Line Modeling Strategy

Based on the above analysis, the proposed ALD-based network instruction detection modeling strategy consists of two phases, which are off-line training and on-line updating. It is shown in Fig. 1.

In Fig. 1, $\boldsymbol{X}_k = \{\boldsymbol{x}_l\}_{l=1}^k = \{x_1^o, \ldots, x_p^o\}_{l=1}^k$ and $\boldsymbol{Y}_k = \{y^o\}_{l=1}^k$ represent the off-line input and output data, respectively; $\boldsymbol{x}_{k+1} = \{x_1^o, \ldots, x_p^o\}_{k+1}$ and y_{k+1}^o represent the new input and output sample; $\{z_l\}_{l=1}^k = \{\{z_1, \ldots, z_{h'}\}_l\}_{l=1}^k$ stand for the selected latent features; h' indicates the number of the latent features; $\hat{\boldsymbol{Y}}_k = \{\hat{y}^o\}_{l=1}^k$ and $\hat{y}_{k+1}^o$ are the

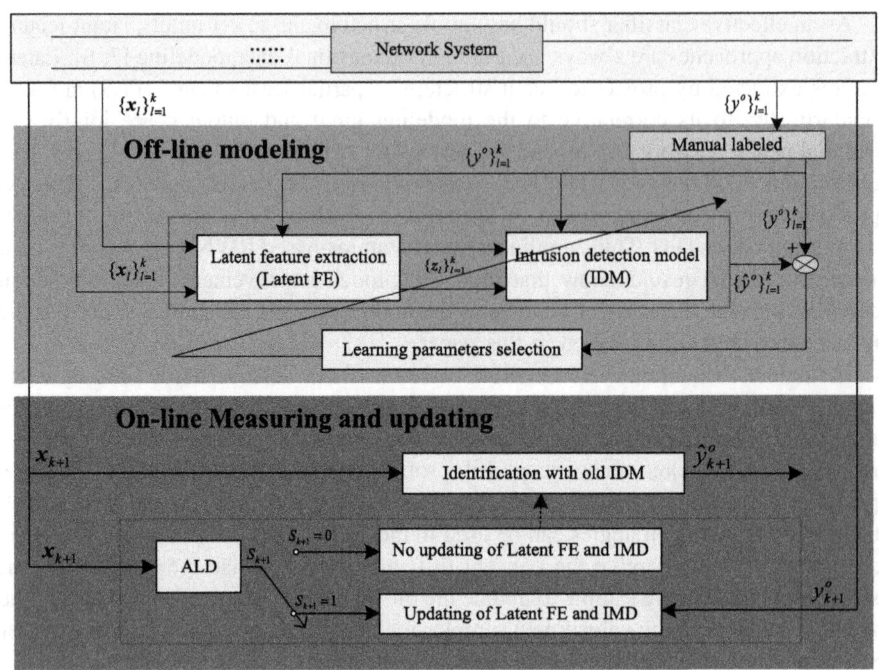

Fig. 1. The proposed on-line modeling strategy

prediction outputs of the off-line and on-line models; S_{k+1} is used to judge whether to update the old IDM or not.

Figure 1 shows that there are two major phases in the proposed strategy, i.e., the off-line modeling phase, the on-line measuring and updating phase. The off-line phase includes latent feature extraction (Latent FE) module and intrusion detection model (IDM) module, whose function is to use the off-line data $\boldsymbol{X}_k$ and $\boldsymbol{y}_k$ to construct classification model. The on-line measuring and updating phase includes two sub-models: the former is the on-line identification based on the old IMD using the new input data; and the later one is the judgments whether to update the old IMF using the ALD value and the updating of the old IMD.

3 On-Line Modeling Algorithm Realization

3.1 Latent Feature-Based Intrusion Detection Model (IDM)

The input data $\boldsymbol{X}_k$ and output data $\boldsymbol{Y}_k$ can be decomposed into (1) and (2) using PLS:

$$\boldsymbol{X}_k = \boldsymbol{T}_k\boldsymbol{P}_k^{\mathrm{T}} + \boldsymbol{E}_h \tag{1}$$

$$\boldsymbol{Y}_k = \boldsymbol{T}_k\boldsymbol{B}_k\boldsymbol{Q}_k^T + \boldsymbol{F}_h \tag{2}$$

The extracted latent features from training and testing samples can be denoted as:

$$Z_k = [t_1, t_2, \ldots, t_{h'}] \tag{3}$$

$$Z^{test} = x^{test} W_k (P_k^T W_k)^{-1} \tag{4}$$

The latent features are used as inputs the random weights neural networks (RWNN). The IDM model constructed with RWNN can be represented as:

$$f_k^{\mathrm{IDM}}(z; \boldsymbol{\beta}) = \sum_{i=1}^{L} \beta_i g(\mathbf{w}_i^{\mathrm{T}} z + b_i) \tag{5}$$

where $\boldsymbol{\beta}_k^{\mathrm{IDM}} = [\beta_1, \beta_1, \ldots, \beta_L] \in R^L$ is the output layer weights; L is the hidden nodes' number; $z \in R^{h'}$ is the input features vector; $w \in R^{h'}$ and $\mathbf{b} \in R$ are the input weights and hidden layer's biases with certain ranges $[-\alpha, \alpha]$, respectively; h' is the number of the input features, i.e., the number of RWNN network inputs.

Given training data set, let $w \in R^{h'}$ and $\boldsymbol{b} \in R$ be chosen randomly from the uniform distribution and fixed in advance, the output weights can be estimated:

$$\hat{\boldsymbol{\beta}}_k^{\mathrm{IDM}} = \underset{\beta}{\arg\min} \frac{1}{k} \sum_{l=1}^{k} \frac{1}{2} (f(z_l) - y_l)^2 \tag{6}$$

The solution can be analytically determined by solving least square problem. However, the least squares problem is usually ill condition. The regularized RWNN model is normally employed to find a solution to overcome the ill-posed problem, which can be formulated as:

$$\min_{\beta} \sum_{l=1}^{k} \left(f(z_l) - \sum_{i=1}^{L} \beta_i g(z_l; w_i, b_i) \right)^2 + \lambda \parallel \boldsymbol{\beta}_k^{\mathrm{IDM}} \parallel_2^2 \tag{7}$$

Thus, the generalization performance of learner model is improved further. Its solution can be obtained in terms of improved generalization performance and stability:

$$\hat{\boldsymbol{\beta}}_k^{\mathrm{IDM}} = (\boldsymbol{H}^T \boldsymbol{H} + \lambda \boldsymbol{I})^{-1} \boldsymbol{H}^{\mathrm{T}} \boldsymbol{Y} \tag{8}$$

3.2 Updating Samples Identification Based on ALD

The off-line IMD $f_k^{\mathrm{IDM}}(\cdot)$ constructed with $\{\boldsymbol{x}_l\}_{l=1}^{k}$ and $\boldsymbol{y}_k$ cannot represent the current conditions of the actual network system. The input/output relation at time m_n can be represented as:

$$y_{m_n} = f'(\boldsymbol{x}_{m_n}),\ m_n = k+1, k+2, \ldots, \tag{9}$$

where $f'(\cdot)$ is the new IDM of network system with concept drift; $\boldsymbol{x}_{m_n}$ is the input at time m_n.

The ALD value between the new sample and old modeling samples can be used to identify the above concept drift, which is calculated with:

$$\delta_{k+1} = \min\left\| \sum_{l=1}^{k} \alpha_l \boldsymbol{x}_l - \boldsymbol{x}_{k+1} \right\|^2, \tag{10}$$

Then, with the δ_{k+1} and pre-set threshold value v, we can decided that which new samples is used to update the old IDM. The relative ALD (RALD) value can be calculated with:

$$\delta_{k+1}^{\text{RALD}} = \frac{\delta_{k+1}}{\left(\sum_{l=1}^{k-1} \delta_l^{\text{ALD}} \right) \Big/ k} \tag{11}$$

where δ_l^{ALD} is the ALD value of the lth old sample to all the other $k-1$ training samples. In this paper, $\delta_{k+1}^{\text{RALD}}$ is used to compare with pre-set threshold. Then, there are two conditions in the identification function:

$$S_{k+1} = F_{\text{ALD}}(\delta_{k+1}^{\text{RALD}}, v) = \begin{cases} 1 & \delta_{k+1}^{\text{RALD}} \geq v \\ 0 & \delta_{k+1}^{\text{RALD}} < v \end{cases} \tag{12}$$

where $S_{k+1} = 1$ represent that the $\boldsymbol{x}_{k+1}$ is used to update the old IDM.

3.3 On-Line Intrusion Detection Model (IDM)

At first, the new input sample should be on-line scaled with the old means and variances. It is shown as follows:

$$\boldsymbol{x}_{k+1}^{\text{old}} = (\boldsymbol{x}_{k+1} - \mathbf{1}_k \boldsymbol{u}_k^{\text{T}}) \cdot \sum\nolimits_k^{-1} \tag{13}$$

where $\mathbf{u}_k$ and $\sum_k$ represent the means and variances of the old modeling data $\{\boldsymbol{x}_l\}_{l=1}^{k}$. And the extracted latent features are represented as:

$$\boldsymbol{z}_{k+1}^{\text{old}} = \boldsymbol{x}_{k+1}^{\text{old}} \boldsymbol{W}_k^{\text{old}} \left((\boldsymbol{P}_k^{\text{old}})^{\text{T}} \boldsymbol{W}_k^{\text{old}} \right)^{-1} \tag{14}$$

where $\boldsymbol{W}_k^{\text{old}}$ and $\boldsymbol{P}_k^{\text{old}}$ are obtained based on the old PLS extraction model.

The identification output based on the old IDM using the new input sample is calculated with:

$$\hat{y}_{k+1}^{0} = f_k(z_{k+1}^{\text{old}}) \tag{15}$$

Secondly, the RALD values of the new sample are calculated with (11). If $S_{k+1} = 0$, there isn't updating of the latent FE and IDM; and if $S_{k+1} = 1, \boldsymbol{x}_{k+1}$ should be scaled with the new means and variances.

The on-line updating of $\boldsymbol{x}_{k+1}$ is realized by:

$$\boldsymbol{x}_{k+1} = (\boldsymbol{x}_{k+1}^{0} - \mathbf{1} \cdot \boldsymbol{u}_{k+1}^{\mathrm{T}}) \cdot \sum_{k+1}^{-1} \tag{16}$$

where,

$$\boldsymbol{u}_{k+1} = \frac{k}{k+1}\boldsymbol{u}_k + \frac{1}{k+1}(\boldsymbol{x}_{k+1}^{0})^{\mathrm{T}} \tag{17}$$

$$\sigma_{(k+1)\cdot i_p}^{2} = \frac{k-1}{k}\sigma_{k\cdot i_p}^{2} + \Delta\boldsymbol{u}_{k+1}^{2}(i_p) + \frac{1}{k}\left\|\boldsymbol{x}_{k+1}^{0}(i_p) - \boldsymbol{u}_{k+1}(i_p)\right\|^2 \tag{18}$$

Thus, the new PLS latent FE model is updated as:

$$\{\mathbf{X}_{k+1}, \mathbf{Y}_{k+1}\} \longrightarrow \text{PLS}\{\mathbf{T}_{k+1}, \mathbf{W}_{k+1}, \mathbf{P}_{k+1}, \mathbf{B}_{k+1}, \mathbf{Q}_{k+1}\} \tag{19}$$

Therefore, the new extracted features are represented as:

$$z_{k+1} = \boldsymbol{x}_{k+1}\boldsymbol{W}_{k+1}\left((\boldsymbol{P}_{k+1})^{\mathrm{T}}\boldsymbol{W}_{k+1}\right)^{-1} \tag{20}$$

Finally, as RRWNN has faster learning speed, the new IDM is retrained with input $\{\{z_l\}_{l=1}^{k}, z_{k+1}\}$ and output $(\{y_l^o\}_{l=1}^{k}, y_{k+1}\}$. The updated new model is denoted as $f_{k+1}^{\text{IDM}}(\cdot)$, and its outputs weighting coefficients is denoted as $\hat{\boldsymbol{\beta}}_{k+1}^{\text{IDM}}$.

4 Experimental Results

4.1 Data Description

KDD CUP99 data are used to validate the proposed method. The data are divided into five categories, which are normal, denial of service (DoS), unauthorized access from a remote machine (Remote to Local, R2L), unauthorized access to local supervisor privileges (User to Root, U2R) and Probe. Each network record contains 41 attributes, of which 34 attributes are continuous and 7 ones are discrete. These discrete attributes should be converted to numerical attributes before being used. Take "protocol type", "service" and "flag" for example, the transform codes are shown in Table 1.

Table 1. Transform codes of the "protocol type", "service" and "flag" attributes

	Discrete attributes	Numerical attributes
Protocol type	TCP, UDP, ICMP	1001–1003
Service	'auth', 'bgp', 'courier', 'csnet_ns','ctf', 'daytime',..., 'exec', 'finger', 17'ftp', 'ftp_data', 'gopher', 'harvest', 'hostnames', 'http',	100001–100070
Flag	'OTH', 'REJ', 'RSTO', 'RSTOS0', 'RSTR', 'S0', 'S1', 'S2', 'S3', 'SF', 'SH'	1001–1011

In this study, the training and testing samples are obtained by random sampling 0.05% and 0.1% from the original training and testing data with size 247 and 311.

4.2 Results

Based on the former studies, the following parameters are used: the number of LV is 4, the number of hidden nodes is 200, the ranges of random width and bias is 1, and the regularized factor is 0.2.

The modeling process is running 10 times. Prediction accuracy based on online testing samples is exploited to evaluate model performance, which is defined as

$$Accuracy = \frac{Num\left\{\left((y_l^o - \hat{y}_l^o) = 0\right)_{l=1}^{k_{\text{test}}}\right\}}{k_{\text{test}}} \tag{21}$$

Feature extraction results with one of the 10 times based on PLS for training samples are shown in Table 2.

Table 2. Percent Variance Captured by PLS Model

LV #	X-Block		Y-Block	
	This LV	Total	This LV	Total
1	13.82	13.82	14.14	14.14
2	27.21	41.03	0.85	14.99
3	20.72	61.75	0.73	15.72
4	11.42	73.18	0.44	16.16
5	9.30	82.48	0.15	16.31
6	2.99	85.46	0.34	16.65
7	2.85	88.31	0.38	17.03
8	4.00	92.31	0.16	17.19
9	2.25	94.55	0.07	17.26
10	2.01	96.56	0.05	17.31

Table 2 shows that only 17.31% variance of the output data is relative to 96.56% that of the input data. Thus is to say, with the linear FE method, most of the latent information cannot be extracted from input data. For comparisons, contributions of the former 10 kernel LVs (KLVs) with different kernel parameters (e.g. $P_{\text{ker}} = 0.1$, 1, 10 and 100) with radius basis function (RBF) using kernel PLS (KPLS) are shown in Fig. 2.

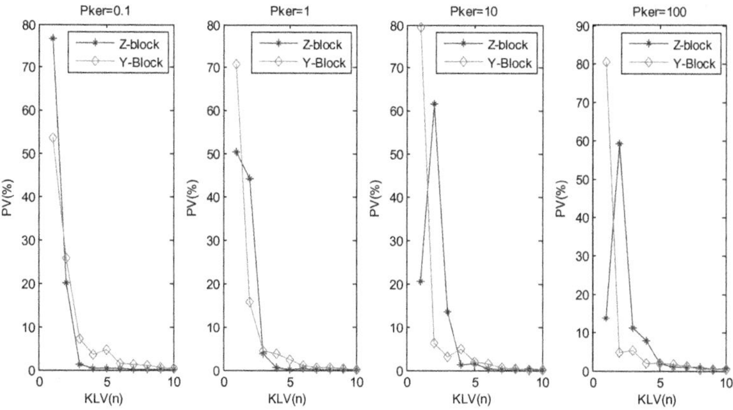

Fig. 2. Contributions of the form 10 KLVs with different kernel parameters

Figure 2 shows that a few of the nonlinear KLVs) can represent most of changes of the original input features and output variable. However, prediction accuracy results of the off-line model with methods based on PLS and KPLS are almost same. Thus, further research should be focused on the detailed modeling approach.

The RALD values of the testing samples to the original training samples are calculated. In order to show the RALD values clearly, the $\log(\delta_{k+1})$ values of RALD are shown in Fig. 3.

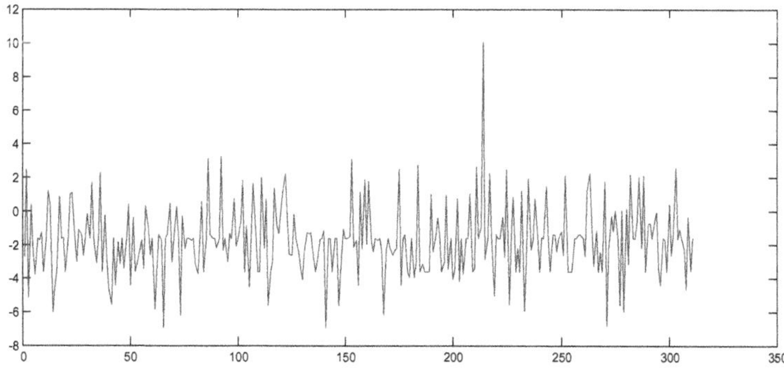

Fig. 3. ALD values of the testing samples to the original training samples

Figure 3 shows that most of the $\log(\delta_{k+1})$ values are around at −2, and only one of $\log(\delta_{k+1})$ value is 10. That is to say, many of the testing samples are similar as of the original training samples in this dataset. It is known that the training samples are random produced from the data set. Therefore, how to select some important samples as the original training samples is an open issue for any actual application problem.

As shown in Fig. 3, the ranges of RALD values are very widely. Thus, these $\delta_{k+1}^{\text{RALD}}$ values are scaled between −3 and +3. Then, the proposed method is repeated 10 times with different RALD threshold values. Statistical results are shown in Table 3.

Table 3. Statistical results of 10 times with different RALD threshold values

	Off-line training			On-line testing			Updating times
	Max	Mean	Min	Max	Mean	Min	
$v = -1$	0.9260	0.9003	0.8681	0.9260	0.9000	0.8745	9
$v = -2$	0.9228	0.9009	0.8327	0.9260	0.9045	0.8553	33
$v = -2.5$	0.9292	0.8938	0.8295	0.9324	0.8954	0.8327	92
$v = -3$	0.9389	0.8954	0.8263	0.9292	0.8926	0.8553	3000

Table 3 shows that the prediction accuracies and updating times are difference with different RALD values. With $v = -2$ and $v = -2.5$, the updating times are 33 and 92, and the maximum prediction accuracy are increased from 0.9228 to 0.9260 and from 0.9292 to 0.9324, respectively. This shown that there is not evident improvement in terms of prediction accuracy. One of the main reasons is the little concept drift among the modeling data as shown in Fig. 3. Moreover, with $v = -3$, 3000 samples are used to update the off-line model; however, only the minimum prediction accuracy is improved. Thus, some old modeling samples are also need to be removed. Thus, there are much improvements of the proposed method. More researches would be done fatherly.

5 Conclusion

Aiming at network intrusion detection model (IDM) construction problem, a new on-line IDM building method combined approximate linear dependent condition and linear latent feature-based regularized random weights neural networks is proposed. Off-line IDM is constructed with the original training samples firstly. Then, the new samples with concept drift are identified. At last, these valued samples are used to update the off-line old model. Simulate results based on KDD99 data show that there is not much improvement in terms of prediction accuracy. This research conclusion does not consist of the theoretical analysis. Therefore, several researches should be focuses in the future, such as how to select the training samples, how to update the learning parameters, how to recursive update the random weights neural networks and how to use the nonlinear feature to construct effective learning model.

Acknowledgments. This work is partially supported by National Natural Science Foundation of China (61640308, 61573364, 61503066, 61503054, 61573249), State Key Laboratory of Synthetical Automation for Process Industries (PAL-N201504), and the Project Funded by the Priority Academic Program Development of Jiangsu Higer Education Institutions (PAPD) and Jiangsu Collaborative Innovation Center on Atmospheric Environment and Equipment Technology (CICAEET) fund.

References

1. Xia, Z.H., Wang, X.H., Sun, X.M., Wang, B.W.: Steganalysis of least significant bit matching using multi-order differences. Secur. Commun. Netw. **7**, 1283–1291 (2014)
2. Weller-Fahy, D.J., Borghetti, B.J., Sodemann, A.: A Survey of distance and similarity measures used within network intrusion anomaly detection. IEEE. Comm. Surv. Tut. **44**, 66–83 (2014)
3. Gianluigi, F., Pietro, S.: Ensemble based collaborative and distributed intrusion detection systems: a survey. J. Netw. Comp. App. **66**, 1–16 (2016)
4. Zhou, Z.L., Wang, Y.L., Wu, J.Q.M., Yang, C.N., Sun, X.M.: Effective and efficient global context verification for image copy detection. IEEE T. Inf. Foren. Sec. **12**, 48–63 (2017)
5. Li, J., Li, X.L., Yang, B., Sun, X.M.: Segmentation-based image copy-move forgery detection scheme. IEEE T. Inf. Foren. Sec. **10**, 507–518 (2015)
6. Xia, Z.H., Wang, X.H., Zhang, L.G., Qin, Z., Sun, X.M., Ren, K.: A privacy-preserving and copy-deterrence content-based image retrieval scheme in cloud computing. IEEE T. Inf. Foren. Sec. **11**, 2594–2626 (2016)
7. Tang, J., Chai, T.Y., Liu, Z., Yu, W.: Selective ensemble modeling based on nonlinear frequency spectral feature extraction for predicting load parameter in ball mills. Chin. J. Chem. Eng. **23**, 2020–2028 (2015)
8. Tang, J., Chai, T.Y., Yu, W., Zhao, L.J.: Feature extraction and selection based on vibration spectrum with application to estimate the load parameters of ball mill in grinding process. Control Eng. Pract. **20**, 991–1004 (2012)
9. Tang, J., Chai, T.Y., Zhao, L.J., Yu, W., Yue, H.: Soft sensor for parameters of mill load based on multi-spectral segments PLS sub-models and on-line adaptive weighted fusion algorithm. Neurocomputing **78**, 38–47 (2012)
10. Wang, G., Hao, J.X., Ma, J., Huang, L.H.: A new approach to intrusion detection using artificial neural networks and fuzzy clustering. Expert Syst. Appl. **37**, 6225–6232 (2010)
11. Cao, F.L., Wang, D.H., Zhu, H.: An iterative learning algorithm for feedforward neural networks with random weights. Inform. Sciences. **328**, 546–557 (2016)
12. Soares, S.G., Araujo, R.: An on-line weighted ensemble of regressor models to handle concept drifts. Eng. Appl. Artif. Intel. **37**, 392–406 (2015)
13. Tang, J., Yu, W., Chai, T.Y., Zhao, L.J.: On-line principal component analysis with application to process modeling. Neurocomputing **82**, 67–178 (2012)
14. Tang, J., Chai, T.Y., Yu, W., Liu, Z., Zhou, X.J.: Adaptive ensemble modelling approach based on updating sample intelligent identification algorithm. Acta Automat. Sinica. **42**, 1040–1052 (2016)

Differential Direction Adaptive Based Reversible Information Hiding

Feipeng Lin, Bo Wang(✉), and Yabin Li

School of Information and Communication Engineering, Dalian University of Technology, Dalian 116024, Liaoning, China
{lewcom,yabinli}@mail.dlut.edu.cn, bowang@dlut.edu.cn

Abstract. In order to reversibly hide information in images with high capacity, an self-adaptive method is proposed in this paper by optimally selecting the differential direction. By dividing image into blocks, differences for adjacent pixel pairs in each blocks are computed in multi-directions. Based on the statistics of these differences, the optimal and self-adaptive strategy for increasing embedding capacity is introduced. The experimental results demonstrate that a significant improvement of embedding capacity is achieved, while the qualities of images is maintained.

Keywords: Reversible information hiding · High capacity · Differential direction

1 Introduction

With the rapid development of communication technology, internet has became one of the most important tools in our daily life. Internet information security becomes an increasing important issue with the widely application of internet. Individuals are worried about the safety of the information transmitted via the internet. In this scenario, information hiding technology attracts much attention and becomes one of the most popular research aspects in information security field, in recent years. As an important branch of the information hiding, reversible information hiding, which can extract the embedded data from the multimedia while restoring the original cover medium after data extraction, has widely applied in military, medical and the other fields. Due to the wide use and spread of digital images, the image reversible information hiding has become one of the hottest issues in multimedia content security, and more and more researchers focus on this topic.

In this decade, several impressive works are carried out and numerous significant algorithms are proposed. All of these reversible information hiding algorithms can be divided into several classes according to different standards. Considering the operation domain, reversible information hiding algorithms could be composed by embedding information in spatial domain, transform domain and compressed domain, for instance. The designers of these algorithms, without

X. Sun et al. (Eds.): ICCCS 2017, Part II, LNCS 10603, pp. 346–356, 2017.
https://doi.org/10.1007/978-3-319-68542-7_29

exception, try their best to balance the image quality, the capacity and the algorithm complexity. The reversible information hiding algorithms based on spacial domain, due to the low complexity, high capacity and good image quality, have been widely discussed and studied. The spacial algorithms are generally realized in three kinds of approaches:

(1) Lossless compression based algorithm. In these approaches, partial data of the cove image, LSB (Least Significant Bit) for instance, is lossless compressed, and the secret information is embedded as the redundancy. For example, Zhang *et al.* [1,2] proposed a method which claimed close to the optimal embedding performance, by compressing the features containing the vast majority of the energy in an image. In [3], Qian *et al.* proposed an algorithm which use 162 different variable length encoding methods defined in the JEPG for embedding messages. Higher capacity of this algorithm is achieved, when the higher compression rate is used, and as a result, a lower quality of the image is expected. To avoid commonly used LSB removal or replacement attack, Shabir *et al.* [4] used Intermediate Significant Bit Substitution (ISBS) to embed watermark data and checksum data, which is capable of providing high quality embedded images.
(2) Difference expansion based algorithm. Considering the correlation of adjacent pixels, the difference expansion based algorithms modify the differences of adjacent pixels to embed secret messages. A typical method is proposed by Tian [5] to embed data into adjacent pixel pairs, while Alattar [6] improves the capacity by using the pixel group with various dimension instead of pixel pair. Based on the difference expansion, Lee et al. [7] proposes an self-adaptive data embedding method, which select smooth areas to carry more information. Comparing with the other algorithms, this method have a better performance in capacity, while a location map is required, which is used to rebuild the cover image.
(3) Histogram shifting based algorithm. This kind of algorithms expands the value of pixels at the peak of the histogram, and uses the pixels, which are located among the zero and peak values, for shifting and furthermore for message embedding. Ni *et al.* [8] proposed to embed data into the interspace of the histogram in early phase. Hu *et al.* [9] constructed the Laplace-Like statistical histogram by prediction error. By shifting the Laplace-Like histogram, they received distinguishing results. Wang *et al.* [10] avoided the unnecessary pixels shifting by selecting the pixels according to the size of embedding data. In [11], Hwang *et al.* embedded messages into multi-pixels. They improved the capacity of the histogram shifting based algorithms, by using two different thresholds to select pixels to embed secret message. The thresholds are typically obtained according to the embedding capacity. Obviously, this method is a content adaptive algorithm, which means the capacity is unstable and highly related to the content of the cover image. Chen *et al.* [12] provided a new perspective of histogram shifting based reversible information hiding. They calculated multiple prediction errors for each pixel embedded data by combining the maximum and minimum error histograms.

Experimental result showed that embedding capacity is improved while the quality of watermarked images is maintained. As a recent work in [13], Lu *et al.* employed an edge sensitivity analysis method proposed in [14] before asymmetric-histogram shifting , to reduce the prediction error, and made it more suitable for both smooth block prediction and complex block prediction by expanding the edge sensitivity analysis method.

Lee *et al.* [15], Thodi and Rodriguez [16] and Weng *et al.* [17] proposed three new algorithms separately, by combining the difference expansion and histogram shifting. They believe the high coherence of the adjacent pixels in cover images, thus propose the difference histogram shifting based reversible information hiding methods. These methods markedly improved the embedding capacity because the peaks in the difference histogram are distinctly more than that in the original histogram.

In this paper, we focus on further improving the capacity of the difference histogram shifting based reversible information hiding algorithm. The paper is organized as follows. In Sect. 2, the previous difference histogram based algorithms are introduced. The proposed method, which is based on adaptive differential direction, is described in Sect. 3. The experiments are demonstrated and analyzed in Sect. 4. Finally the paper is concluded in Sect. 5.

2 Difference Histogram Shifting Based Algorithms

Considering the overflow in the embedding, the cover image have to be preprocessed in the difference histogram shifting based algorithms. A typical approach is as follows. For reversible information hiding based on difference histogram shifting algorithm, cover medium must be pretreated which can avoid overflowing when embed secret data. Cover image, which is denoted as I, is scanned into one dimensional sequences a vector $P = \{x_1, x_2, ..., x_L\}$, with the length of L. Pixels in the vector are modified according to Eq. (1), to generate a new vector $P' = \{x_1', x_2', ..., x_L'\}$, in which the range of pixel values is limited in [1,254] while the pixel values in P vary from 0 to 255. Meanwhile, the location map Q is generated and compressed using run-length coding. As a kind of header information, the location map Q is embedded into the cover image in conjunction with the secret messages.

$$x_i' = \begin{cases} x_i + 1, \ if \ x_i = 0 \\ x_i - 1, \ if \ x_i = 255 \\ x_i, \quad else \end{cases}, \ Q = \begin{cases} 0, x_i \neq 0 \ and \ x_i \neq 255 \\ 1, x_i = 0 \ \ or \ \ x_i = 255 \end{cases}. \tag{1}$$

2.1 Information Embedding

We divide P' into two non-overlapping pixel pairs (p, q), with odd-index and even-index separately, and calculate the corresponding differences $D = \{d_1, d_2, ..., d_{L/2}\}$ between the pairs, according to $d_j = q_j - p_j, j \in [1, L/2]$. The secret messages are embedded by modifying the pixel pairs according to the differences. The algorithms of Lee *et al.* [15], Thodi and Rodriguez [16] and Weng *et al.* [17] could be described as Eq. (2–4).

$$Lee: \quad (\tilde{p},\tilde{q}) = \begin{cases} (p, \ q+1), \ if D(j) > \ 1 \\ (p, \ q-1), \ if D(j) < -1 \\ (p, q-M), \ if D(j) = -1 \\ (p, q+M), \ if D(j) = \ 1 \\ (p, \ q), \ if D(j) = \ 0 \end{cases} . \tag{2}$$

$$Thodi: \quad (\tilde{p},\tilde{q}) = \begin{cases} (p, \ q+1), \ if \ D(j) \geq \ 1 \ and \ odd \\ (p-1, \ q), \ if \ D(j) \geq \ 1 \ and \ even \\ (p+1, \ q), \ if \ D(j) < -1 \ and \ odd \\ (p, \ q-1), \ if \ D(j) < -1 \ and \ even \\ (p+M, q), \ if \ D(j) = -1 \\ (p-M, q), \ if \ D(j) = 0 \end{cases} . \tag{3}$$

$$Weng: \quad (\tilde{p},\tilde{q}) = \begin{cases} (p-1, \ \ q+1), if \ D(j) > \ 1 \\ (p+1, \ \ q-1), if \ D(j) < -1 \\ (p+M, q-M), if \ D(j) = -1 \\ (p-M, q+M), if \ D(j) = 0 \ or \ 1 \end{cases} . \tag{4}$$

Obviously, Lee *et al.* [15] uses the pixel pairs with differences $D \in \{1, -1\}$ and Thodi and Rodriguez [16] selects differences $D \in \{0, -1\}$, to embed data M. Different from these two methods, the pixel pairs with differences $D \in \{1, 0, -1\}$ are chosen for embedding.

2.2 Information Extraction

For extracting the embedded data, the stego image is scanned into a vector P_N and also the differences $D_N = \{y_1, y_2, ..., y_{L/2}\}$ is generated, where $y_j = \widetilde{q_j} - \widetilde{p_j}, j = 1, 2, ..., L/2$. The different extraction methods [15–17] are explained in Eqs. (5) to (7).

$$Lee: M_N = \begin{cases} 1, if \ |D_N = 2| \\ 0, if \ |D_N = 1| \end{cases} . \tag{5}$$

$$Thodi: M_N = \begin{cases} 1, if D_N = -2 \ or \ D_N = 1 \\ 0, if D_N = -1 \ or \ D_N = 0 \end{cases} . \tag{6}$$

$$Weng: M_N = \begin{cases} 1, if \ |D_N| = 3 \ or \ D_N = 2 \\ 0, if \ |D_N| = 1 \ or \ D_N = 0 \end{cases} . \tag{7}$$

The extracted data M_N is divided into two parts: header information H and secret data m. To recover the cover image, the pixels should be shifted according to the differences D_N. And also, the under-flow and over-flow pixels could be recovered by the location map Q, which is assumed to be extracted as the header information.

Considering the capacity of the three approaches, Weng's method [17] advantages in the embedding capacity because the more pixels pairs with differences $D \in \{1, 0, -1\}$ are used, while simultaneously the quality of the stego image is relatively low. By using the pixel pairs with differences $D \in \{1, -1\}$ [15] and $D \in \{0, -1\}$ [16], a high visual quality and PSNR of stego image is guaranteed. Considering that the number of differences of 0 is bigger than the differences of 1, the embedding capacity of Thodi's method is higher than that of Lee's. Meanwhile, the modification of all pixel pairs in [16] results in a larger location map, compared with the even-index pixel modification in [15].

3 Differential Direction Adaptive Method

Considering the embedding capacity of difference histogram shifting method, the higher peak is in the difference histogram, the more bits could be embedded in the cover image. To our best knowledge, the previous approaches scan the images horizontally and furthermore obtain the difference histogram. Actually, the differences of pixel pairs denote the textures of the images. Therefore, different difference histograms are expected in differential direction, for various texture images. For instance, three difference histograms are obtained for Lena, using horizontal, vertical and Zig-zag scanning, as Fig. 1 demonstrated. The peaks in the histograms are 11621, 15041 and 10670 separately. This inspires us that the embedding capacity could be improved by generating difference histogram adaptively, according to the differential direction of the texture in the image.

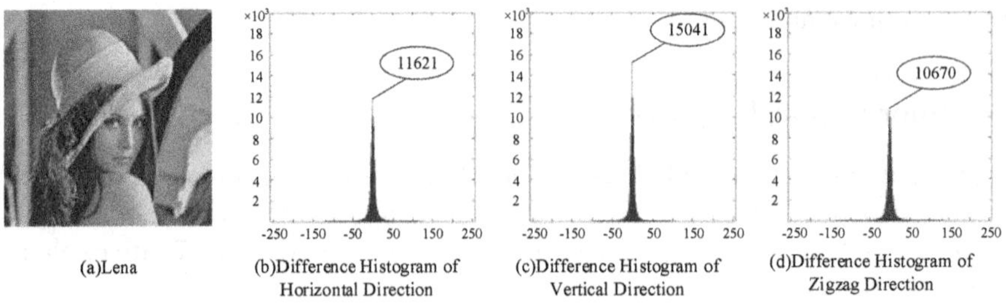

Fig. 1. Image lena and difference histograms: (b) horizontal; (c) vertical and (d) Zig-zag scanning.

In this paper, a differential direction adaptive approach is proposed to improve the embedding capacity by using several preset difference directions, according to the distribution of pixels in the cover image. In our method, four representative differential directions are introduced as follows.

(1) Horizontal direction: The image is scanned horizontally from the top to the bottom, as illustrated in Fig. 2(a).

(2) Vertical direction: We vertically scan the image from the left to the right, as illustrated in Fig. 2(b).
(3) Zig-zag direction: Similar with the Zig-zag scanning using in the JPEG coding, the image is scanned in diagonal direction, as illustrated in Fig. 2(c).
(4) Hilbert direction: Hilbert curve, which was proposed in 1891, can traverse all of the pixels in the image uniformly. Also the Hilbert curve shows the relativity between the neighbor pixels. Considering different origins, four Hilbert curve can be generated [18], as illustrated in Fig. 2(d) to (g).

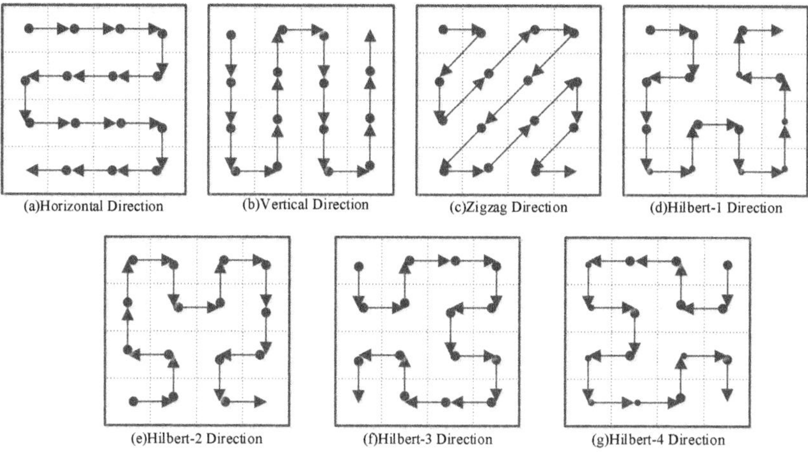

Fig. 2. Different scanning directions.

The differences along the four kinds of directions aforementioned could indicate the relativity in specific direction. For example, the horizontal coherence is enhanced in horizontal scanning, while the vertical and Zig-zag scanning could enlarge the vertical and diagonal correlation in the image. The Hilbert curve scanning balances the relativities in arbitrary direction. Therefore, the embedding capacity for the same image differs because of the different scanning directions.

For increasing the capacity, an intuitionistic approach is finding a specific scanning direction, which could obtain the maximum peak in the difference histogram of the cover image. Hence, we propose a new adaptive differential direction based method, which optimizes the scanning direction in each block of the cover image to achieve a higher embedding capacity.

The algorithm could be described as follows.

(1) Divide the cover image I into several $n \times n$ non-overlapping blocks.
(2) Each image block is scanned to seven vectors $P_i = \{x_1, x_2, ..., x_l\}, i = 1, 2, ..., 7$ with length $l = n \times n$, according to the pre-install seven kinds of difference directions, as Fig. 2 illustrated.

(3) Divide the pixels in the vectors P_i into two non-overlapping pixel pairs with length 1/2 and calculate their differences $D_i = \{y_1, y_2, ..., y_{l/2}\}, i = 1, 2, ..., 7$, where $y_j = x_{2j} - x_{2j-1}, j = 1, 2, ..., l/2$.
(4) The numbers of differences, −1, 0, and 1, which are used for embedding in these methods, are accumulated and denoted as S_a, S_b, S_c. Subsequently, the sum is calculated as $S_i = S_a + S_b + S_c, i = 1, 2, ..., 7$.
(5) The optimal scanning direction is selected by $S_m = max\{S_i\}, i = 1, 2, ..., 7$, where S_m obtain the biggest number of differences in i_{th} scanning direction.
(6) A scanning mode index vector is generated to record all of the optimal scanning directions in each image blocks. And also, the index vector is embedded into the cover image as a header information for extracting the embedded data.

4 Experimental Results

All of the experiments in this paper are carried out using MATLAB 2014a on a desktop computer. We evaluate the proposed method on 96 grayscale images of size 512 × 512, with the methods proposed by Lee *et al.* [15], Thodi and Rodriguez [16] and Weng *et al.* [17] as baselines. Figure 3 demonstrates samples of the test images. For each test images, the maximum Embedding Capacity (EC) and Peak Signal to Noise Ratio (PSNR) are calculated as the criteria to evaluate the performance of the reversible information hiding method. The PSNR is computed as Eq. (8) shows, where $M \times N$are the resolution of the cover image. The Mean Square Error, MSE is estimated by the pixels $I_0(i, j)$

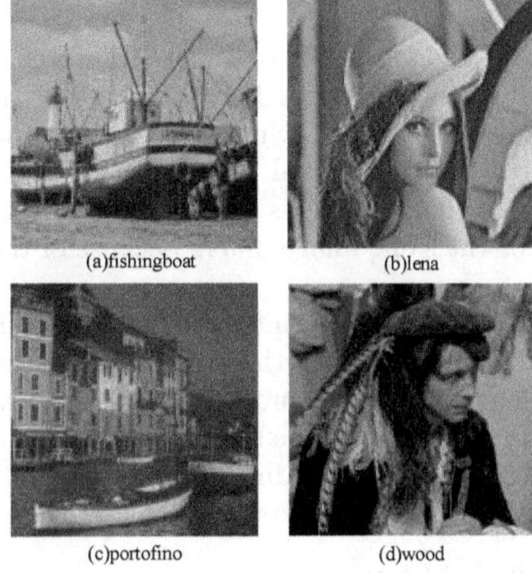

Fig. 3. Four samples of the test images.

and $I_1(i,j)$, which are the values of the pixel located at i_{th} row and j_{th} column before and after embedding.

$$\begin{cases} MSE = \frac{1}{M \times N} \sum_{i=1}^{M} \sum_{j=1}^{N} \left(I_0(i,j) - I_1(i,j)\right)^2 \\ PSNR = 10\lg\left(\frac{255^2}{MSE}\right) \end{cases} . \quad (8)$$

In the experiments, each image is divided into six different sizes of blocks with resolutions of 512×512, 256×256, 128×128, 64×64, 32×32, and 16×16. Each block is processed by the proposed self-adaptive method to select the differential direction for information hiding, and a single fixed difference direction method is also carried out on the full size image as a baseline to show the validity of propose direction selecting method. Then the three aforementioned methods are applied to embed secret data in order to show the wide applicability of our method. The experimental results are demonstrated in Table 1.

Table 1. Average embedding capacity and PSNR of different block sizes

	Block size	Lee		Thodi		Weng	
		EC	PSNR	EC	PSNR	EC	PSNR
Differential direction self-adaption	512×512	11784	52.98	34455	51.92	40323	49.04
	256×256	11871	53.00	34750	51.92	40659	49.05
	128×128	11955	53.04	35160	51.93	41110	49.06
	64×64	12003	53.10	35656	51.94	41632	49.07
	32×32	12019	53.18	36387	51.96	42372	49.08
	16×16	12024	53.29	37518	51.98	43504	49.10
Single differential direction	512×512	11498	52.93	33417	51.90	39141	49.02

If we use a single fixed difference direction, for instance horizontal direction of difference, the difference of the cover image do not change with the size of block due to the single direction of difference. But for self-adaption difference direction, each block has different direction. With the decreasing of block size, the number of image block is increasing and the description of the texture direction in each block becomes more accurate. More pixels can be used to embed data, higher embedding capacity is expected. However, the complexity of computation also increases.

Experiments also show that the proposed method out-perform the single fixed difference direction method in the term of embedding capacity and PSNR, when the same information hiding strategy is used. As Table 2 demonstrated, the embedding capacity and PSNR is obviously higher than that of seven other difference directions, when the cover image is divided into 16 blocks with the size of 128×128. We can naturally get the conclusion that for the three different embedding methods, our self-adaptive difference direction method can im-prove the PSNR of the stego image and maintain, even improve the embedding capacity slightly. Compared with the horizontal direction of difference methods of Lee,

Table 2. Average embedding capacity and PSNR of different directions

	Lee		Thodi		Weng	
	EC	PSNR	EC	PSNR	EC	PSNR
Horizontal	11498	52.93	33417	51.90	39141	49.02
Vertical	11917	52.80	32923	51.88	38858	49.01
Zigzag	10674	52.60	29149	51.81	34458	48.93
Hilbert-1	11712	52.85	33170	51.89	38996	49.02
Hilbert-2	11713	52.85	33176	51.89	39004	49.02
Hilbert-3	11705	52.84	33163	51.89	38997	49.02
Hilbert-4	11700	52.84	33173	51.89	39001	49.02
Differential direction self-adaption	11955	53.04	35160	51.93	41110	51.93

Table 3. The best difference direction of partial test images

		Fishingboat	Lena	Protofino	Wood
Lee	Horizontal	22481	20307	14133	14005
	Self-adaption	25820	23288	16316	15529
	Growth rate	14.9%	14.7%	15.4%	10.9%
Thodi	Horizontal	23020	21703	14060	14527
	Self-adaption	26996	26724	16302	16225
	Growth rate	17.3%	23.1%	15.9%	11.7%
Weng	Horizontal	34445	31928	21143	20406
	Self-adaption	39894	38353	24414	22891
	Growth rate	15.8%	20.1%	15.5%	12.2%
Optimal difference direction in blocks		2, 2, 2, 2,	2, 2, 2, 2,	2, 7, 2, 2,	1, 5, 1, 2,
		2, 2, 2, 2,	5, 2, 7, 2,	2, 2, 2, 2,	6, 2, 7, 2,
		2, 2, 5, 2,	2, 2, 2, 2,	7, 2, 2, 7,	6, 2, 2, 4,
		1, 1, 6, 4	2, 2, 2, 2	1, 1, 5, 6	2, 2, 2, 2

Thodi and Weng, the self-adaptive difference direction method achieves a promotion of 4.0%, 5.2% and 5.0% in the term of embedding capacity, respectively.

Table 3 shows the optimal directions of all blocks in the sample test images, fishingboat, lena, portofino and wood, as shown in Fig. 3. All of these cover images are divided into 16 blocks with the size of 128 × 128 in this experiments. We explore the optimal difference directions automatically selected by the proposed method for all of the blocks. Number 1 to 7 in the last row of Table 3 denotes the horizontal, vertical, Zig-zag and four Hilbert curves scanning respectively. We can learn from the table that, it is not horizontal that most of the optimal difference directions in the 16 blocks are. Therefore, compared with the single fixed horizontal direction method, the embedding capacity of the proposed self-adaptive direction method significantly increases more than 10%, as shown in Table 3.

5 Conclusion

For the difference histogram shifting based reversible information hiding, a new self-adaptive method is proposed in this paper. By dividing the cover image into several blocks, optimal differential directions are selected to improve the embedding capacity and the PSNR of the stego image. Experimental results show that our algorithm maintains PSNR of the stego image, meanwhile improve the embedding capacity, compared with the baselines with single fixed difference direction methods.

Acknowledgments. This work is supported by the National Science Foundation of China (No. 61502076) and the Scientific Research Project of Liaoning Provincial Education Department (No. L2015114).

References

1. Zhang, W., Chen, B., Yu, N.: Improving various reversible data hiding schemes via optimal codes for binary covers. IEEE Trans. Image Process. **21**, 2991–3003 (2012)
2. Zhang, W., Hu, X., Li, X., Yu, N.: Recursive histogram modification: establishing equivalency between reversible data hiding and lossless data compression. IEEE Trans. Image Process. **22**, 2775–2785 (2013)
3. Qian, Z., Zhang, X.: Lossless data hiding in JPEG bitstream. J. Syst. Softw. **85**, 309–313 (2012)
4. Parah, S.A., Ahad, F., Sheikh, J.A., Bhat, G.M.: Hiding clinical iinformation in medical images: a new high capacity and reversible data hiding technique. J. Biomed. Informatics. **66**, 214–230 (2017)
5. Tian, J.: Reversible data embedding using a difference expansion. IEEE Trans. Circuits Syst. Video Technol. **13**, 890–896 (2003)
6. Alattar, A.M.: Reversible watermark using the difference expansion of a generalized integer transform. IEEE Trans. Image Process. **13**, 1147–1156 (2004)
7. Lee, C.C., Wu, H.C., Tsai, C.S., Chu, Y.P.: Expansion, adaptive lossless steganographic scheme with centralized difference. Pattern Recogn. **41**, 2097–2106 (2008)
8. Ni, Z., Shi, Y.Q., Ansari, N., Su, W.: Reversible data hiding. IEEE Trans. Circuits Syst. Video Technol. **16**, 354–362 (2006)
9. Hu, Y., Lee, H.K., Li, J.: DE-based reversible data hiding with improved overflow location map. IEEE Trans. Circuits Syst. Video Technol. **19**, 250–260 (2008)
10. Wang, C., Li, X., Yang, B.: Efficient reversible image watermarking by using dynamical prediction-error expansion. In: 17th IEEE International Conference on Image Processing, pp. 3673–3676. IEEE Press, Hong Kong (2010)
11. Hwang, H.J., Kim, H.J., Sachnev, V., Joo, S.Y.: Reversible watermarking method using optimal histogram pair shifting based on prediction and sorting. KSII Trans. Internet Inform. Syst. **4**, 655–670 (2010)
12. Chen, X., Sun, X., Sun, H., Zhou, Z., Zhang, J.: Reversible watermarking method based on asymmetric-histogram shifting of prediction errors. J. Syst. Softw. **86**, 2620–2626 (2013)
13. Lu, T.C., Tseng, C.Y., Wu, J.H.: Asymmetric-histogram based reversible information hiding scheme using edge sensitivity detection. J. Syst. Softw. **116**, 2–21 (2016)

14. Lukac, R., Martin, K., Platanoitis, K.N.: Digital camera zooming based on unified CFA image processing steps. IEEE Trans. Consum. Electron. **50**, 15–24 (2004)
15. Lee, S.K., Suh, Y.H., Ho, Y.S.: Reversible image authentication based on watermarking. In: IEEE International Conference on Multimedia and Expo, pp. 1321–1324. IEEE Press, Toronto (2006)
16. Thodi, D.M., Rodriguez, J.J.: Expansion embedding techniques for reversible watermarking. IEEE Trans. Image Process. **16**, 721–730 (2007)
17. Weng, S., Zhao, Y., Pan, J.S., Ni, R.: Reversible watermarking based on invariability and adjustment on pixel pairs. IEEE Signal Process. Lett. **15**, 721–724 (2008)
18. Mo, L.: Research on Reversible Information Hiding Algorithm Based on Airspace. GuilinCollege of Computer Science and Information Technology, Guangxi Normal University (2013)

Detection of Jitterbug Covert Channel Based on Partial Entropy Test

Hao Wang[1], Guangjie Liu[1(✉)], Weiwei Liu[1], Jiangtao Zhai[2], and Yuewei Dai[2]

[1] School of Automation, Nanjing University of Science and Technology, Nanjing 210094, China
whaanog@gmail.com, gjieliu@gmail.com, lwwnjust5817@gmail.com

[2] School of Electronics and Information, Jiangsu University of Science and Technology, Zhenjiang 212003, China
jiangtaozhai@gmail.com, dywjust@163.com

Abstract. Jitterbug is a typical delay-based covert timing channel and supplies reliable covert communication in a passive manner. The existing entropy-based detection scheme based on training samples may suffer from model mismatching, which results in detection performance deterioration. In this paper, a new detection method for Jitterbug based on partial entropy test is proposed. A fixed binning strategy without training samples is used to obtain bins distribution feature. The first-order entropy is calculated for several sets of partial successive bins and the weighted mean is used to calculate the final entropy value to distinguish Jitterbug from legitimate traffic. Furthermore, the influence of detection performance caused by network jitter is also discussed. Experimental results show that the proposed detection method achieves high detection performance and is less affected by network jitter.

Keywords: Jitterbug · Covert channel detection · Timing channel · Partial entropy

1 Introduction

For a well-protected local network, the information leakage can commonly be prevented by inspecting the incoming and outgoing traffic on some security equipments, such as network firewalls, intrusion detection systems or other traffic checking devices, which can identify the unauthorized or abnormal network traffic. To evade the check from these security equipments, a network covert channel is constructed to hide the information into authorized normal traffic and conceals the very existence of the secret data transmission. The network covert channel is a stealthy communication technique utilizing redundancies of network protocols or packet-sequence characteristics to transfer secret message. Similar to the concept of covert channel in multi-level security (MLS) systems, network covert channel can also be divided into storage and timing channels [1]. Network covert storage channel is constructed by modifying some unused or insensitive bits of protocol header in network packets. Network covert timing

X. Sun et al. (Eds.): ICCCS 2017, Part II, LNCS 10603, pp. 357–368, 2017.
https://doi.org/10.1007/978-3-319-68542-7_30

channel is constructed by modulating secret message into packet rates/inter-packet delays (IPDs). Besides the time sequence, other covert channels based on characteristics of packet-sequence are usually considered as the timing case [2].

Network covert timing channel is the focus issue of current research. Padlipsky *et al.* [3] firstly described the principle of the on/off timing channel in which the sender either transmits or stays silent in each time interval to represent 0 or 1. Girling [4] also proposed a covert timing channel which can transmit secret message by particular delays between successive transmissions imposed by a sender. Delay-based timing channel does not require synchronized clock while an on/off timing channel needs synchronization mechanism to ensure decoding accuracy. Thus, Cabuk *et al.* [5, 6] implemented the on/off timing channel which introduces SOF (Start of frame) and Silent intervals to synchronize between sender and receiver. The modulation of IPDs may change overt communication pattern and made itself more exposed. To solve this problem, Gianvecchio *et al.* [7] proposed a model-based covert timing channel called MBCTC. In their scheme the channel mimics the observed behavior of legitimate network traffic to evade detection. Liu *et al.* [8] proposed a simple binary covert timing channel based on Gianvecchio's framework, this method is more practical in encoding/decoding and has lower bit error rate. Although these covert channels can resist detection based on statistical properties, the algorithms are usually complicated with low date rate and not easy to be deployed in a real network.

Making the covert timing channels detected is also a challenge issue and researchers have made lots of endeavors. Cabuk et al. [5] proposed a detection method against on/off covert timing channel, in which two measures, *regularity* (i.e. patterns in the variance) and *ε-similarity* (i.e. similarity between adjacent inter-arrival times), were defined to judge whether the traffic was a covert one. Gianvecchio and Wang [9, 10] proposed an entropy-based detection approach which makes use of entropy (EN) and corrected conditional entropy (CCE) to describe abnormal shape or abnormal regularity separately. The approach is able to detect most of the existing covert timing channels but needs legitimate traffic samples to determine the bin ranges. In practice, due to the large dynamics of network traffic, it is no easy to choose proper traffic samples and the detection performance may discount. Shrestha *et al.* [11] proposed a machine learning framework for detecting covert timing channel. However, the four training features were proposed by previous studies for different detection purposes and the combine of them may not obtain maximum profit. Moreover, the results show that the classifier is not effective in detecting Jitterbug covert channel.

This paper is focused on a typical delay-based covert timing channel named Jitterbug [12] which is originally designed as a keyboard device to leak typed messages by creating a passive covert timing channel. The interactive communication applications may be applied as overt channel for Jitterbug which makes it become the very practical covert channel to leak information over Internet. Some improved covert timing channel methods such as Liquid [13], Mimic [14] also have the same basic encoding/decoding scheme. Thus, the reliable detection for Jitterbug is a significant issue. For implementing detection of Jitterbug, we count the bins distribution of IPDs in a fixed binning strategy and then calculate the first-order entropy of partial bins (denoted as Partial Entropy, PEN) which belong to a significant region. After that, these PEN values are utilized to distinguish between normal traffic and Jitterbug traffic.

The remainder of this paper is organized as follows. Section 2 introduces the principle of Jitterbug and corresponding analysis. Section 3 gives our detection scheme. Section 4 presents the experimental results. Section 5 concludes the whole paper.

2 Background and Related Work

2.1 Review of Jitterbug Covert Channel

Shah *et al.* [12] designed Jitterbug covert channel as a hardware interception device installed between the computer and its keyboard. The covert timing channel performed by Jitterbug is a passive one because there are no additional traffics need to be generated for transmitting secret message. The Jitterbug device embeds information into the keystroke timing in the form of small supplementary jitters. If each keystroke is sent within a single packet, the timing information will retain in the IPDs. Therefore, the overt channel of Jitterbug must be an interactive network application (e.g. Telnet, SSH) in which each keystroke corresponds to a packet. The receiver monitors the packet flows of these applications and decodes the secret message from the manipulated IPDs. The mechanism of keyboard Jitterbug can also be extended to a useful covert channel method when a compromised host is obtained. In this scenario, a special driver for NIC (Network Interface Card) is considered to add timing information instead of hardware device. The secret message can be encoded by adding extra packet delays just in the software manner. In this case, the choice of overt channel can be extended to the applications containing continued traffic session (e.g. VoIP).

For the Jitterbug covert channel, the IPDs are manipulated to satisfy certain properties depending on the secret message to be sent. In a binary encoding case, letting b_i denote a bit sequence and w (in millisecond) denote the Jitterbug timing window which is used to determine the delays how to represent encoding symbols, IPD sequence denoted as δ_i should be manipulated to satisfy Eq. (1).

$$(\delta_i - s_i) \bmod w = \begin{cases} 0 & \textit{if } b_i = 0 \\ \lfloor w/2 \rfloor & \textit{if } b_i = 1 \end{cases} \tag{1}$$

where $\delta_i = \delta_i' + \Delta t_i + s_i$ with δ_i' being original inter-packet delay between the packet p_{i+1} and p_i, and Δt_i being the added delays to satisfy modulo operation. To prevent the IPDs clustering around multiples of $w/2$, a pseudo-random sequence s_i with integer millisecond value from 0 to $w-1$ is additionally added, and this sequence is assumed only to be known by the sender and receiver.

After the transmission on the Internet link, the packet p_{i+1} and p_i arrive at the receiver end. The modulated IPD δ_i is changed to $\hat{\delta}_i$ due to the link delay jitters. The receiver decodes the message bit $\hat{b}_i$ with the shared s_i according to Eq. (2).

$$\hat{b}_i = \begin{cases} 0 & \textit{if } (\hat{\delta}_i - s_i) \bmod w \in [0,\ w/4) \cup [3w/4,\ w) \\ 1 & \textit{if } (\hat{\delta}_i - s_i) \bmod w \in [w/4,\ 3w/4) \end{cases} \tag{2}$$

2.2 The Limitation of Entropy-Based Detection Method

Except EN test [10], most of current detection algorithms mentioned in Sect. 1 fail to distinguish Jitterbug from normal traffic. The first-order entropy is estimated in EN test to measure the shape of the investigated traffic. Due to finite number of samples, the empirical probability density function based on the method of histogram is employed to replace probability density function. More importantly, the equiprobable binning strategy based on the normal training IPD samples is used to decide how to partition tested IPDs. Actually, EN test is designed to measure how closely the tested IPDs fit the normal reference traffic by the fine-grain binning with as many as 65536 columns. Although Jitterbug just adds tiny delays to original IPDs, the changes of distribution in the bins are still perceived due to the fine-grain binning strategy. Commonly, EN test scores of normal traffic approaches the upper-bound value of the first-order entropy and the lower EN test scores imply the possible existence of Jitterbug covert channel.

However, there are some restrictions for deploying EN test in a real network environment. As mentioned above, the detection performance significantly depends on the binning strategy determined by training IPD samples, Due to the various manners of network traffic, it is hard to choose proper training samples to adapt to all of the cases, and the threshold setting is also a great challenge. For instance, there are three SSH traffic sets. The first two sets are from the same traffic source while the third set is from a different source and the IPDs of it have a significant different distribution. The first set is chosen as training samples and the Jitterbug traffics are generated based on the other two sets. So there are two SSH-Jitterbug traffic pairs to be detected. The EN test performs well to distinguish first SSH-Jitterbug traffic pair while it fails to distinguish the second pair. For the first pair, the training samples have good indication to obtain proper bins and lead to ideal detection results because they are from the same traffic source. For the second pair, the SSH traffic has a notable deviation from training samples and gets low EN test scores and Jitterbug traffic also gets low EN test scores. Consequently, it is hard to separate them by a constant threshold and the training samples become invalid for guiding binning. We called this state a model (i.e. binning strategy based on training samples) mismatching case of EN test. In our previous work, the model mismatching case also has been verified by an experiment [15].

To solve the model mismatching problem, a possible solution is to build enough models for adapting to the diversity of the network application traffic. However, the IPDs are not only related to the network application but also the network connection environment and the processing ability of the computer, thus the solution is infeasible in the real Internet detection scenario. The other solution is to study the detection methods based on the features of the covert channels themselves. With the limitation just valid to specific covert channel method, these kinds of detection methods are more reliable. It is also the main motivation of this paper.

3 Proposed Method

3.1 Binning Strategy

Based on Eq. (1), Jitterbug firstly adds tiny delays Δt_i to the original inter-packet delays δ'_i, which will cause that IPDs cluster around $mw/2$ (m = 1, 2, 3,…). To smooth the obvious clustering abnormality, the pseudo-random sequence s_i is additionally added to scatter each clustered IPDs over all integer millisecond values in the range [$mw/2$, $(m + 2)w/2$). To discover and investigate the fine change of the IPD histogram, the following binning strategy is adopted in this paper.

$$\begin{aligned} &[L, L+B), [L+B, L+2B), \ldots, [L+(n-1)B, L+nB] \\ &L = \frac{\lfloor 1000 d_{\min} \rfloor}{1000} - \frac{B}{2} \\ &n = \lceil (d_{\max} - L)/B \rceil \end{aligned} \tag{3}$$

where B is the width of each bin and is set to 0.001 s, $d_{\max}$ and $d_{\min}$ denote the maximum and minimum values of observed successive IPDs, respectively.

An experiment is performed to observe the effect of binning strategy on Jitterbug. Skype-VoIP traffic between Nanjing and Beijing is captured and total 10,000 IPDs are recorded. Based on the binning strategy defined by Eq. (3), the statistical result of normal traffic is shown in Fig. 1(a). Processing these IPDs according to the Jitterbug method with the parameter w = 15 ms and 20 ms, then the statistical result of Jitterbug traffic with different w values is shown in Fig. 1(b) and (c). It is clear that Jitterbug will cause the approximately equal bin values in some regions, while the characteristic does not occur in the histogram of normal traffic. This characteristic is also unsurprising according to the principle of Jitterbug. Compared with EN test, the application of fixed binning strategy removes the dependence of training samples and avoids the model mismatching problem. Moreover, the EN test also can-not work well under this binning strategy due to the lack of reference entropy value (the original reference value is calculated by training samples) to distinguish Jitterbug from normal traffic.

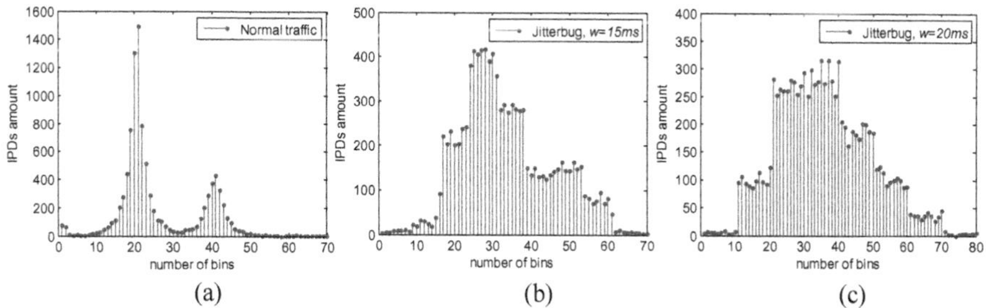

(a) (b) (c)

Fig. 1. Histogram of normal traffic and Jitterbug traffic.

3.2 Detection Based on Partial Entropy

Partial entropy (PEN) in our paper is used to represent the first-order entropy of partial successive bins. The range of partial successive bins is called significant regions. According to the characteristic mentioned above, the PEN values of the significant regions in the histogram of Jitterbug traffic are expected to be larger than that of most regions in the histogram of normal traffic. The selection of significant regions is the most critical step in our detection scheme. It is especially hard for this step because of the finite samples. It is worth nothing that 10,000 samples counted in Fig. 1 are only for distinct illustration, the actual detection window needs to be much smaller for a quick responding. The significant regions are selected by two principles, one is that the region must contain enough proportion of the samples, and the other is that the region must start at a proper position in order to obtain the remarkable feature of samples. The width of region, which is denoted as S (i.e. the total number of bins in the region) must less than $\lfloor w/2 \rfloor$(in ms), is set to 7, because values of w less than 15 ms may cause significant bit error rate according to Table 1 of Ref. [12]. A sliding window with the same width is used to select significant regions and the detection process can be described as follows.

First, in a detection window W, count the histogram of IPDs under the binning strategy mentioned above, and then obtain a sequence of IPDs amount in each bin.

$$t = (t_1, t_2, \ldots, t_n) \tag{4}$$

Second, slide the PEN computation window (i.e. the width of significant region, S) on t, and obtain a new sequence $\hat{t}$ based on Eq. (5).

$$\hat{t} = (\hat{t}_1, \hat{t}_2, \ldots, \hat{t}_{n-S+1}), \quad \hat{t}_i = \sum_{j=i}^{i+S-1} t_j \tag{5}$$

The position set l of peak points of $\hat{t}$ is written as Eq. (6). The position set $\hat{l}$ of remarkable points of $\hat{t}$ is written as Eq. (7). Then the set l^* is obtained using Eq. (8) which is taken as the start positions of each significant region.

$$l = \{l_1, l_2, \ldots, l_x\}, \quad \hat{t}_{l_i} > \hat{t}_{l_i+1} \text{ and } \hat{t}_{l_i} > \hat{t}_{l_i-1} \tag{6}$$

$$\hat{l} = \{\hat{l}_1, \hat{l}_2, \ldots, \hat{l}_y\}, \quad \hat{t}_{\hat{l}_i} > 0.1\,W \tag{7}$$

$$l^* = l \cap \hat{l} = \{l_1^*, l_2^*, \ldots, l_z^*\} \tag{8}$$

Third, the partial entropy of each significant region is calculated by Eq. (9).

$$\begin{aligned} P_{ij} &= \frac{t_{l_i^*+j-1}}{\hat{t}_{l_i^*}}, \quad i = 1,2,\ldots,z, \ j = 1,2,\ldots,S \\ PEN_i &= -\sum_{j=1}^{S} P_{ij} \log_2 P_{ij} \end{aligned} \tag{9}$$

Fourth, the weighted mean of all computed *PEN*s is obtained by Eq. (10) and the weighted coefficient related to IPDs amount of significant region is written as Eq. (11).

$$\overline{PEN} = \sum_{i=1}^{z} \hat{w}_i PEN_i \tag{10}$$

$$\hat{w}_i = \hat{t}_{l_i^*} \Big/ \sum_{j=1}^{z} \hat{t}_{l_j^*}, \quad i = 1,2,\ldots,z \tag{11}$$

Finally, a threshold T is utilized to distinguish Jitterbug from normal traffic. If $\overline{PEN} > T$, the traffic within W is considered to be a Jitterbug covert communication.

4 Experimental Results

4.1 Datasets and Threshold Determination

To evaluate the effectiveness of our detection scheme, several different types of normal traffic are prepared as overt channels. Since VoIP traffic is considered to be a suitable overt channel for network covert communication [17–19], Skype and QQ (the most widely used instant messaging software in China) are chosen to generate overt VoIP traffic. We started voice communications from our laboratory (Nanjing) to outside locations (Beijing, Shanghai, Chengdu) by two kinds of software separately and captured these traffics in our laboratory's gateway to make up two sets named Skype set and QQ set. The SSH set was obtained from the traffic archive of WIDE Project [16], which the traffic was captured from the samplepoint-F of WIDE backbone. Each of these sets contains over 600,000 packets.

Jitterbug traffic was generated based on the three normal traffic sets. We replayed the packets of each set and added delays according to the encoding scheme of Jitterbug. It is considered to be a software implementation of Jitterbug that manipulates IPDs directly. We also captured these traffics in the gateway and obtained three sets named Jitterbug-SSH, Jitterbug-Skype, and Jitterbug-QQ. Moreover, changing the encoding parameter w will generate more Jitterbug traffic for testing.

To find a proper value of threshold T, the PEN values of normal traffic and Jitterbug traffic are calculated separately. The normal traffic is combined by Skype, QQ, and SSH sets. The packet number of the combined set is as many as 500,000, and the tested Jitterbug traffic is combined by the corresponding Jitterbug-Skype, Jitterbug-QQ, and

Jitterbug-SSH. The packet number of Jitterbug traffic is the same as that of normal traffic. In the threshold determination test, the detection window was set to 1,000, and the Jitterbug encoding windows size w was set to 15 ms, 20 ms, 25 ms, and 30 ms. The distribution of PEN values is shown in Fig. 2. The PEN values of two types of traffic have few overlaps and the PEN values of Jitterbug traffic maintain in a stable range which are also less affected by the change of w value. The threshold T to distinguish these two kinds of traffic was chosen as 2.75, which results in the average detection error rate to not be larger than 2%.

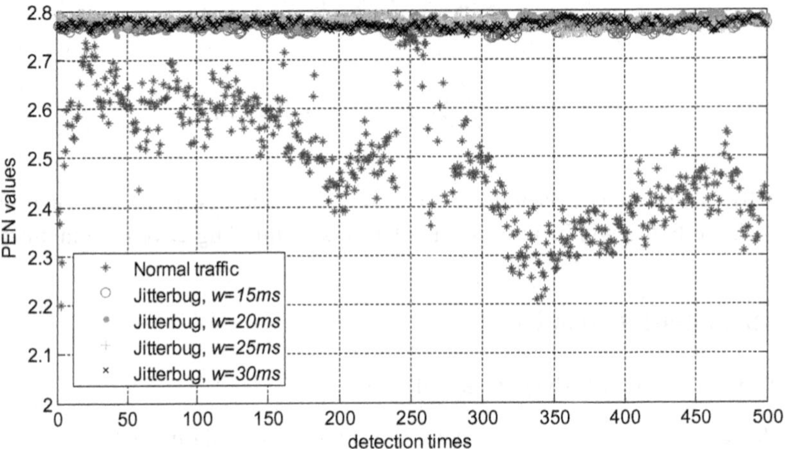

Fig. 2. PEN values of normal traffic and Jitterbug traffic with different w.

4.2 Results and Analysis

Detection performance. The detection performance under different detection windows, different encoding parameters and different overt channels were evaluated. The detection window W was chosen as 1,000, 1,500, and 2,000, while timing window w of Jitterbug was set to 15 ms, 20 ms, 25 ms, and 30 ms, respectively. With the fixed threshold 2.75, the detection rate (denoted as TP) and false alarm rate (denoted as FP) were obtained by sliding the non-overlapped detection window on each test set. The Jitterbug sets were generated 10 times for each w value and the test was repeated 10 times to obtain average TP value. The detection results are summarized in Table 1. The table shows that our scheme is reliable to detect Jitterbug traffic in all cases. It is obvious that the larger detection window size is helpful to make more accuracy detection. Furthermore, the timing window w utilized in the table has little effect on detection results. Although a larger value of w needs more IPD samples for accurate detection (i.e. a larger detection window), it is not often used in Jitterbug covert channel because of the lower data rate.

Table 1. Detection results on different states.

W	w (in ms)	Jitterbug-Skype	Skype	Jitterbug-QQ	QQ	Jitterbug-SSH	SSH
		TP	FP	TP	FP	TP	FP
1,000	15	98.3%	1.3%	97.8%	1.2%	97.7%	1.7%
	20	97.4%		98.2%		98.1%	
	25	98.7%		98.0%		97.5%	
	30	98.3%		97.7%		97.2%	
1,500	15	99.1%	0.5%	99.5%	0.8%	97.7%	1.0%
	20	99.2%		99.2%		98.2%	
	25	98.6%		100%		98.6%	
	30	98.2%		98.9%		98.3%	
2,000	15	100%	0.3%	99.2%	0.7%	98.7%	0.7%
	20	99.4%		99.8%		99.2%	
	25	99.7%		100%		99.0%	
	30	100%		100%		98.5%	

In some cases, the secret message is very short and the successive packets of covert traffic may be less than 1,000. Thus, the detection performance under short detection window should be investigated. In our previous work [15], a detection method based on coefficient of variation (CV test) has been proposed to detect Jitterbug covert channel. Both PEN test and CV test can achieve high detection performance at a proper detection window. Then, we compare them under shorter detection windows. Since parameter w has little effect on detection results, the covert traffic set is combined by different types of Jitterbug traffic with different values of w and the overt traffic set are also mixed. For each detection window, we make the FP of both tests to be constant 1% and obtain the corresponding thresholds. Then, the detection rate of both tests is shown in Fig. 3. The figure shows that PEN test has higher detection rate than CV test under

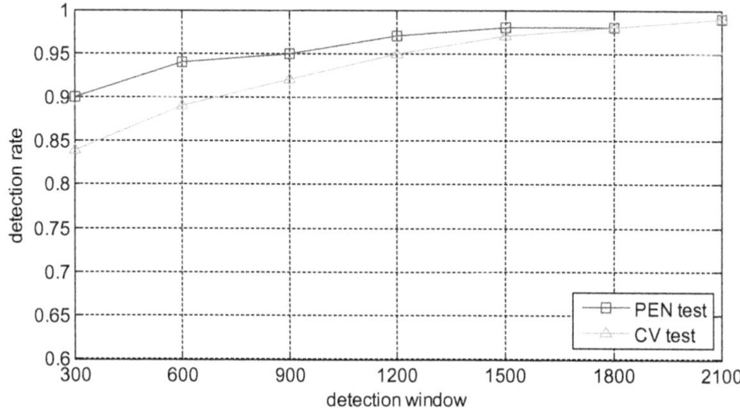

Fig. 3. The detection rate of PEN test and CV test for different detection window.

short detection window. Although both tests are designed based on the similar feature of Jitterbug, the values of PEN metrics are more centralized and easy to be distinguished under short detection window.

Robustness against network jitter. Commonly, the network covert channel detector is used to prevent the data leakage from inside to outside. Hence the detector is always deployed at the network boundary which is close to the sender. When the detector is close enough to the sender (within several routers), the captured IPDs will not suffer from the influence of network jitter. When the detector has to inspect the potential covert channel communication of users in a district, the detector has to be deployed in a backbone network. Therefore, the captured IPDs are unavoidably affected by network jitter caused by the forwarding equipments (e.g. routers). So, the detection performance resisting network jitter should be tested in the latter scenario. To simulate the network jitter, we add a network link emulator between Jitterbug sender and the detector. The network emulator was implemented on Linux host with double NICs. The Netem was used to simulate packet losses, delays, delay jitters, and so on. For $W = 1500$, w = 15 ms, 20 ms, 25 ms, and $T = 2.75$, the detection rate and Jitterbug bit error rate (BER) are investigated under different intensity of jitters. Since there is no acknowledged model for network jitter, the normal distribution with zero mean and standard deviation σ is used to model the network jitter. And 3σ (in ms) is used to measure the intensity of jitters.

As shown in Fig. 4, with the increased the network jitter intensity, the BER of Jitterbug becomes larger and larger, which reflects that Jitterbug is not robust enough to resist network jitter. For fixed network jitter intensity, the smaller Jitterbug timing window is more sensitive than the larger one and results in a greater BER value. Fortunately, the detector's performance is always acceptable. The detection rate maintains high performance under minor network jitter, and it is still over 70% despite the BER is as high as 50%. Although the network jitter may change the distribution of IPDs, the proposed feature based on partial successive bins can still represent Jitterbug's characteristic. Thus, the detection method is robust to resist network jitter.

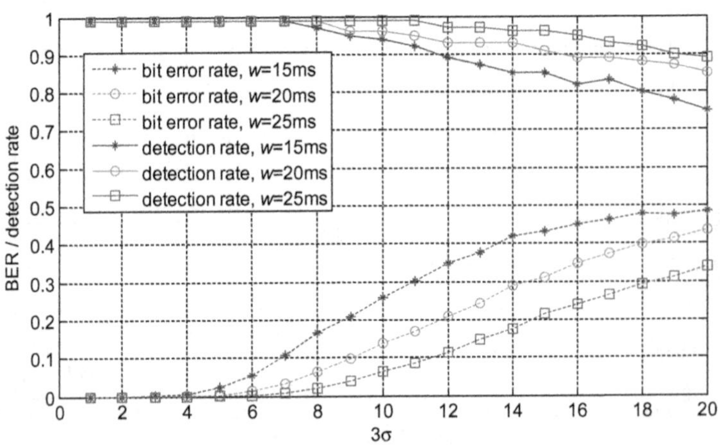

Fig. 4. Influence of network jitter.

5 Conclusion

Although the entropy-based detection method can detect most covert timing channels, the binning strategy based on training samples may cause the model mismatching issue and cut down detection performance. In this paper, a new detection method for Jitterbug is proposed based on partial entropy test, in which the fixed binning strategy works without reference samples. Experimental results show that our scheme achieves high detection performance for different Jitterbug traffic and has higher detection rate than CV test under short detection window. Minor network jitter has little influence on detection rate while major network jitter also makes Jitterbug invalid. In the future, we will focus on the detection problems of the Jitterbug variants, such as Liquid and Mimic.

Acknowledgment. This work is supported by the NSF of China (Grant Nos. 61472188, 61602247, U1636117), the NSF of Jiangsu province (Grant Nos. BK20150472, BK20160840), the Fundamental Research Funds for the central Universities (Grant Nos. 30920140121006, 30915012208) and the CCF-Venustech Hongyan Research Initiative (Grant No. 2016011). The authors also gratefully acknowledge the helpful comments and suggestions of the reviewers, which have improved the presentation.

References

1. National Computer Security Center, US DoD: Trusted computer system evaluation criteria, Technical report DOD 5200.28-STD, National Computer Security Center (1985)
2. Zander, S., Armitage, G., Branch, P.: A survey of covert channels and countermeasures in computer network protocols. IEEE Commun. Surv. Tutor. **9**(3), 44–57 (2007)
3. Padlipsky, M.A., Snow, D.W., Karger, P.A.: Limitations of end-to-end encryption in secure computer networks. Technical report ESD-TR-78-158, Mitre Corporation (1978)
4. Girling, C.G.: Covert channels in LAN's. IEEE Trans. Softw. Eng. **SE-13**(2), 292–296 (1987)
5. Cabuk, S., Brodley, C.E., Shields, C.: IP covert timing channels: design and detection. In: Proceedings of the 11th ACM Conference on Computer and Communications Security, pp. 178–187 (2004)
6. Cabuk, S.: Network covert channels: design, analysis, detection, and elimination. Ph.D. thesis, Purdue University, West Lafayette, USA (2006)
7. Gianvecchio, S., Wang, H., Wijesekera, D., Jajodia, S.: Model-based covert timing channels: automated modeling and evasion. In: Lippmann, R., Kirda, E., Trachtenberg, A. (eds.) RAID 2008. LNCS, vol. 5230, pp. 211–230. Springer, Heidelberg (2008). doi:10.1007/978-3-540-87403-4_12
8. Liu, G., Zhai, J., Dai, Y.: Network covert timing channel with distribution matching. Telecommun. Syst. Model. Anal. Des. Manag. **49**(2), 199–205 (2012)
9. Gianvecchio, S., Wang, H.: Detecting covert timing channels: an entropy-based approach. In: CCS 2007, Alexandria, Virginia, USA (2007)
10. Gianvecchio, S., Wang, H.: An entropy-based approach to detecting covert timing channels. IEEE Trans. Dependable Sec. Comput. **8**(6), 785–797 (2011)

11. Shrestha, P.L., Hempel, M., Rezaei, F., Sharif, H.: A support vector machine-based framework for detection of covert timing channels. IEEE Trans. Dependable Sec. Comput. **13**(2), 274–283 (2016)
12. Shah, G., Molina, A., Blaze, M.: Keyboards and covert channels. In: Proceedings of the 15th conference on USENIX Security Symposium, pp. 59–75 (2006)
13. Walls, R.J., Kothari, K., Wright, M.: Liquid: a detection-resistant covert timing channel based on IPD shaping. Comput. Netw. **55**(6), 1217–1228 (2011)
14. Kothari, K., Wright, M.: Mimic: an active covert channel that evades regularity-based detection. Comput. Netw. **57**(3), 647–657 (2013)
15. Wang, H., Liu, G., Zhai, J., Dai, Y.: Detection and parameter estimation for Jitterbug covert channel based on coefficient of variation. KSII Trans. Int. Inf. Syst. **10**(4), 1927–1943 (2016)
16. Packet traces from WIDE backbone. http://mawi.wide.ad.jp/mawi/. Accessed 8 May 2016
17. Mazurczyk, W., Karaś, M., Szczypiorski, K.: SkyDe: a skype-based steganographic method. Int. J. Comput. Commun. Control **8**(3), 389–400 (2013)
18. Fu, Z., Sun, X., Liu, Q., Zhou, L., Shu, J.: Achieving efficient cloud search services: multi-keyword ranked search over encrypted cloud data supporting parallel computing. IEICE Trans. Commun. **E98**(B1), 190–200 (2015)
19. Zielińska, E., Mazurczyk, W., Szczypiorski, K.: Trends in steganography. Commun. ACM **57**(3), 86–95 (2014)

Multimedia Applications

Frame-Deletion Detection for Static-Background Video Based on Multi-scale Mutual Information

Yanjia Zhao, Tianming Pang, Xiaoyun Liang, and Zhaohong Li(✉)

School of Electronic Science and Technology, Beijing Jiaotong University, Beijing 100044, China
{14291127,14273039,16120011,zhhli2}@bjtu.edu.cn

Abstract. Due to enormous free video editing software on the Internet, tampering of digital videos has become very easy. Authenticating the integrity of videos and detecting any video forgery is a big challenge to researchers. In this paper, an algorithm based on the normalized mutual information feature is proposed to detect the frame-deleting videos which are hardly identified by human visual. The proposed method is composed of two parts: feature extraction and abnormal point detection. Firstly, based on information theory, the normalized mutual information is defined on the single scale visual content of adjacent frames. After using the Gaussian pyramid transform on every frame, the description operator of multi-scale normalized mutual information is computed by linear combination. In the stage of discontinuity point detection, video forgery is identified and the tampering point is localized by performing modified generalized ESD test.

Keywords: Video forensics · Multi-scale analysis · Mutual information · Similarity degree · Abnormal degree

1 Introduction

With the development of capturing devices and network transmission techniques, digital video has become an important media for people to satisfy their demands for information and entertainment. However, more and more digital videos are manipulated for nefarious purposes. For example, digital forgers can use available video editing software to alter the original content in a digital video and mislead the audience. These behaviors seriously affect people's life and social stability. Therefore, the integrity and authenticity of digital video contents cannot be taken for granted, especially when they are used as supporting evidence and historical records in numerous applications. These applications may be related to law enforcements, surveillance and journalistic photography and so on. These aspects are having a high demand for automatic forensic algorithms to determine the trustworthiness of a video.

To detect the manipulation of digital video, great efforts have been devoted from domestic and foreign scholars. However, the video forensic technology is not really mature yet, not merely on account of video's diversity and complicacy but because of

X. Sun et al. (Eds.): ICCCS 2017, Part II, LNCS 10603, pp. 371–384, 2017.
https://doi.org/10.1007/978-3-319-68542-7_31

sophistication of tampering. Video forgery may be performed in intra-frame or inter-frame levels. In comparison with intra-frame forgery that the contents of video frames are tampered, inter-frame forgery comprises frame insertion, deletion and duplication.

For inter-frame forgery, two kinds of passive forensics techniques can authenticate it. One is related to video codec. Now, video coding standards based on image coding standards, the current mainstream video coding standards are MPEG-x and H.26x series. The new generation of video coding standard H.265/HEVC was officially confirmed in 2013. For reducing the computational complexity of the H.265/HEVC encoder, Pan et al. proposed a content property based fast *ME* method [1] and he proposed fast reference frame selection based on content similarity [2]. Yet, H.264/MPEG-4 is still the most widely used video coding standard. In real forensics scenarios, most of tampering processes are conducted on decompressed domain and tampered videos have to undergo the recompression process. Therefore the analysis of double compression can be regarded as the first step of video forensics and it has become a mainstream of forensics about video codec. The doubly MPEG compressed video will demonstrate different intrinsic characteristics from the MPEG video which is compressed only once. Specifically, the probability distribution of the first digits of the non-zero MPEG quantized AC coefficients will be disturbed. The statistical disturbance is a good indication of the occurrence of double video compression, and may be used as tampering evidence [3, 4]. An improved video tampering detection model based on MPEG double compression is proposed by Wang and Farid [5]. With the disturbance to Discrete Cosine Transform (DCT) coefficients and a serial Support Vector Machine (SVM) architecture to estimate original bit rate scale in doubly compressed video. Stamm et al. [6] developed a theoretical model of the forensically detectable fingerprints that frame deletion or addition leaves behind and improved upon the video frame deletion or addition detection technique proposed by Wang and Farid by using the model. Gironi et al. [7] proposed a method which is applicable even when different codecs are used for the first and second compression, and performs well even when the second encoding is as strong as the first one.

The other one is independent of video codec, which transform the compressed video into image sequence. And it is the key of this paper. A novel video inter-frame forgery detection scheme based on optical flow consistency is proposed by Chao et al. [8]. Frame to frame optical flows and double adaptive thresholds are applied to detect frame deletion forgery. An efficient method based on quotients of correlation coefficients between local binary patterns LBPs coded frames is proposed by Zhang et al. [9]. Because each frame of a video is coded by LBP, quotients of correlation coefficients among sequential LBP-coded frames can be calculated. The shortcoming of above mentioned methods is that the falsified videos were generated by random manipulation which left visible traces in forgeries. In contrast, Wang et al. [10] calculated optical flow variation sequence and adopted anomaly detection scheme to locate discontinuity points. And Wu et al. [11] proposed a new algorithm to detect surveillance video inter-frame forgery based on the consistency of velocity field. However this approach is block-based, so it couldn't determine the manipulated location at frame level, and its video database only contains 10 videos. Later, Zhang et al. [12] enlarged the video dataset by combining the static-background videos included in Refs. [10, 11] and proposed a algorithm based on motion vector pyramid (MVP) and its variation factor (VF) to detect frame deletion and duplication. Nowadays, a large number of video set are needed to be authenticated as well as most delicate tampered videos left less visible traces, and it is more difficult for eyes to observe. Therefore in this paper, we propose a more efficient algorithm to carry out video forensics.

Wang constructed the first open inter-frame forgery database and later Wu constructed another. However, the video dataset of Wang and Wu are small which only contain 20 and 10 videos respectively, while the background of their datasets are single which only contain the scenes of elevator and airport. Simultaneously, the video datasets before Wang are synthetically generated by random forgery which left visible traces. Therefore, a larger, richer and more subtle falsified video set is needed to evaluate our algorithm. In real life, most of the tampered videos are implemented by frame-deletion, so this paper just focuses on "meaningful" frame-deleting forgery. "Meaningful" means that the video dataset is tampered without any trace, such as some events or some scenes are deleted, and we will introduce it specifically in Sect. 2.2. We construct our own video set contains 40 original videos and 40 corresponding delicate frame-deleting videos with 4 static scenes. Due to the characteristics of information theory, this paper introduces the mutual information to video tamper detection and proposes a video content similarity measure model that it is called normalized mutual information abbreviated as *NMI*. Furthermore, the mutual information between frames is analyzed from multi-scale perspective based on the "scale invariance" feature of human vision, Multi-scale *NMI* (*MNMI*) descriptor is introduced to characterize the inter-frame's content similarity. Thus, a new algorithm is proposed for frame-deleting videos detection in this paper. The main procedures of the proposed algorithm are: (1) calculate the normalized mutual information between the adjacent two frames, (2) construct Gaussian pyramid to calculate the description operator of multi-scale normalized mutual information, (3) modify the description operator by reducing the periodic effect caused by GOP structure, (4) suppress the influence of video content variation, (5) detect and locate the discontinuity points by using modified Generalized ESD test [13]. Experimental results show that the proposed algorithm can not only distinguish frame-deleting videos from original videos effectively, but also locate accurately at frame level.

The rest of the paper is organized as follows. Section 2 reviews the features of the proposed algorithm and its feasibility are introduced. Section 3 describes the proposed identification algorithm in detail. Experimental results are illustrated in Sect. 4, and conclude the paper in Sect. 5.

2 Content Similarity Measure of Adjacent Frames

For static-background video sequence, one characteristic is that adjacent frames are of high similarity. The similarity would be reduced greatly if inter-frame forgery operation occurs between two frames, even though the forgery operation is delicate and leaves few obvious traces. Motivated by this consideration, we use the normalized mutual information to measure the similarity of adjacent frames. Furthermore, Gaussian pyramid was adopted when calculating the description operator of multi-scale normalized mutual information abbreviated as *MNMI*. The following section will demonstrate the extraction of *MNMI* in detail.

2.1 *MNMI* Extraction in the Video

After constructing video dataset, the first step of *MNMI* extraction is decompressing video into image sequences and transforming them into grayscale images. After that, *MNMI* are calculated between every two consecutive frames. The major steps are as follows:

1. Calculate the normalized mutual information (*NMI*) between the adjacent frames.

In the information theory, communication system which consists of the source (sender), the sink (receiver), the channel (transmission medium) and other components is used to complete the information transmission process of the technical system. In 1948 Shannon [14] pointed out that any information is redundant and that redundancy is associated with every symbol's probability of occurrence or uncertainty in the message. In the source, the uncertainty of a symbol is not taken into account, but the average uncertainty of all possible occurrences of the source is taken into account. Therefore, Shannon proposed that the exclusion of redundant information in the average amount of information known as the "information entropy", and gave the mathematical expression of information entropy, shown as Eq. 1, which E is the average uncertainty of the source, and source symbol can be expressed as $U_1, U_2, \cdots U_n$, the corresponding probability is $p_1, p_2, \cdots p_n$, lb is a logarithm of 2.

$$H(U) = E(-\mathrm{lb}\, p_i) = -\sum_{i=1}^{n} p_i \ \mathrm{lb}\ p_i \tag{1}$$

Mutual information (*MI)* is another useful information measure, it refers to the correlation between the two event sets. The mutual information of two events X and Y is defined as Eq. 2, which $H(X, Y)$ is joint entropy, defined as Eq. 3.

$$I(X;Y) = H(X) + H(Y) - H(X,Y) \tag{2}$$

$$H(X,Y) = -\sum_{x}\sum_{y} p(x,y)\ \mathrm{lb}\ p(x,y) \tag{3}$$

From the above, we can see that the mutual information of two events X and Y in information theory can be used to described the content similarity of two adjacent frames. Therefore, we speculate that information theory can be applied to video authentication even if the human eyes can not see the difference between original video and falsified video. We proposed a communication system consists of two adjacent frames F_t $(t = 1, 2, \cdots, M-1)$ and F_{t+1}, we regard F_t and F_{t+1} as source and sink, respectively. Frame image is described as a time sequence, F_t is the tth grayscale image, L is the total number of gray level, then I_i $(i = 1, 2, \cdots, L)$ is source symbol. Thus we can use the information entropy to measure the information content of F_t, shown as Eq. 4, where $p(I_i(F_t))$ denote the probability of I_i appearing on frame F_t.

$$H(F_t) = -\sum_{i=0}^{L-1} p(I_i(F_t)) \times \mathrm{lb}\, p(I_i(F_t)) \tag{4}$$

Then the information between adjacent two frames can be measured by joint entropy, shown as Eq. 5, where $p\left(I_i(F_t), I_j(F_{t+1})\right)$ denote the probability which means the gray value pair $\left(I_i, I_j\right)$ appearing on the corresponding pixel position of F_t and F_{t+1}.

$$H(F_t,\ F_{t+1}) = -\sum_{i=0}^{L-1}\sum_{j=0}^{L-1} p\left(I_i(F_t), I_j(F_{t+1})\right) \times lb\, p\left(I_i(F_t), I_j(F_{t+1})\right) \tag{5}$$

For the communication system which consist of source F_t and sink F_{t+1}, the average value of F_t can be obtained from F_{t+1}, and it can be measured by average mutual information abbreviated as $MI(F_t, F_{t+1})$, shown as Eq. 6.

$$MI(F_t, F_{t+1}) = H(F_t) + H(F_{t+1}) - H(F_t,\ F_{t+1}) \tag{6}$$

Obviously, the greater $MI(F_t,\ F_{t+1})$, the greater average mutual information. It means the higher similarity between adjacent frames. Therefore, it is reasonable to use average mutual information $MI(F_t,\ F_{t+1})$ to measure the similarity of visual content between adjacent frames. Due to the value range of $MI(F_t,\ F_{t+1})$ is not between 0 and 1, we use normalized mutual information abbreviated as $NMI(F_t,\ F_{t+1})$ to define the single scale visual content similarity of adjacent frames, shown as Eq. 7.

$$NMI(F_t, F_{t+1}) = \begin{cases} 0 & H(F_t, F_{t+1}) = 0 \\ \frac{H(F_t) + H(F_{t+1})}{2H(F_t, F_{t+1})} & H(F_t, F_{t+1}) \neq 0 \end{cases} \tag{7}$$

2. Calculate multi-scale normalized mutual information (*MNMI*) between the adjacent two frames.

The Gaussian pyramids consists of low-pass filtered which can decrease spatial sampling density with increased smoothing and then produce various scales. Due to different scale spatial analysis of the image can obtain different details of the image, which make the analysis of the image more accurate. Therefore, this paper proposed applying Gaussian pyramids to image feature extraction. In consideration of the computational complexity of the algorithm increasing greatly with the number of pyramid layers, we choose 3-layer Gaussian pyramids in our algorithm. Take the $t^{th}(t = 1, 2, \cdots, M-1)$ frame and the $(t+1)^{th}$ frame for example, where M denote the total number of frames in the video. As shown in Fig. 1, the left column represents the Gaussian pyramid of the tth frame, and the right column represents that of the $(t+1)^{th}$ frame. At the bottom of the pyramid are the two original frames denoted as $F_t(0)$. For $F_t(0)$, first Gaussian low-pass filtering, followed by interlaced column resampling, the result is Gaussian pyramid of the first layer, denoted as $F_t(1)$, other and so on.

Fig. 1. Gaussian pyramid of the tth frame and the $(t+1)^{th}$ frame

After calculating *NMI* of Gaussian pyramids, the sum of *NMI* can be expressed as $\rho(t)$, shown as Eq. 8 concretely.

$$\rho(t) = \sum_{k=0}^{3} w_k \times NMI(F_t(k), F_{t+1}(k)) \tag{8}$$

where $w_k(k = 0, 1, 2, 3)$ denotes the weight of the kth layer pyramid. Considering the define of *NMI*, $\rho(t)$ can denote visual content similarity of adjacent frames and it was denoted as *MNMI*. In general, visual content similarity sequence $\{\rho(1), \rho(2), \cdots, \rho(M-1)\}$ can be extracted from the image sequence $\{F_1, F_2, \cdots, F_M\}$. As a result, the discontinuity point introduced by inter-frame forgery will be highlighted in the *MNMI*.

2.2 Traces in *MNMI* Sequence

In this paper, we only take inter-frame deletion forgery into consideration and we focus on meaningful forgeries detection. Figure 2 demonstrates an example of meaningful frame deletion forgery. Note that the frames containing foreground moving object (a woman who walk across the hall) was deleted and few obvious traces would be left in the forgery video.

Fig. 2. (a) Is the frames of 700–1100 in original video and (b) is the frames of 700–1100 in frame-deleted video

Our basic idea is that visual content similarity sequence of original videos are approximately consistent, while abnormal points could be detected on inter-frame falsified videos. Figure 3 illustrates the *MNMI* sequence of a given video. As we can see in Fig. 3, the *MNMI* sequence has periodicity because of GOP structure.

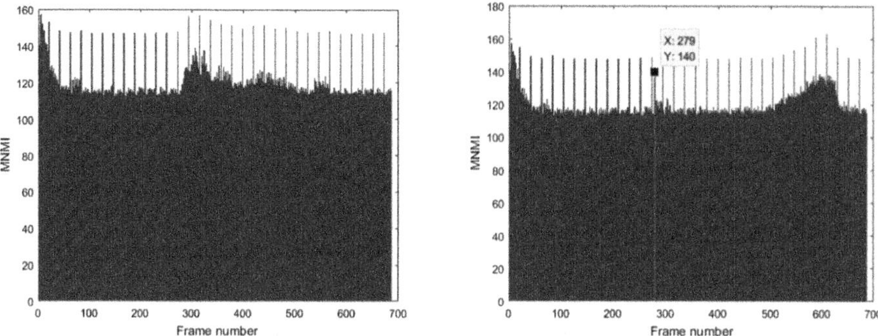

Fig. 3. The *MNMI* of original video (left) and the *MNMI* of frame-deleted video (right)

Reduce the periodic effect caused by GOP structure. Firstly, we review some background of encoding a video. When encoding a video sequence, such as MPEG-x and H.264 encoder, the sequence is segmented into sets of frames named 'group of pictures' (GOP). In each GOP, I frames are encoded independently and without any other predication frames. P frames and B frames are predicted with respect to the initial I frame either directly or indirectly. The fact that the prediction process does not occur across GOPs result in larger difference between the last frame of one GOP and the first I frame of the next GOP. Then we combine the background with *MNMI* calculation. When we calculate the *MNMI* between the last frame of one GOP and the first I frame of the next GOP, take Fig. 4 as an example, the last P frame of GOP1 will be used as the prediction frame of the first I frame of GOP2. As a result, a larger *MNMI* will be emerged at this location. The circumstance happens periodically with a period T $(T = 21)$ equal to the number of frames within one GOP. As the location where larger *MNMI* occurs is considered as suspicious manipulated position, we suppress the *MNMI* at the periodic location in order to reduce false alarm rate. Therefore, we get $MNMI'$ after reducing periodic effect, shown as Eq. 9, where T_{cor} denotes the coefficient of eliminating periodic effects, and $n = 0, 1, \cdots, m$, $m = floor((M - 1)/T)$.

$$MNMI'(t) = \begin{cases} T_{cor} \times MNMI(t), & t = n \times T \\ MNMI(t), & otherwise \end{cases} \tag{9}$$

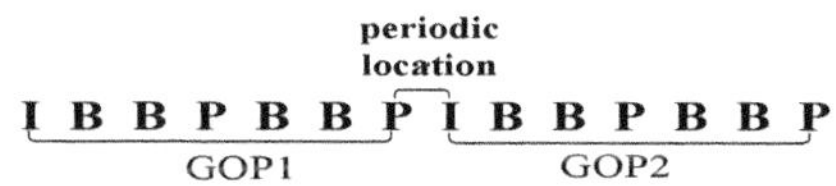

Fig. 4. Illustration of period effect

Figure 5 illustrates the $MNMI'$ sequence of original video and frame-deleted video respectively. We can see that the periodicity of GOP structure has been eliminated, but the sequence is still not smoothness because of the variation of video content.

Suppress the influence of video content variation. For a video with moving foreground, the $MNMI'$ of this part will be increased, which may result in false alarm. To reduce this kind of phenomenon, we propose to use $MNMI''$ to represent the relative changes of $MNMI'$ sequence, shown as Eq. 10.

$$\begin{aligned} MNMI''(t) = & \frac{MNMI'(t)}{MNMI'(t-1)} + \frac{MNMI'(t)}{MNMI'(t+1)} + \frac{MNMI'(t)}{MNMI'(t-2)} + \frac{MNMI'(t)}{MNMI'(t+2)} \\ & + \frac{MNMI'(t)}{MNMI'(t-3)} + \frac{MNMI'(t)}{MNMI'(t+3)} + \frac{MNMI'(t)}{MNMI'(t+4)} + \frac{MNMI'(t)}{MNMI'(t+4)} \end{aligned} \tag{10}$$

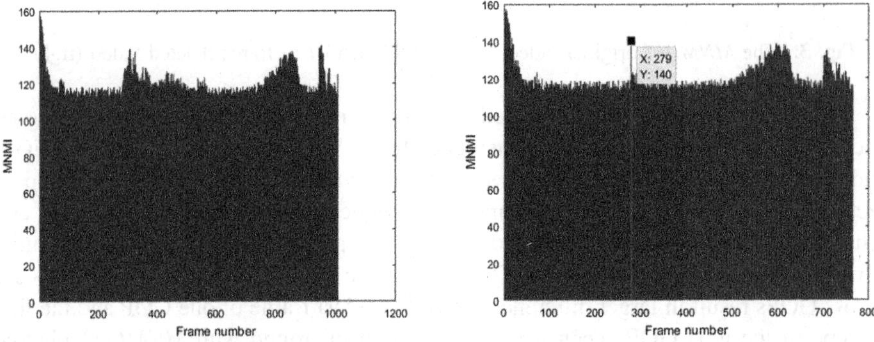

Fig. 5. The $MNMI'$ of original video (left) and the $MNMI'$ of frame-deleted video (right)

As a result, we can get the $MNMI''$ sequence of original video and frame-deleted video respectively, shown as Fig. 6. The discontinuity point introduced by frame-deletion forgery will be highlighted in the $MNMI''$ sequence $\{MNMI''(t)|\ t = 5, 6, \cdots, M-4\}$.

From Fig. 6, we can see that the $MNMI''$ sequence of original video is approximately continuous and an obvious outlier occurs in frame-deleted video because of the deletion process. In frame-deleted video, two originally non-adjacent frames become neighbors, which results in a discontinuity point in the corresponding $MNMI''$ sequence. Therefore, we can use this feature to differentiate between original video and frame-deleted video.

Furthermore, localization of tampered frame is possible. Suppose the tth position of $MNMI''$ sequence is determined as the abnormal point, then the $(t+3)^{th}$ frame of the video sequence will be the tampered frame.

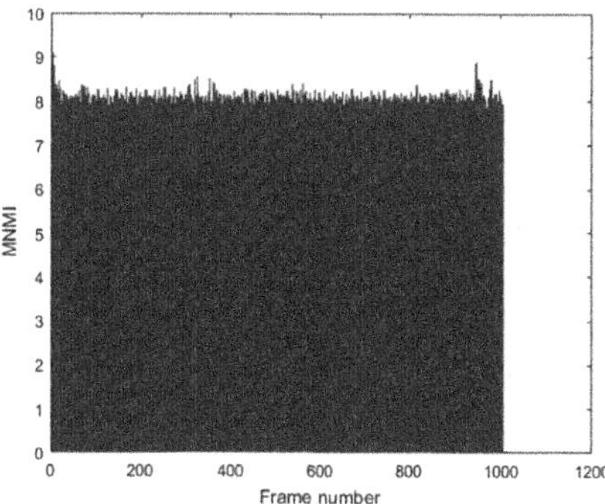

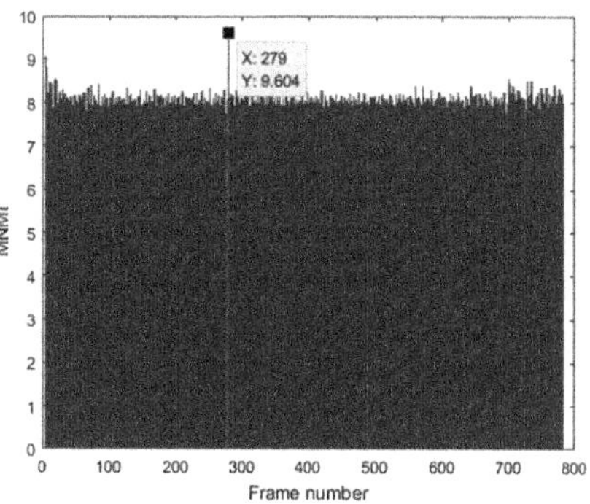

Fig. 6. The *MNMI*″ of original video (left) and the *MNMI*″ of frame-deleted video (right)

3 Video Forgery Identification

According to Sect. 2, discontinuity point indicates the occurrence of frame-deletion forgery operation. In this section, we firstly extract discontinuity points in *MNMI* sequence by using the modified generalized ESD test and then identify the frame-deletion.

3.1 Extraction of Discontinuity Point

Generalized ESD test is known as an outliers-detection method for random variable which follows approximately normal distribution. Since *MNMI* sequence is approximately normally distributed, generalized ESD test is suitable for discontinuity-points extraction of *MNMI* sequence.

There are two significant parameters in the test, the maximum number of outliers r and significance level α. Since there are one discontinuity point in *MNMI* sequence generally, according to Sect. 2, we define $r = 1$. The decision threshold in the test is denoted as λ_i $(i = 1, 2, \cdots, r)$. In this paper, we modified it as Wu et al. [9] did:

$$\lambda_i = TS \times \frac{t_{(p,n-i+1)} \times (n-i)}{\sqrt{\left(n-i-1+t^2_{(p,n-i-1)}\right) \times (n-i+1)}}, \quad i = 1, 2, \cdots, r \tag{11}$$

$$p = 1 - \frac{\alpha}{2 \times (n-i+1)} \tag{12}$$

where n denotes the number of samples in the dataset, $t_{(p,n-i-1)}$ represents the pth percentile of a t distribution with $(n-i+1)$ degrees of freedom and TS is our fine-tuned coefficient.

3.2 Identification Algorithm

After extraction of discontinuity point of *MNMI* sequence according to Sect. 3.1, identification process shown in Fig. 7 is carried out. Frame-deleted forgery is detected. Take the *TS* as fine-tuned coefficient in generalized ESD test and extract the corresponding discontinuity points of *MNMI* sequence. Let N denotes the number of discontinuity points. If $N \geq 1$, the given video is authenticated as frame-deleted forgery. Otherwise, the given video is authenticated as original video.

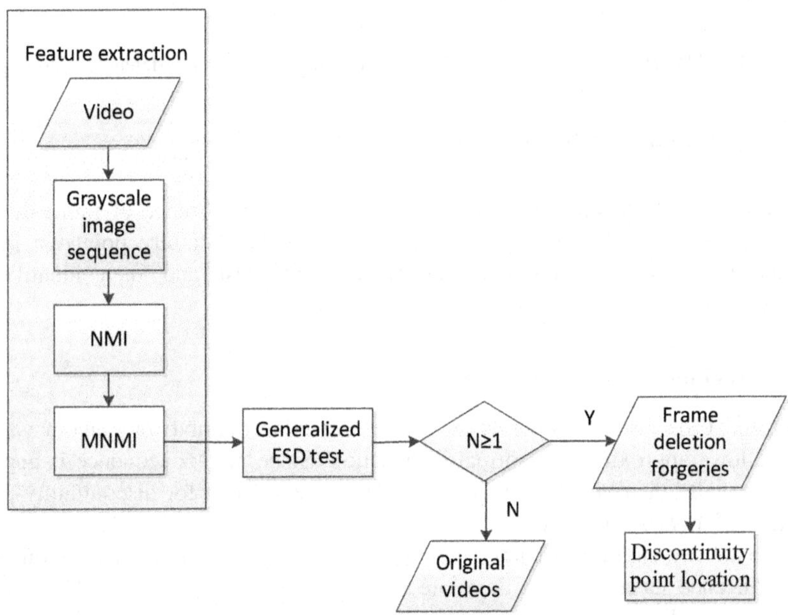

Fig. 7. Flowchart of identification algorithm

4 Experimental Results

4.1 Video Dataset

To the best of our knowledge, there is no both large, rich and subtle video database for inter-frame forgery detection. We hence shoot 40 real-life videos which contain four scenes: hall, lab, floor and stair and each clip contains about 1000 frames with resolution 640×480. For each original video clip, we make delicate frame deletion: successive frames in the original video clip are deleted. The tampering operations were done on decoded frame sequences. Those frames after forgery were then re-encoded with the same coding standard (H.264) and parameters. In this way, we have 40 original video clips and 40 frame-deleted video clips in total. The original video's and frame-deleted video's GOP size is 12 and 21, respectively.

4.2 Results and Analysis

Through the experiment, we can set the parameters of the proposed algorithm as follows: the weight of the $k^{th}(k = 0, 1, 2, 3)$ layer pyramid are $w_0 = 1$, $w_1 = 0.571$, $w_2 = 0.286$, $w_3 = 0.143$; the coefficient of eliminating periodic effects is $T_{\text{cor}} = 0.8$; maximum number of outliers is $r = 1$; significance level is $\alpha = 0.05$; fine-tuned coefficients for deletion detection is $TS = 1.1$.

The experimental results are given as follows.

- Result from frame-deleted video:

We get a frame-deleted video by deleting the frames 280 to 524 of the original video. And the $MNMI''$ sequence of the frame-deleted video shown as Fig. 8. We can see that most values of $MNMI''$ is less than nine except the 279th frame. Actually, the value of $MNMI''$ in the 277th frame and the 278th frame is close which means that frames 277, 278 and 279 are similar. The value of $MNMI''$ in the 279th frame illustrates that the difference between frame 279 and 280 is large. It can be argued that there is a tampering between the 279th frame and the 280th frame. This position matches the deletion of frames 280 to 524 of the original video. Thus, this algorithm detects the falsified position is valid and correct.

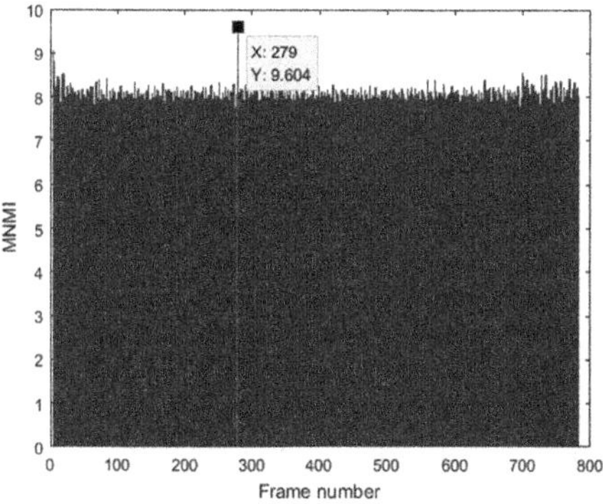

Fig. 8. The $MNMI''$ of frame-deleted video

- Identification accuracy:

An efficient method to detect inter-frame forgery based on motion vector pyramid (*MVP*) was proposed in Reference [12]. For fair comparison, we applied the algorithm proposed in Ref. [12] to our own video dataset as well as set optimized parameters for it. The parameters of Ref. [12] are: the coefficient of eliminating periodic effects is $T_{\text{cor}} = 0.13$; fine-tuned coefficients for deletion detection is $TS = 0.8$.

This experiment is to test the sensitivity of our algorithm by computing the detection accuracies when frames were deleted. Identification accuracies are presented in Table 1. In 40 frame-deleted videos, the proposed algorithm has one misjudgement and it is acceptable. The results demonstrates that our identification algorithm is effective in recognizing frame-deletion. Note that if we only care about whether a video is forged or not, the detection accuracies in Ref. [12] and proposed algorithm are 100% and 97.5%, respectively.

- Localization accuracy of forgery:

The localization accuracies for correctly identified frame-deleted videos are given in Table 2. Here, we only consider the tampered videos which are correctly identified. All the locations of detected peaks in forged videos are identified due to the statistics based generalized ESD algorithm. As we can see, the proposed algorithm can locate tampering point more precisely than the algorithm in Ref. [12].

- Program running time:

In the process of running these two programs, we find that their running time gap is very large. The specific values are shown in Table 3. The operating speed of proposed algorithm is ten time that of Ref. [12]'s.

According to the above comparison, both of these two algorithms have high identification accuracy, while the proposed algorithm has higher localization accuracy and it runs much faster. Therefore, we can draw the conclusion that our algorithm has obvious advantages in frame-deleted video forensics. What's more, maybe much of this algorithm can be applied to daily video forensics for ordinary people.

Table 1. Identification accuracy.

Video type	Ref. [12]	Proposed algorithm
Original	100% (40/40)	100% (40/40)
Deletion	100% (40/40)	97.5% (39/40)

Table 2. Localization accuracy.

Algorithm	Localization accuracy
Ref. [12]	77.5% (31/40)
Proposed algorithm	82.1% (32/39)

Table 3. Running time (s/f).

Algorithm	Running time
Ref. [12]	6.9
Proposed algorithm	0.63

5 Conclusion

This paper proposed a new algorithm for detecting delicately built frame-deleted forgeries with static background. Our basic idea is identifying discontinuity points in the *MNMI* sequence of frame-deleted forgeries. Through the modified generalized ESD test, the frame-deleted forgery can be identified, and the tamper point can be localized precisely. Experiments have demonstrated the high accuracy and effectiveness for video frame-deleted detection. In the future, we will focus on increasing the localization accuracy and extending algorithm on other types of video tampering.

Acknowledgement. We would like to thank Zhenzhen Zhang and Dongdong Li for their kindness by providing us with their codes. We also show our appreciation to Zhaohong Li for the fruitful technical discussion. This work was supported by the Fundamental Research Funds for the Nanjing University of the Information Science and Technology (W16M00060), and SRF for ROCS, SEM (W15C300020).

References

1. Pan, Z., Lei, J., Zhang, Y., Sun, X., Kwong, S.: Fast motion estimation based on content property for low-complexity H.265/HEVC encoder. IEEE Trans. Broadcast. **62**(3), 675–684 (2016)
2. Pan, Z., Jin, P., Lei, J., Zhang, Y., Sun, X., Kwong, S.: Fast reference frame selection based on content similarity for low complexity HEVC encoder. J. Vis. Commun. Image Represent. **40**(Part B), 516–524 (2016)
3. Chen, W., Shi, Y.Q.: Detection of double MPEG compression based on first digit statistics. In: Kim, H.-J., Katzenbeisser, S., Ho, A.T.S. (eds.) IWDW 2008. LNCS, vol. 5450, pp. 16–30. Springer, Heidelberg (2009). doi:10.1007/978-3-642-04438-0_2
4. Milani, S., Bestagini, P., Tagliasacchi, M., Tubaro, S.: Multiple compression detection for video sequences. In: IEEE 14th International Workshop on Multimedia Signal Processing, pp. 112–117 (2012)
5. Wang, W.H., Farid, H.: Exposing digital forgeries in video by detecting double MPEG compression. In: Proceedings of the 8th ACM Workshop on Multimedia and Security, no. NCET-10-0569, pp. 37–47 (2016)
6. Stamm, M.C., Lin, W.S., Liu, K.J.R.: Temporal forensics and anti-forensics for motion compensated video. IEEE Trans. Inf. Forensics Secur. **7**(4), 1315–1329 (2012)
7. Gironi, A., Fontani, M., Bianchi, T., Piva, A., Barni, M.: A video forensic technique for detecting frame deletion and insertion. In: 2014 IEEE International Conference on Acoustics, Speech and Signal Processing (ICASSP), pp. 6226–6230 (2014)
8. Chao, J., Jiang, X., Sun, T.: A novel video inter-frame forgery model detection scheme based on optical flow consistency. In: Shi, Y.Q., Kim, H.-J., Pérez-González, F. (eds.) IWDW 2012. LNCS, vol. 7809, pp. 267–281. Springer, Heidelberg (2013). doi:10.1007/978-3-642-40099-5_22
9. Zhang, Z.Z., Hou, J.J., Ma, Q.L., Li, Z.H.: Efficient video frame insertion and deletion detection based on inconsistency of correlations between local binary pattern coded frames. Secur. Commun. Netw. **8**(2), 311–320 (2014)
10. Wang, W., Jiang, X., Wang, S., Wan, M., Sun, T.: Identifying video forgery process using optical flow. In: Shi, Y.Q., Kim, H.-J., Pérez-González, F. (eds.) IWDW 2013. LNCS, vol. 8389, pp. 244–257. Springer, Heidelberg (2014). doi:10.1007/978-3-662-43886-2_18
11. Wu, Y.X., Jiang, X.H., Sun, T.F., Wang, W.: Exposing video inter-frame forgery based on velocity field consistency. In: 2014 IEEE International Conference on Acoustics, Speech and Signal Processing (ICASSP), pp. 2674–2678 (2014)

12. Zhang, Z., Hou, J., Li, Z., Li, D.: Inter-frame forgery detection for static-background video based on MVP consistency. In: Shi, Y.-Q., Kim, H.J., Pérez-González, F., Echizen, I. (eds.) IWDW 2015. LNCS, vol. 9569, pp. 94–106. Springer, Cham (2016). doi:10.1007/978-3-319-31960-5_9
13. Iglewicz, B., Hoaglin, D.C.: How to Detect and Handle Outliers (E-Book), vol. 16. ASQC Quality Press, Milwaukee (1993)
14. Shannon, C.E.: A Mathematical Theory of Communication, pp. 3–55. McGraw-Hill, New York (1974)

Learning Based Fast H.264/AVC to HEVC INTRA Video Transcoding for Cloud Media Computing

Yun Zhang[1(✉)], Na Li[1], and Zongju Peng[2]

[1] Shenzhen Institutes of Advanced Technology, Chinese Academy of Science, Shenzhen 518055, People's Republic of China
{yun.zhang,na.li1}@siat.ac.cn

[2] Faculty of Information Science and Engineering, Ningbo University, Ningbo 315211, People's Republic of China
pengzongju@nbu.edu.cn

Abstract. Cloud video transcoding enable to convert the video standards and properties from one to another so as to adapt to different user end devices and network capacity, especially in sharing massive video contents in cloud environment. High Efficiency Video Coding (HEVC) and H.264/Advanced Video Coding are two recent high performance video coding standards that are widely used and co-existing in video industry. Video transcoding is desirable to bridge the standard gap. To effectively transcode video stream from H.264/AVC to HEVC for higher compression efficiency and meanwhile maintaining low computational complexity, a learning based fast H.264/AVC to HEVC transcoder is proposed for cloud media computing. We firstly analyze the correlation of block partition sizes between these two standards and then present a fast Coding Unit (CU) decision algorithm, in which three levels of binary classifiers are used to predict different CU sizes in HEVC intra coding and the optimal parameters are determined by statistical experiments. The experimental results show that the proposed transcoder achieves 44.3% time saving on average with only negligible quality degradation when compared with the original cascaded transcoder and is also superior than the state-of-the-art benchmarks in terms of complexity reduction and rate-distortion performance.

Keywords: HEVC · Video transcoding · Machine learning · CU decision · Cloud computing

1 Introduction

Various video coding standards have been developed in the past decades, including the AVS China, VP6, DIRAC and VC-1, ITU-T H.26x series, the MPEG series. Digital videos may either co-exist in different video format, standards or different properties, such as video resolutions, bit rates and scalability, in different specific applications or systems. However, different computing platforms such

X. Sun et al. (Eds.): ICCCS 2017, Part II, LNCS 10603, pp. 385–395, 2017.
https://doi.org/10.1007/978-3-319-68542-7_32

as laptop computer, smart TV or mobile devices have different requirements and specifications on computing resources and networks bandwidth, video transcoding is thus desirable to encode or convert the video format or standards from one to another while sharing the massive video contents, especially in cloud environment. Cloud video transcoding, as a new coming service, allows user to reach out to a multitude of devices with minimal infrastructure costs, in comparison with the traditional video encoding model.

High Efficiency Video Coding (HEVC) [1] and H.264/AVC are two most recent and advanced coding standards in the video community and have been widely used in the multimedia community and industry. However, HEVC double the compression performance comparing with the H.264/AVC at the cost of extremely high computational complexity, which leads to extreme high computational working loads during transcoding or encoding the HEVC bit rate for videos, especially for processing massive videos in cloud environment. Thus, low complexity coding optimization algorithms for HEVC encoder and transcoder are highly desired for cloud video computing. To reduce the computational complexity, many researchers have been investigating fast algorithms for HEVC. For instance, Shen *et al.* [2] proposed a fast Coding Unit (CU) size decision algorithm for HEVC intra coding, in which the adjacent encoded CU's information was utilized to predict the CU depth. Pan *et al.* [3] presented an early termination scheme for low complexity motion search. In [4], a novel fast CU encoding scheme based on spatio-temporal encoding parameters for HEVC inter coding was proposed, which consists of an improved early CU SKIP detection method and a fast CU splitting decision method. In addition, many researchers have devoted their efforts to video transcoding from other hybrid compression standards to HEVC. Lin *et al.* [5] proposed a fast H.264/AVC to HEVC intra transcoder based on Discrete Cosine Transform (DCT) coefficients and prediction modes, in which depth limitation and early termination were utilized to simplify HEVC re-encoding process. However, these above mentioned schemes simply use the information extracted from H.264/AVC stream to form the mapping of mode decision between H.264/AVC and HEVC with thresholds or categories, but different thresholds or categories will lead to different performances for video transcoder.

Recently, in order to develop more sophisticated and reliable coding schemes, Machine Learning (ML) algorithm has been introduced. In [6,7], a content-based ML solution was used for CU depth prediction of inter frames. In this transcoder, full re-encoding was utilized to find a mapping from incoming H.264/AVC stream information to outgoing HEVC CU depths. Besides, the statistical thresholds [7] were also integrated to the ML based framework to improve the accuracy. Zhang *et al.* [8] proposed an hierarchical early termination structure and a three-output joint classifier based on Support Vector Machine (SVM) for fast CU decision. In addition, feature selection algorithms were developed for SVM based CU decision in the inter frame transcoding [9]. Basically, these schemes were developed for CU decision in inter frames, and the CU decision in intra coding optimization shall be further investigated.

In this paper, a low-complexity H.264/AVC to HEVC intra frame transcoder based on on-line SVM learning is proposed to predict CU sizes for fast video transcoding in the cloud environment.

2 Motivations and Analyses

Since H.264/AVC and HEVC are both block based hybrid video coding standards, there must be a high correlation between the block partition sizes of the two standards. In H.264/AVC [10], the MB is the coding unit, and it can be partitioned into block sizes of 16×16, 8×8, or 4×4 for intra prediction, as shown in Fig. 1(a). In HEVC, the concept of Coding Tree Unit (CTU) is similar to MB in H.264/AVC. However, the Largest CU (LCU) size of the CTU is set as 64×64 in HEVC. A CU can be recursively split into four sub-CUs of the same size, until the minimum CU size, *i.e.*, 8×8, as shown in Fig. 1(b). In addition, 8×8 can be further split into four 4×4 blocks, which is conceptually in prediction unit level. Since only the CU mode decision is considered, 4×4 block mode is not considered in this work. For convenience, the CU sizes of 64×64 to 8×8 are defined as Depth 0 to Depth 3. Since both H.264/AVC and HEVC are block based hybrid video coding standards, there are high similarity between the block partitions from H.264/AVC and HEVC.

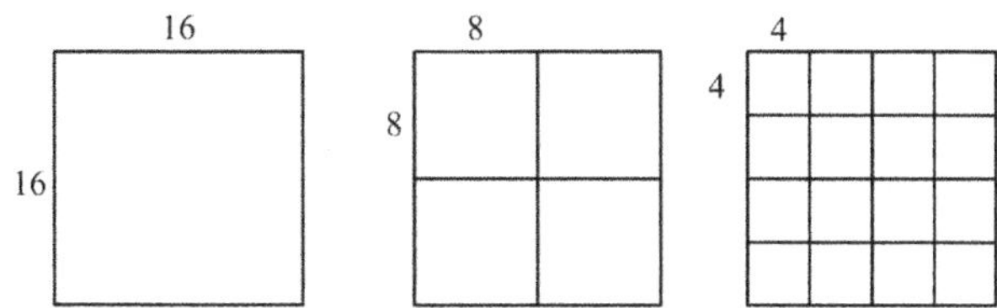

(a) H.264/AVC INTRA block partition

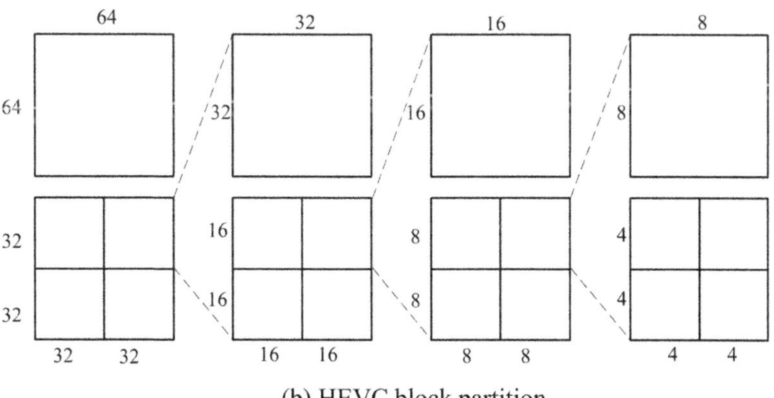

(b) HEVC block partition

Fig. 1. MB partitions in H.264/AVC.

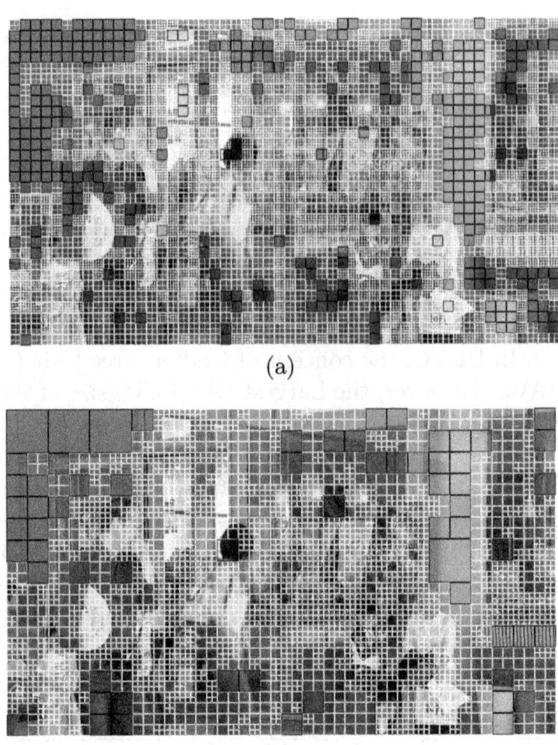

Fig. 2. INTRA block partitions for H.264/AVC and HEVC. (a) H.264/AVC; (b) HEVC.

To analyze the block correlation between H.264/AVC and HEVC, different sequences are encoded by H.264/AVC and HEVC independently. For H.264/AVC, we define the block size of 16×16 as the large block mode, and the block size of 8×8 or 4×4 as the small block mode. For HEVC, if a block size is larger than 16×16, it is defined as a large mode; otherwise, it is a small block mode. An example of INTRA block partitions for H.264/AVC and HEVC are shown in Fig. 2, in which the small and large blocks are painted with white and black rectangles, respectively. The first frame of BQMall sequences are encoded with INTRA and QP 37 by H.264/AVC and HEVC, respectively. We can observe that if the H.264/AVC select the small block mode (white), there is a high probability of selecting the small block partition (white) for HEVC, and vice versa. It illustrates that there are high similarity between the block partition between H.264/AVC and HEVC.

In addition, more precise statistical analyses are performed for observing the block partition correlation. If the block partition is the same (either large or small) while encoded by both H.264/AVC and HEVC, it is denoted as the correlation. The block size correlation between H.264/AVC and HEVC is shown in Fig. 3, where the y-axis represents the correlation. We find that the

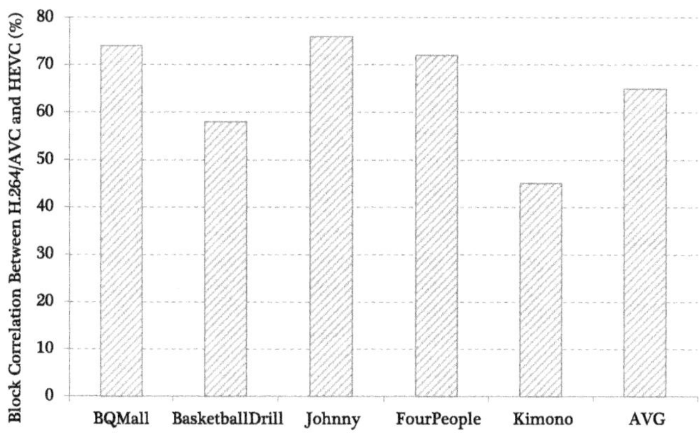

Fig. 3. Block size correlation between H.264/AVC and HEVC.

average percentage correlation over different frames, QPs and sequences reaches 66.5%, which demonstrates that there is a high block size correlation between H.264/AVC and HEVC. Therefore, the mode correlation can be used to facilitate the transcoding process.

As we know, there are only three types of block size in H.264/AVC INTRA coding and the largest block size is 16×16. However, in HEVC, there are four depth levels and the block size can vary from 64×64 to 8×8. They are checked and searched exhaustively to select the best Rate-Distortion (RD) performance in the original JM or HM model, which achieves good compression efficiency at the cost of extremely high computational complexity. Thus, it is essential to propose a transcoder from H.264/AVC to HEVC to significantly reduce the computational complexity. According to the above analyses, the block correlation between H.264/AVC and HEVC can and shall be efficiently exploited to facilitate the transcoding.

3 Proposed Learning Based Fast H.264/AVC to HEVC Transcoding

Inspired by [6–9], CU decision between two adjacent depths can be modeled as a binary classification problem, namely splitting into four sub-CUs or non-splitting, and then could be solved by learning based classification tools. Therefore, we propose a learning based CU depth decision framework for H.264/AVC to HEVC INTRA transcoding, which consists of three hierarchical CU depth decision levels; then, effective learning algorithm and feature selections are presented to solve the binary classification in each CU decision level; In addition, an optimal parameter is introduced to have a good trade-off between transcoding complexity and compression efficiency.

In this paper, we use three levels of SVM classifiers to predict the CU sizes and achieve a trade-off between complexity reduction and RD performance. For

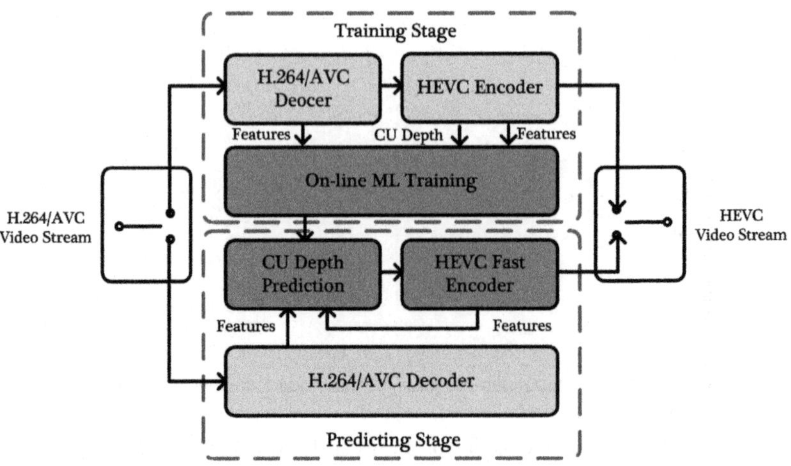

Fig. 4. Proposed framework of video transcoding.

different CUs, different levels of classifiers are utilized to predict splitting or non-splitting. The proposed framework of video transcoding is shown in Fig. 4. The framework is composed of two stages, on-line training stage and predicting stage. At the training stage (*i.e.* the switcher switches upward), the bitstream were decoded by the original H.264/AVC decoder and then encoded by the original HEVC encoder, *i.e.* cascaded transcoder. Then, the optimal CU partition of the transcoded videos are generated as ground truth for on-line learning. Then, the SVM models are trained, which will be used for CU depths prediction at predicting stage. At the predicting stage (*i.e.* the switcher switches downward), the CU partition will be determined by the SVM classifiers with split or non-split prediction. Some unnecessary checking can be skipped or early terminated at the predicting stage of the transcoder, which consist of the original H.264/AVC decoder and the proposed fast HEVC encoder. The proposed framework can effectively reduce complexity in comparison with the full Rate Distortion Optimization (RDO) process. In addition, the trained models for the SVM classifier can be retrained and updated by periodically switching to the training stage. Frequent training call can obtain more accurate models; However, it may leads to less complexity reduction, since the training stage cannot reduce the coding complexity and has complexity overhead from model training and feature extraction.

3.1 Feature Extraction

Training stage consists of features extraction and mode parameters training. For the classifier in ML, feature extraction may lead to complexity overhead, and feature selection is critical for the final prediction accuracy. A reasonable set of features could bring better prediction outputs as well as low complexity. Otherwise, the prediction result will be affected negatively [9,11]. In this paper, totally ten features are selected for the SVM classifiers. Some of the features are from H.264/AVC stream information, including Coded Block Patterns (CBP), MB types and DCT coefficient since they are mostly correlated to the block size of intra coding. If the CBP and DCT coefficient approaches zero, it is of high probability to select large blocks as the best CU partition. In addition, if the MB types of H.264/AVC bit is small block, it is of high probability to select small CU partition, which has been analyzed in section II. These three features are denoted as x_{CBP}, x_{type}, $x_{nonzero-DCT}$, $x_{energy-DCT}$, respectively. Additionally, the video content and by-product HEVC coding information are also adopted as the key features for CU size prediction. The video content related features include the variance of luminance, the number of edge pixel, the mean of gradient, the variance of gradient, which are denoted as $x_{variance-luminance}$, x_{edge}, $x_{mean-gradient}$, $x_{variance-gradient}$. Larger $x_{variance-luminance}$, x_{edge}, $x_{mean-gradient}$ or $x_{variance-gradient}$ values usually indicate the current CU is located in texture area and smaller CU partition is more probable to be chosen. The by-product HEVC coding information includes the CU depth and RD cost of neighboring CUs, which are denoted as x_{depth} and x_{RDcost}, respectively. Due to spatial correlation of the video content, x_{depth} of neighboring CUs may reflect the CU depth of current CU. Also, the current CU may probable select large CU partition if the x_{RDcost} of neighboring CUs is small.

3.2 SVM Based CU Decision Algorithm for Video Transcoding

The ML algorithm of SVM is concerned in this paper. As a widely used ML algorithm, SVM [11] is derived from the idea of Structural Risk Minimization (SRM) and has been successfully applied to solve many real-world numerical problems. The SVM decision function can be written as:

$$y(\mathbf{x}) = sgn(\omega^T \phi(\mathbf{x}) + b) = \begin{cases} +1, \omega^T \phi(\mathbf{x}) + b > 0 \\ -1, \omega^T \phi(\mathbf{x}) + b \le 0 \end{cases}, \tag{1}$$

where ω is the normal vector to a hyper-plane of classification, function $\phi(\mathbf{x})$ maps $\mathbf{x}$ into a higher-dimensional space, and b is a bias term.

In video transcoding, taking into account the complexity and transcoding performance of the CU prediction process, the decision function in Eq. (1) can be rewritten as:

$$Y(\mathbf{x}) = \begin{cases} -1, \omega^T \phi(\mathbf{x}) + b < -T_0 \\ 0, \quad -T_0 \le \omega^T \phi(\mathbf{x}) + b \le T_0, \\ +1, \omega^T \phi(\mathbf{x}) + b > T_0 \end{cases} \tag{2}$$

where T_0 is a positive threshold. If $Y(\mathbf{x})$ is -1, it indicates that the current CU shall not be spilt; if $Y(\mathbf{x})$ is $+1$, it indicates that the current CU will be spilt into four sub-CUs; if $Y(\mathbf{x})$ is 0, it indicates that the decision is of high risk and uncertainty, and the current CU will be encoded with full RDO (checking all CU depths) and determine the CU depth by RD cost comparison.

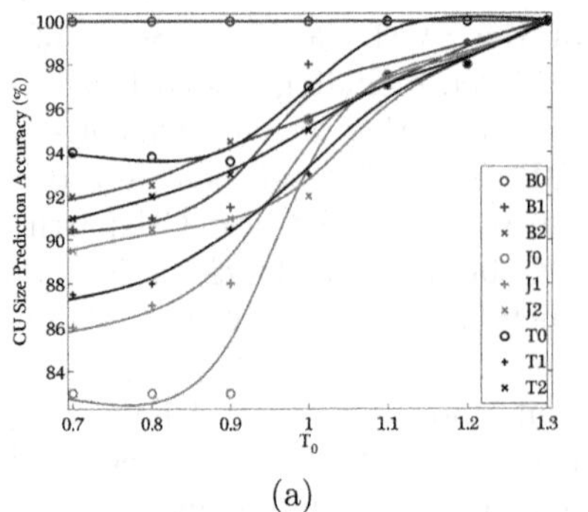

(a)

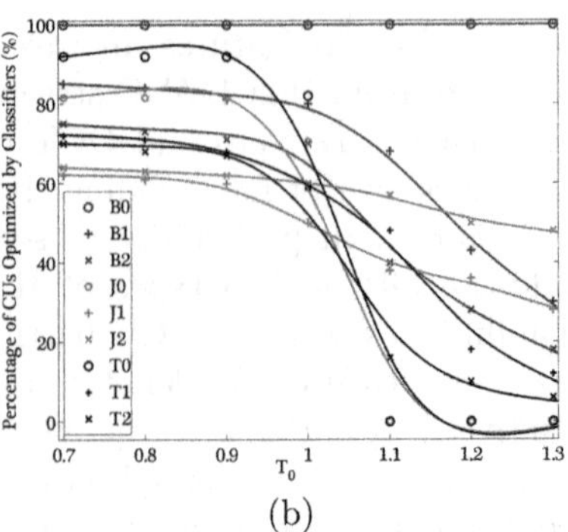

(b)

Fig. 5. Prediction accuracy and complexity reduction over different T_0. (a) Prediction accuracy; (b) Complexity reduction.

3.3 Optimal Parameter Selection

To determine the optimal threshold T_0, statistical experiments were conducted to analyze the relationships of the CU prediction accuracy and complexity reduction over different T_0, as shown in Fig. 5. Three sequences, BQMall, Johny and Tennis, were encoded with different T_0 and QPs. The legend B, J, T denote test sequences BQMall, Johny and Tennis, respectively; The number 0, 1 and 2 indicate CU depth level of the SVM classifiers. For example, B0, B1, B2 demonstrate Classifier 0, Classifier 1 and Classifier 2 for BQMall, respectively. Figure 5(a) shows that the prediction accuracy increases as the parameter T_0 increases from 0.7 to 1.3. In addition, the prediction accuracies over different sequences and QPs are all higher than 90% when T_0 is larger than 1.0, which means that the proposed method is highly accurate and the caused RD degradation will be negligible. Figure 5(b) shows complexity reduction over different T_0 that could be achieved by the proposed fast transcoding algorithm. We can observe that the complexity reduction decreases as T_0 increases. In addition, when T_0 is larger than 1.0, the achieved complexity reduction decrease dramatically. It is mainly because more CUs are determined by the exhaustive full RDO comparison. To have a good trade-off between the RD performance and complexity reduction, the optimal threshold T_0 is set as 1.0 in the experiment.

3.4 Overall Algorithm

Finally, the proposed SVM based CU decision algorithm for H.264/AVC to HEVC transcoding is summarized as follows:

Step 1: Extract the features for the current CU.
Step 2: Predict the CU depth with the trained SVM models by Eq. (2) and the optimal parameters;
Step 3: If the prediction is positive (+1), skip checking the current CU and only check the current CU with four sub-CU mode;

Step 4: If the prediction is negative (−1), only check the current CU depth, then go to Step 1 for next CU;
Step 5: If the prediction is 0, check the CU with current depth and four sub-CUs, go to Step 1 for next CU.

4 Experimental Results and Analyses

To testify the effectiveness of the proposed transcoder, comparative experiments and analyses were performed. Two state-of-the-art schemes Shen's method [2] and Lin's method [5] were adopted as benchmarks. Seventeen test video sequences [12] with different resolutions and contents were adopted and 97 frames each sequence were transcoded. In the experiment, H.264/AVC streams of different sequences were generated by JM 18.6 encoder where the Quantization Parameter (QP) is 22. The proposed algorithm and reference schemes were implemented on the reference software of HEVC, namely HM version 14.0, to transcode the H.264/AVC stream. QPs are set as 22, 27, 32 and 37 for the HEVC transcoder. It should be noted that for the proposed method, only the first four frames encoded by the original HEVC encoder and output CU partitions were used as training data. Then, the rest frames were transcoded with fast algorithm. At the predicting stage of the proposed transcoder, the value of T_0 was set as 1.0. The configuration file of HEVC is encoder_intra_main.

Table 1 shows the results of Shen's method, Lin's method and the proposed method compared with the original cascaded transcoder. The RD performances

Table 1. Complexity reduction and RD performance comparison between the proposed transcoder and the benchmark schemes [Units: %/dB/%]

Sequence	Shen [2]			Lin [5]			Proposed		
	BDBR	BDPSNR	TS	BDBR	BDPSNR	TS	BDBR	BDPSNR	TS
PeopleOnStreet	0.713	−0.043	29.9	0.581	−0.034	23.3	1.154	−0.057	35.7
Traffic	0.896	−0.052	30.3	0.813	−0.043	23.2	1.180	−0.067	38.6
BasketballDrive	1.654	−0.054	33.8	2.642	−0.119	43.0	2.096	−0.066	51.7
BQTerrace	0.918	−0.061	32.3	0.977	−0.076	34.6	0.587	−0.033	33.5
Cactus	0.744	−0.037	29.3	0.835	−0.044	26.0	1.102	−0.046	38.7
Kimono1	0.947	−0.048	42.5	7.352	−0.367	20.9	2.379	−0.121	71.8
ParkScene	0.326	−0.039	48.1	0.269	−0.027	49.8	−0.013	0.003	52.2
BQMall	1.098	−0.070	21.8	1.098	−0.066	18.3	1.633	−0.106	31.6
PartyScene	0.277	−0.024	20.7	0.017	−0.001	20.1	0.180	−0.014	28.4
RaceHorsesC	0.461	−0.032	20.9	0.387	−0.025	19.1	0.520	−0.033	33.0
BasketballDrill	0.622	−0.027	24.6	0.433	−0.014	19.8	1.071	−0.049	34.2
FourPeople	0.875	−0.053	32.6	0.638	−0.034	22.6	1.146	−0.072	42.7
Johnny	2.011	−0.094	40.9	4.259	−0.180	26.5	1.498	−0.068	56.5
KristenAndSara	2.152	−0.121	37.3	2.350	−0.122	24.2	1.300	−0.076	54.1
Vidyo1	1.663	−0.083	32.4	1.946	−0.095	19.0	1.705	−0.094	50.0
Vidyo3	2.193	−0.126	31.8	2.586	−0.144	19.7	1.629	−0.101	51.2
Vidyo4	2.074	−0.101	30.8	2.325	−0.103	19.1	1.632	−0.076	49.5
Average	**1.154**	**−0.063**	**31.8**	**1.736**	**−0.088**	**25.2**	**1.223**	**−0.063**	**44.3**

are measured by Bjønteggard Delta Bit Rate (BDBR) and Bjøntegaard Delta Peak Signal to Noise Ratio (BDPSNR) [13]. TS denotes time saving ratio comparing with the cascaded transcoder consists of original JM decoder and HM encoder. In Table 1, we can observe that Shen's method saves 31.8% encoding time on average when compared with the original JM-HM cascaded transcoder. The average BDBR and BDPSNR are 1.154% and −0.063 dB, respectively. Shen's method only considers the correlation between adjacent CUs to predict the range of current CU, few of CU sizes are skipped and time reduction is limited. Lin's method can achieve 25.2% complexity reduction on average, while the average BDBR and BDPSNR are 1.736% and −0.088 dB, respectively. For the proposed algorithm, it can achieve computational complexity reduction from 28.4% to 71.8%, and 44.3% on average, which is 12.5% and 19.1% better than those of Shen's and Lin's schemes. Meanwhile, the average BDBR and BDPSNR are 1.223% and −0.063 dB, respectively, which is negligible. The proposed H.264/AVC to HEVC transcoder can achieve more complexity reduction while maintaining high RD performance.

5 Conclusions

In this paper, a learning based low-complexity H.264/AVC to HEVC intra frame transcoder is proposed, which exploits the block correlation between two recent coding standards. The proposed transcoder adopts three different levels of classifiers to predict CU sizes. Besides, an optimal parameter determination approach for the SVM based video transcoding is also presented, which can achieve a trade-off between complexity reduction and RD performance. The proposed method reduces 44.3% of transcoding complexity at the cost of negligible RD degradation. It has proved that the proposed algorithm is capable of improving video transcoding efficiency for high quality cloud media computing services.

Acknowledgments. This work was supported in part by the National Natural Science Foundation of China under Grant 61471348, in part by the Guangdong Natural Science Funds for Distinguished Young Scholar under Grant 2016A030306022, in part by the Project for Shenzhen Science and Technology Development under Grant JSGG20160229202345378, in part by the PhD Start-up Fund of Natural Science Foundation of Guangdong Province under grant No. 2015A030310262, in part by Guangdong Special Support Program for Youth Science and Technology Innovation Talents under Grant 2014TQ01X345.

References

1. Sullivan, G.J., Ohm, J.-R., Han, W.-J., Wiegand, T.: Overview of the High Efficiency Video Coding (HEVC) standard. IEEE Trans. Circ. Syst. Video Technol. **22**(12), 1649–1668 (2012)
2. Shen, L., Zhang, Z., An, P.: Fast CU size decision and mode decision algorithm for HEVC intra coding. IEEE Trans. Consum. Electron. **59**(1), 207–213 (2013)

3. Pan, Z., Lei, J., Zhang, Y., Sun, X., Kwong, S.: Fast motion estimation based on content property for low-complexity H.265/HEVC encoder. IEEE Trans. Broadcast. **62**(3), 675–684 (2016)
4. Ahn, S., Lee, B., Kim, M.: A novel fast CU encoding scheme based on spatiotemporal encoding parameters for HEVC inter coding. IEEE Trans. Circ. Syst. Video Technol. **25**(3), 422–435 (2015)
5. Lin, C., Yang, W., Su, C.: FIFD: Fast intra transcoding from H.264/AVC to high efficiency video coding based on DCT coefficients and prediction modes. J. Vis. Commun. Image Represent. **38**, 130–140 (2016)
6. Shanableh, T., Peixoto, E., Izquierdo, E.: MPEG-2 to HEVC video transcoding with content-based modeling. IEEE Trans. Circ. Syst. Video Technol. **23**(7), 1191–1196 (2013)
7. Peixoto, E., Shanableh, T., Izquierdo, E.: H.264/AVC to HEVC video transcoder based on dynamic thresholding and content modeling. IEEE Trans. Circ. Syst. Video Technol. **24**(1), 99–112 (2014)
8. Zhang, Y., Kwong, S., Wang, X., Yuan, H., Pan, Z., Xu, L.: Machine learning based coding unit depth decisions for flexible complexity allocation in high efficiency video coding. IEEE Trans. Image Process. **24**(7), 2225–2238 (2015)
9. Zhu, L., Zhang, Y., Li, N., Jiang, G., Kwong, S.: Machine learning based fast H.264/AVC to HEVC transcoding exploiting block partition similarity. J. Vis. Commun. Image Represent. **38**, 824–837 (2016)
10. Kalva, H.: The H.264 video coding standard. IEEE Multimedia **13**(4), 86–90 (2006)
11. Chang, C.-C., Lin, C.-J.: LIBSVM: a library for support vector machines. ACM Trans. Intell. Syst. Technol. **2**(3), 1–27 (2011)
12. Bossen, F.: Common Test Conditions and Software Reference Configurations. JCTVC-J1100, JCTVC of ISO/IEC and ITU-T, Stockholm, SE (2012)
13. Bjøntegaard, G.: Calculation of average PSNR differences between RD-curves. ITU-T Video Coding Experts Group (VCEG), document M33, Austin, TX (2001)

A Perceptual Encryption Scheme for HEVC Video with Lossless Compression

Juan Chen[1], Fei Peng[2(✉)], and Min Long[3]

[1] Department of Information Engineering, Hunan Engineering Polytechnic, Changsha 410151, Hunan, China
[2] School of Computer Science and Electronic Engineering, Hunan University, Changsha 410082, Hunan, China
eepengf@gmail.com
[3] School of Computer and Communication Engineering, Changsha University of Science and Technology, Changsha 410012, Hunan, China

Abstract. Aiming to protect the video content and facilitate online video consumption, a perceptual encryption scheme is proposed for high efficiency video coding (HEVC) video. Based on RC4 algorithm, a key stream generation method is constructed, whose proportion of "1" and "0" can be regulated. During HEVC encoding, four kinds of syntax elements including motion vector difference (MVD)' sign, MVD's amplitude, sign of the luma residual coefficient and sign of the chroma residual coefficient, are encrypted by the regulated key stream. Experimental results and analysis show that the proposed scheme has good perceptual protection for the video content, and some advantages such as low computational cost, format-compliance and no bitrate increase can be achieved. It provides an effective resolution for the paid video-on-demand services in smart cities.

Keywords: Video encryption · Perceptual encryption · HEVC · RC4

1 Introduction

In order to protect the security of the video content, video encryption is usually adopted as a safety measure to avoid unauthorized watching. Nevertheless, as the encrypted video is completely unwatchable for customers, the desire of buying the watching service cannot be stimulated. For this reason, many online video providers offer some video highlighting clips or initial part of the video for free watching. It can stimulate consumers paying to watch the complete video to an extent, but it is still unable to give full information about the video to the potential customers. Therefore, researchers have proposed perceptual encryption for this kind of situation [1]. The video quality after perceptual encryption is not drastically reduced, and the basic video information can be maintained. After understanding the essential video content, interested customers will pay for the content provider to get the best watching experience.

In recent years, a growing number of ultra-high-definition videos are used in various social fields. Thus, H.264/AVC [2], which is currently the most widely used video

X. Sun et al. (Eds.): ICCCS 2017, Part II, LNCS 10603, pp. 396–407, 2017.
https://doi.org/10.1007/978-3-319-68542-7_33

coding standard, cannot meet the requirements of massive videos compression and storage. In 2013, H.265/HEVC was developed as a new generation of video coding standard [3], which can improve approximately 50% compression ratio compared with H.264. Although some works have been done to selective encryption for H.264 [4–10], perceptual H.264 video encryption [11, 12] and selective coefficient sign encryption for HEVC [12], the security is still questionable. In order to strengthen the security of HEVC videos, a perceptual encryption scheme is proposed in this paper. The main contributions include:

- A controllable key stream generation method is constructed. By using RC4, a key stream whose proportion of "1" and "0" can be regulated in a delicate designed mechanism, which is used to accomplish the perceptual video encryption.
- By properly selecting syntax elements for encryption, lossless compression is achieved in the proposed scheme.
- A perceptual encryption policy is recommended according the differences of the sensitivity of different syntax elements in encryption.

The rest of the paper is organized as follows. The perceptual encryption for HEVC videos with lossless compression is presented in Sect. 2. Experimental results and analysis are provided in Sect. 3. Finally, some conclusion are drawn in Sect. 4.

2 The Perceptual Encryption Scheme for HEVC

To perceptually protect HEVC video, four kinds of syntax elements, including MVD's sign, MVD's amplitude, sign of the luma residual coefficient and sign of the chroma residual coefficient, are selected for encryption. By using the controllable key stream, the percentage of the syntax elements can be controlled, which can meet the requirements of different environments.

2.1 Construction of the Controllable Key Stream Generator

RC4 has been proved to be a secure stream cipher [14] and it has been widely implemented in different applications. Here, based on RC4, a key stream with controllable proportion of "1" and "0" is constructed. The basic idea is: for the key stream generated from RC4, every 8 bits are grouped, and every group can be converted to a decimal fraction. Ideally, the decimal fractions are uniformly distributed from the range of [0, 1]. Assuming the probability of the generation of every decimal fraction is the same, the percentage of the number of decimal fractions is 1-Per ($0 < \text{Per} < 1$) when the decimal fractions are greater than the threshold Per. The procedure of the construction is as follows.

Step 1: Set a key K for RC4 and predefine a threshold Per, which represents the proportion of bit "1".
Step 2: With the key K, key stream key' is generated from RC4.
Step 3: Every 8 bits in key' forms a group, and every group is converted to a decimal fraction $decn$.

Step 4: Generation of the key stream *key*. For each decimal fraction *decn*, compare its value with *Per*. If *decn* is greater than *Per*, the corresponding bit of the *key* will be 0. Otherwise, the corresponding bit will be 1.

The pseudo-code of the above process is shown in Fig. 1.

```
Input: K, Per
Begin
  Initializing S and T
for i = 0 to 255
  S[i]←i
  T[i]←K[i mod strlen(key) ]
  end
  Initializing S
for i = 0 to 255
  S[i]←i
  j←( j+S[i]+T[i] ) mod 256
 swap(S[i],S[j])
end
// Generating RC4 stream cipher key'
Initializing i and j
for r= 0 to len //8*len is the length of key'
     i←(i+1) mod 256;
     j←(j+S[i])mod 256;
     swap(S[i],S[j]);
     t←(S[i]+S[j])mod 256;
     key'[r]←S[t];
   end
// Generating controllable key stream key
     dec←0;
    for i= 0 to len // len is the length of key
     for j= 0 to 8
     dec←dec+key'[i*8+j]*2(-i)
     end
     if dec < Per
      key[i]←1;
     else key[i]←0;
    end
end
Output: key
```

Fig. 1. The pseudo-code of generating key stream with controllable percentage of "1" and "0"

2.2 The Proposed Perceptual Encryption Scheme

Encryption of MVD

During the intra prediction of HEVC coding, one or two motion vectors (MVs) are encoded in a prediction unit (PU). Therefore, many motion vectors need to be encoded.

For the compression of these video data, HEVC facilitate the correlation between MVs in neighboring PUs to predict the current MV. Thus, only motion vector prediction and MVD are both encoded can guarantee the correct decoding of MV.

As MVD's sign and MVD's amplitude are two different syntax elements, they are encoded separately. For this reason, two syntax elements are encrypted with different methods in our scheme.

The encryption of MVD's sign is described as:

$$en\_MVDSign = MVDSign \oplus key_1, \tag{1}$$

where key_1 represents a controllable key stream, *MVDsign* and *en_MVDSign* represent the original MVD's sign and the encrypted MVD's sign, respectively, and $\oplus$ represents XOR operation.

After encryption, some MVD' signs are changed, which will produce wrong predicting direction of MVs.

A MVD contains a horizontal component x and a vertical component y, which respectively represent the horizontal direction and the vertical direction of a video image. The motion vector can be accurately predicted when both x and y are correct.

Generally, the amplitudes of x and y are different. If the amplitude of x swaps with that of y, MVD will become completely different. Therefore, the encryption of the amplitude of MVD is swapping x and y. It is described as:

$$\begin{cases} en\_MVDHorAbs = MVDVerAbs \\ en\_MVDVerAbs = MVDHorAbs \end{cases} (key_2 = 1) \quad , \quad \begin{cases} en\_MVDHorAbs = MVDHorAbs \\ en\_MVDVerAbs = MVDVerAbs \end{cases} (key_2 = 0) \tag{2}$$

where key_2 represents a controllable key stream, *MVDHorAbs* and *en_MVDHorAbs* respectively represent the amplitude of x and the encrypted amplitude of x, and *MVDVerAbs* and *en_MVDVerAbs* respectively represent the amplitude of y and the encrypted amplitude of y.

Encryption of Residual Coefficient

Predictive coding plays an important role in video coding. The spatial redundancy and temporal redundancy can be removed by intra prediction and inter prediction, meanwhile the predictive residual is produced. After transform and quantization, the predictive residual becomes the residual coefficient. According the color space of video coding, residual coefficient is further divided into luma coefficient and chroma coefficient. Two types of residual coefficient are respectively selected to be encrypted to scramble the texture of the video.

The encryption of luma coefficient is described as:

$$en\_LumaCoefSign = LumaCoefSign \oplus key_3, \tag{3}$$

where key_3 represents a controllable key stream. *LumaCoefSign and en_LumaCoefSign* represent the original sign of luma coefficient and the encrypted sign of luma coefficient, respectively.

The encryption of chroma coefficient is described as:

$$en\_ChromaCoefSign = ChromaCoefSign \oplus key_4, \tag{4}$$

where key_4 represents a controllable key stream. *ChromaCoefSign and en_ ChromaCoefSign* represent the original sign of chroma coefficient and the encrypted sign of chroma coefficient, respectively.

As for the decryption, it is carried out in decoding process, and it is just a reverse of encryption.

3 Experimental Results and Analysis

Experiments are performed on HEVC test Model 12.0 (HM 12.0), whose encoding mode is encoder_lowdelay_main [15]. 9 video sequences with CIF format (352 $\times$ 288) are selected to be tested in our scheme. In the experiments, every video sequence is encoded 100 frames, whose quantization parameters (QP) are set as 28.

3.1 Analysis of Cryptosystem Security

Cryptosystem security refers to the security of the cipher used in the encryption scheme. In this paper, the key stream is generated from RC4. Thus, the cryptosystem security is depended on the security of RC4. As RC4 is one of the most widely used stream ciphers, the S-box of it is high nonlinear and no short cycle is produced inside it. Meanwhile, in the proposed scheme, 4 key streams are respectively generated with different *K* and *Per*. Therefore, it can guarantee the security of the proposed perceptual video encryption.

3.2 Analysis of Perceptual Security

Perceptual security is the perception of video contents from human eyes. The more difficult to understand and identify the encrypted video contents is, the better the perceptual security is. In order to evaluate the perceptual security of the proposed scheme, all tested video sequences are encrypted with 50% of the syntax elements to measure the degree of scrambling. The results are shown in Fig. 2.

As seen from Fig. 2, it can be found that the scrambling results for 50% syntax elements are obvious, and the video quality is significantly reduced. In addition, PSNR and SSIM [16] are used to evaluate the perceptual security, and the results are shown in Table 1.

As seen from Table 1, compared with the standard encoding results, the PSNR and SSIM of the encrypted results with the proposed scheme have decreased in varying degrees. Among them, the reduction of PSNR-Y is 23.91, which is the largest. While the reduction of PSNR-U and PSNR-V are 18.12 and 18.91, respectively. In YUV

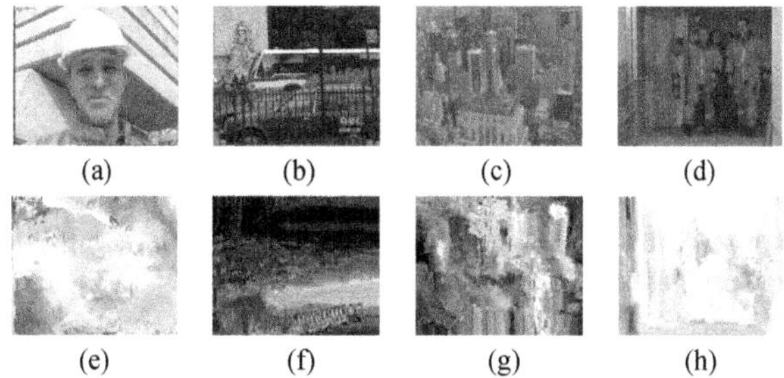

Fig. 2. The perceptual encryption results of Foreman, Bus, City and Crew (a)–(d) represent the original video sequences; (e)–(h) represent the encrypted video sequences

Table 1. PSNR and SSIM of the standardly encoded videos and encrypted videos

Sequences	PSNR-Y		PSNR-U		PSNR-V		SSIM	
	Standard	Encryption	Standard	Encryption	Standard	Encryption	Standard	Encryption
Bus	33.84	10.58	39.97	27.01	41.89	26.23	0.9403	0.1477
City	34.95	13.18	42.16	31.07	43.75	29.37	0.9439	0.1495
Crew	36.41	5.61	41.09	26.23	39.75	20.73	0.9312	0.2464
Football	35.25	13.30	39.42	22.54	35.25	13.30	0.9369	0.2173
Foreman	36.67	10.24	41.26	16.01	43.72	24.67	0.9403	0.2942
Husky	30.86	11.38	39.02	19.00	42.57	27.93	0.9587	0.0528
Mobile	33.03	9.36	36.99	13.94	36.59	9.86	0.9708	0.0922
Soccer	35.15	13.04	42.10	23.74	43.79	20.74	0.9188	0.2619
Stefan	34.46	8.78	38.08	17.46	38.44	22.70	0.9749	0.1138
Average	34.51	10.61	40.01	21.89	40.64	21.73	0.9462	0.1751

color space, as human visual system is more sensitive to luminance than chrominance, the dramatically decrease of luminance component PSNR-Y shows the good performance in scrambling. Meanwhile, the average SSIM of 9 encrypted videos is only 0.1751, and the decrease from the standard encoding is 0.7711, which demonstrates the good perceptual security of the proposed scheme.

3.3 Analysis of Perception of Syntax Element

To analyze the perception of different syntax elements, every syntax element is selected for encryption with different proportion. The experimental results are shown in Figs. 3 and 4.

As seen from Fig. 3, after the encryption of MVD's sign and the MVD's amplitude, the distortion in the encrypted videos are varied with different proportions, and the distortion is more significant as the encryption proportion is increased. As seen from Fig. 4, the encryption of the sign of the luma residual coefficient changes the brightness of the video, while the encryption of the sign of chroma residual coefficient change the color of the video. The encrypted Foreman's PSNR and SSIM of different syntax elements with different proportions are shown in Table 2.

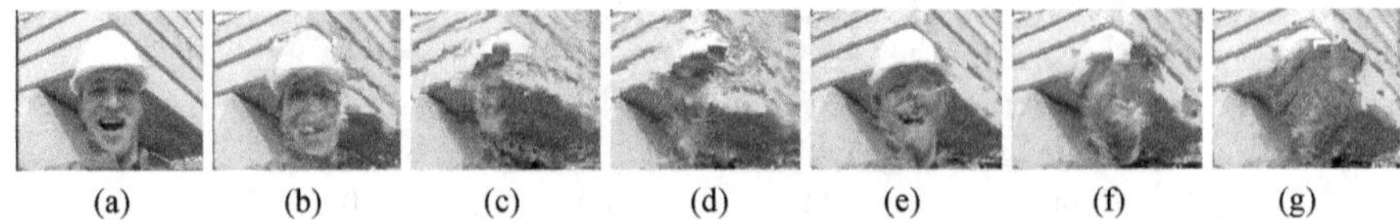

Fig. 3. The encryption results of different syntax elements of MVD with different proportions (Foreman) (a) Original video (b) Encryption results of 10% MVD's sign; (c) Encryption results of 30% MVD's sign; (d) Encryption results of 50% MVD's sign; (e) Encryption results of the 10% amplitude of MVD; (f) Encryption results of the 30% amplitude of MVD; (g) Encryption results of the 50% amplitude of MVD.

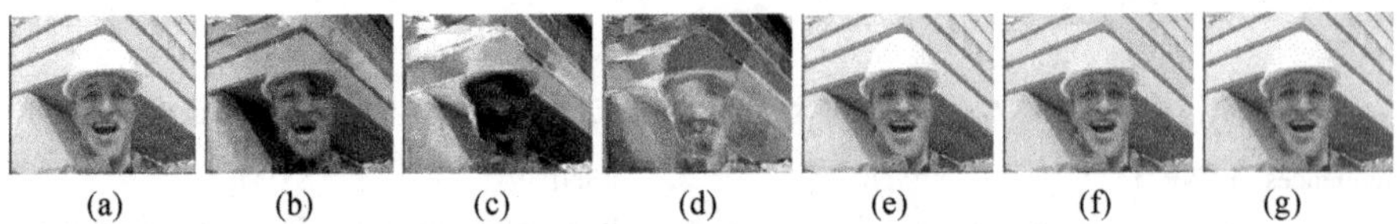

Fig. 4. The encryption results of the sign of luma residual coefficient and the sign of chroma residual coefficient with different proportions (Foreman) (a) Original video; (b) Encryption results of 10% the sign of the luma residual coefficient; (c) Encryption results of 30% the sign of the luma residual coefficient; (d) Encryption results of 50% the sign of the luma residual coefficient; (e) Encryption results of 10% the sign of the chroma residual coefficient; (f) Encryption results of 30% the sign of the chroma residual coefficient; (g) Encryption results of 50% the sign of the chroma residual coefficient.

As seen from Table 2, the decrease of PSNR and SSIM of only encrypting MVD'sign or the MVD's amplitude is obviously larger than those of only encrypting the sign of the luma residual coefficient or the sign of the chroma residual coefficient. Therefore, by encrypting a small proportion of motion information, the quality of the

Table 2. Foreman's PSNR and SSIM of different syntax elements with different proportions

Syntax element	Proportion	PSNR-Y		PSNR-U		PSNR-V		SSIM	
		Standard	Encryption	Standard	Encryption	Standard	Encryption	Standard	Encryption
MVD's sign	10%	36.67	16.97	41.26	34.20	43.72	33.42	0.9403	0.4561
	30%	36.67	15.65	41.26	33.18	43.72	31.90	0.9403	0.3998
	50%	36.67	14.91	41.26	32.68	43.72	31.52	0.9403	0.3568
Amplitude of MVD	10%	36.67	18.56	41.26	36.23	43.72	35.77	0.9403	0.5918
	30%	36.67	15.67	41.26	34.23	43.72	33.17	0.9403	0.4240
	50%	36.67	15.45	41.26	33.58	43.72	32.47	0.9403	0.4106
Sign of the luma residual coefficient	10%	36.67	12.89	41.26	41.26	43.72	43.72	0.9403	0.6879
	30%	36.67	11.67	41.26	41.26	43.72	43.72	0.9403	0.4503
	50%	36.67	10.18	41.26	41.26	43.72	43.72	0.9403	0.3005
Sign of the chroma residual coefficient	10%	36.67	36.67	41.26	33.99	43.72	33.37	0.9403	0.9403
	30%	36.67	36.67	41.26	25.25	43.72	20.94	0.9403	0.9403
	50%	36.67	36.67	41.26	23.72	43.72	20.94	0.9403	0.9403

video can be degraded. Meanwhile, it can be found that encryption of the sign of the luma residual coefficient can reduce the PSNR-Y, and encryption of the sign of the chroma residual coefficient can effectively reduce the PSNR-U and PSNR-V. What's more, the encryption of the sign of the chroma residual coefficient can change the color of the video, but it cannot change the texture structure, so there is no influence on the value of SSIM.

Considering the encrypted video should have a certain perception to attract potential customers' attention and interest, it cannot be completely unidentifiable. According to the above experimental results and analysis, it is recommended that the encryption proportion of MVD's sign or the MVD' amplitude is less than 10%, the encryption proportion of the sign of the luma residual coefficient is less than 30%, and the encrypting proportion of the sign of the chroma residual coefficient is less than 50%. The results with recommended proportions are shown in Fig. 5.

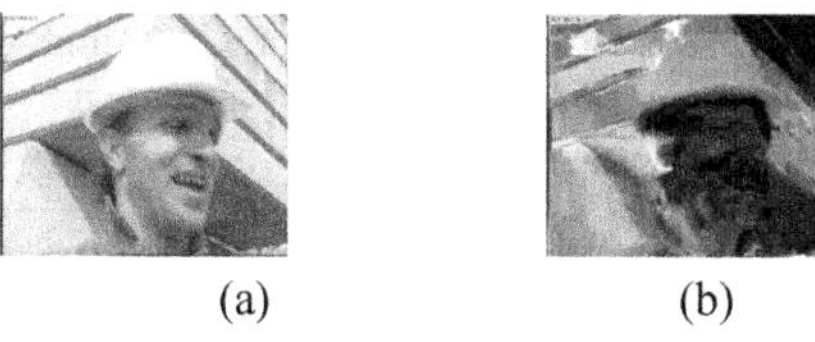

(a) (b)

Fig. 5. Perceptual encryption results of Foreman with recommended proportion (a) Original Video (b) Encrypted results with 7% MVD's sign, 8% MVD's amplitude, 26% sign of the luma residual coefficient and 47% sign of the chroma residual coefficient.

3.4 Analysis of Compression Performance

To analyze the compression performance of proposed scheme, the size of the encoded encrypted videos is compared with that of the standard encoding, the results are shown in Table 3.

Table 3. Comparison of the size of the videos

Sequences	Standard B_1 (Bit)	Encryption B_2 (Bit)	$B_2 - B_1$
Bus	2123136	2123136	0
City	767224	767224	0
Crew	1102592	1102592	0
Football	2966352	2966352	0
Foreman	685552	685552	0
Husky	8620256	8620256	0
Mobile	2467304	2467304	0
Soccer	1195720	1195720	0
Stefan	1697008	1697008	0

As seen from Table 3, the size of the encoding of encrypted videos is just the same as that of the standard encoding, because MVD's sign and the sign of the residual coefficient are coded by the bypass mode during entropy encoding. What's more, for the encryption of MVD's amplitude, the operation is only swapping x and y, their values have no modification, which impose no influence on the entropy coding compression.

3.5 Analysis of Computation Complexity

Computation complexity is a key factor for influencing video encoding efficiency. Generally, low computation complexity of the encryption scheme would not affect the real-time performance of coding. Experiments are made to evaluate the time consumption of the standard encoding and encoding with perceptual encryption, and the results are shown in Table 4.

Table 4. Comparison of encoding time

Sequences	Standard T_1 (Sec)	Encryption T_2 (Sec)	T_2/T_1
Bus	653.313	657.232	1.006
City	559.869	558.749	0.998
Crew	656.568	657.224	1.001
Football	790.848	796.383	1.007
Foreman	570.453	565.318	0.991
Husky	876.867	882.128	1.006
Mobile	661.385	654.109	0.989
Soccer	561.883	566.378	1.008
Stefan	565.262	567.523	1.004
Average	–	–	1.001

As seen from Table 4, the difference between direct coding time T_1 and the time T_2 for encoding with perceptual encryption is very small, which indicates that the proposed encryption scheme does not hinder the real-time performance of encoding. The main reason is that only some simple operations such as Xor and swapping are used in the encryption, and the computation complexity of these operations is very low.

3.6 Analysis of Encryption Space

Encryption space refers to the proportion of bits in the video stream that can be utilized for encryption. The number of bits of each syntax element and the number of bits of the whole encoding video are calculated, and they are listed in Table 5.

From Table 5, the video encryption spaces are varied from 12.68% to 20.26%, and the average value is 15.89%. So it can effectively resist against brute force attacks.

Table 5. Encryption space of every video sequence

Sequences	MVD (bits)	Luma residual sign (Bit)	Chroma residual sign (Bit)	Video Stream (Bit)	Encryption space
Bus	45672	301751	5280	2123136	16.61%
City	23036	81977	820	767224	13.79%
Crew	25516	120550	13070	1102592	14.43%
Football	45956	433677	32429	2966352	17.26%
Foreman	22852	61503	2551	685552	12.68%
Husky	101898	1635469	9111	8620256	20.26%
Mobile	72914	294840	20991	2467304	15.76%
Soccer	29926	150246	3445	1195720	15.36%
Stefan	38138	231254	16055	1697008	16.82%
Average	–	–	–	–	15.89%

3.7 Analysis of Format-Compliance and Operability

According to the proposed perceptual encryption scheme, it does not change the format and control information of the video in the process of encryption. Therefore, the encrypted HEVC video completely fulfills the HEVC standard. Meanwhile, the encrypted video stream file can be decoded by general decoders, which is able to execute any video operations such as play, pause, fast-forward and etc. So the proposed perceptual encryption has good format-compliance and operability.

3.8 Performance Comparison

Here, a comprehensive comparison is made between the method in [13] and the proposed scheme, and the results are listed in Table 6.

Table 6. Comparison of existing scheme and the proposed scheme

Scheme	Syntax elements for perceptual encryption	Cipher	Bitrate increase	Encryption space	Real-time	Format compliance
Method in [13]	Sign of the luma residual coefficient	Not mentioned	No	General	No influence	No influence
Proposed method	MVD's sign, amplitude of MVD, sign of the chroma residual coefficient, and sign of the luma residual coefficient	Key stream generated from RC4	No	Good	No influence	No influence

From Table 6, compared with the scheme in [13], more syntax elements are used for perceptual encryption. At the same time, the implementation of RC4 also contributes to the security of the proposed scheme.

4 Conclusion

A novel perceptual encryption scheme for HEVC video is proposed. Four kinds of syntax elements including MVD's sign, MVD's amplitude, sign of luma residual coefficient and sign of chroma residual coefficient are selected for encryption. The perceptual encryption is carried out by using a key stream with controllable percentage of "1" and "0", which is generated from RC4. Experimental results and analysis show that the proposed scheme has good cryptosystem security and perceptual encryption performance. It has no side effect on the video compression, and real-time performance of HEVC coding is guaranteed. At the same time, it has good format-compliance and operability.

Acknowledgements. This work was supported in part by project supported by National Natural Science Foundation of China (Grant Nos. 61370225, 61572182), project supported by Hunan Provincial Natural Science Foundation of China (Grant No. 15JJ2007).

References

1. Stutz, T., Uhl, A.: A survey of H.264 AVC/SVC encryption. IEEE Trans. Circuits Syst. Video Technol. **22**(3), 325–339 (2012)
2. Wiegand, T., Sullivan, G.J., Bjøntegaard, G., et al.: Overview of the H.264/AVC video coding standard. IEEE Trans. Circuits Syst. Video Technol. **13**(7), 560–576 (2003)
3. Sullivan, G.J., Ohm, J.R., Han, W.J., et al.: Overview of the high efficiency video coding (HEVC) standard. IEEE Trans. Circuits Syst. Video Technol. **22**(12), 1649–1668 (2012)
4. Shahid, Z., Chaumont, M., Puech, W.: Fast protection of H.264/AVC by selective encryption of CABAC. In: IEEE International Conference on Multimedia and Expo, pp. 1038–1041. IEEE, New York City (2009)
5. Shahid, Z., Chaumont, M., Puech, W.: Fast protection of H.264/AVC by selective encryption of CABAC for I and P frames. IEEE Trans. Circuits Syst. Video Technol. **21**(5), 565–576 (2011)
6. Wang, Y., O'Neill, M., Kurugollu, F.: A tunable encryption scheme and analysis of fast selective encryption for CAVLC and CABAC in H.264/AVC. IEEE Trans. Circuits Syst. Video Technol. **23**(9), 1476–1490 (2013)
7. Van Wallendael, G., Boho, A., De Cock, J., et al.: Encryption for high efficiency video coding with video adaptation capabilities. In: IEEE International Conference on Consumer Electronics (ICCE), Las Vegas, USA (2013)
8. Van Wallendael, G., Boho, A., De Cock, J., et al.: Encryption for high efficiency video coding with video adaptation capabilities. IEEE Trans. Consum. Electron. **59**(3), 634–642 (2013)
9. Van Wallendael, G., De Cock, J., Van Leuven, S., et al.: Format-compliant encryption techniques for high efficiency video coding. In: IEEE International Conference on Image Processing, pp. 4583–4587. IEEE, Melbourne (2013)
10. Shahid, Z., Puech, W.: Visual protection of HEVC video by selective encryption of CABAC binstrings. IEEE Trans. Multimedia **16**(1), 24–36 (2014)
11. Yeung, S.-K.A., Zeng, B.: A new design of multiple transforms for perceptual video encryption. In: 19th IEEE International Conference on Image Processing (ICIP 2012), pp. 2637–2640. IEEE, Florida (2012)

12. Zeng, B., Yeung, S.K.A., Zhu, S., et al.: Perceptual encryption of H.264 videos: embedding sign-flips into the integer-based transforms. IEEE Trans. Inf. Forensics Secur. **9**(2), 309–320 (2014)
13. Hofbauer, H., Uhl, A., Unterweger, A.: Transparent encryption for HEVC using bit-stream-based selective coefficient sign encryption. In: IEEE International Conference on Acoustics, Speech and Signal Processing, pp. 2005–2009. IEEE, Kyoto (2014)
14. Stallings, W.: The RC4 stream encryption algorithm. In: Cryptography and Network Security (2005)
15. Joint Collaborative Team on Video Coding (JCT-VC) of ITU-T SG16 WP 3 and ISO DEC JTC I/SC29/WG11: HEVC Reference Software Manual. JCTVC-F634, 6th Meeting, Torino, IT (2011)
16. Wang, Z., Bovik, A.C., Sheikh, H.R., Simoncelli, E.P.: Image quality assessment: from error visibility to structural similarity. IEEE Trans. Image Process. **13**(4), 600–612 (2004)

Spatial-Temporal Correlation Based Multi-resolution Hybrid Motion Estimation for Frame Rate Up-Conversion

Bingyu Ji[1], Ran Li[1,2(✉)], and Changan Wu[1]

[1] School of Computer and Information Technology, Xinyang Normal University, Xinyang 464000, China
liran358@163.com
[2] School of Computer and Software, Nanjing University of Information Science and Technology, Nanjing 210044, China

Abstract. This paper presents a method applied in frame rate up-conversion (FRUC) to estimate the motion vector (MV) based on spatial-temporal motion vectors, which have a high correlation with the interpolated block. Meanwhile, a hierarchical structure is employed to generate a series of low-resolution images for motion estimation (ME) aimed to reduce computation complexity. After using ME in the lowest resolution image, there are several relatively accurate MVs picked to transmit down to the next level for further calculation. Then the initial motion vector field (MVF) is generated by calculating the sums of absolute difference (SAD) of the candidate MVs. To refine the MVF, an outliers detecting criterion is set up to smooth the MVF and obtain a more accurate MVF at the same time. The motion compensated (MC) will not perform until the termination of MVF refinement level-by-level. Experimental reveals that the proposed method find a tradeoff between accuracy and complexity, because the peak signal-to-noise ratio (PSNR) is promoted to 4.69 dB and the processing time is quite fast.

Keywords: Frame rate up-conversion · Multi resolution · Motion vector refinement

1 Introduction

Generally, a successive video sequence can be compressed by frame skipping strategy before transmission, but it will degrade the quality of video and generate a discontinuous sequence. Furthermore, there is a similar puzzle in high-definition videos, with the lack of high-speed camera, low-rate videos may result in ghost artifacts especially in liquid crystal display [1]. In order to conquer the problem from these situations, a technique capable of converting video frame rates should be adopted. FRUC has been an effective method to increases the frame rate of videos, which can reduce the motion blur effect and motion jerkiness. ME and motion compensation interpolation (MCI) are the crucial component of FRUC algorithms. ME is the procedure of estimating the motion trajectory between two adjacent frames, hence, the MVs of object can be calculated, and then MCI part can utilize the MVs to insert the median frames.

X. Sun et al. (Eds.): ICCCS 2017, Part II, LNCS 10603, pp. 408–417, 2017.
https://doi.org/10.1007/978-3-319-68542-7_34

The accuracy of MV is dramatically affected by ME and has a high correlation with the quality of interpolated frames. Block matching algorithm (BMA) is the typical method among various ME algorithms, it has a superiority of low complexity when comparing with pixel-wise ME [2–8]. The bidirectional ME (BME) was prior introduced for the acquirement of MVs in [7] to replace the unidirectional ME (UME). And then lots of research has been performed to obtain more accurate MVs: [2] proposed a blended method combined UME and BME; [3] uses UME in the ME part and uses BME to refine the MVF; [6] proposed a feature based method. But the computation complexity has been gradually elevated with the improvement of accuracy, hence, a low complexity MC was present [9]. [10, 11] utilize hierarchical structure to reduce the processing time, which enlighten us as well. To further decrease calculation time, MVs contained spatial and temporal information are regard as candidates of the undetermined block instead of full search [12–15], which result in both low complexity and precision. In order to rectify the incorrect MVF, MV refinement is considered as a common means to get rid of MVs with great error [16–19].

In this paper, in order to correct the inaccurate MVs by utilizing the spatial and temporal information, we propose a novel hybrid method derived from 3-D recursive search (3-D RS) [12]. Although the introduction of spatial-temporal candidate MVs can reduce computation time, the mixture with hierarchical structure will further gain the effect of low complexity [10, 11]. Gaussian pyramid is provided with the hierarchical property, because it can generate multi-resolution images from the original image. To guarantee the precision, we will utilize the MV refinement level-by-level to correct the outliers on the basis of calculating the distance between the current MV and the median MV, which is acquired from the neighboring blocks of current block.

The rest of this paper is organized as follows. Section 2 elaborate the proposed algorithm, and Sect. 3 exhibits the comparison experiment with existing methods. Section 4 makes a conclusion finally.

2 Proposed Motion Estimation Method

The flowchart of the proposed motion estimation algorithm is shown in Fig. 1. Two adjacent original frames are selected as reference frames to construct the Gaussian pyramid. At top level, a modified 3-D RS algorithm is used to generate candidate MVs, then the initial MV with low matching error is picked from candidates at the second pyramid level by adopting BME. In order to achieve a relatively smooth MVF, the initial MVs must be detected and the outliers will be corrected by MV refinement part. After that, the MVF is propagated to the next level unless the current level is the bottom of pyramid, and the procedure of MV refinement is contributed to smoothen the MVF.

2.1 Modified 3-D RS at Top Level

To establish the hierarchical structure, Gaussian Pyramid is employed with the advantage of reducing noise in the images rather than directly using sub sample, and its structure is shown as Fig. 2. It is need to emphasized that the bottom image comes from original frame and the level number of pyramid is not stationary, but we suggest that the levels is better to set no more than 3 for a tradeoff between accuracy and complexity.

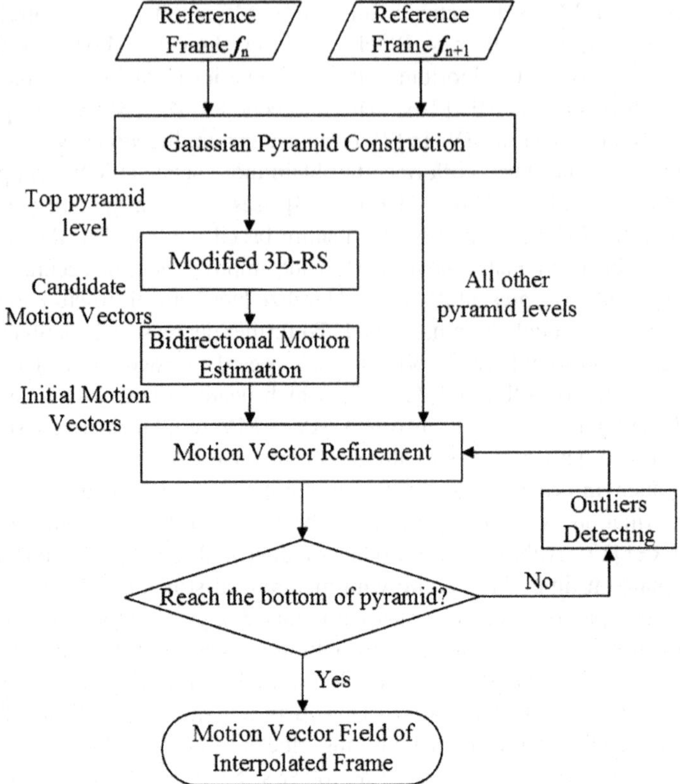

Fig. 1. Flowchart of the proposed motion estimation algorithm.

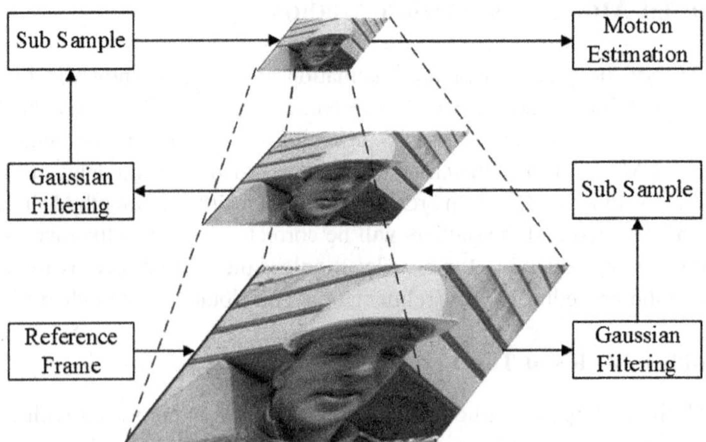

Fig. 2. Construction of Gaussian pyramid

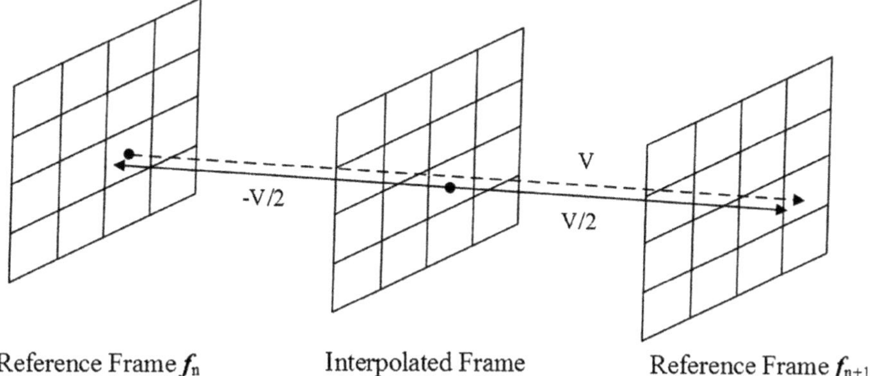

Fig. 3. A hybrid ME method used for estimate the MV of the current block.

The proposed method introduces the 3-D RS algorithm with a slightly modification in the ME part and only utilizes it at top pyramid level to acquire the candidate MVs, which are relative precise. As Fig. 3 shown, the forward frame and the backward frame in the original video sequence is respectively regard as reference frame f_n and f_{n+1} from the viewpoint of the interpolated frame. Meanwhile, the dotted line represents the MV of the reference block in the previous frame with the same coordinate of current block in the interpolated frame, and the full line with two arrows denotes the MV of current block. As the similar trajectory, the MV of reference block is frequently considered as the MV of interpolated block, but a hybrid ME method with 3-D RS is utilized in the proposed algorithm instead of the conventional method: the MV of the block in the forward frame is first calculated by UME and then the MV of the block in the present position is computed by BME refer to the MVF in previous frame. These two fundamentally different criterions can be elucidated respectively as

$$SUAD_n(\boldsymbol{v}_n^{(t)}, \boldsymbol{B}_n^{(t)}) = \sum_{\boldsymbol{p} \in \boldsymbol{B}_n^{(t)}} \left| f_n^{(t)}(\boldsymbol{p}) - f_{n+1}^{(t)}(\boldsymbol{p} + \boldsymbol{v}_n^{(t)}) \right|, \tag{1}$$

$$SBAD_I(\boldsymbol{v}_I^{(t)}, \boldsymbol{B}_I^{(t)}) = \sum_{\boldsymbol{p} \in \boldsymbol{B}_I^{(t)}} \left| f_n^{(t)}(\boldsymbol{p} - \frac{\boldsymbol{v}_I^{(t)}}{2}) - f_{n+1}^{(t)}(\boldsymbol{p} + \frac{\boldsymbol{v}_I^{(t)}}{2}) \right|, \tag{2}$$

where SUAD denotes the unidirectional SAD, and SBAD denotes the bidirectional SAD, the superscript (t) represents the top level, $\boldsymbol{B}_n^{(t)}$ and $\boldsymbol{B}_I^{(t)}$ respectively denotes the current block in the forward frame and interpolated frame at the top pyramid level containing pixel p, $\boldsymbol{v}_n^{(t)}$ and $\boldsymbol{v}_I^{(t)}$ are the candidate MV in different frames. Although the individually employment of the Eq. (1) can provide a fine MV, the mixture with Eq. (2) can generate a more accurate MV.

2.2 Spatial and Temporal Correlation

When calculating the MV of interpolated block, the MVs of blocks in spatial and temporal neighboring positions are regard as reference due to the high correlation. Therefore, three pairs of MVs with such character are selected for the candidates and the illustration of relative location is exhibited in Fig. 4. The spatial-temporal MVs can be directly obtained from the specific blocks with a certain MV, in the meantime, the update MV will be calculated as

$$\boldsymbol{UPG} = \left\{ \begin{pmatrix} 0 \\ 0 \end{pmatrix}, \begin{pmatrix} 0 \\ \pm 1 \end{pmatrix}, \begin{pmatrix} 0 \\ \pm 2 \end{pmatrix}, \begin{pmatrix} \pm 1 \\ 0 \end{pmatrix}, \begin{pmatrix} \pm 3 \\ 0 \end{pmatrix} \right\}, \tag{3}$$

$$\boldsymbol{v}_U^{(t)} = \boldsymbol{v}_S^{(t)} + \boldsymbol{UPG}(N_i \bmod L_{UP}), \tag{4}$$

where $\boldsymbol{UPG}$ denotes the collection of update parameter group, $\boldsymbol{UP}(\bullet)$ denotes the selected one, N_i is the iteration times of the current block in the single frame processing, and L_{UP} is the amount of the update parameter group, $\boldsymbol{v}_S^{(t)}$ is the MV of the block at the upper left or upper right position from the viewpoint of current block. Hence, the update vector $\boldsymbol{v}_U^{(t)}$ can be computed with addition of $\boldsymbol{UPG}$ on the basis of $\boldsymbol{v}_S^{(t)}$. After 3-D RS terminated, the MV with the minimized SBAD is treated as the representative MV for the reference of other blocks, and no less than two MVs are picked for the computation in the second level while the ceiling is set to the half number of the top level candidates for the balance.

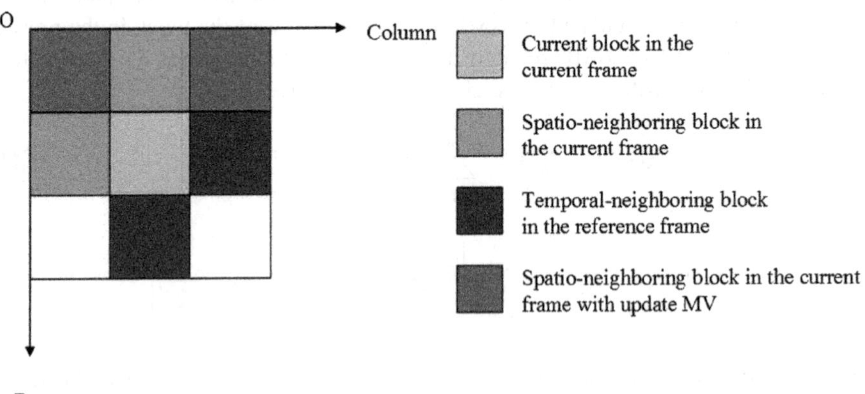

Fig. 4. The position of spatial and temporal blocks. (Color figure online)

2.3 Non-top MVF Refinement

When the referential vector collection is transmitted to the second level, a straightforward BMA chooses the MV with the lower SBAD as the initial MV of the current block. It is necessary to detect the existence of the outliers in the primal MVF, thereby, the MV refinement method is proposed to discover the unreasonable MV and anew calculate the SBAD of neighboring blocks to replace the current MV with the nearby MV. The fast detection criterion is inspired from median filtering [20] as

$$\boldsymbol{v}_m = \arg\min\left\{\sum_{i=1}^{N}\left\|\boldsymbol{v}_i - \boldsymbol{v}_j\right\|_2\right\}, j = 1, 2, \ldots, N, \tag{5}$$

$$\boldsymbol{v}_c = \begin{cases} \boldsymbol{v}_{MS}, & \left\|\boldsymbol{v}_c - \boldsymbol{v}_m\right\|_2 > T \\ \boldsymbol{v}_c, & \left\|\boldsymbol{v}_c - \boldsymbol{v}_m\right\|_2 \leq T \end{cases}, \tag{6}$$

where N is the whole number of the blocks adjoined the current block, $\boldsymbol{v}_i$ and $\boldsymbol{v}_j$ denotes the MVs of these neighboring blocks, $\boldsymbol{v}_m$ denotes the median MV in the contiguous domain of the current block. For the formula (6), the current vector $\boldsymbol{v}_c$ will be substituted by the MV of adjacent blocks with the minimized SBAD, i.e., $\boldsymbol{v}_{MS}$, only in the situation that $\|\boldsymbol{v}_c - \boldsymbol{v}_m\|_2$ exceed threshold T. At each level of the pyramid except top level, the MV refinement will perform and the final MVF will be utilized to interpolate the median frame by using overlapped block motion compensation (OBMC).

3 Experiments

In this section, the result of performance comparison between the proposed algorithm, method 1 [2] and method 2 [3] will be gradually enumerated. The test sequences contain *Mother*, *Foreman*, *City*, *Flower*, *Stefan*, *Mobile*, *Bus*, *Football* and *Soccer*, which are all in CIF format at 30 Hz. 150 odd frames of each video are removed in the experiment and then the quality of the reconstructed frames are evaluated by subjective visual perception and objective value. It is need to explain that the block size at bottom level in our method is set to 16 × 16, the size will be zoomed out by half scale with the elevation of the level. In addition, the experimental platform is MATALB R2014b with Intel Core i7-4900 processor at 3.60 GHz.

To be equitable, we extract the same reconstruction frames to compare, which are the 33rd frame in *City*, the 73rd frame in *Bus* and the 67th frame in *Mobile*. As the Figs. 5, 6 and 7 shown, the subjective visually quality of three group images can be immediately and distinctly caught due to the obviously difference. The buildings in Fig. 5(b) and (c) from *Bus* sequence can be found with the distortion in both compared algorithms, while the proposed method provides more elaborate details with less distortion in Fig. 5(d). What is more, the numbers on the wall calendar in Fig. 6(b) and (c) from *Mobile* are blurring, and the iron handrail in Fig. 7(b) and (c) from *Bus* are apparently malposition, which all generate from the two methods. In contrast, the proposed method offers a clearer reconstruction video sequence in Figs. 6(d) and 7(d) with less mapping error.

Tables 1 and 2 show the objective evaluation from two indicators, which are PSNR and the average processing time of constructing one frame. Compared with two reference methods, it can be found that the proposed algorithm improves the holistic PSNR values of the nine videos ranged from 0.11 to 4.69. Especially, the PSNR of

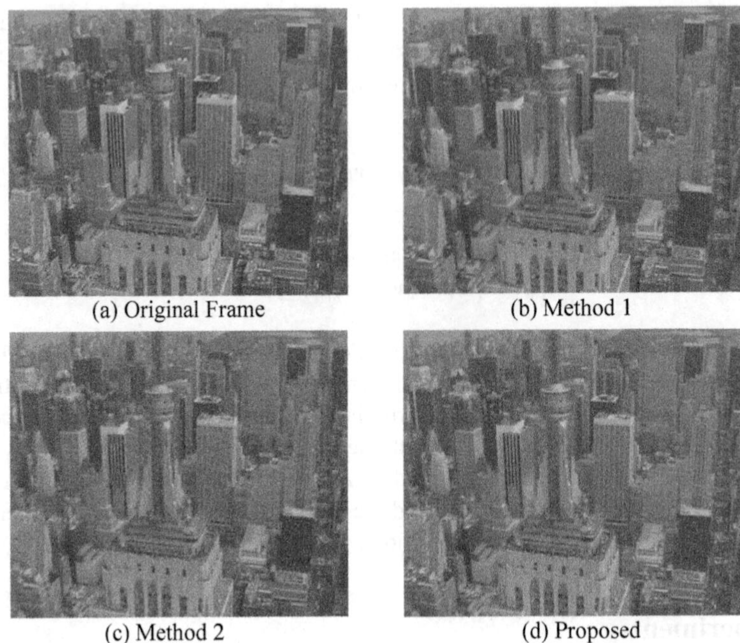

(a) Original Frame (b) Method 1

(c) Method 2 (d) Proposed

Fig. 5. Visual comparison of *City* sequence between the three methods

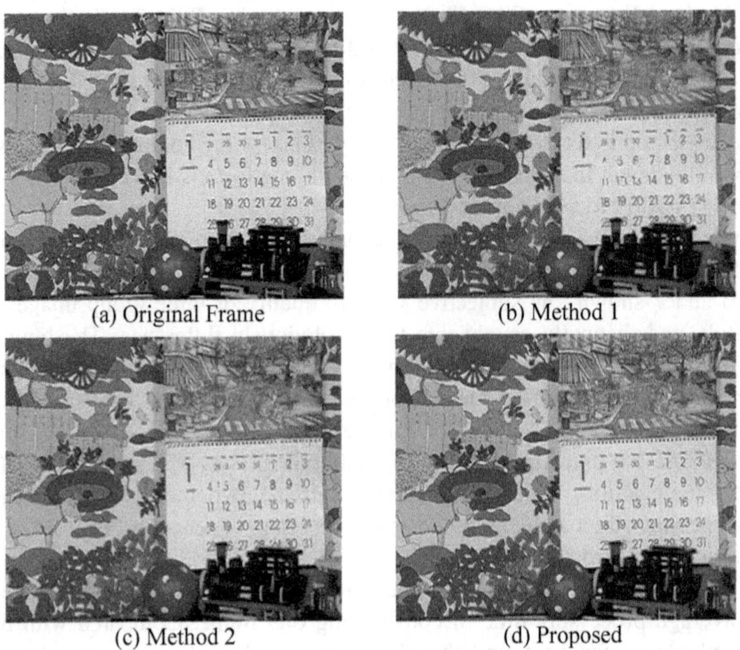

(a) Original Frame (b) Method 1

(c) Method 2 (d) Proposed

Fig. 6. Visual comparison of *Mobile* sequence between the three methods

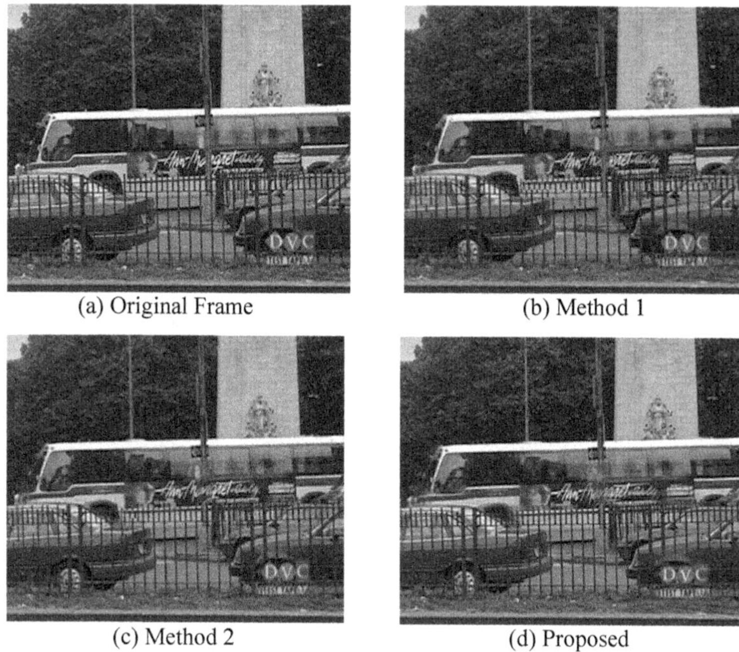

(a) Original Frame (b) Method 1 (c) Method 2 (d) Proposed

Fig. 7. Visual comparison of *Bus* sequence between the three methods

Mobile rises up nearly 20% by using the proposed method, which verifies the advantage of MV prediction based on spatial-temporal information. From Table 2, the proposed method provides a better algorithm structure with low computation complexity than other two methods reflecting in the less time consumption. Through calculation and comparison, the result reveals that the process time of one frame by different method are noticeable different: method 2 spends the most time, method 1 follows and the proposed method outperform them with the low time consumption.

Table 1. Average PSNRs (dB) of test sequences for the proposed and existing ME algorithms.

Sequences	Method 1		Method 2		Proposed
	PSNR (dB)	Δ (dB)	PSNR (dB)	Δ (dB)	PSNR (dB)
Mother	40.81	−1.29	40.92	−1.15	42.07
Foreman	32.37	−2.54	32.29	−2.62	34.91
City	31.94	−2.09	32.64	−1.39	34.03
Flower	28.75	−1.92	29.58	−1.09	30.67
Stefan	27.03	−1.07	27.99	−0.11	28.10
Mobile	25.33	**−4.69**	25.68	**−4.34**	30.02
Bus	25.02	−1.62	25.71	−0.93	26.64
Football	22.78	−0.39	22.79	−0.38	23.17
Soccer	25.96	−2.36	26.26	−2.06	28.32
Average	28.89	−2.00	29.32	−1.56	30.88

Table 2. Average time consumption(s) of test sequences for the proposed and existing ME methods.

Sequences	Method 1		Method 2		Proposed
	S/Frame	Δ (S)	S/Frame	Δ (S)	S/Frame
Mother	0.241	0.110	0.657	0.526	0.131
Foreman	0.329	0.171	0.819	0.661	0.158
City	0.315	0.158	0.787	0.630	0.157
Flower	0.307	0.160	0.762	0.615	0.147
Stefan	0.422	0.268	0.868	0.714	0.154
Mobile	0.304	0.157	0.733	0.586	0.147
Bus	0.358	0.199	0.817	0.658	0.159
Football	0.547	0.273	0.868	0.694	0.174
Soccer	0.318	0.159	0.843	0.684	0.159
Average	0.349	0.184	0.795	0.641	0.154

4 Conclusions

In this paper, we proposed a spatial and temporal algorithm with multi-resolution and level-by-level MV refinement. The algorithm mixes the SUAD and SBAD for matching a more exact MV, and the MV refinement part can detect the incorrect MVs and replace them with a better one, which guarantees the validity of the MV. The experiments also testify the properties of low computation and high reconstruction quality by utilizing the proposed method when compared with two existing methods.

Acknowledgments. This work was supported in part by the National Natural Science Foundation of China, under Grants no. 61501393, in part by the Key Scientific Research Project of Colleges and Universities in Henan Province of China, under Grant 16A520069, and in part by Youth Sustentation Fund of Xinyang Normal University, under Grant no. 2015-QN-043, and in part by Scientific Research Foundation of Graduate School of Xinyang Normal University, under Grant no. 2016KYJJ10.

References

1. Huang, Y.L., Chen, F.C., Chien, S.Y.: Algorithm and architecture design of multi-rate frame rate up-conversion for ultra-HD LCD systems. IEEE Trans. Circ. Syst. Video Technol. (2016)
2. Kang, S.J., Yoo, S., Kim, Y.H.: Dual motion estimation for frame rate up-conversion. IEEE Trans. Circ. Syst. Video Technol. **20**(12), 1909–1914 (2010)
3. Yoo, D.G., Kang, S.J., Kim, Y.H.: Direction-select motion estimation for motion-compensated frame rate up-conversion. J. Disp. Technol. **9**(10), 840–850 (2013)
4. Pan, Z., Lei, J., Zhang, Y., Sun, X., Kwong, S.: Fast motion estimation based on content property for low-complexity H.265/HEVC encoder. IEEE Trans. Broadcast. **62**(3), 675–684 (2016)
5. Pan, Z., Zhang, Y., Kwong, S.: Efficient motion and disparity estimation optimization for low complexity multiview video coding. IEEE Trans. Broadcast. **61**(2), 166–176 (2015)

6. Guo, D., Shao, L., Han, J.: Feature-based motion compensated interpolation for frame rate up-conversion. Neurocomputing **123**, 390–397 (2014)
7. Choi, B.T., Lee, S.H., Ko, S.J.: New frame rate up-conversion using bi-directional motion estimation. IEEE Trans. Consum. Electron. **46**(3), 603–609 (2000)
8. Pan, Z., Jin, P., Lei, J., Zhang, Y., Sun, X., Kwong, S.: Fast reference frame selection based on content similarity for low complexity HEVC encoder. J. Vis. Commun. Image Represent. **40**(Part B), 516–524 (2016)
9. Jiefu, Z., Keman, Y., Jiang, L., et al.: A low complexity motion compensated frame interpolation method. In: International Symposium on Circuits and Systems 2005, pp. 4927–4930. IEEE Press, Kobe, Japan (2005)
10. Heinrich, A., Bartels, C., van der Vleuten, R.J., et al.: Optimization of hierarchical 3DRS motion estimators for picture rate conversion. Sig. Process. **5**(2), 262–274 (2011)
11. Tsai, T.H., Shi, A.T., Huang, K.T.: Accurate frame rate up-conversion for advanced visual quality. IEEE Trans. Broadcast. **62**(2), 426–435 (2016)
12. De Haan, G., Biezen, P.W.A.C., Huijgen, H., et al.: True-motion estimation with 3-D recursive search block matching. IEEE Trans. Circ. Syst. Video Technol. **3**(5), 368–379, 388 (1993)
13. Dar, Y., Bruckstein, A.M.: Motion-compensated coding and frame rate up-conversion: models and analysis. IEEE Trans. Image Process. **24**(7), 2051–2066 (2014)
14. Vinh, T.Q., Kim, Y.C., Hong, S.H.: Frame rate up-conversion using forward-backward jointing motion estimation and spatio-temporal motion vector smoothing. In: International Conference on Computer Engineering and Systems, pp. 605–609. IEEE Press, Cairo, Egypt (2009)
15. Kim, D.Y., Park, H.: An efficient motion-compensated frame interpolation method using temporal information for high-resolution videos. J. Disp. Technol. **11**(7), 580–588 (2015)
16. Zhao, Y., Sun, G., Liu, J., et al.: An improved FRUC scheme based on motion vector refinement. In: International Conference on Signal Processing, pp. 981–986. IEEE Press, Hangzhou, China (2015)
17. Lee, H.S., Kang, S.J., Kim, Y.H.: Motion vector smoothing of boundary of moving object for frame rate up-conversion. In: International SoC Design Conference, pp. 41–42. IEEE Press, Jeju, Korea (2016)
18. Yang, X., Liu, J., Feng, Z., et al.: Frame rate up-conversion based on depth guided extended block matching for 3D video. In: Visual Communication and Image Processing. IEEE Press, Chengdu, China (2016)
19. Guo, Y., Chen, L., Gao, Z., et al.: Frame rate up-conversion using linear quadratic motion estimation and trilateral filtering, motion smoothing. J. Disp. Technol. **12**(1), 1 (2015)
20. Astola, J., Haavisto, P., Neuvo, Y.: Vector median filters. Proc. IEEE **78**(4), 678–689 (1990)

A Robust Seam Carving Forgery Detection Approach by Three-Element Joint Density of Difference Matrix

Wenwu Gu, Gaobo Yang(✉), Dengyong Zhang, and Ming Xia

School of Information Science and Engineering,
Hunan University, Changsha 410082, China
yanggaobo@hnu.edu.cn

Abstract. Seam carving is a popular content-aware image retargeting technique. However, it can also be used for malicious purposes such as object removal. In this paper, a robust blind forensics approach is proposed for seam-carved forgery detection. Since insignificant pixels along seams are removed for image resizing, the spatial neighborhood relations among pixels will be significantly changed, especially in smooth regions. Thus, joint density is exploited to model the change of spatially adjacent pixels' distribution caused by seam carving, even in the case of low scaling ratios. Specifically, three-element joint density of difference matrix is computed to form general forensics features (GTJD). The GTJD features are combined with existing energy and noise features exacted in LBP domain for classification. Experimental results show that the proposed approach achieves better accuracies for both uncompressed images and JPEG images with different scaling ratios.

Keywords: Blind image forensic · Content-aware image retargeting · Seam carving · Difference matrix · Three-element joint density

1 Introduction

With the proliferation of image editing software, it is becoming much easier than ever for ordinary users to produce faked images without leaving any annoying artifacts. Since original images are usually unavailable in practical forensics cases, passive image forensics is becoming one of the hottest topics in the research field of image information security. Many researchers have done related research in specific field, such as image copy-move forgery detection [1] and image splicing forgery detection [2]. Seam carving is a popular content-aware image resizing technique, which can adapt image display on diverse devices or improve image quality for aesthetic purpose [3]. However, it can also be used for malicious purposes. First, it might be used to correct the composition of a photo, which is a cheating if the resultant image is used for photo competition. Second, it can also be deliberately used to remove an object from an image, which usually changes

X. Sun et al. (Eds.): ICCCS 2017, Part II, LNCS 10603, pp. 418–432, 2017.
https://doi.org/10.1007/978-3-319-68542-7_35

image semantics that an image conveys. Therefore, it is worthy of investigation to design a blind detector capable of exposing resized images by seam carving.

Until now, there exist a few blind detection approaches for seam carving, which can be divided into two categories. The first category is suitable for uncompressed images. Fillion and Sharma [4] made the first attempt to detect seam-carved images, which exploits a set of intuitively motivated features including energy bias and the dispersal of seam behavior. Wei et al. [5] proposed a patch analysis method for seam carving forgery detection. The patch transition probability among three-connected mini-squares is exploited to improve detection accuracy. Ryu et al. [6] also proposed a forensic analysis approach by exploiting energy bias and noise level to expose seam carving. In our recent work [7], an improved detection approach is proposed on the basis of Ryu's work [6], which introduces local binary pattern (LBP) to highlight local texture artifacts caused by seam carving. In the work [8], the author proposed a local derivative pattern (LDP) based forensic framework to detect seam-carved images, which also obtains good detection results. The other category is suitable for seam carved JPEG images. Inspired by the similarity between image steganalysis and forgery detection, Sarkar et al. [9] proposed a forgery detection approach for seam carved JPEG images by exploiting 324-dimensional Markov features. Liu and Chen [10] also proposed an improved approach with calibrated neighboring joint density to steganalysis and seam-carved forgery detection in JPEG Images. Recently, Chang et al. [11] proposed a blind approach by exploiting blocking artifact characteristics matrix (BACM) to detect JPEG image forgery due to seam modifications. The idea behind it is that the original JPEG image has a regular symmetrical data, whereas the symmetrical data is destroyed in a block reconstructed by seam modification.

However, most existing seam carving forgery detection approaches are only effective for either JPEG images or uncompressed images. Moreover, they are still far from satisfaction for seam carved images with low scaling ratios. To further improve the accuracy and robustness of seam carving forgery detection with low scaling ratios, the inherent nature of seam carving should be fully exploited. Since seam carving inevitably changes the neighboring relations of pixels near a deleted seam, we are motivated to use joint density to model the differences between adjacent pixels. However, the differences of neighboring pixels are usually small since seams are firstly removed from smooth region with low energies, especially in the case of low scaling ratio. It is a key issue to expose the pixel-pair with small difference for seam carving forensics. Instead of the conventional two-element joint density, a new terminology of three-element joint density is introduced to model the probability of pixel differences either horizontally or vertically. The idea behind this is that three-element joint density has stronger description capability. It will be easier to capture the changes of pixels' neighborhood relations in smooth regions. Please note that the differences between adjacent pixels do not seriously depend on original pixel values [12], which exhibit similar distributions of natural images. That is, the three-element joint density of pixel differences can effectively capture the natural properties of original images, which is a favorable factor to improve detection accuracy. Moreover, this also applies to the neighboring DCT-coefficients of JPEG images. In this paper, the GTJD features are combined with existing energy and noise features exacted in LBP domain for classification. Experimental results show that the proposed approach achieves better accuracies for both uncompressed images and JPEG images with different scaling ratios.

The rest of this paper is organized as follows: Sect. 2 briefly introduces seam carving, and analyzes the possible traces for seam carving forgery detection. Section 3 presents the proposed approach. Experimental results and analysis are provided in Sect. 4, and we conclude this paper in Sect. 5.

2 Preliminaries of Image Seam Carving

Seam carving is originally proposed as a content-aware image retargeting (CAIR) technique [3]. A seam is defined as an 8-connected path of low energy pixels crossing the image from top to bottom, or from left to right. For an image of size $n \times m$, the vertical seam is defined as Eq. (1), where i and col(i) are the row and column coordinate, respectively. A horizontal seam is also defined similarity.

$$s^v = \{i, col\,(i)\}_{i=1}^{n}, s.t.\forall i, |col(i) - col(i-1)| \leq 1 \tag{1}$$

Let I be the intensity of candidate image. The energy function of each pixel is defined as Eq. (1), where G_x, G_y are the Sobel operators. Thus, the energy function of a seam is defined as Eq. (3).

$$e(I) = \left|\frac{\partial}{\partial x} I\right| + \left|\frac{\partial}{\partial y} I\right| = |G_x| + |G_y| \tag{2}$$

$$E(s) = \sum\nolimits_{i=1}^{n} e(i, col(i)), s.t.\forall i, |col(i) - col(i-1)| \leq 1 \tag{3}$$

To find a seam with the lowest energy $s^* = \min E(s)$, a cumulative minimum energy matrix M is defined as Eq. (4). After obtaining the M, the lowest energy seam s^* is found by back-tracking from the minimum value of the last row in M.

$$M(i,j) = e(i,j) + \min(M(i-1, j-1), M(i-1, j), M(i-1, j+1)) \tag{4}$$

By successively deleting seams with low energies, seam carving preserves well the region of interest. Please note that the effects of seam removal are local. Let a vertical seam be an example. Though all the pixels at the right side of this seam are shifted left to fill in the missing path, the possible visual artifacts merely occur near the removed seam. That is, the rest image keeps intact [7]. Figure 1 is an example of image seam carving. Figure 1(a) is an original image with two parrots in it. Figure 1(b) and (c) are the original image with 3% seams to be carved and the resultant image after seam carving, respectively. Apparently, seams mainly pass through the background region of smooth texture, and there is no visually annoying geometric artifact in the seam carved image. However,

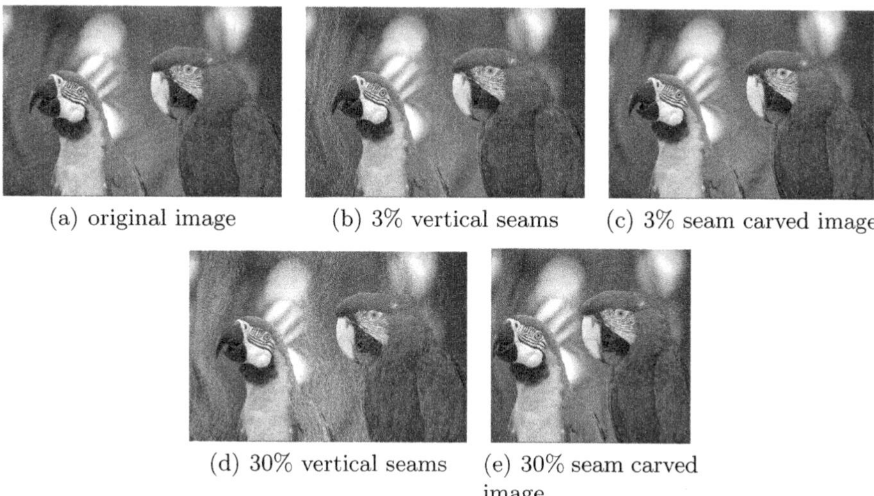

(a) original image (b) 3% vertical seams (c) 3% seam carved image (d) 30% vertical seams (e) 30% seam carved image

Fig. 1. Image seam carving with scaling ratios of 3% and 30% (Color figure online)

when the scaling ratio is up to 30%, seams pass through not only the background region of smooth texture, but also the region of interest (the red parrot) as shown in Fig. 1(d). Moreover, there are also some geometric distortions near the red parrot, as shown in Fig. 1(e). From this example, we are motivated to exploit two traces so as to expose seam carving. One is the statistical distribution of adjacent pixels in smooth region, which will be significantly changed when a nature image is suffered form seam carving. The other one is the local texture change or even possible geometric deformation, especially when the scaling ratio is high for seam carving.

3 Proposed Blind Forensics Approach for Seam Carving

As claimed in the previous section, the change of neighboring relations among those pixels in smooth region is a useful clue to detect seam carving, especially when the scaling ratio is low. Three-element joint density of differences between adjacent pixels is exploited to model this kind of change. In our earlier work [7], local texture variation caused by seam carving is effectively measured in LBP domain, and eighteen energy bias features are defined to achieve desirable detection performance. In this paper, the existing eighteen energy bias features extracted in LBP domain are combined with the proposed GTJD features, so as to enhance the robustness of seam-carved forgery detection for both high and low scaling ratios. Figure 2 is the framework of the proposed approach. First, pre-processing is conducted to consider the seam carved images in either uncompressed or JPEG format. For uncompressed images, pixel intensities are directly computed for analysis. For JPEG images, the quantized DCT-coefficients are extracted for analysis. Second, the image intensities or the quantized DCT-coefficients are sent to difference filter to obtain difference matrix in both horizontal and vertical direction. Third, the three-element joint density is computed from the difference matrix as forensics features (GTJD). Finally, the GTJD features are combined with energy bias features and input into SVM for training and testing.

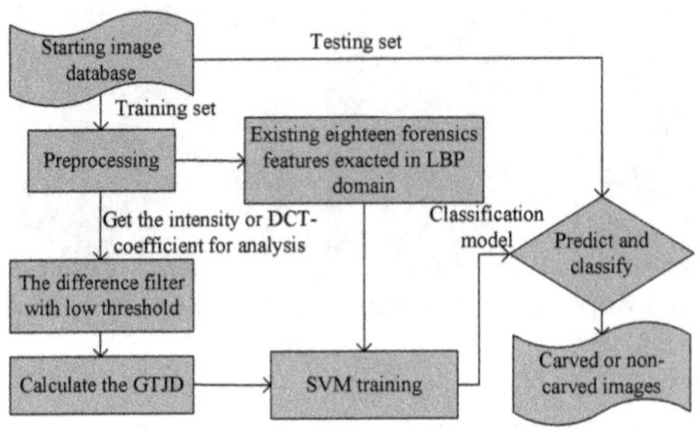

Fig. 2. Framework of the proposed seam carving forgery detection approach

3.1 Difference Matrix

Let I be the intensity of an uncompressed image of size $M \times N$. The difference filter is defined in Eqs. (5) and (6) for horizontal and vertical direction, respectively. If the candidate image is compressed in JPEG, the quantized DCT-coefficients are exploited as the image intensity, and the difference matrix in DCT-domain can be obtained similarly.

$$D^h(i,j) = I(i,j) - I(i,j+1) \tag{5}$$

$$D^v(i,j) = I(i,j) - I(i+1,j) \tag{6}$$

where $i \in \{1,2,\cdots,M\}, j \in \{1,2,\cdots,N-1\}$ in Eq. (5), and $i \in \{1,2,\cdots,M-1\}, j \in \{1,2,\cdots,N\}$ in Eq. (6). Thus, D^h and D^v is the difference matrix of size $M \times (N-1)$ and $(M-1) \times N$ in horizontal and vertical direction, respectively.

Figure 3 is the probability distribution of horizontal difference matrices before and after seam carving. The horizontal axis is the difference value between adjacent pixels in horizontal direction, and the vertical axis represents the probability of difference values. In untouched image, pixel-pairs in smooth area have small difference near zero. Seams are firstly removed from smooth region with low energies, so there is significant change of probability near the difference value of zero in the seam carved image, which is shown in Fig. 3. Specifically, with the increase of scaling ratio, the peak of probability distribution becomes less steep. This motivates us to exploit it as a possible clue to expose seam carving, especially in the cases of low scaling ratios. A threshold T is introduced to highlight the pixel-pairs with small difference. Equation (7) is the difference matrix after thresholding in horizontal direction, which is donated as LD^h. The difference matrix LD^v in vertical direction can also be processed in similar manner.

$$LD^h(i,j) = \begin{cases} -\mathrm{T}, \text{ if } D^h(i,j) \leq -\mathrm{T} \\ \mathrm{T}, \text{ if } D^h(i,j) \geq \mathrm{T} \\ D^h(i,j), \text{ otherwize} \end{cases} \tag{7}$$

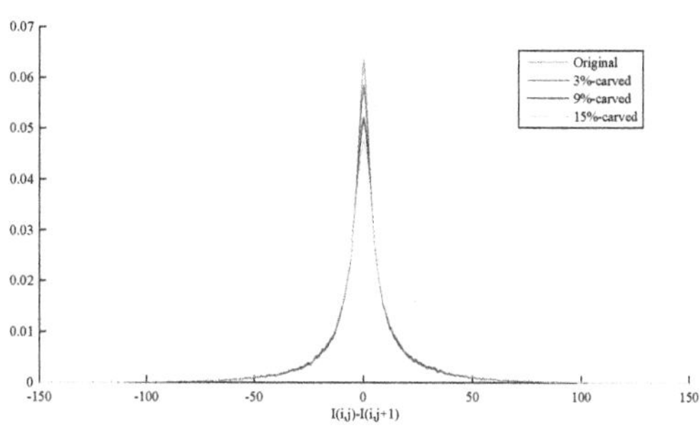

(a) probability distribution of difference matrices

Fig. 3. Probability distribution change of horizontal difference matrices

3.2 Three-Element Joint Density of Difference Matrix

Since neighboring pixels of natural image have strong correlation, the three-element joint density of the differences between adjacent pixels is capable of catching the correlation of neighboring pixels, which might exhibit abnormality for seam carved image. Compared with higher-order pixel-domain descriptor such as co-occurrence matrix, the three-element joint density of difference matrix has many advantages. First, it is independent of image content, which is an important issue for forensics accuracy. Second, the dimension of forensics feature is greatly reduced. Third, it can highlight the statistical changes in smooth regions by selecting appropriate T, which is very important for the detection of seam carving with low scaling ratios.

The three-element joint density of difference matrix is computed in both horizontal and vertical direction, which is denoted as TJD^h and TJD^v in Eqs. (8) and (9), respectively. For an image of size $M \times N$, there are $M \times (N-3)$ overlapping blocks of size 1×3 in horizontal difference matrix to compute TJD^h. Similarly, there exist $(M-3) \times N$ overlapping blocks of size 3×1 in vertical difference matrix to compute TJD^v.

$$TJD^h(x,y,z) = \frac{\sum_{i=1}^{M}\sum_{j=1}^{N-3}\delta(LD^h(i,j)=x, LD^h(i,j+1)=y, LD^h(i,j+2)=z)}{M \times (N-3)} \tag{8}$$

$$TJD^v(x,y,z) = \frac{\sum_{i=1}^{M-3}\sum_{j=1}^{N}\delta(LD^v(i,j)=x, LD^v(i+1,j)=y, LD^v(i+2,j)=z)}{(M-3) \times N} \tag{9}$$

where $x, y, z \in \{-T, -T+1, \cdots, -1, 0, 1, \cdots, T-1, T\}$. And δ is an impulse function, and it equals 1 if its arguments are satisfied, otherwise $\delta = 0$. Then, $TJD^h(x, y, z)$ and $TJD^v(x, y, z)$ are integrated in Eq. (10), which is denoted as GTJD. The dimension of our proposed GTJD feature is $(2 \times \mathrm{T} + 1)^3$. Please note that T is actually a threshold to compromise between feature dimension and detection accuracy.

$$GTJD(x, y, z) = \frac{TJD^h(x, y, z) + TJD^v(x, y, z)}{2} \tag{10}$$

Figure 4 shows the change of three-element joint distribution when a seam is removed from image. For simplicity, an original block of size 4×9 is selected. The pixels along a vertical seam to be removed are marked in blue and their left neighboring pixels are marked in yellow. After removing a seam, the original block is turned into a new block of size 4×8. It is apparent that the right neighboring pixels to those pixel marked in yellow are changed. From the computed three-element joint density of difference matrix, it is sensitive to the change of neighboring pixels in seam carved image.

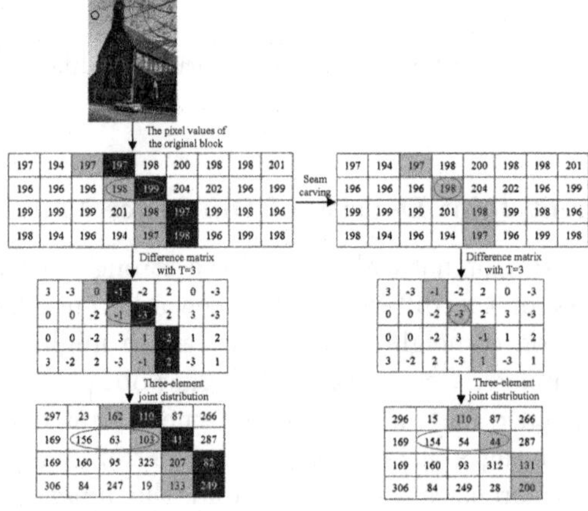

Fig. 4. An example of the change of three-element joint distribution when a seam is removed (Color figure online)

3.3 Existing LBP-Domain Features

LBP is an excellent local texture descriptor for image analysis. It has been verified in our earlier work [7] that the eighteen features extracted in LBP domain are effective for the detection of image seam carving with high scaling ratio. To improve the detection robustness, they are also exploited by the proposed approach to be combined with the GTJD features. Please note that six half-seam features in [7] are not included. Though the half-seam based features are beneficial to the detection of seam carving with low scaling ratios, its contribution is not very prominent. To prove the effectiveness of the proposed GTJD features for seam carving detection with low scaling ratio, the half-seam based features are not included here.

4 Experiment Results and Analysis

4.1 Experiment Setup

To evaluate the detection performance of the proposed approach, a series of experiments have been done for comparisons. The LibSVM [13] with Radial Basis Function (RBF) kernel is used as a classifier, and Python and Gnuplot are exploited for the parameter optimization of SVM. Moreover, $T = 3$ is selected as the threshold to achieve a balance between feature dimension and detection accuracy. This implies that the GTJD features have $(2 \times 3 + 1)^3 = 343$ dimensions, and the final features (343 - GTJD + 18 - LBP) are 361 dimensions. Three state-of-the-art works including energy-based detector [6], LBP-based detector [7] and BACM-based detector [11] are chosen as benchmarks for comparisons. All detectors are running on the same hardware and software environments. In addition, to make fair comparison of experimental results, experimental datasets are divided into two categories: uncompressed images and JPEG images. The uncompressed image database is the same as work [7], and the JPEG image database is same as work [11]. The UCID [14] and the UCUS are used as starting image databases, and the experimental datasets are summarized in Table 1. Please note that the uncompressed image database contains seam carved images of both low scaling ratios and high scaling ratios. To ensure the randomness of the experimental samples, a widely accepted 5-fold cross validation strategy is adopted in the SVM classifier.

4.2 Tamper Detection for Uncompressed Images with High Scaling Ratios

Uncompressed images with four scaling ratios, including 20%, 30%, 40% and 50%, are tested. In each group of experiments, there are 1338 uncompressed images and 1338 seamed carved images with the same scaling ratio. For the 5-fold cross validation strategy, 2676 mixed images are equally divided into five parts. That is, four parts are sent to SVM for training and the remaining part is used for testing. The experimental results are reported in Table 2. Apparently, the proposed detector achieves the best detection accuracy, even though all detectors can achieve desirable detection accuracy. On average, the detection accuracy of our proposed method is about 21.23%, 11.39% and 1.68% higher than BACM-based detector [11], energy-based detector [6], LBP-based detector [7], respectively. The BACM-based detector exploits the symmetric property of blocking artifacts of JPEG compression, which makes it not effective to detect seam carving for uncompressed images.

Table 1. Summary of experiment image database

Experiment image database	Starting image database	Processing	Number of result images
Uncompressed image database	UCID(1338)	High scaling ratios: the UCID images are resized by seam carving with scaling ratios of 20%, 30%, 40% and 50%	$1338 \times (1+4) = 6690$
		Low scaling ratios: the UCID images are resized by seam carving with scaling ratios of 3%, 6%, 9%, 12%, 15%, 18%	$1338 \times (1+6) = 9366$
JPEG image database for seam carving	UCID(1338) and UCUS(1009)	(1) The UCID database is encoded into JPEG images with QF of 75, which are combined with the UCUS database to form original JPEG database with 2347 JPEG images; (2) 2347 JPEG images are decompressed and resized with different scaling ratios of 1%, 2%, 5%, 10%, 20%, 30%, 50%; (3) Seam carved images are recompressed into JPEG images with quality factors of 10, 20, 50, 75 and 100, respectively	$(1338+1009) \times (1+5\times 7) = 84492$
JPEG image database for seam insertion	UCID(1338) and UCUS(1009)	Similar to the second test image set, but images are enlarged by inserting seams, instead of deleting seams in the process of seam carving	$(1338+1009) \times (1+5\times 7) = 84492$

Table 2. Tamper detection results for uncompressed images with high scaling ratios

Scaling ratios	Accuracy (%)				
	BACM-based detector [11]	Energy-based detector [6]	LBP-based detector [7]	GTJD-based detector	Proposed method (GTJD+LBP)
20%	64.94	76.46	92.83	94.54	**97.65**
30%	75.64	85.76	98.24	97.38	**99.51**
40%	81.61	92.45	99.36	98.47	**99.93**
50%	89.91	96.82	99.88	98.95	**99.96**
Average	78.03	87.87	97.58	97.34	**99.26**

4.3 Tamper Detection for Uncompressed Images with Low Scaling Ratios

For low scaling ratios, we choose scaling ratios from 3% to 18% with a step size of 3% for experiments. From Table 3, our proposed method achieves an accuracy of 85.71% on average, which is about 20.85%, 10.22% higher than the energy-based detector [6] and the LBP-based detector [7]. Moreover, we can observe that

Table 3. Tamper detection results for uncompressed images with low scaling ratios

Scaling ratios	Accuracy (%)			
	Energy-based detector [6]	LBP-based detector [7]	GTJD-based detector	Proposed method (GTJD+LBP)
3%	55.16	55.68	61.57	**63.53**
6%	59.27	65.66	76.31	**80.01**
9%	62.67	75.90	83.89	**88.64**
12%	65.02	78.44	85.13	**89.61**
15%	72.27	86.88	91.44	**95.33**
18%	74.78	90.35	93.31	**97.12**
Average	64.86	75.49	81.94	**85.71**

the proposed GTJD-based features achieves better detection accuracies than the LBP-based features about 6%, even though they are effective for seam carving forgery detection.

Figure 5 compares the ROC curves among the three detectors, in which the horizontal axis represents false positive rate (FPR) and the vertical axis represents true positive rate (TPR). FPR and TPR are calculated as the percentage of falsely classified original images and the percentage of correctly classified carved images, respectively. The closer is the curve to the upper left part, the better is

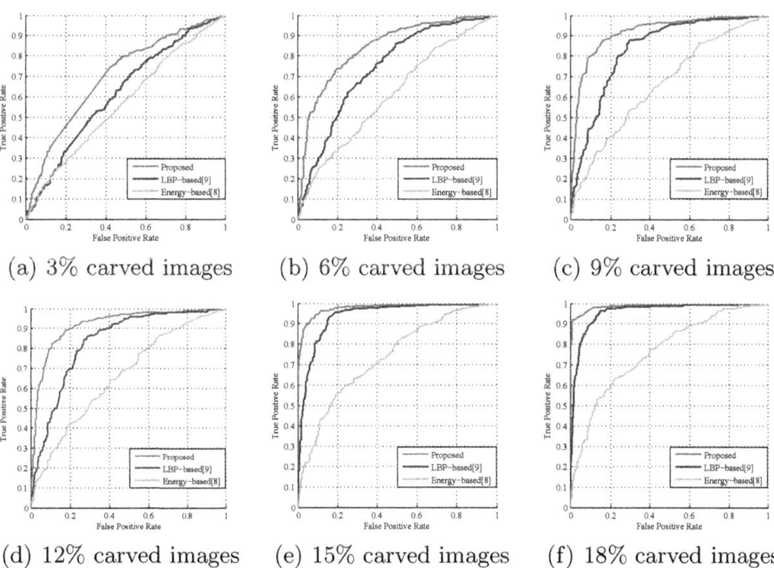

(a) 3% carved images (b) 6% carved images (c) 9% carved images

(d) 12% carved images (e) 15% carved images (f) 18% carved images

Fig. 5. ROC curves of three different detection methods

the classification effect. From Fig. 5, it is also apparent that the proposed approach achieves better detection performance than the LBP-based method [7] and the energy-based method [6]. That is, the proposed approach is more effective for seam carving forgery detection with low scaling ratio.

To prove the robustness of the proposed approach, the resized images with both high and low scaling ratios are mixed for performance evaluation. For the mixed image set, 268 images are randomly selected from the resized images after seam carving with each scaling ratio including 3%, 6%, 9%, 12%, 15%, 18% and 20%, 30%, 40%, 50%. They are combined with 1338 original images to build a test image set of 4018 images. The detection results are reported in Table 4. It is apparent that our proposed approach outperforms the energy-based detector [6] and the LBP-based detector [7] about 15.08% and 7.86%, respectively.

Table 4. Tamper detection results for uncompressed images with mixed scaling ratios

Scaling ratios	Accuracy (%)		
	Energy-based detector [6]	LBP-based detector [7]	Proposed method
Mixed scaling ratios	72.82	80.04	**87.90**

4.4 Seam Carving Detection for JPEG Images with Different Scaling Ratios

An doctored image after seam carving may further suffer from JPEG compression. To prove the robustness of our proposed approach, the JPEG image database after seam carving, which is summarized in Table 1 is also tested. The BACM-based detector [11], which is the state-of-the art work specially designed for the detection of seam carved JPEG images, is chosen as benchmark for comparisons. The experimental results are shown in Table 5. For each scaling ratio, the best detection accuracy is highlighted in bold. For different quality factors (QFs) of JPEG compression including 10, 20, 50 and 100, the proposed approach achieves steady detection accuracies. For seam carved images with JPEG compression of QF75, which are most difficult to be detected, our proposed approach also achieves average detection accuracies of 86.65% and 88.38% for the UCID database and the UCUS database, respectively. Moreover, the proposed approach outperforms the BACM-based detector.

Seam carving can also be used for image enlargement by inserting seams. The proposed method is also tested to verify the effectiveness of detecting seam insertion. The JPEG image database summarized in Table 1 is used for testing, and the BACM-based detector [11] is also chosen as a benchmark. From Table 6, it can be seen that the proposed method achieves better detection accuracy than the BACM-based detector in most cases. There is only one exception for those enlarged images with 1% seam insertion and JPEG compression of QF75. Even

Table 5. Seam carving detection results (%) for JPEG images with different scaling ratios

Scaling factor	(a) BACM-based detector [11] (UCID)					(b) BACM-based detector [11] (UCUS)				
	QF10	QF20	QF50	QF75	QF100	QF10	QF20	QF50	Q75	QF100
1%	98.47	95.67	87.22	71.94	91.41	98.71	97.32	89.35	74.48	94.25
2%	98.28	95.66	84.72	66.26	92.45	98.81	96.70	88.21	68.24	96.38
5%	98.24	94.81	83.74	69.32	95.96	98.61	96.18	84.89	70.17	97.77
10%	97.65	94.36	83.18	79.30	97.61	98.91	95.69	84.69	82.16	99.16
20%	97.46	90.88	79.41	85.50	98.99	98.36	94.45	81.86	86.52	99.45
30%	96.64	87.41	84.27	92.49	99.36	97.77	91.33	86.57	93.41	99.95
50%	96.19	96.75	98.58	99.25	99.70	98.06	96.73	98.61	99.31	**100**
Scaling factor	(c) Our proposed detector (UCID)					(d) Our proposed detector (UCUS)				
	QF10	QF20	QF50	QF75	QF100	QF10	QF20	QF50	Q75	QF100
1%	**99.96**	**99.96**	**99.22**	**73.58**	**100**	**99.95**	**99.85**	**99.45**	**78.10**	**100**
2%	**99.96**	**100**	**99.25**	**77.09**	**100**	**99.95**	**99.85**	**99.45**	**80.23**	**100**
5%	**99.96**	**99.96**	**99.03**	**81.50**	**100**	**99.95**	**99.85**	**99.60**	**83.15**	**100**
10%	**99.96**	**100**	**99.25**	**85.24**	**100**	**99.95**	**99.85**	**99.41**	**86.87**	**100**
20%	**99.96**	**100**	**99.51**	**92.75**	**100**	**99.95**	**99.80**	**99.65**	**93.01**	**100**
30%	**99.96**	**100**	**99.58**	**96.71**	**100**	**99.95**	**99.80**	**99.80**	**97.37**	**100**
50%	**99.96**	**100**	**99.96**	**99.66**	**100**	**99.95**	**99.85**	**99.85**	**97.90**	**100**

in this case, our detection accuracy is very close to that of the BACM-based detector. For QFs of 10, 20, 50 and 100, our proposed approach achieves steady detection accuracies, which are more than 98%. For QF of 75, our proposed method achieves detection accuracy of 86.69% and 88.99% on average for the UCID and UCUS databases, respectively.

4.5 Discussion

In this paper, seam carving forgery detection is achieved by the proposed GTJD features and the LBP-based features in our earlier work. That is, the proposed approach considers the change of neighborhood pixels, global energy distribution and local texture distortion. This leads to superior detection accuracy over the existing approaches for both uncompressed images and JPEG images. For seam carving with low scaling ratios, the proposed approach improves detection accuracy about 10.22% on average compared with the LBP-based detector. Because the proposed GTJD features mainly consider the change of difference values between adjacent pixels, which are more sensitive to the slight change of pixel neighborhood relations caused by seam carving with low scaling ratio. For seam carving detection of JPEG image, the doctored images re-compressed with different quality factors will further change the difference between adjacent DCT-coefficients.

Table 6. Seam insertion detection results (%) for JPEG images with different scaling ratios

Scaling factor	(a) BACM-based detector [11] (UCID)					(b) BACM-based detector [11] (UCUS)				
	QF10	QF20	QF50	QF75	QF100	QF10	QF20	QF50	Q75	QF100
1%	98.06	95.29	86.92	**73.36**	87.78	98.66	96.48	88.55	**76.51**	91.38
2%	97.68	94.66	86.62	67.34	89.28	98.41	96.63	90.34	72.40	92.96
5%	98.09	95.74	88.79	70.22	92.38	98.61	97.03	89.89	72.99	95.69
10%	98.28	96.19	90.88	76.35	95.70	99.01	97.67	93.46	80.43	97.42
20%	98.21	97.12	94.47	84.01	98.32	98.86	98.46	95.59	86.82	99.06
30%	98.65	97.42	96.56	90.10	99.07	99.41	98.76	97.32	92.52	99.70
50%	98.95	98.39	98.21	94.88	99.29	99.36	99.16	98.61	97.32	99.90
Scaling factor	(c) Our proposed detector (UCID)					(d) Our proposed detector (UCUS)				
	QF10	QF20	QF50	QF75	QF100	QF10	QF20	QF50	Q75	QF100
1%	**99.96**	**99.96**	**98.99**	73.06	**100**	**99.95**	**99.80**	**98.81**	76.07	**100**
2%	**99.96**	**99.96**	**99.33**	**76.49**	**100**	**99.90**	**99.80**	**98.85**	**81.07**	**100**
5%	**99.96**	**100**	**99.10**	**83.18**	**100**	**99.95**	**99.80**	**99.01**	**86.47**	**100**
10%	**99.96**	**99.96**	**99.18**	**86.88**	**100**	**99.95**	**99.80**	**98.96**	**89.45**	**100**
20%	**99.96**	**100**	**99.47**	**92.94**	**100**	**99.95**	**99.80**	**99.21**	**94.15**	**100**
30%	**99.96**	**100**	**99.66**	**96.19**	**100**	**99.95**	**99.85**	**99.60**	**97.13**	**100**
50%	**99.96**	**100**	**99.74**	**98.06**	**100**	**99.95**	**99.85**	**99.80**	**98.61**	**100**

For uncompressed images with low scaling ratios(3%–18%), we also compare average detection results by two-element and three-element joint density with different thresholds, which are summarized in Table 7. From the first three columns, we can observe that the average detection accuracy of three-element joint density with $T = 3$ improves about 22.03% compared with two-element joint density. That is, three-element joint density is more effective to detect seam carving than two-element joint density, since it provides stronger description capability. From the last two columns, we know that T is actually a threshold to compromise between feature dimension and detection accuracy. The average detection accuracy of $T = 4$ is 1.92% higher than that of $T = 3$. We finally choose $T = 3$ as the threshold in this paper, because it has much less feature dimensions.

Table 7. Average detection results (%) of two-element and three-element joint density with different thresholds

Two-element joint density (T = 3)	Two-element joint density (T = 4)	Three-element joint density (T = 3)	Proposed approach (T = 3)	Proposed approach (T = 4)
59.91	62.33	81.94	85.71	87.63

5 Conclusions and Future Work

Seam carving is an excellent content-aware image retargeting technique. It usually does not leave any visible distortions, especially when the scaling ratios are low. Even seams to be deleted always goes through relatively smooth regions, it still changes the spatial relations among the pixels near the seam. In this paper, three-element joint density of difference matrix is exploited to detect seam carving. The proposed GTJD features can achieve desirable detection accuracies for both uncompressed images and JPEG images after seam carving. Particularly, the proposed GTJD features are combined with existing LBP-based features to significantly improve the robustness of detection performance for seam carving with either high or low scaling ratios. However, the detection result is only a binary decision about whether an image has been seam carved or not. For future research, we will investigate tampering location. A possible solution is to borrowing idea from image steganalysis by LSB matching [15,16], which is claimed to be effective to model the differences between nonadjacent pixels and multi-order differences.

Acknowledgements. This work is supported in part by the National Natural Science Foundation of China (61572183, 61379143, 61672222), the Specialized Research Fund for the Doctoral Program of Higher Education (SRFDP) under grant 20120161110014, the Priority Academic Program Development of Jiangsu Higer Education Institutions (PAPD) and Jiangsu Collaborative Innovation Center on Atmospheric Environment and Equipment Technology (CICAEET).

References

1. Li, J., Li, X., Yang, B., Sun, X.: Segmentation-based image copy-move forgery detection scheme. IEEE Trans. Inf. Forensics Secur. **10**(3), 507–518 (2015)
2. Li, C., Ma, Q., Xiao, L.: Image splicing detection based on Markov features in QDCT domain. Neurocomputing **228**, 29–36 (2017)
3. Avidan, S., Shamir, A.: Seam carving for content-aware image resizing. ACM Trans. Graph. (TOG) **26**(3), 10–16 (2007)
4. Fillion, C., Sharma, G.: Detecting content adaptive scaling of images for forensic application. In: Media Forensics and Security, p. 75410Z (2010)
5. Wei, J.D., Lin, Y.J., Wu, Y.J.: A patch analysis method to detect seam carved images. Pattern Recogn. Lett. **36**, 100–106 (2014)
6. Ryu, S.J., Lee, H.Y., Lee, H.K.: Detecting trace of seam carving for forensic analysis. IEICE Trans. Inf. Syst. **97**(5), 1304–1311 (2014)
7. Yin, T., Yang, G., Li, L.: Detecting seam carving based image resizing using local binary patterns. Comput. Secur. **55**, 130–141 (2015)
8. Ye, J., Shi, Y.-Q.: A local derivative pattern based image forensic framework for seam carving detection. In: Shi, Y.Q., Kim, H.J., Perez-Gonzalez, F., Liu, F. (eds.) IWDW 2016. LNCS, vol. 10082, pp. 172–184. Springer, Cham (2017). doi:10.1007/978-3-319-53465-7_13
9. Sarkar, A., Nataraj, L., Manjunath, B.S.: Detection of seam carving and localization of seam insertions in digital images. In: Proceedings of the 11th ACM Workshop on Multimedia and Security, pp. 107–116 (2009)

10. Liu, Q., Chen, Z.: Improved approaches with calibrated neighboring joint density to steganalysis and seam-carved forgery detection in JPEG images. ACM Trans. Intelligent Syst. Technol. **5**(4), 63–93 (2015)
11. Wattanachote, K., Shih, T.K., Chang, W.L.: Tamper detection of JPEG image due to seam modifications. IEEE Trans. Inf. Forensics Secur. **10**(12), 2477–2491 (2015)
12. Pevny, T., Bas, P., Fridrich, J.: Steganalysis by subtractive pixel adjacency matrix. IEEE Trans. Inf. Forensics Secur. **5**(2), 215–224 (2010)
13. LibSVM: a library for support vector machines. http://www.csie.ntu.edu.tw/cjlin/libsvm
14. Schaefer, G., Stich, M.: UCID: an uncompressed color image database. Storage Retrieval Methods Appl. Multimedia **5307**, 472–480 (2004)
15. Xia, Z., Wang, X., Sun, X., Xiong, N.: Steganalysis of LSB matching using differences between nonadjacent pixels. Multimedia Tools Appl. **75**(4), 1947–1962 (2016)
16. Xia, Z., Wang, X., Sun, X., Wang, B.: Steganalysis of least significant bit matching using multi-order differences. Secur. Commun. Netw. **7**(8), 1283–1291 (2014)

Chinese Remainder Theorem-Based Secret Image Sharing for (k, n) Threshold

Xuehu Yan(✉), Yuliang Lu, Lintao Liu, Song Wan, Wanmeng Ding, and Hanlin Liu

Hefei Electronic Engineering Institute, Hefei 230037, China
publictiger@126.com

Abstract. In comparison with Shamir's original polynomial-based secret image sharing (SIS), Chinese remainder theorem-based SIS (CRTSIS) overall has the advantages of lossless recovery, low recovery computation complexity and no auxiliary encryption. Traditional CRTSIS methods generally suffer from no (k, n) threshold, lossy recovery, ignoring the image characteristics and auxiliary encryption. Based on the analysis of image characteristics and SIS, in this paper we propose a CRTSIS method for (k, n) threshold, through dividing the gray image pixel values into two intervals corresponding to two available mapping intervals. Our method realizes (k, n) threshold and lossless recovery for gray image without auxiliary encryption. Analysis and experiments are provided to indicate the effectiveness of the proposed method.

Keywords: Secret image sharing · Chinese remainder theorem · Lossless recovery · (k, n) threshold

1 Introduction

Secret image sharing (SIS) scheme for (k, n) threshold splits the secret image into n noise-like shadow images i.e., shares or shadows, which are then distributed to n participants. The secret can be reconstructed by k or more shadow images while less than k shadow images gain nothing about the secret. SIS may be applied in many scenarios, such as, access control, information hiding, authentication, watermarking, transmitting passwords, distributed storage and computing etc. [4,11,12]. For sharing gray image, there are Shamir's polynomial-based scheme [7], Chinese remainder theorem-based SIS (CRTSIS) [1,6,13] and so on.

Shamir's original polynomial-based SIS [7] for (k, n) threshold generates the secret image into the constant coefficient of a random $(k-1)$-degree polynomial to get n shadow images, which are then as well distributed to n participants. The secret image can be disclosed with high-resolution by means of Lagrange interpolation by any k or more shadow images. Inspired by Shamir's original scheme, utilizing all the k coefficients of the polynomial and the participant order to embed secret based on modular 251 and secret image encryption, Thien and Lin [9]

X. Sun et al. (Eds.): ICCCS 2017, Part II, LNCS 10603, pp. 433–440, 2017.
https://doi.org/10.1007/978-3-319-68542-7_36

reduced the shadow image size $1/k$ times to the original secret image (namely Shamir's polynomial-based SIS with smaller shadow size). Following Thien and Lin's research, some researchers [5,14] proposed more Shamir's polynomial-based schemes to possess more features. Although Shamir's polynomial-based SIS with smaller shadow size only needs k shadow images for reconstructing the distortion-less secret image, it is generally lossy recovery with high computation complexity and auxiliary encryption. Since the secret is decoded by modular 251 which is less than max gray value 255, the recovery image will be lost if the pixel value of the secret image exceeds 251 and Shamir's polynomial-based SIS has a little bit of loss. Due to Lagrange interpolations in the recovery phase, it requires $O(k \log^2 k)$ operations [1], i.e., complicated computations, to decrypt each one secret pixel. Auxiliary original secret image encryption is usually applied prior to sharing processing which results in auxiliary encryption.

CRTSIS overall may acquire the advantages of lossless recovery, low recovery computation complexity (the modular only $O(k)$ operations [1] to decrypt each one secret pixel) and no auxiliary encryption, which is therefore studied by other researchers [2,8,10,13]. Yan *et al.* firstly [13] introduced CRT in SIS, which may has a little information leakage as well as may be lossy. Shyu and Chen [8] proposed a threshold CRTSIS based on Mignotte's scheme by pseudo random number generator which has auxiliary encryption. Ulutas *et al.* [10] introduced a modified SIS based on Asmuth Bloom's secret sharing scheme by dividing the gray image pixel values into two possible intervals. The random number range may be not suitable so that the (k, n) threshold may be not obtained. Furthermore, it doesn't consider pixel value 2 times or more to the parameter. Hu *et al.* [3] gave a CRTSIS based on the chaotic map which leads to auxiliary encryption. Chuang *et al.* [2] presented a simple CRTSIS and illustrated (3, 5) threshold for RGB color images. Their method is lossy or least significant bits pre-stored. In addition, their sharing parameters condition is different from the explicit parameters in the experiment. Finally, most existing CRTSIS schemes do not provide applicable explicit parameters for the implementations according to the image characteristics. As a result, traditional CRTSIS methods generally suffer from no (k, n) threshold, lossy recovery, ignoring the image characteristics and auxiliary encryption.

In this paper we propose a CRTSIS method for (k, n) threshold, through dividing the gray image pixel values into two intervals corresponding to two available mapping intervals. Our method realizes (k, n) threshold and lossless recovery for gray image without auxiliary encryption. The contributions of this paper lie in, our (k, n) threshold CRTSIS is lossless recovery for gray image without auxiliary encryption as well as provides applicable explicit parameters for the implementations according to the image characteristics. Analysis and experiments are provided to indicate the effectiveness of the proposed method.

The rest of the paper is organized as follows. Section 2 introduces some basic requirements for the proposed method. In Sect. 3, four security levels are presented in detail. Section 4 is devoted to experimental results. Finally, Sect. 5 concludes this paper.

2 Preliminaries

In this section, we straightforward some preliminaries for our work. For (k, n) threshold SIS, the original secret image S is encrypted among n shadow images $SC_1, SC_2, \cdots SC_n$, and the decrypted secret image S' is reconstructed from t $(k \leq t \leq n, t \in \mathrm{Z}^+)$ shadow images.

2.1 Chinese Remainder Theorem (CRT)

CRT has a long history, which can be traced back to the time of Han Xin. It aims to solve a set of linear congruence equations. A set of integers $m_i (i = 1, 2, \cdots, k)$ is chosen subject to $\gcd(m_i, m_j) = 1, i \neq j$.

Then there exists only one solution

$y \equiv \left(a_1 M_1 M_1^{-1} + a_2 M_2 M_2^{-1} + \cdots + a_k M_k M_k^{-1}\right) \pmod{M},\ y \in [0, M-1])$ for the following linear congruence equations

$$\begin{aligned} y &\equiv a_1 \pmod{m_1} \\ y &\equiv a_2 \pmod{m_2} \\ &\cdots \\ y &\equiv a_{k-1} \pmod{m_{k-1}} \\ y &\equiv a_k \pmod{m_k} \end{aligned} \tag{1}$$

where $M = \prod_{i=1}^{k} m_i$, $M_i = {}^{M}/_{m_i}$ and $M_i M_i^{-1} \equiv 1 \pmod{m_i}$.

$\gcd(m_i, m_j) = 1, i \neq j$ results in that every equation in Eq. (1) will not be eliminated by other equations.

We remark that in $[0, M-1]$ there exists exactly one solution. If only the first $k-1$ equations in Eq. (1) are collected, we can obtain only one solution satisfying the first $k-1$ equations in $[0, \prod_{i=1}^{k-1} m_i - 1]$, denoted as y_0. While in $[0, M-1]$, $y_0 + b\prod_{i=1}^{k-1} m_i$ for $b = 1, 2, \cdots, m_i - 1$ are also the solutions for the first $k-1$ equations in Eq. (1). Thus, there are another $m_i - 1$ solutions in $[\prod_{i=1}^{k-1} m_i - 1, M-1]$, other than only one, which will be utilized in the proposed scheme to possess (k, n) threshold.

2.2 The Feature Analysis of Image

Digital image differs from pure electronic data. The image is composed of pixels, and there exists some correlations between pixels, such as structure, texture, edge and other related information. Thus, SIS should scramble not only the pixel values but also the correlations between adjacent pixels.

The pixel value of the gray image is in $[0, 255]$, which should be considered in the SIS design, such as, the secret pixel value should be in the range as well as $m_i \leq 256$.

3 The Proposed CRTSIS Method for (k, n) Threshold

We present the proposed CRTSIS method for (k, n) threshold based on the original secret image S resulting in n output shadow images $SC_1, SC_2, \cdots SC_n$ and corresponding privacy modular integers $m_1, m_2, \cdots m_n$. Our generation Steps are described in Algorithm 1. And the recovery Steps are presented in Algorithm 2.

Algorithm 1. The proposed SIS CRTSIS method for (k, n) threshold

Input: The original secret image S with size of $H \times W$

Output: n shadow images $SC_1, SC_2, \cdots SC_n$ and corresponding privacy modular integers $m_1, m_2, \cdots m_n$

Step 1: Choose a set of integers $\{128 \le p < m_1 < m_2 \cdots < m_n \le 255\}$ subject to

1. $\gcd(m_i, m_j) = 1, i \ne j$.
2. $\gcd(m_i, p) = 1$ for $i = 1, 2, \cdots, n$.
3. $M > pN$

where $M = \prod_{i=1}^{k} m_i$, $N = \prod_{i=1}^{k-1} m_{n-i+1}$ and p is public among all the participants

Step 2: Compute $T = \left[\frac{\left\lfloor \frac{M}{p} - 1 \right\rfloor - \left\lceil \frac{N}{p} \right\rceil}{2} + \left\lceil \frac{N}{p} \right\rceil \right]$ and T is public among all the participants as well. For each position $(h, w) \in \{(h, w) | 1 \le h \le H, 1 \le w \le W\}$, repeat Steps 3–4

Step 3: Let $x = S(h, w)$

If $0 \le x < p$, pick up a random integer A in $\left[T + 1, \left\lfloor \frac{M}{p} - 1 \right\rfloor\right]$ and let $y = x + Ap$

Else pick up a random integer A in $\left[\left\lceil \frac{N}{p} \right\rceil, T\right)$ and let $y = x - p + Ap$.

Step 4: Compute $a_i \equiv y \pmod{m_i}$ and let $SC_i(h, w) = a_i$

Step 5: Output n shadow images $SC_1, SC_2, \cdots SC_n$ and their corresponding privacy modular integers $m_1, m_2, \cdots m_n$

For Algorithms 1 and 2, we remark that.

1. In Step 1 of our Algorithm 1, $\{128 \le p < m_1 < m_2 \cdots < m_n \le 255\}$ is given by image pixel value range and $pN < M$. We suggest that p is as small as possible for security as well as m_i is as large as possible so that the pixel values in shadow images can randomly lie in large range. $\gcd(m_i, m_j) = 1$ and $\gcd(m_i, p) = 1$ aim to satisfy CRT conditions.
2. In Step 3 of our Algorithm 1, we know A is randomly picked up from $\left[\left\lceil \frac{N}{p} \right\rceil, \left\lfloor \frac{M}{p} - 1 \right\rfloor\right]$, thus $0 \le y < M$ in order to obtain (k, n) threshold for y as explained in Sect. 2.1.
3. In Step 3 of Algorithm 1, T divides interval $\left[\left\lceil \frac{N}{p} \right\rceil, \left\lfloor \frac{M}{p} - 1 \right\rfloor\right]$ into two parts with a view to classify $0 \le x < p$ or $p \le x \le 255$ according to Step 3 of Algorithm 2. As a result, x can be losslessly recovered for arbitrary $x \in [0, 255]$.
4. In Step 3 of Algorithm 1, A is randomly picked up for every x, therefore $y = x + Ap$ can enlarge x value so as to scramble not only the pixel value but also the correlations between adjacent pixels without auxiliary encryption.
5. In Step 3 of Algorithm 1, $y = x + Ap$ and $x < p$ can determine only one x based on $x \equiv y \pmod{p}$.

Algorithm 2. Secret image recovery of the proposed scheme.

Input: k shadow images $SC_{i_1}, SC_{i_2}, \cdots SC_{i_k}$, their corresponding privacy modular integers $m_1, m_2, \cdots m_n$, p and T.

Output: A $H \times W$ recovered secret image S'.

Step 1: For each position $(h, w) \in \{(h, w)|1 \leq h \leq H, 1 \leq w \leq W\}$, repeat Steps 2-3.

Step 2: Let $a_{i_j} = SC_{i_j}(h, w)$ for $j = 1, 2, \cdots, k$. To solve the following linear equations by the Chinese remainder theorem.

$$\begin{aligned} y &\equiv a_1 \pmod{m_1} \\ y &\equiv a_2 \pmod{m_2} \\ &\cdots \\ y &\equiv a_{k-1} \pmod{m_{k-1}} \\ y &\equiv a_k \pmod{m_k} \end{aligned} \tag{2}$$

Step 3: Compute $T^* = \left\lfloor \frac{y}{p} \right\rfloor$. If $T^* \geq T$, let $x \equiv y \pmod{p}$. Else let $x \equiv y \pmod{p} + p$. Set $S'(h, w) = x$.

Step 4: Output the recovered binary secret image S'

4 Experimental Results and Analyses

In this section, experiments and analyses are performed to evaluate the effectiveness of our method.

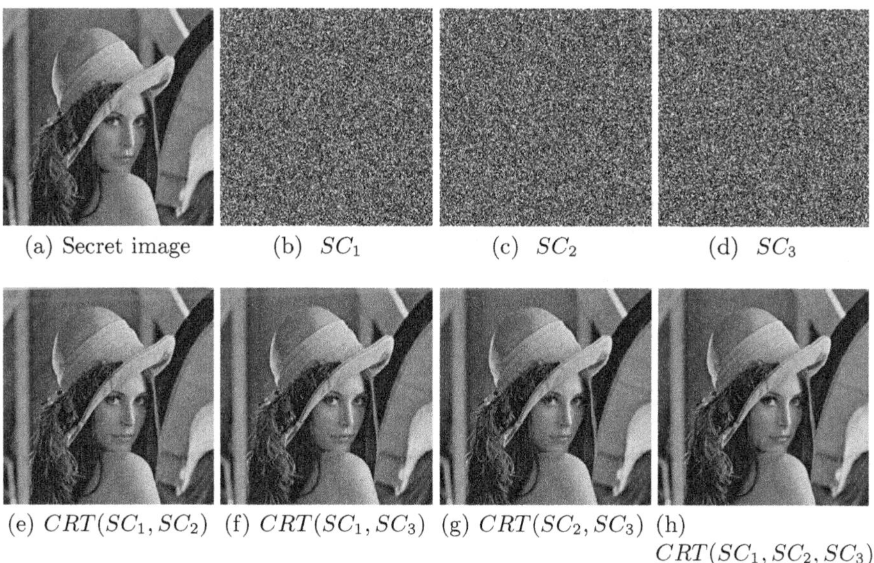

(a) Secret image (b) SC_1 (c) SC_2 (d) SC_3

(e) $CRT(SC_1, SC_2)$ (f) $CRT(SC_1, SC_3)$ (g) $CRT(SC_2, SC_3)$ (h) $CRT(SC_1, SC_2, SC_3)$

Fig. 1. Experimental example of CRTSIS method for (k, n) threshold, where $k = 2, n = 3$

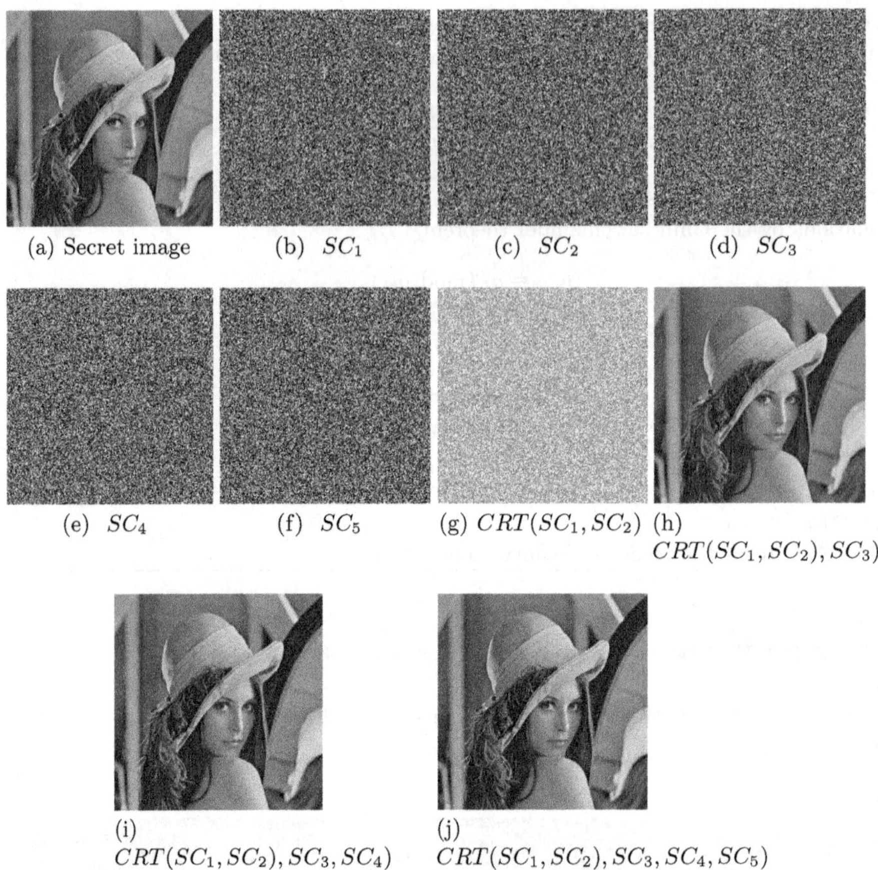

(a) Secret image (b) SC_1 (c) SC_2 (d) SC_3 (e) SC_4 (f) SC_5 (g) $CRT(SC_1, SC_2)$ (h) $CRT(SC_1, SC_2), SC_3)$ (i) $CRT(SC_1, SC_2), SC_3, SC_4)$ (j) $CRT(SC_1, SC_2), SC_3, SC_4, SC_5)$

Fig. 2. Experimental example of CRTSIS method for (k, n) threshold, where $k=3, n=5$

Figure 1 gives the experimental results for $(2, 3)$ threshold, where $p = 128, m_1 = 251, m_2 = 253, m_3 = 255$ and the gray secret image is in Fig. 1(a). Figure 1(b–d) illustrate the 3 shadow images SC_1, SC_2, SC_3, which are noise-like. Figure 1(e–h) exhibit the recovered secret images with any 2 or 3 shadow images based on CRT, from which the secret image recovered from $k = 2$ or more shadow images are lossless by CRT, where $CRT(SC_1, SC_2)$ indicates the recovered secret image from SC_1, SC_2 by CRT.

The next example, we only give the results by the first t th shadow images for saving pages.

Figure 2 gives the experimental results for $(3, 5)$ threshold, where $p = 128, m_1 = 245, m_2 = 247, m_3 = 249, m_4 = 251, m_5 = 253$ and the gray secret image is presented in Fig. 1(a). Figure 2(b) shows one of the 5 shadow images, which is also noise-like. Figure 2(c–f) illustrate the recovered binary secret image with any $t\,(2 \le t \le 5)$ (taking the first t shadow images as an example) by

CRT recovery. When $t < k$ shadow images are collected, there is no clue about the secret image. While when k or more shadow images are collected, the secret image are reconstructed losslessly by CRT.

Based on the above results we can conclude that:

- The shadow images are noise-like, therefore the proposed scheme has no cross interference of secret image in single shadow image.
- When $t < k$ shadow images are collected, there is no information of the secret image could be gained, which shows the security of the proposed scheme.
- When $t(k \leq t \leq n)$ shadow images are recovered by CRT, the secret image could be reconstructed losslessly by CRT.
- CRTSIS method for (k, n) threshold is achieved.

5 Conclusion

In this paper, based on the study of image feature and Chinese remainder theorem (CRT), we propose a CRTSIS method for (k, n) threshold, through dividing the gray image pixel values into two intervals corresponding to two available mapping intervals. Our method realizes (k, n) threshold and lossless recovery for gray image without auxiliary encryption. Experimental results of typical SIS schemes further show the effectiveness of our work. Parameters evaluating and analyzing will be our future work.

Acknowledgments. The authors would like to thank the anonymous reviewers for their valuable comments. This work is supported by the National Natural Science Foundation of China (Grant Number: 61602491).

References

1. Asmuth, C., Bloom, J.: A modular approach to key safeguarding. IEEE Trans. Inf. Theory **29**(2), 208–210 (1983)
2. Chuang, T.W., Chen, C.C., Chien, B.: Image sharing and recovering based on Chinese remainder theorem. In: International Symposium on Computer, Consumer and Control, pp. 817–820 (2016)
3. Hu, C., Liao, X., Xiao, D.: Secret image sharing based on chaotic map and Chinese remainder theorem. Int. J. Wavelets Multiresolut. Inf. Process. **10**(3), 1250023 (2012). [18 pages]
4. Fu, Z., Ren, K., Shu, J., Sun, X., Huang, F.: Enabling personalized search over encrypted outsourced data with efficiency improvement. IEEE Trans. Parallel Distrib. Syst. **27**(9), 2546–2559 (2016)
5. Li, P., Ma, P.J., Su, X.H., Yang, C.N.: Improvements of a two-in-one image secret sharing scheme based on gray mixing model. J. Vis. Commun. Image Represent. **23**(3), 441–453 (2012)
6. Mignotte, M.: How to share a secret. In: Beth, T. (ed.) EUROCRYPT 1982. LNCS, vol. 149, pp. 371–375. Springer, Heidelberg (1983). doi:10.1007/3-540-39466-4_27
7. Shamir, A.: How to share a secret. Commun. ACM **22**(11), 612–613 (1979)

8. Shyu, S.J., Chen, Y.R.: Threshold secret image sharing by Chinese remainder theorem. In: IEEE Asia-Pacific Services Computing Conference, pp. 1332–1337 (2008)
9. Thien, C.C., Lin, J.C.: Secret image sharing. Comput. Graph. **26**(5), 765–770 (2002)
10. Ulutas, M., Nabiyev, V.V., Ulutas, G.: A new secret image sharing technique based on Asmuth Bloom's scheme. In: International Conference on Application of Information and Communication Technologies, AICT 2009, pp. 1–5 (2009)
11. Xia, Z., Wang, X., Sun, X., Liu, Q.: Steganalysis of LSB matching using differences between nonadjacent pixels. Multimedia Tools Appl. **75**(4), 1947–1962 (2016)
12. Xue, Y., Jiang, J., Zhao, B., Ma, T.: A self-adaptive artificial bee colony algorithm based on global best for global optimization. Soft Comput. **8**, 1–18 (2017)
13. Yan, W., Ding, W., Dongxu, Q.: Image sharing based on Chinese remainder theorem. J. North China Univ. Tech. **12**(1), 6–9 (2000)
14. Yang, C.N., Ciou, C.B.: Image secret sharing method with two-decoding-options: lossless recovery and previewing capability. Image Vis. Comput. **28**(12), 1600–1610 (2010)

Kernel Searching Strategy for Recommender Searching Mechanism

Li Zhou[1(✉)], Weiwei Yuan[1,2], Kangya He[1], Chenliang Li[1], and Qiang Li[1]

[1] College of Computer Science and Technology, Nanjing University of Aeronautics and Astronautics, Nanjing, China
lizhou165@outlook.com, {yuanweiwei,qiangli}@nuaa.edu.cn, kangyahe@gmail.com, lcljoric@gmail.com

[2] Collaborative Innovation Center of Novel Software Technology and Industrialization, Nanjing, China

Abstract. A trust-aware recommender system (TARS) is widely used in social media to find useful information. Recommender searching mechanism is an important research issue in TARS. We propose a new searching strategy for recommender searching mechanism of TARS, which named kernel searching strategy. A kernel, which consists of hub nodes of the trust network, is involved in trust propagations. The kernel can be obtained from node degree or node betweenness, take these hub nodes as active users and then finds the recommenders via trust propagations from the kernel, most of the nodes in the network will be covered. Comparing the results of these two methods, the coverage rate of these hub nodes which is obtained from the node degree is almost less than that obtained from the node betweenness. To get better coverage rate, we take both degree and betweenness into consideration. The results show that the combination can get better coverage rate only compared with the node degree. However, the combination has better convergence effect compared with the node betweenness.

Keywords: Kernel searching · Degree · Betweenness · Trust-aware recommender system

1 Introduction

With the rapid development of the internet, information has increased at an unprecedented rate which exacerbates the severity of the information overload problem for online users [1]. Recommender systems are used to solve the problem of information overload, they try to find the items of interest to users based on their preferences, such as books or movies. This personalized recommendation is effective, especially in the online world where we are constantly faced with too much choice. Commonly used recommendation techniques include collaborative filtering (CF) and content-based (CB). When this recommendation is related to new users or new projects, they will face cold start problems. The trust-aware recommender system (TARS) is widely used in social media to give recommendations based on trusts between users. Compared with strangers, users are

X. Sun et al. (Eds.): ICCCS 2017, Part II, LNCS 10603, pp. 441–449, 2017.
https://doi.org/10.1007/978-3-319-68542-7_37

more likely to accept recommendations made by their trusted friends, because users can be influenced by their trustworthy friends. So, trust-aware recommender system (TARS) employs trust information to enhance recommender system [2].

Recommender searching mechanism is one fundamental research issue in TARS [3]. In our paper, we propose a new searching strategy for recommender searching mechanism of Trust-Aware Recommender Systems, which named kernel searching strategy. A kernel, which means a combination of some hub nodes in trust networks, is built for trust propagations. Recommenders are searched via the kernel: this search first propagates the active users' trusts to the kernel, and then finds the recommenders via trust propagations from the kernel. As is known to all, centrality measures indicate the importance, interestingness of the nodes and they play a crucial role in many solutions to practical problems. We use two centrality measures: node degree and node betweenness to get the hub nodes in the trust network. Degree centrality is defined as the number of links incident upon a node. Betweenness centrality expresses the importance or influence of individual vertices (or edges) in a network in terms of the fraction of shortest paths that pass through them [4–7].

We do experiments on the epinions dataset, select different nodes as subsets and the trust data in the same subset should be pretreated. Then, we calculate the degree and betweenness of nodes in the network separately, sort the results in descending order and select nodes from top to bottom. Top m nodes would be chosen as hub nodes according to the value of degree or betweenness, take them as active users in the kernel. Propagate trust and then find the recommenders via trust propagations from the kernel. Exclude the hub nodes and take their recommenders as active users, do trust propagations as before. The coverage rate of nodes in the network will be calculated respectively after every trust propagation. From the experimental results, the hub nodes obtained from degree may be different from the hub nodes obtained from betweenness, and the coverage rate of the kernel which is obtained from the node degree is almost lower than the nodes obtained from the node betweenness during several experiments, regardless of the value of the variable m. Would the combination of betweenness and degree get better coverage rate? We conduct further experiments to confirm our ideas. The experimental results confirm that the combination can also get better coverage rate compared with only take degree into consideration. However, there was no significant change in the results compared with the betweenness. From the perspective of convergence, the combination of both has a good effect. It can use less nodes to represent the whole network.

The rest of the paper is organized as follows. In Sect. 2, a brief description of the related works is presented. Section 3 presents our proposed kernel searching strategy in details. Next, in Sect. 4 the results of our experiments based on the public dataset Epinions are delineated. Finally, Sect. 5 concludes this paper and points out future directions.

2 Related Works

Recommender systems are introduced to solve the problem of information overload. Recommender systems can be defined as information filtering systems, because they aim to provide users with the most suitable items that consistent with users' preferences and interests. Recently, these systems have gained a lot of interest with the enormous increase in the use of social networking applications. Recommender systems are applied in a variety of applications including recommending products, social links, and digital items. With the rapidly growing amount of available information on the web, it is necessary to use tools to filter this information in order to find items that are more likely to be of interest to the users.

In literature, popular techniques of recommender systems can be classified into two major classes: content-based models and collaborative filtering approaches. Content-based recommender systems try to match user profiles against item description, and they use items' and users' features to create a profile for each item or user. User profile includes demographic information and users' interests. Compare each item's attributes with the user profile, items will be recommended when they are very similar to the user profile. These systems can distinguishes between items likely to be of interest to the user and those likely to be uninteresting. However, in Content-based recommender systems, the cold start problem is intense as ratings are not available for new users. The models depend on the performance of content analysis methodology they adopt [1, 10, 11]. Collaborative filtering-based recommendation techniques help people to make choices based on the opinions of other people who share similar interests. CF recommendation systems rely on the user's past behavior to find similar users or items and utilize this information in order to find the items of interests to the user. It is based only on the judgments of the user community. This algorithm suffers expensive computation, because they need search all the user profiles to find the best set of neighbors [8–10].

According to the active users' trusts on the recommenders, the Trust-Aware Recommender System (TARS) suggests the worthwhile information to the users. TARS has superior rating prediction coverage than the traditional recommender system by taking advantages of the trust's transitive property. Various recommendations are important to reflect the quality of items from different aspects. So it is fundamental for TARS to find as many recommenders as possible for active users.

3 Proposed Method

Social network analysis has recently gained a lot of interest because of the advent and the increasing popularity of social media, such as blogs, social networking applications, microblogging, or customer review sites. The Trust-Aware Recommender System (TARS) is the recommender system that suggests the worthwhile information to the users on the basis of trust. In this environment, trust is becoming an essential quality among user interactions and the recommendation for useful content and trustful users is crucial for all the members of the network. Trust-aware recommender systems employ trust information to enhance recommender systems. Merging trust information and recommender systems can improve the accuracy of recommendation as well as the users' experience. Recommender searching mechanism is a research issue of fundamental importance to TARS.

In this paper, we propose a kernel searching strategy for recommender searching mechanism of Trust-Aware Recommender Systems. The architecture of our proposed method is shown as Fig. 1. The kernel is composed of some hub nodes in trust networks, is involved in trust propagations. It is a directional relationship from the trustor (the user that evaluates its trust on the target user) to the trustee (the user that is the target of the trust evaluation). This search first propagates the active users' trusts to the kernel, and then finds the recommenders via trust propagations from the kernel. One of the most important factors in our proposed kernel searching strategy is the choice of hub nodes. We use centrality measures to get the hub nodes in the trust network, because centrality measures indicate the importance, interestingness of the nodes. Then, we calculate the degree and betweenness of nodes in the network separately, sort the results in descending order and select nodes from top to bottom. We obtain the kernel from node degree or node betweenness, take these hub nodes as active users and then find their trusted users via trust propagations. The algorithm can be seen in Table 1. After several

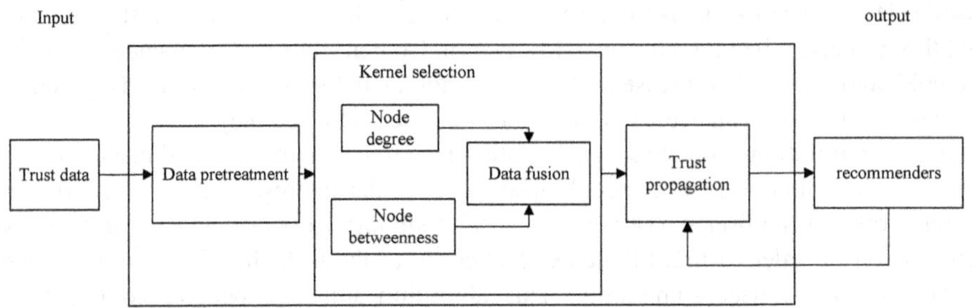

Fig. 1. System framework.

Table 1. Our proposed kernel searching strategy.

Input: *Trust data*, which contains id of the users and trust relationships between all users of the trust network

Output: *Recommenders*

Parameter:ψd: trust propagation distance; *d*max: maximum allowable trust propagation distance from the active user in the kernel; *kernelUserID*: ID of the user in the selected kernel; *selectedUserID*: ID of the user selected at each step of the trust propagation; *trusteeID*: ID of the user trusted by *selectedUserID*

```
Kernel Searching Strategy:
  d=0;
  d++;
  if (d≤ dmax);
      for (all users trusted by kernelUserID)
        selectedUserID= trusteeID;
        Recommenders= selectedUserID;
        Terminate searching;
  d++;
  if (d≤ dmax);
     for (all users trusted by kernelUserID)
     selectedUserID= trusteeID;
        for (all users trusted by selectedUserID)
           selectedUserID= trusteeID;
           Recommenders= selectedUserID;
           Terminate searching;
  ......do until d = dmax.....
```

times of trust propagations, most of the nodes in the network will be covered. We consider that the combination of node degree and node betweenness can get better effect in the network. The conclusion is to be proven by further experiments. We take both degree and betweenness into consideration, get the hub nodes according to this combination. In my submission, these nodes have higher status in the network. Find the best kernel, we can grasp the whole network more quickly.

4 Experiments

Experiments are held on the publicly released dataset Epinions to verify our proposed kernel searching strategy. www.epinions.com is a general consumer review site. Users in this product review site can share their reviews about products. Also they can establish their trust networks from which they may seek advice to make decisions. The Epinions dataset consists of 49 288 users and 487 183 trust statements. Its trust data are divided into several subsets. Our experiments were carried out on above trust data. Kernel is consists of hub nodes of the trust network, we use two centrality measures: node degree and node betweenness to obtain the kernel. We can also take the combination of degree and betweenness into consideration. In our experiments, data pretreatment is necessary. First, we must eliminate some nodes whose in-degree are zero,

Table 2. Experiment 1, coverage rate based on degree, betweenness and the combination.

Kernel size	Hops	Coverage rate		
		Node degree	Node betweenness	Combination
5	1	0.0647	0.0863	0.0863
	2	0.2527	0.4481	0.9121
	3	0.5942	0.7875	0.7875
	4	0.8429	0.9121	0.9121
10	1	0.1140	0.1368	0.1429
	2	0.4237	0.5458	0.9251
	3	0.7440	0.8372	0.8319
	4	0.8995	0.9259	0.9251
15	1	0.1323	0.1917	0.1954
	2	0.4591	0.6272	0.9316
	3	0.7611	0.8681	0.8689
	4	0.9039	0.9316	0.9316
20	1	0.1449	0.2243	0.2304
	2	0.4782	0.6602	0.9341
	3	0.7688	0.8795	0.8767
	4	0.9064	0.9357	0.9341
25	1	0.1697	0.2572	0.2593
	2	0.5120	0.6862	0.9377
	3	0.7875	0.8893	0.8869
	4	0.9105	0.9377	0.9377

because these nodes are not in the same trust network with most of other nodes. According to trust data, we calculate the degree and betweenness of each node, and then normalize the results to get the important nodes for the combination. We select nodes in the kernel by the descending order. The kernels obtained by these three ways are not the same, and users in these kernels are different. Propagate the users' trusts and then find their recommenders via trust propagations from the kernel. After several times trust propagation, most users are covered. Make comparisons of coverage rate between the kernels obtained by different ways. We choose different size of the kernel and the results are shown in the following tables.

From Tables 2 and 3, we can see that the coverage rate of the kernel which is obtained from the node degree is almost less than that obtained from the node betweenness or the combination, regardless of the size of the kernel. However, there was no significant change in the results between node betweenness and the combination. And the results didn't shown that the combination has better coverage rate every time. We conduct further experiments to find a better way between the two. More sizes of the kernel are chosen to carry out experiments, and we can see the results from the following Fig. 2.

Table 3. Experiment 2, coverage rate based on degree, betweenness and the combination.

Kernel size	Hops	Coverage rate		
		Node degree	Node betweenness	Combination
5	1	0.0470	0.0713	0.0841
	2	0.1397	0.2188	0.2416
	3	0.2708	0.3799	0.3863
	4	0.4163	0.4783	0.4790
10	1	0.1076	0.1155	0.1269
	2	0.2545	0.3093	0.3158
	3	0.4163	0.4355	0.4419
	4	0.4975	0.5246	0.5267
15	1	0.1504	0.1447	0.1440
	2	0.3136	0.3350	0.3371
	3	0.4362	0.4669	0.4640
	4	0.5075	0.5445	0.5431
20	1	0.1803	0.1575	0.1632
	2	0.3286	0.3656	0.3621
	3	0.4426	0.4939	0.4833
	4	0.5110	0.5624	0.5488
25	1	0.2117	0.1739	0.1910
	2	0.3642	0.3770	0.3877
	3	0.4740	0.4996	0.5110
	4	0.5232	0.5681	0.5674

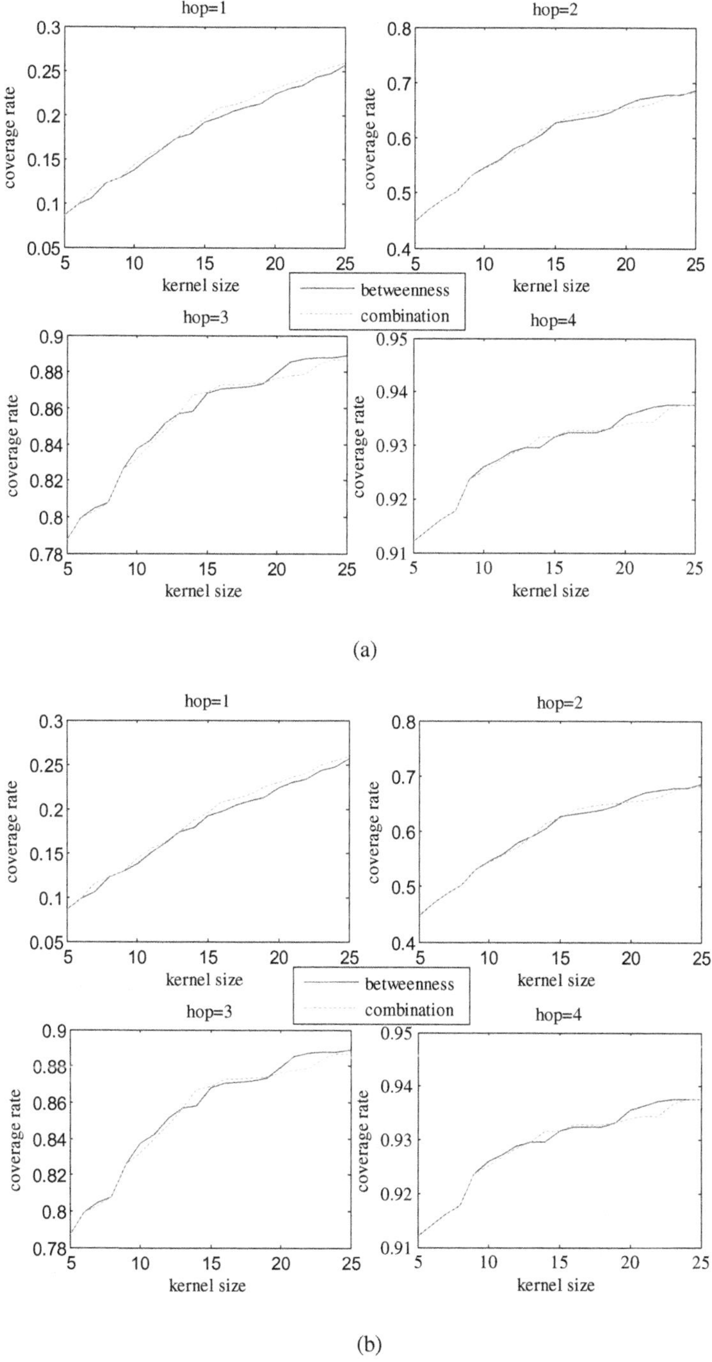

Fig. 2. The coverage rate based on betweenness or the combination of betweenness and degree for each trust propagation, and the experiments were conducted on three different trust data.

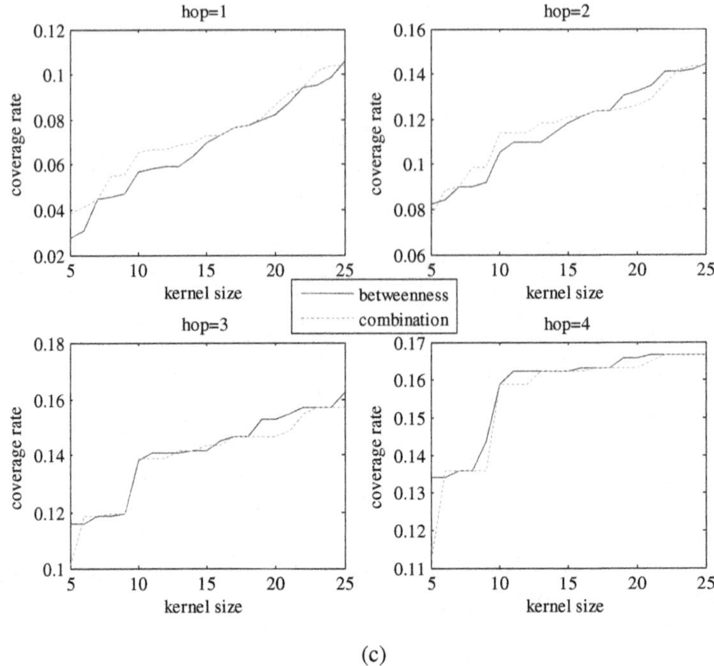

(c)

Fig. 2. (*continued*)

When trust is passed only once, the combination of node degree and node betweenness has higher coverage than betweenness, it means that this situation can get more recommenders, and cover more users. However, with the increase of the number of trust propagation times, this advantage is reduced or even disappeared. From the perspective of convergence, the combination of both has a better effect only in the case of ignoring the small coverage difference between the two. In the vast majority of cases, the method of betweenness can use less nodes to get higher coverage rate, represent the whole network.

5 Conclusions

Recommender systems aim to overcome the information overload problem in a way that covers users' preferences and interests. Trust-aware recommender systems are an attempt to incorporate trust information into classical recommender systems to improve their recommendations. Kernel searching is a newly proposed recommender searching mechanism for TARS. It builds up a kernel for recommender searching, and the kernel composes hub nodes of the trust network. The recommenders are found via trust propagation: the active users' trusts are first propagated according to our known trust data, and then find their recommenders via trust propagations from the kernel. One fundamental process of kernel searching is to propagate active users' trusts to find the recommenders efficiently. Hub nodes are chosen by node degree or node betweenness. According to the experiment analysis of several groups of different trust data, the results of the analysis show that the simple combination of node degree and node betweenness can't get obvious excellent effect. I am sure that the search strategy which considers both node properties will get better results. In our future work, we will mainly focus on combinatorial optimization of degree and betweenness.

Acknowledgments. This research was supported by Nature Science Foundation of China (Grant No. 61672284), China Postdoctoral Science Foundation (Grant No. 2016M591841). This work was also supported by the Priority Academic Program Development of Jiangsu Higher Education Institutions (PAPD) and Jiangsu Collaborative Innovation Center on Atmospheric Environment and Equipment Technology (CICAEET), Open Project Foundation of Information Technology Research Base of Civil Aviation Administration of China (Grant No. CAAC-ITRB-201501 and Grant No. CAAC-ITRB-201602).

References

1. Abbasi, M.A., Tang, J., Liu, H.: Trust-aware recommender systems. In: Machine Learning Book on Computational Trust. Chapman and Hall/CRC Press (2014)
2. Eirinaki, M., Louta, M.D., Varlamis, I.: A trust-aware system for personalized user recommendations in social networks. IEEE Trans. Syst. Man Cybern. Syst. **44**(4), 409–421 (2014)
3. Yuan, W., Guan, D., Lee, S., Wang, J.: Skeleton searching strategy for recommender searching mechanism of Trust-Aware Recommender Systems. Comput. J. **58**(9), 1876–1883 (2015)
4. Riondato, M., Kornaropoulos, E.M.: Fast approximation of betweenness centrality through sampling. Data Min. Knowl. Disc. **30**(2), 438–475 (2016)
5. Kósa, B., Balassi, M., Englert, P., Kiss, A.: Betweenness versus linerank. Comput. Sci. Inf. Syst. **12**(1), 33–48 (2015)
6. Nasre, M., Pontecorvi, M., Ramachandran, V.: Betweenness centrality – incremental and faster. In: Csuhaj-Varjú, E., Dietzfelbinger, M., Ésik, Z. (eds.) MFCS 2014. LNCS, vol. 8635, pp. 577–588. Springer, Heidelberg (2014). doi:10.1007/978-3-662-44465-8_49
7. Bergamini, E., Meyerhenke, H.: Fully-dynamic approximation of betweenness centrality. In: Bansal, N., Finocchi, I. (eds.) ESA 2015. LNCS, vol. 9294, pp. 155–166. Springer, Heidelberg (2015). doi:10.1007/978-3-662-48350-3_14
8. Yuan, W., Guan, D., Lee, Y.K., Lee, S., Hur, S.J.: Improved trust-aware recommender system using small-worldness of trust networks. Knowl.-Based Syst. **23**(3), 232–238 (2010)
9. Lu, J., Wu, D., Mao, M., Wang, W., Zhang, G.: Recommender system application developments: a survey. Decis. Support Syst. **74**, 12–32 (2015)
10. Lika, B., Kolomvatsos, K., Hadjiefthymiades, S.: Facing the cold start problem in recommender systems. Expert Syst. Appl. **41**(4), 2065–2073 (2014)
11. Champiri, Z.D., Shahamiri, S.R., Salim, S.S.B.: A systematic review of scholar context-aware recommender systems. Expert Syst. Appl. **42**(3), 1743–1758 (2015)

A Robust Quantum Watermark Algorithm Based on Quantum Log-Polar Images

Zhiguo Qu[1(✉)], Zhenwen Cheng[2], and Mingming Wang[3]

[1] Jiangsu Engineering Center of Network Monitoring, Nanjing University of Information Science and Technology, Nanjing 210044, People's Republic of China
qzghhh@126.com

[2] School of Electronic & Information Engineering, Nanjing University of Information Science and Technology, Nanjing 210044, People's Republic of China
czw381576996@163.com

[3] School of Computer Science, Xi'an Polytechnic University, Xi'an 710048, People's Republic of China
bluess1982@126.com

Abstract. Copyright protection for quantum image is an important research branch of quantum information technology. In this paper, based on quantum log-polar image (QUALPI), a new quantum watermark algorithm is proposed to better protect copyright of quantum image. In order to realize quantum watermark embedding, the least significant qubit (LSQb) of quantum carrier image is replaced by quantum watermark image. Compared to previous quantum watermark algorithms, the new algorithm effectively utilizes two important properties of log-polar sampling, i.e., rotation and scale invariances. These invariances make quantum watermark image extracted have a good robustness when stego image was subjected to various geometric attacks, such as rotation and scaling. Experimental simulation based on MATLAB shows that the new algorithm has a good performance on robustness, transparency and capacity.

Keywords: Quantum watermark algorithm · Quantum log-polar image · Least significant qubit · Robustness

1 Introduction

With the rapid development of quantum communication network, in order to achieve safe and efficient transmission of quantum image information in quantum communication network, people began to study using quantum states to store and transfer digital image information in the decades. Moreover, with widespread applications of quantum image in quantum communication network, quantum watermark also has emerged to protect copyright of quantum image, which is fulfilled by embedding watermark image consisting of the information related to copyright owner into carrier image. So far, quantum image representation methods and quantum watermark algorithms have made a lot of achievements.

X. Sun et al. (Eds.): ICCCS 2017, Part II, LNCS 10603, pp. 450–460, 2017.
https://doi.org/10.1007/978-3-319-68542-7_38

At present, the major achievements of quantum image representation methods, i.e., Qubit Lattice [1], Entangled Image [2], Real Ket [3], flexible representation of quantum images (FRQI) [4], novel enhanced quantum representation (NEQR) [5], quantum log-polar image (QUALPI) [6] and novel quantum representation of color digital images (NCQI) [7], have been proposed. Among of them, quantum images of QUALPI representation can easily perform some complex geometric transformations, such as rotation and scaling. With the increasing importance of images in people's daily life, color image analysis by quaternion Zernike moments (QZMs) [8], content-based image retrieval (CBIR) [9] and digital image forensics [10] also have been widely studied.

In the aspect of quantum watermark algorithms, analysis and improvement of the watermark strategy for quantum images based on quantum Fourier transform [11] was proposed by Yang et al. In 2013 and 2014, Song et al. put forward two dynamic watermarking schemes for quantum image based on quantum wavelet transform [12] and Hadamard transform [13], respectively. This two quantum watermark algorithms have a larger capacity and good transparency. The least significant bit (LSB [14]) modification is one of the most important methods in classical digital watermark, which has advantages of easy operation and large amount of information hiding. In 2016, a least significant qubit (LSQb) algorithm for quantum image based on NCQI representation [15] was proposed by Sang.

From the achievements given above, it can be found out that the current quantum watermark technology is still on the early stage of its development. Most of algorithms have not yet begun to discuss the robustness of watermark image, especially on geometric attacks. In view of widespread applications and universality of geometric distortion attacks in quantum image processing, most of watermarked quantum images are invulnerable to resist this kind of attacks. In order to make up for the drawbacks of existing quantum watermark algorithms, this paper proposes a novel robust quantum watermark algorithm based on the QUALPI representation. By combining the QUALPI representation model with the LSQb modification technique, the new algorithm enables to effectively resist geometric distortions or attacks, so as to better protect copyright of quantum image.

The rest of the paper is organized as follows. Section 2 introduces the preliminary knowledge related to the new algorithm. In Sect. 3, the novel robust quantum watermark algorithm is described in detail. The simulation results and performance analysis are given in Sect. 4. Finally, a conclusion and the future work are provided in Sect. 5.

2 Preliminaries

2.1 The QUALPI Image Representation and Rotation Transformation

In QUALPI, the sampling resolutions of the log-radius and the angular orientations of a log-polar image are assumed to be 2^m and 2^n respectively. For this image, the quantum image representation can be expressed as shown in the following equation:

$$|I\rangle = \frac{1}{\sqrt{2^{m+n}}} \sum_{\rho=0}^{2^m-1} \sum_{\theta=0}^{2^n-1} (|g(\rho,\theta)\rangle \otimes |\rho\rangle \otimes |\theta\rangle) \tag{1}$$

The position information of a pixel is represented by (ρ, θ), where ρ denotes the log-radius and θ represents the angular position. The gray scale of the corresponding pixel is represented by $g(\rho, \theta)$. The gray range of this image is assumed to be 2^q. Thus the gray scale can be encoded by binary sequence $C_{q-1}C_{q-2}\cdots C_1C_0$ as follow:

$$g(\rho,\theta) = C_{q-1}C_{q-2}\cdots C_1C_0, g(\rho,\theta) \in \left[0, 2^{q-1}\right] \tag{2}$$

Reference [6] discusses the quantum arbitrary rotation transformation of the QUALPI quantum image model. Assume that a rotation transformation R_x for quantum image will be operated and the rotation angle can be encoded by binary sequence $r_{n-1}r_{n-2}\cdots r_1r_0$ as follow:

$$R_x = r_{n-1}r_{n-2}\cdots r_1r_0, r_i \in \{0,1\}, R_x \in [0, 2^n - 1] \tag{3}$$

Thus, when R_x rotation is performed, the procedure can be divided into n sub-operations. If $r_i = 0$, none operation will be done for the ith sub-operation. Otherwise, a 2^i rotation R_{2^i} will be performed on quantum image.

The quantum 2^k rotation U_{2^k} will add the angular positions of every pixel by 2^k (mod 2^n). Specifically, this operation aims to make a unit shift for the highest $(n - q)$ qubits of the angular sequence $|\theta\rangle$ in the QUALPI quantum image.

2.2 Quantum Bit Comparator

In order to embed watermark image into carrier image by using LSQb modification, it is necessary to compare the state of the last qubit of a pixel in the same position of those two images by using quantum bit comparator. According to the results of the comparator, the corresponding unitary operation is performed on carrier image. Consequently, this section describes a specific quantum bit comparator.

In 2012, Wang et al. gave a quantum comparator to judge whether two qubits are same or not in Ref. [16]. As shown in Fig. 1, $|a\rangle, |b\rangle$ are the input qubits and $|c\rangle, |d\rangle$ denote the outputs of the corresponding states.

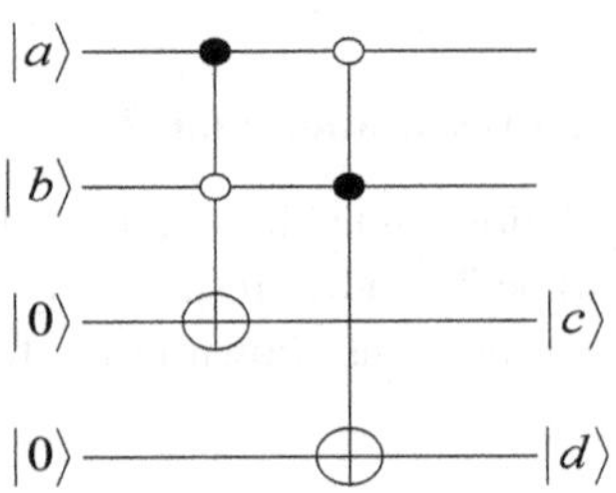

Fig. 1. Two qubit comparator.

If $|c\rangle|d\rangle = |1\rangle|0\rangle$ or $|c\rangle|d\rangle = |0\rangle|1\rangle$, then quantum state $|a\rangle$ is not equal to quantum state $|b\rangle$. If $|c\rangle|d\rangle = |0\rangle|0\rangle$, then quantum state $|a\rangle$ is equal to quantum state $|b\rangle$.

3 A Robust Quantum Watermark Algorithm

In this section, the main steps of new algorithm including embedding watermark process and extracting watermark process are presented in details. The embedding process is mainly based on the QUALPI representation and the LSQb modification technique, and the extracting process is the inverse of the embedding process.

3.1 Embedding Watermark Process

The flow chart of the embedding process is shown in Fig. 2 and steps of the embedding process are given as follows:

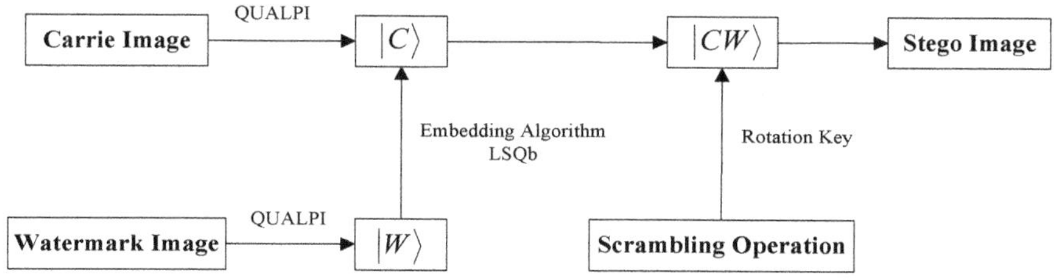

Fig. 2. The flow chart of embedding watermark process.

Step (1): In this paper, the size of carrier image is equal to the size of watermark image. The QUALPI expressions of carrier image and watermark image are shown in Eqs. (4) and (5), respectively:

$$|C\rangle = \frac{1}{\sqrt{2^{m+n}}} \sum_{\rho=0}^{2^m-1} \sum_{\theta=0}^{2^n-1} |c_{q-1}c_{q-2}\cdots c_1 c_0\rangle|\rho\theta\rangle \tag{4}$$

$$|W\rangle = \frac{1}{\sqrt{2^{m+n}}} \sum_{\rho=0}^{2^m-1} \sum_{\theta=0}^{2^n-1} |w_0\rangle|\rho\theta\rangle \tag{5}$$

where $|c_{0_{ji}}\rangle$ and $|w_{0_{ji}}\rangle$ denotes the state of the last qubit of the (ρ_j, θ_i) pixel in carrier image and watermark image, respectively, which are used as inputs into the quantum comparator. According to the results of the comparator, the corresponding unitary operation is performed on carrier image to complete the LSQb modification.

Step (2): If the outputs from the quantum comparator are equal, then it will do nothing about carrier image. In this case, the following unitary transformation will be performed.

$$U_{S_{ji}} = I^{\otimes q} \otimes \left(\sum_{\rho=0}^{2^m-1} \sum_{\theta=0}^{2^n-1} |\rho\theta\rangle\langle\rho\theta| \right) \tag{6}$$

Step (3): However, if the outputs are different, the following unitary transformation will be performed on the state of quantum carrier image.

$$U_{D_{ji}} = I^{\otimes q-1} \otimes U \otimes |ji\rangle\langle ji| + I^{\otimes q} \otimes \left(\sum_{\rho=0}^{2^m-1} \sum_{\theta=0,\rho\theta\neq ji}^{2^n-1} |\rho\theta\rangle\langle\rho\theta| \right) \tag{7}$$

where

$$U = \sigma_X = \begin{bmatrix} 0 & 1 \\ 1 & 0 \end{bmatrix} \tag{8}$$

It is obvious that the unitary U is the CNOT gate. Next, the concrete derivation process is given.

$$\begin{aligned} U_{D_{ji}}(|C\rangle) = & \left(I^{\otimes q-1} \otimes U \otimes |ji\rangle\langle ji| + I^{\otimes q} \otimes \sum_{\rho=0}^{2^m-1} \sum_{\theta=0,\rho\theta\neq ji}^{2^n-1} |\rho\theta\rangle\langle\rho\theta| \right) \\ & \left(\frac{1}{\sqrt{2^{m+n}}} \sum_{\rho=0}^{2^m-1} \sum_{\theta=0}^{2^n-1} \left| c_{q-1}c_{q-2}\cdots c_1c_0 \right\rangle |\rho\theta\rangle \right) \\ = & \frac{1}{\sqrt{2^{m+n}}} \left(I^{\otimes q-1} \otimes U \otimes |ji\rangle\langle ji| + I^{\otimes q} \otimes \sum_{\rho=0}^{2^m-1} \sum_{\theta=0,\rho\theta\neq ji}^{2^n-1} |\rho\theta\rangle\langle\rho\theta| \right) \\ & \left(\left| c_{q-1}^{ji}c_{q-2}^{ji}\cdots c_1^{ji}c_0^{ji} \right\rangle |ji\rangle + \sum_{\rho=0}^{2^m-1} \sum_{\theta=0,\rho\theta\neq ji}^{2^n-1} \left| c_{q-1}c_{q-2}\cdots c_1c_0 \right\rangle |\rho\theta\rangle \right) \\ = & \frac{1}{\sqrt{2^{m+n}}} \left(\left| c_{q-1}^{ji}c_{q-2}^{ji}\cdots c_1^{ji}\overline{c}_0^{ji} \right\rangle |ji\rangle + \right. \\ & \left. \sum_{\rho=0}^{2^m-1} \sum_{\theta=0,\rho\theta\neq ji}^{2^n-1} \left| c_{q-1}c_{q-2}\cdots c_1c_0 \right\rangle |\rho\theta\rangle \right) \end{aligned} \tag{9}$$

where

$$\left| \overline{c}_0^{ji} \right\rangle = \begin{cases} |0\rangle, \left| c_0^{ji} \right\rangle = 1 \\ |1\rangle, \left| c_0^{ji} \right\rangle = 0 \end{cases} \tag{10}$$

Step (4): By repeating the three steps above, watermark image is embedded into carrier image by the LSQb modification. Finally, as it is described in Sect. 2.1, stego image will be made a rotation transformation R_x. The rotation angle can be determined according to the key, named as K_1, shared by two parties of communication in advance.

3.2 Extracting Watermark Process

The flow chart of the extracting process is shown in Fig. 3. Its main steps can be described as follows.

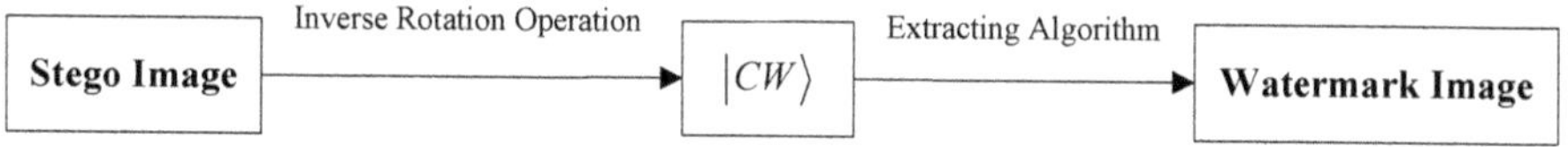

Fig. 3. The flow chart of extracting watermark process.

Step (1): According to the K_1, two parties of communication will share an another key, named as K_2, in order to restore the original stego image. Another rotation transformation can be performed on stego image.

Step (2): It is clear that the LSQb of stego image is a complex vector in Hilbert space which the size is 2^{q+m+n}. So let decompose the vector into the direct product of color and correspondingly position firstly. Taking a $2^1 \times 2^2$ log-polar image with gray rang 2^q as an example, the stego image vector is Q. Then the disintegrated vector Q is given as the following form:

$$Q = a_0 \otimes \begin{pmatrix} 1 \\ 0 \\ 0 \\ \vdots \\ 0 \\ 0 \end{pmatrix} + a_1 \otimes \begin{pmatrix} 0 \\ 1 \\ 0 \\ \vdots \\ 0 \\ 0 \end{pmatrix} + \cdots + a_6 \otimes \begin{pmatrix} 0 \\ 0 \\ 0 \\ \vdots \\ 1 \\ 0 \end{pmatrix} + a_7 \otimes \begin{pmatrix} 0 \\ 0 \\ 0 \\ \vdots \\ 0 \\ 1 \end{pmatrix} \tag{11}$$

Obviously, this step can be realized because the vector Q and the binary encoding of position are known. After converting every first part (color information) of the direct product to binary data, the number of binary bit is equivalent to the number of bits of the stego image's color encoding. In this example, it means converting $a_0, a_1, \cdots, a_6, a_7$ to the appropriate binary data $a_{0_b}, a_{1_b}, \cdots, a_{6_b}, a_{7_b}$. The a_{i_b} stands for the gray's binary sequence of the ith pixel in stego image.

Step (3): The last step is to extract the last bit of every binary data. According to the preparation of QUALPI state in Ref. [6], these bits information is restored to the original watermark image.

In general, the extracting process of watermark image is an inverse process of embedding watermark.

4 The Experiment Result and Performance Analysis

This section gives some simulation-based experiments and analysis of the results and performance of the proposed quantum watermark algorithm. All experiments are simulated on the MATLAB R2012a.

There are three factors of performance evaluation for quantum watermark algorithms, including robustness, transparency and capacity, respectively. Robustness shows that watermark image can be extracted effectively from stego image after various attacks. Transparency represents the similarity between carrier image and stego image. Capacity is the maximum amount of watermark information embedded into carrier image without affecting its normal use. It can be represented by the number of bits of watermark information contained in the unit carrier image pixel. Three images "Baboon", "Cameraman" and "Lena" are used in the experiments as carrier images. Four images "Eagle", "Recycling", "Thumbs-up" and "HTC" are used as watermark images. The image sizes for carrier and watermark are all $2^7 \times 2^8$.

4.1 Robustness

In defending various geometric attacks, the new algorithm effectively utilizes two important properties of log-polar sampling, i.e., rotation and scale invariances. These invariances make quantum watermark image extracted have a good robustness when stego image was subjected to various geometric attacks, such as rotation, vertical axisymmetry, horizontal axisymmetry and scaling.

In order to prove the above argument, Figs. 4, 5, 6 and 7 are given respectively to represent above-mentioned geometric attacks. The experimental results show that watermark image can be extracted effectively after a variety of attacks, and has a high image quality. It means that the new algorithm has good robustness.

Fig. 4. Rotation attack. (a) The stego image attacked by rotation, (b) the stego image restored by the quantum image registration algorithm, (c) the watermark image extracted from (b).

Fig. 5. Vertical axisymmetry. (a) The stego image attacked by horizontal axisymmetry, (b) the stego image restored, (c) the watermark image extracted from (b).

Fig. 6. Horizontal axisymmetry. (a) The stego image attacked by vertical axisymmetry, (b) the stego image restored, (c) the watermark image extracted from (b).

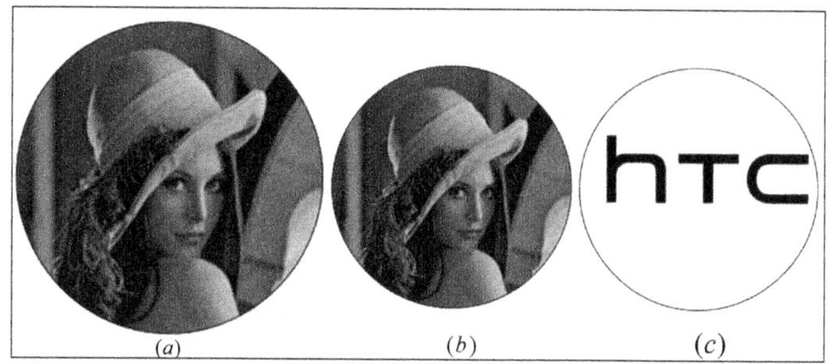

Fig. 7. Scaling attack. (a) The stego image attacked by scaling, (b) the stego image restored, (c) the watermark image extracted from (b).

4.2 Transparency

At present, there is no specific evaluation standard for visual quality index of the quantum image. Therefore, in this paper, the classical PSNR (Peak Signal-to-Noise Ratio) is applied to evaluate transparency of the quantum watermark.

Assuming there are two $2^m \times 2^n$ images I and J with gray range 2^q (I is the original carrier image, J is the embedded carrier image). $I(\rho, \theta)$ and $J(\rho, \theta)$ represents the pixel values of the (ρ, θ) pixel. MSE (Mean Squared Error) and PSNR are defined as Eqs. (12) and (13), respectively:

$$MSE = \frac{1}{mn} \sum_{\rho=0}^{2^m-1} \sum_{\theta=0}^{2^n-1} [I(\rho, \theta) - J(\rho, \theta)]^2 \tag{12}$$

$$PSNR = 20 \times \log_{10}\left(\frac{MAX_I}{\sqrt{MSE}}\right) \tag{13}$$

Here, MAX_I is the maximum possible pixel value of the image.

From the experimental results in Fig. 8, it is easy to know that stego image and the original carrier image are incapable to be identified by the naked eye of human being.

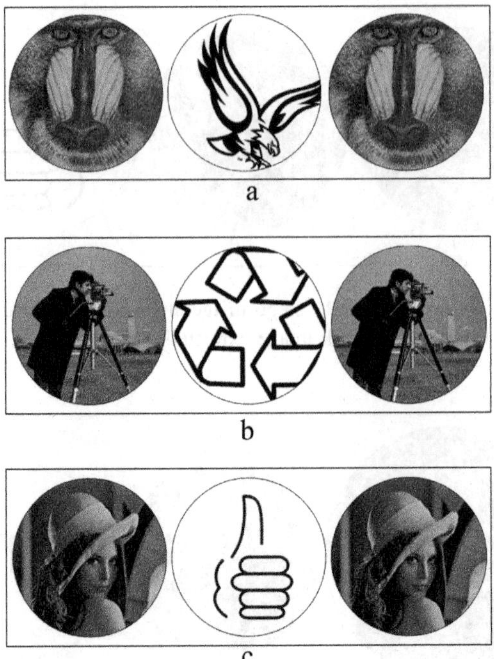

Fig. 8. In three groups of pictures, the left are the original carrier images, the middle are the watermark images, the right are the embedded carrier images.

Table 1 lists out the PSNR values of stego image obtained by embedding different watermark images into the same carrier image, respectively. And Fig. 9 shows the change of PSNR values of Table 1. It can be found that the PSNR values of stego images are much higher than the image quality standard of 38 dB, which proves they have high image qualities. Therefore, the new algorithm can obtain good transparency.

Table 1. PSNR values of stego images in our simulation.

PSNR(dB) — Watermark iamge / Carrier image	Eagle	Recycling	Thumbs-up	HTC
Baboon	46.1551	46.1515	46.1482	46.1454
Cameraman	46.1133	46.0789	46.0832	46.1029
Lena	46.1051	46.1064	46.1074	46.0977

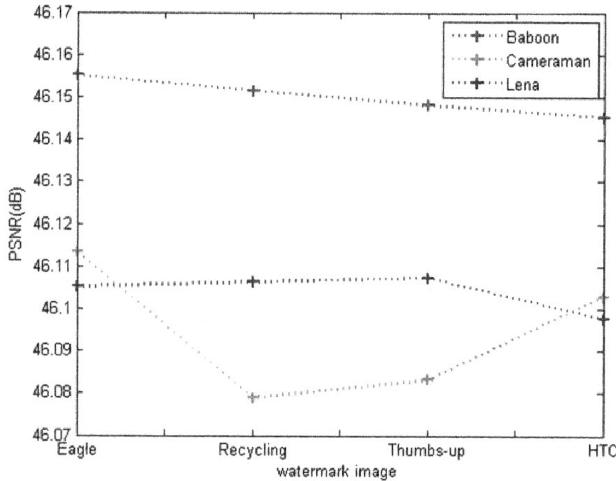

Fig. 9. The change of PSNR values of Table 1.

4.3 Capacity

Capacity can be accurately calculated by the embedding rate, which is denoted by the number of bits embedded divided by all the least significant qubits of the carrier image in this paper. It is easy to know the embedding rate of the new algorithm is equal to 1. Furthermore, based on LSQb modification in our algorithm, the modifying rate of the algorithm is 0.5, which means that half of the qubits need to be modified, and the other half is not. Comparing with the previous achievements, the embedding rate and them modifying rate of our algorithm is rather good.

5 Conclusion

In this paper, a novel robust watermarking algorithm is proposed. By combining the QUALPI representation model with the LSQb modification technique, new algorithm enables to effectively resist geometric distortion or rotation attacks, so as to better protect the copyright of quantum image. The simulation results based on MATLAB show that the new algorithm has a good performance in robustness and transparency. On the basis of the capacity analysis to the new algorithm, the embedding rate of our algorithm is 1 and the modification rate is 0.5.

The robustness of the quantum watermark image against geometric attacks has been improved in this paper. But it does not discuss more complex attacks, such as geometric zooming and tailoring. Therefore, the next research will be focused on the design of quantum robust watermark algorithm to deal with these complex attacks in the future.

Acknowledgments. This work was supported by the National Natural Science Foundation of China (Nos. 61373131, 61303039, 61232016, 61501247), Sichuan Youth Science and Technique Foundation (No. 2017JQ0048), NUIST Research Foundation for Talented Scholars (2015r014), PAPD and CICAEET funds.

References

1. Venegas-Andraca, S.E., Bose, S.: Storing, processing and retrieving an image using quantum mechanics. In: Proceedings of the SPIE Conference on Quantum Information and Computation, vol. 5105, pp. 1085–1090 (2003)
2. Venegas-Andraca, S.E., Ball, J.L., Burnett, K., Bose, S.: Processing images in entangled quantum systems. Quantum Inf. Process. **9**, 1–11 (2004)
3. Latorre, J.I.: Image compression and entanglement. Computer Science (2005)
4. Le, P.Q., Dong, F.Y., Hirota, K.: A flexible representation of quantum images for polynomial preparation, image compression, and processing operations. Quantum Inf. Process. **10**, 63–84 (2011)
5. Zhang, Y., Lu, K., Gao, Y.H.: NEQR: a novel enhanced quantum representation of digital images. Quantum Inf. Process. **12**, 2833–2860 (2013)
6. Zhang, Y., Lu, K., Gao, Y.H., Xu, K.: A novel quantum representation for log-polar images. Quantum Inf. Process. **12**, 3103–3126 (2013)
7. Sang, J.Z., Wang, S., Li, Q.: A novel quantum representation for color digital images. Quantum Inf. Process. **16**, 16–42 (2016)
8. Chen, B.J., Shu, H.Z., Coatrieux, G., Chen, G., Sun, X.M., Coatrieux, J.L.: Color image analysis by quaternion-type moments. J. Math. Imaging Vis. **51**, 124–144 (2015)
9. Xia, Z.H., Wang, X.H., Zhang, L.G., Qin, Z., Sun, X.M., Ren, K.: A privacy-preserving and copy-deterrence content-based image retrieval scheme in cloud computing. IEEE Trans. Inf. Forensics Secur. **11**, 2594–2608 (2016)
10. Wang, J.W., Li, T., Shi, Y.Q., Lian, S.G., Ye, J.Y.: Forensics feature analysis in quaternion wavelet domain for distinguishing photographic images and computer graphics. Multimedia Tools Appl. 1–17 (2016)
11. Yang, Y.G., Jia, X., Xu, P., Tian, J.: Analysis and improvement of the watermark strategy for quantum images based on quantum Fourier transform. Quantum Inf. Process. **12**, 793–803 (2013)
12. Song, X.H., Wang, S., Liu, S., El-Latif, A.A., Niu, X.M.: A dynamic watermarking scheme for quantum images using quantum wavelet transform. Quantum Inf. Process. **12**, 3689–3706 (2013)
13. Song, X.H., Wang, S., El-Latif, A.A., Niu, X.M.: Dynamic watermarking scheme for quantum images based on Hadamard transform. Multimedia Syst. **20**, 379–388 (2014)
14. Shailender, G., Bhushan, A.G.: Information hiding least significant bit steganography and cryptography. Int. J. Mod. Educ. Comput. Sci. **4**, 27–34 (2012)
15. Sang, J.Z., Wang, S., Li, Q.: Least significant qubit algorithm for quantum images. Quantum Inf. Process. **15**, 1–20 (2016)
16. Wang, D., Liu, Z.H., Zhu, W.N., Li, S.Z.: Design of quantum comparator based on extended general Toffoli gates with multiple targets. Comput. Sci. **39**, 302–306 (2012)

Adaptive Hybrid Wavelet Regularization Method for Compressive Imaging

Lingjun Liu[1,2], Weiyu Yu[1,2(✉)], and Cui Yang[1]

[1] School of Electronic and Information Engineering, South China University of Technology, Guangzhou 510641, China
{eeljliu, yuweiyu, yangcui}@scut.edu.cn

[2] School of Electronic and Information Engineering, Nanjing University of Information Science & Technology, Ningliu Road, Nanjing 210044, China

Abstract. This paper proposes a hybrid method that simultaneously considers sparsity in wavelet domain and image self-similarity by using wavelet L1 norm, nonlocal wavelet L0 norm regularization in image compressive sensing (CS) recovery. An auxiliary variable is then introduced to decompose this composite constraint problem into two simpler regularization sub-problems. Based on Fast Iterative Shrinkage-Thresholding Algorithm (FISTA), the sub-problems corresponding to the wavelet L1 norm and the nonlocal wavelet L0 norm are then solved by soft thresholding and adaptive hard thresholding respectively. The threshold of the later is decreased according to the energy of measurement error, leading to an adaptive hybrid regularization method. Experimental results show that it outperforms several excellent CS techniques.

Keywords: Composite regularizations · Adaptive thresholding · Compressive sensing · Nonlocal wavelet L0 norm regularization

1 Introduction

Exploiting a prior knowledge of the original signals is critical to the success of com-pressive sensing (CS) [1, 2] recovery. For CS imaging applications, methods that seek only wavelet-sparsity [3, 4] often fail to recover the image, since images are not sparse enough in the wavelet domain. Researchers have noticed this weakness and have therefore explored the use of more complicated signal models, such as minimal total variation (TV) [5–7], wavelet trees [8, 9], Markov mixture models [10] and non-local regularization [11–16].

Such models can be enforced by using penalty functionals to encourage solutions of a certain form [6, 8, 13, 16, 17], or explicit models [10, 18]. In FCSA (Fast Composite Splitting Algorithm) [6], composite sparsity penalty terms in wavelet and gradient domain are used jointly to constrain the solution space for a good reconstruction result; while WaTMRI (Wavelet Tree sparsity Magnetic Resonancce Imaging) [8] superadds the tree sparse regularization to the objective function of FCSA, further forcing the parent-child wavelet coefficients to be zeros or non-zeros together. On the other hand,

X. Sun et al. (Eds.): ICCCS 2017, Part II, LNCS 10603, pp. 461–470, 2017.
https://doi.org/10.1007/978-3-319-68542-7_39

graphical models are usually used to describe the relationship between measurements and the original signal in Bayesian CS [10, 18], the prior knowledge is embodied with the probability distribution of the nodes.

Nonlocal sparsity-based algorithms [13, 16, 18] which exploit the self-repetitive structure exhibited often in natural images have shown great potential in image CS recovery. NLR-CS (CS via Nonlocal Low-Rank Regularization) [13] builds a patch-based low-rank regularization model to enforce the low-rank property over the sets of nonlocal similar patches; while RCoS (CS recovery via collaborative sparsity) [16] uses a 3D sparsity term to maintain image nonlocal consistency. On the contrast, D-AMP (Denoising-based Approximate Message Passing) algorithm [18] exploits the image self-similarity through the use of nonlocal based denoisers, such as BM3D (Block-matching and 3D filtering) denoiser [19], which performs hard or soft thresh-olding with a 3D orthogonal dictionary (3D filtering) on 3D image blocks built by stacking similar patches together (Block-matching). However, they are ad hoc, e.g. D-AMP, which strongly depends on the denoiser and thus has difficulty in combining with other prior information; or not enough adaptive since most of them are with fixed regularization parameters, in addition, both NLR-CS and RCoS are based on the alternating direction method, resulting in a relatively slow convergence rate.

In this paper, we propose a hybrid wavelet regularization model for image CS recovery, which combines wavelet sparsity and nonlocal wavelet sparsity seamlessly, and solve this problem based on the fastest proximal method FISTA [20]. In the frame of FISTA, the original composite regularization problem is firstly decomposed into two simpler sub-problems by using an auxiliary variable; then each of them is separately solved by thresholding methods. Soft thresholding is used to solve the sub-problem corresponding to the wavelet L1 norm; while adaptive hard thresholding is used to solve the sub-problem corresponding to nonlocal wavelet L0 norm. The threshold of the later can be dynamically tuned according to the energy of measurement error, leading to an adaptive sparse model. Experimental results show that it impressively outperforms previous methods in terms of reconstruction accuracy, and also achieves competitive advantage in computation complexity.

2 Compressive Sensing and FISTA Algorithm

The compressive sensing recovery method recovers a signal $x_0 \in \mathbb{C}^n$ from its randomized linear measurements $y = \mathbf{A}x_0$, $y \in \mathbb{C}^m$, where $\mathbf{A} \in \mathbb{C}^{m \times n}$ is the measurement matrix. Since $m < n$, it is an underdetermined problem. More than one solution can yield the same measurements, thus the prior knowledge of x is needed. If x is sparse or sparse in a transform domain, such as wavelet domain, we can recover the original signal by pursuing the sparsest signal x that satisfies $y = \mathbf{A}x$. One can solve the following L1 minimization problem:

$$\widehat{x} = \arg\min_{x} \frac{1}{2} \|y - \mathbf{A}x\|_2^2 + \lambda \|x\|_1, \tag{1}$$

where λ is a regularization parameter.

The above problem can be efficiently solved by various methods [21–25], one of which is ISTA (iterative shrinkage-thresholding algorithm) [25]. Specifically, the general step of ISTA can be summarized in Algorithm 1, where $f = \|y - \mathbf{A}x\|_2^2/2$ and $\nabla f(x^k) = \mathbf{A}^*(\mathbf{A}x^k - y)$ denotes the gradient of the function f at the point x^k; $\mathbf{A}^*$ denotes the conjugate transpose of $\mathbf{A}$; c is a step size. The undersampled Fourier matrix $\mathbf{A} = \mathbf{SF}$ is used as the measurement matrix, where $\mathbf{F}$ is the 2D Fourier transform and $\mathbf{S}$ is a selection matrix containing m rows of the identity matrix. Step (b) is a proximity operator. It has a close form solution, which can be expressed as:

$$x^k = soft(x_g, \lambda c) = \operatorname{sgn}(x_g) \cdot \max(abs(x_g) - \lambda c, 0). \tag{2}$$

Algorithm 1. ISTA [25]

Input: $y, \mathbf{A}, \lambda, x^0 = 0$
for $k = 1$ **to** K **do**
(a) $x_g = x^k - c\nabla f(x^k)$
(b) $x^k = \arg\min_x \{\lambda \|x\|_1 + \|x - x_g\|_2^2 / (2c)\}$
end for

FISTA [20] offers an accelerated version of ISTA by adding an accelerated step (step (c)), which is summarized in Algorithm 2.

Algorithm 2. FISTA [20]

Input: $y, \mathbf{A}, \lambda, x^0 = r^1 = 0$
for $k = 1$ **to** K **do**
(a) $x_g = r^k - c\nabla f(r^k)$
(b) $x^k = \arg\min_x \{\lambda \|x\|_1 + \|x - x_g\|_2^2 / (2c)\}$
(c) $t^{k+1} = \dfrac{(1 + \sqrt{1 + 4(t^k)^2})}{2}$; $r^{k+1} = x^k + (\dfrac{(t^k - 1)}{t^{k+1}})(x^k - x^{k-1})$
end for

3 CS via Composite Regularizations and Adaptive Thresholding

3.1 The New Composite Model

Images are generally sparse in wavelet domain, although not strictly. Moreover there exist abundant similar image patches in natural images. These sparse priors can be utilized by using two regularizations wavelet sparse and nonlocal wavelet regularization. The composite regularization problem can be formulated as follows:

$$\widehat{x} = \arg\min_{x} \frac{1}{2}\|y - \mathbf{A}x\|_2^2 + \alpha\|\mathbf{\Psi}x\|_1 + \beta\sum_{i \in G}\|\mathbf{\Gamma}_{3D}x_i\|_0, \tag{3}$$

where $\mathbf{\Psi}$ represents the wavelet transform; α and β are two regularization parameters. The first item is the fidelity term; while the last two items are priori constraint terms, denoting wavelet L1 norm and nonlocal wavelet L0 norm respectively. We characterize the image self-similarity by means of the last item derived from BM3D [19], which is used to seek patch correlation in image denoising. To obtain $\mathbf{\Gamma}_{3D}x_i$, we first stack similar image patches to a 3D group, x_i is the i-th group and G is the total number of groups; then 3D wavelet transform $\mathbf{\Gamma}_{3D}$ is conduct on x_i, which is achieved by conducting 2D wavelet transform on each patch and then conducting 1D wavelet transform along the third axis. The proposed composite model considers both the nonlocal self-similarity of patches and the overall sparsity in wavelet domain.

3.2 AHWR_CS Algorithm for Solving the Composite Constraint Problem

The above composite regularization problem (3) can't be solved directly by iterative shrinkage algorithm, thus an auxiliary variable z is introduced to decompose the original problem into two simpler sub-problems and solve each of them by FISTA. Let $z = \mathbf{\Psi}x$, (3) can be rewritten as:

$$\widehat{x} = \arg\min_{x,z} \frac{1}{2}\|y - \mathbf{A}x\|_2^2 + \beta\sum_{i \in G}\|\mathbf{\Gamma}_{3D}x_i\|_0 + \alpha\|z\|_1 + \frac{\mu}{2}\|z - \mathbf{\Psi}x\|_2^2. \tag{4}$$

The z-subproblem in (4) can be written as:

$$z = \arg\min_{z} \frac{\mu}{2}\|z - \mathbf{\Psi}x\|_2^2 + \alpha\|z\|_1. \tag{5}$$

It has a closed form solution by soft thresholding:

$$z = \mathit{soft}(\mathbf{\Psi}x, \alpha/\mu) = \mathrm{sgn}(\mathbf{\Psi}x) \cdot \max(\mathit{abs}(\mathbf{\Psi}x) - \alpha/\mu, 0). \tag{6}$$

For the x-subproblem,

$$\widehat{x} = \arg\min_{x,z} \frac{1}{2}\|y - \mathbf{A}x\|_2^2 + \frac{\mu}{2}\|z - \mathbf{\Psi}x\|_2^2 + \beta\sum_{i \in G}\|\mathbf{\Gamma}_{3D}x_i\|_0 \tag{7}$$

Let $h(x) = (\|y - \mathbf{A}x\|_2^2 + \mu\|z - \mathbf{\Psi}x\|_2^2)/2.$, then it can be solved efficiently by FISTA. Algorithm 3 outlines the solving procedure of our algorithm named as AHWR_CS (CS via Adaptive Hybrid Wavelet Regularization). In step (b), $\nabla h(r^k) = \mathbf{A}^*(\mathbf{A}r^k - y) + \mu\mathbf{\Psi}^{\mathrm{T}}(\mathbf{\Psi}r^k - z)$ with $\mathbf{\Psi}^{\mathrm{T}}$ denotes the inverse wavelet transform. The key to success in solving (3) is to compute step (c). We use a lemma in [26], namely, the minimization problem

$$\widehat{x} = \arg\min_{x} \frac{1}{2}\|x - a\|_2^2 + \lambda\|x\|_0, \tag{8}$$

has a closed form solution, which can be expressed as:

$$\widehat{x} = hard(a, \sqrt{2\lambda}) = \begin{cases} a, & if abs(a) - \sqrt{2\lambda} > 0 \\ 0, & \text{otherwise} \end{cases}. \tag{9}$$

Algorithm 3. AHWR_CS

Input: $y, \mathbf{A}, \alpha, c, x^0 = r^1 = 0$
for $k = 1$ **to** K **do**
(a) $z = \text{soft}(\boldsymbol{\Psi}x, \alpha / \mu)$
(b) $x_g = r^k - c\nabla h(r^k)$
(c) $x^k = \arg\min_{x}\{\beta\sum_{i\in G}\|\Gamma_{3D}x_i\|_0 + \|x - x_g\|_2^2 / (2c)\}$
(d) $t^{k+1} = \frac{(1+\sqrt{1+4(t^k)^2})}{2}$; $r^{k+1} = x^k + (\frac{(t^k - 1)}{t^{k+1}})(x^k - x^{k-1})$
end for

Since the orthogonal transform $\boldsymbol{\Gamma}_{3D}$ has the property of energy conservation, step (c) can be written as:

$$x^k \approx \arg\min_{u}\left\{\beta\sum_{i\in G}\|\boldsymbol{\Gamma}_{3D}x_i\|_0 + \frac{\sum_{i\in G}\|\boldsymbol{\Gamma}_{3D}x_i - \boldsymbol{\Gamma}_{3D}(x_g)_i\|_2^2}{2cN}\right\}, \tag{10}$$

and its solution is:

$$\begin{aligned}(x^k)_i &= hard(\boldsymbol{\Gamma}_{3D}(x_g)_i, \sqrt{2\beta cN}) \\ &= \begin{cases} \boldsymbol{\Gamma}_{3D}(x_g)_i, & if\ abs(\boldsymbol{\Gamma}_{3D}(x_g)_i) - \sqrt{2\beta cN} > 0 \\ 0, & \text{otherwise} \end{cases},\end{aligned} \tag{11}$$

where x_i and $(x_g)_i$ are the i-th similar patches 3D group, which are repetitively computed in the last item of (7), since a patch may be assigned to several 3D groups. According to the Law of Large Numbers, the average number of repetitive computation for the i-th 3D group can be computed by N. However, it is not need to compute N, for the reason that in the implementation we do need the threshold $\delta = \sqrt{2\beta cN}$ which can be set by selecting an appropriate regularization parameter β. The regularization parameters of most regularized image regularization methods [1, 2, 4, 5] are fixed and set empirically. The regularization parameter β is relevant to the denosing threshold $\delta = \sqrt{2\beta c N}$ (see (11)), apparently the threshold should be reduced along with the iteration. Thus we set the threshold proportional to the observation residual:

$$\delta = s\sqrt{\|y - \mathbf{A}x_g\|_2^2 / m} \tag{12}$$

where s is a scale factor and can be set empirically. We obtain an adaptive model for the regularization parameter β is changed adaptively.

4 Experiments

To evaluate reconstruction performances of the proposed algorithm in items of average PSNR, runtime and visual quality, we compare our algorithm with four excellent algorithms (FCSA [6], WaTMRI [8], Turbo-AMP [10] and D-AMP [18]). Three experiments are carried on eight natural images (Cameraman, Lena, Barbara, Boat, House, Peppers, Baboon and Man) and four MR images (Brain, Chest, Heart and Shoulder, which can be found in Fig. 1) with size 256 × 256 at four sampling ratios (18%, 20%, 22%, and 25%). The undersampled Fourier matrix is generated by following the previous works [8, 10], which randomly choose more Fourier coefficients from low frequency and less on high frequency. All experiments are on a desktop with 3.80 GHz AMD A10-5800K CPU. Matlab version is 7.11 (R2010b).

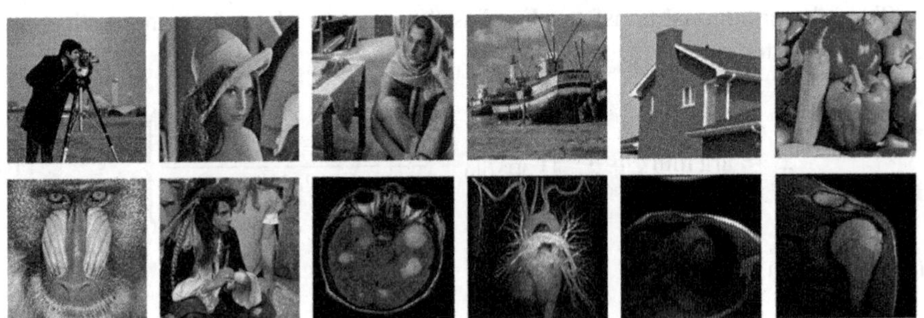

Fig. 1. The 12 widely used test images.

We set the maximum iterations $K = 10$ for Turbo-AMP and set $K = 50$ for the rest algorithms. For our algorithm AHWR_CS, we use the setting $\alpha = 0.002$, $c = 1$. The scale factor in (12) s is set to 30 in the first 20 iterations, and then is fixed at 5 after 20 iterations, since the estimated threshold δ has already been a small valve in the later iterations. The 3D wavelet transform $\boldsymbol{\Gamma}_{3\mathrm{D}}$ is composed of 2-D bior1.5 and 1-D Haar. To construct 3D groups by stacking similar patches, we need to set the following parameters: the size of each patch is 8 × 8; the size of window for searching matched patches is 25 × 25; the number of best matched patches is 16; and the sliding step to process every next reference patch is set to 6. To speed up the algorithm, step (c) is only carried out every 3 iterations (step (c) becomes $x^k = x_g$, if it is not carried out) expect the first 5 iterations. For the rest algorithms, the default setting in their codes is used.

4.1 Quantitative Evaluation

We carry all algorithms on the twelve test images with various sampling ratios, the average PSNR results by running each image five times are listed in Table 1, from which we can see that the nonlocal sparsity-based methods AHWR_CS and D-AMP are better than others. Particularly, the proposed algorithm AHWR_CS achieves the highest PSNR results, and averagely outperforms the second-best algorithm D-AMP by 0.54 dB, validating the superiority of the proposed algorithm in objective quality.

Table 1. Average PSNR (dB) comparisons on the test images with various sampling ratios.

Sampling ratio	18%	20%	22%	25%
FCSA	26.32	28.13	30.16	31.67
WaTMRI	26.97	28.95	31.06	32.68
Turbo-AMP	25.75	27.27	28.74	30.13
D-AMP	29.69	32.21	34.07	36.66
AHWR_CS	29.95	32.52	34.43	37.25

Table 2 gives the average CPU time of different algorithms carried on the twelve test images by running each image five times. FCSA spends the least CPU time; however, its PSNR results in Table 1 are relatively poor. Note that AHWR_CS spends 62.05% less CPU time to achieve higher PSNR than D-AMP, which is the second-best algorithm in PSNR.

Table 2. Average CPU time (sec) comparisons on the twelve test images with various sampling ratios.

Sampling ratio	18%	20%	22%	25%
FCSA	2.07	2.17	2.18	2.41
WaTMRI	2.49	2.44	2.53	2.76
Turbo-AMP	8.62	8.47	8.70	8.92
D-AMP	23.06	23.26	23.68	25.46
AHWR_CS	8.79	9.18	9.47	9.13

The convergence speed of these algorithms with 20% sampling is presented in Fig. 2, the proposed algorithm AHWR_CS always achieves more accurate result after six seconds. Since AHWR_CS is based on the FISTA algorithm, it can converge faster than another nonlocal sparsity-based algorithm D-AMP, which is a Bayesian method.

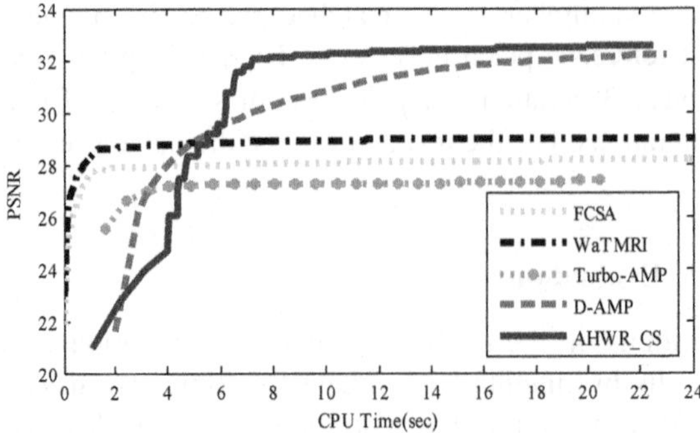

Fig. 2. Performance comparison (CPU time vs. PSNR) with 20% sampling.

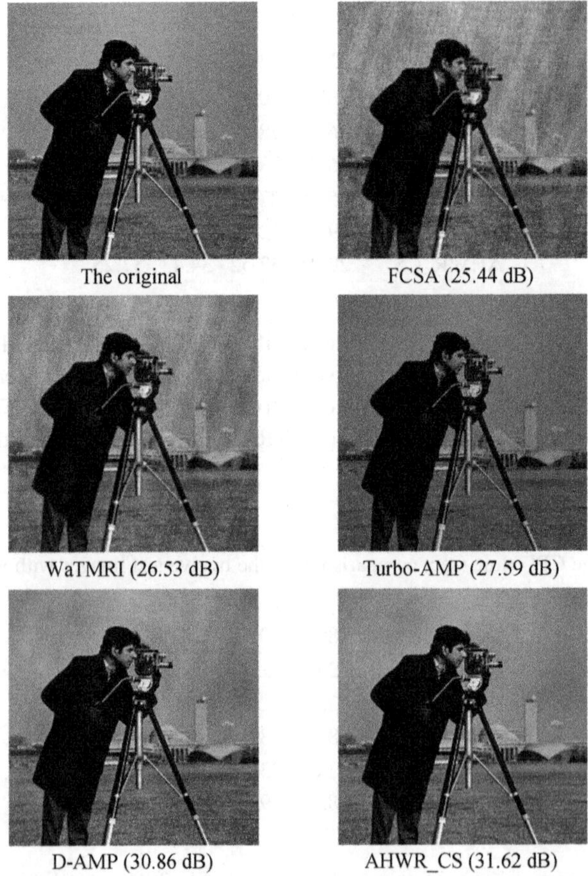

Fig. 3. Visual results of Cameraman image reconstruction with 20% sampling.

4.2 Visual Quality Evaluation

The reconstructed Cameraman images by the test algorithms are shown in Fig. 3, from which we can clearly see that the nonlocal sparsity-based methods AHWR_CS and D-AMP are still better than others. Moreover the proposed algorithm enjoys great advantages over other competing algorithms in producing more clean screens, e.g. on the area of sky. Due to the adaptive thresholding strategy, the elimination of artifacts can be handled more properly by AHWR_CS.

5 Conclusion

We have proposed an adaptive hybrid wavelet regularization method for the compressed image reconstruction. This composite constraint problem consisted of wavelet L1 norm and nonlocal wavelet L0 norm is solved with a new efficient algorithm AHWR_CS based on the FISTA algorithm. To deal with the nonlocal wavelet sparse constraint sub-problem more properly, an adaptive thresholding strategy is designed. In the experiments, our algorithm is shown to outperform four excellent algorithms in reconstructed quality, and also achieve competitive advantage in runtime.

Acknowledgments. This work is partially supported by the National Natural Science Foundation of China (No. 61302120), the Science and Technology Planning Project of Guangdong Province (No. 2017A020214011), the Fundamental Research Funds for the Central Universities (No. 2017MS039), the Specialized Research Fund for the Doctoral Program of Higher Education (No. 20130172120045), and the supports of the Priority Academic Program Development of Jiangsu Higher Education Institutions, Jiangsu Collaborative Innovation Center on Atmospheric Environment and Equipment Technology (No. KJR16237). The authors also gratefully acknowledge the helpful comments and suggestions of the reviewers, which have improved the presentation.

References

1. Donoho, D.L.: Compressed sensing. IEEE Trans. Inf. Theory **52**, 1289–1306 (2006)
2. Candes, E.J., Romberg, J., Tao, T.: Robust uncertainty principles: exact signal reconstruction from highly incomplete frequency information. IEEE Trans. Inf. Theory **52**, 489–509 (2006)
3. Wu, J., Liu, F., Jiao, L.C., Wang, X.: Multivariate compressive sensing for image reconstruction in the wavelet domain: using scale mixture models. IEEE Trans. Image Process. **20**, 3483–3494 (2011)
4. Tan, J., Ma, Y., Baron, D.: Compressive imaging via approximate message passing with image denoising. IEEE Trans. Sig. Process. **63**, 2085–2092 (2015)
5. Rudin, L.I., Osher, S., Fatemi, E.: Nonlinear total variation based noise removal algorithms. In: Eleventh International Conference of the Center for Nonlinear Studies on Experimental Mathematics: Computational Issues in Nonlinear Science: Computational Issues in Nonlinear Science, pp. 259–268. Elsevier, Amsterdam (1992)
6. Huang, J., Zhang, S., Metaxas, D.: Efficient MR image reconstruction for compressed MR imaging. Med. Image Anal. **15**, 670–679 (2011)

7. Xia, Z., Lv, R., Zhu, Y., Ji, P., Sun, H., Shi, Y.: Fingerprint liveness detection using gradient-based texture features. Sig. Image Video Process. **11**, 381–388 (2017)
8. Chen, C., Junzhou, H.: Exploiting the wavelet structure in compressed sensing MRI. Magn. Reson. Imaging **32**, 1377–1389 (2014)
9. Wang, M., Wu, X., Jing, W., He, X.: Reconstruction algorithm using exact tree projection for tree-structured compressive sensing. IET Sig. Process. **10**, 566–573 (2016)
10. Som, S., Schniter, P.: Compressive imaging using approximate message passing and a Markov-Tree prior. IEEE Trans. Sig. Process. **60**, 3439–3448 (2012)
11. Zhang, X., Bai, T., Meng, H., Chen, J.: Compressive sensing-based ISAR imaging via the combination of the sparsity and nonlocal total variation. IEEE Geosci. Remote Sens. Lett. **11**, 990–994 (2014)
12. Dong, W., Shi, G., Wu, X., Zhang, J.: A learning-based method for compressive image recovery. J. Vis. Commun. Image Represent. **24**, 1055–1063 (2013)
13. Dong, W., Shi, G., Li, X., Ma, Y., Huang, F.: Compressive sensing via nonlocal low-rank regularization. IEEE Trans. Image Process. **23**, 3618–3632 (2014)
14. Metzler, C.A., Maleki, A., Baraniuk, R.G.: From denoising to compressed sensing. IEEE Trans. Inf. Theory **62**, 5117–5144 (2016)
15. Metzler, C.A., Maleki, A., Baraniuk, R.G.: BM3D-AMP: a new image recovery algorithm based on BM3D denoising. In: IEEE International Conference on Image Processing (ICIP), pp. 3116–3120. IEEE Press, New York (2015)
16. Zhang, J., Zhao, D., Zhao, C., Xiong, R., Ma, S., Gao, W.: Image compressive sensing recovery via collaborative sparsity. IEEE J. Emerg. Sel. Top. Circuits Syst. **2**, 380–391 (2012)
17. Zhou, Z., Wang, Y., Wu, Q., Yang, C., Sun, X.: Effective and efficient global context verification for image copy detection. IEEE Trans. Inf. Forensics Secur. **12**, 48–63 (2017)
18. Metzler, C.A., Maleki, A., Baraniuk, R.G.: From denoising to compressed sensing. IEEE Trans. Inf. Theory **62**, 5117–5144 (2014)
19. Dabov, K., Foi, A., Katkovnik, V., Egiazarian, K.: Image denoising by sparse 3D transform-domain collaborative filtering. IEEE Trans. Image Process. **16**, 2080–2095 (2007)
20. Beck, A., Teboulle, M.: A fast iterative shrinkage-thresholding algorithm for linear inverse problems. SIAM J. Imaging Sci. **2**, 183–202 (2009)
21. Hosseini, M.S., Plataniotis, K.N.: High-accuracy total variation with application to compressed video sensing. IEEE Trans. Image Process. **23**, 3869–3884 (2014)
22. Ling, Q., Shi, W., Wu, G., Ribeiro, A.: DLM: decentralized linearized alternating direction method of multipliers. IEEE Trans. Sig. Process. **63**, 4051–4064 (2015)
23. Yin, W., Osher, S., Goldfarb, D., Darbon, J.: Bregman iterative algorithms for L1-minimization with applications to compressed sensing. SIAM J. Imaging Sci. **1**, 143–168 (2008)
24. Qiao, T., Li, W., Wu, B.: A new algorithm based on linearized Bregman Iteration with generalized inverse for compressed sensing. Circ. Syst. Sig. Process. **33**, 1527–1539 (2014)
25. Daubechies, I., Defriese, M., DeMol, C.: An iterative thresholding algorithm for linear inverse problems with a sparsity constraint. Commun. Pure Appl. Math. **57**, 1413–1457 (2004)
26. Afonso, M., Bioucas-Dias, J., Figueiredo, M.: Fast image recovery using variable splitting and constrained optimization. IEEE Trans. Image Process. **19**, 2345–2356 (2010)

Registration of OCT Fundus Images with Color Fundus Images Based on Invariant Features

Ping Li[1], Qiang Chen[1,2(✉)], Wen Fan[3], and Songtao Yuan[3]

[1] School of Computer Science and Engineering, Nanjing University of Science and Technology, Nanjing 210094, China
Cassie_lp@126.com, chen2qiang@njust.edu.cn
[2] Fujian Provincial Key Laboratory of Information Processing and Intelligent Control, Minjiang University, Fuzhou 350121, China
[3] Department of Ophthalmology, The First Affiliated Hospital with Nanjing Medical University, Nanjing 210029, China
fanwen1029@163.com, yuansongtao@vip.sina.com

Abstract. Disease diagnosis and treatment are often supported by multiple images acquired from the same patient. Multimodal retinal fundus image registration techniques are fundamental to integrate the information gained from several fundus images for a comprehensive understanding. In this paper, we proposed an algorithm for registration of OCT fundus images (OFIs) with color fundus photographs (CFPs) based on invariant features. The local similarity function is defined based on the blood vessel ridges of retinal fundus images. According to the local maximum similarity function, we can extract effective image blocks and then acquire the feature matching points. We can finally achieve the registration by utilizing the quadratic surface model to calculate the transformation matrix parameters. The proposed algorithm was tested on a sample set containing 3 normal eyes and 18 eyes with age-related macular degeneration. The experiment demonstrates that the proposed method has high accuracy (root mean square error is 111.06 μm) in different qualities for both of color fundus images and OCT fundus images.

Keywords: Multimodal retinal image registration · Color fundus images · OCT fundus images · Similarity function · Quadratic surface model

1 Introduction

The retinal fundus image is an important basis for diagnosing of eye diseases such as diabetes, glaucoma, hypertension, coronary heart disease and so on. The characteristics of retinopathy usually relate to the symptom of many diseases. Retinal images from different modalities can provide complementary information of structure and function. Hence, doctors always need to gather multi-source image information during diagnose and treatment for joint inspection. The retinal image registration is the premise for image fusing and lesion detection, and the registration result have important auxiliary role for diagnosing many diseases. The purpose of retinal image registration is to align

X. Sun et al. (Eds.): ICCCS 2017, Part II, LNCS 10603, pp. 471–482, 2017.
https://doi.org/10.1007/978-3-319-68542-7_40

the two or more retinal images in area space which is clinically beneficial for ophthalmologists in the process of diagnose and treatment, track prediction, and surgical navigation for retina diseases [1].

Spectral Domain Optical Coherence Tomography (SD-OCT) is a new ophthalmic imaging technology of high resolution, which can display the three-dimensional structure of retina [2]. Compared with the traditional time-domain OCT using six rays scanning mode, SD–OCT uses 128 rays to scan images. The fundus images and SD-OCT volume data are showed in Figs. 1(a) and (b). It can be seen that fundus images only provide plane structure, while SD-OCT can capture the 3D image data (called cube). The resolution of SD-OCT images is 512 × 128 × 1024. OCT fundus images are 2D images formed by calculating the average of all gray values of every A-Scan in the B-Scan image (Figs. 1(b) and (c)). OCT fundus images provide a new window for ophthalmologists to relearn and rediscovery retinal diseases from a new angle. The registration between OCT fundus images and retinal images of other modalities a crucial complementary technique for auxiliary retinal diseases diagnosis and treatment, which is helpful to consistency evaluation, pathological characteristics analysis and tracking of retinal diseases. Studying the key problem of retinal image registration is crucial to the clinical practice. A method of registration of OCT fundus images with color images based on invariant features is proposed in this paper.

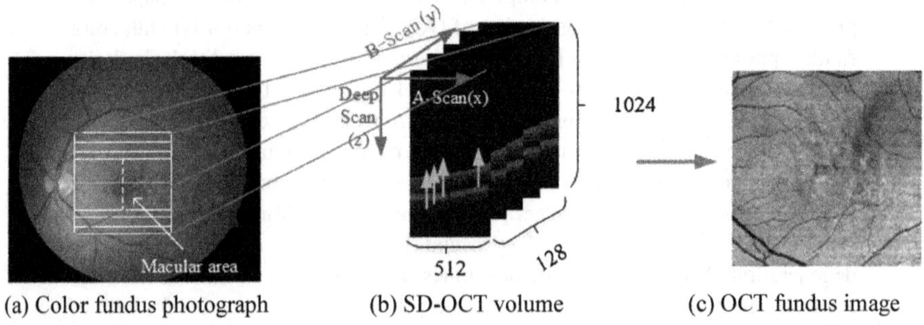

(a) Color fundus photograph (b) SD-OCT volume (c) OCT fundus image

Fig. 1. Imaging principle of OCT fundus images (Color figure online)

Existing image registration methods roughly include two kinds: gray based [3] and features based [4–6] methods. Registration method based on gray measures the similarity between two images by the gray scale of the whole image, such as mutual information and mutual correlation and then finds the points with maximum or minimum similarity, so as to determine the parameters of the transformation matrix between two images. Registration methods based on gray can only handle the gray scale and usually are applied only to monomodal image registration. Compared with image registration methods based on gray, methods based on image features are more suitable for retinal image registration which register images mainly by extracting their corners, outlines, and other local image features. This kind of method is able to be faster and can be used for multimodal image registration, and thus becomes a research focus on medical image registration. The blood vessel is considered to be a relatively robust feature in retinal image registration. Existing retinal image registration methods are basically dependent on the structure of retinal vessels to automatically registering images. [2, 5]. In addition, some researchers have done a lot of work on retinal registration methods without the dependence of retinal blood vessels. Although Scale Invariant Feature Transform (SIFT) algorithm [7] has no need for image pre-segmentation or extraction of feature points of specific structure and has invariance in translation, rotation and scale. It has some disappointments in the application of multimodal retinal image registration [8]. For instance, it needs higher dimension vector feature which leads to the low computing speed. And the saliency of the feature is quite limited leading to the failure of some images of indistinctive structure feature. The method proposed in [9] is based on fast robust features (Speed-up Robust Feature, SURF) while it is only suitable for mono-modal retinal image registration.

At present, the mono-modal retinal image registration method is relatively infinite [4, 5, 9], while the research of multimodal retinal image registration is relatively limited. Hence we proposed a new registration method between OCT image and color fundus image based on invariant features. We utilize the Hessian matrix to extract ridges of retinal blood vessels, and the similarity function is defined based on the overlap ratio of the blood vessels. Then we calculate the maximum of the similarity function to extract feature matching points and estimate the transform coefficient.

2 Method

Given one pair of retinal images, one is the reference image I_R and the other is the target image I_T. We will take I_R to be the color fundus photograph (CFP) and I_T to be the OCT fundus image (OFI) (see Fig. 2). Our goal is to find the optimal transformation that maximizes the similarity function in the appropriate space. The algorithm can be divided in several four steps including: (1) preprocessing, (2) blood vessel extraction, (3) local feature matching points detection and (4) transformation parameter estimation and registration. The overall flowchart of the proposed method is depicted in Fig. 3.

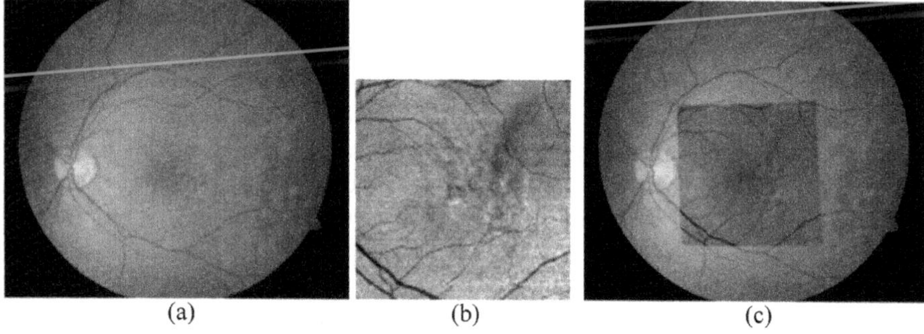

Fig. 2. (a) Color fundus image. (b) OCT fundus image. (c) Registration result by the automatic algorithm. (Color figure online)

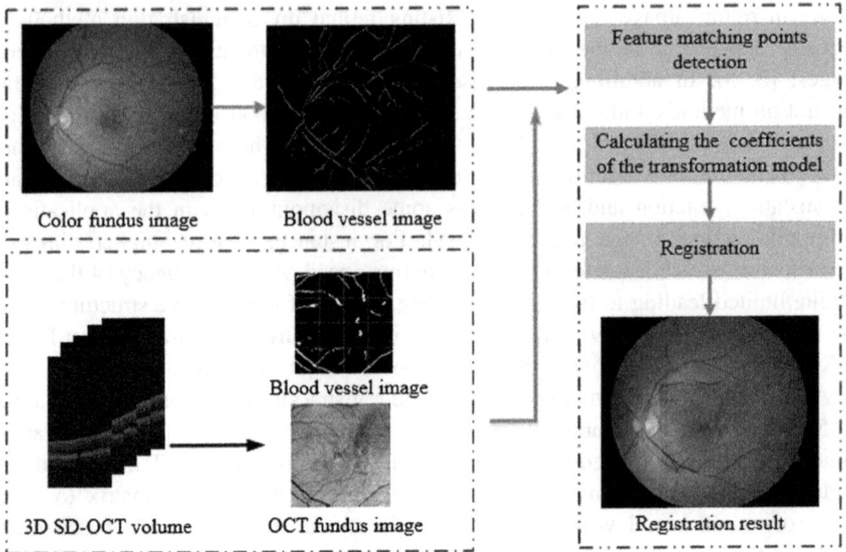

Fig. 3. Flow chart of the registration of SD-OCT fundus image with color fundus photograph. (Color figure online)

2.1 Preprocessing

Preprocessing was first applied to CFP. It will increase the difficulty of vessel segmentation because of the low contrast caused by uneven illumination and the reflection of blood vessel centerline. The green channel of the CFP is used because of its high contrast of blood vessels and then the Contrast Limited Adaptive Histogram equalization (CLAHE) is employed to enhance the contrast between vessels and their backgrounds. Moreover, due to the presence of heavy noise, we utilize the method proposed in [10] to remove noise in OCT fundus images.

2.2 Blood Vessel Extraction

Although retinal vessel segmentation has been widely studied, it is still a challenging problem because of three major reasons: (a) The quality of retinal images is quite different and the segmentation methods face the challenge of low contrast or high inhomogeneity of illumination conditions. (b) The complexity of vascular structures (different scales and orientations) causes most existing methods to be difficult to enhance multi-scale vessel-like structures with various linear orientations. (c) It is difficult to find the most optimum model or method which is the most appropriate for variety of data.

At present, there are many methods for extracting blood vessels of retinal fundus images [11, 12]. The hierarchical graph-based segmentation proposed in [11] is for blood vessel detection in digital retinal images which employs some of perceptual Gestalt principles: similarity, closure, continuity, and proximity to merge segments into coherent connected vessel-like patterns. The integration of Gestalt principles is based on object-based features (e.g., color and black top-hat (BTH) morphology and context) and Graph-Analysis algorithms (e.g., Dijkstra path). Another blood vessel detection method in [12] used a novel synergistic combination of the vesselness filter with high sensitivity and the matched filter with high specificity is obtained using orientation histogram. However, both of the methods above are only applicable to color fundus images.

The algorithm used to extract blood vessel of retinal fundus images in this paper improves the preprocessing step based on the algorithm used by Li [13]. And compared to the methods [11, 12], our method can not only extract the blood vessels of color fundus images, but also performs well on OCT fundus images. The proposed blood vessel segmentation method includes the following 5 steps.

Step 1: Ridge image calculation

A ridge point is defined as a location for which the intensity has a local extremum in the direction of the largest curvature. The blood vessels have a tree-shaped structure, of which the topology structure is mainly composed of line segments and strongly consecutive. This linear structure can be well described by the eigenvalues and eigenvectors of Hessian matrix composed of the second order partial derivatives of multivariate functions. Therefore, we use Hessian matrix to extract blood vessel ridges in this paper. For one pixel with a scale of σ at point x = (u, v) on image I, the Hessian matrix is defined as follows.

$$H(X,\sigma) = \begin{bmatrix} L_{xx}(X,\sigma) & L_{xy}(X,\sigma) \\ L_{xy}(X,\sigma) & L_{yy}(X,\sigma) \end{bmatrix} \tag{1}$$

where $L_{xx}(X,\sigma)$ indicates the convolution of Gaussian second-order partial derivative with the image I at the point x. $L_{xy}(X,\sigma)$ and $L_{yy}(X,\sigma)$ have similar meaning. Hessian matrix has two eigenvalues and two eigenvectors among which the eigenvector with the largest absolute eigenvalue is the direction of the largest surface curvature. Along this direction, we can find the local extremum of curvatures on the image and set it as a ridge point.

Step 2: Pixel-based ridge feature vector computation

A feature vector is designed for each ridge pixel. The features are based on the profile along the direction of the largest surface curvature. The profile is sampled equally with 1 pixel distance and has 12 pixels on each side (Fig. 4(a)). Edges of the profile are defined as the place among these 12 pixels where the absolute value of the gradient reaches the maximum. With one edge on each side of the profile, there are two edges for the profile (Fig. 4(b)).

The pixel-based ridge feature vector has four components (features): (1) The width of the vessel, i.e. the distance between the two edges. (2) The gradient value of one edge point. (3) The gradient value of the other edge point. (4) The difference between the normal direction of the ridge pixel and that of the previous ridge pixel. The normal direction of one ridge pixel is the direction of the largest curvature at this pixel determined by the Hessian matrix.

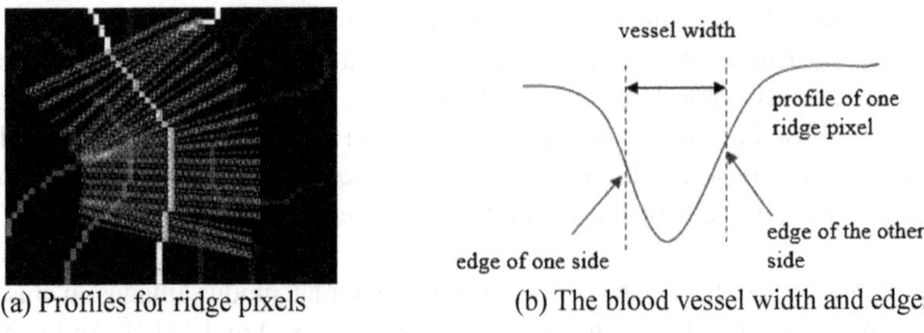

(a) Profiles for ridge pixels (b) The blood vessel width and edges

Fig. 4. Calculate "pixel-based ridge features"

Step 3: Segment-based ridge feature vector computation

Pixel-based ridge feature vectors focus only on the properties of one pixel. Hence, a segment-based feature vector is defined to combine the information of other ridge pixels. We consider 13 consecutive pixels as a segment length and make the investigated ridge pixel as central as possible (Fig. 5). The 13 ridge pixels generate 13 feature vectors of four dimensions. We compute the 13 feature vectors for each ridge pixel (acquired in step 2), and consider the average for each dimension of the 13 feature vectors as the value of segment-based feature vectors for each dimension. Thus, segment-based feature vectors are also vectors of four dimensions including: (1) The average width of vessels. (2) The average of the gradient value for the edge of one side. (3) The average of the gradient value for the edge of the other side. (4) The average of the difference between the normal direction of the investigated ridge pixel and that of the previous one.

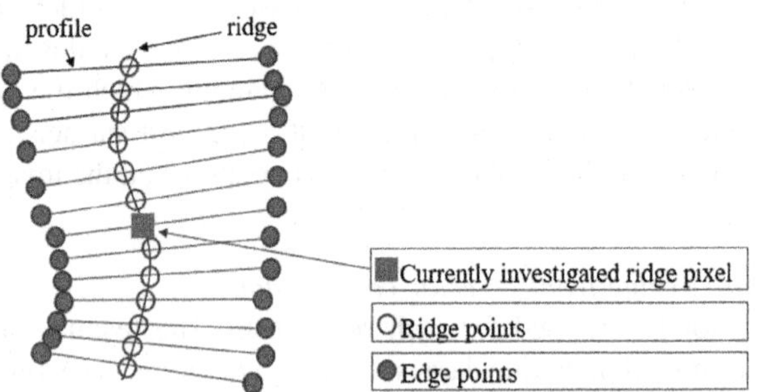

Fig. 5. Determine "segment-based ridge features"

Step 4: Ridge pixels to vessel ridge pixel and non-vessel ridge pixel classification

For each feature in the Segment-Based Ridge Feature vector, a threshold is defined and a true-or-false judgment based on the threshold is made. If all judgments are true, we classify the ridge pixel as a vessel ridge pixel, and vice versa. The four judgment rules are as follows (Note that in the computation program we use width square instead of width for computational convenience): (1) "The average of width square of the vessel" is from 10 to 400. (2) "The average of the gradient value for the edge of one side" is less than 0.6. (3) "The average of the gradient value for the edge of the other side" is less than 0.6. (4) "The average of the difference between the normal direction of the investigated ridge pixel and that of the previous one" is less than 0.5. Figure 6 presents the extracted blood vessel ridge images.

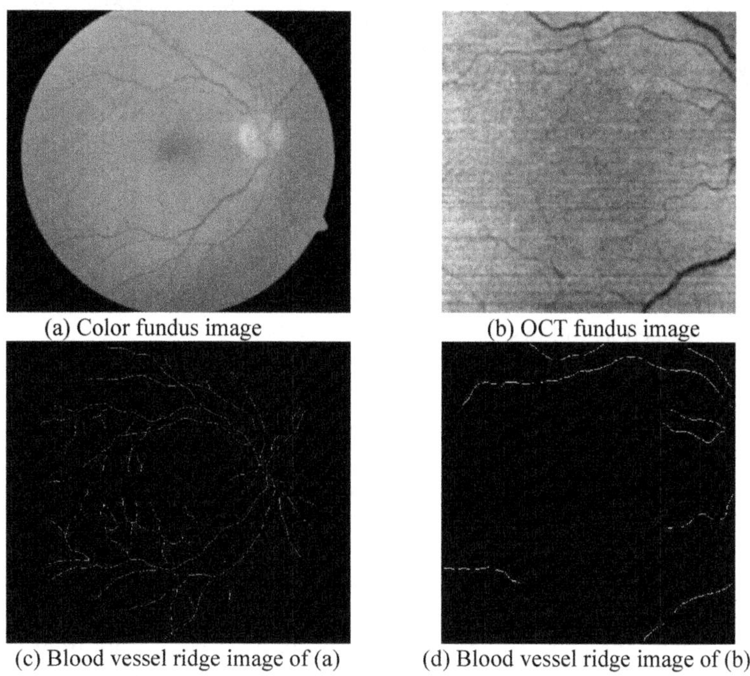

(a) Color fundus image
(b) OCT fundus image
(c) Blood vessel ridge image of (a)
(d) Blood vessel ridge image of (b)

Fig. 6. Examples of blood vessel ridges detection (Color figure online)

Step 5: Blood vessel extraction

As in Step 2, for each investigated ridge pixel, we have a ridge segment with 13 ridge pixels, and therefore 26 edge pixels. We get 12 edge pixels with the 12 largest edge gradient values. We sort these 12 edge pixels according to their intensity values and get the third largest intensity value as the intensity threshold value associated with the investigated ridge pixel. For one pixel in the neighborhood of this investigated ridge pixel, if its intensity is lower than the threshold value, this pixel is classified into vessel segments. Figures 7(a) and (b) show the blood vessel images corresponding to Figs. 6 (a) and (b) respectively.

2.3 Local Feature Matching Point Detection

We utilized the blood vessel as the main features and the local feature matching point detecting method is similar to the one used by Niu in [14]. An OCT-fundus image (512 $\times$ 512) is evenly divided into 16 small patches of the same size (4 $\times$ 4) and each

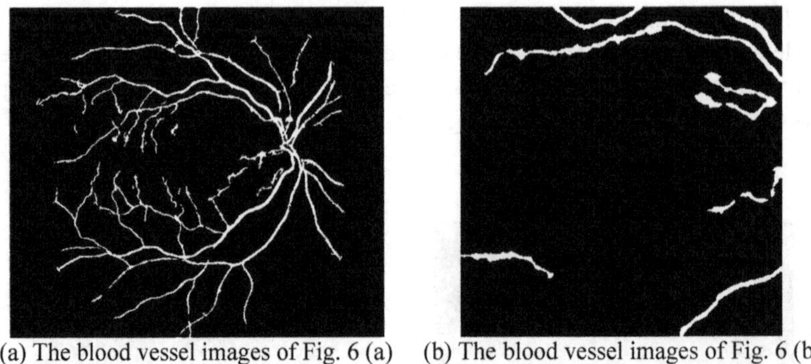

(a) The blood vessel images of Fig. 6 (a) (b) The blood vessel images of Fig. 6 (b)

Fig. 7. The blood vessel images of Fig. 6

patch considered as a window is used to traverse the whole CFP for detecting local matching points based on the local maximization similarity. The local similarity function is defined as follows.

$$S(M) = \frac{A_{actual\_overlap}}{A_{desired\_overlap}}. \tag{2}$$

where $A_{actual\_overlap}$ indicates the actual overlap area, and $A_{desired\_overlap}$ is the expected overlap area.

The extracted image blocks will be classified as an "effective image block" if $S(M)$ is not less than the predefined threshold *th*. According to our experiments the threshold is set here between 0.25 and 0.33. The "effective image block" is used for extracting matching points. We extract three non-adjacent matched point pairs from the blood vessel ridge image block that is corresponded to "effective image block". Note that the matching point pairs of each image block may affect the registration result, matching point pairs are extracted by the nearest distance between the image blocks and the matched pixel pairs for the "non-effective image block" ($S(M) < th$).

2.4 Transformation Coefficients Estimation and Registration

A quadric model [9] is employed in this paper to estimate the transformation coefficients due to the curving anatomical characteristics of fundus images. Assume that $\mathbf{x} = (x, y)^T$ is the coordinate of one feature point in the reference image I_R (CFP) and $\mathbf{x}' = (x', y')^T$ is the coordinate of the corresponding matching point in the target image I_T (OFI), the non-linear transformation in the two-dimensional space can be defined as follows.

$$\begin{bmatrix} x' \\ y' \end{bmatrix} = \begin{bmatrix} \theta_{11} & \theta_{12} & \theta_{13} & \theta_{14} & \theta_{15} & \theta_{16} \\ \theta_{21} & \theta_{22} & \theta_{23} & \theta_{24} & \theta_{25} & \theta_{26} \end{bmatrix} \begin{bmatrix} x^2 \\ xy \\ y^2 \\ x \\ y \\ 1 \end{bmatrix}. \tag{3}$$

where θ_{11}–θ_{26} are the 12 free parameters to be calculated. As shown in Eq. (3), the transformation model requires at least six pairs of matching points. In the experiment, we choose 6 to 20 pairs of matching points detected previously to estimate the transformation parameters. And then we can achieve the registration after transformation model being calculated.

3 Experimental Results and Analysis

We used the dataset containing 3 normal eyes and 18 eyes with age-related macular degeneration to test the performance of our algorithm. Each image pair in our datasets (16 eyes) includes one CFP (2392 × 2048 pixels) and one OFI (512 × 512 pixels) obtained by intensity summation along A-scans of SD-OCT volumetric data. All of the datasets were obtained using a Cirrus SD-OCT device (Carl Zeiss Meditec, Inc., Dublin, CA) at the same time.

In order to assess the accuracy of the registration we decided to select 10 pairs of manually matched point pairs (matched points are normally blood vessel branching points or crossovers) on the registered retinal reference and target images I_R and I_T, and then compute the Root Mean Square Error (RMSE) of manually labeled control point pairs. The larger the RMSE, the worse the registration performance. The advantage with this assessment method is that control points are supposed to be real corresponding feature. However, note that the value of RMSE can be affected by inaccurate locations of manually labeled control points and by the distribution of control points. Figure 8 shows the registration results of our method for different quality images, where we can see that our method has a strong robustness.

We compared our registration results with the results of Niu method [14] and Golabbakhsh method [15]. Figure 9 shows the comparison of the results of the three algorithms, which proves that the registration accuracy of our algorithm is relatively high. Figure 10 presents the root mean square error of the three algorithms.

Table 1 gives the average and standard deviations of RMSE values for the registration of the sample datasets using the three methods. It can be seen from the results that the error of our method (root mean square error is 111.06 μm) is less than Golabbakhsh method (root mean square error is 272.08 μm) and Niu method (root mean square error is 151.96 μm).

These three methods are all based on blood vessels, so the extraction of blood vessels will have much influence on registration results. Blood vessels of OCT fundus images are more difficult to extract compared to the color fundus images because of the

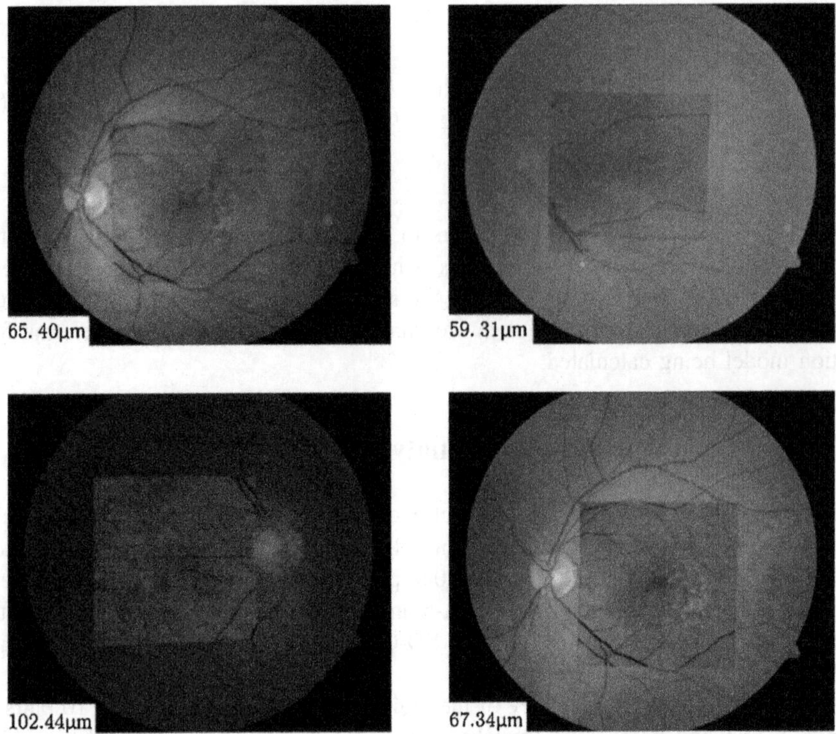

Fig. 8. The registration results of our method for different quality images

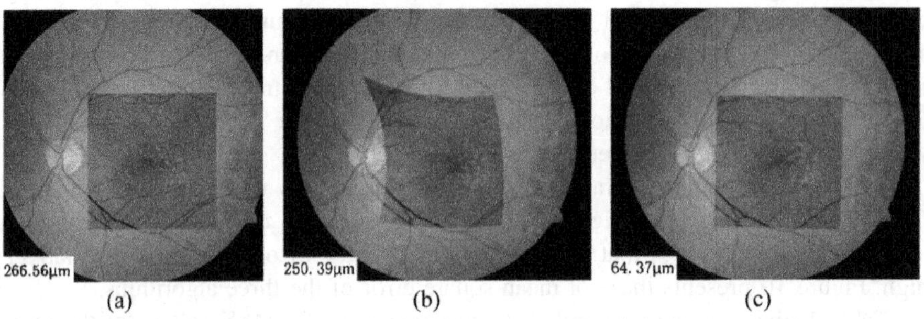

Fig. 9. The comparison of the results of the three algorithms: Golabbakhsh method [15] (a), Niu method [14] (b) and our method (c).

low contrast and diseases. In our method special preprocessing of the OCT fundus images is used so that the blood vessels detection results are better than the other two methods and the final registration results are relatively better.

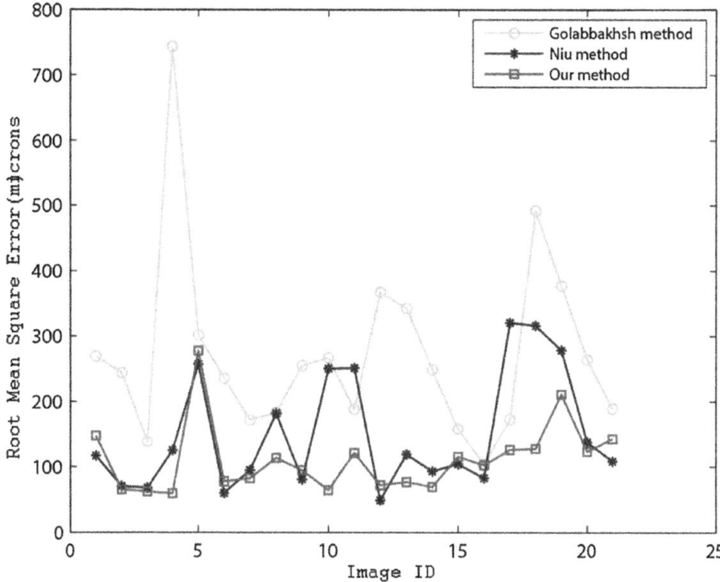

Fig. 10. RMSE of the three methods

Table 1. The average and standard deviations of RMSE values and pixel number error for the registration of the sample datasets using the three method

Method	Average of RMSE (microns)	Standard deviations of RMSE (microns)	Average of pixel number error (pixel)	Standard deviations of pixel number error (pixel)
Golabbakhsh method	272.08	141.55	23.22	12.08
Niu method	151.96	91.46	12.08	7.80
Our method	**111.06**	**53.39**	**9.48**	**4.56**

4 Conclusion

In this paper, we present an automatic registration algorithm based on feature invariance between OFIs and CFPs. The retinal blood vessel is considered as the basic feature of registration, and the matching point pairs are extracted by searching the local maximization of the similarity function between the two blood vessel images. Then we used the extracted feature matching points to calculate the coefficients of the quadratic transformation model and complete the registration. The experimental results show that our method performs well for the images with different quality, such as images with much noise and age-related macular degeneration and so on.

However, the quality of vessel extraction blood has much influence on registration results because vessels are utilized as the main feature in this paper. Therefore, the registration accuracy can be relatively low when the blood vessels are less.

This supplies us a direction to our future works. Furthermore, our method is time consuming and most of the computing time is spent performing two tasks: the blood vessel detection and the brute force search for the maximum of the similarity function. Therefore, we need to apply the parallel computing to optimize the MATLAB code for enhancing the computation speed in the future.

Acknowledgements. This work was supported by the National Science Foundation of China (61671242), a grant from the Fundamental Research Funds for the Central Universities (30920140111004), a six talent peaks project in Jiangsu Province (2014-SWYY-024), and the Open Fund Project of Fujian Provincial Key Laboratory of Information Processing and Intelligent Control (Minjiang University) (No. MJUKF201706).

References

1. Zhao, H.F., Lu, M., Bu, L.B.: Medical image registration based on feature points and Rényi Mutual Information. Chin. J. Comput. **38**(6), 1212–1221 (2015). (in Chinese)
2. Li, Y., Gregori, G., Knighton, R.W.: Registration of OCT fundus images with color fundus photographs based on blood vessel ridges. Opt. Express **19**(1), 7–16 (2011)
3. Pluim, J.P.W., Maintz, J.B.A., Viergever, M.A.: Mutual-information-based registration of medical images: a survey. IEEE Trans. Med. Imaging **22**(8), 986–1004 (2003)
4. Zang, P., Liu, G., Miao, Z.: Automated motion correction using parallel-strip registration for wide-field en-face OCT angiogram. Biomed. Opt. Express **7**(7), 2823–2836 (2016)
5. Chen, L., Huang, X., Tian, J.: Retinal image registration using topological vascular tree segmentation and bifurcation structures. Biomed. Signal Process. Control **16**, 22–31 (2014)
6. Ghassabi, Z., Shanbehzadeh, J., Mohammadzadeh, A.: A structure-based region detector for high-resolution retinal fundus image registration. Biomed. Signal Process. Control **23**, 52–61 (2015)
7. Lowe, D.G.: Distinctive image features from scale-invariant keypoints. Int. J. Comput. Vis. **60**(2), 91–110 (2004)
8. Xing, Y., Zheng, J., Xu, M.: Multimodal retinal image registration based on local feature description (in Chinese). Appl. Res. Comput. **27**(9), 3567–3569 (2010). (in Chinese)
9. Cattin, P.C., Bay, H., Van Gool, L., Székely, G.: Retina mosaicing using local features. In: Larsen, R., Nielsen, M., Sporring, J. (eds.) MICCAI 2006. LNCS, vol. 4191, pp. 185–192. Springer, Heidelberg (2006). doi:10.1007/11866763_23
10. Buades, A., Coll, B., Morel, J.M.: A non-local algorithm for image denoising. In: IEEE Computer Society Conference on CVPR, vol. 2, pp. 60–65. IEEE (2005)
11. Shehhi, R.A., Marpu, P.R., Wei, L.W.: An automatic cognitive graph-based segmentation for detection of blood vessel in retinal images. Math. Probl. Eng. **2016**, 1–15 (2016)
12. Chakraborti, T., Jha, D.K., Chowdhury, A.S.: A self-adaptive matched filter for retinal blood vessel detection. Mach. Vis. Appl. **26**(1), 55–68 (2015)
13. Li, Y., Hutchings, N., Knighton, R.W.: Ridge-branch-based blood vessel detection algorithm for multimodal retinal images. In: Proceedings of SPIE, vol. 7259, 72594K-12 (2009). IEEE Transactions on Image Processing
14. Niu, S.J., Chen, Q., Shen, H.: Registration of SD-OCT en-face images with color fundus photographs based on local patch matching. In: OMIA in MICCAI, pp. 25–32 (2014)
15. Golabbakhsh, M., Rabbani, H.: Vessel-based registration of fundus and optical coherence tomography projection images of retina using a quadratic registration model. IET Image Proc. **7**(8), 768–776 (2013)

View-Based 3D Model Retrieval Based on Distance Learning

Yang Shi, Nannan Liu(✉), Xingjian Long, and Lei Xu

School of Electrical and Information Engineering, Tianjin University, Tianjin 300072, China
hssy03180669@163.com, liunannan985@163.com, tdlxj@tju.edu.cn, xulei03@foxmail.com
http://media.tju.edu.cn

Abstract. As information technologies develop, 3D model retrieval is paid more and more attentions by researchers. But the limitations of image features poses a great challenge to view-based 3D model retrieval. In this paper, a novel 3D model retrieval method based on distance learning is introduced. The objective function with respective to two latent variables was formulated especially. The variables are the clique information in the original graph and the pairwise clique correspondence constrained by the one-to-one matching. The proposed method has the following benefits: (1) the local and global attributes of a graph with the designed structure can be preserved; (2) redundant and noisy information can be eliminated by strengthening inliers and suppressing outliers; and (3) the difficulty of defining high-order attributes and solving hyper-graph matching can be avoided. By extensive experiments on ETH, NTU60 and MV-RED datasets with Zernike moments, Histograms of Oriented Gradients (HoG) and convolutional neural networks (CNN) features, the effectiveness of the proposed method could be tested.

Keywords: 3D model retrieval · View-based · Clique-graph · Distance learning

1 Introduction

Nowadays, a technologies of 3D models being widely used in diverse fields grows rapidly. It has been used in computer-aided design [1], bioinformatics [2], medicine [3], the entertainment industry [5] and so on. Due to the great amount of 3D objects, 3D model retrieval [7,8] is gaining more growth than ever before. The expansion of the utilized occasion of virtual model and improvement of the efficiency of resource use require an effective and efficient 3D model retrieval method. These methods can be sorted into two categories: view-based methods and model-based methods.

View-based 3D object retrieval methods has been widely studied because it is very flexible and easy to implement using multiple views for object representation [9]. In this scheme, we describe a 3D object by a set of views with different

X. Sun et al. (Eds.): ICCCS 2017, Part II, LNCS 10603, pp. 483–493, 2017.
https://doi.org/10.1007/978-3-319-68542-7_41

features, examining primordial characteristics, such as surface distributions [12], Zernike moment [13], and HOG descriptors [16]. Then we compare the features in different feature spaces, seek for the object which is the most close one to the query.

Many view-based methods have been presented to solve 3D model retrieval problem [19]. We computed the light field descriptor (LFD) [24] from 10 silhouettes which were obtained from the vertices of a dodecahedron over a hemisphere. The spatial structure information from different views was described by this image set. In LFD, we adopted Zernike moments and Fourier descriptors of the 3D model as the features of each image. The best match was found by this method between two LFDs as the similarity between two 3D models. We adopted five circular camera arrays, including four vertical and one horizontal camera arrays, to acquire representative views of 3D models in [22]. We modeled each group of views (acquired by a circle set of cameras) as a Markov chain (MC). In MC, there were two levels in 3D model comparison: in the view set level and in the model level. In the MC framework, we used 3D model retrieval to find the maximal a posterior (MAP) in the 3D database given the query model. The Elevation Descriptor (ED) feature was proposed by Shih et al. [20], and it was invariant to translation and scaling of 3D models. An optimal selection of 2D views from a 3D model was proposed by Ankerst et al. [25], and it focused on numerical characteristics obtained from the 3D model representative features. But it is not available for the 3D model containing a set of 2D images. A Bayesian modelbased method for 3D object search was proposed by Ansary et al. [26], and it exploited X-means [24] to filter characteristic views and utilized the Bayesian model to compute the similarity between different models.

According to Bu et al. [6], high-level shape features was extracted, and learned via deep belief networks for view representation. The performance of 3D model retrieval was significantly augmented. View-based and model-based relevance in a graph-based framework for 3D object retrieval were jointly explored by Lu et al. [10]. The view-based methods are proved to have better performance than model-based methods according to literature reports.

However, when it comes to eliminating redundant and noisy data, these methods are not robust and effective enough. Both the missed inliers (the related views that should't be eliminated but did) and the existence of outliers (the non-related views that should be eliminated but not) will reduce the effectiveness and accuracy on distance matching. The distance learning methods can usually perform better than the statistical method based on model because of its structural constraints. The limited ability of preserving the global geometrical structure of the graph by the node-to-node mapping of the bipartite graph-based methods [15], or the difficulty of high-order attribute discovery and hyper-graph matching of the hyper-graph-based methods [11], usually restricts the performance of the current distance learning methods.

To fix these problems, we present a distance learning method which exploit global structure and local structure. We summarized the main contributions of the method as follows:

- We can consider the proposed distance learning as the generalized form of both classic graph and hypergraph. The arbitrary order attributes can be conveyed by individual clique to represent the local structure;
- Based on the discovery of both unary and pairwise correspondence between pairwise nodes/edges, the local similarity measure is unique. The difficulty in discovering the node order of each hyper-edge for hyper-edge similarity measure can be overcome.

Due to the rapid development of RGB-D camera and machine vision technology, the ever-growing 3D models make the acceleration progress of 3D model retrieval necessary. Two paradigms for existing 3D object retrieval methods are utilized generally: retrieval based on model and retrieval based on view.

Shape distribution, shape histogram, and other 3D spatial information model-based methods were applied to represent a 3D model. For example, 3D shape histograms was introduced by Ankerst et al. [25] as intuitive feature vectors. The histograms were based on the space partition. The use of completed 3D information was proposed by Vandeborre et al. They represented the 3D objects as mesh surfaces and used 3D shape descriptors. A novel depth image-based method to handle action retrieval problem was proposed by Zhao et al. A matching technique to compute the similarity between two models based on the shape matching of their multiresolutional Reeb Graphs was developed by Hilaga et al. 3D objects by applying graph-matching techniques to match their skeletons was compared by Murugappan et al. [4].

More attention has been attracted by view-based techniques recently. A group sparse coding method to handle object retrieval problem was proposed by Wang and Nie [23], and the reconstruction error was utilized to compute the similarity. A novel 3D model descriptor was proposed by Gao et al. [21], by which the spatial information of virtual 3D object can be converted into 2D perspective images and traditional image processing methods were applied for 3D model retrieval. A novel compact multi-view descriptors (CMVDs) for 3D model representation was proposed Daras and Axenopoulos [27]. He utilized graph matching to handle similarity measure.

The random walk based models were proposed by Gori et al. [28], by which the graph topological features at node level can be enhanced, and a polynomial algorithm for the classic graph isomorphism problem was introduced, under the constraints of dealing with Markovian spectrally distinguishable graphs. The graph matching was converted into the ranking problem and the random walk for solution was utilized by Minsu et al. A novel projections onto convex sets (POCS) graph matching algorithm was introduced by Van Wyk and Van Wyk [29], in which it enforced two-way assignment constraints without using elaborate penalty terms, graduated nonconvexity, or sophisticated annealing mechanisms to escape from poor local minima.

We organize the rest of the paper as follows. The distance learning method will be explained in detail in Sect. 2 and the experimental results is presented in Sect. 3. Section 4 concludes this paper.

2 Our Approach

2.1 Similarity Measure

We represented each 3D object by a group of multi-view 2D images. A classic graph $G = (V, E, A)$ includes the node set $V = \{v_i\}_{i=1}^{I}$, the edge set $E = \{e_j\}_{j=1}^{J}$, and the attribute set $A = \{a_j\}_{j=1}^{J}$ related with the corresponding edges. We realized the relation between two attribute graphs $G^p = (V^p, E^p, A^p)$ and $G^q = (V^q, E^q, A^q)$ by leveraging the unary attribute with respect to individual node, the pairwise attribute with respect to individual edge, and the high-order attributes with respect to various scales of local structures. Based on the class concept, each clique was regarded as the basic unit for matching and the novel method for distance learning was further presented. In a clique-graph $\tilde{G} = (\tilde{V}, \tilde{A})$ we can represent each clique $\tilde{V_i} \in \tilde{V}$ by a star model and $\tilde{A_i} \in \tilde{A}$ is the attribute of the ith clique. The center of the clique, k leaf nodes pf the clique and k edges linking the center node and k leaf nodes were denoted respectively by the elements in star model $\tilde{V_i} = \{\tilde{c_i}, \{\tilde{l_{ij}}\}_{j=1}^{k}, \{\tilde{e_{ij}}\}_{j=1}^{k}\}$. $\tilde{A_i} \in \tilde{A}$ is the attribute of the ith clique, by which the importance of this clique in the entire clique-graph was represented.

Given two clique-graphs, $G^p = (V^p, A^p)$ and $G^q = (V^q, A^q)$, we can represent the similarity measure of both by $J(X, \tilde{G^p}, \tilde{G^q})$ where $\tilde{G^p}$ and $\tilde{G^q}$ are their structure characteristics, X means the clique-to-clique correspondence. Therefore, we can formulate the similarity calculation when maximize the score function $J(X, \tilde{G^p}, \tilde{G^q})$:

$$(X, \tilde{G^p}, \tilde{G^q})^* = arg \max_{X, \tilde{G^p}, \tilde{G^q}} J(X, \tilde{G^p}, \tilde{G^q}) \tag{1}$$

2.2 Object Function and Optimization

According to the graph matching idea, we can realize the original graph matching by achieving the correspondences between each pair of centers, which is consistent with the discovered clique-to-clique correspondence. The similarity vector S consists of $\{S_{i,m}\}_{i=1,\ldots,N^p, m=1,\ldots N^q} \in R^{N^p N^q \times 1}$ where the clique numbers in $\tilde{G^p}$ and $\tilde{G^q}$ were respectively denoted by N^p and N^q.

We define the relationship between two cliques as a binary indicator matrix $\bar{X} \in \{0,1\}^{N^p \times N^q}$, which means if $\tilde{V_i} \in \tilde{G^p}$ matches to $\tilde{V_m} \in \tilde{G^q}$, $X_{i,m} = 1$, otherwise, $X_{i,m} = 0$.

Therefore, we can formulate the similarity function as the following objective function:

$$\begin{gathered}(X, \tilde{G^p}, \tilde{G^q})^* = arg \max_{X, \tilde{G^p}, \tilde{G^q}} J(X, \tilde{G^p}, \tilde{G^q}), \\ s.t.\ \bar{X} \cdot 1_{N^q \times 1} \leq 1_{N^p \times 1},\ \bar{X}^T \cdot 1_{N^p \times 1} \leq 1_{N^q \times 1}\end{gathered} \tag{2}$$

By considering the individual node of one clique-graph as the center of one clique, we can construct the clique with the center and its neighbors. We can represent each center node by the feature vector $f_i (f_i \in R^d)$ so that we can express all nodes as $\{f_i\}_{i=1}^{I}$. Given an individual node f_i, we can reconstruct it by the other nodes $F = \{f_j\}_{j=1,\ldots,I,j\neq i}$:

$$f_i = Fr_i \quad s.t.\ r_{ii} = 0, \tag{3}$$

where $r_i \triangleq [r_{i1}\ r_{i2} \ldots r_{iI}]^T$.

Therefore, minimizing the tightest convex relaxation of the $L0$-norm of r_i with $L1$-norm is considered. We can formulate the objective functions as:

$$\min\|R\|_1 \quad s.t.\ F = FR, diag(R) = 0, \tag{4}$$

where $r_i \triangleq [r_1\ r_2 \ldots r_I]$, whose i^{th} column corresponds to the sparse representation of f_i.

We can calculate the clique-wise similarity measure with the cosine distance for node-wise similarity measure by:

$$U_{v_s v_a} = \frac{f_s^p \cdot f_a^q}{\|f_s^p\|_2 \cdot \|f_a^q\|_2} \tag{5}$$

where the features of nodes v_s and v_a from graph $\tilde{G^p}$ and $\tilde{G^q}$ can be represented by f_s^p and f_a^q.

We can calculate the pairwise similarity between two edges e_{et} and e_{ab} by:

$$E_{e_{st}e_{ab}} = exp(-\|e_{st} - e_{ab}\|^2/\varepsilon^2) \tag{6}$$

where $\forall e_{st} \in \tilde{V}_i^p$ and $\forall e_{ab} \in \tilde{V}_i^q$, the scaling factor ε^2 is set to 0.15 empirically.

With both unary and pairwise similarity measure, we can re-write the similarity between two cliques from different graphs in the quadratic form by the one-to-one mapping:

$$\begin{aligned} S_{i,m}(Z) = & \tilde{A}_i^p \cdot \tilde{A}_m^q \cdot \{\sum_{v_s v_a} z_{v_s v_a} U_{v_s v_a} + \\ & \sum_{\substack{v_s \neq v_t \\ v_a \neq v_b \\ v_s \,\&\, v_t \in \tilde{V}_i^p, \\ v_a \,\&\, v_b \in \tilde{V}_m^q}} z_{v_s v_t} z_{v_a v_b} E_{e_{st}e_{ab}}\} \\ s.t.\ & Z \cdot 1_{K_i \times 1} \leq 1_{K_m \times 1}, Z^T \cdot 1_{K_m \times 1} \leq 1_{K_i \times 1} \end{aligned} \tag{7}$$

where the matrix $Z(Z \in \{0,1\}^{K_i K_m})$ means the node correspondence, i.e., $z_{v_s v_a} = 1$ if the v_s node of the graph $\tilde{G^p}$ corresponds to the v_a node of the graph $\tilde{G^q}$.

3 Experiment

3.1 Dataset

We evaluate the proposed method on following datasets:

- **ETH** [18]**:** The ETH dataset consists of real-world multi-view 3D objects. 80 objects classified into 8 categories are contained, and each category includes 10 objects. 41 multiple views for each object space evenly over the upper viewing hemisphere, and we determine all positions for cameras by subdividing the faces of an octahedron to the third recursion level.
- **The National Taiwan University 3D Model Database (NTU)** [24]**:** 500 objects in total are contained in the NTU dataset. We employed virtual cameras to capture initial views for 3D objects. 60 cameras are contained in the camera array, and they are set on the vertices of a polyhedron with the same structure with Buckminsterfullerene (C60). Therefore, each object has 60 views.
- **Multi-view RGB-D Object Dataset (MV-RED):** A real-world 3D object dataset with multimodal views was contributed by us, the Multi-view RGB-D Object Dataset (MV-RED). 505 objects from 60 categories are contained in the MV-RED dataset. For each object, we record information on both the RGB and depth simultaneously by 3 Microsoft Kinect sensors along 3 directions. Some examples are shown in Fig. 1.

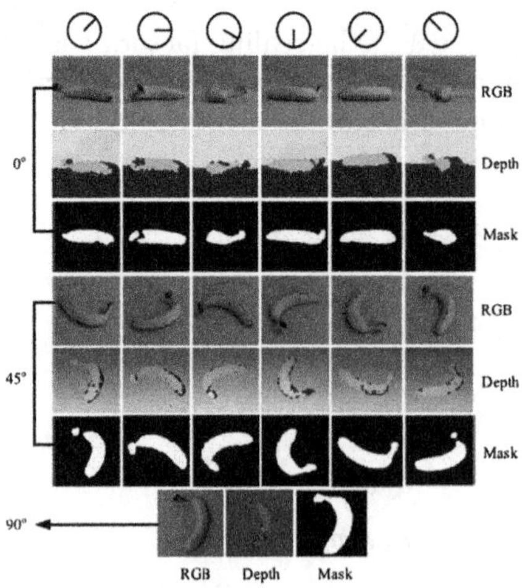

Fig. 1. Examples of MV-RED.

3.2 Evaluation

To evaluate the 3D model retrieval performance, we employ following popular criteria as the measures of the retrieval performance in our experiments.

- Retrieval performance was demonstrated comprehensively by Precision-Recall Curve; We assess it in terms of average recall and average precision, and use it widely in multimedia applications.
- Retrieval accuracy of the first returned result was by evaluated Nearest Neighbor (NN).
- We defined FT as the recall of the top τ results, where τ is the number of relevant objects for the query and it is set as 20.
- We defined ST as the recall of the top 2τ results.
- The precision and the recall of top returned results were jointly evaluated by F-measure (F). In this work, we utilize top 20 retrieved results for evaluation.
- Discounted Cumulative Gain (DCG) assigns relevant results at the top ranking positions with higher weights, assuming that a user is less likely to consider lower results. It is a statistic.
- The ranking information of relevant objects among the retrieved objects was considered by Average Normalized Modified Retrieval Rank (ANMRR), which was a rankbased measure. A lower ANMRR value indicates a better performance was indicated by a lower ANMRR. i.e., relevant objects rank at top positions.

3.3 Comparison Methods

The proposed method is termed as DL. Several popular 3D model retrieval methods are implemented for comparison.

- Nearest Neighbor (NN): HAC was implemented for view clustering and the smallest distance one was selected from the rest of the views in each cluster as the representative view;
- Adaptive views clustering (AVC) [26]: An optimal selection of 2D views from a 3D model was provided by the adaptive views clustering method. Then, we conducted the probabilistic matching to measure the similarity between query object and candidate object;
- Bipartite graph matching (WBGM) [15]: In this method, we represented each multiview object by a set of 2D views. We extracted representative views from query object and candidate object. We conducted the bipartite graph with these selected 2D views. Finally, we utilize the matching results to measure the similarity between two different objects;
- Camera constraint-free view-based (CCFV) method [30]: The CCFV model is created from the basis of the query Gaussian models by combining the positive matching model and the negative matching model. The constraint of static camera array setting for view capturing can be removed by this method and we can apply it to any view-based 3D object database.

3.4 Experimental Results and Discussions

Figures 2, 3, 4, 5, 6 and 7 show the experimental results. The precision-recall curves on ETH, NTU and MV-RED are respectively shown in Figs. 2, 4 and 6

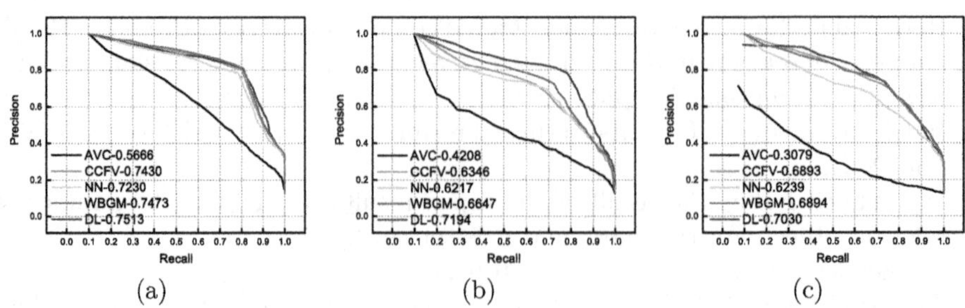

Fig. 2. The precision-recall curves of ETH dataset with different features. (a) Zernike (b) HoG (c) CNN

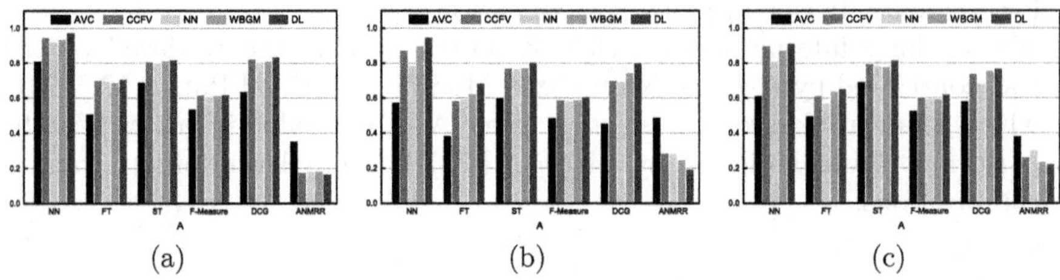

Fig. 3. The performance of ETH dataset with different features. (a) Zernike (b) HoG (c) CNN

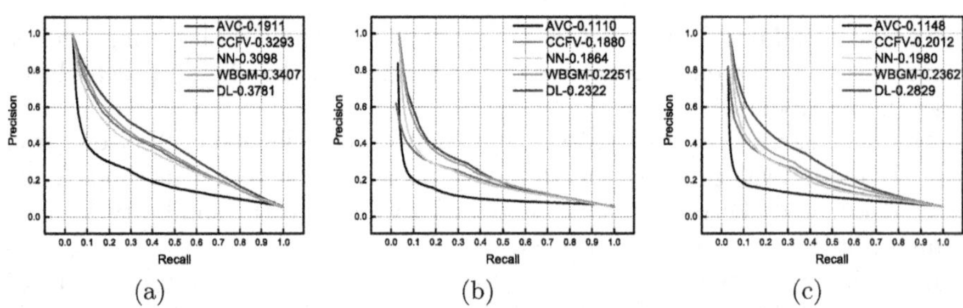

Fig. 4. The precision-recall curves of NTU60 dataset with different features. (a) Zernike (b) HoG (c) CNN

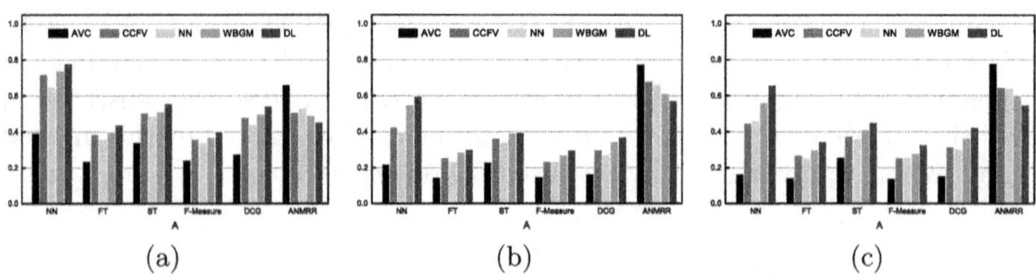

Fig. 5. The performance of NTU60 dataset with different features. (a) Zernike (b) HoG (c) CNN

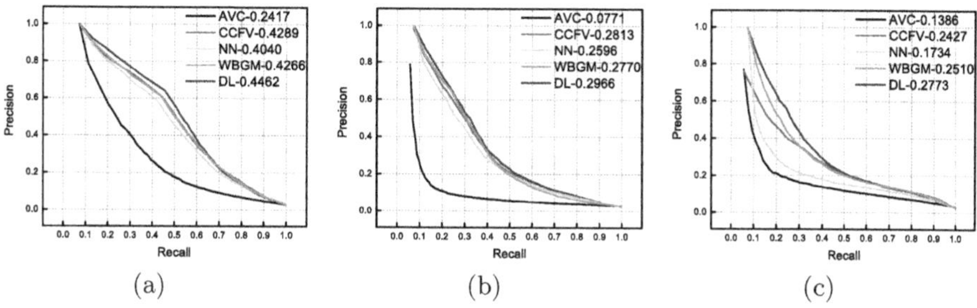

Fig. 6. The precision-recall curves of MV-RED dataset with different features. (a) Zernike (b) HoG (c) CNN

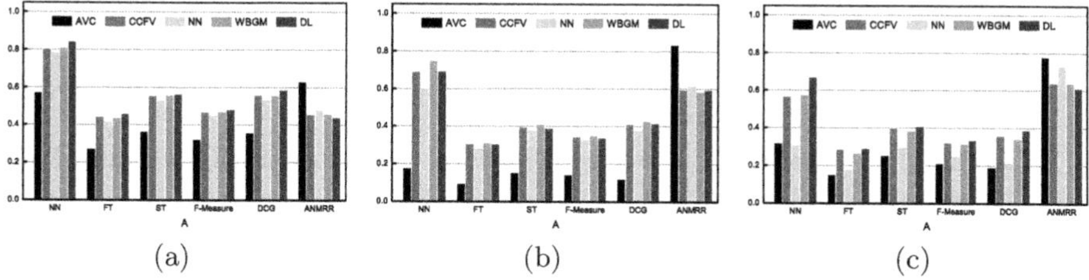

Fig. 7. The performance of MV-RED dataset with different features. (a) Zernike (b) HoG (c) CNN

while the performances by different methods with Zernike moments in (a), Histograms of Oriented Gradients (HoG) in (b) and convolutional neural networks (CNN) in (c) are shown in Figs. 3, 5 and 7. From these experimental results, the proposed method performs better than the other comparative methods, by which the superiority of our approach is also demonstrated.

4 Conclusion

In this paper, a novel framework for multi-view object retrieval was proposed. The clique-graph was proposed originally. The distance learning method by preserving global and local structures was presented and optimized by decomposing it into two consecutive steps, clique-to-clique similarity measure and the graph-to-graph similarity measure. The novel method for 3D object representation was also applied. The superiority of this method is also demonstrated by the extensive experiments on ETH, NTU and MV-RED.

Acknowledgments. This work was supported in part by the National Natural Science Foundation of China (61472275, 61502337), the Tianjin Research Program of Application Foundation and Advanced Technology (15JCYBJC16200), the grant of China Scholarship Council (201506255073), the grant of Elite Scholar Program of Tianjin University (2014XRG-0046).

References

1. Regli, W.C., Cicirello, V.A.: Managing digital libraries for computer-aided design. Comput. Aided Des. **32**, 119–132 (2000)
2. Yeh, J., Chen, D., Chen, B., Ouhyoung, M.: A web-based three-dimensional protein retrieval system by matching visual similarity. BMC **21**, 3056 (2005)
3. Guetat, G., Maitre, M., Joly, L., Lai, S.L., Lee, T., Shinagawa, Y.: Automatic 3-D grayscale volume matching and shape analysis. IEEE Trans. Inf. Technol. Biomed. **10**, 362–376 (2006)
4. Vinayak, Murugappan, S., Liu, H., Ramani, K.: Shape-it-up: hand gesture based creative expression of 3D shapes using intelligent generalized cylinders. Comput. Aided Des. **45**, 277–287 (2013)
5. Wong, H., Ma, B., Yu, Z., Yeung, P.: 3-D head model retrieval using a single face view query. IEEE Trans. Multimedia **9**, 1026–1036 (2007)
6. Bu, S., Liu, Z., Han, J., Wu, J., Ji, R.: Learning high-level feature by deep belief networks for 3-D model retrieval and recognition. IEEE Trans. Multimedia **16**, 2154–2167 (2014)
7. Del Bimbo, A., Pala, P.: Content-based retrieval of 3D models. ACM Trans. Multimedia Comput. Commun. Appl. **2**, 20–43 (2006)
8. Wang, F., Li, F., Dai, Q.: View-based 3D object retrieval and recognition using tangent subspace analysis. In: Proceedings of SPIE, vol. 6822, pp. 68220I–68220I-11 (2008)
9. Li, W., Bebis, G., Bourbakis, N.G.: 3-D object recognition using 2-D views. IEEE Trans. Image Process. **17**, 2236–2255 (2008)
10. Lu, K., He, N., Xue, J., Dong, J., Shao, L.: Learning view-model joint relevance for 3D object retrieval. IEEE Trans. Image Process. **24**, 1449 (2015)
11. Gao, Y., Wang, M., Tao, D., Ji, R., Dai, Q.: 3-D object retrieval and recognition with hypergraph analysis. IEEE Trans. Image Process. **21**, 4290–4303 (2012)
12. Osada, R., Funkhouser, T., Chazelle, B., Dobkin, D.: Shape distributions. ACM Trans. Graph. **21**, 807–832 (2002)
13. Kim, W.Y., Kim, Y.S.: A region-based shape descriptor using Zernike moments. Signal Process.-Image Commun. **16**, 95–102 (2000)
14. Paquet, E., Rioux, M., Murching, A., Naveen, T., Tabatabai, A.: Description of shape information for 2-D and 3-D objects. Signal Process.-Image Commun. **16**, 103–122 (2000)
15. Gao, Y., Dai, Q., Wang, M., Zhang, N.: 3D model retrieval using weighted bipartite graph matching. Signal Process.-Image Commun. **26**, 39–47 (2011)
16. Dalal, N., Triggs, B.: Histograms of oriented gradients for human detection. In: 18th Computer Vision and Pattern Recognition, pp. 886–893. IEEE Press, San Diego (2005)
17. Nie, W., Liu, A., Gao, Z., Su, Y.: Clique-graph matching by preserving global and local structure. In: 28th Computer Vision and Pattern Recognition, pp. 4503–4510. IEEE Press, Boston (2015)
18. Leibe, B., Schiele, B.: Analyzing appearance and contour based methods for object categorization. In: 16th Computer Vision and Pattern Recognition, pp. 409–415. IEEE Press, Boston (2003)
19. Hu, B., Liu, Y., Gao, S., Sun, R., Xian, C.: Parallel relevance feedback for 3D model retrieval based on fast weighted-center particle swarm optimization. Pattern Recognit. **43**, 2950–2961 (2010)

20. Shih, J., Lee, C., Wang, J.: A new 3D model retrieval approach based on the elevation descriptor. Pattern Recognit. **40**, 283–295 (2007)
21. Gao, Y., Dai, Q., Zhang, N.: 3D model comparison using spatial structure circular descriptor. Pattern Recognit. **43**, 1142–1151 (2007)
22. Gao, Y., Tang, J., Li, H., Dai, Q., Zhang, N.: View-based 3D model retrieval with probabilistic graph model. Neurocomputing **73**, 1900–1905 (2010)
23. Wang, X., Nie, W.: 3D model retrieval with weighted locality-constrained group sparse coding. Neurocomputing **151**, 620–625 (2015)
24. Chen, D., Tian, X., Shen, Y., Ming, O.: On visual similarity based 3D model retrieval. Comput. Graph. Forum **22**, 223–232 (2010)
25. Ankerst, M., Kastenmüller, G., Kriegel, H.-P., Seidl, T.: 3D shape histograms for similarity search and classification in spatial databases. In: Güting, R.H., Papadias, D., Lochovsky, F. (eds.) SSD 1999. LNCS, vol. 1651, pp. 207–226. Springer, Heidelberg (1999). doi:10.1007/3-540-48482-5_14
26. Ansary, T.F., Daoudi, M., Vandeborre, J.P.: A Bayesian 3-D search engine using adaptive views clustering. IEEE Trans. Multimedia **9**, 78–88 (2007)
27. Daras, P., Axenopoulos, A.: A 3D shape retrieval framework supporting multimodal queries. IEEE Trans. Multimedia **9**, 78–88 (2007)
28. Gori, M., Maggini, M., Sarti, L.: Exact and approximate graph matching using random walks. IEEE Trans. Pattern Anal. Mach. Intell. **27**, 1100–1111 (2005)
29. Van Wyk, B.J., Van Wyk, M.A.: A POCS-based graph matching algorithm. IEEE Trans. Pattern Anal. Mach. Intell. **26**, 1526–1530 (2004)
30. Gao, Y., Tang, J., Hong, R., Yan, S., Dai, Q., Zhang, N., Chua, T.S.: Camera constraint-free view-based 3-D object retrieval. IEEE Trans. Image Process. **21**, 2269–2281 (2012)

PCANet for Color Image Classification in Various Color Spaces

Jiasong Wu[1,2,3,4(✉)], Shijie Qiu[1,4], Rui Zeng[1,4], Lotfi Senhadji[2,3,4], and Huazhong Shu[1,4]

[1] LIST, The Key Laboratory of Computer Network and Information Integration, Ministry of Education, Southeast University, Nanjing, China
jswu@seu.edu.cn
[2] INSERM, U 1099, 35000 Rennes, France
[3] Laboratoire Traitement du Signal et de l'Image, Université de Rennes 1, Rennes, France
[4] Centre de Recherche en Information Biomédicale Sino-français, Nanjing 210096, China

Abstract. Principal component analysis network (PCANet), which is a recently proposed novel deep learning algorithm, has aroused the interest of a wide variety of researchers. In this paper, we evaluate the performance of PCANet in various color spaces on different types of color image dataset. Experimental results on CURet texture database, UC Merced land use database, and Georgia Tech face database show that Luminance and Chrominance based principal component analysis network outperforms other color spaces in the vast majority of cases. Therefore, when dealing with the problem of color image dataset classification, Luminance and Chrominance based principal component network is recommended.

Keywords: PCANet · Deep learning · Color image dataset · Color spaces

1 Introduction

Color information plays a key role in image processing, including image classification, recognition, and segmentation [1–3]. For example, Cheng and Chen [1] showed that the utilization of color information in color image can obtain higher classification accuracy than that of gray-scale image. Gevers and Smeulders [2] proposed some color invariants to a substantial change in viewpoint, object geometry and illumination, to arrive at recognition of multicolored objects. Tremeau and Borel [3] proposed a color image segmentation algorithm in which the region growing process is based on color similarity and spatial proximity. All the aforementioned algorithms empirically verify that color image contains more information than gray-scale image.

Deep learning [4, 5] is a very hot spot in recent year and it achieves the state-of-the-art results in many image dataset classification, including handwritten digit classification, phonetic classification, and face recognition [6, 7], etc. Recently, convolutional neural networks (CNNs) [8, 9] become the mainstream deep learning structure for dealing with the color image classification, for example, AlexNet [10],

X. Sun et al. (Eds.): ICCCS 2017, Part II, LNCS 10603, pp. 494–505, 2017.
https://doi.org/10.1007/978-3-319-68542-7_42

GoogleNet [11], VGGNet [12], ResNet [13], DenseNet [14], etc. Mallat proposed a wavelet scattering network (ScatNet) [15] and applied it to gray-scale image classification [16]. Oyallon et al. [17] classified color images using scattering network (ScatNet) in YUV color space. Wu et al. [18] performed a comparative study of ScatNet in image texture classification in various color spaces. Liu et al. [19] combined color recognition algorithm through boundary detection and deep neural network for image segmentation. Sun and Qi [20] performed image retrieval based on deep belief networks. More recently, Chan et al. [21] proposed a new deep learning algorithm called principal component analysis network (PCANet), which achieves the state-of-the-art performance in many gray image dataset although is constructed from the most basic units, that is, principal component analysis (PCA) filter banks, binarization, and block-wise histogram. Linear discriminate analysis network (LDANet) [21] was also proposed as a variant of PCANet, which arouses the interest of many researchers in this field. For example, Gan et al. proposed compressive sensing network (CSNet) [22] and graph embedding network (GENet) [23] for image classification. Hu et al. [24] proposed Kernel PCA network for the recognition of facial expression. A discriminative locality alignment network (DLANet) was proposed by Feng et al. [25] for scene classification. Shi et al. [26] proposed a histopathological image classification method based on PCANet and matrix-form classifier. Huang and Yuan [27] proposed a weighted-PCANet to solve the face recognition problem. Hao and Zhao [28] presented an incremental PCANet. Zheng et al. [29] investigated a deep learning technique, named deep learning with PCANet (DLPCANet), to estimate human age. Zeng et al. [30] proposed a quaternion principal component analysis network for color image classification. Wu et al. [31] proposed a Grassmann average network (GANet) algorithm to improve the robustness of learned features from images. Zeng et al. proposed a multilinear discriminate analysis network (MLDANet) [32], which is the tensor extension of LDANet for tensor object classification. We et al. proposed a multilinear principal component analysis network (MPCANet) [33], which is the tensor extension of PCANet for tensor object classification. Wu et al. [34] tried to explained the PCANet in energy perspective. However, the performance of PCANet in various color spaces is not studied by the researchers yet.

In this paper, we perform PCANet on different color image datasets, including CURet texture database [35], UC Merced land use database [36], and Georgia Tech face database [37], in various color spaces and try to find the best color spaces for the utilization of PCANet.

The rest of the paper is organized as follows. The PCANet is briefly reviewed in Sect. 2. Section 3 introduces various color spaces. The performance of PCANet in different types of color image dataset in various color spaces has been studied in Sect. 4. Section 5 concludes the paper.

2 Review of Principal Component Analysis Network

In this section, we briefly review the two-stage PCANet (PCANet-2) [21]. The architecture of PCANet-2 is summarized in Fig. 1.

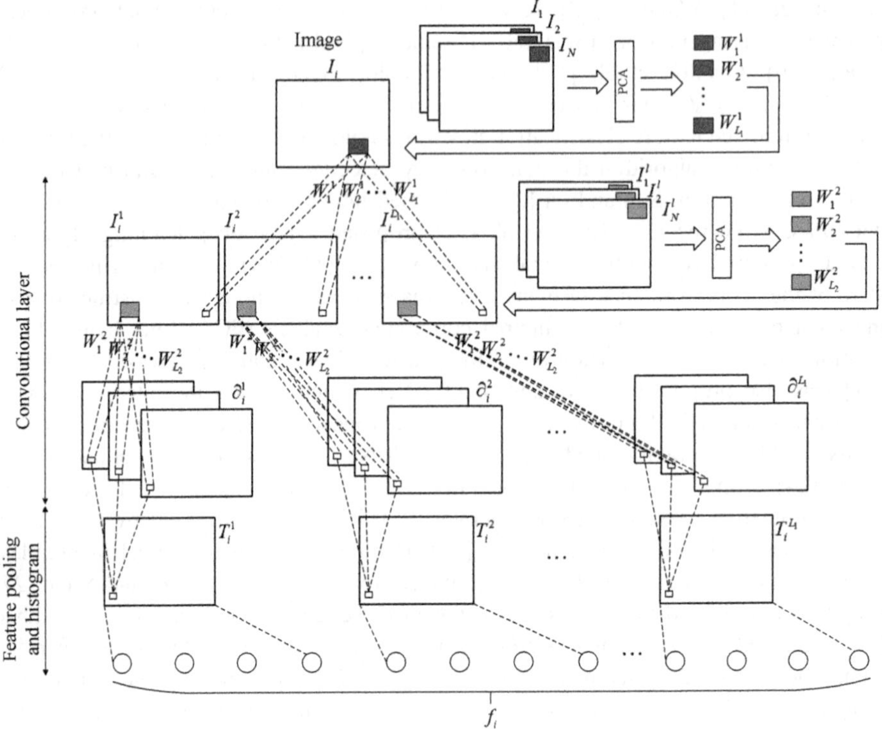

Fig. 1. The architecture of two-stage PCANet (PCANet-2)

In the framework of PCANet, only the principal component analysis (PCA) filters need to be learned from the input images. Assuming that we have N input training color images $\{I_i\}_{i=1}^{N}$ of size $m \times n$ and the number of PCA filters in ℓ th stage is L_ℓ.

At the first stage, we collect all mn patches of size $k_1 \times k_2$ around each pixel from I_i, and obtain $\mathbf{p}_{i,1}, \mathbf{p}_{i,2}, \ldots, \mathbf{p}_{i,mn} \in \mathbb{R}^{k_1 k_2}$, where $\mathbf{p}_{i,j}$ denotes the j th vectorized patch in I_i. We then subtract patch mean from each patch, and get $\bar{\mathcal{P}}_i = [\bar{\mathbf{p}}_{i,1}, \bar{\mathbf{p}}_{i,2}, \ldots, \bar{\mathbf{p}}_{i,mn}]$, where $\bar{\mathbf{p}}_{i,j}$ is a mean-removed patch. We construct a matrix to further collect these patches of all images, i.e.,

$$\mathcal{P} = [\bar{\mathcal{P}}_1, \bar{\mathcal{P}}_2, \ldots, \bar{\mathcal{P}}_N] \in \mathbb{R}^{k_1 k_2 \times Nmn}. \quad (1)$$

PCA is then utilized to minimize the reconstruction error as follows

$$\min_{\mathcal{V} \in \mathbb{R}^{k_1 k_2 \times L_1}} \left\| \mathcal{P} - \mathcal{V}\mathcal{V}^T \mathcal{P} \right\|_F^2, \ \text{s.t.} \mathcal{V}^T \mathcal{V} = \mathcal{I}_{L_1}, \quad (2)$$

where $\mathcal{I}_{L_1}$ is an unit matrix of size $L_1 \times L_1$. The optimal solution $\tilde{\mathcal{V}}^1$ of (2) is known as the first L_1 principal eigenvectors of $\mathcal{P}\mathcal{P}^T$. The PCA filters in the first stage can then be expressed as

$$\mathcal{W}_l^1 = \text{Mat}_{k_1,k_2}(\tilde{\mathcal{V}}_l^1) \in \mathbb{R}^{k_1 \times k_2}, l = 1, 2, \ldots, L_1. \tag{3}$$

where $\tilde{\mathcal{V}}_l$ denotes the l th principal eigenvector of $\tilde{\mathcal{V}}$, and $\text{Mat}_{k_1,k_2}(\sqsubseteq)$ is a function that maps a vector $\sqsubseteq \in \mathbb{R}^{k_1 k_2}$ to a matrix $\mathcal{W} \in \mathbb{R}^{k_1 \times k_2}$. The l th output feature map of the first stage is $I_i^l = I_i * \mathcal{W}_l^1, i = 1, 2, \ldots, N$, where $*$ denotes two-dimensional (2D) convolution.

At the second stage, just like the first stage, we collect all the patches of I_i^l and then subtract patch mean from each patch, and for each image we can get $\bar{\mathcal{Q}}_i^l = [\bar{\mathbf{q}}_{i,l,1}, \bar{\mathbf{q}}_{i,l,2}, \ldots, \bar{\mathbf{q}}_{i,l,mn}] \in \mathbb{R}^{k_1 k_2 \times mn}$. Then for all N input image, we obtain $\mathcal{Q}^l = [\bar{\mathcal{Q}}_1^l, \bar{\mathcal{Q}}_2^l, \ldots, \bar{\mathcal{Q}}_N^l] \in \mathbb{R}^{k_1 k_2 \times Nmn}$. We then concatenate $\boldsymbol{Q}^l, l = 1, 2, \ldots, L_1$ together and obtain $\mathcal{Q} = [\mathcal{Q}^1, \mathcal{Q}^2, \ldots, \mathcal{Q}^{L_1}] \in \mathbb{R}^{k_1 k_2 \times L_1 Nmn}$.

We can get the PCA filters of the second stage by repeating the same process as the first stage, i.e.,

$$\mathcal{W}_\ell^2 = \text{Mat}_{k_1,k_2}(\tilde{\mathcal{V}}_\ell^2) \in \mathbb{R}^{k_1 \times k_2}, \ell = 1, 2, \ldots, L_2. \tag{4}$$

where $\tilde{\mathcal{V}}_l^2 = \mathcal{Q}\mathcal{Q}^T$. Therefore, for each input I_i^l of the second stage, we will have a set of feature maps, which are composed of L_2 outputs

$$\partial_i^l = \{I_i^l * \mathcal{W}_\ell^2\}_{\ell=1}^{L_2}. \tag{5}$$

Obviously, the number of outputs of I_i in the second stage is $L_1 L_2$. One can build more stages if a deeper architecture is found to be beneficial for color image classification.

At the output stage, we first use the function $H(\cdot)$, whose value is one for positive entries and zero otherwise, to binarize the results of the second PCA stage, and then convert the L_2 outputs in ∂_i^l back into a single integer-valued "image":

$$T_i^l = \sum_{\ell=1}^{L_2} 2^{\ell-1} H(I_i^l * \mathcal{W}_\ell^2). \tag{6}$$

Note that each pixel value in "image" T_i^l is an integer in the range $[0, 2^{L_2-1}]$. We then use B blocks to split these feature maps and compute the histogram (with 2^{L_2} bins) of the decimal values in each block. We denote the result of this process as $\text{Bhist}(T_i^l)$. We concatenate all the histograms into one vector and obtain the final feature of PCANet:

$$f_i = [\text{Bhist}(T_i^1), \ldots, \text{Bhist}(T_i^{L_1})]^T \in \mathbb{R}^{(2^{L_2})L_1 B}. \tag{7}$$

Note that the local block can be either overlapping or non-overlapping depending on application [21].

3 Color Spaces

In this section, we briefly review five different types of color space: (1) RGB and I1I2I3; (2) Luminance and Chrominance; (3) Hue and Saturation; (4) Tristimuli, Chromaticity and Colorimetric systems; (5) Opponent theory. Table 1 lists all color spaces which are considered in this paper. For a more deep insight in color spaces, we refer to [38, 39].

Table 1. The description about color spaces category and their representative case.

Description	Color spaces
Red, Green, Blue	RGB, I1I2I3
Luminance, Chrominance	YUV, YIQ, YPbPr, YCbCr, JPEG-YCbCr, and YDbDr
Hue, Saturation, Value/Lightness/Intensity	HSI, HSV, HSL
Trustumuli, Chromaticity, and colorimetric system	CIE XYZ, CIE Luv, CIE LCH, CIE Lab,, and CAT02 LMS
Opponent theory	Opponent RGB [27] and Double Opponent RGB [28]

We only give some commonly used formulas of color space change in the following Eqs. (8)–(15):

(1) RGB to I1I2I3:

$$\begin{bmatrix} I_1 \\ I_2 \\ I_3 \end{bmatrix} = \begin{bmatrix} 1/3 & 1/3 & 1/3 \\ 1/2 & 0 & -1/2 \\ -1/4 & 1/2 & -1/4 \end{bmatrix} \begin{bmatrix} R \\ G \\ B \end{bmatrix}. \tag{8}$$

(2) RGB to YUV:

$$\begin{bmatrix} Y \\ U \\ V \end{bmatrix} = \begin{bmatrix} 0.299 & 0.587 & 0.114 \\ -0.147 & -0.289 & 0.436 \\ 0.615 & -0.515 & -0.100 \end{bmatrix} \begin{bmatrix} R \\ G \\ B \end{bmatrix}. \tag{9}$$

(3) RGB to HSI:

$$\begin{gathered} H = \begin{cases} \theta, & G \geq B \\ \theta + \pi, & G < B \end{cases}, \\ \max = \max(r, g, b), \ \min = \min(r, g, b), \\ \theta = \frac{\pi}{2} - \tan^{-1}\left(\frac{2R - G - B}{\sqrt{3}(G - B)}\right), \end{gathered} \tag{10}$$

$$S = \frac{2}{\sqrt{6}} \times \sqrt{(R-G)^2 + (R-B)(G-B)}, \tag{11}$$

$$I = \frac{R+G+B}{\sqrt{3}}. \tag{12}$$

RGB to CIE XYZ:

$$\begin{bmatrix} X \\ Y \\ Z \end{bmatrix} = \frac{1}{0.177} \begin{bmatrix} 0.49 & 0.31 & 0.20 \\ 0.177 & 0.812 & 0.011 \\ 0.00 & 0.01 & 0.99 \end{bmatrix} \begin{bmatrix} R \\ G \\ B \end{bmatrix}, \tag{13}$$

(4) RGB to Opponent RGB [40]:

$$\begin{bmatrix} O_{11} \\ O_{12} \\ O_{13} \end{bmatrix} = \begin{bmatrix} 1/\sqrt{2} & -1/\sqrt{2} & 0 \\ 1/\sqrt{6} & 1/\sqrt{6} & -2/\sqrt{6} \\ 1/\sqrt{3} & 1/\sqrt{3} & 1/\sqrt{3} \end{bmatrix} \begin{bmatrix} R \\ G \\ B \end{bmatrix}, \tag{14}$$

(5) RGB to double Opponent RGB [41]:

$$\begin{bmatrix} O_{21} \\ O_{22} \\ O_{23} \\ O_{24} \end{bmatrix} = \begin{bmatrix} 1/\sqrt{2} & -1/\sqrt{2} & 0 \\ 2/\sqrt{6} & -1/\sqrt{6} & -1/\sqrt{6} \\ 1/\sqrt{6} & 1/\sqrt{6} & -2/\sqrt{6} \\ 1/\sqrt{3} & 1/\sqrt{3} & 1/\sqrt{3} \end{bmatrix} \begin{bmatrix} R \\ G \\ B \end{bmatrix}. \tag{15}$$

4 Experimental Results

In this section, a set of experiments have been performed on various types of color image dataset, including CURet texture dataset [35], UC Merced land use dataset [36], and Georgia Tech face dataset [37]. The performance of PCANet in different types of color image dataset in various color spaces has been revealed.

4.1 The Performance of PCANet on CURet Texture Database

We evaluate the performance of PCANet in various color spaces on CURet texture database, which contains surface images of 61 materials that we commonly see in our environment. Each class is composed of 92 RGB color images of 200 × 200 pixels. Some examples are shown in Fig. 2(a). We transfer them from RGB color space to various other color spaces which we showed in Table 1. To reduce the computational complexity, all color images are linearly scaled to 32 × 32 pixels. The database is randomly split into a training set and a testing set, with 23 training images for each class.

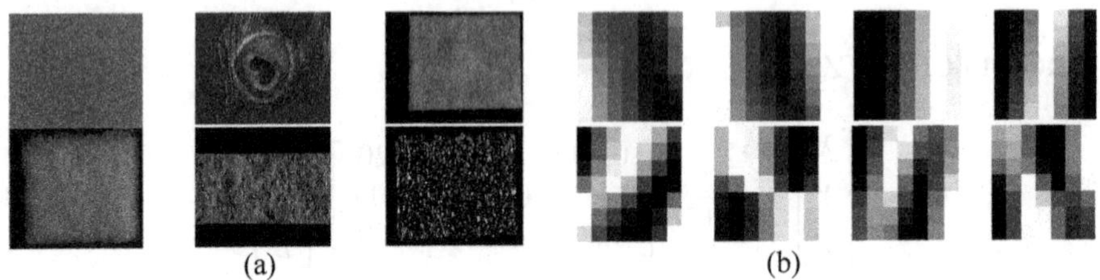

Fig. 2. (a) Some representative samples in CURet texture dataset. (b) The color feature maps learned by PCANet on RGB based CURet dataset.

We use the optimal parameters model in PCANet [21] for these experiments. PCANet-2 is trained with a number of filters $L_1 = L_2 = 8$. The overlapping ratio is set to 0.5 and the block size is fixed as 8 × 8. Patch size varies from 3 × 3 to 7 × 7 to search the optimal parameters model like [21]. SVM is then used to classify the features from PCANet.

The average recognition rates over 5 different random splits in terms of various color spaces are given in Table 2. One can see that the conventional RGB space generally do not achieve the best performance. It is also observed that the PCANet in YUV and YIQ color spaces gets the best accuracy on CURet texture database. It means that PCANet in luminance and chrominance type color space is suitable for texture classification task. Under such configuration of PCANet-2, we can see that color space consisted of hue, saturation, value, lightness, intensity (HSV, HSL, HSI) performs the worst. The feature extracted from these color spaces have poor classification ability. The opponent color space, which is a recently proposed color space, has a middle-level classification performance.

We also show the feature maps learned by CURet texture database with the patch size 7 × 7 in Fig. 2(b) from which we can easily get a direct impression on the color feature maps we learned. We can see that only a few feature maps reveal the affinity of color channels, however, other black-white feature maps learn the texture structure of CURet texture dataset. The reason could be that color texture image recognition mainly depends on the texture structure and less depends on the supplementary color information.

4.2 The Performance of PCANet on UC Merced Land Use Database

In this subsection, we evaluate the performance of PCANet in terms of various color spaces on UC Merced land use dataset. The pictures in UC Merced land use dataset is manually extracted from large images from the USGS national map urban area imagery collection for various urban areas around the country. All RGB images in the dataset

Table 2. Classification accuracy (%) of PCANet in various color spaces on CURet texture dataset, UC Merced land use dataset, Georgia Tech face database.

Accuracy \ Size / Col	CURet Dataset			UC Merced Land Use Dataset			Georgia Tech Face Dataset		
	3 × 3	5 × 5	7 × 7	3 × 3	5 × 5	7 × 7	3 × 3	5 × 5	7 × 7
Gray	93.70	96.56	96.20	66.67	58.81	56.90	99.20	99.20	99.20
RGB	96.36	98.08	98.03	73.33	67.14	63.10	99.20	98.80	99.60
I1I2I3	96.27	97.62	97.41	70.48	63.33	57.38	99.20	99.60	99.60
YUV	97.46	98.17	98.05	73.81	67.38	64.29	100.0	98.80	98.80
YIQ	97.46	98.31	97.74	73.81	70.95	65.71	99.60	99.20	99.20
YPbPr	97.32	98.17	97.96	74.29	68.33	64.29	100.0	99.20	99.60
YCbCr	96.82	97.74	97.51	74.29	72.86	74.29	99.60	99.60	99.60
JPEG-YCbCr	96.53	97.70	97.48	75.24	70.00	66.19	99.2	99.60	100.0
YDbDr	94.70	96.84	96.08	74.76	70.71	61.67	99.60	99.60	99.60
HSI	39.38	41.82	42.58	53.33	48.33	44.76	80.00	86.40	87.20
HSV	39.70	42.20	42.55	53.10	49.29	45.00	79.20	86.00	87.60
HSL	39.77	42.01	42.41	53.57	48.33	44.76	80.00	86.40	87.20
CIE XYZ	95.32	97.53	97.01	73.10	61.19	60.00	99.20	100.0	99.60
CIE Luv	93.21	95.72	95.89	76.90	71.43	63.57	99.20	99.60	99.60
CIE LCH	47.52	61.66	69.21	61.90	59.29	54.76	93.20	92.00	93.60
CIE Lab	90.14	92.99	90.14	76.19	71.43	65.71	99.20	98.80	99.60
CAT02 LMS	96.34	95.51	92.44	73.10	60.95	60.48	99.20	100.0	100.0
Opponent RGB	93.59	95.98	95.82	69.52	60.48	56.43	99.60	99.20	98.80
Double Opponent	95.08	97.01	96.13	70.24	61.43	57.86	99.60	99.60	99.20

are of size 256 × 256 with pixel resolution of one foot. Each color image in the dataset is mannually partitioned into 21 classes, with each class containing 100 images. Some examples are shown in Fig. 3(a).

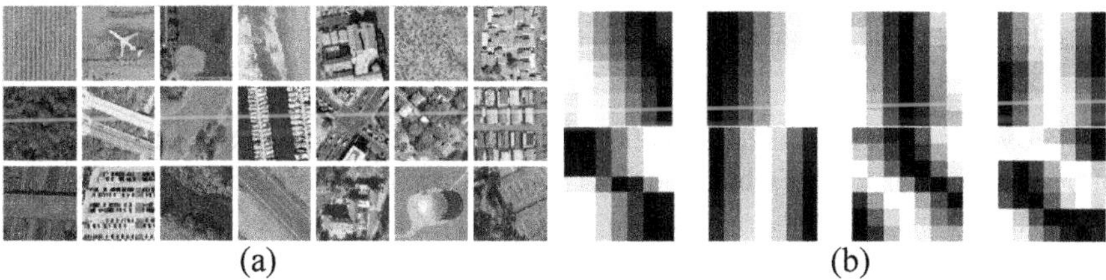

Fig. 3. (a) Some representative examples of classes in the UC Merced land use database. (b) The color feature maps learned by PCANet on RGB based UC Merced land use database with patch size 7 × 7.

In the experiment of this dataset, we first convert the images from RGB space to various other color spaces and then resize them to 32 × 32 pixels. The optimal parameters are the same as the aforementioned section. The experiment results are given in Table 2, which shows that the CIE Luv space outperforms other color spaces on UC Merced land use database. Note also that YCbCr belongs to the Trustumuli, Chromaticity, and Colorimetric System type color space. HSV, HSL, and HIS perform the worst comparing with other color spaces. The opponent color space still get a mediocre recognition accuracy. Although Luminance and Chrominance type color spaces do not gain the best performance, they also have done very well. The color feature maps of UC Merced land use database are shown in Fig. 3(b).

4.3 The Performance of PCANet on Georgia Tech Face Dataset

Georgia Tech face database contains color images of 50 people. Each individual is collected with 15 images at the Center for Signal and Image Processing at Georgia Institute of Technology. The size of all images in the dataset is 640 × 480 pixels, and the faces in each picture are average 150 × 150 pixels. Almost all images are taken into two different sessions, including the variations in illumination conditions, and facial expression.

In these experiments, we crop all the face images with 128 × 160 pixels to maintain consistency. To reduce the computational complexity, we resize these color images to 64 × 64 pixels. Some typical individual faces are shown in Fig. 4(a). We randomly select 10 face images for training and the others for testing, in terms of each individuals. In these experiments, we use one-stage PCANet (PCANet-1) since it already achieves high performance in this dataset. The parameters are the same as the aforementioned section except that the overlap ratio is set to 0 (non-overlapping).

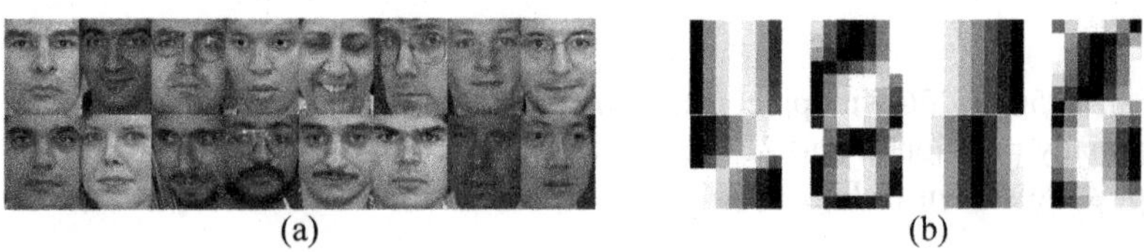

Fig. 4. (a) Sixteen color images of Georgia Tech face database. (b) Eight color feature maps learned by RGB based Georgia Tech face dataset with patch size 7 × 7.

The average accuracy of classifications over 5 times experiments are listed in Table 2. Surprisingly, both JPEG-YCbCr and CAT02 LMS achieve the state-of-the art accuracy 100% with patch size 7 × 7. HIS, HSV, and HSL still perform the worst as before. The performance of Luminance and Chrominance type color spaces is also admissible. Eight color feature maps of Georgia Tech Face Database are given in Fig. 4(b).

Table 2 also compares the results of PCANet in color space with PCANet in gray-scale space. We can see that PCANet in color space is generally performs better than PCANet in gray-scale space except for Hue-Saturation based color spaces (HSI, HSV, HSL). Therefore, we can conclude that although the color information is supplemental compared to the structure information of image, it is still very important for color image classification.

5 Conclusions

In this paper, we study the performance of PCANet in various color space in terms of different types of dataset. We find that Luminance and Chrominance type color spaces are superior to that of other color spaces in most cases. Therefore, the PCANet in Luminance and Chrominance type color spaces (YUV, YIQ, YPbPr, YCbCr, JPEG-YCbCr, and YDbDr) is recommended when we do not obtain the prior knowledge of the color image dataset. It is also worth mentioning that Hue-Saturation based color spaces (HSI, HSV, HSL) have low classification performance, therefore, these color spaces are not recommended.

Acknowledgments. This work was supported by the National Key R&D Program of China (2017YFC0107900), by the National Natural Science Foundation of China (Nos. 61201344, 61271312, 61401085, 31571001, 31640028, 31400842, 61572258, 11301074) and by the Project Sponsored by the Scientific Research Foundation for the Returned Overseas Chinese Scholars, State Education Ministry, by the Qing Lan Project and the '333' project (BRA2015288), by the Open Fund of China-USA Computer Science Research Center (KJR16026), and by the Short-term Recruitment Program of Foreign Experts (WQ20163200398).

References

1. Cheng, Y.C., Chen, S.Y.: Image classification using color, texture and regions. Image Vis. Comput. **21**, 759–776 (2003)
2. Gevers, T., Smeulders, A.W.M.: Color-based object recognition. Pattern Recogn. **32**, 453–464 (1999)
3. Tremeau, A., Borel, N.A.: Region growing and merging algorithm to color segmentation. Pattern Recogn. **30**, 1191–1203 (1997)
4. Hinton, G.E., Salakhutdinov, R.R.: Reducing the dimensionality of data with neural networks. Science **313**, 504–507 (2006)
5. Hinton, G.E., Osindero, S., Teh, Y.W.: A fast learning algorithm for deep belief nets. Neural Comput. **18**, 1527–1554 (2006)
6. Bengio, Y., Courville, A., Vincent, P.: Representation learning: a review and new perspectives. IEEE Trans. Pattern Anal. Mach. Intell. **35**, 1798–1828 (2013)
7. LeCun, Y., Bengio, Y., Hinton, G.E.: Deep learning. Nature **521**, 436–444 (2015)
8. LeCun, Y., Bottou, L., Bengio, Y., Haffner, P.: Gradient based learning applied to document recognition. Proc. IEEE **86**, 2278–2324 (1998)
9. LeCun, Y., Kavukcuoglu, K., Farabet, C.: Convolutional networks and applications in vision. In: Proceedings of 2010 IEEE International Symposium on Circuits and Systems, pp. 253–256. IEEE Press, Paris (2010)
10. Krizhevsky, A., Sutskever, I., Hinton, G.E.: ImageNet classification with deep convolutional neural networks. In: Advances in Neural Information Processing Systems, pp. 1097–1105, Lake Tahoe, Nevada (2012)
11. Szegedy, C., Liu, W., Jia, Y., Sermanet, P.: Going deeper with convolutions. In: IEEE Conference on Computer Vision and Pattern Recognition (CVPR), pp. 1–9. IEEE Press, Boston (2015)
12. Simonyan, K., Zisserman, A.: Very deep convolutional networks for large-scale image recognition. arXiv:1409.1556 (2014)

13. He, K., Zhang, X., Ren, S., Sun, J.: Deep residual learning for image recognition. In: IEEE Conference on Computer Vision and Pattern Recognition (CVPR), pp. 770–778. IEEE Press, Las Vegas (2016)
14. Huang, G., Liu, Z., Weinberger, K.Q.: Densely connected convolutional networks. arXiv: 1608.06993v3 (2016)
15. Mallat, S.: Group invariant scattering. Commun. Pure Appl. Math. **65**, 1331–1398 (2012)
16. Bruna, J., Mallat, S.: Invariant scattering convolution networks. IEEE Trans. Pattern Anal. Mach. Intell. **35**, 1872–1886 (2013)
17. Oyallon, E., Mallat, S., Sifre, L.: Generic deep networks with wavelet scattering. arXiv: 1312.5940 (2013)
18. Wu, J.S., Jiang, L.Y., Han, X., Senhadji, L., Shu, H.Z.: Performance evaluation of wavelet scattering network in image texture classification in various color spaces. J. Southeast Univ. Engl. vers. **31**, 46–50 (2015)
19. Liu, Y., Yang, J., Guo, B.Z., Yang, J.J., Zhang, X.: A novel image segmentation combined color recognition algorithm through boundary detection and deep neural network. Int. J. Multimedia Ubiquit. Eng. **11**, 87–96 (2016)
20. Sun, T., Qi, Y.C.: Image retrieval based on deep belief networks. Int. J. Multimedia Ubiquit. Eng. **11**, 331–342 (2016)
21. Chan, T.H., Jia, K., Gao, S., Lu, J., Zeng, Z., Ma, Y.: PCANet: a simple deep learning baseline for image classification? IEEE Trans. Image Process. **24**, 5017–5032 (2015)
22. Gan, Y., Zhuo, T., He, C.: Image classification with a deep network model based on compressive sensing. arXiv:1409.7307 (2014)
23. Gan, Y., Yang, T., He, C.: A deep graph embedding network model for face recognition. arXiv:1409.7313 (2014)
24. Hu, D., Ye, A., Li, L., Zhang, L.: Recognition of facial expression via kernel PCA network. Appl. Mech. Mater. **631–632**, 498–501 (2014)
25. Feng, Z., Jin, L., Tao, D., Huang, S.: DLANet: a manifold-learning-based discriminative feature learning network for scene classification. Neurocomputing **157**, 11–21 (2015)
26. Shi, J., Wu, J., Li, Y., Zhang, Q., Ying, S.: Histopathological image classification with color pattern random binary hashing based PCANet and matrix-form classifier. IEEE J. Biomed. Health Inf., pp. 1–1 (2016)
27. Huang, J., Yuan, C.: Weighted-PCANet for face recognition. In: Arik, S., Huang, T., Lai, W., Liu, Q. (eds.) Neural Information Processing. LNCS, vol. 9492, pp. 246–254. Springer, Cham (2015)
28. Hao, W.L., Zhang, Z.: Incremental PCANet: a lifelong learning framework to achieve the plasticity of both feature and classifier constructions. In: Liu, C.L., Hussain, A., Luo, B., Tan, K.C., Zeng, Y., Zhang, Z. (eds.) BICS 2016. LNCS, vol. 10023, pp. 298–309. Springer, Cham (2016). doi:10.1007/978-3-319-49685-6_27
29. Zheng, D., Du, J., Fan, W., Wang, J., Zhai, C.: Deep learning with PCANet for human age estimation. In: Huang, D.S., Jo, K.H. (eds.) ICIC 2016. LNCS, vol. 9772, pp. 300–310. Springer, Cham (2016). doi:10.1007/978-3-319-42294-7_26
30. Zeng, R., Wu, J.S., Shao, Z.H., Chen, Y., Chen, B.J., Senhadji, L., Shu, H.Z.: Color image classification via quaternion principal component analysis network. Neurocomputing **216**, 416–428 (2016)
31. Wu, J., Shi, J., Ying, S., Zhang, Q., Li, Y.: Learning representation for histopathological image with quaternion Grassmann average network. In: Wang, L., Adeli, E., Wang, Q., Shi, Y., Suk, H.I. (eds.) MLMI 2016. LNCS, vol. 10019, pp. 122–129. Springer, Cham (2016). doi:10.1007/978-3-319-47157-0_15

32. Zeng, R., Wu, J.S., Senhadji, L., Shu, H.Z.: Tensor object classification via multilinear discriminant analysis network. In: IEEE 40th International Conference on Acoustics, Speech and Signal Processing (ICASSP), pp. 1971–1975. Brisbane, Australia (2015)
33. Wu, J.S., Qiu, S.J., Zeng, R., Kong, Y.Y., Senhadji, L., Shu, H.Z.: Multilinear principal component analysis network for tensor object classification. IEEE Access **5**, 3322–3331 (2017)
34. Wu, J.S., Qiu, S.J., Kong, Y.Y., Jiang, L.Y., Senhadji, L., Shu, H.Z.: PCANet: an energy perspective. arXiv:1603.00944 (2016)
35. Dana, K.J., Van Ginneken, B., Nayar, S.K., Koenderink, J.J.: Reflectance and texture of real-world surfaces. ACM Trans. Graph. **18**, 1–34 (1999)
36. Yang, Y., Newsam, S.: Bag-of-visual-words and spatial extensions for land-use classification. In: Proceedings of the 18th SIGSPATIAL International Conference on Advances in Geographic Information Systems, pp. 270–279. ACM, California (2010)
37. Georgia Tech face database. http://www.anefian.com/research/face_reco.html
38. Ford, A., Roberts, A.: Colour Space Conversions. Westminster University, pp. 1–31 (1998)
39. Color space transformations website. http://www.getreuer.info/home/colorspace
40. Van de Sande, K.E.A., Gevers, T., Snoek, C.G.M.: Evaluating color descriptors for object and scene recognition. IEEE Trans. Pattern Anal. Mach. Intell. **32**, 1582–1596 (2010)
41. Zhang, J., Barhomi, Y., Serre, T.: A new biologically inspired color image descriptor. In: Fitzgibbon, A., Lazebnik, S., Perona, P., Sato, Y., Schmid, C. (eds.) ECCV 2012. LNCS, vol. 7576, pp. 312–324. Springer, Heidelberg (2012). doi:10.1007/978-3-642-33715-4_23

A Method of Group Behavior Analysis for Enhanced Affinity Propagation

Xinning Li(✉), Zhiping Zhou, and Lele Liu

Engineering Research Center of Internet of Things Technology Applications Ministry of Education, Jiangnan University, Jiangsu, China
18861825208@163.com, {zzp,6141918006}@jiangnan.edu.cn

Abstract. With the popularity of mobile phones, it is necessary to mine and analyze the user habits, network applications and other data, which can help provide users with a strong adaptability of information services. On the basis of acceleration sensor and touch screen data, we analyze the behaviors of browsing the web, chatting, making calls and playing game. The traditional Affinity Propagation algorithm analyzes all the characteristics of the data as an equal role in group behavior analysis, which has some limitations. In this paper, an Adaptive Feature Weighting based on Affinity Propagation (AFWAP) Group Behavior Analysis Algorithm is proposed, which introduces feature weight into the AP algorithm. The proposed method makes different contribution to the class center in each iteration process, and assigns a new weight for each dimension attribute then to update the feature weight adaptively. In the clustering process, the importance of different features can be measured, which solves the shortcomings of the traditional AP algorithm using equal weight. Finally we apply the proposed method to group behavior analysis.

Keywords: Feature weighting · Affinity propagation · Mobile sensors · Group behavior

1 Introduction

With the in-depth study of pervasive computing, user behavior recognition has received more and more attention [1]. The rapid development of micro-electromechanical systems, so that various types of sensors are widely used for user behavior recognition. In many types of sensors, the sensors built into the smart phone, such as accelerometers, touch screen sensors, which has the advantages of high sensitivity, low cost, easy to carry, and make up for the limitation of computer vision [2, 3] monitoring and the environmental variables.

In recent years, many researchers have achieved good results by using mobile sensors to identify user behavior. Kwapisz et al. [4] used 29 users' data for unified modeling to identify daily activities such as walking, running, and going downstairs. Altun et al. [5] take 5 inertial measurement units (Inertial, Measurement, IMU) set on the pedestrian to identify different behaviors. Wang et al. [6] put a tri-axial acceleration module on the subject's wrist to collect data of daily activities, including lying, sitting, standing, walking, upstairs and downstairs, and the deep belief network (DBN) is

X. Sun et al. (Eds.): ICCCS 2017, Part II, LNCS 10603, pp. 506–517, 2017.
https://doi.org/10.1007/978-3-319-68542-7_43

utilized to identify the behavior. The above method is mainly for individual user behavior analysis, while ignoring the user group behavior information. Roggen et al. [7, 8] studied the behavior of groups such as queuing users, narrow corridors, and crowding, using mobile sensors to identify user behaviors within a certain period of time. By calculating the similarity coefficients of each user's behavior sequence, the similarity degree matrix is constructed, and the behavior of the user group is analyzed by graph clustering. On the basis of Roggen, Yu et al. [9] proposed a multi pattern fusion clustering algorithm to analyze the user behavior, which can adaptively select the mobile sensor detection model. However, in work [7–9], the number of clustering classes needs to be pre-set in the analysis of group behavior, which determines the non-self-adaptability of the algorithm. Meanwhile, in the process of clustering, the works consider each feature as an equal function and does not take into account the limitations of different features on clustering.

In this work, affinity propagation algorithm is utilized to analyze the behavior of user groups based on the sequence of users' behavior. For solving the shortcomings of traditional AP algorithm that the weights of the feature weights are regarded as equal to each other. A new algorithm that adaptive feature weighting based on Affinity Propagation (AFWAP) is proposed for Group Behavior Analysis, which makes different contribution to the class center in each iteration process, and assigns a new weight for each dimension attribute then to update the feature weight adaptively.

The remainder of this paper is organized as follows. In Sect. 2, gives a brief review of signal acquisition an feature extraction which is important for user behavior recognition and experiment section. We detail the newly proposed Adaptive Feature Weighting based on Affinity Propagation in Sect. 3. Section 4 shows the experimental results on the UCI data and group behavior data. Finally, concluding remarks and suggestions for future work are presented in Sect. 5.

2 Signal Acquisition and Feature Extraction

In this work, we use mobile phone acceleration sensor and touch screen sensor to analyze the users' Browsing Web (BW), Chatting Type (CT), Picking Up (PU), Playing Games (PG) and Free Time (FT) for behavior analysis. The sampling frequency of the sensor is set at 50 Hz, and the data are preprocessed by the moving average filter to reduce the noise interference while retaining the original gesture information. Further processing of the signal window, the window length is 500 sampling points, and the adjacent window data is overlapped by 50%. For making the intercepted gesture signal can recognize the behavior effectively, we need to extract the feature of the acceleration signal and touch screen gesture signal, set up the feature vector set. The features of the extracted acceleration signal include 4 kinds, which are divided into time domain and frequency domain. The time domain features include: the signal energy, the peak value and the number of peaks. Frequency domain features include the FFT (Fast Fourier Transform) of each sliding window data in the first 32 dimensions. The characteristics of the touch screen signal are extracted, such as sliding speed, sliding direction, gesture sliding and so on [10]. In order to regulate the range of similar features, the z-score [11] is utilized to normalize the set of feature vectors.

The feature vectors are extracted from the acceleration signal and the touch screen gesture signal by using the sliding window. The feature vectors are processed by principal component analysis (PCA), and the SVM classification algorithm is utilized to identify the reduced feature vectors. At this time can be obtained within the time T to the user's behavior sequence, as shown in Fig. 1.

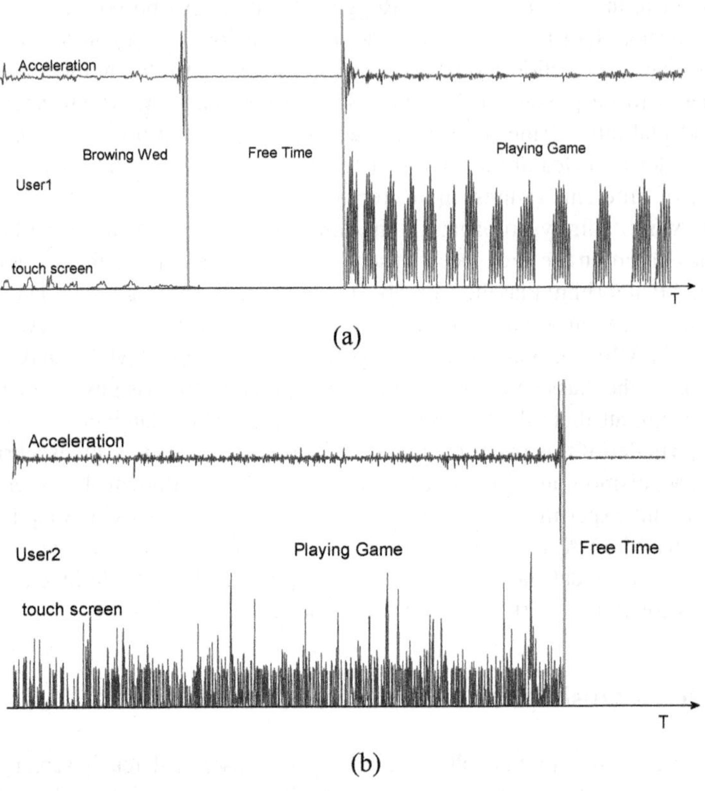

Fig. 1. Behavior sequence within each user's in time T.

The data used in this paper comes from the daily user behavior data, because there are many kinds of complex data in the data source, we need to extract the data from the database, such as the user browsing the web, chatting, picking up, playing games and free time. The proportion of BW, CT, PU, PG and FT can be obtained by Fig. 1 in the time T. With the above five behaviors as data attributes, the data set $\boldsymbol{X}$ can be obtained for n users, and the AP algorithm is applied to the acquired user data set $\boldsymbol{X}$. The $\boldsymbol{X}$ is divided into k clusters by the AP algorithm, according to the characteristics of the data object, the behavior of user groups is analyzed.

3 The AFWAP Algorithm

3.1 Affinity Propagation

AP [12] algorithm is a new unsupervised clustering algorithm, which firstly sets all data points as potential cluster centers then establishes attraction information passing among data points to find clusters. The data set $\boldsymbol{X}$ is n data in space R^d, it is divided into k clusters, and the center of each cluster is denoted by $\boldsymbol{c}_k$. Each data point corresponds to only one cluster center point, then the definition of clustering error function is:

$$J(C) = \sum_{\mathbf{x} \in C_k} \sum_{l=1}^{d} (x_l - x_{kl})^2 \tag{1}$$

The goal of the AP algorithm is to find the optimal set of representative points so that the error function is minimized.

$$C^* = \arg\min[J(C)] \tag{2}$$

3.2 Adaptive Feature Weighted Based on AP

The traditional AP algorithm has some limitations when analyzing the behavior data, and all of the features of the data are considered to be equal to the role of analysis. In this work, we propose a feature-weighted AP algorithm, which assigns different weights to the sample features during the clustering process and updates the feature weights in the iterative process. Assume that the data set consists of n samples of $\boldsymbol{x}_1, \boldsymbol{x}_2, \ldots, \boldsymbol{x}_n$, and each sample has a d-dimensional attribute. We use $\boldsymbol{w}_i = (w_{i1}, w_{i2}, \ldots, w_{id})^T$ to represent the weight of each dimension and calculate the similarity between data points i and k, as following:

$$s(i,k) = -\sum_{l=1}^{d} w_{kl}^{\beta} (x_{il} - x_{kl})^2 \tag{3}$$

where $\sum_{l=1}^{d} w_{il}^{\beta} = 1$, $w_{il} \geq 0$, $l = 1, 2, \ldots, d$, x_{il} and x_{ik} are the l-th component of points $\boldsymbol{x}_i$ and $\boldsymbol{x}_k$. $\beta > 1$, and the parameter β further controls the importance of each attribute.

Since the AP clustering process is performed by minimizing the objective function, AFWAP can be considered as an optimization problem. This optimization problem is a typical quadratic programming problem and has an analytic solution. The functional expression L can be expressed as (4):

$$L = \sum_{x \in C_k} \sum_{l=1}^{d} w_{kl}^{\beta} (\mathbf{x}_l - x_{kl})^2 + \varepsilon \sum_{l=1}^{d} w_{kl}^{\beta} - \gamma\left(\sum_{l=1}^{d} w_{kl} - 1\right) \tag{4}$$

where ε is a small positive real number, for the control type denominator is not 0, and we set $\varepsilon = 10^{-6}$. Finding the partial derivative of L with respect to w_{kl} and make it to be 0, and then get the formula about the weight of the feature, as follows:

$$\frac{\partial L}{\partial w_{kl}} = \beta w_{kl}^{\beta-1}\left[(x_{il} - x_{kl})^2 + \varepsilon\right] - \gamma = 0 \tag{5}$$

$$w_{kl} = \left(\frac{\gamma}{\beta(V_{kl} + \varepsilon)}\right)^{1/(\beta-1)} \tag{6}$$

The V_{kl} representation is as shown in Eq. (7):

$$V_{kl} = \sum_{\mathbf{x} \in C_k} (\boldsymbol{x}_l - x_{kl})^2 \tag{7}$$

By the formula (6) and the constraint condition of the $w_{kh} \in [0, 1]$, $\sum_{h=1}^{d} w_{kh} = 1$ can be obtained:

$$\sum_{h=1}^{d} \left(\frac{\gamma}{\beta(V_{kh} + \varepsilon)}\right)^{1/(\beta-1)} = 1 \tag{8}$$

Solving Eq. (8) can be calculated γ formula:

$$\gamma = \left[\sum\nolimits_{h=1}^{d} [\beta(V_{kh} + \varepsilon)]^{-1/(\beta-1)}\right]^{-(\beta-1)} \tag{9}$$

Furthermore, the formula (9) can be substituted into the formula (6) to obtain the characteristic weight w_{kl}. The final update formula is:

$$w_{kl} = \left(\sum\nolimits_{h=1}^{d} \left(\frac{V_{kl} + \varepsilon}{V_{kh} + \varepsilon}\right)^{1/(\beta-1)}\right)^{-1} \quad k = 1, 2, \ldots, n \quad l = 1, 2, \ldots, d \tag{10}$$

Equation (10) is used to obtain the weight of feature, and it is brought into formula (3) to calculate the similarity between data point i and class center point k. At the beginning of AFWAP, we initialize all the weights to be equal, i.e., $w_{ik} = 1/d$ for i = 1,2,…, n and k = 1,2,…, d. There are two kinds of message exchanged between data points, the responsibility $r(i,k)$ and the availability $a(i,k)$, which take different kinds of competition into account respectively. For the point x_i, when $a(i,k) + r(i,k)$ reach the maximum, it is more likely that the point x_k is the final cluster center. When $a(i,k) + r(i,k)$ remains invariant, the message-passing procedure will stop. By iteration, the sample points are competing to obtain the final clustering center. The responsibility $r(i,k)$ and the availability $a(i,k)$ are shown in Eqs. (11) and (12).

$$r^{(t)}(i,k) = \lambda r^{(t-1)}(i,k) + (1-\lambda) \cdot \left(s(i,k) - \max_{i,j \neq k}\{a(i,j) + s(i,j)\} \right) \tag{11}$$

$$a^{(t)}(i,k) = \begin{cases} \lambda a^{(t-1)}(i,k) + (1-\lambda) \\ \cdot \min\left\{ 0, r(k,k) + \sum_{j \notin \{i,k\}} \max\{0, r(j,k)\} \right\}, \; i \neq k \\ \lambda a^{(t-1)}(k,k) + (1-\lambda)\left(\sum_{j \neq k} \max\{0, r(j,k)\} \right), \; i = k \end{cases} \tag{12}$$

For the point x_i, x_k is calculated for satisfying the condition $\arg\max_k (a^{(t)}(i,k) + r^{(t)}(i,k))$, and the point x_k is taken as the class representative point. Then according to Eq. (10), the weight of each feature is calculated, and the feature weight is updated adaptively. The AFWAP is based on the AP algorithm framework, except that the algorithm adds a step of calculating feature weight differences and redefines the calculation formulas for each iteration step. Since the AFWAP updates the feature weights by adaptively, the following conditions are satisfied in the iterative process: the maximum number of iterations is exceeded; the amount of information change is lower than a fixed threshold; the selected class representative points remain stable during the iterative process. So the AFWAP continues the iterative convergence condition of AP algorithm.

The AFWAP algorithm can be summarized as follows:

(1) **Input:** the data set $\mathbf{X}_{n \times d} = \{\mathbf{x}_1, \mathbf{x}_2, \ldots, \mathbf{x}_n\}$, the similarity matrix $\mathbf{S}(i,j)$, the number of iterations $t_{\max}$, the damping factor λ, the convergence iteration coefficient *conv*.

while true do

(2) Calculate responsibilities according to Eq. (11), Calculate availabilities according to Eq. (12), finding the class center point of each point;
(3) the feature weight w_{kl} is updated according to Eq. (10).
(4) The similarity $s(i,k) = -\sum_{l=1}^{d} w_{kl}^{\beta}(x_{il} - x_{kl})^2$ is calculated and update the similarities between every exemplar and other data points.

end while

(5) **Output:** Finding the exemplars and their corresponding attribute weights.

The complexity of the algorithm is analyzed from the iterative process, the computational complexity of AP clustering depends on the construction of similarity matrix, and the similarity matrix is $O(n^2)$. The AFWAP algorithm through the formula (3) to build the similarity matrix, and the computational complexity is $O(n^2)$. According to formula (10), the calculation complexity of updating the feature weight is

$O(n \cdot d)$, where d is the attribute of the sample, $d \ll n$. The computational complexity of the AFWAP algorithm is $O(n^2 + n \cdot d)$, which is equal to the computational complexity of AP.

4 Experiments and Results Analysis

4.1 Abbreviations and Acronyms

This section mainly compares the clustering performance of AP and the AFWAP to test the effectiveness of the proposed algorithm. The clustering results were evaluated and compared by F-Measure [13], ACC (accuracy) [14] and RI (rand index) [15]. In this paper, 10 common data sets from UCI are selected for experiment, whose characteristics are shown in Table 1.

Table 1. UCI datasets.

Datasets	Classes	Dimensions	Size
Air	3	64	359
Vehicle	4	18	846
Wine	3	13	178
Heart	2	13	270
Diabetes	2	8	768
Australian	2	14	690
Sonar	2	60	208
WDBC	2	30	569

4.2 Results Comparison and Analysis

In order to analyze the clustering performance of AFWAP algorithm, the Kcenters, Fuzzy C-means (FCM), AP and AFWAP are compared in this section in terms of F-Measure, ACC and RI. The experiments run by MATLAB2014b, and the hardware configuration of the computer is: Intel Core 3230 M, CPU 2.60 GHz, 4 GB RAM. The maximum number of iterations Maxgen is set to 500 for AP and AFWAP. At the beginning of the algorithm, the responsibilities and availabilities are initialized to 0, the bias parameter is set to the median value of the similarity matrix S. The AP and AFWAP algorithms use the same damping factor $\lambda = 0.9$, and the β is set to 3 for AFWAP. Take AFWAP adaptive clustering as the number of clusters in Kcenters and FCM algorithms, each algorithm running 100 times independently. We calculate the average of F-Measure, ACC and RI and the corresponding standard deviation in parentheses. The experimental results are shown in Table 2, where the optimal index value for each data is bold.

Firstly, it can be seen from Table 2 that in most cases the AFWAP algorithm is significantly improved relative to the AP, thus the feasibility of using feature weighting to improve the algorithm is verified. According to the F-Measure index of each algorithm in

Table 2. Comparison of algorithm performance.

Data sets	Method	F-Measure	ACC	RI
Sonar	AP	0.206	0.120	0.473
	FCM	0.362(0.071)	0.329(0.006)	0.470(0.077)
	Kcenters	0.288(0.030)	0.184(0.024)	0.492(0.020)
	AFWAP	**0.586**	**0.380**	**0.499**
Wine	AP	**0.511**	0.365	0.395
	FCM	0.494(0.009)	0.357(0.006)	0.675(0.098)
	Kcenters	0.489(0.029)	0.359(0.035)	**0.693**(0.093)
	AFWAP	0.503	**0.399**	0.347
Air	AP	0.319	0.206	0.503
	FCM	0.291(0.057)	0.260(0.021)	0.579(0.187)
	Kcenters	0.173(0.021)	0.097(0.014)	**0.675**(0.145)
	AFWAP	**0.463**	**0.292**	0.341
Heart	AP	0.220	0.130	0.489
	FCM	0.206(0.011)	0.117(0.006)	**0.552**(0.076)
	Kcenters	0.234(0.023)	0.139(0.016)	0.544(0.093)
	AFWAP	**0.620**	**0.452**	0.505
WDBC	AP	0.306	0.185	0.496
	FCM	0.259(0.019)	0.151(0.014)	0.494(0.188)
	Kcenters	0.278(0.023)	0.165(0.017)	0.521(0.187)
	AFWAP	**0.678**	**0.619**	**0.545**
Australian	AP	0.291	0.187	0.473
	FCM	0.283(0.019)	0.180(0.015)	0.501(0.079)
	Kcenters	0.138(0.006)	0.077(0.004)	0.476(0.013)
	AFWAP	**0.652**	**0.535**	**0.513**
Diabetes	AP	0.177	0.100	**0.606**
	FCM	0.198(0.005)	0.111(0.003)	0.568(0.088)
	Kcenters	0.181(0.026)	0.103(0.017)	0.590(0.115)
	AFWAP	**0.651**	**0.546**	0.535
Vehicle	AP	0.327	0.222	**0.675**
	FCM	0.280(0.005)	0.177(0.005)	0.674(0.053)
	Kcenters	0.332(0.027)	**0.260**(0.020)	0.596(0.017)
	AFWAP	**0.398**	0.255	0.253

the table, the AFWAP algorithm outperforms the AP, FCM and Kcenters algorithm in addition to the data set Wine, among which the 5 data sets of Sonar, WDBC, heart, Australian, diabetes have obvious advantage. For the ACC index, the AFWAP algorithm outperforms the other three algorithms on the 8 UCI datasets, except for the dataset Vehicle. While for the data set Vehicle, the ACC index of K centers is 0.260, only 0.005 higher than AFWAP. For the RI index, the proposed algorithm has advantages over the other three algorithms on Sonar, WDBC and Australian data sets, which is 5.50%, 9.87% and 8.46% higher than the AP. Comparisons show that, except for a few cases, the clustering index of AFWAP is the largest and has been marked in Table 2.

Relative to FCM and K centers, AP and AFWAP can effectively overcome the initial center-sensitive issues, without pre-specified class center. By the responsibilities and availabilities can automatically determine the class center, after setting the parameter preference, the AP and AFWAP can automatically determine the number of clusters, which reflecting the advantages of AP and AFWAP. The AFWAP makes different contribution to the class center in each iteration process, and assigns a new weight for each dimension attribute then to update the feature weight adaptively. In the clustering process, the importance of different features can be measured. Compared with AP, AFWAP can update the feature weight adaptively, and distinguish the effect of different features on clustering, so it can be concluded that AFWAP has the best clustering performance.

4.3 Group Behavior Data Analysis

In this work, the data are from the daily user behavior, we select the simulation of 108 experiments to collect their mobile phone sensor data records. During the recording process, a set of sensor record data for 7 consecutive days is obtained, and we sampled 3 h early in the evening to analyzed the sensor data. The sensor data is preprocessed and extracted, the SVM is utilized to identify the user behavior. Further, we can obtain the proportion of the time occupied by each user BW, CT, PU, PG and FT behavior. With the above 5 kinds of behavior as the data attributes, we can get 108 user behavior data sets.

This section is divided into two parts, the first part is that the performance analysis of the AFWAP and AP algorithm in the real data. The second part uses the AFWAP algorithm to analyze the behavior of the group and dig the potential information between the groups. In first part we use Silhouette index [16] to analyze the performance of AFWAP. The Silhouette index can reflect the intracluster compactness and inter cluster separation of the clustering structure. The values are between 0 and 1, and the larger the clustering results are, the better value is. When Silhouette is greater than 0.5, which shows that each class can be clearly separated. When Silhouette is less than 0.5, showing that some classes have overlapping situations, while when the value is less than 0.2, which shows that the lack of substantive clustering structure.

In Fig. 2, the group behavior data is analyzed by AP clustering algorithm, and the Silhouette index is 0.224, which shows that there are some cases of overlapping in the clustering process. The Silhouette performance index is 0.519 by AFWAP, indicating

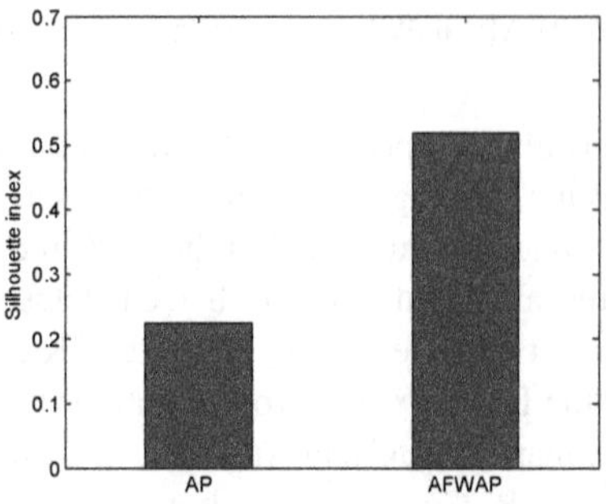

Fig. 2. Clustering results

that each class can be clearly separated. The experimental results show that the proposed algorithm performance is better than the AP algorithm. Further the AFWAP is utilized to analyze the behavior of user groups. The clustering results are shown in Fig. 3.

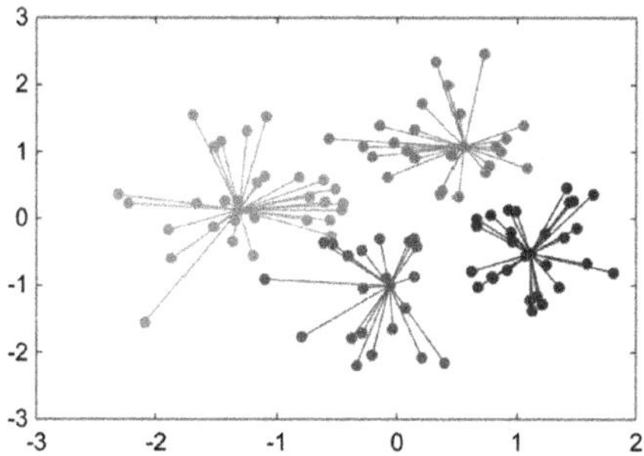

Fig. 3. AFWAP clustering effect diagram.

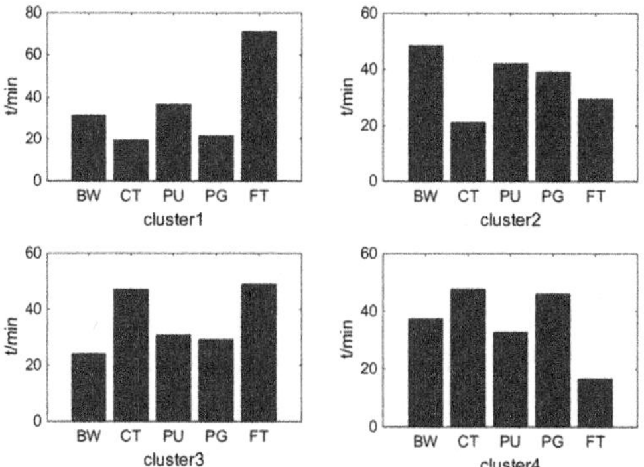

Fig. 4. The effect of cluster.

It can be seen from Fig. 3 that the AFWAP algorithm can automatically cluster the group behavior data into four categories. Each category corresponds to the average value of each attribute as shown in Fig. 4, which corresponds to the characteristics of each category:

Cluster 1: This category contains 31 users, and accounting for 28.70% of the 108 users. Among them, the free time of the cluster 1 is the highest compared with the other 3 cluster on free time, and the total time is up to 43%. These users are not highly dependent on the phone, who are in a relatively stable low-activity state, but still maintain business use. In the browsing Web, chatting, picking up and play games, the main activity is to call and play games.

Cluster 2: This category contains 26 users, and accounting for 24.07% of the 108 users. The user in cluster 2 is more balanced than the other cluster, who belong to balanced users. Among them, these users tend to browse Web and make phone calls. Decision-makers can provide call packages, traffic concessions and other services according to the characteristics of such user behavior.

Cluster 3: This kind of user's free time is second only to category 1, the proportion of time is 27.25%. These users spend time in browsing Web, picking up the phone and playing games is basically the same, and they are more keen to use mobile chatting. In contrast, these users have a greater market potential, decision-makers should strengthen guidance, through the activities of marketing, product upgrades and other methods to develop into high-value users.

Cluster 4: This category contains a total of 29 users, these users spend the least time outside the phone, indicating that such users have a strong dependence on the phone. Except for the time to pick up the phone, they browse the web, chatting, playing game compared to the other 3 categories of users, these users account for a higher proportion using the time on the phone. Decision makers can seize the opportunity to recommend to the user social application class App, or provide preferential application push message and other value-added services according to the characteristics of such user behavior.

5 Conclusion

This work proposed an adaptive feature weighted Affinity Propagation algorithm based on analysis of user behavior, which can be applied to group behavior analysis. The proposed method makes different contribution to the class center in each iteration process, and assigns a new weight for each dimension attribute then to update the feature weight adaptively. In the clustering process, the importance of different features can be measured, which solves the shortcomings of the traditional AP algorithm using equal weight. Compared with the clustering algorithm on UCI dataset, the AFWAP algorithm has better clustering performance. Using the proposed algorithm to evaluate the clustering results on the real population behavior data, which can predict the direction of users' development and help the decision makers formulate marketing strategies to provide different services or products for different users' needs.

Acknowledgments. This work is supported by the Special Funds of Basic Research Business Expenses of Central University under Grant No. JUSRP51510.

References

1. Li, M., Rozgica, V., Thatte, G., et al.: Multimodal physical activity recognition by fusing temporal and cepstral information. IEEE Trans. Neural Syst. Rehabil. Eng. **18**(4), 369–380 (2010)
2. Tang, C., Wang, W., Li, W.: Multi-learner co-training model for human action recognition. J. Softw. **26**(11), 2939–2950 (2015)

3. Yao, B., Hagras, H., Alhaddad, M., et al.: A fuzzy logic-based system for the automation of human behavior recognition using machine vision in intelligent environments. Soft Comput. **19**(2), 499–506 (2015)
4. Kwapisz, J., Weiss, G.M., Moore, S.A.: Activity recognition using cell phone accelerometers. ACM SIGKDD Explor. Newslett. **12**(2), 74–82 (2011)
5. Altun, K., Barshan, B., Tunçel, O.: Comparative study on classifying human activities with miniature inertial and magnetic sensors. Pattern Recogn. **43**(10), 3605–3620 (2010)
6. Wang, L.: Recognition of human activities using continuous autoencoders with wearable sensors. Sensors **16**(2), 189 (2016)
7. Roggen, D., Wirz, M., Tröster, G., et al.: Recognition of crowd behavior from mobile sensors with pattern analysis and graph clustering methods. Netw. Heterogen. Media **6**(3), 521–544 (2011)
8. Gordon, D., Wirz, M., Roggen, D., et al.: Group affiliation detection using model divergence for wearable devices. In: Proceedings of the 2014 ACM International Symposium on Wearable Computers, pp. 19–26. ACM press (2014)
9. Yu, N., Zhao, Y., Han, Q., et al.: Identification of partitions in a homogeneous activity group using mobile devices. Mob. Inf. Syst. **4–26**, 1–14 (2016)
10. Feng, T., Liu, Z., Kwon, K.A., et al.: continuous mobile authentication using touchscreen gestures. In: IEEE Conference on Technologies for Homeland Security (HST), pp. 451–456. IEEE press, Boston (2012)
11. Altman, E.I., Laitinen, E.K., Suvas, A.: Financial distress prediction in an international context: a review and empirical analysis of Altman's Z-score model. J. Int. Financ. Manag. Acc. **28**(2), 131–171 (2016)
12. Frey, B.J., Dueck, D.: Clustering by passing messages between data points. Science **315**(5814), 972–976 (2007)
13. Liu, H., Liu, T., Wu, J., et al.: Spectral ensemble clustering. In: The 21th ACM SIGKDD International Conference on Knowledge Discovery and Data Mining, pp. 715–724. ACM press (2015)
14. Sun, L., Guo, C., Liu, C., et al.: Fast affinity propagation clustering based on incomplete similarity matrix. Knowl. Inf. Syst., 1–23 (2016)
15. Rand, W.M.: Objective criteria for the evaluation of clustering methods. J. Am. Stat. Assoc. **66**(336), 846–850 (1971)
16. Wang, C.D., Lai, J.H., Suen, C.Y., et al.: Multi-exemplar affinity propagation. IEEE Trans. Pattern Anal. Mach. Intell. **35**(9), 2223–2237 (2013)

A Median Filtering Forensics Approach Based on Machine Learning

Bin Yang(✉), Zhenyu Li, Weifeng Hu, and Enguo Cao

School of Design, Jiangnan University, Wuxi, Jiangsu, China
yewind2002@163.com, 150245114@qq.com,
153337724@qq.com, 24942849@qq.com

Abstract. Today manipulation of digital images has become easy due to powerful computers, advanced photo-editing software and high resolution capturing devices. Verifying the integrity of images without extra prior knowledge of the image content is an important research field. Since some general post-operations, like widely used median filtering, can affect the reliability of forensic methods in various ways, it is also significant to detect them. Current image median filtering forensics algorithms mainly extract features manually. In this paper, we present a new image forgery detection method based on machine learning, which utilizes a convolutional neural networks (CNN) to automatically learn hierarchical representations from the input images. A modified CNN architecture is specifically designed to identify traces left by the manipulation. The experimental results on several public datasets show that the proposed CNN based model outperforms some state-of-the-art methods.

Keywords: Deep learning · Median filtering forensics · Convolutional neural networks · Forgery detection · Approach design

1 Introduction

Image security and authentication are playing a critical role in our society. Recent years, the field of digital forensics has emerged to help restore some trust to digital images. Digital watermarking has a drawback that a watermark must be inserted into an image first. On the contrary, Blind forensics techniques [1] do not need any explicit priori information about the image. They work in the absence of any digital watermark or signature [2]. Generally, lots of forensic methods concentrate on intentional content forgeries of the image, which mainly include copy-move forgery [3–7] and image splicing [8]. However, most of these approaches can only deal with one type of tempering, e.g. clone and splicing due to the complexity of the image splicing localization problem itself. Most of them are based on some certain assumptions or some prior knowledge of the questioned image, which restricts its practical usage. For example; we do not know the forgery type of a test image before further examinations are made. Since the forger always makes some additional postprocessed processes to conceal the trace of tampering. Widely employed as a popular noise removal and image enhancement tool, median filtering has the properties of nonlinearity and preserving edge information of an image. These characters have been utilized by anti-forensics

X. Sun et al. (Eds.): ICCCS 2017, Part II, LNCS 10603, pp. 518–527, 2017.
https://doi.org/10.1007/978-3-319-68542-7_44

methods, e.g., removing statistical traces of blocking artifacts left by the JPEG compression [9], or destroying linear correlations between adjacent pixels for the purpose of hiding the trace of re-sampling [10].

Recent years, many related works confined to median filtering forensics [11–16] have been carried out. Kirchner and Fridrich [11] developed an artifacts and subtractive pixel adjacency matrix (SPAM) features to detect median filtering in bitmap and JPEG post-compressed images, respectively. In the same year, Cao et al. [12] developed an approach to identify the median filtering statistical fingerprint by detecting the zero values on the first order difference map in texture regions. Kang et al. [14] utilized a feature from the autoregressive (AR) model of median filter residual (MFR) to improve detection performance for nearly saturated images. Zhang et al. [16] using a second-order local ternary pattern (LTP) operator to detect median filtering; and the kernel principal component analysis (KPCA) is exploited to reduce the dimensionality of the proposed feature set. However, most existing methods manually extract reliable features, and then feed them into a classifier like the support vector machine (SVM), which has been trained with lots of labeled images, for detection [15].

Motivated by the rapid developing of machine learning, deep neural networks, such as Deep Belief Network [17], Deep Auto Encoder [18] and Convolutional Neural Network (CNN) [19], have shown to be capable of extracting complex statistical dependencies from high-dimensional sensory inputs and efficiently learning their hierarchical representations. Machine learning based approaches have been proposed in the passive image forensics. Chen et al. [20] made an attempt to adopt a deep learning method based on the same MFR and achieved significant improvement with a high-dimensional feature. Bayar and Stamm [21] proposed a new form of convolutional layer that will force the CNN to learn manipulation detection features from images without requiring any preliminary feature extraction or pre-processing.

In this paper, a novel universal CNN based approach is proposed for the image forgery forensic. The approach could automatically learning the tempering traces left in the forgery. However, the conventional CNN framework may not be directly applied to image forgery detection. Since the forgery images tend to closely resemble the authentic ones not only visually but also statistically [22, 23]. We modified the conventional CNN model by adding a filter layer to suppress the main content of the input image. A specific CNN architecture for median filtering forensics is proposed. Extensive experiments have shown that the proposed method can achieve better detection performance than the state-of-the-art schemes.

2 Proposed CNN Model

In the computer vision and machine learning fields, deep neural networks architectures have recently gained significant attention. Convolutional neural networks (CNN) are one of the most popular architectures used in computer vision problems because of their reduced number of parameters compared to fully connected models and intuitive structure, which allows the networks to learn translation invariant features [24]. As shown in Fig. 1, a typical CNN consists of convolutional layers, pooling layers, fully connected layers and Classification layer.

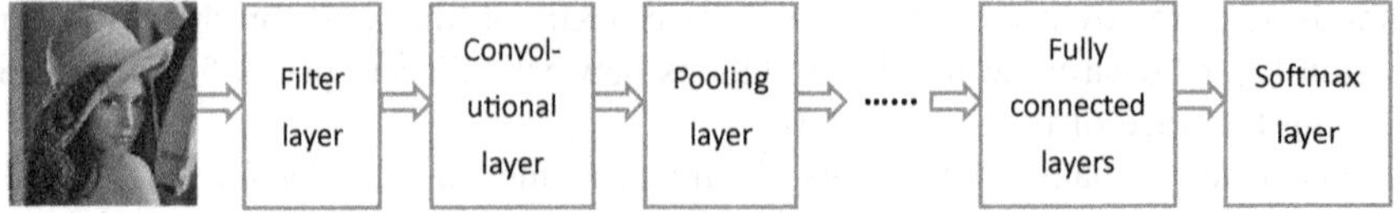

Fig. 1. A conventional CNN model

As the convolutional layers will extract features of an image's content instead of learning filters that identify traces of the tempering. We used the raw image pixels as inputs to conventional CNN models directly in the former test, and obtained a poor performance. The traces caused by median filtering is heavily affected by image edges and textures. Thus, a filter layer is added into the conventional CNN in our modified architecture. As depicted in Fig. 2, the proposed networks contains 1 filter layer, 2 convolutional layers, 2 max-pooling layers and 3 fully-connected layers.

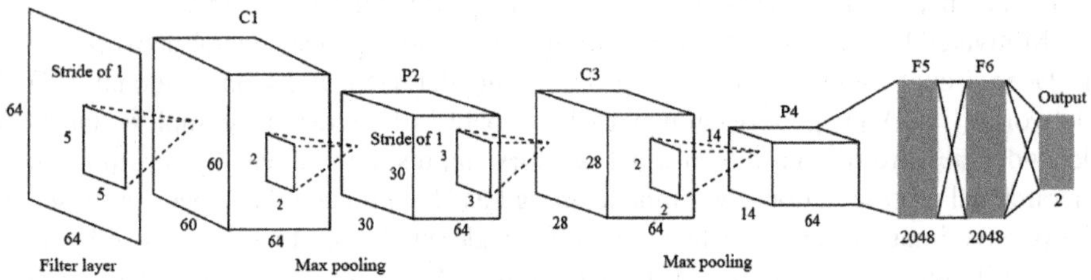

Fig. 2. Architecture of the proposed CNN

2.1 Filter Layer

The filter layer is important in the proposed method since it can suppress the interference caused by image edges and textures, as shown in [1]. With eliminating/ suppressing the interference of irrelevant information (e.g., image edges and textures), the trace left by median filtering can be investigated. An additional filter layer is added to the conventional CNN to increase the performance in median filtering forensics. The frequency residual of median filtering (FRMF) is obtained when the image is put into this filter layer. The FRMF is then fed into the conventional networks.

Median filtering works by replacing the center pixel with the median of gray levels in a $w \times w$ window which slides pixel by pixel over the entire image. A 2D median filter is defined as:

$$Y(i,j) = med_w(X(i,j)) \tag{1}$$

where $X(i, j)$ is the original image and $Y(i, j)$ is the median filtered one. The size of the square filter window is mostly set to an odd number, e.g., $3 \times 3, 5 \times 5, \ldots$

Many approaches detect features from the difference between a median filtered version of an image and the image itself to suppress both image content and block artifacts. The difference is called median filter residual (MFR), which is defined as:

$$d(i,j) = med_w(X(i,j)) - X(i,j) = Y(i,j) - X(i,j) \tag{2}$$

However, we discover that the median filter residual in frequency domain is easier learned by CNN. As demonstrated in Fig. 3, the residual features from frequency domain have stronger identifiability compared to MFR. Therefore, the FRMF of an image is calculated in the filter layer. FRMF is defined as:

$$F(i,j) = FFT2(med_w(X(i,j))) - FFT2(X(i,j)) \tag{3}$$

$$FRMF(i,j) = \log(|F(i,j)| + 1)$$

where FFT2 is 2-D Fast Fourier Transform.

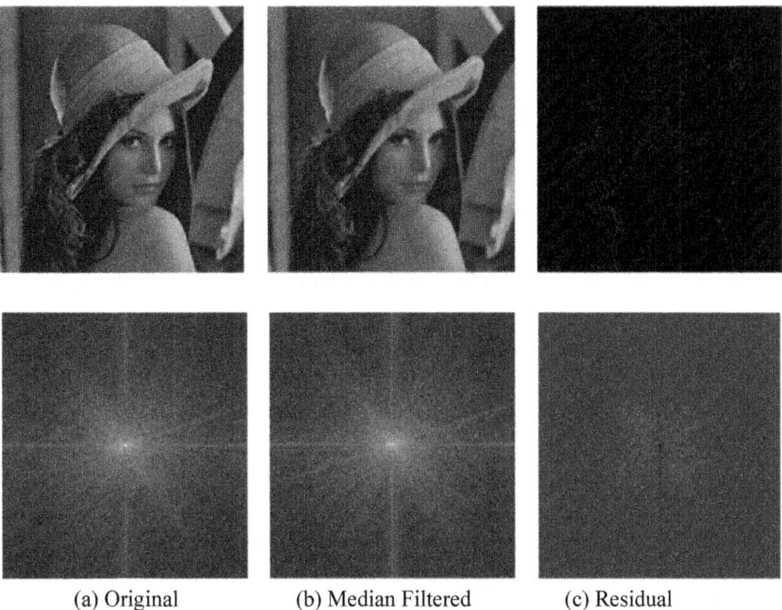

(a) Original (b) Median Filtered (c) Residual

Fig. 3. The residual of median filtering in spatial domain (first row) and frequency domain (second row). The filter size is 5 * 5

Since the spectral values in the low-frequency region are much bigger than other values in the medium- and high-frequency region. The spectral value is converted into a log-scale-form to ensure the values in the same order of magnitude for further analysis. Thus, FRMF is redefined as:

$$F(i,j) = \log(|FFT2(med_w(X(i,j))) - FFT2(X(i,j))| + 1) \tag{4}$$

2.2 Convolutional Layers

A conventional convolutional layer consists of two operations: convolution and non-linearity. Neurons in convolutional layers are connected to only a small region of the input to perceive local correlation. Every entry in the output can thus be regarded as the output of a neuron which perceives a sub-region in the input and shares weights with the same kernel (or filter). The convolution operation can be denoted as:

$$x_j^l = \sum_{l=1}^{n} x_i^{l-1} * k_{ij}^{l-1} + b_j^l \tag{5}$$

where * denotes convolution, x_j^l is the j-th output map in layer l, the convolutional kernel k_{ij}^{l-1} (also called weight) can be updated by training. It connecting the i-th output map in layer l − 1 and the j-th output map in layer l. b_j^l is the trainable bias parameter of the j-th output map in layer l. Each low level feature is extracted from only a subset of the input, the numbers of pixels in connection is controlled.

The non-linearity operation is obtained by applying an element-wise non-linear activation function (sigmoid, tanh, etc.) to each element of feature maps. Even with unsupervised pre-training and large training sets, wide and deep neural networks are still vulnerable to overfitting. Dropout [25] is a wildly used technique for avoiding overfitting in neural networks. Therefore, the Rectified linear units (ReLUs) [26] and dropout are used in our proposed CNN architecture. Based on Eq. (5), the operation is expressed as

$$f_{m,n} = \max\left(x_{m,n}^l, 0\right) \tag{6}$$

where $x_{m,n}$ is for the input patch centered in the feature map point (m, n) in layer l.

2.3 Pooling Layers

There are several nonlinear functions to implement pooling, among which max pooling is the most common. The overlapping max-pooling layer is used to reduce the resolution of the feature map in our approach. By using the pooling layer, the feature map would be robust to variations for previous learned features. Explicitly, this method consists of computing the maximum value in each neighborhood at different positions. It divides each output map from the previous layer into a set of non-overlapping sub regions and outputs their maximums. As presented in Fig. 2, the size of the feature map in C1 is reduced from 60 × 60 × 64 to 30 × 30 × 64 after the first max-pooling layer. Through this operation, the possibility of overfitting to some extent in feature maps would be reduced greatly.

2.4 Classification Layer

Finally, after several repeated sections of alternating convolutional and max pooling layers, the higher level representation will be acquired. In general, the classification layer consists of a few fully connected layers. Following by a softmax loss layer, these fully connected layers is used for classification. The back propagation algorithm is used to train the CNN. As described in [27], the weights and the bias can be renewed adaptively in the convolutional and fully connected layers following the error propagation procedure. In this way, the classification result can be fed back to guide the feature extraction automatically and the learning mechanism can be established.

2.5 Parameter Settings

In this work, we address the challenge of detecting median filtering from a small-sized and compressed image block. We consider two sizes of an input image, i.e. 64 × 64 and 32 × 32 pixels. For the sake of brevity, we only explain one size choice in detail. Let us take a gray scale image of size 64 × 64 as the input to the architecture shown in Fig. 2. Firstly, the filter layer gets the FRMF of an image. Then the first convolutional layer convolves them with 32 kernels of size 5 × 5. The size of the output (C1) is 60 × 60 × 32, which means the number of feature maps is 32 and the resolution of feature maps is "60 × 60". It is followed by an max pooling layer with filters of size 2 × 2, to decrease the size of feature maps to 30 × 30. The third convolution layers apply convolutions with 64 kernels of size 3 × 3, which is followed by an max pooling layer with filters of size 2 × 2. The Rectified Linear Units (ReLUs) is applied to the output of every convolutional layer. Each of the fully-connected layers (F5 and F6 in Fig. 2) has 2048 neurons. A recently-introduced technique, i.e., dropout [28] is used in both fully-connected layers. The last fully connected layer has two neurons. Its output is fed to a two-way softmax.

When the size of an input image is 32 × 32 pixels, the only difference of the architecture settings is that there is no max pooling layer followed the C1 convolutional layer. Other settings remain the same as in the 64 × 64 case.

3 Experiments

3.1 Experimental Setup

To evaluate the performance of the proposed model and compare its performance with other methods, we test on a composite image database containing 15352 images. These images are from five widely used image databases: the BOSSbase 1.01 [29], the UCID database [30] and CASIA v1.0 and v2.0 [31]. BOSSbase database contributes 7000 images and the rest of 2 databases contributes 2112 images. All images are converted to gray-scale images before any further processing. Each image from the original composite database belongs to the negative class and its median filtered version belongs to the positive class. The training set contains half number of images in each class, while the other half of images compose the testing set. Detection accuracy (Ac) is used to evaluate the performance:

$$\mathrm{Ac} = \frac{c}{n} \tag{7}$$

where c is the number of correctly predicted samples and n is the number of total testing images. We compare the proposed model with existing works: median filter feature (MFF) method [13], the AR method [14] and MFR method [20]. We perform SVM training and testing for the two conventional methods. We also generate the CNN model in [20] for the comparison. For the proposed model, all experiments are conducted on GPU using the C++ programming language.

3.2 Detecting Median Filtering from JPEG Compressed Image Blocks

We first crop image blocks with size of 64 × 64 and 32 × 32 from the center of a full-resolution image, and then build a corresponding training set and testing set. 3 × 3 median filtering (MF3 in short form) and 5 × 5 median filtering (MF5 in short form) are considered in our experiments. The detection accuracy results are reported in Table 1. "JPEG60" denotes that the image without median filtered but JPEG compressed with quality factor (QF) of 60, "MF3 + JPEG60" denotes that the image with composite operation of median filtering and JPEG compression with QF 60. It is noted that the proposed model performs the best in all cases. Considering that the detection accuracy of the proposed model is about 3%–20% better than that of the state-of-the-art methods in different cases, we believe that the deep learning feature representations are effective. It is clear that the filter layer for obtaining FRMF is important in the proposed CNN model.

Table 1. Detection accuracy (%) for median filtering detection against JPEG compression.

Image size	Method	MF3 + JPEG60	MF3 + JPEG90	MF5 + JPEG60	MF5 + JPEG90
64 * 64	Proposed	90.58	95.87	93.28	96.41
	MMF [13]	77.54	84.57	85.41	87.62
	AR [14]	81.94	90.23	83.84	91.16
	MFR [20]	83.22	93.81	91.07	95.33
32 * 32	Proposed	87.45	94.83	94.62	95.11
	MMF [13]	70.59	76.36	80.12	84.78
	AR [14]	76.28	81.45	78.87	88.92
	MFR [20]	79.22	88.41	86.31	92.75

3.3 Splicing Forgery Detection

The ability to detect median filtering in low-resolution images and image windows is essential for detecting forgeries. Most splicing forgeries use smooth filtering to reduce the discontinuity between the forged regions and the rest of the image, for the purpose of appearing more realistic. Thus, the ability to detect median filtering is essential in copy-move and splicing forgery detection.

An example of splicing forgery and the corresponding forensic detection results are shown in Fig. 4. Figure 4(a) shows the 3 × 3 median filtered image from which an object (the boat) was pasted. Figure 4(b) shows the unaltered image into which the cut object was pasted. Figure 4(c) shows the composite image, which was JPEG compressed using

QF 60. In order to detect the forgery, the composite image was first segmented into 64 × 64 pixel blocks, and then each block was tested for evidence of locally applied median filtering. In this example, each detection method was trained on corresponding training images, i.e. the JPEG 60 compressed images with size of 64 × 64. Blocks corresponding to median filtering detections were marked by white blocks. Figure 5(a) shows the result of block-wise detections on the composite image using our proposed CNNs method. Figure 5(b) shows the result using the MFR method in [20]. Figure 5(c) shows the result with the AR method in [14]. Note that, the CNN-based method [20] achieves a score as close to ours, which confirms the efficacy of CNN-based technique in image forensic. However, as method [20] used median filtering in spatial domain, some image blocks are mismatched due to the low differences between filtered and unfiltered image. This example illustrates that the proposed CNN-based approach outperforms the three state-of-the-art approaches in the splicing forgery detection.

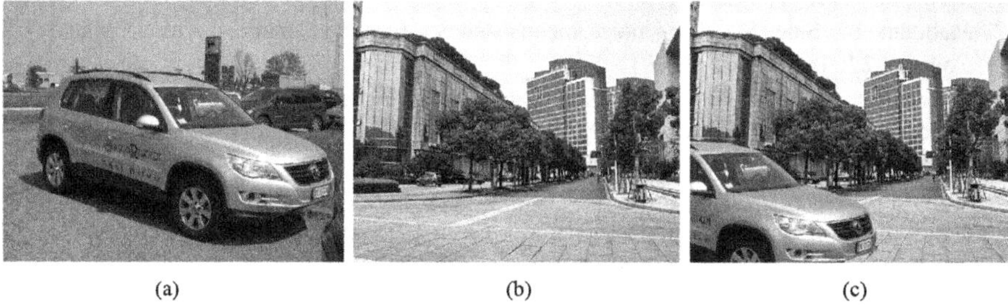

(a) (b) (c)

Fig. 4. A cut and paste forgery detection example, showing (a) the median filtered image from which an object is cut; (b) the unaltered image into which the cut object is pasted; (c) the composite image which is JPEG compressed using a quality factor of 60.

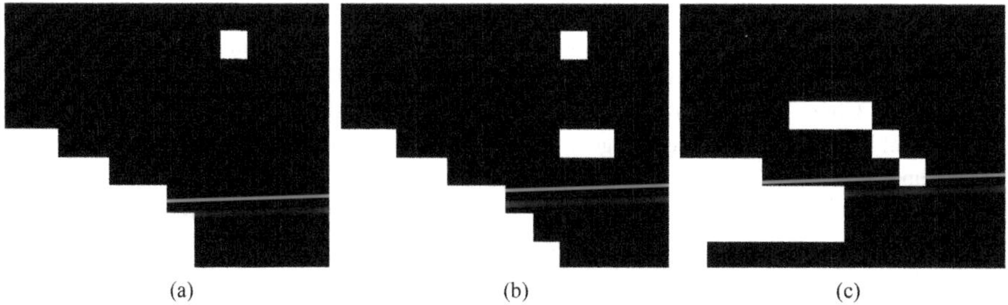

(a) (b) (c)

Fig. 5. Detection results of (a) the proposed approach; (b) the MFR method [20]; and (c) the AR method [14]. Detected forged patches are marked by white blocks.

4 Conclusions

In this paper, we propose a novel method of median filtering forensics based on deep learning technique. We capture median filtered image blocks by adding a filter layer in front of a conventional CNN model. A modified CNN-based approach is developed to automatically learn the residual feature median filtering in frequency domain. Experiments demonstrates that the proposed CNN-based approach is able to detect median filtering in small and JPEG compressed image blocks. In the future, we would try to extend the approach by involving more types of filtering operations.

Acknowledgements. This work is supported in part by the National Natural Science Foundation of China (Grant NO. 51505191), Jiangsu Province Natural Science Foundation of China (Grant NO. BK20150161), the Fundamental Research Funds for the Central Universities (NOs. JUSRP11534, JUSRP51642A).

References

1. Amerini, I., Ballan, L., Caldelli, R., Del Bimbo, A., Serra, G.: A SIFT-based forensic method for copy-move attack detection and transformation recovery. IEEE Trans. Inf. Forensics Secur. **6**, 1099–1110 (2011)
2. Mahdian, B., Saic, S.: Using noise inconsistencies for blind image forensics. Image Vis. Comput. **27**, 1497–1503 (2009)
3. Fu, Z., Ren, K., Shu, J., Sun, X., Huang, F.: Enabling personalized search over encrypted outsourced data with efficiency improvement. IEEE Trans. Parallel Distrib. Syst. **27**, 2546–2559 (2016)
4. Qu, Z., Keeney, J., Robitzsch, S., Zaman, F., Wang, X.: Multilevel pattern mining architecture for automatic network monitoring in heterogeneous wireless communication networks. Chin. Commun. **13**, 108–116 (2016)
5. Xue, Y., Jiang, J., Zhao, B., Ma, T.: A self-adaptive artificial bee colony algorithm based on global best for global optimization. Soft Comput. **8**, 1–18 (2017)
6. Yang, B., Sun, X., Guo, H., Xia, Z., Chen, X.: A copy-move forgery detection method based on CMFD-SIFT. Multimedia Tools Appl. 1–19 (2017)
7. Yang, B., Sun, X., Xin, X., Hu, W., Wu, Y.: Image copy–move forgery detection based on sped-up robust features descriptor and adaptive minimal–maximal suppression. J. Electron. Imag. **24**, 063016 (2015)
8. Yang, B., Sun, X., Chen, X., Zhang, J., Li, X.: Exposing photographic splicing by detecting the inconsistencies in shadows. Comput. J. **58**, 588–600 (2014)
9. Liu, Q., Chen, Z.: Improved approaches with calibrated neighboring joint density to steganalysis and seam-carved forgery detection in JPEG images. ACM Trans. Intell. Syst. Technol. **5**, 1–30 (2014)
10. Mahdian, B., Saic, S.: Blind authentication using periodic properties of interpolation. IEEE Trans. Inf. Forensics Secur. **3**, 529–538 (2008)
11. Kirchner, M., Fridrich, J.: On detection of median filtering in digital images. In: Media Forensics and Security II, p. 754110 (2010)
12. Cao, G., Zhao, Y., Ni, R., Yu, L., Tian, H.: Forensic detection of median filtering in digital images. In: IEEE International Conference on Multimedia and Expo, pp. 89–94 (2010)
13. Yuan, H.D.: Blind forensics of median filtering in digital images. IEEE Trans. Inf. Forensics Secur. **6**, 1335–1345 (2011)
14. Kang, X., Stamm, M.C., Peng, A., Liu, K.J.R.: Robust median filtering forensics using an autoregressive model. IEEE Trans. Inf. Forensics Secur. **8**, 1456–1468 (2013)
15. Liu, A., Zhao, Z., Zhang, C., Su, Y.: Smooth filtering identification based on convolutional neural networks. Multimedia Tools Appl. 1–15 (2016)

16. Zhang, Y., Li, S., Wang, S., Shi, Y.Q.: Revealing the traces of median filtering using high-order local ternary patterns. IEEE Sig. Process. Lett. **21**, 275–279 (2014)
17. Peter, O.C., Daniel, N., Liu, S.C., Tobi, D., Michael, P.: Real-time classification and sensor fusion with a spiking deep belief network. Frontiers Neurosci. **7**, 178 (2013)
18. Deng, L., Seltzer, M.L., Yu, D., Acero, A., Mohamed, A.R., Hinton, G.E.: Binary coding of speech spectrograms using a deep auto-encoder. In: INTERSPEECH 2010, Conference of the International Speech Communication Association, pp. 1692–1695, Makuhari, Chiba, Japan, September 2010
19. Kalchbrenner, N., Grefenstette, E., Blunsom, P.: A convolutional neural network for modelling sentences. Eprint Arxiv, vol. 1 (2014)
20. Chen, J., Kang, X., Liu, Y., Wang, Z.J.: Median filtering forensics based on convolutional neural networks. IEEE Sig. Process. Lett. **22**, 1849–1853 (2015)
21. Bayar, B., Stamm, M.C.: A deep learning approach to universal image manipulation detection using a new convolutional layer. In: ACM Workshop on Information Hiding and Multimedia Security, pp. 5–10 (2016)
22. Zhang, Y., Win, L.L., Goh, J., Thing, V.L.L.: Image region forgery detection: a deep learning approach (2016)
23. Yang, B., Sun, X., Chen, X., Zhang, J., Li, X.: An efficient forensic method for copy-move forgery detection based on DWT-FWHT. Radioengineering **22**, 1098–1105 (2013)
24. Li, S., Liu, Z.Q., Chan, A.B.: Heterogeneous multi-task learning for human pose estimation with deep convolutional neural network. Int. J. Comput. Vis. **113**, 19–36 (2015)
25. Srivastava, N., Hinton, G., Krizhevsky, A., Sutskever, I., Salakhutdinov, R.: Dropout: a simple way to prevent neural networks from overfitting. J. Mach. Learn. Res. **15**, 1929–1958 (2014)
26. Nair, V., Hinton, G.E.: Rectified linear units improve restricted Boltzmann machines. In: International Conference on Machine Learning, pp. 807–814 (2010)
27. Haykin, S., Kosko, B.: Gradient based learning applied to document recognition. Wiley-IEEE Press (2009)
28. Krizhevsky, A., Sutskever, I., Hinton, G.E.: ImageNet classification with deep convolutional neural networks. In: International Conference on Neural Information Processing Systems, pp. 1097–1105 (2012)
29. Bas, P., Filler, T., Pevný, T.: "Break our steganographic system": the ins and outs of organizing BOSS. In: Filler, T., Pevný, T., Craver, S., Ker, A. (eds.) IH 2011. LNCS, vol. 6958, pp. 59–70. Springer, Heidelberg (2011). doi:10.1007/978-3-642-24178-9_5
30. Schaefer, G., Stich, M.: UCID: an uncompressed color image database, vol. 5307, pp. 472–480 (2004)
31. Dong, J., Wang, W., Tan, T.: CASIA image tampering detection evaluation database. In: IEEE China Summit and International Conference on Signal and Information Processing, pp. 422–426 (2013)

Spatiotemporal Radio Tomographic Imaging with Bayesian Compressive Sensing for RSS-Based Indoor Target Localization

Baolin Shang[1], Jiaju Tan[2], Xiaobing Hong[1], Xuemei Guo[1], Guoli Wang[1(✉)], Gonggui Liu[3], and Shouren Xue[3]

[1] Key Laboratory of Machine Intelligence and Advanced Computing, Ministry of Education, School of Data and Computer Science, Sun Yat-sen University, Guangzhou, China
isswgl@mail.sysu.edu.cn

[2] Tianjin Key Laboratory of Intelligent Robotics, Institute of Robotics and Automatic Information System, Nankai University, Tianjin, China

[3] Vkan Certification and Testing Co. Ltd, Guangdong, China

Abstract. Wireless sensor network based device-free localization (DFL) is now widely used in security and monitoring systems for indoor and outdoor areas. Multipath fading induced noises often degrade the performance of the DFL security system. To address this problem, the paper firstly presents a spatiotemporal radio tomographic imaging (RTI) approach for the enhancement of localization. Specifically, the task of RTI can be formulated into a sparse Bayesian learning problem. In addition, two robust sparse Byesian learning algorithms are developed to handle with the low signal-to-noise-ratio (SNR) with heterogeneous noise. The proposed spatiotemporal RTI approach performs much better than traditional RTI with lower average errors in our four diverse cluttered indoor scenes. The localization results also highlight advantages of applying proposed robust sparse Bayesian learning algorithms in addressing missing estimations and outlier errors, and finally improving indoor target DFL performance.

Keywords: Radio tomographic imaging · Target localization · Sparse bayesian learning · Wireless sensor network

1 Introduction

Accurate localization of people in the environment is the key requirement of the security surveillance and attention-getting AmI [1] system, which aims to show location of people in a building during hostage situations, fire alarms, and other emergences. RTI based security system can help law enforcement and responders to know where they should pay attention through walls and to reduce injury. Many enforcement officers are injured every year since they lack the ability of

X. Sun et al. (Eds.): ICCCS 2017, Part II, LNCS 10603, pp. 528–540, 2017.
https://doi.org/10.1007/978-3-319-68542-7_45

detection and tracking offenders within a building. Most existed security system are mainly based on camera, infrared ray or others [2,3]. Cameras are usually ineffective in the cases of obstruction, light illumination and others. Infrared ray system works when people cross a boundary while fails to locate or track the intruder. Our proposed spatiotemporal RTI system could serve both as a camera based- and infrared ray based- system.

In this paper, we present our research with higher localization accuracy using received signal strength (RSS) based on RF sensor network. With numbers of peer-to-peer sensor nodes, recorded RSS measurements contain amounts of information about the environment the target locates in. When links pass through the target, they will experience shadowing losses. The way the radio signal transmitted by nodes is also changed by reflecting, diffracting, or scattering a subset of their multipath component [4]. Due to this reason, RSS measurements may tend to be unpredictable and uninformative especially when the non-target induced multipath interferences greatly affect measurements of links.

The spatiotemporal RTI, structured by a multitask CS [5] scheme, could be mathematically depicted by a multiple measurement vectors (MMV) model. Among MMV algorithms, multiple response of extension of standard sparse Bayesian learning (MSBL) [6] is extended straightforwardly from SBL for single measurement vector model and FOCUSS [7] belongs to iterative reweighed algorithm family. However, existed algorithms ignore the ground-truth fact that the noise of real-life scenario is heterogeneous, especially in RTI application that the environment is heavily obstructed and rich in multipath components. Most of works focus on how to benefit from priors model over signal space in RVM framework, while further research is expected to exploit the advantage from noises self-tuning. For this end, the heterogeneous noise model is precisely built for every communication cycle of all individual links under Bayesian compressive sensing framework and two robust statistical sparse learning rules are accordingly derived for the performance enhancement.

The paper is organized as follows. In Sect. 2, we formulate the spatiotemporal RTI approach. In Sect. 3, the heterogeneous noise in real-life scene is illustrated and learning rules are derived. Numerical trails on synthetic signal and the real-life experimental studies in the context of DFL are conducted to evaluate the improved algorithms and the proposed RTI approach in Sect. 4. The conclusion is drawn finally.

2 Problem Statement

In this section, traditional RTI is presented briefly, and our proposed spatiotemporal RTI is formulated in the context of Bayesian compressive sensing.

2.1 Radio Tomographic Imaging

RTI proposed by Wilson and Patwari [8] adopts computed tomography methods to reconstruct an image of the object in the sensing area. If P is the number of sensors deployed along the perimeter, there are $N = P(P-1)/2$ communication links that cover the sensing area. In RSS-based human detection, the RSS on a single link $i \in \{1, 2, \cdots, N\}$ at time t can be modelled in logarithmic(dB) scale as [4]

$$s_{it}(\varpi) = s_i(o) + \Delta s_{it}(\varpi) \tag{1}$$

where ϖ is the current state of the link, and $s_i(o) = E[s_{it}(\varpi = o)]$ when o is the human-free state. The additive deviation $\Delta s_{it}(\varpi)$ models the body-induced perturbation. In RTI scheme, the body-induced perturbation is mostly ascribed to the shadow fading of a target, which is approximated as a spatial integral of the sensing area. Thus, the RSS variation for link i can be described as

$$\Delta s_{it}(\varpi) = \sum_{j=1}^{N} \Phi_{ij} w_j + \varepsilon_i \tag{2}$$

where $w = [w_1, w_2, \cdots, w_M]^T$ denotes the fading distribution of pixels, Φ_{ij} is the weight of pixel j for link i and ε_i represents observation noise.

Now we take all links into consideration to formulate the tomographic imaging with single period signal, that is

$$s = \Phi w + \varepsilon \tag{3}$$

where $s \in R^N$ is the response signal due to the target's presence, $\Phi \in R^{N \times M}$ is the measurement matrix depending on the weights model.

The goal is to estimate w given s and Φ. Of particular attention is the case that single period measurements are usually contaminated by amounts of "noise" since they experience various levels of measurement uncertainties, and worse estimation or outlier error will be more likely to occur in a real-time security system. We focus on a Bayesian approach to solve the compressive sensing based RTI problem in this paper, which can provide a more degree of freedom for dealing with the contamination thus improving the performance of DFL.

2.2 Spatiotemporal Radio Tomographic Imaging

Suppose that measurement vectors from multiple periods are collected by sensors deployed around the monitoring area. As an extension of CS in (3), the multitask one is given by

$$\mathrm{Y} = \Phi\ X + V \tag{4}$$

where $Y = [Y_{\cdot 1}, \ldots, Y_{\cdot L}] \in R^{N \times L}$ is the variation of RSS in L periods before and after the presence of a target. $\mathrm{X} = [\mathrm{X}_{\cdot 1}, \ldots, \mathrm{X}_{\cdot L}] \in R^{M \times L}$ is the solution matrix to be reconstructed and V is the noise matrix. As the communication time for token transmission among all sensors is in tens of milliseconds, it is reasonable to make an assumption that the target nearly remains static in multiple periods, that is, indexes of the nonzero pixels or the sparsity profile does not change. Thus supports of $\mathrm{X}_{\cdot j}$ in X is identical and sparse Bayesian learning is desirable for the localization issue. Similar to (3), the number of nonzero rows in X is small enough to ensure a unique and global solution.

The sparse image signal $X_{i\cdot}$ is assumed to be Gaussian, and RSS measurements from all links in same period are independent

$$p(X_{i\cdot}|\gamma_i B_i) \sim N(X_{i\cdot}|0, \gamma_i B_i) \tag{5}$$

where B_i is a positive definite matrix that captures the possible correlation in RSS measurements between L periods. Similar to Eq. (3) in Bayesian approach, γ is a hyperparameter that controls the row sparsity of X.

The prior for image signal X can be rewritten

$$p(X) \sim N(0, \Sigma_0) \tag{6}$$

where Σ_0 is (we empirically replaced B_i with B, see details [6])

$$\Sigma_0 = \begin{pmatrix} \lambda_1 B & 0 & 0 \\ 0 & \ddots & 0 \\ 0 & 0 & \lambda_N B \end{pmatrix} \tag{7}$$

Combining prior and likelihood, we use the Bayesian inference to obtain the posterior density of X

$$\mathrm{p}(X|Y, \Xi) \sim N(\mu_x, \Sigma_x) \tag{8}$$

with mean and covariance given by

$$\mu_x = \frac{1}{\lambda}\Sigma_x D^T \mathbf{y} \tag{9}$$

$$\Sigma_x = (\frac{1}{\lambda}D^T D + \Sigma_0^{-1})^{-1} \tag{10}$$

where Ξ represents all hyperparameters that need to be estimated and λ is the noise variance. $D = kron(\Phi, I) = \Phi \otimes I = [d_1, d_2 \cdots, d_{NL}]^T$ represents the Kronecker product of the observation matrix Φ and a identity matrix. x and y is the vectorization of X^T and Y^T respectively.

In sparse Bayesian learning framework, it can be seen that Σ_0 controls sparsity of the image signal, which indicates where attenuation in the image or network is occurring, and therefore, where is location of the target. Just like the Bayesian methodology solving Eq. (3), when $\gamma_i = 0$, the associated ith entry becomes zero and this associated location is not in our concern. Of special note is that we assume all elements in noise have same variance λ while what we measure in real-life scenario doesn't meet the expectation. Unfortunately, the improper estimation of noise would degrade the RTI performance with more outlier errors in localization. The following we will show the measured noises and our robust learning rules.

3 The Robust Learning Rule

3.1 Noise Observation

We deployed 16 sensors along the perimeter of a 4.8 m × 5 m heavily obstructed target-free indoor office. As suggested in [9], the transmission power for all sensor nodes is set as −45 dBm. About 10000 measurements were collected for each link. Figure 1(a) shows the RSS variance of all unidirectional links covered monitoring area. The red and black triangle represent the RSS variance of two directional lines, respectively. Figure 1(b) presents a typical link, (5, 15), in 10000 samples. It can be seen that the RSS fluctuates around −70 dBm, and changes significantly at some samples. The frequency histograms and fitted curves of two links are shown in Figs. 1(c), (d) for detailed illustration that variances on different links vary in different values.

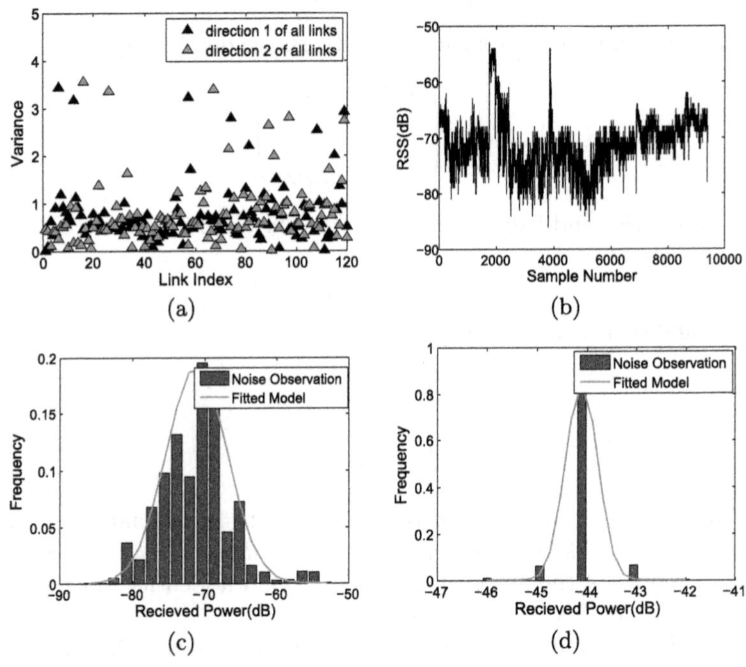

Fig. 1. (a) The noise variance of all links, (b) RSS variation of link between (5, 15), (c) Frequency histogram and fitted model of noise, (d) Frequency histogram and fitted model of noise. Variances on different links vary in different values. (Color figure online)

As described, RSS measurements are easily contaminated by "noise" in a real-time RTI system with the fact that any disruption from outside and inside would change the power of the link since the phase or amplitude of the multi-path component is altered. Thus, the proper estimation of "noise" is in striking importance to reduce outlier errors and improve RTI performance.

3.2 Noise Learning Rules

To address the exceptions and singularities, [10] proposes a robust regularization path algorithm for ν-support vector classification. In [11], C_n is measured as the noise covariance during the calibration phase when no extrinsic motion is in the signal. It can be seen that noise estimation is mostly depend on empirical RSS samples of target-free area. Thus manual tuning of C_n is inevitable for diverse environments, while different with these referred researches, our works focus on, firstly, building a heterogeneous noise model precisely for every communication cycle of all individual links under Bayesian compressive sensing framework, and secondly, on the iteration step, the algorithm automatically estimates the posterior probability of noises by statistical sparse learning method. It shows highly adaptive in self-tuning.

Noise Model: HBSBL. The prior of image signal x is described in previous section and the prior of noise matrix is assumed to be Gaussian, given by

$$p(n|\sigma) = \prod_{i=1}^{ML} N(n_i|0, \sigma_i^2) \tag{11}$$

where σ_i is the variance of noise component n_i, a parameter needs to be estimated. Based on the prior probability given above, we obtain a Gaussian posterior of signal with the mean and the covariance matrix of form

$$\begin{aligned} \mu_x &= \Sigma_x D^T C y \\ &= \Sigma_0 D^T (C^{-1} + D\Sigma_0 D^T)^{-1} y \end{aligned} \tag{12}$$

$$\begin{aligned} \Sigma_x &= (\Sigma_0^{-1} + D^T C D)^{-1} \\ &= \Sigma_0 - \Sigma_0 D^T (C^{-1} + D\Sigma_0 D^T)^{-1} D\Sigma_0 \end{aligned} \tag{13}$$

where $C = diag(\beta_1, \beta_2 \cdots \beta_i) = diag(\sigma_1^{-2}, \sigma_2^{-2} \cdots \sigma_i^{-2})$, $i = [1, 2 \cdots, N]$. In order to estimate the parameter of noise, a Type II Maximum Likelihood or Expectation-Maximisation is employed in the update procedure. Here we use EM formulation by treating image signal x as the "hidden" variables and maximise the following

$$\begin{aligned} Q(\beta) &= E_{x|y,\beta^{old}}[logp(y|x;\beta)] \\ &\propto \frac{1}{2}\log C - \frac{C}{2} E_{x|y,\beta^{old}}[||y - Dx||_2^2] \\ &\propto \frac{1}{2}\log C - \frac{C}{2}[||y - D\mu_x||_{fro} \\ &+ E_{x|y,\beta^{old}}[||D(x - \mu_x)||_2^2] \\ &\propto \frac{1}{2}\log C - \frac{C}{2}[||y - D\mu_x||_{fro} \\ &+ (diag(\Sigma_x))^T d_i^2] \end{aligned} \tag{14}$$

By setting the derivative in (14) to zero, we have the learning rule for β_i

$$\beta_i = \frac{1}{(y_i - d_i^T \mu_x)^2 + (diag(\Sigma_x))^T d_i^2} \tag{15}$$

Here, *diag* denotes a vector with elements being from the diagonal of *diag()*. From the learning rule procedure, we can see the extended space for seeking parameter of noise to obtain an optimal solution could provide more degree of freedom for data fitting.

Noise Model: BHSBL. As we discussed in previous section, measurements of all radio links are collected from L periods in wireless sensor network. To avoid the high dimension of model in (15) we introduced before, a block heterogeneous noise sparse Bayesian learning algorithm with a parameter controlling the row of noise matrix is developed, which not only reduces parameters that needs to be estimated, but also exploits the possible RSS correlation between different communication cycles.

Similar to HBSBL, the noise is assumed to be Gaussion

$$p(n;\lambda_i,C_i) \sim N(n|0,\Sigma_{noise}) \tag{16}$$

where Σ_{noise} is

$$\Sigma_{noise} = \begin{pmatrix} \lambda_1 C_1 & & 0 \\ & \ddots & \\ 0 & & \lambda_N C_N \end{pmatrix}$$

where C_i is covariance matrix depicted the possible structure of the noise. Based on the prior probability given above, we obtain a Gaussian posterior of signal as previous section with the mean and the covariance matrix of form

$$\begin{aligned} \mu_x &= \Sigma_x D^T \Sigma_{noise}^{-1} y \\ &= \Sigma_0 D^T (\Sigma_{noise} + D\Sigma_0 D^T)^{-1} y \end{aligned} \tag{17}$$

$$\begin{aligned} \Sigma_x &= (\Sigma_0^{-1} + D^T \Sigma_{noise}^{-1} D)^{-1} \\ &= \Sigma_0 - \Sigma_0 D^T (\Sigma_{noise} + D\Sigma_0 D^T)^{-1} D\Sigma_0 \end{aligned} \tag{18}$$

From prior probability in (16), we can see that λ_i is a noise variance parameter controlling the block row in n to reduce the number of parameters, and C_i captures the possible noise covariance structures in the rows. Actually, instead of C_i, a same C for each row is empirically adopted as previous. Here, C is a $L \times L$ positive definite matrix

$$\Sigma_{noise} = \begin{pmatrix} \lambda_1 C & 0 & 0 \\ 0 & \ddots & 0 \\ 0 & 0 & \lambda_N C \end{pmatrix} \tag{19}$$

$$\Gamma_{noise} = diag(\lambda_1 \cdots \lambda_N)$$

Also, we use EM formulation by treating image signal x as the "hidden" variables and maximise the following

$$Q(\lambda, C) = E_{x|y,\Theta^{old}}(\log p(y|x;\Sigma_{noise})) \tag{20}$$

In our target detection application, the prior probability of RSS measurement y from radio links with respect to image signal and measurement matrix is given by

$$\log p(y|x;\lambda,C) \propto -\frac{1}{2}\log|\Sigma_{noise}| - \frac{1}{2}(y-Dx)^T\Sigma_{noise}^{-1}(y-Dx)$$

Substitute it into (20)

$$\begin{aligned} Q(\lambda,C) &\propto -\frac{L}{2}\log|\Gamma_{noise}| - \frac{N}{2}\log|C| \\ &- \frac{1}{2}E_{x|y,\Theta^{old}}[Tr(\Sigma_{noise}^{-1}(y-Dx)(y-Dx)^T)] \\ &\propto -\frac{L}{2}\log|\Gamma_{noise}| - \frac{N}{2}\log|C| \\ &- \frac{1}{2}Tr(\Sigma_{noise}^{-1}[(y-D\mu_x)(y-D\mu_x)^T) \\ &+ E_{x|y,\Theta^{old}}[D(x-\mu_x)(x-\mu_x)^T D^T]) \\ &\propto -\frac{L}{2}\log|\Gamma_{noise}| - \frac{N}{2}\log|C| \\ &- \frac{1}{2}Tr({\Gamma_{noise}}^{-1}\otimes C^{-1}[(y-D\mu_x)(y-D\mu_x)^T) \\ &+ D\Sigma_x D^T]) \end{aligned} \tag{21}$$

Setting the relative derivations to zero

$$\frac{\partial Q}{\partial \lambda_i} = 0$$

$$\frac{\partial Q}{\partial C} = 0$$

The learning rules for λ_i and C are the following

$$\lambda_i \leftarrow \frac{Tr(C^{-1}[(y^i-D^i\mu_x)(y^i-D^i\mu_x)^T) + D^i\Sigma_x(D^i)^T])}{L} \tag{22}$$

$$C \leftarrow \frac{1}{N}\sum_{i=1}^{N}\frac{(y^i-D^i\mu_x)(y^i-D^i\mu_x)^T) + D^i\Sigma_x(D^i)^T]}{\lambda_i} \tag{23}$$

The notations of y^i and D^i are defined as

$$y^i \triangleq y[(i-1)*L+1 : i*L]$$

$$D^i \triangleq D[(i-1)*L+1 : i*L, :]$$

4 Experiment Results

4.1 Experimental Setting

All experiments are performed in chaotic offices, and a variety of "noise" is the most challenging to localization issue. Next we will briefly introduce these four diverse experimental scenes.

- ***Scene 1: Slightly Cluttered Environment.*** The cluttered indoor environment is located in room 415 of the Information Science and Technology building in Sun Yat-sen University. The sensors are placed along the perimeter of a 4 m × 5.8 m rectangle area with 16 nodes at a height of one meter from the floor. As shown in Fig. 2(a), the sensing area is surrounded by walls and equipments.
- ***Scene 2: Severely Obstructed Environment.*** The heavily obstructed indoor environment is located in our laboratory 421 of the same building in SYSU. As we can see in Fig. 2(b), amounts of chairs, desks and computers are blocking radio links, leading to extensively rich multipath. Sixteen RF nodes are deployed to form a 4 m × 4 m area with the height of one meter from the floor.
- ***Scene 3: Cluttered Through-wall Environment.*** The cluttered through-wall area in Fig. 3(a), divided by a wooden wall (the thickness is about 8 cm) into two part, is located in the same office 415. A 24 peer-to-peer network was placed in a rectangular perimeter of 7 m × 8 m, and there are many other obstructions inside and outside the sensing area.

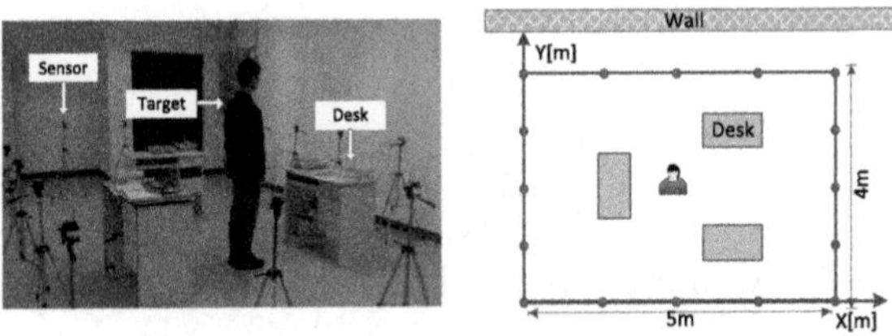

(a) Slightly Cluttered Environment, $20m^2$

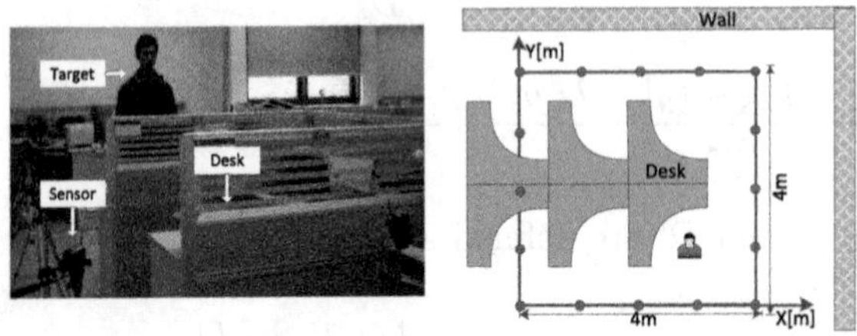

(b) Severely Obstructed Environment, $16m^2$

Fig. 2. (a) and (b) are two different scenes (left) and their corresponding sketches (right), Scene 1 and Scene 2 respectively.

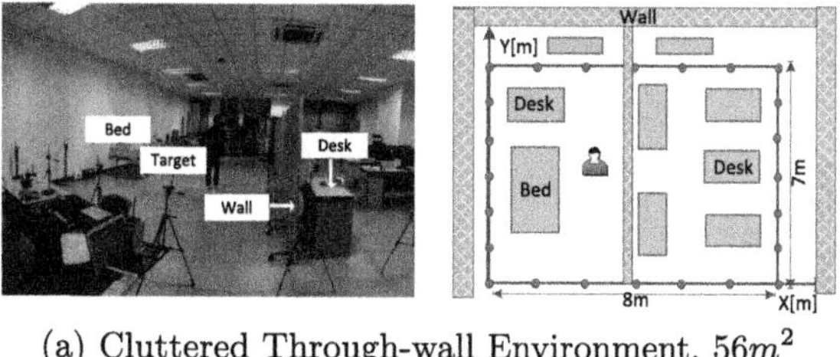

(a) Cluttered Through-wall Environment, $56m^2$

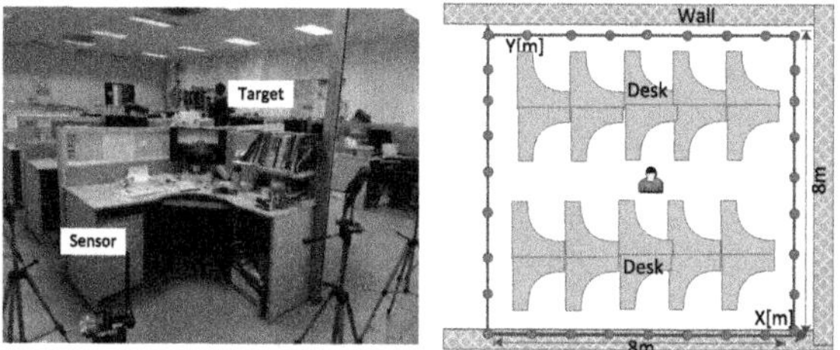

(b) More Challenging Obstructed Environment, $64m^2$

Fig. 3. (a) and (b) are two different experimental scenes (left) and their corresponding sketches (right), Scene 3 and Scene 4 respectively.

- ***Scene 4: More Challenging Obstructed Environment.*** This more challenging obstructed one is in our laboratory 421 with 30 nodes deployed around the perimeter of the whole room to form a $8\,\text{m} \times 8\,\text{m}$ area. As shown in Fig. 3(b), the height of each node is much less than tables', and RF waves travel through many dense objects from transmitter to receiver.

Besides, we use the optimal mass transfer (OMAT) [12] metric to evaluate the localization performance.

4.2 Localization Results

Results of single and multiple target experiments are presented in this subsection. It should be known that, instead of averaging measurements for tens of seconds to increase the SNR during the off-line analysis in traditional RTI which is impractical in real-time detection for a LBS or AmI system, we extract three-single period measurements for localization in our experiments, forming spatiotemporal RTI method. Therefore, when a target stands on a specific location for seconds, there will be dozens of measurement vectors. All of them are utilized for detection, and all OMAT errors (about 50 estimations on a specific location) are averaged to be the final localization error of the target at this location.

In this part, localization results with spatiotemporal RTI using MSBL, TMSBL, HBSBL and BHSBL are reported. In Fig. 4, it shows that the performance of RTI using HBSBL and BHSBL algorithms we extended is improved significantly since averaged OMAT errors of all locations are under 0.5 m or less

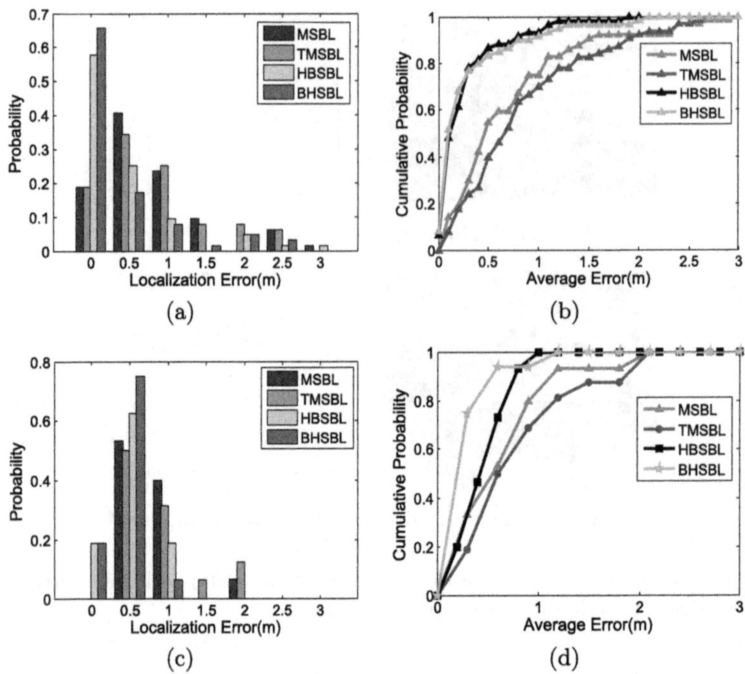

Fig. 4. (a) Statistical histogram of OMAT errors and (b) Cumulative Probability in scenario 1, (c) Statistical histogram of OMAT errors and (d) Cumulative Probability in scenario 2. The OMAT error is averaged from above 50 results at a specific position and proposed algorithms have much less outlier errors.

in both scene 1 and scene 2, whereas others are much worse with averaged errors above 1 m or higher. For instance, OMAT errors of HBSBL and BHSBL in scene 1 are mostly confined in a range of $0 \sim 0.5$ m with a relatively small number of missing estimations compared to MSBL and TMSBL algorithms.

The OMAT error in statistical histograms and cumulative distribution functions for scene 3 and scene 4 are shown in Fig. 5. In office through-wall experiment, most OMAT errors from HBSBL and BHSBL are under 1 m, while only about half of errors from MSBL and TMSBL are under 2 m, and the average error for HBSBL is 1.03 m and 0.73 m for BHSBL, while others are larger than 2 m, achieving 50% improvement at least. For experiment performed in scene 4, the average error of HBSBL is 1.23 m and BHSBL is 1.18 m. Compared to 2.56 m for MSBL and 2.43 m for TMSBL, our algorithm shows better adaptability and more robustness to environment noise. These large errors are due to the through-wall attenuation and objects induced noises, particularly, in scene 4 there are many metallic obstruction in the office and links cross all of them to complete the communication cycle. Results of multiple targets situation are presented in Table 1.

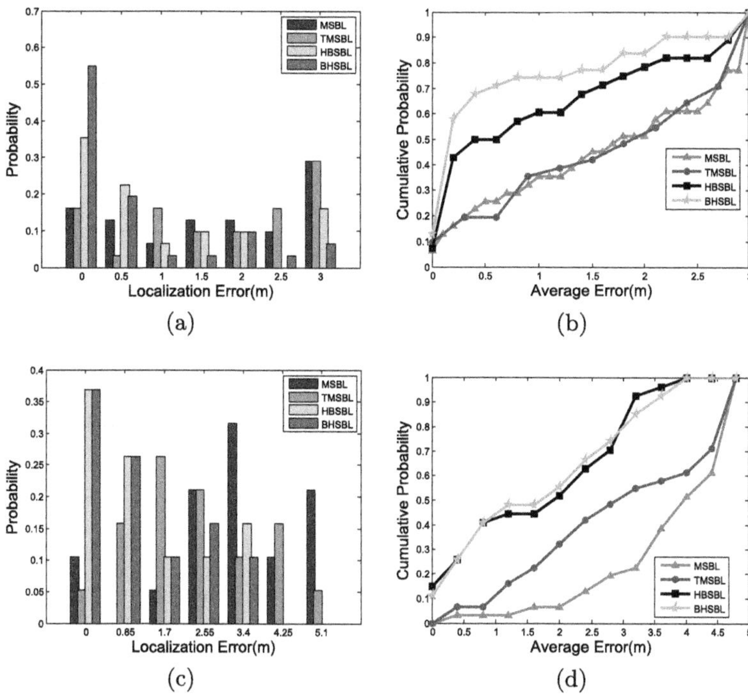

Fig. 5. (a) Statistical histogram of OMAT errors and (b) Cumulative Probability in scenario 3, (c) Statistical histogram of OMAT errors and (d) Cumulative Probability in scenario 4. The OMAT error is averaged from above 50 results at a specific position and proposed algorithms have much less outlier errors.

Table 1. Localization performances in meter: average OMAT errors (m) (S: single target M: mutiple targets (2–4))

List	Targets	RTI	Spatiotemporal RTI			
		SBL	MSBL	TMSBL	HBSBL	BHSBL
Scene 1	S	1.40	0.75	0.87	0.43	0.46
	M	1.45	0.94	1.00	0.48	0.50
Scene 2	S	1.05	0.80	0.93	0.58	0.48
	M	1.14	1.03	1.07	0.80	0.73
Scene 3	S	2.20	1.99	2.07	1.03	0.73
	M	1.65	1.58	1.71	1.16	0.97
Scene 4	S	2.47	2.56	2.43	1.23	1.18
	M	2.52	2.50	2.28	1.67	1.49

5 Conclusion

To address the problem that the Multipath fading induced noises in cluttered environment degrade the performance of indoor target localization in a real-time system with plenty of missing estimations, this paper presents a spatiotemporal RTI approach to explore the RSS correlation between different communication cycles. Further, better models handling with the outlier estimations for robust localization are precisely built for every communication cycle of all individual links under Bayesian compressive sensing framework. We conduct experimental applications in four diverse indoor cluttered environments, and localization results demonstrate that proposed RTI approaches outperform others in our system.

Acknowledgement. This work was supported by the National Natural Science Foundation of P.R. China under Grant No. 61375080, and the Key Program of Natural Science Foundation of Guangdong, China under Grant No. 2015A030311049. The Guangzhou science and technology project under Grant Nos. 201510010017 and 201604010101. The Special Project of Sharing Large Scientific Instruments and Equipments with the Public under Grant No. 2015B030304001.

References

1. Suryadevara, N.K., Mukhopadhyay, S.C., Wang, R.: Forecasting the behavior of an elderly using wireless sensors data in a smart home. Eng. Appl. Artif. Intell. **26**, 2641–2652 (2013). Elsevier
2. Xia, Z., Wang, X., Zhang, L., Qin, Z., Sun, X., Ren, K.: A privacy-preserving and copy-deterrence content-based image retrieval scheme in cloud computing. IEEE Trans. Inf. Forensics Secur. **11**, 2594–2608 (2016)
3. Fu, Z., Ren, K., Shu, J.: Enabling personalized search over encrypted outsourced data with efficiency improvement. IEEE Trans. Inf. Forensics Secur. **27**, 2546–2559 (2016)
4. Savazzi, S., Sigg, S., Nicoli, M., Rampa, V., Kianoush, S., Spagnolini, U.: Device-free radio vision for assisted living: leveraging wireless channel quality information for human sensing. IEEE Signal Process. Mag. **33**, 45–58 (2016)
5. Ji, S., Dunson, D., Carin, L.: Multitask compressive sensing. IEEE Trans. Signal Process. **57**, 92–106 (2009)
6. Wipf, D.P., Rao, B.D.: An empirical Bayesian strategy for solving the simultaneous sparse approximation problem. IEEE Trans. Signal Process. **557**, 3704–3716 (2007)
7. Gorodnitsky, I.F., Rao, B.D.: Sparse signal reconstruction from limited data using FOCUSS: a re-weighted minimum norm algorithm. IEEE Trans. Signal Process. **45**, 600–616 (1997)
8. Wilson, J., Patwari, N.: Radio tomographic imaging with wireless networks. IEEE Trans. Mob. Comput. **9**, 621–632 (2010)
9. Luo, Y., Huang, K., Guo, X., Wang, G.: A hierarchical RSS model for RF-based device-free localization. Pervasive Mob. Comput. **31**, 124–136 (2016)
10. Guo, B., Sheng, V.S.: A robust regularization path algorithm for ν-support vector classification. IEEE Trans. Neural Netw. Learn. Syst. **99**, 1–8 (2016)
11. Zhao, Y., Patwari, N.: Robust estimators for variance-based device-free localization and tracking. IEEE Trans. Mob. Comput. **14**, 2116–2129 (2011)
12. Schuhmacher, D., Vo, B.-T., Vo, B.-N.: A consistent metric for performance evaluation of multi-object filters. IEEE Trans. Signal Process. **56**, 3447–3457 (2016)

Detection in SAR Images Based on Histogram and Improved Elitist Genetic Fuzzy Clustering

Ronghua Shang(✉), Weitong Zhang, and Licheng Jiao

Key Laboratory of Intelligent Perception and Image Understanding of Ministry of Education, International Research Center for Intelligent Perception and Computation, Joint International Research Laboratory of Intelligent Perception and Computation, Xidian University, Xi'an 710071, Shaanxi, China
rhshang@mail.xidian.edu.cn

Abstract. Change detection in Synthetic Aperture Radar Images has been an important technique for Synthetic Aperture Radar Images. In this paper, a novel unsupervised change detection algorithm based on histogram and improved elitist genetic fuzzy clustering is proposed. First, a difference image is generated by multiplying transform fusion. Second, we use the characteristics of the histogram to deal with the difference image. Then, the new algorithm is proposed to partition these characteristics into changed and unchanged regions. The proposed algorithm has the following merits: 1. FCM is employed to initialize the population and to calculate the fitness function of the genetic algorithm. 2. The optimal solution is selected by an elitist selection strategy based on population concentration and the optimal solution will be the initial clustering center of FCM, which significantly increases the convergence speed. 3. The histogram is utilized to reduce the sample points of images. Compared with the state-of-the-art algorithms, the experimental results demonstrate the effectiveness in processing of change detection in SAR images.

Keywords: SAR images · FCM algorithm · Histogram · Elitist genetic fuzzy clustering

1 Introduction

The image retrieval has been widely applied in medical imaging, environmental monitoring, disaster estimation, land utilization, deforestation monitoring, etc. [1]. The change detection of the SAR images is a process aimed at identifying changes in images of the same geographical area which are taken at different times [2]. The change detection in remote sensing images generally consists of the following processes: (1) obtain the images to be processed; (2) preprocess images by radiation correction, geometric correction, image registration, etc.; (3) generate difference image; (4) analyze difference image and produce the results of change detection [3].

Many change detection algorithms have been proposed. Shang et al. mainly summarized a comprehensive exploration of all the major change detection approaches implemented [2]. Rignot and van Zyl proposed that SAR images follow Gamma distribution and they proposed the change detection based on the irrelevance of spots [4].

X. Sun et al. (Eds.): ICCCS 2017, Part II, LNCS 10603, pp. 541–553, 2017.
https://doi.org/10.1007/978-3-319-68542-7_46

Bruzzone and Prieto proposed an adaptive parcel-based technique for unsupervised change detection [5]. It adaptively exploits the spatial-contextual information contained in the neighborhood of each pixel to reduce the effects of noise. Su et al. proposed an algorithm based on locally fitting model and semi-EM (expectation-maximization) algorithm [6]. The locally fitting model orientated to deal with the unchanged class is put forward to reach a best fit, and the semi-EM algorithm for the changed class is used to tackle the phenomenon of overlapping. Moser and Serpico proposed the change detection based on generalized minimum error threshold [7]. Celik proposed a novel change detection algorithm based on improved genetic algorithm (GA) [8]. The change detection problem has been transferred to calculate the maximal value of an objective function. Although it can obtain the enhanced results of change detection in SAR images, the operation needs long time because of the large number of iterations required.

Clustering is another option. Gong et al. proposed FLICM algorithm which is called Reformulated Fuzzy Local-Information C-Means [3]. Ghosh et al. proposed the improved Simulated Annealing and Gustafson-Kessel Clustering (SA-GKC) algorithm for image change detection based on FCM and genetic algorithm [9]. But the algorithm is computationally complex. FCM and the improved fuzzy c-means algorithms randomly select the initial clustering center. The change detection based on FCM will cost much time. And selection of the best threshold value is not a trivial task. Considering this, histogram thresholding for unsupervised change detection is proposed in reference [10], several non-fuzzy and fuzzy histogram thresholding techniques are investigated for the change detection problem [11, 12].

To address these existing problems, we propose a change detection algorithm based on histogram and improved elitist genetic fuzzy clustering. The proposed algorithm has the following improvements: (1) We employ genetic algorithms to select the initial clustering centers of FCM algorithm, which avoids the FCM algorithm to fall into local optimum. We combine the merits of genetic algorithm, which has a good global search capability, and FCM, which has a good local search capability. It significantly improves the convergence of the algorithm. Moreover, we use FCM to initialize genetic algorithm, which overcomes the difficulty in determining the fitness function of the genetic algorithm. (2) Because the conventional genetic algorithm may have the premature convergence or no convergence, we employ an improved genetic algorithm based on elitist strategy in optimizing blind source separation with guided genetic algorithms [12], which introduce Reduction Operators and the Elitist GA. The improved genetic algorithm resorts to the roulette to select the populations of the local optimal solution. Crossover and mutation are two common genetic operators. Crossover operates on two individuals at one time and creates new individuals by combining parts from two individuals. So the offspring produced by the crossover combine the features of both of the two individuals. The Cross generational elitist, Heterogeneous recombination and Cataclysmic mutation (CHC) algorithm [13] is adopted during the crossover operation, which replaces the location of individuals from two parents. The crossover operator randomly selects from 0–$c/2$ (c is the clustering number) to carry out the cross, but others does not cross. This operation effectively protects the optimal individual. The mutation operator is the main operator in the GA, which produces random changes in various individuals. So it can increase the diversity of the population and speed up the convergence. And the individual is updated only when the mutation probability is less than a certain value in Real-coded genetic algorithms and interval-schemata. This can not only maintain the diversity of the solution, but can also avoid the damage to the optimal solution to some extent. Finally, we compare a population of offspring after crossover and mutation with the saved the parent population, and the elitist selection strategy based on population concentration, which compares offspring population with parent population and uses the individual of offspring population whose fitness value is greater than the fitness value of parent population to replace the individual of parent population, is used to select the optimal population. The optimal population will be used as the initial clustering center of FCM to update the next iteration of the initial population and the fitness function of genetic algorithm. It will speed up the algorithm convergence. (3) Addressing the difficulties arising from huge dataset of the remote sensing images, we apply the simplest feature description method of histogram-remote sensing image change detection method based on pixel gray level distribution [14]. We can obtain the accurate solution in a relatively short period of time.

2 The Background and Preliminaries

2.1 The Fuzzy C-Means Clustering Algorithm

Fuzzy c-means clustering algorithm is applied to the pixels of the difference image in image change detection. The clustering of the difference image $Y = \{y_1, y_2, \cdots, y_i, \cdots, y_n\}$ is divided into c classes and the clustering is achieved by optimizing the clustering objective function J [4]:

$$J = \sum_{i=1}^{c} \sum_{k=1}^{n} \mu_{ik}^{m} d_{ik}^{2} \tag{1}$$

where, the y_i is the ith gray value of the respective stack pixel in this paper; c is the clustering number; the mth pixel is the weight of fuzzy degree; μ_{ki}^{m} is the fuzzy membership of the gray value k with respect to the ith cluster, which satisfies the constraint conditions:

$$0 \leq \mu_{ik} \leq 1 \text{ and } \sum_{i=1}^{c} \mu_{ik} = 1, i = 1, 2, \cdots, n \tag{2}$$

d_{ik} is the distance from the sample y_k to the clustering center v_i, which is:

$$d_{ik}^{2} = \|y_k - v_i\|^2 = (y_k - v_i)^T A (y_k - v_i) \tag{3}$$

When $A = I$, d_{ik} is the Euclidean distance. y_k is the kth sample of Y and v_i is the ith clustering center.

In order to obtain the best clustering results, we will carry out much iteration to acquire the optimal solution of J, namely obtain the minimum value of J. A solution of the objective function J can be gained through an iterative process that updates the membership degree matrix $U = [\mu_{ik}]_{c \times n}$ and the clustering center $V = [v_i]_{c \times n}$ (μ_{ik} represents the fuzzy membership of the gray value k with respect to the ith cluster; v_i is the ith clustering center; c represents the clustering number; n represents the number of data items).

2.2 The FCM Algorithm Based on Histogram

The computational complexity of FCM is O($L \times c \times n + L \times c$), where, n represents the time taken for each iteration. Due to large number of images data, extensive computation will be needed when processing the difference image. As a consequence, FCM algorithm based on histogram will be introduced.

The histogram that represents the information of figure pixel (usually in gray value) is $h(k)$. L is a maximum of grey value and k = 0–L, k is the number of the same grey value of pixel. According to Eq. (3), the distance from the kth samples to the ith class is changed to:

$$d_{ik}^2 = \|k - v_i\|^2, k = 0, 1, \cdots, L \tag{4}$$

3 Change Detection in Synthetic Aperture Radar Images Based on Histogram and Elitist Genetic Fuzzy Clustering

3.1 Generating Difference Images Using Image Fusion

The algorithm in this paper adopts non-local filtering to construct difference map [15]. The construction of difference map based on non-local filtering makes better use of spatial information and similarity information in gray field to suppress noise and overcomes the inherent shortcomings in existing methods.

Suppose that we have two images taken at different times in the same place, image taken at T_1 time is $Y_1 = \{y_1(i, j)|1 \leq i \leq N, 1 \leq j \leq M\}$ and it taken at T_2 time is $Y_2 = \{y_2(i, j)|1 \leq i \leq N, 1 \leq j \leq M\}$.

We use neighborhood subtraction to generate the difference image Y_{d1} from images Y_1 and Y_2, which is given as follows:

$$Y_{d1} = 255 - \frac{\left|\sum Y_1^H(i,j) - \sum Y_2^H(i,j)\right|}{H \times H} \tag{5}$$

where, $Y_1^H(i,j)$ and $Y_2^H(i,j)$ represent respectively the neighborhood collection of images Y_1 and Y_2 in the same pixels (i, j), whose sizes are all $H \times H$.

We use neighborhood ration to generate the difference image Y_{d2} from images Y_1 and Y_2, which is given as follows:

$$Y_{d2} = 255 \times \frac{\sum_{i=1}^{L\times L} \min\{N_1(y_i), N_2(y_i)\}}{\sum_{i=1}^{L\times L} \max\{N_1(y_i), N_2(y_i)\}} \tag{6}$$

where, $N_1(y_i)$ and $N_2(y_i)$ represent respectively the neighborhood collection of images Y_1 and Y_2 in the same location y pixels, whose sizes are all $L \times L$.

The difference map based on neighborhood subtraction generally large errors in high-gray areas than in low-gray scale ones, which is unfavorable for constructing level histogram. The neighborhood ratio method converts multiplicative speckle noise to additive one, to some extent, which suppresses the impact of noise. However, it weakens the contour information in regions of variation and increases the detection errors. Considering the inherent merits and drawbacks of the neighborhood subtraction method and neighborhood ratio method, we use a multiplying transform fusion to combine neighborhood subtraction method and neighborhood ratio method to generate the difference map Y:

$$Y(x,y) = \frac{\sum_{(i,j)\in N_{y,z}} m(i,j) Y_{d2}(i,j)}{\sum_{(i,j)\in N_{y,z}} m(i,j)} \tag{7}$$

where, $M_{y,z}$ represents the neighborhood of the center pixel whose size is $(2L+1) \times (2L+1)$ in the pixel (i, j). $m(i, j)$ is determined as follows:

$$m(i,j) = m_v(i,j) \times m_u(i,j) \tag{8}$$

$$m_v(i,j) = e^{\frac{|h_1(i,j) - h_1(y,z)|^2}{2\delta_v^2}} \tag{9}$$

where, $h_1(i, j)$ represents the grey value of the image Y_{d1} in the pixel (i, j), $|h_1(i,j) - h_1(y,z)|^2$ represents the Euclidean distance of the grey value from $h_1(i, j)$ with $h_1(y, z)$. δ_v is the parameter.

$$m_u(i,j) = e^{\frac{|i-y|^2 + |j-z|^2}{2\delta_u^2}} \tag{10}$$

where $|i-y|^2 + |j-z|^2$ represents the Euclidean distance from the pixel (i, j) of image Y_{d1} with the cluster center (y, z). δ_u is the parameter.

3.2 Initialization and Fitness Evaluation of Histogram and Improved Elitist Genetic Fuzzy Clustering

In this paper, the population $\boldsymbol{X} = [x_1, \cdots, x_i, \cdots, x_n]^T$ is derived by FCM based on histogram, where x_i represents the ith individual of population, and $x_i = v_i$, v_i is the ith clustering center. First, we randomly generate the initial clustering center v_0 and then repeat n times to initialize chromosome (using the FCM algorithm based on histogram to update n times clustering center v_i and the objective function J, where, J is defined in Sect. 2.1,) until the initial population $\boldsymbol{X} = [x_1, \cdots, x_i, \cdots, x_n]^T$ and the fitness function $f = [f_1, \ldots, f_n]^T$ are generated. What's more, the size of population is n and n is generally ranging from 30 to 100. That's why if the population is too small, we may not find out the solution. On the other hand if the population is too large, we may make the computation too complex. So here, n = 30, $x_1 = [x_{11}, \cdots, x_{1c}]$, ..., $x_i = [x_{i1}, \cdots, x_{ic}]$ ..., $x_n = [x_{n1}, \cdots, x_{nc}]$, and c = 2. According to Eq. (1), the fitness function of genetic algorithm is defined as:

$$f = \frac{1}{1 + J} \tag{11}$$

3.3 Selection Operator of Histogram and Improved Elitist Genetic Fuzzy C-Means

The selection operator of histogram and elitist genetic fuzzy c-means is to guarantee that better chromosome can be kept to the next generation of group. We use the roulette method to select. Roulette wheel selection is based on the population of individual fitness value to calculate the probability of each individual in the offspring. Then the appropriate the offspring population individuals $\boldsymbol{X}^{(1)}$ is generated according to the probability. The individuals have better fitness values have high probability to be selected.

The selection process of the initial population $\boldsymbol{X}$ is given in Table 1. The fitness value of x_j = {122 21} is selected 27 times. x_2 = {96 242} is selected 2 times. x_{30} = {152 150} is selected 1 time because the fitness value is small. The x_j is the jth individual of initial population X, x_{j1} and x_{j2} are genes of the jth individual, where $j \in [1, 30]$.

Table 1. Selection process of initial population $\boldsymbol{X}$

X	x_{j1} x_{j2}	Fitness value f	Selection number	Selection result $\boldsymbol{X}^{(1)}$
x_1	131 83	9.37e-06	0	122 21
x_2	96 242	0.0073	2	152 150
⋮	⋮	⋮	⋮	⋮
x_j	122 21	0.6383	27	96 242
⋮	⋮	⋮	⋮	⋮
x_{30}	152 150	6.80e-05	1	122 21

3.4 Crossover Operator of Histogram and Improved Elitist Genetic Fuzzy C-Means

The crossover operator of histogram and improved elitist genetic fuzzy c-means is based on crossover probability P_c of two chromosomes to exchange some genes in some manner and form two new individual. Crossover operator is the important feature of the genetic algorithm which is different from other evolutionary algorithms. It plays a key role in genetic algorithm and is the main method to generate new individual. In this paper, because the clustering center $\boldsymbol{v}$ is regarded as chromosome, it makes the two chromosome information correlated. The conventional crossover algorithm may lead to that the fitness of new individuals is poorer. In order to solve this problem, we randomly select from 0–c/2 parent individuals (c is the different digits of two parent individuals, and c also is the clustering number) to cross. The rest of positions have no crossover operation, which can effectively protect the individuals [13]. Because of large value of P_c may make high fitness individuals destroyed and small value of P_c may stop search process, the crossover probability P_c is generally in range of 0.2–0.8. Crossover process of population $\boldsymbol{X}^{(1)}$ is given in Table 2.

Table 2. Crossover process of population $X^{(1)}$

Selection result $\boldsymbol{X}^{(1)}$	$x_{j1}^{(1)} x_{j2}^{(1)}$	Crossover condition	Crossover result $\boldsymbol{X}^{(2)}$
$x_1^{(1)}$	122 21	$x_1^{(1)} \to x_j^{(1)}$	96 21
$x_2^{(1)}$	152 150	$x_2^{(1)} \to x_1^{(1)}$	122 150
⋮	⋮	⋮	⋮
$x_j^{(1)}$	96 242	$x_j^{(1)} \to x_{30}^{(1)}$	122 242
⋮	⋮	⋮	⋮
$x_{30}^{(1)}$	122 21	$x_{30}^{(1)} \to x_j^{(1)}$	122 21

As shown in Table 2, crossover is operated between $x_1^{(1)}$ with $x_j^{(1)}$, $x_2^{(1)}$ with $x_1^{(1)}$, $x_j^{(1)}$ with $x_{30}^{(1)}$, and $x_{30}^{(1)}$ with $x_j^{(1)}$. Because only two individuals in 0–c/2 cross when $c = 2$, only the first of each individual genes crosses. Here, $x_j^{(1)}$ is the jth individual of the population $\boldsymbol{X}^{(1)}$, and $x_{j1}^{(1)}$ and $x_{j2}^{(1)}$ are genes of the jth individual, $j \in [1, 30]$.

3.5 Mutation Operator of Histogram and Improved Elitist Genetic Fuzzy C-Means

Mutation operator of histogram and improved elitist genetic fuzzy c-means is based on the mutation probability P_m to change some genes of individual coding series, and thus form a new individual. Mutation operator is important method to produce new individual. It determines the local search ability of genetic algorithm and ensures the diversity of solution. In order to make sure that better individuals are not destroyed, we mutate and update individuals only when the mutation probability P_m is smaller than a certain value [13]. Because of large value of P_m may make genetic algorithm a random search algorithm and small number of P_m can't generate new population, the mutation probability P_m is generally in the range of 0.01–0.1. Mutation process of population $\boldsymbol{X}^{(2)}$ is given in Table 3.

Table 3. Mutation process of population $X^{(2)}$

Crossover result $X^{(2)}$	$x_{j1}^{(2)}$ $x_{j2}^{(2)}$	Random number *rand*	Mutation result $X^{(3)}$
$x_1^{(2)}$	96 21	136	96 21
$x_2^{(2)}$	122 150	80	122 150
⋮	⋮	⋮	⋮
$x_j^{(2)}$	122 242	58	58 58
⋮	⋮	⋮	⋮
$x_{30}^{(2)}$	122 21	207	122 21

In Table 3, $x_j^{(2)} = \{122\ 242\}$ execute mutation operation. The random number 58 replaces $x_j^{(2)}$ with the gene values of 122 and 242. Here, $x_j^{(2)}$ is the *j*th individual population of $X^{(2)}$. $x_{j1}^{(2)}$ and $x_{j2}^{(2)}$ are genes of the *j*th individual where $j \in [1,30]$.

3.6 Elitist Strategy of Histogram and Improved Elitist Genetic Fuzzy C-Means

In order to make sure that better solutions can be saved, we add in the idea of elitist selection strategy based on population concentration. If the elitist selection probability *Pr* is smaller than the random number between 0 and 1, it compares offspring population $X^{(3)}$ with parent population $X^{(1)}$ and uses the individual of offspring population whose fitness value f^* is greater than the fitness value f of parent population to replace the individual of parent population, and then to generate the new population of $X^{(4)}$. $X^{(4)}$ will be regarded as the next iteration initial clustering center v of FCM. The selection probability *Pr* is given as follows:

$$P_r = \delta_a \times R \times \left|1 - \frac{f}{\max(f)}\right| + \delta_b \times \frac{f}{\max(f)} \tag{12}$$

where, δ_a, δ_b and R all are the parameters between 0 and 1. The elitist selection of offspring population $X^{(3)}$ and parent population of $X^{(1)}$ is given in Table 4.

Table 4. Elitist selection mechanism of offspring population $X^{(3)}$ and parent population $X^{(1)}$

Parent population $X^{(1)}$	Offspring population $X^{(3)}$	The fitness values f	The fitness values f^*	Selection probability Pr	Elitist selection result $X^{(4)}$
122 21	96 21	9.37e-06	3.98 e-04	0.1659	96 21
152 150	122 150	0.0073	0.0081	0.5000	152 150
⋮	⋮	⋮	⋮	⋮	⋮
96 242	58 58	0.6383	3.41e-05	0.2348	96 242
⋮	⋮	⋮	⋮	⋮	⋮
122 21	122 21	6.80e-05	2.34e-04	0.1502	122 21

In Table 4, only the fitness value f^* of the first individual offspring population is greater than the fitness value f of parent population. Hence, we use the first individual {96 21} of the offspring to replace the first individual {122 21} of parent population.

3.7 Change Detection in Synthetic Aperture Radar Images Based on Histogram and Improved Elitist Genetic Fuzzy C-Means

As described above, the detailed steps of the change detection in SAR images based on histogram and improved elitist genetic fuzzy c-means algorithm are given as follows:

Step 1: Input the image Y_1 and image Y_2;
Step 2: Generate difference image Y according to Eqs. (5)–(10);
Step 3: Set the fuzzy weighting parameter m, the clustering number c, the maximum number of evolution T and the termination condition ε;
Step 4: Generate the initial population $\boldsymbol{X}$;
Step 5: Calculate the fitness function f according to Eqs. (1) and (11);
Step 6: The selection of initial population $\boldsymbol{X}$;
Step 7: The crossover of population $\boldsymbol{X}^{(1)}$;
Step 8: The mutation of population $\boldsymbol{X}^{(2)}$;
Step 9: The elitist selection from population $\boldsymbol{X}^{(1)}$ with offspring population $\boldsymbol{X}^{(3)}$, generating new offspring population $\boldsymbol{X}^{(4)}$;
Step 10: Update the initial population $\boldsymbol{X}$ and the fitness function $\boldsymbol{f}$ by the FCM algorithm based on histogram;
Step 11: If the maximum value of fitness function f is less than ε or the maximum number of evolution T, then go to Step 12; otherwise, go to Step 6;
Step 12: Obtain the segmentation threshold t, and finally segment the difference image Y. Where, t is the index value of $u(i)$ when $u(i)$ gets the minimum.

4 The Experimental Results and Analyses

4.1 Evaluating Criteria and Experimental Parameter

The quantitative analysis of the change detection results in SAR images are from [3]. T represents the times of the complete process besides of generating the difference image for each algorithm. The percentage of correct classification (PCC) is given by: 1 - TE/N; N is the total number of pixels. TE is the total error. FN represents the false negatives which is the pixel number that reference data pixels change but the change detection results don't change; FP represents the false positives which is the pixel number that the reference data pixels don't change but the change detection results change. T represents the running time of the algorithms.

The experimental parameter as shown follows. For each method, the fuzzy weight parameter $m = 2$, the clustering number $c = 2$, the maximum number of iterations T = 100, termination conditions threshold $\varepsilon = 0.001$. For the proposed algorithm, the size of population is n = 30. For FACMs-GA, the experimental parameters are given in [16].

4.2 Experiments and Analyses

The proposed algorithm will be compared with the FCM algorithm [17], the FLICM algorithm [17], the RFLICM algorithm [3] and the FACMs-GA algorithm [16]. We select two groups of SAR images for evaluation: The Switzerland Bern and the Feltwell. Figure 1 shows the five final maps are obtained by using FCM, FLICM, RLICM and the proposed algorithm on Ottawa dataset and the reference data image.

As shown in Fig. 1(a), the simulation result of FCM contains lots of noise spots. It can be seen from Figs. 1(b) and (c), the simulation results of FLICM and RFLICM still have more noise spots compared with that of the proposed algorithm shown in Fig. 1 (e). The resulting image of the proposed algorithm is the nearest one to the reference data image (Fig. 1(f)). The quantitative change detection results obtained from different algorithms for input the Bern data set are shown in Table 5.

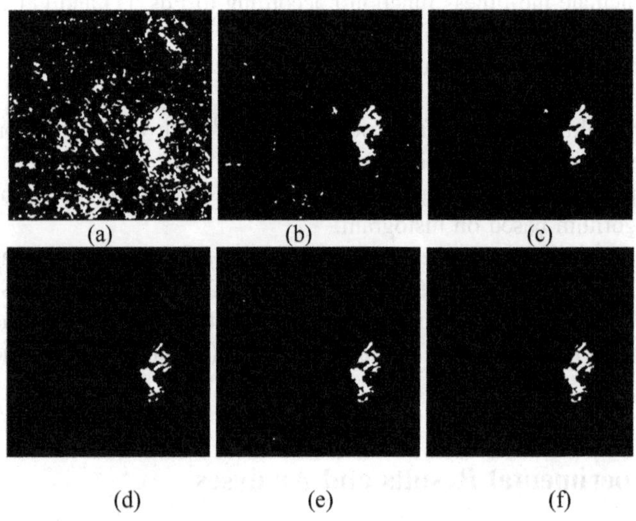

Fig. 1. Change detection results of Bern achieved by (a) FCM, (b) FLICM, (c) RFLICM, (d) FACMs-GA, (e) the proposed algorithm, (f) the reference data image.

As shown in Table 5, FCM achieves the worst result. Compared with FLICM and RFLICM, TE of the proposed algorithm is lower and PCC is much higher than these methods. These are mainly due to the fact that FCM, FLICM and RFLICM easily obtain a local optimal solution, but the proposed algorithm use genetic algorithm to overcome this defect. This also speeds up the convergence of due the proposed algorithm. So the proposed algorithm uses the least time. Especially, the time of FACMs-GA is far bigger than the proposed algorithm.

Figure 2 shows the five final maps are obtained by using FCM, FLICM, RLICM and the proposed algorithm on Feltwell data set and the reference data image. For FCM, FLICM and RFLICM, the change detection maps are illustrated in Figs. 2 (a), (b) and (c). These maps have some noise spots, with the fact that the missed alarms

Table 5. The simulation results of Bern

Algorithms	FN	FP	TE	PCC	T/s
FCM	609	10060	10669	88.22%	2.8786
FLICM	157	392	549	99.39%	795.11
RFLICM	126	144	270	99.70%	1127.5
FACMs-GA	127	140	267	99.70%	1349.6
The proposed algorithm	**85**	**19**	**104**	**99.89%**	**0.8627**

caused by FCM, FLICM and RFLICM randomly select the initial clustering center so that these algorithms easily fall into local optimum.

As shown in Fig. 2(d), the map of FACMs-GA loses more detail texture information of image. The Feltwell data sets are quantitative analysis of the experimental results are shown in Table 6.

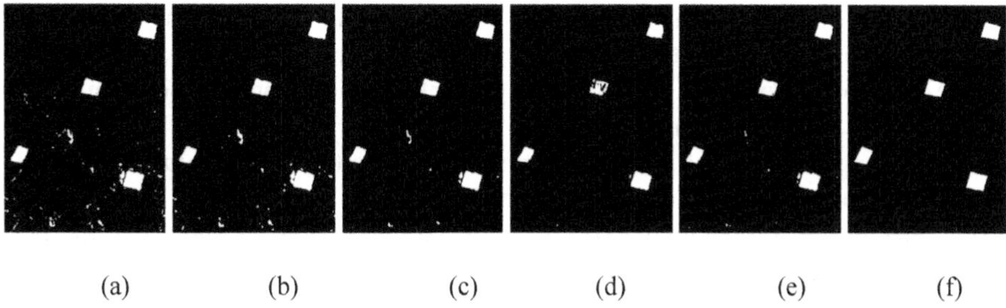

(a) (b) (c) (d) (e) (f)

Fig. 2. Change detection results of Feltwell are achieved by (a) FCM, (b) FLICM, (c) RFLICM, (d) FACMs-GA, (e) the proposed algorithm, (f) the reference data image.

As shown in Table 6, concerning the total errors, the proposed algorithm obtains the smallest error pixels. The proposed algorithm results in the highest PCC. Moreover, the proposed algorithm obtains the best solution with the shortest time. The proposed algorithm is superior to the other algorithms.

Table 6. The simulation results of Feltwell

Algorithm	FN	FP	TE	PCC	T/s
FCM	943	745	1688	98.93%	4.4493
FLICM	710	535	1245	99.21%	1103.0
RFLICM	378	287	665	99.58%	1975.0
FACMs-GA	470	335	847	99.41%	2757.9
The proposed algorithm	**344**	**248**	**592**	**99.62%**	**0.9659**

By the qualitative analysis to assess the subjective pictures and the quantitative analysis to analyze the data in the tables, the detection total errors rate of the proposed algorithm almost is the lowest when comparing it with the reference algorithms, e.g.,

FCM algorithm, FLICM algorithm and RFLICM algorithm. In addition, compared with FCM, FLICM and RFLICM, the proposed algorithm can find the optimal solution with the least time consumption. Although the proposed algorithm has better change detection results in the SAR images change detection than that of FACMs-GA, the proposed algorithm spends far less times on the two SAR images. By evaluating the experimental results from both figures and tables, we have demonstrated that the proposed algorithm is a novel change detection algorithm with better performance to some extent.

5 Conclusions

In this paper, we have reviewed both the merits and drawbacks of FCM algorithm and improve over it. We have proposed a change detection algorithm based on histogram and elitist genetic fuzzy c-means. The proposed algorithm retains the optimal solution for every population by updating and replacement. This proposed method not only keeps the characteristics of the original population, and can also make the evolution of the optimal solution without loss. At the same time, the offspring population will replace the parent population timely which guarantees that the optimal solution can be acquired more quickly. It accelerates the convergence speed of the algorithm. In addition, the employment of FCM algorithm to calculate the initial population and the fitness function makes the genetic algorithm simpler. The integration of histogram can also accelerate the computational speed. The experimental results show that the proposed algorithm performs significantly better in enhancing the detection precision and in reducing the computational time.

Acknowledgments. This work was partially supported by the National Natural Science Foundation of China, under Grants 61371201 and 61272279, the National Basic Research Program (973 Program) of China under Grant 2013CB329402.

References

1. Shang, R.H., Qi, L.P., Jiao, L.C., Stolkin, R., Li, Y.Y.: Change detection in SAR images by artificial immune multi-objective clustering. Eng. Appl. Artif. Intell. **31**, 53–67 (2014)
2. Shang, R.H., Tian, P.P., Jiao, L.C., Stolkin, R., Feng, J., Hou, B., Zhang, X.R.: A spatial fuzzy clustering algorithm with kernel metric based on immune clone for SAR image segmentation. IEEE J. Sel. Top. Appl. Earth Obs. Remote Sens. **9**(4), 1640–1652 (2016)
3. Gong, M.G., Zhou, Z.Q., Ma, J.J.: Change detection in synthetic aperture radar images based on image fusion and fuzzy clustering. IEEE Trans. Image Process. **21**(4), 2141–2151 (2012)
4. Rignot, E.J.M., van Zyl, J.J.: Change detection techniques for ERS-1 SAR data. IEEE Trans. Geosci. Remote Sens. **31**(4), 896–906 (1993)
5. Bruzzone, L., Prieto, D.F.: An adaptive parcel-based technique for unsupervised change detection. Int. J. Remote Sens. **21**(4), 817–822 (2000)
6. Su, L.Z., Gong, M.G., Sun, B., Jiao, L.C.: Unsupervised change detection in SAR images based on locally fitting model and semi-EM algorithm. Int. J. Remote Sens. **35**(2), 621–650 (2014)

7. Moser, G., Serpico, S.B.: Generalized minimum-error thresholding for unsupervised change detection from SAR amplitude imagery. IEEE Trans. Geosci. Remote Sens. **44**(10), 2972–2982 (2006)
8. Celik, T.: Change detection in satellite images using a genetic algorithm approach. IEEE Geosci. Remote Sens. Lett. **7**(2), 386–390 (2010)
9. Ghosh, A., Mishra, N.S., Ghosh, S.: Fuzzy clustering algorithms for unsupervised change detection in remote sensing images. Inf. Sci. **181**(4), 699–715 (2011)
10. Krinidis, S., Chatzis, V.: A robust fuzzy local information C-means clustering algorithm. IEEE Trans. Image Process. **19**(5), 1328–1337 (2010)
11. Shang, R.H., Wen, A.L., Zhang, K., Jiao, L.C.: Synthetic aperture radar image change detection based on improved bilateral filtering and fuzzy C mean. J. Appl. Remote Sens. **10** (4), 046017 (2016)
12. Elsayed, S.M., Sarker, R.A., Essam, D.L.: A new genetic algorithm for solving optimization problems. Eng. Appl. Artif. Intell. **27**, 57–69 (2014)
13. Gorriza, J.M., Puntonetb, C.G., Rojas, F.: Optimizing blind source separation with guided genetic algorithms. Neurocomputing **69**, 1442–1457 (2006)
14. Eshelman, L.J., Shaffer, D.J.: Real-coded genetic algorithms and interval-schemata. In: Whitley, D.L. (ed.) Foundations of Genetic Algorithms, vol. 2, pp. 187–202. Morgan Kaufman, San Mateo (1993)
15. Bezdek, J.: Pattern Recognition with Fuzzy Objective Function Algorithms. Plenum, New York (1981)
16. Furtuna, R., Curteanu, S., Leon, F.: An elitist non-dominated sorting genetic algorithm enhanced with a neural network applied to the multi-objective optimization of a polysiloxane synthesis process. Eng. Appl. Artif. Intell. **24**(5), 772–785 (2011)
17. Shi J., Wu J.J., Paul A., Jiao L.C., Gong M.G.: Change detection in synthetic aperture radar images based on fuzzy active contour models and genetic algorithms. Math. Probl. Eng. **2014**, 15 p. (2014). Article ID 870936

Research on Cognitive Radio Spectrum Sensing Method Based on Information Geometry

Qiang Chen[1], Pin Wan[1], Yonghua Wang[1,2(✉)], Jiangfan Li[1], and Yirui Xiao[1]

[1] School of Automation, Guangdong University of Technology, Guangzhou 510006, China
bypb_chen@163.com, wanpin2@163.com, sjzwyh@163.com, 13726926816@163.com, xiaoyirui@163.com

[2] Key Laboratory of Machine Intelligence and Advanced Computing (Sun Yat-Sen University), Ministry of Education, Guangzhou 510006, China

Abstract. Making using of the emerging information geometry theory, we analyze the statistical properties of wireless spectrum signals received by secondary users, and propose a cognitive radio spectrum sensing method based on information geometry. We introduce a new detection structure, using the sample covariance matrix and corresponding to the points on the statistical manifold, by calculating the distance between them and make a decision, thus transforming the statistical detection problem into the geometric problem on the manifold. We also used two solutions: Constant False Alarm Rate (CFAR) Detector and Distance Detector (DD). The simulation results reveal that the performance of the information geometry method is superior to the traditional spectrum sensing algorithm, and research results will help us to explore the spectrum sensing problem from a new perspective.

Keywords: Information geometry · Cognitive radio · Spectrum sensing · Statistical manifold

1 Introduction

The development of wireless communication and the popularity of mobile devices in recent years have imposed increasing stress on the fixed and limited radio spectrum. Dynamic spectrum allocation has been considered as an effective way to remedy the shortage of spectrum. Cognitive radios [1], which are typically built on the software defined radio (SDR) technology, have been identified as a key enabler for dynamic spectrum access networks. In cognitive radio networks, secondary users (SU) can sense spectra and tune their transmitters to available channels [2, 3], which are premised on the fact that their communication does not bring interference to primary users (PU), so spectrum sensing plays a central role in cognitive radio technology. Existing classical spectrum sensing methods include matched filter detection, energy detection, cyclostationary feature detection, etc. Matched filter detection is optimized when the PU signal is known [4]. Although energy detection is easy to implement, it depends on

X. Sun et al. (Eds.): ICCCS 2017, Part II, LNCS 10603, pp. 554–564, 2017.
https://doi.org/10.1007/978-3-319-68542-7_47

accurate estimation of noise power which is difficult to obtain under low SNR environment [5]. Cyclostationary feature detection also has huge complexities and is unable to distinguish the PU signal from the noise which is also cyclostationary [6]. Eigenvalue based detection can be exploited for different signal detection applications with unknown signals and unknown noise power [7–9]. Eigenvalue based detection is based on eigenvalues of covariance matrix of received signal. Some schemes for eigenvalue based detection include maximum eigenvalue detection (MED), maximum-minimum eigenvalue (MME) detection, and energy with minimum eigenvalue (EME) detection, etc. Their studies are mainly focus on the combination and improvement of spectrum sensing methods, and the detection performance is also need to be improved [10].

In order to improve the detection performance and explore the spectrum sensing problem from a new perspective, we propose a spectrum sensing method based on information geometry theory. Traditionally, Euclidean geometry, normed space and linear algebra are treated as mathematical foundation of signal processing. However as the problem being more complex, it urgently needs new concepts and mathematical tools to confront the revolution of signal processing theory. Information geometry is a set of theoretical systems, which is based on the study of the intrinsic geometric properties of the probability distribution manifold [11]. Some scholars at home and abroad have studied the application of information geometry in information resolution, signal detection, parameter estimation, sensor network and other signal processing problems. Ever since the introduction by Rao in 1945 of the Fisher information metric on a family of probability distributions there has been interest among statisticians in the application of differential geometry to statistics [12–14]. Japanese scientist Amari has also done a lot of research [15–17], enriching the theory and has produced many applications. In [18], a Constant False Alarm Rate (CFAR) detector structure based on information geometry is proposed for radar echo detection, which however measured by only geodesic distance (GD). The author of [19] proposed a distance detector based on Kullback-Leibler Divergence (KLD), which does not satisfy the symmetry. In [20], the author use the square of the geodesic distance instead of KLD, which has better properties, such as symmetry, satisfying triangle inequality and the performance is better than geodesic.

In this paper, we use the idea of information geometry to spectrum sensing with two solutions CFAR and DD, adopt the optimization algorithm to process the sampling data and use Symmetrized Kullback-Leibler Divergence (SKLD) to measure distance on the manifold which also satisfy symmetry and other properties. Section 2 presents the system model of spectrum sensing in cognitive wireless network and two different detector structures. In Sect. 3, we discuss the calculation method of GD and SKLD under Gaussian distribution, use gradient descent algorithm to obtain the Riemannian mean of multiple covariance matrices and finds thresholds for the proposed detectors. Performance evaluations and comparisons are given in Sect. 4. Finally, the conclusions of this paper are drawn in Sect. 5.

2 System Model

2.1 Spectrum Sensing Scheme

In this paper, we use two kinds of detection schemes, one is constant false alarm rate (CFAR) detector, and another is the distance detector (DD). CFAR detector method needs to detect the noise environment, and then realize spectrum sensing by calculating the difference between the corresponding two points on the manifold that perceived wireless spectrum signal and the noise environment, respectively. Distance detector method requires a priori information about the signal as a reference, the observations of H_0 (noise only) and H_1 (mixed with noise) are assumed to the two corresponding points $\mathbf{R}_w$ and $\mathbf{R}_s + \mathbf{R}_w$ on the statistical manifold $\mathbf{S}$, respectively. By calculating the difference between the corresponding points of the perceived spectrum signal on $\mathbf{S}$ and the distance between these two points, the purpose of spectrum sensing is realized. Here we use the geodesic distance detector (GDD) and Symmetrized Kullback-Leibler Divergence Detector (SKLDD). Two kinds of detection schemes of spectrum sensing are shown in Figs. 1 and 2, respectively.

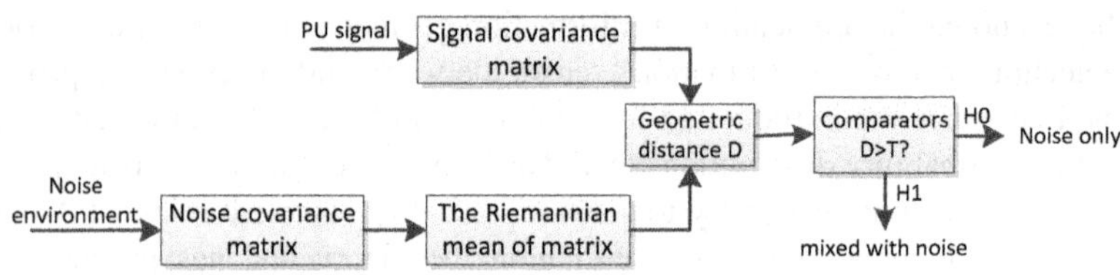

Fig. 1. CFAR detector

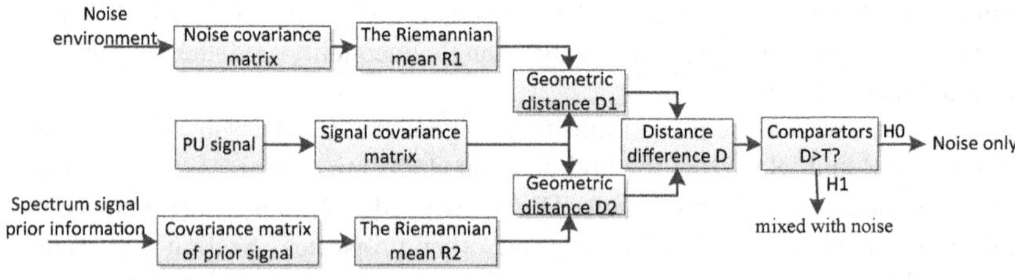

Fig. 2. Distance detector

2.2 Signal Model

In cognitive radio network, the situation of single secondary user (SU) detects whether a primary user (PU) is present can be represented by the binary hypothesis model in statistics as:

$$\mathrm{x(k)} = \begin{cases} n(\mathrm{k}), & \mathrm{H_0} \\ s(\mathrm{k}) + n(\mathrm{k}), & \mathrm{H_1} \end{cases}, \qquad \mathrm{k} = 1, 2, \ldots, \tag{1}$$

Here, x(k) is the signal received by SU at time index k, the vectors s(k) and n(k), describe the received PU signal (if present) and the noise, respectively. Assuming that n(k) represent the additive white Gaussian noise, s(k) is the signal transmitted by PU, Then under the two assumptions, the data x(k) are respectively subject to the distribution $N(0, \mathbf{R}_n)$ and $N(0, (\mathbf{R}_s + \mathbf{R}_n))$, Where $\mathbf{R}_n$ and $\mathbf{R}_s$ represent the covariance matrix of the noise vector n(k) and the random signal s(k), respectively [21].

Assuming that there are M SUs in the cognitive network, By combining N sample vectors into the sample matrix $\mathbf{X} = [\mathbf{x}_1, \ \mathbf{x}_2, \ \ldots, \ \mathbf{x}_M]$, we can grasp the model in a convenient matrix. Where $\mathbf{x}_i = [x_i(1), \ x_i(2), \ \cdots, \ x_i(N)]^T$ denotes the signal received by the ith SU. Thus, X is a matrix of $N \times M$ dimensions:

$$\mathbf{X} = [\mathbf{x}_1, \ \mathbf{x}_2, \ \ldots, \ \mathbf{x}_M] = \begin{bmatrix} x_1(1), & x_2(1), & \cdots, & x_M(1) \\ x_1(2), & x_2(2), & \cdots, & x_M(2) \\ \vdots & \vdots & \ddots & \vdots \\ x_1(N), & x_2(N), & \cdots, & x_M(N) \end{bmatrix} \tag{2}$$

For any n-dimensional vector x, if it follows the zero mean Gauss distribution, its distribution expression is given by

$$\mathrm{p}(\mathrm{x}|\mathbf{R}) = \frac{1}{\sqrt{(2\pi)^n \det R}} \exp\left(-\frac{1}{2}\mathrm{x}^T \mathbf{R}^{-1} \mathrm{x}\right) \tag{3}$$

Consider the probability distribution family $\mathbf{S} = \{\mathrm{p}(\mathbf{x}|\mathbf{R}) | \mathbf{R} \in C^{n \times n}\}$, it is parameterized by the covariance matrix $\mathbf{R} \in C^{n \times n}$, where C is the open set of $n \times n$-dimensional vector spaces, according to the information geometry theory, it can compose a manifold in a certain topological structure. The manifold is called statistical manifold [15], $\mathbf{R}$ is the coordinates of the manifold. Since the parameters of the manifold $\mathbf{S}$ are covariance matrices, then it can be called matrix manifold [21]. The two hypothetical distributions $\mathrm{p}(\mathrm{x}|\mathbf{H}_0)$ and $\mathrm{p}(\mathrm{x}|\mathbf{H}_1)$ correspond to two points on the manifold, respectively, and the coordinates of these two points are $\mathbf{R}_w$ and $\mathbf{R}_s + \mathbf{R}_w$. The distance between two points on the manifold increases with the increase of SNR, if the distance is greater than the threshold, then there is a signal exists, on the contrary, noise only.

3 Information Geometry Tool

3.1 Geodesic Distance and SKLD

The distance between two probability distributions on statistical manifold can be approximated with a variety of metrics, here we introduce the calculation method of geodesic distance and SKLD of Gaussian distribution.

Consider the family of multivariate normal distributions with common mean vector but different covariance matrices. The geodesic distance between two members of the family with covariance matrices Σ_1 and Σ_2 is given by [16]

$$\mathrm{D}(\Sigma_1, \Sigma_2) = \sqrt{\frac{1}{2}\mathrm{trlog}^2\left(\Sigma_1^{-\frac{1}{2}}, \Sigma_2\Sigma_1^{-\frac{1}{2}}\right)} = \sqrt{\frac{1}{2}\sum_{i=1}^{n}\log^2\eta_i} \tag{4}$$

where η_i denote the n eigenvalues of the matrix $\Sigma_1^{-\frac{1}{2}}\Sigma_2\Sigma_1^{-\frac{1}{2}}$.

In information geometry, closeness between two probability distributions usually measured by the KLD, however, for the two points on the manifold far away, KLD does not consider the shortest path connecting two points, that is, the structure of the manifold. Therefore, there is a difference between KLD and Fisher information distance (geodesic distance) for the distant points on the manifold. For the two points P and Q on the manifold, the KLD from P to Q is given by [17]

$$\mathrm{KL}(\mathbf{P}, \mathbf{Q}) = \mathrm{tr}\left(\mathbf{Q}^{-1}\mathbf{P} - \mathbf{I}\right) - \mathrm{logdet}\left(\mathbf{Q}^{-1}\mathbf{P}\right) = \sum_{i}^{n}(\lambda_i - \log\lambda_i - 1) \tag{5}$$

where λ_i denote the n eigenvalues of the matrix $\mathbf{Q}^{-1}\mathbf{P}$. We emphasize here the fact that the KLD does not define a distance on the space of positive-definite matrices as it is neither symmetric with respect to its two arguments nor does it satisfy the triangle inequality. Its symmetrical form $\mathrm{KL_S}(\mathbf{P}, \mathbf{Q}) = \frac{1}{2}(\mathrm{KL}(\mathbf{P}, \mathbf{Q}) + \mathrm{KL}(\mathbf{Q}, \mathbf{P}))$ can be expressed as

$$\mathrm{KL_S}(\mathbf{P}, \mathbf{Q}) = \frac{1}{2}\mathrm{tr}\left(\mathbf{Q}^{-1}\mathbf{P} + \mathbf{P}^{-1}\mathbf{Q} - 2\mathbf{I}\right) \tag{6}$$

or, in terms of the λ_i's, as

$$\mathrm{KL_S}(\mathbf{P}, \mathbf{Q}) = \frac{1}{2}\sum_{i=1}^{n}\left(\sqrt{\lambda_i} - \frac{1}{\sqrt{\lambda_i}}\right)^2 \tag{7}$$

By conclusion, unlike KLD, the symmetrized Kullback-Leibler Divergence (SKLD) has better properties, such as symmetry, and it is invariant under inversion, i.e., $\mathrm{KL_S}\left(\mathbf{P}^{-1}, \mathbf{Q}^{-1}\right) = \mathrm{KL_S}(\mathbf{P}, \mathbf{Q})$.

3.2 Riemannian Mean of Matrix

We define a mean [17, 18] relative to a distance (or a divergence) of a finite set of symmetric positive-definite (SPD) matrices $\mathbf{R}_k(\mathrm{k} = 1, 2, \ldots, \mathrm{N})$ to be the SPD matrix $\mathbf{R}$ that minimizes

$$J(\mathbf{R}) = \frac{1}{N}\sum_{K=1}^{N} D^2(\mathbf{R}_k, \mathbf{R}) \tag{8}$$

that is,

$$\bar{\mathbf{R}} = \arg\min_{\mathbf{R}\in\Theta} J(\mathbf{R}) \tag{9}$$

For the case of two points $\mathbf{R}_1$ and $\mathbf{R}_2$ on the manifold, $\bar{\mathbf{R}}$ is equal to the midpoint of the geodesic line connecting A and B, and the Riemannian mean can be written as

$$\bar{\mathbf{R}} = R_1^{1/2}\left(R_1^{-1/2}R_2R_1^{-1/2}\right)^{1/2}R_1^{1/2} \tag{10}$$

For the case of N (N > 2) points, the Riemannian mean is more difficult to find, in [19, 22], the iterative method of $\bar{\mathbf{R}}$ is given by using the gradient descent algorithm, the final expression of the Riemann mean is given by

$$\bar{\mathbf{R}}_{i+1} = \bar{\mathbf{R}}_i^{1/2} e^{\frac{\tau}{N}\sum_{k=1}^{N}\log\left(\bar{\mathbf{R}}_i^{-1/2}\mathbf{R}_k\bar{\mathbf{R}}_i^{-1/2}\right)}\bar{\mathbf{R}}_i^{1/2}, \quad 0 \le \tau \le 1 \tag{11}$$

where τ is the iterative step.

To estimate the performance of the algorithm, we simulate the change of the average geodesic distance $\frac{1}{N}\sum_{K=1}^{N} D(\mathbf{R}_k, \mathbf{R})$ and the average SKLD $\frac{1}{N}\sum_{K=1}^{N} D_{KLs}(\mathbf{R}_k, \mathbf{R})$ following the number of iterative step in Fig. 3. It can be seen from the figure that the performance of the gradient descent algorithm is superior to the direct average method, and the average geodesic distance and the average SKLD trends down with the increasing of iterative step number, and when the number increases to a certain value the variance will be almost invariable.

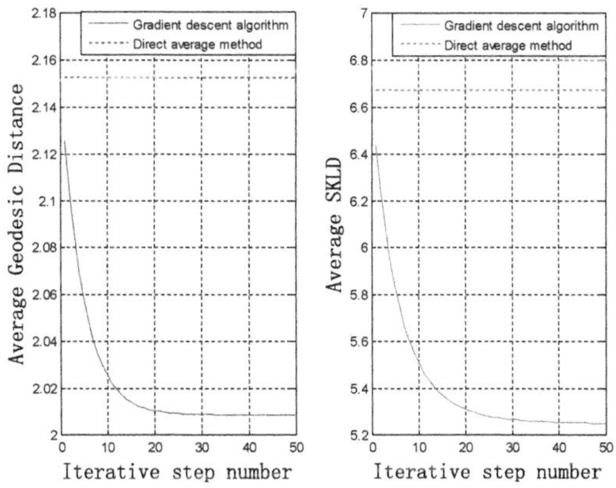

Fig. 3. Gradient descent algorithm performance graph.

3.3 Threshold

The detection performance of the proposed two detectors depends on many factors. In this section, we get the decision threshold of CFAR detector by Monte-Carlo simulation method. The main process is as follow:

(1) We obtain the N + 1 noise covariance matrix by simulation under H_0, and one of them is the matrix R to be detected.
(2) Compute the Riemannian mean R_d of N sample covariance matrices by gradient descent method.
(3) Obtain the geometric distance $D(R_d, R)$ on the manifold.
(4) Assume that the probability of false alarm is $10^{-2}(Pf = 10^{-2})$, repeat steps (1)–(3) L times (as high as possible), and sort L geometric distances in descending order. The threshold corresponds to the value of L * Pf position of the descending sequence
(5) It should be noted that the geometric distance $D(R_d, R)$ can be measured by many ways, and it should be consistent with the metric used previously.

In Table 1, we approximate the threshold of the computing method proposed above. We specify sample number N, cooperative SUs M and the probability of false alarm Pf, and then we get threshold of two kinds of detectors by use different metrics. T_{GD} and T_{SKLD} are the thresholds in CFAR detector by using geodesic and SKLD to compute geometric distance. T_{GDD} and T_{SKLDD} are the thresholds in DD scheme by using geodesic and SKLD to compute geometric distance.

Table 1. Simulated Threshold of Detectors

(N, K, Pf)	T_{GD}	T_{SKLD}	T_{GDD}	T_{SKLDD}
(200, 5, 10^{-2})	0.4059	0.1748	0.4132	0.4639
(500, 5, 10^{-2})	0.2562	0.0682	0.5422	0.5559
(200, 8, 10^{-2})	0.5679	0.3252	0.4872	0.8054
(500, 8, 10^{-2})	0.3579	0.1284	0.6311	0.9004

4 Simulation and Analysis

In this section, the paper presents the simulation results of information geometry and maximum and minimum eigenvalue (MME) algorithms. Under the two system models introduced in Sect. 2, we adopt two ways to measure the geometric distance on the manifold, geodesic distance and SKLD. We compare from four aspects, SNR, the number of samples, the number of cooperative SUs, the probability of false alarm (Pf), and 3000 Monte-Carlo simulations are performed each time. GD and SKLD are CFAR detector by using geodesic and SKLD to compute geometric distance. GDD and SKLDD are DD scheme by using geodesic and SKLD to compute geometric distance.

In Fig. 4, we shows probability of detection (Pd) as a function of SNR with $P_{fa} = 0.01$, N = 500, M = 5. From Fig. 4, we can see with the growth of SNR, the detection performance of all algorithms is improved rapidly, and the two methods based on distance detector are more obvious. The two methods of CFAR are slightly better than the MME algorithm. It should be noted that, although the geodesic distance is a more accurate measurement method than SKLD, its detection performance is poor. This is because geodesic distance is the shortest distance between two points on the manifold, when SNR changes, the distance of this change is not large, and it's easy to cause false alarm. Sometimes we use the square of geodesic distance to replace it.

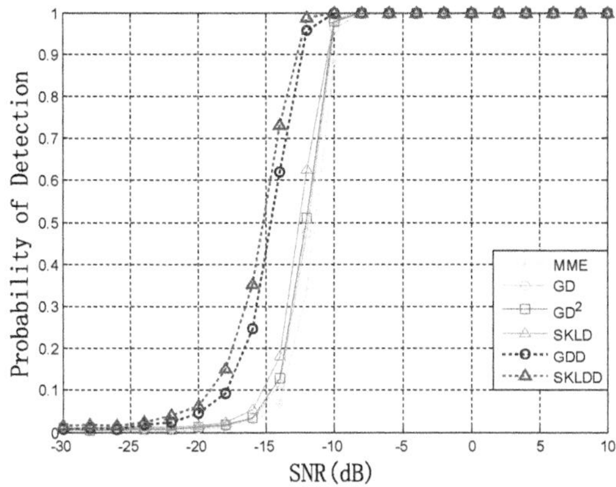

Fig. 4. Pd vs SNR curve with $P_{fa} = 0.01$, N = 500, M = 5.

Figure 5 present simulation results by varying number of samples with $P_{fa} = 0.01$, M = 5, SNR = −14 dB. From Fig. 5, we know that with the growth of the number of samples, the detection performance of all algorithms is improved. With more samples, in general, the noise can be averaged out when calculating which improves overall SNR and finally improve detection performance. The two methods of the distance detector model are superior to the CFAR detection method and the MME algorithm at the fixed number of samples.

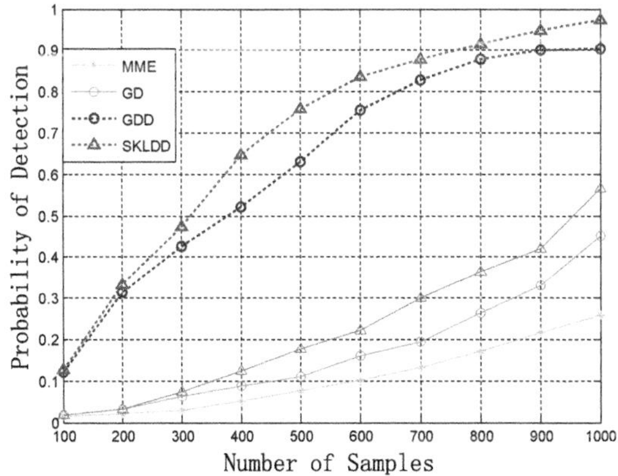

Fig. 5. Pd vs samples curve with $P_{fa} = 0.01$, SNR = −14 dB, M = 5.

In Fig. 6, we plot Pd as a function of the number of cooperative SUs with $P_{fa} = 0.01$, N = 500, SNR = −14 dB. In our signal model, the number of cooperative SUs has an effect on the rank of the covariance matrix. The figure shows that with the growth of the number of the cooperative SUs, the detection performance of all algorithms is improved, and the proposed detector outperforms the MME algorithm.

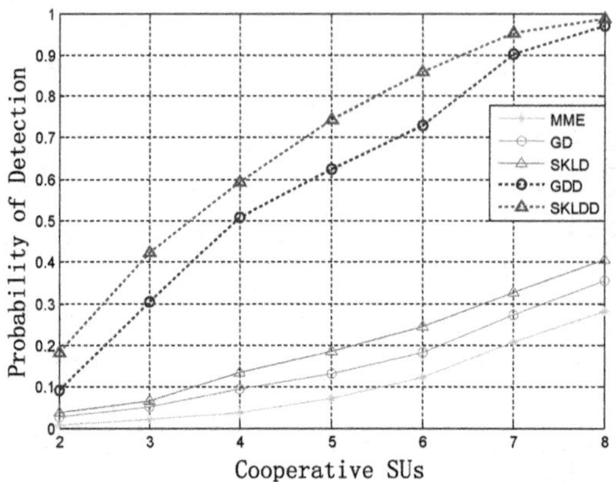

Fig. 6. Pd vs SUs curve with $P_{fa} = 0.01$, SNR = −14 dB, N = 500.

Figure 7 above is the ROC (Receiver Operating Characteristics) which shows the relationship between Pd and Pf with M = 5, N = 500, SNR = −14 dB. Increasingly Pf causes the miss detection probability decreases thus increasing Pd.

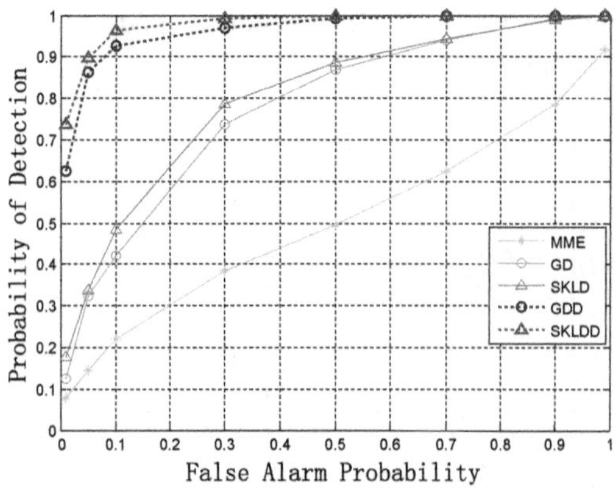

Fig. 7. ROC curve: N = 500, M = 5, SNR = −14 dB

5 Conclusions

Based on the emerging information geometric theory in recent years, this paper proposes a spectrum sensing structure and two kinds of detectors: CFAR detector and distance detector. This method achieves the purpose of spectrum sensing by calculating the distance between the points corresponding to the observation data on the statistical manifold. We compute the geometric distance by geodesic distance and SKLD, and obtain matrix mean by gradient descent algorithm. Through theoretical analysis, we obtain the decision threshold by simulation method. The simulation results show that it has better detection performance than traditional methods in some scenarios. Information geometry not only has a broad application prospects in the spectrum signal processing, there are more problems to be solved. If the noise environment is uncertain, will lead to performance degradation, which is the future study needs to focus on the solution.

Acknowledgements. This work was supported in part by the Science and Technology Program of Guangdong Province under Grant No. 2016B090918031, Degree and Graduate Education Reform Project of Guangdong Province under Grant No. 2016JGXM_MS_26, Foundation of Key Laboratory of Machine Intelligence and Advanced Computing of the Ministry of Education under Grant No. MSC-201706A and Higher Education Quality Project of Guangdong Province.

References

1. Mitola, J.I., Maguire, G.Q.: Cognitive radio: making software radios more personal. J. IEEE Pers. Commun. **6**, 13–18 (1999)
2. Akyildiz, I.F., Lee, W.Y., Vuran, M.C., Mohanty, S.: A survey on spectrum management in cognitive radio networks. IEEE Commun. Mag. **46**, 40–48 (2008)
3. Kong, Y., Zhang, M., Ye, D.: A belief propagation-based method for task allocation in open and dynamic cloud environments. Knowl. Based Syst. J. **115**, 123–132 (2016)
4. Tandra, R., Sahai, A.: Fundamental limits on detection in low SNR under noise uncertainty. In: International Conference on Wireless Networks, Communications and Mobile Computing, pp. 464–469. IEEE, Maui (2005)
5. Tandra, R., Sahai, A.: SNR walls for signal detection. IEEE J. Sel. Top. Signal Process. **2**, 4–17 (2008)
6. Sutton, P.D., Nolan, K.E., Doyle, L.E.: Cyclostationary signatures in practical cognitive radio applications. IEEE J. Sel. Areas Commun. **26**, 13–24 (2008)
7. Zeng, Y., Liang, Y.C.: Maximum-minimum eigenvalue detection for cognitive radio. In: International Symposium on Personal, Indoor and Mobile Radio Communications, pp. 1–5. IEEE, Athens (2007)
8. Zeng, Y., Koh, C.L., Liang, Y.C.: Maximum eigenvalue detection: theory and application. In: IEEE International Conference on Communications, ICC 2008, Beijing, China, 19–23 May, pp. 4160–4164. DBLP (2008)
9. Zeng, Y., Liang, Y.C.: Eigenvalue based spectrum sensing algorithms for cognitive radio. IEEE Trans. Commun. **57**, 1784–1793 (2009)
10. Yucek, T., Arslan, H.: A survey of spectrum sensing algorithms for cognitive radio applications. IEEE Commun. Surv. Tutor. **11**, 116–130 (2009)

11. Amari, S.I.: Information geometry of statistical inference - an overview. In: Proceedings of the IEEE Information Theory Workshop (2002)
12. Liu, J.K., Wang, X.S., Tao, W., et al.: Application of information geometry to target detection for pulsed-doppler radar. Guofang Keji Daxue Xuebao/J. Natl. Univ. Def. Technol. **33**, 77–80 (2011)
13. Zhao, X., Wang, S.: An information geometric method for radar target detection. Signal Process. Chin. **6**, 631–637 (2015)
14. Xiang, L.: Information Geometry Method for Radar Signal Processing. Science Press in Chinese (2014)
15. Amari, S., Nagaoka, H.: Methods of Information Geometry. American Mathematical Society (2000)
16. Calvo, M., Oller, J.M.: A distance between multivariate normal distributions based in an embedding into the Siegel group. J. Comput. Appl. Math. **35**, 223–242 (1990)
17. Moakher, M., Batchelor, P.G.: Symmetric positive-definite matrices: from geometry to applications and visualization. In: Weickert, J., Hagen, H. (eds.) Visualization and Processing of Tensor Fields, pp. 285–298. Springer, Heidelberg (2006)
18. Pennec, X.: Intrinsic statistics on Riemannian manifolds: basic tools for geometric measurements. J. Math. Imaging Vis. **25**, 127–154 (2006)
19. Lenglet, C., Rousson, M., Deriche, R., et al.: Statistics on the manifold of multivariate normal distributions: theory and application to diffusion tensor MRI processing. J. Math. Imaging Vis. **25**, 442–444 (2006)
20. Lu, Q., Yang, S., Liu, F.: Wideband spectrum sensing based on riemannian distance for cognitive radio networks. Sens. Chin. **17**, 661 (2017)
21. Li, X.: Information Geometry Method for Radar Signal Processing. Science Press in Chinese (2014)
22. Moakher, M.: A differential geometric approach to the geometric mean of symmetric positive-definite matrices. SIAM J. Matrix Anal. Appl. **26**, 735–747 (2005)

Android Malware Detection Using Hybrid Analysis and Machine Learning Technique

Fan Yang, Yi Zhuang(✉), and Jun Wang

College of Computer Science and Technology,
Nanjing University of Aeronautics and Astronautics, Nanjing, China
yfwork@outlook.com, {zyl6, feihen1991}@nuaa.edu.cn

Abstract. This paper proposes a two-stage Android malware detection and classification mechanism based on machine learning algorithm. In this paper, we use the static analysis method to extract the software's package features, permission features, component features and triggering mechanism. Then we use the dynamic analysis tools to obtain the dynamic behavior characters of the software, and format the static and dynamic features. Finally, we use the machine learning algorithm to deal with the feature eigenvectors in two stages, and then we will get the malicious classification of the software. The experimental results show that in the data set used in this paper the proposed method based on the combination of dynamic and static malicious code detection is more accurate than the common detection engine, and the ability of classifying malicious family is much stronger.

Keywords: Android · Malware detection · Dynamic analysis · Static analysis · Machine learning

1 Introduction

Android system is the world's most popular mobile operating system. Gartner data shows that in the last quarter of 2016, 82% of the global sales of smart phones is based on the Android operating system [1]. The popularity of the Android system not only promoted the development of the smart phone market, but also provided an active site for many malicious code developers. Kaspersky found a total number of 296,177 malicious packages and 884,774 new mobile malwares in the Kaspersky Lab in 2015. Among them, the number of new malware increased three times [2] compared with the previous year. Meanwhile the malicious software technology is also evolving and the malwares become more and more complex in order to avoid detection. While Google has provided the Bouncer mechanism for Google Play to ensure that the submitted software is not malware, the attacker is still able to bypass the mechanism by well-designed software [3]. In addition, a large number of third-party application stores and active Android software forums are supervised chaotically, providing more opportunities for malware spread.

At present, malicious code detection technology includes two methods of static detection and dynamic detection. Malware detection technology based on static analysis mainly analyzes the features of software installation package, the use of decompilation

X. Sun et al. (Eds.): ICCCS 2017, Part II, LNCS 10603, pp. 565–575, 2017.
https://doi.org/10.1007/978-3-319-68542-7_48

technology as well as the control flow and code flow based on smali intermediate code to detect malicious code. But it is difficult to deal with code obfuscation, encryption, and the problem of decoding malicious code in dynamic execution. Researchers have considered techniques of encryption, dynamic loading of code, dynamic loading of native code in static analysis, such as Riskranker [4] and DroidRanger [5]. Although these methods can reflect the behavior of the software to some extent, but they can't get its actual operating logic. Android software dynamic analysis method installs the software in the Android system, and collects the information of the behavior of the application in its operation process. Dynamic analysis method has inherent advantages in dealing with code confusion, encryption and other issues. In the malicious code detection based on dynamic analysis we usually select features which include system calls [6], network behavior [7], system status [8] and so on. To extract the dynamic behavior of the software, the software to be analyzed is usually installed in a real device [8, 9] or sandbox environment [6, 10]. The use of dynamic stain analysis method can conduct software's behavior tracking and API monitoring. This method can make a real-time dynamic stain analysis of the system, and report sensitive information leakage and other events. The use of dynamic stain analysis technology can effectively obtain the malicious behavior of the software, typical research includes Droidbox [11] and Mobile-Sandbox [10] and so on. The above research work laid the foundation for the research of this paper.

The existing research selected all the samples of malware for analysis and use it as a basis for judging the malicious nature of the software. The malware of the same malware family has similar malicious behavior [12]. And malware belonging to different families have different malicious behaviors, and their malicious characteristics are also different. Malware detection which can give the software's families while determining its malicious is known as multi-label detection. The existing malware detection tool for malicious software is weak in multi-label detection, such as when McAfee detects a malicious sample in the Genome dataset, there will be more than 90% of the samples are detected as Trojan or Downloader, but in fact the samples belong to different malware families (such as DroidDream) [13]. To solve the problems mentioned above, this paper first uses the hybrid method to extract the characteristics of the software, and then designs the two-stage detection method based on machine learning to realize the multi-label detection of malware. In this paper we determine the malicious software at first, and then we determine the malware samples for further analysis to determine which Android malware family they belong to. Finally, multi-label detection of malware is implemented. To validate the effectiveness of this method, 3378 malware samples and 2140 benign software samples were tested. The results show that the proposed method can be used effectively for the multi - label detection of malware, and the accuracy of malware detection and malicious family classification is 95.9% and 94.8% respectively.

2 Overview

This paper first puts forward the multi-label detection method of Android malware based on static and dynamic combination method, and then designs the detection framework of malicious code. Finally, through the comparison experiment, this paper shows the superiority of the proposed method.

The Android malicious code detection framework based on the combination of static and dynamic method is shown in Fig. 1. The static analysis module mainly completes the software static feature extraction and triggering mechanism analysis, and the extracted features are formatted and stored locally. We use the tools to decompile the malware installation package and then use the python scripting tool to parse the resulting AndroidManifest.xml file. Then we will get the authority characteristics and component characteristics as a basis for judging the maliciousness of the software. Furthermore, the analysis of the software's malicious load triggering mechanism can provide guidance for the dynamic analysis process.

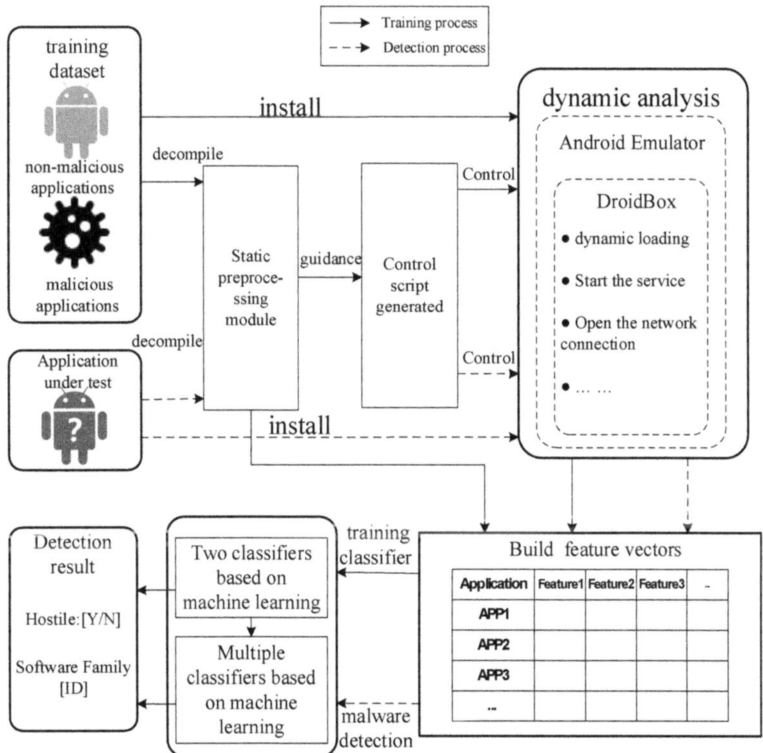

Fig. 1. Framework of malicious code detection

Dynamic behavior analysis module uses Android software dynamic analysis tool DroidBox to obtain the dynamic behavior of the software. We manipulate the software by learning the malicious load triggering mechanism of the software, and format the dynamic behavior of the acquired software to generate the feature vector. We construct the control script based on the analysis result of the static processing module to realize the automatic analysis of the software. Then we structure the above obtained static and dynamic features.

We use malicious and benign software to obtain the feature vector through the static processing and dynamic processing, and we use these feature vectors to train the classifier of the random forest algorithm. Then we pretreat the software which will be tested, and classifies the software according to the extracted software characteristics. In order to achieve multi-label detection of malicious software, this paper first determines whether the software is malware, and then determines which family the malware belongs to.

3 Feature Extraction Using Hybrid Analysis

In order to extract the characteristics of the software effectively, we use a mixed method to analyze the software which will be tested. There are static and dynamic analysis of the software features and their extracted methods.

3.1 Static Analysis

Android software static analysis mainly completes the progresses of the software static feature extraction and triggering mechanism analysis, and the extracted features are formatted and stored locally. Malware relies on the software package features, permission features and component features when executing malicious loads, and activated by different triggering mechanisms. Using static analysis method to obtain the software package features, permissions features and component features can be used as a basis for malicious judgments and could analyze the malicious load's triggering mechanism. At the same time, it can provide guidance for the dynamic analysis process.

Definition 1. The static features extracted by the static analysis module can be expressed as follows:

$$F_{static} = (E_f, E_p, E_c, E_a) \quad (1)$$

In formula (1):

(1) E_f is the set of software package features;
(2) E_p is the set of permissions for the software application;
(3) E_c is the set of components for the software claiming;
(4) E_a is the set of events for software monitoring.

Software package features can be obtained by decompiling the malware installation package. We use decompile tools to decompile the software installation package. In the decompiled package, we can get whether the package contains so library files, root explicit files, subroutines or exception.

The software's permissions features and component features can be obtained by decompiling the malware installation package in its AndroidManifest.xml file. To get the AndroidManifest.xml file, we can use anti-compiler tools to decompile the software installation package. Then we use the Python tool to parse the file to get the permissions for the software application and the components that are declared.

Malicious behavior of malware triggers typically involves triggering at startup, clicking, and listening system events. Malware behavior which automatically triggered by malicious loads at startup can be detected directly from the results of dynamic analysis. Click-triggered software is executed to trigger a malicious load when clicked on the appropriate location in the interface. This article uses the way of random click and drag to simulate the software click behavior. Malware triggered by monitoring the system event will perform its malicious load in a specific system state. This article will consider the system event as a software feature. And we use the adb command to simulate these system events in dynamic analysis.

3.2 Dynamic Analysis

In the dynamic analysis phase, first we use the Android SDK to create Android virtual device (Android Virtual Device, AVD), and start the Android system modified by DroidBox through the Android emulator. The software to be tested is installed in the Android emulator and the main active object of the software is activated by the script. Then we perform the MonkeyRunner script and the adb shell script constructed in the static analysis to simulate users' clicks and system events. Finally, we uninstall the software and record the analysis results of DroidBox and then restore the system to the initial state.

This article uses the Android software dynamic analysis tool DroidBox [11] which developed based on TaintDroid [14] to get the software running behavior. TaintDroid could provide track on message-level, variable-level, function-level and file-level. Meanwhile TaintDroid can do the real-time dynamic stain analysis to the system, and report sensitive information leaks and other events. TaintDroid tracks the stain spread behavior by marking the stains and capturing inter-process communication (IPC) of the Binder mechanism in Android, and prompting when a sensitive information leak occurs in an untrusted application.

We divides software behavior which obtained by the DroidBox into 10 categories, including: dynamic loading, starting services, receiving network data, sending network data, reading and writing files, opening network connections, closing network connections, sending text messages, making calls, using encryption algorithms.

Definition 2. We formalize the behavior of the software described above, then we can get the following formula:

$$F_{dynamic} = (E_{dl}, E_{ss}, E_{rnd}, E_{snd}, E_{rw}, E_{on}, E_{cnc}, E_{sm}, E_{mc}, E_{ua}) \tag{2}$$

In formula (2):

(1) E_{dl} is dynamic loading behavior, including dynamic load of dex files and jar files, and record the file names of the dynamic load;

(2) E_{ss} refers to staring the service, indicating the services of the software started during the dynamic process of operation;
(3) E_{rnd} refers to receiving network data and we will record the IP address and port number of the data receiving server;
(4) E_{snd} refers to sending network data and we will record the IP address and port number of the data sending server;
(5) E_{rw} refers to reading and writing file;
(6) E_{on} refers to opening the network connection and we will record the IP address and port number of the server;
(7) E_{cnc} refers to closing the network connection;
(8) E_{sm} refers to sending text messages and we will record the number and content of the message;
(9) E_{mc} refers to making a call and we will record the dialed number;
(10) E_{ua} refers to using the encryption algorithm and we will record the type of encryption algorithm and encryption keys.

4 Learning-Based Multi-label Detection

This section describes the malicious code detection based on machine learning. In order to make the static and dynamic feature of the software can match the input data format of the classifier, we introduce the software feature representation firstly. Then, according to the characteristics of software malicious determination and malicious family classification, we use the random forest algorithm to classify.

4.1 Embedding in Vector Space

Machine learning algorithm requires formatted input data, so we need to format the static and dynamic features of the software.

Definition 3. The feature vectors of the sample can be calculated from the static feature F_{static} and the dynamic feature $F_{dynamic}$. The definition is as following:

$$F = (F_{static}, F_{dynamic}) \tag{3}$$

For the extracted permissions feature, we consider the common permissions of malicious software given by Zhou [15] and Talha [16], as well as 22 dangerous rights in the Android software permissions provided by Google in its developer documentation. Then we remove the duplicates and permissions used infrequently, and finally we get 32 permissions to form a 32-dimensional vector.

For the component features, we extract the declaration of the service component and the broadcast receiver component. These declarations which have a total of four fields include the number of service components, which contains the number of service components in the <intent-filter> field, and include the number of declared broadcast receiver components, which contains the number of broadcast receiver components of the <intent-filter> field.

The software monitoring events extracted by the static analysis phase can reflect the triggering mechanism of malicious load. This paper constructs a feature vector containing 10 fields based on the system events which the malware usually listens to represent the system events that the software monitor.

For the dynamically extracted features, it is preferred to use 13 fields to indicate whether the dynamic behavior of the monitoring is present. And then to express the dynamic behavior of the subsidiary information and reflect the frequency of behavior, this paper uses the bag model (Bag-of-words Model) to build software dynamic behavior characteristics. At the same time, in order to reduce the dimension of dynamic behavior vector, this paper ignores three fields of the file name in the read and write files, network data in the receiving and transmitting network, and remove the records of opening the software in dynamic load.

4.2 Learning-Based Detection

To achieve multi-tag detection of malicious code, it is necessary to use a machine learning algorithm that supports multiple classification. And the accuracy of malicious code detection will decline if we use multiple classifiers for classification directly on all malicious and benign samples. Therefore, this paper proposes a two-stage classification mechanism based on machine learning algorithm. On the first stage we use a random forest-based two classifiers to determine the malicious nature of the software; on the second stage we use a random forest-based multi-classifier to determine the family which the malware belongs to.

5 Experiments and Evaluation

In order to verify the validity of the malicious code detection mechanism based on the combination of static and dynamic, this paper has carried out a series of experiments. This section gives the data set used in the experiment and the hardware and software environment, introduces the analysis effect of static and dynamic combination, and analyzes the detection effect of the method in the data set used.

5.1 Dataset and Experiment Setup

In our evaluation, Drebin [17] is used as our malware samples. This malware set is one of the largest and newest datasets of Android malwares which are publicly available today. It contains 5560 samples belonging to 179 families. To perform our statistical analysis we remove some families with few samples. And abnormal samples are removed since they can't run in Android emulator successfully. Finally, our malware dataset consists of 3378 instances belonging to 20 families. To build a benign dataset, we downloaded popular apps from Google Play. And we sent these apps to the VirusTotal service for inspection. The final benign dataset consists of 2140 samples. We conduct our experiment on a desktop with 3.4 GHz Intel® Core™ i7-3770 CPU and 16 GB of memory. The operating system is Ubuntu 16.04 LTS.

5.2 Malware Detection Results

At first, we experiment the method of the first stage of the malicious decision. We use the features extracted by the combination of static and dynamic method proposed previously to conduct a classification effect test for the common learning algorithms such as Random Forest (RF), Support Vector Machine (SVM), Naïve Bayes, Logistic Regression (LR), Decision Tree J48. The evaluation criteria of the selected machine learning include the True Positive Rate (TPR), also called Recall Rate, False Positive Rate (FPR), Precision, F-Measure and AUC (Area Under the Curve).

We use the above evaluation indicators to test different machine learning algorithms. Firstly, we extract the static and dynamic characteristics of all samples and store the eigenvectors of all the samples in the local file. We use the feature representation proposed in this paper to express the experimental results as a 256-dimensional eigenvector. Meanwhile, the sample feature vectors are marked according to the malicious nature of the software. We use the WEKA tool to test the 3778 malware sample features and 2140 benign software sample features using 10-fold cross-validation, and the test results are shown in Fig. 2.

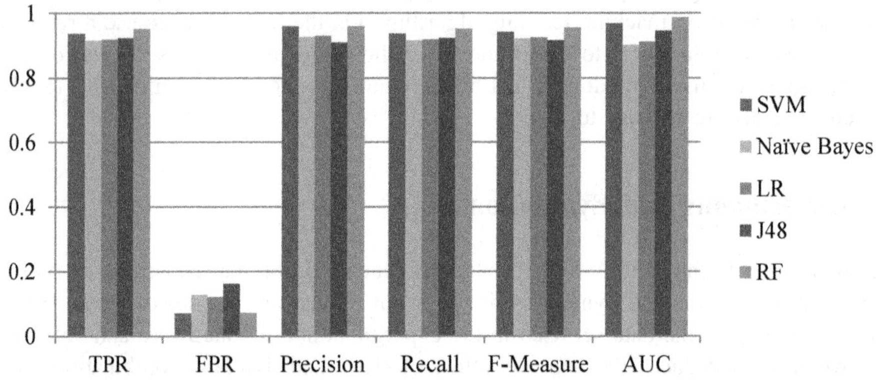

Fig. 2. Detection results of machine learning algorithms

Among the selected evaluation criteria such as TPR, FPR, Precision, Recall, F-Measure and AUC, AUC can correctly reflect the relationship between TPR and FPR. The higher the AUC value represents the superior performance of the selected classifier. In this paper, the random forest can achieve the highest AUC value, and the other indicators only FPR value is slightly lower than the SVM classifier. Therefore, the optimal performance of random forest is the best. Using the combination of static and dynamic methods designed to detect Android malicious code, we achieve a higher detection accuracy (95.9%) and recall rate (95.1%).

5.3 Malware Family Classification Results

The second stage of malicious code detection is experimented and analyzed to verify the accuracy of the proposed method based on random forest classification.

Since the second stage only deals with samples of the first stage that have been identified as malware, there is no need for a benign sample dataset in training the model. We randomly selected 70% (2644) of the malicious samples as the training set for this phase. The malicious feature vector of the first stage structure is further processed, and in order to realize the multi-class classification each sample is marked as the malicious family to which it belongs. The remaining 1134 malicious samples in the data set are used as test sets. The classification results are shown in Table 1. The table shows the results of 10 families with a large number of samples in the data set, other family test results are given together. The first column in the table is the malware family and the second column is the number of samples for each family in the test set. FN in this table indicates that the number of samples belong to the malware family F but is judged as benign or other family. FP represents the number of samples which not belong to the malware family F, but classified as the malware family F.

Table 1. Android malware family classification results

Family ID	TP	FN	FP	Accuracy	Recall
FakeInstaller	236	4	1	98.5%	98.5%
Opfake	181	4	2	98.2%	98.3%
DroidKungFu	156	5	1	99.6%	96.8%
BaseBrige	97	3	0	100.0%	96.9%
Plankton	85	1	1	99.1%	98.8%
Iconosys	45	2	2	96.2%	95.7%
Kmin	44	1	3	94.9%	97.9%
FakeDoc	38	2	4	90.9%	95.2%
DroidDream	25	3	3	89.3%	89.3%
Gappusin	17	3	2	88.9%	84.2%
Others	210	32	43	83.7%	87.4%
Total	1134	60	62	94.8%	95.0%

The experimental results show that the accuracy of the malicious family classification based on random forest is 94.8% and the recall rate is 95.0%. And it can solve the problem that Drebin can't detect the Gappusin family. Through the analysis of the data, we can find that the classification accuracy and recall rate of the malicious families are higher when there are more samples. And when the number of detection samples is more than 85 (the number of training samples is 237) as a result the detection accuracy is more than 98% and the recall rate is higher than 96%. On the other hand, the less sample of the malicious family results detection effect is relatively poor. By observing the number of samples of different malicious families, we can see that the data processed in this experiment is imbalance data. Random forest algorithm to sample fewer family can only receive less training samples when the sample is returned to the samples, causing a decrease in classification accuracy. As in the Android malicious code detection, we focus on the effectiveness of the detection method, rather than solve the impact of unbalanced data on the detection effect, so we can improve the random forest classification accuracy by collecting more malicious family samples.

We submitted the 1134 samples of the test dataset to the VirusTotal online test. After removing the 13 engines with poor performance, the accuracy of the remaining 45 detection engines for all samples was 78.4% and the classification accuracy was 34.7%. If we use all the results of the test engine to vote on the way to determine the malicious nature of any sample, the detection accuracy is 94.5%. The comparisons between the test results of our method and the test results of the eight anti-virus engines (Ad-Aware, AVG, Avira, BitDefender, DrWeb, F-Secure, GData, Kaspersky) are shown in Table 2.

Table 2. Comparison with AVs

Precision (%)	AV1	AV2	AV3	AV4	AV5	AV6	AV7	AV8	Ours
Detection	95.6	92.9	87.8	93.8	91.5	94.6	92.8	91.8	95.9
Classification	46.8	41.7	49.2	58.1	46.7	54.2	56.7	70.8	94.8

As can be seen from Table 3, by using the Android malicious code detection method based on the combination of static and dynamic design, the detection accuracy of the data set used in this paper is slightly higher than that of the common detection engine, and the classification ability of the malicious family is stronger.

6 Conclusions and Feature Work

This paper presents an Android malicious code detection mechanism based on static and dynamic combination. According to the characteristics of different stages of malicious code in multi-label detection, this paper designs the Android malicious code detection framework based on static and dynamic combination, and obtains the software features through static preprocessing and dynamic feature extraction. And then we construct the static and dynamic feature vector of software, and propose a malicious code detection method based on random forest algorithm. The experimental results show that the use of static and dynamic analysis of the method can obtain the malicious behavior of the software accurately. Through the malicious code detection based on static and dynamic characteristics, we can achieve higher detection accuracy. In the next work, we will try to analyze some of the connection between software dynamic behaviors. We hope that the real-time decision of the malicious software not only limited to use statistical methods, but also through some malicious software attack mode.

Acknowledgments. This work is supported by the National Natural Science Foundation of China (General Program) under Grant No. 61572253, the Aeronautical Science Foundation of China under Grant No. 2016ZC52030.

References

1. Gartner. http://www.gartner.com/newsroom/id/3323017
2. Securelist. https://securelist.com/analysis/kaspersky-security-bulletin/73839/mobile-malware-evolution-2015/
3. Maier, D., Muller, T., Protsenko, M.: Divide-and-conquer: why android malware cannot be stopped. In: Ninth International Conference on Availability, Reliability and Security, pp. 30–39 (2014)
4. Grace, M., Zhou, Y., Zhang, Q., Zou, S., Jiang, X.: RiskRanker: scalable and accurate zero-day android malware detection. In: International Conference on Mobile Systems, Applications, and Services, pp. 281–294 (2012)
5. Zhou, Y., Wang, Z., Zhou, W., Jiang, X.: Hey, you, get off of my market: detecting malicious apps in official and alternative android markets. In: Proceedings of Annual Network & Distributed System Security Symposium, pp. 50–52 (2012)
6. Dimja, M., Atzeni, S., Ugrina, I., Rakamaric, Z.: Evaluation of android malware detection based on system calls. In: ACM on International Workshop on Security and Privacy Analytics, pp. 1–8 (2016)
7. Shabtai, A., Tenenboim-Chekina, L., Mimran, D., Rokach, L., Shapira, B., Elovici, Y.: Mobile malware detection through analysis of deviations in application network behavior. Comput. Secur. **43**, 1–18 (2014)
8. Shabtai, A., Kanonov, U., Elovici, Y., Glezer, C., Weiss, Y.: "Andromaly": a behavioral malware detection framework for android devices. J. Intell. Inf. Syst. **38**, 161–190 (2012)
9. Burguera, I., Zurutuza, U., Nadjm-Tehrani, S.: Crowdroid: behavior-based malware detection system for Android. In: ACM Workshop on Security and Privacy in Smartphones and Mobile Devices, pp. 15–26 (2011)
10. Spreitzenbarth, M., Schreck, T., Echtler, F., Arp, D., Hoffmann, J.: Mobile-Sandbox: combining static and dynamic analysis with machine-learning techniques. Int. J. Inf. Secur. **14**, 141–153 (2015)
11. Lantz, P., Desnos, A., Yang, K.: DroidBox: android application sandbox (2012)
12. Yang, C., Xu, Z., Gu, G., Yegneswaran, V., Porras, P.: DroidMiner: automated mining and characterization of fine-grained malicious behaviors in android applications. In: Kutyłowski, M., Vaidya, J. (eds.) ESORICS 2014. LNCS, vol. 8712, pp. 163–182. Springer, Cham (2014). doi:10.1007/978-3-319-11203-9_10
13. Zhang, M., Duan, Y., Yin, H., Zhao, Z.: Semantics-aware android malware classification using weighted contextual API dependency graphs. In: Proceedings of the 2014 ACM SIGSAC Conference on Computer and Communications Security, pp. 1105–1116 (2014)
14. Enck, W., Gilbert, P., Han, S., Tendulkar, V., Chun, B.-G., Cox, L.P., Jung, J., McDaniel, P., Sheth, A.N.: TaintDroid: an information-flow tracking system for realtime privacy monitoring on smartphones. ACM Trans. Comput. Syst. (TOCS) **32**, 5 (2014)
15. Zhou, Y., Jiang, X.: Dissecting Android malware: characterization and evolution. In: 2012 IEEE Symposium on Security and Privacy, pp. 95–109 (2012)
16. Talha, K.A., Alper, D.I., Aydin, C.: APK auditor: permission-based android malware detection system. Digit. Invest. **13**, 1–14 (2015)
17. Arp, D., Spreitzenbarth, M., Hübner, M., Gascon, H., Rieck, K.: DREBIN: effective and explainable detection of android malware in your pocket. In: Network and Distributed System Security Symposium (2014)

Workload-Aware Page-Level Flash Translation Layer for NAND Flash-Based Storage Systems

Huibing Wang[1], Mingwei Lin[2], Jinbo Xiong[2], Li Lin[1], and Ruliang Xiao[1(✉)]

[1] College of Mathematics and Informatics, Fujian Normal University, Fuzhou 350108, China
wanghbfjnu@163.com, llfjfz@163.com, xiaoruliang@163.com

[2] Fujian Engineering Research Center of Public Service Big Data Mining and Application, Fuzhou 350108, China
linmwcs@163.com, jinbo810@163.com

Abstract. Demand-based flash translation layer is an efficient page-level flash translation layer, which can effectively reduce the RAM (Random Access Memory) footprint of NAND flash-based storage systems. However, this demand-based flash translation layer does not consider the spatial locality of workloads. In this paper, a new workload-aware page-level flash translation layer is proposed for NAND flash-based storage systems. The proposed flash translation layer maintains three caches in RAM to cache mapping entries, which are the on-demand mapping entry cache, frequent mapping entry cache, and dirty mapping entry cache. Considering both temporal locality and spatial locality of workloads, the on-demand mapping entry cache is designed to store the on-demand mapping entries and sequential mapping entries. Considering the access frequency of workloads, the frequent mapping entry cache is designed to cache the most frequently accessed mapping entries. To decrease the number of updates to translation pages, the dirty mapping entry cache is designed to cache the dirty mapping entries and flush the dirty mapping entries belonging to the same translation page to NAND flash memory in a batch mode. The experimental results show that the proposed flash translation layer performs better than existing page-level flash translation layers.

Keywords: Flash translation layer · Temporal locality · Spatial locality · Access frequency

1 Introduction

Because of the mechanical nature of hard disks [1], the performance gap between CPU and hard disk based storage systems has increased exponentially in recent years. The hard disk based storage system has become the performance bottleneck of computer systems. To meet the needs of today's performance hungry applications, a variety of clever approaches have been used to bridge this performance gap. These approaches

X. Sun et al. (Eds.): ICCCS 2017, Part II, LNCS 10603, pp. 576–588, 2017.
https://doi.org/10.1007/978-3-319-68542-7_49

range from using the very limited amounts of expensive cache memory to various RAID schemes and intelligent firmware [2]. Although these approaches can greatly improve the I/O performance of hard disk based storage systems, the I/O performance of hard disk based storage systems still cannot keep up with the I/O performance of CPU [3–6].

NAND flash memory is an electronic non-volatile storage medium that can retain its data even when it is not powered electrically [7]. It has a large number of advantages such as non-volatility, fast access speed, strong shock resistance, small size, and low power consumption [8]. It has become the dominant data storage medium for consumer electronics. With the rapid progress of semiconductor manufacturing technology, the storage capacity of a single NAND flash memory chip is increasing, while the cost-per-bit is decreasing dramatically. This improvement makes NAND flash memory be used to improve the I/O performance of enterprise-scale storage systems [9]. For example, Facebook and Google companies have introduced NAND flash memory based solid state drives (SSD) to be a part of their storage systems.

However, NAND flash memory shows very different physical characteristics from hard disks and traditional file systems are optimized for hard disks. Hence, traditional file systems cannot be employed for NAND flash memory directly. In this case, a large number of flash translation layers have been proposed for NAND flash memory to hide its unique physical characteristics. The flash translation layer is deployed between the traditional file system and NAND flash memory in the storage systems [10]. It emulates NAND flash memory as a block device like hard disks and then traditional file systems can operate and also manage NAND flash memory smoothly by using flash translation layer without any modification. It usually has three main functions, which are the address translation, garbage collection, and wear leveling. The address translation translates logical addresses from file systems to physical addresses in NAND flash memory [11]. The garbage collection is triggered to reclaim the garbage in terms of invalid pages caused by the out-of-place update and then obtain free space for NAND flash memory [12]. The wear leveling is employed to wear out all the blocks as evenly as possible and then extend the lifetime of NAND flash memory [13].

To perform the address translation between logical addresses and physical addresses, the flash translation layer needs to maintain a huge mapping table in the RAM (Random Access Memory). The mapping table is composed of mapping entries that record the mappings from logical addresses to physical addresses. With the increasing storage capacity of NAND flash memory, the mapping table becomes bigger and bigger. However, because of the high cost of RAM, the size of RAM is severely constrained and then the mapping table greatly degrades the overall performance of flash translation layer. In order to address this problem, an efficient demand-based flash translation layer called DFTL has been proposed for NAND flash-based storage systems to store the whole mapping table in NAND flash memory and then selectively cache the on-demand mapping entries in the RAM [14]. However, DFTL only considers the temporal locality of workloads and does not consider the spatial locality and access frequency of workloads. Moreover, it usually incurs many updates to translation pages, especially for write-intensive workloads. A large number of updates to translation pages will incur massive write operations and garbage collection operations. Both of them are energy-consuming and time-consuming.

To deal with the problems of demand-based flash translation layer, a new workload-aware page-level flash translation layer is proposed for NAND flash-based storage systems in this paper. The proposed flash translation layer maintains three caches in the RAM to selectively cache the mapping entries, which are the on-demand mapping entry cache, frequent mapping entry cache, and dirty mapping entry cache. In order to consider both temporal locality and spatial locality of workloads, the on-demand mapping entry cache is employed to cache the on-demand mapping entries and sequential mapping entries. Because of the access frequency of workloads, the frequent mapping entry cache is used to cache the most frequently accessed mapping entries. To decrease the number of updates to translation pages, the dirty mapping entry cache is employed to cache the dirty mapping entries and flush the dirty mapping entries belonging to the same translation page into the NAND flash memory in a batch mode. The experimental results show that the proposed flash translation layer obtains better performance than previous page-level flash translation layers in terms of cache hit ratio, translation page read count, translation page write count, block erase count, and average system response time.

The rest of this paper is organized as follows. Section 2 shows the overview of NAND flash memory. Section 3 briefly reviews existing works on flash translation layer. Section 4 presents the detailed implementation of the proposed workload-aware page-level flash translation layer. The performance evaluation is given in Sect. 5. Finally, conclusions are drawn in Sect. 6.

2 Overview of NAND Flash Memory

Flash memory is a kind of electronic non-volatile computer storage medium, which can retain the stored data even when it is not powered electrically. There are two main types of flash memory, which are the NOR flash memory and NAND flash memory. They shows very different structures of the interconnections between the individual memory cells and then they have different physical characteristics [15].

In NOR flash memory, the individual memory cells are connected in parallel to the bit lines, which allows the NOR flash memory to be accessed randomly at the byte level. NOR flash memory has an execute-in-place capability, which enables the applications to be executed in NOR flash memory directly instead of loading them into the main memory. This makes it a suitable replacement for storing the BIOS of computers or firmware of consumer electronics, which rarely needs to be updated. However, it is more expensive than NAND flash memory and it has very small storage capacity. Therefore, NOR flash memory is typically employed for code storage and direct execution [16].

In NAND flash memory, a group of individual memory cells are connected in series just like a NAND gate. The series connection of NAND flash memory consumes less space than the parallel connection of NOR flash memory. This makes NAND flash memory have greater storage density and lower cost-per-bit than NOR flash memory. It also has up to ten times the endurance of NOR flash memory. Hence, NAND flash memory is usually employed for data storage in portable consumer electronics. For example, some notebook computers are equipped with NAND flash memory based solid state drives as their secondary storage devices [17].

A NAND flash memory chip is composed of a fixed number of blocks. Each block also consists of a fixed number of pages. Each page has two parts, which are the main area and spare area. The main area is used for storing the user data and the spare area is used to store the error correction code checksum [18]. There are three basic operations that can be performed on a NAND flash memory chip, namely read, write, and erase. Read operation is used to read the data from a page and write operation is performed to write the data to a target page. Hence, the basic unit of read operation and write operation is a page. Erase operation is performed to erase a victim block after its valid data are migrated to a free block. Therefore, the basic unit of erase operation is a block.

NAND flash memory exhibits three unique characteristics [19]. First, it shows an erase-before-write hardware constraint. It often introduces an out-of-place update scheme to deal with this hardware constraint. The out-of-place update scheme writes the new data to the free space and then invalidates the original data as invalid. Second, It has the asymmetric costs for three basic operations. The write operation cost is higher than the read operation cost, the erase operation cost is higher than the write operation cost. Third, the number of erase count allowed to each block is very limited, typically 10,000–100,000. If the number of erase count of a block is exceeded, this block will suffer from frequent write errors. Hence, a number of wear leveling algorithms have been proposed for NAND flash memory to erase all the block as evenly as possible and then the lifetime of NAND flash memory can be extended.

3 Related Work

In order to avoid the unique physical characteristics of NAND flash memory, a number of flash translation layers have been proposed for NAND flash-based storage systems. There are mainly three types of flash translation layers, which are the page-level flash translation layer, block-level flash translation layer, and hybrid flash translation layer.

In the page-level flash translation layer, a mapping table is maintained to store the mapping information between the logical page number and the physical page number. When a request is sent from the file system to the NAND flash-based storage device, its logical page number can be translated into any physical page in NAND flash memory. Hence, it obtains the high space utilization of blocks in NAND flash memory. However, it should maintain a large mapping table in the main memory [20]. Due to the high cost-per-bit, the storage capacity of main memory is small. Hence, the large mapping table could degrade the performance of NAND flash-based storage systems.

In the block-level flash translation layer, the mapping table is introduced to store the translation information between logical block number and physical block number [21]. When a request is sent from the file system to the NAND flash memory, its logical page number is divided into two parts: logical block number and offset. The logical block number can be translated into the physical block number by using the mapping table and then the physical block, which serves the request, is determined. Finally, the offset is employed to further locate the page, which serves the request, in the located physical block. The mapping table in the block-level flash translation layer only maintains the translation information between the logical block number and physical block number, so the block-level flash translation layer exhibits less memory footprint than the page-level flash translation layer. However, its space utilization of blocks within the NAND flash memory is very low, especially for strong locality of references. Then the time-consuming and energy-consuming garbage collection is frequently incurred to reclaim garbage.

To overcome the shortcomings of above two flash translation layers, the hybrid flash translation layer is introduced to achieve a trade-off between the main memory footprint and address translation efficiency. It divides the entire NAND flash memory into two types of blocks logically, which are the data block and log/update block, respectively [22–26]. The data blocks are used to store the original data and they are mapped using the block-level mapping scheme. The log blocks are employed to store the update data of the original data within the data blocks and their pages are mapped using the page-level mapping scheme. Since the percentage of log/update blocks is very small, the hybrid flash translation layer can reduce the memory footprint efficiently. Using the page-level mapping scheme to map the pages within the log/update blocks can also improve the space utilization of blocks within the NAND flash-based storage device. However, it incurs a large amount of garbage collection overhead.

In recent years, a demand-based flash translation layer (DFTL) is proposed, which is a kind of page-level flash translation layer. DFTL stores the entire mapping table in the NAND flash memory and then selectively caches the on-demand mapping entries in the main memory. DFTL not only reduces the main memory footprint significantly, but also obtains a high space utilization of blocks. However, DFTL only considers the temporal locality of workloads and does not consider the spatial locality and access frequency of workloads. Moreover, it usually generates many updates to the translation pages, especially for write-intensive workloads. A large number of updates to translation pages will incur a large number of write operations and garbage collection operations, which are energy-consuming and time-consuming [14].

4 Workload-Aware Page-Level Flash Translation Layer

In this section, a efficient workload-aware page-level flash translation layer called WPFTL is put forward for NAND flash-based storage systems.

4.1 Design Overview

The system architecture of the proposed WPFTL is illustrated in Fig. 1. In WPFTL, the physical pages within the NAND flash-based storage device are categorized into two types, which are the data pages and translation pages. The data pages are used to store the real data that are accessed or updated by I/O requests and they are mapped by the page-level address translation scheme. The translation pages are employed to store the data page mapping table that stores the translation information between the logical data page number (DLDPN) and the physical data page number (DPDPN). They are mapped using the page-level address translation scheme. Their corresponding translation page mapping table stores the translation information between the virtual translation page number (TVTPN) and the physical translation page number (TPTPN) and it is maintained in the main memory.

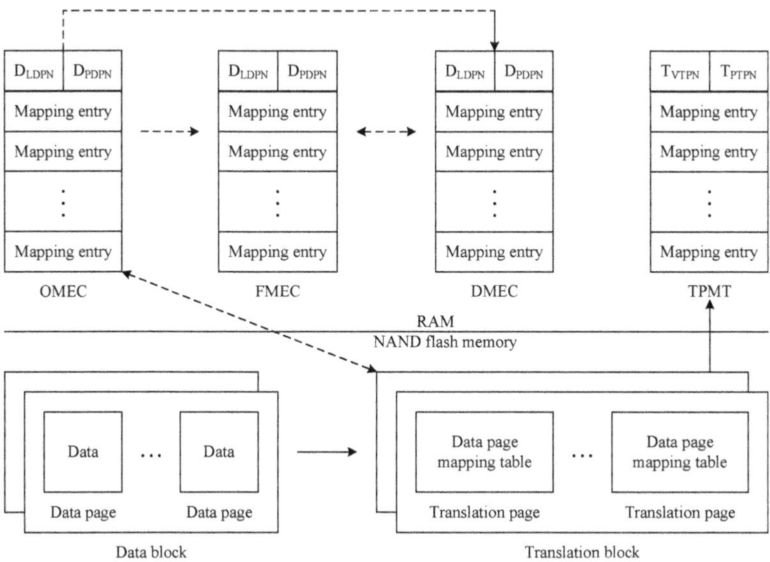

Fig. 1. System architecture of WPFTL.

As illustrated by the single-ended arrow with a solid line in Fig. 1, the data page mapping table is stored in the translation pages, while the translation page mapping table is stored in the main memory. In order to exploit the locality of references and decrease the number of updates to translation pages, the proposed WPFTL maintains three caches in the RAM, which are the on-demand mapping entry cache (OMEC), frequent mapping entry cache (FMEC), and dirty mapping entry cache (DMEC). The on-demand mapping entry cache is employed to cache the on-demand mapping entries and sequential mapping entries. The frequent mapping entry cache is used to cache the most frequently accessed mapping entries. The dirty mapping entry cache is used to cache the dirty mapping entries that are evicted from the on-demand mapping entry cache or frequent mapping entry cache. Different cache replacement policies are proposed for different caches.

4.2 Address Translation Process

Algorithm 1 describes the address translation process when the proposed WPFTL services a request from the file system. The proposed WPFTL first searches for the requested mapping entry in the caches in the order of frequent mapping entry cache, on-demand mapping entry cache, and dirty mapping entry cache. If the requested mapping entry hits in the caches, the corresponding translation information will be obtained and then the request will be serviced directly. Otherwise, WPFTL needs to fetch the requested mapping entry from NAND flash memory as follows (Fig. 2).

WPFTL determine if the size of the request is larger than a predefined threshold or not. If yes, WPFTL exploits the spatial locality of references and loads the requested

Algorithm 1 Address_Translation

```
Input: The logical page number of the request (request_lpn)
       The size of the request (request_size)
Output: NULL
while request_size≠0 do
   if request_lpn is in FMEC then
         service the request;
   else if request_lpn is in OMEC then
         service the request;
         if FMEC is full then
                evict a mapping entry from FMEC;
                remove the requested mapping entry from OMEC to FMEC;
         end
   else if request_lpn is in DMEC then
         service the request;
         if the FMEC is full then
                evict a mapping entry from FMEC;
                remove the corresponding mapping entry from DMEC to FMEC;
         end
   else if request_size ≥Threshold then
         if OMEC is full then
                evict eight mapping entries from OMEC;
         end
         load the requested mapping entry and its following seven mapping entries into OMEC;
         service the request;
   else
         if OMEC is full then
                evict a mapping entry from OMEC;
         end
         load the requested mapping entry into OMEC;
         service the request;
   end
   request_size--;
end
```

Fig. 2. Address translation process.

mapping entry and its following seven mapping entries into the on-demand mapping entry cache. Otherwise, WPFTL exploits the temporal locality of references and only loads the requested mapping entry into the on-demand mapping entry cache.

4.3 Cache Replacement Policies

In the OMEC, an efficient update-aware LRU (UALRU) replacement algorithm is designed to evict a mapping entry for obtaining free space. The UALRU replacement algorithm first selects the LRU mapping entry as the victim mapping entry candidate. If the victim mapping entry candidate has not been updated, it will be evicted from OMEC directly. Otherwise, it will be removed from OMEC to DMEC and then select a new victim mapping entry candidate. FMEC also employs the UALRU replacement algorithm. First evicting the mapping entry that is not updated and storing the updated mapping entry in the DMEC can reduce the number of updates to translation pages.

In the DMEC, an efficient classification-based replacement algorithm is introduced to evict a group of mapping entries and obtain the free space. It classifies all the mapping entries in the DMEC by grouping the mapping entries belonging to the same translation page into a cluster. When DMEC is full, the classification-based replacement algorithm evicts the cluster having the most mapping entries from the DMEC and then all the mapping entries in this cluster are written back to the NAND flash-based storage device.

5 Performance Evaluation

In this section, the experimental setup and performance metrics are described in Sect. 5.1. Section 5.2 presents the experimental results.

5.1 Experimental Setup and Performance Metrics

To evaluate the performance of the proposed WPFTL, FlashSim is employed to conducted a series of trace-driven simulation experiments. FlashSim is a simulator of solid state disk and it is developed by enhancing the DiskSim, which is a disk drive simulator. In the simulation experiments, a 1 GB NAND flash memory device is simulated and its simulation parameters are listed in Table 1. The WPFTL is compared with the demand-based flash translation layer (DFTL) and they are implemented in the FlashSim.

Table 1. Simulation parameters of NAND flash memory.

Basic operation	Access granularity	Access time
Read	Page (2 KB)	130.9 μs
Write	Page (2 KB)	405.9 μs
Erase	Block (128 KB)	1.5 ms

A mixture of real-world and synthetic traces are employed to study the performance of these two flash translation layers under various enterprise-scale workloads. Table 2 presents the characteristics of these traces. Fin1 and Fin2 are two Financial traces collected from OLTP applications running at a financial institution. Web1 and Web2 are two read-dominant Web search engine traces. All these four traces are provided by the Storage Performance Council. Syn1 and Syn2 are two synthetic traces, which are produced by DiskSim. Five performance metrics that are used in the simulation experiments, which are the cache hit ratio, translation page read count, translation page write count, block erase count, and average system response time.

Table 2. The characteristics of traces.

Traces	Number of requests	Write (%)	Average request size (kb)	Average arrive time (ms)
Fin1	5344983	76.84	3.38	8.19
Fin2	3699194	17.65	2.39	11.08
Web1	85111	0.12	16.90	37.03
Web2	348439	0.14	17.13	44.18
Syn1	400000	34.18	7.10	16.02
Syn2	450000	63.98	8.42	19.98

5.2 Experimental Results

Figure 3 shows the experimental results for various flash translation layers in terms of cache hit ratio. The WPFTL exploits the temporal locality, spatial locality, and access frequency of workloads, while the DFTL only exploits the temporal locality of workloads. Therefore, the proposed WPFTL gets higher cache hit ratio than the DFTL, especially for Web1 and Web2 traces, which exhibit strong spatial locality.

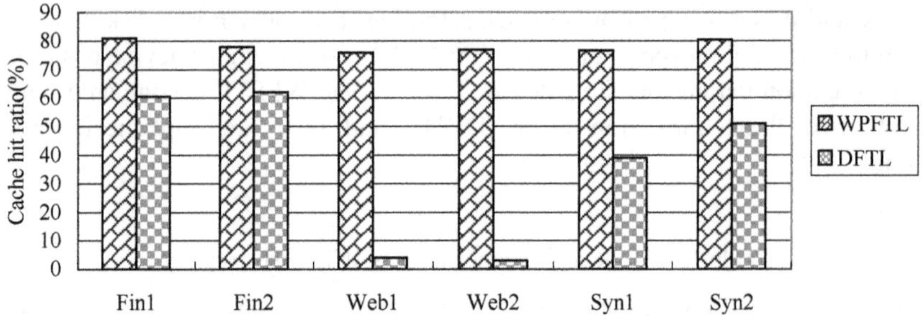

Fig. 3. Cache hit ratios for various flash translation layers.

Figure 4 shows the normalized translation page read count for various flash translation layers. If the requested mapping entry is not cached in the RAM, the WPFTL and DFTL will read the translation page that contains the requested mapping entry. Hence, the normalized translation page read count of each flash translation layer depends on its cache hit ratio. Since WPFTL gets higher cache hit ratio than DFTL, it incurs less translation page read count than DFTL.

Figure 5 shows the normalized translation page write count for various flash translation layers. The proposed WPFTL gives the mapping entries that have been updated a second chance to stay in the dirty mapping entry cache and then the translation page write count can be reduced. In order to further decrease the translation page write count, the dirty mapping entry cache groups the mapping entries belonging to the same translation page into a cluster and evicts all the mapping entries in the cluster that has the most mapping entries in a batch mode. Hence, the proposed WPFTL incurs less translation page write count than DFTL.

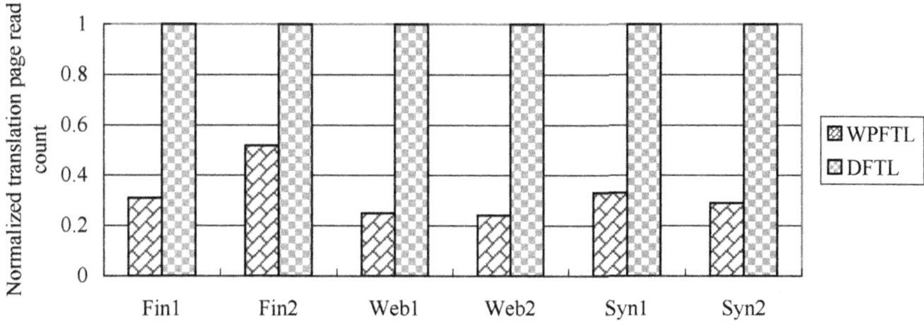

Fig. 4. Normalized translation page read counts for various flash translation layers.

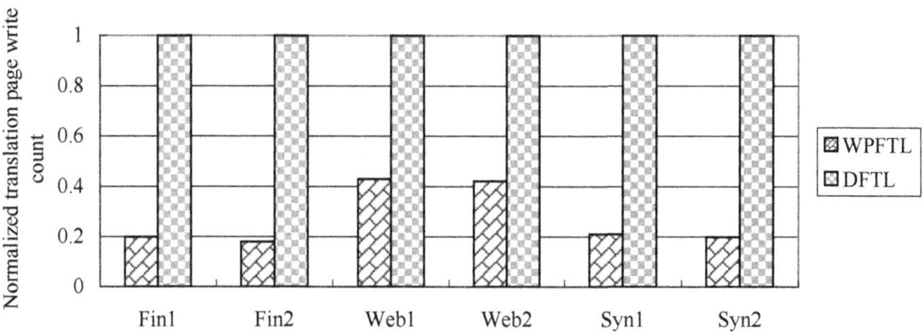

Fig. 5. Normalized translation page write count for various flash translation layers.

Table 3 lists the block erase counts for various flash translation layers. Because the erase operation is executed during the garbage collection operation, the block erase count depends on the number of garbage collection operations. The proposed WPFTL shows less translation page write count than DFTL, so it generates less garbage collection operations than DFTL and then it incurs less block erase count than DFTL.

Table 3. Block erase count for various flash translation layers.

Traces	WPFTL	DFTL
Fin1	276383	356655
Fin2	32235	42770
Web1	10	12
Web2	39	50
Syn1	48305	64821
Syn2	106220	142082

Figure 6 shows the experimental results for various flash translation layers in terms of average response time. The average response time is an important metric, which is used to assess the performance of various flash translation layers and it mainly depends on the cache hit ratio, translation page read count, translation page write count, and erase count. Since the WPFTL exhibits higher cache hit ratio, less translation page read count, translation page write count, and block erase count than DFTL, it takes WPFTL less average response time than DFTL.

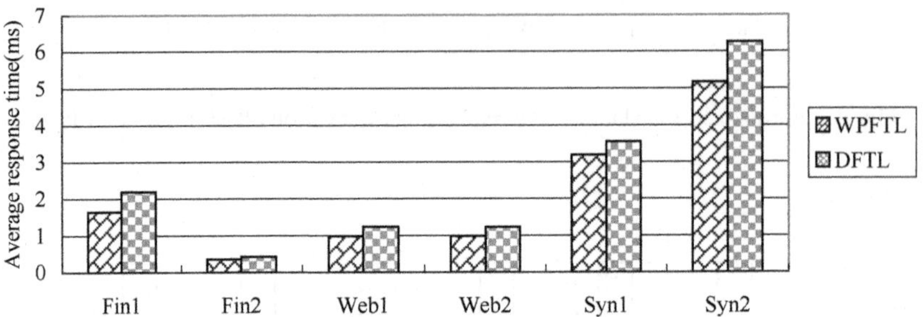

Fig. 6. Average response time for various flash translation layers.

6 Conclusion

In this paper, a novel workload-aware page-level flash translation layer called WPFTL is proposed for NAND flash-based storage systems. It stores the entire mapping table in NAND flash-based storage device like the demand-based flash translation layer. It maintains three caches in the main memory, which are the on-demand mapping entry cache, frequent mapping entry cache, and dirty mapping entry cache. The on-demand mapping entry cache is used to cache the on-demand mapping entries and sequential mapping entries. The frequent mapping entry cache is used to cache the most frequently accessed mapping entries. The dirty mapping entry cache is used to cache the mapping entries that are evicted from the on-demand mapping entry cache and frequent mapping entry cache and flush mapping entries in a batch mode. A series of simulation experiments have been conducted and encouraging results are obtained.

Acknowledgments. This work was supported by the National Natural Science Foundation of China under Grant Nos. 61502102, 61402109, and 61502103; Natural Science Foundation of Fujian Province, China under Grant Nos. 2016J05149, 2015J05120, and 2017J01737; Fujian Provincial Key Laboratory of Network Security and Cryptology Research Fund (Fujian Normal University) (No. 15008); and Distinguished Young Scientific Research Talents Plan in Universities of Fujian Province (2017).

References

1. Xia, Y., Zhou, M., Luo, X., Pang, S., Zhu, Q.: A stochastic approach to analysis of energy-aware DVS-enabled cloud datacenters. IEEE Trans. Syst. Man Cybern. Syst. **45**(1), 73–83 (2015)

2. Fu, Z., Ren, K., Shu, J., Sun, X., Huang, F.: Enabling personalized search over encrypted outsourced data with efficiency improvement. IEEE Trans. Parallel Distrib. Syst. **27**(9), 2546–2559 (2016)
3. Xia, Y., Zhou, M., Luo, X., Pang, S., Zhu, Q.: Stochastic modeling and performance analysis of migration-enabled and error-prone clouds. IEEE Trans. Ind. Inf. **11**(2), 495–504 (2015)
4. Ren, Y., Shen, J., Wang, J., Han, J., Lee, S.: Mutual verifiable provable data auditing in public cloud storage. J. Internet Technol. **16**(2), 317–323 (2015)
5. Guo, P., Wang, J., Geng, X.H., Kim, C.S., Kim, J.U.: A variable threshold-value authentication architecture for wireless mesh networks. J. Internet Technol. **15**(6), 929–936 (2014)
6. Shen, J., Tan, H., Wang, J., Wang, J., Lee, S.: A novel routing protocol providing good transmission reliability in underwater sensor networks. J. Internet Technol. **16**(1), 171–178 (2015)
7. Zhang, Q., Li, X., Wang, L., Zhang, T., Wang, Y., Shao, Z.: Lazy-RTGC: a real-time lazy garbage collection mechanism with jointly optimizing average and worst performance for NAND flash memory storage systems. ACM Trans. Design Autom. Electron. Syst. **20**(3), Article No. 43 (2015)
8. Huang, M., Liu, Z., Qiao, L.: Asymmetric programming: a highly reliable metadata allocation strategy for MLC NAND flash memory-based sensor systems. Sensors **14**(10), 18851–18877 (2014)
9. Nam, B.W., Na, G.J., Lee, S.W.: A hybrid flash memory SSD scheme for enterprise database applications. In: Proceedings of the 12th Asia-Pacific Web Conference, Busan, Korea, pp. 39–44 (2010)
10. Chung, T.S., Park, D.J., Park, S., Lee, D.H., Lee, S.W., Song, H.J.: A survey of flash translation layer. J. Syst. Archit. **55**(5–6), 332–343 (2009)
11. Ma, D., Feng, J., Li, G.: A survey of address translation technologies for flash memories. ACM Comput. Surv. **46**(3), Article No. 36 (2014)
12. Kwon, O., Koh, K., Lee, J., Bahn, H.: FeGC: an efficient garbage collection scheme for flash memory based storage systems. J. Syst. Softw. **84**(9), 1507–1523 (2011)
13. Liao, J., Zhang, F., Li, L., Xiao, G.: Adaptive wear-leveling in flash-based memory. IEEE Comput. Archit. Lett. **14**(1), 1–4 (2015)
14. Gupta, A., Kim, Y., Urgaonkar, B.: DFTL: a flash translation layer employing demand-based selective caching of page-level address mappings. ACM SIGPLAN Not. **44**(3), 229–240 (2009)
15. Qin, Z., Wang, Y., Liu, D., Shao, Z.: A two-level caching mechanism for demand-based page-level address mapping in NAND flash memory storage systems. In: Proceedings of the 17th IEEE Real-Time and Embedded Technology and Applications Symposium, Chicago, IL, USA, pp. 157–166 (2011)
16. Chang, Y.H., Hsieh, J.W., Lin, J.H., Kuo, T.W.: A strategy to emulate NOR flash with NAND flash. ACM Trans. Storage. **6**(2), Article No. 5 (2010)
17. Guan, Y., Wang, G., Wang, Y., Chen, R., Shao, Z.: BLog: block-level log-block management for NAND flash memorystorage systems. ACM SIGPLAN Not. **48**(5), 111–120 (2013)
18. Park, S.O., Kim, S.J.: An efficient multimedia file system for NAND flash memory storage. IEEE Trans. Consum. Electron. **55**(1), 139–145 (2009)
19. Liu, D., Wang, Y., Qin, Z., Shao, Z., Guan, Y.: A space reuse strategy for flash translation layers in SLC NAND flash memory storage systems. IEEE Trans. Very Large Scale Integr. VLSI Syst. **20**(6), 1094–1107 (2012)
20. Kim, Y., Gupta, A., Urgaonkar, B.: A temporal locality-aware page-mapped flash translation layer. J. Comput. Sci. Technol. **28**(6), 1025–1044 (2013)

21. Choudhuri, S., Givargis, T.: Performance improvement of block based NAND flash translation layer. In: Proceedings of International Conference on Hardware/Software Codesign and System Synthesis, pp. 257–262 (2007)
22. Lee, S.W., Park, D.J., Chung, T.S., Lee, D.H., Park, S., Song, H.J.: A log buffer-based flash translation layer using fully-associative sector translation. ACM Trans. Embed. Comput. Syst. **6**(3), Article No. 18 (2007)
23. Kim, J., Kim, J.M., Noh, S.H., Min, S.L., Cho, Y.: A space-efficient flash translation layer for CompactFlash systems. IEEE Trans. Consum. Electron. **48**(2), 366–375 (2002)
24. Kang, J.U., Jo, H., Kim, J.S., Lee, J.: A superblock-based flash translation layer for NAND flash memory. In: Proceedings of the 6th ACM and IEEE International Conference on Embedded Software, Seoul, Korea, pp. 161–170 (2006)
25. Lee, S., Shin, D., Kim, Y.J., Kim, J.: LAST: locality-aware sector translation for NAND flash memory-based storage systems. Oper. Syst. Rev. ACM **42**(6), 36–42 (2008)
26. Shen, Z., Jia, Z., Li, X., Cai, X., Ju, L.: A data-driven superblock-based flash translation layer. Optik **126**(20), 2735–2742 (2015)

Biclustering Evolutionary Spatiotemporal Community in Global Trading Network

Leiming Yan[1,2(✉)], Zeyu Chen[2], and Ping Zang[2]

[1] Jiangsu Engineering Center of Network Monitoring,
Nanjing University of Information Science and Technology, Nanjing, China
yan_leiming@163.com
[2] School of Computer and Software, Nanjing University of Information Science and Technology, Nanjing, China
2650317451@qq.com, 2044549972@qq.com

Abstract. Detecting evolving communities in dynamic weighted networks are significant for understanding the evolutionary patterns of complex networks. In this paper, a novel algorithm is proposed to detect overlapping evolutionary spatiotemporal communities in the global trading network, a dynamic weighted network. This algorithm is capable of discovering those edges with similar evolving trend in a weighted community, and revealing the evolutionary of nodes and edge weight vectors simultaneously. Experiments on the global trading network show that the proposed algorithm can discover more evolving behaviors and properties which hide in those seemingly stable community structures.

Keywords: Link community · Weighted complex network · Community evolution · Biclustering

1 Introduction

Community detection is a fundamental task in complex networks analysis, especially in analyzing social networks evolutionary. In general, there are mainly two kinds of communities: nodes-community and link-communities. For nodes-community, community is defined as a group of nodes in unweighted networks, where the nodes in a community have higher degrees and those between different communities have lower density [1]. At present, most of community detection algorithms aim to find this kind of communities and focus on finding how the nodes evolve in a community [2–8]. However, if a network is with a very large size, it is so difficult and challenging to observe the evolving patterns with notable significance. Normally, we just obtain some large and dense communities with thousands of nodes and millions of edges by traditional algorithms. We couldn't see directly the detailed sub-structure in this kind of large communities, and it doesn't make any sense to find which node is deleted or which new edge is added.

While for link community [7], it is considered as a set of closely interrelated links or edges. Some algorithms are introduced to discover stable and consistent link communities [8–11]. These methods think the structure of link communities should not dramatically evolve from one timestep to the next timestep. The link community could

X. Sun et al. (Eds.): ICCCS 2017, Part II, LNCS 10603, pp. 589–598, 2017.
https://doi.org/10.1007/978-3-319-68542-7_50

be used to analyze the very large dynamic networks and other application areas [12–17]. However, these algorithms omit the edges' weight values. In fact, lots of real networks could be modeled as weighted networks. For example, in the world trading network [18], the link weight values reflect the relationship strength between two different countries. Although the structure of a trade community looks like stable, while in fact, the total exports or imports between some countries are fluctuating dramatically.

Here, we propose Spatiotemporal Community to describe the evolutionary of a community from both of the perspectives of space and time simultaneously. Inspired by link communities and biclustering algorithms [19–22], we propose a novel method to focus on detecting link communities with evolving weight values from dynamic weighted networks, especially from dense large networks.

The remainder of this paper is organized as follows. In Sect. 2, we describe some concepts and definitions related to the evolutionary community detection. Section 3 proposes a two-stage community detection algorithm. Then Sect. 4 demonstrates the experiment setting and the results of spatiotemporal community detection. Finally, Sect. 5 is the conclusion.

2 Preliminaries

To facilitate our elaborations, some fundamental concepts and notations are introduced as follow.

2.1 Dynamic Weighted Networks

Let $G_t = (V_t, E_t)$ be a network snapshot at time t, where $V_t = \{V_t^1, V_t^2, \cdots, V_t^N\}$ is the set of vertices in the network snapshot G_t, and E_t is the set of weighted edges. A dynamic weighted network can be denoted as a sequence of subgraph G_t, $G = \{G_1, G_2, \cdots, G_t, \cdots G_{|T|}\}$, where T is the set of time steps, $t \in |T|$.

If at least one G_t is a weighted network, the whole weighted network G can be denoted as $G = (E, T)$, where E is the set of all of edges between vertex v_i and v_j. There is mapping $E \times T \rightarrow W_{ET}$, $W_{ET} = \left(w_{ij}^t\right) = \left(e_k^t\right), e_k \in E$.

2.2 Spatiotemporal Community

Ahn et al. [7] proposed the concept of link community in unweighted dynamicnetwork. A dynamic network can be denoted as a set of communities $C_t = \{C_t^1, C_t^2, \cdots, C_t^n\}$ at time t, where $C_t^i \cap C_t^j = \emptyset, i \neq j$, which means there is no any nodes belonging to two different communities simultaneously. The original link community is defined as none-overlapping community. A link community is still a static sub-network at a timestep t. We have to trace the topological structure so as to observe which nodes and edges have joined or left a community at a period of time. Moreover, the concept of link community neglects the evolving behaviors of edge weights in a community over times.

Here, we propose Spatiotemporal Community to describe the evolutionary of a community from both of the perspectives of space and time simultaneously.

Let $C(G^m, T^n, W')$ be a dynamic link community in a weighted network, where time interval $T^n = [t_s, t_e]$, start time step $t_s \in T$ and $t_e \in T$, G^m is a subgraph, $S(\cdot)$ is a similar function, W' is a sub-matrix of the community's weight matrix in time interval T^n.

Intuitively, if $S(W') \leq \delta$, where δ is a similarity threshold, then community C is a spatiotemporal community.

That means, a spatiotemporal community is such a community with well-connected nodes and similar temporal evolving weight vectors of edges.

3 Methodology

In this subsection, we propose a community detection algorithm, which consists of two main stages: (i) biclustering dynamic weighted network to obtain spatiotemporal sub-networks with similar evolving trend, (ii) extracting overlapping communities in spatiotemporal sub-networks.

3.1 Bipartite Weighted Graph Matrix

We denote a dynamic weighted network $G = \{G_1, G_2, \cdots, G_t, \cdots G_{|T|}\}$ as one bipartite graph $G_B = (E, T)$. As Fig. 1. Shows, the time set T is one part, and the set of all of weighted edges E is another part. If an edge vertex e_i appear in time vertex t_k, then link edge e_i and time t_k.

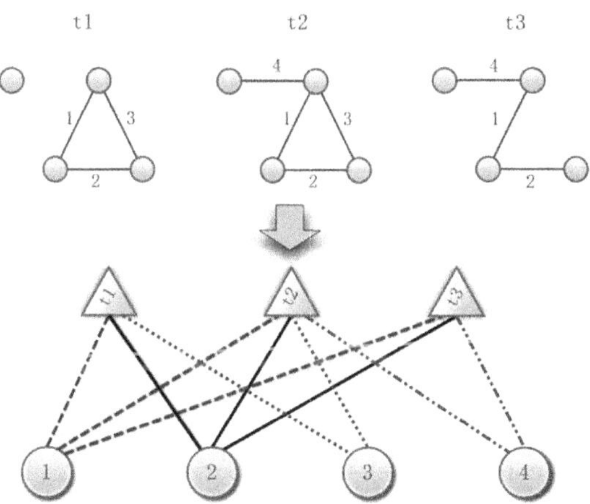

Fig. 1. Transform dynamic subgraphs into a Bipartite Graph

Therefore, a series of weighted graph can be put into the same data matrix no matter the network is directed or undirected (Fig. 2a). The different columns in the data matrix correspond to different subgraphs G_t in G. In Fig. 2b, from time t1 to t3, the weight vectors of edge e1, e2 and e3 show similar evolving trend.

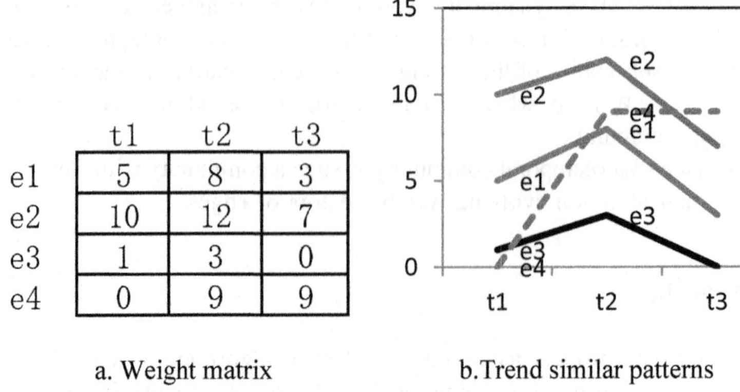

	t1	t2	t3
e1	5	8	3
e2	10	12	7
e3	1	3	0
e4	0	9	9

a. Weight matrix b. Trend similar patterns

Fig. 2. Bipartite Weighted Graph Matrix and similar patterns.

3.2 Extracting Temporal Similar Sub-graphs

Here, we define the temporal similar sub-graph based on mean squared residue score, which was introduced to measure the coherence of genes and conditions in a sub-matrix of a DNA array [19].

Let $A_{IJ} = \left(A_1, A_2, \cdots, A_t, \cdots, A_{|J|}\right)$ be a sub matrix of the bipartite graph matrix, where the column vector $A_t = \left(e_{1t}, e_{2t}, \cdots, e_{it}, \cdots, e_{|I|t}\right)'$, I is a subset of edges, $I \subseteq E$, $t \in J$, J is a subset of time step, $J \subseteq T$, the similar score is

$$\mathrm{Score}(A_t, A_{t+1}) = \frac{1}{|I|} \sum\nolimits_{i \in I} \left(e_{i,t+1} - e_{i,t} - e_{I,t+1} + e_{I,t}\right)^2 \tag{1}$$

where $e_{I,t} = \frac{1}{|I|} \sum_{i \in I} e_{i,t}$.

If the similarity $\mathrm{Score}(A_t, A_{t+1})$ is less than a threshold δ, the pattern (A_t, A_{t+1}) is a temporal similar sub-graphs pattern.

A consecutive of temporal similar sub-graphs can construct a spatiotemporal network with similar evolving trend.

Given a spatiotemporal network $G_{IJ} \subseteq G_B(E, T)$, $I \subseteq E$, $J \subseteq T$, $|J| > 2$, a threshold $\delta > 0$, $\mathrm{Score}(A_{IJ}) < \delta$, where

$$\mathrm{Score}(A_{IJ}) = \frac{1}{|J| - 1} \sum\nolimits_{j=1}^{|J|-1} Score\left(A_j, A_{j+1}\right) \tag{2}$$

According to the definition above, biclustering in a bipartite weighted graph matrix is equivalent to extracting the maximum edge bicliques, which is a NP-complete problem [23]. We propose a biclustering algorithm to extract temporal similar sub-graphs. The detail of the clustering algorithm is described in algorithm 1.

Algorithm 1: Extracting Temporal Similar Sub-graphs

Input: Bipartite graph matrix, threshold δ
Output: all temporal similar sub-graphs
begin
  foreach $t \in T$ **do**
    sort all (A_t, A_{t+1}) by ascendence;
    initial each edge as a cluster $C_i^t \leftarrow \{(e_{i,t}, e_{i,t+1})\}$;
  end
  foreach $t \in T$ **do**
    /* expand one row into C_i^t */
    foreach C_i^t **do**
      if $score(C_i^t \cup C_{i+1}^t) < \delta$
      and $score(C_i^t \cup C_{i+1}^t) \leq score(C_{i+1}^t \cup C_{i+2}^t)$ **then**
        $C_i^t \leftarrow C_i^t \cup C_{i+1}^t$
      end
      /* expand one column into C_i^t */
      if $score(C_i^{t,t+1}) < \delta$ **then**
        $C_i^t \leftarrow C_i^{t,t+1}$
      else
        reslut_set.append(C_i^t)
      end
    end
  end
  return *result_set*;
end

3.3 Extracting Overlapping Communities

Here, we use bipartite graph to describe spatiotemporal sub-networks (Fig. 3.), and then detect communities based on the clique percolation method (CPM) [5].

k-cliques are defined as fully connected subgraphs of k vertices. If two k-cliques share k−1 vertices, these two cliques are adjacent. A k-clique-community is defined as the union of all k-cliques that can be reached from each other through a series of adjacent k-cliques [5].

The basic features of such communities are that their node members can be reached through well connected subgraphs, and thus the communities may overlap because of sharing nodes with each other.

In this stage, the biclustering results in first stage, spatiotemporal sub-networks, are treated as unweighted and undirected networks. Then, we use the k-cliques [5] method to obtain the final spatiotemporal communities.

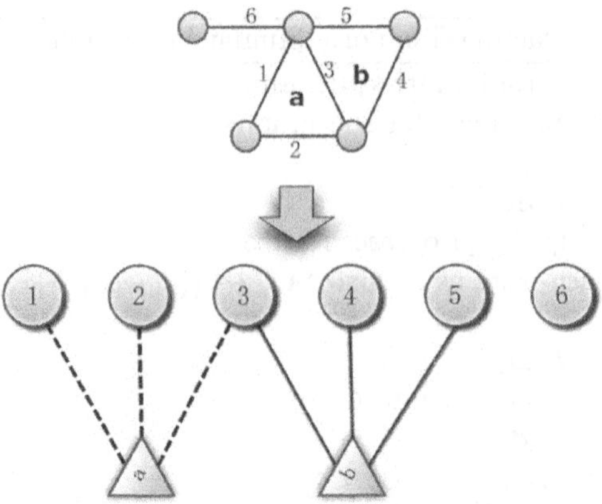

Fig. 3. Extracting cliques from bipartite graph.

4 Experimental Results

In this subsection, we use a real dataset to evaluate and validate the effectiveness of our method.

4.1 Global Trading Network

These data provide estimates of trade flows between independent states (1948–2000) and GDP per capita of independent states (1950–2000) [24]. We use the export data, which include 1158458 records, corresponding to the total export between different countries in the world from 1948 to 2000. This dataset covers many political crises and financial crises, such as the financial crisis in Asia in 1997.

In our experiment, the original export network data are converted into a bipartite graph of 5361 weight vectors with 53 years.

4.2 Results Analysis

When the clique k is set as 10, threshold $\delta = 0$, we obtained 198 spatiotemporal communities. Some results are shown in Fig. 4.

In Fig. 4, the left graphs are the topological structures of communities, whose solid lines with arrows (the red lines) are those edges with similar evolving trend and similar score is less than the threshold. The right figures next to communities' structures show the evolving trends of their edges' weight vectors over time. Take the community 189 as instance, which shows some countries export to China and China export to Philippines from year 1991 to 2000. We can find that in that period, the export to China witnessed a slight fluctuation when the financial crisis of Asia breaking out, whereas the export USA to Mexico kept a rapid increase (the uppermost line in Fig. 4d). In stark contrast to Fig. 4e and f, in the community 193 and 195, most of the total export of these countries underwent dramatic decreases in 1997. These countries include South Korea, Iceland, Brazil, Paraguay, Netherland, German, and so on.

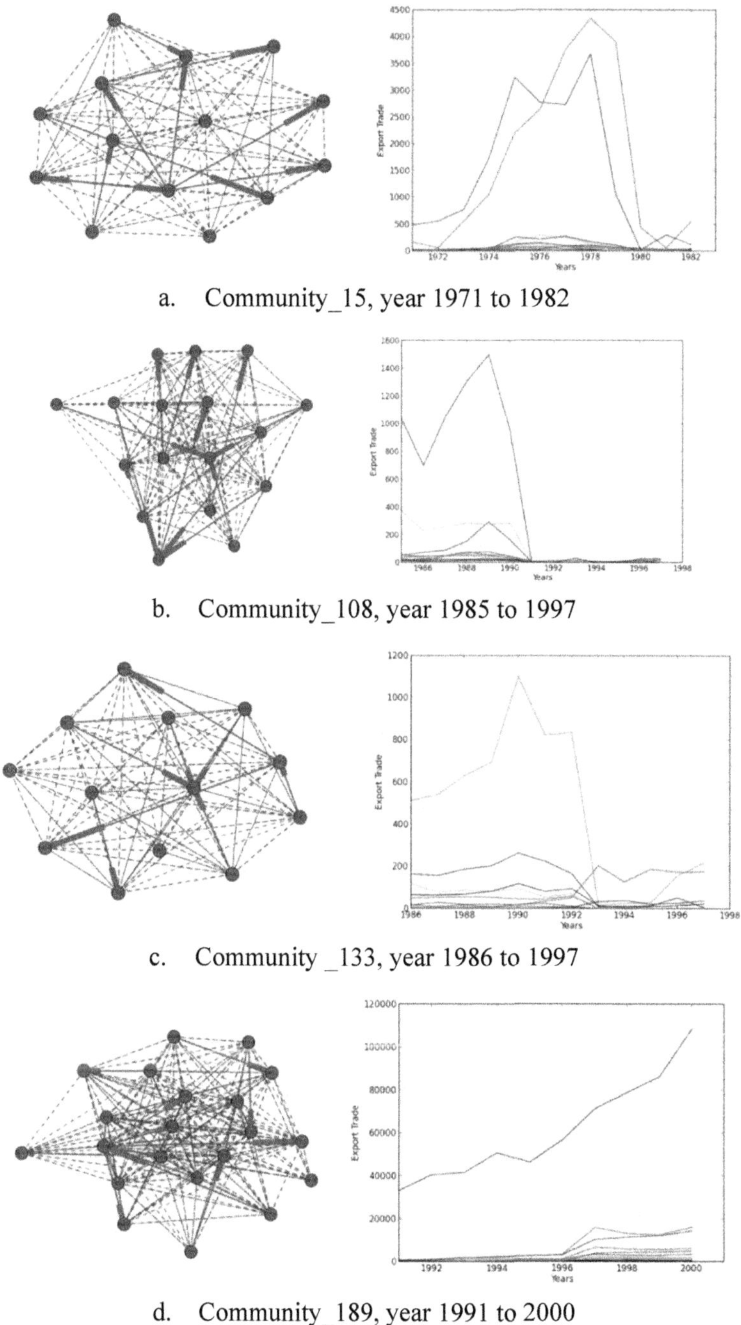

a. Community_15, year 1971 to 1982

b. Community_108, year 1985 to 1997

c. Community _133, year 1986 to 1997

d. Community_189, year 1991 to 2000

Fig. 4. Some spatiotemporal communities results (Color figure online)

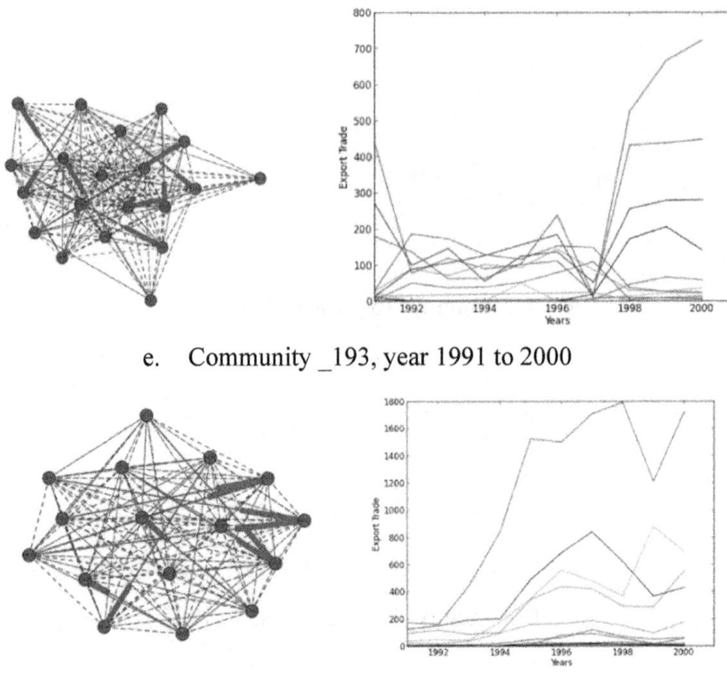

e. Community _193, year 1991 to 2000

f. Community _195, year 1991 to 2000

Fig. 4. (*continued*)

Comparing with the results of literature [18], the spatiotemporal communities found by our method are no longer limited in the same geographical area, but crossing inter-continental area, and are more suitable for revealing the temporal evolving mechanism.

5 Conclusion

In this paper, we propose a method to detect evolutionary spatiotemporal communities in dynamic weighted networks. This kind of communities can uncover the evolving behaviors at two dimensions: nodes and edge weights when communities are changing with time passing. Besides, our method can find the overlapping communities both at structure and time dimensions. In addition, our method could be directly applied to directed networks without any modification. Our experimental results also demonstrate evolutionary spatiotemporal communities can discovery more evolving information than traditional communities.

Acknowledgements. This work is supported by the NSFC [grant numbers 61573191, 61602254]; Jiangsu Province Natural Science Foundation [grant number BK2160968]; the Priority Academic Program Development of Jiangsu Higher Education Institutions (PAPD) and Jiangsu Collaborative Innovation Center on Atmospheric Environment and Equipment Technology (CICAEET).

References

1. Newman, M.E.: Finding community structure in networks using the eigenvectors of matrices. Phys. Rev. E: Stat. Nonlin. Soft Matter Phys. **74**(3 Pt 2), 036104 (2006)
2. Chen, Y., Wang, X., Xiang, X., et al.: Overlapping community detection in weighted networks via a Bayesian approach. Phys. A Stat. Mech. Appl. **468**, 790–801 (2017)
3. Takaffoli, M., Sangi, F., Fagnan, J., et al.: Community evolution mining in dynamic social networks. Procedia Soc. Behav. Sci. **22**(22), 49–58 (2011)
4. Nadakuditi, R.R., Newman, M.E.: Graph spectra and the detectability of community structure in networks. Phys. Rev. Lett. **108**(18), 188701 (2012)
5. Palla, G., Barabási, A.L., Vicsek, T.: Quantifying social group evolution. Nature **446**(446), 664–667 (2007)
6. Guo, C., Wang, J., Zhang, Z.: Evolutionary community structure discovery in dynamic weighted networks. Phys. A **413**(11), 565–576 (2014)
7. Ahn, Y.Y., Bagrow, J.P., Lehmann, S.: Link communities reveal multiscale complexity in networks. Nature **466**(7307), 761 (2010)
8. Folino, F., Pizzuti, C.: An evolutionary multiobjective approach for community discovery in dynamic networks. IEEE Trans. Knowl. Data Eng. **99**(8), 1 (2014)
9. Liu, Q., Liu, C., Wang, J., et al.: Evolutionary link community structure discovery in dynamic weighted networks. Phys. A **466**, 370–388 (2016)
10. Bai, X., Yang, P., Shi, X.: An overlapping community detection algorithm based on density peaks. Neurocomputing **207**, 264–275 (2016)
11. Cordeiro, M., Rui, P.S., Gama, J.: Dynamic community detection in evolving networks using locality modularity optimization. Soc. Netw. Anal. Min. **6**(1), 1–20 (2016)
12. Qu, Z., Keeney, J., Robitzsch, S., Zaman, F., Wang, X.: Multilevel pattern mining architecture for automatic network monitoring in heterogeneous wireless communication networks. China Commun. **13**(7), 108–116 (2016)
13. Xue, Y., Jiang, J., Zhao, B., Ma, T.: A self-adaptive artificial bee colony algorithm based on global best for global optimization. Soft Comput. (2017). doi:10.1007/s00500-017-2547-1
14. Chen, Y., Hao, C., Wu, W., Wu, E.: Robust dense reconstruction by range merging based on confidence estimation. Sci. China Inf. Sci. **59**(9), 1–11 (2016). doi:10.1007/s11432-015-0957-4
15. Liu, Q., Cai, W., Shen, J., Fu, Z., Liu, X., Linge, N.: A speculative approach to spatial-temporal efficiency with multi-objective optimization in a heterogeneous cloud environment. Secur. Commun. Netw. **9**(17), 4002–4012 (2016)
16. Zhang, Y., Sun, X., Baowei, W.: Efficient algorithm for K-barrier coverage based on integer linear programming. China Commun. **13**(7), 16–23 (2016). doi:10.1109/CC.2016.7559071
17. Wang, T.S., Lin, H.T., Wang, P.: Weighted-spectral clustering algorithm for detecting community structures in complex networks. Artif. Intell. Rev. **47**, 463–483 (2016)
18. Lupu, Y., Traag, V.A.: Trading communities, the networked structure of international relations and the kantian peace. J. Conflict Resolut. **57**(6), 1011–1042 (2013)
19. Cheng, Y., Church, G.M.: Biclustering of expression data. In: International Conference on Intelligent Systems for Molecular Biology, p. 93 (2000)
20. Denitto, M., Farinelli, A., Figueiredo, M.A.T., et al.: A biclustering approach based on factor graphs and the max-sum algorithm. Pattern Recogn. **62**, 114–124 (2016)
21. Liu, M., Shi, J., Li, Z., et al.: Towards better analysis of deep convolutional neural networks. IEEE Trans. Visual Comput. Graph. **23**(1), 91 (2016)

22. Veroneze, R., Banerjee, A., Zuben, F.J.V.: Enumerating all maximal biclusters in numerical datasets. Inf. Sci. **379**, 288–309 (2017)
23. Peeters, R.: The maximum edge biclique problem is NP-complete. Discrete Appl. Math. **131**(3), 651–654 (2003)
24. Gleditsch, K.S.: Expanded trade and GDP data. J. Conflict Resolut. **46**(5), 712–724 (2002)

Optimization and Classification

Cost Optimization for Time-Bounded Request Scheduling in Geo-Distributed Datacenters

Xiaohui Wei, Lanxin Li, Xingwang Wang(✉), and Yuanyuan Liu

College of Computer Science and Technology,
Jilin University, Changchun, China
weixh@jlu.edu.cn,
{lilx15,wangxw2109,liuyuanyuan16}@mails.jlu.edu.cn

Abstract. To cope with the growing service requests, a large number of cloud services are deployed in geographically distributed datacenters for better performance. Currently, how to optimize the monetary expenditure spent on VM (Virtual Machine) rental has been widely concerned. Especially, the diversities of the rental prices and service capabilities in geo-distributed regions make the problem more complicated. In this paper, the time restriction of requests and load balance are both taken into account when optimizing the VM rental cost. A two-layer geo-distributed request scheduling algorithm is presented respectively for internal and external datacenters to reduce the VM rental cost. To provide datacenter-level load balance and SLA (Service-Level Agreement) assurance, the proposed algorithm not only considers new arrival requests, but also re-dispatches requests being served to other datacenters. Finally, our work is evaluated and compared with the previous scheduling algorithms in small and large scale. Experimental results demonstrate the effectiveness of the proposed algorithm.

1 Introduction

With the popularity of infrastructure-as-a-service (IaaS) computing paradigm, service providers can easily deploy their services by renting VM instances from infrastructure providers. Owing to the globalization and regionalization of service customer, service providers are more inclined to deploy datacenters across multiple regions. For example, Google owns 13 datacenters over 8 countries in 4 continents. Modern datacenters are virtualization-based and a tenant can rent a handful of virtual resources, e.g., virtual machines [9]. Therefore, different from the single datacenter structure used in literatures [1–4], we consider a more common circumstance that datacenters are deployed in geo-distributed regions.

As shown in Fig. 1, customers submit their requests to the nearest datacenter which has the required service, and the service provider rents a certain number of VMs in different regions according to historical information. In some cases, for instance, a sudden request increase or peak of service, servers needed in these datacenters will be tight, while in other datacenters may be relatively light. In order to provide a

X. Sun et al. (Eds.): ICCCS 2017, Part II, LNCS 10603, pp. 601–610, 2017.
https://doi.org/10.1007/978-3-319-68542-7_51

cost-effective and resource-efficient processing, it's crucial for service providers to appropriately schedule real-time requests. Therefore, how to effectively schedule requests becomes an attractive problem for service providers.

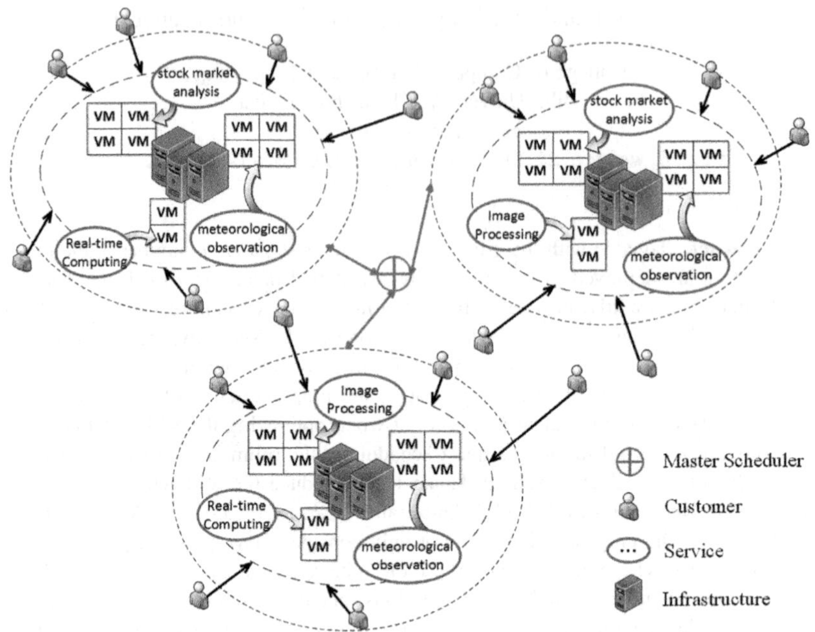

Fig. 1. The three roles of geo-distributed cloud datacenter

In this paper, we focus on scheduling strategies from the perspective of service providers. According to the heterogeneity of user requests and real-time system load, our approach not only effectively utilizes virtual resource to schedule service requests in bounded time, but also remaps serving requests to consolidate resource for satisfying more requests with load balance.

Our contributions can be summarized as follows:

(1) We address the cost-effective problem that providers concern and take global load balance, data-stream latency and price diversity into consideration. With these, a constrained optimization problem is modeled in this paper.
(2) Then, we propose a two-layer geo-distributed request scheduling algorithm respectively for internal and external datacenters. These scheduling strategies consider both new arrival and serving requests to ensure the global system efficiency.
(3) Compared with a local optimal and a random scheduling algorithm, the effectiveness of the proposed algorithm has been validated. Conclusive results show that our algorithm achieves global load balance and SLA assurance with lower cost.

2 Related Work

In this section, we introduce the previous work on monetary cost concerned by service providers, which correlates with the SLA, stream processing latency, and datacenter-level load balance assurance.

Monetary cost and SLA. In order to improve the profit of service providers, FI Popovici et al. proposed profit-based scheduling and admission control policies, but ignored the consideration of user requirements [5]. Therefore, to guarantee the SLA of users, two scheduling algorithms [1] and a double-quality-aware renting scheme [6] were proposed to make a trade-off between profit and customer satisfaction. However, these two researches cannot completely fit for geo-distributed datacenters since they considered little transfer latency between datacenters. Considering the above factors, a cost-aware service request scheduling algorithm, CSRSGA was presented to process user service requests more cost-effectively without any SLA violation [7], but this work paid little attention to the heterogeneity of price.

Stream processing latency. With the increasing requirements of low latency in big data stream computing services, a real-time, energy-efficient resource scheduling and optimization framework, named Re-Stream was proposed to meet their low response time and strict deadlines [8]. Facing the problem of abundant communication cost, Gu et al. investigated big data stream processing problem through exploring the inter-DC traffic latency diversities in geo-distributed DCs [9]. However, in these researches, the diversity of VMs rental price is not discussed.

Datacenter-level load balance. From a high-level resource management view, datacenter-level load balance has attracted a lot of attention on the cost optimization problems [10, 11]. These studies considered homogenous datacenters where servers are identical, which is far from the current situations [12]. Although Lin et al. considered heterogeneous datacenters comprised of servers with different system configuration and performance [13], this work neglected the heterogeneity of VMs.

Different from the above works, we concentrate on these three factors: the model we developed considers global load balance and data-stream processing requirements; the algorithm we designed can handle different types of VM resource with diverse prices; this work schedules both serving and arriving requests efficiently.

3 Problem Formulation

In this section, the rental cost optimization for the service provider in geo-distributed datacenters is formulated. We first model the problems of the datacenter-level load balance and request latency respectively.

3.1 Notations

Assume that a service provider deploys S kinds of services in geo-distributed datacenters, denoted as D. Each datacenter supplies multiple virtual machines with different prices. The customers locate in G regions. At each time slot t, customers submit their requests to the nearest datacenter with the required service. Table 1 summarizes some notations mentioned throughout this paper.

Table 1. The key parameters in our model

Parameters	Notes
V	The type of VMs set
Q_g	The received requests set from location g
P_d^v	The price of type v VMs in datacenter d
R_{gsd}	The submitted requests from location g for service s in datacenter d
M_{sd}^v	The number of rental type v VMs for service s in datacenter d
M_d^v	The number of rental type v VMs in datacenter d

3.2 Datacenter-Level Load Balance

In geographical datacenters, we enhance customer satisfaction by balancing workloads across the datacenters. In each time slot t, when the load rate in datacenter d exceeds the limit value, it will notify master scheduler to route some requests to other datacenters with lighter loads. Given received request number $A(t)$, the master scheduler makes a decision that routes some requests to the datacenter d, denoted as $R_d(t)$. Therefore, we have:

$$\sum_{d=1}^{N} R_d(t) = A(t), R_d(t) \geq 0 \quad (1)$$

3.3 Request Latency

Due to the low latency requirements of big data stream services, service providers should limit the total latency within the maximum delay time T_s^{max} for each service s. In this paper, we mainly focus on the transferring, queueing and processing latency.

Generally, users submit their requests to the nearest datacenter for the required service, the datacenter communicates with master scheduler for dispatching requests according to the current state. To simplify the formula definition, we directly utilize the distance between user location and master scheduler to replace the distance from user to datacenter and datacenter to master scheduler. Hence, the total transferring latency is affected by dis_{gm} and dis_{gd}, where d is the dispatched datacenter. The previous studies have shown that the round-trip network latency can be obtained through active measurements or other means in practice [14]. Empirical studies have also demonstrated that the round-trip network latency can be approximated by geographical distance multiplying 0.02 ms/km [15]. In our model, the latency L_{gs} of the user in location g for service s can be formulated:

$$L_{gs} = \left(dis_{gm} + dis_{gd}\right) \times 0.02\,\text{ms/km}, \quad (2)$$

Suppose there are $|S_d|$ types of services and $|S_d|$ numbers of queues are ordered in datacenter d. Without loss of generality, we assume that there are M_{sd} servers, customers arrive at a Poisson distribution with a parameter of λ_{sd}, the service time for each customer follows a negative exponential distribution with a parameter of μ_{sd} for service s in datacenter d. When a customer request arrives, the request will be dispatched to an available server, otherwise it will wait in a queue. Based on the M/M/c queueing model, we calculate the queueing latency W_{sd} for a request as follow:

$$\begin{aligned} W_{sd} &= QL_{sd}/\lambda_{sd} \\ &= \left(M_{sd}\rho_{sd} + \frac{\rho_{sd}PR_{sd}^{\infty}}{1-\rho_{sd}}\right)\Big/\lambda_{sd} \\ &= \left(M_{sd}\rho_{sd} + \frac{\rho_{sd}(M_{sd}\rho_{sd})^{M_{sd}}PR_{sd}^{0}}{M_{sd}!(1-\rho_{sd})^2}\right)\Big/\lambda_{sd} \\ PR_{sd}^{0} &= \left\{\left[\sum_{n=0}^{M_{sd}-1}\frac{(M_{sd}\rho_{sd})^n}{n!}\right] + \left[\frac{(M_{sd}\rho_{sd})^{M_{sd}}}{M_{sd}!(1-\rho_{sd})}\right]\right\}^{-1}, \rho_{sd} = \frac{\lambda_{sd}}{M_{sd}\mu_{sd}} \end{aligned} \tag{3}$$

where QL_{sd} is the mean queue length of service s in datacenter d. In order to obtain QL_{sd}, we need calculate the probability that all the servers are busy PR_{sd}^{∞} and the service intensity ρ_{sd}. PR_{sd}^{∞} is derived based on the probability PR_{sd}^{0} that all the servers are idle.

Therefore, we get the total latency formula as follows:

$$TL = L_{gs} + W_{sd}. \tag{4}$$

3.4 Problem Statement

With the objective of minimizing rental cost of the service provider, the optimization problem is modeled:

$$\begin{aligned} &\min \sum_{d\in D}\sum_{v\in V} M_d^v \times P_d^v, \\ s.t.\quad &\sum_{d=1}^{N} R_d(t) = A(t),\ R_d(t) \geq 0, && (a) \\ &L_{gs} + W_{sd} \leq T_s^{\max}, \forall s \in S, g \in G, d \in D, && (b) \\ &\sum_{g\in G}\sum_{s\in S} R_{gsd} \times M_{sd}^v \leq M_d^v, \forall d \in D, \forall v \in V, && (c) \\ &\sum_{s\in S}\sum_{d\in D} R_{gsd} \times x_{gsd} = Q_g,\ \forall g \in G, x_{gsd} = 0\, or\, 1. && (d) \end{aligned} \tag{5}$$

In Eq. (5), our defined objective function is to minimize the total rental cost of the service provider. Constraint 5(a) is the datacenter-level load balance constraint that the received requests of master scheduler are equal to the sum of requests required to be routed to other datacenters. Constraint 5(b) specifies that the total latency including data transferring, queueing and processing latency is not more than the maximum latency for service s. The third constraint illustrates that the total used number of VMs from all locations does not exceed the sum of rented VMs for each VM type in each datacenter. The last constraint assures that the number of scheduled requests must equal to the number of total received requests for each location g. If the request from location g is dispatched to datacenter d, the equation $x_{gsd} = 1$, otherwise $x_{gsd} = 0$. Besides, it can assure one request can only be scheduled to one datacenter.

4 Algorithm Design

Algorithm 1: TRSA-LS (Local Scheduler)

```
Get requests set RS from master scheduler;
Sort requests in RS in ascending order according to remaining time rt=T_s^max - wt ;
for each request in RS do
  if there are available VMs then
    Dispatch this request to the available VM with minimal price;
  else
    Rent more VM to process this request;
  end if
end for
for each arriving request r_s ∈ R do
  Record the set IVS of available VMs in local datacenter d ;
  if IVS ≠ NULL then
    Dispatch r_s to the VM with minimal price in IVS ;
  else
    Put r_s in the end of queue_s ∈ queue and record waiting time wt ;
  end if
end for
if load rate LR=U/M ≥ β or any waiting request T_s^max - wt ≤ δ then
  Put waiting and serving requests into SR to make LR < β ;
end if
Submit load rate LR_d , total ability M_d , SR to master scheduler.
```

Algorithm 2: TRSA-MS (Master Scheduler)

```
Get load rate LR_d , total ability M_d , SR from each datacenter;
Initial total residual ability TA ;
for each datacenter d do
  if LR_d < β then
    Calculate residual ability RA_d = (β - LR_d) × M_d not exceed β ;
    TA = TA + RA_d ;
    Put d into datacenter set DS ;
  end if
end for
Calculate average load rate μ = (1/N) Σ_{d=1}^{N} LR_d and the standard deviation sd = sqrt( (1/N) Σ_{d=1}^{N} (LR_d - μ)^2 ) ;
if sd > α then
  Sort DS in descending order according to RA_d / LR_d ;
end if
Sort requests in SR in descending order according to remaining time (T_s^max - wt) ;
Put requests in SR (total needResource < TA) into RS_d (d ∈ DS) according to RA_d ;
Put remaining requests in SR according to location distance into RS_d (d ∈ D) ;
Submit requests set RS_d to each datacenter d ;
```

Since the exhaustive search method is not feasible for the minimum problem defined above in large-scale circumstance, a two-layer algorithm respectively for internal datacenter and external master scheduler is developed to reduce rental cost. The details of the methods are shown in *TRSA (Two-layer Request Schedule Algorithm).*

The proposed algorithm adopts the traditional FCFS queueing method, and each datacenter intercommunicates with the master scheduler for exchanging information. Since the most request processing is stateless in practical applications, the algorithm is designed with a premise that migrating serving requests to other VMs has no effect for computational results. For each service request entering the system, the system begins recording its waiting time and the available server set. The requests are assigned to the server with minimal price in the order of arrival times. Each datacenter tries their best to serve serving and arriving requests internally, but when the load rate exceeds the upper limit β or the maximal request limit reaches, the datacenter will inform the master scheduler to dispatch some requests to other datacenters. To meet the datacenter-level load balance and request latency requirements, the master scheduler gathers information such as load rate, total serving ability and so on from each datacenter, and then schedules requests to them according to these indicators properly.

5 Performance Evaluation

In order to verify the effectiveness of *TRSA*, we conduct the following simulation experiments. The experimental settings and performance metrics for evaluation are presented. Finally, we compare with two existing baseline algorithms to demonstrate the superiority of the proposed algorithm.

5.1 Settings and Metrics

In our experiments, we set up our test sets similar to [16] for small-scale and large-scale problems, and multiple types of servers are deployed in datacenters. The arriving requests with different locations and service demand follow a Poisson distribution. Since the time bound of each service request is different, we set it a random distribution. The results presented in the following are averaged over 10 independent runs.

A service provider leases VM instances from infrastructure provider to handle user requests. Under this circumstance, the type and number of rental servers all affect the cost of service provider. Load balance is vital for the stability of system and user experience. Therefore, we focus on the following performance measurement metrics to evaluate our algorithm:

1. *Rental Cost*: the total cost of rental VMs to process requests in a time slot.
2. *Leased Number*: the number of rented VM instances in a time slot.
3. *Unbalance Degree*: the standard deviation of the load rate in each datacenter.

5.2 Compared Algorithms

Local Optimum (LO): the algorithm is a basic method in single datacenter. When a request arrives, the system searches available servers in local datacenter. If there are many available servers, it chooses one with the lowest price. Otherwise, the request will be putted at the end of queue. When the maximum request latency is reaching, the system will rent temporary server for it.

Random Schedule (RS): the algorithm is the most common method in multi-datacenters. When a request arrives, it will be dispatched to the available server with the lowest price, otherwise queued. When reaching the maximum request latency, the algorithm will randomly choose a datacenter which has available servers to schedule requests.

5.3 Compared Results

Figure 2 shows the performance of three algorithms by comparing the rental cost and Fig. 3 shows the number of VM instances rented by each algorithm with small-scale (Fig. 3a) and large-scale (Fig. 3b) conditions respectively. By taking the VM instances price, type and processing ability diversities into account, these algorithms have little difference in small-scale condition. But when the problem scale is relatively large, *LO* fails to save cost and the customer requests are not processed timely within the limited capacity, while our method obtains a more optimized result in Fig. 2b. Hence, the proposed two-layer algorithm, *TRSA*, achieves a lower rental cost and builds appropriate instances to handle these requests via dispatching requests to the proper datacenters, which outperforms *LO* and *RS* greatly.

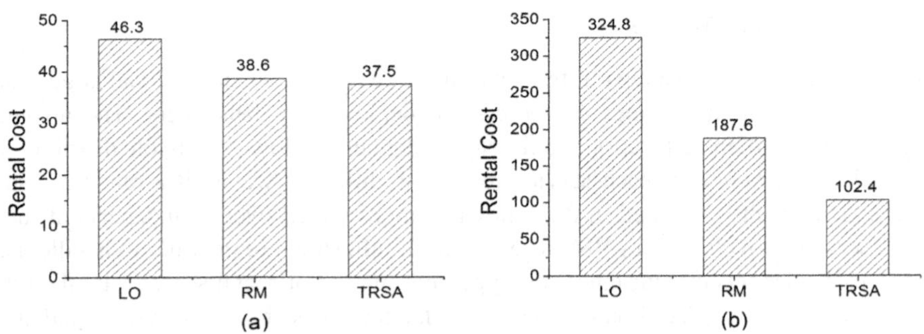

Fig. 2. The comparison of rental cost

In order to evaluate the global load balance degree, we adopt the standard deviation of the load in each datacenter to reflect it. The smaller the standard deviation is, the better load balance the system gains. As illustrated in Fig. 4, in small-scale condition (Fig. 4a), these algorithms almost achieve the same experimental performances. But on a large-scale problem (Fig. 4b), our algorithm significantly outperforms the other two algorithms.

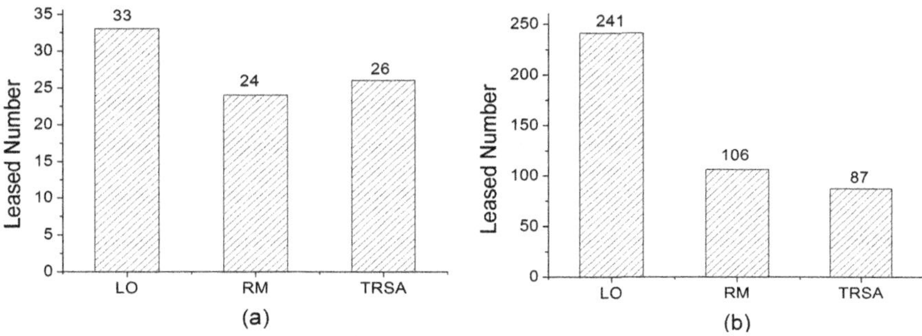

Fig. 3. The comparison of leased VMs numbers

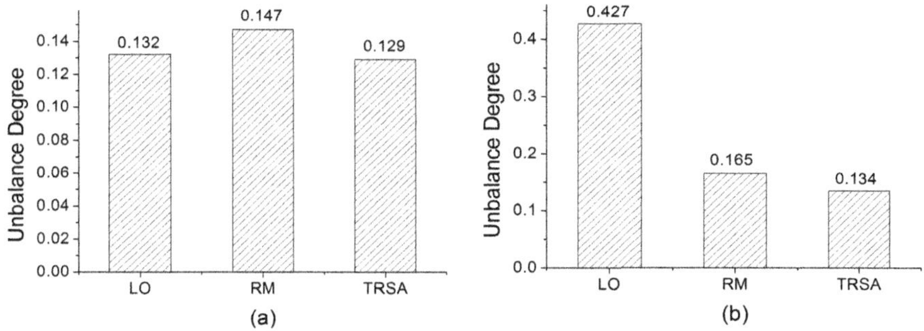

Fig. 4. The comparison of unbalance degree

Our algorithm reduces more monetary cost than these two baseline algorithms. In addition, it uses less VM servers to process requests and obtains a lower unbalance degree. Therefore, these performance results demonstrate our proposed methods perform better in many aspects.

6 Conclusion

In this paper, we investigate the problem of minimizing service provider rental cost with the SLA in geo-distributed datacenters. To formulate our issue as a constrained optimization problem we take both the datacenter-level load balance and data-stream bounded time constrains into account. We propose a two-layer heuristic algorithm to dispatch serving and arriving requests. With the consideration of price diversity, the presented algorithm can efficiently reduce rental cost while ensuring the QoS. Conclusive results show that our algorithm can save rental cost about 68% than *LO* and 45% than *RM* in large-scale problem.

Acknowledgments. This work is supported by the National key research and development program of China (Grant No.2016YFB0201503, No.2016YFB0701101), National Natural Science Foundation of China (NSFC) (Grants No.61602205, No.51627805, No.61170004),

Specialized Research Fund for the Doctoral Program of Higher Education (20130061110052), Major Special Research Project of Science and Technology Department of Jilin Province (20160203008GX), Key Science and Technology Research Project of Science and Technology Department of Jilin Province (20140204013GX). Jilin Scientific and Technological Development Program (20170520066JH), Graduate Innovation Fund of Jilin University.

References

1. Chen, J., Wang, C., Zhou, B.B., et al.: Tradeoffs between profit and customer satisfaction for service provisioning in the cloud. In: Proceedings of the 20th International Symposium on High Performance Distributed Computing, pp. 229–238. ACM, New York (2011)
2. Huang, D., Yang, D., Zhang, H., et al.: Energy-aware virtual machine placement in data centers. In: Global Communications Conference (GLOBECOM), pp. 3243–3249. IEEE, Anaheim (2012)
3. Anand, A., Lakshmi, J., Nandy, S.K.: Virtual machine placement optimization supporting performance SLAs. In: IEEE 5th International Conference on Cloud Computing Technology and Science (CloudCom), pp. 298–305. IEEE, Bristol (2013)
4. Fang, W., Liang, X., Li, S., et al.: VMPlanner: Optimizing virtual machine placement and traffic flow routing to reduce network power costs in cloud data centers. J. Comput. Netw. **57**, 179–196 (2013)
5. Popovici, F.I., Wilkes, J.: Profitable services in an uncertain world. In: Proceedings of the 2005 ACM/IEEE Conference on Supercomputing, p. 36. IEEE Computer Society, Seattle (2005)
6. Mei, J., Li, K., Ouyang, A., et al.: A profit maximization scheme with guaranteed quality of service in cloud computing. J. IEEE Trans. Comput. **64**, 3064–3078 (2015)
7. Liu, Z., Wang, S., Sun, Q., et al.: Cost-aware cloud service request scheduling for SaaS providers. J. Comput. J. **57**, 291–301 (2013)
8. Sun, D., Zhang, G., Yang, S., et al.: Re-Stream: real-time and energy-efficient resource scheduling in big data stream computing environments. J. Inf. Sci. **319**, 92–112 (2015)
9. Gu, L., Zeng, D., Guo, S., et al.: A general communication cost optimization framework for big data stream processing in geo-distributed data centers. J. IEEE Trans. Comput. **65**, 19–29 (2016)
10. Rao, L., Liu, X., Xie, L., et al.: Minimizing electricity cost: optimization of distributed internet data centers in a multi-electricity-market environment. In: 2010 IEEE INFOCOM Conference, pp. 1–9. IEEE, San Diego (2010)
11. Stanojevic, R., Shorten, R.: Distributed dynamic speed scaling. In: 2010 IEEE INFOCOM Conference, pp. 1–5. IEEE, San Diego (2010)
12. Goudarzi, H., Pedram, M.: Geographical load balancing for online service applications in distributed datacenters. In: IEEE CLOUD, pp. 351–358. IEEE, USA (2013)
13. Lin, M., Liu, Z., Wierman, A., et al.: Online algorithms for geographical load balancing. In: International Green Computing Conference (IGCC), pp. 1–10. IEEE, California (2012)
14. Szymaniak, M., Presotto, D., Pierre, G., et al.: Practical large-scale latency estimation. J. Comput. Netw. **52**, 1343–1364 (2008)
15. Qureshi, A.: Power-Demand Routing in Massive Geo-distributed Systems. Massachusetts Institute of Technology (2010)
16. Jing, C., Zhu, Y., Li, M.: Customer satisfaction-aware scheduling for utility maximization on geo-distributed cloud data centers. In: 2013 IEEE 10th International Conference on HPCC_EUC, pp. 218–225. IEEE, Zhangjiajie (2013)

The Application of Naive Bayes Classifier in Name Disambiguation

Na Li[(✉)] and Jin Han

School of Computer and Software, Nanjing University of Information Science and Technology, Nanjing 210044, China
757165407@qq.com, 284615715@qq.com

Abstract. Name repetition exists in the academic resource management system, which brings difficulties to academic evaluation, information retrieval, citation analysis and so on. According as different authors use function words in different habits, the Naive Bayes classifier was used to study in this paper. Based on the assumption of feature independence, this paper selects 26 common function words with high frequency as statistical frequency standard, use Naive Bayes classifier to classify texts. Experiments show that the method has a high accuracy rate.

Keywords: Naive Bayes classifier · Feature independence · Function words analysis · Name disambiguation

1 Introduction

The authors of many scientific papers have same name, some authors' names change with time or living environment, these problems bring difficulties to academic evaluation, information retrieval, citation analysis and so on. Joint Conferences Digital Libraries is held for this issue, it began in 2001 in the United States, has been successfully held 16 sessions.

In order to solve name repetition in web search, some systems have been developed. In 2007, Chen and Martin proposed a robust unsupervised name disambiguation method, developed the Poly UHK system [1]. Ikeda and Ono developed an ITC_UT system [2], using two-step clustering, the first step using hierarchical clustering, the second step based on hybrid keyword clustering algorithm. Romano and Buza developed a XMedia system [3], the system used the quality threshold clustering algorithm and used machine learning methods on the similarity comparison.

In recent years, some new name disambiguation algorithm is proposed. The first kind is a similarity calculation-based clustering disambiguation method, such as Huang proposed an algorithm for the same name differentiation based on multi-view non-negative matrix decomposition [4]. The second is a hierarchical-based clustering disambiguation approach, such as Zhang used hierarchical clustering algorithm to solve the multi-document ambiguity issue of Chinese names [5]. Huang put forward person

X. Sun et al. (Eds.): ICCCS 2017, Part II, LNCS 10603, pp. 611–618, 2017.
https://doi.org/10.1007/978-3-319-68542-7_52

name disambiguation based on hierarchical clustering and web page relationship [6]. The third is a clustering disambiguation method based on the specific relationships. For example, Li presented a name disambiguation approach based on the relationship of document collaborators [7].

Most of above are clustering algorithms, which use the metadata of the papers as the basis of clustering, calculate the similarity between the papers, and then use the appropriate clustering algorithm to cluster the papers according to the similarity degree. But these algorithms depend on a lot of conditions. When the conditions are less or often changes, the test accuracy rate will be greatly reduced. In addition, the application of this kind of algorithm is narrow. But the algorithm of name disambiguation in this paper is based on the frequency of using function words, so that it eliminates the dependence on a lot of conditions, has a wider scope of application and performs good in name disambiguation.

2 The Principle of Naive Bayes Classifier

In the construction method and theory of many classifiers, the Naive Bayes classifier has been widely used because of its computational efficiency, high accuracy and solid theoretical basis. The basis of the idea is as follows: For the given items to be classified, solve the probability of occurrence of each category under the conditions in which this item occurs, and sort this item as the category whose probability is the largest. Each training sample data is decomposed into one-dimensional eigenvector X and decision category variable C, and it is assumed that the components of the eigenvector are independent of each other.

The specific definition is as follows:

$x = \{a_1, a_2, \ldots, a_m\}$ is a feature to be classified, and each "a" is a characteristic attribute of x, $C = \{y_1, y_2, \ldots, y_n\}$ is a decision category variable, calculate $P(y_1|x), P(y_2|x), \ldots, P(y_n|x)$.

If $P(y_k|x) = max\{P(y_1|x), P(y_2|x), \ldots, P(y_n|x)\}$, then $x \in y_k$.

According to Bayes theorem:

$$P(y_i|x) = \frac{P(x|y_i)P(y_i)}{P(x)}. \tag{1}$$

Because the denominator is constant for all categories, we only need to maximize the molecules can be. And because the characteristic attributes are conditional independent, so there are:

$$P(x|y_i)P(y_i) = P(a_1|y_i)P(a_2|y_i)\ldots P(a_m|y_i)P(y_i) = P(y_i)\prod_{j=1}^{m} P(a_j|y_i). \tag{2}$$

Therefore, it is only necessary to solve the conditional probability of each characteristic attribute under each category, put the result into the above formula, and then we can get the probability of occurrence of each category under the condition of the item to be classified, compare out the maximum value, and classify the item to be classified as the category that the maximum probability represents.

3 Key Technology and Algorithm Process

3.1 Feature Extraction

At present, there are seven kinds of methods of feature extraction: mutual information, expected cross entropy, information gain, text evidence, probability ratio, word frequency method and CHI. In this paper, word frequency method is used to calculate the frequency of the function words. According to statistical results, there is a great difference in the frequency of the function words used by different authors (Fig. 1.). The object of this study is Chinese scientific papers. For a paper, calculate the number of the words that need to be counted in this paper, and then divide the total number of words in the paper to get the frequency of the statistical function words needed in the paper. In this paper, 26 commonly used Chinese function words with highest frequency are selected as the standard of statistical frequency.

Since the value of the frequency is continuous, the value of each feature attribute is infinite, so Naive Bayes classifier can not be applied to this problem. In this paper, according to the distribution of the calculated frequency, the accuracy of the frequency will be reduced to 2, 3 or 4 bits after the decimal point, and take reduced precision frequency as the value of the characteristic attribute.

The extracted feature vector format is as follows:

$$[a1,\ a2,\ a3, \ldots\ldots,\ a24,\ a25,\ a26,\ \text{type}]$$

"a1–a26" is the frequency of 26 words, "type" is the category that the feature vector represents (yes or no).

This paper selects some now commonly used Chinese function words, including prepositions, conjunctions, adverbs, auxiliary words, through the statistics of 452 papers in the frequency, select the 26 function words of highest frequency. The 26 selected function words are as follows: {"进而", "但", "且", "而且", "按", "及", "以及", "和", "同", "因此", "于", "与", "假如", "如果", "当", "并且", "或","根据", "然而", "跟", "但是", "或者", "因而", "在", "按照", "从而", "一样"}.

3.2 Algorithm Process

3.2.1 Data Input

The program enters a path that contains all the papers of a given scholar, and uses the tika plugin to extract the pdf format of the paper into a string. And use ansj to divide the

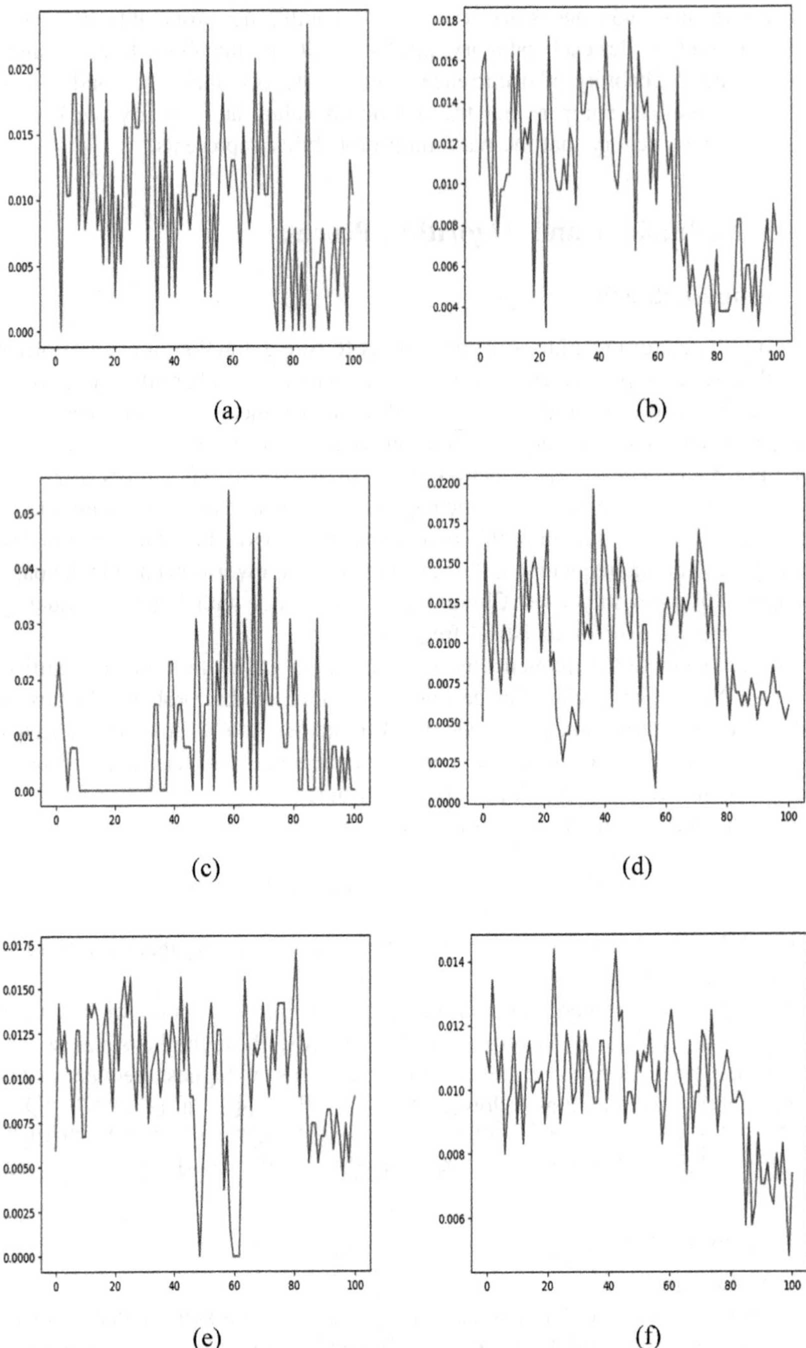

Fig. 1. Distribution of function words in papers from six different authors

text into word segmentation, extract the function words, calculate the frequency of each function word. The final output of these papers as a two-dimensional array of data. Each line represents a paper, marked with "yes", take a small number of papers as a test sample. In the same way, take the equivalent of another author's paper, marked the category with "no", constitute a complete sample in this way.

3.2.2 Process

For each test sample, calculate the probability that each feature attribute of the sample appears in the "yes" category, multiply the product of these probabilities with the probability of "yes" in the training sample to obtain the result P1. Calculate the probability P2 which represents "no" in the same way, compare P1 and P2, and classify the test sample as the category represented by the larger value of the two.

Due to some feature of the training sample value does not appear in the experimental process, resulting $P(a|y) = 0$, so that the quality of the classifier greatly reduced. In order to solve this problem, we introduce Laplace calibration, the idea is very simple, that is, all the categories under the division of the count plus 1, to avoid the embarrassing situation caused by the frequency of 0 (Fig. 2).

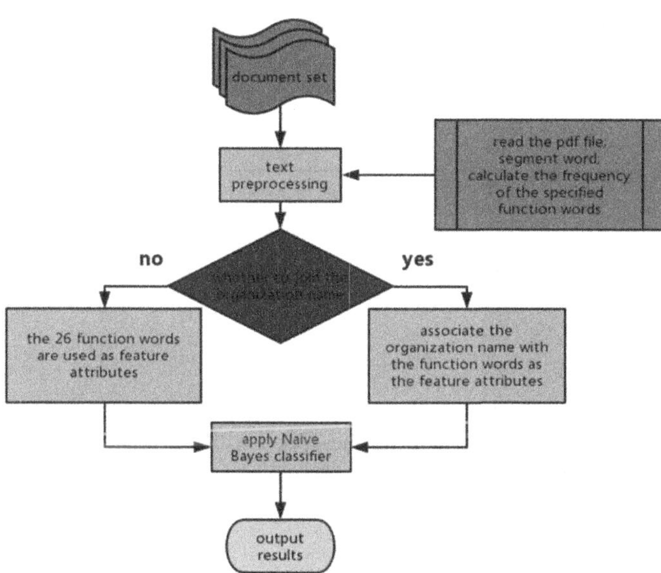

Fig. 2. Algorithm flow chart

3.2.3 Core Pseudo-Code of the Algorithm

```
Algorithm 1 Realization of Naive Bayes Classifier
BEGIN
The training samples were divided into two groups according to the results of yes or no,
  put groups into resultMap;
    Traversal resultMap{
          If the key is "yes"{
           Assign the proportion of the sample with the result of "yes" in the total
           training sample to yesCurrent;
              Traversal testList{
           yesCurrent=yesCurrent* The probability of the current feature attribute
           value in the testList that appears in the "yes" sample;
         }
       }
         If the key is "no"{
             Assign the proportion of the sample with the result of "no" in the total
           training sample to noCurrent;
              Traversal testList{
           noCurrent=noCurrent* The probability of the current feature attribute value
           in the testList that appears in the "no" sample;
         }
       }
       If yesCurrent>noCurrent
           return "yes";
       Else return"no";
    }
END
```

4 Experiment

4.1 Data Sources

The data studied in this paper are the Chinese periodicals downloaded from CNKI. In order to ensure that the sample will not be doped with the scholar who has the same name, those papers were all published by scholars on the home page. A total of 52 scholars and 1282 papers were studied.

4.2 Experiment Result

This paper has studied 52 samples, the average accuracy rate of classification without organization name is 85.273%, the average accuracy rate of classification with organization name is 93.074%.

The selected 6 representative data are as follows (Table 1):

Table 1. Partial experiment data

Subject (author)	Training samples (articles)	Test sample (articles)	Correct rate % (without organization)	Correct rate % (with organization)
Zhuge Jianwei	17	5	100.00	100.00
Wu Libing	19	5	80.00	100.00
Li Wei	28	7	85.71	85.71
Deng Zhengchun	54	11	72.73	90.91
Ni Ming	105	13	84.62	92.31
Xu Zeshui	167	21	95.24	95.24

As is shown in the table, when use the organization name as a characteristic attribute, the correct rate of classification will be significantly improved, which is consistent with the real situation in life that the probability that the author has the same name will be very low in the same organization. Thus it can be seen that organization name can be used as an important indicator of the name disambiguation.

At the same time, by observing the experimental results and training samples, this paper found that the higher the correct rate of several groups of data, the emergence of high frequency words is more. Therefore, it is concluded that the classifier realized in this paper has a better classification effect on those papers in which the frequency of the function words that this paper select is relatively high.

5 Conclusion

Many algorithms regard name disambiguation as a clustering problem. The field, the title, the author, the journal, and the abstract of the paper are used as the basis of clustering. By applying a similarity function to the document attributes to measure the similarity between the paper and the paper or the collection of papers and the collection of papers, and then use the appropriate clustering algorithm to cluster the paper according to the calculated similarity. The well-performed algorithm of the name disambiguation needs to rely on a large number of document metadata attributes, but some attributes in the actual academic resource platform is missing or difficult to obtain, which led to the poor practical application of these algorithms and poor scalability.

This paper mainly studies the common same name problem in academic resource platform, and proposes a new algorithm of name disambiguation based on function words analysis and organization name. The algorithm eliminates the dependence of the algorithm on the field, the title, the collaborators, etc., and focuses on the author's habit of using the function words. The experiment has fully demonstrated that the algorithm based on the function words has a high accuracy, can be applied to combat writing paper for others. For some ancient books whose author is absent, we can take some authors who study the same direction with the ancient books in the same age as the categories, extract some representative function words, modify the classifier into a multi-classifier, then we can find possible author of these ancient books. When the organization name is added to the algorithm of the function words analysis, the average accuracy of the algorithm is improved by 7.8%, which can be used to track the experts of different disciplines, identify and study the hot topics in different fields. In summary, this algorithm saves a lot of human resources, achieve a certain accuracy, and have better flexibility and scalability.

References

1. Chen, Y., Martin, J.: Towards robust unsupervised personal name disambiguation. In: Proceedings of the 2007 Joint Conference on Empirical Methods in Natural Language Processing and Computational Natural Language Learning (EMNLP-Co NLL) (2007)
2. Ikeda, M., Ono, S., Sato, I.: Person name disambiguation on the web by two stage clustering. In: Second Web People Search Evaluation Workshop, WWW 2009 (2009)
3. Romano, L., Buza, K., Giuliano, C.: XMedia: Web people search by clustering with machinely learned similarity measures. In: Second Web People Search Evaluation Workshop, WWW 2009 (2009)
4. Huang, Z.: Research on name disambiguation algorithm based on multi-view nonnegative matrix factorization. Dalian University of Technology. Master thesis (2015)
5. Zhang, S., You, L.: Chinese people name disambiguation by hierarchical clustering. New Technol. Libr. Inf. Serv. **2010**(11), 64–68 (2010)
6. Li, Q.: Person name disambiguation based on hierarchical clustering and web page relationship. Shan Dong University. Master Thesis (2012)
7. Li, W.J.: The research and application of name disambiguation algorithm based on multi-level clustering. Dalian University of Technology. Master Thesis (2013)
8. Yang, Y.L., Zhou, J., Li, B.C.: Name disambiguation algorithm based on ensemble. Appl. Res. Comput. **33**(9), 2716–2720 (2016)
9. Chen, C., Wang, H.F.: Social network based cross-document personal name disambiguation. J. Chin. Inf. Process. **25**(5), 75–82 (2011)
10. Guo, S.: Research on author name disambiguation algorithm in the literature database. New Technol. Libr. Inf. Serv. **29**(Z1), 69–74 (2013)
11. Gu, B., Sun, X.M., Sheng, V.S.: Structural minimax probability machine. IEEE Trans. Neural Netw. Learn. Syst. (2016). doi:10.1109/TNNLS.2016.2544779
12. Zhou, Z.L., Wang, Y.L., Wu, Q.M.J., Yang, C.N., Sun, X.M.: Effective and efficient global context verification for image copy detection. IEEE Trans. Inf. Forensics Secur. **12**(1), 48–63 (2017). doi:10.1109/TIFS.2016.2601065
13. Gu, B., Sheng, V.S., Tay, K.Y., Romano, W., Li, S.: Incremental support vector learning for ordinal regression. IEEE Trans. Neural Netw. Learn. Syst. **26**(7), 1403–1416 (2015)
14. Tian, Q., Chen, S.C.: Cross-heterogeneous-database age estimation through correlation representation learning. Neurocomputing **238**, 286–295 (2017)
15. Li, X., Xie, H., Chen, L., Wang, J., Deng, X.: News impact on stock price return via sentiment analysis. Knowl.-Based Syst. **69**, 14–23 (2014)
16. Xie, H., Li, X., Wang, T., Chen, L., Li, K.: Personalized search for social media via dominating verbal context. Neurocomputing **172**, 27–37 (2016)
17. Rao, Y.H., Li, Q., Wu, Q., Wang, T.: A multi-relational term scheme for first story detection. Neurocomputing (2017). doi:10.1016/j.neucom.2016.06.089

Mobility Prediction-Based Service Scheduling Optimization Algorithm in Cloudlets

Lei Shi, Xi Fu, and Jing Li(✉)

School of University of Science and Technology of China, Hefei 235500, Anhui, China
{sl950313,fuxi}@mail.ustc.edu.cn, lj@ustc.edu.cn

Abstract. Cloudlet is an emerging technology in mobile cloud computing. However users may be far away from cloudlets due to the mobility of mobile users, which leads to a poor network connectivity, thus, user experience will be poor. While a user moves across multiple cloudlets areas, issues of service scheduling between cloudlets to better support user experience become important. In this paper, we consider a latency-sensitive and stateful service scheduling problem in cloudlets. We propose a novel cloudlet service model and formulate the problem with the goal of finding the optimal service running sequence which minimizes the average service response time during the whole running process of the service for a user. To solve this problem, we propose an algorithm called Mobility Prediction-based Markov Decision Process (MPMDP). The proposed algorithm takes user's mobility prediction into account, and makes an decision based on Markov Decision Process to decide on which cloudlet the service should run for a user each time. Finally, we evaluate the effectiveness of the proposed MPMDP algorithm by simulations with real-world users' traces. The simulation result shows our algorithm achieves a lower average response time compared with previous schemes.

Keywords: Cloudlets · Mobile cloud computing · Service scheduling · Mobility prediction · Markov Decision Process

1 Introduction

Many emerging applications, such as real-time face recognition, require high data processing capability and low response time [1]. However, portable devices are generally limited by their size and battery life, which makes them incapable of performing complicated computational tasks. The solution to this problem is to use Cloudlet [2] (This concept has also been termed as Follow Me Cloud [3], edge computing [4]). By deploying services on cloudlets, users can request these services from cloudlets to reduce the consumption of mobile device resources.

In reality, a poor network connectivity between users and cloudlets will occur due to users' mobility. An important issue in cloudlets is service scheduling caused by the mobility of users. Consider such scenario, in an area

X. Sun et al. (Eds.): ICCCS 2017, Part II, LNCS 10603, pp. 619–630, 2017.
https://doi.org/10.1007/978-3-319-68542-7_53

(city, school etc.) where multiple cloudlets are deployed and a latency-sensitive and stateful service such as interactive high-definition video game is deployed in cloudlets. At the begin, a user requests service provided by the nearby cloudlet, with the user's movement, the user may be far from the cloudlet and get a high delay while interacting with the service. A solution is to schedule the service from original cloudlet to a new cloudlet near to the user, a procedure of scheduling is to migrate the service data related to the user. However, the scheduling procedure usually takes lots of time because of a large amount of service data and low bandwidth between cloudlets through WAN, the user's requests will not be processed in time during the scheduling. And the user may frequently switch among different areas covered by cloudlets, thus it is challenging to decide whether to schedule the service to better support user experience when the user location changes each time during the whole service running time for the user [5].

In this paper, we propose a novel cloudlet service model, on which we formulate the service scheduling problem with the goal of finding the optimal service running sequence which minimizes average response time during the service running time for a user. A mobility prediction-based cloudlet service optimization algorithm is proposed based on the model, called MPMDP (Mobility Prediction-based Markov Decision Process).

The main contributions of this paper are twofold:

- We develop the service model in cloudlets for service scheduling, the model considers the response time in different running status of a service.
- We propose a mobility prediction-based service scheduling optimization algorithm for the service scheduling problem. The algorithm first predicts a user's state transition probability between different locations and the dwell time of each location, then formulates the scheduling decisions as an MDP model and get results by solving the bellman equation of MDP model.

2 Related Work

Service scheduling between cloudlets is a new branch of research in mobile cloud computing [5], and user mobility becomes a key factor in cloudlets [6]. Ksentini et al. [7] first studied this problem and proposed a framework based on Markov Decision Process [8], a reinforcement learning algorithm, to study this issue, but the work defines the user mobility model as a simple one-dimensional random walk mobility model. Therefore, this model can not be applied well in real scene, and the model of service scheduling between cloudlets can not be used in real-world scenarios as well. Wang et al. [9–11] improved the work in [7], by proposing an improved approach for MDP value iteration algorithm, a general scheduling cost model and an approach based on predicting the cost of a service. In these work, user mobility is defined as a random work which can not stand for the real behaviors of a user. In a real scene, the user's history of movement information is usually very full (like GPS, etc.), we can avoid a lot of unnecessary service scheduling and reduce user response time through reasonably predicting the mobility of the user. Typical patterns are as follows, a user stays for a few minutes after moving to a new cloudlet area and returns to the previous cloudlet area or the user has a very short dwell time in a cloudlet area, and quickly moves to the next cloudlet area. If the prior knowledge can be understood by learning from historical mobility information, the user experience will be greatly improved by avoiding twice service scheduling during those kind of movements. This leads to a smaller average response time of service.

3 Preliminaries

3.1 System Model

User Mobility Definition. The user is active in a cloudlets system. The set of possible user locations is given by Γ, where Γ is assumed to be finite (but arbitrarily large) and each location in Γ is covered by an access point (AP). We use tuple (l, t, dt) to represent that a user enters location l at time t and the dwell time is dt. Then the mobility of a user can be defined as $Trace : (l_i, t_i, dt_i)$ where $1 \leq i \leq n$, and we assume that $dt_i = t_{i+1} - t_i$, where $1 \leq i \leq n - 1$.

Cloudlets Architecture. We consider a cloud computing system with multiple cloudlets, where the cloudlets are indexed by $m \in \{1, 2, \ldots, N\}$, the cloudlets are co-located at APs in the network, and all cloudlets are connected with each other via certain topology T, where $T_{i,j} = 1$ represents the directed connect and $T_{i,j} = 0$ represents not directed connect, each cloudlet can host and provide services. Users can request from service in cloudlet and get response. The bandwidth between the cloudlets is denoted by $d \in \mathbb{R}^{N \times N}$, where $d_{i,j}$ represents the data transfer bandwidth between the cloudlet i and the cloudlet j, and the bandwidth between a cloudlet and a user which directly connect to the cloudlet is $\hat{d}$.

Service in Cloudlets. We consider a latency-sensitive and stateful service which continually interacts with users, the service is deployed in all cloudlets. When a user first requests the service in a nearby cloudlet, the service will be initialized to the user. Then each time the user requests the service, it responds to the request based on the user's current request data and the state data associated with the user.

A time-slotted service running system as shown in Fig. 1 is considered, where the slots $t \in \{1, 2, \ldots, T_{max}\}$ can be either evenly or unevenly spaced. The expectations of interactions between user u and the service served u in a time slot is defined as E. The total number of slots T_{max} matches with the time duration that the service runs for user u. The service may run in two statuses, Response Status (RS) or Scheduling Status (SS). Requests from users can be processed quickly in response status, and requests can not be processed by service when the service is in scheduling status, those requests will be processed after service status turns into SS again. Following we will describe the two statuses in detail.

For status RS, service will add incoming requests to its own queue for processing, a $M/M/n$ queue can be used to model the service in cloudlet, where each

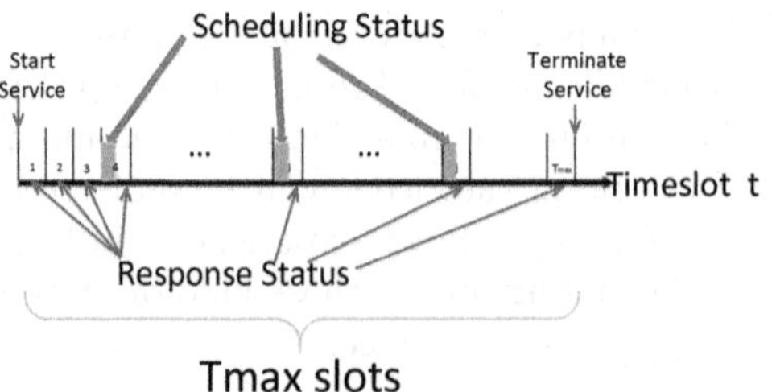

Fig. 1. Service running statuses

cloudlet $i \in \{1, 2, \ldots, N\}$ has n_i services with the service rate μ_i in cloudlet i. Due to the rapidly changing nature of users' demands, the rate of incoming requests can fluctuate wildly at each cloudlet over time. Therefore, we assume that the incoming users' requests at cloudlet i randomly arrive according to the Poisson process with arrival rate λ_i, the response time of requests at cloudlet i consists of queuing time, processing time and delay from the cloudlet to user u.

Denoted by T_i, a function of a given request arrival rate λ to calculate the queuing time and the processing time of requests at cloudlet i,

$$T_i(\lambda) = \frac{C\left(n_i, \frac{\lambda}{\mu_i}\right)}{n_i\mu_i - \lambda} + \frac{1}{\mu_i} \tag{1}$$

where $C(n, p)$ is calculated by Erlang C formula [12].

Denoted by T_{net}, a function of a given cloudlet i where the service served user u belong to and cloudlet j where user u locate in to calculate the delay from service to user u.

$$T_{net}(i, j) = \frac{D_1}{d\lfloor i \rightarrow j \rfloor} \tag{2}$$

where we assume the response package of user's request has the same size D_1, $d\lfloor i \rightarrow j \rfloor$ represents the minimum throughput during the shortest path from cloudlet i to cloudlet j and $d\lfloor i \rightarrow i \rfloor = \hat{d}$ for $i \in 1, 2, \ldots, N$. The shortest path can be obtained by Dijkstra algorithm [13]. Then the response time of a request which is received in RS at time t denoted by $R_{rs}(i, j, t)$ is defined as follow:

$$R_{rs}(i, j, t) = T(\lambda_i) + T_{net}(i, j) \tag{3}$$

.

For status SS, service will add incoming request to its own queue for waiting as well, but they will be processed after the scheduling procedure is over. We define the time of service scheduling from cloudlet i which hosts the service served user u to cloudlet j where user u locates in at time t denoted by $M(i, j, t)$.

$$M(i, j, t) = \begin{cases} \frac{D_2}{d\lfloor i \rightarrow j \rfloor} & i \neq j \\ 0 & i = j \end{cases} \tag{4}$$

where D_2 represents the migration data of service(service data related to user u). After service is scheduled to cloudlet j that is near to user u, its status will turn into response status again, therefore, the response time of a request which is received in SS at time t denoted by $R_{ss}(i,j,t)$ is defined as follow:

$$R_{ss}(i,j,t) = M(i,j,t) + R_{rs}(j,j,t) \tag{5}$$

we normalize the response time of a request as follow:

$$R(i,j,t) = \begin{cases} R_{rs}(i,j,t), t \in T_{RS} \\ R_{ss}(i,j,t), t \in T_{SS} \end{cases} \tag{6}$$

where T_{RS} represents the time of response status, and T_{SS} represents the time of scheduling status.

3.2 Problem Definition

The Cloudlet Service Scheduling Optimization problem is defined as follows. Given a set of cloudlets $\{1,2,\ldots,N\}$, the topology of cloudlets is T, bandwidth between cloudlets is d, service in each cloudlet i has request arrival rate λ_i and n_i services with processing rate μ_i for all $i \in \{1,2,\ldots,N\}$, the expected interaction between user and service in each time slot is E. And given a user's historical mobility information $Trace : (l_i, t_i, dt_i), 1 \le i \le n$, the problem is to find a service running sequence $(t_i, cl_i, rt_i), 1 \le i \le n$ for the user to minimize the average response time, each (t_i, cl_i, rt_i) means the user gets response from cloudlet cl_i from time t_i and lasts for rt_i. That is, our optimization objective is to

$$minimize \frac{1}{E \cdot T_{max}} \sum_{t=1}^{T_{max}} (R(i_t, j_t, t)) \tag{7}$$

subject to T, d, λ, μ, n, E, $Trace$.

4 Algorithm

In this section, we propose an optimization algorithm MPMDP (Mobility Prediction-based Markov Decision Process). The idea is to get the state transition probability matrix which represents the transition probability between different location and dwell time of each location according to the historical movement through mobility prediction scheme first, then make the optimal decision (schedule the service or not at current time-slot) by optimal service scheduling MDP based on current state. The details are given in Algorithm 1. The following we introduce the mobility prediction scheme and optimal service scheduling MDP.

Algorithm 1. Mobility Prediction-based Markov Decision Process

Input: The task arrival rate λ_i, the number of server n_i, and the service rate μ_i of each cloudlet $i \in \{1, 2, \ldots, N\}$; the network topology matrix $T_{i,j}$, and bandwidth matrix $d_{i,j}$, $(i, j \in \{1, 2 \ldots, N\})$;user's historical mobility data $Trace : (l_i, t_i, dt_i)$, $i \in \{1, 2, \ldots, n\}$; service's response data size D_1 and migration data size D_2.
Output: service running sequence (t_i, cl_i, rt_i), $i \in \{1, 2, \ldots, times\}$

Get the cloudlet which user first request for service $firstCl$,
$curT \leftarrow 1$, $times \leftarrow 1$, $curCl \leftarrow firstCl$, $servCl \leftarrow firstCl$
Get the location transition probability matrix *pro* and ω by Mobility Prediction Scheme which introduced in Section. *A* from $Trace : (l_i, t_i, dt_i), i \in \{1, 2, \ldots, n\}$
for $t \leftarrow 1$ to T_{max} **do**
    Get the cloudlet Cl corresponding to the current user location p_t
    if $Cl \neq curCl$ **then**
        Get decision $action_t$ by Optimal MDP which introduced in Section. *B*
        if $action_t = SCHEDULE$ **then**
            $(t_i, cl_i, rt_i) \leftarrow (curT, servCl, t - curT)$
            $curT \leftarrow t$, $servCl \leftarrow CL$, $times \leftarrow times + 1$
        end if
    end if
    $curCl = CL$
end for
return (t_i, cl_i, rt_i), $i \in \{1, 2, \ldots, times\}$

4.1 Mobility Prediction Scheme

In this section, we propose a mobility prediction scheme to estimate the transition probability between different locations and the dwell time in each location by $Trace$. We model the user mobility as a continuous-time stochastic process $\{X(t), t \geq 0\}$, state space is $\{\Gamma = l_n, n \geq 0\}$. Based on the analysis of user mobility, we assume that the transition of the user location is only related to the current location, which is described as follow:

$$P(X(t_{n+1}) = l_{n+1} | X(t_i) = l_i,\ 1 \leq i \leq n) = P(X_{n+1} = l_{n+1} | X(t_n) = l_n) \quad (8)$$

This is well known as a Continuous-time Markov Chain (CTMC) [14]. We generally formate the transition probability as *pro*, defined as follow: $pro_{i,j}(s, t) = P(X_{s+t} = j | X(s) = i)$. which represents the transition probability from state i to state j at time s and last for t. we also assume the markov chain is a Homogeneous Markov Chain, thus the transition probability *pro* can be simply defined: $pro_{i,j}(s, t) = pro_{i,j}(t)$. There is an important property of CTMC that the dwell time in each state i is subject to exponential distribution, and the expectation of the exponential distribution is ω_i. Furthermore we can get the *pro* and ω by learning from user's history mobility $Trace$. The transition probability $pro_{i,j}$ is defined as the probability of occurrence when the state is i and the next state is j, defined as follow:

$$pro_{i,j} = \frac{\sum_{l_k = i, l_{k+1} = j, 1 \leq k \leq n} 1}{\sum_{l_k = i, 1 \leq k \leq n} 1} \quad (9)$$

we define ω_i as the average dwell time in state i, defined as follow:

$$\omega_i = \frac{\sum_{l_j=i,1\leq j\leq n} dt_i}{\sum_{l_j=i,1\leq j\leq n} 1} \tag{10}$$

4.2 Optimization MDP Formulation

In this section, we propose a model based on MDP to describe the optimal service scheduling problem in each time-slot. First, we define the state and action spaces of the service scheduling. State transition matrices and reward matrices are then derived. Afterward, the MDP optimization problem is expressed by a Bellman equation, and solved by employing a value iteration algorithm.

State Space and Action Space. The state space of the mobile user u and service in the cloudlets system is defined as follow:

$$\Theta = \{S = (c', c)\,|c', c \in \{1, 2, \ldots, N\}\} \tag{11}$$

where c' is the cloudlet which hosts the service for the user u, and c is the cloudlet which user u directly connects. All c' and c are in the cloudlets system.

The action space is

$$\mathbf{A} = \{a = 0, a = 1\} \tag{12}$$

denoting that a service can make a decision to be scheduled to another cloudlet (i.e., $a = 1$), or not be scheduled to any other cloudlet (i.e., $a = 0$).

Transition Matrices. In the following, we derive the transition matrices P for the states Θ and actions $\mathbf{A}$.

We consider the scheduling transitions without scheduling failure, if fail, the service will be not scheduled. When the cloudlet schedules service at $S = (c', c)$ $(A = 1)$, which represents user u's nearby cloudlet is c and cloudlet which hosted service for user u is c', the service will be scheduled from cloudlet c' to c for a better performance, and the state S becomes S' where $S' = (c, c)$. so the transaction probability is: $P\left(S|\left(a = 1, S'\right)\right) = 1$ we normalize as follow:

$$P\left(S|\left(a = 1, S'\right)\right) = \begin{cases} 1, & c_1 = {c_2}' = c_2 \\ 0, & else \end{cases} \tag{13}$$

where $S = ({c_1}', c_1)$ and $S' = ({c_2}', c_2)$.

By contrast, if the action is not to schedule the service($a = 0$), we assume user u's current location is l_i and the nearby cloudlet is cl_i. Thanks to the mobility predicting algorithm, we know that user u will move to $l_j(j = 1, 2, \ldots, n)$ with a probability of $pro(l_i, l_j)$, and the nearby cloudlet to those locations are c_i. Then we can get the transition matrices of action(not schedule) $P\left(S' = (c', c)|\left(a = 0, S = (c, c_i)\right)\right)$ as follows:

$$P\left(S' = (c', c)|\left(a = 0, S = (c_i, c)\right)\right) = pro(l_i, l') \tag{14}$$

Reward. For an action A, the state $S = ({c_1}', c_1)$ will transit to $S' = ({c_2}', c_2)$, an immediate reward $R(S', S, a)$ will be incurred to the user u, it defines as follows:

$$R\left(S', S, a\right) = \begin{cases} C_S\left(S', S\right), & a = 1 \\ C_N\left(S', S\right), & a = 0 \end{cases} \tag{15}$$

where $C_S\left(S', S\right)$ is the immediate reward of scheduling service to user u's nearby cloudlet, and $C_N\left(S', S\right)$ is the immediate reward of not scheduling. We present general definitions of $C_M\left(S', S\right)$ and $C_N\left(S', S\right)$.

The $C_S\left(S', S\right)$ is the immediate reward of transiting from state $S = ({c_1}', c_1)$ to $S' = ({c_2}', c_2)$, we define it as the reduction of total service response time between scheduling and no scheduling during the dwell time in location l which is covered by cloudlet ${c_2}'$. The response time with no scheduling is defined as follows:

$$RT_{NS}(l) = \omega_l \cdot E \cdot R({c_1}', c_1, t) \tag{16}$$

where ω_l is the expected dwell time in l, E is the expected number of interactions and $R(i, j, t)$ is the response time when user u in cloudlet region j and the service is hosted in cloudlet i for each interaction at time t.

The response time after scheduling at location l has two situations, when service is in Scheduling Status or Response Status. For Scheduling Status, the total response time of interacting during the dwell time in l is defined as follow:

$$T_{SS}(l) = M({c_1}', {c_2}', t) \cdot E \cdot (R({c_2}', c_2, t) + M({c_1}', {c_2}', t)) \tag{17}$$

where $M(i, j, t)$ is the service scheduling time from cloudlet i to cloudlet j. For Response Status, the total response time is defined as follow:

$$T_{RS}(l) = (\omega_l - M({c_1}', {c_2}', t)) \cdot E \cdot R({c_2}', c_2, t) \tag{18}$$

where l is user $u's$ current location, ω_l is the expected dwell time in l. So the response time with scheduling is defined as: $RT_{SD}(l) = T_{SS}(l) + T_{RS}(l)$. Thus, the immediate reward $C_M\left(S', S\right)$ is defined as follows

$$C_S\left(S', S\right) = RT_{NS}(l) - RT_{SD}(l) \tag{19}$$

As there is no benefits from no scheduling, so we define: $C_N\left(S', S\right) = 0$

Solving the Optimal Policy for the MDP. Given the proposed MDP, a policy for the MDP is denoted as $\Phi\left(S, A\right)$, which is the action A taken at state S. To obtain the optimal policy, the following Bellman equation based on the defined state space and derived transition matrices has to be solved:

$$V\left(S\right) = min_{\Phi(S,A)} \left\{ R\left(S, A\right) + \gamma \sum_{S' \in \mathbf{S}} P^S(S, S'|A)V(S') \right\} \tag{20}$$

$$\phi^*\left(S\right) = argmin_{\Phi(S,A)} V(S) \tag{21}$$

$V(S)$ is a *value function* of the mobile user u. $\phi^*(S)$ denotes the optimal policy. $\gamma \in [0, 1)$ is a discount factor of future states. $R(S, A)$ is the immediate reward to the state S and $P(S, S'|A)$ is the transition probability of the mobile user from the current state S to the next state S', which can be obtained from the transition matrices, these two is which we define before. The Bellman equation can be solved numerically by employing the value iteration algorithm [8], and finally get the optimization strategy $\phi^*(S)$.

5 Simulation

In this section, we evaluate the performance of the proposed algorithm MPMDP in terms of average response time during a service running for a user. We compare the performances of the proposed MPMDP algorithm with the algorithm used in [10] which MDP is used but mobility prediction is not considered (furthermore we call it OMDP) and other three baseline schemes:

- Always scheduling scheme (AMS). The service is always scheduled to a new cloudlet that user u enter.
- Never scheduling scheme (NMS). The service is never scheduled, which means the service will run on original cloudlet all the time.
- Myopic scheme (MYO). The service makes a short-sighted decision only based on immediate rewards of the current decision period. The decision is defined as follows:

$$A = \begin{cases} 0, & for\ C_S(S', S) < C_N(S', S) \\ 1, & for\ C_S(S', S) >= C_N(S', S) \end{cases} \tag{22}$$

  where $C_M(S', S)$ and $C_N(S', S)$ is the immediate rewards of scheduling service and not scheduling the service.

Then we explain the simulation settings and evaluate the performance of the proposed algorithm.

5.1 Simulation Environment

We first study a hypothetical structure of a cloudlet network. We adopt University of Science and Technology of China (USTC)'s AP deployment topology as cloudlets' distribution, a service is deployed on those cloudlets which users can request. We assign the network bandwidth between each pair of directly connected cloudlets randomly, according to the Normal distribution: $0.5 \leq \mathbf{N}(1.5, 1) \leq 2.5$. For bandwidth between cloudlets and users in the same AP area, we assume it as 20, the unit is MB/s.

We use real mobility data, acquired from USTC's network information laboratory's database, and select information of a student which includes nearly a month of the campus network access records and the use of the school card, this information contains the location of one day the user appears and the time at that location.

Table 1. Default simulation settings

Notation	N	$d_{i,j}$	$\hat{d}$	λ_i	μ_i	n_i	D_1	D_2	E	ζ	γ
Default	20	1.5	20	15	5	3	1.5	20	4	2	0.9

For service hosted in each cloudlet i, we assign its service rate μ_i by obeying the Normal distribution $\mathbf{N}(5, 2) > 0$, and the number of servers by sampling the Poisson distribution with a mean of 3. The task arrival rate λ_i at cloudlet i is determined by the Normal distribution $0 < \mathbf{N}(15, 6) < \mu_i \cdot n_i - 1$. This is due to the infinite queuing time required to meet $\lambda_i \leq \mu_i \cdot n_i$. For service response and migration data size, we assign the response data size D_1 as $1.5M$ and the migration data size D_2 as $20M$, the expected number of interactions E is 4. Table 1 shows the total default simulation settings.

5.2 Simulation Results

We first count the average response time of a day while the service was running for the user. Figure 2a shows the actual response time at different time of the day, the fluctuation is because of different network load. We can see that the proposed method MPMDP outperforms alternative placement methods including AMS, NMS, MYO and OMDP. MPMDP provides an average of 3.10 s during the whole running time while OMDP provides an average of 3.40 s (9.6% than MPMDP), MYO provides an average of 3.49 s (12.6 % than MPMDP), NMS and AMS provides an average of 3.81 s (22.9% than MPMDP) and 3.84 s (23.8% than MPMDP).

Furthermore, in order to intuitively understand the advantages of the algorithm MPMDP in reducing the scheduling times, we count the total response time (and distributions of response time in both Response Status and Scheduling Status) at several time points (0:00–24:00, interval is four hours) shown

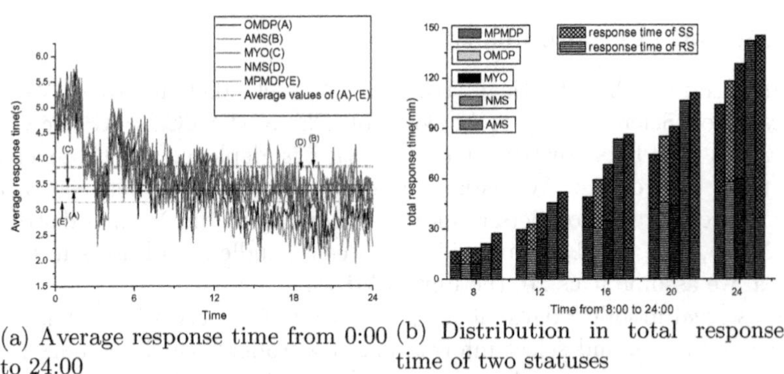

(a) Average response time from 0:00 to 24:00

(b) Distribution in total response time of two statuses

Fig. 2. Response time of simulation result

in Fig. 2b. It shows that compared to OMDP, MYO, NMS or AMS, MPMDP always has the smallest total response time, by using MPMDP we reduced the total response time of service interaction by approximately more than 20% of the total running time of the day. And we can see more information about the distributes in total response time, AMS has the smallest response time in response status but the largest scheduling time in scheduling status, resulting in the largest overall response time. The response time of requests in scheduling status of NMS is 0, but the response time in response status is the largest, and the overall response time is almost equal to AMS. The response times of MPMDP, OMDP and MYO in response status are almost the same, but the response time in scheduling status of MPMDP is about 20% smaller than OMDP and MYO. So this is a full verification of our proposed algorithm MPMDP that it can avoid certain schedulings and ensure the response time of the service in response status by rationally utilizing the mobility of users.

Finally, we analyze the impact of predictive accuracy on various strategies. We use the data size of the original mobility data as an indicator of the accuracy of the prediction, data of 2–10 weeks were used as training data, respectively, the result is shown in Fig. 3. It can be seen that with the increase of the size of training set, the use of mobility prediction can reduce the total response time of the service, which indicates that the accuracy of the prediction is higher with the increasing size of the training set, thus achieves a better effect. But when the size of training set achieves a sufficient amount (10 weeks), the average response time becomes larger than it previous is. A reasonable explanation is that the prediction on the data set is over-fitted. In summary, the mobility prediction can help reduce the total response time, and the accuracy of the prediction is positively correlated with the results without overfitting.

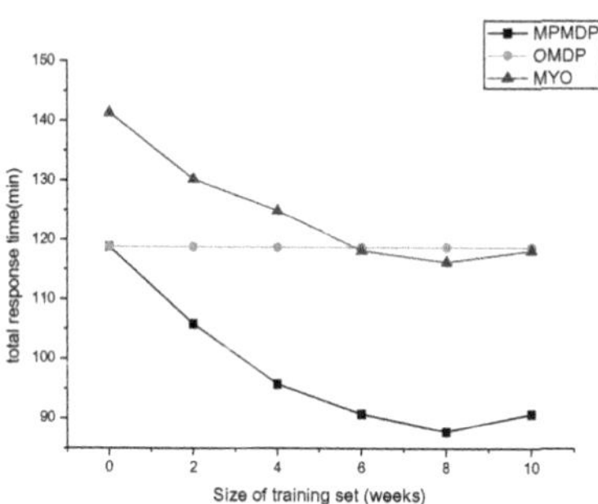

Fig. 3. The effect of training set size on decision

6 Conclusion

In this paper, we have studied the service scheduling problem for cloudlets, we formulate the problem by a novel model and propose an algorithm called

MPMDP (Mobility Prediction-based Markov Decision Process) to solve the problem in the model. The algorithm MPMDP consists of two core parts, (1) a mobility prediction algorithm that aims to estimate the transition probability between different locations and the dwell time of each location, (2) an MDP-based decision algorithm that aims to decide on which cloudlet the service should run for a user. The simulation results did show that our scheme achieves the lowest service response time compared with previous scheme and baseline schemes.

References

1. Soyata, T., Muraleedharan, R., Funai, C., Kwon, M., Heinzelman, W.: Cloud-vision: real-time face recognition using a mobile-cloudlet-cloud acceleration architecture. In: 2012 IEEE Symposium on Computers and Communications (ISCC), pp. 000059–000066. IEEE (2012)
2. Satyanarayanan, M., Bahl, P., Caceres, R., Davies, N.: The case for VM-based cloudlets in mobile computing. IEEE Pervasive Comput. **8**(4), 14–23 (2009)
3. Taleb, T., Ksentini, A.: An analytical model for follow me cloud. In: 2013 IEEE Global Communications Conference (GLOBECOM), pp. 1291–1296. IEEE (2013)
4. Davy, S., Famaey, J., Serrat, J., Gorricho, J.L., Miron, A., Dramitinos, M., Neves, P.M., Latré, S., Goshen, E.: Challenges to support edge-as-a-service. IEEE Commun. Mag. **52**(1), 132–139 (2014)
5. Zhang, W., Tan, S., Xia, F., Chen, X., Li, Z., Qinghua, L., Yang, S.: A survey on decision making for task migration in mobile cloud environments. Pers. Ubiquit. Comput. **20**(3), 295–309 (2016)
6. Fernando, N., Loke, S.W., Rahayu, W.: Mobile cloud computing: a survey. Future Gener. Comput. Syst. **29**(1), 84–106 (2013)
7. Ksentini, A., Taleb, T., Chen, M.: A Markov decision process-based service migration procedure for follow me cloud. In 2014 IEEE International Conference on Communications (ICC), pp. 1350–1354. IEEE (2014)
8. Puterman, M.L.: Markov decision processes. Handb. Oper. Res. Manag. Sci. **2**, 331–434 (1990)
9. Wang, S., Urgaonkar, R., He, T., Zafer, M., Chan, K., Leung, K.K.: Mobility-induced service migration in mobile micro-clouds. In 2014 IEEE Military Communications Conference, pp. 835–840. IEEE (2014)
10. Wang, S., Urgaonkar, R., Zafer, M., He, T., Chan, K., Leung, K.K.: Dynamic service migration in mobile edge-clouds. In: IFIP Networking Conference (IFIP Networking), pp. 1–9. IEEE (2015)
11. Wang, S., Urgaonkar, R., Chan, K., He, T., Zafer, M., Leung, K.K.: Dynamic service placement for mobile micro-clouds with predicted future costs. In: 2015 IEEE International Conference on Communications (ICC), pp. 5504–5510. IEEE (2015)
12. Kleinrock, L.: Queueing systems volume i: theory (1975)
13. Skiena, S.: Dijkstra Algorithm. Implementing Discrete Mathematics: Combinatorics and Graph Theory with Mathematica, pp. 225–227. Addison-Wesley, Reading (1990)
14. Isaacson, D.L., Madsen, R.W.: Markov Chains, Theory and Applications, vol. 4. Wiley, New York (1976)

Single Appliance Recognition Using Statistical Features Based k-NN Classification

Qi Liu[1], Hao Wu[2(✉)], Xiaodong Liu[3], and Nigel Linge[4]

[1] Jiangsu Collaborative Innovation Center of Atmospheric Environment and Equipment Technology (CICAEET), School of Computer and Software, Nanjing University of Information Science and Technology, Nanjing, China
[2] School of Computer and Software, Jiangsu Engineering Centre of Network Monitoring, Nanjing University of Information Science and Technology, Nanjing, China
yoerking@163.com
[3] School of Computing, Edinburgh Napier University, Edinburgh, UK
[4] School of Computing Science and Engineering, University of Salford, Salford, UK

Abstract. Recognizing the appliance according to the flowed electric current through it is quite a meaningful work which can help the electric management system to make effective policy of energy conservation. We designed an algorithm based on an improved k-nearest neighbor which can classify the unlabelled appliances' running power data into its most similar data clusters. In other words, this algorithm is able to recognize the appliance only according to its running power data series. The classification is based upon the multifarious features extracted from the time series data sensed from the running appliance with the power metering sensors. Appliance recognition is performed with a mean accuracy over 90% in five-class classification problem.

Keywords: Appliance recognition · Feature extraction · k-NN

1 Introduction

Electricity power is one of the most widely used energy sources for it has been applied into all aspects of production and living. However, the waste of electricity is serious in clivil and service industry. Some objective factors, such as disorderly growth of high energy-consuming industries, weak awareness of energy conservation and old energy saving technology of public and home appliances, lead to the serious electricity waste.

With the continuous consumption of non-renewable energy sources, the generation of electric energy will be more and more difficult which means that the use of electricity needs to be more and more efficient. Therefore, monitoring the hole process of electricity consumption, analysing the data of electricity consumption and looking for the points where we can save energy are quite efficient ways of saving energy in general.

X. Sun et al. (Eds.): ICCCS 2017, Part II, LNCS 10603, pp. 631–640, 2017.
https://doi.org/10.1007/978-3-319-68542-7_54

On the other hand, the current intelligent home industry and power industry do not take advantage of the maximum value of the data of users' electricity consumption. They have not fully mining the value of the data generated from household electric appliances. Many valuable information can be inferred from the data of the running appliances in a region, such as conjecturing users' behavior, screening high-energy-consuming appliances and assessing the level of regional electricity consumption. These information can be the effective reference for the decisions of saving electricity and electrical safety.

This paper focuses on the study of the sequent data sensed from the third part sensors set on the circuit of the appliances. The purpose of the method proposed in this paper is recognizing the working appliances according to the electricity consumption data. This paper proposes an efficient method integrated with the classic k-NN algorithm and statistical features which can realize the classification of appliance electricity consumption data. On the other words, this method is able to recognize the different class of the appliance only depend on the time series data of electricity consumption.

2 Related Work

2.1 Appliance Recognition

In the present, appliance recognition have two popular main ideas which are invasive appliance recognition and non-invasive appliance recognition. The invasive method have the advantage of very high accuracy. But the heavy transformation cost cases its hardly application because some label chips need to be embed into the appliance. The non-invasive method is more popular in the field of appliance recognition for its lower transformation cost [1]. For example, Gulati et al. utilize the radio frequency interference emissions from electronic appliances to recognize the appliance. Appliance detection is performed with a mean accuracy of 71.9% across seven-class classification problem [2]. The data analysis method is also important. Antonio Ridi al. use the hidden Markov Models to realize the application and its state recognition at low frequency electrical signatures [3]. Barriquello al. use the vector projection length and Stockwell transform method which was used in the image processing field to realize the home appliance recognition. The mean recognition accuracy is close to 90% [4].

2.2 k-NN Overview

There are a lot of data analysis methods in the machine learning field. In this study, we use the classic k-NN algorithm for its excellent classification ability in time-series data. The core idea of k-NN algorithm can be described that: an unknown sample's class can be identified as the majority of the top k most similar known samples. Specifically, there is a set of data sample, which is called training set. The samples in the set have been classificated. It means that each data has a category label. The unlabelled data was input into the algorithm.

And the algorithm will compare the each feature of the data with the known sample's features. The most k similar samples will be extracted from the training set which can be identified as a subset of samples. At last, the algorithm will count each category's occurrence number. The most frequent category can be identified as the unknown sample's class.

3 k-NN Based Classification for Single Appliance Recognition

The process of single appliance recognition is just the process of the classification of the data generated from the working appliance. The category of the time series data of the appliance electricity consumption is the category of the appliance. The data analyzed in this study is sensed by the sensor periodically when the appliances work.

3.1 Challenges in the Classification of Time-Series Data

In the actual situation, the data sensed from the working appliances have these characteristics. First, it is a sequence of continuous time and power value pairs. Second, it's difficult to make the acquisition period exact. However, this algorithm need them to be relatively stable. If not, the data can resample after draw the curve with the original data. This kind data is called time series data usually. According to the previous study, classifying the time series data with the k-NN algorithm is an efficient method. Therefore, this study adapts the same idea to deal with the data in order to realize the appliance recognition. But the effect of the k-NN depends on the select of the features. The representative features can lead to a good result. At the same time, too many features will not improve the accuracy of the algorithm and slow down the efficiency instead. In order to solve or avoid the questions, this study proposed another improvement based on the statistical features. The algorithm proposed in this paper achieves a better accuracy and efficiency in terms of the single appliance recognition.

3.2 Feature Extraction and Adaption for k-NN Classification

According to the principle of the k-NN algorithm, the quality of the features decide the accuracy of the algorithm. Therefore, the selection of the features from the samples is very important.The question of how to select the representative and differentiated features is the topic of this section. At the same time, this section introduces some improvements of the k-NN algorithm in detail according to the scene of appliance recognition in order to increase the accuracy.

The following Fig. 1 describes a typical appliance(electric kettle)'s working data which is a line chart drawn with a lot of time and its power value pairs.

In order to express expediently, this paper calls the data collected throw the sensors when the appliance is working as the appliance electricity consumption data.It is periodic and constructed with a series time and corresponding instantaneous power value pairs which changes with the time.

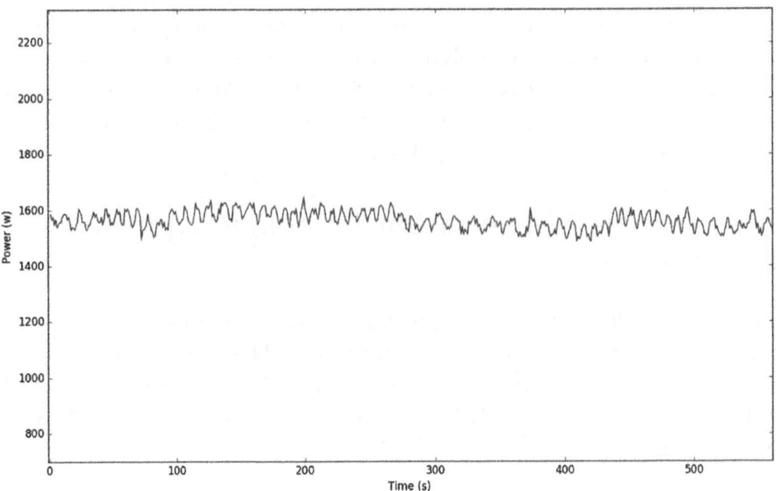

Fig. 1. Electricity consumption data curve of a electric kettle

If we compare the appliance electricity consumption data sample with the data in the sample set directly and compute similarity straight, the following two main problems will be encountered:

1. *Excessive computation cost.* In general, a piece of data consists of hundreds of time points. Therefore, the computation cost will become very giant when the sample set has thousands pieces of data or even more. It will be a quite hard task for the ordinary computer.
2. *Fitting difficulty.* The fast fitness of unknown sample curve with the known samples in the set will be very difficult for the too much computation cost and complexity of algorithm. The electricity consumption data of the same model have the extreme similarity. But it's hard to decide where the two data begin. Otherwise, it's very easy to shift or offset. In this way, the similarity will be small although they are very similar in the fact. On the other hand, the electricity consumption data of different model appliances have a lot of differences which is not suitable for fitness computation in principle.

Therefore, in order to solve the two problems above, this study adopts the statistical feature extract method. The cure of appliance electricity consumption can be described with few statistical features from analysis of the data series. The offset problem of cure fitness can be avoided skillfully. At the same time, the data quantity of the statistical features are so small than the original data that can result in the distinct improvement of algorithm efficiency.

1. The appearance of outliers requires minimal impact on the statistics.
2. The size of statistical feature values are not affected by sample size as much as possible.

3. The statistical features need have university when the data are from the same category.
4. The statistical features need have distinction when the data are from the different category.

Based on the three principles above, this study proposes thirteen different ways of feature extraction in the view of statistics. Details are follows:

First, in general, a sampe can be represented with vector **a**:

$$\mathbf{a} = (f_1, f_2, f_3, \cdots, f_n, l), n \in \mathbf{N}_+$$

1. ***Mean***, represented with $\overline{m}$. It is the average value of appliance electricity consumption data in a period of time.
2. ***Maximum***, represented with v_{max}. It is the maximum value of a piece of appliance electricity consumption data in a period of time.
3. ***Minimum***, represented with v_{min}. It is the Minimum value of a piece of appliance electricity consumption data in a period of time.
4. ***The difference between the maximum and minimum values***, represented with $d_{max-min}$. It is the difference between the maximum and minimum values of a piece of appliance electricity consumption data in a period of time.
5. ***The proportion of rise gradient values***, represented with G_{up}. There are two continuous pieces of data. If the previous data is smaller than the latter one, the later one is called rise gradient. G_{up} is represented the proportion of this kind of data.
6. ***The proportion of decline gradient values***, represented with G_{down}. There are two continuous pieces of data. If the previous data is larger than the latter one, the later one is called decline gradient. G_{down} is represented the proportion of this kind of data.
7. ***The proportion of peak values***, represented with P_{peak}. There are three continuous pieces of data. If the first one is smaller than the middle one and the last one is also smaller than the middle one, the middle one is called peak value. P_{peak} is represented the proportion of this kind of data.
8. ***The proportion of valley values***, represented with P_{valley}.There are three continuous pieces of data. If the first one is larger than the middle one and the last one is also larger than the middle one, the middle one is called valley value. P_{valley} is represented the proportion of this kind of data.
9. ***The mean value of peak values***, represented with $\overline{m}_{peak}$. It is the average value of the peak values of the data in a period of time.
10. ***The mean value of valley values***, represented with $\overline{m}_{valley}$. It is the average value of the peak values of the data in a period of time.
11. ***The proportion of outliers values***, represented with $P_{outlier}$. There is a point whose value is far larger than the other points. This point is called outlier. $P_{outlier}$ is represented the proportion of this kind of data.
12. ***The mean value of outliers***, represented with $\overline{m}_{unoutlier}$. It is the average value of the outliers.
13. ***Fluctuation range without the outliers***, represented with $d_{unoutlier}$. It is the difference between the maximum and minimum values of a period data without the outliers.

The thirteen statistical values constitute a vector of a piece of appliance electricity consumption data:

$$\mathbf{a} = (\overline{m}, v_{max}, v_{min}, d_{max-min}, G_{up}, G_{down}, P_{peak},$$
$$P_{valley}, \overline{m}_{peak}, \overline{m}_{valley}, P_{outlier}, \overline{m}_{unoutlier}, d_{unoutlier})$$

All samples in the sample set can transform with this method. In this way, the storage of the samples can be saved a lot and the speed of similarity computation will be accelerated. Besides this, this method can ignore the fitness of different data.

3.3 Normalization Processing for Unaligned Data

In practical applications, the normalization of each dimension of the vectors is very important. The normalization operation can remove the effect of the large values to the small values. For example, the difference between the maximum value and the minimum value would be very large such as air-condition, which may be thousand watt, and it would be very small such as lamp, which may be several watt. When the Euclidean distance is computed, the large feature values will usually flood the effects of the small feature values.

4 Experiment and Performance

In order to verify the effectiveness of the algorithm, we designed an inexpensive electrical monitoring devices. This device includes electricity sense and measurement module, Wi-Fi module, power adapter module and so on. This device can be embedded in a common socket inside in order to realize the function of monitor the work of appliances. The appliance electricity consumption data can be collected conveniently with the device and the supplementary supporting software systems.

The test method are single data cross-validation and single-class data cross-validation.

Single Data Cross-Validation
Getting a piece of data one by one from the n pieces data in the sample data set as the unknown sample, and the left n-1 pieces data are as the known data. Then the system tests whether each data is successfully classified. This test method can verify the accuracy of the classification of known appliances.

Single-Class Data Cross-Validation
Getting all data (10 pieces) of each model appliance one by one from the sample data set as the unknown samples, and the left n-10 pieces data are as the known data. Then the system tests whether each data of the same model appliance is successfully classified. This test method can verify the accuracy of the classification of unknown model appliance (Fig. 2).

All the tests are based on the full 300 s length data of appliance electricity consumption after the feature extract finished.

Fig. 2. Electricity consumption monitoring device

4.1 Experimental Results

The main purpose of this experiment is testing the classification accuracy of the algorithm. The k value of the k-NN algorithm is set as 3 because of the not too much data in the sample set.The final experimental results are as follows.

The overall accuracy rate of single data cross-validation was 92.0%. The results are shown in Table 1.

Table 1. Accuracy rate of single data cross-validation

Category	Model	Data count	Accurate count	Accuracy	Integrated accuracy
Electric kettle	MK-17S18H	10	9	90%	93.3%
	AUX-12A15	10	9	90%	
	AUX-12A16	10	10	100%	
Lamp	MT-6040	10	10	100%	90.0%
	TC609	10	8	80%	
	P-ZD-70023-30	10	9	90%	
Cell phone charger	A1443	10	8	80%	90.0%
	ETA-U90CBC	10	9	90%	
	CH-P002	10	10	100%	
Laptop power adapter	ADP-150NB	10	10	100%	96.7%
	ADP-90DDB	10	10	100%	
	A1435	10	9	90%	
Heater	NPS7-13T	10	10	100%	90.0%
	NS8-13F	10	8	80%	
	NDK20-17DW	10	9	90%	
Total		150	138		92.0 %

Table 2. Accuracy rate of single-class data cross-validation

Category	Model	Data count	Accurate count	Accuracy	Integrated accuracy
Electric kettle	MK-17S18H	10	8	90%	83.3%
	AUX-12A15	10	8	90%	
	AUX-12A16	10	9	100%	
Lamp	MT-6040	10	6	100%	70.0%
	TC609	10	7	80%	
	P-ZD-70023-30	10	8	90%	
Cell phone charger	A1443	10	7	80%	73.3%
	ETA-U90CBC	10	7	90%	
	CH-P002	10	8	100%	
Laptop power adapter	ADP-150NB	10	8	100%	86.70%
	ADP-90DDB	10	9	100%	
	A1435	10	9	90%	
Heater	NPS7-13T	10	9	100%	83.3%
	NS8-13F	10	8	80%	
	NDK20-17DW	10	8	90%	
Total			119		79.3%

What needs to be emphasized is that this classification method is classifying the data into the category of the appliance instead of the model of the appliance.

According to the experiment results above, the proposed algorithm have a very heigh accuracy when the training sample set contains the appliance's data.

However, in the practical application, it is not possible to collect all the appliances' data in the world into the sample data set. So, it's much valuable to test the accuracy of the classification of the unknown model appliance's data. In other words, whether the algorithm is able to classify the unknown model appliance into its category correctly.

Specific experiment results are shown in Table 2.

The experiment result shows that the overall accuracy rate of single class data cross-validation was 79.3%. This result shows that the algorithm has the ability of recognition of unknown model appliance for the unknown model appliances' classification accuracy is still comparative heigh.

4.2 Detailed Performance Analysis

The proposed algorithm based on the statistical feature extraction is sensitive to the quantity of the data. More stable statistical features can be extracted when the data is much and the features will be more representative. In order to prove this, the study designs another experiment. The experiment tests the accuracies of different length of data. The experiment still adopts the single data cross-validation and single-class data cross-validation. However, the different aspect is the data length. The data length are 30 s, 60 s, 120 s, 180 s, 240 s and 300 s.The accuracies change with the different data length are shown as the Figs. 3 and 4:

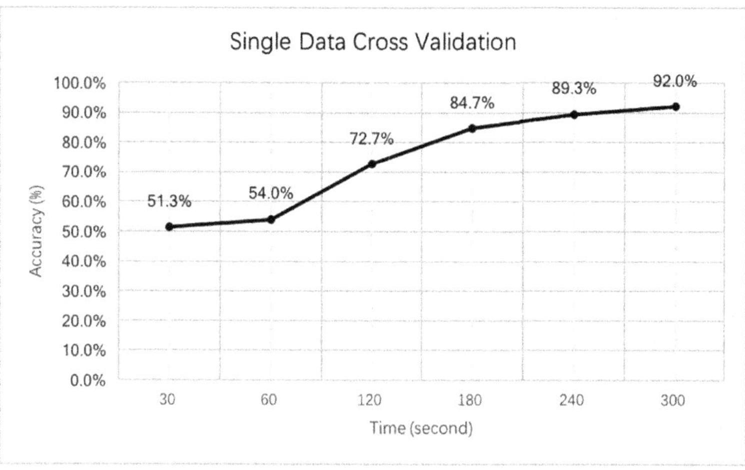

Fig. 3. Recognition accuracy changes with the data length of single data

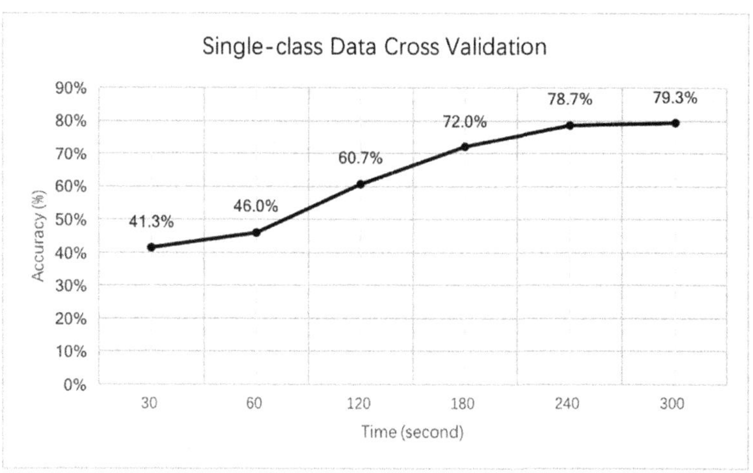

Fig. 4. Recognition accuracy changes with the data length of single class

Some conclusions can be concluded from the two result figures above. The less data was collected, the accuracy of classification will be lower. When the amount of data is increasing, the accuracy of the algorithm will increase distinctly. However, when the amount of data get to a specific value, the accuracy increase will not change distinctly. Because the values of statistical features are going to be stable and the accuracy of the classification is also going to be stable relatively.

5 Conclusion

This study proposed an appliance recognition method based on the classic k-NN algorithm. It can not only recognize the known appliance according to the appliance electricity consumption data but also recognize the unknown appliance. This study proposed an efficient feature extraction method based on the statistics which can reduce the complexity of computation. The experiment results show that the proposed method has a heigh accuracy of classification. On the other hand, the experiment proves that the same category appliance electricity consumption data have some similarities in some statistics and the different category appliance data have differences. Therefore, different category appliances have the possibility to be classified.

Acknowledgments. This work is supported by Marie Curie Fellowship (701697-CAR-MSCA-IF-EF-ST), the NSFC (61300238 and 61672295), the 2014 Project of six personnel in Jiangsu Province under Grant No. 2014-WLW-013, and the PAPD fund.

References

1. Cho, W.T., Chiu, Y.S., Wang, L.C., Lai, C.F.: A lightweight appliance recognition approach for smart grid. In: IEEE International Conference on Dependable, Autonomic and Secure Computing, pp. 469–474 (2013)
2. Gulati, M., Singh, V.K., Agarwal, S.K., Bohara, V.A.: Appliance activity recognition using radio frequency interference emissions. IEEE Sens. J. **16**(16), 6197–6204 (2016)
3. Ridi, A., Gisler, C., Hennebert, J.: Appliance and state recognition using Hidden Markov models. In: IEEE International Conference on Data Science and Advanced Analytics (2015)
4. Borin, V.P., Barriquello, C.H., Campos, A.: Approach for home appliance recognition using vector projection length and stockwell transform. Electron. Lett. **51**(24), 2035–2037 (2016)
5. Ridi, A., Gisler, C., Hennebert, J.: A survey on intrusive load monitoring for appliance recognition. In: IEEE International Conference on Pattern Recognition, vol. 94, pp. 3702–3707 (2014)
6. Fu, Z., Sun, X., Liu, Q., Zhou, L., Shu, J.: Achieving efficient cloud search services: multi-keyword ranked search over encrypted cloud data supporting parallel computing. IEICE Trans. Commun. **E98–B**(1), 190–200 (2015)
7. Liu, Q., Cai, W., Shen, J., Fu, Z., Liu, X., Linge, N.: A speculative approach to spatial-temporal efficiency with multi-objective optimization in a heterogeneous cloud environment. Secur. Commun. Netw. **9**(17), 4002–4012 (2016)
8. Xia, Z., Wang, X., Sun, X., Wang, B.: Steganalysis of least significant bit matching using multi-order differences. Secur. Commun. Netw. **7**(8), 1283–1291 (2014)

Performance Measurement and Configuration Optimization of Virtual Machines Based on the Bayesian Network

Jia Hao, Binbin Zhang(✉), Kun Yue, Juan Wang, and Hao Wu

School of Information Science and Engineering, Yunnan University, Kunming 650500, China
zhangbinbin@gmail.com

Abstract. It is significant to accurately measure the performance of virtual machines (VMs) and reasonably allocate resources according to users' requirements for both users and cloud resource providers in IaaS cloud computing. In this paper, we propose a Bayesian network based model, called PPBN, to describe uncertain relationships among properties and performance of VMs and then measure VM performance in the form of probabilities. Further, we design a linear optimization approach to minimize resource cost and improve host resource utilization at the same time. Experimental results show that our method can measure VM performance accurately and the achieved configuration can meet users' performance requirements well.

Keywords: Virtual machine · Performance measurement · Configuration optimization · Bayesian network

1 Introduction

IaaS (Infrastructure as a Service), as the cloud computing service model, provides computing resources to users in the form of virtual machines (VMs) [1]. Users can require and pay for a VM configured on demand, while resource providers should supply VMs to meet the demands of users. Therefore, it is significant to measure the performance of VMs accurately and allocate resources reasonably according to users' requirements for both users and cloud resource providers [2].

Currently, when users plan to rent a VM, they can customize the VM by setting the resource configuration. For example, Amazon Elastic Compute Cloud (Amazon EC2) provides quite a lot of VM types comprising different combinations of CPU, memory, storage, and networking capacity [3]. The customers can choose and pay for the appropriate VM to fit the performance requirement of their applications.

However, it is difficult for customers to form opinions about the performance of the VMs according to the resource properties mentioned above, which is mainly reflected in following challenges.

First, there are many other properties that may affect the performance of a VM, it is difficult to analyze and quantify the relationships between them. E.g., the resource competition among multiple VMs and how VM's virtual CPUs (vCPUs) pin to

X. Sun et al. (Eds.): ICCCS 2017, Part II, LNCS 10603, pp. 641–652, 2017.
https://doi.org/10.1007/978-3-319-68542-7_55

physical CPUs (it describes the mappings from vCPUs to CPUs) certainly impact on VM performance, but their impacts are hard to quantify. Second, the performance of a VM fluctuates and presents uncertainty due to the unpredictable load changes from other VMs hosted on the same host. It is difficult for existing performance measurement approaches to quantify the performance fluctuations [4].

To respond to the challenges, we first try to find out the properties of a VM that may have effect on its performance, including hardware, software, configuration and runtime environmental properties. The hardware and software properties describe the infrastructure of the virtualization environment, while the configuration and runtime environmental properties can reflect the resource usage and suggest resource competition. They can provide more details for performance measurement. Furthermore, we propose a performance measurement approach based on Bayesian network (BN) in this paper. BN is a directed acyclic graphic widely adopted as the framework for uncertainty representation and reasoning [5]. It has a great advantage to solve complex problems caused by uncertainty and relevance. Thus, we propose to construct a Property Performance Bayesian Network (PPBN) to represent relationships between VMs properties and performance. We can also use the PPBN to quantify the uncertainty of the performance of a VM. Based on PPBN, the performance of a VM with particular configuration can be measured by a probabilistic form quantitatively.

Moreover, in order to help users to configure a VM according to the performance requests, we can use the PPBN to produce multiple VMs configurations satisfying customers' performance requirements. We further propose a VM configuration optimization approach to minimize the resource cost and optimize the resource utilization on the premise of meeting the VM performance requirements.

The remainder of this paper is organized as follows: Sect. 2 introduces related work. Section 3 introduces PPBN construction. Section 4 introduces VM performance measurement and configuration optimization based on PPBN. Section 5 introduces experiments to evaluate our proposed model. Section 6 is the conclusion and future work.

2 Related Work

Wang [6], and Xiong and Wang [7] proposed linear models to describe the relationships between VM properties and performance. However, there exist complex relationships between VM properties and VM performance which cannot be abstracted by a simple linear relationship.

Li et al. [8], Kraft et al. [9], Kundu et al. [10] and Kousiouris et al. [11] collected the memory, CPU, I/O and network bandwidth usage as properties and respectively use SVD algorithm, Artificial Neural Networks (ANNs) and queuing theory to establish non-linear models to analyze the relationship between properties and performance to measure the performance of a VM. Kong et al. [12] proposed a decentralized belief propagation based method, which aimed at accelerating the online response, improving the resilience from the unpredicted changing in the environments, and reducing the message passing for task allocation. However, due to the resource competition between VMs, performance of a VM fluctuates. It is difficult to measure the fluctuation ranges of the performance by the above mentioned methods.

Meanwhile, there are many BN based research findings for cloud resource usage and optimization. Zhang et al. [13] predicted QoS posterior probability based on BN reasoning method clique tree propagation. Ramezani et al. [14], Shyam et al. [15] and Bashar [16] collected massive data from cloud data center (Google CE, Amazon EC2), and then measured performance based on BN. In Bayesian-Network modeling, the method mentioned above mainly considered the properties for the data center, such as types of the workloads, resource availabilities, and resource utilities. But we pay more attention to VM's own properties about the virtualization infrastructure and the configuration, and the runtime environmental properties of the VM.

3 Bayesian Network for Properties and Performance of Virtual Machines

There are many properties which may have an effect on VM performance, illustrated in Table 1.

Table 1. VM properties classification

Hardware	Software	Configuration	Runtime environment
CPU type; Memory type; Storage type	Hypervisor type; CPU, memory, I/O devices virtualization technology; Scheduling algorithms	Number of vCPUs; vCPU-CPU pinning; VM memory capacity; Virtual block disk type	Number of VMs running at the same time; Type of workload running on the other VMs

When we are to measure a particular virtualization environment, we first select properties that may affect the VM performance from this virtualization environment and set up multiple different VMs by assigning different values to these properties. Then, we run benchmarks to get the corresponding results which indicate VM performance. We use the samples of property assignments and benchmark results to construct a PPBN. This training set is denoted by D. Definition 1 defines a PPBN.

Definition 1. The PPBN denoted by $G_{PPBN} = (U, E)$ is a probabilistic directed acyclic graphic, where the set of nodes $U = \{V, T\}$. $V = \{V_1, V_2, \ldots, V_n\}$ represent VM property nodes where V_k $(1 \leq k \leq n)$ represents a property, while T is the performance node. The set of edges E represents their conditional dependencies between nodes, in which $e(U_i, U_j)$ is the edge from node U_i to U_j $(U_i, U_j \in U, i \neq j)$. Each node of a PPBN is associated with a Conditional probability table (CPT) in a PPBN to give the probability of each value when given assignments of its parents. The CPT for the performance node is used to quantify how much performance depends on its parent property nodes.

In line with the generic steps for BN construction [17], to construct a PPBN is to construct the structure, followed by parameter calculation.

3.1 Constructing the Structure of PPBN

The structure of PPBN indicates if there is causal relationship between every two nodes. In this paper, we believe that all the properties in a resource suite provided by the current IaaS cloud service, e.g. Amazon EC2, have a direct impact on the performance of VMs. That is to say, there are directed edges from these property nodes to VM performance node. Thus we can get an initial structure for PPBN. And we use a property and performance matrix (*PPM*) to mark the edges in the initial structure. Each element in *PPM* is denoted by $\mathrm{R}(U_i, U_j)$, which indicates whether there is an edge from node U_i to U_j. The possible values of $\mathrm{R}(U_i, U_j)$ is defined as:

a. $\mathrm{R}(U_i, U_j) = 1$: there is a directed edge from U_i to U_j.
b. $\mathrm{R}(U_i, U_j) = 0$: there is no directed edge from U_i to U_j.
c. $\mathrm{R}(U_i, U_j) = \alpha(\alpha \neq 0, \alpha \neq 1)$: to be determined.

The *PPM* is initialized according to the initial structure. Then we only need to determine if there is an edge from U_i to U_j when $\mathrm{R}(U_i, U_j) = \alpha$. We use a dependency analysis method based on mutual information [19] to do this according to the training set *D*.

Mutual information can represent the dependency between two variables [18]. The mutual information of nodes U_i and U_j is denoted by $I(U_i; U_j)$, which is calculated by Eq. (1).

$$I(U_i, U_j) = \sum\nolimits_{u_i} \sum\nolimits_{u_j} P(u_i, u_j) \mathrm{lb} \frac{P(u_i, u_j)}{P(u_i) * P(u_j)} \tag{1}$$

where $P(u_i, u_j)$ is the joint distribution for u_i and u_j, which is the values of U_i and U_j, and the marginal distributions of u_i and u_j are $P(u_i)$ and $P(u_j)$. If $I(U_i; U_j) = 0$, then U_i and U_j are independent of each other and there is no edge from U_i to U_j. If $I(U_i; U_j) > \mathcal{E}$, then we add an edge from U_i to U_j, where $\mathcal{E}$ is a given threshold value. Thus we get an approximate structure of PPBN. Then we check the structure to delete edges to remove cycles and redundant edges. Algorithm 1 describes the structure construction of PPBN:

```
Algorithm.1. Structure construction of PPBN
Input: R(U_i, U_j)[]: the initial PPM
    U={V,T}: VM property and performance nodes
    E=∅: the initial PPBN edge set;
    E_staging=∅: the staging edge set;
    ε: threshold of mutual information;
    n: the total number of property and performance nodes.
Output: G_PPBN=(U, E), the structure of PPBN.
Steps:
for i←n to 1 do
for j←n-1 to 1 do
 switch (R(U_i, U_j))
    case 0 :  // No directed edge from U_i to U_j.
       break;
    case 1 : // There is a directed edge from U_i to U_j.
       E_staging ← E_staging∪e(U_i, U_j)
       break;
    case α : // to be determined.
       if I(U_i; U_j)<ε
       break;
        else if I(U_i; U_j)>ε
         E_staging ← E_staging∪e(U_i, U_j);
       break;
end for
end for
check_and_remove(E_staging, E); //to delete edges to
   remove cycles and redundant edges.
return G_PPBN =(U, E);
```

When half elements in *PPM* are 0 or 1, we need to calculate the mutual information $n^2/2$ times, reducing by half comparing with the traditional method to calculate mutual information n^2 times for each pair of nodes U_i and U_j.

3.2 Determining the Parameters of PPBN

For a node U_i in PPBN we denote its parameters in CPT as ϑ_i. If U_i doesn't have any parent, we use priori probability to represent ϑ_i. Else, take the performance node as an example of U_i. There are r property nodes as its parents and there are m cases for the values of its parent nodes. The performance node T has n possible values u_{i1}, $u_{i2} \ldots u_{in}$. Then ϑ_i could be represented by a table of $m*n$ entries, each entry is denoted by ϑ_{ijt}, $1 \le j \le m$, $1 \le t \le n$. ϑ_{ijt} is the conditional probability of T taking the value u_{it} when the values of its parent nodes are in case j. We can use our training set D and the maximum likelihood estimation (MLE) [17] to estimate each ϑ_{ijt} using Eq. (2).

$$\theta_{ijt} = \frac{Num(U_i = u_{it}, \pi(U_i) = j)}{Num(\pi(U_i) = \mathrm{j})} \tag{2}$$

In Eq. (2), $Num(U_i = u_{it}, \pi(U_i) = j)$ is the number of samples which satisfy $U_i = u_{it}$ and $\pi(U_i) = j$ (the values of the parent nodes are in case j) in D, while $Num(\pi(U_i) = j)$ is the number of samples which satisfy $\pi(U_i) = j$ in D. For each U_i in PPBN, we sequentially use Eq. (2) to calculate each ϑ_{ijt}. Thus, CPT of node U_i is a matrix ϑ_i, each row of which is $\vartheta_{ij} = (\vartheta_{ij1}, \vartheta_{ij2} \ldots \vartheta_{ijn})$, $j = 1, 2, \ldots, m$.

When the values of parent property nodes are in case j, each ϑ_{ijt} quantify the possibility for the performance node to take the value u_{it}. So the performance fluctuation can be measure by ϑ_{ij}.

4 PPBN Based Performance Measurement and Configuration Optimization

4.1 PPBN Based Performance Measurement

In a PPBN, the structure presents the dependency between VM properties and performance, and the CPT of the performance node contains all the conditional probabilities of each possible value. So given a specific VM, we can assign the values to property nodes which are the parents of the performance node in PPBN. Then we can look up the CPT of the performance node to find out the row according to the parents assignments. The conditional probabilities in this row are used to quantify the performance of this VM.

Then we take the performance value with the greatest probability as the final performance measurement result of the VM. And the other values with their probabilities can illustrate the performance fluctuation of the VM when the probabilities are not 0. The values range means the fluctuation range, while the probability distribution indicates the fluctuation possibility.

4.2 PPBN Based Configuration Optimization

When a user specifies the performance requirement for a VM, the corresponding conditional probability for each value of each property can be calculated based on the parameters of PPBN. The probability of a property value reflects the possibility of taking this value to meet the performance requirement. There may be more than one value with a high probability for a same property. So there may be more than one configuration satisfying the performance requirement. In order to find out the VM with the minimal resource cost from these candidates, in this section we propose a linear optimization approach.

Selecting Candidate Values for Each Property. When given a specific VM performance requirement, we can calculate the probability of satisfying the performance requirement when V_i taking the value v_{ij}.

Given a performance value t_k, by using Bayesian formula and chain rules of probability theory, the conditional probability of configuration vector V can be represented through Eq. (3):

$$P(V|T_k) \propto \prod_{i=1}^{n} P(V_i) * P(T_k|V_i) \quad (3)$$

The greater the $P(V \mid T_k)$ value, there is a greater possibility for meeting users' requirement. $P(V \mid T_k)$ is directly proportional to each $P(V_i) * P(T_k|V_i)$. So when $i = 1, 2, \ldots, n$, we try to make each $P(V_i) * P(T_k|V_i)$ as greater as possible. Each $P(V_i) * P(T_k|V_i)$ can be calculated using parameters in CPT.

In this paper, we select candidate values for each property as follows:

a. If a value v_{ij} of the property V_i makes $P(V_i) * P(T_k|V_i)$ the maximum, we make v_{ij} as a candidate value for V_i. The maximal value of $P(V_i) * P(T_k|V_i)$ is denoted by *MAX*.
b. If another value v_{il} of the property V_i makes $P(V_i) * P(T_k|V_i)$ the second maximum and the second maximum value is denoted by *SEC*, we make v_{il} as another candidate value for V_i only if $MAX\text{-}SEC \leq 10\%$.
c. If there are two values make $P(V_i) * P(T_k|V_i)$ the second maximum, we only make the small one as the candidate.

Thus, we can get one or two candidate values for each property, which are most likely to meet the performance requirement.

We combine all these candidate property values as candidate configurations of VMs. These VMs can meet user's performance requirement with high probability.

Minimizing Resource Cost according to Hardware Prices. In order to help users lower costs, we propose a linear optimization approach to select the minimal-cost configuration, in which we use hardware unit cost to measure the resource cost Y. So,

Optimization objective: $Y_{\min} = aV_1 + bV_2 + cV_3 \ldots + nV_n$.

where $a, b, \ldots, n$ represent the unit cost of the properties ($V_1, V_2, \ldots, V_n$) respectively.

If the number of properties is not very large, we only need to calculate the resource cost for all of the possible configurations successively and find the minimal-cost one.

5 Experimental Results

5.1 Experiment Setup

We used two physical hosts to stimulate cloud servers. The first is configured with an AMD-A10 7850 k Quad-Core 3.6 GHz processor, 16 GB 1866 GHz DDR3 memory, 500 GB SATA hard drive and 120 GB SSD. The second is configured with an Intel i5-6600 Quad-Core 3.3 GHz processor, 16 GB 2133 GHz DDR4 memory, 500 GB SATA hard drive and 120 GB SSD. Both hosts run Xen-4.6, and each of them hosts two VMs. Each VM runs Centos-7 with Linux kernel 3.18.34–20.el7.x86_64.

We select six main properties which influence VM performance under our experimental environment. They are type of CPU(CPUTYPE), hard disk drive type (HDD), the number of vCPUs(vCPUNUM), vCPU-CPU pinning (vCPU-pinning), memory size (MEM) and the application type on the other VM (LoadTYPE). CPUTYPE and HDD describe the hardware differences which will affect VM performance in our environment. vCPUNUM, vCPUpinning and Memory are main configuration properties which can reflect CPU and memory usage of a VM. vCPU-pinning and LoadTYPE reflect the resource competition. Table 2 illustrates the value ranges of these properties.

Table 2. Properties and their value ranges

Properties	CPUTYPE	HDD	vCPUNUM	vCPU-pinning	MEM	LoadTYPE
Range	AMD	SATA	1	None	512	CPU-intensive
	Intel	SSD	2	Competitive	1024	Memory-intensive
			3	Noncompetitive	2048	

We set up VMs according to the configurations which are combinations of these properties values. Then we select some programs in benchmark PARSEC [20] to stimulate different applications. They are *bodytrack*, *freqmine*, *x264* and *streamcluster*. We use their wall clock execution time to represent the VM performance. We run each program 100 times on each VM and collect all the property values and corresponding performance results as a training set D to construct a PPBN.

5.2 Accuracy of Performance Measurement

In order to evaluate the accuracy of our proposed PPBN based performance measurement model, we compare the performance results measured by PPBN with that measured by a linear model Z. $Z = \alpha_1 V_1 + \alpha_2 V_2 + \alpha_3 V_3 + \alpha_4 V_4 + \alpha_5 V_5 + \alpha_6 V_6 + \alpha_7$, where V_1 to V_6 are different VM properties in Table 2. We use least square method to estimate the parameters α_1 to α_7 using the same training set D collected in 5.1.

We randomly choose eight different VMs with configurations denoted by $C1$ to $C8$. On each VM we first run four benchmark programs 1000 times, and the value repeated most often in the results is denoted as E_r. Then we use PPBN model to measure the most likely performance value of the same VM and denote it as P_r. Finally we use the linear model Z to measure its performance, and the result is denoted by L_r.

The comparison of E_r, P_r and L_r is illustrated in Fig. **1**.

It is observed from Fig. **1** that P_r is closer to E_r compare to L_r results most of the time, that is, the measurement results of our proposed PPBN model are closer to the experiment results compare to linear model.

Moreover, the PPBN model can measure VM performance fluctuations, while the linear model cannot do that. To evaluate the measurement of performance fluctuations, we do the following experiment.

We randomly assign a value to each property, e.g., CPUTYPE is Intel. HDD is SATA. The VM uses 3 vCPUs, which are noncompetitively pinned to CPU cores. The memory capacity is 512 MB. The application type on the other VM is memory-intensive. These

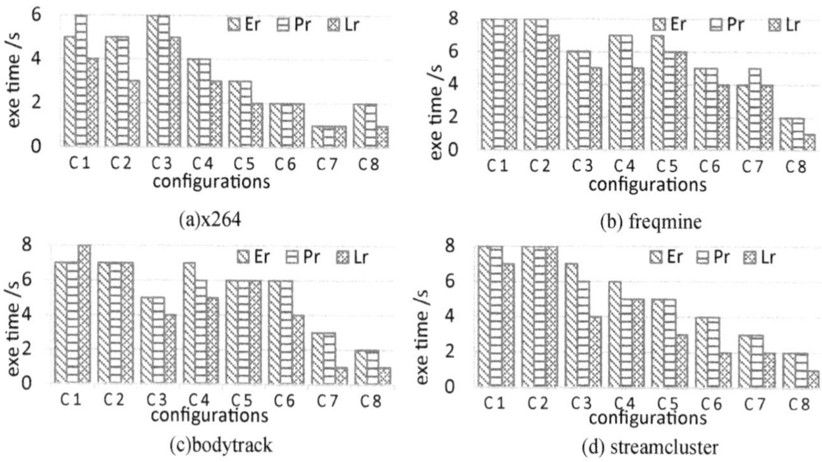

Fig. 1. Experimental results compared with PPBN and linear model results

assignments describe a specific VM's configuration and its runtime environment. To measure its performance, we can look up the CPT of the performance nodes in PPBN and find the probability distribution of the performance results.

We set up this VM and run each PARSEC program (bodytrack, freqmine, x264 and streamcluster) 1000 times to collect the performance results and calculate the probability distribution. We use P_m to denote the probability measured by PPBN, and P_r to denote the probability calculated by experimental results. Figure 2 shows the performance ranges and probability distributions derived from the experimental results and that from the PPBN.

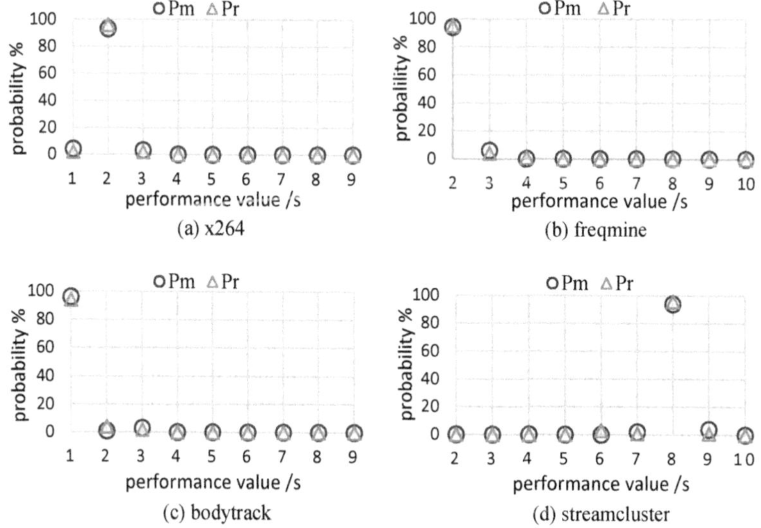

Fig. 2. PPBN measured results compared with the experimental results

We can conclude from Fig. 2 that the greatest possible performance values measured by PPBN are exactly the same as the experimental results. The ranges of performance values derived from PPBN are the same as the experimental results, and the fluctuations have the same trend.

Table 3 shows the differences between the greatest probabilities measured by PPBNs (P_m) and the maximum probabilities derived from experiments (P_r). In Table 3, $error = P_m - P_r$, $relative\ error = |P_m - P_r| / P_r$.

Table 3. The errors of PPBN measured and experimental probabilities

Program	Exe time/s	P_m	P_r	Error	Relative error
Freqmine	2	0.94	0.95	−0.01	1.05 %
Bodytrack	1	0.96	0.94	0.02	2.12 %
x264	2	0.95	0.97	−0.02	2.06 %
Streamcluster	8	0.94	0.97	−0.03	3.09 %

We can see from Table 3 that the greatest absolute error is 0.03 and the smallest is 0.01. The mean relative error for the four Parsec programs is 2.08% and mean square error (MSE) is 0.00045. The evaluation illustrates that the measured results are very close to the experimental ones, including the performance ranges and their probability distributions, our proposed PPBN model can effectively measure the performance and also the performance fluctuation which is important in virtualization environments.

5.3 Effectiveness of Configuration Optimization

In our experimental environment, when a user specifies the performance requirement for a VM, e.g., the run time of freqmine is specified as 8 s, the candidate VM properties values can be got through PPBN and combined into the following VM configurations:

*C*1 = {AMD, SATA, 1, competitive, 512, cpu-intensive};
*C*2 = {AMD, SATA, 1, competitive, 1024, cpu-intensive};
*C*3 = {Intel, SATA, 1, competitive, 512, cpu-intensive};
*C*4 = {Intel, SATA, 1, competitive, 1024, cpu-intensive};

We believe the four candidate VMs with these configurations *C*1–*C*4 can satisfy the user's performance requirement with a higher probability than any VM with any other configuration. Thus, we first evaluate whether the candidate VMs can satisfy the performance requirement. We run freqmine 1000 times on each candidate VMs and record the run time. The results are illustrated in Fig. 3.

In Fig. 3, we can see that execution time equals to 8 s in most tests. That is, any of the candidates can satisfy the performance requirement with a high probability (>71%).

In this paper, we use hardware price to represent hardware unit cost and calculate the resource cost. We respectively calculate the resource cost of VMs with the configurations *C*1 to *C*4, and the minimal is *C*3. In Fig. 3, we found the performance of *C*3 VM can satisfy the user's requirement. The experiments show that our proposed PPBN and linear optimization approach can measure the VM performance results accurately and obtain a VM with the minimal resource cost on the premise of satisfying the user's performance requirements.

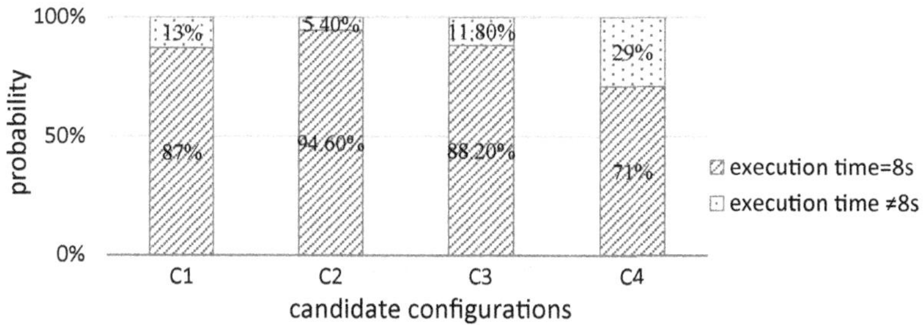

Fig. 3. Performance of the VMs with candidate configurations

6 Conclusions and Future Work

When applications run on VMs, there are many properties that affect its performance. Some properties' effects are uncertain. So it's hard to measure their performance. We propose a Bayesian-Network based model (PPBN) to find out the dependency relationships between the properties and performance of VMs from the massive testing data. Based on PPBN we can measure how much each property affects the performance, and also we can measure the performance of a VM according to its configuration. The measurement results can express the fluctuation of performance by its range and probabilities. This performance measurement approach can help customers to form opinions about the performance of a VM in detail according to the properties which include hardware, software, configuration, and runtime environment characteristics.

Based on PPBN, when users specify performance requirement, a set of configurations which can meet the requirement can be calculated through the probability reasoning. So we propose a linear optimization approach to find out a minimal recourse cost configuration. It can help users to reduce the cost based on the premise of satisfying the performance requirements.

However, we will try to find out more properties to further analyze the influence on performance, especially the impact of resource competition among VMs on performance. And using the parallel and incremental approach for BN learning [21], we can try to bring in some runtime properties to model PPBN and measure performance of VMs online.

Acknowledgements. This paper was supported by the National Natural Science Foundation of China (Nos. 61402398, 61472345, 61562090, 61462056), Natural Science Foundation of Yunnan Province (No. 2014FA023), Program for Innovative Research Team in Yunnan University (No. XT412011), Program for Excellent Young Talents of Yunnan University (No. WX173602), and the Innovation Research Foundation for Graduate Students of Yunnan University.

References

1. Danilov, A., Andersen, J., Molodkina, E., Polukarov, Y., Miller, P.: The NIST definition of cloud computing. Commun. ACM **53**, 50 (2011)

2. Armbrust, M., Fox, A., Griffith, R., Joseph, A., Katz, R., Konwinski, A., Lee, G., Patterson, D., Rabkin, A.: Above the clouds: a Berkeley view of cloud computing. Eecs Department University of California Berkeley, vol. 53, pp. 50–58 (2009)
3. Amazon EC2 Instance Types. http://aws.amazon.com/ec2/instance-types
4. Dillon, T., Chen, W., Chang, E.: Cloud computing: issues and challenges. In: Proceedings of the 24th IEEE International Conference on Advanced Information Networking and Applications, pp. 27–33. IEEE Computer Society, Washington (2010)
5. Zhang, L., Guo, H.: Introduction of Bayesian Network. Science Press, Beijing (2005)
6. Wang, R.: A virtual data center design and implementation of dynamic performance control system. Shanghai Jiao Tong University (2011)
7. Xiong, H., Wang, C.: Cloud application classification and fine-grained resource provision based on prediction. J. Comput. Appl. **33**(6), 1534–1539 (2013)
8. Li, F., Yang, D., Zhou, P., Wu, Y.: Modeling application performance in a virtualized environment. Comput. Syst. Appl. **24**, 9–15 (2015)
9. Kraft, S., Casale, G., Krishnamurthy, D.: I/O performance prediction in consolidated virtualized environments. In: Proceedings of the 2nd ACM/SPEC International Conference on Performance engineering, pp. 295–306. ACM Press, New York (2011)
10. Kundu, S., Rangaswami, R., Dutta, K.: Application performance modeling in a virtualized environment. In: 16th International Symposium on High Performance Computer Architecture, pp. 1–10. IEEE Press, New York (2010)
11. Kousiouris, G., Cucinotta, T., Varvarigou, T.: The effects of scheduling, workload type and consolidation scenarios on virtual machine performance and their prediction through optimized artificial neural networks. J. Syst. Softw. **84**(8), 1270–1291 (2011)
12. Kong, Y., Zhang, M., Ye, D.: A belief propagation-based method for task allocation in open and dynamic cloud environments. Knowl.-Based Syst. **115**, 123–132 (2016)
13. Zhang, P., Han, Q., Li, W.: A novel QoS prediction approach for cloud service based on bayesian networks model. In: IEEE International Conference on Mobile Services, pp. 111–118. IEEE Press, San Francisco (2016)
14. Ramezani, F., Naderpour, M., Lu, J.: Handling uncertainty in cloud resource management using fuzzy Bayesian networks. In: 2015 IEEE International Conference on Fuzzy Systems, pp. 1–8. IEEE Press, Istanbul (2015)
15. Shyam, G., Manvi, S.: Virtual resource prediction in cloud environment: a Bayesian approach. J. Netw. Comput. Appl. **65**, 144–154 (2016)
16. Bashar, A.: Autonomic scaling of cloud computing resources using BN-based prediction models. In: The 2nd International Conference on Cloud Networking (CloudNet), pp. 200–204. IEEE Press, San Francisco (2013)
17. Stephenson, T.: An Introduction to Bayesian Network Theory and Usage. IDIAP Research Report, 00-03 (2000)
18. Mukherjee, T., Jung, G.: System and process to recommend cloud service cloud configuration based on service similarity. U.S. Patent Application 13/795, 566 (2013)
19. Cheng, J., Greiner, R.: Learning Bayesian networks from data: an information-theory based approach. Artif. Intell. **137**, 43–90 (2002)
20. The PARSEC Benchmark Suite. http://parsec.cs.princeton.edu/overview.htm
21. Yue, K., Fang, Q., Wang, X., Li, J., Liu, W.: A parallel and incremental approach for data-intensive learning of Bayesian networks. IEEE Trans. Cybern. **45**(12), 2890–2904 (2015)

Image Recapture Detection Through Residual-Based Local Descriptors and Machine Learning

Jian Li(✉) and Guojing Wu

School of Computer and Software, Nanjing University of Information Science and Technology, Nanjing 210044, China
Ljian20@gmail.com

Abstract. At present, the tamper evidence would be invalid in recaptured image in terms of most of the digital image forensics, so the authenticity of the image detection is a security threat. Since dense local descriptors and machine learning have been successfully applied in steganalysis and forgery detection, we propose a new image recapture detection method based on these two techniques. The local descriptors were recently proposed in the field steganalysis, and some descriptors are selected by greedy strategy in the experiments. Support vector machine and ensemble classifier are utilized as the classifier in the proposed method. The experimental results show that the proposed method achieves a good performance rate that exceeds 99.61% of recaptured images and 96.40% for single captured images on the open source database.

Keywords: Image forensics · Image recapture detection · Machine learning

1 Introduction

Nowadays, high resolution images can be easily obtained by digital cameras. However, if such a high quality digital camera is used to recapture an image from a good quality print or a high resolution LCD monitor, it is difficult for people to recognize whether the image is single captured or recaptured.

With the wide application of image processing software, anyone can modify digital images and spread widely on the Internet. Because the tamper evidence would be invalid in recaptured image, an attacker may choose to recapture a forged image. So the authenticity of the image detection is a security threat.

Recapture detection is to detect whether a given image was a single capture of natural scene or whether it was recaptured with a digital camera from an LCD monitor or a high quality print. Many image recapture detection approaches have been proposed in the recent years. Yu et al. [1] analyzed the recaptured image from print paper and the texture information was considered to be reflected from the specularity component of a recaptured image, so they detect recaptured images using specularity component. Bai et al. [2] applied this method on images with high resolution and got a good result. Gao et al [3] proposed a method based on a set of physical features such as the contexture background information, the spatial distribution of specularity, the color information

X. Sun et al. (Eds.): ICCCS 2017, Part II, LNCS 10603, pp. 653–660, 2017.
https://doi.org/10.1007/978-3-319-68542-7_56

and contrast etc. Cao et al [4] studied the recaptured photographs on LCD screen. They did a test of detecting the recaptured images by human eye. The results of the experiment show that the recaptured image has the threat of potential confusion in the human eye and the forensic system. They took advantage of texture features, the loss-of-fine-details characteristics and the color as features, and got good classification results. Recently, Thongkamwitoon et al [5] proposed a recapture detection algorithms based on edge blurriness. The line spread functions of selected edges were used to train single capture and recapture dictionaries following the K-SVD approach. Only using dictionary approximation errors and the mean edge spread width, an SVM classifier was established. They also showed how to eliminate aliasing by setting the capture parameters and built a public database for the benchmarking of forensic methods for recapture detection. Finally, besides this group, they are many others researchers, such as [10–12], who are interested in reducing the complexity of coding.

In this paper, we propose a recapture detection method based on dense local descriptors. As we know, due to the relatively low display resolution of the monitor compared to the camera's image sensor, the process to recapture an image will accompany with some aliasing, blurriness and distortion. Then some texture or edge feature extraction methods could be useful in recapture detection. Dense local descriptors and machine learning have been successfully applied in several applications, like classification of textures, steganalysis, and forgery detection. Drawing from the relevant literature in the field of steganalysis, and some descriptors are selected by greedy strategy in the experiments. The approach is tested on the public open source database [6]. Support vector machine and ensemble classifier are utilized as the classifier in the proposed method. The experimental results show that the features extracted using steganalysis method have a good performance in detecting recaptured images.

The rest of this paper is organized as follows. We specify the implemented method which contains the residual-base local descriptors and machine learning in Sect. 2. In Sect. 3, we will describe the dataset and provide experimental results. Finally, we give the conclusions of the paper in Sect. 4.

2 Implemented Method

The local descriptors (feature vectors) proposed in this article use the same family of high-pass residuals as the SRM [7]. In order to make this paper self-contained, we briefly describe the SRM residual family as well as the SRM feature vector while focusing on the conceptual part without going into details, which can be found in the original publication.

The main processing steps can be summarized as follows:

(1) Computation of the residuals;
(2) Truncation and quantization;
(3) Feature extraction based on co-occurrence matrices of selected neighbors;
(4) Design of a suitable classifier on the training set.

2.1 High-Pass Residuals

Since the image content does not help detecting local alterations and should be completely suppressed, and modeling the residuals rather than the pixel values are suitable for recapture detection. In the context of recapture detection, especially considering that recapture inevitably introduces aliasing and blurriness, it is reasonable to characterize statistically some edge image, and it can also be the output of a simple high-pass filter, like a derivative of first order. As a further advantage, the residual image has a much narrower dynamic range than the original one, allowing for a compact and robust statistical description by means of co-occurrences.

Each residual is tied to a pixel predictor $\widehat{x}_{ij}$. The noise residual corresponding to this predictor is a matrix $R = \left(r_{ij}\right) \in \mathbb{R}_{n_1 \times n_2}$ with elements r_{ij} can be computed using the following form:

$$r_{ij} = \widehat{x}_{ij}\left(\mathrm{N}_{ij}\right) - x_{ij}, \quad 1 \leq i \leq n_1, \quad 1 \leq n_2 \leq j, \tag{1}$$

where N_{ij} is a local neighborhood of pixel x_{ij}, $x_{ij} \notin \mathrm{N}_{ij}$, and $\widehat{x}_{ij}(\cdot)$ is a predictor of x_{ij} defined on N_{ij}.

The residuals are computed using two types of pixel predictor – linear and non-linear. For each linear predictor, we can use the following form to calculate the residuals,

$$R = K * X - X, \tag{2}$$

where K is a kernel matrix that estimates the value of central pixel from its local neighborhood, and the symbol '$*$' denotes the convolution.

For nonlinear predictors, each one contains two or more linear predictors, so these kind of residuals can be obtained by taking the minimum or maximum of the output of two or more residuals obtained using linear predictors. Therefore, there will be two residuals for a nonlinear predictor. For example, the first order symmetric nonlinear predictor is defined by

$$r_{ij} = \min\left[\left(x_{ij+1} - x_{ij}\right), \left(x_{i+1j}, -x_{ij}\right)\right]. \tag{3}$$

2.2 Truncation and Quantization

For the residuals, they must be truncated and quantized so as to suppress the residual dynamic range to allow their description using co-occurrence matrices and to make the residual more sensitive to changes at spatial discontinuities in the images (at edges and textures). As [7], we use

$$\widehat{r}_{ij} = trunc_T\left(round\left(r_{ij}/q\right)\right), \tag{4}$$

where q is a quantization step, and T is the truncation value. We keep using $T = 2$ to limit the matrix size and consider all three quantization steps $q \in \{1, 1.5, 2\}$ to make the residuals more sensitive to changes caused by recapture.

Each quantization residual can eventually take on 5 values, from −2 to +2.

2.3 Co-occurrence Matrices and Sub-models

Then, we compute co-occurrence matrices from four neighboring values of the quantization residuals. According to [7], the average correlation between neighboring pixels in the diagonal/minor diagonal directions fall faster than the horizontal/vertical direction with increasing distance between pixels. Thus, we compute co-occurrences of pixels along the horizontal and vertical directions. Through co-occurrence matrices computing, we will obtain 625 entries. Finally, the symmetries of natural images are leveraged to decrease the feature dimension and better populate the feature vector.

After symmetry operations, each individual sub-model consists of 169 features for linear residual or 325 features for nonlinear residual, which are obtained from the union of co-occurrences from min/max nonlinear residuals. Further, the authors of the SRM combined the features of two linear sub models into one "sub-model". After that, all sub-models have approximately the same dimension (338 or 325) and can thus be fairly ranked by their individual detection performance.

There are a total of 39 sub-models if only one quantization step is considered (its dimension is 12753). However, we take all three quantization steps into consideration and there are totally 106 sub-models. Its dimension is 34671.

2.4 Designing of Classifier

In the classification phase, we deviate from the reference technology. For each sub-model, we train a SVM classifier on the training set to test its actual performance. Then we attempt to merge the features of a limited number of sub-models to improve the accuracy of recapture detection. However, if the merged features are too large, the SVM classifier is not suitable to carry out a meaningful training and would lead to over fitting problem. In [8], this problem was dealt with by means of an ensemble classifier, so we choose the ensemble classifier when the merged features are large.

3 Experimental Results

In this section, in order to validate the effectiveness of our recaptured image detection method, we use the publicly available database [6] for experiments. The database is constructed using a wide range of consumer digital cameras recently which are high quality single capture and alias-free recaptured images. They eliminate the aliasing of recaptured images by setting the capture parameters to predetermined values and this makes the task of recapture detection more difficult. Figure 1 shows some examples from the database. The first column of Fig. 1 is the real-scene images, while the second column of Fig. 1 is the corresponding recaptured images. The success rate of the observers in the image classification was only 61.31% tested by authors of [5]. This shows that it is a difficult task to detect the recaptured images in the dataset by visual inspection.

(b) Indoor scene

(a) Recapture Indoor scene

(d) Architectural scene

(c) Recapture architectural scene

Fig. 1. Images from the recapture database showing examples of single captured and recaptured scenes.

The recapture database consists of 900 single capture images taken using nine different cameras. Each camera was used to capture 100 images. Out of each set of 100 images, of which there are 20 images containing scenes that were common over all nine cameras. Thus, the total number of images containing common scenes was 180. Each image in the set of common single captured images was then recaptured using eight different cameras. This resulted in a total of 1440 recaptured images.

We decide to test each sub-model separately. In each experiment, we randomly select 1/6 of the single captured images (that is 150) and 150 recapture images for training. The remaining images of each class (that is 750 and 1290 for each) are then used for testing. After extracting the features of each image, we train a support vector machine (SVM) classifier using LIBSVM tools [9]. The parameters of the LIBSVM are decided using 10 times cross validation to reduce the test error and gain a stable classifier. To reduce the randomness, each experiment is repeated 10 times, randomly selected the training and testing set, and results are eventually averaged. Figure 2

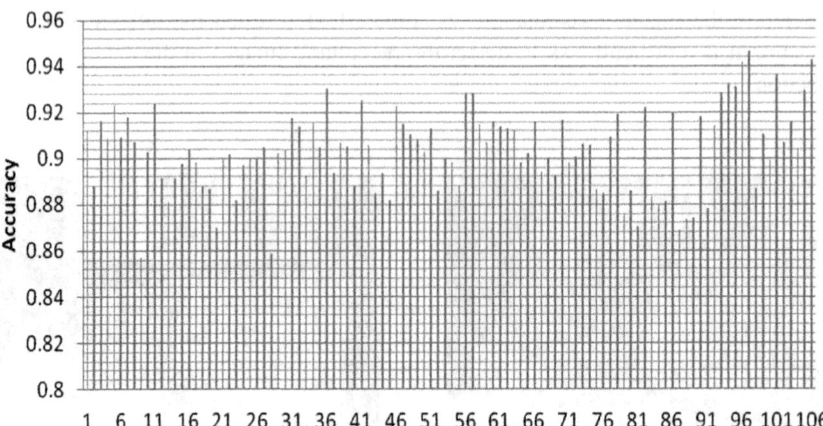

Fig. 2. Detection accuracies for all 106 sub models. The vertical axis represents the detection accuracy while the horizontal axis represents each sub-model labeled from 1 to 106.

shows the detection results of all the 106 sub-models. The following formula is used to calculate the test error:

$$error = \frac{|\{\text{images of missing detection}\}| + |\{\text{images of false alarm}\}|}{|\{\text{total test images}\}|}, \quad (5)$$

where the missing detection is defined as testing the recaptured image to the original class, while false alarm is defined as testing the single captured image to recaptured class. The detection accuracy is defined as

$$Accuracy = 1 - error. \quad (6)$$

The highest detection accuracy obtained from no. 97 sub-model is 0.9461. The sub-model corresponds to the model s3_spam14hv_q2 in SRM [7].

Then we try to merge the features of a limited number of sub-models. The greedy strategy is used in our merging process. From the highest detection accuracy of the single sub-model, the optimal detection accuracy can be obtained after each merging of model. It is found that the detection accuracy is 0.9672 when three sub-models are merged. The three sub-models are no. 97, no. 88 and no. 48, corresponding to s3_spam14hv_q2, s5x5_minmax24_q2 and s3_minmax34h_q15, respectively. Results are shown in Tables 1 and 2 in terms of accuracy obtained before and after merging. It should be noted that the performance improves a lot after merging.

Table 1. The comparison of detection performance of three individual sub-models

Submodel	Type	Dimension	Accuracy
97	s3_spam14hv_q2	338	0.9461
88	s5x5_minmax24_q2	325	0.8735
48	s3_minmax34h_q15	325	0.9025

Table 2. Detection accuracy obtained before and after merging by the three sub-models

Submodel	Accuracy	Sub models/merge.	Dimension/merge.	Accuracy/merge.
97	0.9461	88, 48	988	0.9672

When using this greedy strategy to merge 10 sub-models, the dimension of features is 3276 after merging. Since the features are too large for SVM classifier to carry out a meaningful training which we discussed above, we choose ensemble classifier instead of LIBSVM classifier. The ensemble classifier used the same introduced in [8].

This time, the detection performance improves to 0.9843, which is greater than the performance of most methods proposed recently. Table 3 shows the performance comparison results based on the same set of test images. Note that although the number of features of the method Learning Dictionaries of Edge Profiles is 2, the computational complexity of the method is not low.

Table 3. The comparison of performance of the algorithms in classifying original and recaptured images.

Method	Number of features	Success rate (%)		Overall accuracy
		Original captured	Recaptured	
MSWS + LBP + color features	129	83.67	92.02	87.85
Higher-order wavelet statistics	216	87.56	90.04	88.80
Learning dictionaries of edge profiles	2	93.00	99.31	96.72
Proposed	3276	96.40	99.61	98.43

4 Conclusions

In this paper, we propose a recapture detection method based on dense local descriptors and machine learning. The local descriptors are recently proposed in the field of steganalysis and some descriptors are selected by greedy strategy in the experiments. For the aspect of machine learning, our SVM classifier and ensemble classifier use the merge of all the features of selection descriptors and train on the training set. The experimental results indicate that the proposed method performs well on open source database, and achieves a 98.43% accuracy rate. The performance of the proposed method is comparable to that of the early work. In the future research, we plan to explore additional features to detect recaptured images.

Acknowledgements. This work is supported by NSFC (61502241), Natural Science Foundation of the Universities in Jiangsu Province (14KJB520024), Natural Science Foundation of Jiangsu Province of China (Grant Nos. BK20160971, BK20141006) and the Startup Foundation for Introducing Talent of NUIST (Grant No. 2241101301061).

References

1. Yu, H., Ng, T.T., Sun, Q.: Recaptured photo detection using specularity distribution. In: IEEE International Conference on Image Processing (ICIP), pp. 3140–3143 (2008)
2. Bai, J., Ng, T.T., Gao, X., Shi, Y.Q.: Is physics-based liveness detection truly possible with a single image. IEEE International Symposium on Circuits and Systems (ISCAS), pp. 3425–3428 (2010)
3. Gao, X., Ng, T.T., Qiu, B.: Single-view recaptured image detection based on physics-based features. In: IEEE International Conference on Multimedia & Expo (ICME), pp. 1469–1474 (2010)
4. Cao, H., Kot, A.C.: Identification of recaptured photographs on LCD screen. In: IEEE Conference on Acoustis, Speech, and Signal Processing, pp. 1790–1793 (2010)
5. Thongkamwitoon, T., Muammar, H., Dragotti, P.L.: An image recapture detection algorithm based on learning dictionaries of edge profiles. In: IEEE Transactions on Information Forensics and Security, pp. 953–968 (2015)
6. Recapture Image Database. http://www.commsp.ee.ic.ac.uk/~pld/research/Rewind/Recapture/
7. Fridrich, J., Kodovsky, J.: Rich models for steganalysis of digital images. IEEE Trans. Inf. Forensics Secur. **7**(3), 868–882 (2012)
8. Fridrich, J., Kodovsky, J.: Ensemble classifiers for steganalysis of digital media. IEEE Trans. Inf. Forensics Secur. **7**(2), 432–444 (2012)
9. Chang, C.C., Lin, C.J.: LIBSVM–a library for support vector machines. http://www.csie.ntu.edu.tw/~cjlin/libsvm
10. Pan, Z., Lei, J., Zhang, Y., Sun, X., Kwong, S.: Fast motion estimation based on content property for low-complexity H.265/HEVC encoder. IEEE Trans. Broadcast. **62**(3), 675–684 (2016)
11. Pan, Z., Zhang, Y., Kwong, S.: Efficient motion and disparity estimation optimization for low complexity multiview video coding. IEEE Trans. Broadcast. **61**(2), 166–176 (2015)
12. Pan, Z., Jin, P., Lei, J., Zhang, Y., Sun, X., Kwong, S.: Fast reference frame selection based on content similarity for low complexity HEVC encoder. J. Vis. Commun. Image Representat. **40**(Part B), 516–524 (2016)

A Method Towards Community Detection Based on Estimation of Distribution Algorithm

Yawen Chen[1(✉)], Wenan Tan[1,2], and Yibo Pan[1]

[1] Nanjing University of Aeronautics and Astronautics, Nanjing, China
{cwwaty, wtan, cloudsky_pan}@foxmail.com
[2] Shanghai Polytechnic University, Shanghai, China

Abstract. Estimation of Distribution Algorithm (EDA) is a stochastic optimization algorithm based on statistical theory. It has strong global search ability, but it is easy to fall into the local optimal solution and can not get good results in community detection. In order to solve this problem, we propose a community detection algorithm based on Estimation of Distribution Algorithm, named EDACD, whose basic framework refers EDA and the target function is modularity. EDACD keeps population diversity by adding crossover mutation operation of Genetic Algorithm as well as the improvement of probability model. Genetic Algorithm is based on "micro" level of gene, which has good local optimization ability; EDA uses the evolutionary method based on "macro" level of search space, which has strong global search ability and fast convergence speed. Taking advantage of the two methods, EDACD can used to improve the search ability of algorithm from "micro" and "macro" two levels. Finally, by experimenting on some typical real-world networks and computer-generated networks, the experimental results show that the proposed algorithm can detect the community division accurately, and has higher clustering precision compared with some representative algorithms. In addition, the proposed algorithm also has a fast convergence rate.

Keywords: Complex network · Community detection · Distribution estimation · Genetic Algorithm

1 Introduction

With the rapid development of information technology, research of complex network has gradually become a hot topic in the academic field. Many systems in real world exist in the form of network, such as the interpersonal network, the gene regulatory network, the World Wide Web, etc. Because of high complexity of these networks, they are called "complex networks". Juxtaposed with the small world [1], scale-free [2] and other basic statistical characteristics, cluster structure is one of the most important topology attributes of complex network. This structural feature shows that there is a community structure in complex networks, that is, link between the same communities is dense, and link between different communities is sparse [3].

X. Sun et al. (Eds.): ICCCS 2017, Part II, LNCS 10603, pp. 661–671, 2017.
https://doi.org/10.1007/978-3-319-68542-7_57

Research of community structure in complex networks has a lot of practical significance. Community detection technology can simplify the complexity and improve the performance of network. At present, there are many kinds of complex network community detection algorithms, which can be roughly classified into two kinds [4]: the method based on optimization and heuristic method. In the former, complex network community detection problem is transformed into an optimization problem. The latter transforms the problem into design of predefined heuristic rules.

The classical community detection algorithms based on optimization technique are Kernighan-Lin algorithm (KL) [5], Fast-Newman algorithm (FN) [6] and Guimera-Amaral algorithm (GAA) [7], etc. These algorithms include 3 basic parts: objective function, search strategy of candidate solution and search strategy of optimal solution. The classical heuristic algorithms are Girvan-Newman algorithm (GN) [3], Finding and Extracting Communities algorithm (FEC) [8] and Label Propagation Algorithm (LPA) [9]. Then many improved algorithms have been proposed, such as Jin et al. [10] used structural similarity to replace the number of edges in GN, which reduces the time complexity compared with GN. Zhang et al. [11] in order to solve the weakness of the randomness in LPA, they selected the label that has a local ring with the node to be updated when there are many different optimal labels in their paper. In another work, by Peng et al. [12] proposed to consider the variance and average node energy of each node in the process of label propagation. Liu et al. [13] proposed a combination of local information, subordinate function about point to community and effective mutation method in order to solve the problem that Genetic Algorithm (GA) is easy to fall into the local optimal solution.

As a new stochastic optimization algorithm, Estimation of Distribution Algorithm (EDA) [14] has opened up a new way to solve the problem of community detection from the perspective of optimization. This paper proposes a community detection algorithm based on EDA. The first step is to use LPA to optimize the randomly generated individual. Second step is to use EDA for learning and sampling. In the third step, we use the idea of crossover mutation of GA to cross some dominant groups and then form a new population with the remaining dominant groups and new individuals. Repeat above steps to achieve population evolution. EDA is a modeling of biological evolution from "macro" level; GA is a simulation of biological evolution from "micro" level. Combination of the two can optimize target from "macro" and "micro" two levels. In next chapter, we will introduce the LPA and the EDA in detail.

2 Related Algorithms

2.1 Label Propagation Algorithm

The main idea of Label Propagation Algorithm (LPA) [9] is the similar data should have the same label. The specific algorithm flow is as follows: when the initialization, each node carries a unique label, and then updates the label of the node, so that the label is the same as the label of most of its neighbors. Iterate the process of label propagation until the label of each node no longer changes.

LPA has the advantages of simple and near linear time complexity, although there are some problems of shock and randomness [15]. In this paper, we use the idea of LPA to modify individuals in population, so that individuals in population have higher degree of fitness.

2.2 Estimation of Distribution Algorithm

Estimation of Distribution Algorithm (EDA) is a combination of statistical learning and evolutionary algorithms. EDA uses the evolutionary method based on search space, not only has strong global search ability and fast convergence speed, but also can grasp the evolution direction from the "macro" and solve difficult optimization problem more effectively [16]. The EDA algorithm is as follows: At first, initialing population; secondly, selecting the dominant group from population; and then constructing probability model from dominant group; next, random sampling and generating a new population; at last looping until the termination condition is satisfied.

However, in the process of evolution, EDA in the process of building probability model is easy to be over fitted. It will cause the probability model constructed by algorithm cannot accurately express the information of solution space. After several iterations of algorithm, probability model will no longer produce the diversity of solution, which will affect the performance of algorithm. The simple EDA has a rapid decline in population diversity. In order to maintain population diversity, crossover mutation of GA is added. The reasons are as follows:

The evolution of GA is based on "micro" level of gene, which has good local optimization ability, but its global search ability is poor and convergence speed is slow. EDA bases on "macro" level of search space, which has stronger global search ability and faster convergence speed. Taking advantage of the two methods, EDA was used to optimize the population and improve convergence speed as well as the genetic variation of GA was added to improve the global search ability in EDACD.

3 Community Detection Based on EDA

3.1 Related Knowledge

Assume that the number of nodes in network is n; the number of communities to be divided into k, the following are some of relevant knowledge in proposed algorithm.

Definition 1. The state variables of population and individual. The population is expressed by X and the number of individuals is m. $X = \{X_1, X_2, \cdots, X_m\}$, X consists of m individuals (solutions), each of which corresponds to a division situation.$X_i = [X_{i1}, \cdots, X_{in}]$, $X_{it} \in \{1, 2, \cdots, k\}$ while X_{it} represents the community of node t.

Definition 2. Dominant group. In this paper, we select evaluating index function Q to estimate the individual. Modularity Q is typically used to access the quality of community detection. The higher module value is, the higher similarity of the nodes in the same community. Modularity is defined as:

$$Q = \frac{1}{2m}\sum\nolimits_{vw}\left(A_{vw} - \frac{k_v k_w}{2m}\right)\sigma(c_v, c_w) \tag{1}$$

Where A_{vw} is an element of the adjacency matrix in the network, it is defined as: if the node V and W are adjacent, A_{vw} is 1, otherwise it is 0. The value of function $\sigma(c_v, c_w)$ is defined as: if V and W in the same community, then $\sigma(c_v, c_w) = 1$, otherwise equal to 0. m is the total number of edges in the network. k_v represents the degree of point v.

The first 30% individuals were selected as the dominant group through function Q, the first 10% individuals were the optimal group, and 10%–30% individuals were the suboptimal group.

Definition 3. Normalization. In order to calculate the probability distribution matrix, community number must correspond with the actual community. The normalized operation can make different individuals use the uniform number to represent the same community. The concept of an individual is defined in Definition 1 above. Assume that $X_1 = [0, 0, 0, 1, 1,]$ and $X_2 = [1, 1, 1, 0, 0,]$, it is obvious that individual X_1 and X_2 represent the same result, so it is necessary to normalize all individuals in population. The main process is to select an individual as a template firstly, then match each individual with the template to calculate confusion matrix, and finally each individual is normalized according to the confusion matrix.

Definition 4. Probability model matrix. The probability model matrix is established according to the information of dominant group, which is expressed as a matrix of $k * n$ dimension:

$$P = \begin{bmatrix} P_{11} & \cdots & P_{1n} \\ \vdots & \ddots & \vdots \\ P_{k1} & \cdots & P_{kn} \end{bmatrix} \tag{2}$$

Where P_{ij} represents the probability that node j belongs to community i. In order to prevent premature convergence of EDA, this paper makes a correction to the original probability formula, which ensures that each value of probability model matrix is not equal to 0. For example: there are x nodes which node j belongs to the community i in the sample with a total of y. The original formula is

$$P_{ij} = \frac{x}{y} \tag{3}$$

In this paper the formula is

$$P_{ij} = \frac{x+1}{y+k} \tag{4}$$

In this way, we can ensure that there is no 0 value in probability model matrix, which can maintain the diversity of the population to a certain extent.

Definition 5. Crossover operation. Randomly select an individual X_i from the optimal group and select an individual X_j from the suboptimal group. New individual X_{new-i} generated by cross consists of two parts, the first half is provided by the first $\lceil \frac{n}{2} \rceil$ parameters from X_i, the latter half is provided by the latter $\lfloor \frac{n}{2} \rfloor$ parameters from X_j. The crossover operation produces $20\% \cdot m$ individuals.

Individuals generated by crossover operation have a certain probability which is controlled by parameter α to mutate. There are two kinds of mutation, which are self-mutation and substitution mutation.

Definition 6. Self-mutation operation. Selecting a node randomly, transforming the community number which the node belongs to, and then change its neighbors' community to the same as it. As shown in Fig. 1(a), Node 6 is selected for the self-mutation operation, then the community number of node 6 changes from 1 to 2, at the same time, the community number of neighbors of node 6 whose community number are also required to change to 2, there are node 3, 7 and 9. Since node 9 is already part of community 2, there is no need to change. The results are shown in Fig. 1(b).

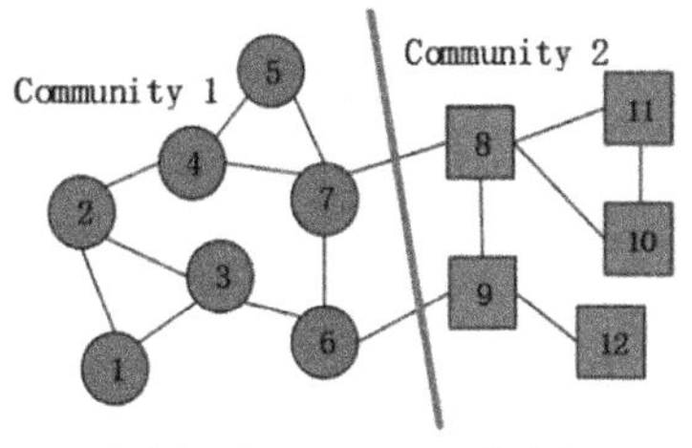

(a) Original community division

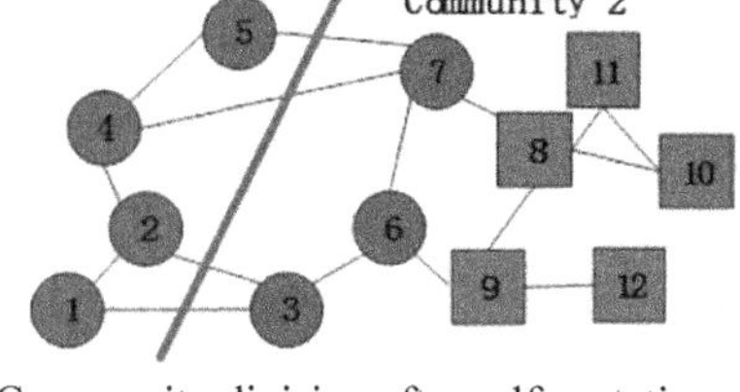

(b) Community division after self-mutation

Fig. 1. Schematic diagram of self-mutation operation

Definition 7. Substitution mutation operation. Selecting two nodes randomly, exchanging the community number of them and their neighbors. As shown in Fig. 2(a). Swapping node 1 and node 11, then the community of node 1, 2 and 3 should be changed from 1 to 2; the community of node 8, 10 and 11 should be changed from 2 to 1. The results are shown in Fig. 2(b).

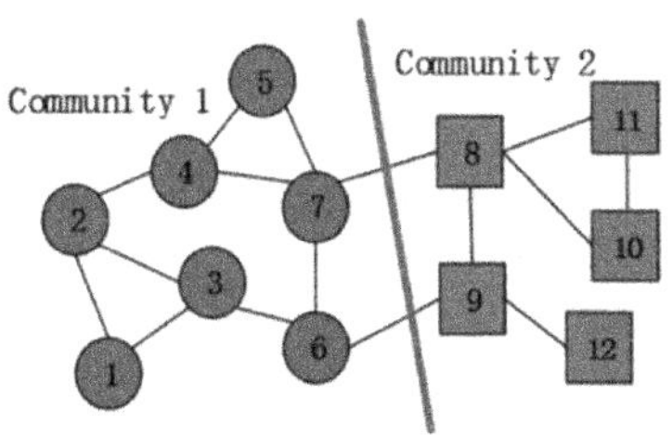

(a) Original community division

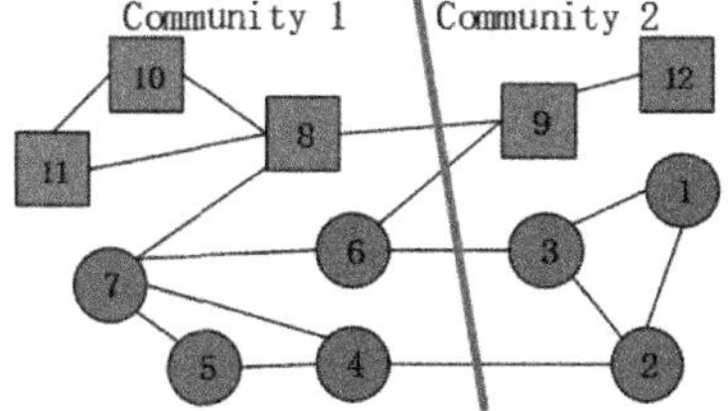

(b) Community division after substitution

Fig. 2. Schematic diagram of substitution mutation operation

3.2 Description of Community Detection Based on Estimation of Distribution Algorithm

The flow of the proposed algorithm is basically consistent with traditional EDA, but only crossover mutation operation of GA is introduced in the process of building a new generation of population. Pseudo code of proposed algorithm is as follows:

```
Algorithm: EDACD

Input: The individual number, m; Iteration times, λ.
Output: The best result of community detection
1. for i=1 to m do
2.    Generate X_i randomly;
3.    LPA_Correct(X_i);
4.    Calculate the modularity Q_i;
5. Sort X by modularity Q;
6. Normalizing X;
7. for i=1 to λ do
8.    Old_X=X;
9.    Old_Q=Q;
10.    Constructing probability matrix P with the top
         0.3*m X;
11.    for j=1 to 0.1*m do
12.      X_j=Old_X_j;
13.      Q_j=Old_Q_j;
14.    for j=0.1*m+1 to 0.3*m do
15.      Xj=Cross(X_j,X_1);//X_1 is selected from the top 0.1*m
                                randomly
16.      Calculate the modularity Q_j;
17.    for j=0.3*m+1 to m do
18.      Generate X_j with the probability matrix P;
19.      LPA_Correct(X_j);
20.      Calculate the modularity Q_j;
21.    Sort X by the modularity Q;
22. Output the best result X_0;
```

Description

Steps 1 to 4 are initialization and fitness calculation of population, in which the idea of label propagation is used to correct each individual in population initialization. Then, in steps 5 and 6, initial population is normalized and sorted by fitness. Steps 7–22 simulate the evolution of population for λ times. At first, to construct the probability model matrix of population according to dominant group; next, the optimal population kept directly to the next generation; and then new 20% * *m* individuals are generated by suboptimal and optimal groups through crossover and mutation, adding new individuals to the next generation and calculating the fitness degree; Finally, the remaining 70% * *m* individuals in the next population are generated according to the probability model matrix of the current population, at the same time, LPA is modified and fitness is calculated for these $70\% * m$ individuals. Repeat steps 7 to 22 to simulate population evolution, the proposed algorithm can output the best individual in population.

Time complexity of population initialization is $O(mn)$, time complexity of individual normalization is $O(mK)$, where m is the number of individuals in population, K is the number of communities. Time complexity of crossover and mutation is $O(n)$. Finally, because the time complexity of computing modularity is $O(n^2)$, the time complexity of EDACD can be expressed as $O(n^2)$.

4 Experiment and Analysis

EDACD is compared with other typical community detection algorithms to verify its effectiveness and feasibility on some real-world networks and computer-generated networks. The experimental results show that the proposed algorithm is feasible and has high precision. EDACD not only can detect community structure but has a fast convergence speed.

4.1 Real-World Network

In this paper, we select five real-world networks, and analyze Karate Club network in detail. The information of five networks is shown in Table 1.

Table 1. The information of five networks

Network name	The number of nodes	The number of edges
Karate Club network	34	78
American college football	115	613
Dolphin social network	62	159
Krebs polbooks network	105	441
Jazz musicians network	198	2742

Karate Club network was built by Zachary through a two-year observation of an American College karate club. It takes the 34 members in club as nodes, if two members are friends, then they will have an edge between their vertices. Later, due to differences in opinion, the club eventually split into two new clubs, the cores are respectively node 1 and node 34.

Figure 3(a) shows the real community structure of karate club network; Fig. 3(b) shows the result of EDACD. The proposed algorithm divides the network into two communities, only the node 10 is different from actual situation. Through observation we found that there is only an edge between node 10 and two communities, therefore this paper considers the result of EDACD is in agreement with actual situation.

Table 2 shows the experimental results of proposed algorithm and classical algorithm GN, FN and LPA. Repeat experiment over 100 runs on above five networks. It can be seen from Table 1 that the Q value of EDACD in this paper is higher than the other three algorithms, which indicates that EDACD divides the community to a higher quality.

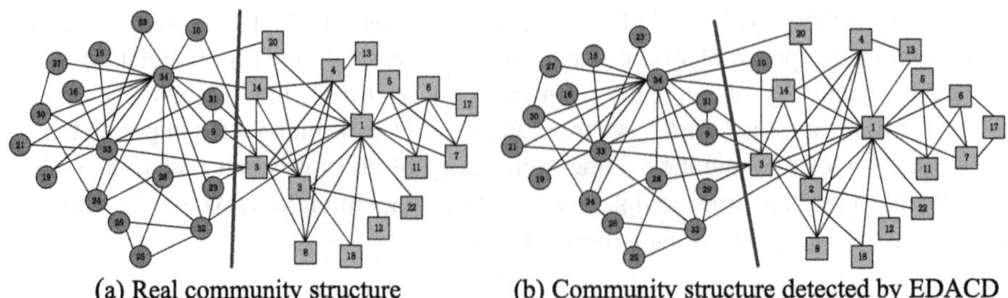

(a) Real community structure (b) Community structure detected by EDACD

Fig. 3. Karate club network community structure

Table 2. Comparing EDACD with GN, FN and LPA in term of function Q

Q-value	Karate	Dolphin	Football	Polbooks	Jazz
GN	0.4052	0.5220	0.5981	0.4938	0.3082
FN	0.3718	0.3854	0.3616	0.4772	0.4030
LPA	0.3744	0.4806	0.5743	0.4986	0.3854
EDACD	0.4188	0.5268	0.6044	0.5269	0.4444

Figure 4 is the relationship between iteration times and modularity on above five networks of EDACD. From Fig. 4, we can see that in the framework of EDA, the convergence speed of population is fast, and the population tends to be stable after 20 generations of evolution.

4.2 Computer-Generated Networks

GN benchmark network [3] and LFR benchmark network [17] are always used to evaluate the performance of community detection algorithms in computer-generated networks. LFR benchmark network has the characteristic of "the node degree and the scale of community is a power-law distribution", which is similar to the real network, Therefore, we use LFR benchmark network to generate artificial networks. As for the computer-generated networks, Normalized Mutual Information (NMI) [18] is widely used as evaluation index for community detection results. NMI is defined as follows:

$$\mathrm{NMI}(A,B) = \frac{-2\sum_{i=1}^{C_A}\sum_{j=1}^{C_B} C_{ij}\log\left(\frac{C_{ij}N}{C_{i.}C_{.j}}\right)}{\sum_{i=1}^{C_A} C_{i.}\log\left(\frac{C_{i.}}{N}\right) + \sum_{j=1}^{C_B} C_{.j}\log\left(\frac{C_{.j}}{N}\right)} \tag{5}$$

Where A is the real community structure of network, B is a community detection result obtained, C_A is the number of communities in real detection, C_B is the number which community detection algorithm obtained. C is confusion matrix, the element C_{ij} in matrix C represents the number of nodes that were supposed to be part of A's community i appeared in B's community j. $C_{.i}$ represents sum of all elements of row i in matrix C, $C_{.j}$ represents sum of all elements of column j in matrix C, NMI compares similarity degree between real community structure and community structure detected

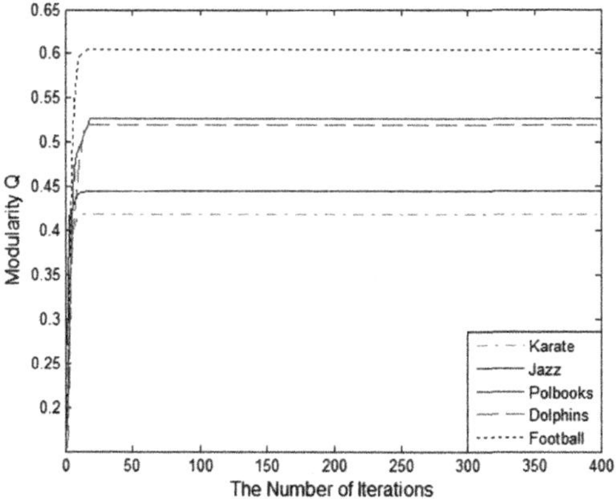

Fig. 4. Analysis the convergence of EDACD

by algorithm, the range of NMI is 0 to 1. If real community structure is as same as community structure detected by algorithm, then $\mathrm{NMI}(\mathrm{A},\mathrm{B}) = 1$, if A and B are completely different, then NMI $(\mathrm{A},\mathrm{B}) = 0$. Therefore, the value of NMI is large, which means that community structure detected by algorithm is similar to real community structure, the effect of community detection is good.

In this paper, parameters of LFR benchmark network are settled as follows. Network size $n = 5000$; minimum for the community sizes $C_{min} = 10$ or 20; mixing parameter is increased from 0 to 0.8, with an interval of 0.1. At the same time, keeping the other parameters unchanged: the average degree $d = 20$; maximum degree $d_{max} = 2.5 * d$; maximum for the community sizes $C_{max} = 5 * C_{min}$; minus exponent for the degree sequence $\tau_1 = 2$; minus exponent for the community size distribution $\tau_2 = 1$. Two benchmark networks are generated with this parameter. GN algorithm is slow and only suitable for small size network [19], so here only contrast LPA and FN. The result of $C_{min} = 10$ is showed in Fig. 5(a) and the result of $C_{min} = 20$ is showed in Fig. 5(b).

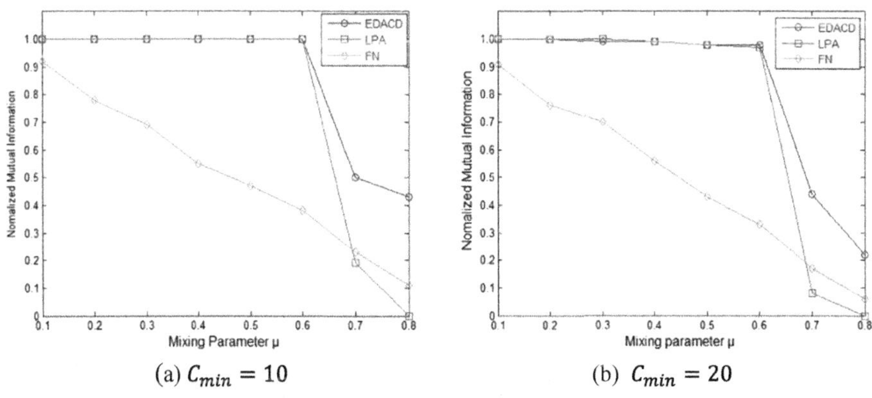

(a) $C_{min} = 10$ (b) $C_{min} = 20$

Fig. 5. NMI comparison of LPA, FN and EDACD on computer-generated networks

From Fig. 5 we can see when community structure is obvious, the NMI of EDACD and LPA are both high, but with mixing parameter increases, community structure becomes more and more blurred, the difficulty of community detection also increases gradually. At this point, the NMI of EDACD, LPA and FN show a downward trend. However, by selecting dominant population and maintaining population diversity, the accurate of EDACD is significantly higher than LPA and FN when the community structure is not obvious ($\mu > 0.6$), which shows that the proposed algorithm on computer-generated networks can achieve better results when compared to classical community detection algorithm such as LPA and FN.

The experimental results on real-world networks and computer-generated networks showed that the proposed algorithm can find better results in community detection when compared with representative algorithm, such as LPA, GN and FN. At the same time, EDACD can inherit the advantage of high convergence of EDA.

5 Conclusion

In this paper, a community detection algorithm based on EDA is proposed, the idea of distribution estimation is applied to community detection. In order to solve the problem of that EDA is too easy to over fit the solution space, crossover mutation operation of GA is introduced to realize parallel optimization of two aspects from “macro” to “micro”. The experimental results on real-world networks and computer-generated networks showed that EDACD can quickly and accurately find network communities, at the same time is better than the classical algorithm, such as LPA, GN and FN.

However, in real social network, many nodes usually belong to multiple communities. The applicability of overlap community will be more widely. Therefore, the follow-up work of this paper is mainly focused on the extension of algorithm to detect community on directed, weighted and overlapping network.

Acknowledgements. This work is supported in part by Foundation of Graduate Innovation Center in Nanjing University of Aeronautics and Astronautics under Grant No. kfjj20161608, the National Natural Science Foundation of China under Grant No. 61672022, Key Disciplines of Computer Science and Technology od Shanghai Polytechnic University under Grant No. XXKZD1604, the Fundamental Research Funds for the Central Universities and Foundation of Graduate Innovation of Shanghai Polytechnic University.

References

1. Watts, D.J., Strogatz, S.H.: Collective dynamics of ‘small-world’ networks. Nature **393**(6684), 440–442 (1998)
2. Adamic, L.A., et al.: Power-law distribution of the world wide web. Science **287**(5461), 2115 (2000)
3. Girvan, M., Newman, M.E.J.: Community structure in social and biological networks. Proc. Natl. Acad. Sci. U.S.A. **99**(12), 7821–7826 (2002)
4. Yang, B., et al.: Complex network clustering algorithms. J. Softw. **20**(1), 54–66 (2009)

5. Newman, M.E.J.: Detecting community structure in networks. Eur. Phys. J. B **38**(2), 321–330 (2004)
6. Newman, M.E.J.: Fast algorithm for detecting community structure in networks. Phys. Rev. E: Stat. Nonlin. Soft Matter Phys. **69**(6 Pt 2), 066133 (2004)
7. Guimerà, R., Amaral, L.A.N.: Functional cartography of complex metabolic networks. Nature **433**(7028), 895–900 (2005)
8. Yang, B., Cheung, W., Liu, J.: Community mining from signed social networks. IEEE Trans. Knowl. Data Eng. **19**(10), 1333–1348 (2007)
9. Raghavan, U.N., Albert, R., Kumara, S.: Near linear time algorithm to detect community structures in large-scale networks. Phys. Rev. E: Stat. Nonlin. Soft Matter Phys. **76**(3 Pt 2), 036106 (2007)
10. Jin, D., et al.: k-Nearest-neighbor network based data clustering algorithm. Pattern Recog. Artif. Intell. **23**(4), 546–551 (2010)
11. Zhang, X., et al.: Label propagation algorithm based on local cycles for community detection. Int. J. Mod. Phys. B **29**(5), 1550029 (2015)
12. Peng, H., et al.: An improved label propagation algorithm using average node energy in complex networks. Phys. A **460**, 98–104 (2016)
13. Liu, H.: Genetic algorithm optimizing modularity for community detection in complex networks. In: Proceedings of the 35th Chinese Control Conference (CCC), pp. 1252–1256. IEEE (2016)
14. Larrañaga, P., Lozano, J.A.: Estimation of Distribution Algorithms, vol. 64, no. 5, pp. 1140–1148. Springer, Boston (2002)
15. Liu, G.S., Zhang, H.L., Meng, K., et al.: Non-random label propagation community detection algorithm. J. Shanghai Jiao Tong Univ. **49**(8), 1168–1173 (2015)
16. Izquierdo, C.E., Velarde, J.L.G., Batista, B.M., Moreno-Vega, J.M.: Estimation of distribution algorithm for the quay crane scheduling problem. In: Pelta, D.A., Krasnogor, N., Dumitrescu, D., Chira, C., Lung, R. (eds.) Nature Inspired Cooperative Strategies for Optimization, NICSO 2011, vol. 387, pp. 4063–4076. Springer, Heidelberg (2011). doi:10.1007/978-3-642-24094-2_13
17. Lancichinetti, A., Fortunato, S.: Benchmarks for testing community detection algorithms on directed and weighted graphs with overlapping communities. Phys. Rev. E: Stat. Nonlin. Soft Matter Phys. **80**(1), 016118 (2009)
18. Danon, L., et al.: Comparing community structure identification. J. Stat. Mech. Theory Exp. **2005**(9), 09008 (2005)
19. Liu, D., Jin, D., He, D., Huang, J., Yang, J., Yang, B.: Community mining in complex networks. J. Comput. Res. Dev. **50**(10), 2140–2154 (2013)

Sentiment Analysis with Improved Adaboost and Transfer Learning Based on Gaussian Process

Yuling Liu[1(✉)], Qi Li[1], and Guojiang Xin[2]

[1] College of Computer Science and Electronic Engineering, Hunan University, Changsha 410082, China
yuling_liu@126.com, qili5207@hnu.edu.cn
[2] College of Management and Information Engineering, Hunan University of Chinese Medicine, Changsha 410208, China
lovesin_guojiang@126.com

Abstract. Sentiment analysis is an increasingly important area in NLP to extract opinions and sentiment expressed by humans. Traditional methods are often difficult to tackle the problems of different sample distribution and domain dependence, which seriously limits the development of sentiment classification. In this paper, a novel sentiment analysis method is proposed by combining improved Adaboost and transfer learning based on Gaussian Processes to solve these two problems. A Paragraph Vector Model is employed to obtain the continuous distributed vector representations. Then, Adaboost method is used to choose the most important training features in source training data and auxiliary data. Finally, an asymmetric transfer learning classifier is introduced in Gaussian Processes. It is shown that, compared with the existing algorithms, our method is more effective for the different sample distribution and domain dependence.

Keywords: Sentiment analysis · Adaboost · Gaussian processes · Transfer learning · Paragraph Vector Model

1 Introduction

With the development of cloud computing and big data, people pay more attention to information security and information hiding technology [1–3]. The explosive growth of social media, such as blogs and social networking sites, has enabled individuals and organizations to write about their personal experience, express opinions and share life. Naturally, the extraction of expressed opinions or implied sentiments with the most accurate method has become increasingly important for businesses, politics and researchers.

Sentiment analysis refers to the process of the extraction of textual polarity, and capture the latent information of people's opinion [4]. There exist two main approaches for the sentiment analysis, the unsupervised lexicon-based approach and the supervised machine learning method. The former involves calculating orientation for a document from the semantic orientation of words or phrases in the document [5]. The later extracts features from texts and then trains the classifier with a human-coded corpus [6]. Recently, the sentiment analysis method based on deep neural network has become a

X. Sun et al. (Eds.): ICCCS 2017, Part II, LNCS 10603, pp. 672–683, 2017.
https://doi.org/10.1007/978-3-319-68542-7_58

hot-spot and achieved some remarkable results. Conventional machine learning requires a large amount of training samples in order to train a reliable model, however, it's expensive and sometimes even impossible to get enough labeled training data. Moreover, a major assumption in many machine learning and data mining algorithms is that the training and test data must be in the same feature space and has the same distribution [7]. However, in many practical applications, this assumption may not hold.

In this paper, we propose a sentiment analysis method with improved Adaboost and Transfer Learning based on Gaussian Processes. First, we obtain the continuous distributed vector representations with the Paragraph Vector Model (Doc2vec). Then, we put forward an asymmetric transfer learning method based on Deep Gaussian process and improved Adaboost, which employ the improved Adaboost method to automatically adjust the weight of source domain data and aid domain data to acquire a high-quality training features to implement sentiment classification. This method allow us to learn an accurate model under the condition that the source training data, the auxiliary data and the target test data have different distributions, thus the proposed approach might improve the accuracy of classifier. We also evaluate the proposed approach on the corpus from The sixth Chinese Opinion Analysis Evaluation (COAE2014) in comparison with other current sentiment analysis methods, and the results confirm the competitive and robustness of the proposed approach.

The rest of paper are organized as follows. Related work is presented next in Sect. 2, followed by our method in Sect. 3. Experimental evaluation is presented and discussed in Sect. 4, followed by conclusions and future work in Sect. 5.

2 Related Work

Sentiment analysis is the field of study that analyzes people's opinions, evaluations, attitudes, and emotions towards entities such as products, services, organizations, individuals, topics, and their attributes. Since early 2000, sentiment analysis has grown to be one of the most active research area in natural language processing and data mining [4]. In general, sentiment analysis has been investigated mainly at three different levels: document level, sentence level, and aspect level [8]. Based on the above three levels, there are two main types of sentiment analysis method: Lexicon-based methods and machine learning techniques. The former is an aspect level method which involves the application of a sentiment lexicon of opinion-related positive or negative terms to evaluate text in an unsupervised fashion [5]. And the latter utilizes a textual feature representation coupled with machine learning algorithms to derive the relationship between features of the text segment and the opinions expressed in the writing in a supervised fashion [6].

For these two methods, researchers have developed various improvement to find the most accurate manner for the opinion mining. Taboada et al. [9] proposed that shifting the sentiment score of a term in a negated context towards the opposite polarity by a fixed amount. Soon, Moreo et al. [10] proposed a lexicon-based comment-oriented news sentiment analyzer to deal with the non-standard language and the opinions in a multi-domain scenario. Milagros et al. [11] proposed an approach based on an unsupervised text classification method based on dependency parsing, and it leveraged the sentiment lexicons created by means of a semiautomatic polarity in order to improve accuracy. While lexicon-based methods can calculate the overall sentiment orientation of a given document, they often suffer from low coverage, and fail to capture more latent manifestations of sentiment and emotion.

On the other hand, machine learning techniques usually extract sentiment features from text and then train the classifier with a manual labeled corpus. Hu et al. [12] used the labeled data to train a sentiment classifier to classify the new microblog messages. Later, a more accurate classification model was proposed to mine the contextual knowledge of words from the unlabeled data [13]. To detect sentiment out of textual snippets faster, Giatsoglou et al. [14] proposed a methodology in which text documents were represented by some vectors and used for training a polarity classification model. In recent years, some sentiment analysis approaches based on Deep Neural Networks (DNN) and representation leaning have been widely used. In 2014, a deep Convolutional Neural Network (CNN) was proposed by exploiting information from character-level to sentence-level to perform sentiment analysis of short texts [15]. Similarly, Cai et al. [16] used two individual CNN architectures for learning textual features and visual features, which could be integrated as input of another CNN architecture for exploiting the internal relation between text and image. Shortly afterwards, Sun et al. [17] combined posts and related comments into a microblog conversation for features extension, and employed a DNN model which was stacked with several layers of Restricted Boltzmann Machine (RBM) to analyze short microblog textual sentiment. Machine learning method successfully captures syntactic and semantic regularities encountered in written language, and has proven to be extremely useful on sentiment classification. However, machine learning requires that the training and test data should be under the same distribution, and in fact, training data and test data are difficult to satisfy the assumption of independent identically distribution, thus the performance of the classification method may get worse.

Transfer learning (TL) is a method which allows training data and test data with different domains, tasks, and distributions [7], and aims to solve the problem by training models on one dataset (the source domain) to adapt to sparsely labeled data in another domain (the target domain). Based on whether the sample of the source and target domains are labeled and the tasks are same, TL can be divided into three categories: inductive transfer learning, transductive transfer learning, and unsupervised transfer learning [18]. Inductive transfer learning transfer knowledge by extracting the samples from the training set which suit for the test data. Dai et al. [19] used boosting by automatically adjusting the weights of training instances to filter out the diff-distribution training data that were very different from the same-distribution data. In the transductive transfer learning setting, there is no labeled data in the target domain, and requires the model to employed the source and target data from different domains. Huang et al. [20] utilized the availability of unlabeled data to direct a sample selection and presented a nonparametric method which directly produces resampling weights without distribution estimation. The unsupervised transfer learning focuses on handling unsupervised learning tasks in the target domain and there is no labeled data available in both the source domain and the target domain. Dai et al. [21] proposed a co-clustering method based on self-taught clustering algorithm, which allow the feature representation from the auxiliary data to influence the target data through a common feature sets by clustering the target and auxiliary data simultaneously.

Transfer learning is enable to tackle the problems of insufficient labeled data and cross-domain sentiment classification in the field of data mining and sentiment analysis. The sentiment classifier trained in one domain may not perform well in another domain [22]. Therefore, how to select useful features and samples in different domain has become vital. Jiang and Zhai [23] proposed a two-stage approach to pick up useful features specific to the target domain. Similarly, Gu et al. [24] studied the multi-task clustering, and aimed to learn a subspace shared by all tasks in which the knowledge could transfer to each other.

3 Methodology

In this section we introduce two important components used in our sentiment analysis method, and give the complete steps of our algorithm in Sect. 3.3. Figure 1 illustrates the framework of the method. First, we use the Doc2vec model to map each paragraph into a unique vector, represented by a column in matrix, and each word is also mapped to a unique vector. And then, using the improved Adaboost method to get the high weight features from the source training data and the auxiliary data, which have the most similar distribution with the target test features. Finally, an Asymmetric Transfer Learning with Deep Gaussian Process (ATL-DGP) model are trained and tested by all features.

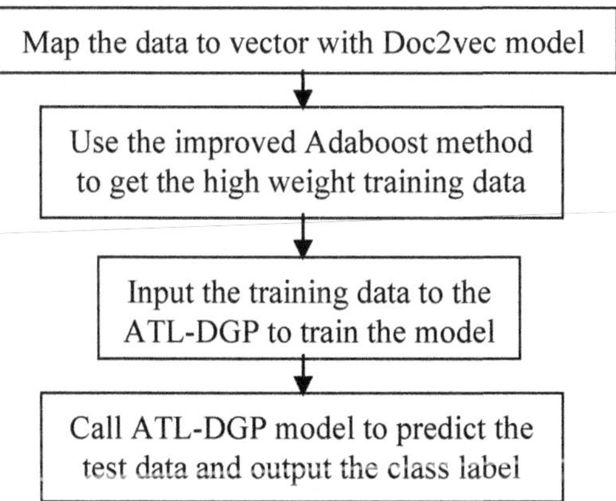

Fig. 1. the framework of the proposed method

3.1 Improved Adaboost Method

In fact, the traditional machine learning algorithms has performed well when the training data and test data have the same distribution, but the performance might be terrible if they are from different feature space. To solve this problem, Dai et al. [17] provided a Tradaboost framework, which extended Adaboost for transfer learning. In this method, the source training data and test data had the same distribution, and the auxiliary training data, whose distribution may be different from the test data. And in the Tradaboost, Adaboost was still applied to the source training data to build the model, but for the auxiliary training data, a mechanism was proposed to decrease the weights of instances which were wrongly predicted by the learning model to weaken their impacts, since those instances could be the most dissimilar to the source training data. They intended to use the auxiliary training data from different domain to implement transfer the knowledge from an old domain to a new domain.

But in most cases, we have not enough labeled training data, and the distribution is different from that in test data, on the other hand, the limited training samples are unable to cover the entire features space, which might result in the problem of sample bias. Therefore, we proposed an improved Adaboost method to solve the above problems.

Formally, let D_s be the source training instance space, D_a be the auxiliary training instance space, and $L = \{0, 1\}$ be the set of category labels. A concept is a boolean function f mapping from D to L, where $D = D_s \cup D_a$. The test space is denoted by D_t, and the data in D_t are unlabeled. The auxiliary training data, the source training data and the test data are respectively represented by $T_a = \{(d_i^a, f(d_i^a))\}$, $T_s = \left\{\left(d_j^s, f\left(d_j^s\right)\right)\right\}$ and $T_t = \{(d_k^t)\}$, there have $d_i^a \in D_a (i = 1, \ldots, n)$, $d_j^s \in D_s (j = 1, \ldots, m)$ and $d_k^t \in D_t (k = 1, \ldots, r)$, n, m and r are the size of T_s T_a and T_t, respectively. $f(d)$ returns the label for the data instance d. The combined training set $T = \{(d_i, f(d_i))\}$ is defined as follows:

$$d_i = \begin{cases} \mathrm{d_i^a}, & \mathrm{i} = 1, \ldots, \mathrm{n}; \\ \mathrm{d_i^s}, & \mathrm{i} = \mathrm{n} + 1, \ldots, \mathrm{n} + \mathrm{m}. \end{cases} \tag{1}$$

Here, T_a and T_s correspond to some labeled data from different domain which we try to fully utilize, however, there is no way we can know which part of T_a and T_s are useful for us. The T_t can be employed to find out the useful part. The problem that we are trying to solve is: given a small number of labeled source training data T_s, many labeled auxiliary data T_a and some unlabeled test data T_t, they are all from different domain, the objective is to select the part of useful data in T_a and T_s for sentiment analysis.

In our modified Adaboost method, which is different from Tradaboost, Hedge(β) is applied to decrease the weight of the instance in T_a and T_s, which might be the most dissimilar to the distribution of the test. In each iteration round, if an instance is mistakenly predicted, the instance may conflicts with the test data. Then, we decrease its training weight to reduce its effect through multiplying its weight by $\beta^{|h_t(x_i) - f(x_i)|} \in (0,\ 1]$. After several iterations, the instances which have same distribution with test data will have larger weights, and then, we can choose the first fixed number of the higher-weight training data from the source training data and the auxiliary data. And these instances will help the learning algorithm to build a better classifier. The detailed steps of the method are described as follows:

Step 1. Given the two labeled data sets T_a and T_s, the unlabeled data set T_t, a Learner, and the maximum number of iterations N.

Step 2. Initialize the weight vector, that $w^1 = \left(\omega_1^1, \ldots, \omega_{n+m}^1\right)$, we allow the user to specify the initial values for w^1.

Step 3. For $t = 1,\ldots N$, set $p^t = w^t / \left(\sum_{i=1}^{n+m} \omega_i^t\right)$; Call Learner, providing it the combined training set T with the distribution p^t over T and the unlabeled dataset T_t, Then get back a hypothesis $\mathrm{h_t} : D \rightarrow L$. So calculate the error of h_t on T:

$$\epsilon_t = \sum_{i=n+1}^{n+m} \frac{\omega_i^t |h_t(d_i) - f(d_i)|}{\sum_{i=n+1}^{n+m} \omega_i^t},$$

and set $\beta_t = \in_t / (1 - \in_t)$ note that $\in_t$, required to be less than 1/2; Update the new weight vector:

$$\omega_i^{t+1} = \omega_i^t \beta_t^{|h_t(d_i) - f(d_i)|}, 1 \leq i < n+m.$$

Step 4. Select the first fixed number of high weight source training data and auxiliary data set T_s' and T_a' respectively.

3.2 Asymmetric Transfer Learning by Deep Gaussian Processes

Gaussian processes (GPs), also called normal stochastic process, which satisfies the normal distribution, is a generalization of a probability distribution. By using GPs, it turns out that the computation with high-dimension and non-linear function become relatively easy. Moreover, the output of the GPs can be mapped to a probability value on the classification model, and these values represent the probability of the corresponding output class. Kandemir [25] proposed an ATL-DGP model, which adopted a two-layer feed-forward deep Gaussian process as the task learner of source and target domain, and achieved a state-of-the-art in benchmark real-world image categorization task. Figure 2 illustrates the idea. Generally, the process of image categorization is similar to the textual sentiment analysis, both of which can use the vector representation as input to the classifier, therefore, the model of image categorization can also be used in sentiment analysis. In this paper, we benefit from the ATL-DGP, and intend to employ it to sentiment classification.

In this section, we set X_i as the $N_i \times$ D dimensional data matrix for task i with N_i instances of D dimensions in its rows, and Y_i is the $N_i \times$ C matrix having the corresponding outputs. We set $T_s = \{X_s, Y_s\}$, $T_a = \{X_a, Y_a\}$, and construct two Gaussian processes classification models $F = \{F_a, F_s\}$. According to the ATL-DGP, F_a can be expressed as follows:

$$p(Y_a|F_a) = N\left(Y_a|F_a, \beta^{-1}I\right), \quad (2)$$

$$p(F_a|D_a) = N(F_a|0, K_{D_aD_a}), \quad (3)$$

$$p(D_a|B_a) = \prod_{i=1}^{H} N(d_a^i|b_a^i, \alpha^{-1}I), \quad (4)$$

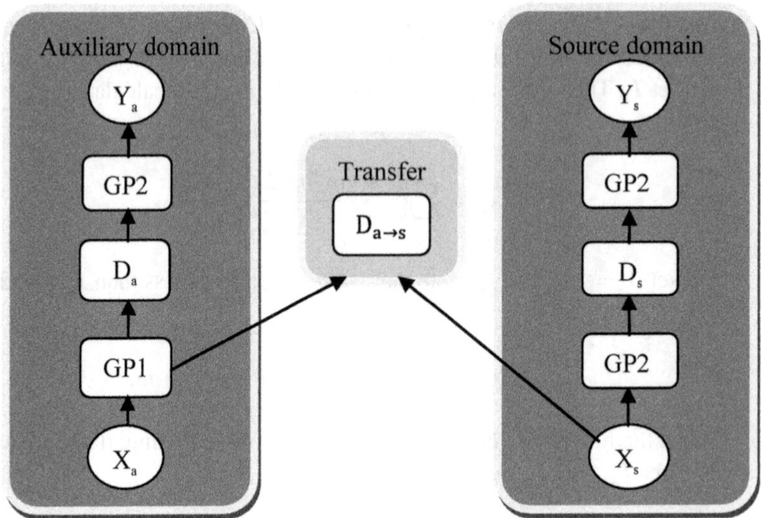

Fig. 2. Asymmetric transfer learning with deep gaussian process model

$$p(B_a|X_a) = \prod_{i=1}^{H} N(b_a^i|0, K_{X_aX_a}), \tag{5}$$

Where Y_a and F_a are decision margins, D_a is latent representations of input data. Here, B_a is the representation of auxiliary instances on the latent non-linear manifold. K_{XX} is Gram matrix with $[K_x](ij) = k(x_i, x_j)$, $K_{D_aD_a}$ is the Gram matrix generated by the first Gaussian process model layer with the F_a and $D_aK_{X_aX_a}$ is the Gram matrix generated by the second Gaussian process model layer with the B_a and X_a $p(\cdot)$ represents the density function, $N(x|\mu, \varepsilon)$ is the multivariate normal density with mean μ and covariance ε. α, β in Eqs. (1), (3) and λ in the following are precisions of normal densities. R represents the number of latent nodes.

Similarly, for F_s there are:

$$p(Y_s|F_s) = N\left(Y_s|\, F_s,\, \beta^{-1}I\right), \tag{6}$$

$$p(F_s|D_s) = N(F_s|\,0, \mathrm{K}_{D_sD_s}), \tag{7}$$

$$p(D_s|B_s, B_{a\to s}, \pi) = \prod_{k=1}^{N_s} N(d_s^k|\pi b_{a\to s}^k + (1-\pi)b_s^k, \alpha^{-1}I), \tag{8}$$

$$p(\pi) = Beta(\pi|e,f), \tag{9}$$

$$p([B_s; B_{a\to s}]|X_a, X_s) = \prod_{i=1}^{H} N([b_a^i; b_s^i|0, K_{[X_a;X_s][X_a;X_s]}), \tag{10}$$

$$p(B_s|X_s) = \prod_{i=1}^{H} N(b_s^i|0, K_{X_sX_s}). \tag{11}$$

Note that there is additional term $B_{a \to s}$ in the target task, which is the projection of the target instances onto the latent source space. The mixture weight π follows a Beta distribution hyperparameterized by e and f. For both tasks, the second layer GP takes D_i as input and maps it to the output labels Y_i [25]. The part responsible for the process of knowledge transfer are shown in (7) and (8).

3.3 The Proposed Algorithm

In the field of sentiment analysis, when the training data, especially the labeled training data are too insufficient to produce an accurate classification model, the final result of sentiment analysis will be unsatisfactory. In addition, the training data and test data might be under different distribution because the training samples can not cover the entire feature space. Labeling the new data can be costly and it would also be a waste to throw away the old data. In this paper, we propose a method of sentiment analysis with improved Adaboost and transfer learning based on Gaussian processes. Traditional bag-of-words lose the order of the word and they also ignore semantics of the words, it suffers from data sparsity and high dimensionality. Le and Mikolov [26] proposed an unsupervised framework named Paragraph Vector (Doc2vec) that learned continuous distributed vector representations for piece of texts, this method can be applied to variable-length pieces of texts. In order to handle the dataset better, we use the Doc2vec model to map all features to paragraph vector and word vector. Moreover, making the best of the auxiliary training data will improve the performance of the classification model. But the auxiliary training data might also have different distribution from test data. Thus the purpose of the improved Adaboost method is to choose the most helpful training data from auxiliary and source data. After the feature selection, we get the high weight source training data and auxiliary dataset T_s' and T_a'. Here, T_s' and T_a' are features which have the most similar distribution with target test features. Finally, for the sake of knowledge transfer, ATL-DGP are trained and tested by all features from T_a, T_s, T_s', T_a' and T_t. A description of our method is given in Algorithm 1.

Algorithm 1. The proposed method

Input: the source training dataset T_s and the auxiliary training dataset T_a, the target test dataset T_t, Doc2vec model, the number of hidden nodes R, and the maximum number of Adaboost iterations N.

Output: the label of target test dataset T_t.

Steps:

Step 1: Map the T_s, T_a, T_t to paragraph vectors and word vectors with Doc2vec model;

Step 2: Call GPs model, use the improved Adaboost method to get the high weight source training data and auxiliary dataset T_s' and T_a' respectively;

Step 3: Input T_a, T_s, T_s', T_a' to the ATL-GDP to train the model;

Step 4: Call ATL-DGP model to predict T_t and output the class label.

4 Experimental Evaluation

4.1 Experimental Settings

To evaluate our approach, we take the training data and the test data from the benchmark of the sixth Chinese Opinion Analysis Evaluation (COAE2014) Chinese Microblog viewpoint recognition task, the training dataset is set as the source training data, the test dataset is set as the target test data. There are 1840 training instances from the same topic, which include 1005 manually labeled positive instances and 835 negative instances, and 7000 testing instances from three different domains of mobile, insurance and emerald, which include 3776 positive instances and 3224 negative instances.

Moreover, we take the auxiliary data from the benchmark of the Natural Language Processing & Chinese Computing (NLPCC2014) Sentiment Classification with Deep Learning task, there are 10000 training instances from different domain such as book, digital video etc., 5000 positive instances and 5000 negative instances are included.

Several preprocessing steps were taken. Firstly, JieBa[1] Chinese text segmentation is applied to word segmentation, POS Tagging and stopword removement. Then, Doc2vec[2] is used to project all data set to the vector representation, and screen out the helpful training features from the source and auxiliary features by the improved Adaboost method. Finally, enter the source training features which concatenate the source and auxiliary features and target test features into ATL-GDP model to obtain the class result. All the parameters required for the experiment are shown in Table 1.

Table 1. Parameter setting

Model	Name	Value
Doc2vec	Min_count	1
	Window size	10
Hedge(β)	Dimension of word vector	300
	Number of training	10
	Learning rate	0.025
	Maximum number of iterations	10
ATL-DGP	Initial weight	1
	Number of inducing points	10
	Number of hidden units(source)	5
	Number of hidden units(target)	5
	Maximum number of iterations	1
	Starting learning rate	0.001

[1] https://github.com/fxsjy/jieba.

[2] https://radimrehurek.com/gensim/models/doc2vec.

4.2 Results and Analysis

In this section, we evaluate the performance of our approach by comparing it with a series of baseline methods with the help of the benchmark datasets. After the text are converted to vector representations, these vector matrices are considered as input for the following four different algorithms for classification purpose. Support Vector Machine (SVM) [3], which separates the document vectors in one class from other classes and the separation is maintained to be large as possible. RBMDNN [14] employs a DNN model which is stacked with several layers of RBM, to analyze short microblog textual sentiment. In order to more fully compare these methods, only the source training data is used as training samples in ATL-DGP1, and the combined training features which concatenate the source training data and auxiliary data are used as training data in SVM, RBMDNN, ATL-DGP2 and Adaboost ATL-DGP(A-ATL-DGP), and the target test data is used as the test data.

Generally, the performance of sentiment classification is evaluated using four indexes, namely: Accuracy, Precision (P), Recall (R) and F1-score(F). The performances of different methods are shown in Table 2. In the Table 2, the performance of the method which employed the transfer learning technique is superior to the traditional machine learning algorithm like NB, SVM and RBMDNN.

Table 2. The performance of different methods

Method		SVM	RBMDNN	ATL-DGP1	ATL-DGP2	A-ATL-DGP
Accuracy (%)		79.95	81.50	**85.17**	84.02	**87.70**
Positive	P	0.7880	0.8469	0.8523	0.8159	0.8750
	R	0.7924	0.7967	0.8309	0.8581	0.8803
	F	0.7902	0.8210	0.8415	0.8365	0.8776
Negative	P	0.7916	0.7750	0.8172	0.8046	0.8914
	R	0.7820	0.8000	0.8060	0.8255	0.8774
	F	0.7868	0.7873	0.8116	0.8149	0.8843

Moreover, although there are auxiliary data in ATL-DGP2, compared with the ATL-DGP1, the accuracy of the ATL-DGP2 decreased 1.15%. It shows that the addition of the training dataset might benefit to the classifier, but it may also lower the performance, for there are many noisy data in the auxiliary data, and the distribution of the auxiliary data might different from the test data, this phenomenon is called negative transfer.

In the contrast, if we perform selection on the auxiliary data, as our method mentioned above, the performance of the classifier would be greatly improved. Obviously, compared with the ATL-DGP2, the accuracy of the A-ATL-DGP algorithm increased 3.68%, and it is also 2.53% higher than ATL-DGP1.

5 Conclusion

In this paper, we have proposed a novel sentiment analysis approach which combined the Adaboost algorithm with an Asymmetric Transfer Learning model based on Deep Gaussian Processes. The experimental results show that the proposed method is particularly effective and efficient, because the most useful different distribution instances are selected as the additional training data for predicting the labels of test data. The performance could be further improved in the following aspects: the nature of positive transfer can be used to find a better approach to avoid negative transfer; meanwhile, we may proceed from the domain similarity and develop a simpler algorithm for domain similarity measurement.

Acknowlegements. This work is partially supported by National Natural Science Foundation of China (No. 61103215, 61502242).

References

1. Zhangjie, F., Kui, R., Jiangang, S., Xingming, S., Fengxiao, H.: Enabling personalized search over encrypted outsourced data with efficiency improvement. IEEE Trans. Parallel Distrib. Syst. **27**, 2546–2559 (2016)
2. Zhiguo, Q., John, K., Sebastian, R., Faisal, Z., Xiaojun, W.: Multilevel pattern mining architecture for automatic network monitoring in heterogeneous wireless communication networks. China Commun. **13**, 108–116 (2016)
3. Xue, Y., Jiang, J., Zhao, B., Ma, T.: A self-adaptive articial bee colony algorithm based on global best for global optimization. Soft Comput. 1–18 (2017)
4. Liu, B.: Sentiment Analysis and Opinion Mining. Morgan & Claypool, San Francisco (2012)
5. Turney, P.D.: Thumbs up or thumbs down? Semantic orientation applied to unsupervised classification of reviews. In: Proceedings of Annual Meeting of the Association for Computational Linguistics, pp. 417–424 (2002)
6. Pang, B., Lee, L., Vaithyanathan S.: Thumbs up? Sentiment classification using machine learning techniques. In: Proceedings of Emnlp, pp. 79–86 (2002)
7. Pan, S.J., Yang, Q.: A survey on transfer learning. IEEE Trans. Knowl. Data Eng. **22**, 1345–1359 (2010)
8. Feldman, R.: Techniques and applications for sentiment analysis. Commun. ACM **56**, 82–89 (2013)
9. Taboada, M., Brooke, J., Tofiloski, M., Voll, K., Stede, M.: Lexicon-based methods for sentiment analysis. Comput. Linguist. **37**, 267–307 (2011)
10. Moreo, A., Romero, M., Castro, J.L., Zurita, J.M.: Lexicon-based comments-oriented news sentiment analyzer system. Expert Syst. Appl. Int. J. **39**, 9166–9180 (2012)
11. Fernández-Gavilanes, M., Álvarez-López, T., Juncal-Martínez, J., Costa-Montenegro, E.: Unsupervised method for sentiment analysis in online texts. Expert Syst. Appl. Int. J. **58**, 57–75 (2016)
12. Hu, X., Tang, L., Tang, J., Liu, H.: Exploiting social relations for sentiment analysis in microblogging. In: Proceedings of ACM International Conference on Web Search and Data Mining, ACM, pp. 537–546 (2013)

13. Wu, F., Song, Y., Huang, Y.: Microblog sentiment classification with contextual knowledge regularization. In: Proceedings of the Twenty-Ninth AAAI Conference on Artificial Intelligence (2015)
14. Giatsoglou, M., Vozalis, M.G., Diamantaras, K., Vakali, A., Sarigiannidis, G.: Sentiment analysis leveraging emotions and word embeddings. Expert Syst. Appl. **69**, 214–224 (2017)
15. Dos Santos, C.N., Gattit, M.: Deep convolutional neural networks for sentiment analysis of short texts. In: Proceedings of International Conference on Computational Linguistics (2014)
16. Cai, G., Xia, B.: Convolutional neural networks for multimedia sentiment analysis. In: Li, J., Ji, H., Zhao, D., Feng, Y. (eds.) NLPCC 2015. LNCS, vol. 9362, pp. 159–167. Springer, Cham (2015). doi:10.1007/978-3-319-25207-0_14
17. Sun, X., Li, C., Ren, F.: Sentiment analysis for Chinese microblog based on deep neural networks with convolutional extension features. Neurocomputing **210**, 227–236 (2016)
18. Weiss, K., Khoshgoftaar, T.M., Wang, D.D.: A survey of transfer learning. J. Big Data **3**, 9 (2016)
19. Dai, W., Yang, Q., Xue, G.R., Yu, Y.: Boosting for transfer learning. In: Proceedings of International Conference on Machine Learning, pp. 193–200. ACM (2007)
20. Huang, J., Smola, A.J., Gretton, A., Borgwardt, K.M., Scholkopf, B.: Correcting sample selection bias by unlabeled data. IN: Proceedings of International Conference on Neural Information Processing Systems, pp. 601–608. MIT Press (2006)
21. Dai, W., Yang, Q., Xue, G.R., Yu, Y.: Self-taught clustering. In: Proceedings of International Conference, pp. 200–207. DBLP (2008)
22. Wu, F., Huang, Y.: Sentiment domain adaptation with multiple sources. In: Proceedings of Meeting of the Association for Computational Linguistics, pp. 301–310 (2016)
23. Jiang, J., Zhai, C.X.: A two-stage approach to domain adaptation for statistical classifiers. In: Research Collection School of Information Systems, pp. 401–410 (2007)
24. Gu, Q., Zhou, J.: Learning the shared subspace for multi-task clustering and transductive transfer classification. In: Proceedings of the Ninth IEEE International Conference on Data Mining, pp. 159–168. DBLP (2009)
25. Kandemir, M.: Asymmetric transfer learning with deep gaussian processes. In: Proceedings of International Conference on Machine Learning, pp. 730–738 (2015)
26. Le, Q.V., Mikolov, T.: Distributed representations of sentences and documents. Comput. Sci. **4**, 1188–1196 (2014)

HL-HAR: Hierarchical Learning Based Human Activity Recognition in Wearable Computing

Yan Liu(✉), Wentao Zhao, Qiang Liu, Linyuan Yu, and Dongxu Wang

College of Computer, National University of Defense Technology, Changsha 410073, Hunan, People's Republic of China
642293721@qq.com, {wtzhao,qiangliu06}@nudt.edu.cn, 809932887@qq.com, wangdongxuking61@gmail.com

Abstract. In recent years there have been many successes of recognizing the human activity using the data collected from the wearable sensors. Besides, many of these applications use the data from the smartphone. But it is also a challenge in practice for two reasons. Most method can achieve a high precision in the cost of increasing memory consumption, or asking for complicated data source. In this paper, (1) Utilizing Plus-L Minus-R selection to single out the optimal combination from the feature vector extracted; (2) Introducing a fast classification method named H-ELM to resolve the problem of the highly memory consumption in the process of calculation. The main benefit of this factor is to reduce memory usage and increase recognition accuracy with a brief feature vector so that a wearable device can identify activities all by itself. And the wearable device can recognize the sample activities even if keeping away from cellphone. Our results show that this method leads to that we can recognize object activities with the overall accuracy of 93.7% in a very short period of time on the dataset of Human Activity Recognition Using Smartphones Dataset. The selected 25-dimension feature vector nearly contains all the information and after many times of test, it can achieve very high percentage of accuracy. Moreover, the method enables the learning velocity to outperform the state-of-the-art on the Human Activity Recognition domain.

Keywords: Activity Recognition · Wearable devices · Machine learning · Hierarchical extreme learning

1 Introduction

During the past years, the Human Activity Recognition (HAR) based on wearable devices has been becoming an increasingly significant research topic. The fundamental reason is that more and more people are progressively interested in health-conscious [1]. And with the grow of life expectancy and the ageing population, it becomes a challenge to make the elderly more independent and safer. Likewise, patients with some mental pathologies need to be monitored to

X. Sun et al. (Eds.): ICCCS 2017, Part II, LNCS 10603, pp. 684–693, 2017.
https://doi.org/10.1007/978-3-319-68542-7_59

prevent negative effects [2]. The wearable sensors are good choices to monitor Activities of Daily Living due to that the development of electronic technology that makes the sensors smaller in size and much more powerful [3]. Meanwhile, comparing to the data from the field of computer vision, it is more conducive to protect personal privacy and hardly to be interfered by the environment. A plenty of intelligent devices appear on the market at present, such as Millet bracelet, Apple Watch and so on. Mostly devices take advantage of acceleration to record daily walking-steps, further figure up the body movement energy expenditure. Whereas it is rarely refer to the Human Activity Recognition.

The high precision of recognition generally relies on the original data that including fully integrated information, or extracting the high-dimensional feature vector. The focus in these recent advances has been on improving accuracy by wearing various kinds of sensors or a type of sensors putted in different positions on body. In [4], Mannini and Sabatini do the activity classification using data from 5 biaxial accelerometers fixed in different part of the body. Finally, they achieve the accuracy of 98.4% by the HMM based on sequential classifier. Four accelerometers [5] are made use and positioned in the waist, thigh, ankle and arm to collect data. Using the AdaBoost method and decision trees C4.5, the authors gain the classifier accuracy of 99.4%. Xinlong Jiang [6] presents a system named AIR which using infrared (IR) sensors to measure distance from the feet. Their results show that AIR obtains much higher accuracy and better generalization in recognizing activity than approaches that rely primarily on accelerometers. Other recent successes including [7,8] collect data from the smartphone. In [7], Ghosh classifies activities based on the fusion of signal streams, including audio card, accelerometers, and gyroscope embedded in a smartphone. And they show that performance of the multi stream human activity recognition is higher preciser and robuster at the same time. Korpela [8] presents an energy-aware method for recognition through selecting the optimal tree in the random forests which has lower energy consumption as well as higher recognition accuracy, then partitioning the tree across the wearable device and smartphone. Extreme Learning Machine (ELM) has been verified a term of classification accuracy and calculating speed in the applications of HAR [9]. In the paper [10], the author adopts support vector machine (SVM) with a 561-dimensions feature vector, achieving an overall accuracy of 96%. Other researchers attempt to recognize the activities only by wearable devices [11]. The proposed method is a novel bag-level human activity classification method in an accuracy level of 85%. The high precision relies on the original data including fully integrated information or high-dimensional feature extracting in general.

Although part of the experimental data is disposed by wearable devices, but rarely devices can recognize the different activities independently on account of the limited compute capacity. The key reason is that some traditional learning algorithms, e.g., the single hidden layer feed forward networks (SLFNs), the parameters in the learning process need to be adjusted through iterative analysis calculated, which requires a certain amount of computing power. And some excellent algorithms, like support vector machine (SVM), the memory consumption and operation time have grown at rates more than the growth rate of the sample size. The existing wearable devices are hardly to meet requirements, both in CPU and the battery life.

The main contributions of this paper are summarized as follows: (1) Select the optimal combination from the feature vector extracted utilizing Plus-L Minus-R selection; The influence is obvious of feature vector to the final classification result. The suitable feature vector can not only advance the accuracy but also accomplish modeling in a shorter time. (2) An effective and efficient method named hierarchical ELM (H-ELM) [12] is introduced to classify the activities. The H-ELM is multilayer framework based on ELM for perceptron multilayer perceptron. In recent years, ELM [13,14] is a hotpoint on account of its good performance in the field of velocity and generalizing function. Unlike the shallow structure in ELM, H-ELM is multilayer so that it is validity of natural signals. Meanwhile, H-ELM inherits the advantages of ELM that can achieve better generalization performance in a shorter period of time.

The rest of this paper is organized as follows: Sect. 2 introduces the H-ELM framework and the concepts in details. Section 3 describes our method step by step, including how to extract the optimal feature vector and how to classify using H-ELM. Section 4 compares the performance of the proposed HL-HAR and other state-of-the-art method. Section 5 draws in the conclusion finally.

2 Introduction of Hierarchical Extreme Learning Machine

To achieve in terms of both highly recognition accuracy and learning velocity, we introduce the H-ELM algorithm to construct the classifier. The framework of H-ELM is proposed for multilayer perceptron. Since framework of ELM is a single layer architecture, the performance may be descended when is dealing with nature signal despite of increasing the number of the hidden nodes. H-ELM covers this shortage, improve the generalization performance and learning speed besides.

In the H-ELM, every layer is identical to the ELM, and each hidden layers is independent of each other. Every layer can transform the input data into an ELM random feature space. In this way, a N-layer learning is executed to get the high-level sparse features finally. As the increasing of the layers, the features become more and more compact. The information contained in high-level is much more than in low-level. The theory and application [15] demonstrate that high-dimensional and non-line conversion in feature extraction can advance the classification accuracy obviously.

The H-ELM is based on and further improving the performance of ELM, so understanding the framework of H-ELM must comprehend the theory of ELM at first.

ELM is proposed for the Single-hidden Layer Feed forward Neural Network (SLFNs). The traditional function approximation theories need adjust import weights and hidden layer biases by iterative calculation and analysis. But in the paper [15], a large number of experiments show that it makes no sense to modulate the input weights and hidden layer biases over and over again. In the meantime, modulation will slow the calculation speed down. So the input is generated randomly in the ELM algorithm and the process can be simply described as follows:

Given the training sample set $\mathbf{X} = \{(\mathbf{x}_i, \mathbf{t}_i) \mid \mathbf{x}_i \in \mathbf{R}^n, \mathbf{t}_i \in \mathbf{R}^m\}_{i=1}^N$, where $\mathbf{x}_i$ denotes the ith input, and t_i denotes the ith output, and the activation function $g(x)$, the number of the nodes in hidden layer is L, the standard model in math of SLFNs is:

$$\sum_{i=1}^{L} g(\boldsymbol{\omega}_i \cdot \mathbf{x}_j + b_i)\boldsymbol{\beta}_i = \boldsymbol{o}_j, j = 1, 2, \cdots, N \tag{1}$$

Step 1: Generate input parameters $\boldsymbol{\omega}_i$ and b_i $(i = 1, 2, \cdots, L)$ randomly;
Step 2: Calculate the output matrix of the hidden layer:

$$\mathbf{H} = \mathbf{H}(\mathbf{W}, \mathbf{b}) = (h_{ij})_{N \times L}, h_{ij} = g(\boldsymbol{\omega}_i \cdot \boldsymbol{x}_j + b_i) \tag{2}$$

Step 3: Calculate the matrix of the output weight:

$$\boldsymbol{\beta} = \boldsymbol{H}^{\dagger}\boldsymbol{T}, \tag{3}$$

where $\mathbf{T} = [\boldsymbol{t}_1, \cdots, \boldsymbol{t}_L]^{\mathrm{T}}$, $\mathbf{H}^{\dagger}$ is the Moore-Penrose (MP) generalized inverse of matrix $\mathbf{H}$, i.e.,

$$\mathbf{H}^{\dagger} = \mathbf{H}^{\mathrm{T}} \left(\frac{1}{\lambda} + \mathbf{H}\mathbf{H}^{\mathrm{T}} \right)^{-1}. \tag{4}$$

MP is calculated by the orthogonal projection, and $\frac{1}{\lambda}$ is the positive value to the diagonal on the theoretical basis of the ridge regression.

H-ELM is a multilayered structure ELM. Each layer of the H-ELM determine the parameters as same as ELM. And the relationship between the current layer and the last layer is calculated by using the following formula:

$$\mathbf{H}_i = g\left(\mathbf{H}_{i-1} \cdot \boldsymbol{\beta}\right). \tag{5}$$

Because every layer is independent of each other, the weights and parameters randomly assigned of the current hidden layer will be fixed. The whole system does not need to be retrained iteratively. This is a significance reason why the training velocity would be much faster than other traditional algorithms.

3 The Proposed HL-HAR Method

3.1 Overall Framework

The overall framework of the proposed HL-HAR method is shown in Fig. 1. At first, carry out a set of experiments to gain experimental data, then by using the method of sampling, filter to do the data preprocessing. The next step is extracting the features that you think would be effective to improve the precision, then choose a new brevity but robust feature vector from the extracted features by the Plus-L Minus-R Selection (LRS) method. At last, feed into the classifier to establish model and classify after formatting the feature vector.

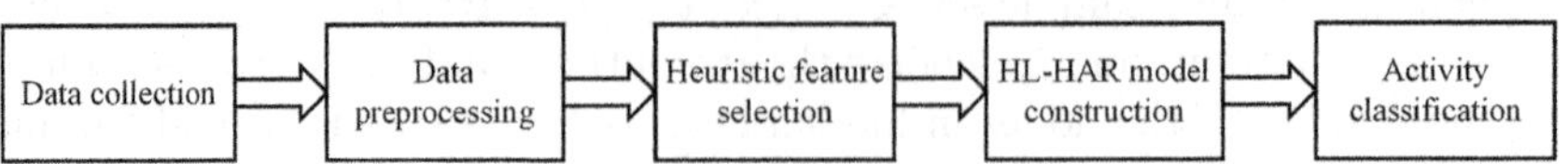

Fig. 1. The overall framework of the proposed HL-HAR method

3.2 Data Preprocessing

Pick a wearable devices which are embedded a tri-axial accelerometer and a tri-axial gyroscope to collect data. Then utilizing a Butterworth low-pass filter with the cutoff frequency of 0.3 Hz, the body acceleration is separated from the gravity. So every sample contained 9 sets of data which are the body-acceleration-XYZ, the gravity-acceleration-XYZ, and the angular-velocity-XYZ. All the data is sampled in fixed-width sliding windows of 2.5–3 s and 50% overlap. The length of time window wants moderate, if taking a shorter rectangular window, it may not be containing a complete walking cycle or increasing the amount of calculation. And if taking a longer rectangular window, it will appear serious delays for the real-time systems. The window of 2.5–3 s almost is the fourfold of one walking cycle.

The features are extracted on each group data of each sample separately. The features contain both time and frequency domain, and many have proved to be available, such as mean, standard deviation, velocity, frequency, energy of coefficients of wavelet decomposition, median absolute value, largest values in array, smallest value in array and so on.

3.3 Heuristic Feature Selection

When selecting the best features, we usually try to extract many features and test their efforts. Even so, many features are redundant, because a wealth of information in different features is correlation. So in this paper, we select features by Plus-L Minus-R selection (LRS). LRS is a type of heuristic search algorithms. Comparing the full-search, it is faster and actually aiming at specific issues. There are several types of heuristic search algorithms, e.g., sequential forward selection, sequential backward selection, bidirectional search, Plus-L Minus-R selection, sequential floating selection, decision tree method. Other types beside sequential floating selection do not take the correlation of different features into consideration. The LRS is more simple and faster than sequential floating selection.

Algorithm 1. *The proposed HL-HAR method*

Input: The training set of data $\mathbf{X} = \{\mathbf{x}_i, t_i\}_{i=1}^{N}$, the number of layers M.
Output: The output weight matrix $\boldsymbol{\beta}$.
1. $\boldsymbol{t} = 1$;
2. Random Assign to the input randomly weights $\omega = [\omega_1, \cdots, \omega_N]$ and bias $\mathbf{B} = [b_1, \cdots, b_N]$;
3. Calculate the output matrix $\mathbf{H}_1$ of the hidden layer according to (2);
4. Calculate the output weights $\boldsymbol{\beta}_1$ according to (3);
5. **while** $\boldsymbol{t} < \boldsymbol{M}$
6. $\quad \mathbf{H}_{t+1} = g(\mathbf{H}_t \cdot \boldsymbol{\beta}_t)$;
7. $\quad$ Calculate the output weights $\boldsymbol{\beta}_{t+1}$ according to (3);
8. $\quad \boldsymbol{t} = \boldsymbol{t} + 1$;
9. **end while**

Eventually the feature vector must be standardized and fed to the classifier. Data standardization is the critical process of bringing data into a common format that allows for research. It can eliminate effects of the parameters with different units and scales. We have two known methods to rescale data, 0–1 scaling and Z-score scaling. In this paper, we apply the Z-score scaling method. The classifier will automatically build the model by the feature vector and output the classified result of testing data.

3.4 Human Activity Recognition Based on H-ELM

In summary, the work flow of the proposed HL-HAR method is shown in Algorithm 1.

4 Performance Evaluation

4.1 Experimental Settings

In this paper, we select the data from Human Activity Recognition Using Smartphones Data Set. The data set is separated into the gravity composition and the body acceleration composition, and it is sampled in fixed-width sliding windows of 2.56 s and 50% overlap (128 readings/window). For collecting data, the author invites 30 participants to perform six activities. And when they do the activities, every participant carries about a smartphone embedded with a tri-axial accelerometer and a tri-axial gyroscope on the waist. The six activities are Walking, Walking-Upstairs, Walking-Downstairs, Sitting, Standing, and Lying. Then the author takes sample at the rate of 50 Hz. The data from 70% participants generates the training data and other test data. In this dataset, the author affords to the whole 561-dimensions feature vector so that it is easy to use.

In all the simulation below, we use the Matlab R2014b in the system of Win7 Sp1 64 to test different classifiers. And the testing computers CPU is Intel Core i7-4790 CPU @ 3.60 GHz, the RAM is 16.0 GB.

The process of choosing the feature vector by LRS is divided into two steps due to the feature vector is too large in dimensions. At first, set the L = 1 and R = 0 (equal to take without putting back) to choose a 45-dimensions feature vector. The following step, set the L = 2 and R = 1 to choose a 20-dimensions feature vector, a 25-dimensions feature vector and a 30-dimensions feature vector in the 45-dimensions feature vector. There are 200 hidden nodes of ELM and 80,80,200 hidden nodes of H-ELM. The number of H-ELM layer is 3.

4.2 Comparative Results and Analysis

Performance Comparison in Terms of Accuracy. We conduct some experiments on the dataset to compare the performance between our method and others. The comparative results of ELM, kNN and SVM are shown in [11], it demonstrated that the method using ELM achieves superior performance compared with kNN, SVM, and previous multi-instance learning methods like mi-SVM and MI-SVM in terms of the classification accuracy and the classification time. Therefore, in this paper, we mainly compare the performance of ELM and H-ELM. After 10 repeated tests, the mean and standard deviation to the results of classification accuracy are shown in Table 1. It can be seen that the performance of classification in accuracy rise up when the feature vector transforms from the feature vector of the mean and standard deviation to that selected by our method. The simulations prove that the feature vector selected by LRS includes more information of the activities. Comparing the difference between the second and third line, we can get the result that confronting with ELM classifier, H-ELM classifier also can improve the accuracy. Meanwhile, the consequence variations is pretty stable and with less difference among tests.

Table 1. Featurel represent the 18-dimensional feature vector contain the mean and standard deviation to every sample, and the feature2 represent the 20-dimensional feature vector selected by our method

		Walking	Upstairs	Downstairs	Sitting	Standing	Lying
ELM+featurel	μ	79.78%	66.26%	80.86%	79.96%	82.35%	99.20%
	σ	0.000159	0.000136	0.000275	0.000179	9.5E−05	2.64E−05
ELM+feature2	μ	88.37%	87.54%	86.71%	85.72%	88.78%	99.53%
	σ	0.000225	0.000109	0.000388	0.001014	0.000953	1.2E−05
H-ELM+feature2	μ	**93.02%**	**91.82%**	**88.00%**	**89.76%**	**89.76%**	**100%**
	σ	5.72E−05	3.26E−05	0.000127	0.000417	0.000973	0

To estimate the generalized accuracy to every activity by H-ELM with different feature vectors, we conduct an experiment of the various combination of H-ELM and feature vectors. Average results of 20 repeat trials of simulations with each feature vector are obtained and the result is shown in Fig. 2. As observed from Fig. 1, general speaking, the 20-dimensions feature vector, 25-dimensions feature vector and 30-dimensions feature vector obtain similar performance in precision, which is slightly lower than 561-dimensions feature vector in many cases. And the 25-dimensions feature vector for best performer. But the feature vector of mean and standard deviation obtains lower precision in any activity. It turns out that the feature vector of selected from the original feature vector includes nearly equal information. And after the feature selection, the running time of classifier has improved significantly. The mean of overall accuracy with 25-dimensions feature vector is 93.7%.

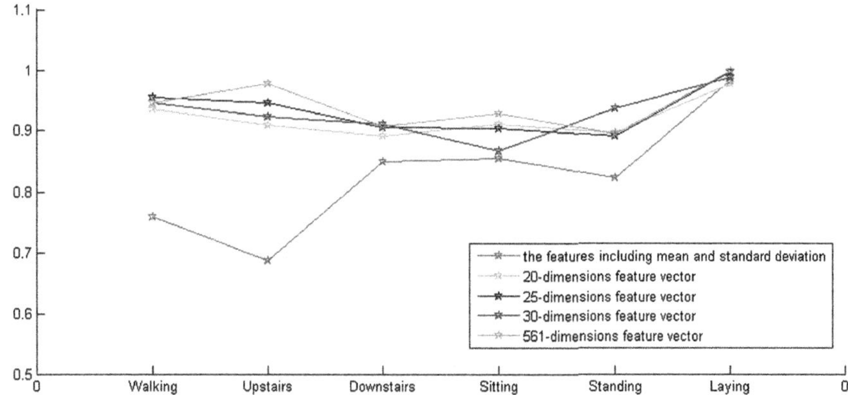

Fig. 2. The comparative results of the classification accuracy regarding each activity with different feature vectors, the ordinate represents the recognition accuracy

Performance Comparison in Terms of Time. Comparing with other classifiers such as SVM and KNN, ELM has obvious advantage in training and testing rate [11]. The speed of ELM is at least ten fold faster than the other two methods. To further demonstrate the advantages of our method, we compare the time spent in classification of H-ELM and ELM with a 25-dimensions feature vector, and the Table 2 shows result. Note that both the training time and testing time reduce significantly in the comparative results. The ELM is known for the speed, and the speed of H-ELM is much least.

Based on the experiments above, we can see that HL-HAR is obviously superior performance in term classification accuracy, operation time, and robust. While other classification algorithms take more time to achieve a high performance, our method can be easily with a wearable device.

Table 2. The training time and testing time of the ELM and H-ELM, the mean and standard deviation for 10 repeated tests

		Training time	Testing time
ELM	μ	2.3509	0.1513
	σ	0.0276	0.0008
H-ELM	μ	**0.1971**	**0.0438**
	σ	4.03E−05	1.4E−06

5 Conclusions

In this paper, we have proposed a novel HL-HAR to classify the human activities, which exploits LRS to select the optimal feature vector and a bag-level human activity classification method (H-ELM) to recognize target from the feature vector. The proposed HL-HAR achieves a terms of both high precision and fast learning speed because of two reasons. First, we remove the redundant elements to select a more efficient, more compact and briefer feature vector from the original features by LRS. Then we introduce the classification method H-ELM. Experimental results show that the new feature vector contains more informations. And comparing with ELM, H-ELM achieves much faster speed and higher learning accuracy.

However, rooms for improvements exist: while dynamic activities can be efficiently classified but non-dynamic actions still present misclassification overlaps. And the high accuracy thanks to the newly features selected by LRS, but this a algorithm need a longer operation time. Hence, these two respects are the next main work.

References

1. Van Laerhoven, K., Schmidt, A., Gellersen, H.: Multi-sensor context aware clothing. In: IEEE International Symposium on Wearable Computers (ISWC), IEEE Computer Society, October 2002
2. Lara, O.D., Labrador, M.A.: A survey on human activity recognition using wearable sensors. IEEE Commun. Surv. Tutor. **15**(3), 1192–1209 (2013)
3. Aggarwal, J.K., Ryoo, M.S.: Human activity analysis - a review. ACM Comput. Surv. **43**(3), 1–43 (2011)
4. Mannini, A., Sabatini, A.M.: Machine learning methods for classifying human physical activity from on-body accelerometers. Sensors **10**, 1154–1175 (2010)
5. Ugulino, W., Cardador, D., Vega, K., Velloso, E., Milidiú, R., Fuks, H.: Wearable computing: accelerometers' data classification of body postures and movements (2012)
6. Jiang, X., Chen, Y., Liu, J., Hayes, G.R., Hu, L., Shen, J.: Air: recognizing activity through IR-based distance sensing on feet. In: Proceedings of the 2016 ACM International Joint Conference on Pervasive and Ubiquitous Computing: Adjunct, ser. UbiComp 2016, pp. 97–100. ACM, New York (2016)
7. Ghosh, A., Riccardi, G.: Recognizing human activities from smartphone sensor signals. In: Proceedings of the 22nd ACM International Conference on Multimedia, ser. MM 2014, pp. 865–868. ACM, New York (2014)
8. Korpela, J., Takase, K., Hirashima, T., Maekawa, T., Eberle, J., Chakraborty, D., Aberer, K.: An energy-aware method for the joint recognition of activities and gestures using wearable sensors. In: Proceedings of the 2015 ACM International Symposium on Wearable Computers, ser. ISWC 2015, pp. 101–108. ACM, New York (2015)
9. Minhas, R., Baradarani, A., Seifzadeh, S., Jonathan Wu, Q.M.: Human action recognition using extreme learning machine based on visual vocabularies. Neurocomputing **73**(10–12), 1906–1917 (2010)

10. Anguita, D., Ghio, A., Oneto, L., Parra, X., Reyes-Ortiz, J.L.: A public domain dataset for human activity recognition using smartphones. In: 21th European Symposium on Artificial Neural Networks, Computational Intelligence and Machine Learning, ESANN 2013, Bruges, Belgium (2013)
11. Yin, J., Zhu, C., Zhou, S., Yuan, L., Liu, Q., Lu, M.: A highly efficient human activity classification method using mobile data from wearable sensors. Int. J. Sens. Netw. **1**(1), 1 (2016)
12. Tang, J., Deng, C., Huang, G.B.: Extreme learning machine for multilayer perceptron. IEEE Trans. Neural Netw. Learn. Syst. **27**(4), 809–821 (2016)
13. Huang, G.B., Zhu, Q.Y., Siew, C.K.: Extreme learning machine: a new learning scheme of feedforward neural networks. In: Proceedings of the International Joint Conference Neural Network, pp. 985–990 (2006)
14. Huang, G.-B., Zhu, Q.-Y., Siew, C.-K.: Extreme learning machine: a new learning scheme of feedforward neural networks. In: 2004 IEEE International Joint Conference on Neural Networks (IEEE Cat. No. 04CH37541), vol. 2, pp. 985–990, July 2004
15. Huang, G.B., Chen, L., Siew, C.K.: Universal approximation using incremental constructive feedforward networks with random hidden nodes. IEEE Trans. Neural Netw. **17**, 879–892 (2006)

An Improved Quantum-Inspired Evolutionary Algorithm for Knapsack Problems

Sheng Xiang[1,3], Yigang He[1(✉)], Liuchen Chang[1,3], Kehan Wu[1], and Chaolong Zhang[1,2(✉)]

[1] School of Electrical Engineering and Automation, Hefei University of Technology, Hefei 230009, China
zhangcl@aqnu.edu.cn, 18655136887@163.com
[2] School of Physics and Electronic Engineering, Anqing Normal University, Anqing 246011, China
[3] Department of Electrical and Computer Engineering, University of New Brunswick, Fredericton E3B 5A3, Canada

Abstract. As a well-known combinatorial optimization problem, knapsack problems commonly arise in security areas. In this paper, an improved quantum-inspired evolutionary algorithm (PEQIEA) is proposed to solve knapsack problems. In PEQIEA, in each iteration, the state preference of the elite group is used to update the group. The elite group of each iteration consists of a certain number of individuals which are selected by their fitness values. A state preference is proposed to improve the efficiency of the algorithm. A new quantum-inspired gate is obtained by the elite group and their state preference. The Q-gate is then used to make the evolution of the group. The parameters in PEQIEA, which affect the accuracy and efficiency of the algorithm, are discussed empirically. The performance of PEQIEA is then evaluated through extensive experiments.

Keywords: Quantum-inspired evolutionary algorithm · Elite group · State preference · Knapsack problem

1 Introduction

As a well-known NP-complete combinatorial optimization problem, knapsack problems are critical in security fields [1–3]. In recent decades, many methods had been proposed to solve knapsack problems. Evolutionary algorithm (EA) compares two feasible solutions of each iteration, selecting the best solution until specific requirements are met [4]. Being superior to other algorithms in terms of convergence and quality [5], EA has proven to be useful. Many quantum computing concepts and principles are introduced in evolutionary algorithm (QIEA), such as quantum bits, quantum gates in [6] and in [7, 8], a quantum gate (Q-gate) and a probabilistic observation are used to specify QIEA's steps and structure. The main characteristic of QIEA is that each individual consists of a string of Q-bits, so it can not only represent a linear superposition of states, but can also use a small number of individuals to explore the search place, speeding up the convergence. Hence, a QIEA has better performance

X. Sun et al. (Eds.): ICCCS 2017, Part II, LNCS 10603, pp. 694–708, 2017.
https://doi.org/10.1007/978-3-319-68542-7_60

than EAs [6, 7, 9]. A number of QIEAs have been researched in literature dealing with accuracy and speed [10–33].

To solve knapsack problems, a good performance in convergence and accuracy is required. In [1], a new QIEA with local and global migrations has shown good performance in solving knapsack problems. One downside of EAs with knapsack problems is that is easy to fall into a local optimum. Han used an Hϵ gate (HQIEA) in [13], Li used crossover and mutation operators [18]. Zhang used a novel update method for Q-gates and a catastrophe operator [19]. Immune operator and particle swarm optimization have also been used to solve knapsack problems in literature [20, 21]. An improved QIEA (IQIEA) has been proposed in [22], where the quantum rotation rate gate adaptive calculation was obtained by the probability amplitude ratio of the quantum states. A variant of QIEA (FQIEA) was proposed by Vlachogiannis [12], where the value of Q-gate angle was obtained by comparing each individual and the global best individual. In [23], a P system was proposed with a novel hybrid algorithm (QEPS). A comprehensive learning strategy was proposed as CLQIEA in [24]. In [28], a novel quantum-inspired artificial immune system (MOQAIS) is presented. A hybrid quantum inspired harmony search algorithm is proposed to solve 0–1 optimization problems [29]. Chiang used a quantum-inspired table research algorithm for optimization problems in [30]. A QIEA-PSA is presented in literature [31], based on size reduction for each new generation. All of these QIEAs use only one Q-bit individual to affect the Q-gate.

In literature [33], an elite group guidance was proposed in EQIEA, where the elite group was selected by fitness values in the current iteration. All the individuals in the elite group were then cooperated together to influence Q-gates to produce next iteration improving the performance. However, the speed of convergence should be improved and the accuracy of solutions should be further enhanced.

In this paper, PEQIEA is proposed to solve the knapsack problems. As a modified EQIEA, PEQEIA introduces a state preference updating approach, where Q-gates push the genes of individuals to evolve toward state ‘1’, as with [33]. A number of experiments have been used to test the performance of PEQIEA. Experimental results show that PEQIEA has superior performance for knapsack problems.

This paper consists of 5 parts. Section 2 describes PEQIEA in detail. Section 3 presents comparative experiments and results. The parameters in PEQIEA and EQIEA are discussed in Sect. 4. In Sect. 5, conclusions are provided.

2 PEQIEA

As an enhanced version of QIEA for solving the knapsack problems, the main characteristic of PEQIEA is the guidance of the elite group and state performance. The main objective is to get the best solution. In each iteration, a certain number of individuals which have good fitness values are selected as the elite group. Generally, various types of QIEAs such as the QIEA in [1], HQIEA in [11], QEPS in [21], did not use any state preference in Q-gates, i.e., $\phi_0 = \phi_1$ in Table 1. If we apply the combination of a state preference strategy in Q-gates and a greedy repair, the quality of solutions can be greatly improved when knapsack problems are considered. This is the motivation for introduction of PEQIEA. In PEQIEA, a state preference, $\phi_0 < \phi_1$, and a greedy repair are employed to push the genes of individuals to evolve toward state '1' when Q-gates are used to update Q-bit individuals.

On the basis of QIEA, two special steps are inserted in PEQIEA. Figure 1 is the pseudo-code of PEQIEA, where Steps (vii) and (x) are described in detail as follows:

```
Begin
         t=0;
(i)      initialize Q(t);
(ii)     make P(t) by observing the states of Q(t);
(iii)    evaluate P(t);
(iv)     store the best solutions among P(t) into B(t);
(v)      while(not termination criterion) do
             t=t+1;
(vi)         make P(t) by observing the states of Q(t-1);
(vii)        greedy repair P(t);
(viii)       evaluate P(t);
(ix)         select E(t) from P(t);
(x)          update Q(t) using Q-gates with a guidance of E(t)
             and a state preference updating approach;
(xi)         store the best solutions among B(t-1)  and P(t) into B(t);
(xii)        store the best solution b among B(t);
         end-while
End
```

Fig. 1. The pseudo-code algorithm of the PEQIEA.

(i) In this step, *Q(t)* is generated, in order to make all possible states equal probability of occurring at the beginning, $(sign(rand[0,1] - 0.5) * 1/\sqrt{2}, sign(rand[0,1] - 0.5) * 1/\sqrt{2})$ is used to initialize all the Q-bits, *sign*(.) is the symbolic function and *rand* (.) is the function generating random values between '0' and '1'. Where $Q(t) = \{\boldsymbol{q}_1^t, \boldsymbol{q}_2^t, \ldots, \boldsymbol{q}_n^t\}$, n is the population size, every individual q_i^t is combine with m Q-bits.

(ii) A binary solutions set, $P(t) = \{\boldsymbol{x}_1^t, \boldsymbol{x}_2^t, \ldots, \boldsymbol{x}_n^t\}$ is obtained by observing the states of *Q*(*t*), an observed value of the Q-bit q_i^{t-1} is store as a binary bit as '0' or '1', $\boldsymbol{x}_i^t$ is a binary solution.

(iii) An evaluation function is used to calculate the fitness value of each binary solution, and all fitness value are stored in $F(t) = \{f_1^t, f_2^t, \ldots, f_n^t\}$, where f_i^t is the fitness of the ith individual.

(iv) Choose the best solutions among *P*(*t*) with fitness value, then store them into *B*(*t*).

(v) The maximal prescribed number of iterations is used as the termination condition, and if the conditions are met, the program will be end, else continuing.

(vi) Binary solutions *P(t)* by observing the states of *Q(t − 1)*.

(vii) In this step, when the weight of a candidate solution exceeds the knapsack capacity, a greedy repair is used to adjust the solution to satisfy the knapsack capacity. In this repair, all items in the knapsack are sorted in a decreasing order of their profit to weight ratio and the selection procedure always chooses the last item for deletion [1]. It is worth pointing out that PEQIEA can use various repair strategies, not solely the greedy repair.

(viii) An evaluation function is used to calculate the fitness value of each binary solution, all the fitness value are stored in $F(t) = \{f_1^t, f_2^t, \ldots, f_n^t\}$.

(ix) A certain number of individuals are selected from *P(t)* by their fitness values, then stored in to an elite group *E(t)*.

The details are as follows:

(a) At first, the worst individual of ith iteration is found by fitness value, called *min (F(t))*, then the fitness difference of ith iteration between *min(F(t))* is obtained as $\tilde{f}_i^t (i = 1, 2, \ldots, n)$,

$$\tilde{f}_i^t = abs(f_i^t - min(F(t))) \tag{1}$$

where abs(*X*) is the function for calculating the absolute value of *X*.

(b) The probability of the ith individual $\boldsymbol{x}_i^t$ $(i = 1, 2, \ldots, n)$ which is chosen into *E(t)* can be obtained by formula (2),

$$S(t) = \{s_1^t, \ldots, s_i^t, \ldots, s_n^t\} \text{ and } s_i^t = \tilde{f}_i^t \Big/ \sum_{i=1}^{n} \tilde{f}_i^t \tag{2}$$

(c) Finally, a roulette wheel method is used to select a certain number of individuals from *P(t)* based on S*(t)*, and those individuals are stored into the elite group *E(t)*, $E(t) = \{e_1^t, e_2^t, \ldots, e_p^t\}$, where *p* is the number of elite individuals, dependent on the selection time. In Sect. 4, how to choose *p* is discussed.

(x) A Q-gate $U(\Delta\theta_{ij}^t)$ is used to update *Q(t)*, the Q-gate $U(\Delta\theta_{ij}^t)$ $(i = 1, 2, \ldots, n;$ $j = 1, 2, \ldots, m)$ is an adjustable angle as follows:

$$U(\Delta\theta_{ij}^t) = \begin{bmatrix} \cos(\Delta\theta_{ij}^t) & -\sin(\Delta\theta_{ij}^t) \\ \sin(\Delta\theta_{ij}^t) & \cos(\Delta\theta_{ij}^t) \end{bmatrix} \tag{3}$$

In here, $\Delta\theta_{ij}^t$ is obtained through (4),

$$\Delta\theta_{ij}^t = sign(\alpha_{ij}^t \beta_{ij}^t) \frac{1}{p} \sum_{k=1}^{p} \Delta\phi_{ij}^k \tag{4}$$

where $sign(\alpha_{ij}^t \beta_{ij}^t)$ can be '1' or '−1', when the Q-bit of each iteration is located in the first or third quadrant, $sign(\alpha_{ij}^t \beta_{ij}^t) = 1$, otherwise, $sign(\alpha_{ij}^t \beta_{ij}^t) = -1$.

$$sign(\alpha_{ij}^{t}\beta_{ij}^{t}) = \begin{cases} 1 & 1,3 \ quadrant \\ -1 & 2,4 \ quadrant \end{cases} \tag{5}$$

To improve the performance of PEQIEA, all the individuals in the elite group *E(t)* of each iteration cooperate together, $\frac{1}{p}\sum_{k=1}^{p}\Delta\phi_{ij}^{k}$ is obtained as the rotation angle, through the rotation angle the current individuals Q-bit will evolve toward better individuals, proving a better solution.

The value of $\Delta\phi_{ij}^{k}$ can be obtained from Table 1.

Table 1. Look-up table of $\Delta\phi_{ij}^{k}$ in Peqiea

x_{ij}^{t}	e_{ij}^{t}	$f(x_i^t) \leq f(e_k^t)$	$\Delta\phi_{ij}^{k}$
*	*	False	0
0	0	True	0
0	1	True	ϕ_1
1	0	True	ϕ_0
1	1	True	1

where x_{ij}^{t} is the ith Q-bit of the jth iteration Q-bit individual; e_{kj}^{t} is the ith Q-bit of the jth iteration Q-bit individual in elite group *E(t)*; '*' can be '0' or '1'; ϕ_0 and ϕ_1 are two different rotation angle, the values will be discussed in Sect. 4. As shown in Table 1, ϕ_0 and ϕ_1 are used to increase or decrease the probability of the state of the current Q-bit. When the state of the current Q-bit is '1', we decrease the value of ϕ_0 to reduce the possibility of state '1' to evolve toward state '0'. Otherwise, the state of the current Q-bit is '0', we increase the value of ϕ_1 to enhance the possibility of state '0' to evolve toward state '1'. This idea pushes the genes of individuals to evolve toward state '1'. Thus, the number of candidate solutions which violate the capacity constraint will go up, so the number of the repair of the candidate solutions will correspondingly rise. According to the description of Step (vii), the quality of the solution can be greatly improved.

(xi) In this step, the best solutions are selected from $B(t-1)$ and $P(t)$, then they are stored into $B(t)$.

(xii) The best solution in *B(t)* is compare with the best solution ***b***, if it is better than ***b***, let it to be the best solution ***b***.

3 Experiment Results

Section 3.1 describes knapsack problems. Section 3.2 presents experimental results of PEQIEA.

3.1 Knapsack Problems

As well-known combinatorial optimization problem, knapsack problems [1] are critical in practical applications. In this paper, 0–1 knapsack problems are considered the same as literature [29], and also have limited capacity [25]. Search maximize the profit $f(x)$

$$f(x) = \sum_{i=1}^{m} p_i x_i \quad \text{Subject to} \sum_{i=1}^{m} \omega_i x_i \leq C \tag{6}$$

where x_i in $\boldsymbol{x}$, $x = (x_1, x_2, \ldots, x_m)$, $i = 1, 2, \ldots, m$, each individual x_i is '0' or '1', if $x_i = 1$, it means that the ith item is selected for the knapsack, $x_i = 0$ means not selected. So $\boldsymbol{x}$ is a string of '0' or '1', it is a solution of knapsack problems by a certain method. C is the capacity of the knapsack; p_i represents the profit of the ith item and ω_i is the weight of the ith item,

$$\omega_i = \text{uniformly random}[1,v] \tag{7}$$

$$p_i = \omega_i + r \tag{8}$$

where $v = 10$ and $r = 5$.

3.2 Experiments of PEQIEA

In this subsection, a new criterion is introduced to evaluate the convergence speed of PEQIEA and how good the solutions obtained by PEQIEA are. To clearly understand the new criterion, we first present two points: the solution obtained by using a greedy algorithm, which is called GS in this paper, and an ideal upper-limit (UL) of the solution of a knapsack problem. In the process of searching for the optimal solution, a greedy algorithm always chooses the item with the biggest ratio of its profit to weight for the given knapsack. Although the solution obtained by using a greedy algorithm for a specific knapsack problem can be regarded as a good one, it may be not the optimal one. On the basis of the solution obtained by using a greedy algorithm, we insert the item with an ideal weight into the given knapsack so that the knapsack is completely full. The item with an ideal weight is obtained from the critical item, which is the first item that the greedy algorithm cannot put into the knapsack. So the item with an ideal weight can be considered as a part of the critical item. It is evident that UL is always above GS. Based on this assumption, the actual optimal solution of a knapsack problem will fall into the range between GS and UL. In what follows we give the definition of the new criterion TC as

$$TC = GS + k * (UL - GS) \tag{9}$$

where the parameter $k (0 \leq k \leq 1)$ is a coefficient for measuring the distance between GS and UL.

To clearly understand the criterion TC, the best solutions (i.e., BS) and the mean of best solutions (i.e., MBS), which are obtained by PEQIEA, of 13 knapsack problem are used to draw the figure shown in Fig. 2, where the vertical axis is the ratio of each of GS, MBS and BS to UL and UL for each problem is fixed as 1.

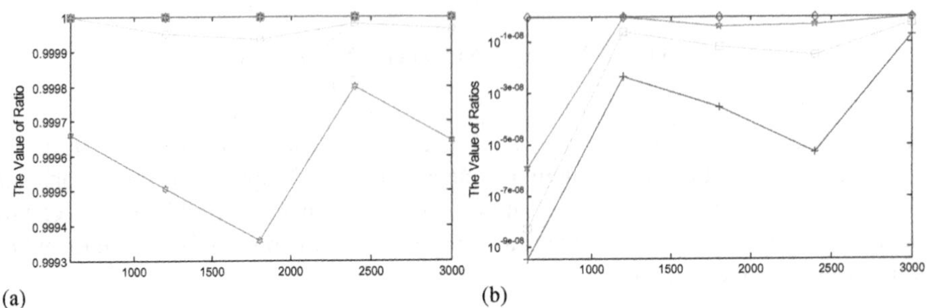

Fig. 2. Results of GS, UL, BS and MBS of PEQIEA

The results in Fig. 2 show that the gaps between BS (or MBS) of PEQIEA and GS, between BS (or MBS) of PEQIEA and UL, become bigger as the number of items goes up. Therefore the criterion can be used to evaluate the quality of solutions obtained by applying various algorithms. Through adjusting the parameter k, TC can also be used as a termination condition for an algorithm to measure its convergence speed.

To test PEQIEA performance, five different knapsack problems with the items varying from 600 to 3000 with an interval 600 are applied to conduct experiments. Benchmark algorithms include seven variants of QIEAs, QIEA [1], HQIEA [11], IQIEA [20], FQIEA [10], QEPS [21], CLQIEA [22], and EQIEA [27]. The greedy repair method in [1] is used in the eight algorithms. In those algorithms, let the population size n to be 20 and the number of independent runs be set to 30; In order to avoid an infinite loop, if there has 1000 iterations the loop should be ended. To evaluate the algorithm performance, the best solution (BS), the mean of best solutions (MBS), the worst solution (WS) and their standard deviation (STD) are used. Table 2 shows the experimental results, where GS, TC and UL for each problem are also listed. To test the convergence of PEQIEA, TC with the parameter $k = 0.9$ and if there has 1000 iterations the loop should be ended for each algorithm. In Table 2, NoI, AL, MNI, BS, MBS and WS represent the number of items in a knapsack problem, algorithms, and the mean number of iterations when each run reaches TC, BS, MBS and WS, respectively.

As shown in Table 2, for the knapsack problem with 600 items, PEQIEA achieves the best BS, MBS and WS among the eight algorithms, but its MNI is more than that of PEQIEA; when the number of items is 1200, 1800, 2400 or 3000, PEQIEA obtains better results than EQIEA and other six variants of QIEAs; BS of PEQIEA nearly approaches UL and MNI of PEQIEA is the smallest among the eight algorithms. Specially, MNI of PEQIEA for the knapsack problem with 3000 items is only 324, which is far less than the other seven algorithms. Therefore, PEQIEA has better ability to balance exploration and exploitation for knapsack problems, and has better convergence.

Table 2. Experimental results of eight algorithms.

NoI	AL	MNI	BS	MBS	WS	GS/TC/UL
600	QIEA	10000	3676.1290	3675.6275	3671.1261	GS = 3679.8790
	HQIEA	10000	3676.1280	3670.6278	3666.1266	TC = 3681.0041
	IQIEA	10000	3666.1287	3663.1251	3656.1290	UL = 3681.1291
	FQIEA	7814	3681.1258	3679.2501	3670.9387	
	QEPS	10000	3631.1214	3617.6242	3596.1278	
	CLQIEA	10000	3676.1289	3676.1277	3676.1256	
	EQIEA1	2961	3681.1289	3681.1238	3681.1179	
	EQIEA2	582	3681.1291	3681.1289	3681.1288	
	PEQIEA	173	3681.1286	3681.1284	3681.1283	
1200	QIEA	10000	7365.4952	7357.9944	7355.4917	GS = 7371.8498
	HQIEA	10000	7340.4905	7334.4700	7320.4842	TC = 7375.1315
	IQIEA	10000	7320.4867	7310.9122	7295.1624	UL = 7375.4961
	FQIEA	8894	7375.4902	7370.6721	7363.1028	
	QEPS	10000	7230.4937	7208.9874	7185.4958	
	CLQIEA	10000	7365.4959	7363.4941	7360.4930	
	EQIEA1	7335	7375.4927	7374.9195	7370.4909	
	EQIEA2	876	7375.4960	7375.4956	7375.4940	
	PEQIEA	216	7375.4961	7375.4960	7375.4957	
1800	QIEA	10000	11023.6642	11007.6652	10978.6658	GS = 11036.5618
	HQIEA	10000	10963.6448	10942.1029	10913.6130	TC = 11042.9555
	IQIEA	10000	10893.3635	10864.4902	10848.6453	UL = 11043.6659
	FQIEA	8271	11043.6588	11039.4819	11025.4341	
	QEPS	10000	10743.6641	10711.1526	10653.6633	
	CLQIEA	10000	11028.6620	11021.6642	11008.6656	
	EQIEA1	9882	11043.6470	11040.0167	11038.6201	
	EQIEA2	1321	11043.6639	11043.6637	11043.6613	
	PEQIEA	1100	11043.6658	11043.6656	11043.6650	
2400	QIEA	10000	14699.7198	14679.7188	14649.7187	GS = 14746.7553
	HQIEA	10000	14579.6499	14546.8915	14494.5388	TC = 14749.4237
	IQIEA	10000	14403.3049	14376.8923	14344.2411	UL = 14749.7202
	FQIEA	9699	14749.6244	14739.5228	14723.7171	
	QEPS	10000	14274.7198	14206.6810	14164.7197	
	CLQIEA	10000	14709.7199	14703.7185	14684.7152	
	EQIEA1	10000	14739.2400	14735.6317	14734.3871	
	EQIEA2	2036	14749.7196	14749.7097	14749.6996	
	PEQIEA	353	14749.7201	14749.7197	14749.7184	
3000	QIEA	10000	18301.2696	18280.2692	18246.2699	GS = 18374.7172
	HQIEA	10000	18061.2126	18031.8713	17984.6050	TC = 18380.6155
	IQIEA	10000	17816.0103	17777.0292	17736.2377	UL = 18381.2708
	FQIEA	10000	18379.8046	18370.6711	18357.2014	

(*continued*)

Table 2. (*continued*)

NoI	AL	MNI	BS	MBS	WS	GS/TC/UL
	QEPS	10000	17721.2648	17628.2355	17570.9420	
	CLQIEA	10000	18321.2701	18310.7693	18301.2676	
	EQIEA1	10000	18366.1046	18362.3927	18360.5100	
	EQIEA2	2037	18381.2706	18381.2500	18381.1844	
	PEQIEA	324	18381.2708	18381.2707	18381.2705	

4 Discussions

As an improved algorithm, PEQIEA shares similarities with EQIEA, and in the following, the parameters of the two algorithms are discussed. This section first discusses how to choose the number p of individuals in $E(t)$ and the value of ϕ (let $\phi_0 = \phi_1$ in Table 1 and $\phi = \phi_0 = \phi_1$) in EQIEA. Next, the parameter setting of PEQIEA is discussed.

4.1 Parameter Setting of EQIEA

To investigate the effects of the parameters p and ϕ on the EQIEA performance, two experiments are conducted on the knapsack problems with 1400 items. In the two experiments, the termination condition is defined as the maximum number of iterations should be no more than 1000. In the first experiment, the population size n is set to 5, 10, 20, 30 and 40, respectively. The value 0.04π of ϕ is fixed. 30 independent runs are performed for each case. Experimental results are shown in Fig. 3, where MBS in the vertical axis is the mean of best solutions over 30 independent runs. In the second experiment, the population size n is set to 20; the parameter p varies from 1 to 19 with an interval 2; and the value of ϕ varies from 0.01π to 0.08π with an interval 0.005π. Experimental results are shown in Fig. 4, where MBS and ET in the vertical axis are the mean of best solutions over 30 independent runs and the mean of elapsed time per run, respectively.

As shown in Fig. 3, the trends of MBS with different values of p have similar changes when the population size n has different values; when the population size n varies from 5 to 40, MBS with different values of p has a fast increase and then stays at a relatively steady level; for each value of n, as the value of p increases from 1 to 40, MBS goes through a rapid rise and quickly turns to a steady value. Thus, it is better that the values of n and p be assigned with values more than 20. The experimental results in Fig. 4(a) and (b) show that MBS with different ϕ takes on a similar trend when the value of p varies from 1 to 19 and that for each value of p, MBS goes through a fast increase and then a slow decrease and the maximum can be obtained at $\phi = 0.04\pi$. The experimental results in Fig. 4(c) and (d) show that ET with different values of ϕ has a similar trend when the value of p varies from 1 to 19, and that for each value of p, as ϕ rises from 0.01π to 0.08π, ET decreases at a relatively slow speed. Through trading off the quality of solutions and the elapsed time, the values of p and ϕ would be assigned as 20 and 0.04π, respectively.

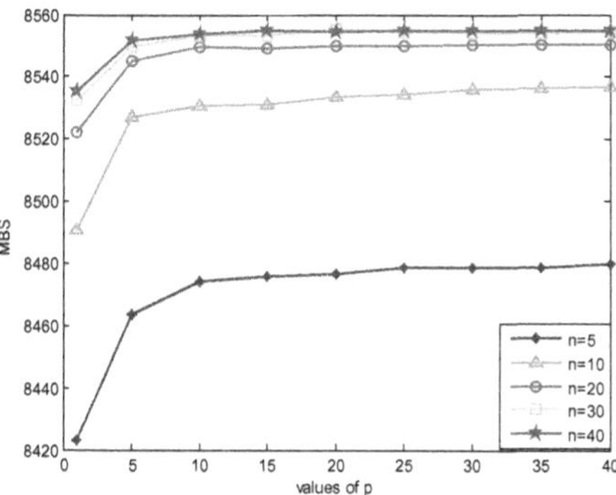

Fig. 3. Experiment results of different p and n

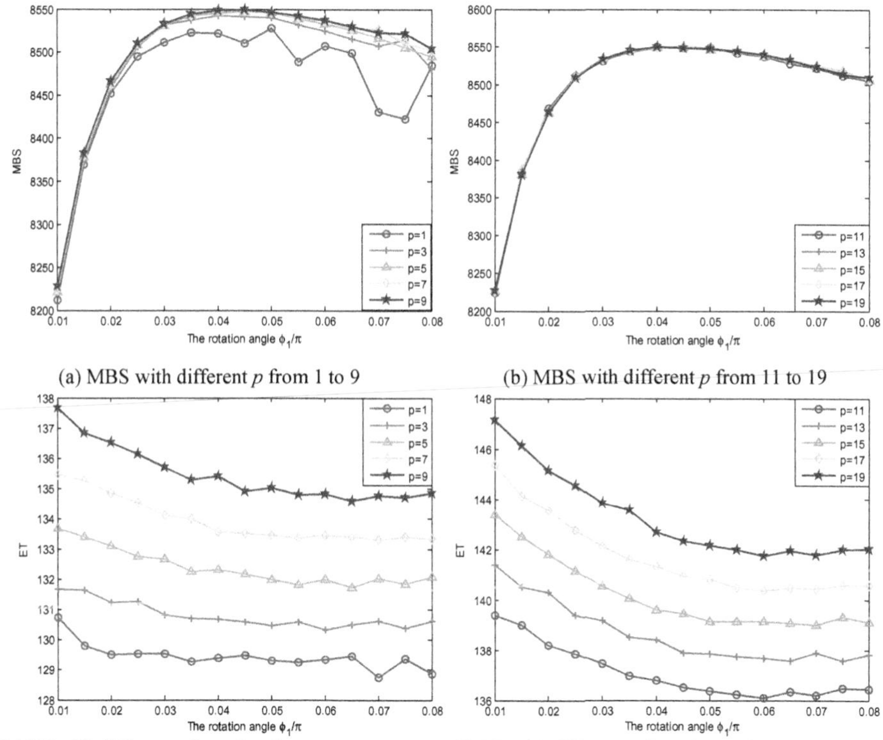

(a) MBS with different p from 1 to 9

(b) MBS with different p from 11 to 19

(c) ET with different p from 1 to 9

(d) ET with different p from 11 to 19

Fig. 4. Experiment results of different p and ϕ

4.2 Parameter Setting of PEQIEA

In this subsection, we first discuss how to choose the values of ϕ_0 and ϕ_1 in Table 1 and then in turn discuss the choice of k mentioned in Sect. 3.2.

In the discussion of ϕ_0 and ϕ_1, the knapsack problem with 200 items is used as an example to conduct experiments. Let both ϕ_0 and ϕ_1 vary from -0.1π to 0.1π with an increasing interval 0.01π. The population size is set to 20, the parameter p is set to 20 and the maximal number of iterations is set to 1000. For each case 30 independent runs are performed and MBS is recorded. Experimental results are shown in Fig. 5.

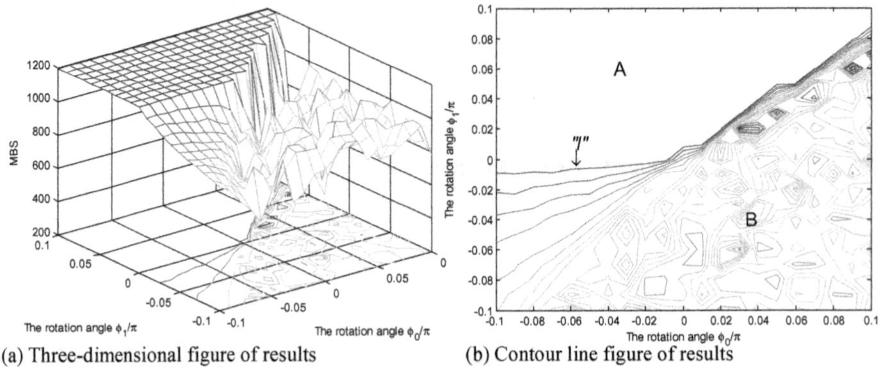

(a) Three-dimensional figure of results (b) Contour line figure of results

Fig. 5. Experimental results of 200 items with different ϕ_0 and ϕ_1

As shown in Fig. 5, better results are obtained when $\phi_0 \geq 0$ and $\phi_1 \geq \phi_0$, which is clearer in Fig. 5(b), where the plane is divided into two regions by the line "*l*"; the results in region *A* are much better than those in region *B*; the standard deviations of solutions in region *A* are much smaller than those in region *B*. It is clear that many combinations of ϕ_0 and ϕ_1 can be used in the experiments. To further discuss the choices of ϕ_0 and ϕ_1, we fix $\phi_1 = 0.04\pi$ and conduct two kinds of experiments to investigate the effects of different values of ϕ_0 on the convergence performance of this algorithm.

First, knapsack problems with various items are considered to investigate the effect of ϕ_0 on the PEQIEA performance. The population size is set to 20, the parameter p is set to 20 and the maximum number of iterations is set to 1000. The rotation angle $\phi_1 = 0.04\pi$. ϕ_0 varies from -0.04π to 0.04π with an interval 0.01π. The parameter k in TC is set to 0.95, where TC is described in Sect. 3.2. The average number of iterations over 30 independent runs for each test are recorded and shown in Fig. 6 when the algorithm stops.

The experimental results in Fig. 6(a) show that the average iterations for the knapsack problems with 400, 600, 800 and 1000 items steadily increase with the value of ϕ_0 going up, but the average iterations for the knapsack problems with 200 items are 2936, 2481, 2261 and 2115 when the $\phi_0 = -0.04\pi$, -0.03π, -0.02π and -0.01π, respectively. This phenomenon indicates that PEQIEA quickly traps into at a local optimal solution when ϕ_0 is too small. In Fig. 6(b), the average iterations for the knapsack problems with 1600 items is 10000 when $\phi_0 \leq -0.01\pi$, and the average iterations gradually reduce as ϕ_0 increases, but the average iterations of $\phi_0 = 0.04\pi$ is greater than the ones of $\phi_0 = 0.03\pi$. These results illustrate that PEQIEA easily falls

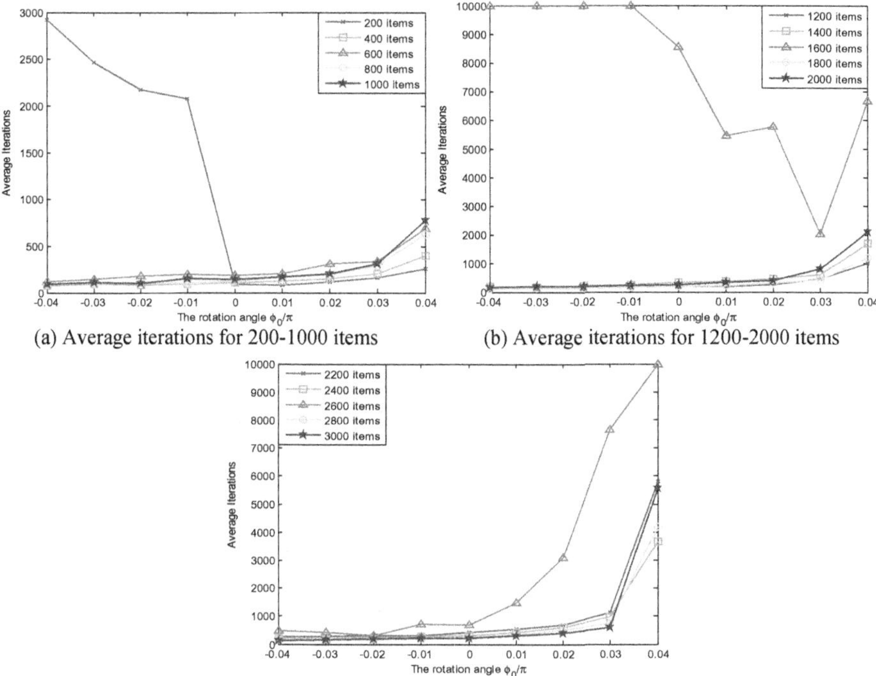

(a) Average iterations for 200-1000 items (b) Average iterations for 1200-2000 items

Fig. 6. Average iterations for knapsack problems with different items

into a local optimal solution, but the convergence speed can be accelerated when ϕ_0 is too small. The average iterations of the rest of the knapsack problems have steady increases with the value of ϕ_0 rising, indicting PEQIEA has a fast convergence speed.

In the second experiment, to test the convergence speed of PEQIEA with different TCs, the knapsack problems with 1600 items are used. Experimental results are shown in Fig. 7.

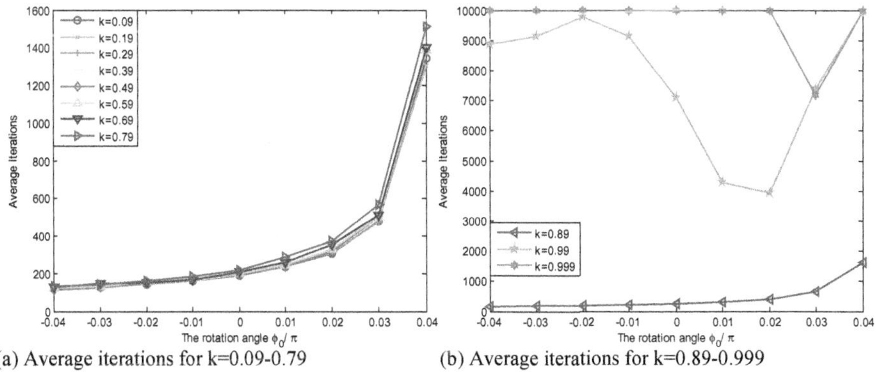

(a) Average iterations for k=0.09-0.79 (b) Average iterations for k=0.89-0.999

Fig. 7. Average iterations obtained by PEQIEA with different *k* in TC

Figure 7 shows that the average iterations with various k increase at a fast speed as ϕ_0 goes up from 0 to 0.04π. However, when $k = 0.99$ or 0.999, this trend does not exist and the average iterations first has a decreasing trend and then an increasing one. In Fig. 7(b), when $k = 0.99$, the average iterations with $\phi_0 \leq 0.01\pi$ are more than that with $\phi_0 = 0.02\pi$; the average iterations with $\phi_0 = 0.03\pi$ or $\phi_0 = 0.04\pi$ are greater than that with $\phi_0 = 0.02\pi$; the average iterations with $\phi_0 = 0.03\pi$ is the least when $k = 0.999$; the average iterations with $\phi_0 \leq 0.02\pi$ or $\phi_0 = 0.04\pi$ are the maximal number 10000 iterations.

5 Conclusion

This paper proposes an improved quantum-inspired evolutionary algorithm, PEQIEA for solving knapsack problems by introducing an elite group and state preference updating approach for Q-gates and applying the greedy repair. Extensive experimentation on multiple knapsack problems is performed with discussion on how to choose proper parameters for EQIEA and PEQIEA and verify the performance of PEQIEA's. The results show that PEQIEA is superior to seven alternate typical QIEAs. PEQIEA can not only obtain better solutions than others QIEAs, but also has better convergence as it takes advantage of special characteristics of knapsack problems. Following this work, more real-world applications will be considered.

Acknowledgments. This work was supported by the National Natural Science Foundation of China under Grant Nos. 51577046, 51607004, the State Key Program of National Natural Science Foundation of China under Grant No. 51637004, the national key research and development plan "important scientific instruments and equipment development" Grant No. 2016YFF0102200, Anhui Provincial Natural Science Foundation No. 1608085QF157, and Key projects of Anhui Province university outstanding youth talent support program No. gxyqZD2016207. This work was supported by the China Scholar Council.

References

1. Rastaghi, R.: New approach for CCA2-secure post-quantum cryptosystem using knapsack problem. Comput. Sci. (2012)
2. Fu, Z., Ren, K., Shu, J., Sun, X., Huang, F.: Enabling personalized search over encrypted outsourced data with efficiency improvement. IEEE Trans. Parallel Distrib. Syst. **27**(9), 2546–2559 (2016)
3. Qu, Z., Keeney, J., Robitzsch, S., Zaman, F., Wang, X.: Multilevel pattern mining architecture for automatic network monitoring in heterogeneous wireless communication networks. Chin. Commun. **13**(7), 108–116 (2016)
4. Xue, Y., Jiang, J., Zhao, B., Ma, T.: A self-adaptive artificial bee colony algorithm based on global best for global optimization. Soft Comput. (2017)
5. Holland, J.: Adaptation in Natural and Artificial System. University of Michigan Press, Ann Arbor (1975)
6. Han, K.H., Kim, J.H.: Quantum-inspired evolutionary algorithm for a class of combinatorial optimization. IEEE Trans. Evol. Comput. **6**, 580–593 (2002)

7. Zhang, G.X.: Quantum-inspired evolutionary algorithms: a survey and empirical study. J. Heuristics **17**, 303–351 (2011)
8. Zhang, G.X.: Time-frequency atom decomposition with quantum-inspired evolutionary algorithms. Circ. Syst. Sig. Process. **29**, 209–233 (2010)
9. Manju, A., Nigam, M.J.: Applications of quantum inspired computational intelligence: a survey. Artif. Intell. Rev. (2012)
10. Narayanan, A., Moore, M.: Quantum-inspired genetic algorithms. In: Proceedings of the ICEC, pp. 61–66, Nagoya, Japan (1996)
11. Zhang, G.X., Li, N., Jin, W.D.: Novel quantum genetic algorithm and its application. Frontiers Electr. Electron. Eng. Chin. **1**, 31–36 (2006)
12. Vlachogiannis, J.G., Lee, K.Y.: Quantum-inspired evolutionary algorithm for real and reactive power dispatch. IEEE Trans. Power Syst. **23**, 1627–1636 (2008)
13. Han, K.H., Kim, J.H.: Quantum-inspired evolutionary algorithms with a new termination criterion, Hε gate, and two-phase scheme. IEEE Trans. Evol. Comput. **8**, 156–169 (2004)
14. Zhang, G.X., Rong, H.N.: Parameter setting of quantum-inspired genetic algorithm based on real observation. In: Proceedings of the RSKT, vol. 4481, pp. 492–499, Toronto, Ont, Canada (2007)
15. Liu, H.W., Zhang, G.X., Liu, C.X., Fang, C.: A novel memetic algorithm based on real-observation quantum-inspired evolutionary algorithms. In: Proceedings of the ISKE, pp. 486–490, Xiamen, China (2008)
16. Abs da Cruz, A.V., Hall Barbosa, C.R., Pacheco, M.A.C., Vellasco, M.: Quantum-inspired evolutionary algorithms and its application to numerical optimization problems. In: Pal, N. R., Kasabov, N., Mudi, R.K., Pal, S., Parui, S.K. (eds.) ICONIP 2004. LNCS, vol. 3316, pp. 212–217. Springer, Heidelberg (2004). doi:10.1007/978-3-540-30499-9_31
17. Babu, G.S.S., Das, D.B., Patvardhan, C.: Real-parameter quantum evolutionary algorithm for economic load dispatch. IET Gener. Transm. Distrib. **2**, 21–31 (2008)
18. Li, N., Du, P., Zhao, H.J.: Independent component analysis based on improved quantum genetic algorithm: application in hyperspectral images. In: IGARSS, vol. 6, pp. 4323–4326 (2005)
19. Zhang, G., Rong, H.: Improved quantum-inspired genetic algorithm based time-frequency analysis of radar emitter signals. In: Yao, J., Lingras, P., Wu, W.-Z., Szczuka, M., Cercone, N.J., Ślęzak, D. (eds.) RSKT 2007. LNCS, vol. 4481, pp. 484–491. Springer, Heidelberg (2007). doi:10.1007/978-3-540-72458-2_60
20. Li, Y., Zhang, Y.N., Zhao, R.C., Jiao, L.C.: The immune quantum-inspired evolutionary algorithm. In: IEEE ICSMC, vol. 4, pp. 3301–3305, Xi'an, China (2004)
21. Wang, L., Feng, X.Y., Huang, Y.X., Pu, D.B., Zhou, W.G., Liang, Y.C., Zhou, C.G.: A novel quantum swarm evolutionary algorithm and its applications. Neurocomputing **70**, 633–640 (2007)
22. Zhang, R., Gao, H.: Improved quantum evolutionary algorithm for combinatorial optimization problem. In: ICMLC, vol. 6, pp. 3501–3505, Hong Kong, China (2007)
23. Zhang, G.X.: A quantum-inspired evolutionary algorithm based on p systems for knapsack problem. Fundam. Inform. **87**, 93–116 (2008)
24. Qin, Y., Zhang, G., Li, Y., Zhang, H.: A comprehensive learning quantum-inspired evolutionary algorithm. In: Qu, X., Yang, Y. (eds.) IBI 2011. CCIS, vol. 268, pp. 151–157. Springer, Heidelberg (2012). doi:10.1007/978-3-642-29087-9_22
25. Garey, M.R., Johnson, D.S.: Computers and Intractability: A Guide to the Theory of NP-Completeness. Freeman, Oxford (1979)
26. Kim, J.H., Myung, H.: Evolutionary programming techniques for constrained optimization problems. IEEE Trans. Evol. Comput. **1**, 129–140 (1997)

27. Michalewicz, Z.: Genetic Algorithms + Data Structures = Evolution. Springer, New York (1999). doi:10.1007/978-3-662-03315-9
28. Garcia, S., Molina, D., Lozano, M., Herrera, F.: A study on the use of non-parametric tests for analyzing the evolutionary algorithms' behaviour: a case study on the CEC'2005 special session on real parameter optimization. J. Heuristics **15**, 617–644 (2009)
29. Layeb, A.: A hybrid quantum inspired harmony search algorithm for 0–1 optimization problems. Appl. Math. Comput. **253**, 14–25 (2013)
30. Gao, J., He, G., Liang, R., Feng, Z.: A quantum-inspired artificial immune system for the multiobjective 0–1 knapsack problem. Appl. Math. Comput. **230**, 120–137 (2014)
31. Chiang, H.-P., Chou, Y.-H., Chiu, C.-H., Kuo, S.-Y., Huang, Y.-M.: A quantum-inspired Tabu search algorithm for solving combinatorial optimization problems. Soft. Comput. **18**, 1771–1781 (2014)
32. Patvardhan, C., Bansal, S., Srivastav, A.: Quantum-inspired evolutionary algorithm for difficult knapsack problems. Memet. Comput. **7**, 135–155 (2015)
33. Xiang, S., He, Y.G.: A quantum-inspired evolutionary algorithm with elite group guided. In: Applied Mechanics and Materials, vol. 738–739, pp. 323–333 (2015)

Output-Based Sampled Data Control for Linear Systems: A Measurement Error Estimation Approach

Yuelin Shen[1] and Wenbing Zhang[2(✉)]

[1] School of Mechanical Engineering, Nantong Institute of Technology, Nantong 226002, China
115195443@qq.com

[2] Department of Mathematics, YangZhou University, Yangzhou 225002, Jiangsu, China
zwb850506@126.com

Abstract. In this paper, the output based sampled data control problem for linear systems is investigated. First, based on the measured output, a closed-loop system with measurement error has been obtained. Then, in order to obtain the maximum upper bound of the sampling interval, a measurement error model has been derived to estimate the measurement error. By using the Gronwall-Lemma and the Lyapunov stability theory, the control gain matrix and the maximum upper bound of the sampling interval has been explicitly given.

Keywords: Output-based · Sampled data · Measurement error

1 Introduction

During the past decades, networked control systems have aroused many research attention due to their wide applications in many fields [1], such as mobile sensor networks [2], haptics collaboration over the Internet [3], and automated highway systems and unmanned aerial vehicles [4,5]. There are fruitful results have been obtained on stabilization of networked control systems. For instance, finite capacity stabilization problem was investigated for nonlinear systems in [6]. In [7], a new method was derived to investigate the stabilization problem of networked control systems with random delays. In [8], a Bernoulli distributed white sequence was introduced to model packet dropouts in networked control systems, and the stochastic stabilization problem was investigated. Further, in [9], based on the information of system output, an output based stabilization problem for a class of networked control systems with packet dropouts was investigated. In [10], first of all, an asynchronous dynamic system was used to model packet dropouts, and then based on this asynchronous dynamic system, the stability problem was investigated. In [11], the Robust H_∞ problem was investigated for a class of networked control systems with parameter uncertainty.

X. Sun et al. (Eds.): ICCCS 2017, Part II, LNCS 10603, pp. 709–716, 2017.
https://doi.org/10.1007/978-3-319-68542-7_61

As mentioned above, fruitful results have been reported on networked control systems. However, it should be mentioned that the above mentioned results are based on the assumption that the system state can be obtained continuously. Actually, nowadays, the data transmission between a physical plant and a controller is completed through a digit network. Therefore, it is difficult to obtain the network states continuously. Thus sampled data control strategy is more practical than the feedback controller. In the past few years, sampled data stabilization of networked control systems has received increasing research attention [12–15]. In [13], an input delay approach was proposed to investigate the stabilization problem of networked control systems. In [14], a hybrid system approach was presented to study the stability problem of networked control system with uncertain sampled data, and in [15], a lifting technique (discrete-time approach) was proposed for linear periodic sampled data systems. In most existing results, it is assumed that the states of systems are fully measurable and the sampled data control can be realized. However, in practise, it is very difficult to obtain the full state of the system state, and usually, we can only obtain partial state of the system state [19]. Thus, it is interesting to investigate the output-based sampled data control of networked control systems. Recently, there are some results have been obtained on this interesting topic, see [20] and the references therein. It is worth pointing out that in most existing results, linear matrix inequality (LMI) approach was used to derive the main results. As the dimension of the network state grows, the size of LMI grows exponentially, which will give rise to heavy burden of computations. Thus, it is of great interesting to find another method to reduce the decision numbers of LMIs.

Based on the above discussions, in this paper, a measurement error estimation method will be presented to investigate the output-based stabilization problem of networked control systems. By means of the Lyapunov function method and the Gronwall-inequality, a sufficient condition ensuring the stabilization of networked control systems was obtained. Then an algorithm is proposed to solve the controller gain matrix. Finally, a numerical example is given to illustrate the effectiveness of the theoretical results.

2 Preliminaries

Consider the following linear system

$$\begin{cases} \dot{x}(t) = Ax(t) + Bu(t) \\ y(t) = Cx(t), \end{cases} \tag{1}$$

where $x(t) \in R^n$ is the state vector, $u(t) \in R^m$ and $y(t) \in R^p$, respectively, the control input and the measured output. $A \in R^{n\times n}$, $B \in R^{n\times m}$ and $C \in R^{p\times n}$ are constant real matrices. In this paper, the following output-based sampled data controller will be used to control linear system

$$u(t) = Ky(t_k), t \in [t_k, t_{k+1}), \tag{2}$$

where $t_0 < t_1 < \ldots < t_k < t_{k+1} < \ldots$ are the sampling instants. t_0 is the initial time, without loss of generality, we assume that $t_0 = 0$. K is the controller needs to be designed under which the following closed-loop system is stable.

$$\dot{x}(t) = Ax(t) + BKCx(t_k). \tag{3}$$

In the following, we will use the measurement error estimation method to investigate the stabilization problem of (3). Let the measurement error be $e(t) = x(t) - x(t_k)$, then, the following model can be obtained.

$$\dot{x}(t) = Ax(t) + BKCx(t) - BKCe(t). \tag{4}$$

$$\dot{e}(t) = Ae(t) + (A + BKC)x(t_k). \tag{5}$$

In what follows, we aim to investigate the stabilization problem of the system (1) via the estimation of $e(t)$. Thus, the following definition and lemma are needed to obtain the main results.

Definition 1. *Consider the linear control system (1) with output-based sampled data based control law $u(t) = BKCx(t_k)$, if there exist constants $M > 0$ and $\lambda > 0$ such that the following inequality is satisfied:*

$$\|x(t)\| \leq Me^{-\lambda t}, \forall t > 0 \tag{6}$$

then the closed-loop system is globally stable.

Lemma 1 (Gronwall-Belleman Lemma). *Let I denote an interval of the real line of the form $[a, +\infty)$ or $[a, b]$ or $[a, b)$ with $a < b$. Let α, β and v be real-valued continuous functions defined on I. Assume that β and v are continuous and that the negative part of α is integrable on every closed and bounded subinterval of I.*

If β is non-negative and if v satisfies the integral inequality

$$v(t) \leq \alpha(t) + \int_a^t \beta(s)v(s)ds, \qquad t \in I, \tag{7}$$

then

$$v(t) \leq \alpha(t) + \int_a^t \alpha(s)\beta(s)\exp(\int_s^t \beta(r)dr)ds, \tag{8}$$

for all $t \in I$. If, in addition, the function α is non-decreasing, then

$$v(t) \leq \alpha(t)\exp(\int_a^t \beta(r)dr). \tag{9}$$

Lemma 2. *For a positive definite matrix P, the following inequality holds*

$$x^T x \leq \lambda_{\max}(P^{-1})x^T Px. \tag{10}$$

3 Main Results

In this section, the output-based sampled data stabilization problem for the linear system in (1) will be investigated. By virtue of the Gronwall-Belleman Lemma, the upper bound of the measurement error $e(t)$ will be first estimated. Then, by virtue of the Lyapunov function method, the stabilization problem will be investigated, where the upper bound of the sampling interval and an algorithm for solving the control gain matrix will be given.

Lemma 3. *The measurement error $e(t)$, system state $x(t)$ and $x(t_k)$ satisfy the following inequality*

$$\begin{aligned} \|e(t)\| &\leq \gamma \|x(t_k)\|, \\ \|x(t)\| &\leq (1+\gamma)\|x(t_k)\|, \\ \|x(t_k)\| &\leq \frac{\|x(t)\|}{1-\gamma}, \end{aligned}$$

where $\gamma = (t_{k+1} - t_k)\|A + BKC\|e^{(t_{k+1}-t_k)\|A\|}$.

Proof. Applying Lemma 1 to the error system (5) yields

$$\begin{aligned} \|e(t)\| &\leq \|x(t_k)\|\|A + BKC\|(t - t_k)e^{\int_{t_k}^{t} \|A\| ds} \\ &\leq \|x(t_k)\|\|A + BKC\|(t - t_k)e^{(t-t_k)\|A\|}. \end{aligned} \tag{11}$$

Then, it can be easily obtained from (11) that

$$\|e(t)\| \leq \gamma \|x(t_k)\|. \tag{12}$$

From (12), one can easily get:

$$\|x(t)\| = \|e(t) + x(t_k)\| \leq \|e(t)\| + \|x(t_k)\| \leq (1+\gamma)\|x(t_k)\| \tag{13}$$

and

$$\|x(t_k)\| \leq \|x(t)\| + \|e(t)\| \leq \gamma\|x(t_k)\| + \|x(t)\|, \tag{14}$$

which further means that

$$\|x(t_k)\| \leq \frac{\|x(t)\|}{1-\gamma}. \tag{15}$$

Thus, the proof is complete.

Till now, we have obtained the estimations of $e(t)$, $x(t)$ and $x(t_k)$ and in what follows, we will prove the stabilization problem of system (1) by using these estimations.

Theorem 1. *If the controller gain matrix K is known and if there exists a positive definite matrix P and a positive scalar $\eta > 0$ such that the following matrix inequalities holds*

$$A^T P + PA + C^T K^T B^T P + PBKC + \eta P < 0, \tag{16}$$

$$\eta - 2\lambda_{\max}(P^{-1})\frac{\gamma}{1-\gamma}\|PBKC\| > 0. \tag{17}$$

Then, the linear system in (1) with output-based sampled data controller (2) is globally stable.

Proof. Consider the following Lyapunov function

$$V(t) = x^T(t)Px(t), \tag{18}$$

where P is a positive definite matrix. Taking the derivative of $V(t)$ along system (4), we get

$$\begin{aligned}\dot{V}(t \leq & x^T(t)[A^T P + PA + C^T K^T B^T P + PBKC]x(t) \\ & - x^T(t)PBKCe(t) - e^T(t)C^T K^T B^T Px(t) \\ \leq & -\eta V(t) - 2\|x(t)\|\|PBKC\|\|e(t)\| \\ \leq & -\eta V(t) + 2\frac{\gamma}{1-\gamma}\|PBKC\|\|x(t)\|^2. \end{aligned} \tag{19}$$

From Lemma 2, it is easy to see that

$$\|x(t)\|^2 \leq \lambda_{\max}(P^{-1})V(t). \tag{20}$$

In view of (19) and (20), it is easy to see that

$$\dot{V}(t) \leq -\eta V(t) + 2\lambda_{\max}(P^{-1})\frac{\gamma}{1-\gamma}\|PBKC\|. \tag{21}$$

From (17), we know that $-\eta + 2\lambda_{\max}(P^{-1})\frac{\gamma}{1-\gamma}\|PBKC\| < 0$. Let $\beta = \eta - 2\lambda_{\max}(P^{-1})\frac{\gamma}{1-\gamma}\|PBKC\|$, from (21), we can conclude that for $t \in [t_k, t_{k+1})$

$$V(t) \leq e^{-\beta(t-t_k)}V(t_k) \leq e^{-\beta(t-t_0)}V(t_0). \tag{22}$$

The proof is complete.

In Theorem 1, the output-based sampled data stabilization problem was solved for the linear system in (1). However, it should be mentioned that the controller gain matrix K is assumed to be known. Thus, in what follows, an algorithm will be presented to solve this problem by using the convex optimization method.

Theorem 2. *Suppose that that rank(B) = rank(B, inv(P) ∗ C), if there exists a positive definite matrix P and a positive scalar $\eta > 0$ such that the following matrix inequalities holds*

$$A^T P + PA - 2C^T C + \eta P < 0, \tag{23}$$

$$\eta - 2\lambda_{\max}(P^{-1})\frac{\gamma}{1-\gamma}\|PBKC\| > 0. \tag{24}$$

then the linear system in (1) with output-based sampled data controller (2) is globally stable and K can be solved by solving the following matrix equation

$$BK = -inv(P) * C^T.$$

Proof. *It can be obtained from* $BK = inv(P) * C^T$ *that* $PBKC = -C^T C$ *and* $C^T K^T B^T P = -C^T C$. *Then, the rest proof is the same to the proof of Theorem 1.*

4 Numerical Example

In this section, a numerical example is provided to illustrate the effectiveness of the theoretical results in the above section. Consider the following linear system:

$$\begin{cases} \dot{x}(t) = Ax(t) + Bu(t) \\ y(t) = Cx(t), \end{cases} \tag{25}$$

where $A = \text{diag}\{0.5, 0.5\}$, $B = \begin{bmatrix} 1 & 0.2 \\ 0.2 & 0.1 \end{bmatrix}$ $C = \begin{bmatrix} 1 & 0 \\ 0 & 1 \end{bmatrix}$. Let $\eta = 1$, by solving Theorem 2, we can get

$$P = \begin{bmatrix} 0.5319 & 0 \\ 0 & 0.5319 \end{bmatrix}$$

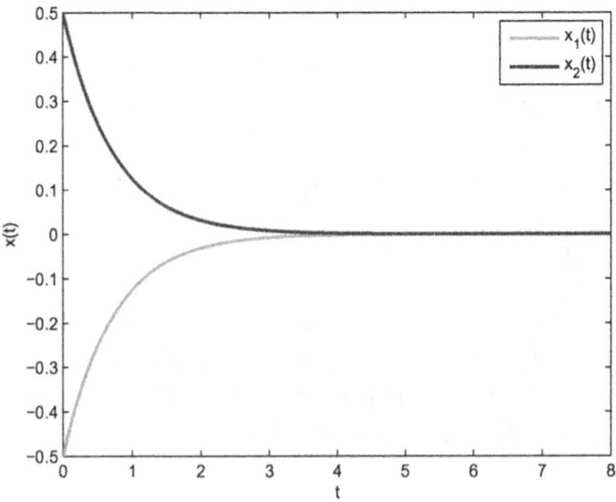

Fig. 1. State trajectories of $x(t)$ of the linear system in (1).

and by solving $BK = -inv(P) * C^T$, we get that

$$K = \begin{bmatrix} -1.9586 & 0.3917 \\ 0.3917 & -1.9586 \end{bmatrix}.$$

Then, we can get $t_{k+1} - t_k < 0.3102$. Let $t_{k+1} - t_k = 0.31$, then the state trajectories of the linear system in (1) with output-based sampled data controller (2) is plotted in Fig. 1, from which we can see that the simulation result confirms our theoretical results well.

5 Conclusion

In this paper, the output-based sampled data stabilization problem has been investigated. Different from existing results, an measurement error based approach was presented to reduce the decision number of LMIs. First of all, by means of the Gronwall inequality, the upper bound of the measurement error has been obtained. Then, based on the estimation and the Lyapunov function method, a sufficient condition is obtained to ensure the stabilization problem of networked control systems, where the upper bound of the sampling interval is give. In addition, the control gain matrix is also solved by an algorithm. It is interesting to use the methods in [16–18] to collect sampled-data.

Acknowledgements. This work was supported in part by the National Natural Science Foundation of China under Grant No. 61503328.

References

1. Hespanha, J.P., Naghshtabrizi, P., Xu, Y.: A survey of recent results in networked control systems. Proc. IEEE **95**, 138–162 (2007)
2. Ogren, P., Fiorelli, E., Leonard, N.E.: Cooperative control of mobile sensor networks: adaptive gradient climbing in a distributed environment. IEEE Trans. Autom. Control **49**, 1292–1302 (2004)
3. Shirmohammadi, S., Woo, N.H.: Evaluating decorators for haptic collaboration over the Internet. In: Proceedings of the 3rd IEEE International Workshop on Haptic, Audio and Visual Environments and their Applications, pp. 105–109 (2004)
4. Seiler, P., Sengupta, R.: Analysis of communication losses in vehicle control problems. In: Proceedings of the 2001 American Control Conference, pp. 1491–1496 (2001)
5. Seiler, P., Sengupta, R.: An H_∞ approach to networked control. IEEE Trans. Autom. Control **50**, 356–364 (2005)
6. Liberzon, D., Hespanha, J.P.: Stabilization of nonlinear systems with limited information feedback. IEEE Trans. Autom. Control **50**, 910–915 (2005)
7. Zhang, L., Shi, Y., Chen, T., Huang, B.: A new method for stabilization of networked control systems with random delays. IEEE Trans. Autom. Control **50**, 1177–1181 (2005)
8. Wang, Z., Ho, D.W.C., Liu, X.: Variance-constrained filtering for uncertain stochastic systems with missing measurements. IEEE Trans. Autom. Control **48**, 1254–1258 (2003)

9. Zhang, W.A., Yu, L.: Output feedback stabilization of networked control systems with packet dropouts. IEEE Trans. Autom. Control **52**, 1705–1710 (2007)
10. Zhang, W., Branicky, M.S., Phillips, S.M.: Stability of networked control systems. IEEE Control Syst. **21**, 84–99 (2001)
11. Yue, D., Han, Q.L., Lam, J.: Network-based robust H_∞ control of systems with uncertainty. Automatica **41**, 999–1007 (2005)
12. Xiong, J., Lam, J.: Stabilization of networked control systems with a logic ZOH. IEEE Trans. Autom. Control **54**, 358–363 (2009)
13. Fridman, E., Seuret, A., Richard, J.P.: Robust sampled-data stabilization of linear systems: an input delay approach. Automatica **40**, 1441–1446 (2004)
14. Naghshtabrizi, P., Hespanha, J.P., Teel, A.R.: Exponential stability of impulsive systems with application to uncertain sampled-data systems. Syst. Control Lett. **57**, 378–385 (2008)
15. Bamieh, B., Pearson, J.B., Francis, B.A.: A lifting technique for linear periodic systems with applications to sampled-data control. Syst. Control Lett. **17**, 79–88 (1991)
16. Fu, Z., Sun, X., Ji, S., Xie, G.: Towards efficient content-aware search over encrypted outsourced data in cloud. In: Proceedings of the 35th Annual IEEE International Conference on Computer Communications (IEEE INFOCOM), San Francisco, CA (2016). doi:10.1109/INFOCOM.2016.7524606
17. Chen, Y., Hao, C., Wu, W., Wu, E.: Robust dense reconstruction by range merging based on confidence estimation. Sci. China Inf. Sci. **59**, 1–11 (2016)
18. Kong, Y., Zhang, M., Ye, D.: A belief propagation-based method for task allocation in open and dynamic cloud environments. Knowl.-Based Syst. **115**, 123–132 (2016)
19. He, Y., Wu, M., Liu, G.P., She, J.H.: Output feedback stabilization for a discrete-time systems with a time-varying delay. IEEE Trans. Autom. Control **53**, 2372–2377 (2008)
20. Zhang, X., Han, Q.L.: Output feedback stabilization of networked control systems with a logic zero-order-hold. Inf. Sci. **381**, 78–91 (2017)

Adaptive Firefly Algorithm with a Modified Attractiveness Strategy

Wenjun Wang[1], Hui Wang[2,3](✉), Jia Zhao[2,3], and Li Lv[2,3]

[1] School of Business Administration, Nanchang Institute of Technology, Nanchang 330099, China

[2] Jiangxi Province Key Laboratory of Water Information Cooperative Sensing and Intelligent Processing, Nanchang Institute of Technology, Nanchang 330099, China

huiwang@whu.edu.cn

[3] School of Information Engineering, Nanchang Institute of Technology, Nanchang 330099, China

Abstract. The performance of firefly algorithm (FA) is seriously affected by its parameters. Recently, we proposed a new FA with adaptive control parameters (ApFA), in which the step factor is dynamically updated and the attractiveness oscillates in a fixed interval. In this paper, we present a modified version of ApFA, namely MApFA, which introduces a new strategy to change the attractiveness. Simulation results on several benchmark functions show that MApFA can achieve more accurate solution than ApFA.

Keywords: Firefly algorithm (FA) · Adaptive parameter · Dynamic attractiveness · Optimization

1 Introduction

In the past decades, several new optimization techniques have been proposed by the inspiration of swarm intelligence, such as artificial bee colony (ABC) [1–4], bat algorithm (BA) [5–7], firefly algorithm (FA) [8–10], cuckoo search (CS) [11, 12], fruit fly optimization (FFO) [13], and artificial plant optimization algorithm [14, 15]. FA has become a popular tool in swarm intelligence optimization community [8]. It mimics the mating flashing behaviour of fireflies in summer night sky. The concept of FA is simple, yet powerful. Recently, the study of FA attracted a lot of attention, and it was widely used to solve various optimization problems.

Although FA has shown good search capacities, it has some drawbacks. For instance, the performance of FA is seriously affected by its parameters, step factor α and light absorption coefficient γ. To overcome this issue, some excellent methods were proposed. In [16], a memetic FA (MFA) was designed to handle combination optimization problems, in which α is adaptively updated. The attractiveness β is constrained in a short range. Results show that MFA performs better than hybrid evolutionary algorithm (HEA) and Tabucol on graph 3-coloring problems. Some recent studies proved that MFA also achieved good results on continuous optimization problems [17]. In [9], MFA was combined with random attraction and Cauchy

X. Sun et al. (Eds.): ICCCS 2017, Part II, LNCS 10603, pp. 717–726, 2017.
https://doi.org/10.1007/978-3-319-68542-7_62

mutation. Computational results show that the new MFA (namely RaFA) significantly improve the performance of MFA. Compared to MFA and other improved FA variants, RaFA has lower computational time complexity. In [10], a neighbourhood attraction model was introduced to MFA. Similar to the random attraction model, the neighborhood attraction achieves a balance to avoid fast convergence. In [18], different chaotic maps were employed to update α and γ. Wang et al. [19] analyzed the convergence behavior of FA and pointed out α should tend to 0 when FA converges to a point. Then, an adaptive FA (ApFA) was designed. In ApFA, the parameter α is gradually decreased with the growth of iterations. Moreover, the weight of the attractiveness β_0 is oscillated between 0 and 1. This is helpful to avoid the unchanged attractiveness between fireflies.

In this paper, a modified ApFA (called MApFA) is proposed, in which a new strategy is employed to dynamically adjust the attractiveness. Six famous benchmark functions are used for evaluating the performance of MApFA. Results show the performance of MApFA is superior to ApFA.

2 Firefly Algorithm

Like other population based optimization algorithms, FA also starts with an initial population having N solutions ($X_i, i = 1, 2, \ldots, N$), where N is the population size. Through multiple iterations, the population is continually updated and better solutions are found. In general, the initial population can be generated as follows.

$$x_{ij}(t) = lb + (ub - lb) \cdot rand(0, 1), \tag{1}$$

where $t = 0, j = 1, 2, \ldots, D$, D is the dimensional size, t is the index of generation, lb and ub are lower and upper boundaries, respectively, and $rand(0, 1)$ represents a random value in the interval [0, 1].

The updating of solutions is based on the attraction movement of fireflies. For any two fireflies X_i and X_j, their attractiveness β is computed by [8]

$$\beta(r_{ij}) = \beta_0 \cdot e^{-\gamma r_{ij}^2}, \tag{2}$$

where β_0 is the attractiveness at $r = 0$, γ is called light absorption coefficient, and r_{ij} is the distance between X_i and X_j. The distance r_{ij} is calculated as follows [8].

$$r_{ij} = \|X_i - X_j\| = \sqrt{\sum_{d=1}^{D} (x_{id} - x_{jd})^2}, \tag{3}$$

If X_j is better than X_i, X_i will move to X_j by the attraction. In the standard FA, the attraction movement is formulated as follows [8].

$$x_{id}(t+1) = x_{id}(t) + \beta(r_{ij}) \cdot \left(x_{jd}(t) - x_{id}(t)\right) + \alpha\left(rand - \frac{1}{2}\right), \tag{4}$$

where x_{id} and x_{jd} are the dth dimensions of X_i and X_j, respectively, $\alpha \in [0, 1]$ is called step factor, and *rand* is randomly generated in the interval [0, 1].

Figure 1 shows the framework of the standard FA, where *FEs* means the number of function evaluations, and *MaxFEs* indicates the maximum value of *FEs*. The standard FA consists of two procedures. The first one is population initialization (Steps 2–3), and the second one is the attraction movement (Steps 5–13). For each firefly, it is compared with other all fireflies. If the compared fireflies are better than the current one, the current firefly will move toward the compared ones.

Algorithm 1: The Standard FA

```
1:  Begin
2:      Initialize the population according to Eq. (1);
3:      FEs=N;
4:      while FEs <= MaxFEs do
5:          for i=1 to N do
6:              for j=1 to i do
7:                  if f(Xj)<f(Xi) then
8:                      Move Xi towards Xj according to Eq. (4);
9:                      Evaluate the new solution Xi;
10:                     FEs++:
11:                 end if
12:             end for
13:         end for
14:     end while
15: End
```

Fig. 1. The framework of the standard FA.

3 Proposed Approach

In [19], we analyzed the convergence characteristics of FA and concluded that the parameter α must satisfy $\lim_{t\to\infty} \alpha = 0$. Based on this condition, we proposed an adaptive FA (called ApFA), in which the parameter α is defined by

$$\alpha(t+1) = \left(1 - \frac{t}{T_{\max}}\right) \cdot \alpha(t), \tag{5}$$

where t is the generation number, and T_{max} is the maximum number generations. By the suggestions of [19], the initial $\alpha(0)$ is set to 0.5. It can be seen that α is gradually decreased with increasing of generations.

When the population tend to be convergent, the distance between two fireflies become zero.

$$\lim_{t \to \infty} r_{ij} = 0. \tag{6}$$

According to Eq. (2), we can deduce

$$\lim_{t \to \infty} \beta(r_{ij}) = \lim_{t \to \infty} \beta_0 \cdot e^0 = \beta_0. \tag{7}$$

From Eq. (7), the attractiveness β between two fireflies will become a constant value. In some literature, β_0 is set to 1.0. So, the attractiveness β will increase to 1.0 and keep unchangeable. To prevent this case, a simple method was used to disturb β_0 as follows [19].

$$\beta_0(t+1) = \begin{cases} rand_1, & \text{if } rand_2 < 0.5 \\ \beta_0(t), & \text{Otherwise} \end{cases}. \tag{8}$$

where $rand_1$ and $rand_2$ are two independent random values in the interval [0,1]. It is obvious that the attractiveness β will be oscillated between 0 and 1.0. The initial $\beta_0(0)$ is set to 1.0.

Although Eq. (8) can prevent the attractiveness β from being a constant value, the random oscillation may not be effective. In this paper, we propose a modified attractiveness strategy. Like Eq. (8), the attractiveness β is also dynamically changed with the growth of generations.

$$\beta^*(r_{ij}) = \left(1 - \frac{t}{T_{\max}}\right) \cdot \beta_0 \cdot e^{-\gamma r_{ij}^2}, \tag{9}$$

where t is the number of generations, T_{max} is the maximum number generations. To clearly illustrate the characteristic of the new strategy, Fig. 2 shows the changes of the attractiveness β between two fireflies based on Eq. (9). As seen, the attractiveness β quickly increases. At t = 30, the attractiveness β is up to the maximum value. Then, the attractiveness β gradually decreases with increasing generations.

As suggested in [8], the step factor α is multiplied by the length of the search range. Then, the new attraction movement equation is used as follows.

$$x_{id}(t+1) = x_{id}(t) + \beta^*(r_{ij}) \cdot \left(x_{jd}(t) - x_{id}(t)\right) + \alpha(t) \cdot s_d \cdot \left(rand - \frac{1}{2}\right), \tag{10}$$

where s_d is the length of the search range for the dth dimension, and $\beta^*(r_{ij})$ is defined by Eq. (9).

Figure 3 presents the framework of the proposed MapFA. It can be seen that Step 5 aims to update the parameter α. The new attractiveness β is calculated in Step 9. For Step 10, the new movement operation is executed. Compared to the standard FA (described in Fig. 1), no extra loop calculation operations are added in MapFA. Thus, both MApFA and FA have the same computational time complexity.

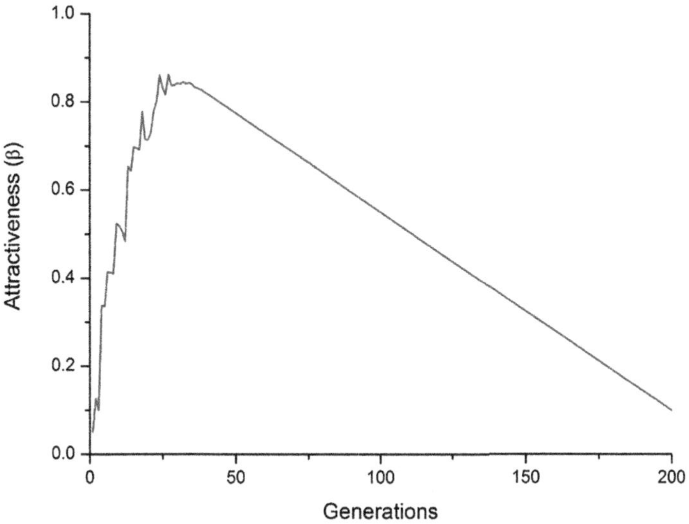

Fig. 2. The changes of the attractiveness β based on the new model.

Algorithm 2: Proposed MApFA

```
Begin
    Randomly initialize the population according to Eq. (1);
    FEs=N;
    while FEs <= MaxFEs do
        Update the parameter α according to Eq. (5);
        for i=1 to N do
            for j=1 to i do
                if f(X_j)<f(X_i) then
                    Calculate the attractiveness according to Eq. (9);
                    Move X_i towards X_j according to Eq. (10);
                    Evaluate the new solution X_i;
                    FEs++:
                end if
            end for
        end for
    end while
End
```

Fig. 3. The framework of the MApFA.

4 Experimental Study

4.1 Experiment Setup

In this paper, there are six benchmark functions used in the experiment to evaluate the performance of MApFA. These test functions were considered in the literature [20–24]. All these functions are minimization problems, and their brief descriptions are displayed in Table 1. The details of these functions can be referred to [20].

Table 1. Six test functions.

Functions	Search range	Global minimum
Sphere (f_1)	$[-100, 100]$	0
Schwefel 2.22 (f_2)	$[-10, 10]$	0
Schwefel 1.2 (f_3)	$[-100, 100]$	0
Rastrigin (f_4)	$[-5.12, 5.12]$	0
Ackley (f_5)	$[-32, 32]$	0
Griewank (f_6)	$[-600, 600]$	0

In the experiment, we mainly investigate whether the proposed strategy can improve the performance of ApFA. Thus, we only compare the performance of MApFA with ApFA. For ApFA and MApFA, the same settings are used for common parameters. Detailed parameter settings are listed in Table 2. For each test function, both ApFA and MApFA are independently run 30 times.

Table 2. Parameter settings for ApFA and MApFA.

Parameters	ApFA	MApFA
MaxFEs	2.0E + 05	2.0E + 05
N	30	30
α	N/A	N/A
$\alpha(0)$	0.5	0.5
β_0	N/A	1.0
$\beta_0(0)$	1.0	N/A
γ	$1/\Gamma^2$	$1/\Gamma^2$

4.2 Results

Table 3 gives the mean function values of ApFA and MApFA, where "Mean" is the mean function value, and "Std" indicates the standard deviation. The best results between ApFA and MApFA are shown in bold. From the results, it is obvious that MApFA achieve more accurate solutions than ApFA on all six test functions. It demonstrates that the proposed dynamic attractiveness strategy is effective and can improve the performance of FA.

Table 3. Computational results achieved by ApFA and MApFA.

Functions	ApFA		MApFA	
	Mean	Std	Mean	Std
f_1	3.41E − 16	2.76E − 16	**2.41E − 21**	**3.83E − 21**
f_2	2.19E − 05	4.23E − 05	**3.32E − 07**	**5.26E − 07**
f_3	4.30E + 01	1.67E + 01	**2.86E + 01**	**1.29E + 01**
f_4	3.49E + 01	1.36E + 01	**2.19E + 01**	**7.34E + 00**
f_5	7.32E − 09	6.13E − 09	**2.87E − 11**	**1.12E − 11**
f_6	1.35E − 05	3.91E − 05	**2.14E − 07**	**4.57E − 07**

To compare the convergence speed of ApFA and MApFA, Figs. 4, 5, 6 and 7 present their convergence graphs on 4 test functions. As shown, MApFA is faster than ApFA. It can be found that ApFA and MApFA have the same convergence behaviour at the beginning of the search. For Fig. 4, both ApFA and MApFA almost show the same convergence curves when *FEs* is less than 8.0E + 04. At the middle and last stages of the search, MApFA can find more accurate solutions and converge faster than ApFA. For Fig. 5, the convergence process of MApFA is similar to ApFA before *FEs* = 7.0E + 04. At the middle and last stages, MApFA is faster than ApFA. For Figs. 6 and 7, we can get similar conclusions. The main reason is that the decreasing attractiveness in MApFA can improve the local search and find more accurate solutions.

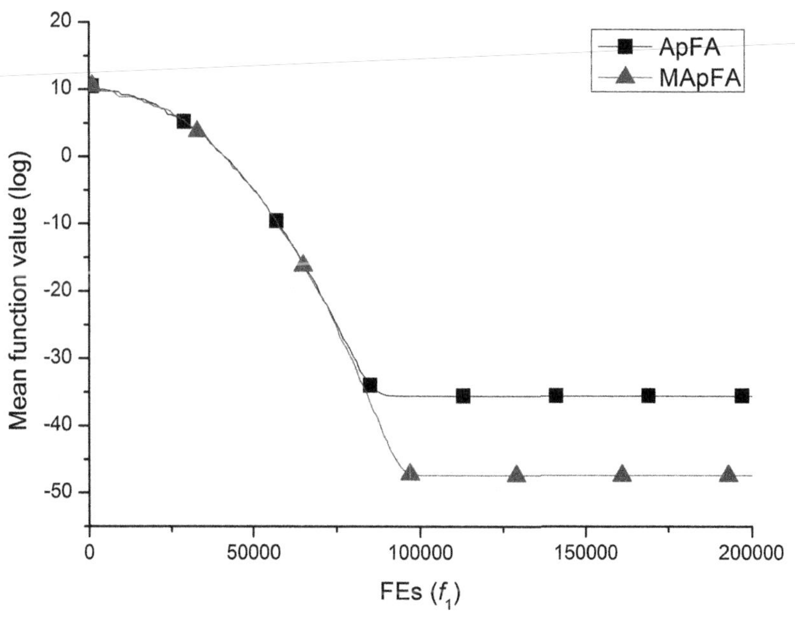

Fig. 4. The convergences graphs of ApFA and MApFA on function f_1.

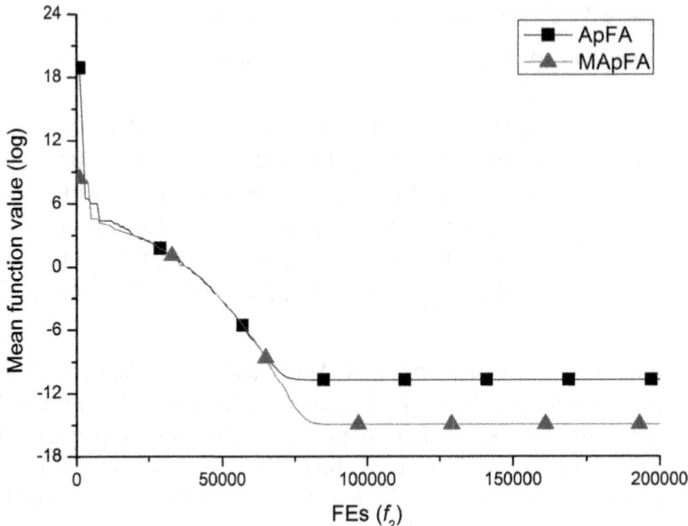

Fig. 5. The convergences graphs of ApFA and MApFA on function f_2.

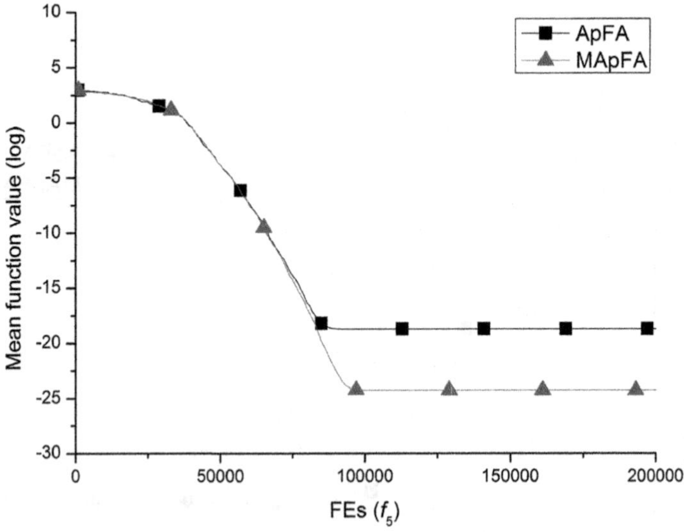

Fig. 6. The convergences graphs of ApFA and MApFA on function f_5.

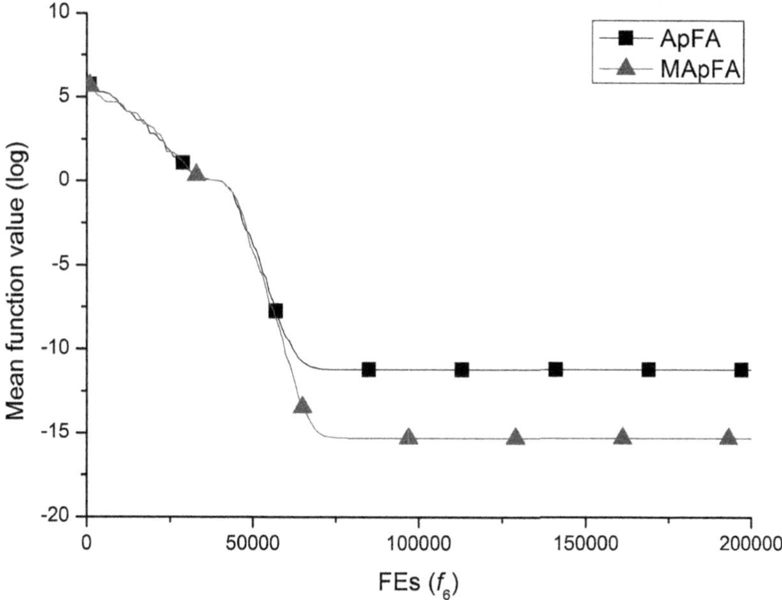

Fig. 7. The convergences graphs of ApFA and MApFA on function f_6.

5 Conclusions

In this paper, a modified ApFA (called MApFA) is proposed, in which a new strategy is employed to dynamically adjust the attractiveness. Six famous benchmark functions are used in the experiments to evaluate the performance of MApFA. Results show MApFA achieves more accurate solutions and faster convergence rate than ApFA. The improvement of MApFA is due to the decreasing attractiveness at the middle and last stages of the search. This is beneficial for enhancing local search and searching more accurate solutions.

Acknowledgements. This work is supported by the Science and Technology Plan Project of Jiangxi Provincial Education Department (No. GJJ161115), the National Natural Science Foundation of China (No. 61663028), the Natural Science Foundation of Jiangxi Province (No. 20171BAB202035), and the Open Research Fund of Jiangxi Province Key Laboratory of Water Information Cooperative Sensing and Intelligent Processing (No. 2016WICSIP015).

References

1. Sun, H., Wang, K., Zhao, J., Yu, X.: Artificial bee colony algorithm with improved special centre. Int. J. Comput. Sci. Math. **7**(6), 548–553 (2016)
2. Yun, G.: A new multi-population-based artificial bee colony for numerical optimization. Int. J. Comput. Sci. Math. **7**(6), 509–515 (2016)

3. Lv, L., Wu, L.Y., Zhao, J., Wang, H., Wu, R.X., Fan, T.H., Hu, M., Xie, Z.F.: Improved multi-strategy artificial bee colony algorithm. Int. J. Comput. Sci. Math. **7**(5), 467–475 (2016)
4. Lu, Y., Li, R.X., Li, S.M.: Artificial bee colony with bidirectional search. Int. J. Comput. Sci. Math. **7**(6), 586–593 (2016)
5. Cai, X., Gao, X.Z., Xue, Y.: Improved bat algorithm with optimal forage strategy and random disturbance strategy. Int. J. Bio-Inspired Comput. **8**(4), 205–214 (2016)
6. Xue, F., Cai, Y., Cao, Y., Cui, Z., Li, F.: Optimal parameter settings for bat algorithm. Int. J. Bio-Inspired Comput. **7**(2), 125–128 (2015)
7. Cai, X., Wang, L., Kang, Q., Wu, Q.: Bat algorithm with Gaussian walk. Int. J. Bio-Inspired Comput. **6**(3), 166–174 (2014)
8. Yang, X.S.: Nature-Inspired Metaheuristic Algorithms. Luniver Press, Beckington (2008)
9. Wang, H., Wang, W.J., Sun, H., Rahnamayan, S.: Firefly algorithm with random attraction. Int. J. Bio-Inspired Comput. **8**(1), 33–41 (2016)
10. Wang, H., Wang, W.J., Zhou, X.Y., Sun, H., Zhao, J., Yu, X., Cui, Z.: Firefly algorithm with neighborhood attraction. Inf. Sci. **382–383**, 374–387 (2017)
11. Cui, Z., Sun, B., Wang, G., Xue, Y.: A novel oriented cuckoo search algorithm to improve DV-Hop performance for cyber-physical systems. J. Parallel Distrib. Comput. **103**, 42–52 (2017)
12. Wang, G.G., Gandomi, A.H., Yang, X.S., Alavi, A.H.: A new hybrid method based on krill herd and cuckoo search for global optimization tasks. Int. J. Bio-Inspired Comput. **8**(5), 286–299 (2016)
13. Zhang, Y.W., Wu, J.T., Guo, X., Li, G.N.: Optimising web service composition based on differential fruit fly optimisation algorithm. Int. J. Comput. Sci. Math. **7**(1), 87–101 (2016)
14. Cui, Z., Fan, S., Zeng, J., Shi, Z.Z.: APOA with parabola model for directing orbits of chaotic systems. Int. J. Bio-Inspired Comput. **5**(1), 67–72 (2013)
15. Cui, Z., Fan, S., Zeng, J., Shi, Z.Z.: Artificial plant optimisation algorithm with three-period photosynthesis. Int. J. Bio-Inspired Comput. **5**(2), 133–139 (2013)
16. Fister Jr., I., Yang, X.S., Fister, I., Brest, J., Memetic firefly algorithm for combinatorial optimization (2012). arXiv preprint arXiv:1204.5165
17. Wang, H., Cui, Z.H., Sun, H., Rahnamayan, S., Yang, X.S.: Randomly attracted firefly algorithm with neighborhood search and dynamic parameter adjustment mechanism. Soft Comput. **21**(18), 5325–5339 (2017). doi:10.1007/s00500-016-2116-z
18. Gandomi, A.H., Yang, X.S., Talatahari, S., Alavi, A.H.: Firefly algorithm with chaos. Commun. Nonlinear Sci. Numer. Simul. **18**(1), 89–98 (2013)
19. Wang, H., Zhou, X.Y., Sun, H., Yu, X., Zhao, J., Zhang, H., Cui, L.Z.: Firefly algorithm with adaptive control parameters. Soft Comput. **21**(17), 5091–5102 (2017). doi:10.1007/s00500-016-2104-3
20. Wang, H., Wu, Z.J., Rahnamayan, S., Liu, Y., Ventresca, M.: Enhancing particle swarm optimization using generalized opposition-based learning. Inf. Sci. **181**(20), 4699–4714 (2011)
21. Wang, H., Rahnamayan, S., Sun, H., Omran, M.G.H.: Gaussian bare-bones differential evolution. IEEE Trans. Cybern. **43**(2), 634–647 (2013)
22. Guo, Z.L., Wang, S.W., Yue, X.Z., Yin, B.: Enhanced social emotional optimisation algorithm with elite multi-parent crossover. Int. J. Comput. Sci. Math. **7**(6), 568–574 (2016)
23. Yu, G.: An improved firefly algorithm based on probabilistic attraction. Int. J. Comput. Sci. Math. **7**(6), 530–536 (2016)
24. Xue, Y., Jiang, J.M., Zhao, B.P., Ma, T.H.: A self-adaptive artificial bee colony algorithm based on global best for global optimization. Soft Comput. (2017, in press). doi:10.1007/s00500-017-2547-1

Newton Method for Interval Predictor Model with Sphere Parameter Set

Xuan Xiao[1,2(✉)], Peng Wang[1], and Jian-Hong Wang[1]

[1] Computer Department, Jing-De-Zhen Ceramic Institute, Jing-De-Zhen 333403, China
jdzxiaoxuan@163.com, 1182643454@qq.com, 936258635@qq.com

[2] School of Computer and Software, Nanjing University of Information Science and Technology, Nanjing 210044, China

Abstract. In this paper, we study the construction of interval prediction model. After introducing the family of models and some basic information, we present the computational results for the construction of interval predictor models, using linear regression structures which regression parameters are included in a sphere parameter set. Given a size measure to scale the average amplitude of the predictor interval, one optimal model that minimizes a size measure is efficiently computed by solving a linear programming problem, firstly we apply the active set approach to solve the linear programming problem and propose one Newton iterative form of the optimization variables. Based on these optimization variables, the predictor interval of the considered model with sphere parameter set can be directly constructed. Secondly as for a fixed non-negative number from the size measure, we propose a better choice by using the Karush-Kuhn-Tucker optimality conditions.

Keywords: Interval predictor model · Newton method · Sphere · Optimization

1 Introduction

In the classical system identification theory, one parametric model structure corresponding to the identified system is selected firstly, then the parameters in the parametric model structure are estimated using the measured input-output data. In the system identification process, many identification methods are proposed to identify these unknown parameters, for example the classical least squares method, instrumental variable method, maximum likelihood estimation method, prediction error method, Bayesian method. one common property in these identification methods is that the prior information about noise is known. Based on some probabilistic assumptions on noise, the unknown parameters are identified as the specific numerical values. But the probabilistic assumptions on noise are not realistic and it means these probabilistic assumptions are not realized in reality. So in order to relax the probabilistic assumptions on noise, we always assume that the noises are unknown but bounded. This unknown but bounded assumption is weaker than the formal probabilistic assumption. Because it needs not any prior distribution of noise. The common used method used to

X. Sun et al. (Eds.): ICCCS 2017, Part II, LNCS 10603, pp. 727–737, 2017.
https://doi.org/10.1007/978-3-319-68542-7_63

solve the unknown but bounded case is called set membership identification. In set membership identification, the obtained result is not a numerical value, but a guaranteed interval with respect to each parameter. This guaranteed interval means that each parameter can be included in the interval with one guaranteed accuracy which is assessed by some probability inequalities.

From the idea of set membership identification, after the unknown parameters are identified, the identified parametric model may be applied to determine one predicted value for the output of the system, together with probabilistic intervals of confidence around the prediction [1]. As we expect the interval of confidence can accurately describe the actual probability that the future prediction will fall into the obtained interval. The future predictor is important in the next controller design and state estimation, so in reference [2], a novel approach for the construction of prediction models is proposed. The advantage of this novel approach is that instead of using a standard identification way where one constructs a parametric model by minimizing an identification cost, and uses the identified model to design the prediction interval; this novel approach directly considers interval models and applies measured data to ascertain the reliability of such interval predictor model [3]. It means that we directly obtain the interval predictor model from measured data and avoid the identification process of the parametric model structure. The interval predictor model is combined with a multilevel pattern mining architecture to support automatic network management. Further interval predictor model can be used to eliminate the influence of modification traces in secret communication. In future classical optimization algorithm will be replaced by efficient cloud search services, but here we still use classical optimization to devise the interval predictor model.

In this paper, we follow a deep research for the construction of interval prediction model. After introducing the family of models under study and some basic information about the interval prediction model, we present the computational results for the construction of interval predictor models, using linear regression structures which regression parameters are included in a sphere. Given a size measure to scale the average amplitude of the predictor interval, one optimal model that minimizes a size measure is efficiently computed by solving a linear programming problem, our contributions of this paper are that firstly we apply the active set approach to solve the linear programming problem and propose one Newton iterative form of the optimization variables. Based on these optimization variables, the predictor interval of the considered model with sphere parameter set can be directly constructed. Secondly as for a fixed non-negative number coming from the size measure, we propose a good choice by using the Karush-Kuhn-Tucker (KKT) optimality conditions.

2 Interval Predictor Model

Internal predictor model returns an interval as output. The following concepts can be seen in references [2, 4]. Define $\Phi \subseteq R^n$ and $Y \subseteq R$ be given sets, and they are denoted as the instance set and outcome set. The interval predictor model is a rule that assigns to each instance vector $\varphi \in \Phi$ a corresponding output interval. An interval predictor model is a set valued map.

$$I : \varphi \rightarrow I(\varphi) \subseteq Y \tag{1}$$

where φ is a regression vector, $I(\varphi)$ is the prediction interval, also $I(\varphi)$ is called an informative interval.

Consider the parametric model family M, the output of a system is expressed as $y = M(\varphi, q)$, for some parameters $q \in Q \subseteq R^{n_q}$. Through selecting a feasible set Q, an interval predictor model is obtained as the following relation.

$$M = \{y = M(\varphi, q), q \in Q \subseteq R^{n_q}\} \tag{2}$$

In a dynamic setting, at each time instant the instance vector φ may contain past values of input and output measurements, then behaving as a linear regression function. From standard auto-regressive structures, a parametric interval predictor model is derived.

$$y(k) = \varphi^T(k)\theta(k) + e(k), \; |e(k)| \leq \gamma \tag{3}$$

where $y(k)$ and $\varphi(k)$ denote the output measurement and regression vector at time instant k, $\theta(k) \in R^n$ is the time varying unknown parameter, $e(k)$ is the external noise. But here any prior probability information of noise $e(k)$ is unknown. We only assume that noise $e(k)$ is unknown but bounded and γ is its magnitude bound.

Assume time varying unknown parameter $\theta(k) \in R^n$ satisfies.

$$\theta(k) \in \Delta \subseteq R^n \tag{4}$$

where Δ is one assigned bounded set. Here in this paper we assume Δ is a sphere with center θ and radius r.

$$\Delta = \{\theta + \delta : \theta, \delta \in R^n, \|\delta\| \leq r\} \tag{5}$$

By combining Eqs. (2), (3) and (5), the parameters indicating the feasible set Q are the center θ and radius r of sphere Δ, and the magnitude bound γ on noise $e(k)$.

By substituting (5) into (3), we obtain the output of the system.

$$y(k) = \varphi^T(k)(\theta + \delta) + e(k) = \varphi^T(k)\theta + \varphi^T(k)\delta + e(k) \tag{6}$$

By using the bounded radius r and magnitude bound γ, regression vector $\varphi(k)$, the output of the parametric model is one interval.

$$I(\varphi(k)) = \left[\varphi^T(k)\theta - (r\|\varphi(k)\| + \gamma), \;\; \varphi^T(k)\theta + (r\|\varphi(k)\| + \gamma)\right] \tag{7}$$

Equation (7) is one interval model, it contains the output of the parametric model $y(k)$ with some guaranteed probability. When the observations are collected in the data sequence $D_N = \{\varphi(k), y(k)\}_{k=1}^{N}$, whatever open or closed loop, the following relation holds.

$$y(k) \in I(\varphi(k)),\ for\ k = 1, 2 \cdots N \tag{8}$$

where Eq. (8) means that the interval $I(\varphi(k))$ is consistent with a given data sequence D_N.

By observing the interval (7) again, we see that this interval is dependent on three parameters-(θ, r, γ). So if these three parameters are identified, the interval can be constructed based on Eq. (7). In order to obtain three parameters, one linear programming problem is constructed [5].

Introducing a size measure $\mu = \gamma + ar$, where a is a fixed non-negative number, the optimal model that minimize μ can be derived by solving a linear programming problem.

Theorem 1: Given an observed data sequence $D_N = \{\varphi(k), y(k)\}_{k=1}^{N}$, a model order n, and a size objective $\mu = \gamma + ar$, three parameters used to construct the optimal interval predictor model are computed by solving the following linear programming problem with respect to three variables.

$$\begin{cases} \min\limits_{\theta,\gamma,r} \quad \gamma + ar \\ subject\ to \\ \varphi^T(k)\theta - r\|\varphi(k)\| - \gamma \leq y(k) \\ -\varphi^T(k)\theta - r\|\varphi(k)\| - \gamma \leq -y(k),\ k = 1, 2 \cdots N \\ \theta \in R^n, \gamma, r \end{cases} \tag{9}$$

According to linear programming problem (9), there are no any references about how to solve it, so here the main contributions of the next two sections are about how to solve this linear programming problem and how to choose an appropriate fixed non-negative number.

3 One Choice of a Fixed Non-negative Number

In the linear programming problem (9), as the optimization variables r and γ denote the radius of sphere Δ and magnitude bound on noise $e(k)$, so these two optimization variables must satisfy that.

$$r \geq 0\ and\ \gamma \geq 0 \tag{10}$$

By combining linear programming problem (9) and inequality constraints (10), we rewrite the new linear programming problem as that.

$$\begin{cases} \min\limits_{\theta,\gamma,r} \quad \gamma + ar \\ subject\ to \\ \varphi^T(k)\theta - r\|\varphi(k)\| - \gamma \leq y(k) \\ -\varphi^T(k)\theta - r\|\varphi(k)\| - \gamma \leq -y(k),\ k = 1, 2 \cdots N \\ r \geq 0\ and\ \gamma \geq 0 \end{cases} \tag{11}$$

Define the Lagrangian function L corresponding to the above linear programming problem by

$$L(\theta,\gamma,r,\lambda_1,\lambda_2,\mu_k^+,\mu_k^-)=\gamma+ar-\lambda_1\gamma-\lambda_2 r-\sum_{k=1}^{N}\mu_k^+\left(y(k)-\varphi^T(k)\theta+r\|\varphi(k)\|+\gamma\right)$$
$$-\sum_{k=1}^{N}\mu_k^-\left(-y(k)+\varphi^T(k)\theta+r\|\varphi(k)\|+\gamma\right) \quad (12)$$

We refer to $\lambda_1,\lambda_2,\{\mu_k^+,\mu_k^-\}_{k=1}^N$ as the Lagrangian multipliers. By applying the optimality KKT sufficient and necessary condition on Lagrangian function, then some equality relations for the optimal solution hold.

$$\frac{\partial L}{\partial\theta}=\sum_{k=1}^{N}(\mu_k^+-\mu_k^-)\varphi(k)=0 \quad (13)$$

$$\frac{\partial L}{\partial\gamma}=1-\lambda_1-\sum_{k=1}^{N}(\mu_k^++\mu_k^-)=0 \quad (14)$$

$$\frac{\partial L}{\partial r}=a-\lambda_2-\sum_{k=1}^{N}(\mu_k^++\mu_k^-)\|\varphi(k)\|=0 \quad (15)$$

$$\lambda_1\gamma=0,\quad \lambda_2 r=0 \quad (16)$$

$$\mu_k^+\left(y(k)-\varphi^T(k)\theta+r\|\varphi(k)\|+\gamma\right)=0 \quad (17)$$

$$\mu_k^-\left(-y(k)+\varphi^T(k)\theta+r\|\varphi(k)\|+\gamma\right)=0 \quad (18)$$

Also as optimization variables r and γ denote the radius of sphere Δ and magnitude bound on noise $e(k)$ respectively, if $\gamma=0$, then that $|e(k)|=0$ means no noise exists in the standard auto-regressive structure (3). If $r=0$, then sphere Δ reduces to its center θ, so here for interval predictor model, we want to satisfy that.

$$r>0 \textit{ and } \gamma>0 \quad (19)$$

When r and γ are all equal to zero, then $I(\varphi(k))$ is not an interval, but a fixed output value.

$$I(\varphi(k))=\varphi^T(k)\theta$$

By comparing (16) and (19), we see that Eq. (16) holds unless Lagrangian multipliers $\{\lambda_1,\lambda_2\}$ must satisfy by.

$$\lambda_1 = \lambda_2 = 0 \tag{20}$$

Further in Eq. (13), assume regression vectors $\varphi(1), \varphi(2) \cdots \varphi(N)$ at different instants are linearly independent. So in order to let Eq. (13) hold, the $\{\mu_k^+, \mu_k^-\}_{k=1}^N$ need to satisfy by.

$$\mu_k^+ = \mu_k^- = \mu_k,\ k = 1, 2 \cdots N \tag{21}$$

By substituting (20) and (21) into (14) and (15), we obtain the following simplified forms.

$$\begin{cases} \sum\limits_{k=1}^{N} \mu_k = \frac{1}{2} \\ \sum\limits_{k=1}^{N} \mu_k \|\varphi(k)\| = \frac{a}{2} \end{cases} \tag{22}$$

From the idea of Eq. (22), one choice of this fixed non-negative number a is given here. As $\sum\limits_{k=1}^{N} \mu_k = \frac{1}{2}$ holds, we can set $\mu_k = \frac{1}{2N}$. Then after substituting $\mu_k = \frac{1}{2N}$ into equality $\sum\limits_{k=1}^{N} \mu_k \|\varphi(k)\| = \frac{a}{2}$, we have.

$$\frac{1}{2N}[\|\varphi(1)\| + \|\varphi(2)\| + \cdots \|\varphi(N)\|] = \frac{a}{2} \tag{23}$$

It means that

$$a = \frac{1}{N}[\|\varphi(1)\| + \|\varphi(2)\| + \cdots \|\varphi(N)\|] \tag{24}$$

Equation (24) is one of the choices of that fixed non-negative number a. As regression vectors $\{\varphi(k)\}_{t=1}^N$ and the number of data are given, so the form (24) of a can be computed easily.

4 Newton Method for Interval Predictor Model

Because interval predictor model (7) is dependent of the linear programming problem (11) with respect to three kinds of optimization variables $\{\theta, \gamma, r\}$, so the important step in constructing interval predictor model (7) is to solve that linear programming problem (11). First we rewrite the linear programming problem (11) as its standard form.

Define a new vector $x \in R^{n+2}$ as $x = \{\theta, \gamma, r\}$. Based on the new optimization vector $x \in R^{n+2}$, the cost function in (11) can be rewritten as.

$$\gamma + ar = \begin{pmatrix} 0 & 1 & a \end{pmatrix} \begin{pmatrix} \theta \\ \gamma \\ r \end{pmatrix} = C^T x \qquad C = \begin{pmatrix} 0 & 1 & a \end{pmatrix} \tag{25}$$

Also each inequality can be rewritten as.

$$\begin{cases} \varphi^T(k)\theta - r\|\varphi(k)\| - \gamma \le y(k) \Leftrightarrow \begin{pmatrix} \varphi^T(k) & -1 & -\|\varphi(k)\| \end{pmatrix} \begin{pmatrix} \theta \\ \gamma \\ r \end{pmatrix} \le y(k) \\ -\varphi^T(k)\theta - r\|\varphi(k)\| - \gamma \le -y(k) \Leftrightarrow \begin{pmatrix} -\varphi^T(k) & -1 & -\|\varphi(k)\| \end{pmatrix} \begin{pmatrix} \theta \\ \gamma \\ r \end{pmatrix} \le -y(k) \\ r \ge 0 \Leftrightarrow \begin{pmatrix} 0 & 0 & -1 \end{pmatrix} \begin{pmatrix} \theta \\ \gamma \\ r \end{pmatrix} \le 0, \quad \gamma \ge 0 \Leftrightarrow \begin{pmatrix} 0 & -1 & 0 \end{pmatrix} \begin{pmatrix} \theta \\ \gamma \\ r \end{pmatrix} \le 0 \end{cases} \tag{26}$$

Define some matrices to merge all inequities in Eq. (26).

$$A = \begin{bmatrix} 0 & -1 & 0 \\ 0 & 0 & -1 \\ \varphi^T(1) & -1 & -\|\varphi(1)\| \\ \vdots & \vdots & \vdots \\ \varphi^T(N) & -1 & -\|\varphi(N)\| \\ -\varphi^T(1) & -1 & -\|\varphi(1)\| \\ \vdots & \vdots & \vdots \\ -\varphi^T(N) & -1 & -\|\varphi(N)\| \end{bmatrix}, \quad B = \begin{bmatrix} 0 \\ 0 \\ y(1) \\ \vdots \\ y(N) \\ -y(1) \\ \vdots \\ -y(N) \end{bmatrix} \tag{27}$$

where $A \in R^{(2N+2)\times 3}, B \in R^{(2N+2)\times 1}$. Given regression vector $\{\varphi(k)\}_{k=1}^N$ and output measured data $\{y(k)\}_{k=1}^N$, the above two matrices A, B are known.

Applying two matrices A, B, all inequities in Eq. (26) are obtained in a simplified form.

$$Ax \le B \tag{28}$$

Then based on (26) and (29), the formal linear programming problem (11) can be formulated into a standard linear programming form.

$$\begin{cases} \min\limits_x \quad C^T x \\ subject\ to\ Ax \le B \end{cases} \tag{29}$$

Now we propose a Newton method to solve the above standard linear programming problem. Our Newton method introduces the active set approach into classical Newton approach.

The active set approach to be introduced is based on a transformation by means of which the optimality KKT condition are converted into a system of nonlinear equations.

Firstly for a fixed scalar $c > 0$, consider the open set $S_c^* \subset R^{2N+2} \times R^{2N+2}$ defined by.

$$S_c^* = \{(x.m)/m_j + cA_j x \neq, j = 1, 2 \cdots 2N+2\} \tag{30}$$

where A_j is the j column of matrix A, and the system of equations on S_c^*.

$$\begin{cases} C + \nabla_x g^+(x, m, c)m = 0 \\ g^+(x, m, c) = 0 \end{cases} \tag{31}$$

where the function $g^+(x, m, c)$ is defined by.

$$g^+(x, m, c) = \begin{bmatrix} g_1^+(x, m_1, c) \\ \vdots \\ g_{2N+2}^+(x, m_{2N+2}, c) \end{bmatrix}$$
$$g_j^+(x, m_j, c) = \max\left\{A_j x, -\frac{m_j}{c}\right\}, j = 1, 2 \cdots 2N+2 \tag{32}$$

Note that $g^+(x, m, c)$ is differentiable on S_c^* as $Ax - B$, so the Eqs. (31), (32) are well defined. We think that $g^+(x, m, c)$ appears in the definition of the augmented Lagrangian function which takes the form.

$$L_c(x, m, c) = C^T x + m' g^+(x, m, c) + \frac{1}{2} c |g^+(x, m, c)|^2$$

Secondly now consider the implementation of Newton approach. Define for $(x.m) \in S_c^*$.

$$\begin{gathered} L^+(x, m, c) = C^T x + m' g^+(x, m, c) \\ A_c(x, m) = \left\{j / A_j x - B_j > -\frac{m_j}{c}, j = 1, 2 \cdots 2N+2\right\} \end{gathered} \tag{33}$$

Assume without loss of generality that $A_c(x, m) = \{1 \cdots p\}$ for one integer p. This integer p depends on x and m. We view $A_c(x, m)$ as the active index set, in the sense that indices in $A_c(x, m)$ are predicted by the algorithm to be active at the solution. By differentiation in Eq. (31), we propose that Newton method consists of the iteration.

$$\bar{x} = x + \Delta x, \quad \bar{m} = m + \Delta m \tag{34}$$

where $(\Delta x, \Delta m)$ is the solution of the following system.

$$\begin{bmatrix} \nabla^2_{xx}\{m'g^+(x,m,c)\} & N(x,m,c) & 0 \\ N(x,m,c) & 0 & 0 \\ 0 & 0 & -\frac{1}{c}I \end{bmatrix} \begin{bmatrix} \Delta x \\ \Delta m_1 \\ \vdots \\ \Delta m_p \\ \Delta m_{p+1} \\ \vdots \\ \Delta m_{2N+2} \end{bmatrix} = -\begin{bmatrix} C+\nabla_x\{m'g^+(x,m,c)\} \\ g_1^+(x,m,c) \\ \vdots \\ g_p^+(x,m,c) \\ g_{p+1}^+(x,m,c) \\ \vdots \\ g_{2N+2}^+(x,m,c) \end{bmatrix} \tag{35}$$

where $N(x,m,c)$ is the $(2N+2)\times p$ matrix having as columns the gradients $A_j, j\in A_c(x,m)$, I is the $(2N+2-p)\times(2N+2-p)$ identity matrix, and the zero matrices have appropriate dimension. Since we see that.

$$g_j^+(x,m,c) = -\frac{m_j}{c},\ \forall j \notin A_c(x,m)$$

It follows that

$$\bar{m}_j = 0, \forall j \notin A_c(x,m)$$

It follows from Eq. (35) that the remaining variables Δx and $\Delta m_1 \cdots \Delta m_p$ are obtained by solving the reduced system.

$$\begin{bmatrix} \nabla^2_{xx}\{m'g^+(x,m,c)\} & N(x,m,c) \\ N(x,m,c) & 0 \end{bmatrix} \begin{bmatrix} \Delta x \\ \Delta m_1 \\ \vdots \\ \Delta m_p \end{bmatrix} = -\begin{bmatrix} C+\nabla_x\{m'g^+(x,m,c)\} \\ A_1x-B_1 \\ \vdots \\ A_px-B_p \end{bmatrix} \tag{36}$$

where we make use of the fact that.

$$\begin{aligned} g_j^+(x,m,c) &= g_j(x), \forall j\in A_c(x,m) \\ \nabla_x L^+(x,m,c) &= C + \sum_{j\in A_c(x,m)} (A_j - B_j)m_j \end{aligned} \tag{37}$$

From above equations, we see that the proposed Newton iteration can be described in a simpler manner.

5 Simulation

Now we propose a simple simulation example to illustrate the nature of the above results. In this simulation example, the unknown regressive structure is assumed as follows.

$$\begin{aligned} y(k) &= 0.1u(k-1) + 0.2u(k-2) + e(k) \\ &= \begin{pmatrix} u(k-1) & u(k-2) \end{pmatrix} \begin{pmatrix} 0.1 \\ 0.2 \end{pmatrix} + e(k) \end{aligned} \tag{38}$$

Setting regression vector as $\varphi^T(k) = \begin{pmatrix} u(k-1) & u(k-2) \end{pmatrix}$, and seek an explanatory interval predictor model of the form.

$$y(k) = \varphi^T(k)\theta(k) + e(k), \ |e(k)| \leq \gamma$$

In order to fit this above interval predictor model to the measured data, we choose $u(k) = \cos(k)$ and collect $N = 500$ observations as the data sequence $D_N = \{\varphi(k), y(k)\}_{k=1}^N$.

Choosing that size measurement as $\mu = \gamma + 0.8r$, and solving the linear programming problem by Newton method on the basis of our measured data $D_N = \{\varphi(k), y(k)\}_{k=1}^N$, we obtain one optimal center $\theta = \begin{pmatrix} 0.1 \\ 0.18 \end{pmatrix}$ with bounded radius $r = 0.2$, and level of magnitude bound $\gamma = 0.1$. The resulting interval predictor model in shown in Fig. 1, with the measured data are also clustered around at the point $\theta = \begin{pmatrix} 0.1 \\ 0.18 \end{pmatrix}$.

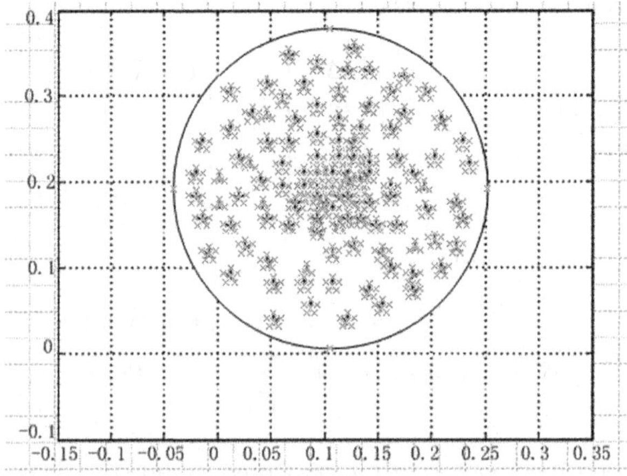

Fig. 1. Given regression vector, the resulting interval predictor model is used to predict the additional outputs

6 Conclusion

In this paper, we study the problem of interval predictor model with sphere parameter set. After introducing some parameters, this interval predictor model is dependent of three unknown parameters. In identifying these three unknown parameters, one linear programming problem is constructed. The main contributions are that we propose to choose one fixed non-negative number in size measure and give a Newton method to solve that linear programming problem. But the confidence level of our interval predictor model is not considered, so this is our next subject.

Acknowledgments. This work was partially supported by the National Nature Science Foundation of China (No. 31560316), the Department of Education of JiangXi Province (GJJ160866), Natural Science Foundation of Jiangxi Province, China (20171ACB20023).

References

1. Campi, M.C., Kumar, P.R.: Learning dynamical systems in a stationary environment. Syst. Control Lett. **16**(3), 125–132 (1998)
2. Campi, M.C., Calafiore, G., Garatti, S.: Interval predictor models: identification and reliability. Automatica **45**(2), 382–392 (2009)
3. Campi, M.C., Vidyasagar, M.: Learning with prior information. IEEE Trans. Autom. Control **46**(11), 1682–1695 (2001)
4. Vidyasagar, M., Karandikar, R.L.: A learning theory approach to system identification and stochastic adaptive control. J. Process Control **18**(3–4), 265–302 (2005)
5. Campi, B.M.C.: Uncertain convex programs: randomized solutions and confidence levels. Math. Program. **102**(1), 25–46 (2005)

A Conjugate Gradient Algorithm with Yuan-Wei-Lu Line Search

Gonglin Yuan[1,2(✉)], Wujie Hu[1], and Zhou Sheng[1]

[1] College of Mathematics and Information Science, Guangxi University, Nanning 530004, Guangxi, People's Republic of China
yuangl0417@126.com, glyuan@gxu.edu.cn, 15578093929@163.com, szhou03@live.com

[2] School of Computer and Software, Nanjing University of Information Science and Technology, Nanjing 210044, People's Republic of China

Abstract. This paper presents a three term conjugate gradient algorithm and it has the following properties: (i) the sufficient descent property is satisfied; (ii) the algorithm has the global convergence for nonconvex functions; (iii) the numerical results are more effective than that of the normal algorithm.

Keywords: Conjugate gradient algorithm · Optimization · Line search · Convergence

1 Introduction

In this paper, consider the following optimization problems

$$\min\{f(x) \mid x \in \Re^n\}, \tag{1}$$

the function $f : \Re^n \to \Re$ and $f \in C^2$. The model can be found in many other similar fields (see [6,7,11–13,18,20,21,25–27] etc.). The numerical method is used by the following formula for (1)

$$x_{k+1} = x_k + \alpha_k d_k,\ k = 0,\ 1,\ 2, \cdots \tag{2}$$

where x_k is the current iteration point, α_k is the so called stepsize, and d_k is the named search direction. The search direction d_k generated by conjugate gradient (CG) algorithm is defined by

$$d_{k+1} = \begin{cases} -g_{k+1} + \beta_k d_k, & \text{if } k \geq 1 \\ -g_{k+1}, & \text{if } k = 0, \end{cases} \tag{3}$$

where $\beta_k \in \Re$ and it will generate different CG algorithms (see [2–4,8,9,14–16,19,22–24,28–31,33] etc.). The well-known PRP algorithm [22,23] has the following form

$$\beta_k^{PRP} = \frac{g_{k+1}^T(g_{k+1} - g_k)}{\|g_k\|^2}. \tag{4}$$

X. Sun et al. (Eds.): ICCCS 2017, Part II, LNCS 10603, pp. 738–746, 2017.
https://doi.org/10.1007/978-3-319-68542-7_64

where $g_k = g(x_k) = \nabla f(x_k)$ and $g_{k+1} = g(x_{k+1}) = \nabla f(x_{k+1})$ are the gradient at x_k and x_{k+1}, respectively. The PRP algorithm is very effective for large-scale optimization problems, but fails to the global convergence for nonconvex function under the following weak Wolfe-Powell (WWP) line search technique for α_k

$$f(x_k + \alpha_k d_k) \leq f_k + \delta \alpha_k g_k^T d_k \tag{5}$$

and

$$g(x_k + \alpha_k d_k)^T d_k \geq \sigma g_k^T d_k, \tag{6}$$

where $\delta \in (0, 1/2)$ and $\sigma \in (\delta, 1)$. To solve this open problem, Yuan et al. [32] give a modified WWP line search technique

$$f(x_k + \alpha_k d_k) \leq f_k + \delta \alpha_k g_k^T d_k + \alpha_k \min[-\delta_1 g_k^T d_k, \delta \frac{\alpha_k}{2} \|d_k\|^2] \tag{7}$$

and

$$g(x_k + \alpha_k d_k)^T d_k \geq \sigma g_k^T d_k + \min[-\delta_1 g_k^T d_k, \delta \alpha_k \|d_k\|^2], \tag{8}$$

where $\delta \in (0, 1/2)$, $\delta_1 \in (0, \delta)$, and $\sigma \in (\delta, 1)$. Moreover, they also solve another open problem which is the global convergence of the BFGS quasi-Newton algorithm for general functions. In this paper, we call it Yuan-Wei-Lu (YWL) line search technique. Motivated by this technique and the PRP algorithm, we will make a further study. Then a new three term CG algorithm is proposed and it has the following properties:

- The search direction possesses the sufficient descent property.
- The new algorithm combining with the YWL line search has the global convergence for the general functions.
- The new algorithm has better numerical results than that of the PRP algorithm for large scale problems.

This paper is organized as follows. The new section states the inspiration and algorithm. The sufficient descent property and the global convergence is proved in Sect. 3. Section 4 reports the tested numerical results. Throughout this paper, $f(x_k)$ and $f(x_{k+1})$ are replaced by f_k and f_{k+1}, $\|\cdot\|$ is the Euclidean norm.

2 Inspiration and Algorithm

The PRP algorithm has not the global convergence for general functions, one main reason is the sufficient descent property that can not be satisfied. Touati-Ahmed and Storey [1], Al-Baali [2], Gilbert and Nocedal [10], and Hu and Storey [17] hinted that the sufficient descent condition is very crucial for conjugate gradient methods to ensure the global convergence. Thus, a three term conjugate gradient formula is designed by

$$d_{k+1} = \begin{cases} -\gamma_k g_{k+1} + \beta_k^{PRP} d_k - \frac{d_k^T g_{k+1} y_k}{\|g_k\|^2}, & \text{if } k \geq 1 \\ -g_{k+1}, & \text{if } k = 0, \end{cases} \tag{9}$$

where $\gamma_k = \frac{\theta_k}{\min\{\eta_1 s_k^T y_k, \eta_2 \theta_k\}}$, $\theta_k = \frac{s_k^T y_k}{\|s_k\|^2}$, $s_k = x_{k+1} - x_k$, $\eta_1 \in (0, 1)$, and $\eta_2 \in (0, 1)$. The algorithm is stated as follows.

Algorithm 1 (The new three term PRP CG algorithm).
Step 0: Choose point $x_0 \in \Re^n$, $\varepsilon \in (0,1)$ $\delta \in (0,\frac{1}{2})$, $\delta_1 \in (0,\delta)$, $\sigma \in (\delta,1)$, $\eta_1 \in (0,1)$, and $\eta_2 \in (0,1)$. Let $d_0 = -g_0 = -\nabla f(x_0)$, $k := 0$.
Step 1: the algorithm will stop if $\|g_k\| \leq \varepsilon$.
Step 2: Compute α_k using the YWL line search (7) and (8).
Step 3: Set $x_{k+1} = x_k + \alpha_k d_k$.
Step 4: If $\|g_{k+1}\| \leq \varepsilon$ holds, the algorithm stops.
Step 5: Update the search direction by (9).
Step 6: Let $k := k+1$ and go to Step 2.

3 Descent Property and Convergence

The following assumption about the general functions is needed to obtain the global convergence of Algorithm 1.

Assumption A. (i) The level set $\Omega = \{x \in \Re^n \mid f(x) \leq f(x_0)\}$ is bounded.

(ii) The function f has a lower bound, is differentiable, and its gradient g is Lipschitz continuous, namely,

$$\|g(x) - g(y)\| \leq L\|x - y\|, \ \forall \ x, y \in \Omega \tag{10}$$

holds, where $L > 0$ is a constant.

Now we prove the sufficient descent property of the search direction d_k of (9).

Lemma 1. *The search direction d_k of (9) has the following condition*

$$d_{k+1}^T g_{k+1} \leq -\eta \|g_{k+1}\|^2 \tag{11}$$

where $\eta \geq 1$ is a constant.

Proof. If $k = 0$, we have $g_0^T d_0 = -\|g_0\|^2$ and (11) is true. If $k \geq 1$, we turn to prove that (11) holds too. By (9), we have

$$\begin{aligned} g_{k+1}^T d_{k+1} &= g_{k+1}^T[-\gamma_k g_{k+1} + \beta_k^{PRP} d_k - \frac{d_k^T g_{k+1} y_k}{\|g_k\|^2}] \\ &= -\gamma_k \|g_{k+1}\|^2 + \frac{g_{k+1}^T y_k}{\|g_k\|^2} g_{k+1}^T d_k - \frac{d_k^T g_{k+1} g_{k+1}^T y_k}{\|g_k\|^2} \\ &= -\gamma_k \|g_{k+1}\|^2 \\ &\leq -\frac{1}{\eta_2} \|g_{k+1}\|^2, \end{aligned} \tag{12}$$

where the last inequality follows the relation $\gamma_k = \frac{\theta_k}{\min\{\eta_1 s_k^T y_k, \eta_2 \theta_k\}} \geq \frac{\theta_k}{\eta_2 \theta_k} = \frac{1}{\eta_2}$, letting $\eta = \frac{1}{\eta_2} > 1$ generates (11). The proof is complete.

The following theorem is the global convergence of Algorithm 1.

Theorem 1. *Let Assumption A hold and $\|d_k\| \le c\|g_k\|$ is true with a constant $c > 0$. We have*

$$\lim_{k\to\infty} \|g_k\| = 0. \tag{13}$$

Proof. By (11) and (8), we have

$$g(x_k + \alpha_k d_k)^T d_k \ge \sigma g_k^T d_k + \min[-\delta_1 g_k^T d_k, \delta\alpha_k \|d_k\|^2] \ge \sigma g_k^T d_k.$$

Using (10), we have

$$-(1-\sigma) g_k^T d_k \le g_{k+1}^T d_k - g_k^T d_k \le \|g_{k+1} - g_k\| \|d_k\| \le \alpha_k \|d_k\|^2. \tag{14}$$

So we obtain $\alpha_k \ge \frac{-(1-\sigma)g_k^T d_k}{\|d_k\|^2} \ge \frac{\eta(1-\sigma)\|g_k\|^2}{\|d_k\|^2} \ge \frac{\eta(1-\sigma)}{c}$. By Assumption A, (11), (14), and (7), we get

$$\begin{aligned} f(x_k + \alpha_k d_k) &\le f_k + \delta\alpha_k g_k^T d_k + \alpha_k \min[-\delta_1 g_k^T d_k, \delta\frac{\alpha_k}{2}\|d_k\|^2] \\ &\le f_k + (\delta - \delta_1)\alpha_k g_k^T d_k \\ &\le f_k - \eta(\delta - \delta_1)\alpha_k \|g_k\|^2 \\ &\le f_k - \frac{\eta^2(\delta - \delta_1)(1-\sigma)}{c}\|g_k\|^2. \end{aligned}$$

Summing the above inequalities from $k = 0$ to ∞, we have

$$\sum_{k=0}^{\infty} \|g_k\|^2 \le f_0 - f_\infty.$$

Since $f(x)$ is bounded, we get $\|g_k\| \to 0$. This completes the proof.

4 Numerical Results

In this section, we report the numerical results of Algorithm 1 and the three-term conjugate gradient algorithm [35] (so called ZZL). The test problems can be found from [36] and listed in Table 1. To show the performance of Algorithm 1 for the test problems in Table 1, we will compare with ZZL. The following *Himmeblau* stop rule [34] is used: If $|f(x_k)| > e_1$, let $stop1 = \frac{|f(x_k) - f(x_{k+1})|}{|f(x_k)|}$, or $stop1 = |f(x_k) - f(x_{k+1})|$. If the conditions $\|g(x)\| < \epsilon$ or $stop1 < e_2$ are satisfied, the algorithm is stopped, where $e_1 = e_2 = 10^{-5}$, $\epsilon = 10^{-6}$. The algorithm is also stopped if the number of iterations is greater than 1000. The test problems whose dimension has been chosen in the range [3000, 9000]. All the programs were written in MATLAB 7.10 and run on a PC with a 1.80 GHz CPU and 4.00 GB of memory running the Windows 7 operating system. The columns of the Table 1 have the following meanings: "No.": the number of the tested problems in Table 1. "Problem" denotes the name of problems.

Table 1. Test problems

No.	Problem	No.	Problem
1	Extended Freudenstein and Roth Function	38	ARWHEAD Function (CUTE)
2	Extended Trigonometric Function	38	ARWHEAD Function (CUTE)
3	Extended Rosenbrock Function	40	NONDQUAR Function (CUTE)
4	Extended White and Holst Function	41	DQDRTIC Function (CUTE)
5	Extended Beale Function	42	EG2 Function (CUTE)
6	Extended Penalty Function	43	DIXMAANA Function (CUTE)
7	Perturbed Quadratic Function	44	DIXMAANB Function (CUTE)
8	Raydan 1 Function	45	DIXMAANC Function (CUTE)
9	Raydan 2 Function	46	DIXMAANE Function (CUTE)
10	Diagonal 1 Function	47	Partial Perturbed Quadratic Function
11	Diagonal 2 Function	48	Broyden Tridiagonal Function
12	Diagonal 3 Function	49	Almost Perturbed Quadratic Function
13	Hager Function	50	Tridiagonal Perturbed Quadratic Function
14	Generalized Tridiagonal 1 Function	51	EDENSCH Function (CUTE)
15	Extended Tridiagonal 1 Function	52	VARDIM Function (CUTE)
16	Extended Three Exponential Terms Function	53	STAIRCASE S1 Function
17	Generalized Tridiagonal 2 Function	54	LIARWHD Function (CUTE)
18	Diagonal 4 Function	55	DIAGONAL 6 Function
19	Diagonal 5 Function	56	DIXON3DQ Function (CUTE)
20	Extended Himmelblau Function	57	DIXMAANF Function (CUTE)
21	Generalized PSC1 Function	58	DIXMAANG Function (CUTE)
22	Extended PSC1 Function	59	DIXMAANH Function (CUTE)
23	Extended Powell Function	60	DIXMAANI Function (CUTE)
24	Extended Block Diagonal BD1 Function	61	DIXMAANJ Function (CUTE)
25	Extended Maratos Function	62	DIXMAANK Function (CUTE)
26	Extended Cliff Function	63	DIXMAANL Function (CUTE)
27	Quadratic Diagonal Perturbed Function	64	DIXMAAND Function (CUTE)
28	Extended Wood Function	65	ENGVAL1 Function (CUTE)
29	Extended Hiebert Function	66	FLETCHCR Function (CUTE)
30	Quadratic Function QF1 Function	67	COSINE Function (CUTE)
31	Extended Quadratic Penalty QP1 Function	68	Extended DENSCHNB Function (CUTE)
32	Extended Quadratic Penalty QP2 Function	69	DENSCHNF Function (CUTE)
33	A Quadratic Function QF2 Function	70	SINQUAD Function (CUTE)
34	Extended EP1 Function	71	BIGGSB1 Function (CUTE)
35	Extended Tridiagonal-2 Function	72	Partial Perturbed Quadratic PPQ2 Function
36	BDQRTIC Function (CUTE)	73	Scaled Quadratic SQ1 Function
37	TRIDIA Function (CUTE)	74	Scaled Quadratic SQ2 Function

Table 2. Numerical results for total NI, NFG and CPU-time

Algorithm	NI	NFG	CPU-time
Algorithm 1	1689	7002	139.527277
ZZL	1792	14578	291.534656

In numerical results, Algorithm 1 requires the total number of iterations of 1,689 times, running 139.527277 s to solve these problems of Table 1, and the number of the function and gradient evaluations is 7,002. However, ZZL algorithm than the Algorithm 1 in the total number of iterations 103 times, running time more than 152.007379 s, in the number of the function and gradient evaluations of more than 7,000 times.

The algorithm of Dolan and Moré [5] will be used to analyze the profiles of these two algorithms. Figures 1, 2 and 3 show the performance of these four methods related to NI, NFG, and CPU-time, respectively, where NI: the total number of iterations, NFG: the number of the function and gradient evaluations, CPU-time: the CPU time in second. Figure 3 shows that Algorithm 1 is competitive to the ZZL algorithm.

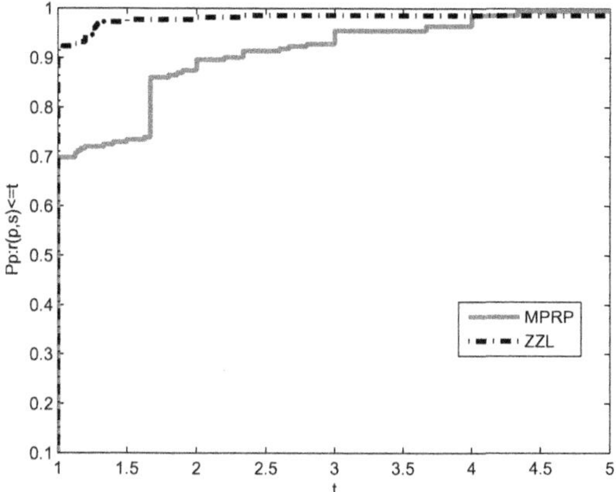

Fig. 1. Performance profiles of these methods (NI)

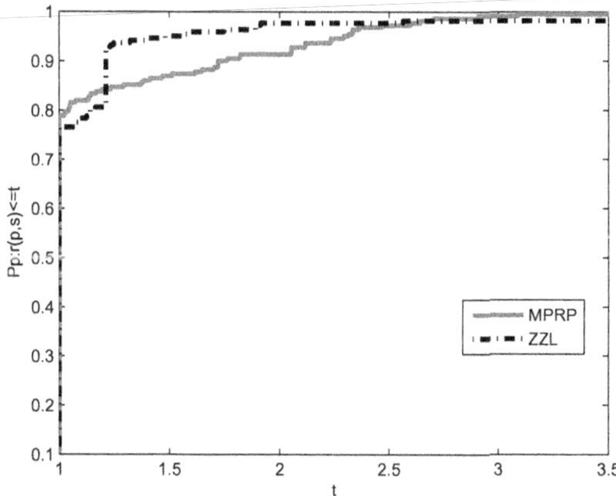

Fig. 2. Performance profiles of these methods (NFG)

From the Figs. 1, 2, On the one hand, we will safely arrive a conclusion that Algorithm 1 (MPRP) solves a great variety of problems since the numerical result

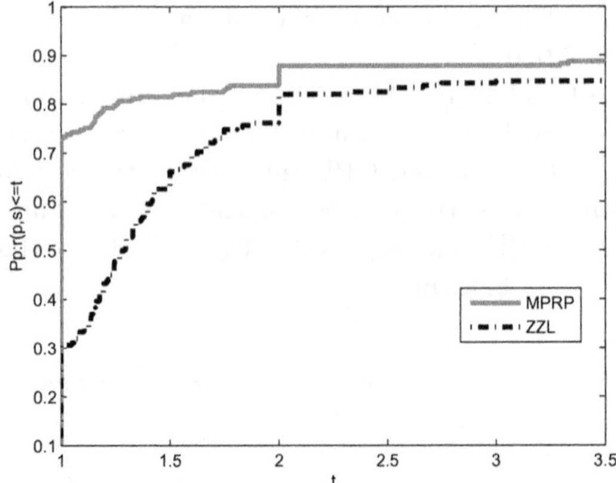

Fig. 3. Performance profiles of these methods (CPU-time)

of Y-axis equals 1 when coming to an end. On the other hand, the method of ZZL fails to address some problems to some extent because the largest value of corresponding curve extends to 1 rather than 1.

From the Fig. 3, the convergence of MPRP is much superior to ZZL. Firstly, the speed of convergence is obviously efficient. There is more point that the corresponding value of algorithm MPRP is more acceptable and stable.

Acknowledgments. We would like to thank all anonymous reviewers for their helpful advice and comments. This work is supported by the Guangxi Science Fund for Distinguished Young Scholars (No. 2015GXNSFGA139001), the National Natural Science Foundation of China (Grant Nos. 11261006 and 11161003).

References

1. Touati-Ahmed, D., Storey, C.: Efficient hybrid conjugate gradient techniques. J. Optim. Theory Appl. **64**, 379–397 (1990)
2. Al-Baali, A.: Descent property and global convergence of the Flecher-Reeves method with inexact line search. IMA J. Numer. Anal. **5**, 121–124 (1985)
3. Dai, Y., Yuan, Y.: A nonlinear conjugate gradient with a strong global convergence properties. SIAM J. Optim. **10**, 177–182 (2000)
4. Daniel, J.W.: The conjugate gradient method for linear and nonlinear operator equations. SIAM J. Numer. Anal. **4**, 10–26 (1967)
5. Dolan, E.D., Moré, J.J.: Benchmarking optimization software with performance profiles. Math. Program. **91**, 201–213 (2002)
6. Fu, Z., Ren, K., Shu, J., Sun, X., Huang, F.: Enabling personalized search over encrypted out-sourced data with efficiency improvement. IEEE Trans. Parallel Distrib. Syst. (2015). doi:10.1109/TPDS.2015.2506573
7. Fu, Z., Wu, X., Guan, C., Sun, X., Ren, K.: Towards efficient multi-keyword fuzzy search over encrypted outsourced data with accuracy improvement. IEEE Trans. Inf. Foren. Secur. (2016). doi:10.1109/TIFS.2016.2596138

8. Fletcher, R.: Practical Methods of Optimization, 2nd edn. Wiley, Chichester (1987)
9. Fletcher, R., Reeves, C.M.: Function minimization by conjugate gradients. Comput. J. **7**, 149–154 (1964)
10. Gilbert, J.C., Nocedal, J.: Global convergence properties of conjugate gradient methods for optimization. SIAM J. Optim. **2**, 21–42 (1992)
11. Gu, B., Sheng, V.S.: A robust regularization path algorithm for ν-support vector classification. IEEE Trans. Neural Netw. Learn. Syst. (2016). doi:10.1109/TNNL-S. 2016.2527796
12. Gu, B., Sheng, V.S., Tay, K.Y., Romano, W., Li, S.: Incremental support vector learning for ordinal regression. IEEE Trans. Neural Netw. Learn. Syst. **26**, 1403–1416 (2015)
13. Gu, B., Sun, X., Sheng, V.S.: Structural minimax probability machine. IEEE Trans. Neural Netw. Learn. Syst. (2016). doi:10.1109/TNNLS.2016.2544779
14. Hager, W., Zhang, H.: A new conjugate gradient method with guaranteed descent and an efficient line search. SIAM J. Optim. **16**, 170–192 (2005)
15. Hager, W., Zhang, H.: Algorithm 851: $CG_DESCENT$, a conjugate gradient method with guaranteed descent. ACM Trans. Math. Softw. **32**, 113–137 (2006)
16. Hestenes, M.R., Stiefel, E.: Method of conjugate gradient for solving linear equations. J. Res. Nation. Bur. Stand. **49**, 409–436 (1952)
17. Hu, Y.F., Storey, C.: Global convergence result for conjugate method. J. Optim. Theory Appl. **71**, 399–405 (1991)
18. Li, J., Li, X., Yang, B., Sun, X.: Segmentation-based image copy-move forgery detection scheme. IEEE Trans. Inf. Foren. Secur. **10**, 507–518 (2015)
19. Liu, Y., Storey, C.: Efficient generalized conjugate gradient algorithms part 1: theory. J. Appl. Math. Comput. **69**, 17–41 (1992)
20. Pan, Z., Zhang, Y., Kwong, S.: Efficient motion and disparity estimation optimization for low complexity multiview video coding. IEEE Trans. Broadcast. **61**, 166–176 (2015)
21. Pan, Z., Lei, J., Zhang, Y., Sun, X., Kwong, S.: Fast motion estimation based on content property for low-complexity H.265/HEVC encoder. IEEE Trans. Broadcast. (2016). doi:10.1109/TBC.2016.2580920
22. Polak, E.: The conjugate gradient method in extreme problems. Comput. Math. Mathem. Phys. **9**, 94–112 (1969)
23. Polak, E., Ribière, G.: Note sur la convergence de directions conjugees. Rev. Fran. Inf. Rech. Opérat. **3**, 35–43 (1969)
24. Wei, Z., Yao, S., Liu, L.: The convergence properties of some new conjugate gradient methods. Appl. Math. Comput. **183**, 1341–1350 (2006)
25. Xia, Z., Wang, X., Sun, X., Wang, Q.: A secure and dynamic multi-keyword ranked search scheme over encrypted cloud data. IEEE Trans. Parallel Distrib. Syst. **27**, 340–352 (2015)
26. Xia, Z., Wang, X., Sun, X., Liu, Q., Xiong, N.: Steganalysis of LSB matching using differences between nonadjacent pixels. Multimed. Tools Appl. **75**, 1947–1962 (2016)
27. Xia, Z., Wang, X., Zhang, L., Qin, Z., Sun, X., Ren, K.: A privacy-preserving and copy-deterrence content-based image retrieval scheme in cloud computing. IEEE Trans. Inf. Foren. Secur. (2016). doi:10.1109/TIFS.2016.2590944
28. Yuan, G., Lu, X.: A modified PRP conjugate gradient method. Ann. Oper. Res. **166**, 73–90 (2009)
29. Yuan, G., Lu, X., Wei, Z.: A conjugate gradient method with descent direction for unconstrained optimization. J. Comput. Appl. Math. **233**, 519–530 (2009)

30. Yuan, G., Meng, Z., Li, Y.: A modified Hestenes and Stiefel conjugate gradient algorithm for large-scale nonsmooth minimizations and nonlinear equations. J. Optim. Theory Appl. **168**, 129–152 (2016)
31. Yuan, G., Wei, Z., Li, G.: A modified Polak-Ribière-Polyak conjugate gradient algorithm for nonsmooth convex programs. J. Comput. Appl. Math. **255**, 86–96 (2014)
32. Yuan, G., Wei, Z., Lu, X.: Global convergence of BFGS and PRP methods under a modified weak Wolfe-Powell line search. Appl. Math. Model. **47**, 811–825 (2017). doi:10.1016/j.apm.2017.02.008
33. Yuan, G., Zhang, M.: A three-terms Polak-Ribire-Polyak conjugate gradient algorithm for large-scale nonlinear equations. J. Comput. Appl. Math. **286**, 186–195 (2015)
34. Yuan, Y., Sun, W.: Theory and Methods of Optimization. Science Press of China, Beijing (1999)
35. Zhang, L., Zhou, W., Li, D.H.: A descent modified Polak-Ribiè-Polyak conjugate gradient method and its global convergence. IMA. J. Num. Anal. **26**, 629–640 (2006)
36. Andrei, N.: An unconstrained optimization test function collection. Adv. Model. Optim. **10**, 147–161 (2008)

IU-PMF: Probabilistic Matrix Factorization Model Fused with Item Similarity and User Similarity

Yilong Shi(✉), Hong Lin, and Yuqiang Li

School of Computer Science and Technology, Wuhan University of Technology, Wuhan 430061, China
798266215@qq.com, 1934636310@qq.com, 17954183@qq.com

Abstract. Probabilistic Matrix Factorization has been proven a very successful model for recommending because of scalability, accuracy and the ability to handle sparsity problem. However, many studies have demonstrated that PMF alone is poor to reveal local relationships which can be captured by neighborhood-aware methods. In this paper we present the IU-PMF model fusing Item Similarity and User Similarity in PMF, which combines the merits of both methods. The IU-PMF model consists of two phases: the Item and User similarity matrices computation phase not needing to be applied frequently; the fused PMF model solving phase which scales linearly with the number of observations. The IU-PMF model incorporates Item similarities and User similarities abstracted from User-Item ratings into the PMF model, which helps to overcome the often encountered problem of data sparsity, scalability and prediction quality. Experiments on three real-world datasets and the complexity analysis show that IU-PMF is scalable and outperforms several state-of-the-art methods.

Keywords: Recommender systems · Collaborative filtering · PMF · Similarity

1 Introduction

With the coming of digital era, recommender systems have gained more and more attention and become one of the most effective tool to deal with "information overload" problem [1]. Correspondingly, a number of effective techniques and methods for recommendation have been proposed and many have been successfully applied to business systems during the last decade.

Typically, collaborative filtering is the most active in the field of recommendation in recent years, mainly because it is simple and effective and has played an important role in Netflix competition. Underlying the hypothesis that the similar users have the same hobbies and similar items have the same fans [1, 2], the memory-based collaborative filtering algorithms, such as User-KNN (K nearest neighbor algorithm based on user rating similarity) [3–5] and Item-KNN (K nearest neighbor algorithm based on item rating similarity) [6, 7], are widely studied and applied in many commercial systems, such as Amazon and eBay. However, these methods suffer from the inherent weakness that the sparsity of the user-item rating matrix (the available ratings of a

X. Sun et al. (Eds.): ICCCS 2017, Part II, LNCS 10603, pp. 747–758, 2017.
https://doi.org/10.1007/978-3-319-68542-7_65

business system is typically less than 1%) make them fail to find similar users and items. Recently, model-based collaborative filtering algorithms have gained more and more attention mainly due to that they are scalable and have some ability of solving sparsity problem. In model-based algorithms, a predefined model is trained using observed ratings and other available information. The representative model-based algorithms contain Singular Value Decomposition (SVD) [1], SVD++ [1], and Probabilistic Matrix Factorization (PMF) [8] and so on, which achieves some good results, but still cannot perform well when the observed data is sparse.

Recently, many scholars [9–15] have put forward a lot of fused collaborative filtering algorithms by using the social information of users and structure information of items, and have achieved good results especially when there is a sparsity problem. Ma et al. [9] recognized the prediction quality, scalability and data sparsity problem, and proposed a novel social recommendation algorithm based on PMF, which outperforms several baselines. Lei et al. [14] consider the influence of item relations, and fuse item relations in social recommendation on the basis of Ma's research. However, how to obtain and measure the social and structure information is the key challenge, which may have a lot of influence on the recommendation results. The current solution mainly includes the following types: (1) Using the explicit social network information for recommendation; (2) Calculating the similarities among users (items) by using implicit label information. But in reality, it is difficult to get the social network information or enough implicit label information of the users (items).

In order to overcome the above mentioned defects, underlying the idea that item similarity and user similarity can affect one's personal behaviors, and historical behaviors on web can reflect item similarity and user similarity, we proposed a novel two-phase recommender framework named IU-PMF, which abstract item similarity and user similarity attributes from user-item ratings firstly, and then fuse them with PMF model to make more personalized and accurate recommendations. Although this idea of fusing similarity in matrix factorization may not be very new, to the best of our knowledge, IU-PMF is most concise, and the complexity analysis shows that IU-PMF is more scalable than other state-of-the-art similarity fused models, such as NHPMF [16] and SBMF [17]. Additionally, the experiments on three real-world datasets shows that IU-PMF is outstanding in terms of RMSE.

The remainder of the paper is organized as follows. In the next section we describe the related work. The IU-PMF model and complexity analysis are presented in Sect. 3. Section 4 displays and analyses the experimental result. Finally the conclusion and future work have been presented in Sect. 5.

2 Related Work

In this section, we explore the latest development of the relevant research content. Specifically, PMF, several latest MF based recommendation algorithms and other state-of-the-art similarity fused models are displayed.

Based on ordinary matrix factorization model, Mnih et al. [8] presented PMF, which assumes that the user-item rating matrix, the derived user latent matrix and item latent matrix obey Gaussian distribution, and combines the three organically with the

Bayesian principle. Their experimental results demonstrate that PMF performs well on Netflix that is sparse, large and very imbalanced. While many studies have demonstrated that PMF alone is poor to reveal local relationships [1].

In these years, in order to further promote the performance, PMF is widely studied and used for social recommendation and context-aware recommendation. By employing both user-item rating records and users' social network information, Ma et al. [9] proposed a novel social recommender approach based on PMF named SoRec. In SoRec, they introduced latent factor feature matrix, and combined it with the latent user feature matrix and latent item feature matrix in a single Bayesian equation, which helped to improve prediction accuracy and solve the data sparsity problem, especially when users have few or no ratings. Based on the research content of Lei et al. [14] presented PMFUI model incorporating Item Relations to Social Recommendation based on the idea that related items are more likely to be enjoyed by the same user. Specifically, PMFUI considers the influence of user connections and item relations simultaneously and utilizes the shared latent feature space to constrain the objective function. And their experimental results show that their method outperforms SoRec on 2012 KDD Cup dataset. Sun et al. [18] noticed the sequential correlations among users and items, and proposed a PMF based method to capture the sequential behaviors of items and users, which can help find neighbors that are most influential to the given items (users). Furthermore, the method successfully combined the recommendation process with the influential neighbors based on PMF, and achieved good results.

Although the methods mentioned above have achieved good results, most of them require additional social information or implicit label information, which are usually not available in reality. To overcome the weakness, recent researches have focused on similarity fusion, which combines the advantages of neighborhood-aware methods and matrix factorization model. Wu et al. [16] proposed NHPMF, a novel two-stage recommendation model, which firstly uses tagging data to select neighbors of each users and items, and then incorporate them into the factorization. Although the proposed can improve rating accuracy a lot when applied to extra tagging data, it performs not well when there only exists rating data. Wang et al. [17] suggested SBMF which establishes the clusters of users and items using rating data and then incorporates the cluster information into Matrix factorization, the idea is effective, while the clusters computation phase is time consuming, and thus reduces the scalability. Observed the above defects, this paper mainly simply mines Item similarities and User similarities from User-Item ratings, and then incorporates them into PMF using a concise fused model which have high scalability, to promote the performance of recommendation.

3 IU-PMF

In this section, we first present the notations and description of IU-PMF. Then we introduce the User (Item) similarity matrix computation method. After that, the IU-PMF model is demonstrated in detail. Finally, the complexity analysis is shown.

3.1 Notations and Description of IU-PMF

Suppose we have *N* users, *M* items, and integer user-item rating values ranging from *1* to *K*. To make our model more adaptable, we propose to use the function $t(x) = (x-1)/(K-1)$ to map the ratings to interval *[0,1]*. Let $R_{i,j}$ be the rating of user *i* for item *j*. Let $U \in R^{L \times N}$ and $V \in R^{L \times M}$ be latent user and item feature matrices, with column vectors U_i and V_j representing user-specific and item-specific latent feature vectors respectively. Let $D \in R^{N \times N}$ and $S \in R^{M \times M}$ abstracted from User-Item ratings be user similarity matrix and item similarity matrix respectively. We connect user similarity, item similarity and user-item ratings data in shared user latent feature space and shared item latent feature space in IU-PMF, and the graphical model for IU-PMF is shown in Fig. 1.

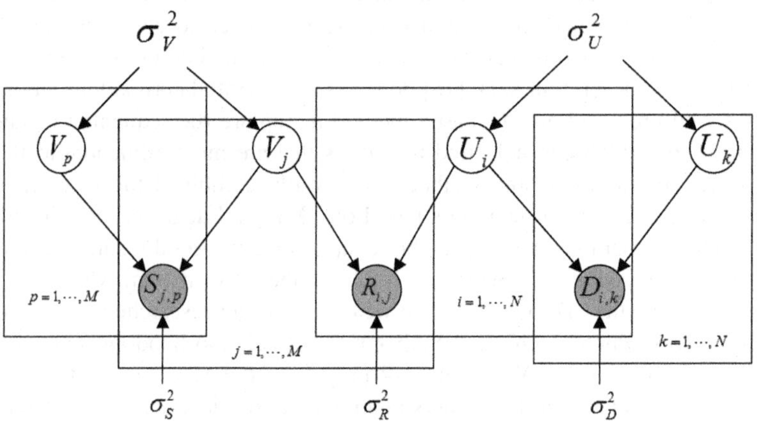

Fig. 1. Graphical model for IU-PMF

3.2 User (Item) Similarity

In IU-PMF, we need to model user (item) similarity, and due to that we connect user similarity, item similarity and user-item ratings that we map to interval *[0,1]* in shared user and item latent feature space, the output of the similarity measure function must lie in *[0,1]*. In statistics, the similarity of two samples can be measured by linear and non-linear ways, such as Cosine similarity [19], Pearson correlation coefficient (PCC) [20] and Radial basis function (RBF) [21] etc. Among these methods, PCC is the most commonly used for rating evaluation [1], while Cosine similarity is simpler than PCC and it has been stated that cosine similarity is a better measure function for top-N recommendation [1]. Additionally, thus to simplify modeling, we proposed to model user (item) similarity based on PCC and Cosine similarity respectively, and explore their ultimate performance in the experiment section.

The range of similarity measured by PCC or Cosine similarity is [*−1, 1*], so we use the scale function $t(x) = (1 + x)/2$ to scale it to [*0, 1*]. Although the idea is simple and rough, as we demonstrate in our experimental results section, it brings good performance.

3.3 IU-PMF Model

Similar to PMF, the conditional distribution of IU-PMF over the observed user-item ratings is defined as:

$$p(R|U,V,\sigma_R^2) = \prod_{i=1}^{N}\prod_{j=1}^{M} N(R_{i,j}|g(U_i^T V_j),\sigma_R^2)^{I_{i,j}^R} \tag{1}$$

where $N(x|\mu,\sigma^2)$ is the Gaussian distribution density function with variance σ^2 and mean μ, $g(x)$ is the logistic function and $g(x) = 1/(1 + \exp(-x))$, $I_{i,j}^R$ is the indicator function returning 1 if user i rated item j and 0 otherwise.

The conditional distribution over the user similarity matrix D is defined as:

$$P(D|U,\sigma_D^2) = \prod_{i=1}^{N}\prod_{k=1}^{N} N(D_{i,k}|g(U_i^T U_k),\sigma_D^2)^{I_{i,k}^D} \tag{2}$$

where $I_{i,k}^D$ is the indicator function returning 1 if the similarity between user i and k can be calculated and 0 otherwise.

Similar to user similarity, the conditional distribution over the item similarity matrix S is defined as:

$$P(S|V,\sigma_S^2) = \prod_{j=1}^{M}\prod_{p=1}^{M} N(S_{j,p}|g(V_j^T V_p),\sigma_S^2)^{I_{j,p}^S} \tag{3}$$

where $I_{j,p}^S$ is the indicator function returning 1 if the similarity between item j and p can be calculated and 0 otherwise.

We also assume that U and V are subject to spherical Gaussian priori distribution with zero-mean:

$$\begin{aligned} P(U|\sigma_U^2) &= \prod_{i=1}^{N} N(U_i|0,\sigma_U^2 \mathrm{I}) \\ P(V|\sigma_V^2) &= \prod_{j=1}^{M} N(V_j|0,\sigma_V^2 \mathrm{I}) \end{aligned} \tag{4}$$

So, by a simple Bayesian derivation, the posterior distribution function is as follows:

$$
\begin{aligned}
&P(U,V|R,D,S,\sigma_R^2,\sigma_D^2,\sigma_S^2,\sigma_U^2,\sigma_V^2)\\
&\propto P(R|U,V,\sigma_R^2)*P(D|U,\sigma_D^2)*P(S|V,\sigma_S^2)*P(U|\sigma_U^2)*P(V|\sigma_V^2)\\
&=\prod_{i=1}^{N}\prod_{j=1}^{M}N(R_{i,j}|g(U_i^TV_j),\sigma_R^2)^{I_{i,j}^R}\times\prod_{i=1}^{N}\prod_{k=1}^{N}N(D_{i,k}|g(U_i^TU_k),\sigma_D^2)^{I_{i,k}^D}\\
&\quad\times\prod_{j=1}^{M}\prod_{p=1}^{M}N(S_{j,p}|g(V_j^TV_p),\sigma_S^2)^{I_{j,p}^S}\times\prod_{i=1}^{N}N(U_i|0,\sigma_U^2\mathrm{I})\times\prod_{j=1}^{M}N(V_j|0,\sigma_V^2\mathrm{I})
\end{aligned}
\tag{5}
$$

And the log of the posterior distribution (Eq. 5) is given by:

$$
\begin{aligned}
&\ln P(U,V|R,D,S,\sigma_R^2,\sigma_D^2,\sigma_S^2,\sigma_U^2,\sigma_V^2)\\
&=-\frac{1}{2\sigma_R^2}\sum_{i=1}^{N}\sum_{j=1}^{M}I_{i,j}^R(R_{i,j}-g(U_i^TV_j))^2-\frac{1}{2\sigma_D^2}\sum_{i=1}^{N}\sum_{k=1}^{N}I_{i,k}^D(D_{i,k}-g(U_i^TU_k))^2\\
&\quad-\frac{1}{2\sigma_S^2}\sum_{j=1}^{M}\sum_{p=1}^{M}I_{j,p}^S(S_{j,p}-g(V_j^TV_p))^2-\frac{1}{2\sigma_U^2}\sum_{i=1}^{N}U_i^TU_i-\frac{1}{2\sigma_V^2}\sum_{j=1}^{M}V_j^TV_j\\
&\quad-\frac{1}{2}(MN\ \ln\sigma_R^2+N^2\ \ln\sigma_D^2+M^2\ \ln\sigma_S^2+ND\ \ln\sigma_U^2+MD\ \ln\sigma_V^2)+C
\end{aligned}
\tag{6}
$$

where C is a constant not depending on any parameters. Maximizing the log-posterior function (Eq. 6) over U and V with parameters kept fixed is equivalent to minimizing the following sum-of-squared-errors objective functions:

$$
\begin{aligned}
E=&\frac{1}{2}\sum_{i=1}^{N}\sum_{j=1}^{M}I_{i,j}^R(R_{i,j}-g(U_i^TV_j))^2+\frac{\sigma_R^2}{2\sigma_D^2}\sum_{i=1}^{N}\sum_{k=1}^{N}I_{i,k}^D(D_{i,k}-g(U_i^TU_k))^2\\
&+\frac{\sigma_R^2}{2\sigma_S^2}\sum_{j=1}^{M}\sum_{p=1}^{M}I_{j,p}^S(S_{j,p}-g(V_j^TV_p))^2+\frac{\lambda_U}{2}\sum_{i=1}^{N}U_i^TU_i+\frac{\lambda_V}{2}\sum_{j=1}^{M}V_j^TV_j
\end{aligned}
\tag{7}
$$

where $\lambda_U=\sigma_R^2/\sigma_U^2$, $\lambda_V=\sigma_R^2/\sigma_V^2$. By performing gradient descent in U_i and V_j, a local minimum of the above objective function can be found.

$$
\begin{aligned}
\frac{\partial E}{\partial U_i}=&\sum_{j=1}^{M}I_{i,j}^R(g(U_i^TV_j)-R_{i,j})g'(U_i^TV_j)V_j\\
&+\frac{2\sigma_R^2}{\sigma_D^2}\sum_{k=1}^{N}I_{i,k}^D(g(U_i^TU_k)-D_{i,k})g'(U_i^TU_k)U_k+\lambda_UU_i\\
\frac{\partial E}{\partial V_j}=&\sum_{i=1}^{N}I_{i,j}^R(g(U_i^TV_j)-R_{i,j})g'(U_i^TV_j)U_i\\
&+\frac{2\sigma_R^2}{\sigma_S^2}\sum_{p=1}^{M}I_{j,p}^S(g(V_j^TV_p)-S_{j,p})g'(V_j^TV_p)V_p+\lambda_VV_j
\end{aligned}
\tag{8}
$$

where $g'(x) = \exp(x)/(1 + \exp(x))^2$ and it is the derivative of the logistic function. To reduce the model complexity, we set $\lambda_U = \lambda_V$ in all the experiments in Sect. 4.

3.4 Complexity Analysis

The IU-PMF model consists of two phases: the Item and User similarity matrices *D* and *S* computation phase, and the phase of minimizing the objective function Eq. (7). The first phase doesn't need to be applied frequently, due to that it is able to receive a good effect as long as 80% of the observations are involved in the phase (means that when a handful of new data arrives, we do not need to calculate the similarity matrices again), which is demonstrated in Subsect. 4.4. Suppose we have *T* observations, *N* users and *M* items, the average number of ratings for each user is T/N, so for every two users, the complexity of computing their similarity is $O(T/N)$, and the complexity of computing similarity matrix *D* is $O(N * N * (T/N)) = O(NT)$. Similarly, the complexity of computing similarity matrix *S* is $O(MT)$. The second phase is similar to PMF which scales linearly with the observations. Due to the sparsity of matrices *R*, *D* and *S*, the computational complexity of evaluating the object function *E* is $O(\rho_R + \rho_D + \rho_S)$, and the computational complexities for gradients $\frac{\partial E}{\partial U}$ and $\frac{\partial E}{\partial V}$ are $O(\rho_R + \rho_D)$ and $O(\rho_R + \rho_S)$ respectively, where ρ_R, ρ_D and ρ_S are the numbers of nonzero entries in matrices *R*, *D* and *S*, respectively. Therefore, the total computational complexity in one iteration is $O(\rho_R + \rho_D + \rho_S)$, which indicates that the computational time of our method is linear with respect to the number of observations. This complexity analysis demonstrates that our proposed approach can be applied efficiently in very large datasets.

4 Experimental Evaluation

In this section, we firstly describe the experimental dataset, and then the effectiveness comparison with other state-of-the-art approaches has been showed. After that, we analyze the influence of parameters on IU-PMF and further explore its ability of solving sparsity problem. Finally we study the effect of similarity matrices on IU-PMF.

4.1 Experimental Datasets

We use three real-world datasets in our experiment. The first dataset is Movielens-1M released in February 2013 by *Movie Lens*, which consists 1,000,209 ratings from 6,040 anonymous users on 3,952 movie titles. The other two datasets is Book and Music rating datasets crawled from *DouBan* website, and users and items with less ratings (only three ratings) which make no sense in statistics are deleted, finally we obtain 1,030,701 valid book ratings from 4,705 users on 3,876 book names, and 1,173,540 valid music ratings from 7,924 users on 4,759 music titles. The description of the three datasets are shown in Table 1.

Table 1. The description of the experimental datasets

Dataset	User	Item	Sparsity
MovieLens-1M	6,040	3,952	95.8098%
Book	4,705	3,876	94.3482%
Music	7,924	4,759	96.8880%

4.2 Effectiveness Comparison

In order to assess the performance of IU-PMF, we compare the following models. Among them, only NHPMF needs extra tagging data, to ensure fairness, we use the rating data instead of tagging data to select neighbors in NHPMF. If the similarity function is not specified, PCC is default.

1. Item-KNN: this is the regular K nearest neighbor algorithm based on item similarity.
2. User-KNN: this is the regular K nearest neighbor algorithm based on user similarity.
3. PMF: regular probabilistic matrix factorization model which is popular and widely used recently.
4. NHPMF: this is a neighborhood-aware PMF model needing tagging data.
5. SBMF: A novel similarity fusion model based on Matrix Factorization.
6. IU-PMF (CS): our proposed model using cosine similarity.
7. IU-PMF (PCC): our proposed model using PCC to compute similarity.

In the comparison experiment, we spit the datasets into two parts. 90% is for training and the left 10% is for testing, and we use five-fold cross validation on the training set to select optimal parameters. For Item-KNN and User-KNN, we select the optimal neighbor size from {5, 10, 15, 20, 25,..., 100}. We use batch gradient descent to train the MF based methods, in which the learn ratio we set is 0.001 and the regularization parameters are selected from {0.0005, 0.01, 0.05, 0.1, 0.2, 0.4, 0.8, 1.2}. We employ RMSE for assessing the quality of the recommendation when $L = 10$ and $L = 20$, and Table 2 displays the comparison results.

Table 2. The effectiveness comparison results

Models	MovieLens-1M		Book		Music	
	10	20	10	20	10	20
Item-KNN	0.9317		0.9297		0.9236	
User-KNN	0.9498		0.9468		0.9425	
PMF	0.8819	0.8948	0.8576	0.8621	0.8477	0.8524
NHPMF	0.8673	0.8794	0.8341	0.8415	0.8297	0.8376
SBMF	0.8667	0.8787	0.8337	0.8407	0.8242	0.8354
IU-PMF (CS)	0.8559	**0.8693**	0.8224	0.8309	0.8147	0.8246
IU-PMF (PCC)	**0.8548**	0.8697	**0.8219**	**0.8306**	**0.8133**	**0.8245**

From Table 2, we can observe that Item-KNN outperforms User-KNN, and the performance of MF based approaches when $L = 10$ is better than when $L = 20$ on the three datasets. We also discover that MF based models performs much better than neighborhood-aware methods in terms of RMSE, which further proves the effectiveness of MF assumption. Table 2 also tells us that NHPMF which combines the advantages of neighborhood-aware methods and PMF model, reduces the average RMSE over PMF by 0.0187 when $L = 10$ and 0.0169 when $L = 20$, which demonstrates that it is effective to incorporate similarity information in PMF model. However, we can find that SBMF outperforms NHPMF in each case, which indicates the effectiveness of integrating local preference information in MF. As for our IU-PMF model, we can find that IU-PMF using PCC obviously reduces RMSE than IU-PMF using cosine similarity in many case. As a conclusion, PCC is more suitable for IU-PMF in our experiments. Additionally, we observe that IU-PMF is able to outperform other state-of-the-art methods obviously. Therefore, we can conclude that the similarity relationship hidden in User-Item ratings has an important influence on the recommendation results, and IU-PMF which concisely maps similarity relationship to latent feature space is more effective than any other baseline models on the three datasets.

4.3 Impacts of Parameters λ_U and λ_V

In IU-PMF model, parameters λ_U and λ_V play an important role in countering over-fitting problem. In this subsection, we will explore the impacts of parameters λ_U and λ_V. To simplify the complexity, in the experiment, we set $\lambda_U = \lambda_V = \lambda$, which is enumerated from $\{0.0005, 0.01, 0.05, 0.1, 0.2, 0.4, 0.8, 1.2\}$, and we only probe the performance in the optimal circumstances (when $L = 10$ meanwhile PCC is used according to the experimental results in the last subsection), additionally, the other experimental conditions remain unchanged.

Figure 2 show the impacts of λ_U and λ_V on RMSE. We observe that the values of λ_U and λ_V impact the recommendation results significantly. When λ increases with initialization of 0.0005, RMSE gradually decreases (the lower the better). However when they reach a certain threshold, RMSE starts to increase. From Fig. 2 we can also see that IU-PMF's ability of countering under-fitting is superior to its ability of countering over-fitting (when λ exceed the threshold, the model's performance goes bad relatively slowly), which may because that the IU-PMF model's incorporating similarity into rating data improves its learning ability.

4.4 The Effect of Similarity Matrices *D* and *S*

The main advantage of our IU-PMF model is that it incorporates the similarity information abstracted from User-Item ratings in PMF, which helps the model grasp the hidden information of User-Item ratings. From the complexity analysis (Subsect. 3.4), we know that the computation of Item and User similarity matrices is expensive. In order to probe the scalability of IU-PMF, we conduct the experiment to explore the effect that different proportion of the training data applied in similarity matrices computation phase has on IU-PMF. In the experiment, we select the first 60%, 65%,

70%, 75%, 80%, 85%, 90%, 95% and 100% of the training data in chronological order for the calculation of the similarity matrices (we use chronological order in this place because we want verify that when a handful of new data arrives, the similarity matrices computed using historical data do not need to be computed again), and then apply the full training set to train IU-PMF model, finally evaluate the RMSE performance on the testing set. Additionally, the other experimental conditions are same as the experiment in Subsect. 4.3.

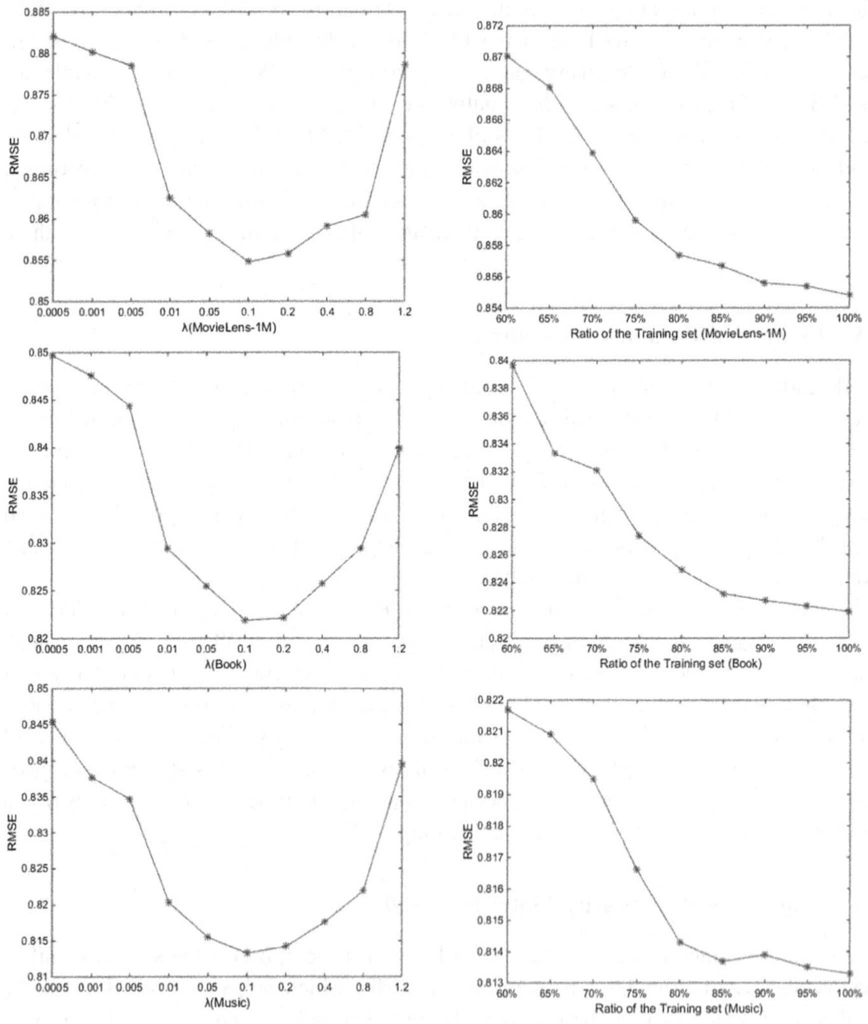

Fig. 2. Impacts of parameters λ_U and λ_V

Fig. 3. The effect of similarity matrices on IU-PMF

From Fig. 3, we can observe that the similarity matrices have a great influence on recommendation results (On average, the more training samples are involved in the calculation of the similarity matrices, the lower the corresponding RMSE is). Additionally, Fig. 3 shows that when there is 80% or above of the training set involved in the similarity matrices computation phase, IU-PMF model is able to receive good effects. We can conclude that similarity matrices don't need to be computed frequently, and so the efficiency of the IU-PMF model is determined by the training time of the fused PMF model, which scales linearly with the number of observations.

5 Conclusion and Future Work

In this paper, based on the intuition that item similarity and user similarity can affect the users' behaviors on the items, we present a novel and concise recommender framework incorporating item similarity and user similarity abstracted from observed user-item ratings into PMF model. The experimental results show that our approach outperforms the state-of-the-art baseline models, and the complexity analysis indicates it is scalable to large datasets.

One of the core part of the IU-PMF model is user (item) similarity computation, which has a great influence on recommendation results. In this paper, we roughly compare PCC with cosine similarity in terms of RMSE, and finally select PCC to compute similarity matrices. Although the proposed similarity computation method achieves good results, we believe it is worthy of further study. Specifically, we could use a kernel function, such as Gaussian Kernel or a Polynomial Kernel, which maps the relations of two vectors into a nonlinear space, and thus would further enhance the nonlinear learning ability of IU-PMF. Additionally, in the form, our model could also be used with similarities computed from content-based features, and so we will conduct further research on content-based features to use our model for content-based recommendation.

References

1. Ricci, F., Rokach, L., Shapira, B.: Recommender Systems Handbook. Springer, New York (2011). doi:10.1007/978-0-387-85820-3
2. Ma, H., King, I., Lyu, M.R.: Effective missing data prediction for collaborative filtering. In: Proceedings of the 30th Annual International ACM SIGIR Conference on Research and Development in Information Retrieval, pp. 39–46. ACM, New York (2007)
3. Breese, J.S., Heckerman, D., Kadie, C.: Empirical analysis of predictive algorithms for collaborative filtering. In: Proceedings of the 14th Conference on Uncertainty in Artificial Intelligence, pp. 43–52. Morgan Kaufmann Publishers Inc., San Francisco (1998)
4. Herlocker, J.L., Konstan, J.A., Borchers, A.: An algorithmic framework for performing collaborative filtering. In: Proceedings of the 22nd Annual International ACM SIGIR Conference on Research and Development in Information Retrieval, pp. 230–237. ACM, New York (1999)
5. Koohi, H., Kiani, K.: User based collaborative filtering using fuzzy C-means. Measurement **91**, 134–139 (2016)

6. Deshpande, M., Karypis, G.: Item-based top-N recommendation algorithms. ACM Trans. Inf. Syst. **22**, 143–177 (2004)
7. Linden, G., Smith, B., York, J.: Amazon.com recommendations: item-to-item collaborative filtering. IEEE Internet Comput. **7**, 76–80 (2003)
8. Mnih, A., Salakhutdinov, R.: Probabilistic matrix factorization. In: 20th Annual Conference on Neural Information Processing Systems, pp. 1–8, Sierra Nevada (2011)
9. Ma, H., Yang, H., Lyu, M.R.: SoRec: social recommendation using probabilistic matrix factorization. In: ACM Conference on Information and Knowledge Management, pp. 931–940. ACM, Napa Valley (2008)
10. Ma, H., King, I., Lyu, M.R.: Learning to recommend with social trust ensemble. In: International ACM SIGIR Conference on Research and Development in Information Retrieval, pp. 203–210. ACM, Boston (2009)
11. Wu, L., Chen, E., Liu, Q.: Leveraging tagging for neighborhood-aware probabilistic matrix factorization. In: ACM International Conference on Information and Knowledge Management, pp. 1854–1858. ACM, New York (2012)
12. Jamali, M., Ester, M.: TrustWalker: a random walk model for combining trust-based and item-based recommendation. In: ACM SIGKDD International Conference on Knowledge Discovery and Data Mining, pp. 397–406. ACM, New York (2009)
13. Liu, Q., Chen, E., Xiong, H.: Enhancing collaborative filtering by user interest expansion via personalized ranking. IEEE Trans. Syst. Man Cybern. **42**, 218–233 (2011)
14. Lei, G., Jun, M.A., Chen, Z.M.: Incorporating item relations for social recommendation. Chin. J. Comput. **37**, 219–228 (2014)
15. Tan, F., Li, L., Zhang, Z., Guo, Y.: A multi-attribute probabilistic matrix factorization model for personalized recommendation. In: Dong, X.L., Yu, X., Li, J., Sun, Y. (eds.) WAIM 2015. LNCS, vol. 9098, pp. 535–539. Springer, Cham (2015). doi:10.1007/978-3-319-21042-1_57
16. Wu, L., Chen, E., Liu, Q.: Leveraging tagging for neighborhood-aware probabilistic matrix factorization. In: ACM International Conference on Information and Knowledge Management. pp. 1854–1858. ACM, Hawaii (2012)
17. Wang, X., Xu, C.: SBMF: similarity-based matrix factorization for collaborative recommendation. In: IEEE 26th International Conference on Tools with Artificial Intelligence. pp. 379–383. IEEE, Limassol (2014)
18. Sun, G.F., Wu, L., Liu, Q.: Recommendations based on collaborative filtering by exploiting sequential behaviors. J. Softw. **24**, 2721–2733 (2014)
19. Alewiwi, M., Orencik, C., Sava, E.: Efficient top-k similarity document search utilizing distributed file systems and cosine similarity. Cluster Comput. **19**, 109–126 (2016)
20. Ahlgren, P., Jarneving, B., Rousseau, R.: Requirements for a cocitation similarity measure, with special reference to Pearson's correlation coefficient. J. Am. Soc. Inf. Sci. Technol. **54**, 550–560 (2003)
21. Fornberg, B., Larsson, E., Flyer, N.: Stable computations with Gaussian radial basis functions. SIAM J. Sci. Comput. **33**, 869–892 (2011)

New Delay-Dependent Stability for Neutral Systems with Its Application to Partial Circuit Model

Tao Li[1(✉)], Ting Wang[2], Jin Deng[1], and Li Zhang[1]

[1] School of Automation Engineering, Nanjing University of Aeronautics and Astronautics, Nanjing 211106, People's Republic of China
autolitao@nuaa.edu.cn

[2] School of Information Science and Technology, Nanjing Forestry University, Nanjing 210042, People's Republic of China

Abstract. The issue on robust stability for a class of uncertain linear neutral systems with time-varying delays is studied. Together with multiple integral functional technique and using some novel integral inequalities, the much tighter estimation on derivative of Lyapunov functional is presented and one stability criterion is presented in terms of linear matrix inequalities (LMIs), in which those previously ignored information can be reconsidered. Especially, the multiple Lyapunov functional terms include the interconnection between neutral delay and state one. Finally, some comparing results with application to partial element circuit model can show the benefits of our conditions.

Keywords: Neutral systems · Time-varying delay · Robust stability · Partial element equivalent circuit · LMI approach

1 Introduction

Owing to great potential applications, the stability issue on neutral systems has received a considerable amount of attention [1–27]. In [1–3], by choosing some special Lyapunov-Krasovskii (L-K) functionals and using LMI approach, the asymptotical stability for a class of neutral systems has been studied together with constant time-delay and in [4], a necessary and sufficient condition on exponential stability has been derived, in which time-varying delay was involved. In many practical cases, owing to that accurate mathematical model cannot be easily obtained, these systems in present works always assume that there exist the uncertainties on the parameters. On one hand, in [5–9,14–17], some LMI criteria on robust stability for uncertain neutral systems have been deeply established. On the other hand, in [10–17], through treating the nonlinearity as system's disturbance, some delay-dependent criteria have been presented in terms of LMIs. Meanwhile, some researchers have studied the robust stability for neutral systems with distributed delays [7–9,12–16]. Furthermore, by using

X. Sun et al. (Eds.): ICCCS 2017, Part II, LNCS 10603, pp. 759–771, 2017.
https://doi.org/10.1007/978-3-319-68542-7_66

various delay-partitioning ideas, the works [17–19] have established some less conservative results and the conservatism can be greatly general form of modeling partial e reduced with thinning delay intervals. There also exist some works considering the effect of other factors, such as stochastic disturbance [20–22], leakage delays with impulse [23,24], neutral proportional delays [25], H_∞ performance with Markov jumping [26], and application to partial element equivalent circuit [11,27]. It is worth pointing out that, since triple integral Lyapunov approach was put forward, it has received considerable attention and improvements in [28,29]. Yet, there always exist both neutral delay and state one in neutral system simultaneously. However, most present works respectively employed each time-delay to derive the relevant results. In practical cases, the neutral delay is always different from the state one. Yet, few existent works have utilized their interconnection during the studying, which would unavoidably reduce the conservatism. Though the works [3,9] has given some preliminary discussions on this point, there still exists much room waiting for the further research. Especially, the Lyapunov functional terms in [3,9] seem to be simple and they cannot efficiently represent and employ the interconnected relationship between the neutral delay and state one. Overall, some more effective techniques need to be put forward.

Motivated by the discussion above, in this work, the robust stability for a class of time-delay neutral systems will be deeply studied. Together with the interconnection between two kinds of time-varying delays, an improved Lyapunov-Krasovskii functional including multiple Lyapunov terms will be constructed and some novel integral inequalities will be utilized to estimate the much tighter upper bound of L-K functional's derivative. The derived criteria are presented in terms of LMIs and can be easily tested. Finally, one numerical example will be presented to illustrate the derived results.

Notations: The term L-K functional is the abbreviation of Lyapunov-Krasovskii functional; $\mathbf{sym}\{X\} = X + X^T$; and $\begin{bmatrix} X & Y \\ Y^T & Z \end{bmatrix} = \begin{bmatrix} X & Y \\ * & Z \end{bmatrix}$.

2 Problem Descriptions

In this work, we consider uncertain time-delayed neutral systems as

$$\dot{x}(t) - [C + \Delta C(t)]\dot{x}(t - \tau_1(t)) = [A + \Delta A(t)]x(t) + [B + \Delta B(t)]x(t - \tau_2(t)), \quad (1)$$

where $x(t) \in \mathbf{R}^n$ is the state of system (1) and A, B, C are constant matrices of appropriate dimensions with $\| C + \Delta C(t) \| < 1$.

The following assumptions on the system (1) are made throughout this paper.

H1. The functions $\tau_i(t)$ $(i = 1, 2)$ denote the time-varying delays satisfying

$$0 \le \tau_i(t) \le \tau_i, \quad \upsilon_i \le \dot{\tau}_i(t) \le \mu_i \quad (i = 1, 2) \quad (2)$$

Denote $\bar{\tau}_i(t) = \tau_i - \tau_i(t)$, $\bar{\mu}_i = \mu_i - \upsilon_i, \tau_{21} = \tau_2 - \tau_1$, $\Delta_{21} = \tau_2^2 - \tau_1^2, \theta_{21} = \tau_2^3 - \tau_1^3$.

H2. The uncertainties $\Delta A(t), \Delta B(t), \Delta C(t)$ satisfy the following conditions

$$\left[\Delta A(t)\ \Delta B(t)\ \Delta C(t)\right] = F\Delta(t)\left[E_1\ E_2\ E_3\right];\ \Delta(t) = \Lambda(t)[I - J\Lambda(t)]^{-1}, \quad (3)$$

in which F, J, E_i $(i = 1, 2, 3)$ are known constant matrices of appropriate dimensions, $\Lambda(t)$ satisfies $\Lambda^T(t)\Lambda(t) \le I$, and $I - J^TJ > 0$.

3 Delay-Dependent Stability Criteria

In order for the simplification, some denotations will be presented as

$$\varphi_i(t) = \frac{1}{\tau_i(t)}\int_{t-\tau_i(t)}^{t} x(s)ds,\quad \nu_i(t) = \frac{2}{\tau_i^2(t)}\int_{t-\tau_i(t)}^{t}\int_{t-\tau_i(t)}^{s} x(u)duds\ (i = 1, 2); \quad (4)$$

$$\varrho_i(t) = \frac{1}{\bar{\tau}_i(t)}\int_{t-\tau_i}^{t-\tau_i(t)} x(s)ds,\quad \omega_i(t) = \frac{2}{\bar{\tau}_i^2(t)}\int_{t-\tau_i}^{t-\tau_i(t)}\int_{t-\tau_i}^{s} x(u)duds\ (i = 1, 2); \quad (5)$$

$$\alpha(t) = \frac{1}{\tau_{21}}\int_{t-\tau_2}^{t-\tau_1} x(s)ds,\quad \beta(t) = \frac{2}{\tau_{21}^2}\int_{t-\tau_2}^{t-\tau_1}\int_{t-\tau_2}^{s} x(u)duds; \quad (6)$$

$$\gamma(t) = \frac{2}{\delta_{21}}\int_{-\tau_2}^{-\tau_1}\int_{t+s}^{t} x(u)duds;\quad e_i^T = \left[0_{n\times(i-1)n}\ I_n\ 0_{n\times(19-i)n}\right]\ (1 \le i \le 19); \quad (7)$$

$$\Lambda = \left[e_1\quad e_4\quad 0_{19n\cdot 2n}\quad \tau_{21}e_{17}\right];\quad \$ = \left[e_{14}\quad e_{16}\quad e_1 - e_4\quad e_1 - e_5\quad e_4 - e_5\right]; \quad (8)$$

$$\Phi_i = \left[0_{19n\cdot(i+1)n}\quad e_{5+i}\quad 0_{19n\cdot(3-i)n}\right]\quad (i = 1, 2); \quad (9)$$

$$\Psi_j = \left[0_{19n\cdot(j+1)n}\quad e_{7+j}\quad 0_{19n\cdot(3-j)n}\right]\quad (j = 1, 2); \quad (10)$$

$$\Pi_{i1} = e_1 - e_{i+1},\quad \Pi_{i3} = e_1 + e_{i+1} - 2e_{2(i+2)}\ (i = 1, 2); \quad (11)$$

$$\Pi_{i5} = e_1 - e_{i+1} - 6e_{2(i+2)} + 6e_{2(i+4)}\ (i = 1, 2); \quad (12)$$

$$\Pi_{j2} = e_{j+1} - e_{j+3},\ \Pi_{j3} = e_{j+1} + e_{j+3} - 2e_{2(j+2)+1}\quad (j = 1, 2); \quad (13)$$

$$\Pi_{j5} = e_{j+1} - e_{j+3} - 6e_{2(j+2)+1} + 6e_{2(j+4)+1}\quad (j = 1, 2); \quad (14)$$

$$\Pi_7 = e_4 - e_5,\ \Pi_8 = e_4 + e_5 - 2e_{17},\ \Pi_9 = e_4 - e_5 - 6e_{17} + 6e_{18}; \quad (15)$$

$$\begin{aligned}\eta^T(t) = \big[&x^T(t)\quad x^T(t-\tau_1(t))\quad x^T(t-\tau_2(t))\quad x^T(t-\tau_1)\quad x^T(t-\tau_2)\quad \varphi_1^T(t)\quad \varphi_2^T(t)\\ &\varrho_1^T(t)\quad \varrho_2^T(t)\quad \nu_1^T(t)\quad \nu_2^T(t)\quad \omega_1^T(t)\quad \omega_2^T(t)\quad \dot{x}^T(t)\quad \dot{x}^T(t-\tau_1(t))\quad \dot{x}^T(t-\tau_1)\\ &\alpha^T(t)\quad \beta^T(t)\quad \gamma^T(t)\big]. \end{aligned} \quad (16)$$

In what follows, some lemmas will be given for the proof procedure.

Lemma 1 [28]**.** Let $x(\cdot)$ be a differential function: $[a, b] \to \mathbf{R}^n$. For the positive matrices $M \in \mathbf{R}^{n\times n}$, and $N_1, N_2, N_3 \in \mathbf{R}^{4n\times n}$, the following inequality holds:

$$-\int_a^b \dot{\varphi}^T(s)M\dot{\varphi}(s)ds \le \chi^T\Omega\chi,$$

where $\Omega = \mathbf{sym}\{N_1\Theta_1 + N_2\Theta_2 + N_3\Theta_3\} + (b-a)\left(N_1M^{-1}N_1^T + \frac{1}{3}N_2M^{-1}N_2^T + \frac{1}{5}N_3M^{-1}N_3^T\right)$, $e_i = \left[0_{n\times(i-1)n}\quad I_n\quad 0_{n\times(4-i)n}\right]$ $(i = 1, 2, 3, 4)$, and

$$\Theta_1 = e_1 - e_2;\quad \Theta_2 = e_1 + e_2 - e_3;\quad \Theta_3 = e_1 - e_2 - 6e_3 + 6e_4;$$

$$\chi = \left[\varphi^T(b)\quad \varphi^T(a)\quad \frac{1}{b-a}\int_a^b \varphi^T(s)ds\quad \frac{2}{(b-a)^2}\int_a^b\int_a^s \varphi^T(u)duds\right]^T.$$

Lemma 2 [29]. For an any constant matrix $M > 0$, the following inequalities hold for all continuously differentiable function φ in $[a, b] \rightarrow \mathbf{R}^n$:

$$-(b-a)\int_a^b \varphi^T(s)M\varphi(s)ds \leq -\Big(\int_a^b \varphi(s)ds\Big)^T M\Big(\int_a^b \varphi(s)ds\Big) - 3\Theta^T M\Theta,$$

$$-\frac{b^2-a^2}{2}\int_a^b\int_{t+\theta}^t \varphi^T(s)M\varphi(s)dsd\theta \leq -\Big(\int_a^b\int_{t+\theta}^t \varphi(s)dsd\theta\Big)^T M\Big(\int_a^b\int_{t+\theta}^t \varphi(s)dsd\theta\Big),$$

$$-\frac{b^3-a^3}{6}\int_{-b}^{-a}\int_{\varrho}^{0}\int_{t+\theta}^t \varphi^T(s)M\varphi(s)dsd\theta d\varrho$$
$$\leq -\Big(\int_{-b}^{-a}\int_{\varrho}^{0}\int_{t+\theta}^t \varphi(s)dsd\theta d\varrho\Big)^T M\Big(\int_{-b}^{-a}\int_{\varrho}^{0}\int_{t+\theta}^t \varphi(s)dsd\theta d\varrho\Big),$$

where $\Theta = \int_a^b \varphi(s)ds - \frac{2}{b-a}\int_a^b\int_a^s \varphi(u)duds$.

Lemma 3 [29]. For an any constant matrix $M > 0$, the following inequality holds for all continuously differentiable function φ in $[a, b] \rightarrow \mathbf{R}^n$:

$$-\frac{(b-a)^2}{2}\int_a^b\int_a^s \varphi^T(u)M\varphi(u)duds \leq -\Big(\int_a^b\int_a^s \varphi(u)duds\Big)^T M\Big(\int_a^b\int_a^s \varphi(u)duds\Big)$$
$$-2\Theta^T M\Theta,$$

where $\Theta = \int_a^b\int_a^s \varphi(u)duds - \frac{3}{b-a}\int_a^b\int_a^s\int_a^u \varphi(v)dvduds$.

Lemma 4 [30]. Suppose that $\Omega, \Xi_{ij}, \Xi_{mn}$ $(i, m = 1, 2, 3, 4; j, n = 1, 2)$ are the constant matrices, $\alpha \in [0, 1], \beta \in [0, 1], \gamma \in [0, 1]$, and $\delta \in [0, 1]$, then

$$\Omega + \big[\alpha\Xi_{11} + (1-\alpha)\Xi_{12}\big] + \big[\beta\Xi_{21} + (1-\beta)\Xi_{22}\big] + \big[\gamma\Xi_{31} + (1-\gamma)\Xi_{32}\big]$$
$$+\big[\delta\Xi_{41} + (1-\delta)\Xi_{42}\big] < 0$$

holds, if and only if the following inequalities hold simultaneously,

$$\Omega + \Xi_{ij} + \Xi_{mn} < 0 \quad (i, m = 1, 2, 3, 4; j, n = 1, 2).$$

Lemma 5 [31]. Let $I - G^TG > 0$ define the set $\Upsilon = \{\Delta(t) = \Sigma(t)[I - G\Sigma(t)]^{-1}, \Sigma^T(t)\Sigma(t) \leq I\}$, for given appropriate matrices H, J and R and symmetrical one H, then $H + J\Delta(t)R + R^T\Delta^T(t)J^T < 0$, iff there exists $\rho > 0$ such that

$$H + \begin{bmatrix} \rho^{-1}R \\ \rho J^T \end{bmatrix}^T \begin{bmatrix} I & -G \\ -G^T & I \end{bmatrix}^{-1} \begin{bmatrix} \rho^{-1}R \\ \rho J^T \end{bmatrix} < 0.$$

Now we give one novel stability criterion for nominal system of (1).

Theorem 1. For any given scalars $\tau_i \geq 0, \mu_i, \upsilon_i, \bar{\mu}_i$ $(i = 1, 2), \tau_{21}, \delta_{21}, \theta_{21}$ in **H1**, the nominal system of (1) is asymptotically stable, if there exist $5n \times 5n$ matrix $P > 0, n \times n$ matrices $Q_i > 0$ $(i = 1, \cdots, 6), N_i$ $(i = 1, 2, 3, 4), X_i > 0,$

$Y_i > 0$ $(i = 1, 2), U > 0, V > 0, W > 0, X > 0, Y > 0$, and $19n \times n$ matrices H_{ij} $(i = 1, 2; j = 1, \cdots, 6), H_l$ $(l = 7, 8, 9)$ such that the LMIs in (17) hold

$$\begin{bmatrix} \mathbf{\Omega} + \Xi(i,j,m,n) & \mathbf{\Gamma} & \mathbf{\Gamma}_{ij} \\ * & -\mathbf{\Delta} & 0 \\ * & * & -\mathbf{\Delta}_i \end{bmatrix} < 0 \quad \forall\, i, j, m = 1, 2; n = 5, 6, \tag{17}$$

where $\mathbf{\Gamma} = \tau_{21}\begin{bmatrix} H_7 & H_8 & H_9 \end{bmatrix}, \mathbf{\Gamma}_{ij} = \begin{bmatrix} H_{ij} & H_{i(j+2)} & H_{i(j+4)} \end{bmatrix}, \mathbf{\Delta} = \text{diag}\big(V,\ 3V,\ 5V\big), \mathbf{\Delta}_i = \text{diag}\big(X_i,\ 3X_i,\ 5X_i\big)$, and

$$\begin{aligned} \Xi(i,j,m,n) &= \mathbf{sym}\big[\varLambda P\$^T + \sum_{i=1}^{2}\sum_{l=1}^{6} H_{il}\varPi_{il} + \tau_{21}\sum_{l=7}^{9} N_l\varPi_l\big] + \tau_i\mathbf{\Upsilon}_i + \tau_j\mathbf{\Theta}_j \\ &\quad + \bar{\mu}_1\big[e_2^T Q_m e_2 + e_{15}^T Q_{m+2} e_{15}\big] + \bar{\mu}_2 e_3^T Q_n e_3, \\ \mathbf{\Upsilon}_i &= \mathbf{sym}\{\varPhi_i P\$^T\} - e_{i+5}^T Y_i e_{i+5} - 3(e_{i+5} - e_{i+9})^T Y_i (e_{i+5} - e_{i+9}) \\ &\quad - (e_{i+1} - e_{i+3})^T \frac{Z_i}{2\tau_i}(e_{i+1} - e_{i+3}); \\ \mathbf{\Theta}_j &= \mathbf{sym}\{\varPsi_j P\$^T\} - e_{j+7}^T Y_j e_{j+7} - 3(e_{j+7} - e_{j+11})^T Y_j (e_{j+7} - e_{j+11}) \end{aligned}$$

with e_i $(i = 1, 2, \cdots, 19)$ defined in (7) and $\mathbf{\Omega} = \big[\mathbf{\Omega}_{ij}\big]_{19n \times 19n}$ with its elements listed as

$$\begin{aligned}
&\mathbf{\Omega_{11}} = \tau_1 Y_1 - 0.5Z_1 + \tau_2 Y_2 - 0.5Z_2 + Q_1 + Q_5 + \tau_{21}^2 W + N_1^T A + A^T N_1 - \tau_{21}^2 X \\
&\qquad -0.25\delta_{21}^2 Y, \\
&\mathbf{\Omega_{22}} = (\upsilon_1 - 1)Q_1 + (1 - \mu_1)Q_2 - 1.5Z_1, \\
&\mathbf{\Omega_{33}} = (\upsilon_2 - 1)Q_5 + (1 - \mu_2)Q_6 - 1.5Z_2 + N_4^T B + B^T N_4,\ \mathbf{\Omega_{44}} = \tau_{21}U - Q_2 - Z_1, \\
&\mathbf{\Omega_{55}} = \tau_{21}U - Q_6 - Z_2, \quad \mathbf{\Omega_{66}} = \mathbf{\Omega_{88}} = -3Z_1, \quad \mathbf{\Omega_{77}} = \mathbf{\Omega_{99}} = -3Z_2, \\
&\mathbf{\Omega_{10,10}} = \mathbf{\Omega_{12,12}} = -4.5Z_1, \quad \mathbf{\Omega_{11,11}} = \mathbf{\Omega_{13,13}} = -4.5Z_2, \\
&\mathbf{\Omega_{14,14}} = \tau_1 X_1 + \tau_2 X_2 + 0.25(\tau_1^2 Z_1 + \tau_2^2 Z_2 + \delta_{21}^2 X) + Q_3 + \tau_{21}^2 V - N_2 - N_2^T + \frac{\theta_{21}^2}{36} Y, \\
&\mathbf{\Omega_{15,15}} = N_3^T C + C^T N_3 + (\upsilon_1 - 1)Q_3 + (1 - \mu_1)Q_4, \quad \mathbf{\Omega_{16,16}} = -Q_4, \\
&\mathbf{\Omega_{17,17}} = -\tau_{21}^2(4W + X), \mathbf{\Omega_{18,18}} = -3\tau_{21}^2 W, \\
&\mathbf{\Omega_{19,19}} = -0.25\delta_{21}^2 Y; \quad \mathbf{\Omega_{13}} = N_1^T B + A^T N_4, \quad \mathbf{\Omega_{16}} = \mathbf{\Omega_{28}} = -Z_1, \\
&\mathbf{\Omega_{17}} = \mathbf{\Omega_{39}} = -Z_2, \quad \mathbf{\Omega_{1,10}} = \mathbf{\Omega_{2,12}} = 1.5Z_1, \quad \mathbf{\Omega_{1,11}} = \mathbf{\Omega_{3,13}} = 1.5Z_2, \\
&\mathbf{\Omega_{1,14}} = A^T N_2 - N_1^T, \quad \mathbf{\Omega_{1,15}} = N_1^T C + A^T N_3, \ \mathbf{\Omega_{1,17}} = \tau_{21}^2 X, \\
&\mathbf{\Omega_{1,19}} = 0.25\delta_{21}^2 Y, \mathbf{\Omega_{26}} = \mathbf{\Omega_{48}} = Z_1, \quad \mathbf{\Omega_{37}} = \mathbf{\Omega_{59}} = Z_2, \\
&\mathbf{\Omega_{3,14}} = B^T N_2 - N_4^T, \quad \mathbf{\Omega_{3,15}} = B^T N_3 + N_4^T C, \quad \mathbf{\Omega_{6,10}} = \mathbf{\Omega_{8,12}} = 3Z_1, \\
&\mathbf{\Omega_{7,11}} = \mathbf{\Omega_{9,13}} = 3Z_2, \quad \mathbf{\Omega_{14,15}} = N_2^T C - N_3, \quad \mathbf{\Omega_{17,18}} = 3\tau_{21}^2 W.
\end{aligned}$$

Proof. Now setting $\zeta^T(t) = \big[x^T(t)\ x^T(t - \tau_1)\ \int_{t-\tau_1}^{t} x^T(s)ds\ \int_{t-\tau_2}^{t} x^T(s)ds\ \int_{t-\tau_2}^{t-\tau_1} x^T(s)ds\big]$ and using the assumption **H1**, we can construct the L-K functional:

$$V(x_t) = V_1(x_t) + V_2(x_t) + V_3(x_t) + V_4(x_t), \tag{18}$$

where

$$\begin{aligned}
V_1(x_t) &= \zeta^T(t)P\zeta(t),\\
V_2(x_t) &= \int_{t-\tau_1(t)}^{t} \left[x^T(s)Q_1x(s) + \dot{x}^T(s)Q_3\dot{x}(s)\right]ds + \int_{t-\tau_1}^{t-\tau_1(t)} \left[x^T(s)Q_2x(s)\right.\\
&\quad \left.+ \dot{x}^T(s)Q_4\dot{x}(s)\right]ds + \int_{t-\tau_2(t)}^{t} x^T(s)Q_5x(s)ds + \int_{t-\tau_2}^{t-\tau_2(t)} x^T(s)Q_6x(s)ds,\\
V_3(x_t) &= \sum_{i=1}^{2}\Big\{\int_{-\tau_i}^{0}\int_{t+s}^{t} \left[\dot{x}^T(\theta)X_i\dot{x}(\theta) + x^T(\theta)Y_ix(\theta)\right]d\theta ds\\
&\quad + \frac{1}{2}\int_{t-\tau_i}^{t}\int_{t-\tau_i}^{\varrho}\int_{t-\tau_i}^{\theta} \dot{x}^T(s)Z_i\dot{x}(s)dsd\theta d\varrho\Big\},\\
V_4(x_t) &= \tau_{21}\int_{t-\tau_2}^{t-\tau_1} x^T(s)Ux(s)ds + \tau_{21}\int_{-\tau_2}^{-\tau_1}\int_{t+s}^{t} \left[\dot{x}^T(\theta)V\dot{x}(\theta) + x^T(\theta)Wx(\theta)\right]d\theta ds\\
&\quad + \frac{\delta_{21}}{2}\int_{-\tau_2}^{-\tau_1}\int_{\varrho}^{0}\int_{t+\theta}^{t} \dot{x}^T(s)X\dot{x}(s)dsd\theta d\varrho\\
&\quad + \frac{\theta_{21}}{6}\int_{-\tau_2}^{-\tau_1}\int_{\mu}^{0}\int_{\varrho}^{0}\int_{t+\theta}^{t} \dot{x}^T(s)Y\dot{x}(s)dsd\theta d\varrho d\mu.
\end{aligned}$$

Firstly, we can easily check that for $i = 1, 2, \int_{t-\tau_i}^{t} x(s)ds = \tau_i(t)\varphi_i(t) + \bar{\tau}_i(t)\varrho_i(t)$. Then based on the denotations in (8)–(15), the derivative of $V_i(x_t)$ ($i = 1, 2, 3$) along the nominal system of (1) can be directly computed out as follows:

$$\dot{V}_1(x_t) = \eta^T(t)\mathbf{sym}\Big\{\varLambda P\$^T + \sum_{i=1}^{2}\tau_i(t)\varPhi_i P\$^T + \sum_{j=1}^{2}\bar{\tau}_j(t)\varPsi_j P\$^T\Big\}\eta(t); \tag{19}$$

$$\begin{aligned}
\dot{V}_2(x_t) &= \left[x^T(t)(Q_1 + Q_5)x(t) + \dot{x}^T(t)Q_3\dot{x}(t)\right] - \left[x^T(t-\tau_1)Q_2x(t-\tau_1)\right.\\
&\quad \left.+ \dot{x}^T(t-\tau_1)Q_4\dot{x}(t-\tau_1)\right] - [1-\dot{\tau}_1(t)]\Big[x^T(t-\tau_1(t))(Q_1 - Q_2)x(t-\tau_1(t))\\
&\quad + \dot{x}^T(t-\tau_1(t))(Q_3 - Q_4)\dot{x}(t-\tau_1(t))\Big] - [1-\dot{\tau}_2(t)]\\
&\quad \times x^T(t-\tau_2(t))(Q_5 - Q_6)x(t-\tau_2(t)) - x^T(t-\tau_2)Q_6x(t-\tau_2);
\end{aligned} \tag{20}$$

$$\begin{aligned}
\dot{V}_3(x_t) &= \sum_{l=1}^{2}\Big\{\tau_i\left[\dot{x}^T(t)X_i\dot{x}(t) + x^T(t)Y_ix(t)\right] + \frac{\tau_i^2}{4}\dot{x}^T(t)Z_i\dot{x}(t) - \int_{t-\tau_i}^{t} \dot{x}^T(\theta)X_i\dot{x}(\theta)d\theta\\
&\quad - \int_{t-\tau_i}^{t} x^T(\theta)Y_ix(\theta)d\theta - \frac{1}{2}\int_{t-\tau_i}^{t}\int_{t-\tau_i}^{\theta} \dot{x}^T(s)Z_i\dot{x}(s)dsd\theta\Big\}.
\end{aligned} \tag{21}$$

Now as for any $19n\times n$ matrices H_{ij} ($i = 1, 2; j = 1, \cdots, 6$), we use Lemmas 1–3 and denotations (4)–(16) to give some estimations on the integral terms in (21). Firstly, we can derive that

$$
\begin{aligned}
&-\int_{t-\tau_i}^{t} \dot{x}^T(\theta)X_i\dot{x}(\theta)d\theta = -\Big[\int_{t-\tau_i(t)}^{t} + \int_{t-\tau_i}^{t-\tau_i(t)}\Big]\dot{x}^T(\theta)X_i\dot{x}(\theta)d\theta \\
&\leq \eta^T(t)\Big[\mathbf{sym}\Big\{\sum_{l=1}^{6} H_{il}\Pi_{il}\Big\} + \tau_i(t)\big(H_{i1}X_i^{-1}H_{i1}^T + \frac{1}{3}H_{i3}X_i^{-1}H_{i3}^T + \frac{1}{5}H_{i5}X_i^{-1}H_{i5}^T\big) \\
&\quad + \bar{\tau}_i(t)\big(H_{i2}X_i^{-1}H_{i2}^T + \frac{1}{3}H_{i4}X_i^{-1}H_{i4}^T + \frac{1}{5}H_{i6}X_i^{-1}H_{i6}^T\big)\Big]\eta(t);
\end{aligned} \tag{22}
$$

$$
\begin{aligned}
&-\int_{t-\tau_i}^{t} x^T(\theta)Y_i x(\theta)d\theta = -\Big[\int_{t-\tau_i(t)}^{t} + \int_{t-\tau_i}^{t-\tau_i(t)}\Big]x^T(\theta)Y_i x(\theta)d\theta \\
&\leq -\tau_i(t)\varphi_i^T(t)Y_i\varphi_i(t) - 3\tau_i(t)\big[\varphi_i(t)-\nu_i(t)\big]^T Y_i\big[\varphi_i(t)-\nu_i(t)\big] \\
&\quad - \bar{\tau}_i(t)\varrho_i^T(t)Y_i\varrho_i(t) - 3\bar{\tau}_i(t)\big[\varrho_i(t)-\omega_i(t)\big]^T Y_i\big[\varrho_i(t)-\omega_i(t)\big];
\end{aligned} \tag{23}
$$

$$
\begin{aligned}
&-\frac{1}{2}\int_{t-\tau_i}^{t}\int_{t-\tau_i}^{\theta} \dot{x}^T(s)Z_i\dot{x}(s)dsd\theta \\
&\leq -\Big[x(t-\tau_i(t)) - x(t-\tau_i)\Big]^T\Big[\frac{\tau_i(t)Z_i}{2\tau_i}\Big]\Big[x(t-\tau_i(t)) - x(t-\tau_i)\Big] \\
&\quad -\Big[\varphi_i(t) - x(t-\tau_i(t))\Big]^T Z_i\Big[\varphi_i(t) - x(t-\tau_i(t))\Big] - \Big[\varrho_i(t) - x(t-\tau_i)\Big]^T Z_i \\
&\quad \times\Big[\varrho_i(t) - x(t-\tau_i)\Big] - \Big[\frac{x(t)}{2} + \varphi_i(t) - \frac{3}{2}\nu_i(t)\Big](2Z_i)\Big[\frac{x(t)}{2} + \varphi_i(t) - \frac{3}{2}\nu_i(t)\Big] \\
&\quad -\Big[\frac{1}{2}x(t-\tau_i(t)) + \varrho_i(t) - \frac{3}{2}\omega_i(t)\Big]^T(2Z_i)\Big[\frac{1}{2}x(t-\tau_i(t)) + \varrho_i(t) - \frac{3}{2}\omega_i(t)\Big].
\end{aligned} \tag{24}
$$

In what is the next, we can derive $\dot{V}_4(x_t)$ as follows:

$$
\begin{aligned}
\dot{V}_4(x_t) &= \tau_{21}\Big[x^T(t-\tau_1)Ux(t-\tau_1) - x^T(t-\tau_2)Ux(t-\tau_2)\Big] \\
&\quad + \tau_{21}^2\Big[\dot{x}^T(t)V\dot{x}(t) + x^T(t)Wx(t)\Big] + \dot{x}^T(t)\Big(\frac{\delta_{21}^2}{4}X + \frac{\theta_{21}^2}{36}Y\Big)\dot{x}(t) \\
&\quad - \tau_{21}\int_{t-\tau_2}^{t-\tau_1}\big[\dot{x}^T(\theta)V\dot{x}(\theta) + x^T(\theta)Wx(\theta)\big]d\theta \\
&\quad - \frac{\delta_{21}}{2}\int_{-\tau_2}^{-\tau_1}\int_{t+\theta}^{t}\dot{x}^T(s)X\dot{x}(s)dsd\theta - \frac{\theta_{21}}{6}\int_{-\tau_2}^{-\tau_1}\int_{\varrho}^{0}\int_{t+\theta}^{t}\dot{x}^T(s)Y\dot{x}(s)dsd\theta d\varrho,
\end{aligned} \tag{25}
$$

then based on Lemmas 1–2 and any $19n \times n$ matrices H_l ($l = 7, 8, 9$), we can estimate the integral terms in (25) as

$$
\begin{aligned}
-\tau_{21}\int_{t-\tau_2}^{t-\tau_1}\dot{x}^T(\theta)V\dot{x}(\theta)d\theta &\leq \eta^T(t)\Big[\mathbf{sym}\Big\{\tau_{21}\sum_{l=7}^{9}H_l\Pi_l\Big\} \\
&\quad + \tau_{21}^2\big(H_7V^{-1}H_7^T + \frac{1}{3}H_8V^{-1}H_8^T + \frac{1}{5}H_9V^{-1}H_9^T\big)\Big]\eta(t);
\end{aligned} \tag{26}
$$

$$
\begin{aligned}
&-\tau_{21}\int_{t-\tau_2}^{t-\tau_1} x^T(\theta)Wx(\theta)d\theta \\
&\qquad \leq -\tau_{21}^2\alpha^T(t)W\alpha(t) - 3\tau_{21}^2\big[\alpha(t)-\beta(t)\big]^T W\big[\alpha(t)-\beta(t)\big];
\end{aligned} \tag{27}
$$

$$
-\frac{\delta_{21}}{2}\int_{-\tau_2}^{-\tau_1}\int_{t+\theta}^{t}\dot{x}^T(s)X\dot{x}(s)dsd\theta \leq -\tau_{21}^2\Big[x(t)-\alpha(t)\Big]^T X\Big[x(t)-\alpha(t)\Big]; \tag{28}
$$

$$
-\frac{\theta_{21}}{6}\int_{-\tau_2}^{-\tau_1}\int_{\varrho}^{0}\int_{t+\theta}^{t}\dot{x}^T(s)Y\dot{x}(s)dsd\theta d\varrho \leq -\frac{\delta_{21}^2}{4}\Big[x(t)-\gamma(t)\Big]^T Y\Big[x(t)-\gamma(t)\Big]. \tag{29}
$$

For any $n \times n$ matrices N_i $(i = 1, 2, 3, 4)$, it follows that

$$\begin{aligned}0 = 2\big[x^T(t)N_1^T + \dot{x}^T(t)N_2^T + \dot{x}^T(t-\tau_1(t))N_3^T + x^T(t-\tau_2(t))N_4^T\big] \\ \times\big[-\dot{x}(t) + C\dot{x}(t-\tau_1(t)) + Ax(t) + Bx(t-\tau_2(t))\big]. \qquad (30)\end{aligned}$$

Now combining with the terms from (19) to (30), $\dot{V}(x_t)$ satisfies

$$\begin{aligned}\dot{V}(x_t) \le \eta^T(t)\Big\{&\mathbf{\Omega} + \mathbf{\Gamma}\mathbf{\Delta}^{-1}\mathbf{\Gamma}^T + \mathbf{sym}\Big[\Lambda P\$^T + \sum_{i=1}^{2}\sum_{l=1}^{6} H_{il}\Pi_{il} + \tau_{21}\sum_{l=7}^{9} N_l\Pi_l\Big] \\ &+ [\dot{\tau}_1(t) - \upsilon_1]\big[e_2^TQ_1e_2 + e_{15}^TQ_2e_{15}\big] + [\mu_1 - \dot{\tau}_1(t)]\big[e_2^TQ_3e_2 + e_{15}^TQ_4e_{15}\big] \\ &+ [\dot{\tau}_2(t) - \upsilon_2]e_3^TQ_5e_3 + [\mu_2 - \dot{\tau}_2(t)]e_3^TQ_6e_3 \\ &+ \sum_{i=1}^{2}\tau_i(t)\Big[\mathbf{sym}\{\Phi_iP\$^T\} - (e_{i+1} - e_{i+3})^T\frac{Z_i}{2\tau_i}(e_{i+1} - e_{i+3}) \\ &- e_{i+5}^TY_ie_{i+5} - 3(e_{i+5} - e_{i+9})^TY_i(e_{i+5} - e_{i+9}) + \mathbf{\Gamma}_{i1}\mathbf{\Delta}_i^{-1}\mathbf{\Gamma}_{i1}^T\Big] \\ &+ \sum_{j=1}^{2}\bar{\tau}_j(t)\Big[\mathbf{sym}\{\Psi_jP\$^T\} - 3(e_{j+7} - e_{j+11})^TY_j(e_{j+7} - e_{j+11}) \\ &- e_{j+7}^TY_je_{j+7} + \mathbf{\Gamma}_{j2}\mathbf{\Delta}_j^{-1}\mathbf{\Gamma}_{j2}^T\Big]\Big\}\eta(t) \doteq \eta^T(t)\tilde{\mathbf{\Phi}}(t)\eta(t), \qquad (31)\end{aligned}$$

where $\mathbf{\Omega}, \mathbf{\Gamma}, \mathbf{\Delta}, \mathbf{\Gamma}_{ij}, \mathbf{\Delta}_i$ $(i, j = 1, 2)$ are presented in (17). Now based on definition on Schur-complement, one can easily derive that the LMIs in (17) guarantee the following matrix inequalities can be true,

$$\mathbf{\Omega} + \mathbf{\Xi}(i,j,m,n) + \mathbf{\Gamma}\mathbf{\Delta}^{-1}\mathbf{\Gamma}^T + \mathbf{\Gamma}_{ij}\mathbf{\Delta}_i^{-1}\mathbf{\Gamma}_{ij}^T < 0\ \forall\ i,j,m = 1,2; n = 5,6 \qquad (32)$$

with $\mathbf{\Xi}(i,j,m,n)$ defined in (17). That is to say, for $i, j, m = 1, 2; n = 5, 6$,

$$\begin{aligned}&\mathbf{\Omega} + \mathbf{sym}\Big[\Lambda P\$^T + \sum_{i=1}^{2}\sum_{l=1}^{6} H_{il}\Pi_{il} + \tau_{21}\sum_{l=7}^{9} N_l\Pi_l\Big] + \mathbf{\Upsilon}_i + \mathbf{\Theta}_j + \mathbf{\Gamma}\mathbf{\Delta}^{-1}\mathbf{\Gamma}^T \\ &+ \mathbf{\Gamma}_{ij}\mathbf{\Delta}_i^{-1}\mathbf{\Gamma}_{ij}^T + \bar{\mu}_1\big[e_2^TQ_me_2 + e_{15}^TQ_{m+2}e_{15}\big] + \bar{\mu}_2e_3^TQ_ne_3 < 0. \qquad (33)\end{aligned}$$

Then according to Lemma 4, the terms in (33) can guarantee $\tilde{\mathbf{\Phi}}(t) < 0$ in (31) to be true. Therefore, it can be concluded that as the conditions (17) hold simultaneously, the nominal system of (1) is asymptotically stable.

Then we will use Lemma 5 to obtain the stability criterion on (1).

Theorem 2. For given scalars $\tau_i \ge 0, \mu_i, \upsilon_i, \bar{\mu}_i$ $(i = 1, 2), \tau_{21}, \delta_{21}, \theta_{21}$, in **H1** and the uncertainties satisfying **H2**, the system (1) is robustly stable, if there exist positive scalars $\eta_{ijmn} > 0$ $(i, j, m = 1, 2; n = 5, 6)$, $5n \times 5n$ matrix $P > 0$, $n \times n$ matrices $Q_i > 0$ $(i = 1, \cdots, 6)$, N_i $(i = 1, 2, 3, 4)$, $X_i > 0, Y_i > 0$ $(i = 1, 2)$, $U > 0$,

$V > 0, W > 0, X > 0, Y > 0$, and $19n \times n$ matrices H_{ij} $(i = 1,2; j = 1,\cdots,6), H_l$ $(l = 7,8,9)$ such that the LMIs in (34) hold

$$\begin{bmatrix} \mathbf{\Omega} + \mathbf{\Xi}(i,j,m,n) & \mathbf{\Gamma} & \mathbf{\Gamma}_{ij} & \eta_{ijmn}\bar{\mathbf{\Psi}}_1 & \bar{\mathbf{\Psi}}_2 \\ * & -\mathbf{\Delta} & 0 & 0 & 0 \\ * & * & -\mathbf{\Delta}_i & 0 & 0 \\ * & * & * & -\eta_{ijmn}I & \eta_{ijmn}J \\ * & * & * & * & -\eta_{ijmn}I \end{bmatrix} < 0,\ \forall\ i,j,m = 1,2;\ n = 5,6, \quad (34)$$

where $\mathbf{\Omega}, \mathbf{\Xi}(i,j,m,n), \mathbf{\Gamma}, \mathbf{\Gamma}_{ij}$ are identical to the ones in Theorem 1 and

$$\bar{\mathbf{\Psi}}_1 = \begin{bmatrix} E_1 & 0_{n\cdot n} & E_2 & 0_{n\cdot 11n} & E_3 & 0_{n\cdot 4n} \end{bmatrix}^T;$$
$$\bar{\mathbf{\Psi}}_2 = \begin{bmatrix} F^T N_1 & 0_{n\cdot n} & F^T N_4 & 0_{n\cdot 10n} & F^T N_2 & F^T N_3 & 0_{n\cdot 4n} \end{bmatrix}^T.$$

As illustrated in Ref. [27], the general form of modeling partial element equivalent circuit (PEEC) can be modeled as

$$C_0\dot{y}(t) + G_0 y(t) + C_1\dot{y}(t-\tau) + G_1 y(t-\tau) = Bu(t, t-\tau). \qquad (35)$$

To be consistent with the mathematical notation, the system (35) can be rewritten as the following neutral system

$$\dot{y}(t) = Ay(t) + By(t-\tau) + C\dot{y}(t-\tau). \qquad (36)$$

As we know, a stable numerical solution should be based on a stable model. Therefore, the study of asymptotic stability of a system is an important issue before handling its numerical solution. Thus, the delay-dependent stability of the system (36) was investigated in some works [1–3,27]. Then if we take the parameter uncertainties commonly existing in the modeling of a real circuit and different time-varying delays into account, a more general form of (37) can be described by the system (1) as

$$\dot{y}(t) = [A + \Delta A(t)]y(t) + [B + \Delta B(t)]y(t - \tau_2(t)) + C\dot{y}(t - \tau_1(t)). \quad (37)$$

Thus the derived theorems in this work can be applied to study the stability for the PEEC model with more general forms.

4 Numerical Examples

Example 1. Consider the partial element equivalent circuit (PEEC) model (37) with the following parameters [11,27]

$$A = 100 \times \begin{bmatrix} -2.105 & 1 & 2 \\ 3 & -9 & 0 \\ 1 & 2 & -6 \end{bmatrix},\ B = 100 \times \begin{bmatrix} 1 & 0 & -3 \\ -0.5 & -0.5 & -1 \\ -0.5 & -1.5 & 0 \end{bmatrix},\ C = \frac{1}{72} \times \begin{bmatrix} -1 & 5 & 2 \\ 4 & 0 & 3 \\ -2 & 4 & 1 \end{bmatrix};$$
$$\| \Delta A(t) \| \leq 2,\ \ \| \Delta B(t) \| \leq 2,\ \ \| \Delta C(t) \| = 0.$$

Then we can assume that $F = \text{diag}\{1,1,1\}, E_1 = E_2 = \text{diag}\{2,2,2\}$, and $J = E_3 = 0_{3\times 3}$.

Table 1. The calculated MAUBs $\tau_{\max}$ for different υ_1, μ_1, and $\tau_1(t) = \tau_2(t)$

μ_1	0.4	0.7	1.1
Ren et al. [5]	0.3654	0.2434	–
Liu [6]	0.3686	0.2465	–
Theorem 2 ($\upsilon_1 = -1.1$)	0.3722	0.2520	0.2515
Theorem 2 ($\upsilon_1 = -0.5$)	0.3735	0.2535	0.2533

Firstly, as for the case $\tau_1(t) = \tau_2(t)$, with the existent feasible solution to the LMIs in Theorem 2, the computational results on maximum allowable upper bounds (MAUBs) of time-delays for various υ_1, μ_1 can be computed out and meanwhile, we also obtain the corresponding MAUBs based on the results in [5,6]. Together with all derived MAUBs listed in Table 1, one can check that Theorem 1 can be superior over some present ones. Since different conditions on the theorems are required in [5,6], during the computing, we assume that the lower bound of time-delay is set as 0 in [5] and $\rho = 0.5$ is given in [6]. It is worth noting that, since the upper bound of neutral delay's derivative has to be less than 1, there does not exist the corresponding MAUBs when $\mu_1 > 1$ in [5,6].

Secondly, as for $\tau_1(t) \neq \tau_2(t)$, based on the conditions in [5,6], we can choose $\tau_1(t) = 0.3\sin^2(t)$. Then $\tau_1 = 0.3$ and $\upsilon_1 = -0.3, \mu_1 = 0.3$. In what follows, through setting different υ_2, μ_2, we also can derive the corresponding MAUBs of τ_2 based on the LMIs in Theorem 2 and the results in [5,6], which can be listed in Table 2. From Tables 1 and 2, one can check that our method is less conservative than those existent ones. Therefore, it is of significance to use the interconnection between the neutral delay and state one to construct the Lyapunov functional, especially when two kinds of time-delays are different.

Table 2. The calculated MAUBs $\tau_{\max}$ for different υ_2, μ_2, and $\tau_1(t) \neq \tau_2(t)$

μ_2	0.4	0.7	1.1
Ren et al. [5]	0.3654	0.2434	0.2302
Liu [6]	0.3686	0.2465	0.2335
Theorem 2 ($\upsilon_2 = -1.1$)	0.3770	0.2555	0.2534
Theorem 2 ($\upsilon_2 = -0.5$)	0.3777	0.2572	0.2568

Thirdly, similar to the Refs. [11,27], we choose the matrix $A = 100 \times \begin{bmatrix} \delta & 1 & 2 \\ 3 & -9 & 0 \\ 1 & 2 & -6 \end{bmatrix}$ with $\delta < 0$. Especially, in [11], the unknown nonlinearities can be equivalently transformed as the normal uncertainties in this paper, i.e.,

$$f_1\big(t, x(t)\big) \doteq \Delta A(t)x(t);\; f_2\big(t, x(t-\tau(t))\big) \doteq \Delta B(t)x(t-\tau(t));$$
$$f_3\big(t, \dot{x}(t-\tau(t))\big) \doteq \Delta C(t)\dot{x}(t-\tau(t)).$$

In what follows, in order to better give the comparison, we let $\| \Delta A(t) \| = \| \Delta B(t) \| \leq 0.01$ and $\| \Delta C(t) \| = 0$. Since in [11,27], the upper bound of $\dot{\tau}(t)$ should be less than 1 and thus, we choose $\tau(t) = 0.1 + 0.3\sin^2(0.2t)$. Based on Theorem 2 and Matlab LMI ToolBox, it can be shown that the system is robustly stable for any $\delta \leq -3.445$. However, since $\delta \leq -3.810$ in [11] and $\delta \leq -4.465$ in [27] are needed, these criteria fail to determine the robust stability of the system with $\delta = -3.5$.

5 Conclusions

In this work, one mixed-delay-dependent condition on robust stability has been established for a class of uncertain neutral systems with time-varying delays. Compared with some existing results, the derived results are mainly based on an augmented L-K functional and can effectively reduce the conservatism owing to using some efficient techniques, in which the interconnection between the neutral delay and state one is deeply studied. One numerical example shows the application to partial element equivalent circuit model.

Acknowledgements. This work is supported by National Natural Science Foundation of China (Nos. 61403194, 61473079), Jiangsu Natural Science Foundation (Nos. BK20140836, BK20150888), Natural Science Foundation for Universities in Jiangsu Province (No. 15KJB12004), and Fundamental Research Fund for Central Universities (Nos. NS2016030, NJ20160024).

References

1. Samli, R., Arik, S.: New results for global stability of a class of neutral-type neural systems with time delays. Appl. Math. Comput. **210**, 564–570 (2009)
2. Park, J., Kwon, O.: On new stability criterion for delay differential systems of neutral type. Appl. Math. Comput. **162**, 627–637 (2005)
3. Ding, L., He, Y., Wu, M., Ning, C.: Improved mixed-delay-dependent asymptotic stability criteria for neutral systems. IET Control Theory Appl. **9**, 2180–2187 (2015)
4. Alaviani, S.: Delay-dependent exponential stability of linear time-varying neutral delay systems. IFAC-PapersOnLine **48**, 177–179 (2015)
5. Ren, Y., Feng, Z., Sun, G.: Improved stability conditions for uncertain neutral-type systems with time-varying delays. Int. J. Syst. Sci. **47**, 1982–1993 (2016)
6. Liu, P.: Improved results on delay-interval-dependent robust stability criteria for uncertain neutral-type systems with time-varying delays. ISA Trans. **60**, 53–66 (2016)
7. Qian, W., Liu, J., Sun, Y., Fei, S.: A less conservative robust stability criteria for uncertain neutral systems with mixed delays. Math. Comput. Simul. **80**, 1007–1017 (2010)

8. Lu, R., Wu, H., Bai, J.: New delay-dependent robust stability criteria for uncertain neutral systems with mixed delays. J. Frankl. Inst. **351**, 1386–1399 (2014)
9. Chen, Y., Qian, W., Fei, S.: Improved robust stability conditions for uncertain neutral systems with discrete and distributed delays. J. Frankl. Inst. **352**, 2634–2645 (2015)
10. Liu, S., Xiang, Z.: Exponential H_∞ output tracking control for switched neutral system with time-varying delay and nonlinear perturbations. Circuits Syst. Signal Process. **32**(1), 103–121 (2013)
11. Liu, Y., Ma, W., Mahmoud, M., Lee, S.: Improved delay-dependent exponential stability criteria for neutral-delay systems with nonlinear uncertainties. Appl. Math. Model. **39**, 3164–3174 (2015)
12. Wang, W., Nguang, S., Zhong, S., Liu, F.: Delay-dependent stability criteria for uncertain neutral system with time-varying delays and nonlinear perturbations. Circuits Syst. Signal Process. **33**(9), 2719–2740 (2014)
13. Qiu, F., Cao, J., Hayat, T.: Delay-dependent stability of neutral system with mixed time-varying delays and nonlinear perturbations using delay-dividing approach. Cogn. Neurodyn. **9**, 75–83 (2015)
14. Cheng, J., Zhu, H., Zhong, S., Li, G.: Novel delay-dependent robust stability criteria for neutral systems with mixed time-varying delays and nonlinear perturbations. Appl. Math. Comput. **219**, 7741–7753 (2013)
15. Qiu, F., Cui, B., Ji, Y.: Further results on robust stability of neutral system with mixed time-varying delays and nonlinear perturbations. Nonlinear Anal.: Real World Appl. **11**, 895–906 (2010)
16. Lakshmanan, S., Senthilkumar, T., Balasubraman, M.: Improved results on robust stability of neutral systems with mixed time-varying delays and nonlinear perturbations. Appl. Math. Model. **35**, 5355–5368 (2011)
17. Hui, J., Kong, X., Zhang, H., Zhou, X.: Delay-partitioning approach for systems with interval time-varying delay and nonlinear perturbations. J. Comput. Appl. Math. **281**, 74–81 (2015)
18. Han, Q.: Improved stability criteria and controller design for linear neutral systems. Automatica **45**, 1948–1952 (2009)
19. Qiu, F., Cui, B.: A delay-dividing approach to stability of neutral system with mixed delays and nonlinear perturbations. Appl. Math. Model. **34**, 3701–3707 (2010)
20. Chen, H., Wang, L.: New result on exponential stability for neutral stochastic linear system with time-varying delay. Appl. Math. Comput. **239**, 320–325 (2015)
21. Obradovic, M., Milosevic, M.: Stability of a class of neutral stochastic differential equations with unbounded delay and Markovian switching and the Euler-Maruyama method. J. Comput. Appl. Math. **309**(1), 244–266 (2017)
22. Liu, L., Zhu, Q.: Mean square stability of two classes of theta method for neutral stochastic differential delay equations. J. Comput. Appl. Math. **305**(15), 55–67 (2016)
23. Balasubramaniam, P., Krishnasamy, R.: Robust exponential stabilization results for impulsive neutral time-delay systems with sector-bounded nonlinearity. Circuits Syst. Signal Process. **33**(9), 2741–2759 (2014)
24. Raja, R., Zhu, Q., Senthilraj, S., Samidurai, R.: Improved stability analysis of uncertain neutral type neural networks with leakage delays and impulsive effects. Appl. Math. Comput. **266**, 1050–1069 (2015)
25. Yu, Y.: Global exponential convergence for a class of neutral functional differential equations with proportional delays. Math. Methods Appl. Sci. (2016). doi:10.1002/mma.3880

26. Xiong, L., Zhang, H., Li, Y.: Improved stability and H infinity performance for neutral systems with uncertain Markovian jumpinging. Nonlinear Anal.: Hybrid Syst. **19**, 13–25 (2016)
27. Yue, D., Han, Q.: A delay-dependent stability criterion of neutral systems and its application to a partial element equivalent circuit model. IEEE Trans. Circuits Syst.-II **51**, 685–689 (2004)
28. Zeng, H., He, Y., Wu, M., She, J.: New results on stability analysis for systems with discrete distributed delay. Automatica **63**, 189–192 (2015)
29. Park, M., Kwon, O., Park, J., Lee, S.: Stability of time-delay systems via Wirtinger-based double integral inequality. Automatica **55**, 204–208 (2015)
30. Li, T., Wang, T., Song, A., Fei, S.: Delay-derivative-dependent stability for delayed neural networks with unbounded distributed delay. IEEE Trans. Neural Netw. **21**, 1365–1371 (2010)
31. Li, T., Song, A., Fei, S.: Robust stability of stochastic Cohen-Grossberg neural networks with mixed time-varying delays. Neurocomputing **73**, 542–551 (2009)

A Quantitative Evaluation Method of Surveillance Coverage of UAVs Swarm

Wei Li[1(✉)], Changxin Huang[1], Kaimin Chen[2], and Songchen Han[1]

[1] School of Aeronautics and Astronautics, Sichuan University, No. 24, South Section 1, Yihuan Road, Chengdu 610065, China
Li.wei@uestc.edu.cn

[2] School of Computer Science, Sichuan University, No. 24, South Section 1, Yihuan Road, Chengdu 610065, China

Abstract. Small unmanned aerial vehicles (UAVs) have native advantages in wide area surveillance. Pursuing the spreading of the UAV swarm as dispersive as possible is an effective method of improve the performance of surveillance. In this paper, quality of deployment issue is surveyed and analyzed in term of a novel measure - deployment entropy. The idea of deployment entropy comes from Shannon's information entropy. Deployment entropy could help operators to obtain the whole understanding of the interested region from describing the circumstances of every sub region. The more dispersive UAVs are deployed, the greater the deployment entropy we can get. From numerical simulation, results show that by computing the value of deployment entropy, it is possible to evaluate the distribution of UAVs in a wide area, and the burden of calculation is less than traditional evaluation method.

Keywords: UAV · Deployment entropy · Surveillance coverage

1 Introduction

Recent advances in technology are encouraging the use of small unmanned aerial vehicles (UAVs) for intelligence, surveillance and reconnaissance missions. However, small UAVs are designed to be inexpensive and therefore include low quality sensors and poor navigation algorithms, leading to feeble performance of the individual UAV. The concept of swarm UAVs is introduced in order to overcome these problems. Individual small UAV may be less capable than any large sophisticated one under development today, but through communications across the swarm of UAVs, the group exhibits behaviors and capabilities that can exceed those demonstrated by more large sophisticated systems that do not employ communications between UAVs.

A future reconnaissance task is envisioned to be comprised of a large number of collaborating unmanned and manned systems with a small group human operators or users that simultaneously manage teams of heterogeneous vehicles at a supervisory level to find out potential target. Small UAVs are uniquely suited for these tasks, with advantages over larger vehicles that include superior stealth, the ability to field many vehicles over a wide area to create a distributed sensor or communications network, and relatively small acquisition and operating costs [1]. In this perspective, small

X. Sun et al. (Eds.): ICCCS 2017, Part II, LNCS 10603, pp. 772–782, 2017.
https://doi.org/10.1007/978-3-319-68542-7_67

UAVs swarm would exert extraordinary effects on surveillance mission. How we evaluate the performance of surveillance? In general, surveillance coverage is a vital evaluation measure. For current UAVs systems, surveillance coverage mission is begun by assuming the environment to have a specific simple shape. The UAVs then execute a simple coverage path until they discover potential targets. However, this strategy neglects uncertainty of the environment where pop-up threats and moving threats/targets happen [2, 3]. Area surveillance task requires managing a dynamic spatiotemporal configuration of UAVs over the interested area, in other words, it is required to keep situation awareness at any moment, in order to maintain the complete coverage and reconnaissance of the interested area in real time. The spatial distribution of the UAV swarm determines the performance of the reconnaissance. The more dispersedly the UAVs are deployed, the more the surveillance area is accumulated, and the clearer the operator knows about the interested area [4].

From this perspective, pursuing the spreading of the UAV swarm as dispersive as possible is an effective method to improve the performance of surveillance. Once a set of UAVs is deployed for, say, region surveillance, how can one be sure that the deployment provides the necessary coverage level? To analyze if the requirement is met, one needs a measure that represents the quality of deployment. Consequently, it is reasonable to find an available quantitative measurement of the spreading of the small UAVs swarm to help the human operators to scatter UAVs over the interested area, or to make strategies for the UAV swarms to accomplish surveillance coverage mission of the interested area.

The available method is coverage extent measurement, whose idea is to sum up all the detected area of each UAV, then divided by the total area of interested region, which could be symbolized as follows [5]:

$$C = \frac{\bigcup\limits_{i=1\ldots n} A_i}{A} \tag{1}$$

where C is the degree of region coverage; Ai is the detected area of UAVs in the ith sub region; A is the total area of the interested region; N is the number of sub regions. The coverage extent is measured by C. If a great value of C is acquired, one can get the understanding that UAVs exhibit good coverage over the interested region. However, this type of method is hampered by its computational expense. It takes a large amount of time to calculate the detected area, in which the redundant part of detected areas of each UAV has to be removed. Moreover, when the positions of UAVs change, the calculation process has to been repeated. Therefore, that cannot provide evaluation results immediately, neither adapt with the uncertain environment. The main objective of this paper is to present a novel quantitative evaluation method with little calculation expense for computing extent of the spreading of the UAVs swarm to meet the requirement of the surveillance coverage of the interested region in real time.

2 Deployment Entropy

This study is motivated by a mission scenario in which a group of autonomous air vehicles with proximity restricted communications are tasked to provide cooperative surveillance for a large region of interest. We want to find a measure of how dispersive that UAVs are located in the region is or how well the surveillance coverage is.

To assess the quality of UAV deployment, appropriate measures that reveal the detail situation in the interested region can be employed. It is reasonable to decompose the interested region into several sub regions. If we can find a proper method to provide the information of distribution of UAVs in each sub region, and a mechanism to synthesize the information together, we could obtain the whole understanding of the interested region from describing the circumstances of every sub region.

Based on the above consideration, we provide a novel quantitative evaluation methodology - deployment entropy - to realize the above objective with little calculation burden. The essential inspiration of deployment entropy comes from the information entropy which was introduced by Shannon. He invented the information entropy to be a method to measure the information. Similarly, we provide the deployment entropy to measure the distribution of UAVs.

The form of information entropy is:

$$H = -\sum_{i=1}^{n} p_i \ln p_i \tag{2}$$

where p_i is the probability of a system being in cell i of its phase space. A noticeable characteristic is that any change toward equalization of probability $p_1, p_2, \ldots p_n$ increase H [6]. Thus, if we suppose that p_i represents the distribution of ith sub region, the whole deployment of UAVs in the interested area could be expressed by H. When the distributions of each sub region are equal, we can get the maximum H. According to this idea, the definition of deployment entropy is described as follows:

$$H = -\sum_{i=1}^{n} p_i \ln p_i \tag{3}$$

where,

$$p_i = \frac{ratio_i}{\sum_{k=1}^{n} ratio_k} \tag{4}$$

$$ratio_i = \frac{N_i}{S_i} \tag{5}$$

$$N_{total} = \sum_{i=1}^{n} N_i \tag{6}$$

$$S_{total} = \sum_{i=1}^{n} S_i \tag{7}$$

N_i is the amount of UAVs in the ith sub region. S_i is the area of the ith sub region; $ratio_i$ is the ratio of the amount of UAVs over the area of the ith sub region; P_i is the unitary proportion of the ith ratio in the sum of all ratios; N_{total} is the total number of all the UAVs; S_{total} is the total area of the interested region; n is the number of sub regions that the interested region is composed of. Since differentiations are involved in the assumption argument process, the base e is more useful. The quantity H has some interesting properties which further substantiate it as a reasonable measure of deployment of UAVs or other agents.

Theorem 1: If and only if each $ratio_i$ equals to N_{total}/S_{total}, H will achieve the maximum value.

Proof: In order to prove the theorem, let us demonstrate the validity of the follow inequation firstly:

$$\ln x \leq x - 1, x > 0 \tag{8}$$

Given the assumption that:

$$f(x) = \ln x - (x - 1) \tag{9}$$

Then we can get the first order differential result:

$$f'(x) = \frac{1}{x} - 1 \tag{10}$$

Hence, when $x = 1$, $f(x) = 0$ is the extremum of $f(x)$.
And since

$$f''(x) = -\frac{1}{x^2} < 0 \quad (x > 0) \tag{11}$$

This extremum is a maximum value. It is easily shown that:

$$f''(x) = -\frac{1}{x^2} < 0 \quad (x > 0) \tag{12}$$

By this inequation, it is easier to prove the Theorem 1. The process of proving is as follows.

From the definition of p_i:

$$p_i = \frac{ratio_i}{\sum_{k=1}^{n} ratio_k}, \; q_i = \frac{ratio_i}{\sum_{k=1}^{n} ratio_k}, \; \sum_{i=1}^{n} p_i = 1, \; \sum_{i=1}^{n} q_i = 1 \tag{13}$$

Combined with inequation (8), we can get:

$$\ln\frac{p_i}{q_i} \leq \frac{p_i}{q_i} - 1 \tag{14}$$

Then,

$$\sum_{i=1}^{n} p_i \ln\frac{q_i}{p_i} \leq \sum_{i=1}^{n} p_i\left(\frac{q_i}{p_i} - 1\right) = \sum_{i=1}^{n} q_i - \sum_{i=1}^{n} p_i \tag{15}$$

According to the known condition:

$$\sum_{i=1}^{n} p_i = \sum_{i=1}^{n} q_i = 1 \tag{16}$$

Then,

$$-\sum_{i=1}^{n} p_i \ln p_i \leq -\sum_{i=1}^{n} p_i \ln q_j \tag{17}$$

Therefore,

$$H \leq -\sum_{i=1}^{n} p_i \ln q_i \tag{18}$$

While $p_i = q_i$, the equal mark of the above formula comes into existence. Hence

$$ratio_i = ratio_j = \frac{N_i + N_j}{S_i + S_j} = \frac{\sum_{i=1}^{n} N_i}{\sum_{i=1}^{n} S_j} = \frac{N_{total}}{S_{total}} \tag{19}$$

Thus it can be seen that the Theorem 1 is correct. Therefore, it is proven that we could get the maximum value of H if all the sub-regions have the uniform *ratio*.

Theorem 2: H is a strictly convex function.

Based on definition of convex function, it is assumed that

$$f(x_1, x_2, \ldots, x_n) = f(x). \tag{20}$$

For every positive number a $(0 < a < 1)$ that is less than 1, and for any two vectors x and y in domain, if

$$f[ax + (1-a)y] \geq af(x) + (1-a)f(y) \tag{21}$$

Then f is defined as a convex function. Furthermore, if

$$f[ax+(1-a)y] > af(x)+(1-a)f(y) \quad (x \neq y) \tag{22}$$

f is a strictly convex function.

The prove process that H is a kind of strictly convex function is given as follows:

$$\sum_{i=1}^{n} p_i = \sum_{i=1}^{n} q_i = 1,\ (i = 1, 2, \ldots, n) \tag{23}$$

$$H[ap+(1-a)q] = -\sum_{i=1}^{n} [ap_i+(1-a)q_i] \ln[ap_i+(1-a)q_i] \tag{24}$$

According to the Theorem 1 and known condition that the two latter parts in the above expression is greater than zero ($p_i \neq q_i$), then we get

$$H[ap+(1-a)q] > aH(p)+(1-a)H(q) \tag{25}$$

Therefore, it is proven that H has the property of strictly Convexity.

Based on the Theorem 2, it is known that when $ratio_i$ equals to N_{total}/S_{total}, $p_i = 1/n$, $a > b$, then

$$H_1(p_1, p_2, \ldots, p_n - a, a) = -\sum_{i=1}^{n-1} p_i \ln p_i - (p_n - a)\ln(p_n - a) - a \ln a \tag{26}$$

$$H_2(p_1, p_2, \ldots, p_n - b, b) = -\sum_{i=1}^{n-1} p_i \ln p_i - (p_n - b)\ln(p_n - b) - b \ln b \tag{27}$$

$$H_1 - H_2 < 0 \tag{28}$$

As a result, the less uniform the $ratio_i$ is, the less the value of H is. And here it becomes evident that, by computing the value of H, it is possible to evaluate the distribution of UAV agents in the interested area. Furthermore, utilizing H, we can assess the quality of UAVs' surveillance coverage.

3 Simulation Results

In this section, we present results produced with MATLAB to justify the above assumption that the deployment entropy could evaluate the distribution of UAVs. A simulation of a simple area surveillance scenario is developed. The detail is assumed as follows: 50 UAVs are randomly located in a 100 * 100 2D region, illustrated as Fig. 1. The red '+'s represent the UAVs. Utilizing the Voronoi partition method, the 2D region is divided into 10 sub-regions.

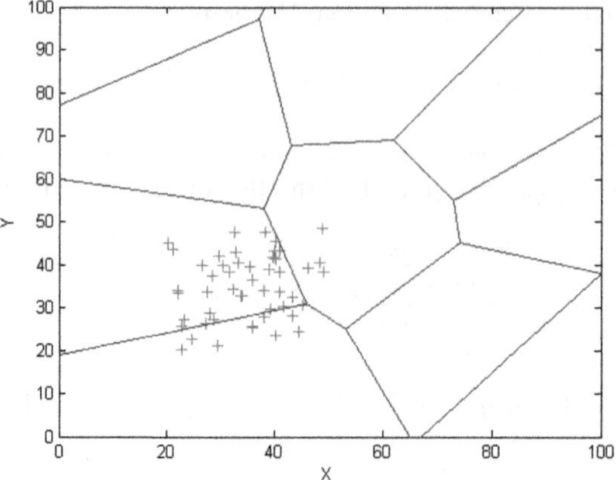

Fig. 1. UAVs spread in a relative small region (Color figure online)

Scenario 1: Same Partition, Different Deployments

In this section, we present a simulation scenario that calculates the value of H for the different deployments of UAVs in the same partition of the region. There are 5 deployments: the first and the fifth are random distributions in relative small regions; in the second and the fourth deployment, UAVs are spread in the whole region randomly; the third one is an approximate uniform distribution that UAVs scatter in the whole region. All the distributions are illustrated in the Figs. 1, 2, 3, 4 and 5.

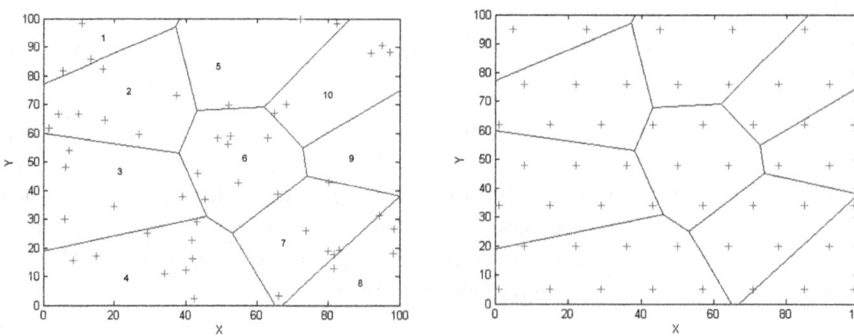

Fig. 2. UAVs spread randomly over whole area

Fig. 3. UAVs spread in an approximate uniform distribution form

Put the areas of each sub-region and the numbers of UAVs into the formula of the deployment entropy, we can get the results of H which is illustrated in the Fig. 6. From the computation results, it is shown that the scenario of approximate uniform distribution obtains the maximum H, whereas, the scenario of random distributions in relative small region get the minimum value. Therefore, random deployment schemes in a relative small region may yield large poorly sensed areas, where redeployment may

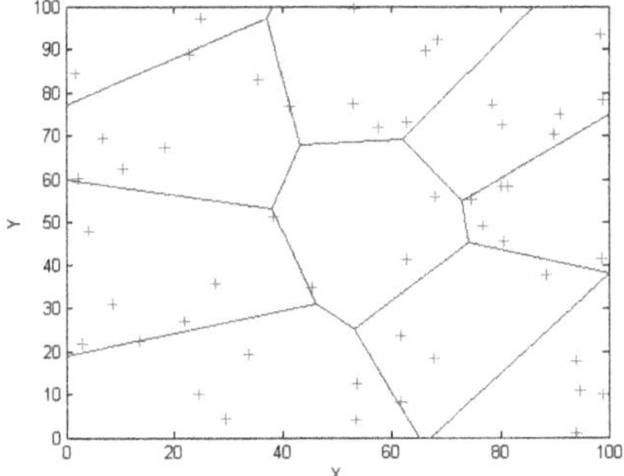

Fig. 4. UAVs spread randomly in another distribution form over whole area

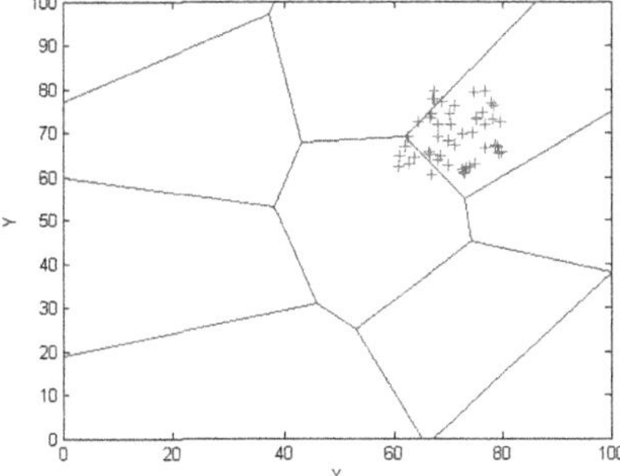

Fig. 5. UAVs spread in a relative small region in another form

be necessary. And, the value of H that is obtained from random distribution in the whole region is close to that given by the approximate uniform distribution. Therefore, it could be verified that deployment entropy H can measure the distribution of UAVs in the interested area. The more dispersant UAVs are, the greater the value of H will be obtained. Consequently, deploying UAVs to execute surveillance mission, or adjusting the reconnaissance position of UAVs in real time, it is reasonable to use deployment entropy H as reference, that is to say, choosing the strategy with a greater value of H.

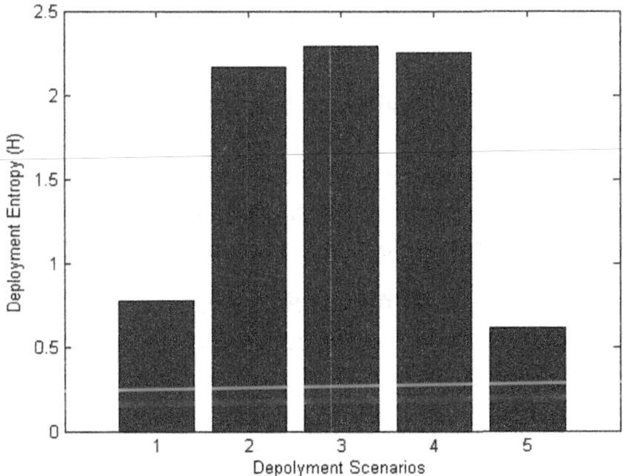

Fig. 6. Deployment entropy results comparison

It is worth pointing out that, in practice, it is hard to obtain the theoretical maximum H, in this case presented in the simulation, $H_{max} = 2.3026$. The reason is that we have not taken the strategy where the interested region is made up with equal parts. Therefore, for every sub-region, it is very likely that fraction number of UAVs may occur, while in practice, the number of UAV could only be in integral. Therefore, in actual case, we could only obtain the maximum value, rather than the theoretical greatest value.

Scenario 2: Same Deployment, Different Partitions

In this section, we present a simulation scenario that calculates the value of *H* for the same deployments of UAVs in the different partitions of the region. The partition in the simulation 1 is served as a reference, shown as Fig. 2. The other partition generates

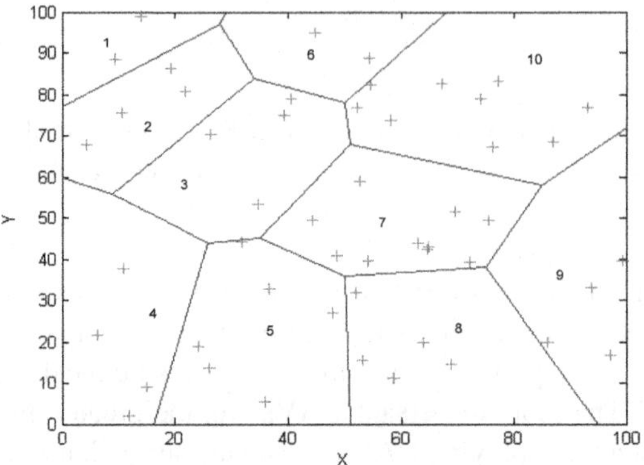

Fig. 7. UAVs spread over the area in another partition

from Voronoi method, illustrated as Fig. 7. The distributions of UAVs in the two scenarios are the same.

From deployment entropy computation, in the first partition, *H* is 2.2482, and in the other one, *H* is 2.2489. This difference shows that although the distributions of UAVs are the same, distinct partition strategies would influence the value of *H*. As a result, when the distribution is under evaluation, all scenarios should take a same partition method. Otherwise, it is hard to reflect the surveillance coverage of UAVs.

Scenario 3: Same Deployment, Different Sub Regions

In this section, we mainly focus on the calculation of *H* with distinct numbers of sub regions while the distribution of UAVs is exactly the same. It is assumed that the distribution of UAV is as same as that of simulation 2. In this section, the interested area is divided into 5 pieces, which is also utilizing Voronoi partition method, illustrated as Fig. 8.

Put the known conditions into the formula of *H*, we can get that $H = 1.5831$, while in the other partition strategies which include 10 pieces, the value of *H* is generally greater than 2 in the same distribution. Therefore, we can get a result: in a same distribution, different partition strategy could bring the dramatically distinct values of *H*. This result can be obtained from theoretical analysis. When the interested area is divided into 5 pieces, the theoretical maximum value of *H* is 1.6094, while the greatest value of *H* is 2.3026 in the 10 pieces partition in theory. And when the area is divided into 100 pieces, the theoretical maximum value is 4.6052. Consequently, in general, in the same distribution, the more pieces the interested area is divided into, the greater the value of

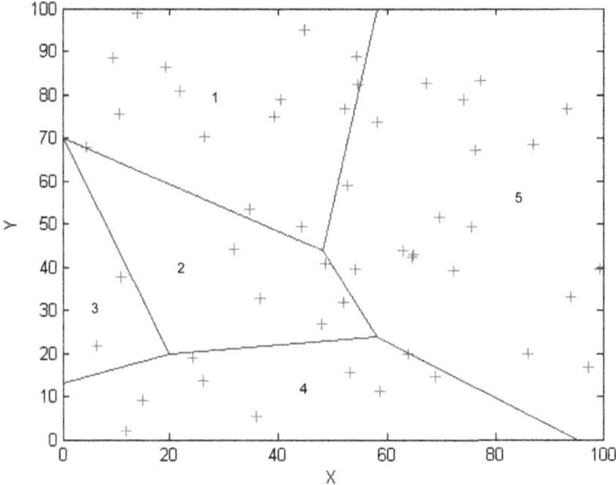

Fig. 8. Deployment entropy results comparison

H will be, and accordingly, the more accurate the evaluation of surveillance coverage of UAVs is.

4 Conclusions

We considered the problem of surveillance coverage evaluation undertaken by the measure the dispersing of UAVs. In this perspective, this paper described deployment entropy, a novel quantitative measure of distribution of UAVs when they execute surveillance coverage mission. The properties of deployment entropy make it as reasonable method to measure the distribution. Some simulation results reveal that the deployment entropy could estimate the distribution of UAVs under distinct scenarios: different partition strategy with same UAVs deployment, the same partition strategy with various deployment models, the uniform deployment with different number of sub regions, etc. In general, deployment entropy could provide the distribution information of UAVs in real time without calculation burden, as well as could be regarded as a basis of decision making in establishing control strategy of surveillance mission of UAVs.

Acknowledgement. This work was supported by "National Natural Science Foundation of China, No. 61403065" and "Project of Sichuan Science and Technology Bureau, No. 2015JY0084".

References

1. Bamberger, R.J., Watson, D.P., Scheidt, D.H., Moore, K.L.: Flight demonstrations of unmanned aerial vehicle swarming concepts. Johns Hopkins APL Tech. Dig. **27**(1), 41–55 (2006)
2. Liu, Y., Cruz, J.B., Sparks, A.G.: Coordinating networked uninhabited air vehicles for persistent area denial. In: 43rd IEEE Conference on Decision and Control, Paradise Island, Bahamas, pp. 3351–3356 (2004)

3. Frazzoli, E., Bullo, F.: Decentralized algorithms for vehicle routing in a stochastic time-varing environment. In: 43rd IEEE Conference on Decision and Control, Paradise Island, Bahamas, pp. 3351–3356 (2004)
4. Moore, B.J., Passino, K.M.: Distributed balancing of AAVs for uniform surveillance coverage. In: 44th IEEE Conference on Decision and Control, and The European Control Conference, Seville, Spain, pp. 7060–7065 (2005)
5. Gage, D.W.: Command control for many-robot systems. In: 19th Annual AUVS Technical Symposium, Huntsville, pp. 22–24 (1992)
6. Zhang, Z., Wang, X., Sun, L.: Mobile payment anomaly detection mechanism based on information entropy. IET Netw. **5**(1), 1–7 (2016)

Chaos Prediction of Fast Fading Channel of Multi-rates Digital Modulation Using Support Vector Machines

Yijing Ren[1,2] and Ren Ren[2(✉)]

[1] Internet of Thing, Beijing University of Posts and Telecommunications, Beijing 100876, China
Renyijing1996_@bupt.edu.cn

[2] Department of Optics Information, Xi'an Jiaotong University, Xi'an 710054, China
renr01@163.com

Abstract. According to the support vector domain properties, the paper establishes vector domain predictive models of chaos channel as well as chaos phase trace of non-linear map, the chaotic fading channel model was established based on Takens phase space delay reconstructing theory. Self-learning makes error least upper bound of generalization model to be minimum. The non-linear higher dimension map was realized by the squares support vector domain. The future fading channel data was predicted from training data set. The predictive error changes with the increase of embed dimension to a constant. The experiment result indicates that the support vector domain needs little support vector with fast convergence rate. With the small sample and unknown probability density, the multi-path predictive series consisted with true value series in Doppler fast fading channel. Under the conditions of small sample, the predicted series is in concordance with the channel true value.

Keywords: Interpersonal communication · Support vector machines · Communication network · Fast fading · Least square · Chaos predictive

1 Introduction

Interpersonal media communication is one of the important social activities existing in human society. Support vector domain can make sample point error and error least upper bound of generalization model to be minimum at the same time, improving the generalization ability of the model especially when the sample is small [1, 7]. A variety of automatic identification of the multi-speed modulation model is one of the key problems need to be solved in the software radio system [2–6]. In the research of classifying modulation method, a general method is for pattern recognition and statistical decision theory. Nandi adopted 6 kinds of digital modulation mode to increase recognition correct rate to more than 90% with the method of statistical decision, but the deficiency of the algorithm is to determine the decision threshold [3]. Azzouz identified analog and digital modulation mode using the neural network respectively, under the signal-to-noise ratio is more than 10 dB, realizing recognition correct rate of

X. Sun et al. (Eds.): ICCCS 2017, Part II, LNCS 10603, pp. 783–790, 2017.
https://doi.org/10.1007/978-3-319-68542-7_68

over 90% for all kinds of modulation mode [4]. Due to limited samples, the neural network algorithm are easily seen and owe learning as well as the local minimum point problem, the neural network algorithm is restricted. The support vector machine of SVD has simple structure and is independent of mathematical model. It also has the ability of adjustment through self-learning. Consequently, it has excellent ability of prediction and identification when it is used in solving small sample, non-linear problems or in the field of density estimation and high-dimensional pattern recognition [1, 14–27].

2 Methods

2.1 Model I

Support vector domain is a kind of regional classification based on support vector machine (SVM) which produces objects from the small sample provided with the object set that have existed and the domain description model. Therefore, Support vector domain is a kind of machine learning method that has been developed [8–13].

We carry out the training of classification with classification points, the description boundary of this kind of data will be got from the minimum ultra-spherical boundary, and then the other two kinds of data can be classified based on the description boundary.

When the Support vector domain classifier is applied for the classification of a group of sample set, the slack variable ξ_i is used for excluding the singular point from the interface of the ultra-sphere with the minimum radius of the array. The constraint condition of the best ultra-sphere interface is $(x_i - a)^T(x_i - a) \leq R^2 + \xi^2$; while minF (R, a, ξ_i) = min $\left|R^2 + C\sum_i \xi_i\right|$, $\xi \geq 0$. The coefficient C can be determined through ultra-sphere interface and the refused domain. The optimal solution of this optimization problem is provided by the saddle point of Lagrangian functional, that is

$$\mathrm{L}(\mathrm{R},\ \mathrm{a},\ \alpha_i, \xi_i) = \sum_i \{\alpha_i[R^2 + \xi_i - (x_i^2 - 2ax_i + a^2)]\} + \sum_i v_i\xi_i - C\sum_{i=1}^{l} \xi_i - R^2 \quad (1)$$

Where α_i is the Lagrangian coefficient, which is actually the support vector, ξ_i is the slack valuable. We can define a nonlinear mapping $\phi(x)$ from L(R, a, α_i, ξ_i), which can map the input space to a high-dimensional Hilbert space, $y(x) = w^T\Phi(x) + b$, where w is the weight vector and b is the deviation. It is ensured through training that the distance between the separating plane and the sample points which are closest to the optimal separating hyper-plane is the maximum.

Compared with the traditional SVM method, the SVD needs less data and support vector because SVD establishes the optimal separating hyper-plane from part of the data. The input space is mapped to a high-dimensional space through the non-linear map $\Phi(x)$. As for the training set $(x_1, y_1), \cdots, (x_i, y_i), x_i \in R^n, y_i \in \{+1, -1\}$, $i = 1, 2, \cdots, l$ if x_i belongs to the first category, then $y_i = +1$, otherwise $y_i = -1$. The expression of the optimization problem of the sample set whose $y_i = +1$ is the expression (1). The restrictive conditions are that $0 \leq a_i \leq C, \sum a_i = 1$. In this case, we can get the solutions of the optimal separating hyperplane by ordering derivative for the parameters R, a and ξ. The value of R, a, ξ can be got according to the Karush-Kuhn-Tucker optimum conditions α, R and ξ:

$$\frac{\partial L}{\partial R} = 0 \rightarrow \sum_i \alpha_i = 1 \tag{2}$$

$$\frac{\partial L}{\partial a} = 0 \rightarrow \sum_i \alpha_i x_i = a, and \quad a = \frac{\sum_i \alpha_i x_i}{\sum_i \alpha_i} \tag{3}$$

$$\frac{\partial \mathrm{L}}{\xi} = 0 \rightarrow \mathrm{C} = \alpha_i + \nu_i \rightarrow 0 < \alpha_i < \mathrm{C} \tag{4}$$

3 Experiments

3.1 Model Comparisons Between Communication in the Past and Now

The wireless fading channel obtains the narrowband channel coefficient series through motivating low-pass network with the orthogonal complex Gaussian white noise sequence, and then the wireless channel data is generated through the interpolation according to need. The complex Gaussian noise complies with Rayleigh probability density distribution. The Doppler frequency shift of the channel performs as received Doppler spectrum [1, 14–37].

The simulation is designed for 2G downlinks, the maximum Doppler frequency shifts are respectively 222.222 Hz, the sampling frequency of the channel is 40000 Hz. The number of frequency sampling points is 1024, the length of the non-interpolated channel is designed as 3023 points, the first 300–500 points of the data are designed as training data, based on which the following 1500–2000 points of the channel coefficient sequence are predicted. The frequency of the carrier is 2 GHz, and the data are from both the channel data of Jakes model and the actual measured data of the outdoor and interior broadband channel by UWB of the IMAT company. Both the radial basis kernel function and SVD prediction and classification of channels are used [27–37].

When the embedding dimension is 6, the delay time $\tau = 3$, the predicted value and the prediction result of true value are indicated by Figs. 1, 2. The deviation between the true value and the predicted value is revealed in Fig. 1. When the velocity is 80 km/h, the prediction results are indicated in Figs. 1, 2.

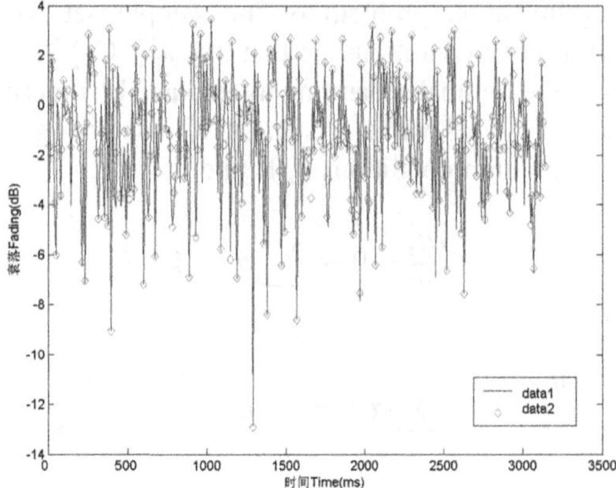

Fig. 1. Mobile rates 80 km/hr, Doppler frequency 74.074 Hz, The channel predict valve and true value comparing

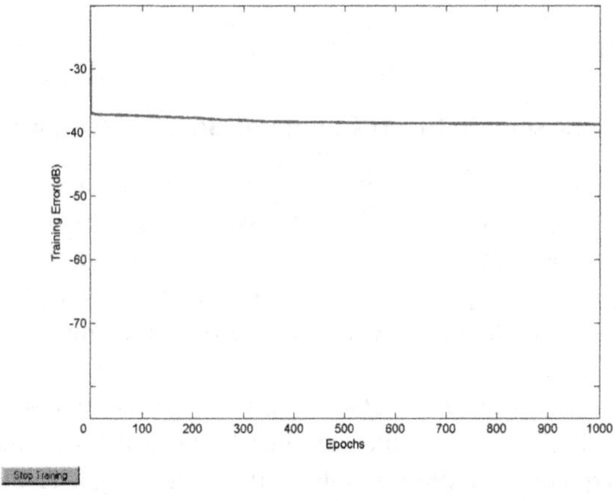

Fig. 2. Channel steps prediction error and learning curve at mobile rates 80 km/hr, Doppler frequency 74.074 Hz, Channel predict valve and true value.

4 Discussion and Results

The prediction result is shown in Fig. 1 when the actually measured wireless broadband channel data is used, the velocity is 80 km/h, the sampling frequency is 4000 Hz, and the carrier frequency is 2 GHz. Considering the situation of high-speed movement, if the velocity increases, the performance when the Doppler frequency shift is increased. From the analysis above, with the increase of embedding dimension, when m = 70, the correlation dimension does not tend to be constant. However, the actually measured data by UWB indicates that the correlation dimension tend to be a constant when the embedding dimension increases. The result of the analysis indicates that the partial relevance of Jakes model is relatively weak. We also reveals that the correlation dimensions tend to be a constant with the increase of embedding dimension. However, different from the determined system, the correlation dimension of the noise sequence does not converge when the embedding dimension increases, and its degree of freedom is infinite. The minimum embedding dimension is about 70.

The experiment compared the actual measured interior embedding dimension of the fading channel with that outdoor, m = 70, and the system correlation dimension converges to a determined value. We can see that when the embedding dimension of the channel is minimum, the phase space has fully expanded, with limited dimension [38–41]. Polynomial kernel function, two-tier neutral network kernel function and radial basis kernel function are respectively be chosen as the kernel function for the experiment contrast between the error rate and the choice of kernel function. The result is: SVD radial basis support vector method can establish more network point for signal prediction with less support vector. Compared with polynomial and two-tier neutral network, SVD and SVM have smaller error probability and can obtain the support of more support vector for function approximation. However, the higher of the approximation precision required is, the more support vector needed is [27–30].

The prediction time, the number of support vectors, the convergence step and the maximum mean square error are indicated in table [31–38]. We compare the convergence step, prediction time and the prediction accuracy rate of different amount of the kernel function support vector. The amount of support vector and sample needed by support vector domain SVD is only half of the SVM, polynomial and neutral network, but its accuracy rate decreases by only less than 2%. The convergence step and prediction time improve significantly compared with the original situation, improving by about 15.7%. The result indicates that the study efficiency of SVD is higher than that of SVM. In one hand, this is because SVD have to search less sample and support vector, the range needs to be searched is small. In the other hand, SVD avoids the numerous recursive least squares matrix vector computing of the sample in SVM [19–37].

This paper compared the minimum embedding dimension in fading channels of Jakes model with that of interior and outdoor actually measured non-looking straight ahead data. The amount of support vector needed by SVD is nearly one time less than that of SVM, while the number of its network points of prediction channel response increases by more than 10 times. It needs only a little time for training and is favorable for the online real-time channel estimation and detection. In the experiment the deep fading channels of different Doppler frequency shift and velocity were predicted, the classification error rate was reduced and the error comparison was accomplished [42].

5 Conclusion

The Internet network and channel prediction have sure brought great changes for us. According to the feature of irregular and fully disordered chaotic attractors in fast fading channels, using SVM and the reconstruction theory of phase space delay, we establish the predictive model of wireless channel. By the SVM training of the small sample, The channel data of the training set is mapped to a high-dimensional feature space through a nonlinear method $\Phi(h)$, and the prediction of the channel data of the predicted set is accomplished. The correlation dimension of strange attractors in wireless channels is discussed. The prediction indicates that the wireless channel has minimum embedding dimension, different from noise, the closer to the minimum embedding dimension, the smaller the relative error, mean square error of prediction is. The experimental observation and the theoretical analysis indicate that the method of SVM chaotic phase space estimation and prediction of fading channels is feasible, and is of important application value for auto-adapted adjustment, auto-adapted bit speed setting, power control and the effective use of channel resources.

Acknowledgements. Supported by the National Natural Science Foundation of China under Grant No 61574115. Shaanxi Natural Science Basic Research Plan in Shaanxi Province of China (2016JM1029), and a Project Funded by the Priority Academic Program Development of Jiangsu Higher Education Institutions, PAPD, CICAEET.

References

1. Fu, Z., Ren, K., Shu, J., Sun, X., Huang, F.: Enabling personalized search over encrypted outsourced data with efficiency improvement. IEEE Trans. Parallel Distrib. Syst. **27**(9), 2546–2559 (2016). doi:10.1109/TPDS.2015.2506573
2. Zhou, Z., Wang, Y., Jonathan Wu, Q.M., Yang, C.-N., Sun, X.: Effective and efficient global context verification for image copy detection. IEEE Trans. Inf. Forensics Secur. **12**(1), 48–63 (2017). doi:10.1109/TIFS.2016.2601065
3. Nandi, A.K., Azzouz, E.E.: Automatic modulation recognition: I. Sig. Process. **46**(2), 211–222 (1995)
4. Nandi, A.K., Azzouz, E.E.: Modulation recognition using artificial neural networks. Sig. Process. **56**(1), 165–175 (1997)
5. Fu, Z., Wu, X., Guan, C., Sun, X., Ren, K.: Toward efficient multi-keyword fuzzy search over encrypted outsourced data with accuracy improvement. IEEE Trans. Inf. Forensics Secur. **11**(12), 2706–2716 (2016). doi:10.1109/TIFS.2016.2596138
6. Zhou, Z., Yang, C.-N., Chen, B., Sun, X., Liu, Q., Jonathan Wu, Q.M.: Effective and efficient image copy detection with resistance to arbitrary rotation. IEICE Trans. Inf. Syst. **E99-D**(6), 1531–1540 (2016). doi:10.1587/transinf.2015EDP7341
7. Tax, D., et al.: Data domain description using support vectors. In: Proceedings of the European Symposium Artificial Neural, p. 251 (1999)
8. David, M.J., et al.: Support vector domain description. Pattern Recogn. Lett. **20**, 1191–1199 (1999)
9. Louvier, H., et al.: Maintenance of transient chaos using a neural-network-assisted feedback control. Phys. Rev. E **65**(1), 016203 (2002)
10. Jackes, W.C.: Microwave Mobile Communication. IEEE press, Hoboken (1993)
11. Costamagna, E.: Block-error probabilities for mobile radio channels derived from chaos equations. IEEE Commun. Lett. **3**(3), 66–68 (1999)
12. Costamagna, E.: Multipath channel modeling with chaotic attractors. Proc. IEEE **90**(5), 842–859 (2002)
13. Metzler, R.: Information flow through a chaotic channel: prediction and postdiction at finite resolution. Phys. Rev. E **70**(2), 026205 (2004)
14. Xia, Z., Wang, X., Zhang, L., Qin, Z., Sun, X., Ren, K.: A privacy-preserving and copy-deterrence content-based image retrieval scheme in cloud computing. IEEE Trans. Inf. Forensics Secur. **11**(11), 2594–2608 (2016). doi:10.1109/TIFS.2016.2590944

15. Li, J., Li, X., Yang, B., Sun, X.: Segmentation-based image copy-move forgery detection scheme. IEEE Trans. Inf. Forensics Secur. **10**(3), 507–518 (2015). doi:10.1109/TIFS.2014.2381872
16. Xia, Z., Wang, X., Sun, X., Wang, Q.: A secure and dynamic multi-keyword ranked search scheme over encrypted cloud data. IEEE Trans. Parallel Distrib. Syst. **27**(2), 340–352 (2015). doi:10.1109/TPDS.2015.2401003
17. Shen, J., Moh, S., Chung, I.: Comment: "Enhanced novel access control protocol over wireless sensor networks". IEEE Trans. Consum. Electron. **56**(3), 2019–2021 (2010). doi:10.1109/TCE.2010.5606360
18. Gu, B., Sun, X., Sheng, V.S.: Structural minimax probability machine. IEEE Trans. Neural Netw. Learn. Syst. **1**, 1–11 (2016). doi:10.1109/TNNLS.2016.2544779
19. Gu, B., Sheng, V.S., Tay, K.Y., Romano, W., Li, S.: Incremental support vector learning for ordinal regression. IEEE Trans. Neural Netw. Learn. Syst. **26**(7), 1403–1416 (2015). doi:10.1109/TNNLS.2014.2342533
20. Fu, Z., Huang, F., Sun, X., Vasilakos, A.V., Yang, C.-N.: Enabling semantic search based on conceptual graphs over encrypted outsourced data. IEEE Trans. Serv. Comput. (2016). ISSN 1939,99,1. doi:10.1109/TSC.2016.2622697
21. Pan, Z., Lei, J., Zhang, Y., Sun, X., Kwong, S.: Fast motion estimation based on content property for low-complexity H.265/HEVC encoder. IEEE Trans. Broadcast. **62**(3), 675–684 (2016). doi:10.1109/TBC.2016.2580920
22. Pan, Z., Zhang, Y., Kwong, S.: Efficient motion and disparity estimation optimization for low complexity multiview video coding. IEEE Trans. Broadcast. **61**(2), 166–176 (2015). doi:10.1109/TBC.2015.2419824
23. Yuan, C., Sun, X., Lv, R.: Fingerprint liveness detection based on multi-scale LPQ and PCA. Chin. Commun. **13**(7), 60–65 (2016). doi:10.1109/CC.2016.7559076
24. Zhang, Y., Sun, X., Baowei, W.: Efficient algorithm for k-barrier coverage based on integer linear programming. Chin. Commun. **13**(7), 16–23 (2016). doi:10.1109/CC.2016.7559071
25. Ma, T., Zhang, Y., Cao, J., Shen, J., Tang, M., Tian, Y., Al-Dhelaan, A., Al-Rodhaan, M.: KDVEM: a k-degree anonymity with vertex and edge modification algorithm. Computing **70**(6), 1336–1344 (2015)
26. Xia, Z., Wang, X., Sun, X., Liu, Q., Xiong, N.: Steganalysis of LSB matching using differences between nonadjacent pixels. Multimed. Tools Appl. **75**(4), 1947–1962 (2016). doi:10.1007/s11042-014-2381-8
27. Gu, B., Sheng, V.S., Wang, Z., Ho, D., Osman, S., Li, S.: Incremental learning for ν-support vector regression. Neural Netw. **67**, 140–150 (2015). doi:10.1016/j.neunet.2015.03.013
28. Liu, Q., Cai, W., Shen, J., Fu, Z., Liu, X., Linge, N.: A speculative approach to spatial-temporal efficiency with multi-objective optimization in a heterogeneous cloud environment. Secur. Commun. Netw. **9**(17), 4002–4012 (2016). doi:10.1002/sec.1582
29. Xia, Z., Wang, X., Sun, X., Wang, B.: Steganalysis of least significant bit matching using multi-order differences. Secur. Commun. Netw. **7**(8), 1283–1291 (2014). doi:10.1002/sec.864
30. Kong, Y., Zhang, M., Ye, D.: A belief propagation-based method for task allocation in open and dynamic cloud environments. Knowl.-Based Syst. **115**, 123–132 (2016). doi:10.1016/j.knosys.2016.10.016
31. Pan, Z., Jin, P., Lei, J., Zhang, Y., Sun, X., Kwong, S.: Fast reference frame selection based on content similarity for low complexity HEVC encoder. J. Vis. Commun. Image Represent. **40**(Part B), 516–524 (2016). doi:10.1016/j.jvcir.2016.07.018
32. Chen, Y., Hao, C., Wu, W., Wu, E.: Robust dense reconstruction by range merging based on confidence estimation. Sci. Chin. Inf. Sci. **59**(9), 1–11 (2016). doi:10.1007/s11432-015-0957-4

33. Chen, X., Chen, S., Wu, Y.: Coverless information hiding method based on the chinese character encoding. J. Internet Technol. **18**(2), 91–98 (2017). doi:10.6138/JIT.2017.18.2.20160815
34. Tian, Q., Chen, S.: Cross-heterogeneous-database age estimation through correlation representation learning. Neurocomputing **238**, 286–295 (2017)
35. Xue, Y., Jiang, J., Zhao, B., Ma, T.: A self-adaptive artificial bee colony algorithm based on global best for global optimization. Soft. Comput. **22**(3), 1–18 (2017). doi:10.1007/s00500-017-2547-1
36. Yuan, C., Xia, Z., Sun, X.: Coverless image steganography based on SIFT and BOF. J. Internet Technol. **18**(2), 209–216 (2017)
37. Qu, Z., Keeney, J., Robitzsch, S., Zaman, F., Wang, X.: Multilevel pattern mining architecture for automatic network monitoring in heterogeneous wireless communication networks. Chin. Commun. **13**(7), 108–116 (2016). doi:10.1109/CC.2016.7559082
38. Zhang, J., Tang, J., Wang, T., Chen, F.: Energy-efficient data-gathering rendezvous algorithms with mobile sinks for wireless sensor networks. Int. J. Sens. Netw. **23**(4), 248–257 (2017)
39. Sun, Y., Feihong, G.: Compressive sensing of piezoelectric sensor response signal for phased array structural health monitoring. Int. J. Sens. Netw. **23**(4), 258–264 (2017)
40. Zhangjie, F., Huang, F., Ren, K., Weng, J., Wang, C.: Privacy-preserving smart semantic search based on conceptual graphs over encrypted outsourced data. IEEE Trans. Inf. Forensics Secur. **12**(8), 1874–1884 (2017)
41. Shen, J., Shen, J., Chen, X., Huang, X., Susilo, W.: An efficient public auditing protocol with novel dynamic structure for cloud data. IEEE Trans. Inf. Forensics Secur. **18**(5), 1 (2017). doi:10.1109/TIFS.2017.2705620
42. Shen, J., Tan, H., Moh, S., Chung, I., Liu, Q., Sun, X.: Enhanced secure sensor association and key management in wireless body area networks. J. Commun. Netw. **17**(5), 453–462 (2015)

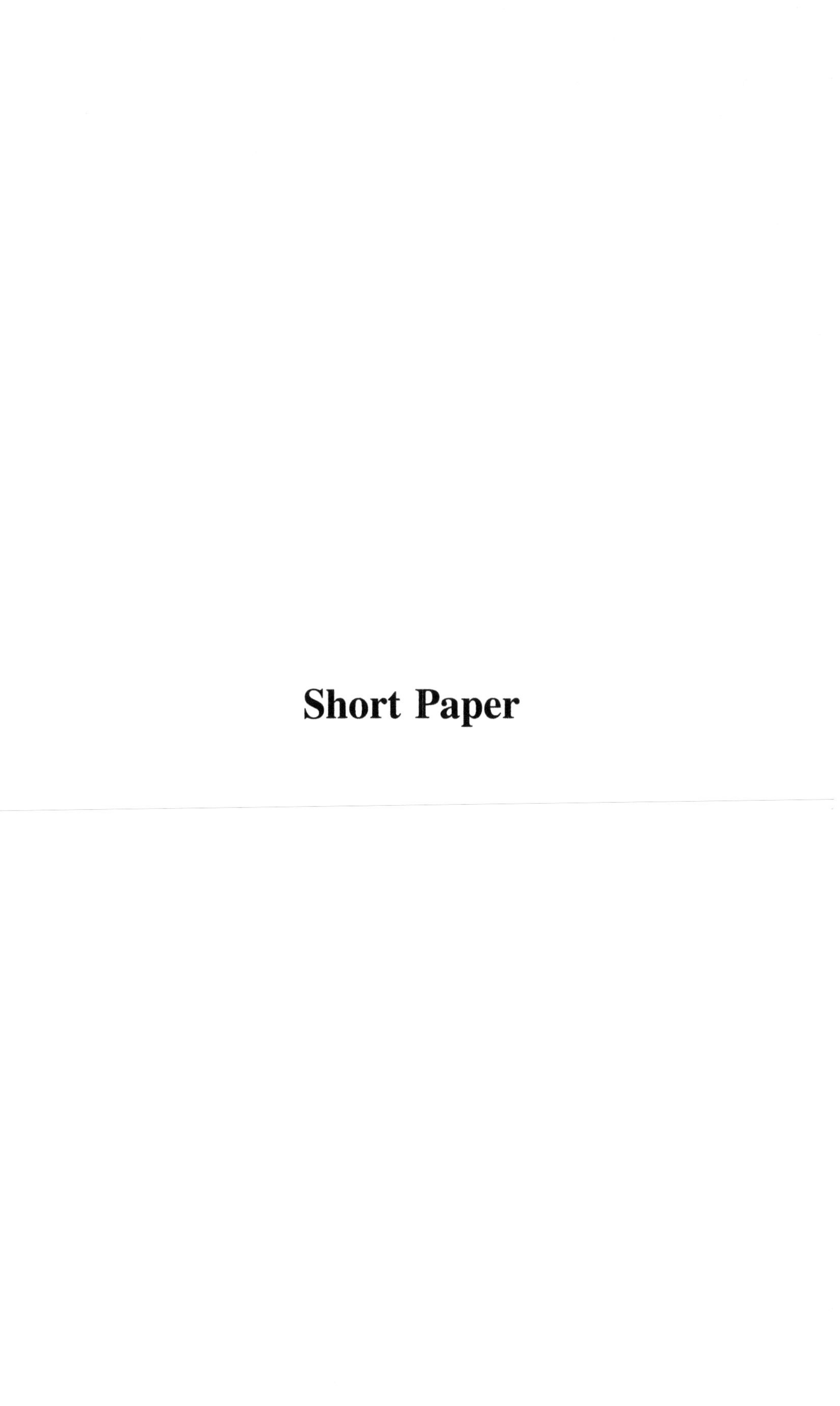

Short Paper

System Log-Based Android Root State Detection

Junjie Jin and Wei Zhang(✉)

College of Computer Science, Nanjing University of Posts and Telecommunications, Nanjing 210023, Jiangsu, China
zhangw@njupt.edu.cn

Abstract. Android rooting enables device owners to freely customize their own devices. However, rooting system weakens the security of Android devices and opens the backdoor for malware to obtain privileged access easily. For this reason, some developers have introduced detection mechanisms for sensitive or high-value mobile apps to mitigate the potential security risks. Nevertheless, the existing root prevention and detection methods generally lack universality. In this paper, we studied the existing Android root detection methods and found the both parties have ignored the traces of the relevant behavior in the log. Thus, we proposed the system log based root state detection method. In the method, we directly use the existing log information to find clues to verify the system root state on one hand, on the other hand, to use the triggering features of some special operations to update and enrich the log information. The results show that, even be deliberately erased, some log information is still remained which can be used to verify whether system was rooted or not.

Keywords: Android security · Root detection · System log

1 Introduction

With android system share in the global market upgrade, Android system is facing more serious security problems. In Android security-related research, the inherent security mechanisms, such as permissions mechanism, process isolation (sandbox) mechanism are the focus of researchers' attention [1]. While Android's security vulnerabilities have a more detailed study, many researchers specifically for the root exploit use a number of ways to break the Android inherent security mechanism. Android system is based on the Linux kernel but root privileges are not open to the normal user. However, many users keen to obtain the root privileges of the device to cut the phone pre-installed applications or customize mobile optimization programs. Hackers are also keen to find vulnerability in the Android system to obtain root privileges. Currently, Google does not open the root privileges to the user. It is a fact that some system vulnerabilities can be employed to get Android system root privileges. Through these vulnerabilities, malware can obtain root privileges to bypass the Android own protection mechanisms or third-party advanced security mechanism.

For the rooted system risk, some researchers have analyzed in their articles. Sun et al. [2] mentioned that some applications would check the system root status at the

X. Sun et al. (Eds.): ICCCS 2017, Part II, LNCS 10603, pp. 793–798, 2017.
https://doi.org/10.1007/978-3-319-68542-7_69

first installation. Evans et al. [3] described several common methods to implement root and proposed the corresponding detection methods. Google proposed the CTS (Compatibility Test Suite) framework [4] in the Android platform. During the compatibility test, CTS also analyzes the system root state.

Most of the existing detection methods focus on the discovery of single trace or several traces combined. These methods cannot deal with the deliberate deletion, or change for the traces to circumvent the detection. Some well-known anti-detection frameworks have been able to avoid most of the existing detection contents. Google Play Store and some of the Android hacking community also provided a variety of root state hidden software. Xposed Framework [5] is one of the most widely used software which used hook API technology and can dynamic bypasses most of the existing traces of root detection function.

In this paper, based on the research of the existing methods of Android system root trace detection, we present a more general method based on the system log information of Android, and demonstrates the detail process of detecting root traces. Sections 1 and 2 introduces the root principles and some basic detection methods. Section 3 describes the root trace in the log items analysis. Section 4 discusses the criterion of system root traces detection. Section 5 summarizes our work and concludes the paper.

2 Background and Related Work

Nowadays, the root processing of Android devices is more popular and easier. According to the most recent Google Android security report [14], about 3–4% of the devices in the Chinese market exists root applications. Moreover, many cheap devices are shipped with customized image that allow root access by default. The vulnerability code is free to download in the XDA forum [12] and other hacker communities.

In the Android system, Google does not take into account the management issues of the root privileges. Many programmers have developed a similar superUser.apk permissions management program to deal with root privileges request. Using a customized su file, through SuperUser.apk to respond, grant other applications root privileges. In the process of getting root permissions, the actions of adding files or modifying the system directory will create the new trace log. Some of the changes are essential, while some appearance unconsciously.

These traces of intentionally or unintentionally will constitute the main contents of the system root trace detection. There are many different root system exploits. Since these developers do not mine and utilize the same vulnerabilities, everyone's code is different. So the traces are not the same.

Based on the above, we divided the existing root traces detection methods of Android into three categories: traces detection that require permission response, traces detection that does not require permission response [2, 3] and the Google CTS detection framework [4]. The first category requires su permission response. If the user for some reason refused to grant the highest authority to apply detection, it may result in the misjudgment of root trace detection. The detection method without relying on the su response to the traces is more adaptable. It only relies on the basic permissions granted by the first installation, without the need of human intervention, and is more efficient and reliable. Google CTS framework is compatible with all versions of the Android API with a unified user experience, and the developed applications can run on all compatible devices. In order to prevent its SDK API compatibility, CTS completes the verification of some key parts of the system, which contains the detection of system root state.

Trace-detection method without su permission response: Check the installed apps, Check the existing files, Check the build tags, Check the specific system properties, Check the list of currently running processes.

Trace-detection method requires su permission response: Check the shell command execution, Check the disk remount state.

Google CTS: Signature testing, Platform API testing, Dalvik perform format testing, platform data model testing, Intents, Permissions, Resources testing.

3 Detection Based on System Log

3.1 Root Trace Information Acquisition

When the user uses the root software to modify the system, it leaves many traces of traceability. For a long time, a large number of mobile phone applications are made by individuals and third-party companies, which have large technical level differences. Application crashes and unresponsive situations have occurred, or even that has become the norm. Android system records these special events in background and intends to provide the log to the software developers to enhance the user experience. However, the root program developers and root traces of detectors have ignored the value of the log information [6–8].

Because some operations, such as Android system restricts the log storage, the user restarts the system or deliberately use the clean-up optimization software, will cause some relevant existing log information to be cleared. However, we found that after the device restarted, new traces information is generated automatically which includes initialization of various applications, response to commands, error messages, network information, and update information.

3.2 Based on the Information to Determine the Root State

General log analysis. In the process of detecting the root state of the mobile phone, regardless of the user to restart the device and deliberately delete the log behavior, we called the method of matching traces of root left in the log as the regular log analysis.

For example, in Fig. 1, we find supersu permission management software traces, which obviously contains: supolicy, sukernel, su daemon, su and other relevant output information. Then we match the known package name, the specific string information: su, supersu, busybox, etc., to determine the device was rooted and owned the highest administrator privileges.

Trace analysis of traces triggered. In the process of detecting the root state of the device, the user may reboot the system or use the log cleaning software. If the required key log of detection is less or the available information is ambiguous, not enough to support our log analysis. In this situation, we invoke a number of existing root state detection methods mentioned in the previous section, triggering the response of the relevant application in the system. Then, the log certainly contains traces of our trigger response, regardless of success or failure of the execution results. Finally, determine whether the system is rooted. We call this method as trace-triggered log analysis.

```
I/ActivityManager( 789): Displayed eu.chainfire.supersu/ .PromptActivity: +156ms
D/SuperSU][APK( 1554): [SuperSU][APK][Installer] su --> 277
D/SuperSU][APK( 1554): [SuperSU][APK][Installer] su backup --> 277
D/SuperSU][APK( 1554): [SuperSU][APK][Installer] su daemon --> 277
D/SuperSU][APK( 1554): [SuperSU][APK][Installer] sugote --> 277 / 1 /1
D/SuperSU][APK( 1554): [SuperSU][APK][Installer] supolicy --> 277
D/SuperSU][APK( 1554): [SuperSU][APK][Installer] sukernel --> -3
D/SuperSU][APK( 1554): [SuperSU][APK][Installer] su old --> -2
D/SuperSU][APK( 1554): [SuperSU][APK][Installer] app_process --> 0
D/SuperSU][APK( 1554): [SuperSU][APK][Installer] sdk == 19
```

```
I/PackageManager( 764): Running dexopt on: com.example.nss.testfor
D/PackageBroadcastService( 975): Received broadcast
action=android.intent.action.PACKAGE_ADDED and uri=com.example.nss.testfor
I/ActivityManager( 764): Displayed com.example.nss.testfor/ .MainActivity:
+278ms (total +1s749ms)

v/abcd (2876): su exec not success
I/ActivityManager( 764): Displayed com.example.nss.testfor/ .MainActivity:
+283ms
D/SuperSU][APK( 2846): [SuperSU][APK][Installer] detect(278)
D/SuperSU][APK( 2846): [SuperSU][APK][Installer] su --> 278
D/SuperSU][APK( 2846): [SuperSU][APK][Installer] su backup --> 278
D/SuperSU][APK( 2846): [SuperSU][APK][Installer] su daemon --> 278
```

Fig. 1. Basic log analysis samples and trigger log analysis samples.

In Fig. 1, right side line 4 indicates a failed exec(su) operation. Regardless of the success or failure of the implementation, it will return to a large number of operations responses or the process traces. According to these traces, we can determine the device's current rooted status.

Determination criterion of analysis. The detection decision includes two steps. The commonality of detection is our first concern. We do not check some certain strings. Instead, we assume that all suspicious things might indicate the existence of root behavior. When the log contains little useful information or was deliberately erased or covered by a third party application, the result is vague. In this situation, we can install our pre-designed experimental application. The application will artificially trigger some high-power operation to cause the system to record more reliable response information for log analysis.

Due to the fragmentation phenomenon of Android system, most of the third-party ROM providers make some changes to the application and performance. Meanwhile, the modification of the log system is relatively small, thus the originality of log system is preserved. Therefore, the information generated by the log system has high credibility. The method based on system logs, avoiding the disadvantages of regular detections. It uses ignored system log clues to find root-related applications, which indicates the current root state of the system. In the hypothetical case to restart and remove information, we can use trigger mechanism to enrich the log information. The method mentioned in the paper compared to other detection scheme has obvious superiority.

4 Experiment and Analysis

In our experiments, we perform root operations on Google Nexus 5, Android 4.4, and install applications such as Supersu, Busybox, Titanium Backup, Xposed framework [9–13] to check for log traces.

The goal of the test is clear, that is to check whether there are some log items associated with the root privileges of the application package name, operating traces, error records. If some items are detected that require root privileges to work properly installed in the system, we believe that the system was rooted.

Through the power process and the system initialization process, we extract the related system logs to check the appropriate clues. As shown in the following:

```
I/am_proc_start( 776):
[0,1554,10075,eu.chainfire.supersu,broadcast,eu.chainfire.supersu/
.BootCompleteReceiver]
I/am_proc_bound( 776): [0,1554,eu.chainfire.supersu]
I/am_create_service( 776): [0,1119590600,SuperUserIntentService,10075,1554]
I/notification_cancel( 776): [eu.chainfire.supersu,1,NULL,0,0,64]
I/am_kill( 776): [0,1554,eu.chainfire.supersu,15,empty #17]
I/am_proc_died( 776): [0,1554,eu.chainfire.supersu]
```

```
W/PackageManager( 776): Unknown permission android.permission.READ_MEDIA_STORAGE in package
com.keramidas.TitaniumBackup
W/PackageManager( 776): Not granting permission android.permission.WRITE_MEDIA_STORAGE to package
com.keramidas.TitaniumBackup (protectionLevel=18 flags=0x8be44)
W/PackageManager( 776): Not granting permission android.permission.BROADCAST_SMS to package
com.keramidas.TitaniumBackup (protectionLevel=2 flags=0x8be44)
W/PackageManager( 776): Not granting permission android.permission.REBOOT to package eu.chainfire.supersu
(protectionLevel=18 flags=0x83e05)
I/ActivityManager( 766): Start proc eu.chainfire.supersu for broadcast eu.chainfire.supersu/
.BootCompleteReceiver: pid=1554 uid=10075 gids{50075}
I/ActivityManager( 766): Killing 1554:eu.chainfire.supersu/u0a75 (adj 15): empty #17
```

Fig. 2. Events log analysis and system log analysis.

Through the analysis of the experimental data, we found traces of the general information about the process info, package manager, debug, warning, and other information recorded by the system response of the various applications. It provides extremely useful information for finding root-related traces. In Fig. 2, we found the trace of super user permission management application for some operations, such as, startup process, create services, kill process. In Fig. 2, right side, we found Titanium backup application in the permission granted error message. In Fig. 3, we found debugging information outputted by supersu application and the time of elapsed displayed by Activity interface. When occurred the above mentioned similar information, we can consider the device is rooted.

```
I/ActivityManager( 789): Displayed eu.chainfire.supersu/ .PromptActivity: +156ms
D/SuperSU][APK( 1554): [SuperSU][APK][Installer] su --> 277
D/SuperSU][APK( 1554): [SuperSU][APK][Installer] su backup --> 277
D/SuperSU][APK( 1554): [SuperSU][APK][Installer] su daemon --> 277
D/SuperSU][APK( 1554): [SuperSU][APK][Installer] sugote --> 277 / 1 /1
D/SuperSU][APK( 1554): [SuperSU][APK][Installer] supolicy --> 277
D/SuperSU][APK( 1554): [SuperSU][APK][Installer] sukernel --> -3
D/SuperSU][APK( 1554): [SuperSU][APK][Installer] su old --> -2
D/SuperSU][APK( 1554): [SuperSU][APK][Installer] app_process --> 0
D/SuperSU][APK( 1554): [SuperSU][APK][Installer] sdk == 19
```

Fig. 3. Main log analysis.

5 Summary

Aiming at the deficiency of existing detection methods, we propose a root trace detection method based on log analysis. This method is based on several key clues in the system log to determine whether the system has been rooted. In the case of relatively small amount of the log information, we use the trigger application to increase the amount of useful information and draw a conclusion. The experimental results show that the method is credible and effective. Our next work is to analyze root traces hidden mechanism, improve the detection accuracy.

Acknowledgments. Project supported by the National Natural Science Foundation of China (No. 61272422, 61202353).

References

1. Evans, N.S., Benameur, A., Shen, Y.: All your root checks are belong to us: the sad state of root detection. In: Proceedings of the 13th ACM International Symposium on Mobility Management and Wireless Access (MobiWac 2015), pp. 81–88, New York (2015)
2. Sun, S.-T., Cuadros, A., Beznosov, K.: Android rooting: methods, detection, and evasion. In: Proceedings of the 5th Annual ACM CCS Workshop on Security and Privacy in Smartphones and Mobile Devices (SPSM 2015), pp. 3–14, New York (2015)
3. Ho, T.-H., Dean, D., Gu, X., Enck, W.: PREC: practical root exploit containment for android devices. In: Proceedings of the 4th ACM Conference on Data and Application Security and Privacy (CODASPY 2014), pp. 187–198, New York (2014)
4. Zhang, H., She, D., Qian, Z.: Android root and its providers: a double-edged sword. In: Proceedings of the 22nd ACM SIGSAC Conference on Computer and Communications Security (CCS 2015), pp. 1093–1104, New York (2015)
5. Wang, X., et al.: DeepDroid: Dynamically Enforcing Enterprise Policy on Android Devices. NDSS (2015)
6. Zhang, Z., Wang, Y., Jing, J., Wang, Q., Lei, L.: Once root always a threat: analyzing the security threats of android permission system. In: Susilo, W., Mu, Y. (eds.) ACISP 2014. LNCS, vol. 8544, pp. 354–369. Springer, Cham (2014). doi:10.1007/978-3-319-08344-5_23
7. Google Compatibility Test Suite. https://source.android.com/compatibility/cts/
8. cyanogenmod. http://www.cyanogenmod.org/
9. supersu. https://www.chainfire.eu/
10. Xposed Framework. http://www.cydiasubstrate.com/
11. titanium-backup. http://www.titaniumtrack.com/titanium-backup.html
12. xda-developers. http://forum.xda-developers.com/apps/supersu
13. compatibility. http://source.android.com/compatibility
14. Google Android Security 2015 Report. https://source.android.com/zh-CN//security/reports/Google_Android_Security_2015_Report_Final.pdf

Quantified Attribute Access Control Model for Cloud Storage Platform

DongMin Li[1], Jing Li[1(✉)], Sai Liu[2], and Chao Wang[1]

[1] College of Computer Science and Technology, Nanjing University of Aeronautics and Astronautics, Nanjing 211106, China
jingli@nuaa.edu.cn

[2] NARI Group Corporation, Nanjing 210003, China
liusai1010@126.com

Abstract. Recently, cloud computing is the most domain studies in information technology. At the same time, the security of cloud computing becomes an important challenge. Existing access control models are poor on the granularity of the model elements and the dynamics which leads the security of the resource in cloud computing is limited. In this paper, a quantified attribute-based access control (QABAC) model is proposed. The concept of quantified attribute and trust degree is defined. Three attribute quantization functions are proposed for dynamically calculation, and the security degree of the access will be obtained. Finally the authorization policy determines final permission according to the trust degree. Compared with other traditional models, QABAC is flexible, extensible and dynamic. It will not only protect the security of resource among potential attack from network, but also has the capacity to meet the performance requirement in practical applications.

Keywords: Access control · Dynamic authorization · Cloud computing security

1 Introduction

Cloud computing is an emerging computing paradigm. It is Internet-centric and provides all the resources as services such as storage, computation and communication. Cloud computing is a unique combination of capabilities and innovation technologies [1], which can offer an extensible and powerful environment for growing amounts of data and services, and make full use of computing resources of each computer through a ubiquitous and low-cost platform. At the same time, the client's burden from management and maintenance can be relieved. Thus it soon attracts a large number of researchers and companies.

Security is one of the primary challenges to adopt cloud computing. Three major issues in cloud storage platform security are listed below.

(1) Control ability of the database owner is limited.
(2) Access right will be adjusted with time [2].
(3) Hence data faces issues like privacy and unauthorized access [3].

X. Sun et al. (Eds.): ICCCS 2017, Part II, LNCS 10603, pp. 799–804, 2017.
https://doi.org/10.1007/978-3-319-68542-7_70

Hence, access control (AC) should be introduced into cloud computing to protect sensitive data in terms of access policy [4]. The research of access control model began in the last century in 70s. At first, it was responsible for sharing data of large computer access authorization management. The role-based access control (RBAC) model is one of the most classical models in the traditional access control model [5]. Then some attributes such as user attribute, object attribute and environment attribute are introduced to the model. New access control models such as task-based access control (TBAC) [6, 7] and action-based access control (ABAC) [8] were proposed.

The model is mainly improved in two aspects, which are model element and the reliability calculation.

(1) Extending traditional access control models. New model elements are incorporated into model, which are used to supplement the subject and object attributes.
(2) Three mapping functions are proposed. The value of the attribute is mapped to a numerical value with a unified standard of measurement, further the confidence interval of the user behavior is evaluated by these values.

The rest of the paper is organized as follows. Section 2 gives the details of QABAC model and process of authorization. Section 3 analyzes our model and shows the performance of it in cloud storage platform. Section 4 concludes this method.

2 Our Access Control Model

The structure of QABAC, which is an extended from RBAC for generality, is illustrated in Fig. 1. The concept of the action control is introduced based on role, environment and temporal, and they work together to evaluate the access. Trust degree of the access is calculated by quantification, and then proper permission is granted according it.

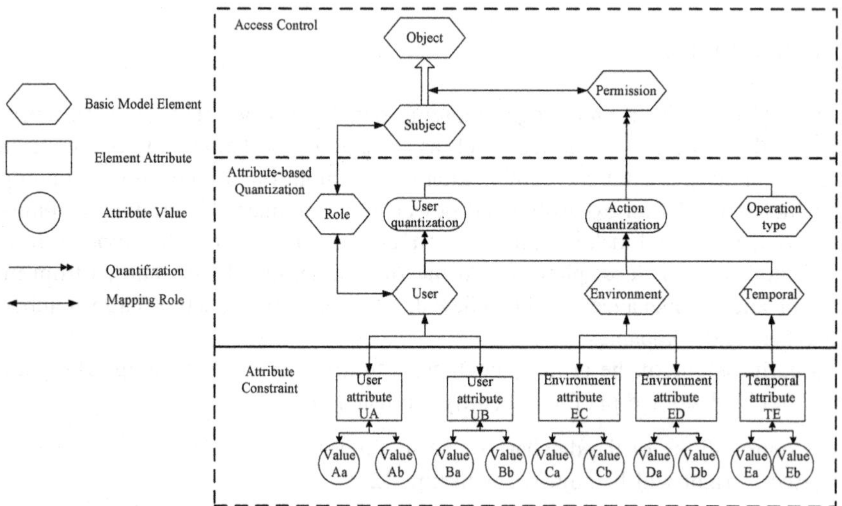

Fig. 1. Structure of model access control

2.1 Model Basic Elements

QABAC model comprehensively restricts the access from the perspective of subject and object, it can be expressed as $QABAC = \{U, R, O, Action,\ opc\}$.

Subject (U): Data resource requester. $U = \{user_1, user_2, \ldots user_n\}$, each user is defined the related properties and identified by the user *ID*.

Role (R): A collection formed by users with same identity attributes.

Object (O): Services offered by cloud storage platform such as storage, computation and communication.

Environment (E): A collection contains network environment and terminal platform information of subjects.

Calendar (C): Calendar is used to describe temporal, it is an infinite set of periodic continuous time sets such as hour, day, month and year [9].

Temporal (T): Given a set of calendar *C1*...*Cn*. Corresponding temporal can be defined as $T = \sum_{i=1}^{n} C_i \triangleright r \circ C_d$. The previous part before $\triangleright$ represents the starting time and the later part represent the duration.

Action (Action): A relationship between subject and object. This element is represented by symbol $Action = R \times E \times T$.

Operation type (OPC): Users will operate resource in different ways. Operation type is defined by the follow formulate. $Opc = \{read, write, delete, update\}$.

2.2 Mapping Rules

Users are restricted through roles and access objects during authorizing. Corresponding mapping rules are defined to associate different elements.

Permission Assignment (PA): The relationship between permission with three elements of role, action and operation type. Corresponding mapping function is (1).

$$P_{assigned}(r) = \{p \in P | (p, <role, action, opc>) \in PA\} \tag{1}$$

User Attribute Map (UAM): One to multi mapping relationship of user and attribute. The content of role attribute is mapped to a certain value according to the mapping function, which is shown as (2).

$$AttrMap_{uattr} = (\forall attr \in Attr | (u, attr) \in UAM) \tag{2}$$

Environment Attribute Map (EAM): One to multi mapping relationship between environment and attribute, the content of environment attribute is mapped to a numerical value. Corresponding mapping function is (3).

$$AttrMap_{eattr} = (\forall attr \in Attr | (e, attr) \in EAM) \tag{3}$$

Temporal Attribute Map (TAM): One to multi mapping relationship between temporal and attribute, the content of environment attribute is mapped to a certain value. Corresponding mapping function is (4).

$$AttrMap_{tattr} = (\forall attr \in Attr|(t, attr) \in TAM) \tag{4}$$

2.3 Attribute Quantification

Quantify attribute: According to the mapping function, the values of user attribute domain is converted to the numerical value, and put these values into the trust computation function to calculate user trust [10]. User and action trust computation function is shown as (5) and (6).

$$qtyU(Uattr) = \sum_{i=1}^{n} w_i V(uattr_i) \tag{5}$$

$$qtyA(Aattr, t) = \sum_{i=1}^{n} w_i V(uattr_i) + \sum_{j=1}^{m} w_j V(eattr_j) + \sum_{k=1}^{z} w_k V(tattr_k) \tag{6}$$

where $V(eattr_j)$ is the value of the environment attribute and $V(tattr_k)$ is the value of the temporal attribute, w_j and w_k are the weights of the corresponding attribute. t means the moment of the calculation.

Final trust: The calculation of the final trust is based on the evaluation results of these two kinds of attributes, and the calculation function of final trust is defined as (7).

$$\gamma(Uattr, Aattr, t) = qtyU * qtyA \tag{7}$$

Permission granted: Access control model determines permission of user access based on the dynamic authorization strategy. The access is adopted if the security level of user access is higher than the minimum required for the type of operation on the resource file, otherwise the access will be denied [11].

3 Security Analysis and Performance Evaluation

QABAC model is implemented using C++. Experiments were run on Intel Core 4 processors with 3.3 GHz and 4G RAM on Windows 7. This article had a total five group data, which contained ten thousand accesses. Figure 2 shows authorization time trend with the increase in the number of accesses. It is obvious that the access time showed a linear growth trend and ten million-scale visit can be authorized at the same time.

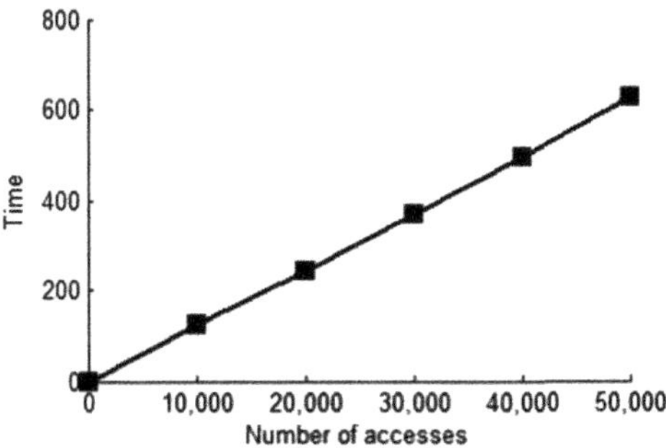

Fig. 2. The trend of authorization time under multiple accesses

QABAC and RBAC model are used to grant the permissions for these access behaviors and the correct rate of two models is calculated by (8).

$$C = \frac{n}{N} \tag{8}$$

where C is the correct rate. n means the correctly authorized access number, correct authorization includes both cases that allow legitimate access and denial of unlawful access. N is total number of access.

Figure 3 shows the authorization correct rate between two models, in which the x axis represents the number of access behavior and y axis represents the authorization correct rate. QABAC is close to the true accuracy when the number of access behaviors is increasing, and it is significantly higher than the RBAC model.

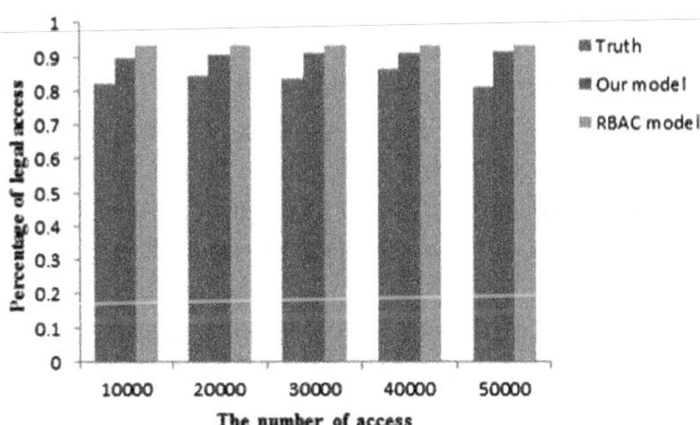

Fig. 3. Authorized correct rate trend with the change of the number of access behavior (Color figure online)

4 Conclusions

An access control model for cloud computing is proposed in this paper. It facilitates the role and task principles to make assigning privileges very dynamic and easy. Temporal and environment is introduced into model elements. Corresponding attributes are designed which include category and value for these elements. The calculation result of each access by the dynamic quantization function divides these accesses into different security levels. Proved by experiments, it can fulfill the access control requirements in cloud computing.

Acknowledgments. Supported by National Power Grid Corp headquarters project of science and technology: research and application of heterogeneous disaster recovery technology (No. 0711-150TL173).

References

1. Beak, J., Vu, Q.H., Liu, J.K., et al.: A secure cloud computing based framework for big data information management of smart grid. IEEE Trans. Cloud Comput. **3**(2), 233–244 (2015)
2. Liu, Q.Y., Sha, H.Z., Shi-Ming, L.I., et al.: An access control method based on quantified services and roles in large scale of network visits. Chin. J. Comput. (2014)
3. Almutairi, A., Sarfraz, M., Basalamah, S., et al.: A distributed access control architecture for cloud computing. IEEE Softw. **29**(2), 36–44 (2011)
4. Xia, Z., Wang, X., Zhang, L., et al.: A privacy-preserving and copy-deterrence content-based image retrieval scheme in cloud computing. IEEE Tran. Inf. Forensics Secur. **11**(11), 2594–2608 (2016)
5. Younis, A., Kifayat, K., Merabti, M.: An access control model for cloud computing. J. Inf. Secur. Appl. **19**(1), 45–60 (2014)
6. Yang, K., Liu, Z., Jia, X., et al.: Time-domain attribute-based access control for cloud-based video content sharing: a cryptographic approach. IEEE Trans. Multimedia **18**(5), 940–950 (2016)
7. Zhang, Y., Sun, X., Wang, B.: Efficient algorithm for k-barrier coverage based on integer linear programming. Chin. Commun. **13**(7), 16–23 (2016)
8. Simmhan, Y., Kumbhare, A.G., Cao, B., et al.: An analysis of security and privacy issues in smart grid software architectures on clouds. In: IEEE International Conference on Cloud Computing, pp. 582–589. IEEE Computer Society (2011)
9. Chakraborty, S., Ray, I.: TrustBAC: integrating trust relationships into the RBAC model for access control in open systems. In: SACMAT 2006, ACM Symposium on Access Control MODELS and Technologies, DBLP, vol. 18, pp. 49–58 (2006)
10. Wu, C.: On web services access control based on quantified-role. Computer Applications and Software (2012)
11. Liu, Q., Cai, W., Shen, J., et al.: A speculative approach to spatial-temporal efficiency with multi-objective optimization in a heterogeneous cloud environment. Secur. Commun. Netw. **9**(17), 4002–4012 (2016)

Dynamically-Enabled Defense Effectiveness Evaluation in Home Internet Based on Vulnerability Analysis

Ting Wang[1], Min Lei[2], Jingjie Chen[2], Shiqi Deng[2(✉)], and Yu Yang[2]

[1] China Information Technology Security Evaluation Center, Beijing, China
[2] Information Security Center, Beijing University of Posts and Telecommunications, Beijing, China
{leimin, chenjingjie, dengshiqi, yangyu}@bupt.edu.cn

Abstract. Current intelligent devices in Home Internet, such as routers and cameras, have suffered malicious attacks from hackers. Therefore, security for Home Internet appears particularly significant. In order to have a quantitative evaluation of security defense ability of Home Internet system, this paper proposes an improved vulnerability scoring method on Home Internet based on Information Security Technology Security Vulnerability Classification Guide. Compared to original scoring method which is mainly based on Internet, this improved scoring performs differently. It's aimed to have a quantitative evaluation on security defense effectiveness of Home Internet system: higher vulnerability score indicates higher threaten degree and relatively weak defense ability. In this paper, the Home Internet system takes dynamically-enabled defense technology (randomly changes system status) to make defense. Through calculating vulnerability scores before and after random changes of system status, this paper succeeds in making a quantitative evaluation on security defense ability of Home Internet system.

Keywords: Family smart terminal · Home Internet · Dynamically-enabled defense · Vulnerability score

1 Introduction

With rapid development of Home Internet, a large number of family smart terminals have accessed the Internet via gateway devices in home [1]. Current intelligent devices in a Home Internet, such as routers and cameras, have suffered malicious attacks from hackers. Therefore, for the purpose of improving security defensive capability of Home Internet, this paper analyzes various security vulnerability existing in Home Internet, takes dynamically-enabled technology to make defense, and evaluates its effectiveness.

X. Sun et al. (Eds.): ICCCS 2017, Part II, LNCS 10603, pp. 805–815, 2017.
https://doi.org/10.1007/978-3-319-68542-7_71

2 Related Work

2.1 Home Internet

A Home Internet takes TV, refrigerator, air conditioning and other smart appliances as the main bearing based on the home environment [2]. It takes responsible for the interconnection and intelligent cooperation among these smart appliances.

A Home Internet is composed of terminals, networks, clouds, and APPs. The general framework of a Home Internet system is shown as Fig. 1.

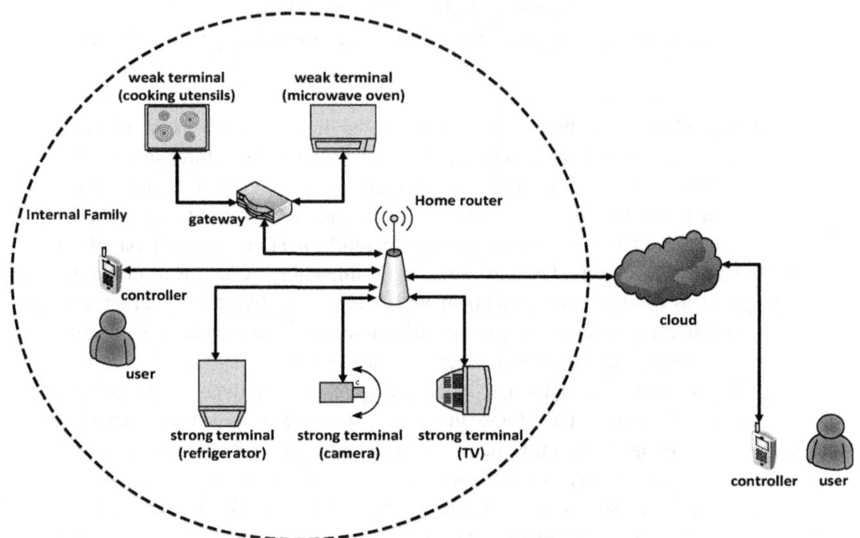

Fig. 1. General framework of Home Internet

As Fig. 1 shown, network nodes conclude control point, equipment, and gateway. The control point is main controller in the network, for example, mobile phone, PAD, and Set-Top Box. Equipment such as TV, refrigerator, smoke stove, switch, curtain, etc., acts as a service provider in the Home Internet. The gateway is special equipment which concludes nature of ordinary equipment, and is able to be an agent of other equipment. Both the control point, equipment and gateway are logic devices. Each physical device can act as equipment, gateway, and control point simultaneously.

The strong terminals (refrigerator, camera, and TV) and controller in internal family are connected to the Home router directly. The weak terminals (cooking utensils and microwave oven) connect to the Home router via the gateway. Another controller outside the internal family network controls equipment through the cloud.

2.2 Ideas of Vulnerability Assessment

The core idea of dynamically-enabled defense technology is to change the state of the system by the randomly changing of the core elements such as software, network, platform and data, so that it is difficult for the attacker to exploit accumulated and outdated system vulnerabilities directly [3]. Theoretically, there are a certain change in the number of vulnerabilities and ease of vulnerability usage between the status of before and after the Home Internet system which is adjusted by taking dynamically-enabled defense technology and the original system status [4]. Besides, only the decline in the number of vulnerabilities and the increase in the ease of vulnerability usage can bring a positive meaning to the dynamic change of the system status [5]. Therefore, analyzing vulnerability distribution before and after the system changes in the Home Internet can accurately evaluate the defense effectiveness of dynamically-enabled defense technology [6].

2.3 Vulnerability Classification

A Home Internet system concludes terminal, network, cloud, and APP. Each module has potential vulnerabilities. According to attack type, attack surface and attack point three aspects, security vulnerabilities of the Home Internet system are classified as Table 1 shown.

2.4 Vulnerability Scoring

According to the diversity of vulnerability assessment results, techniques of vulnerability assessment can be divided into qualitative evaluation and quantitative evaluation. The qualitative evaluation is to determine a threat level for vulnerabilities, such as high, medium, and low, based on vulnerability assessment factors. The quantitative evaluation is to determine a certain threat score for vulnerabilities on the basis of established rating factors, for example, any integer between 0 and 10. Currently, Information Security Technology Security Vulnerability Classification Guide [7] is domestic standardized vulnerability rating criteria. This paper makes some improvement on the basis of this criteria and has a quantitative evaluation on Home Internet system.

2.4.1 Information Security Technology Security Vulnerability Classification Guide

Information Security Technology Security Vulnerability Classification Guide (GB/T 30279-2013) specifies classification elements and hazard degree of information security system vulnerabilities, which is applicable for information security vulnerability management organizations and information security vulnerability issuing agency to evaluate and identify hazard degree of information security system vulnerabilities [8]. It is also a reference for information security products production, technology research and development, system operation and other organizations, institutions in related works [9].

Table 1. Security vulnerability classification in the Home Internet system

Attack type	Attack surface	Attack point
Intelligent terminal	Device storage	User name plaintext storage
		Password plaintext storage
		Insecure key storage
	Web interface	SQL injection
		XSS
		CSRF
		Weak password
		Violence enumeration
		Known default authentication
	Device firmware	Sensitive information leakage
		Backdoor account
		Firmware degradation
	Network service	Unencrypted service
		Insecure OTA firmware update
		Carrier verification deficiency
		Lack of integrity check
	Local data storage	Unencrypted data
		Encryption with a leaked key
		Lack of data integrity detection
		Encryption with static key
	Hardware	Device forgery
		Verification defect
	Renewal mechanism	Unencrypted update
		No-signature update
		Rewritten permitted in update location
		Malicious update
		No-verification update
Communication network	Authentication leakage	Cookie-leak attack
		Session-leak attack
	Unencrypted authentication	Unencrypted authentication between equipment and equipment
		Unencrypted authentication between equipment and terminal
		Unencrypted authentication between equipment and cloud
		Lack of dynamic authentication
		Full-trust in cloud and device
APP	Mobile terminal	Known default account
		Insecure data storage
	Disassembling	No shell
		Bad confusion

(*continued*)

Table 1. *(continued)*

Attack type	Attack surface	Attack point
Cloud	Identity authentication security	SQL injection
		XSS
		CSRF
	Design defect	Violence enumeration
		Weak password
		Account leakage
		Known default account

The criteria give a classification method of security vulnerabilities: users can make a comprehensive judgement of the damage degree of a vulnerability according to the specific deployment of affected system and the vulnerability hazard level given by the criteria [10].

In the criteria, the security vulnerability classification elements include three aspects: access vector, access complexity, and impact degree. The available values of access vector include "local", "adjacent", and "remote". In general, the damage degree of the vulnerability that can be exploited remotely is higher than that which can be exploited adjacently. The available values of access complexity include "simple" and "complex", and the damage degree of the vulnerability that has "simple" access complexity is higher. The available values of impact degree include "completely", "partially", "lightly", and "none". Usually the greater the impact degree of vulnerability, the higher the degree of damage.

From low to high order, the damage degree of security vulnerability is low, medium, high, and super. The specific hazard level is determined by the different values of three elements (access vector, access complexity, and impact degree).

In the evaluation process, Information Security Technology Security Vulnerability Classification Guide first assigns values to access vector, access complexity and impact degree (confidentiality, integrity, and availability). These values reflect the potential impact of the vulnerability itself. And then according to the evaluation values of confidentiality, integrity and availability, the impact degree is calculated. Finally, on the basis of the evaluation values of access vector, access complexity and impact degree, the final hazard level of the vulnerability is determined. The grade assessment made by the criteria is a quantitative assessment.

Figure 2 describes hazard level evaluation process of security vulnerabilities in Information Security Technology Security Vulnerability Classification Guide.

2.4.2 Improved Vulnerability Evaluation Method

Considering the actual situation of the Home Internet system, this paper made some improvements based on Information Security Technology Security Vulnerability Classification Guide. The improved vulnerability evaluation method is more suitable

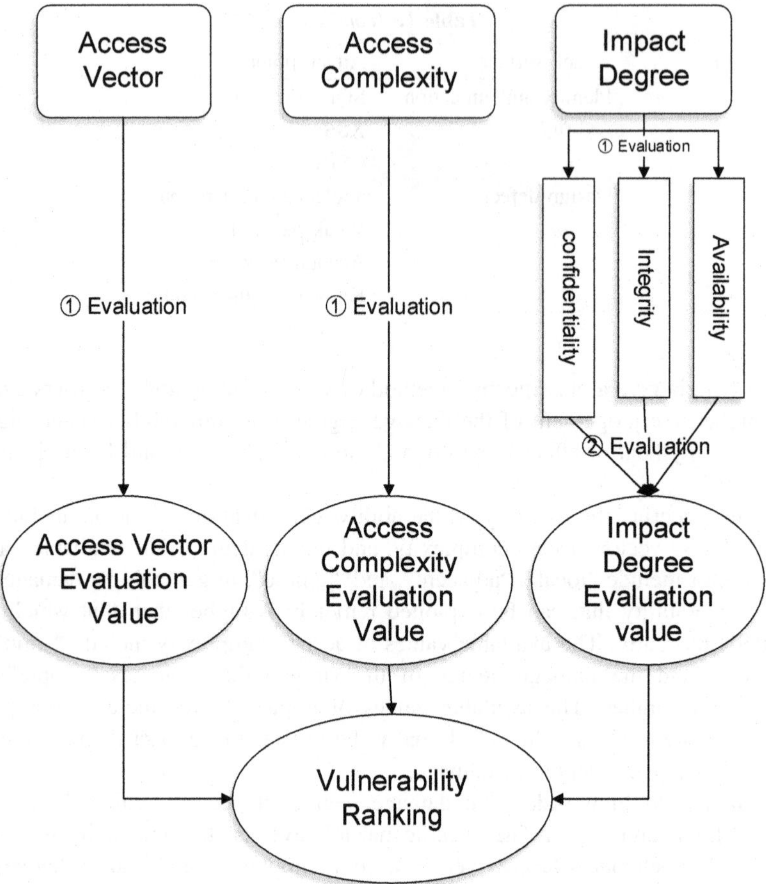

Fig. 2. Hazard level evaluation process of security vulnerability

for vulnerability assessment in the Home Internet system. It's a quantitative assessment method and can describe the damage degree of the vulnerability more accurately. The main changes are as follows:

(1) Add "physical" into the range value of access vector: via the physical paths can directly launch attacks.
(2) Adjust the range value of access complexity to "low", "medium" and "high".
(3) Add corresponding values into related attributes of each vulnerability evaluation factor.
(4) Obtain the evaluation score of impact degree by mathematic formula.
(5) Combine the evaluation score of each factor with the mathematic formula for final vulnerability score to make calculation.

Improved vulnerability evaluation method is shown in Fig. 3.

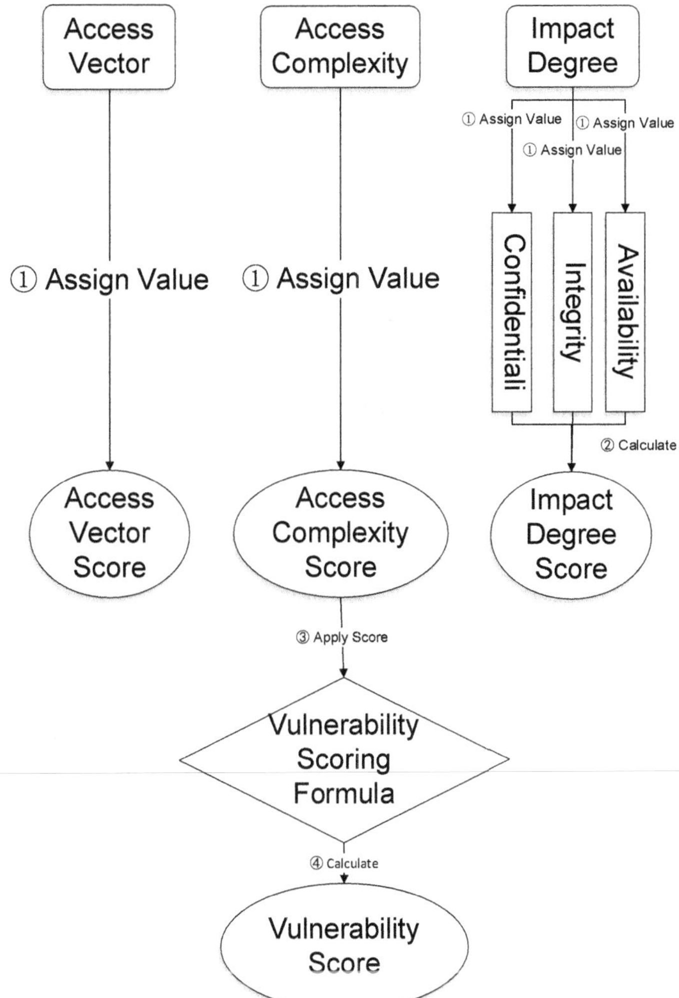

Fig. 3. Improved vulnerability evaluation method

The indicators and their value of improved vulnerability evaluation method are shown in Tables 2, 3 and 4.

Table 2. Value range in access vector

Symbol	Optional value	Evaluation standards
AccessVector	Physical/local/adjacent/remote	0.7/0.8/0.9/1.0

Table 3. Value range in access complexity

Symbol	Optional value	Evaluation standards
AccessComplexity	Low/medium/high	1.0/0.9/0.8

Table 4. Value range in impact degree

Symbol	Optional value	Evaluation standards
ComfImapact	None/partially/completely	0/0.7/1.0
IntegImapact	None/partially/completely	0/0.7/1.0
AvailImapact	None/partially/completely	0/0.7/1.0

In improved vulnerability evaluation method, the mathematic formula for calculating the score of impact degree factor is:

$$\begin{aligned} \text{Impact} = {} & \text{ConfImpact} \times \text{ConfImpactBias} + \text{IntegImpact} \times \text{IntegImpactBias} \\ & + \text{AvailImpact} \times \text{AvailImpactBias} \end{aligned}$$

The value range of the impact factors in shown in Table 5.

Table 5. Value range of the impact factor

Factor	Symbol	Evaluation standards	
Confidentiality impact factor	ComfImapactBias	Normal	0.33
		Confidentiality	0.50
		Integrity	0.25
		Availability	0.25
Integrity impact factor	IntegImpactBias	Normal	0.33
		Confidentiality	0.50
		Integrity	0.25
		Availability	0.25
Availability impact factor	AvailImpactBias	Normal	0.33
		Confidentiality	0.25
		Integrity	0.25
		Availability	0.50

In the improved vulnerability evaluation method, the mathematic formula for final score of the vulnerability is:

$$\text{Score} = \text{round}(10 \times \text{AccessVector} \times \text{AccessComplexity} \times \text{Impact}).$$

3 Case Analysis

In this paper, improved vulnerability evaluation method is verified by taking a vulnerability of home router as example.

The model number of home router is D-link DIR-645. A vulnerability exists in D-link DIR-645: when fetching the value of the "password" parameter in the "POST" parameter in an authentication script called "authentication.cgi", the attacker can cause a buffer overflow and then get remote command execution rights: when "authentication.cgi" on Web server of the router is visited, the read() function in the authentication_main() function reads the POST parameter into the stack, without verifying that the content-length field in the HTTP protocol exceeds the buffer size, then buffer overflow is caused.

In improved vulnerability evaluation method, the example of the vulnerability in shown in Table 6.

Table 6. Evaluation score of each vulnerability evaluation factor

Symbol	Evaluation value	Score
AccessVector	Remote	1.0
AccessComplextity	Medium	0.9
ConfImpact	Partially	0.7
IntegImpact	None	0
AvailImpact	Completely	1.0

The evaluation score of impact degree factor can be obtained by combining the score of impact factors and Table 5, as is shown in Table 7.

Table 7. Evaluation score of impact factors

Symbol	Score
ConfImpactBias	0.25
IntegImapactBias	0.25
AvailImpact	0.50

Substitute the evaluation score of impact degree factors and impact factors into mathematic formula for impact degree evaluation: $\text{Impact} = 0.7 \times 0.25 + 0 \times 0.25 + 1.0 \times 0.50 = 0.675$. The evaluation score of impact degree is 0.675.

Substitute the evaluation score of access vector, access complexity, and impact degree into mathematic formula for vulnerability evaluation: $\text{Score} = \text{round}(10 \times 1.0 \times 0.9 \times 0.675) = 6.08$. The final evaluation score of the vulnerability is 6.08.

4 Results

On the basis of the dynamic characteristics of the Home Internet system based on dynamically-enabled defense theory, assume the router D-link DIR-645 will switch to another router DIR-818 W at the next moment. However, HNAP (Home Network Administration Protocol) vulnerability (CVE-2016-6563) exists in DIR-818 W, and it will possibly be used to execute remote code. The router includes a pre authentication stack buffer overflow vulnerability which affects the HNAP SOAP protocol, accepts any string of arbitrary length of some XML parameters, and then copies them onto the stack. In the process of executing HNAP login operation, handling SOAP message generated by incorrect format will cause a buffer overflow in the stack. The XML field in the mail body of SOAP that is vulnerable includes: Action, Username, LoginPassword, and Captcha.

In improved vulnerability evaluation method, the evaluation score of each vulnerability evaluation factor and impact factors are shown in Tables 8 and 9.

Table 8. Evaluation score of each vulnerability evaluation factor

Symbol	Evaluation value	Score
AccessVector	Remote	1.0
AccessComplextity	Medium	0.8
ConfImpact	Partially	0.7
IntegImpact	None	0
AvailImpact	Completely	1.0

Table 9. Evaluation score of impact factors

Symbol	Score
ConfImpactBias	0.25
IntegImapactBias	0.25
AvailImpact	0.50

Substitute the evaluation score of impact degree factors and impact factors into mathematic formula for impact degree evaluation:Impact $= 0.7 \times 0.25 + 0 \times 0.25 + 1.0 \times 0.50 = 0.675$. The evaluation score of impact degree is 0.675.

Substitute the evaluation score of access vector, access complexity, and impact degree into mathematic formula for vulnerability evaluation: Score $=$ round $(10 \times 1.0 \times 0.8 \times 0.675) = 5.40$. The final evaluation score of the vulnerability is 5.40.

According to evaluation result, it's clearly indicated that this dynamic defense of system is positive because vulnerability score after system defense is lower than before. It also means that security risk of system after dynamic defense becomes relatively lower.

5 Conclusion

This paper analyzes vulnerability distribution before and after the system changes in the Home Internet in order to accurately evaluate the defense effectiveness of dynamically-enabled defense technology. Through applying improved vulnerability evaluation method based on Information Security Technology Security Vulnerability Classification Guide in D-link DIR-645 and D-link DIR-818 W, vulnerability score of router in the Home Internet system decreased from 6.08 to 5.40. From the attacker's point of view, it becomes more difficult to utilize the vulnerability. It confirms that this dynamic change of the system is of positive significance. On basis of evaluation on defense effectiveness, security personnel are able to improve defense program better.

Acknowledgements. We would like to thank all anonymous reviewers for their helpful advice and comments. This work is supported by the CCF-Venustech Hongyan Research Initiative (2016-009), PAPD fund and the CICAEET fund.

References

1. Yang, Y., et al.: General theory of security and a study case in internet of things. IEEE Internet Things J. **4**(2), 1 (2016)
2. Verma, H., Jain, M., Goel, K., Virkram, A., Verma, G.: Smart home system based on Internet of Things. In: 2016 3rd International Conference on Computing for Sustainable Global Development (INDIACom), pp. 2073–2075. IEEE, 31 October 2016
3. Salamat, B., Jackson, T., Wagner, G., et al.: Runtime defense against code injection attacks using replicated execution. IEEE Trans. Dependable Secure Comput. **8**(4), 588–601 (2011)
4. Lin, Y., Quan, Y.: Dynamially-Enabled Cyberspace Defense, 1st edn. The People's Posts and Telecommunications Press (Posts & Telecom Press), Beijing (2016). pp. 214–215
5. Liu, Y., Hu, S., Ho, T.-Y.: Vulnerability assessment and defense technology for smart home cybersecurity considering pricing cyberattacks. In: Computer-Aided Design (ICCAD), pp. 183-190. IEEE, 08 January 2015
6. Antunes, N., Vieira, M.: Defending against Web Application Vulnerabilities. Computer **45**(2), 66–72 (2011)
7. Liu, Q., Zhang, Y., Zhang, Y., et al.: Research on key technologies of security vulnerability classification. J. Commun. (s1), 79–87 (2012)
8. Srivatsa, M., Liu, L.: Vulnerabilities and security threats in structured overlay networks: a quantitative analysis. In: 2004 20th Annual Computer Security Applications Conference. IEEE, pp. 252–261 (2005)
9. Li, X., Chang, X., John, A.B., et al.: A novel approach for software vulnerability classification. In: 2017 Annual Reliability and Maintainability Symposium (RAMS), pp. 1–7. IEEE, 30 March 2017
10. Jin, S., Wang, Y., Cui, X., et al.: A review of classification method for network vulnerability. In: IEEE International Conference on System, Man and Cybernetics (SMC), pp. 1171–1175. IEEE, 04 December 2009

The Formal Transformation of AADL Based on Z-CoIA

Fugao Zhang(✉) and Zining Cao

College of Computer Science and Technology,
Nanjing University of Aeronautics and Astronautics, Nanjing 210016, China
luwayzhg@163.com, caozn@163.com

Abstract. The Architecture Analysis and Design Language (AADL) is a component-based semi-formal language. This paper proposes an expanded component-interaction automaton with Z language (Z-CoIA) based on the characteristics of AADL, introducing the formal specification Language Z into the component-interaction automata, then the formal transformation rules from AADL to the Z-CoIA is given, which is good for describing the data during system interaction and the attributes in state transitions and data constraints. Finally, a concrete example is shown.

Keywords: AADL · Component-interaction automata · Z language · Model transformation

1 Introduction

With the development of the AADL, the research about the formal verification of the AADL model has become a hot topic. Transforming from the AADL model into the expanded automata is one of the main directions. The literature [1] proposed a series of formal transformation rules converting the subset of the abstract AADL model into a timed automata, and developed the AADL verification tool based on the OSATE. The literature [2] transformed the AADL model into a generalized stochastic Petri net, and evaluated the reliability of the model based on stochastic Petri nets analysis technology. To specify some other aspects which are not limited to behavior and communication, the literature [8] translates AADL to timed abstract state machine for timing and resource aspects of a system. Some other researches such as literature [9] pays attention to the formal verification of distributed real-time systems, it transforms AADL model to another specification formalism like LNT language which is an input to CADP toolbox for formal analysis.

Some early automata like I/O automata and interface automata do not describe the interaction between components, which do not support the interface interaction between components naturally. The literature [3] proposed the component interaction automata, the advantages and disadvantages of component interaction automata and the verification method based on the temporal logic are also mentioned. The literature [4] mentioned a modeling method based on the time component interaction automata and introduced the definition, combination and verification algorithm of the time component

X. Sun et al. (Eds.): ICCCS 2017, Part II, LNCS 10603, pp. 816–822, 2017.
https://doi.org/10.1007/978-3-319-68542-7_72

interaction automata. The literature [5] introduced the qos constraints into the component interaction automata, and put forward a component model based on constraint interaction automata.

AADL is the industry standard language for embedded real-time systems, and is suitable for the specification of hierarchical components architecture. Embedded real-time systems with data constraint are computing system with time constraints and variable data constraints at the same time. Constraints between data variables are certainly included in the requirements of these systems, so in order to describe the constraints between data variables, we use the Z language to describe the states sets, state transition and properties in the model. Z language is a formal specification language based on the first order predicate logic and set theory, and is well suited for describing the states transitions and data constraints. The literature [6] combined Z language and interface automata, and put forward the definition of ZIA. ZIA is in a style of interface automata but its states and operations are described by Z language.

Moreover, AADL is semi-formal and cannot be verified by the formal methods directly, so this paper combines the Z language and the component interaction automata based on the characteristic of AADL. And then transforms the AADL model into the Z-CoIA model based on the formal transformation rules, so as to AADL can be verified by logic formula or any other formal methods in the future work.

2 Component Interaction Automata with Z Language

The formal specification language Z is based on the first-order predicate logic and set theory. Z language adopted strict mathematical theory, thus can produce concise, precise, unambiguous, and provable specifications.

The schema [7] is a kernel notation in Z language that to aid the structuring and modularization of the specification. A schema is constitute of variable declarations and predicates represent the limitation of these variables, and the schema has vertical and horizontal two forms.

Where S is the name of the schema, $D_1; \ldots; D_m$ are the declarations part and $P_1; \ldots; P_n$ are the predicates, and the horizontal form will be: $S \triangleq [D_1; \ldots; D_m | P_1; \ldots; P_n]$.

Furthermore, Z language use the identifier decorations to encode intended interpretations. A variable ending with "?" represents an input variable, and the "!" represents the output. The decoration "'" behind the variable represents the next state. With the decorations, Z language can depict the next state variables and the current state of the relationship between variables. Then the definition of component interaction automata with Z language is as follows, which can be abbreviated by Z-CoIA.

Definition 1. The component interaction automata with Z language can be depict as $M = (Q, Q_0, A, V, \Gamma, F^A, F^V, H)$, where,

(1) Q is a set of states that is finite and not empty, $Q_0 \subseteq Q$ represents the set of the initial states;
(2) A is a set of the actions in the automata, and include the input, output and internal actions respectively;

(3) V is a set of the variables in the automata, and include the input, output and internal variables respectively;
(4) $\Gamma \subseteq Q \times \sum \times Q$ is a set of transitions between states;
(5) F^A is a map, and maps any states in A to a operation schema in Z language, and specifically, the input action maps the input operation schema in Z language, the output action maps an output operation schema in Z language, and the internal maps operation schema in Z language;
(6) F^V is a map, which maps any states in V to a state schema in Z language;
(7) H is a tuple corresponding to a hierarchy of component names.

A component interaction automata with Z language M consists of the following elements, which can be represented by Fig. 1:

(1) $Q = \{q_0, q_1, q_2, q_3\}$;
(2) $Q_0 = \{q_0\}$;
(3) $A^I = \{a, c\}, A^O = \{d\}, A^H = \{b\}$;
(4) $V^I = \{x_1, x_2\}, V^O = \{y\}, V^H = \{z\}$;
(5) $\Gamma = \{(M, a, +), (M, b, M), (M, c, +), (M, d, -)\}$;
(6) $F^V(p_0) = S_0 \triangleq [z : N | z = 0]$,
$F^V(p_1) = S_1 \triangleq [x_1? : N | x_1 \in N; z = 0]$,
$F^V(p_2) = S_2 \triangleq [x_1 : N; z : N | z = x_1]$,
$F^V(p_3) = S_3 \triangleq [x_2? : N; y! : N | x_2 \in N; z = x_1]$,
(7) $F^A(a) = A_a \triangleq [x_1? : N | x_1 \in N]$,
$F^A(b) = A_b \triangleq [x_1? : N; z : N | z' = z + x_1?]$,
$F^A(c) = A_c \triangleq [x_2? : N | x_2 \in N]$,
$F^A(d) = A_d \triangleq [x_2 \in N; y! : N; z : N | y! = z * x_2]$;
(8) $H = \{M\}$;

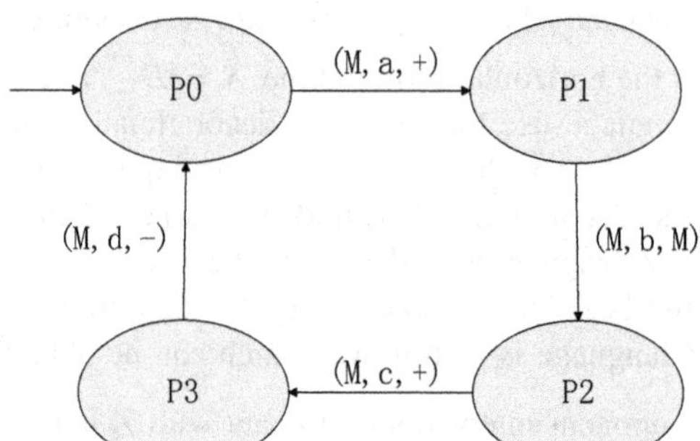

Fig. 1. A component interaction automata with Z language.

The compointernal actions of each component automata is disnent automata is hierarchical and composable if the joint with the action sets of all other component automata.

Definition 2. $S = (Q_C, Q_{C0}, A_C, V_C, \Gamma_C, F_C^A, F_C^V, H_C)$, the Combination of Component Interaction Automata with Z Language is combined by the sets of components where,

(1) $i \in N$ and the set of component name $\{(H_i)\}$ is disjoint of each other;
(2) Q_C, Q_{C0}, is the combined automata states set and the initial states; and the set of actions and variables of the combined automata $A_C = \cup_{i \in N} A$, $V_C = \cup_{i \in N} V$;
(3) $\Gamma_C \subseteq \{X \times A_C \times (X \cup \{\pm\})\}, X \in \{(H_i)\}$ is the set of transitions between states of the combined automata;
(4) F_C^A, F_C^V are maps of actions and states of the combined automata;
(5) $H_C = \{(H_i)\}, i \in N$ is the corresponding to a hierarchy of component names.

When combining this kind of automata, the question that whether the components are matched each other or not should be taken into account. When two components are input and output module with each other, the input and output actions can be matched for an internal action, marked as (X, τ, X). The input part is $M_1 = (Q_1, Q_{10}, A_1, V_1, \Gamma_1, F_1^A, F_1^V, H_1)$, $M_2 = (Q_2, Q_{20}, A_2, V_2, \Gamma_2, F_2^A, F_2^V, H_2)$. The output part is $S = (Q_C, Q_{C0}, A_C, V_C, \Gamma_C, F_C^A, F_C^V, H_C)$. The synchronous actions are combined into the internal action, and the others are interleaving. And there will be the combined set of states Q_C, the set of actions A_C and the set of transitions Γ_C, then the new states and actions can be remapped into the Z language, at last, the component name sets $H_C = (H_1, H_2)$, then the work of the combination of the Z component interaction automata is finished.

3 The Transformation of AADL to Z-CoIA

AADL is a modeling language that supports early and repeated analyses of a system's architecture with respect to performance-critical properties through an extendable notation, a unified framework, and precisely defined semantics. AADL subset includes the components of thread, process, process group, system and the behavior annex. In order to construct data constraint, we use Z schema to extend AADL based on its behavior annex. The formal transformation rules is given in Table 1.

The main transformation rules include: one basic component in AADL to one single Z-CoIA; the in-ports and out-ports in the feature of AADL component to the set of interaction in the Z-CoIA; the states set in the behavior annex to the sets of states in Z-CoIA; the transitions of states in AADL to the sets of states transitions in Z-CoIA; the guard of the states transitions to the input actions of the Z-CoIA; the actions in the behavior annex to the output actions of Z-CoIA; the transitions without the output

Table 1. The transformation rules of the AADL to Z-CoIA.

AADL model	Z-CoIA model
A single component	One component interaction automata
The features of the component	The ports of the Z-CoIA
The states in behavior annex	The sets of states in Z-CoIA
The transitions of the states	The sets of transitions in Z-CoIA
The action of transitions	The actions of Z-CoIA
The component consist of subcomponents	The combined Z-CoIA

actions to the internal actions in Z-CoIA. And the Table 1 is the formal transformation rules of the AADL to Z-CoIA.

4 The Example of AADL Model Transformation

We present a specific metro control system to show our method to transform the AADL to Z-CoIA. The architecture of metro control system can is shown in Fig. 2. It includes metro control system, the metro door control system and the platform door control system. Control system receives the command from the metro control system, and send command to control the open or closed of the metro door after data processing, and at the same time, send the status of the metro door to the metro control system.

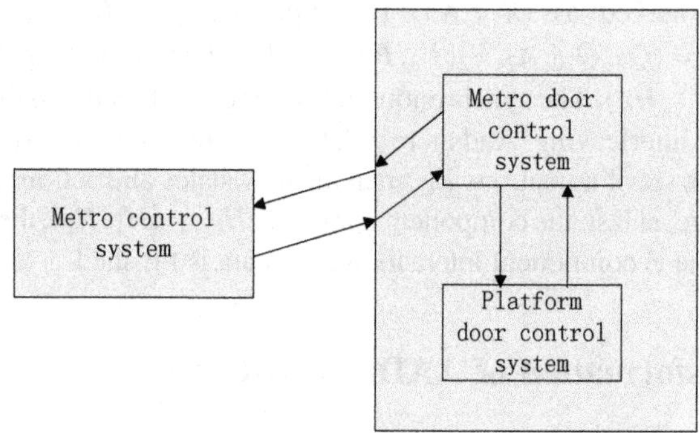

Fig. 2. The architecture of metro control system.

The entire system can be described by the system component metro_system in AADL like Table 2, and consist of two subcomponents, the metro_controller process component and door_system component. Whereby, the system component is consist of door_controller and door process components, and each process component consist of the corresponding thread components. Based on the transformation rules and the specific AADL model, we can transform the AADL model of metro control system into the Z-CoIA model.

The process component metro_controller can be transformed to the Z-CoIA M_1:

$$M_1 = (\{p_0, p_1\}, \{p_0\}, \{a, b\}, \{(M_1, a, +), (M_1, b, -)\}, F^A, F^V, (M_1)).$$

The process component door_controller can be transformed to the Z-CoIA M_2:

$$M_2 = (\{p_0, p_1, p_2, p_3\}, \{p_0\}, \{a, b, c, d\}, \{(M_2, a, +), (M_2, b, -), (M_2, c, +), (M_2, d, -)\}, F^A, F^V, (M_2)).$$

Table 2. The AADL model of metro control system.

```
process door
    features
        x: in data port;
end door;

process door_controller
    features
        current_data: in data port;
        new_feature: out data port;
        new_feature2: out data port;
end door_controller;

process metro_controller
    features
        current_data: out data port;
        new_feature: in data port;
end metro_controller;

system implementation door_system.impl
    subcomponents
        door:process door;
        door_controller: process door_controller;
end door_system.impl;

system implementation metro_system.impl
    subcomponents
        door:system door_part;
        metro_controller: process metro_controller;
end metro_system.impl;
```

The process component door can be transformed to the Z-CoIA M_3:

$$M_3 = (\{p_0, p_1\}, \{p_0\}, \{a, b\}, \{(M_3, a, +), (M_3, b, -)\}, F^A, F^V, (M_3)).$$

The system component can transformed by the combined of the Z-CoIA. The door_system component is combined by the door_controller and door process components, and can be described by M_4:

$$M_4 = (\{p_0, p_1\}, \{p_0\}, \{a, b\}, \{(M_4, a, +), (M_4, b, -)\}, F^A, F^V, (M_4)).$$

5 Conclusion

Based on the modeling language AADL, this paper presents an expended component interaction automata with Z language named Z-CoIA. So as to formally describe large amount of data and data constraints in the system and expend the advantages of Z language with automata, and take advantages of the two formal methods. It can be used for the formal verification of the AADL in the future research work. Then the formal transformation rules from AADL to Z-CoIA are described formally, and apply our method to a specific example of metro control system.

AADL is the industry standard language for embedded real-time systems. When an embedded real-time systems with data constraint is a computing system, we can combine the Z language, at the same time, we can also generate the time component interaction automata to describe the time constraints in the system, which both with time constraints and variable data constraints. Similarly, when combine the component automata, we can expend the process algebraic language to add the description of the relationship between the components. In addition, we can also develop the tool to realize the automatic transformation from AADL to Z-CoIA as a plug of the AADL tool OSATE in the future work.

Acknowledgments. This paper was supported by the Aviation Science Fund of China under Grant No.20150652008, the National Basic Research Program of China (973 Program) under Grant No.2014CB744903 and the National Natural Science Foundation of China under Grant No.61572253.

References

1. Yang, Z., Hu, K., Ma, D., et al.: From AADL to timed abstract state machines: a verified model transformation. J. Syst. Softw. **93**(2), 42–68 (2014)
2. Wu, Y.: The study of formal verification of embedded software based on AADL. Shanxi Normal University (2014)
3. Zimmerova, B., Vařeková, P., Beneš, N., Černá, I., Brim, L., Sochor, J.: Component-interaction automata approach (CoIn). In: Rausch, A., Reussner, R., Mirandola, R., Plášil, F. (eds.) The Common Component Modeling Example. LNCS, vol. 5153, pp. 146–176. Springer, Heidelberg (2008). doi:10.1007/978-3-540-85289-6_7
4. Yangli, J., Zhenling, Z.: Formal model of component real-time interaction behavior based on automata theory. J. Comput. Sci. **37**(9), 151–156 (2010)
5. Yuyu, Z.: The study of component behavior consistency based on constraints interaction automata. Harbin Engineering University (2012)
6. Zining, C.: Temporal logics and model checking algorithms for ZIAs. In: International Conference on Software Engineering and Data Mining, New York, pp. 57–62. IEEE Press (2010)
7. Jonathan, B., Bowen, A.J.: Formal specification and documentation using Z: a case study approach (2003)
8. Hu, K., et al.: Exploring AADL verification tool through model transformation. J. Syst. Archit. **61**(3–4), 141–156 (2015)
9. Mkaouar, H., Zalila, B., Hugues, J., Jmaiel, M.: From AADL model to LNT specification. In: de la Puente, J.A., Vardanega, T. (eds.) Ada-Europe 2015. LNCS, vol. 9111, pp. 146–161. Springer, Cham (2015). doi:10.1007/978-3-319-19584-1_10

Masking Signature Data Errors of Software-Based Control Flow Checking Techniques Employing Redundancy Signature

Liping Liu(✉), Linlin Ci, and Wei Liu

Computer Department, Beijing Institute of Technology, Beijing, China
llp19860623@163.com, cilinlin_bit@126.com,
Liuwei_bit@126.com

Abstract. With technology scaling, transient faults are becoming an increasing threat to hardware reliability. Commodity systems must be made resilient to these in-field faults through very low-cost resiliency solutions. Up to 77% of the transient faults cause Control Flow Errors (CFEs). Software-based control-flow checking techniques have emerged as promising low-cost and effective solutions. The signature monitoring method is the foundation of most of these control flow checking techniques. Some CFEs cannot be detected by previous control flow checking techniques when transient fault hit the software signature. A technique, masking signature data errors of software-based control flow checking techniques employing redundancy signature (CFCRS), with the ability to mask these CFEs is proposed in this paper. In CFCRS, these errors can be detected and corrected by triple redundancy signature. The experimental results demonstrated that CFCRS is able to mask all 2,000 injected faults in software signatures; It is reasonable and feasible to apply this technique on the former software-based control flow checking techniques due to its perfect correction coverage of CFEs caused by incorrect-signature and low overheads.

Keywords: Dynamic measurement · Control-flow errors · Error detection · Signature data error · Coded signature

1 Introduction

Single Event Upsets (SEUs) is a transient fault occurring in the consequence of the impact of charged particles with sensitive areas of integrated circuits. SEUs-induced soft errors have been known as one of the major threats to functionality and reliability of space-borne computers and their host spacecrafts. Soft errors may be explicit bit flips in latches or memories, or glitches in combinational logics that can propagate and be captured in latches [1]. If not handled properly, such errors can cause illegal accesses to peripherals, memory overflow, data corruption, false and sometimes fatal data or action outputs, and so on. Therefore, it is necessary to detect and correct errors in control flows hopefully before damages are caused.

It has been experimentally shown that about 33–77% of the transient faults cause control flow errors (CFE) and the remaining are converted into data errors [2]. It can therefore be concluded that, by the use of new techniques based on control flow

X. Sun et al. (Eds.): ICCCS 2017, Part II, LNCS 10603, pp. 823–828, 2017.
https://doi.org/10.1007/978-3-319-68542-7_73

checking, instead of the traditional techniques of transient fault detection in the application layer, the additional costs of detecting the faults that will finally be ineffective can be avoided. The system efficiency and its cost can thus be reduced [3–5].

Control flow checking (CFC) techniques are widely being applied to detect CFEs since the 1980s. These techniques are categorized into three major groups, software-based [6–8], hardware-based [5, 9] and hybrid [10, 11]. The signature monitoring method is the foundation of the most of these control flow checking techniques.

Existing software-based control flow checking techniques store the run-time signature in a general register. When the signature data are hit by transient fault at the execution time of the program, a mismatch is detected and the control flow is recovered to last correct checkpoint. The performance overhead of recovery is severe and not necessary.

This paper focuses on masking signature errors of control flow checking techniques. The idea behind this paper has two main phases. In the first phase, signatures of the program blocks are coded and in the second phase, signature error checking and correcting instructions are inserted into error handle routine. Implementations of this idea show that it is possible to mask all the signature errors with a slight performance and memory overhead compared to the control flow checking techniques. Our primary contributions can be summarized as follows:

- Redundancy signature data are employed to detect and correct signature data errors.
- The implementation method of proposed technology, which is compatible with existing software-based control flow checking techniques, is described detailed.
- The proposed technology is evaluated in multi measure.

The rest of this paper is organized as follows: in the next section the motivation for this paper is presented, then in Sect. 3 the proposed technique introduced and analyzed in detail. Section 4 shows the fault injection technique, and the experimental results of the proposed method. Finally some conclusions are given in Sect. 5.

2 Motivation

When a SEU fault happens in the signature data, the control flow checking results of software-based control flow checking is not corrected. The fault result is known as false positives. Control flow will be rollback to the last correct point when a false positive occurs. The overhead of rollback is not necessary and sometimes is severe when the number of instructions located between two checking points is great. One of the most important software-based solutions proposed in the literature is the techniques called Control Flow Checking by Software Signatures (CFCSS). Figure 1 shows a hypothetical scenario of CFCSS in order to more clearly describe the fault results model above.

In Fig. 1, we assume that before the execution of the instructions of block1 (B_1), the value of global signature register (G) contained s_1 was equal to 1000 and then a transient fault happened in the location of this signature date in the memory. This fault flipped the first bit of s_1 from 0 to 1 caused the value of s_1 change from 1000 to 1001.

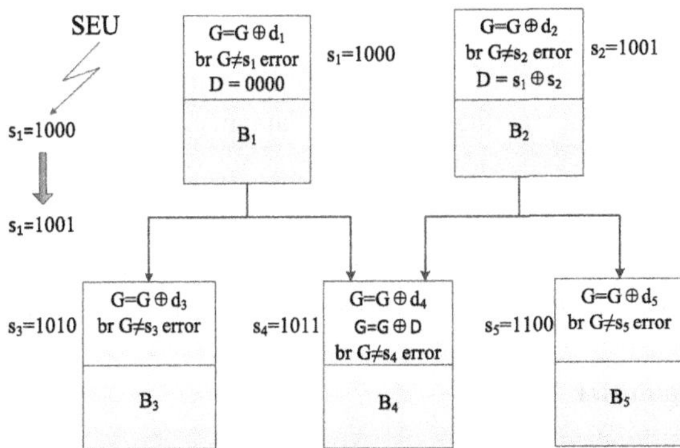

Fig. 1. An example of wrong control flow checking results caused by wrong signature

If the branch $br_{1,3}$ was taken, the value of G was updated by the instruction $G = G \oplus d_3$, $G = G \oplus d_3 = G \oplus s_1 \oplus s_3 = 1001 \oplus 1000 \oplus 1010 = 1011$, then the control flow checking instruction *br* $G \neq s_3$ *error* was executed, control was transferred to the error handling routine due to the value of G was different from s_3. Thus, a legal branch was considered to be illegal.

3 Description of CFCRS

In this paper, we adopt triple-redundant signature data to mask signature data error. Therefore, two clones are being made out of any signature data. The value of the clones will change with the original one at any point of the program that the signature updating instructions alter the value of signature data. CFCRS ensures the correctness of signature data by hiring a voter. Also in case of error occurrence in any signature data, the voter will correct the faulty value keeping the system safe from error propagation.

The implementation of proposed technology is based on previous software-based control-flow checking techniques. Since the proposed technology performs fault detection and recovery in a manner compatible with most previous software-based control-flow checking techniques, it can be easily extended to incorporate complete fault tolerance.

The algorithm of existing software-based control-flow checking techniques can be summarized as the following steps:

1. Identify all basic blocks and build CFG.
2. Assign a signature to each node of CFG.
3. Insert signature updating instructions into each node of CFG.
4. Insert signature checking instructions into nodes where the comparison between the run-time signature and the saved signature is wanted.
5. Handle errors detected by the step 4.

To implement proposed technology, the following works are needed:

- cloning the node signature of Software-based control-flow checking technique;
- insert checking and correcting signature data instructions into the errors handle routine.

In this section the proposed technology is explained in details. Subsection 3.1 explains how to code the signature data and insertion of signature data checking and correcting instructions is described in Subsect. 3.2.

3.1 Cloning Signature Data

The coded signature consists of original signature and two cloned signature. The structure of new signature is shown in Fig. 2. For an instance, a signature data 1001 will be converted to 100110011001. Fault occurrence in any signature data bit can be detected by comparing the original signature and the two cloned signatures. If the value of original signature and one of the two cloned signatures are in agreement it means that no error had happened in any of these two fields; therefore, select anyone of them as the right signature and replace another cloned signature. If the value of the two cloned signatures go along with each other, it means that these two fields are error-free and fault happened at original signature field. It is thoughtful to replace the original signature with any of the two cloned signatures. Thus, the fault is detected and corrected.

Original signature	Cloned signature	Cloned signature

Fig. 2. The structure of new signature

3.2 Inserting Signature Checking and Correcting Instructions

In previous software-based control-flow checking techniques, a signature comparing instruction is executed to detect control flow error. When a mismatch is detected, control flow will be transferred to error handle routine. In the error handle routine, a common approach is to recover the control flow to last correct checkpoint. In our proposed technology, we insert signature checking and correcting instructions into error handle routine to check and correct signature data error. If a signature data error is detected, signature data will be corrected by signature correcting instructions and program can proceed to executing without recovering control flow to last correct checking point.

4 Experimental Evaluation

To evaluate the proposed technique, the experiments were run on an ARM920T microprocessor machine running Linux kernel 2.6.32. The microprocessor possesses a 3 GB SDRAM and runs at a frequency of 400 MHz.

Memory overhead, performance overhead and error detection coverage are imperative parameters for evaluating our approach. So all of these parameters is measured and reported.

In order to assess the effectiveness of CFCRS, four benchmark programs are chosen for the experiment: Quick sort (QS), Bubble Sort (BS), Matrix Multiplication (MM), Fast Fourier Transformation (FFT).

CFCRS is a hardening technique of previous software-based control-flow checking techniques. A typical technique CFCSS [6] is chosen for experimental evaluation. Two versions are considered for each benchmark for fault injection, given here:

- adding CFCSS [6] method to the original code;
- adding CFCSS [6] and CFCRS method to the original code.

To inject signature data errors, the GSR contained signature data will be selected, then one bit of this signature data will be flipped with the XOR operator. Consequently, this process leads the system toward a signature data error. Finally, a signature data fault is injected into the GSR during program execution.

For each program (totally 8), the source file is compiled and assembly code is generated firstly; secondly, checkpoint optimal technique ESoftCheck [12] is applied to reduce the amount of checkpoint without losing fault coverage; thirdly, the resulting assembly code is compiled and executed. Finally, a fault is injected into the GSR during program execution. This process is repeated 2000 times for each of the mentioned versions. Table 1 shows the results of applying the proposed technique on the mentioned benchmarks.

Table 1. Results of signature data errors injection into the programs with CFCSS and CFCRS.

Program	Signature data errors masking (%)	Overheads (%)	
		Performance	Memory
QS	100	3.41	3.02
BS	100	4.14	1.52
MM	100	3.16	1.25
FFT	100	4.22	1.60

As can be seen from the Table 1, CFCRS has the ability to mask all the injected faults completely and incurs extra 1.85% memory overhead and 3.73% performance overhead averagely. The memory overhead and performance overhead are mainly caused by signature checking, signature updating and signature correcting instructions introduced by CFCRS.

5 Conclusions

Existing software-based control flow checking techniques cannot detect signature data errors. In this paper, we proposed a technique named Masking Signature Data Errors of Software-Based Control Flow Checking Techniques Employing Coded Signature

(CFCRS) to harden the existing software-based control flow checking techniques. When a signature data error occurs, CFCRS has the ability to mask all the injected faults completely and incurs extra 1.85% memory overhead and 3.73% performance overhead averagely. Moreover, CFCRS can be easily extended to incorporate complete fault tolerance because it performs fault detection and recovery in a manner compatible with most previous software-based control-flow checking techniques.

Acknowledgements. This research was supported by the National Natural Science Foundation of China under grant No. 61370134, the National High Technology Research and Development Program of China (863 Program) under grant No. 2013AA013901.

References

1. Bhattacharya, K., Ranganathan, N.: RADJAM: a novel approach for reduction of soft errors in logic circuits. In: International Conference on VLSI Design, pp. 453–458 (2009)
2. Zhu, D., Aydin, H.: Reliability effects of process and thread redundancy on chip multiprocessors. In: Dependable Systems and Networks (2006)
3. Jafari-Nodoushan, M., Miremadi, S.G., Ejlali, A.: Control-flow checking using branch instructions. In: International Conference on Embedded and Ubiquitous Computing, pp. 66–72. IEEE Press, Shanghai (2008)
4. Asghari, S.A., Abdi, A., Taheri, H., et al.: SEDSR: soft error detection using software redundancy. J. IJSEA **5**, 664–670 (2012)
5. Asghari, S.A., Abdi, A., Taheri, H., et al.: I2BCFC: an effective intra-inter block control flow checking method against single event upsets. J. Res. J. Appl. Sci. Eng. Tech. **4**, 4367–4379 (2012)
6. Oh, N., Shirvani, P.P., Mccluskey, E.J.: Control-flow checking by software signatures. J. IEEE T Reliab. **51**, 111–122 (2002)
7. Li, A., Hong, B.: On-line control flow error detection using relationship signatures among basic blocks. J. Comput. Electr. Eng. **36**, 132–141 (2010)
8. Mu, Y., Hao, W., Zheng, Y., et al.: Graph-tree-based software control flow checking for COTS processors on pico-satellites. J. CJA **26**, 413–422 (2013)
9. Rajabzadeh, A., Miremadi, S.G.: CFCET: a hardware-based control flow checking technique in COTS processors using execution tracing. J. Microelectron. Reliab. **46**, 959–972 (2006)
10. Wang, N.J., Patel, S.J.: ReStore: symptom-based soft error detection in microprocessors. In: 35th Dependable Systems and Networks, pp. 188–201. IEEE Press, Yokohama (2005)
11. Qureshi, M.K., Mutlu, O., Patt, Y.N.: Microarchitecture-based introspection: a technique for transient-fault tolerance in microprocessors. In: 35th Dependable Systems and Networks, pp. 434–443. IEEE Press, Yokohama (2005)
12. Yu, J., Garzaran, M.J., Snir, M.: ESoftCheck: removal of non-vital checks for fault tolerance. In 2009 International Symposium on Code Generation and Optimization, pp. 35–46. IEEE, Seattle (2009)

The Analysis of Key Nodes in Complex Social Networks

Yibo Pan[1(✉)], Wenan Tan[1,2], and Yawen Chen[1]

[1] Nanjing University of Aeronautics and Astronautics, Nanjing, China
[2] Shanghai Polytechnic University, Shanghai, China
{cloudsky_pan,wtan,cwwaty}@foxmail.com

Abstract. Key nodes play really important roles in the complex socail networks. It's worthy of analysis on them so that the social network is more intelligible. After analyzing several classic algorithms such as degree centrality, betweenness centrality, PageRank and so forth, there indeed exist some deficiencies such as ignorance of edge weights, less consideration on topology and high time complexity in the research on this area. This paper makes three contributions to address these problems. Firstly, a new idea, divide and conquer, is introduced to analyze directed-weighted social networks in different scales. Secondly, the improved degree centrality algorithm is proposed to analyze small-scale social networks. Thirdly, an algorithm named NodeRank is proposed to address large-scale social networks based on PageRank. Subsequently, the effectiveness and feasibility of these two algorithms are demonstrated respectively with case and theory. Finally, two representative basesets with respect to the social networks are adopted to mine key nodes in contrast to other algorithms. And experiment results show that the algorithms presented in this paper can preferably mine key nodes in directed-weighted complex social networks.

Keywords: Social network · Key node · Improved degree centrality · NodeRank

1 Introduction

In the real world, social networks [1] such as QQ, WeChat, networks of interpersonal relationships and the like exist everywhere, which display the characteristics of the complex networks. Social network has evolved from the graph theory in the field of mathematics, thus typically composed of nodes and edges. To better study the social network, we describe a network G as a triple G $<V,E,W>$, in which $V = \{V_1, V_2, ..., V_n\}$ is the collection of nodes in the network, and $E = \{E_{ij}, i, j = 1, 2, ..., n\}$ is the collection of edges in the network, and $W = \{W_1, W_2, ..., W_n\}$ is the collection of edges' weights. Each edge connected with nodes has its own wight which quantizes the strength between two nodes.

X. Sun et al. (Eds.): ICCCS 2017, Part II, LNCS 10603, pp. 829–836, 2017.
https://doi.org/10.1007/978-3-319-68542-7_74

With the rapid development of social networks, the analysis of the key nodes [2] plays a more and more important role, which does contribute a lot to social science and computer science. For instance, in terms of the electronic commerce [3,4], mining the potential customers would have an impact on promoting and popularizing new products. In addition, ranking authors combined with the qualities of papers and the influences between authors contributes a lot to the academic social network [5,6].

From this view, the analysis of key nodes is of great essence to the complex social network. A number of measurements such as degree centrality [7], closeness centrality [8], betweenness centrality [9], eigenvector centrality [10] and PageRank [11] have been broadly used among varieties of areas. These algorithms define node importance from different perspectives, such as node topology, the shortest path or the location a node situates in the network. While there is a common ground that the above mentioned methods either perform inefficiently with high time complexity or neglect the weights of edges.

In this paper, two newly defined algorithms named improved degree centrality and NodeRank, which are specific to the above deficiencies, aiming to address the problem about key nodes in complex social networks are proposed. Given the different scales of complex social networks, this paper introduces the idea of dividing and conquering, which means that we apply improved degree centrality to the small-scale social networks and NodeRank to the large-scale social networks. To prove the accuracy and efficiency of these two algorithms, two datesets with respect to complex social networks, are selected. And we make an detailed analysis of the experimental result compared with other algorithms.

2 Analysis of Key Nodes

2.1 Divide and Conquer

In real-life context with different-scale social networks, a single algorithm generally cann't meet the requirements. As a consequence, different methods, as the paper comes up with thereunder, should be adopted on analyzing the large-scale social networks and the small-scale ones.

For networks with several tens nodes, key nodes can be determined by the means of improved degree centrality based on both degree and weight. While for that networks with more nodes, NodeRank works more efficiently on the premise of guaranteeing lower time complexity. Nevertheless, a base set is required from the network firstly so that avoiding the interference of unimportant nodes. The quantity of base set may be freely ten to twenty percent of all the nodes according to the requirement of study.

2.2 Improved Degree Centrality (IDC)

As is mentioned above, degree centrality is the simplest measurement among existed algorithms, while the nodes found by the means of which is similarly conformant to manual judgement in small-scale network. It is a pity that degree centrality leaves weight out of consideration to directed-weighted social network.

Improved degree centrality introduces a new index, weighted degree. Not only does it acknowledge the significance of degree, but it also takes weight into consideration.

Definition 1. Weighted degree (WD) indicates the product of the degree of a node i and the proportion of the weight of the edge between node i and goal node in the sum of weights of edges between node i and all of its adjacent nodes. The weighted degree of a node is defined as follows:

$$WD(i) = \sum_{j \in M_i} D(j) \times \frac{w_{ji}}{\sum_{k \in L_j} w_{jk}}, \tag{1}$$

where M_i is the set of nodes that direct to node i and L_j is that of nodes which node j directs. Moreover, $WD(i)$ is the weighted degree of node i and w_{ji} is the weight of the edge from node j to node i.

After that, weighted degree is integrated into traditional degree centrality and we get improved degree centrality as follows:

$$IC_D(i) = D(i) \times WD(i) \tag{2}$$

Not only can improved degree centrality mine important nodes from small-scale social network, it also determines the base set of large-scale social network so that providing data to NodeRank.

2.3 NodeRank

PageRank is an excellent algorithm in evaluating pages. However, it's out of action for complex social network because of its ignorance of weight. Relationship strength, which plays a really important role in social networks, needs to be taken into consideration.

Definition 2. With the purpose of measuring node importance, NodeRank based on PageRank and relationship strength is defined by:

$$NR(i) = \sum_{j \in M_i} \frac{s_{ji} NR(j)}{\sum_{k \in L_j} s_{jk}}, \tag{3}$$

where M_i is the collection of nodes that direct to node i and L_j is that of nodes which node j directs. Furthermore, $NR(i)$ is the importance of node i and s_{ji} is relationship strength from node j to node i.

The principle idea of NodeRank is that the importance of one node is assigned to nodes it directs in proportion to the outbound relationship strength. In order to express more concisely, the formula can be transformed into a matrix form.

The NodeRanks of all the nodes can be expressed by matrix R and the proportion of relationship strength can be expressed by w_{ji}. Next let square matrix W store all of w_{ji}. Consequently, definition 2 can be expressed as :

$$R = WR \tag{4}$$

This equation need to be proved solvable next, it's therefore rewritten into another form:

$$(W - I)R = 0, \tag{5}$$

where I is a unit matrix. What's more, a normalization condition, that the sum of all the values of NodeRank should be 1, is needed to be recommended. That means the L1 norm of R is 1. Since R is nonzero, we can learn from Eq. (5) that R is an eigenvector of the matrix W. Accordingly, a sequence as $[1, 1, ..., 1]_N$ can be found to premultiply $W - I$, whose result is a zero vector, which is thus proved the column vector groups of the matrix $W - I$ are linear dependence. Hence, we can derive the determinant of $W - I$ is 0 expressed as:

$$|W - I| = 0 \tag{6}$$

Thereupon, Eq. (4) is proved solvable.

What to do next is to iterate Eq. (4) until the result is convergent. But there exists a problem that the precondition of convergence is that the matrix W is irreducible. In order to address this problem, we utilize a convex combination of both stochastic matrixes W and E . The new matrix U is certainly irreducible, and however the initial value sets, $R(n)$ eventually converges to a stable vector as well. The combined matrix is expressed by:

$$U = \alpha W + (1 - \alpha)E, \tag{7}$$

where α is a constant between 0 and 1, and $E = ee^T/N$.

After initializing the matrix R with $[0, 0, ..., 0]^T$, we can iterate the equation $R = UR$ until the result is convergent. The matrix R we ultimately get is the NR of all nodes. Just ranking the scores completes the analysis of key nodes in complex social network. Thus it can be seen that the time complexity is merely $O(n^2)$.

3 Experimental Evaluation

For purpose of evaluating the effect of algorithms this paper proposes in both small and large scale social networks, two kinds of representative datasets with respect to the social network are adopted for mining key nodes.

3.1 The Analysis of Key Nodes in Small-Scale Social Network

The dataset 1 is offered by the Ref. [12] about an experiment in student government of the University of Ljubljana, which contains 11 nodes and 48 arcs. The

Table 1. The importance ranking of nodes in dateset 1 based on 5 algorithms

Ranking	DC	CC	BC	PR	IDC
1	8	3	7	8	3
2	3	2	3	3	8
3	2	6	6	2	2
4	6	8	9	7	6
5	7	4	5	6	7
6	4	5	8	4	5
7	5	7	10	5	4
8	10	9	11	10	10
9	1	1	2	11	9
10	9	11	4	1	11
11	11	10	1	9	1

analyzed network consisted of communication interactions among 11 members and advisors of the student government at the University of Ljubljana.

As a consequence of simplicity of dataset 1, $IC_D(i)$ of each node can be calculated by Eq. (6). After sorting the values, we can get the sequence of their importance. In order to analyze the validity of IDC, four other algorithms, Degree centrality (DC), closeness centrality (CC), betweenness centrality (BC) and PageRank (PR), are selected to be in contrast. Thus comparison experiment results obtained are shown in Table 1:

As is shown in Table 1, the ranking of IDC is quite different from that of CC and BC, whose essential reason is that they not only ignore the weight of arcs, but also use unique index as ranking criteria. By contrast, the ranking of DC and PR are less different because all of them are based on the topology of social network. While both DC and PR ignore the weight similarly, which indicates the relationship strength can influence the ranking. Nevertheless, the relationship strength may be inferior to network structure in small-scale social network. And the result by the means of IDC more approximately matches subjective assessment of people.

In consideration of the above several points, IDC has the capacity of analyzing small-scale social network and providing baseset for NodeRank.

3.2 The Analysis of Key Nodes in Large-Scale Social Network

The dataset 2 is offered by the Ref. [13] about the user interaction in Facebook, which contains 45813 nodes and 817090 edges. It not only includes social relations among users but also their records of communication. That is, there are approximately 18 edges connected to each node on the average, which means that the relationship strength of this social network is rather high.

Table 2. The top 10 key nodes of dateset 2 based on 3 algorithms

Ranking	EC	PR	NR
1	761	699	2912
2	699	3671	10891
3	1238	3536	19912
4	458	761	30251
5	4992	2000	14792
6	1039	496	4992
7	698	4992	21110
8	845	8060	699
9	2000	698	37519
10	3554	41054	698

On account of the complexity of dataset 2, divide and conquer is supposed to be active on this occasion. In order to mine the key nodes in this social network, a base set of 4000 nodes is determined to be prepared in view of the scale of dataset 2 in the first place. So $IC_D(i)$ of each node ought to be calculated and then choose top 4000 of which into the base set for the next step. It's a crucial step that the core algorithm NodeRank is performed on this base set and the algorithm quicksort is adopted to sort the NR value of each node. Ultimately, the ranking of key nodes is gotten.

Similarly, we select two less different algorithms, PageRank and Eigenvector Centrality, to make a comparative analysis. Due to nodes of large quantity, we can only choose the top 10 representatively key nodes as referenced gist to evaluate the performance of diverse algorithms. The top 10 key nodes based on 3 less different algorithms are shown in Table 2:

Through the analysis of this table, we can conclude that:

(1) The top 10 key nodes enumerated in the Table 2 based on no matter PR or EC are entirely included in our baseset, which indicates the accuracy of IDC and that the topology of social network is of great importance as well.
(2) Since the algorithms neither PageRank nor Eigenvector Centrality consider the weight of edges ,which is relationship strength in this paper, the results of ranking are different to a great extent. This illustrates relationship strength can sharply influence the importance of nodes.
(3) As the Table 2 shows, in spite of numerous similarities between PR and EC based on topology, merely half out of top 10 key nodes are the same, which suggests that there is no strictly right and wrong in the research of social network but conformance to cognition of almost all the people.
(4) The nodes 698, 699 and 4992 appear below NR and they are also regarded as top 10 key nodes by others, which can more convincingly prove that NodeRank performs really well on the structure of the social network to a

great degree. And in the real network, if a node is extremely significant in the aspect of network structure, the relationship strength of the node may be equally matched.
Hence, the experimental result verify the validity of this algorithm which takes not only topology but also relationship strength. And the key nodes mined by NodeRank are more powerfully representative.

4 Conclusion and Future Work

This paper presents a new idea to analyze different-scale social networks and two improved algorithms named IDC and NodeRank, are proposed to address directed-weighted social networks. After analyzing these two algorithms, we respectively demonstrate the effectiveness and feasibility with case and theory. Base on which, two basesets are adopted to mine key nodes in contrast to other algorithms. Experiment results show that the algorithms presented in this paper can preferably mine key nodes in directed-weighted social networks.

In the real world, it's difficult to precisely sample the interaction between nodes. As a result, how to sample effectively and efficiently is our future work. Furthermore, it is also a matter worth studying to combine key nodes found with other ordinary nodes for information dissemination.

Acknowledgements. This work is supported in part by the Foundation of Graduate Innovation Center in Nanjing University of Aeronautics and Astronautics under Grant No. kfjj20161601, the National Natural Science Foundation of China under Grant No. 61672022, Key Disciplines of Computer Science and Technology of Shanghai Polytechnic University under Grant No. XXKZD1604, the Fundamental Research Funds for the Central Universities and Foundation of Graduate Innovation of Shanghai Polytechnic University.

References

1. Oliveira, M., Gama, J.: An overview of social network analysis. Wiley Interdisc. Rev. Data Min. Knowl. Discov. **2**(2), 99–115 (2012)
2. Xu, H., Yang, Y., Wang, L., Liu, W.: Node classification in social network via a factor graph model. In: Pei, J., Tseng, V.S., Cao, L., Motoda, H., Xu, G. (eds.) PAKDD 2013. LNCS, vol. 7818, pp. 213–224. Springer, Heidelberg (2013). doi:10.1007/978-3-642-37453-1_18
3. Dwivedi, A., Dwivedi, A., Kumar, S., Pandey, S.K., Dabra, P.: A cryptographic algorithm analysis for security threats of Semantic E-Commerce Web (SECW) for electronic payment transaction system. In: Meghanathan, N., Nagamalai, D., Chaki, N. (eds.) ACIT. AISC, pp. 367–379. Springer, Heidelberg (2013). doi:10.1007/978-3-642-31600-5_36
4. Qu, Z., Keeney, J., et al.: Multilevel pattern mining architecture for automatic network monitoring in heterogeneous wireless communication networks. China Commun. **13**(7), 108–116 (2016)

5. Li, L., Wang, X., Zhang, Q., Lei, P., Ma, M., Chen, X.: A quick and effective method for ranking authors in academic social network. In: Park, J.J.J.H., Chen, S.-C., Gil, J.-M., Yen, N.Y. (eds.) Multimedia and Ubiquitous Engineering. LNEE, vol. 308, pp. 179–185. Springer, Heidelberg (2014). doi:10.1007/978-3-642-54900-7_26
6. Liu, Q., Cai, W., Shen, J., Fu, Z., Liu, X., Linge, N.: A speculative approach to spatialtemporal efficiency with multiobjective optimization in a heterogeneous cloud environment. Secur. Commun. Netw. **9**(17), 4002–4012 (2016)
7. Kimura, M., Saito, K., Motoda, H.: Blocking links to minimize contamination spread in a social network. ACM Trans. Knowl. Discov. Data **3**(2), 60–61 (2009)
8. Jacob, R., Koschützki, D., Lehmann, K.A., Peeters, L., Tenfelde-Podehl, D.: Algorithms for centrality indices. In: Brandes, U., Erlebach, T. (eds.) Network Analysis. LNCS, vol. 3418, pp. 62–82. Springer, Heidelberg (2005). doi:10.1007/978-3-540-31955-9_4
9. Brandes, U.: A faster algorithm for betweenness centrality. J. Math. Sociol. **25**(2), 163–177 (2004)
10. Zhang, Y., Sun, X., Wang, B.: Efficient algorithm for k-barrier coverage based on integer linear programming. China Commun. **13**(7), 16–23 (2016)
11. Page, L.: The PageRank citation ranking : bringing order to the web. Stanford InfoLab, vol. 9, no. 1, pp. 1–14 (1998)
12. Hlebec, V.: Recall versus recognition: comparison of the two alternative procedures for collecting social network data. In: Developments in Statistics and Methodology, pp. 121–129 (1993)
13. Viswanath, B., Mislove, A., Cha, M., et al.: On the evolution of user interaction in facebook. ACM Workshop Online Soc. Netw. **39**(4), 37–42 (2009)

Novel Schemes for Bike-Share Service Authentication Using Aesthetic QR Code and Color Visual Cryptography

Li Li[1], Lina Li[1], Shanqing Zhang[1(✉)], Zaorang Yang[1], Jianfeng Lu[1], and Chin-Chen Chang[2(✉)]

[1] Institute of Graphics and Image, Hangzhou Dianzi University, Hangzhou 310018, China
{lili2008,sqzhang,jflu}@hdu.edu.cn, 851200613@qq.com, yangzaorang@163.com

[2] Department of Information Engineering and Computer Science, Feng Chia University, Taichung, Taiwan
alan3c@gmail.com

Abstract. To enhance bike-share service authentication, we propose two novel schemes based on aesthetic QR code combining XOR-based visual cryptography scheme (XVCS). In Scheme I, aesthetic QR code based on error correction mechanism and XVCS are combined for authentication. In comparison, Scheme II exploits aesthetic QR code based on XOR mechanism of RS with Positive Basis Vector Matrix (PBVM) and XVCS. The larger region of secret information and the better visual appearance of aesthetic QR code are shown in experiments.

Keywords: Authentication · Aesthetic QR code · Visual cryptography scheme

1 Introduction

Bike-share service is booming, where the QR code is applied. However, there is hidden danger because of tampering or replacement of the QR code, such as personal information leakage and wrong transfer. In order to make bike-share service more reliable and secure, we propose a bike-share service authentication mechanism (Fig. 1). The secret image is preprocessed and then split into shadows (shadow1 and shadow2) according to the visual cryptography scheme (VCS). Shadow1 is stored in the cloud server. Shadow2 is fused with the QR code based on different aesthetic QR code methods. And Scanned-bike QR code (Q) is obtained, posted on the bike. The official web address is the input information of Q. Then users scan Q with smartphone and access the official web address to download shadow1. Finally shadow1 and Q are stacked together to obtain secret information OfO for authentication. Users can pay in security to use the bike after authentication.

X. Sun et al. (Eds.): ICCCS 2017, Part II, LNCS 10603, pp. 837–842, 2017.
https://doi.org/10.1007/978-3-319-68542-7_75

We have proposed multiple schemes for mobile payment authentication in [1]. Extending to color image as the secret image, in this paper, we propose two novel schemes for bike-share service authentication.

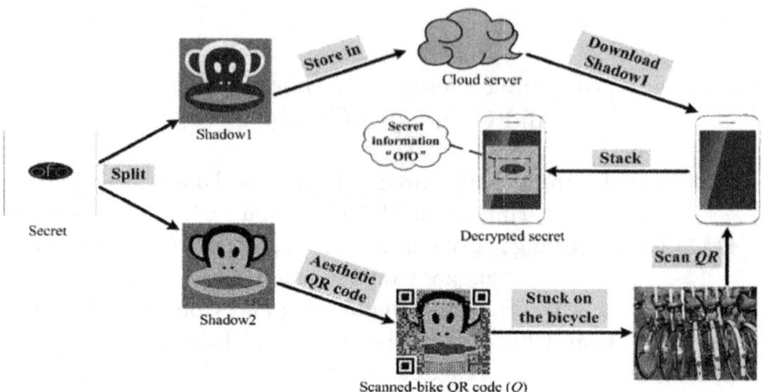

Fig. 1. One practical scenario of bike-share service authentication.

2 Preliminary

QR code versions have four error correction levels: L, M, Q and H, and error correction capacities are 7%, 15%, 25% and 30%, respectively [2]. This performs error correction mechanism of the QR code. A series of RS codes, from Gauss Jordan elimination method [3], formulate a matrix, whose front section is a unit vector matrix. The sub-region of upper left corner of matrix is used to modify the data region. Modification uses XOR mechanism of RS with Positive Basis Vector Matrix (PBVM).

3 Authentication Schemes for Bike-Share Service

The designed (2, 2)-XVCS can be a basis for bike-share service authentication in Subsect. 3.1. In order to achieve further authentication, aesthetic QR code based on error correction mechanism and XOR mechanism of RS are used in Subsect. 3.2 and in Subsect. 3.3, respectively.

3.1 The Designed (2, 2)-XVCS for Color Image

The description of designed (2, 2)-XVCS is as follows: transform color image into R, G, and B halftone images on R, G, and B channels respectively; encrypt each pixel of three halftone images into a $2*2$ block based on XOR operation, and obtain six shadows image ShadowR1, ShadowR2, ShadowG1, ShadowG2 and ShadowB1, ShadowB2; stack ShadowR1, ShadowG1, and ShadowB1 to obtain Shadow1 based on XOR operation, stack ShadowR2, ShadowG2, and ShadowB1 to obtain Shadow2 similarly; decrypt secret image by stack of Shadow1 and

Shadow2. Figure 2 shows a yellow block (1, 1, 0) is broken down into two shadow blocks and how to reconstruct the yellow-like block.

Compared with traditional VCS based on OR operation (OVCS), XVCS performing XOR operation enhances contrast of decrypted secret image. Uniform distribution meets security condition of visual cryptography.

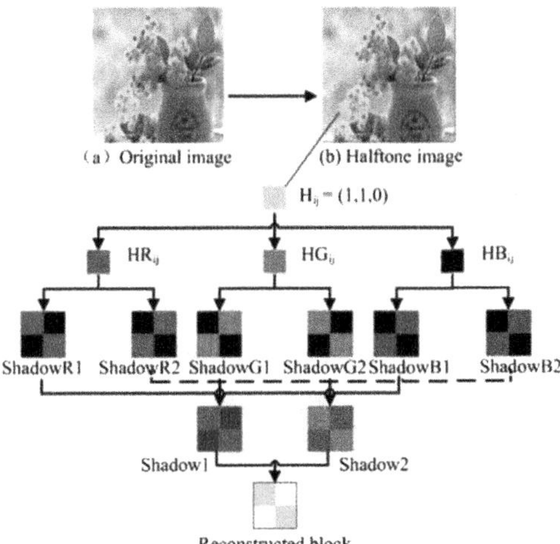

Fig. 2. An example of designed (2, 2)-XVCS (Color figure online)

3.2 Scheme I Based on XVCS and Error Correction Mechanism of QR Code

Scheme I exploits aesthetic QR code based on error correction mechanism. Figure 3 shows the overall framework:

Step 1. The noise pretreatment of S

An adding operation among secret image (S) and random binary image with same size is computed to obtain S_n. The noise pretreatment makes the region of secret information for authentication smooth.

Step 2. The acquisition of saliency map

Secret information in S is thought important, whose region is called salient region. The saliency map is generated by saliency detection.

Step 3. The fusion of Q_1 and B

First positions of modules of original QR code (Q_1) are marked as module layout. Combining saliency map, figure out saliency values and then select appropriate modules as changeable region in QR code. Construct codeword layout based on saliency map in range of error correction. Thus Qr is obtained. Second background image (B) is transformed into binary image and divided onto blocks with the same size of QR module. The average value of each block is calculated. The saliency map is the corresponding the region of background image. Thirdly, there are module values modifications. For changeable region, the

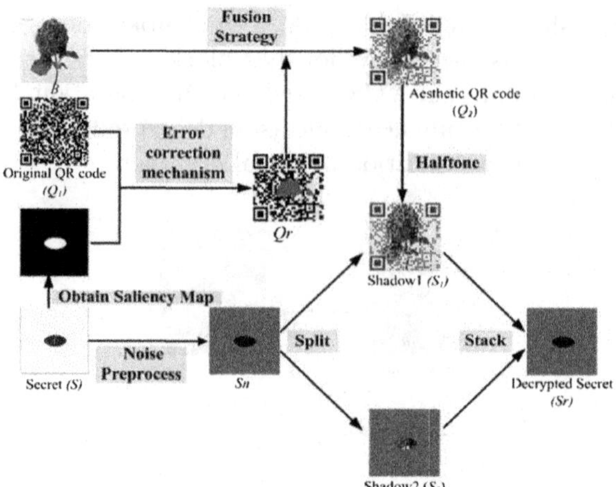

Fig. 3. Flowchart of Scheme I

corresponding module values are directly filled by values of background image blocks. For unchangeable region, there are four cases in Eq. (1).

$$Q = \begin{cases} 0, T_i < T_0 \cap N_i = 0 \\ -1, T_i > T_0 \cap N_i = 0 \\ 1, T_i < T_0 \cap N_i = 1 \\ 0, T_i > T_0 \cap N_i = 1 \end{cases} \tag{1}$$

T_i represents gray average of gray block. T_0 represents binary threshold, which is obtained from Otsus method. $N_i = 1$ represents white block. $N_i = 0$ represents black block. $Q = 0$ represents that background image is completely replaced; $Q = -1$ or 1 represents that the central region of the specified module is replaced by the corresponding region of the QR code, and the other region is replaced by corresponding region of background image. Aesthetic QR code (Q_2) is obtained.

Step 4. The stack of S_1 and S_2

Q_2 is transformed into halftone image as shadow1 (S_1). Shadow2 (S_2) is generated based on (2, 2)-XVCS. Stack S_1 and S_2 to obtain decrypted secret image (S_r). Experimental results are listed in Table 1. The region of secret information OfO accounts for 4% in S. S_1 can be scanned.

Table 1. Experimental results of Scheme I

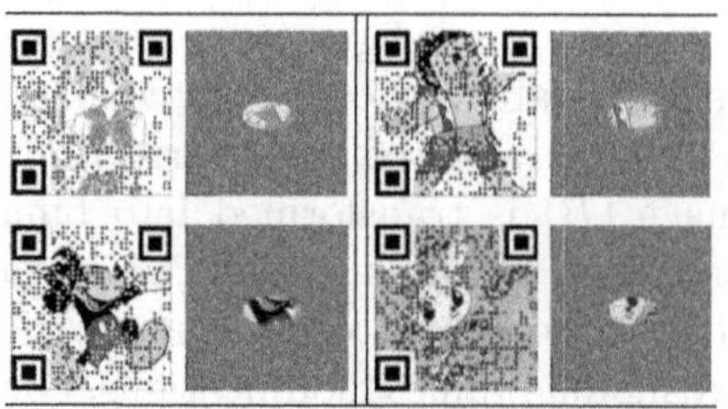

3.3 Scheme II Based on XVCS and XOR Mechanism of RS

With purposes of the larger region of secret information and better visual appearance of the QR code, Scheme II exploits (2, 2)-XVCS combining aesthetic QR code based on XOR mechanism of RS with PBVM. The flowchart is shown in Fig. 4.

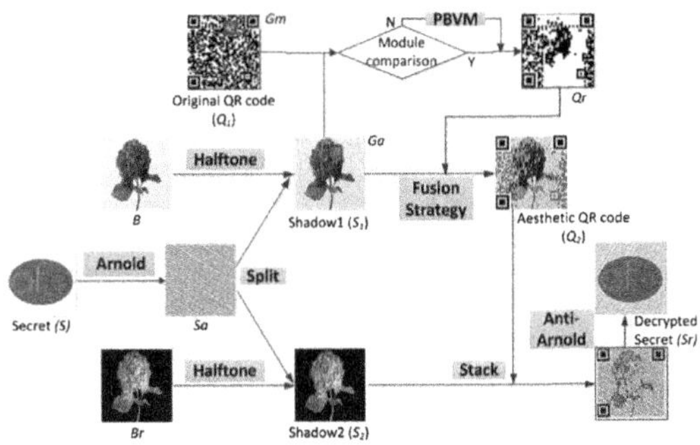

Fig. 4. Flowchart of Scheme II

Step 1. Arnold scrambling preprocess of S

In order to make the region of secret information larger, Arnold scrambling is applied. Rearrange of points in discrete secret image (S) matrix, which makes secret information concealable. Transform S into halftone image, and then halftone image is transformed into binary image (S_a) by Arnold scrambling.

Step 2. Generation of shadows

Select randomly an image (B), and reverse B to obtain the image (B_r). Transform respectively the B and B_r into halftone images. According to (2, 2)-XVCS, Sa combining two halftone images is split into shadow1 (S_1) and shadow2 (S_2).

Step 3. Fusion of S_1 and Q_1

First, S_1 as background image is divided into blocks according to the size of the QR code (Q_1) module. Second the average value (G_a) of each block is calculated and compared with the corresponding value (G_m) of QR code module. If the compared result is inconsistent, XOR operation is executed for the QR code with PBVM to make them same. Thus Q_r is further obtained. Last, the QR code is fused with S_1. Aesthetic QR code (Q_2) is obtained by the fusion strategy formula, which is the same as in Scheme I.

Step 4. Stack of Q_2 and S_2

Based on (2, 2)-XVCS, the stacked result of Q_2 and S_2 is used with anti-Arnold transformation. Decrypted secret (S_r) is obtained.Experimental results are listed in Table 2. S_1 can be scanned. Compared with Scheme I, the larger region of secret information and the better visual appearance of S_1 are shown to enhance authentication.

Table 2. Experimental results of Scheme II

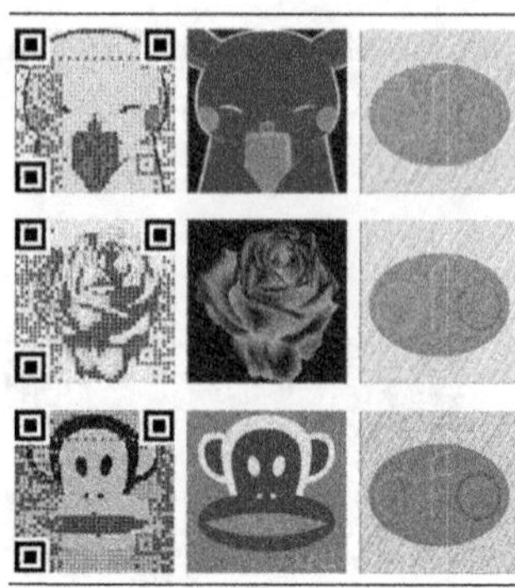

4 Conclusion

In this paper, our schemes can reduce possibility of tampering QR code. Considering convenience and efficiency during authentication, application scenarios will be further explored in the future.

Acknowledgments. This work was mainly supported by National Natural Science Foundation of China (No. 61370218).

References

1. Lu, J.F., Yang, Z.R., Li, L.N., Yuan, W.Q., Li, L., Chang, C.C.: Multiple schemes for mobile payment authentication using QR code and visual cryptography. Mob. Inf. Syst. **2017**, 12 (2017)
2. Li, L., Qiu, J.X., Lu, J.F., Chang, C.C.: An aesthetic QR code solution based on error correction mechanism. J. Syst. Softw. **116**, 85–94 (2016)
3. Cox, R.: Qartcodes. http://research.swtch.com/qart. last Accessed Oct 2012
4. Lu, J.F., Zhang, S.Q., Li, L., Yang, Z.R., Li, Y.Y.: A Self-adaptive Aesthetic QR Code Algorithm Based on Hybrid Basis Vector Matrices. unpublished

An Improved RFID Search Protocol

Ping Wang(✉) and Zhiping Zhou

Engineering Research Center of Internet of Things Technology Applications Ministry of Education, Jiangnan University, Wuxi, Jiangsu, China
6151913006@vip.jiangnan.edu.cn, zzp@jiangnan.edu.cn

Abstract. In this paper, we propose an improved scheme to solve the security risks of S-S's scheme. In order to resist the replay attack, the improved protocol uses the pseudo identifier XOR to encrypt the random number generated by the reader; the random number generated by the reader is added to the tag's response message to resist the tag impersonation attack. In addition, this paper uses Avoine model to analyze the privacy of the improved protocol. The theoretical analysis shows that the proposed scheme can effectively resist against replay attack, tag impersonation attack, and de-synchronization attack. Moreover, the improved scheme can provide forward untraceability and tag untraceability. Compared with the existing RFID tag search protocol, the computational complexity of the tag and gate complexity on the tag side in the improved protocol is lower, the number of interaction with the reader is less, so the search for low-cost tags can be implemented more efficiently.

Keywords: RFID search protocol · Tag impersonation attack · Avoine model

1 Introduction

RFID tag search protocol was first proposed by Tan et al. in 2008 [1]. The scheme put forward by Tan has attracted lots of attention [2, 3]. To reduce the computational complexity of readers, literature [4] proposed a search protocol using error correcting codes. Subsequently, Erguler [5] describe tag tracing attack and other security risks of literature [4] by using linear properties of error correcting code. SDB protocol using distance bounding approach is proposed by literature [6] to overcome relay attack. This scheme could not meet the requirement of low cost tags because of using hash function. Wang et al. [7] proposed a search protocol based on hash collision, however, it can't resist replay and tag tracking attacks, etc. Literature [8] proposed a tag seeking protocol using hash encryption to ensure the security, however, Jeon and Yoon [9] pointed out this scheme is not suitable for low cost tags and vulnerable to reader compromise attack. In 2015, Sundaresan et al. [10] proposed an RFID tag search protocol that is based on pseudo random number generators. This scheme can be well applied to resource constrained low-cost tags, but there are some security risks.

This paper introduces that S-S's scheme [10] is vulnerable to tag impersonation attack because lack the reader's random number in tag's reply message; the unreasonable of reader's request message causes replay and DoS attacks; and then put

X. Sun et al. (Eds.): ICCCS 2017, Part II, LNCS 10603, pp. 843–848, 2017.
https://doi.org/10.1007/978-3-319-68542-7_76

forward the improved scheme. This paper shows the outstanding efficiency and security properties of the improved scheme through detailed analysis and comparisons.

2 Related Work

2.1 The Weaknesses of S-S's Scheme

Tag Impersonation Attack: The attacker blocks (M_3, M_4) to prevent the reader's key from being updated *i*-th round. During the (*i* + 1)-*th* round session, the attacker replays (M_3, M_4) in *i*-th round to the reader, this time the reader calculates $M_3 \oplus PRNG(id_j \oplus M_4 \oplus \beta) = rts_j$, so the message replayed by the attacker is authenticated by the reader, the attacker fake tag successfully.

Replay Attack: In the *k*-th session, the attacker replays *i*-th round message $M_1 = id_j \oplus PRNG(rts_j \oplus r_r)$, $M_2 = r_r \oplus \beta$ to the tag. It is assumed that rts_j has been updated $\alpha(\alpha \geq 1)$ times in the tag side. After received the replay message from the attacker, the tag computes $M_1 \oplus PRNG(rts'_j \oplus M_2 \oplus \beta') = id_j$. It shows that (M_1, M_2) is authenticated by the tag and the attacker replays the message successfully.

De-synchronization Attack: After the replay attack, the key stored in the reader is $PRNG^{\alpha}(rts_j)$ while the tag stores the key as $PRNG^{\alpha+1}(rts_j)$, $PRNG^{\alpha}(rts_j)$. Firstly, the valid reader generates r'_r. It then computes and send (M_1, M_2) to the tag. After received the message, the tag computes $r_r \leftarrow M_2 \oplus \beta' \neq r_r^{-1}$ and $M_1 \oplus PRNG(rts'_j \oplus M_2 \oplus \beta') = id_j$. The tag generates random number t_r to compute (M_3, M_4). After reader receives (M_3, M_4), it computes $M_3 \oplus PRNG(id_j \oplus M_4 \oplus \beta) \neq PRNG^{\alpha}(rts_j)$. Therefore, the legal tag can't be authenticated by the reader.

2.2 The Improved Scheme

The proposed scheme consists of two phases: the setup phase and the search phase. The description for the notation used in the protocol is the same to literature [10].

The Setup Phase: this phase is similar to S-S's scheme. The reader downloads an access list *AL* which contains *n* tags that it is authorized to search. The *AL* stores pseudo identifier $id = h(TID,\ t_s)$, shared key *rts* and counters *ctr*, *ctr*max for each tag. The tag stores its own *id*, current and previous shared reader-tag secrets *rts*, rts^{-1}, counters *ctr*, *ctr*max as well as previous round of reader's random number r_r^{-1} for each reader.

The Search Phase: the specific steps of the search phase are as follows.

Step 1: if $ctr_j < ctr\max_j$, the reader generates random number r_r. Then, it computes $A = id_j \oplus r_r$, $B = id_j \oplus PRNG(rts_j \oplus r_r)$ and broadcasts (A, B) to all the tags in its field. Using pseudo identifier id_j XOR random number to compute message *A* is beneficial to resist the replay attack.

Step 2: upon receiving the reader's message, if $ctr_k \geq ctr\max_k$, the tag will terminate the protocol, otherwise the tag computes r_r as $r_r = A \oplus id_k$, the next process is divided into four cases:

If $r_r = r_{r_k}^{-1}$, it signifies that the message is the previous round message the attacker replays, so the protocol will be terminated.

If $id_k = B \oplus PRNG(rts_k \oplus r_r)$ and $r_r \neq r_{r_k}^{1}$, then tag T_k is the target tag. The tag will generate random number t_r and computes $C = rts_k \oplus PRNG(PRNG(id_k \oplus t_r) \oplus r_r)$, $D = t_r \oplus rts_k \oplus id_k$. T_k transfers respond message (C, D) to the reader and updates: $rts_k^{-1} \leftarrow rts_k$, $rts_k \leftarrow PRNG(rts_k)$, $r_{r_k} \leftarrow A \oplus id_k$, $ctr_k \leftarrow ctr_k + 1$.Adding the reader's random number r_r to the tag response message can resist the tag impersonation attack.

If $id_k = B \oplus PRNG(rts_k^{-1} \oplus r_r)$ and $r_r \neq r_{r_k}^{1}$, it signifies that T_k is the target tag but the shared key rts_j stored in the reader is not updated normally. At this point the tag generates t_r and computes $C = rts_k^{-1} \oplus PRNG(PRNG(id_k \oplus t_r) \oplus r_r)$, $D = t_r \oplus rts_k^{-1} \oplus id_k$. The tag transmits (C, D) to the reader, and updates: $ctr_k \leftarrow ctr_k + 1$, $r_{r_k}^{-1} \leftarrow A \oplus id_k$.

If rts_k and id_k stored in the tag cannot match with the reader's message correctly, it indicates that the tag is the non-target tag. So, the tag generates two random number response the reader with probability $\lambda (0 < \lambda < 1)$ to provide tag location privacy.

Step3: after received the message (C, D), the reader computes $t_r = D \oplus rts_j \oplus id_j$. If $rts_j = C \oplus PRNG(PRNG(id_j \oplus t_r) \oplus r_r)$, then the target tag is present and the reader updates:$rts_j \leftarrow PRNG(rts_j)$, $ctr_j \leftarrow ctr_j + 1$.Otherwise, it signifies that the target tag is absent.

3 The Security and Performance Analysis of the Protocol

3.1 Security Analysis

In this paper, we analyze the privacy of the improved protocol based on the Avoine model [11], the attacker can query $Query(\pi_T^i, m_1, m_3)$, $Send(\pi_R^j, m_2)$, $Execute(\pi_T^i, \pi_R^j)$, $Execute^*(\pi_T^i, \pi_R^j)$, Reveal$(\pi_T^i)$ Oracles.

Theorem 1. The improved protocol is forward untraceable. The attacker can obtain the internal information of the tag at the moment $t_1({}^{t_1}id_k, {}^{t_1}rts_k, {}^{t_1}rts_k^{-1}, {}^{t_1}r_{r_k}^{-1}, {}^{t_1}ctr_k, {}^{t_1}ctr\max_k)$ by calling the Reveal( ) oracle, In addition, the attacker can query *Query*( ), *Send*( ), *Execute*( ) Oracles. In the improved scheme, the tag response message is $C = rts_k \oplus PRNG(PRNG(id_k \oplus t_r) \oplus r_r)$, $D = t_r \oplus rts_k \oplus id_k$. Thus, in order to calculate the message of the time t_2, the attacker must have the knowledge of (rts_k, id_k, t_r, r_r) at time t_2. The key rts_k will be updated after each valid session and the random number generated by each round is different. Therefore, the attacker cannot calculate the messages at the time t_2 of the tag. The protocol is forward untraceable.

- Â requests the Challenger then receives her target T_k.
- Â chooses $I = \{i\}$ and calls $Query(\pi_{T_k}^i, A, B)$, thus receiving (C, D).
- Â calls $Reveal(\pi_{T_k}^i)$ at time t_1, thus receiving ${}^{t_1}rts_k$, ${}^{t_1}rts_k^{-1}$.
- The advantage of Â can calculate ${}^{t_2}C, {}^{t_2}D (t_1 > t_2)$ is 0, that is, $Adv_P^{For-untra}(\hat{A}) = 0$.

Theorem 2. The improved protocol is existential untraceable. In the improved scheme, the tag response message is $C = rts_k \oplus PRNG(PRNG(id_k \oplus t_r) \oplus r_r)$, $D = t_r \oplus rts_k \oplus id_k$. t_r and r_r are random numbers generated by the tag and reader, respectively. Even if the attacker obtains the response information of the tag by calling *Query*( ), *Send*( ), *Execute*( ), however, because in the each session, the tag and the reader will generate a new random number, the response message of the same tag in different sessions is different, so the attacker cannot trace the tag by eavesdropping communication between the reader and the tag. In addition, the reader's request message (A, B) is encrypted using rts_j, so the attacker could not calculate the correct message (A, B) without known of the key to impersonate legal reader. In summary, the improved protocol can meet existential untraceability.

- Â requests the Challenger then receives her target T_k.
- Â chooses $I = \{i\}$ and calls $Query(\pi_T^i, (A, B))$, thus receiving (C, D).
- Â requests the Challenger then receives T_1, T_2.
- Â chooses $I_1 = I_2 = [i+1,\ i+2]$.
- Â calls $Query(\pi_{T_1}^{i+1}, (A', B')) \to (C', D')$, $Query(\pi_{T_1}^{i+2}, *) \to (C'', D'')$.
- If $(C', D') = (C'', D'')$, then Â outputs T_1 else Â outputs T_2.
- The advantage of Â winning the game is 0, that is $Adv_P^{Exis-untra}(\hat{A}) = 0$.

Theorem 3. The improved protocol can resist replay attack. When the attacker replays the last round message (A, B), rts_k^{-1} can be matched with the tag's data, but $r_{r_k}^{-1} = A \oplus id_k$, so that the message cannot be authenticated by the tag. When the attacker replays previous round of the reader's message (A', B'), since the shared key rts has been updated which causes $id_k \neq B' \oplus PRNG(rts_k \oplus r_r)$, so the message cannot be authenticated by the tag.

Theorem 4. The improved protocol can resist tag impersonation attack. In the improved scheme, the *id* stored in the tag and reader is not the true *ID* of the tag, but the hashed form of tag *ID* using tag secret t_s. Therefore, an attacker cannot impersonate the tag through physical method. In addition, the tag uses reader's random number to compute the response message which causes the tag's response message replayed by the attacker cannot be authenticated by the reader. Therefore, the attacker cannot successfully counterfeit the tag by replaying the message.

Theorem 5. The improved protocol can resist de-synchronization attack. After each successful session, both tag's and reader's shared key rts_j are updated. When the tag receives a legitimate request message from reader and updates secret key successfully, the attacker can block the message (C, D) so that the key rts_j stored in the reader cannot be updated. Although the reader's secret key is not update, but in the improved protocol, the tag stores both the updated and un-updated key. As a result, the tag can still authenticate the reader. So our scheme can effectively resist de-synchronization attack (Table 1).

Table 1. Security comparison

Category	Ref [4]	Ref [7]	Ref [8]	Ref [10]	Our scheme
Forward untraceablility	✓	✗	✓	✓	✓
Tag untraceability	✗	✗	✓	✗	✓
Replay attack	✗	✗	✓	✗	✓
Tag impersonation attack	✗	✓	✓	✗	✓
De-synchronization attack	✗	✓	✓	✗	✓
Tag anonymity	✗	✓	✓	✓	✓

3.2 Performance Analysis

The performance of each scheme is shown in Table 2, P_r and P_h represent pseudo-random number and hash function, respectively. This paper set (pseudo) identifier, random number and hash output, shared key, timestamp, *ctr* and *ctr*max as 96bits, 128bits, 24bits, 32bits. *m* is the number of readers, *N* is the number of response tags. On the computational cost of the tag, we only consider the pseudo random function and hash function, the simulation environment is Intel core i5-2.30 GHz, RAM-4 GB; programming language using Java. The hash function and the pseudo-random function take about 0.253 ms and 0.021 ms, respectively. The number of gates of pseudo-random function and hash function is 1435 and 8120, respectively. Low cost tags only can accommodate 3K gates to implement security features.

Table 2. Performance comparison

Category	Ref [4]	Ref [7]	Ref [8]	Ref [10]	Our scheme
Number of interactions	3	3	3	2	2
Gate complexity on the tag side	9555	8120	8120	1435	1435
Computational cost of the tag	3 P_h + 2 P_r	3 P_h	4 P_h	3 P_r	4 P_r
Time-consuming of the tag/ms	0.801	0.759	1.012	0.063	0.084
Storage cost of tag/bits	12512	248	225	448 m+96	448 m+96
Communication cost/B	24(1 + 2N)	(39 + 36N)	36(1 + N)	24(1 + N)	24(1 + N)
EPCC1G2 compliance	✗	✗	✗	✓	✓

4 Conclusion

This paper analyzes the security risks of the S-S's scheme, and proposes an improved RFID secure search protocol. The analysis shows that the proposed scheme can effectively resist replay, tag impersonation, and de-synchronization attacks, etc. In addition, the proposed scheme only uses lightweight pseudo-random function and XOR operation which meet EPCC1G2 Compliance.

Acknowledgements. This work is supported by the Special Funds of Basic Research Business Expenses of Central University under Grant No. JUSRP51510.

References

1. Tan, C.C., Sheng, B., Li, Q.: Secure and server-less RFID authentication and search protocols. IEEE Trans. Wirele. Commun. **7**(4), 1400–1407 (2008)
2. Lee, C.F., Chien, H.Y., Laih, C.S.: Server-less RFID authentication and searching protocol with enhanced security. Int. J. Commun Syst **25**(3), 376–385 (2012)
3. Yoon, E.-J.: Cryptanalysis of an RFID tag search protocol preserving privacy of mobile reader. In: Park, J.J., Zomaya, A., Yeo, S.-S., Sahni, S. (eds.) NPC 2012. LNCS, vol. 7513, pp. 575–580. Springer, Heidelberg (2012). doi:10.1007/978-3-642-35606-3_68
4. Chen, C.M., Chen, S.M., Zheng, X., et al.: A secure RFID authentication protocol adopting error correction code. Sci. World J. **2014**(1), 246–261 (2014)
5. Erguler, I.: A key recovery attack on error correcting code based a lightweight security protocol. IACR Cryptol. ePrint Arch. **2014**(1), 475–485 (2014)
6. Jannati, H., Falahati, A.: An RFID search protocol secured against relay attack based on distance bounding approach. Wirel. Pers. Commun. **85**(3), 711–726 (2015)
7. Wang, X., Jia, Q.X., Gao, X., et al.: Provable security lightweight service-less RFID security search srotocol. J. Hunan Univ. Nat. Sci. **41**(8), 117–124 (2014)
8. Xie, W., Xie, L., Zhang, C., et al.: RFID seeking: finding a lost tag rather than only detecting its missing. J. Netw. Comput. Appl. **42**(6), 135–142 (2014)
9. Jeon, I.S., Yoon, E.J.: An ultra-lightweight RFID seeking protocol for low-cost tags. Appl. Math. Sci. **8**(125), 6245–6255 (2014)
10. Sundaresan, S., Doss, R., Piramuthu, S., et al.: Secure tag search in RFID systems using mobile readers. IEEE Trans. Dependable Sec. Comput. **12**(2), 230–242 (2015)
11. Avoine, G.: Adversarial model for radio frequency identification. IACR Cryptol. ePrint Arch. **2005**(7), 49–62 (2005)
12. Gu, B., Sheng, V.S., Tay, K.Y., et al.: Incremental support vector learning for ordinal regression. IEEE Trans. Neural Netw. Learn. Syst. **26**(7), 1403–1416 (2015)
13. Kong, Y., Zhang, M., Ye, D.: A belief propagation-based method for task allocation in open and dynamic cloud environments. Knowl.-Based Syst. **115**, 123–132 (2017)
14. Chen, Y., Hao, C., Wu, W., et al.: Robust dense reconstruction by range merging based on confidence estimation. Sci. China Inf. Sci. **59**(9), 1–11 (2016)

A Developmental Evolutionary Algorithm for 0-1 Knapsack Problem

Ming Zhong and Bo Xu(✉)

Department of Computer Science and Technology,
Guangdong University of Petrochemical Technology,
Maoming, Guangdong 525000, China
MingZhong@163.com, xubo807127940@163.com

Abstract. In this paper, a developmental evolutionary algorithm (DEA) is proposed, which mainly based on the developmental evolutionary and learning theory. We regarded the chromosome individual that in EC as an autonomous development individual; and developed mental capabilities through autonomous real-time interactions with its environments by using development learning methods under the control of its intrinsic developmental program, when chromosome individual achieved the development objective, genetic operation started immediately, otherwise continue developing. Finally, we used DEA to solve the 0/1 knapsack problem and designed experiment to compare with QEA, ACO. Experimental results showed that DEA has better convergence, and can effectively avoid falling into local optimal solution.

Keywords: Evolutionary computation · Developmental evolutionary theory · Reinforcement learning · Knapsack problem

1 Introduction

Evolutionary computation (EC) is one of the fastest-growing areas in computer science [1]. The field of EC was founded in the 16th and 17th of the twentieth century [2]. The fundamental idea of EC is gleaned from Darwin's theory of evolution by natural selection [3, 4]. EC is suitable for high-dimensional spaces, discontinuous and searching nonlinear, which is being applied to many complex real-world optimization problems to find near-optimal obtain or optimal solutions, and its problem solving capability even exceeds that of humans [5–8]. The fact that not a single optimization method is likely to be able to outperform all other methods on all problems can easily be accepted, which has been formalized by Wolpert and Macready in their No Free Lunch Theorems for search and optimization algorithms [9]. So EC is no exception, and new improved algorithms are constantly being introduced, and researched.

2 Developmental Evolutionary Algorithm

2.1 The Algorithm Framework of Developmental Evolutionary Algorithm (DEA)

The DEA algorithm framework is as follows: (Fig. 1).

X. Sun et al. (Eds.): ICCCS 2017, Part II, LNCS 10603, pp. 849–854, 2017.
https://doi.org/10.1007/978-3-319-68542-7_77

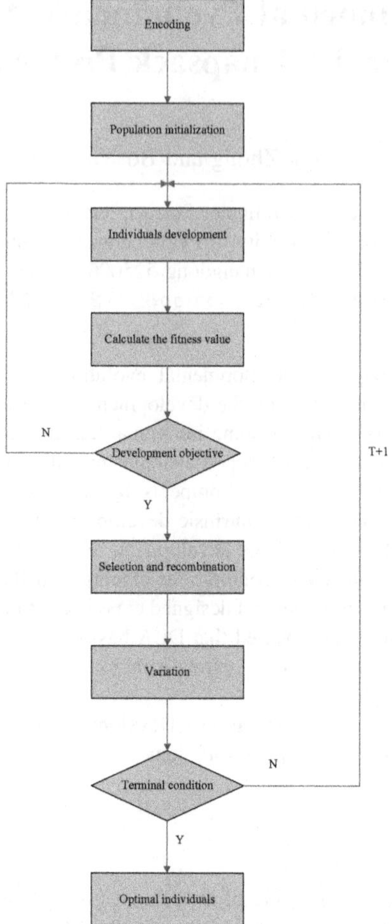

Fig. 1. The algorithm framework of DEA

2.2 Development Objective

Through the previous analysis, we define the development objective mathematical model as follows: the number of individuals is n.

Definition 1: define the average fitness value of generation t as follows

$$avg(t) = \frac{\sum_{i=1}^{n} fitness(i)}{n} \tag{1}$$

Definition 2: define fitness variance $p(t)$ as follows

$$p(t) = \sqrt{\sum_{i=1}^{n} (fitness(i) - avg(t))^2} \tag{2}$$

Definition 3: define $q(t)$ is best fitness individual of generation t as follows

$$q(t) = \max\{fitness(i)\},\ i = 1, 2, \ldots n \tag{3}$$

Definition 4: define the development objective function is as follows

$$objective \quad \max\ (\ c_1 \times \frac{1}{p(t)} + c_2 \times q(t)) \tag{4}$$

where $c_1, c_2 \in [0, 1]$, $c_1 + c_2 = 1$. In Eq. (4) through the reciprocal of fitness variance $\frac{1}{p(t)}$ to judge each individual fitness tends to overall average fitness, and use $q(t)$ to prevent the individuals tend to be low fitness at the same time.

3 Experimental Results and Analysis

A 0/1 knapsack problem is a typical combinational optimization problem, which is well known that the 0-1 knapsack problem is NP-hard. It has become a better test problem for evaluation the performance of EAs. The 0-1 knapsack problem is described as follows: given a set of items and a knapsack, maximize the sum of the values of the items in the knapsack so that the sum of the weights must be less than the knapsack's capacity for each item it have only two choices, namely loading or not loaded backpack, items can not be loaded backpack for many times, given a profit vector p_i, a weight vector w_i and knapsack capacity C. It can be formally defined as follows:

$$Maximize \sum_{i=1}^{n} p_i x_i$$

$$subject\ to \sum_{i=1}^{n} w_i x_i \leq C \tag{5}$$

where $x_i = 0$ or $x_i = 1$, $(i = 1, \ldots, n)$, n is the number of items.

In order to compare with classical algorithms, In all experiments, strongly correlated sets of data were considered

$$w_i = uniformly\, random\, [1,\ 10]$$

$$p_i = w_i + 5 \tag{6}$$

and the following average knapsack capacity was used:

$$C = \frac{1}{2}\sum_{i=1}^{m} w_i \tag{7}$$

The data were unsorted. Four knapsack problems with 100, 250, 500, and 750 items were considered. In this paper, the experiment for knapsack problem independently run algorithm ACO, QEA and DEA. The ACO proposed in [10] is used in this experiment. The parameters are set for ACO as: population size is 20, $\rho = 0.1$, $q_0 = 0.75$, $\beta = 2$, $Q = 1$. The QEA is coded as describing in [11]. The parameters are set for QEA as: population size is 20, and $delta = 0.001^* p_i$, the aberrance probability $P_m = 0.5$. The parameters are set for DEA as: population size is 20, $c_1 = 0.2$, $c_2 = 0.8$.

The procedure is programmed in matlab 7.0 and is run on a personal computer Pentium IV 2.10 GHz for all experiments. Statistical comparisons data of the three algorithms are shown in Table 1. The three algorithms computing convergence curve are shown in Fig. 2. Figure 2 shows the evolution of the mean of the best profits and the mean of average profits of DEA, QEA, ACO over 100 runs in the four knapsack problems. As can be seen from Fig. 2, When QEA algorithm or ACO algorithm solve the problem, in the generation of less than 300, were unable to reach the optimal solution that DEA can achieve. So DEA has better convergence, and can effectively avoid falling into local optimal solution. Table 1 shows the experimental results of the instances. For all the proposed instances, the DEA solves the problem with good results. The series of experimental results demonstrate the superiority and effectiveness of DEA. In comparison with ACO and QEA; DEA can get better results in shorter time.

Table 1. Comparisons of simulation (100 statistics)

Items	Algorithms	Best solution	Average	Worst solution	Run time (s)
100	ACO	581	580.32	577	1.190
	QEA	583	582.11	578	0.987
	DEA	610	609.78	580	0.873
250	ACO	1423	1420.78	1415	2.356
	QEA	1426	1425.86	1420	2.502
	DEA	1488	1488.01	1416	2.203
500	ACO	2617	2617.23	2600	4.659
	QEA	2790	2789.04	2618	4.578
	DEA	2889	2885.33	2819	4.399
750	ACO	3989	3822.01	3783	7.343
	QEA	4115	4110.03	4012	6.987
	DEA	4389	4387.43	4467	6.302

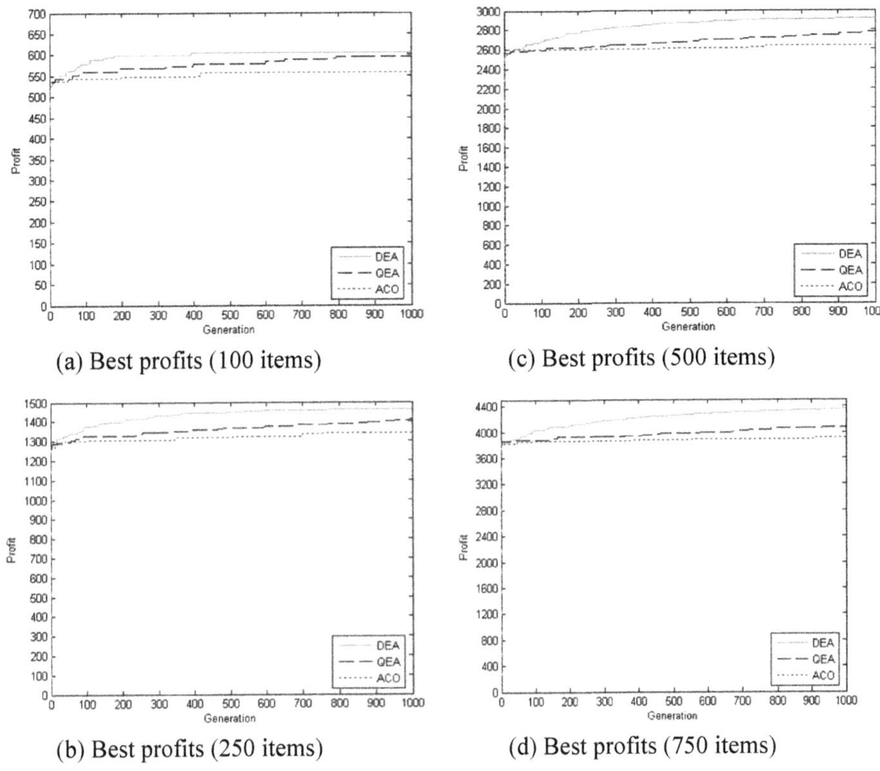

(a) Best profits (100 items)

(b) Best profits (250 items)

(c) Best profits (500 items)

(d) Best profits (750 items)

Fig. 2. DEA, QEA, ACO comparisons (1000 generation)

4 Conclusion

We design our algorithm based on the development evolutionary and learning theory. Finally, we use our method to solve the 0/1 knapsack problem and design experiment to compare with QEA, ACO. Experimental results show that DEA has better convergence, and can effectively avoid falling into local optimal solution.

Acknowledgments. The authors thank all the reviewers and editors for their valuable comments and work. This paper is supported by the Guangdong Provincial Department of education Youth Innovation Talent Project (No. 2015KQNCX099). Science and technology project of Maoming (201532), Natural science research project of Guangdong University of Petrochemical Technology (2012qn0104).

References

1. Zhang, J., Zhan, Z., Lin, Y., et al.: Evolutionary computation meets machine learning: a survey. IEEE Comput. Intell. Mag. **6**, 68–75 (2011)

2. Hu, T., Banzhaf, W.: Evolvability and speed of evolutionary algorithms in the light of recent developments in biology. J. Artif. Evol. Appl. **4**, 1–5 (2010). Article no. 1
3. Wen, X., Shao, L., Xue, Y., et al.: A rapid learning algorithm for vehicle classification. Inf. Sci. **295**, 395–406 (2015)
4. Gould, S.J.: The Structure of Evolutionary Theory. Harvard University Press, Cambridge (2002)
5. Liu, Q., Cai, W., Shen, J., et al.: A speculative approach to spatial-temporal efficiency with multi-objective optimization in a heterogeneous cloud environment. Secur. Commun. Netw. **9**, 4002–4012 (2016)
6. Bin, G., Sheng, V.S., Li, S.: Bi-parameter space partition for cost-sensitive SVM. In: Proceedings of the 24th International Conference on Artificial Intelligence, pp. 3532–3539. AAAI Press (2015)
7. Kong, Y., Zhang, M., Ye, D.: A belief propagation-based method for task allocation in open and dynamic cloud environments. Knowl.-Based Syst. **115**, 123–132 (2016)
8. Xia, Z., Wang, X., Sun, X., et al.: Steganalysis of least significant bit matching using multi-order differences. Secur. Commun. Netw. **7**, 1283–1291 (2014)
9. Wolpert, D.H., Macready, W.G.: No free lunch theorems for optimization. IEEE Trans. Evol. Comput. **1**, 67–82 (1997)
10. Bai, J., Yang, G.K., Chen, Y.W., et al.: A model induced max-min ant colony optimization for asymmetric traveling salesman problem. Appl. Soft Comput. **13**, 1365–1375 (2013)
11. Platel, M.D., Schliebs, S., Kasabov, N.: Quantum-inspired evolutionary algorithm: a multimodel EDA. IEEE Trans. Evol. Comput. **13**, 1218–1232 (2009)

WiSmart : Robust Human Access and Identification for Smart Homes Using WiFi Signals

Shangqing Liu[1,2], Yanchao Zhao[1,2(✉)], and Bing Chen[1,2(✉)]

[1] College of Computer Science and Technology, Nanjing University of Aeronautics and Astronautics, Nanjing, China
{sqliu,yczhao,cb_china}@nuaa.edu.cn

[2] Collaborative Innovation Center of Novel Software Technology and Industrialization, Nanjing, China

Abstract. In smart homes environment, the access and identification of different persons are key enabling technology to make personalized services or intrusion detection. However, most state-of-the-art systems require users to carry or wear dedicated devices which are not user-friendly. In this paper, we present WiSmart, a fine-grained device-free framework that can distinguish different actions and identify persons within a short duration using WiFi signal. The experiments show that we can achieve an average accuracy of human activity model up to 89.14% and human identification model greater than 85.6%.

Keywords: Channel State Information · WiFi · Human activity recognition · Human identification

1 Introduction

The fast evolving of sensing and communication technology has made smart homes becoming a hot spot. People can use sensing technologies to monitor our daily activities, for example fall detection [1], privacy preservation [2] in smart homes. However, these technologies are based on dedicated devices which are intrusive and introduce a great deal of inconvenient to users especially for the elderly and children. Meanwhile, with the ubiquity of WiFi and the recent development of wireless sensing researches, people realized that WiFi signal could be used far beyond data transmission, e.g. sensing small changes in the environment. Hence, we ask whether it is possible to monitor human activities and identify persons by WiFi signals. Using WiFi for environmental perception will greatly promotes the convenience of smart homes.

Person identification is the premise of activity recognition for the reason that if we cannot identify the person, we cannot associate a specific activity to a given person. Such person identification can be applied to many applications.

X. Sun et al. (Eds.): ICCCS 2017, Part II, LNCS 10603, pp. 855–861, 2017.
https://doi.org/10.1007/978-3-319-68542-7_78

For example, when there is someone entering into the room, we can trigger person-specific customization according to the identity we have identified.

In this paper, we propose our system WiSmart, which uses Commercial Off-The-Shelf (COTS) WiFi devices to recognize different human activities and identify a person. Compared to WiWho [3], WFID [4], WiFi-ID [5], FreeSense [6], WiSmart uses the physical features such as the speeds of human walking for person identification. The system of WiSmart is illustrated in Fig. 1. It mainly consists of two parts: a transmitter, which can be a router, continuously sends signals to the receiver. The receiving signals contain the CSI (Channel State Information) values which are the estimation of wireless channel. It describes how a signal propagates from the transmitter to the receiver with the combined effect of scattering, fading with distance. The CSI data are affected by human activities due to the multi-path effect of wireless signals. Hence, we can use the variances in CSI values which mainly caused by human activities to separate different activities. When people is walking in the WiFi environment, we can also use CSI to identify humans according to the unique gaits of humans [7]. Based on this, WiSmart extracts effective information from WiFi signals to perform activity recognition and human identification.

Our contributions are to demonstrate the feasibility of activity recognition and human identification by WiFi and design a WiSmart system, which recognize activities accuracy up to 82% in untrained environment and identify people up to 85.6%.

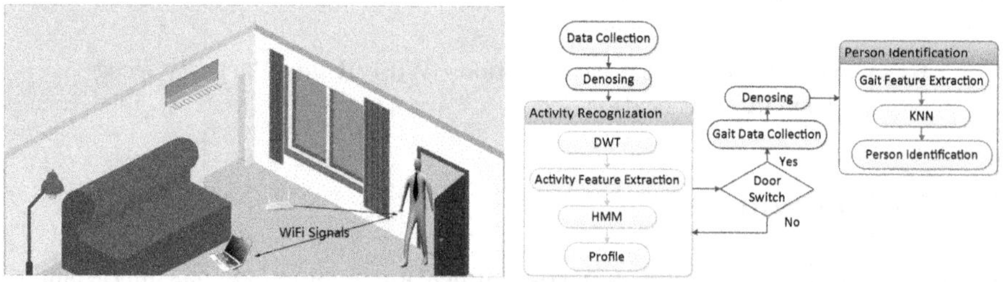

Fig. 1. WiSmart system

Fig. 2. Framework of WiSmart

2 WiFi Signal Processing

From Fig. 2, we find that WiSmart contains two modules: activity recognition module and person identification module. We first collect CSI values from WiFi signals. Second, we remove the noises by Butterworth and PCA filters. Then we judge whether there is an activity of door switch. Here, we define the door switch as two different activities, one is someone open the door and get into the room, the other is someone who close the door and get out of room. For activity recognition, we use DWT and HMM to build activity recognition model. If WiSmart have detected someone entered into room, the gait information will be extracted. We use KNN to separate different people by the features we get.

2.1 CSI Data Collection

WiSmart collects CSI measurements on the receiving end of the WiFi link between transmitter and receiver. In order to get fine-grained information about CSI, we leverage MIMO technology to multiply the capacity of a radio link. Hence we can get $2 \times 3 \times 30 = 180$ CSI values when transmitter has 2 antennas and receiver has 3 antennas and the number of subcarriers is 30. We define the CSI stream as the sequence of CSI values at each subcarrier for a given pair of sending/receiving antenna. WiSmart sends 2500 packets/second, hence in one second, we can get 2500 packets and each packet contains 180 streams.

2.2 Noise Removal

As is shown in Fig. 3(a), raw CSI data contain too many noises, and in our system, the signal changes caused by human activities lie at a low frequency spectrum while the noises caused by hardware have a relatively high frequency spectrum. Hence, we use Butterworth low-pass filter and set a cut-off frequency of 200 Hz to remove high frequency noises. We can find that high frequency noises are removed from Fig. 3(b). In order to reduce low frequency noises and find the correlations between CSI streams, we utilize PCA to calculate the principal components of CSI streams for all subcarriers. Figure 3(c) shows the third PCA component of our method and we find that the signal is much smoother compared to the traditional denoising methods such as Fig. 3(d), the moving average filter.

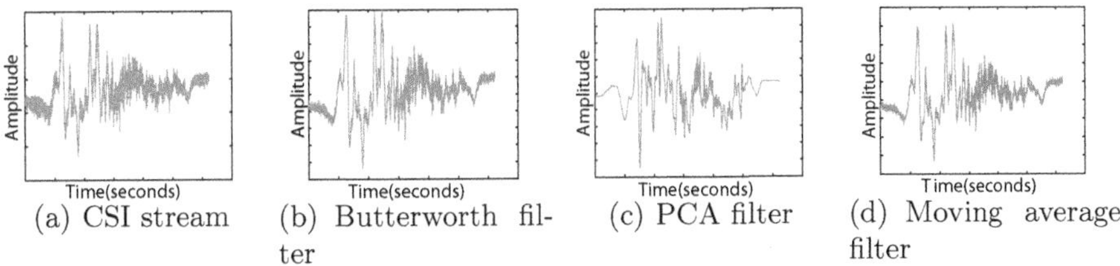

(a) CSI stream (b) Butterworth filter (c) PCA filter (d) Moving average filter

Fig. 3. Noise removal

2.3 Activity Recognition

Now, we effectively remove the noises. Next, we should extract features from activities and take a proper training method to distinguish different activities.

Feature Extraction. The responses of different activities on the frequency spectrum are different. Hence, Discrete Wavelet Transformation (DWT) is a proper choice. In WiSmart, we select the Daubechies D4 wavelet to decompose the PCA components into ten levels which span the frequencies from 1 Hz to 200 Hz. Then, we average the detail coefficients using the time window whose size is 128 in each level to capture the detailed information of different activities.

In each window, we extract the average energy and variance as features. We use the following matrix to represent the feature matrix:

$$\begin{pmatrix} E_{1,1} & E_{1,2} & \cdots & E_{1,n-1} & E_{1,n} \\ \vdots & \vdots & \ddots & \vdots & \vdots \\ E_{10,1} & E_{10,2} & \cdots & E_{10,n-1} & E_{10,n} \\ V_{1,1} & V_{1,2} & \cdots & V_{1,n-1} & V_{1,n} \\ \vdots & \vdots & \ddots & \vdots & \vdots \\ V_{10,1} & V_{10,2} & \cdots & V_{10,n-1} & V_{10,n} \end{pmatrix} \tag{1}$$

where $E_{i,j}$,$V_{i,j}$ represent the average energy and variance at the ith level in the jth time window and n is the number of time windows.

Classification. After above steps, we obtain the feature matrix, which characters different activities. We utilize Hidden Markov Model (HMM) to train the features for the reason that most of human activities can be divided into different phases, for example door switch can be divided into silent, acceleration, deceleration and stop four phases, which corresponding to the concept of states in HMM. Compared to the traditional training methods [8,9] HMM utilizes the transition probability which provides more information.

2.4 Person Identification

When WiSmart recognizes the activity of door switch including entering into the room and leaving the room. Leaving the room means there is nobody in our single person system, the light is automatically extinguished, the air conditioner is automatically turned off and so on. However, entering into the room means there is someone in home, we need to identify the person who he/she is and adjust the indoor environment according to his/her preferences. Hence, we propose our human identification model.

Walking Series Data Extraction. One hard part to extract walking series data is how to separate the walking data with the CSI data after someone entering/leaving the room and switch the gate. Our method is as follows. Normally, when someone entering the room, the walking distance is 1 m to 2 m. Meanwhile the end of door switch and the start of walking has a small static interval. We can use the static interval as judging standard to extract the walking series data because the data sequence before the static interval can be confirmed to some kind of activities by our activity recognition model.

Walking Detailed Information Extraction. We remove the noises when we get the walking series data. For more details about noise removal, please refer to section 2.2. Then we can analysis CSI waveform in the time frequency domain by using the Short Time Fourier Transform (STFT) technique. The spectrogram has three dimensions: time, frequency, and FFT amplitude which reflect more information about people walking. We can use the following equation to estimate the speeds of torso and leg :

$$F(t) = \frac{\sum_0^f A(f,t)}{\sum_0^{f_{\max}} A(f,t)} > \alpha \quad (2)$$

where $A(f,t)$ is the amplitude at frequency f and time t. We set α equals 50% and 90% respectively to predict the torso movement speed and leg speed. Then we get the speed by the equation $V_t = f_t\lambda/2$, where f_t is the frequency we get by the Eq. 2, λ is the radio wavelength. When we get the leg speed, we use the autocorrelation to estimate the gait cycle time.

Train Gait Model. By extracting walking detailed information, WiSmart trains a gait model for the target human subject. The gait model can identify whether the person is the target person or a stranger and who the person is among the given set of users. We use K Nearest Neighbor (KNN) to build the gait model.

3 Implementation and Evaluation

In this section, we will introduce the hardware setup and data set we have collected, then we will evaluate the accuracy of activity recognition and person identification in trained and untrained environment.

3.1 Hardware Setup

WiSmart deploy an Intel NUC D54250WYKH laptop with an Intel 5300 NIC and three antennas as receiver whose operating system is Ubuntu 12.04 and a mini R1C wireless router with two antennas as transmitter. We send 2500 packets per second to receiver by the iperf tool. We performed the experiments in the 5 GHz frequency band with 20 MHz bandwith channels.

3.2 Evaluation Setup

We collected a total of 700 samples from 10 volunteers which include 7 male students and 3 female students for 7 different activities and 100 samples when the room is empty in our activity recognition. Theses activities are listed in Table 1, along with the number of samples for each activity. For person identification, we collected 100 samples for each human subject from 5 volunteers.

Table 1. Activity recognition samples

Activity:	Empty	Walking	Sitting down	Falling	Running	Entering into room	Leaving room	Wavin
Abbreviation:	E	W	S	F	R	O	L	A
Samples:	100	100	100	100	100	100	100	100

3.3 Experiment Results

We first evaluate the accuracy of WiSmart in trained environment with the samples we have collected. Then, we increase the number of training samples to evaluate the impact of training set size. Finally, we apply WiSmart into untrained environment to observe the accuracy.

Accuracy in Trained Environment. We take the 80% of samples in each class as the training set, the rest as the test set. For the training set, we use 10-fold cross validation to get optimal parameters for the activity model including the states in HMM. From Fig. 4(a), we get the average accuracy of activity model is 89.14%. The average accuracy of person identification is up to 85.6%.

Impacts of Training Set Size. To find the effect of training set size on the accuracy of WiSmart, we increase to 200 samples for per activity and 150 samples for per volunteer. We observe the average accuracy of door switch increased from 87.5% to 92.5% and the average accuracy of human identification increased from 85.6% to 86.8%. When we increase the number of samples, we also improve the computational cost of WiSmart.

Accuracy in Untrained Environment. In daily living environment, family members are relatively stable. Hence when WiSmart is applied to a new environment, we need to train the person identification model once for different family members. However, we can use the activity recognition model directly. The average accuracy drops to around 82%, the results indicates that the activity recognition model is robust in the trained and untrained environment.

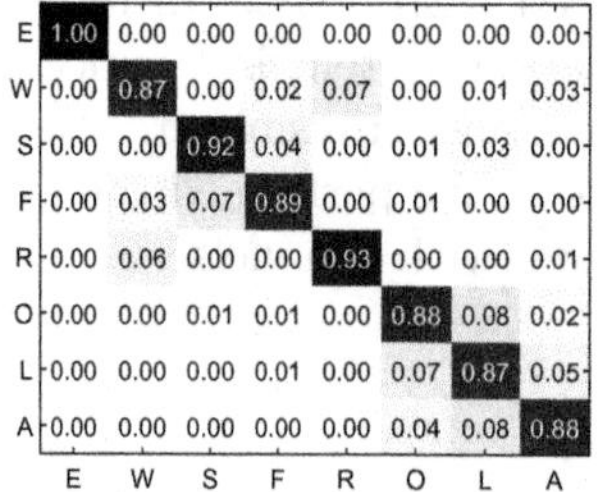

(a) Activity Recognition

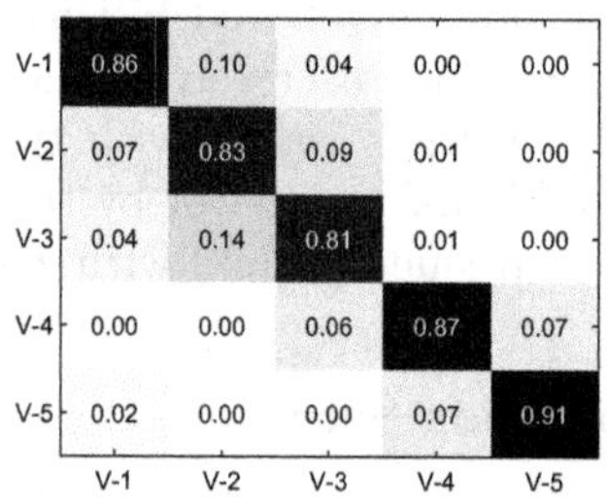

(b) Person Identification

Fig. 4. Accuracy in trained environment

4 Conclusions

In this paper, we present WiSmart, a framework for activity recognition and person identification using CSI information captured by WiFi devices. We can create a smart home environment by WiSmart. We recognize different activities according to the effects of human activities on the CSI data and identify different persons according to the gait information. WiSmart achieves more than 89.14% average activity recognition accuracy and more than 85.6% average human identification accuracy. We plan to explore the possibility to separate multiple users by multiple devices in the future.

References

1. Selvabala, V.S.N., Ganesh, A.B.: Implementation of wireless sensor network based human fall detection system. Procedia Eng. **30**, 767–773 (2012)
2. Xia, Z., Wang, X., Zhang, L., Qin, Z., Sun, X., Ren, K.: A Privacy-preserving and copy-deterrence content-based image retrieval scheme in cloud computing. TIFS **11**(11), 2594–2608 (2016)
3. Zeng, Y., Pathak, P.H., Mohapatra, P.: WiWho: WiFi-based person identification in smart spaces. In: Proceeding of IEEE/ACM IPSN (2016)
4. Hong, F., Wang, X., Yang, Y., Zong, Y., Zhang, Y., Guo, Z.: WFID: passive device-free human identification using WiFi signal. In: Proceeding of MOBIQUITOUS, pp. 47–56 (2016)
5. Zhang, J., Wei, B., Hu, W., Kanhere, S.S.: WiFi-ID: human identification using WiFi signal. In: Proceeding of DCOSS, pp. 75–82 (2016)
6. Xin, T., Guo, B., Wang, Z., Li, M., Yu, Z.: FreeSense: indoor human identification with WiFi signals. In: arXiv:1608.03430
7. Unar, J.A., Seng, W.C., Abbasi, A.: A review of biometric technology along with trends and prospects. Pattern Recogn. **47**(8), 2673–2688 (2014)
8. Gu, B., Sheng, V.S.: A robust regularization path algorithm for v-support vector classification. IEEE Trans. Neural Networks Learn. Syst. **28**(5), 1241–1248 (2016)
9. Fu, Z., Ren, K., Shu, J., Sun, X., Huang, F.: Enabling personalized search over encrypted outsourced data with efficiency improvement. IEEE Trans. Parallel Distrib. Syst. **27**(9), 2546–2559 (2016)

Robust Face Recognition Model with Adaptive Correction Term via Generalized Alternating Direction Method of Multipliers

Can Wu[1], Yunhai Xiao[2(✉)], and Wen-Jie Liu[3]

[1] School of Mathematics and Statistics, Henan University, Kaifeng 475000, People's Republic of China
wucanhello@gmail.com

[2] Institute of Applied Mathematics, School of Mathematics and Statistics, Henan University, Kaifeng 475000, People's Republic of China
yhxiao@henu.edu.cn

[3] Jiangsu Collaborative Innovation Center of Atmospheric Environment and Equipment Technology (CICAEET), Nanjing 210044, People's Republic of China
wenjieliu@nuist.edu.cn

Abstract. During the past few years, face recognition technique has received significant attention in the fields of computer vision, neuroscience, psychology and others. The robust face recognition casts the problem as an ℓ_1-minimization problem to find a sparse representation of the test image in terms of the training set. The main purpose of this paper is to firstly construct an ℓ_1-ℓ_1-minimization model and secondly be solved via a generalized alternating direction method of multipliers. Most importantly, the model proposed therein contains an adaptive correction term to get sparse representation with higher accuracy. Extensive experiments on the simulated data verify that the proposed method is effective.

Keywords: Generalized alternating direction method of multipliers · Robust face recognition model · Adaptive correction term · Augmented Lagrangian function · Dual problem

1 Introduction

With the development of science and technology, face recognition plays an important role in all walks of life. Given sufficient training samples of the i-th object class which arranged as columns of a matrix $A_i = [v_{i,1}, v_{i,2}, \dots, v_{i,n_i}] \in \mathbb{R}^{m\times n_i}$, where n_i is the number of training samples in i-th class. Let $b \in \mathbb{R}^m$ be the identified (test) sample from the same class, which approximately lies in the linear span of the training samples associated with class i, i.e., $b = \alpha_{i,1}v_{i,1} + \alpha_{i,2}v_{i,2} + \dots + \alpha_{i,n_i}v_{i,n_i}$ for some scales $\alpha_{i,j} \in \mathbb{R}$ with $j = 1, 2, \dots, n_i$. If the membership i of the test sample is initially unknown, a new matrix $A = [A_1, A_2, \dots, A_k] \in \mathbb{R}^{m\times n}$ for the entire training set of total k classes should

X. Sun et al. (Eds.): ICCCS 2017, Part II, LNCS 10603, pp. 862–873, 2017.
https://doi.org/10.1007/978-3-319-68542-7_79

be defined, where $n = n_1 + n_2 + \ldots + n_k$. Then the linear representation of b can be written in terms of all training samples as $A\bar{x} = b$, where $\bar{x}$ is a sparse coefficient vector whose entries are zero except those associated with i-th class. For given data A, one can find the associated class of b via solving the linear system of equations $Ax = b$, which emerges in various fields such as vehicle classification [1], homogeneous wireless sensor network [2], image segmentation [3] and others [4–7] and [8]. In robust face recognition, it always has $m \ll n$, which means the system $Ax = b$ is typically "under-determined" and admits infinite solutions.

To find the sparsest solution it is reasonable to solve the following optimization problem

$$\min_{x\in\mathbb{R}^n} \{\|x\|_0 : \; Ax = b\},$$

where $\|x\|_0$ is the so-called ℓ_0-norm which counts the number of nonzero components in x. The ℓ_0 term makes this problem NP-Hard and computationally intractable. On the other hand, the given image b is partially occluded, i.e., $b = A\bar{x} + \gamma$, where $\gamma \in \mathbb{R}^m$ is a vector of errors which a fraction of its entries are nonzero. From [9], it should minimize the residual between b and Ax, i.e.,

$$\min_{x\in\mathbb{R}^n} \|Ax - b\|_0.$$

In summary, seeking a simultaneously sparse solution with respect to x and γ may result in the following minimization problem

$$\min_{x\in\mathbb{R}^n,\gamma\in\mathbb{R}^m} \{\|x\|_0 + \frac{1}{v}\|\gamma\|_0 : Ax + \gamma = b\},$$

where $v > 0$ is a weighting parameter. Recent results show that if the x and γ are sufficiently sparse, then it is equal to minimize the convex relaxation ℓ_1-ℓ_1-norm optimization problem with high probability

$$\min_{x\in\mathbb{R}^n,\gamma\in\mathbb{R}^m} \{\|x\|_1 + \frac{1}{v}\|\gamma\|_1 : Ax + \gamma = b\}. \tag{1}$$

From optimization literature, the problem (1) consists a couple of nonsmooth ℓ_1-norm terms, which cause more challenges for algorithm designing especially in some practical problems. Yang and Zhang [10] reformulate model (1) equivalently as the form of equality constrained ℓ_1-norm minimization

$$\min_{\hat{x}\in\mathbb{R}^{n+m}} \|\hat{x}\|_1, \quad \text{s.t. } \hat{A}\hat{x} = \hat{b}.$$

by setting

$$\hat{A} = \frac{[A\ vI]}{\sqrt{1+v^2}}, \quad \hat{b} = \frac{vb}{\sqrt{1+v^2}}, \quad \text{and} \quad \hat{x} = \begin{pmatrix} vx \\ \gamma \end{pmatrix}.$$

Moreover, Xiao et al. [11] used the alternating direction method of multipliers based on the primal or dual forms to solve (1) directly.

Both reviewed solvers focus on the case $AA^\top = I$ which always holds in compressive sensing. However, in robust face recognition, the matrix "A" is just the data [12,13], and the condition $AA^\top = I$ may not be true. In this study, we focus on the application of a generalized alternating direction method of multipliers (ADMM) with semi-proximal terms from primal and dual approaches to solve the ℓ_1-ℓ_1-norm involved minimization problem (1). Particularly, an adaptive correction term is added to (1) for getting higher accuracy solutions. The subproblems for each variable are minimized inexactly or exactly. Furthermore, we add a relaxation step to make the algorithm more flexible. We proved that the global convergence of the proposed algorithm can be guaranteed from known results in this literature. Extensive experiments indicate that the proposed algorithms are promising and perform well.

The remaining parts of this paper are organized as follows. In Sect. 2, we present some preliminaries for our subsequent developments. In Sect. 3, we construct our algorithm step by step, and establish the algorithm's convergence immediately via relating it with the recent generalized ADMM with semi-proximal terms. In Sect. 4, we report numerical experiments to show the efficiency of the algorithms, and do performance comparisons with other solvers. Finally, we conclude our paper in Sect. 5.

2 Preliminaries

In this section, we quickly review some preliminary results and the semi-proximal generalized ADMM of Xiao et al. [14] for later developments. Let $\mathcal{E}$ be finite dimensional real Euclidean space endowed with an inner product $\langle \cdot, \cdot \rangle$ and its induced norm $\|\cdot\|$. Let $f : \mathcal{E} \to (-\infty, +\infty]$ be a closed proper convex function. A vector x^* is said to be a subgradient of f at point x if $f(z) \geq f(x) + \langle x^*, z - x \rangle$ for all z. The set of all subgradients of f at x is called the subdifferential of f at x and is denoted by $\partial f(x)$. Obviously, $\partial f(x)$ is a closed convex set while it is not empty.

For any closed proper convex function $f : \mathcal{E} \to (-\infty, +\infty]$, the Moreau-Yosida regularization of f at $x \in \mathcal{E}$ with positive scalar $\beta > 0$ is defined by

$$\varphi_f^\beta(x) := \min_{y \in \mathcal{E}} \Big\{ f(y) + \frac{1}{2\beta} \|y - x\|^2 \Big\}. \tag{2}$$

For any $x \in \mathcal{E}$, problem (2) has a unique optimal solution, which is well known as the proximal point of x associated with f and is denoted by $P_f^\beta(x)$, i.e.,

$$P_f^\beta(x) := \operatorname{argmin}_{y \in \mathcal{E}} \Big\{ f(y) + \frac{1}{2\beta} \|y - x\|^2 \Big\}.$$

The Fenchel conjugate function of a convex f at $x \in \mathcal{E}$ is defined as

$$f^\star(y) = \sup_x \{ \langle x, y \rangle - f(x) \} = - \inf_x \{ f(x) - \langle x, y \rangle \}, \quad \forall y \in \mathcal{E}.$$

It is well known that the conjugate function $f^\star$ is always convex and closed, proper if and only if f is proper [15]. For example, given a function $f(x) = \|x\|_1$, its Fenchel conjugate function can be expressed as

$$f^\star(y) = \begin{cases} 0, & \|y\|_\infty \leq 1, \\ +\infty, & \|y\|_\infty > 1. \end{cases}$$

Let $F : \mathbb{R}^n \to \mathbb{R}^n$ be a vector-valued function. The function F is said to be symmetric if

$$F(x) = Q^\top f(Qx),$$

where Q is any signed permutation matrix, i.e., a real matrix that contains exactly one nonzero entry 1 or -1 in each row and column and 0 elsewhere.

Let $\mathcal{X}$, $\mathcal{Y}$, $\mathcal{Z}$ be finite dimensional real Euclidian spaces. Consider the convex optimization problem with the following two-block separable structure

$$\begin{aligned} \min_{y\in\mathcal{Y}, z\in\mathcal{Z}} \quad & f(y) + g(z) \\ \text{s.t.} \quad & \mathcal{F}^* y + \mathcal{G}^* z = c, \end{aligned} \tag{3}$$

where $f : \mathcal{Y} \to (-\infty, +\infty]$ and $g : \mathcal{Z} \to (-\infty, +\infty]$ are closed proper convex functions, $\mathcal{F} : \mathcal{X} \to \mathcal{Y}$ and $\mathcal{G} : \mathcal{X} \to \mathcal{Z}$ are given linear maps with adjoints $\mathcal{F}^*$ and $\mathcal{G}^*$ respectively, and $c \in \mathcal{X}$ is given. Since both ∂f and ∂g are maximal monotone [15], there exist self-adjoint positive semidefinite linear operators $\Sigma_f : \mathcal{Y} \to \mathcal{Y}$ and $\Sigma_g : \mathcal{Z} \to \mathcal{Z}$, such that for any $y, y' \in \mathcal{Y}$ and $z, z' \in \mathcal{Z}$ with $u \in \partial f(y)$, $u' \in \partial f(y')$, $v \in \partial g(z)$, and $v' \in \partial g(z')$,

$$\langle u - u', y - y' \rangle \geq \|y - y'\|^2_{\Sigma_f} \quad \text{and} \quad \langle v - v', z - z' \rangle \geq \|z - z'\|^2_{\Sigma_g}.$$

The Lagrangian function of problem (3) is defined by

$$\text{Ł}(y, z; x) := f(y) + g(z) - \langle x, \mathcal{F}^* y + \mathcal{G}^* z - c \rangle, \ \forall (x, y, z) \in \mathcal{X} \times \mathcal{Y} \times \mathcal{Z}.$$

The dual of problem (3) is given by

$$\min_x \Big\{ -\langle c, x \rangle + f^\star(\mathcal{F}x) + g^\star(\mathcal{G}x) \Big\}. \tag{4}$$

A vector $(\bar{x}, \bar{y}, \bar{z}) \in \mathcal{X} \times \mathcal{Y} \times \mathcal{Z}$ is said to be a saddle point to the Lagrangian function if it is a solution to the following Karush-Kuhn-Tucker (KKT) system

$$\mathcal{F}x \in \partial f(y), \quad \mathcal{G}x \in \partial g(z), \quad \text{and} \quad \mathcal{F}^* y + \mathcal{G}^* z = c. \tag{5}$$

Let $\sigma > 0$ be a given penalty parameter. The augmented Lagrangian function associated with (3) is given as follows:

$$\text{Ł}_\sigma(y, z; x) := f(y) + g(z) - \langle x, \mathcal{F}^* y + \mathcal{G}^* z - c \rangle + \frac{\sigma}{2} \|\mathcal{F}^* y + \mathcal{G}^* z - c\|^2.$$

Throughout this paper, we make the following Assumption which ensures $(\bar{y}, \bar{z})$ is an optimal solution to problem (3) and $\bar{x}$ is an optimal solution to the dual problem (4).

Assumption 1. *There exists a vector* $(\bar{x}, \bar{y}, \bar{z}) \in \mathcal{X} \times ri(dom\ f) \times ri(dom\ g)$ *satisfying the KKT system (5).*

Next, we quickly review a couple of types of ADMM. In order to improve the performance of the classic ADMM with unite step-length, Eckstein and Bertsekas [16] proposed the following generalized ADMM scheme:

$$\begin{cases} y^{k+1} := \operatorname{argmin}_y \mathrm{Ł}_\sigma(y, z^k; x^k), \\ z^{k+1} := \operatorname{argmin}_z \Big\{ g(z) - \langle z^k, \mathcal{G}x^k \rangle + \frac{\sigma}{2} \|\rho \mathcal{F}^* y^{k+1} - (1-\rho)\mathcal{G}^* z^k + \mathcal{G}^* z - \rho c\|^2 \Big\}, \\ x^{k+1} := x^k - \sigma[\rho \mathcal{F}^* y^{k+1} - (1-\rho)\mathcal{G}^* z^k + \mathcal{G}^* z^{k+1} - \rho c], \end{cases} \tag{6}$$

where $\rho \in (0, 2)$ is the relaxation factor. We adopt the notation $\omega := (x, y, z) \in \mathcal{X} \times \mathcal{Y} \times \mathcal{Z}$ for convenience. Chen [17, Sect. 3.2] show that the generalized ADMM scheme (6) is equivalent to the following iterative ADMM scheme:

$$\begin{cases} z^k := \operatorname{argmin}_z \mathrm{Ł}_\sigma(\tilde{y}^k, z; \tilde{x}^k), \\ x^k := \tilde{x}^k - \sigma(\mathcal{F}^* \tilde{y}^k + \mathcal{G}^* z^k - c), \\ y^k := \operatorname{argmin}_y \mathrm{Ł}_\sigma(y, z^k; x^k), \\ \tilde{\omega}^{k+1} := \tilde{\omega}^k + \rho(\omega^k - \tilde{\omega}^k). \end{cases} \tag{7}$$

Observe that the subproblems in the generalized ADMM scheme (6) and (7) may not admit solutions because $\mathcal{F}$ or $\mathcal{G}$ is not assumed to be surjective. For this purpose, Xiao et al. [14] developed the following generalized ADMM with semi-proximal terms:

$$\begin{cases} y^k := \operatorname{argmin}_y \mathrm{Ł}_\sigma(y, \tilde{z}^k; \tilde{x}^k) + \frac{1}{2}\|y - \tilde{y}^k\|^2_{\mathcal{S}}, \\ x^k := \tilde{x}^k - \sigma(\mathcal{F}^* y^k + \mathcal{G}^* \tilde{z}^k - c), \\ z^k := \operatorname{argmin}_z \mathrm{Ł}_\sigma(y^k, z; x^k) + \frac{1}{2}\|z - \tilde{z}^k\|^2_{\mathcal{T}}, \\ \tilde{\omega}^{k+1} := \tilde{\omega}^k + \rho(\omega^k - \tilde{\omega}^k), \end{cases} \tag{8}$$

where $\mathcal{S} : \mathcal{Y} \to \mathcal{Y}$ and $\mathcal{T} : \mathcal{Z} \to \mathcal{Z}$ are chosen such that $\Sigma_f + \mathcal{S} + \mathcal{F}\mathcal{F}^* \succ 0$ and $\Sigma_g + \mathcal{T} + \mathcal{G}\mathcal{G}^* \succ 0$. Meanwhile, for any starting point $(\tilde{x}^0, \tilde{y}^0, \tilde{z}^0) \in \mathcal{X} \times (\text{dom } f) \times (\text{dom } g)$, the convergence of the algorithm (8) can be stated in the following theorem. For its detail proof, one can refer to [14, Theorem 5.1] and the references therein.

Theorem 2 [14]. *Suppose Assumption 2.1 holds. Let* $\{(x^k, y^k, z^k)\}$ *be the sequence generated by algorithm (8). Then the whole sequence* $\{(x^k, y^k, z^k)\}$ *converges to the KKT system (5).*

3 Model and Algorithm

This section is devoted to constructing an efficient augmented Lagrangian method with a specially designed proximal term to solve the more general optimization model (1). Inspired by Miao et al. [18], we added a rank-correction term based on spectral operator $F(\hat{x})$ to the objective function of (1) as the following one:

$$\min_{x \in \mathbb{R}^n, \gamma \in \mathbb{R}^m} \Big\{ \|x\|_1 + \frac{1}{v}\|\gamma\|_1 + \eta\langle F(\hat{x}), x \rangle : Ax + \gamma = b \Big\}, \tag{9}$$

where $F : \mathbb{R}^n \to \mathbb{R}^n$ is a symmetric function, parameter $\eta > 0$, and a typical choic is

$$F_i(x) = \begin{cases} \phi(\frac{x_i}{\|x\|_\infty}), & x \in \mathbb{R}^n \setminus \{0\}, \\ 0, & x = 0, \end{cases} \tag{10}$$

where the scalar function $\phi : \mathbb{R} \to \mathbb{R}$ is defined as

$$\phi(t) = \operatorname{sgn}(t)(1+\tau^\alpha)\frac{|t|^\alpha}{|t|^\alpha + \tau^\alpha}, t \in \mathbb{R},$$

for some positive scalars $\tau > 0$ and $\alpha > 0$. In the subsequent of this section, we turn our attention to constructing a generalized ADMM for solving problem (9) from primal and dual formulations, respectively.

3.1 Generalized ADMM for Primal Model

This subsection is devoted to providing a generalized ADMM for solving the primal problem (9). The augmented Lagrangian function of (9) is defined by

$$Ł_\sigma(x, \gamma; \lambda) = \|x\|_1 + \frac{1}{v}\|\gamma\|_1 + \eta\langle F(\hat{x}), x\rangle - \langle \lambda, Ax + \gamma - b\rangle + \frac{\sigma}{2}\|Ax + \gamma - b\|_2^2,$$

where $\sigma \in 0$ is a penalty parameter. While the generalized ADMM (8) is used, its iterative scheme is listed as follows:

$$\begin{cases} x^k := \operatorname{argmin}_x Ł_\sigma(x, \tilde{\gamma}^k; \tilde{\lambda}^k) + \frac{1}{2}\|x - \tilde{x}^k\|_{\mathcal{S}}^2, \\ \lambda^k := \tilde{\lambda}^k - \sigma(Ax^k + \tilde{\gamma}^k - b), \\ \gamma^k := \operatorname{argmin}_\gamma Ł_\sigma(x^k, \gamma; \lambda^k) + \frac{1}{2}\|\gamma - \tilde{\gamma}^k\|_{\mathcal{T}}^2, \\ \tilde{\omega}^{k+1} := \tilde{\omega}^k + \rho(\omega^k - \tilde{\omega}^k), \end{cases} \tag{11}$$

where $\omega := (x, \gamma, \lambda)$.

We now focus on the solution of the sub-problems involved in (11). Firstly, given $\gamma = \tilde{\gamma}^k$, $\lambda = \tilde{\lambda}^k$, $x = \tilde{x}^k$, $\mathcal{S} = \sigma\big(\frac{1}{\theta}I - A^\top A\big)$. It is easy to see that while $\frac{1}{\theta} \geq \lambda_{\max}(A^\top A)$, then $\mathcal{S}$ is positive semi-definite, where $\lambda_{\max}(\cdot)$ is the largest eigenvalue of a given matrix. Then, the x-subproblem is given by

$$\begin{aligned} x^k &= \operatorname{argmin}_x\Big\{\|x\|_1 + \eta\langle F(\hat{x}), x\rangle - \langle \tilde{\lambda}^k, Ax + \tilde{\gamma}^k - b\rangle + \tfrac{\sigma}{2}\big\|Ax + \tilde{\gamma}^k - b\big\|_2^2 + \\ &\quad \tfrac{1}{2}\big\|x - \tilde{x}^k\big\|_{\mathcal{S}}^2\Big\} \\ &= \operatorname{argmin}_x\Big\{\|x\|_1 + \eta\langle F(\hat{x}), x\rangle + \tfrac{\sigma}{2\theta}\big\|x - \big(\tilde{x}^k - \theta A^\top(A\tilde{x}^k + \tilde{\gamma}^k - b - \tfrac{1}{\sigma}\tilde{\lambda}^k)\big)\big\|_2^2\Big\} \\ &= \operatorname{argmin}_x\Big\{\|x\|_1 + \tfrac{\sigma}{2\theta}\big\|x - \big(\tilde{x}^k - \theta A^\top(A\tilde{x}^k + \tilde{\gamma}^k - b - \tfrac{1}{\sigma}\tilde{\lambda}^k)\big) + \tfrac{\theta\eta}{\sigma}F(\hat{x})\big\|_2^2\Big\} \\ &= P_{\|x\|_1}^{\frac{\theta}{\sigma}}\Big(\tilde{x}^k - \tfrac{\theta\eta}{\sigma}F(\hat{x}) - \theta A^\top\big(A\tilde{x}^k + \tilde{\gamma}^k - b - \tfrac{1}{\sigma}\tilde{\lambda}^k\big)\Big) \\ &= \max\Big\{\Big|\tilde{x}^k - \tfrac{\theta\eta}{\sigma}F(\hat{x}) - \theta A^\top(A\tilde{x}^k + \tilde{\gamma}^k - b - \tfrac{1}{\sigma}\tilde{\lambda}^k)\Big| - \tfrac{\theta}{\sigma}, 0\Big\} \odot \operatorname{sgn}\Big(\tilde{x}^k - \\ &\quad \tfrac{\theta\eta}{\sigma}F(\hat{x}) - \theta A^\top\big(A\tilde{x}^k + \tilde{\gamma}^k - b - \tfrac{1}{\sigma}\tilde{\lambda}^k\big)\Big), \end{aligned}$$

where $|\cdot|$ is component-wise, and "max" is interpreted as componentwise maximum and the convention $0 \cdot 0 \setminus 0 = 0$ is followed, and $\operatorname{sgn}(\cdot)$ is a sign function, and $\odot$ is the dot product.

For $x = x^k$, $\lambda = \lambda^k$ and $\mathcal{T} = 0$ fixed, the γ-subproblem is given by

$$\begin{aligned}\gamma^k &= \mathrm{argmin}_\gamma \left\{ \tfrac{1}{v}\|\gamma\|_1 - \langle \lambda^k, Ax^k + \gamma - b\rangle + \tfrac{\sigma}{2}\|Ax^k + \gamma - b\|_2^2 \right\} \\ &= \mathrm{argmin}_\gamma \left\{ \tfrac{1}{v}\|\gamma\|_1 + \tfrac{\sigma}{2}\left\|Ax^k + \gamma - b - \tfrac{1}{\sigma}\lambda^k\right\|_2^2 \right\} \\ &= P^{\frac{1}{\sigma v}}_{\|\gamma\|_1}\left(b + \tfrac{1}{\sigma}\lambda^k - Ax^k\right) \\ &= \max\left\{ |b + \tfrac{1}{\sigma}\lambda^k - Ax^k| - \tfrac{1}{\sigma v}, 0 \right\} \odot \mathrm{sgn}\Big(b + \tfrac{1}{\sigma}\lambda^k - Ax^k\Big).\end{aligned}$$

We are now ready to state iterative framework of the primal version generalized ADMM method with semi-proximal terms (abbr.PGADMM) for problem (9) as follows.

(PGADMM)

Initialize. Given $\tilde{\omega}^0 := (\tilde{x}^0, \tilde{\gamma}^0, \tilde{\lambda}^0) \in \mathbb{R}^n \times \mathbb{R}^m \times \mathbb{R}^m$. Constants $\rho \in (0, 2)$, $\sigma > 0, v > 0, \eta > 0, \tau > 0, \alpha > 0$ and $\frac{1}{\theta} \geq \lambda_{\max}(A^\top A)$. Set $k = 0$.
Step 1. Compute
$x^k := \max\left\{ \left|\tilde{x}^k - \frac{\theta\eta}{\sigma}F(\hat{x}) - \theta A^\top(A\tilde{x}^k + \tilde{\gamma}^k - b - \frac{1}{\sigma}\tilde{\lambda}^k)\right| - \frac{\theta}{\sigma}, 0 \right\} \odot \mathrm{sgn}\Big(\tilde{x}^k - \frac{\theta\eta}{\sigma}F(\hat{x}) - \theta A^\top\big(A\tilde{x}^k + \tilde{\gamma}^k - b - \frac{1}{\sigma}\tilde{\lambda}^k\big)\Big)$;
$\lambda^k := \tilde{\lambda}^k - \sigma(Ax^k + \tilde{\gamma}^k - b)$;
$\gamma^k := \max\left\{ |b + \frac{1}{\sigma}\lambda^k - Ax^k| - \frac{1}{\sigma v}, 0 \right\} \odot \mathrm{sgn}\big(b + \frac{1}{\sigma}\lambda^k - Ax^k\big)$.
Step 2. Compute
$\tilde{\omega}^{k+1} := \tilde{\omega}^k + \rho(\omega^k - \tilde{\omega}^k)$;
$k := k + 1$.

Finally, we state the convergence result of the algorithm PGADMM according to Theorem 2.

Theorem 3. *Let $\{(x^k, \gamma^k, \lambda^k)\}$ be the sequence generated by algorithm PGADMM. Then the whole sequence $\{(x^k, \gamma^k)\}$ converges to the solution of problem (9) provided that $\frac{1}{\theta} \geq \lambda_{\max}(A^\top A)$.*

3.2 Generalized ADMM for Dual Model

In this subsection, we take a dual generalized ADMM to solve the problem of (9), which makes the algorithm more flexible. The Lagrangian function of (9) is

$$\text{Ł}(x, \gamma; \lambda) = \|x\|_1 + \frac{1}{v}\|\gamma\|_1 + \eta\langle F(\hat{x}), x\rangle - \langle \lambda, Ax + \gamma - b\rangle.$$

Then the Lagrangian dual problem of (9) can be deduced by

$$\begin{aligned} &\max_\lambda \inf_{x,\gamma} \text{Ł}(x,\gamma;\lambda) \\ &= \max_\lambda \inf_{x,\gamma} \left\{ \|x\|_1 + \tfrac{1}{v}\|\gamma\|_1 + \eta\langle F(\hat{x}), x\rangle - \langle \lambda, Ax+\gamma-b\rangle \right\} \\ &= \max_\lambda \left\{ \inf_\gamma \left\{ \tfrac{1}{v}\|\gamma\|_1 - \langle\lambda,\gamma\rangle \right\} + \inf_x \left\{ \|x\|_1 - \langle x, A^\top\lambda - \eta F(\hat{x})\rangle \right\} + \langle \lambda, b\rangle \right\} \\ &= \max_\lambda \left\{ \langle\lambda, b\rangle : \|\lambda\|_\infty \le \tfrac{1}{v}, \|A^\top\lambda - \eta F(\hat{x})\|_\infty \le 1 \right\}. \end{aligned} \tag{12}$$

With an auxiliary variable $u \in \mathbb{R}^n$, the formulation of (12) can be written as

$$\max_{\lambda\in\mathbb{R}^m, u\in\mathbb{R}^n} \left\{ \langle\lambda, b\rangle : A^\top\lambda - \eta F(\hat{x}) = u, \|\lambda\|_\infty \le \frac{1}{v}, \|u\|_\infty \le 1 \right\},$$

or, equivalently,

$$\min_{\lambda\in\mathbb{R}^m, u\in\mathbb{R}^n} \left\{ -\langle\lambda, b\rangle + \delta_{\mathcal{B}^\infty_{\frac{1}{v}}}(\lambda) + \delta_{\mathcal{B}^\infty_1}(u) : A^\top\lambda - \eta F(\hat{x}) = u \right\}, \tag{13}$$

where $\mathcal{B}^\infty_{\frac{1}{v}} = \{\lambda \in \mathbb{R}^m : \|\lambda\|_\infty \le \frac{1}{v}\}$, $\mathcal{B}^\infty_1 = \{u \in \mathbb{R}^n : \|u\|_\infty \le 1\}$, and $\delta_\mathcal{C}(\cdot)$ is an indicator function defined on closed convex set $\mathcal{C}$.

Now, we turn our attention to the construction of a generalized ADMM for solving the dual problem (13). The augmented Lagrangian function of (13) is defined as

$$\text{Ł}_\sigma(\lambda, u; x) := \begin{cases} -\langle\lambda, b\rangle - \langle x, A^\top\lambda - \eta F(\hat{x}) - u\rangle + \\ \frac{\sigma}{2}\|A^\top\lambda - \eta F(\hat{x}) - u\|_2^2, & \text{if } \lambda \in \mathcal{B}^\infty_{\frac{1}{v}},\ u \in \mathcal{B}^\infty_1, \\ +\infty, & \text{otherwise}, \end{cases}$$

where $\sigma > 0$ is a penalty parameter. While the generalized ADMM is used to minimize $\text{Ł}_\sigma(\lambda, u; x)$, its iterative scheme reads

$$\begin{cases} \lambda^k := \text{argmin}_{\lambda\in\mathbb{R}^m} \text{Ł}_\sigma(\lambda, \tilde{u}^k; \tilde{x}^k), \\ x^k := \tilde{x}^k - \sigma(A^\top\lambda^k - \eta F(\hat{x}) - \tilde{u}^k), \\ u^k := \text{argmin}_{u\in\mathbb{R}^n} \text{Ł}_\sigma(\lambda^k, u; x^k), \\ \tilde{\omega}^k := \tilde{\omega}^k + \rho(\omega^k - \tilde{\omega}^k), \end{cases}$$

where $\omega = (\lambda, u, x)$.

Firstly, with fixed $u = \tilde{u}^k$ and $x = \tilde{x}^k$, the λ-subproblem can be obtained by forcing the gradient of Ł_σ with respect to λ to zero, i.e.,

$$\nabla_\lambda \text{Ł}_\sigma(\lambda, \tilde{u}^k; \tilde{x}^k) = -b - A\tilde{x}^k + \sigma A(A^\top\lambda - \eta F(\hat{x}) - \tilde{u}^k) = 0.$$

Noticing that $\lambda \in \mathcal{B}^\infty_{\frac{1}{v}}$, it yields that

$$\lambda^k = \mathcal{P}_{\mathcal{B}^\infty_{\frac{1}{v}}}\left(\frac{1}{\sigma}(AA^\top)^{-1}\left[b + A\tilde{x}^k + \sigma A\big(\eta F(\hat{x}) + \tilde{u}^k\big)\right] \right)$$

where $\mathcal{P}_\mathcal{C}(\cdot)$ is defined as the projection on closed convex set $\mathcal{C}$.

Secondly, for fixed $\lambda = \lambda^k$ and $x = x^k$, the u-subproblem can be derived by

$$\nabla_u \mathrm{L}_\sigma(\lambda^k, u; x^k) = x^k - \sigma(A^\top \lambda^k - \eta F(\hat{x}) - u) = 0.$$

Also noticing that $u \in \mathcal{B}_1^\infty$, we obtain

$$u^k = \mathcal{P}_{\mathcal{B}_1^\infty}\big(A^\top \lambda^k - \eta F(\hat{x}) - \frac{1}{\sigma} x^k\big).$$

In summary, the iterative framework of the dual version generalized ADMM method (abbr.DGADMM) can be listed as follows.

(DGADMM)

Initialization: Given $\tilde{\omega}^0 = (\tilde{\lambda}^0, \tilde{u}^0, \tilde{x}^0) \in \mathbb{R}^m \times \mathbb{R}^n \times \mathbb{R}^n$. Constants $\sigma > 0$, $v > 0$, $\eta > 0$, $\tau > 0$, $\alpha > 0$, and $\rho \in (0, 2)$. Set $k = 0$.
Step 1. Compute
$\lambda^k := \mathcal{P}_{\mathcal{B}_{\frac{1}{v}}^\infty}\Big(\frac{1}{\sigma}(AA^\top)^{-1}\big[b + A\tilde{x}^k + \sigma A(\eta F(\hat{x}) + \tilde{u}^k)\big]\Big);$
$x^k := \tilde{x}^k - \sigma(A^\top \lambda^k - \eta F(\hat{x}) - \tilde{u}^k);$
$u^k := \mathcal{P}_{\mathcal{B}_1^\infty}\big(A^\top \lambda^k - \eta F(\hat{x}) - \frac{1}{\sigma} x^k\big).$
Step 2. Compute
$\tilde{\omega}^{k+1} := \tilde{\omega}^k + \rho(\omega^k - \tilde{\omega}^k);$
$k := k + 1.$

Finally, we present the convergence result of the algorithm DGADMM by Theorem 2.

Theorem 4. *Let $\{(\lambda^k, u^k, x^k)\}$ be the sequence generated by algorithm DGADMM. Then the whole sequence $\{(\lambda^k, u^k)\}$ converges to the solution of problem (13), and the sequence of multiplier $\{x^k\}$ converges to the problem (9).*

4 Numerical Experiments

The purpose of this section is to demonstrate the feasibility and efficiency of the proposed algorithms. For this purpose, we perform a series of experiments concentrating on simulated data. All experiments are performed under Window 10 Premium and Matlab v7.8 (2013b) running on a Lenovo laptop with an Intel Core i5-5200U CPU at 2.2 GHz and 8 GB of memory. In this test, we set $k = 400$, i.e., the total number of classification. We then set $n_i \equiv 5$ for each $i = 1, \cdots, k$, which means there are 5 number of images in each class. In one words, the total number of images in the whole data A is $n = k \times n_i = 2000$. Each image is saved as one column of A with length $m = 300$. Each column of matrix $a_{i,j} \in A$, i.e., the j-th image in class i, is generated randomly by nonnegative integers with interval $[0, 255]$. Moreover, the to be identified image b is chosen randomly from the columns of A. The data A is contaminated by Gaussian white noise, i.e.,

$$a_{i,j} := a_{i,j} + 10^{-2}\epsilon$$

for each i and j, where ϵ is vector with eateries drawn from the standard normal distribution. Moreover, the to be identified image is corrupted by implosive noise, i.e.,

$$b := b + 10^{-2} I_s,$$

where I_s is set to be nonzero at random positions.

To implement algorithms PGADMM and DGADMM, we set the parameters as follows:

$$v = 2, \quad \sigma = 2, \quad \eta = 2, \quad \theta = \frac{1}{20\lambda_{\max}(A^\top A)}.$$

Moreover, in the construction of the correction function (10), we choose $\alpha = 1.2$ and $\tau = 2.0$. In running of both algorithms, we start at zero, and terminate when

$$\frac{\|x_{k+1} - x_k\|_\infty}{\|x_k\|_\infty} \leq tol,$$

where tol is a tolerance and be chosen as $tol = 10^{-6}$ in the following test. Moreover, we also force the iterative process stop while the iterative number achieve 500.

In the first experiment, we test the influence of the correction term contained in our developed model (9). More preciously, we solve a series of corrected model (9) with an initial point which derived from the previous step. In each process, we fix the relaxation factor $\rho = 1$. The numerical results are listed in the following figures. As can be observed from Fig. 1, both algorithms derived similar quality solutions within three loops, and on the other hand, good advantages of the corrected term are clearly achieved. In the second experiment, we test the influence of the relaxation factor ρ in the interval $(0, 2)$ with the fixed three loops. The parameters' values are chosen as the ones previously. The results are displayed

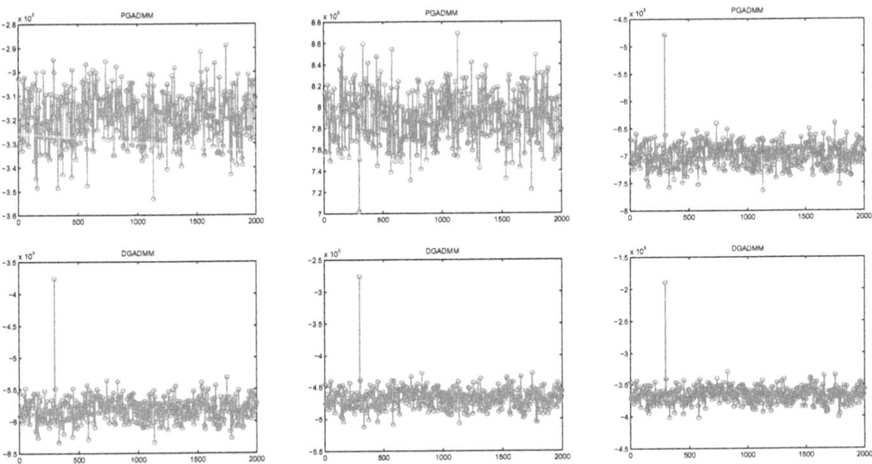

Fig. 1. Numerical results of algorithms PGADMM (top row) and DGADMM (bottom row) based on one loop (left), two loops (middle), and three loops (right).

in Fig. 2. From this figure, we clearly see that both proposed algorithms find the sparse repression of the random data A in the case of $\rho = 1.0$ and 1.3. However, both algorithms cannot achieve the solutions when $\rho = 1.6$ and 1.9, and the case $\rho = 1.9$ is the worst case. These figures also illustrate that both proposed algorithms have good performance if the value of ρ is around one.

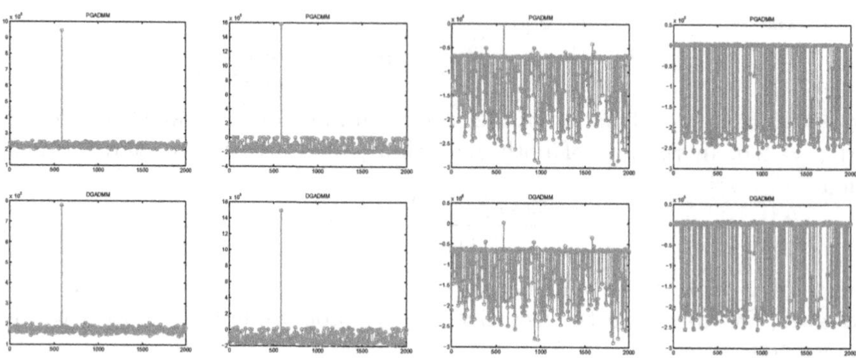

Fig. 2. Numerical results of algorithms PGADMM (top row) and DGADMM (bottom row) based on different relaxation factors. The values of ρ are 1.0, 1.3, 1.6, and 1.9 from left to right.

5 Conclusion

The main contribution of this paper lies in two aspects: firstly, we proposed an adaptive correction term based ℓ_1-ℓ_1-norm model to describe sparse representation to be identified face image; Secondly, we developed a generalized ADMM to solve the model based on primal and dual formulation. Numerical results using simulated data illustrated that the introduced model along with the developed algorithms performs well.

Acknowledgments. The research of Y. Xiao was supported by the National Science Foundation of China (Grant No. 11471101).

References

1. Wen, X., Shao, L., Xue, Y., et al.: A rapid learning algorithm for vehicle classification. Inf. Sci. **295**, 395–406 (2015)
2. Xie, S., Wang, Y.: Construction of tree network with limited delivery latency in homogeneous wireless sensor networks. Wirel. Pers. Commun. **78**, 231–246 (2014)
3. Zheng, Y., Jeon, B., Xu, D., et al.: Image segmentation by generalized hierarchical fuzzy C-means algorithm. J. Fuzzy Syst. **28**, 961–973 (2015)
4. Li, J., Li, X., Yang, B., Sun, X.: Segmentation-based image copy-move forgery detection scheme. IEEE Trans. Inf. Forensics Secur. **10**, 507–518 (2015)

5. Xia, Z., Wang, X., Sun, X., Wang, Q.: A secure and dynamic multi-keyword ranked search scheme over encrypted cloud data. IEEE Trans. Parallel Distrib. **27**, 340–352 (2015)
6. Gu, B., Sun, X., Sheng, V.S.: Structural minimax probability machine. IEEE Trans. Neural Netw. Learn. Syst. **28**(7), 1646–1656 (2017)
7. Xia, Z., Wang, X., Sun, X., Liu, Q., Xiong, N.: Steganalysis of LSB matching using differences between nonadjacent pixels. Multimed. Tools Appl. **75**, 1947–1962 (2016)
8. Chen, B.J., Shu, H.Z., Coatrieux, G., Chen, G., et al.: Color image analysis by quaternion-type moments. J. Math. Imaging Vis. **51**, 124–144 (2015)
9. Wright, J., Yang, A., Ganesh, A., Sastry, S., Ma, Y.: Robust face recognition via sparse representation. IEEE Trans. Pattern Anal. **31**, 210–227 (2009)
10. Yang, J., Zhang, Y.: Alternating direction algorithms for ℓ_1-problems in compressive sensing. SIAM J. Sci. Comput. **33**, 250–278 (2011)
11. Xiao, Y.H., Zhu, H., Wu, S.Y.: Primal and dual alternating direction algorithms for ℓ_1-ℓ_1-norm minimization problems in compressive sensing. Comput. Optim. Appl. **54**, 441–459 (2013)
12. Chen, Y.D., Hao, C.Y., Wu, W., et al.: Robust dense reconstruction by range merging based on confidence estimation. Sci. China Inf. Sci. **59**, 1–11 (2016)
13. Gu, B., Sheng, V.S.: A robust regularization path algorithm for ν-support vector classification. IEEE Trans. Neural Netw. Learn. Syst. **28**, 1241–1248 (2017)
14. Xiao, Y.H., Chen, L., Li, D.: A Generalized Alternating Direction Method of Multipliers with Semi-proximal Terms for Convex Composite Conic Programming (Unpublished)
15. Rockafellar, R.T.: Convex Analysis. Princeton University Press, Princeton (1970)
16. Eckstein, J., Bertsekas, D.P.: On the Douglas-Rachford splitting method and the proximal point algorithm for maximal monotone operators. Math. Program. **55**, 293–318 (1992)
17. Chen, C.: Numerical algorithms for a class of matrix norm approximation problems. Ph.D. thesis, Department of Mathematics, Nanjing University, Nanjing, China (2012). http://www.math.nus.edu.sg/~matsundf/Thesis_Caihua.pdf
18. Miao, W., Pan, S., Sun, D.F.: A rank-corrected procedure for matrix completion with fixed basis coefficients. Math. Program. Ser. A. **159**, 289–338 (2016)

Author Index

Printed in the United States
By Bookmasters